# Orestes A. Brownson

## A DEFINITIVE BIOGRAPHY

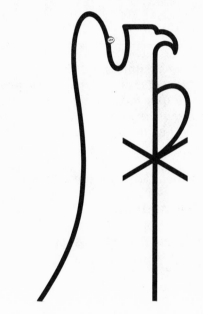

## Thomas R. Ryan C.PP.S.

OUR SUNDAY VISITOR, INC.

ISBN: 0-87973-884-7
Library of Congress Catalog Card Number: 76-29141

Cover Design by James E. McIlrath

Published, printed and bound in the U.S.A. by
Our Sunday Visitor, Inc.
Noll Plaza
Huntington, Indiana 46750

884

# CONTENTS

# ACKNOWLEDGMENTS

For interest shown in this biography, or for being helpful in one way or another, the author makes grateful acknowledgment to Raphael H. Gross, C.PP.S., John E. Byrne, C.PP.S., Edmund L. Binsfeld, C.PP.S., Dominic B. Gerlach, C.PP.S., and Francis H. Corden. Similar appreciation is also expressed to George N. Shuster of the University of Notre Dame and to Leonard T. Gilhooley of the Department of English of Fordham University. Both read many of the chapters and made suggestions.

The author also deeply appreciates the many kindly services extended to him at various centers of research: those of the Congressional Library, Washington, D.C.; those of the Harvard College Library; those of the Library of the University of Notre Dame; those of Charles Stephen Dessain of Newman's Birmingham Oratory, England; and those of Catherine E. Weidle of the Pius XII Memorial Library of St. Louis, Missouri.

Considerable information has also been obtained from various descendants of Brownson, particularly from the late Elizabeth Brownson of Grosse Pointe, Michigan, granddaughter of Brownson, and from Helena H. Odiorne of Toledo, Ohio, his great-granddaughter. Two other descendants of Brownson, Sister M. Arsenia, O.S.F., and Sister M. Margaret Brownson, S.S.N.D., were also helpful.

ACKNOWLEDGMENTS

# INTRODUCTION

This biography may perhaps be regarded as another sign that Orestes A. Brownson is gradually coming more and more into his own. How it happened that he had been for so long and so widely neglected calls for a fuller explanation than can be here entered upon. (It will unfold in the biography.) But one or the other fact might be mentioned by way of a partial explanation. From Octavius Brooks Frothingham we have one reason that has been generally overlooked. The great bulk of Brownson's writings falls into the category of periodical literature, and, as Frothingham said (speaking of the *Dial*): "It is the misfortune of periodical literature to be ephemeral. The magazine sows, but it does not harvest. It brings thoughts suddenly to the light, but buries them in season for the next issue, which must have its turn to live. Volumes that are compiled from magazines have lost their bloom. The chapters have already discharged their virtue, and spent their perfume on the air; the smell of the 'old numbers' clings to the pages, which are not of to-day, but of the day before yesterday."[1] It was for this reason that Sir John (later Lord) Acton urged Brownson in a remarkable letter in 1854 to write more books as a thing of more perennial value. "By means of a review," said Acton, "[a writer] can exert a more constant and prolonged influence on his own times than by sending forth a book. But a journal cannot live like a book. . . . [It] must become after a time a literary curiosity to a certain degree, and cannot continue to have the same effect as a book which is one whole, both in matter and in form as a work of art."[2]

Although Brownson did write half a dozen books, the great bulk of his writings lies buried in the quarterlies he published and which his son Henry gathered together into the twenty volumes of his father's collected *Works*. Added to the disadvantage attending all periodical literature, mentioned by Frothingham, is the other disadvantage that it has been extremely difficult in the past to come by a set of Brownson's *Works*. The set had been out of print for well-nigh a century and was not readily accessible to the public. Latterly, however, the set has been reprinted. But while the price of a book is usually manageable, the price of the set has been enough to frighten off many a prospective buyer.

We find another partial explanation of how it happened that Orestes Brownson faded from national remembrance in the unpopular causes he espoused in his day or the choice of topics upon which he wrote. The *Nation* remarked in 1873: "Had he written for some great newspaper, and on topics in which he and a wide audience had a common interest, it is probable that no writer of the century would have gained a surer popularity."[3] But as Arthur M. Schlesinger, Jr., has pointed out, Brownson wrote on subjects that were unpopular and have not until recently become fashionable for historical treatment.[4] Scholars who determined what should be remembered of nineteenth-century America were little interested in the unpopular causes Brownson had championed — his passionate concern for the fortunes of labor, his protests against the evils incidental to industrialism, or to those incidental to the feminist movement. The most unpopular cause of all he espoused was of course Catholicism. In consequence, he was deliberately ignored rather than casually forgotten after he entered the Catholic Church in 1844. Perry Miller, late professor of Harvard University, informs us that his former associates of the Transcendentalist movement (such men as Emerson, Parker, Hedge, Channing, etc.) "entered into a tacit conspiracy to expunge his name from the record. . . ."[5] His passionate pursuit of truth, as he saw it, evidently outweighed any desire for popularity, acclaim, or worldly advantage.

This biography is an honest attempt to bring into better focus Orestes Brownson than could perhaps have been done in the past. This surely is quite appropriate in this centennial year of his passing, 1976. The more recent biographies of him, that by Arthur M. Schlesinger, Jr., the one by Doran Whalen, and the one by Theodore Maynard, have each their own merits. But much work has been done on various phases of Brownson's thought during the last three decades, including three books, numerous doctoral dissertations at various universities, and an ever-increasing number of articles in a wide variety of publications. Many new and important letters, too, have come to light in the meantime. An attempt has been made to update the record by integrating this new matter into the Brownson narrative. The bibliography will furnish ample evidence of the extensive work done on Brownson's thought during the last three decades.

It was the judgment of the great Newman that the best way in which to write biography is largely by the use of the letters of the subject.[6] He felt that that would be the most reliable way of revealing the subject of the biography and setting forth historical truth. It is on that score that a liberal use of Brownson's letters has been made in this narrative, quoted more fully than by other biographers, except by his son Henry. It is regrettable that an attempt to recover some of Brownson's outlying letters has, in some cases, failed. Others, still unknown, will no doubt be discovered in time.

A distinctive feature of this biography is the juxtaposition, in a measure, of the career of Brownson with that of John Henry Newman inasmuch as they were the two great Catholic apologists in the English-speaking world of the nineteenth century. The similarities of their fortunes, or rather misfortunes, after they had entered the Church, is simply amazing. Both were egregiously misunderstood, both were "under a cloud" at precisely the same time, in the early 1860s. The dramatic circumstances under which Newman wrote his *Apologia* in 1864, but especially the cardinalitial dignity conferred on him by Pope Leo XIII in 1879, had much to do in restoring him to the confidence of the Catholic public in general. Brownson, a layman, was less favored by any such extraordinary events in his career. Yet, as a layman, he did receive warm commendation from the Official Voice of the Church on his gallant role as a Catholic apologist. In May 1849, he received a letter of approbation and encouragement from all the American bishops (signed by each bishop) assembled in plenary council at Baltimore; and another such letter of approbation and encouragement from His Holiness, Pope Pius IX, in April 1854. Some of the similarities between these two great apologists will be noted in the course of this narrative.

In giving references for the letters in the biography, I have often referred to the three-volume *Life* by Henry Brownson as the source rather than to the content of the microfilms. (All Brownson's known letters and other papers in the archives of Notre Dame University were microfilmed in 1966-1967.) This has been done for the reason that the three-volume *Life* is more accessible to the general reader than the microfilms.

Charles Carroll Hollis expresses the novel idea that Brownson "had to be forgotten before he could be placed in whatever niche our history will grant him.'"[7] What does Mr. Hollis mean? Battling heroically for truth and justice, as he saw it, Orestes Brownson brought many a swirling storm about his head during the fifty years of his public career, and never more so than during his career as a Catholic apologist. With him the *fortiter in re* weighed more than the *suaviter in modo* in the battle for the good cause. Deep passions were aroused in some quarters, and perhaps some institutional enemies made. Time has been needed for those storms to blow themselves out and for passions to cool. Now, a hundred years after Brownson's demise, Hollis would seem to be saying, we have the right milieu in which to make a calm, objective appraisal of Orestes A. Brownson and his works.

Thomas R. Ryan, C.PP.S.

# PART
# 1

*ORESTES A. BROWNSON*

(From *United States Magazine and Democratic Review*, April 1843)

# 1

## CHILDHOOD AND YOUTH

*Orestes Augustus Brownson was born only sixteen years after the ratification of the federal Constitution of the United States • His long American ancestry • Speculations on his original ancestry • His father, Sylvester Augustus Brownson, migrated from Hartford County, Connecticut, to Vermont, and settled with his family at Stockbridge • The untimely death of his father • Orestes is "adopted" by an elderly couple in order to relieve the burdens of his mother • His lonely childhood and insatiable appetite for books • The salient traits of his youthful character • His great love of his native state, Vermont • Love of religion: his great passion • He experiences perplexity over the various forms of religion, and seeks the advice of an American anchoress • When fourteen he goes with his mother and family to live in Ballston Spa, New York • He works there in a printing office, and attends an academy briefly • He is instructed in Universalism by an aunt, and falls in with a speckled crowd of misbelievers and nonbelievers • Great confusion of mind results • His random attendance at a Presbyterian service, and his decision to submit himself to some form of authority in religion for guidance.*

Orestes Augustus Brownson was born on September 16 at Stockbridge, Vermont, in the same year that President Thomas Jefferson added the Louisiana tract to the domain of the United States, 1803, and only sixteen years after the ratification of the Constitution of the United States. His life was to span the most exciting domestic period of the nineteenth century, and was to 'come to an end in the Centennial year, 1876. From earliest manhood he was to take an intense and most active interest in those problems of the age which concerned the welfare of his fellowmen. In grappling vigorously with these he often shifted his position, becoming many things by turn. But through it all he was to remain ever a staunch critic and reasoning defender of the American system.

The long line of American ancestry which he could, and did boast, could be claimed by few Americans. On the paternal side he was descended from one of the first settlers with Thomas Hooker of the Hartford colony, Connecticut; on his maternal side, at least collaterally, he could claim kinship with the Mayflower pilgrims.[1] John Brownson, from whom he claimed descent, came to Hartford probably in 1636, and distinguished himself in the bloody Pequot War of the following year, 1637.[2] It may be to this event, at least in part, that he refers when he tells us that he "came of a military family."[3] Certainly the warrior tradition seems to have been inborn, a fact that was to stand him in good stead in many a resounding battle stretching to the very end of his life.

But who was John Brownson, and from where in England did he come? There is little information on this subject. Not even Dr. Henry Bronson (a direct descendant of John Brownson) who wrote *The History of Waterbury, Connecticut* (homeplace of the Bronsons) in 1858, was able to draw on any dossier for John Brownson. When Orestes reviewed Dr. Henry's *History of Waterbury,* in 1860, he noted that the author and the publishers had dropped the *w* in the name, but he insisted that whether spelled Brownson, Bronson, or Brunsun, the bearers of those names, as far as is known, have all descended from the same John Brownson who had come to Hartford in 1636.[4] The surname itself is lost in the mists of English history. Mrs. Harriet Bronson Sibley, however, tells us in her treatise, *The Bronson Lineage (1636-1917),* that the first Brownson of whom we have any knowledge came to England from Scotland as one of the eighteen or twenty followers of Mary Queen of Scots when she fled to England after the battle of Langside, near Glasgow, May 1568. This Brownson finally settled in Derbyshire, England. The motto of the Brownsons or Branstons of Derbyshire was, *"Quod Bonum est Tenete"* *("What I have I hold").* Mrs. Sibley's historical research concerned itself with *The Ancestors and Descendants of Captain William Bronson of the Revolutionary War and other Ancestral Lines.*[5] It would seem not improbable that the original John Brownson may well have come to the New World from Derbyshire, England.

Although the Bronson branch of the John Brownson family (who had dropped the *w*) settled in Waterbury, Connecticut, the Brownson branch settled in New Britain, Hartford County, Connecticut. From there Sylvester Augustus Brownson, father of Orestes, migrated to Vermont. He was apparently following the road of a previous stream of Connecticut Yankees who were looking for more promising land. To acquire land in Vermont at that time, when it was a no-man's-land between New York and New Hampshire, one merely had to establish squatters' rights, a relatively easy matter. Daniel Stiles informs us that in this movement Ethan Allen, a native of Connecticut, played a prominent role:

> This process [i.e., acquisition of Vermont land] was greatly abetted by Ethan Allen . . . who persuaded the Connecticut people that they would be well advised, once the Indian wars were over in 1763, to think of moving to Vermont, and many did, as the repetition of Connecticut place names attests. You paid Ethan Allen for a right or privilege, settled down, then waited for Ethan to defend you, which he did, sometimes against the Yorkers, and sometimes against the less aggressive New Hampshire men, sometimes against both. Ethan's Green Mountain Boys may or may not have been the scourge of the British later on they are reputed to have been, but they performed valiantly against all and sundry who would disturb the nebulous land titles of Vermont. And however questionable the whole enterprise in the eyes of the law, it got Vermont populated, and provided a place for excess Connecticut population.[6]

It has been established that Sylvester A. Brownson was not the first of his family to come to Vermont. Madeline Wilkinson, a Vermont genealogist, has written: "The U.S. census of 1790 for Vermont has 12 heads of household Brownsons; the 1800 has 15, including Sylvester [Orestes's father], and one Bronson."[7] This information explains a reference to a Brownson clan in Vermont. J. Fairfax McLaughlin spoke of the martial cast of the Vermont Brownsons when he wrote: "In the early border wars between the Yorkers and the Green Mountain Boys, known as the Hampshire Grants Controversy, the Brownson clan were stalwart partisans on the Vermont side, and responded with alacrity whenever that whirlwind of a man, Ethan Allen, sounded the summons to battle:

" 'Leave the harvest to rot on the field where it grows,
and for the reaping of wheat the reaping of foes.' "[8]

Perhaps something more than Ethan Allen's personal charism made the Brownsons especially responsive to his influence. Allen had joined the Brownson family back in Connecticut; he had married Mary, the daughter of Cornelius Brownson, on June 23, 1762, in Judea parish, Woodbury. The wedding ceremony cost him four shillings.[9]

In what precise year Sylvester A. Brownson arrived in Vermont is not known. Nor is it known when or where he met and eventually married Relief Metcalf, daughter of Jotham Metcalf, a native of Keene, Cheshire County, New Hampshire. But whether the couple came before or after Vermont had been added to the original thirteen states in 1791, they made their home in Stockbridge, Vermont, Windsor County, a small town on the White River founded in 1783, and numbering scarcely more than a hundred inhabitants. The surrounding countryside, though very picturesque, was rough and mountainous; here Sylvester Brownson accepted the obvious hardship of wresting out a livelihood for himself and family of five — Daniel, Oran, Thorina and the twins, Orestes and Daphne Augusta. Shortly after the birth of the twins, Sylvester Brownson took a bad cold, went into pneumonia, and died, leaving his spouse with the care of five small children.[10]

This irreplaceable loss clearly and understandably affected the development of the young, intelligent and deeply sensitive boy Orestes. In later life he was to lament frequently the unhappy condition of the widow and the orphan when he pleaded with stirring eloquence the cause of the underprivileged classes of society. There is deep pathos in the words he used in adult life to describe the effect on him of William Ellery Channing's sermon "Likeness to God" when read to him by a friend:

> I listened [he said] as one enchanted. A thrill of indescribable delight ran through my whole soul. I could have leaped for joy. I seemed suddenly to have found a father. To me this was much. I had never known an earthly father, and often had I wept when I heard, in my boyhood, my playmates, one after another, say: "my father." But now, lone and deserted as I had felt myself, I too had become a son, and could look up and say, "my father" — around and say, "my brothers."[11]

This passage takes on additional significance in the light of some recent observations of Per Sveino who has seen in Brownson's long and intense life an ardent search for a father. After noting Brownson's never-failing search for a unity or synthesis in all things, beginning especially with his *Society for Christian Union and Progress* in 1836, he observed that "his way to traditional Christianity and, more particularly, to Catholicism was his fervent search for a FATHER. The tragic loss of his father in childhood seemed to motivate to a great extent his desires of believing in a heavenly father." Per Sveino's view is that this search of Brownson strongly motivated his philosophical speculations on the problem of God as evidenced in his article on Cousin's philosophy in 1836. After weaving together a long string of philosophical terms more or less abstract, Brownson imparted warmth to them all when he indicated what they ultimately meant to him: "Hence, from the absolute principles of Causality, Substance, Unity, Intentionality, the Just, and the Beautiful, we obtain the absolute God, Cause of causes, Being of beings, Substance of substances, Unity of unities, Intentionality of intentionalities, morally just, beautiful, righteous — our Father."[12]

At all events, with his father gone, the boy Orestes lived a somber and

17

lonely childhood. His father died intestate, and left the family in difficult circumstances. Relief Metcalf Brownson struggled admirably for some years to keep her children together, but she was finally forced to capitulate to increasing difficulties, and to accept the offer of kind neighborhood friends to take or adopt separately the two youngest, Orestes and Daphne, aged six. The separation of the twins was so painful that Daphne, recalling it in her old age — she lived to be ninety or more — spoke of it as one of the great griefs of her life.[13] Orestes went to live with an elderly couple (their name has never been given) near the town of Royalton, five or six miles north of Stockbridge. They lived on a small farm and supported themselves by their own industry. They were not churchgoing people, but had been reared in New England Congregationalism, and were strictly moral — far more willing to suffer wrong than to do it. They taught him, as he informs us, "to be honest, to owe no one anything but good will, to be frugal and industrious, to speak the truth, never to tell a lie under any circumstances, or to take what was not my own, even to the value of a pin; to keep the Sabbath, and never to let the sun go down on my wrath." They also taught him the Shorter Catechism, the Apostles' Creed, the Lord's Prayer, and a short rhymed evening prayer.[14]

How well the elderly couple succeeded in impressing these moral lessons on the plastic character of the child, may be gathered from his own later words:

> I grew up a healthy, active, well-made and unusually strong boy. I never begged, and never stole the value of a pin, and would have starved or frozen to death sooner than I would have done either: I had no vicious tendencies, and I think I was well disposed, and my heart swelled and my eyes overflowed if any one spoke a gentle word.[15]

But he tells us also in his autobiography that he had an irritable temper, and was not free from violent outbreaks of passion, which, however, he tried hard to control so as not to do or say anything wrong. And he could not remember ever to have allowed the sun to go down on his wrath. He acknowledged that he had his faults, and did many things which were by no means right or excusable; but his conscience, he adds, was always active, he readily felt remorse, and was ready to submit to any humiliation no matter how great, to atone for any fault he had committed, or to repair the wrong done. For he felt that "the next best thing to never doing wrong, was to own the wrong done, and endeavor to undo it."[16]

Living apart with an aging couple, attending no school, young Orestes was largely without playmates as he grew into youth. However he may have felt about it at the time, he was to lament it in later years. He tells us that properly speaking he had no childhood at all, that being brought up with old people, debarred from the sports and frolics of children, he had the manners, the tone and the tastes of an old man before he was a boy. "A sad misfortune," he said, "for children form one another, and should always be suffered to be children as long as possible. Both childhood and youth are quite too short with us, and the morals and manners of the country suffer from it."[17]

But it seems clear that his unusual childhood was not an unmitigated misfortune, for it turned him in his earliest years to reading as a substitute for other pursuits, and developed in him an insatiable appetite for books. In the home in which he lived there was the King James Bible, Watt's *Psalms and Divine Songs, The Franklin Primer,* Edward's *History of the Re-*

*demption* and a few other volumes. Having begun on these — there was no public library in the vicinity — he scoured the neighborhood for what he could find. In the home of one gentleman he found the English classics of Queen Anne's reign, in another home fifty volumes of the English poets, in still another a work on universal history. Further inquiries turned up Locke's *Essay on Human Understanding,* Pope's *Homer,* various monographs of American history, books on the planting of the colonies, on wars with the Indians, *Robinson Crusoe,* Philip Quarles and the *Arabian Nights.* Although he did not understand all that he read, he devoured them all the same; reading was his supreme delight. Whenever he had a moment of leisure, he always had a book in his hand. In later life he was to say: "I have had my joys and sorrows, but I have never known or imagined on earth greater enjoyment than I had as a boy lying on the hearth in a miserable shanty reading by the light of burning pineknots some book I had just borrowed. I felt neither hunger or thirst, and no want of sleep; my book was my meat and drink, home and raiment, friend and guardian, father and mother."[18] Here surely we have kinship with Abe Lincoln.

He considered it fortunate that he never got his hands on children's books in his growing childhood. What is needed, he insisted, are books or reading matter that will severely exercise, toughen and strengthen the mind of the growing child. He wrote:

> There were in those days few children's books and none came my way, for which I have been thankful. Old people may read children's books, and find recreation in them; but they are unprofitable reading for children. It is a damage for children to have thought [ideas] made easy for them. The earlier their intellects are taxed, and the harder they are obliged to struggle to find some meaning in what they read the better for them. Their minds grow by exercise and become strong; but children's books feed their minds on pap and panada, and keep their mental indigestion always weak and incapable of relishing even in after life, healthy and invigorating food. Hence in our day we are obliged to dilute our literature for grown up men and women, and write novels and romances, and to take care that we do not overload them with thought. We no longer train our children to be men, thinking men, or as Emerson says, men thinking. We do their thinking for them, what little there is, and keep them children in understanding all their lifetime. I think it was a great advantage to me that I read books beyond my age, and could think, reason, reflect before I had a beard on my upper lip.[19]

But of all the books that came within his reach, none did he study with more intense interest than the Bible, "all of which," he said, "I had read by the time I was eight, and a great part of which I knew by heart before I was fourteen years of age."[20] The edition of the Bible which he had for reading, as has been noted, was the King James Version.[21] Here one may detect one of the sources of that superb literary style which he was to develop when he later turned to writing. In an article in his *Review* on "The Study and Reading of the Scriptures," 1861, he extolled highly the literary excellence of the King James Version, and asserted that its literary superiority is due to the fact that the translation was made in the sixteenth century when the English language was at its zenith. The English language was then marked by a majestic simplicity, a naturalness, an ease, grace and vigor which it had been gradually losing since; what it had retained of these qualities is due to the influence of the King James Version together with the Book of Common Prayer. Every day, he continued, the English language had been departing more and more from the grandeur, strength and simplicity that had distinguished it in the sixteenth and seventeenth centuries — a proof in itself that the reading of the Scriptures, at least in the King James Version, had grown less and less common, or that the authors who had gained the mastery in the modern literary world, had not modeled their literary tastes after its study.[22] His own close knowledge of that version could not but have exerted considerable influence on the formation of his literary style.

His son Henry tells us that his father early acquired three traits of character which were to dominate the rest of his life. From the elderly couple with whom he lived he absorbed a great love of truth; from the scenery around him, a love of nature's beauties and a patriotic attachment to his boyhood home; from the Bible and the *History of the Redemption,* a love of religion as a matter of the first importance in life. These three loves were to run like golden threads through all the thought and writings of his long life. His son mentions also another trait that distinguished him as a youth, namely, that "he would suffer no one of his age to surpass him in any kind of manual labor."[23] This was prophetic of his future prodigious energy and the extraordinary labors he was to perform during his lifetime.[24]

Again, Henry Brownson suggests the importance of his father's early love of his native Vermont. It was great indeed. To what extent his youthful imagination had been stimulated by the heroic deeds of Ethan Allen and his Green Mountain Boys in the border wars against the Yorkers, or by the long and fierce struggle of Vermont for separate independence, or statehood, we are not told. It is certain that the heroic spirit of the people of what was to become the state of Vermont, their fierce love of freedom and personal independence, was to pass into the sensibility of Orestes A. Brownson and leave with him the characteristics of the "true blue" Vermonter. Few Americans, perhaps, have ever had a deeper attachment to their native state than he. Although he was to leave the state in his early years, its memory was ever nostalgic with him, and he spoke of it with great affection. It was ever to remain for him like a mother from whom he had received so much.

> We feel toward that state [he said in middle age], though it has not been our home for many a year, all the affection of a son for his mother. Amid her Green Hills we drew our earliest breath, and there are all the associations which become all the dearer the farther we recede from them. To Vermont we owe our hardy constitution, our fearless love of freedom, our indomitable spirit of independence; and if, in the restless excitement of youth, or the deeper ambition of manhood, we have ever been touched by that infirmity, "love of fame," it has been that we might leave a memory to our own native state, which she would not be unwilling to preserve. But she needs not this. In the struggle for independence, she was the first to obtain a victory; on her soil was fought the battle that decided the War of the Revolution; and should liberty be driven from all the rest of the Union, she will still make her eyrie in the cliffs of her Green Mountains, and where her eagle-brood shall continue her line through all time.[25]

But whatever the developing characteristics of the boy, it was religion more than anything else that engaged his budding mind. His "greatest pleasure was in conversing, or hearing others converse on religion."[26] The age in which he lived, so different from our own times, was basically religious-minded, too. Religion was taught in the schools of the land, the elementary school, the college and the university. It had a clear and prominent part in the intellectual ambience of nineteenth-century America. The people of those times talked and argued more readily about religion in the home, at the country store, in the railroad car or on the steamboat than we moderns do in our present-day setting, while not abating an interest in politics, athletics, business trends, education and foreign policy. The people of those times were a serious-minded people, for the day was yet far off in which the movement began that was to secularize modern society. The country saw, too, from time to time, great spiritual revivals. The second revival, or Great Awakening, coming in 1800, was to have immediate and lasting effects upon American society generally. As Russell Blaine Nye has remarked:

[The second Great Awakening] meant that the United States, despite the shocks of eighteenth-century rationalism and "infidelity," remained predominantly a religious-minded nation, with an emotional, pietistic, and moralistic thinking for generations to come. The shrewd French traveler, Alexis de Tocqueville, noted this primary fact of American life in 1831, after the Awakening had run its course. "There is no country in the world," he said, "in which the Christian religion retains a greater hold over the souls of men than in America. Religion is the foremost of institutions in the country."[27]

Though engrossed in religion, young Orestes was interested in all that went on around him. When he was nine years old, he was permitted to accompany an older boy to the "middle of the town [probably Royalton]," about four miles from where he lived, to witness a general training of a brigade of militia. On his return, he was asked what of interest he had seen. He replied that he had seen two old men arguing about religion. So interested had he himself become in the discussion that he forgot all about the soldiers, even though he had come from a military family. The card of gingerbread he had brought along almost went uneaten. The discussion turned on free will and election, and the nine-year-old actually took part in it, "stoutly maintaining free will against Edwards, who confounds volition with judgment, and maintains that the will is necessarily determined by the state of the affections and motives presented to the understanding."[28] There is here an early foreshadowing of that astonishing role he was to play in the intellectual arena of the nineteenth century.

His earliest wish was to be a minister of religion, to bring others to a knowledge and love of God. It was for this ambition that he longed to go to school, to pursue learning, to grow up and be a man. "I looked upon myself," he writes, "as one called and set apart for the service of religion."[29] Later he dreamed of becoming a missionary to the heathen, a short-lived dream, it is true; upon reflection he concluded that the warring sects should first settle their differences before offering a Babel of tongues for the gospel message.

His early call to the service of religion reminds one of young John Henry Newman's premonition that God's will demanded for him a celibate life, more or less connected in his mind with the notion that his calling would indeed require such a sacrifice, as, for instance, missionary work among non-Christians to whom he had been strongly drawn for some years.[30] The many striking similarities in the lives of these two great men of the nineteenth century will be noted in the course of this book.

The strong sense of religion that was becoming deeply embedded in the nature of the youth Orestes, urging him to dedicate himself totally to the service of religion, stemmed no doubt from his meditative reading of the Sacred Scriptures. Explaining the effects on him of Bible reading, he said:

The simple story of the Passion of Our Lord, as I read it in the Evangelists, affected me deeply, I hung with delight on the mystery of the Redemption, and my young heart often burned with love to Our Blessed Lord, who had been so good as to come into the world, and to submit to the most cruel death of the

cross that he might save us from our wicked dispositions, and make us happy forever in heaven. I wanted to know all about him, and used to think of him
frequently in the day and the night. Sometimes I seemed to hold long familiar
conversations with him, and was deeply pained when anything occurred to inter-
rupt them. Sometimes, too, I seemed to hold a spiritual intercourse with the
Blessed Mary, and with the holy Angel Gabriel, who had announced to her that
she was to be the mother of the Redeemer. I was rarely less alone than when
alone. I did not speculate on the matter. It all seemed real to me, and I enjoyed
often an inexpressible happiness. I preferred to be alone, for then I was in the
presence of Jesus and Mary, and the holy angels; yet I had not yet been baptized, and had very little instruction except such as I had obtained from the
reading of the Holy Scriptures.[31]

Yet in spite of his ardent leanings toward religion, there seems to have
been no one to explain doctrinal matters to him, such as the necessity of baptism, or the nature and office of the Church in the scheme of salvation. All
that he was told was that he must "get religion," "experience religion,"
"have a change of heart," "be born again." But just how this was to be done,
there was no one to enlighten him. In the town near which he lived there
were Congregationalists, called "the Standing Order," Methodists, Baptists,
Universalists and Christians, or as they insisted on being called, *Christyans*. The Methodists and the Christyans were the more numerous, and it
was to them that he felt himself most drawn. Whenever he went to a religious meeting, it was to one of these two groups. He knew they differed, but
the only difference he could readily notice was that the Methodist preachers
had stronger lungs: when they preached the people shouted more. He gave
them the first place as preachers inasmuch as they made the most noise, and
gave the most spine-tingling descriptions of hellfire and the tortures of the
damned. Yet all he learned from either set of preachers was that he must be
born again or go to hell, get religion or be damned. Apparently nothing was
said about the means of salvation. (This is evidently a case of preachers taking for granted a certain amount of rudimentary religious knowledge in the
audience.) The more he listened the more his fear of hell increased, and the
less he loved God. He was constantly in dread that the devil might come and
carry him off bodily. "I had tried to get religion," he said, "and at times almost made up my mind to submit to the Methodists, and let them bring me
out."[32]

Sadly perplexed at twelve, Orestes decided to seek the counsel of an elderly lady, whose advice was to have considerable influence on his thought
for years to come. She was a Congregationalist, fairly well-educated for
those times, and a person of intelligence and refinement. Now reduced to
penury, she was living alone in a miserable hut on the edge of the farm on
which Orestes lived. He visited this American anchoress one evening, and
unburdened himself as he told her of his perplexities in matters of religion:
which sect should he join? She listened patiently, and then said:

My poor boy, God has been good to you, and has no doubt gracious designs
toward you. He means to use you for a purpose of his own, and you must be
faithful to his inspirations. But go not with the Methodists or any of the sects.
They are New Lights, and not to be trusted. The Christian religion is not new,
and Christians have existed from the time of Christ. These New Lights are of
yesterday. You yourself know the founder of the Christian sect, and I myself
knew personally both George Whitefield and John Wesley, the founders of
Methodism. Neither can be right, for they came too late, and have broken off,
separated from the body of Christians, which subsisted before them. When you

22

join any body calling itself Christian, find out and join one that began with Christ and his Apostles, and has continued to subsist the same without change of doctrine or worship down to our own times. You will find the true religion with that body, and nowhere else. Join it, obey it, and you will find rest and salvation. Beware of sects and New Lights: they will make you fair promises, but in the end will deceive you to your own destruction.[33]

Narrating this incident in his autobiography years later, Brownson says that her words made a deep impression upon him; they struck him as just. But what is to be noted in particular is his statement that her counsel prevented him from "ever being a genuine, hearty Protestant, or a thorough-going radical even." The woman was not a Catholic, but a sincere Congregationalist, and only held the church views of the New England Puritans which were insisted upon in those days by the old Standing Order in New England. As Brownson explained: "However erroneous were the views of the New England Puritans, they retained a conception of the Church of Christ, held that Christ had himself founded a Church, established its order, and given it its ordinances, and taught that it was necessary to belong to it in order to be saved."[34]

When Orestes turned fourteen, his mother left Vermont with her children and went to live at Ballston Spa, Saratoga County, New York. One may only guess at the reasons. It may be that she was practically forced out of the state in the aftermath of the catastrophe which had occurred in Vermont in the year 1816. Winter came in summer; the year became known in Vermont history as the "famine year." On June 8 a foot of snow fell and blew into drifts three or four feet high. There was also some snow in July and August, and on September 10 came a killing frost. Scarcely any crops survived for harvesting. With the failure of the hay crop, much of the livestock perished. Many of the inhabitants had nothing between them and starvation but nettles, wild turnips, hedgehogs and other crude substitutes for normal fare. Never had the people of the territory known such intense physical sufferings and hardships. Many of them struck out for lands of promise in the West, particularly Ohio, toward which many in the New England states were already drifting.[35] Whatever the precise reason for the move, Mrs. Sylvester Brownson may have decided to go at least far enough to get out of the state. All this could be of some significance in determining how soon Orestes may have been able to attend school in Ballston Spa. If the family had been in straitened circumstances because of the hardships of the previous year, any earnings Orestes was able to garner during the first years in New York State may well have been needed for family support.

Henry Brownson mentions the academy at Ballston Spa which Orestes attended, and in which "he acquired some Latin and less Greek, and attained to a fair knowledge, as it was then considered, of the usual branches of English education."[36] Yet it is at least questionable whether Orestes attended the academy immediately after coming to Ballston Spa. Sir John (later Lord) Acton, who had a four-day interview with Brownson, July 1853, on his visit to the United States, stated in a letter to his tutor in Munich, Johann Joseph Ignaz Döllinger, that Brownson had told him — among other things — that although "he learned to read with an old uncle, and soon began to work . . . in his eighteenth year he did not know how to write."[37] Taken *prima facie* the statement would seem to argue that he did not attend the academy his first two or three years at Ballston Spa. Brownson himself mentions that when he joined the Presbyterians (in his fourth year at Ballston Spa), he was at the time pursuing his studies at the academy.[38] In its obituary notice of

Brownson's passing in 1876, the *New York Times* noted: "He was sent to the Ballston Academy, in this state, at the age of nineteen."[39] It seems, then, that his formal education began and ended at this academy — very meager indeed — perhaps one school year, if that.

In Ballston Spa there was also a printing office, owned by James Comstock. Here young Orestes found employment, first as an apprentice, then as a journeyman.[40] Here too (at the printing office and elsewhere), he fell in with a speckled crowd of sectaries, Universalists, deists, atheists, "nothingarians," as they were called, and those professing no particular form of religion. For one with no systematic instruction in religion, the effect was disastrous. He tried desperately to hold on to religion, but his young head became so bewildered by contradictory assertions, by the doubts and denials expressed, that he half persuaded himself that all religion is humbug, the work of priestcraft and statecraft. "I was in a labyrinth of doubt," he later wrote, "with no Ariadne's thread to guide me out to the light of day. I was miserable, and I knew not where to turn for relief. I felt that my own reason was insufficient to guide me; and the more I attempted by it alone to arrive at truth, the further I went astray, and the more . . . perplexed I became."[41]

At this time he became acquainted with a number of Universalist books; he had in fact been instructed in that creed by his mother's sister who had herself listened in her youth to the preaching of Dr. Elhanan Winchester, one of the earliest and most distinguished Universalist preachers in America. Among the several books Winchester had written were his *Dialogues,* his *Lectures on the Prophecies* and an epic poem celebrating the triumph of the empire of Christ.[42] When he was between fourteen and fifteen years of age Orestes had read these works, and, aided, as he tells us, by the brilliant and enthusiastic commentaries of his aunt, they had shaken his faith in the central doctrines of Christianity. A neighbor's gift of a *Treatise on the Atonement* by Hosea Ballou, another distinguished Universalist minister, added to the young man's bewilderment. In this work Ballou "denies free will, denies responsibility, denies a future judgment, denies all rewards and punishments, denies virtue, denies sin, in all except name, and consequently the whole moral order." Never, said Brownson, in after life, had a book issued from the American press been more replete with heresies of the most deadly character, or one that was more calculated to carry away "a large class of young, ingenuous, uninformed minds." If anything was wanting to compound the evil, some popular works "openly warring against all revealed religion, indeed against all religion, whether revealed or natural," came his way at the time.[43] As he had no rule of guidance at all in religion, these books only increased his gnawing doubts and perplexity, and made him despair of ever being able to know what to believe.

In this state of mind, it happened that one Sunday morning, when he was about nineteen, he was passing a Presbyterian meetinghouse in Malta, Saratoga County, New York. He saw people gathering for the service, and he decided to join them. He had not been in a place of worship for some time. While the hymn singing displayed no special art, it did soothe him, even to the point of tears. He listened reverently to the reading of the Scriptures, to the prayer and the sermon. Years later he could recall nothing at all of the sermon. Nevertheless, he went out from that meetinghouse not only deeply touched, but also feeling that he had somehow missed his way in life. As he continued on his journey, he kept asking himself what he had gained by his speculations, why he must stand alone and find no belief to sustain him, why there was no worship to refresh him.

I have, said I, in my communing, done my best to find truth, to experience religion, and to lead a religious life, yet here I am without faith, without hope, without love. I know not what to believe, I know not what to do. My life is like a stream that flows out of darkness. The world is dark to me, and not a ray of light even for one instant relieves it. My heart is sad, and I see nothing to hope for, or to live for. For me heaven is dispeopled, and the earth is a desert, a barren waste. Why is this so? Why does my heart rebel against the speculations of my mind? If doubt is all there is for me, why cannot I discipline my feelings into submission to it? Why this craving to believe when there is nothing to believe? . . . Why this thirst for an unbounded good, when there is no good, when all is mere show, an illusion, and nothing is real? Have I not mistaken my way?

Was I not told at the outset that, if I followed my own reason, it would lead me astray, that I should lose all belief, and find myself involved in universal doubt and uncertainty? Has it not been so? In attempting to follow the light of reason alone, have I not lost faith, lost the light of revelation, and plunged myself into universal darkness? I did not believe what these people said, and, yet, were they not right? They were. They told me to submit my reason to revelation. I will do so. I am incapable of directing myself. I must have a guide. I will hear the church. I will surrender, abnegate my own reason, which hitherto has only led me astray, and make myself a member of the church, and do what she commands me."

These later reflections on the state of his mind at this youthful time of his life were perhaps expressed with a greater clarity than he could have achieved in the very midst of his early confusion. But that we have here an accurate description of the early state of his mind, and his desperate resolve to extricate himself from it, can scarcely be questioned. No doubt he added some coloring at times to facts in general, but there seems no reason to dispute Brownson's recollection of the facts themselves of his early experience. As Augustine Hewit has observed: "Intellect, reason, imagination, and memory were alike powerful faculties of his mind."[45] In any case, it seems clear that at this youthful period he had lost his way in life. Perhaps it was well that he did not know or suspect how long the road and how rocky its travel before he would find an inn for his spirit and the warm fire of his tested conclusions.

# 2

## AN ENCOUNTER WITH CALVINISM
## AND A LOOK AT THE WORLD

*The youth Orestes joins the Presbyterian Church • His experience
as revealed to us in his autobiography and his diary • His explanation in extenso of why he found Calvinism unsatisfactory • He gags
on the Calvinistic doctrine of unconditional election and reprobation • He becomes a no-churchman, and passes from a supernaturalist to a rationalist • He teaches school at Stillwater, Saratoga
County, New York • His desperate struggle to understand the many
grievous evils and glaring inequalities in society leaves him perplexed.*

Acting on his previous resolution to submit to authority in matters of
religion, Orestes Brownson, now nineteen, called upon the Presbyterian
minister of Ballston Spa, New York, the Rev. Reuben Smith, and told him of
the experience he had recently encountered. That same day, at the minister's request, he told it again to the session of the church. Since all present
were apparently satisfied that he had experienced what is called "conversion," he was baptized on the following Sunday and received into the Presbyterian communion. He did not ask at the time, he tells us, whether the Presbyterian Church was the true church or not, for the church question had not
yet surfaced in his mind. But since the Presbyterian Church did not differ essentially from the Standing Order, claimed to be the true church and was
considered respectable, he was at the time satisfied.[1]

Of his Presbyterian experience we have Brownson's account both in *The
Convert* and a diary he kept at the time ("A Notebook of Reflections"). Although, as Arthur M. Schlesinger, Jr., has observed, "the Calvinist dogma
did violence to his innermost impulses,"[2] he seems really to have tried to
adapt himself to Calvinist doctrine and practice — even after having said: "I
saw at once I had made a mistake."[3] There are passages in his diary which
plainly show that he was trying to impose the Calvinist doctrine of total depravity upon his thinking, at least in a fashion. On the last day of the year in
which he had embraced Presbyterianism, 1822, he wrote in his diary:

> Reflect, O my soul, on what has employed thee during this year — on what
> character thou has established and what thy general course of conduct. Canst
> thou look with pleasure on the scenes that have occupied thy attention? Has
> thou done nothing that causes shame and regret? Nothing that makes thee
> mourn and condemn thyself as vile in the sight of God — nothing that makes
> thee abhor thyself "in dust and ashes" and cry "unclean, unclean"? Yes, I have
> sinned every day, every hour, yea, and every breath has been drawn in iniqui-
> ty; every thought, and every imagination of my heart has been evil, only evil,
> and that continually. And yet thou dost exist? What a mercy! Sinned every
> breath, and yet among the living?[4]

With this he also mingled sentiments of deep-felt gratitude to God.

> Art thou not lost in contemplation of that Power which has preserved thee?

Canst but exclaim "thou art all mercy, O Love Divine, who didst not cast me off and appoint my portion with them that go down into the pit"? Dost not feel thy heart glow with gratitude to this great Preserver? Yes, for he has not only preserved my life and loaded me with unnumbered temporal blessings, but has taken my feet from a horrible pit and placed them on a sure foundation. Yea, sought me dashing my speculative brains against the rocks of infidelity, bound up my wounds, and given me a new song, even of praises to the most High God.[5]

Again on Saturday, January 18, 1823, he wrote:

Dead to every sense of pleasure. Feel no life in religion. Can apply no promise of God, none. Hope only because I know he is faithful who has promised. Believe the carnal nature always remains, and that nature is prone to sin, not only prone to sin, but it is evil. All its thoughts and imaginations are evil, only evil, and that continually.[6]

But he did at times experience spiritual solace and elevation when attending Presbyterian services. On May 25, 1823, he wrote:

Attended church. . . . A most precious day. There was exhibited that love, that self-moved love that gave a Savior to a lost and perishing world; there was shown the death and sacrifice of the spotless lamb, the Son of God, the mighty Maker of all we behold. O what heart will not weep when exposed to view the glorious sufferer? Who can repress the tear when up Calvary's rugged way we see him fainting beneath the ponderous wood, or extended between the heavens and the earth? O sin, what hast thou done? Was it not enough to hurl from heaven legions of angels? Must thou rage till the Son, the only Son of the Father descends and dies an ignominious death on the cross? Tremble, O my soul, as thou dost contemplate. All other deeds but this the sun permitted to pass; but ashamed to see his Maker dying he hid his face and shrouded the world in darkness. O hide thy face in shame and confusion, for thou hast murdered the King of Heaven and he forgives thee, grants thee pardon, and bids thee live! O adore His goodness, love his mercy, and praise him forever.[7]

But whatever his efforts to adapt to the Presbyterian doctrine and practice, he did not long abide the company of John Calvin. Had Brownson been precipitate in joining the Presbyterians, or did he leave them without good and sufficient reasons? He had often later been accused of religious instability, of changing "with every moon." In this critical case (his first identification with organized religion) it seems only fair to allow him to state in his own words the reasons for his departure. His original decision to join the Presbyterians had been impulsive, hasty, "a cowardly act, an act of an intellectual desperado," he asserted.[8] Can such a statement be taken literally, or must an honest observer read his motive as shallow and the man as fickle? One should, perhaps, be all the more willing to hear him out in his own defense inasmuch as this is a sort of test case, for having once rejected Presbyterianism, he became a no-churchman, and held for a considerable time that Christ founded no church at all. This position once taken, he could support nothing better than a sort of protean if liberal Christianity, one that questioned and disputed the authority of any and all churches to speak in the name of Christ. If he argued the case more forcefully in later years for leaving the Presbyterians, the reasons given at this point were those which, it seems, honestly decided the matter for him at the time.

His description of a Presbyterian covenant meeting which he attended shortly after he had become a Presbyterian is interesting. The picture he gives us of what he saw is deeply etched in bigotry and intolerance. It is quite credible that he laid the darker tints on a bit too heavily as it was difficult for him to touch any subject lightly. Then, too, zeal may easily become offensive, and there was evidently much misguided zeal in what he saw. What seemingly displeased him most at the meeting was the acceptance by six hundred participants of a program of surveillance among themselves: each one present pledged himself or herself to observe and promote a repressive system of spying upon the others, and to rebuke, admonish, or report them to the Session. Such a program affected him as extremely odious; it cramped all the finer, more genial qualities of the human heart. His "whole life became constrained." "The meeting," he remarked, "was animated by a singular mixture of bigotry, uncharitableness, apparent zeal for God's glory, and a shrewd regard for the interests of this world."[9]

With this as a backdrop, we can now proceed to weigh the reasons he gave for leaving the Presbyterians.

I tried [he said] for a year or two to stifle my discontent, to silence my reason, to repress my natural emotions, to extinguish my natural affections, and to submit patiently to the Calvinistic discipline. I spent much time in prayer and meditation, I read pious books, and finally plunged into my studies with a view of becoming a Presbyterian minister. But it would not do. I had joined the church because I had despaired of myself, and because, despairing of reason, I had wished to submit to authority. If the Presbyterian church had satisfied me that it had authority, was authorized by Almighty God to teach and direct me, I should have continued to submit; but while she exercised the most rigid authority over me, she disclaimed all authority to teach me, and remitted me to the Scriptures and private judgment. . . . While the church refused to take the responsibility of telling me what doctrines I must believe, while she sent me to the Bible and private judgment, she claimed authority to condemn and excommunicate me as a heretic, if I departed from the standard of doctrine contained in her confession.

This I regarded as an unfair treatment. It subjected me to all the disadvantages of authority without any of its advantages. . . . Be one thing or another, said I: either assume the authority and responsibility of teaching me, or leave me with the responsibility of my freedom. If you have authority from God, avow it, and exercise it. I am all submission. I will hold what you say, and do what you bid. If you have not, then say so, and forbear to call me to an account for differing from you, or disregarding your teaching. Either bind me or loose me. Do not mock me with a freedom that is no freedom, or with an authority that is illusory. . . .

My position was a painful one, and I could not endure it. I had gained nothing, but lost much, by joining the Presbyterian church. I had given up the free exercise of my own reason for the sake of an authoritative teacher, and had found no such teacher. I had despaired of finding the truth by my own reason, and had now nothing better, nor so good, because I could not exercise it freely. Certainly I had been too hasty. . . . After all, what reason had I to regard this Presbyterian church as the true church of Christ? "Go not after the New Lights," said my old Congregationalist friend. . . . If Our Lord founded a church and has a church on earth, it must reach back to his time, and come down in unbroken succession from the Apostles. . . .

I was answered that the church of Christ had become corrupt, and been for a series of ages perverted to a papistical and prelatical church, and these men were reformers, and they simply labored to restore the church to its pristine purity and simplicity. But had they a warrant to do that? Or did they act on their own responsibility, without warrant? If you say the former, where is the proof? If you say the latter, how can their act bind me? . . . If they had a right to break from her and set up their private understanding of Scripture, why have I not the right to break from them and the Presbyterian church, follow my private understanding, and set up a church of my own?

It was clear to me that the Presbyterian church, though the church of one class of reformers, was not and could not be the church of Christ, and therefore could have no legitimate authority over me. If Christ had a church on earth which he founded, and which had authority to teach in his name, it is certainly the Catholic Church. But that church, of course, was out of the question. It was everything that was vile, base, odious, and demoralizing. It had been condemned by the judgment of mankind, and the thought of becoming a Catholic found and could find at the time no entrance into my mind. I would sooner have thought of turning Jew, Mahometan [Muhammadan], Gentoo [Hindu], or Buddhist. What, then, was I to do? There was no alternative. . . . Since I cannot be a Catholic, I must be a no-churchman, and deny all churches, and make war on every sect claiming the slightest authority in matters of faith or conscience.

I was at that time about twenty-one years of age. . . . In becoming a Presbyterian on the ground I did, I committed a mistake, and placed myself in a false position, which it took me years to rectify. . . . Not that I was insincere, or governed by bad motives, but because, feeling the insufficiency of my own reason to guide me, I turned my back on reason, and took up with what I supposed to be authority without a rational motive for believing it divinely commissioned. As far as I could, I abnegated my own rational nature, denied reason to make way for revelation, rational conviction to make way for authority.

God gave me reason, I said, in my self-communings. It is my distinguishing faculty, and to abnegate it is to surrender my essential nature as a man, and to sink myself, theoretically, to the level of brute creation. Revelation, if revelation there be, must be made to me as a man, as a rational subject. Take away my reason, and you may as well make a revelation to an ox or a horse, a pig or an ass. It demands reason to receive a revelation, and the natural to receive the supernatural. . . .

I must, then, I continued, revoke the act of surrender which I made of my reason to authority on entering the Presbyterian church; for it was an irrational act. I offered in it no reasonable obedience or submission to God. It was a blind submission, and really no submission of my reason at all. It was a cowardly act, an act of an intellectual desperado, although the motive was good. I reclaim my manhood, and henceforth will, let come what may, be true to reason, and preserve the rights and dignity of my human nature. This resolution, of course, separated me from the Presbyterians.[10]

Brownson tells us further that in joining the Presbyterian Church he had been little concerned about what precise doctrines he was to believe; his real concern was the authority on which he was to believe, or whom he was to obey. Having found reason a wholly inadequate guide, like St. Augustine, his search was for a safe guide in matters of religion. "The important thing with me [he said], from first to last, was, to find out the rule of faith."[11] Yet one Presbyterian doctrine in particular would have caused his rejection of the sect, the doctrine of unconditional election and reprobation. That is, the doctrine that God foreordains the wicked to sin necessarily that he may damn them justly. This doctrine, Brownson wrote, was repugnant to reason, and having settled that Scripture can never contain anything contrary to reason, he rejected the doctrine outright without any thought of investigating whether or not it had any scriptural basis. He did, however, speak about the matter to his pastor, Rev. Reuben Smith. "My pastor," he related, "told me that he regarded that doctrine as a hard doctrine, as revolting to human nature, and he had tried in the General Assembly of the Presbyterian church, to get it modified, or rescinded altogether, but failed by one or two votes."[12]

Theodore Maynard writes that "belief snaps altogether"[13] at this point. He apparently felt that Brownson's memory was at fault. Yet Brownson was here discussing an experience which had left an indelible character on his mind at an impressionable time; further, the experience represents his first contact with organized religion. Deeply religious by nature, he might not easily confuse the details of such a discussion with his pastor. It is of some importance, too, that Brownson had stated this same fact ten years before he wrote *The Convert*. In an article on "The Presbyterian Confession of Faith,"[14] he made the identical statement. It is scarcely thinkable that Brownson would have been careless in any way in setting down such a matter as a definite fact if it were not true.

Indeed, when Brownson published his autobiography in 1857, a general review of it, dealing in particular with his description of the Ballston Spa Presbyterians, appeared in the January issue of the Princeton Review (1858).[15] To all that the reviewer had to say objecting to what Brownson had written, Brownson replied directly: "The facts are as stated in *The Convert*. . . . In regard to the vote on the article or confession touching fore-ordination, the author merely states what his pastor, an old-school Presbyterian, we believe, told him. If the information is incorrect, the fault lies not with him, but with his informant. He never intended to state it as a fact within his own personal knowledge. The reviewer knows better than we what degree of credit is due the statements of a Presbyterian minister."[16]

If the last sentence appears to be a bit churlish on Brownson's part, it is to be observed that he had not found the Presbyterian reviewer overly much the gentleman. In concluding his reply to him, he said: "If the reviewer will leave off personalities, and consent to discuss the questions at issue between him and us, dispassionately, calmly, fairly, on their merits, we shall be happy to meet him again."[17] It is not surprising that there was no second attempt made by the reviewer to meet Brownson's arguments in defense of himself and the Catholic faith.

Per Sveino reminds us that a protracted controversy had broken out between "the Old" and "the New school" Presbyterians already in the 1820s.[18] Nathaniel W. Taylor (1786-1858), professor of theology at the Yale Divinity School (1822-1858), advocated a somewhat modified Calvinism by maintaining that the free will of the sinner is the reason for God's punishment. While he may not have consciously deviated from Calvinist dogma, the church historian, William Warren Sweet, concluded that "the two departures of Taylorism from orthodox Calvinism were its denial that God is the author of sin, and the virtual repudiation of the doctrine of election." Sveino, as it seems to me, correctly concludes that "even in the early 1820's, therefore, Presbyterian congregations and their pastors could not have been completely waterproof to similar doctrinal influences."[19]

One might wonder why Brownson, having become convinced at twenty that truth was with the Catholic Church if any church at all, should have so firmly brushed aside any thought of joining that church. Such an idea could not even enter his head. "I would sooner have thought of turning Jew, Mahometan [Muhammadan], Gentoo [Hindu] or Buddhist," he later wrote. Why? As it appears he had been reared in a rabidly anti-Catholic tradition. He probably had no personal knowledge of Catholics at all; he had never even so much as seen a Catholic church before he was twenty.[20]

Yet it is only in the last issue of *Brownson's Quarterly Review* (October 1875) that he alludes to his early anti-Catholic environment, when he wrote graphically:

> All of us who had the misfortune to be brought up in an exclusively Protestant community, received the impression, as an undoubted fact, that the Catholic church is, and always has been, a persecuting church. . . . We were told that the church was drunk with the blood of the saints, and were admonished against her as the Mystery of Iniquity; and to her were applied all the terrific Biblical denunciations of Babylon. We were told of the reign of "Bloody Queen Mary," and we had the New England primer, in which we had a picture of John Rogers who was burnt at Smithfield, we forget the date of the month, 1555, followed by his wife with nine children and one at her breast.[21]

In spite of such early indoctrination, there is little or nothing malignant in any of Brownson's writings about the Catholic Church during the pre-conversion period of his life. Per Sveino has remarked that despite Brownson's early and general denunciations of "priesthood and priestcraft," he was "surprisingly tolerant of the Catholic church," and "even defended Catholicism."[22] At worst, Brownson at times looked upon the Catholic Church as having done a grand work in the Middle Ages before it had historically outgrown its usefulness. Thus, in this matter, he fared better than John Henry Newman who felt the propriety of abjuring a number of passages in his previous writings at the time of his own conversion.[23]

Having adopted the status of a "no-churchman," as we have noted, Brownson now neither accepted nor rejected the Scriptures outright. If they represented the words of God, obviously they were *in se* infallible, yet infallible only in the sense intended by the Holy Spirit. How did one ascertain that special sense? What was left but the light of one's own reason? If reason, then, was the guide for interpretation, one naturally scouted any authority beyond it, challenged the possibility of inspiration, and, ineluctably passed from a supernaturalist position to that of a rationalist. In an article in his *Review* on "What Reason Can Do" (1855), he spoke of how Calvinism or Presbyterianism had driven him into rationalism: "Calvinism by its exaggerated supernaturalism, by its doctrine of total depravity, and its annihilation of nature for anything good, declaring our best acts done without grace sinful and deserving of eternal damnation, drove us into exaggerated rationalism. Catholicity has redeemed us, and taught us that the supernatural presupposes the natural."[24] His passage at the time from a supernaturalist to a rationalist he called the "first notable change" of his life. He emphasized the religious change less than the fact that it marked, at twenty, the commencment of his intellectual life.[25]

At the same time the young man had been desperately probing for certainty while a Presbyterian, he had also perforce been engaged in providing a livelihood for himself, and in part for his family. Just when he began work in the printshop of James Comstock, and how long he worked there, cannot be determined. In any case, he doubtless gained some valuable knowledge as a printer's assistant — a useful education for the future editor. We know, however, that by the year 1823, Brownson was teaching school in the village of Stillwater, Saratoga County, New York.[26] It is probable that this appointment may have been obtained through his connection with the Presbyterians, and that when he broke with that religious group the appointment was canceled, or had lapsed. Religion and economics were closely related in those days, at least in certain areas. Whatever the exact truth may be, he taught school at Stillwater for one year only.

Perhaps it was Brownson's encounter with the doctrine of total personal depravity that turned his mind in these years to a serious consideration of evil as it was to be found in the current social order. For he began at this time already to rail at the inequalities and inequities of society. Was it not being proclaimed from the tops of houses and mountains that all men are created equal? Why then these glaring differences among the classes of society, the rich and the poor, the high and the low, the learned and the unlearned? Worse yet:

> In one country, rank due to violence, robbery, piracy, successful crimes in peace or war, of some sort, practiced by nearer or remoter ancestors, is worshipped and the crowds throw up their caps and hurrah with all their lungs as it rides or rolls by; in another country, as in our own for instance, titles are not run after indeed, but wealth, more frequently the veriest shadow of wealth, no matter how got or how used, is the real god, the omnipotent Jove, of modern idolatry. The man is nothing without his trappings. Humble virtue is commended in word, for are we not Christians? . . . but disdained, despised, and cast out to die of cold, hunger, and nakedness. Get money, the spirit saith, get rich no matter how, by gambling in stocks, by false pretenses, by extortion, by swindling, by cheating, feeing lawyers, buying up legislators, corrupting incorruptible courts of justice, and you will be great, honored, and followed.[27]

As for himself, he had always been honest, had cultivated his intelligence, had even acquired some learning; an industrious young man, he had wronged no one, and had helped the poor as far as he could. Yet what had those efforts gained him? He could only confess: I am nobody, and if I venture to say anything, the only answer is, he is a poor devil, and has not a red cent in his pocket — heed him not.

When he tried to align all this with the idea of a God of love and justice, he immediately became immersed in waters deep and dark:

> Call you this God's world? To me it is more like the devil's world, in which Ahriman, the prince of darkness, is supreme. If God made it, and is all good and powerful, why does he suffer it to be governed, ruined rather, turned topsy turvy by an enemy whom he could crush, extinguish with a look? Why, if he made all equal, and is equally good to all, does he suffer inequality to prevail everywhere? If he is good, the good itself, and is Maker of heaven and earth and all things therein, visible and invisible, whence comes evil?[28]

Brownson's perplexed words remind a reader of a remarkable passage in Newman's *Apologia*. Newman writes that if he had looked into a mirror and had not seen his own face he would have had the same feeling that came over him when he observed this living, busy world and, far from apprehending a reflection of its Creator, he saw instead the prevalence and intensity of sin, pervasive idolatries, and dreary, hopeless irreligion — all to him a profound mystery "absolutely beyond solution."[29] Unfortunately, there was no one to explain to the young Vermonter the truth of the matter expressed by Newman in his mature years: *"Since* there is a God, the human race is implicated in some terrible aboriginal calamity. It is out of joint with the purposes of its Creator."[30] What Brownson did not seem to understand at the time is that evil is negative rather than positive, the result of the abuse by creatures of free will. Original sin itself was the great primal Pandora's box from which evil has inundated the world. That the mind of Orestes was much engrossed with the problem of evil in these years is further evident from the fact that his diary, kept from 1822-1825, has twenty-four pages of reflections on the Book of Job.[31]

Orestes Brownson had by this time lost whatever of serenity his early youth had known. He had found the world to be of iron, and stern in its blunt reality. Much he saw he knew to be wrong; deep within him smoldered a passion for change, for amelioration. Without sober friend or sound counselor, he was soon to be adrift on a rough sea of speculations. He was to shock and bewilder the so-called orthodox by the logical extremes to which he would boldly, even, perhaps, recklessly push those principles which the comfortable and godly had seldom ever seriously probed. But in the meantime he felt a deep need for a religion of some kind.

# 3

## SAMPLING UNIVERSALISM
## AND A DESCENT INTO AGNOSTICISM

*The various books and persons which inclined Brownson toward Universalism • After becoming a Universalist he struck westward to Detroit with the intention of teaching school • He falls victim to malaria and is confined to his room for well-nigh a year • After his sickness, and with due preparation, he is ordained a Universalist minister • He becomes editor of the* Gospel Advocate and Impartial Investigator, *a Universalist periodical • His reasoning on Universalist doctrine leads to "frightful conclusions" • Afloat on a sea of doubts, he founders into the slough of agnosticism • The arguments for the existence of God "by giants of other days" he finds defective • He calls this period "the winter of his life," but yet sets great store by his experience • He again teaches school at Elbridge, Onondaga County, New York • His marriage to Sally Healy and her influence on him • His doubts of God's existence he settles in a practical fashion • He does not suppress his religious doubts in preaching and writings, and gets into trouble • Passages truly descriptive of his character • His departure from the Universalists.*

To put the matter as clearly and simply as may be, Orestes Brownson left Presbyterianism because, in his view, it had failed miserably to meet his need for an authoritative teacher in matters of religion. He left without an immediate alternative;[1] yet he was not unconscious of a certain personal desolation, an emptiness. "I was unwilling to be an unbeliever," he wrote, "and felt deeply the need of having a religion of some sort."[2] As he was now a no-churchman, and as Universalism is a rather undefined form of what is called "liberal Christianity," his decision now to join that sect is not surprising. It may be remembered that the extreme reaction to Calvinistic Puritanism in New England of the seventeenth and eighteenth centuries had become two-pronged: it had issued on the one hand in Unitarianism via Arminianism, and trailed off, on the other hand, in the direction of Universalism. His first association with Universalism and then later with Unitarianism was a kind of historical rhythm. The similarity in trend of these two sects was expressed by the church historian, William Warren Sweet: "The Unitarians and the Universalists were in fundamental agreement, the Universalists holding that God was too good to damn man; the Unitarians insisting that man was too good to be damned."[3]

Universalism was first preached in this country by John Murray who had migrated from Great Britain in 1770. He had become minister of the First Universalist Congregation in Gloucester, Massachusetts, and eventually pastor of the First Universalist Society in Boston. Yet the real founder of Universalism in the United States, Brownson tells us, was Dr. Elhanan Winchester whose influence on the young Brownson has already been noted. Winchester's endeavor to popularize Universalism was aided by the zeal of a number of other gifted individuals. Dr. Charles Chauncy, son of President Chauncy of Harvard College, and pastor of the First Congregational Church in Boston, contributed his share to its propagation, particularly through his book *The Salvation of All Men Illustrated and Vindicated as a Scripture Doctrine*. The fact that this book was published anonymously in London in 1782 and 1784, may be some evidence that Universalism was making its way only slowly in America. Brownson had also read this book, and seems to have been a bit intrigued by the character of Dr. Charles Chauncy. He relates how vehemently opposed Dr. Charles Chauncy was to George Whitefield, and to the ensuing "enthusiasm" his preaching in this country excited, as well as to episcopacy, which Dr. Chauncy could never tolerate. Whitefield, an Englishman, had been a student at Oxford and a presbyter of the Established Church. He was also one of the original Methodists, and was for a time closely associated with John Wesley. On one of Whitefield's numerous visits to this country, Dr. Chauncy made bold to meet him as he was landing on the wharf of Boston, and taking the Englishman by the hand, said: "Mr. Whitefield, I am sorry you have come to this country. I am sorry to see you here." Replied Whitefield, "No doubt of it, and so is the devil."[4]

Brownson mentioned among others Dr. Joseph Huntington, pastor of the Congregational Church in Coventry, Connecticut, as another propagator of Universalism in the United States. Huntington's book *Calvinism Improved* was familiar to the young American. But Brownson named Hosea Ballou as "the patriarch of American Universalism," and added that at the time that he himself had become a Universalist minister, Ballou "was very nearly its pope." We have already noted that Ballou's teachings were wholly subversive of orthodox Christianity. Indeed, he had given a new trend to Universalism in America, for up to his time and influence "the fathers of modern Universalism," with the single exception of the doctrine of the endless punishment of the wicked, had professed belief in the fundamental mysteries of Christianity, the mysteries of the Trinity, the Incarnation, and the expiatory Atonement. These mysteries Ballou labored to demolish, and in so doing, opened the way for a combination to a large extent of the doctrines of the Universalists with those of the Unitarians. This new turn Ballou gave Universalism influenced Brownson in no small way, and prepared his relatively easy passage from Universalism to Unitarianism.[5]

Having declared himself a Universalist, Brownson struck westward for Detroit, early in the year 1824, with the intention of making his home there. He eventually settled at Springwells, about eleven miles south of Detroit, on the River Rouge, where he again turned to teaching school. Unfortunately, the River Rouge was at the time a spawning bed of virulent malaria, so thick at times that it could be cut with a jackknife, as some put it. The tall, rugged Vermonter became its victim; his condition became so critical that recovery was in doubt. During the latter part of 1824 and a great part of 1825 he was confined to his room, if not to his bed.[6] As an old man he recalled that during this illness a certain Puritan minister came "with unutterable groanings" to visit him. "Not a word of the love and mercy of God had he to say, but talked to us of hell and brimstone, till we could bear it no longer, and were forced to bid him, 'Begone, and suffer us to die in peace.' "[7] Brownson, of course, recovered fully. During this confinement he had devoted himself to the reading of the Scriptures, and such Universalist publications as were available.[8]

Whether it was due to the sobering effects of his illness, or to his assiduous reading of the Scriptures and the Universalist publications, or to both, he now decided, upon his recovery in the fall of 1825, to become a Universalist minister. Accordingly, he applied at once to the Universalist Convention, which met that year at Hartland, Vermont, for a letter of fellowship as a preacher. Upon the receipt of the document, he returned to his native state, and began preaching on Sundays while he otherwise continued his studies preparatory to his ordination as an evangelist. On June 18, 1826, he was "set apart to the work of the ministry by public solemn ordination," at a meeting of the New Hampshire Universalist Association, held that year at Jaffrey, New Hampshire. He was twenty-two.[9]

Brownson's three-year career as a Universalist minister allowed him the double theater of preacher and writer. Brief early efforts in New Hampshire and Vermont prefaced a return in October of 1826 to New York State where he continued his work at such places as Fort Ann and Whitehall. He expanded his activity to Litchfield, in Harkimer County, and then spent a year at Ithaca, a few months in Geneva, and the following year at Auburn.[10] At Ithaca (1828) he wrote a number of articles for *The Gospel Advocate and Impartial Investigator,* a semimonthly publication which, Brownson states, was the most influential Universalist periodical in the country. Its popularity was gained, however, not so much by its advocacy of Universalism as by its opposition to the movement of the Presbyterian and evangelical sects to stop the Sunday mails and to gain a controlling position in national politics.[11] As Hugh Marshall has observed, "In his opposition to the subtle 'establishment of religion,' Brownson stood firmly on the principle of separation of church and state. This marked his first concern for political matters."[12] At the end of the year the editor of the *Gospel Advocate,* Rev. L. S. Everett, moved to Charlestown, Massachusetts, and was succeeded by a former contributor, Orestes A. Brownson, both as editor of the journal and as pastor of the Universalist Congregation at Auburn. Thus began a long and remarkable career of editorship. Of his role as editor of *The Gospel Advocate* he said: "I conducted it for a year, but with more credit to my free, bold, and crude thinking, than to my piety or orthodoxy even as a Universalist. It is a confused medley of thoughts and the germs of nearly all I subsequently held or published till my conversion to the Catholic Church."[13]

At the commencement of his ministerial career, Brownson tried to smother his doubts about divine revelation, but with minimal success. His difficulty was that his ground afforded him no validation of the Bible as a supernatural message to mankind. Upon what authority could infallible assurance be given that the Bible is the word of God? The book, he said, does not validate itself. Granted that the Bible is the word of God, there is the added question: how does one know that he understands it correctly, that is, in the sense intended by the Holy Spirit? A false reading interdicts the word of God. Moreover, the biblical doctrine of "endless vindictive punishment"[14] (as he then understood it) appeared to him a violation of reason. And he could accept no statement that appeared to contradict reason. He admitted that if he had an infallible authority to assure him that such a doctrine is not contrary to reason, the difficulty for him would vanish. But he had reason only by which to judge. He wrote:

> I may believe on competent authority that a doctrine is reasonable, although I do not see its reasonableness; but I cannot, if I try, believe what appears to me unreasonable, on the authority of reason alone. To say that you believe a thing unreasonable is to say that you do not believe it, and that you reject it. Belief always is and must be a reasonable act; in it reason assents, mediately or immediately, to the proposition that it is true. Where that assent

is wanting, belief cannot be predicated. It is a contradiction in terms to say that you believe what you hold to be unreasonable. . . . The Bible, then, without an infallible authority to assert it and deduce its sense, can never be authority sufficient for believing a doctrine to be reasonable, when that reasonableness is not apparent to the understanding. By rejecting the authority of the church as the witness of revelation and the judge of its meaning, I found myself obliged, therefore, to reject, in turn, the authority of the Scriptures.[15]

Although he still paid a certain reverence to the Scriptures in what did not seem to conflict with reason, and even to accept in them what is accounted over and above reason, yet with only reason as a guide, Brownson was eventually led to deny the divinity of Christ, and all belief in future rewards and punishments. His close reasonings on the distinctive doctrines of Universalism issued ultimately in "frightful conclusions" against which his better feelings rebelled, although, indeed, he knew that they "followed logically" from the premises in the case. He summed up sadly: "Thus, I had, following reason, lost the Bible, lost my Savior, lost Providence, lost reason itself, and had left to me only my five senses, and what could fall under their observation: that is, reduced myself to a mere animal."[16]

As a Universalist he had to argue that Jesus saves neither from sin nor its punishment; he was disposed to regard Christian teachings about the Savior as superstitious notions that should be combated. "My Universalism made me," he explained, "so far as logic can go, not only non-Christian but anti-Christian. This was my reasoning at the time, not merely my reasoning now."[17]

There was, however, one particular distinctive Universalist doctrine that undercut for him any possible adherence to Universalism. While endeavoring to combat the scriptural doctrine of future rewards and punishments and to maintain the final salvation of all men, he had finally become convinced that the Scriptures, if interpreted according to their obvious sense, could never be made to teach such a doctrine, no matter by whom twisted or pummeled. Upon close examination he was now satisfied that the arguments which had been used against the adversaries of this particular Universalist doctrine could not stand the incisive test of enlightened criticism — their arguments were in fact "more specious than conclusive." Indeed, if Judas, Pilate and Herod were to receive a crown of life equally bright with that of Peter, James and John, then virtue shall have lost all its meaning, and we are left with a doctrine utterly subversive of all morality.[18]

But things rapidly worsened with him as a Universalist minister. Apparently in the early part of that career he had begun to dig a little more deeply into theology, as he read some of the reputed masters. The result was that while he did not say "there is no God," neither did he say "there is a God."[19] For a brief period he became something of an agnostic. Was his case that of the libertine anxious to avoid the restraints of religion, or might the experience be explained otherwise? Was he still the sincere, earnest seeker after truth? The great increase of professed atheists in our own times invests the matter with renewed interest. As the Second Vatican Council has said in its *Constitution on the Church in the Modern World:* "Atheism must be accounted among the most serious problems of the age, and is deserving of closer examination."[20] Brownson himself was to write a formidable treatise later in life dealing with this same problem under the title *An Essay in Refutation of Atheism.*[21]

But his difficulty at this time was that, rightly or wrongly, he found the arguments for the existence of God as presented by the "giants of other days" defective. The argument from design in particular, he found inconclusive. It will, he said, confirm him who is already a believer, but it will not convince the atheist. John Henry Newman seems to have been in substantial agreement with Brownson on this point. Replying to a critic of his *An Essay in Aid of a Grammar of Assent,* April 13, 1870, Newman said:

> I have not insisted on the argument from *design,* because I am writing for the 19th century, by which, as represented by its philosophers, design is not admitted as proved. And to tell the truth, though I should not wish to preach on the subject, for 40 years I have been unable to see the logical force of the argument myself. I believe in design because I believe in God; not in God because I see design.[22]

Speaking in general of his problem concerning the existence of God, Brownson wrote:

> I can read Clark, Tillotson, Locke, Paley and other giants of other days, and still doubt the existence of God. To me they all seem to have failed to meet the difficulties in the case, and to have taken for granted the very points they should have proved. All I ever read on this subject but increased my doubts, and plunged me deeper and deeper into scepticism.[23]

But again, like Newman, he appealed to his own conscience as an affirmation of the existence of God in one of the more beautiful passages he has written:

> My own experience must count for something for myself. Theology has been to me something more than mere speculation. It engrossed my infant mind. It is connected with all I remember of my early visions, and entwined with all the endearing associations of childhood and youth. When reason first awoke, while thought was unfledged it was to be a subject of deep and cherished feeling. In the early dawn of youth, there was nothing I so much dreaded as that which should divert my thoughts from the Deity, and interrupt my silent but blissful intercourse of soul with the Father of our spirits. I loved the night, for it seemed to shadow him forth and give him a local habitation. I frequented the deep solitude of the forest, I clomb the cragged mountain, stood upon its huge cliffs; I gazed upon nature in her wildest and most fitful moods; for in the lone, wild, grand, sublime scenery around me, I seemed to trace his work, and to feel his spirit reigning, in silent, but now unacknowledged majesty. I was never alone. I felt the Deity was with me. I loved his presence. A consciousness of it created my joy and waked my holier and better feelings. Those were hallowed days! Their memory is deep graven on my heart. As I view them mellowed by time and distance, it is with emotion I say to myself, "They are gone!"
>
> Such was the state of my young affections; such the religious feelings of my childhood and youth. They were not learned from books; they were not produced by human teachers. They were the simple feelings of nature, the child led by instinct to seek the embrace of its parent. But as soon as I entered the school of theology, and began to take my religion from books, I began to doubt. The more I read the stronger grew my scepticism. Inclination, interest, early habit, and even a lively sensibility to devotion, struggled against it in vain. I stood upon the precipice. I looked down the abyss of atheism, ready to take the awful plunge.
>
> I look back with startling horror, upon that eclipse of the soul, that midnight of reason, from which I am but just recovered. Still, my doubts were first awakened by reading Paley's Natural Theology.[24]

Yet he did not seem disposed at this time to allow the full cogency of the various arguments constructed from external nature for the existence of God. On the contrary, he attached more importance to the argument from the voice of conscience as evidence of a Lawgiver and Supreme Ruler. After speaking of what he considered the need of meeting the atheist on other than traditional grounds (to which he hoped in due time to turn his attention), he said:

> For the present, I can only say, the atheist who looks only at external nature for proofs of a God will probably look in vain; but, if he will turn his mind inward and converse with his own spiritual nature, he will hear the still, small, but clear and convincing voice of God to the inner man. I have thus a witness, and having this witness, I can find its testimony corroborated by the whole of external nature. I forgot the spirit, looked only at the flesh, and this witness was unheeded. It was therefore I doubted. I have turned my thoughts inward; I heard the voice of God, I believed — I felt myself again locked in the embrace of my Father.[25]

It was the voice of conscience that Newman, too, used as the great foundation stone for the existence of God in his elaborate apologetic treatise entitled *An Essay in Aid of a Grammar of Assent.*[26]

Of course the cry "infidel" was soon raised against Brownson. But it is possible that all in his case happened quite innocently enough. Newman tells us in his *Apologia* that even two or three years before he had become a Catholic he had come to the conclusion — a thought he felt had been in his mind a long time — "that there is no medium, in true philosophy, between atheism and Catholicity, that a perfectly consistent mind, under those circumstances in which it finds itself here below, must embrace either the one or the other." He went on to say: "There [are] but two alternatives, the way to Rome, and the way to atheism; Anglicanism is the halfway house on the one side, and liberalism [religious] is the halfway house on the other."[27] The young Orestes, at the time of which we write, was a disciple of liberalism, and it was never in his nature to stop at halfway houses. But with what shock and horror he saw himself swept toward the undertow of atheism, we may gather from a passage in his *Charles Elwood* (the complete title is *Charles Elwood: Or the Infidel Converted*):

> Bitter the day when for the first time we look up into the heavens, and see no spirit shining there, over the rich and flowering earth and see no spirit blooming there, abroad over the world of silent, senseless matter, and feel we are — alone. I shall never forget the day; and I have no doubt that I shall see all the objects of sense, one after another, fade away and lose themselves in the darkness of death, with far less shrinking of soul, than I saw my childhood's faith depart, and felt the terrible conviction fastening itself upon me that all must go — God, Christ, immortality, that which my fathers had believed, for which they toiled, lived, suffered, and died — all, all even to the last and dearest article must vanish and be to me henceforth but as a dream which cannot be recalled.[28]

Quite understandably was Brownson to call this episode "the winter of his life."[29] And yet he evidently counted it an experience that had enriched him in its own way. Perhaps it had for him something of the *"felix culpa"* in it. Speaking about his eventual passage from "infidelity to an unwavering belief in God and the supernatural origin of Christianity," he said, in the words of *Charles Elwood:*

In looking back on the long struggle I have had, I must thank God for it. I have been reproached by my Christian brethren; they have tried to make me believe that I was very wicked in being an unbeliever; but I have never reproached myself for being one, nor have I regretted it. I would consent to go through the whole again, rather than not have the spiritual experience I have acquired. I have sinned, but never in having doubted; I have much to answer for, but not for having been an unbeliever. I have no apology to make to the Christian world. I have no forgiveness to ask of it. I have done it no disservice, and it will one day see that I have not been an unprofitable servant. It has never fairly owned me, but I care not for that. Even to this day it calls me an infidel, but that is nothing. . . . I have not lived in vain, nor in vain have I doubted, inquired, and finally been converted. When the scales fell from my eyes and I beheld the light, I followed it: and I have done what was in my power to direct others to it. . . . I say not this in a spirit of vain boasting, but in humble confidence. I say it to express my strong faith in God, and his care for all who attempt to do his will.[30]

It was paradoxical that while he had lost himself in dark agnostic caves, he not infrequently surprised himself by uttering a prayer to God for light and guidance.[31] The difficulties he could not resolve were merely intellectual. There seems to be much truth in what a critic remarked when reviewing Brownson's *Early Life* in *The Nation:* "Apparently his infidelity . . . was much grosser in others' apprehension and in his own than in reality."[32] Whatever the difficulties, he resolved them on practical grounds. Inasmuch as religion is found to have been coeval and coextensive with the human race, it is, he reasoned, either natural to man, or it was originally imposed by a superior power. If it is natural to man, it was folly to fight against it; if it is of supernatural origin and so imposed by a superior power, it is man's duty to accept it. Judging the Christian religion to be the best known to the world, it seemed to him altogether in accordance with reason to accept it. He did not for the moment concern himself as to what precisely might be the authentic form of Christianity — the drowning man seldom tests the buoyancy of straw. Having advanced thus far, his doubts about the existence of God were forever at an end, and he seemed disposed to accept the supernatural origin of the Christian religion.[33]

But he realized, too, that he had not yet obtained a scientific solution to his former doubts. The situation, however, did not disturb him unduly, for he somehow felt certain that such proof must be possible. Characteristically, he wished to come by that secret more for the sake of others than for himself. For he thought that by proclaiming it to the world he might do immense good in saving others from atheism. Little as he cared at the time for philosophy, at which, in fact, he had been accustomed to sneer, he now assumed that the scientific answer to his difficulties must be found somewhere in its mazes. Thus he soon plunged impetuously into metaphysical studies, the early gleanings of which he used to construct his argument for the existence of God in his *Charles Elwood.*[34]

Speaking of the method by which Brownson worked his way up again to the high plateau of a firm belief in God, his son Henry tells us that "there was an influence operating on him which was not that of his own reasoning, and that from that time his downward course ceased."[35] What that influence was, Henry Brownson gives no hint. It seems reasonable to suggest that, in part, at least, a salutary yet silent force may have been Sally Healy.

After Brownson had returned to New York State in the fall of 1825 following his brief period of teaching school in Detroit, he again taught school "for a few months" at Elbridge, Onondaga County, New York. This, it would appear, was during the year 1826-1827. Among his pupils were the two daughters of John Healy, a prosperous farmer of the district. The custom in those days was that the schoolteacher became a guest in the homes of families of the pupils. Brownson was a guest for a time in the Healy household. A lifelong friendship soon developed between Brownson and John Healy; it was to the second daughter of John Healy and Dolly Rude, Sally Healy, that Orestes Brownson was married at Elbridge, June 19, 1827. Born at Elbridge on January 17, 1804, Sally was just a few months younger than Orestes, and was cousin to the Hon. John P. Healy, the law partner of Daniel Webster.[36]

In Henry Brownson's description she was a tall, dark-eyed girl with regular, refined features. Her education was above that common in rural districts of the time, and showed itself in her great fondness for reading, especially in the Bible, history and poetry. She was gifted with an extremely retentive memory, and had learned by heart large passages of Milton, Dryden, Young, Thompson and Watts. She could quote accurately any text she wished to use as an argument or as an illustration in conversation, and was exact in dates and facts she had once learned.[37] But from all we can learn of Sally Healy — we get only glimpses of her in the shadowy background of her husband — these matters are only secondary to a singular nobility of character. One of the greatest blessings Providence ever bestowed on Orestes Brownson was his wife. Of his mother Henry Brownson writes: "Her dignity consisted in being unknown to the world; her glory the esteem of her husband; her pleasure the happiness of her family."[38]

They were married almost precisely one year (June 19, 1827) after Brownson had become a Universalist minister, June 15, 1826. This was the time when Orestes was foundering in the slough of agnosticism. When, therefore, his son Henry tells us that "there was another influence" operating on him besides his reasonings in his efforts to extricate himself from the quagmire of unbelief into which he had fallen, an oblique reference to Sally Healy is easily seen. The angelic creature Elizabeth in *Charles Elwood* (which details his own religious experience) must in some sort of way represent Sally Healy and her influence over Brownson. One passage in particular is significant:

> "O, there is a God," spoken by the sweet lips of eighteen, by her we love and hope in a few days to call our own by the most intimate and sacred ties — it goes well nigh to melt even the atheist. It comes to us as the voice from another world, and wins the heart though it fail to convince the understanding. It is no easy thing to be an atheist when one loves, and is in the presence of the one he loves, and hears her, in the simple, confiding tones of the child, exclaim, "O, there is a God." For a moment I gazed on the beautiful being before me, as upon one inspired. Could I see her, hear her, love her with all my heart, and not believe in the divinity? She seemed sent from a fairer world, to bear witness to the reality of brighter beings than the dull inhabitants of earth.[39]

Brownson asserted that he had written *Charles Elwood* for the very purpose of showing the insufficiency of logic to meet the wants of the soul, or to effect any real change in one's faith. In the narrative there is a subtler influence than logic at work on the infidel, namely, that of love. And had not untoward circumstances separated Charles from Elizabeth, she would no doubt have reconciled him to the Christian faith.

> As a general rule [said Brownson], would you gain the reason you must first win the heart. That is the secret of most conversions. There is no logic like

41

love. And by-the-by, I believe that the heart is not only often stronger than the head, but in general is a safer guide to truth. At any rate, I have not found it difficult to assign plenty of good reasons for doing what my heart prompted me to do.[40]

The mute but uplifting influence of Sally Healy during Brownson's agnostic days is further confirmed by what Henry Brownson tells concerning this matter:

> One of her greatest sorrows was the unchristian character of her husband's writings and speeches assumed a few years after their marriage. She had been taught the so-called orthodox faith and was a devout believer in it; but she knew it was hopeless to try to bring her husband back to his belief by attempting to argue the matter with him. She could only wait and pray, patiently and hopefully.[41]

Although this period of agnosticism occurred during his career as a Universalist minister,[42] he did not give a public account of it until after he had regained a firm belief in the existence of God. *The Philanthropist*, February 14, 1832, carried the story.[43] Belief in divine revelation, however, in any orthodox sense, he did not regain for many years to come.

It was his lack of belief in divine revelation that was to work much mischief for him while a Universalist minister. In such a state of mind, how could he as an honest man present himself before the public as a Christian minister? What to do in the circumstances? Where to turn? In the meantime, however, he neither wrote nor spoke differently from what he thought and felt. But that candor would not do. He could not endure seeming to be what he was not. To continue the role of a Christian minister while he no longer believed as a Christian only increased his irritation at himself — both heart and brain demanded more. Although he was beginning to acquire a prominent place among the Universalists, he now began to consider leaving them. And the moment he was to cut his connection with them, he felt his manhood restored to him, his mind began to recover its balance, and the tone of his feelings toward Christianity changed.[44]

But a few months before he parted company with the Universalists he framed and published "half in mockery, but at bottom in sober earnest" a five-point formulary called "My Creed." It ran:

> Art. I. I BELIEVE that every individual of the human family should be *honest*.
> Art. II. I BELIEVE that every one should be BENEVOLENT and KIND to all.
> Art. III. I BELIEVE that every one should use his best endeavors to procure food, clothing and shelter for himself, and labor to enable others to procure the same to the extent of his ability.
> Art. IV. I BELIEVE that every one should cultivate his mental powers, that he may open to himself a new source of enjoyment, and also be enabled to aid his brethren in their attempts to improve the condition of the human race, and to increase the sum of human happiness.
> Art. V. I BELIEVE that if mankind act on these principles they serve God all they can serve him, that he who has this faith and conforms the nearest to what it enjoins, is the most acceptable to God.
> This, O! ye who accuse me of infidelity, is my creed — read it, obey it, and never again tell me that I am a disbeliever. . . . Now, ye doctors of divinity, hurl your anathemas. Let every one be *honest*.[45]

There is surely nothing especially captivating or prophetic in this creed. Yet, for all its youthful bombast, it merits citation since it reveals the dominant motives which were fuel to his dynamic activities in the years ahead. As far as the present was concerned, it was Article I that was loaded with meaning, if not dynamite: "I BELIEVE that every individual of the human family should be *honest*."

This first article or rule of life was a direct criticism of his brother ministers. When Brownson had entered the Universalist ministry it was as an apostle of liberal inquiry: he invariably spoke his mind plainly, doubts and all. (He was in this case, as he was to be all his life, a plain, blunt, utterly sincere man — some might say that he carried the virtue to the edge of fault.) Quite understandably, and rightly so, some of his fellow ministers deplored this airing of his doubts, even though, as he knew from confidential interviews, there were those who believed not a whit more than he did. They censured him, not precisely because of the doubts he entertained, but because he did not conceal them.[46] Here began a series of lectures to him on prudence, expediency, inopportunism that were to plague him to the end of his life. The growth of years and the concomitant accumulation of pious lectures finally led to some of the more memorable passages in his autobiography. These passages, written in 1857, are a clear index to the whole character of the man. At their writing he may have been smarting from some recent repetitive lectures, but the early strictures of his Universalist brethren seem to have been the source of his ire. He wrote:

> Prudence is a virtue, and rashness is a sin, but my own reason and experience have taught me that truth is a far more trustworthy support than the best-devised scheme of human policy possible. Honesty is the best policy. Be honest with thyself, be honest with the world, be true to thy convictions, be faithful to what truth thou hast, be it ever so little, and never dream of supplying its defect by thy astuteness or craft. Certainly be so if thou believest in a God who is truth itself, and with whom it is impossible to lie. . . . It is comparatively easy to know what is true, what is virtuous; but what, aside from fidelity to truth and virtue is wise policy, or genuine prudence, surpasses the wit of man to say.[47] Never yet has a great man arisen without seeming, to even great and good men in church and state as well as to the wise and prudent men of the world, terribly rash, shockingly imprudent. No one can be a man, and do a man's work, unless he is sincere, unless he is in earnest, terribly in earnest, throwing his whole heart and soul into his work; and whoever does so, may depend upon it that the chief men of his sect, his party, or his school, if not of his church, will be alarmed at his conduct, will accuse him of being ultra, of going too far, of endangering everything by his rashness, his want of prudence, of policy. I am not a saint, and never was, and never shall be a saint.[48] I am not, and never shall be, a great man; but I always had, and I trust I always shall have the honor of being regarded by my friends and associates as impolitic, as rash, imprudent, and impracticable. I was and am, in my natural disposition, frank, truthful, straightforward, earnest; and therefore have had, and, I doubt not, shall carry to the grave with me, the reputation of being reckless, ultra, a well-meaning man, perhaps an able man, but so fond of paradoxes and extremes that he cannot be relied on, and more likely to injure than serve the cause he espouses.[49]

After acknowledging that his personal blunders had been committed only when he had tried the easy tread of the politic, and had prided himself on being the diplomatic Brownson, he urged his countrymen in 1857 (and this seems a rebuke and an admonition addressed to Catholics in particular) to stand firmly by the man who has had the courage to speak clear truth as he saw it:

> If what a man says is true, and it is evidently said with an honest intention, do not decry him, do not disown him, do not beat the life out of him by lectures on prudence: stand by him, and bear with him the odium he may incur by telling the truth, encourage him by your respect for his honesty and candor, and shelter him, as far as in your power, from reproaches of weak and timid brethren; for be assured we live in an age and country where honesty and candor, fidelity to one's honest convictions, and the moral courage in avowing them, are not virtues likely to become excessive. Fidelity to what one believes to be true, moral courage in adhering to our convictions before the world, is the greatest want of our times. The age lacks above all sincerity, earnestness. Give us back the old-fashioned loyalty of heart, and we shall not need to labor long to bring the age to see, own, and obey the truth. The subjective heresy of the age is a far greater obstacle to its conversion than its objective errors. What most men lack is principle, is the feeling that they should be true to the right; and that to be manly is to be ready to follow the truth under whatever guise it may come, to whatever it may lead, to the loss of reputation, to poverty, to beggary, to the dungeon or the scaffold, to the stake or to exile.[50]

What good, then, was accomplished by his own honesty of thought and expression as a Universalist minister? He does not hesitate to affirm that his "honest avowal of unbelief was, under the circumstances, a step that brought me nearer to the kingdom of God."

> Give me rather [he said], the open, honest unbeliever, who pretends to believe nothing more than he does believe, than your sleek, canting hypocrite, who rolls up his eyes in holy horror of unbelief, and makes a parade of his orthodoxy, when he believes not a word of the Gospel, and has a heart which is a cage of unclean beasts, out of which more devils need to be cast than were cast out of Magdalen. The former may never see God, but the latter deserves the lowest place in hell. There is hope of the conversion of a nation of unbelievers; of the conversion of a nation of hypocrites none.[51]

As from a mirror, these passages reflect the real character of Orestes Brownson — more so than anything else he ever wrote. That character, like every character, was an ensemble of traits. But among them all, no trait stood out more prominently than his absolute honesty. Men might carp at his inopportunism, or might dislike the ardor of his temperament, but no man dared impeach his honesty, at least not with any show of reason. With those who knew him, his honesty was beyond all question. This trait was well-demonstrated in the many fierce and protracted battles of intellect in which he was engaged during his long public career. Never, even in the heat, smoke and fog of battle, did he yield to the temptation of taking an unfair advantage, nor did he ever forget that truth and justice were the stones of his quarry. To few men can the line of Alexander Pope be more meaningfully applied: "An honest man's the noblest work of God."[52]

Brownson followed the publication of his five-point "Creed" with an eight-point manifesto called a "Gospel Creed." Its purpose was to gratify the wish of a class of his readers who needed a clarification of his Christian beliefs, especially as he came more and more into disrepute with his Universalist brethren. Although the persuasiveness of his arguments against hell-fire had at first made him popular among his coreligionists, the startling boldness of his speculations on other matters of religion, particularly his questioning of the Bible on rational grounds, not only as to its interpretation, but, more basically, as to its acceptance or rejection, increased others' distrust and even brought against him the charge of deism. In his "Gospel Creed" he made clear enough his divergence from Universalist doctrine; among other things, he said: "Though my heaven has not as much immediate felicity as the Universalist supposes, neither has it the misery of the orthodox hell. I do not like the notion of teaching men they may sin all their lives and be equally happy at death with the most virtuous."[53]

What is perhaps more significant in his "Gospel Creed" at this juncture is his declaration that "Jesus of Nazareth [is] the greatest and best reformer ever vouched us by heaven."[54] All kinds of social theories were beginning at this time to swirl in his head. The glaring social inequalities he saw everywhere jolted him and turned his mind more and more to the problem of reform. He thus began that penetrating analysis of economic factors which he was to bring to greater perfection in his later writings. In an article on "Equality" he wrote: "It will be found the more the laborer produces the poorer he grows. This seems a hard case, that plenty should increase poverty, a surplus should produce want. Yet it is so. The inequality which exists tends to perpetuate and increase itself."[55] A lack of an immediate and effective remedy presaged a class warfare he foresaw and dreaded.

Whatever the difference of opinion Brownson had experienced with his Universalist brethren, he did deeply enjoy his editorship of the *Gospel Advocate* during the years 1828-1829. The work afforded him an easy outlet to his immensely active and inquiring mind. He had come to know something of the exhilaration that comes from reaching so many minds through the printed word, and the concomitant brisk interchange of ideas. But even if he had continued as a Universalist minister, this opportunity would have been lost to him. For, precisely at this time, the proprietor and publisher of the *Gospel Advocate,* Ulysses F. Doubleday, was negotiating for its sale and consolidation with the *Evangelical Magazine,* published at Utica, New York, by Dolphus Skinner.[56] Brownson accompanied Doubleday to Utica and was present when the sale was closed, September 1829. From Utica he went to Boston where he spent some weeks. At Boston he visited the "patriarch of American Universalism," Hosea Ballou, who had a large congregation in the city. Brownson preached to Ballou's congregation on Sunday, both in the morning and in the evening; ". . . in the evening," he said, "to the largest congregation of people to which I have ever spoken."[57] These events climaxed his career as a Universalist minister.

Brownson's statement in *The Convert* that he left the Universalists only after having gained "a prominent position" among them seems to imply that he left them amicably enough.[58] Yet his various accounts of the matter render that judgment uncertain. In 1845, twelve years before he wrote *The Convert,* he said: "We ourselves, many years ago, were excommunicated, without even a hearing or a notice, by the Universalists, for having embraced views not quite in harmony with theirs."[59] The certainty in the case is that near the end of 1829 he left Universalism behind. He well knew that the trend of his thought did not entitle him to tarry any longer; his Universalist brethren no doubt concurred.

A letter has recently come to light in which Brownson not only summarily relates his experiences with the Universalists, but also tells us how he fell in with skeptics and turned to world reform. It will serve as an appropriate conclusion to this chapter and an introduction to the next. It was written to the Rev. Bernard Whitman, June 13, 1841, who later became editor of *The Unitarian.* Speaking of the Universalists, Brownson wrote:

I united with them in 1826, became a preacher among them and for a time a writer and editor. But I was disappointed. I did not find that brotherly love I longed for; I did not witness that salutary moral influence of their doctrine neither on myself nor others I wished. Some of them treated me harshly; I felt a sense of injury. I fell in with some skeptics. My own mind was predisposed to hear them favorably. I read, I thought, I doubted. But as I struggled with my doubts and was doing all I could to overcome them I fell in with a clergyman of my own ardor who solicited me to embark with him on an enterprise infidel in character. He assured me nearly all of the prominent Universalist preachers were skeptics or deists. He was my most valued friend. . . . He had the offer of a good salary to continue as a preacher. He accepted — left me to get rid of my skepticism as I could. I struggled for one year to suppress it in my own mind and in the minds of others but could not. The religious part of the community shunned me, and I found no sympathy but with skeptics. I heard Miss Wright lecture, and finally became a corresponding editor of The Free Enquirer. I remained there but a short time. I now had a chance to look around on skepticism, and being among its friends I saw its deficiency. I liked many of the reforms they proposed and was particularly pleased with the principles of the party known as the Workingmen.[60]

# 4

## TURNED WORLD REFORMER

*Universalism having left him with no reason to concern himself
about man's felicity in the life beyond, Brownson now turned totally
to mundane reform • Three social reformers engage his attention:
Robert Owen, William Godwin and Frances Wright • His practical
but brief collaboration with Frances Wright and the other Free Enquirers in promoting the cause of the Workingmen's party in New
York • The humanitarian side of their program appealed to him •
He becomes editor of the Genesee Republican and Herald of Reform in
support of the Workingmen's party • The reasons why he left the
Workingmen's party • He comes to realize that only religion can
furnish the motives necessary for effecting the needed reforms •
Some sobering thoughts on efforts at world reform and his innocent
incursion into practical politics.*

Disenchanted with Universalism, Orestes Brownson now turned to mundane reform. He had rejected Universalism not only for its false theology, as
he saw it, but also because it could provide him with no real mission in life.
He had never sought truth for its mere apprehension or barren contemplation, but that above all, he might bring its use to some moral or practical
end. Whether or not he would agree with Newman that knowledge is an end
in itself, he sought truth as a practical solvent. In this respect, as he thought,
Universalism had failed him badly. The only practical message he could extract from Universalism was Epicurean: "Let us eat, drink and be merry,
for tomorrow I die, and go — to heaven."[1] For if the salvation of all men was
just as certain without his labors as it was with them, evidently then man's
labors were of little use to his ultimate destiny. Universalism lacked the
power to engage Brownson's practical energies.

It was this same chilling defect in the philosophy of Victor Cousin that he
was to lament so deeply later. To adhere to Cousin's rationalistic pantheism,
he said, would cause us to "fall into a state of absolute indifferency, smoke
our pipe, and say, 'God is great, and what is written will be.' "[2] Against such
a doctrinal defect in religion or philosophy, his soul shouted its protest. Few
men perhaps have lived whose spirit clamored more ardently for some real
mission in life, some appointed work to do, than that of Orestes Brownson.
After Brownson's *alter ego,* Charles Elwood, had turned world reformer,
he said: "Now I had a purpose, an end, an aim — a future, and begin to live
again. No more whimpering, no more sickly sentimentalism; I was a man
now, and had a man's work to do."[3]

Frustrated, then, by the lack of a stronger religious faith from putting
forth thought and effort for the happiness of his fellowmen in a life beyond,
he now resolved to labor earnestly instead for the promotion of the virtue
and happiness of his fellowmen in this world. This by no means satisfied him,
but it was the only alternative left him. The hope of heaven having disappeared with the fear of hell, he now wished to see what he could do for the

amelioration of the plight of his fellowmen here and now.[4] And in that direction certain events in the country were at the time drawing his attention.

Shortly before he had become a Universalist minister (1826), Robert Owen had arrived in America from New Lanark, Scotland. A social reformer, he had been for a quarter of a century the dominant partner and sole manager of the cotton mills of New Lanark, with 1400 to 1500 employees, the largest such establishment in the British Isles. His new system of the management of these cotton mills had brought such decided improvement in the way of cleanliness, order, thrift and the physical comfort of the workers that Owen, deeply convinced that he had a messianic destiny, felt that his methods were not only exportable, but would prove a general benefit to mankind. He had first attempted to interest the statesmen of Europe in his scheme, but without success. In England, however, the movement was by no means without results. H. S. Foxwell writes that "intellectually, perhaps, the Owenite movement was most brilliant and interesting in 1825; but it was in the full tide of its activity for nearly twenty years after that date."[5] It was, therefore, at the very time when his movement was the "most brilliant and interesting" that Robert Owen had come to this country (1825) and laid his plans for social reform before the President, the Congress, and the American people. A man of philanthropic spirit and noble aims, he had at once gained a respectful hearing. Some who listened were completely captivated by his Utopian dreams, and he succeeded in gathering about him an enthusiastic band, some from abroad and some citizens of this country. With these in 1825 he made a settlement in Posey County, Indiana, and called the place "New Harmony." It was provisional in nature, and looked to the later introduction of his complete plan for a communitarian life. It was socialistic in form or might be called inchoate communism.[6]

Although some sixteen communities, either avowedly Owenite or influenced considerably by Owenite ideas, were established in the United States, New Harmony on the banks of the Wabash River was the sun to these lesser planets. In it Robert Owen had put practically the whole of his large fortune. According to J. F. C. Harrison he bought the town from the Rappites for $125,000 and the additional expenditures brought the total price to $200,000. For this money he acquired 20,000 acres of land and the entire village with its houses, churches, four mills, a textile factory, distilleries and brewery, a tanning yard and mechanics' shops. Two thousand acres were already under cultivation, and there were large vineyards and orchards. It seemed a very inviting site for the experiment Owen contemplated, and so, as the former possessors moved out, some nine hundred enthusiastic adventurers moved in, in response to Owen's widespread invitation to "the industrious and well disposed of all nations."[7]

Owen now endeavored to put into operation at this settlement in the New World the results of the experiments he had made in New Lanark. At New Lanark Owen had been very much impressed with the work of Philipp Emanuel von Fellenberg in Hofwyl, near Bern, Switzerland, and had introduced schools there modeled to a degree after those of Fellenberg's. Owen deeply believed in the dynamic role of education in the formation of the child's character. He had established at New Lanark infant schools and in 1816 the Institute for the Formation of Character which had drawn enthusiastic encomiums from a steady stream of visitors. His enthusiasm for gathering children into his school from their earliest years was part of his plan for separating them from parental influence and maximizing the effects of what he considered beneficent environment. His new view of society (expressed in his book, *A New View of Society*) envisaged the abolition of marriage and a whole new educative program extending to all persons of all ages for the introduction of his new moral order (as he called it). Owen brought these educational ideas with him to New Harmony where they were further amplified by his collaborator, William Maclure, who introduced there also a group of Pestalozzian teachers — Madame Fretageot, William Phiquepal and Joseph Neef.[8]

The fundamental theory upon which Owen based his entire system was that man is passive in the formation of his character, that in the past he had been the abject victim of the circumstances in which he was born, lived and developed. (Some scholars have seen here a relationship to John Locke and Helvetius.) What was needed, as Owen saw it, was to abolish the unequal conditions then prevalent in society, remove the trinity of evils (religion, marriage and private property), and create and bring to bear equally upon each and all the same set of circumstances or environment. Then the envisioned golden age would be ushered in. Owen's iridescent dream foresaw an equalitarian society of perfect harmony. Unfortunately, like Karl Marx, Owen had evidently never looked closely into the nature of man, nor asked himself whether his system would really fit the nature of man, his inborn needs, wants and aspirations. His new system was in consequence foredoomed to failure from the beginning.

After a few months, says Brownson, Owen's New Harmony proved to be no harmony at all, only harsh discord instead. (The experiment itself came to an end in 1827.) In his comments years later on Owen's daring venture, it is not to be supposed that Brownson perceived in his young manhood the impracticality of such a scheme with the same perspicacity as he did in later life, but he tells us that he never did fully adopt Owen's theory. For he was unable to understand how it could be that if man in the past had been the helpless victim of his circumstances or environment or both, he yet had it in his power to alter or control those selfsame factors which had held him in unrelenting bondage. Again, if all was to be perfect contentment, freedom and tranquillity in the new order, and man was to know no want, what would stimulate his energies? And even if the plan were to succeed, wrote Brownson, "it would have made men only well-trained and well-fed animals."[9]

Yet it was Robert Owen who had drawn Brownson's attention to the social evils that exist in every land.[10] As the pale tenets of Universalism were fading from his mind, the discourses, publications and movements of Owen had been engaging his attention more and more. Brownson began to see man, even in privileged America, as half free and half slave. Political equality, secured by law, was one thing, but the absence of social equality was to him a glaring contradiction in a democratic society which incessantly preached the equality of all men. Actual social inequality mocked the ideal. Having reasoned himself into the belief that man was not made for God, and could not find his happiness therewith, now, at twenty-seven, he turned to a sort of socialism. He was ready to address himself in deadly earnest to the great task of so remodeling society and its government as to secure for all men a paradise on earth. This was to be the great and glorious work of his life, a task to which he steadily held, he tells us, from 1828 to 1842, when he began to find himself unconsciously tending toward the Catholic Church. Octavius Brooks Frothingham's characterization of Brownson as "an experimenter of systems, a taster of speculations," is accurate during this period of his life.[11] For fourteen years he was taken up wholly with devising, adopting, supporting, testing, and in turn rejecting various theories and plans of world reform, whether social or political, ethical or aesthetic, philosophical or theological. He sought truth, he sought knowledge, he sought virtue — everything for one end only: the creation of the envisaged paradise on earth for all mankind. He wrote:

> My end was man's earthly happiness, and my creed was progress. In regard to neither did I change or swerve in the least, till the truth of the Catholic Church was forced on my mind and heart. During the period of fourteen years, for the greater part of which I was accused of changing at least every three months, I never changed my principles or purpose, and all I did change were my tools, my instruments, or my modes of operation.[12]

It is interesting to what extent socialism can often become a "religion" with its advocates and promoters. Writing as a Catholic, Brownson wished he could feel the fervor, the enthusiasm, in the cause of truth, that he had at one time of his life felt in the socialist cause. Say what you will, he asserted, the sincere socialist is often governed by noble instincts, and generous sentiments which Christianity does not disown, but accepts and consecrates.[13] Elsewhere in his writings he remarked that it is a significant fact that socialism arose in Christian, not pagan lands.[14] The socialist has a truth derived from the Gospel, namely, that there should be a better distribution of the world's goods among the inhabitants of the earth. The Catholic Church has always taught the same, affirming that men are only stewards of their possessions, and that what is superfluous to their state of life should be shared in effective ways with the poor. In his encyclical letter on *The Condition of the Working Classes (Rerum Novarum)*, 1891, Pope Leo XIII reaffirmed the words of St. Thomas Aquinas: "Man must not consider his outward possessions as his own, but as common to all, so as to share them without hesitation when others are in need."[15]

This is a truth the simon-pure socialist and the communist have seized upon, but which they have unfortunately perverted by their denial of the right of private property and their concerted effort to abolish it. The socialist, continued Brownson, has aspects of Christian truth which, without revelation and the operation of Christian charity, he could never have beheld. This is significant in his own case, for he tells us that "it was not in seeking to save my soul, or to please God, or to have true religion, that I was led to the Catholic Church, but [by endeavoring] to obtain the means of gaining the earthly happiness of mankind."[16] That he himself was operating during this period of his life under the influence of the Gospel seems clearly enough indicated in the chapter in *Charles Elwood* titled: "A Paradox."[17]

Robert Owen was not, however, the only social reformer who exerted a considerable influence on Brownson. The English radical, William Godwin (a former Calvinistic dissenting minister), exerted an even greater influence on him. Though the author of a number of books, Godwin is probably best remembered for his book, *An Inquiry Concerning the Principles of Political Justice.* This book Brownson had studied with great care. His early reading carried with it little understanding. Yet he reread it as a Universalist minister, and again after he had turned world reformer. It had more influence on his mind, he tells us, than any other book, the Bible alone excepted. From what he says of the purity, elegance and force of Godwin's diction, its calmness and strength, its repose and energy combined, we may conclude that it had also the greatest influence of all books on the formation of his own literary style, the Scriptures again excepted. This book he looked upon in later years as containing in substance nearly every error to which the human mind has ever fallen victim, being in fact an exposé of nearly all the false and dangerous principles of the French Revolution of 1789 "systematically arranged, developed, and pushed to their last consequences with a merciless logic, chasteness, vigor, grace, and eloquence of language, which I have never," he said, "seen surpassed."[18] The book is, of course, a storehouse of the baldest radicalism. It is significant that Brownson gave it no less than a six-page notice in *The Convert,* and finally tells us that, although Godwin had a powerful influence on his mind, he did not absolutely master it.

To anyone of Brownson's untempered and unsettled mind at this time, certain aspects of Godwin's thought were bound to appeal. Basically, Godwin advocated the sweeping away of the whole social organization, the complete and final emancipation of the individual from any trammels religious, social or political. The whole framework of his thought rests upon the tacit assumptions of the essential integrity of human nature and the indefinite perfectibility of man. Were one to assume these as points of departure, wrote Brownson, Godwin's remedial proposals have "on one side at least, a certain degree of plausibility." Godwin's doctrine that, in justice, property belongs to him who needs it most, rather pleased Brownson, for he himself had less than his share, he claimed, and therefore stood to gain rather than lose by it. But apparently the only instance in which Godwin did influence Brownson in a practical detail was in his attack on schools, especially public schools, inasmuch as they impose, in some form, the opinions of the masters, or through them, of parents and guardians, on their pupils. "This," said Brownson, "seemed to me so reasonable — if the rule of private judgment be adopted — that so long as I remained a Protestant I took care never to give my own children any religious instruction."[19] But Brownson could not go along with Godwin, even in his earlier years, with his sweeping proscription of the reigning social and political organization, and his condemnation of associated wealth. The problem as Brownson saw it was to labor to remodel and perfect the indicted social and political order, and use it as a means to gain the end to which he had consecrated himself.

It is curious that Henry Brownson does not mention Godwin at all; for if we are to trace Brownson's early radical tendencies to a primary source it would seem that Godwin's book must have been the real fountainhead. If there is one source in Brownson's early reading for his well-known "Essay on the Laboring Classes" in 1840, it would seem to be Godwin's book which he had read and reread. Something of its animus must have remained in his system for years to come. Yet Brownson had no real kinship with Godwin's extreme brand of radicalism. Godwin's radicalism, as explained, was destructive in intent and purpose, while Brownson was, at least by and large, no radical at all in the destructive sense. As Brownson said later concerning his own bent of character: "I was not naturally a radical, or even inclined to radicalism, but I had a deep sympathy for the poorer classes of society."[20] This deep sympathy for the downtrodden led him to join the social reformers of the day who were truly endeavoring to ameliorate the distressing condition of the poorer classes of society — yet the association was overly cautious, grave and reserved.

Too strong a believer in law and order to be a lamb-like follower of Godwin, too thorny an individualist to accept the communism of Owen, Brownson watched with increasing interest that other social reformer of the day, Frances Wright, better known as Fanny Wright. Fanny Wright, born in Scotland, had inherited considerable wealth, and was well-educated; as Brownson put it, she was "a woman of rare and original powers, and extensive and varied knowledge." She and her sister Camilla had visited and toured the United States in the years 1818-1820. After returning to England, she published *Views of Society and Manners in America* (1821) in which she gave way to unrestrained praise of the American people and their institutions.[21] The book brought her at once to the attention of the liberals abroad. It attracted, for example, the attention of Jeremy Bentham who sought her friendship and offered her the hospitality of his home in Queen's Square Place. Later that same year, 1822, she received a congratulatory letter from the Marquis de Lafayette, known as General Lafayette, who expressed a wish to meet her. By September she was in France, and was asked by Lafayette to visit La Grange, the beautiful countryseat of the Lafayettes. Here she spent much of her time for the next three years, filling the role of the General's secretary and *confidante*. So fond did Lafayette become of her that he made several attempts to adopt her legally, but he was overruled by the determined opposition of his family. However, when he came to the United States on his triumphal tour in 1824, Fanny and her sister Camilla were a part of the entourage.[22]

On her first visit to the United States Fanny Wright had avoided any visits to the Southern states. To her, as to most Europeans, slavery was odious. But her accompaniment of Lafayette on his tour through the country brought her to the Monticello estate of Thomas Jefferson to which Jefferson himself had invited her. There in consultation with former President Madison, Lafayette and Jefferson — though Jefferson expressed some skepticism about the idea — she devised a cooperative plan whereby black slaves would work out their own freedom while learning a trade which would be a means of livelihood once the person was free.[23] Education was the longer scheme: a process, in short, whereby intelligence could be nurtured and polished, and adequate leadership be ultimately provided. She chose Nashabo, Tennessee, fifteen miles from Memphis, where she bought in November 1825 a 2,000-acre site for her quixotic experiment. Within two years the experiment had failed, partly, as Miss Wright alleged, because of her illness in the meantime, and partly because of her inability to find persons of the requisite managerial ability to direct the venture rightly.

But there were other reasons for the failure. Frances Wright was an ardent admirer of Robert Owen, and had returned with him again in 1825 to the United States. Apparently she had first discussed with him her plan for freeing black slaves in the South. After she and her sister Camilla together with James Richardson and George Flower had gone to live on the estate at Nashabo, she made a second visit to New Harmony. The discussions she had there with Owen and Maclure had convinced her of the necessity of religious and sexual as well as slave emancipation. Thereafter Nashabo became a sort of racially integrated experiment modeled on Owenite ideas. Miscegenation became an accepted idea in the settlement. Such a novel idea at the time soon generated local hostility. Real odium developed, however, when Richardson, the chief manager of Nashabo, took as mistress one of the slave women and then announced the same privileges and rights to the other members of the colony. The cry "brothel" at once went up.[24] This unhappy turn of events at Nashabo was apparently more chargeable to Richardson than to Miss Wright.

But whatever the moral misdemeanors that stained Nashabo, Frances Wright's ingenious attempt to free Southern blacks from slavery cannot be praised too much. In this particular matter her sentiments were much more

Christian than those of many a critic who later castigated her unmercifully for doctrines which were truly heterodox. She was one of the first in the country who made a dramatic attempt to draw attention to the sprawling evil of slavery. Perhaps some of the sentiment she fostered at the time passed later into the Abolition Societies of New England. After her experiment had collapsed, involving the loss of sixteen thousand dollars — more than half of her fortune at the time — she honorably redeemed her promise of emancipating the slaves she had taken under her care, some thirty in number, by colonizing them on the island of Haiti, then a republic under President Boyer.[25] She personally supervised their transfer, sailing with them from New Orleans about the middle of January 1830.[26]

Fanny Wright's brave humanitarian work appealed strongly to Orestes Brownson. But shortly before he left the Universalist ministry, Fanny had embarked on a new kind of world reform. When the Nashabo experiment ended, she became convinced (evidently taking her ideas again from Owen) that the American people at large were the victims of a much more deep-seated complaint than black slavery: she thought them addicted to superstition, and supine subjection to the clergy. No superficial treatment would suffice; the ax must slice the root of the tree. Accordingly she decided on a campaign for the enlightenment of the people, making war in particular on that trinity of evils: religion, marriage and private property. In the autumn of 1828, now in her early thirties, she began a series of provocative lectures on "knowledge" delivered in Cincinnati, Boston, Philadelphia, Albany, Utica, Auburn, Buffalo and at various other centers of the country.[27] These lectures created a great stir at the time.

Brownson first met Frances Wright on this tour. In October 1829, his Universalist days coming to an end, he learned that Miss Wright was to lecture at Utica. He decided to break his homeward trip from Boston and attend the lecture.[28] If charm, intelligence and magnetic eloquence can lend plausibility to doctrine, Fanny Wright had powerful assets. Speaking of her gifts as a lecturer, Brownson wrote:

> Her lectures were eminently popular. Her free, flowing, ornate style — French rather than English — her fine, rich musical voice, highly cultivated and possessing great power, her graceful manners, her tall, commanding figure, her wit and sarcasm, her apparent honesty of purpose, her deep and glowing enthusiasm, made her one of the most pleasing and effective orators, man or woman, that I have ever heard.[29]

The impression made on Brownson by the Utica lecture, his son tells us, was further strengthened by a conversation with the lecturer that evening and still further by a visit of Miss Wright to Auburn soon afterwards where she delivered a course of lectures.[30] But Fanny's visit to Auburn was not a happy one. She had already been humiliated by the clergy at Utica, and had been forced to deliver her lecture in a "dirty old circus,"[31] although originally arrangements had been made for the use of the courthouse. Her position as the avowed enemy of religion, made the clergy her adversaries; the press of the country, too, had been spitefully tilting at her. When she had lectured in New York City, January 8, 1829, the *New York American* declared: "When one thus shamefully obtrudes herself on the public, waiving alike modesty, gentleness, and every amiable attribute of her sex, she also waives all claims to its privileges: she ceases to be a woman, and is no longer aught else than what we take the liberty to call her — 'a female monster.' "[32] Such an excoriation of a woman lecturer in her day is understandable, however regrettable. As a specimen of the reaction of the religious press, the *New York Observer* called her: " 'infidelity in an angel's garb,' concealing her infidel principles under the false species of morality, liberty, equality and the like, aiming at the ridicule of vital religion, and reproaching the pious, faithful preachers of the Gospel."[33] Bitter opposition to her had been mounting as she flitted from platform to platform during the last year. Especially was her opposition to the marriage tie used as a handle by her enemies to cover her with ridicule and scorn.

Yet Brownson, impressed by her humanitarian intentions, had taken her part more than once when he was editor of the *Gospel Advocate*. He wrote:

> We are ashamed of our countrymen that they should exhibit such enmity towards a woman who, whatever may be the correctness of her conclusions, has given no mean proof of an enlightened mind and truly philanthropic heart. And we regret to see the female part of the country so severe on one who adorns their sex and seems anxious to give woman her proper place in society, the rank she ought to fill. Miss Wright may err, and who may not? But abating her views on matrimony, which are probably more censured than understood, and censured by more than believe them ill-founded, we have seen nothing in her ethicks [*sic*] that should be discarded.[34]

Whether or not Brownson had personally invited Miss Wright to lecture at Auburn, where he was a pastor, we do not know, but when she did come in November, the people there probably felt that he had a great deal to do with her coming. Since his own thought during the preceding year or two had been tending more and more toward infidelity, there probably seemed to them a natural link between himself and this notorious lecturer. Whatever the truth of the matter, the more pious of the village determined beforehand that they would let her know clearly how welcome she was. But however unholy her cause, Fanny Wright was a very resourceful individual. Brownson tells us that the Evangelicals had said all manner of things about her, for the most part untrue, and had endeavored, not to disprove what she had said, but to render her personally odious. The hard things said about her finally came to her ears; at the close of one of her lectures, she quietly, and in the sweetest manner imaginable, remarked:

> We have here this evening considered the subject of religion. Tomorrow evening, at half past seven, we will meet again to discuss the subject of morals. I observed in driving through your beautiful city today, the spires of six meeting-houses, belonging to as many different denominations, and I was told that there are two or three other denominations that have not as yet erected meeting-houses for themselves. It is evident that religion must have been well discussed among you, and that you are an eminently religious people. I have travelled much and have visited many countries, and in no place have I been so uncourteously received, or been the subject of so much personal insult, as in your most religious village. Perhaps it will not be inappropriate to spend one evening in the discussion of morals.[35]

It was on the occasion of Miss Wright's visit to Auburn that Brownson agreed to become corresponding editor of the *Free Enquirer* at Auburn.[36] The *Free Enquirer* was a weekly journal that Miss Wright, Robert Dale Owen, the eldest son of Robert Owen, and Robert L. Jennings had started and published at 359 Broome Street, New York City, where they had converted an old meetinghouse into a "Hall of Science," and had "put into operation all the machinery of the most vigorous propagandism."[37] The *Free Enquirer* was really the *New Harmony Gazette* of Robert Owen in a new disguise which Fanny herself had for a time helped to edit at New Harmony, Indiana. In announcing in the December 1829 issue of the journal that Orestes A. Brownson had "held out to her the hand of friendship," and had consented to become corresponding editor at Auburn, Miss Wright further remarked:

> We conceive our readers to be familiar with the name and style of the *Gospel Advocate,* from which publication, since it has been in the hands of the present editor, Orestes A. Brownson, we have made many interesting extracts. With that individual, until a few weeks ago, we had no personal intercourse whatever. But we recognized him by his writings for an honest laborer in the same vine-yard with ourselves; we saw that if nominally attached to a sect, he was neither in thought or feeling sectarian; we saw that he had dropped from the clouds upon the solid earth, and that he had renounced the chair of dogmatism to pursue enquiry in the field of nature and human life.[38]

It was strange company, indeed, in which Orestes Brownson was now getting involved. The Free Enquirers, coming to our shores from abroad, had apparently imported their heterodox notions with them. The tenets of the Wright-Owen partnership most obnoxious to the orthodox were no doubt those on marriage. As a husband and father, Brownson surely did not agree with them. Yet he argued on theoretical grounds that, once the doctrine of almost all modern novelists and romancers was accepted, namely, that love is fatal and irresistible — a doctrine accepted by no small part of American nineteenth-century society — the vows made in marriage were immoral inasmuch as their keeping was beyond the control of those who took them. With the Free Enquirers themselves, however, this matter never went beyond theory.[39] Content with speculation, they never expected an immediate acceptance of their views. Both Miss Wright and her sister Camilla, as well as Robert Dale Owen, abided the marriage conventions of society.

Brownson merely suffered the negative side of Miss Wright's program. But there was a positive side also to her program which enlisted his deep sympathies: that fact helps to explain his brief association with the Free Enquirers. Robert Dale Owen set down a list of what had been the group's objectives in his autobiography, *Threading My Way* (1874):

> We advocated [he said] the abolition of imprisonment for debt and capital punishment; equality for women, social, pecuniary, political; equality of rights for all persons without distinction of color, and the right of every man to testify in a court of justice without inquiry being made as to his religious beliefs. Above all, we urged the importance of a national system of education, free from all sectarian teaching, with industrial schools where the children of the poor might be taught farming or a trade, and obtain, without charge, support as well as education.[40]

Whether or not Robert Owen might have given us more details on the nature of the public schools the Free Enquirers sought to establish, a new system of schools was the great measure upon which they relied for the regeneration of society. They advocated complete "state guardianship" of children from their earliest years. The system proposed they called: "National, Rational, Republican education; Free for All At the Expense of All; Conducted under the Guardianship of the State, And for the Honor, The Happiness, The Virtue, The Salvation of the State."[41] One may see here in this proposal to take very young children for schooling the influence of the ideas that Robert Owen had introduced in his schools in New Lanark, Scotland. Frances Wright may have been also considerably influenced in the formation of her educational program by William Phiquepal whom she had first met at New Harmony. He was a Pestalozzian teacher (whom she was to marry soon after). At least Brownson tells us that this same Phiquepal had a hand in the management of the proposed schools; he was a man whose educational methods Brownson respected as little as the man himself.[42]

Speaking of the system of schools proposed by the Free Enquirers, Brownson said:

> The great measure on which Fanny Wright and her friends relied for ultimate success was the system of schools, which, as I have said, were to include the maintenance, as well as the instruction and education, of all children of the state. These schools were intended to deprive as well as relieve parents of all care and responsibility of their children after a year or two of age. It assumed that parents were in general incompetent to train up their children in the way they should go, to form them with the right sort of characters, tempers, and aims; and therefore it was proposed that the state should take the whole charge of children, provide proper establishments, and teachers and governors for them, till they should reach the age of majority. This would liberate parents, and secure the principal advantage of a community of goods.
>
> This aim was, on the one hand, to relieve marriage of its burdens, and to remove the principal reasons for making marriage indissoluble; and, on the other, to provide for bringing up children in a rational manner to be reasonable men and women, that is, free from superstition, all belief in God and immortality, or regard for the invisible, and make them look upon this life as their only life, this home as their only home, and the promotion of their earthly interests and enjoyments as their only end. The three great enemies to worldly happiness were held to be religion, marriage, or the family, and private property. Once . . . rid of these three institutions, and we may hope soon to realize our earthly paradise. . . . In this we did but follow the popular philosophy of Locke and Condillac, and draw the conclusions warranted by the premises supplied by the age and country. The sensism of Locke and the utilitarian morals of Paley were then taught in nearly all our colleges and universities.[43]

But the more immediate question was how to get the system of schools adopted. A plan was formed to organize the whole nation secretly, patterned somewhat after the operations of the *Carbonari* of Europe, a group about which Brownson knew nothing at the time. Each member of this secret society was to use all possible means, each in his own locality, to form public opinion in favor of the proposed schools, and to get elected to the legislature such men as would favor the adoption of their views. How far this secret organization extended, Brownson appeared ignorant. He added: "But I do know that a considerable portion of the state of New York was organized, for I myself was one of the agents for organizing it. I, however, became tired of the work, and abandoned it after a few months."[44]

The Free Enquirers had to find some effective way to get their educational scheme adopted. Here they perceived the Workingmen's party could be of use. That party had been founded in Philadelphia in 1827. It was, in great part, the result of a strike in the city's building trades and came as a reaction to the letters of Matthew Carey which had depicted the deplorable conditions of seamstresses in large American cities.[45] The chief founders of the Workingmen's party in New York City, with the help of Brownson, were Frances Wright, Robert D. Owen, Robert J. Jennings and George H. Evans. Jennings was on the editorial staff of the *Free Enquirer,* and Evans was the editor of the *Workingman's Advocate,* the first important labor journal in the United States. It was in 1829 that the Free Enquirers got busy organizing and promoting the Workingmen's party in New York City. In an effort to give the party firm support, Brownson became the editor of the Genesee *Republican and Herald of Reform,* published at Leroy, New York.

In conjunction with their own purposes the Free Enquirers endeavored at the time to link the Workingmen's party to the ultra-democratic sentiment of the country, which from the time of Jefferson and Tom Paine, had had a slightly anti-Christian bent.[46] Representing themselves from this supposed vantage point as the radical champions of those oppressed or defrauded by employers, the Free Enquirers had hoped to enlist a sufficient number of the American people on their side to secure the elevation of the Workingmen's party to political power. Thus they might guarantee the eventual adoption of their educational system.

> Into this party I entered with enthusiasm [wrote Brownson]. I established in Western New York a journal in its support, and co-operated with the *Daily Sentinel,* conducted by my friends in the city. But I soon tired of the party, and gave my influence and that of my journal, in the autumn of 1830, to the Jackson candidate, E. T. Troop, against Frank Granger, the candidate of the anti-Masons, for governor. The defection ruined my journal as a party journal, and a few days after the election, I disposed of it to my partner, and ceased to be its editor. The truth is, I never was and never could be a party man, or work in the traces of a party. I abandoned, indeed, after a year's devotion to it the Workingmen's Party, but not the workingmen's cause, and to that cause I have ever been faithful according to my light and ability.[47]

There were evidently more reasons why Brownson "soon tired of the party," or lost faith in it. From its beginning the party had become so torn by internecine bickering as to rob it of a needed forceful unity. Within its first year in New York State it had split into two factions, first over the "agrarian" issue, and then over the "state guardianship" plan of education. In the first meeting of the Mechanics of New York (April 1829), Thomas Skidmore, "a machinist by trade and a dialectician strongly under the influence of Tom Paine," promoted the passage of resolutions in which "the nature of tenure by which all men hold title to their property" was questioned. The plan he formulated called for a "state constitutional convention which should decree an abolition of all debts and all claims to private property within the state." Property was then to be divided between all the adult citizens of the state, "in order," said Skidmore, "that every citizen may enjoy in a state of society substantially the rights which belong to him in the state of nature."[48] His program soon came to be known as "agrarianism," probably from the similarity it bore to Tom Paine's "Agrarian Justice." Although Skidmore apparently had some influence for a time on the Workingmen's party, his agrarian doctrines were vigorously rejected by a majority (January 1829), and he and his followers were practically driven from the party into a short-lived organization of their own. Yet in the meantime Skidmore and his faction had given the Workingmen's party something of the appearance of a wild-eyed project that hinted an ominous threat to a well-ordered society.[49]

With the Skidmores gone, the party's schism scarred over only briefly. For almost immediately the party split again over the "state guardianship" system of education. This division led to a bitter factional struggle which remained until the fall election of 1830.[50] So completely had unity been shattered that prior to the elections there were actually three claimants to be truly the representatives of the Workingmen's party.[51] What chances had such a divided party for success at the polls with their adversaries charging upon them the championship of "anarchical," "agrarian," and "infidel" principles?[52] Such signal handicaps to party unity meant not only defeat at the polls, but presaged a sure and speedy disintegration.

These events must likewise be reckoned among the reasons why Orestes Brownson "soon tired" of the Workingmen's party. One consideration weighed most heavily with him. As sincerely and earnestly as he wished to advance the cause of the workingmen, he quickly saw that little or no good could be effected by appealing to workingmen as a separate class. To excite class warfare was a policy of disaster. "The movement we commenced," he said, "could only excite a war of man against money; and all history and all reasoning prove that in such a war money carries it over man. Money commands the supplies, and can hold out longer than they who have nothing but their manhood. It can starve them into submission."[53] (This, of course, was much more true in a time prior to the powerful labor organizations.) In any case, the true policy, as Brownson now saw it, was not to array class against class, but to induce all classes of society to cooperate for the improvement of the workingmen's lot. "The rich and the poor, the learned and the unlearned, the producers and the consumers, the headworkers and the handworkers, must unite, work together, or no reforms practicable, no amelioration of the condition of any class was to be hoped for."[54] He had begun to see the social body as an organic whole, no member benefiting without all the members benefiting, and no member suffering without all the members suffering. In this view we have something more than a glimmering anticipation of Pope Leo XIII's epochal encyclical on *The Condition of the Working Classes (Rerum Novarum)*, 1891. Warning against class warfare in the economic order, Pope Leo wrote forcefully and clearly:

> The great mistake in regard to the matter under consideration is to take up with the notion that class is naturally hostile to class, and that the wealthy and the workingman are intended by nature to live in mutual conflict. So irrational and so false is this view, that the direct contrary is the truth. Just as the symmetry of the human frame is the resultant of the disposition of the bodily members, so in a State it is ordained by nature that these two classes should dwell in harmony and agreement, and should, as it were, groove into one another, so as to maintain the balance of the body politic. Each needs the other: Capital cannot do without labor, nor labor without capital. Mutual agreement results in pleasantness of life and the beauty of good order; while conflict necessarily produces confusion and savage barbarity.[55]

But where, Brownson was forced to ask himself at this stage, could he find the grand reconciler, the grand harmonizer of society? His previous efforts in behalf of the workingmen had advocated a kind of Lockeism: the belief that all that was necessary was merely to show men the best course for their own interests — and they would follow it. He had yet to learn that although man may be a reasonable being, he is also a bundle of blinding appetites which divert him from the pursuit of those interests. Being at this time no sectarian, Brownson's early religious principles and affections gradually began to reassert themselves; he now saw clearly that the puissant influence of religion was the only great harmonizer. It alone could, as he saw the matter, unite all classes of society into one healthy, coordinate whole.

> The moment I threw off all religion and began to work without it [he confessed] I found myself impotent. I did not need religion to pull down or destroy society; but the moment I wished to build up, to effect something positive, I found I could not proceed a single step without it. Even to move men to seek their own good, I must have some power by which I can overcome what religious people call the flesh, a power that will strengthen the will, and enable men to subdue their passions and control their lusts. Where am I to find this power except in religious ideas and principles, in the belief in God and immortality, in duty, moral accountability.[56]

The Archimedian principle had been that to move anything in this world one must place his fulcrum in another world. In thus speaking of the indispensable role of religion in the building up of a healthy and sound society by furnishing each member with strong motives for fulfilling his duties, whatever they may be, he was again anticipating Leo XIII's *The Condition of the Working Classes*. Pope Leo wrote:

> Now, in preventing such strife as this, and in uprooting it, the efficacy of Christian institutions is marvellous and manifold. First of all, there is no intermediary more powerful than Religion (whereof the Church is the interpreter and guardian) in drawing the rich, and the poor bread-winner, together, by reminding each class of its duties to the other, and especially of the obligations of justice.[57]

These insights into a sounder social philosophy began to separate Brownson from the New Enquirers. Per Sveino believes that his contributions to the *Free Enquirer* had not been numerous and were gentle and moderate in style. He cites Albert Post as suggesting that "Brownson . . . failed to speak out boldly and loudly against superstition, in part because of his youthfulness."[58] This explanation Sveino rightly discards, for Brownson had been forthright in the *Gospel Advocate* and inflammatory in previous writings. Whatever the value of Sveino's suggestion, the real explanation of the matter would seem to be that Brownson had never, after all, given anything more than a lagging, halfhearted commitment to the whole program of the Free Enquirers. There is a possible hint of this in the *Spirit-Rapper* (a book written by Brownson in 1854).[59] It is the common interpretation that a character in the narrative, Priscilla, represents Fanny Wright.[60] As far as the book deals so largely with world reform, the narrator, or the hero of the book, may possibly represent Brownson himself in some measured degree. Near the end of the book the hero realizes his mistake, and then explains why he had associated at all with Priscilla (Fanny Wright) in world reform: "Half in spite, and half under the charm of Priscilla, I embraced philanthropy, but not inwardly, for her sophistry never for a moment deceived me. Never was there a moment when I did not see through the philanthropists, radicals, and revolutionaries with whom I associated, or when with a breath I could not have swept away their cob-web theories. . . ."[61]

Why then did he associate with radicals and world reformers? The narrator replied that he did so partly because he did not know what else to do, and partly because he could not endure absolute idleness. He saw indeed the destructive character of the movements with which he was associated, but he cherished the hope that by making things worse he was really preparing the way for things to become better. The old edifice must be razed, and the rubbish cleared away, before the new and more useful structure could be erected. He readily admitted, too, his own confused state. He had adhered to philanthropy, infidelity and radicalism, not because he loved or believed in them, but rather because he did not see the truth of traditional orthodoxy. The refutations of the orthodox seemed to him to assert either too much or too little, and his perplexity remained.[62]

Whatever be the truth of these speculations, Brownson made it clear enough in *The Convert* that he had never been completely in agreement with the Free Enquirers. He tells us that his motives for supporting the Workingmen's party never precisely matched theirs. He aimed more directly at benefiting the workingmen themselves, and had never more than acquiesced in the proposed system of education. "I was a husband and a father," he said, "and did not altogether relish the idea of breaking up the family and regarding my children as belonging to the state rather than to me."[63] The statement sounds entirely credible. Sally had already borne him two children, Orestes and John Healy Brownson. Moreover, although certain aspects of Brownson's thought do at times seem a bit doctrinaire, the impracticality of the educational system of the Free Enquirers could scarcely have escaped him. Where was the state to get its army of nurses, teachers, governors, and the rest required to take children in their tenderest years, properly feed, clothe and educate them during all their formative years? And what guarantee was there that these officials would do the job better than the parents, although some of these might be far from admirably qualified for the task? And even if these officials of the state did succeed in their system of education, would the result be desirable? Would it be a gain to bring up the children — in the sense of the Free Enquirers — strictly rational, that is, ignorant of all morality resting for its foundation on a belief in God, in immortality, in moral accountability, restricted in all their thoughts and affections to purely material good and sensual pleasures?[64] When he thought about it, Orestes Brownson was probably no more in favor at the time of such a system of education for children in general than for his own children.

Holding these views, so divergent from his associates, Brownson, then, had come to the parting of the ways with the Free Enquirers soon after the fall elections of 1830. Frances Wright herself, with all her roseate dreams unfulfilled, fled to France in July where she married William Phiquepal according to the accepted conventions of society. At her request Phiquepal resumed at the time the family name of D'Arusmont.[65] Robert D. Owen continued as editor of the *Free Enquirer* for a year or two, and then returned to New Harmony, Indiana. From there he went on to a political career, and became a member of Congress (1843-1847); he was finally appointed U.S. Minister to Italy (1855-1858).[66] After disposing of the Genesee *Republican and Herald of Reform,* Orestes Brownson was left quite sobered by his brave attempt at world reform, and its innocent incursion into practical politics.

How did affairs now stand with Orestes Brownson? He had firmly fixed in his mind that his great mission in life was to create a paradise on earth for his fellowmen, and had now been unselfishly devoting all his talents and energies to direct his fellowmen toward the inauguration of that happier state. Yet who was there to appreciate what he was doing? Who cared what sacrifices he might be making? On the contrary, in place of appreciation and gratitude for what he was doing, his portion was only misunderstanding and abuse. This had given him pause. It gradually brought him to such a state of mind that he apparently began to doubt his fitness for the mission in life to which he had felt himself called. There is a passage in *Charles Elwood* that would seem to indicate as much, and as such it is an interesting sidelight on Brownson's character. Insofar as *Charles* speaks for Brownson, he said:

> I was never intended to be a warrior, was never fitted to be a reformer. My natural inclinations and tastes were for a quiet and retired life passed in the midst of a family and a circle of friends. In laboring for mankind, my love for them increased; and in proportion as I became really philanthropic the solitude to which I was doomed became insupportable. I could not bear to feel that in the vast multitude around me, not a single heart beat in unison with my own. I would love and be loved. Not the race only would I love. I wished for some one dearer than all to cheer me on to the combat, and welcome my return. It was doubtless a weakness I was never able to get over. The affections have always had a great power over me, and in fact have always done with me pretty much as they would. Could I have so generalized my affections as to have cared for mankind only in the abstract, and to have had no craving for sympathy with individuals, I would have been a stronger man, perhaps, and might not have failed in my undertaking. But this was not in my nature. I could never live on abstractions, love everybody in general and nobody in particular. I was alone. There was no God in heaven, to whom I could go for succor; there was no spot in earth to which I could retire awhile, throw off my armor and feel myself secure; no sympathizing soul with whom I could talk over my plans, give free utterance to my feelings which I must ordinarily suppress, and find ample amends for the ungenerous scorn of the world. I felt I was wronged, that I was misunderstood. My philanthrophy turned sour, and, I grieve to say, I ended by railing against mankind — a no uncommon case, as I have since learned, with those who set out to be world-reformer.[67]

These thoughts were perhaps only momentary discouragements which came and went, for he was to continue to do unrelenting battle for his earthly paradise right up to the year 1842. Balm in Gilead had not yet failed. If his signal efforts at world reform had been fruitless in the past, had he not now discovered the secret of failure? He had attempted "to make brick without straw."[68] He had left out of his formula for world reform the most important of all ingredients — religion. Might not his dreams still be realized? With the knowledge now that religion is the only power that can infuse into the souls of men that spirit of love, disinterestedness and self-sacrifice so necessary to effect reforms in society, he now turned back in good earnest to enlist the aid of religion to carry through his plans of world reform. This turnabout was in no sense difficult for him. After all, his religious doubts had only been of a speculative sort. Ever would he have clasped to his soul the ennobling truths and principles of religion could he but have established their validity to his own satisfaction. "As much opposed as I am," he put into the mouth of *Charles Elwood,* "to the nonsense and mischief which pass with the multitude under the name of religion, yet ever have I felt that I would give worlds did I but possess them."[69] With the religious sentiments and principles which had been so native to his heart now beginning to reassert their sway over him, he determined to resume his old profession of preacher, though of what particular creed or gospel, he had yet to decide.

# 5

## THE INDEPENDENT PREACHER

*Beginning his religious ministry again, Brownson locates at Ithaca,*
*New York • He adopts the Religion of Humanity, or philanthropy •*
*The aid he received from René de Chateaubriand and Dr. W. Ellery*
*Channing in regaining his former Christian faith • His unabated ef-*
*forts at social reform • His notable Fourth of July oration delivered*
*at Ovid, New York, 1831 • He founds and publishes* The Philanthropist
*• His journey in search of a new pulpit • His letters to wife Sally in*
*the meantime • He accepts a call from the Unitarian Society of Wal-*
*pole, New Hampshire.*

When Orestes Brownson returned to the pulpit, he did so as a free-lance
minister, responsible to no church, sect, or denomination. He was just entering his twenty-eighth year. Something of the granite hills of Vermont was by
this time beginning to surface in his character. A certain grimness, albeit
cheerful enough, marked his features. The air of freedom and independence
which had swept his soul as he had roamed the hills of his native state years
earlier now began to invigorate his person with new power and verve. He already knew something of the reverses and vicissitudes of life and the experience had toughened him. His powerful six-feet-two-inch frame, towering
above others, may have had its psychological effect on his own personality.
"Brownson's originality and force," wrote his son, "were unquestionably
due to his physical and moral temperament."[1] Above all, Brownson had now
come to a turn in his life when he wished to be just himself, and to live out his
life from the center of his own being. From this time on the man was determined to live utterly according to his own inner convictions. There was to be
one Orestes Brownson, individualist nonpareil. Years later Fr. Isaac T.
Hecker was to remark of him: "He was routine in nothing."[2]

While assuming this new stance as an independent minister, he was fully
aware that he had not yet resolved the conflict that had been agitating his
mind over the great questions of religion, but as he did not intend to speak
dogmatically on matters of religion, he did not count this disadvantage a de-
terrent in the case. The day was yet far, far off when he was to regard himself as an assured teacher of mankind. Nothing more than a humble inquirer
after truth when he reascended the pulpit, he renounced any tendency to dog-
matize; his present purpose in examining the Gospel was to stimulate his
hearers to inquire after truth themselves. As he was now, more independently than ever, trying to work out a religious faith for himself by which he
would be willing to live, so he would have each of his listeners discover for
himself a faith, his own genuine belief. That sort of faith alone could be a
*living* faith. Brownson stressed the necessity of such a faith in an article on
"Creeds," published in the *Christian Register;* he wrote: "A borrowed
faith, which is all most people can boast, is constantly directing us to some
external force; carrying us away from ourselves, and constantly urging us to
fix on some one else. There is no abiding principle within; no ever ready
monitor in the beast whose voice may be consulted and whose decisions
obeyed."[3]

In harmony with this new outlook he was determined, however, to keep himself clear of all sects or denominations so as to preserve his mind unfettered in its search after truth. Nevertheless, he was soon to associate himself with the Unitarians after learning that they "were liberal, that they eschewed all creeds and professions, allowed the unrestricted exercise of reason, and left their ministers each to stand on his own private convictions, and to arrange matters each as best he could with his own congregation."[4]

Whether or not he had any difficulty in finding at once a pastoral service, we do not know. (Certainly some of the things a portion of the Universalists had been saying about him after he left their fold could scarcely have been any help to him in finding a new congregation to serve.) Whatever the case, within a reasonably short time he became the pastor of a congregation in Ithaca, New York, where he had formerly preached as a Universalist minister. In his opening sermon, February 1831, he said:

> I belong to no party, I disclaim all sectarian names. . . . I am an independent preacher, accountable to my God, to truth, to my country, to the people of my charge, but to no other tribunal. . . . Truth is the property of no one sect, righteousness is the exclusive boast of no one denomination. All have some truth, all have some errors. To join one, you must support its falsehoods as well as its truths, or they will cast you out of the synagogue. You must study to conceal the faults of your party, and often be compelled to suffer reproach from the misconduct of your associates.
>
> I do not speak at random, my friends, I speak from experience. I was a Universalist — a Universalist minister. I was so unfortunate, in the prosecution of my studies, as to have doubts; I withdrew myself from the denomination to which I belonged, and ceased to preach. What was the consequence? Approbation for my honesty? No, they excommunicated me, and published me from one end of the country to the other as a rejecter of Christianity, as an unprincipled villain.[5] That is the principle by which all sects are governed. What encouragement has one to inquire after truth, or to aspire to any growth in knowledge, after he has united with a sect?
>
> To preach righteousness, then, I do not conceive it necessary to urge you to join a church. I wish you to observe all the good there is in any and all of our churches, to ascertain all they have of truth, and make it your own; but, if you are wise, you will beware how you receive their fetters, and place yourselves in a situation by which you must father their faults as well as their virtues.[6]

It was reflections such as these that had determined him to strike out for himself as a free-lance minister of religion. But it should be noted well, and realistically, that he had still "scarcely the simplest elements of natural religion." The only religion he professed was what he called the Religion of Humanity, that is, philanthropy. "I had put humanity in the place of God," he said. "The only God I recognized was the divine in man, which I supposed to be the real meaning of the Christian doctrine of the Incarnation, the mystery of Emmanuel, or God with us, God manifest in the flesh." His great aim therefore was not to serve God, but man; the love of man, not of God, moved him. He was still passionately bent on social reform, and wished to make religion and all else subservient thereto. As a social reformer, he looked to Christ as "the model man, who sought, by teaching the truth under a religious envelope, and practicing the purist morality, to meliorate the earthly condition of mankind." A social reformer, devoted heart and soul to the promotion of the welfare and happiness of his fellowmen, he thought he might liken himself to Christ, the great reformer, and call himself a Christian. But he assumed the name "Christian," not because he took Christ as his master in all things, but simply because, like Jesus, he was laboring to introduce a new order of things and promote the earthly felicity of his fellowmen.[7]

He stood in the pulpit, then, more as a social reformer than as an evangelist. Little had changed in his thought since the days of his avowed unbelief, except "the tone and temper." He was now at peace with the Christian world, and no longer wished to fight it. He found himself cherishing more and more feelings and sentiments in accordance with, not so much Christianity, as natural religion. This gradual transition from anti-Christian feelings to more congenial Christian feelings, he ascribed in later years partly to the favorable effect on his mind and heart of Chateaubriand's *The Genius of Christianity* which he had read during his days of unbelief. Although, as he himself observed, the argument for Christianity of that celebrated work is not entirely conclusive since it is grounded on human considerations, it did remove his hostility to Christianity, and disposed him to study its evidence without prejudice.[8] Likewise the socioreligious movement in France at the time, led on by Félicité de Lamennais, Jean Baptiste Henri Dominque Lacordaire and the Count de Montalembert, affected him deeply in favor of Christianity. Referring to the experience many decades later, he wrote:

> It was that movement more than any thing else that brought me back to Christianity, inspired me with belief in the possibility of reconciling religion and modern society, and finally prepared me for the recognition and acceptance of the church. [When the movement fell under the ban of the Catholic Church as too revolutionary, he said:] We wept as a child over the death of his mother, made honorable mention of her memory, and followed away the St. Simonian dreamer, the fallen priest, and wasted a dozen years of our life in the endeavor to lay the foundation of a new church.[9]

But in his autobiography Brownson was to mention especially in this connection an eloquent sermon of Dr. William Ellery Channing entitled: "Likeness to God." This sermon was to be of exceptional aid to him in the recovery of his former faith. It was, in fact, that inspiring homily which had moved him to resume his "profession as a Christian minister." "You, Sir," he said in a remarkable letter to Dr. Channing, June 1842, "have been my spiritual Father. Your writings were the first to suggest to me those trains of thought which have finally ended in raising me from the darkness of doubt to the warm sun-light of a living faith in God."[10]

In no less a degree did Dr. Channing come to his aid at this time as a social reformer in another eloquent sermon, "The Dignity of Human Nature." While under the influence of the materialistic philosophy of the Wright-Owen partnership, young Brownson had accepted a rather dark view of man's nature and destiny, and had begun to question the good sense of any arduous labors for his fellowmen. For, as he pointed out:

> If man is a mere animal, born to propagate his species, and die and be no more, why shall I love him, and sacrifice myself for him? Where is his moral worth, his dignity, the greatness and majesty of his nature? What matters it, whether, during the existence of a day, he be happy or miserable, since tomorrow he dies, and it is all the same? For a being so worthless, wherefore devote myself? What is there in him to inspire me with heroism, and enable me in his behalf to dare poverty, reproach, exile, the rack, the dungeon, the scaffold, or the stake?[11]

Channing's sermon on the dignity of human nature was just the answer to all that. Its eloquence, its noble sentiments, its elevated thoughts moved Brownson so powerfully, he tells us, that he almost became a worshiper of man. Such were the glowing terms in which Dr. Channing spoke of man's godlike nature that one of his brother ministers was wont to say that "he [had] made man a great god, and God a little man."[12] The sermon opened up to Brownson new and inspiring views of man's capacity for the good and noble, and made him feel that man's soul could never die, but must live forever. "I saw in man," he said, "more clearly and more vividly than ever before, something worth living for, something one could love, and, if need be, die for . . . something that could serve as a basis to that love of mankind necessary as an agent for introducing the social changes and organizations through which I hoped to obtain my earthly paradise."[13]

The intimations of immortality which the sermon had also afforded him, caused him to write:

> Perhaps it is not unreasonable to infer a future state from the capacity of the soul itself. Few who have contemplated the soul, its mighty powers, its sublimity of feeling, its moral grandeur, its continual aspirations after something it has not, its wish to stretch beyond the narrow circumference of earth, beyond the stars, beyond the farthest limits of space, to rise and hold communion with the Mysterious Power it feels but sees not; few have taken this view of the human soul, and have not deemed it destined to survive the frail tenement of clay in which it is lodged. Who can believe that a being of such varied and extensive powers, so high, so noble, and often so god-like in its aspirations and achievements, is born but for an hour? No, it cannot be.[14]

Whatever the influence of Dr. Channing or others at this time, Brownson had by now become a dedicated crusader for social reform. And he was to remain such, by and large, the rest of his life. But as no party is always right, or always wrong, this man could never commit himself wholeheartedly to any *party*. He might in due course take up with Unitarianism, Transcendentalism or the Democratic party for a time, but he was never to identify himself fully with any of them, or, for that matter, with any party, in any total sense. Higher than loyalty to party was loyalty to those difficult abstracts: truth and justice. He would hold himself free at any cost to accept truth and justice wherever either could be found. No man ever believed more strongly in the right of the human mind to an untrammelled pursuit of truth. And for those things in which he believed so passionately, he was to use pulpit and platform, pen and voice to the edge of his ability. The resultant literary output during the fifty years of his public career has been preserved mainly in the twenty octavo volumes, titled *The Works of Orestes A. Brownson,* collected and arranged by his son Henry. The volumes contain four hundred massive essays, some of booksize length. Charles Carroll Hollis estimates that the twenty volumes contain only about one third of his total literary achievement.[15] Not all his addresses, however, have been preserved to us, though many are still extant.

One of the first and clearly more notable addresses he ever gave was a Fourth of July oration delivered at Ovid, New York, 1831 (a few months after he had returned to the ministry at Ithaca). The very fact that he was the chosen speaker on that occasion is an indication in itself that he was becoming quite well-known as a speaker. The length of the address was fully such as the dignity of the occasion could require. In contrast to the empty bombast so often a staple of such addresses, Brownson made use of the occasion to probe the national spirit that national good might thereby be effected. A few paragraphs — the address is much too long to be quoted in its entirety — may show that young as he was, he had already understood clearly that only a free people makes a free government, and not the other way around. He knew, too, that a people as a rule get a government no better than they deserve — a government that is only a reflection of themselves. Only a people that is morally sound and intelligent will ever beget a government that is morally sound and intelligent, particularly in a democracy or republic. The stream cannot rise above its source. His thoughts on this particular aspect of government are no doubt much more apposite today than in his own day, and warrant a close reading on our part.

> Friends, bear with me. I am most anxious to impress this all important truth, *that our only hope for the full development and perpetuity of our free institutions is in the moral soundness of the people* [italics Brownson's]. Our rulers are men from our midst; they do and will partake of the prevailing passions of the times. They will be creatures of the reigning tone — vice or virtue, of the people from whom they are selected. In the general corruption of morals and manners, they escape not uncontaminated. They drink at the popular fountain, and always will be infected by the disease it generates. To the most stupid and least observant, then, it must be evident that in a government like ours, virtue, high, stern, unbending virtue must be maintained by all our citizens, or else we have not the security desired and needed.
>
> We complain of our public officers, of their want of public spirit, stern integrity, and generous disregard of self, but our complaints are misplaced. Our politicians and public men exhibit only the prevailing spirit of the times; and as it would be hard to find out who would not exhibit the same disregard of the public, the same all-absorbing selfishness, it ill becomes us to complain. True, party spirit rages to an alarming extent, evincing very clearly the diseased state of the public mind; true, all seem scrambling for a place to fatten on its rewards; but are only our rulers and prominent politicians to blame? This were a partial view. The demon that sports with our security and threatens our free institutions, possesses not merely a few individuals; he is the reigning spirit of the times; and you all feel his influence, and in greater or less degree, yield to his unholy dominion.
>
> But the errors to which I have alluded, are not those of the government; they are those of the people. We are prone to charge too much to government, as well as to exact too much from its exertions. Government can cure but few of the evils of any community. Its province is mostly negative, to check the encroachments of individual upon individual, and to secure to each the reward of his industry. The great business of life asks no aid of government. The people as individuals and social beings must conduct it as self-interest prompts, and wisdom or ignorance, vice or virtue, directs. There can be no bad government where the people as individuals, are wise, virtuous and independent. There can be no good government where the people are slaves of ignorance and vice, victims of crime, or votaries of luxury and licentiousness.

In this same extended oration Brownson also laid great stress on the necessity of widespread education among the people in general as a necessary constituent of good government. Only a liberal diffusion of knowledge among the people can qualify them to participate as citizens in the government with sufficient intelligence to guarantee the perpetuity of our free institutions. Only virtue plus knowledge would suffice:

> But as true as a high, uncompromising moral virtue is the only sure pledge for national independence and the perpetuity of our free institutions, so true is it that this virtue can never exist without a high mental cultivation. There is no permanence, no worth, no loveliness in the inspirations of ignorance. There is

no hope, no promise of good from the morality of a people over whom hangs an intellectual night, spreading its leaden influence over all the faculties, benumbing all the energies of the human being. . . . Knowledge, correct and universal must be diffused; the mind must be disciplined; and all its almightiness must be aroused, exerted, to give virtue its finish, and man his felicity. Education must wake up a day in the soul, and give life, activity and energy to the whole intellectual man, or moral excellence is but a dream. . . .

The history of the past demonstrates this. Where now are the nations that fill so much of ancient history? Egypt has fallen and long since passed beneath the barbarian's yoke, and yet Egypt was the nursery of the arts and sciences, and by her genial care many of them were brought to a perfection we emulate in vain. Athens has fallen. The Grove, the Portico, the Lyceum, the Garden, no longer echo with the wisdom and refinement of Plato, the moral sublimity of the Stoic, the deep thought, the extensive research of the Stagerite, nor with the amiable philosophy of the Gargettian. A dark night rests upon the scattered fragments of the earliest and loveliest of republics. But Athens was the seat of learning, the academy of Europe. Her sons were masters of all that belong to deep thought, extensive acquaintance with the phenomena of nature; were rich with the creations of genius, and able to seize, abstract and body forth the beautiful, the lovely, the sublime, in forms that shall remain models to all time to come. Rome, too, once haughty mistress of the world, by her arts and sciences, as well as by her arms, now sits in solitude on her seven hills, sighing over her fallen grandeur and departed dominion.

Why? Because there were wanting men of enlightened minds? Surely not for want of philosophers, sages, heroes, statesmen, or orators. No, my friends, the secret of their fall is not in want of knowledge, correct and extensive of the few; but in that the many were ignorant. . . . It was in that general ignorance, with those millions in worse than Egypt's darkness, that originated the diseases which corrupted the body politic and hurried it on to its ruin. The knowledge of the few was too weak to dispel the surrounding darkness, it gave but a feeble glare, and was soon overpowered by universal night.

Let the past teach us wisdom. Let us avoid the rock on which were wrecked the hopes of all our predecessors. . . . Let me repeat it, there is no security to virtue independent of high mental cultivation. Our moral superstructure must rest on mind — must be supported by understanding, or it will have neither beauty nor permanence. . . . Well does it import us, then, to attend to our schools. Our highest wisdom, our holiest thoughts and wishes should be turned to multiplying the facilities for giving every branch of useful knowledge to all, of all ranks, sexes, or condition. We have already done much. Our citizens have not been indifferent to education; but they may do much more; and they will not have done their duty till the means of a competent education are within the reach of every son and daughter of this republic.[16]

Such thoughtful orations may well have had their share in preparing the public mind for the eventual upbuilding of a system of universal education in the country.

Thus, it appears, Orestes Brownson was beginning a career on the platform which was to form a large part of his activities as a public figure. But his more influential work was to be done on neither the platform nor in the pulpit but through his forceful writing. As Daniel Sargent has remarked: "When he had a pen in his hand he feared no man."[17] His pen, said a contemporary, "is nervous as if of iron. His blows fall like those of the Black Knight on the postern-gate of Ivanhoe."[18] But for him to use the pen to fullest effect it had to be his own. What he most needed was a journal of which he was entirely the master, responsible to no individual or group. At this time, when functioning as an independent minister at Ithaca, he also edited and published *The Philanthropist,* a weekly journal. Now for the first time, apparently, he had a free hand to say precisely what he wanted to say without having to reckon with sectarian complaints. He was now undenominational. When he conducted the *Gospel Advocate* his Universalist brethren spurned his social theories. Yet, if the premises were granted from which he argued, critics would have been hard put to find any flaw in his logic, and could scarcely therefore have refuted him. Again, if they could not refute him, they could deny him his salary, and they did so.[19] Independence, he was learning, has its practical and metaphoric price. But that price he was ever more than willing to pay as a journalist. Late in life he wrote in the October issue of his *Review* (1874): "It is ungenerous to threaten us with the loss of subscribers, for we have never yet written a sentence with the view to win, or escape the loss of, a subscriber, and we do not think we ever shall."[20]

Brownson used the columns of *The Philanthropist* to explain his religious experiences. He spoke of the brush he had had with atheism, his recent convalescence, and suggested a line of thought which he was later to develop in *Charles Elwood*. Some of his more beautiful passages (one or the other already quoted) are to be found in its columns. It was perhaps of other passages, however, that George Ripley spoke when he assured Fr. Isaac Hecker "that there are passages in Dr. Brownson which could not be surpassed in the whole range of English literature."[21] Among the contributors to *The Philanthropist* was William Ellery Channing, one of the leading, if not the foremost philanthropist of the day. When Channing sent in one of his sermons for publication, a correspondence between the minister and editor began, but they did not meet until after Brownson's settlement in Walpole, New Hampshire. *The Philanthropist,* however, was to be short-lived. Its circulation was wide enough, but a number of subscribers having failed to pay their dues, the editor was forced to suspend in the middle of the second volume, June 1832. "We dare not," he said, "contract a debt with our printer that we cannot pay; it would be wronging him."[22] Per Sveino, who has examined *The Philanthropist* incisively, further tells us that in his leave-taking Brownson gave way a bit to self-pity when he exclaimed: "The banner of truth may then be furled, ourself ruined, and the friends of a mild and rational religion be compelled to wait yet longer for the day of redemption." With a pathetic sigh, he proposed to retire to "obscurity."[23]

Evidently this failure marked a traumatic moment in his life. Actually, the fact seems to be that Brownson's fortunes had at this juncture dipped to the lowest ebb they were ever to reach during his entire lifetime. The letters he was soon to write to wife Sally show plainly that not only was he financially embarrassed, but that his health was impaired. His own recent struggles against the loss of faith had been trial enough, but he had also on his mind his late damaging association with the Wright-Owen partnership. He could not wholly escape reproachful repercussions from the sanctimonious, nor the pious vapidities of the backbiters. "Infidel" was an ugly epithet. So far he could look back on nothing but failure. His earnest attempt to find truth in matters of religion, soul-trying as it was, had been rewarded with less than indifferent success; his dedicated efforts to push forward the movements for social reform had practically come to naught. His sole rewards for his labors were his pains. A concomitant melancholy, then, is not inexplicable.

With one of the important sources of his revenue gone (the demise of *The Philanthropist*) Brownson felt compelled to try a change of fortunes elsewhere. He decided to seek a new pulpit. Still unattached to any denomination, he was soon to become an associate of the Unitarians. He had been greatly impressed by Channing's sermons and, as the Unitarians were generally well-educated, distinguished for their pure and temperate lives, their philanthropic works in behalf of all men, particularly of the poor and oppressed, Brownson felt that he would find among them his "real home and natural associates."[24] Accordingly, he set off in July 1832 on his quest for a new pulpit and congregation. Yet it was some months before he could make a decision and get settled. After seeing him off at Ithaca, Sally with the two little boys went back home to her parents in Elbridge. If she was to be separated from her husband for a time, the Healy home was a good haven in the interim. And it was to that address that Orestes forwarded his letters.

As he was moving quickly from place to place on his journey and doing considerable lecturing or preaching, it is not surprising that Brownson's letters were infrequent. The first came from Battleborough, Vermont, which he had reached by August 24, 1832.

> My dear:
> I ought to have written you sooner, but I have been flying about with such rapidity that I could hardly find a stopping place. My health is, in the main, good. I was a little indisposed for a fortnight since, but I was in good harbor at my worthy friend, Dr. Willoughby's, Newport. I have heard from you only once since you left me at Ithaca. I pray God you may be well, and also the little boys; I think of you often; my little boys come to me in my dreams. I embrace you in my sleep, and I awake alone. A kind father above will yet smile upon us.
> The object of my journey, I think, will be answered. My good friends in Trenton gave me a new hat and coat; so I am decently dressed. I preached two lectures at Little Falls, one at Troy, as I believe, to good acceptance. Will spend next Sabbath at Walpole, N.H., a short distance from Charleston where resides your uncle Jesse [whom] I had the pleasure of hearing a few days since. He belongs to a Unitarian parish. I shall visit him, I think, as I promised to preach a Sabbath for the Rev. Mr. Crosby, a minister of his parish. God has prospered me thus far better than I could expect. I am received by those Unitarian clergymen I have met with a warmth, a cordiality, and respect which is peculiarly soothing.
> Rev. Mr. Brown, a Unitarian minister with whom I now stop, received this morning a letter from Troy, New York, which was very pleasing. It informed him that active measures were being made there for me, and requested him to follow me, if I had left, with a line not to engage till I should hear from friends in Troy. The letter intimates a design to have me publish my paper in Troy, and adds, "What a treasure we might obtain in Mr. Brownson." So, it is barely possible that I might locate in Troy. It is a delightful city, and a desirable location.
> It is thought I may easily obtain a parish in New England. I prefer Troy. The New England people are kind, warm-hearted, but fastidious and notional; and I believe New York the field after all for which I am best fitted. Say what you will, New England has not the energy and free view of New York. In science, in literature, in reading, it is before us; but in bold men, in activity of thought, in impatience of restraint, New York is abundant years in advance. With us, the people are in advance of the clergy; here, the clergy are fifty years, yes, a hundred years before the people.
> Do enjoy yourself as much as you can. Make yourself easy about me. I will venture to bid you hope, and I do not say it merely to keep your spirits up; but because I think I can say so with propriety. I feel myself that we shall see better times. God grant we may. Give my love to all the family. Tell the little boys, "Pa wants to see and kiss them." May heaven protect them and you, my dear wife. Of His love feel confident, and of mine passionately and forever.
> Yours in the tenderest of affection,
> O.A. Brownson[25]

In spite of the attractions Troy had at first held for Brownson, he was finally to settle as the pastor of the Unitarian Society in Walpole, New Hampshire. But he first canvassed matters in Walpole very closely. He was scheduled to preach there at least three Sabbaths — on one of which, however, he exchanged pulpits with Rev. Mr. Wilson, pastor of Petersham, Massachusetts. During his visits to Walpole, he had become very fond of the people whom he considered congenial and intelligent. Brownson being a great lover of natural scenery, Walpole had its special charms for him. The village itself is located at the foot of a great slope on the east side of the Connecticut River; the bridge spanning the river leads to Bellow Falls, Vermont, on the other side. "The view from the bridge is highly interesting and sublime. In a distance of half a mile the water descends in cataracts and rapids more than forty feet, though in no place is the fall perpendicular to any considerable extent; but below the junction of Cold River the Connecticut is compressed into a narrow strait between rocks, and for nearly a quarter of a mile is hurried on with great rapidity and roaring."[26]

While still on his journey Orestes wrote Sally another letter telling her of the experiences he had had, and, finally, of the call he had received, all but definite, from the parish in Walpole. The letter, begun at Petersham, Massachusetts, on October 15, was not completed till two weeks later. If one or two sentences seem a bit boastful, it is well to remember the private character of the comments. Little did he dream that his letter would become public property. He wrote:

My dear:

I should have written you sooner, but I have been driven along by such a bustle as is usual with me. I shall write the first part of my letter today, for I feel the mood is for it; but I may not conclude it under some days.

To begin with, my health is not very good just this moment owing to a slight cold, and too great fatigue; but, upon the whole, I am a hundred percent better as to my general health than when I left Ithaca. I hope you and the little boys continue good. You know how much I want to see, and how anxious I think about you.

You may want to know how I came here. Well, I attended an association of Unitarian clergymen in New Salem, about nine miles from this, last Tuesday. The association was very pleasant. There was one public service. A sermon was preached by myself, and, I believe, to general satisfaction. It was criticized pretty closely in council, but pronounced "good." The remark of one aged clergyman was acquiesced in by all. "It," he said, "has not often fallen to my lot to hear a discourse in which I was so well pleased." I went from Salem to Athol, a promising town in Worcester Co., where I preached a lecture for the Rev. Mr. Nevon which I believe was well received. Mr. Nevon brought me here, a distance of 8 miles, to the home of Mr. Wilson, to whom I had letters from Truxton, New York. We negotiated a change. Mr. Wilson went to Walpole, about fifty miles, for me yesterday, and I officiated for him. My congregation was large, and I believe my services were more than acceptable. Today, I go to Templeton to attend another association, and shall aim to be back at Walpole next Sabbath. I have seen no Unitarian parish yet that I could think of in preference to Walpole. Walpole suits me.

You may be curious to know how I find myself by the side of Unitarian clergymen. Well, my dear, pardon my vanity, I shall speak what I believe the truth. I must premise that I have seen only the ordinary class. They are all respectable but with rather narrow views. I have seen no one yet that made me feel small, and the popularity of my discourses proves that people do not deem me inferior. In Walpole, where have preached some of the greatest men of the order, I have been pronounced superior to any of them. Probably this is exaggeration. My own conviction is that I am inferior only in useless browsing, but superior in practical knowledge. I do not think I have met here a clergyman who has so sifted the human heart, and who is so capable of taking enlarged and comprehensive views of religion as myself. I believe it in my power to impart two ideas where I may receive one. My talents are decidedly more popular than most I have met.

His statement that he felt it within his power to impart two ideas where he had received only one is interesting, and perhaps not entirely without some truth. At least what Joseph Henry Allen related of Brownson would seem to lend the assertion some coloring of truth. Speaking of Brownson's reading of Kant, Allen said: "With a curiously slender stock of erudition, he showed an equally extraordinary arrogance and fertility in abstract argument. For example, having toiled with much ado (as he told me) through some fourteen pages of Kant's *Introduction* — having got the idea of it to his own satisfaction — he proceeded to write more than fifty pages of what, I am told by those more competent to judge than I, is really instructive exposition."[27]

Orestes continued his letter to Sally:

The trustees in Walpole say that they want a man that can take high rank among New England clergymen; and they say I can, and they believe will do it. It is most probable you will receive a call there. I will be as expeditious as possible. But I must do my work thoroughly. It is better to suffer a little now from absence that we may be comfortable for a long time together hereafter, than it is to precipitate affairs, and have everything to do over again.

This much of the letter he wrote at Petersham. The last paragraphs were to be added at Walpole, October 29, after the contract establishing him pastor there had been finalized. He now added the happy news to his letter that he was to have the parish he wanted. The yearly salary would be $500 — "not large, but we can live on it."

My love to you and the little boys. Compliments to all. I shall write you soon again; but you must write me once a week, no failure, at peril of giving me great pain.

If John can aid you in obtaining clothes for you and the little ones, I wish he would; as you will need considerable before you come here, I wish it might be furnished by him. Be in good heart. God bless you and protect you, and grant that we meet soon again.

Yours ever,
O. A. Brownson[28]

Having made his choice of place, his mind was at ease. Whether he might have decided more wisely, we do not know. But it does seem that Walpole offered him at this time of his life the milieu and opportunities wholly agreeable to an appropriate cultural preparation favorable to his later more public career. If he had been largely denied any formal education, Walpole was to be his academy wherein he could fill the gaps in his learning, and lay the foundations of a remarkable scholarship.

# 6

## THE YEARS AT WALPOLE

*He begins his study of foreign languages with French • Benjamin Constant and other French philosophers and social reformers engage his close attention • He makes the acquaintance of the prominent Unitarians of the day, Dr. William Ellery Channing, George Ripley, Bernard Whitman and others • Contributes to the popular Unitarian publications of the day,* The Unitarian *and* The Christian Register, *and begins his public addresses and lyceum lectures.*

In the latter part of 1832 Orestes Brownson settled down with his family as pastor of the Unitarian parish in Walpole, New Hampshire. It was to become the closest thing to a haven of peace that he would ever know. Walpole became for him a sort of academy. For the first time he began a systematic study of philosophy and theology. The pleasures of the scholar became so absorbing for him that he "almost forgot his socialistic dreams."[1] French books came his way, and he worked earnestly to master the French language with only a grammar, a dictionary and the Bible to aid him. The first use to which he put his new reading knowledge was a reading of Benjamin Constant's huge work in five octavo volumes, *De la Réligion Considérée dans sa Source, ses Formes et ses Dévelopments (Religion, Considered in Its Origin, Its Forms, and Its Developments)*. Constant's all-pervasive theory is that religion has its origin in a sentiment universal to man, a sentiment which may be called the law of man's nature. Although Brownson was to apply this theory quite elaborately later, his first impulse was to clasp it gratefully to his bosom as a happy confirmation of his own religious faith. Many years later he was to recall the salutary influence the reading of Constant's work had on him at the time:

> Never shall we forget the joy with which my heart bounded, when we fancied that Benjamin Constant had proved that religion has a firm and solid foundation in a law of nature, universal, personal, and indestructible as that nature itself — not indeed because it saved us from the necessity of believing the Bible or of submitting to an external authoritative revelation, but because for the moment it seemed to restore us to communion with the religious world. It was indeed but the straw to which the drowning man clings, but it seemed to us something more, and to give us the right to say, I too am a believer; I too can look up to heaven and say, My Father; around upon mankind and say, My Brothers.[2]

With the reading of Benjamin Constant, Brownson began to see clearly that a knowledge of languages may unlock great treasures. He began a study of German. He later went on as opportunity offered to studies of the principal languages of Europe, particularly Italian and Spanish, and looked to an improvement of his German.[3] While content with a thorough reading knowledge of these languages, his effort was so able that he could in later years criticize the profoundest works in philosophy and theology in those languages. Previously, as his son has told us, he had acquired "some Latin and less Greek" in the academy at Ballston Spa, New York. His knowledge of the classic languages he was to brush up quite thoroughly. In 1844 he was directing his attention to the study of Greek.[4] Matthew Smith, who studied Brownson's *Works* "intensely" for two or three years under the guidance of a theologian, asserted that Brownson read "the Fathers of the Church . . . in the original Latin and Greek."[5]

Brownson's fascinating acquaintance with Benjamin Constant was, however, only the beginning of his absorbing interest in French authors, philosophers and social reformers. Later he was to acknowledge not only the great influence French literature had had in the forming of his own mind and taste, but also the pervasive nature of French influence among the nations:

> Her doctrines have immense influence in England; they reign supreme in this country; Germany reaches us only through France, and from France we import not only our fashions, but our tastes, our principles, our ideas, our philosophy, and our literature. In France is the fountain whose streams flow either to fertilize or to deluge our land. . . . We have spoken kindly . . . of that beautiful country, whose literature has had more to do in the forming of our mind and our taste than that of our mother tongue.[6]

In their turn, after Benjamin Constant, came Comte de Saint-Simon, Theodore Jouffroy, Victor Cousin, Pierre Leroux and others to exert their influences upon him. Brownson made some of these writers the first subjects of his stimulating book reviews in *The Unitarian, The Christian Register,* or the more sedate *Christian Examiner,* to which he contributed many articles for a span of years. In later life he was called "a born reviewer," with little suspicion of the laborious efforts by which he had acquired the ability to analyze an author's thoughts thoroughly. For a dozen years before he began book reviewing it had been his habit when reading an author to set down in a notebook what the author had set out to prove, then to examine the book closely chapter after chapter, and to mark down to what extent the author had succeeded in establishing his points, or in case of failure, to give his judgment on the reason for and the extent of his failure. Through such an analysis of each work he gradually acquired the ability to state an author's views with precise brevity and with at least as much force as the author himself. The notebook method he was to follow for another dozen years until the process became automatic, a habit of mind. His son Henry assures us that it was only by much painstaking endeavor that his father acquired his uncanny ability as a critic or book reviewer.[7]

Leonard J. McCarthy, in his dissertation, *Rhetoric in the Works of Orestes Brownson,* tells us that Brownson's notebook method was really what is called "invention": "Invention is the discovery of valid, or seemingly valid arguments to render one's cause plausible." It also serves as a means of judging the structure of an essay or speech. This method or pattern includes a seven-point division:

1. Identification of the book or article under consideration.
2. Identification of the author.
3. Comments on the author and his style.
4. Exposition: what the author says.
5. Argument: why Brownson agrees or disagrees. Argument from induction, deduction, analogy or retort.
6. Emotional appeal: rare in the logical style.
7. Conclusion.[8]

This is the logical skeleton that underlies all Brownson's literary works as a critic. Following this method he became a highly able critic indeed. In a foreword to *The Literary Criticism of Orestes Brownson,* C. C. Hollis remarks:

> Brownson's literary criticism is important for two reasons, each relating to separate periods of his life. In his liberal period, from 1838 to 1844, the critical reviews of his *Boston Quarterly* are those of a major Jacksonian critic as well as a significant interpreter and critic of New England Transcendentalism. In the second and longer conservative period, from 1844 to the termination of *Brownson's Quarterly Review* in 1875, he was the first Catholic literary critic of the age.[9]

Whatever the process by which he had acquired his unique skill as a literary critic, he considered book reviewing to be, "if one would excel in it, the most difficult species of writing that can be named."[10] It is extremely taxing in that it calls for a wide-ranging knowledge. Through intense and tireless application Brownson did what he could to measure up to that requirement. In time his knowledge became encyclopedic. The story has been handed down that Bishop John B. Fitzpatrick of Boston (Brownson's good friend), and a group of priests, having been greatly impressed by the astonishing range of Brownson's knowledge, and perhaps a bit vexed by his dogmatic tone at times, agreed among themselves to see if they could catch him short on some topic of conversation. To pull it off, they chuckled, would be a good joke on the Old Boy. The next time they met with Brownson they brought up as a topic of conversation a subject so far removed from the ordinary orbit of conversation as the Catholic missions of Iceland, quietly ignoring the Doctor as if the theme was entirely out of his latitude. Brownson was not only *not* caught, but he turned the tables on them by correcting their main leads, and enlarging on the whole theme with an elaborate array of facts. He afterwards disclosed that he had only recently been studying an extensive work on the subject, just issued, and the company despaired of ever being able to overshadow him on any subject.[11]

But a man of Brownson's intense energies could not limit himself in any sense merely to books. He was as typical an American as any that lived, with all the bustling activity and intense practicality of the American. While sedulously reading the French philosophers and social reformers, he was also hammering out from them new religious and social theories for his active program in the years ahead. Closely, too, did he identify himself with the surrounding community. He preached an average of four sermons a week, and gave frequent lyceum lectures and public addresses, mainly in Massachusetts. These were always carefully prepared beforehand, and written out though not committed to memory. The mere writing out of his thoughts impressed them sufficiently upon his memory that he could recall them with substantial accuracy when speaking. He did not, however, follow his manuscript slavishly, but might at any time bring in relevant matter that might occur to him on the spur of the moment.[12]

These public addresses and lyceum lectures of Brownson were a real source of popular instruction in an age when the modern newspaper had not yet the informative role it has today, and libraries were still relatively scarce. Neither the Boston nor New York library was founded until 1854. In 1850, the Harvard Library, with its 72,000 volumes, was, according to Justin Winsor, the largest in the country.[13] With cultural sources thus limited, the public speaker in the first part of the nineteenth century was still one of the principal sources of public instruction. And on special occasions such as the Fourth of July, or Revival Meetings, the public address served also as a chief source of diversion for the people. Formal addresses to the people became a tradition which stimulated them to discuss the information imparted. Alexis de Tocqueville, astonished at the flow of rhetoric he found among the American people, remarked: "Debating Clubs are, to a great extent, a substitute for theatrical entertainment; an American can converse, but he cannot discuss; and his talk falls into a dissertation. He speaks to you as if he were addressing a meeting; and if he should chance to become warm in his discussion, he will say, 'Gentlemen,' to the person with whom he is conversing." Speaking of the importance of the lecture in his day, Ralph Waldo Emerson went so far as to say: "I look upon the lecture-room as the true church of today, and as the home of a richer eloquence than Faneuil Hall or the Capitol ever knew."[14]

It is not surprising, then, that Brownson was not without ambition as a public speaker. He put forth every effort to excel in that art. His son Henry tells us that:

> Although Brownson had never received a regular education in a college or university, he had studied oratory more earnestly and thoroughly than the vast majority of college graduates. He had read attentively all the most applauded orations of ancient and modern times, and had heard the best speakers of his own country, by no means behind others in oratory.[15]

He was to continue to give public lectures and addresses all his life. There was scarcely a small town in New England, or a large one in the Atlantic States, in which he did not eventually lecture. Over the years his lecturing took him as far south as New Orleans and Mobile, as far west as St. Louis, and on to Montreal and Quebec in Canada at the invitation of friends there. Scarcely ever did a Fourth of July pass without Brownson delivering an address in some New England town. Frequently, too, he was called upon to deliver the main address on commencement day at colleges for the graduating class. Whatever the occasion, he always adopted a style and manner in harmony with it. "In sermons and political addresses he was more impassioned, imaginative, declamatory; in academical addresses and lyceum lectures reasoning, argument, and exposition were conspicuous, as a general rule; though in every case he sought to convince the mind before laboring to rouse the feelings."[16]

Fr. Isaac T. Hecker has left us a notable sketch of Brownson as he appeared on the public platform in New York City in 1841. Recalling toward the end of his life the impression Brownson had made on him, Hecker said:

> Dr. Brownson was then in the very prime of his manhood. He was a handsome man, tall, stately, and of grave manners. As he appeared on the platform and received our greetings he was indeed a majestic man, displaying in his manner the power of a mind altogether above the ordinary. But he was essentially a philosopher, and that means he never could be what is called popular. He was an interesting speaker, but he never sought popularity. He never seemed to care much about the reception his words received, but he exhibited anxiety to get his thoughts rightly expressed and to leave no doubt about what his convictions were. Yet among a limited class of minds he always awakened real enthusiasm — among minds, that is, of a philosophical tendency. He never used manuscript or notes; he was familiar with his topic, and his thoughts flowed out spontaneously in good, pure, forcible English. He could control any reasonable mind, for he was a man of great thoughts and never without some

75

grand truth to impart. But to stir the emotions was not in his power, though he sometimes attempted it; he never succeeded in being really pathetic.[17]

One wonders a bit at the last sentence, for Fr. Hecker modified it somewhat when describing the effects of a Fourth of July oration delivered by Brownson in New York City that same year. After telling us that it was he himself and his brothers who had secured Brownson's consent to come to the city for the occasion, Hecker wrote: "Brownson was never more earnest in his life than in that address. I have forgotten the exact matter of the oration, but none who heard him could ever forget his manner. The immense energy, the intense conviction, the great voice, the emphatic gestures, not only aroused our emotions but shook the old hotel to its foundations and made the glass in the windows rattle again."[18]

In an article on Brownson in *The Catholic World,* Virgil Michel has argued that Brownson had everything in his favor as an orator — his towering height, his voice of great power and compass, his imposing figure. He cited O. B. Frothingham's comment: "[He was] a powerful writer and lecturer." Even Brownson's writings, asserted Michel, were of such a magnetic quality that they often carried the reader headlong away, and made it difficult to imagine that the impetuous ardor of the man would not also have imparted a genuine and forceful quality to his public speaking.[19] A writer who had listened to his lectures in St. Louis in 1854, though differing "widely" from his views on different subjects, said of him: "His appearance can hardly be improved upon, and his delivery fills exactly our idea of what it should be in a popular orator."[20]

But Brownson learned the art of effective public speaking only by earnest and persevering effort. It was not a native gift. He used to say that when he preached his first sermon he was under such stress and strain that the perspiration could have been wrung from his clothing before he was through. But by persevering effort and study he learned in time to modulate his voice properly, gesture appropriately, gained perfect control and poise, and could master any audience he faced, even if the group was unfriendly. One such incident occurred in a speech in the Tabernacle of New York City, where Brownson was greeted by hisses and yells. He advanced to the edge of the platform and, growing seemingly bulkier as he advanced, leaned over the edge, and said in a voice that could be heard above the raucous scene: "I came not here to gain your applause or to escape your censure but to tell you the truth; and I *will* tell it." The audience liked this show of bold independence, and there was soon a general outburst of applause.[21]

Brownson could not accept the kind of preaching he found common in New England. It was, he thought, cold and lifeless, stiff and artificial, devoid of that earnestness which should go with the preaching of the great, solemn truths of the Gospel. It lacked warmth and directness, that magnetic spark of communication between preacher and people necessary to make a truth vivid. As C. C. Hollis remarks, he understood the wants of the times. He appealed to his fellow ministers for a change of tone and manner in a letter he contributed to *The Unitarian* entitled "The Coldness of New England Preaching." In the course of his letter, he wrote:

> I know the New England character; I know the New England climate is cold; I know the wind that comes over her bleak hills and granite mountains is cold; I know that the exterior of her sons and daughters is cold; but she has souls of fire. . . . No people can feel genuine eloquence better than the New Englanders. Yet it is not given them; the pulpit knows only coldness. There is

something almost criminal in the coldness of the pulpit. The state of the world demands a ministry that can forget everything save Christ and him crucified. Let us have such a ministry. Let us speak loudly, and earnestly, in strong nervous, bold, glowing, burning language, and cold as is our northern manner, we will put up with it, and thank God for it.[22]

The private life of every great man, perhaps all the more so in the case of a clergyman, is often of intriguing interest — his appearance, if not personally known, his general way of life, his personal manners, habits, likes and dislikes. Fortunately in Brownson's case, his son Henry has handed down to us a thumbnail sketch of his father as a Protestant minister in his early life. One wishes the details were fuller, but there is enough to indicate his general way of life:

> Brownson's personal appearance as a Protestant minister was very different from what he became in later life. Two inches over six feet in height, with broad shoulders and a large frame, his weight was less than 170 pounds. His bodily strength was unusually great, and his vigor was kept up by habitual exercise, both in walking and working in the garden. His hair was black and brushed straight back from his forehead without parting; around his mouth he was shaved, and on the upper part of his cheeks; his eyes seemed black, but were of mixed grey and hazel; his upper lip long, his hands long and broad. His dress, at this time and until he gave up preaching, was broadcloth; he wore a dress coat, what is sometimes called a swallow-tail, at all hours of the day, even in his studies, and a large square white handkerchief folded to a width of three or four inches in front of his neck, crossed behind and tied in front. He slept little, but sat up writing or studying till 2 or 3 o'clock or later. His diet was sparing, his abstinence from wine and spirits total, though he drank strong coffee morning and evening. His total abstinence from alcohol was as much due to taste as to principle, and indeed he never heartily took up the total abstinence fanaticism, though he often addressed temperance societies.[23]

On February 26, 1833, he delivered a full-length address before the Walpole Temperance Society in which he gave the movement all the encouragement and backing his earnest words could impart. Yet he admitted that only slowly had he been won over to an acknowledgment of the good done by temperance societies. He deeply disliked the fanaticism sometimes found in such societies; nor could he accept any movement that tended to swallow the individual to the loss of his personal identity. (His was a prescient hostility to what has developed in later days into mass conformity.) Whatever the less amiable features of these societies, Brownson admitted that temperance societies have done good for society: "This admission has been extorted from me, for I am opposed to self-created societies in general. I do not like the machinery put into operation by this wonder-working age. We have too many wheels within wheels, too many governments within governments. The age tends too much to association; people are beginning to act only in crowds, and the individual is being fast lost in the mass."[24] Much of Brownson's thought here may have some relevance to our own times.

Though a resident of Walpole, Brownson's mind often turned to Boston, where resided so many of the most distinguished leaders of the Unitarian movement, Dr. William Ellery Channing, George Ripley, Bernard Whitman and others. Indeed, he made frequent visits to Boston, ninety miles away by stagecoach, that he might gain a personal acquaintance with the best minds there and carry away with him new inspiration and zest for the work he was trying to do. Years later Augustine F. Hewit remarked: "He [Brownson] came into contact with intellectual and cultured men for the first time in Boston after he joined the Unitarians."[25] While he was making his personal acquaintance with the literati of Boston, they on their part were becoming more and more impressed by his writings which were appearing in the more popular Unitarian publications, *The Unitarian* and *The Christian Register*. It was the gradual beginning of the impact he was to make on the New England mind.

His first contributions were to *The Unitarian,* a monthly journal published in Boston. They appeared in two installments of the magazine under the heading, "Christianity and Reform." His aim was to show that Christianity is the true principle of reform in society since it alone appeals to the whole nature of man, spiritual as well as material, particularly to his higher faculties. Infidelity, on the other hand, is ineffectual to bring about the needed alterations in society, for it addresses man only as a soulless animal and does not enlist his higher powers and aspirations as necessary for effecting salutary reforms. Its appeal leaves out, therefore, a part, and the noblest part, of man's nature. Yet in the past the reform movement has often been allied with the infidel movement. How explain it? Brownson replied:

> When the French reformer rose against the mischievous remains of the feudal system, and the severe exactions of a superannuated tyranny, he found the church leagued with the abuses he would correct. Those who lived upon her revenues bade him retire. The anathema met his advance and repelled his attacks; and he was induced to believe there was no place whereon to erect the palace of liberty and social order, but [only] the ruins of the temple.[26]

Whether or not, or to what extent, the human element in the Church stood in the way of proper reforms in the past, Vatican Council II declared: "Therefore, by virtue of the gospel committed to her, the Church proclaims the rights of man. She acknowledges and greatly esteems the dynamic movements of today by which these rights are everywhere fostered." To which a footnote is appended: "Whatever the regrettable misunderstandings that turned 'the rights of man' into a rallying cry by the Church's bitter foes in the 18th and 19th centuries and entrenched the Church in a role of intransigent resistance to movements for social revolution in many parts of the world, the Council makes it unequivocally plain that the Church intends to play its historic role as champion of human rights and align itself with those who fight for these rights."[27]

Perhaps Brownson was thinking of his own earlier days when he wrote in "Christianity and Reform" that the hostility of the reformer is often directed not at religion itself, but rather at the abuses that go under its name, that have become mixed up with it, and that are so easily identified with it by the vast majority of mankind. He called upon his readers to separate the real Christianity of the Gospel from the incidental abuses that have grown up around it, abuses which were the result of the human element within the Christian pale. It will be readily perceived, he assured them, that Christianity is the real principle of reform: "Did it not, and does it not, appeal directly to the individual heart, and seek to kindle up a strong, undying love of all that is pure, useful, generous and noble in character; and was it not expressly designed to impart the inward power needed to gain it? Is not here the spirit of reform, of radical reform?

"Should every individual become virtuous, acquire that purity of heart, that firmness of purpose, that love to God and man, which the gospel demands, that moral growth which Jesus labored to produce, there could re-

main no institutions of an evil tendency. . . . Make all men good Christians —
and all men can and should be — all governments would become free, all
social institutions beneficial, and man's intercourse with man, harmonious,
pleasing, and endearing."[28]

The Rev. Bernard Whitman, the principal editor of *The Unitarian,* informed Brownson that the editors thought "highly" of his performance, and
assured him that they would be "exceedingly" glad to have a continuance of
*such* articles. He earnestly begged Brownson to begin in the very next edition of *The Unitarian* a series of letters on the Workingmen's party, a subject then awakening interest. "The extemporaneous lectures on the party
which you gave for me," he said, "if cut up into six or eight parts, would furnish suitable matter." Whitman went to some pains to outline a plan for the
letters. Brownson, however, did not follow out the plan, but did contribute an
article on the Workingmen's party in April 1834. Whitman's request to
Brownson shows that Brownson was pretty well associated in the public
mind with the workingmen's cause. Whitman had asked him to draw on his
personal knowledge and experience.

Brownson had also been contributing a series of articles to *The Christian Register,* of Boston, and Whitman ended his letter, saying:

> Your letters in the Register have been much liked and generally read. I
> was however surprised yesterday to find that many in Boston did not know
> their author. Mr. Ripley had Christmas service. We had a goodly collection of
> clergy. Mr. Francis, one of the very first men, spoke in high terms of the let-
> ters, and wished to know if you would not collect them into a volume. Mr.
> Emerson of Boston did not know their author.[29]

Among the articles Brownson contributed to *The Unitarian* was one on
the life and work of the French philosopher, Comte de Saint-Simon, founder
of the Saint-Simonians.[30] Regarded also as the founder of French socialism,
Saint-Simon was to have a tremendous influence on Brownson in the years
ahead, particularly through his teaching that the institutions of society
should be so organized as to aid in the speediest, most effective way the continuous moral, intellectual and physical amelioration of the poorer and more
numerous classes of society. No doctrine could have been more appealing to
the mind and heart of Orestes Brownson. Inasmuch as Saint-Simon had
erected his theories into a hierarchical religion, he was also of service to
Brownson in helping him to overcome any prejudice he may have had to the
hierarchical nature of Catholicity — papacy and all.

Dr. William Ellery Channing, too, was quite favorably impressed by
Brownson's articles in *The Unitarian*, and took pen in hand to write the author his gratification. Brownson had previously written the Doctor expressing his esteem for his writings and his gratitude for the salutary effect they
had had in his own case. (Brownson's esteem for Dr. Channing in these years
was so pronounced that he named his third son after him.) In reply to Brownson's letter to him Dr. Channing told Brownson that he owed the letter being
written him to his communications in *The Unitarian*. "I am much gratified," he said, "to find that you were to treat Christianity as a principle of
*reform*." Yet Channing was rather cautious about what he said in his letter.
He continued: "I have read several of your publications, and though I cannot
subscribe to them without some important modifications, yet the consciousness they breathe of your moral and immortal nature, the sensibility you
express to what is great and good, your spiritual views of religion, your superiority to the artificial distinctions of society and your desire to raise up the

mass of your fellow creatures, have interested me much." Then he added: "I know that a man's writings are not sure tests of his character, and that a stranger, like yourself, not brought up among us, and who has made important changes in religion, cannot be regarded immediately with that entire reliance which we place in a long known and tried friend."[31]

In a way, Channing's words were curiously prophetic. He was not to like all that Brownson was to say and do. There was, after all, a certain unpredictability about Brownson, and Channing sensed that fact. (All that anyone could be sure about in Brownson's case was that he would be as constant as the North Star to what he honestly believed to be right. About the rest, no one could be sure.) As a result he was to remain all his life long an adamantine individualist — fighting in defense of his right to remain Orestes A. Brownson to the end.

*The Unitarian*, a monthly publication, begun in 1834, was short-lived as Whitman, the editor and pastor of the Unitarian Congregation of Waltham, Massachusetts, died in November of 1834. It had as its contributors, besides Brownson, a number of able writers such as Rev. Noah Worcester and James Freeman Clarke. Whitman's aim had been to make Unitarianism popular by giving to *The Unitarian* an easy, plain and direct address such as would appeal to the popular mind and heart. Brownson went further, and endeavored to bring out in his contributions the democratic doctrine latent in the Gospel, for as he believed, it is rather the democratic thought than the plain and easy address that would make a vibrant appeal to the popular mind and heart.[32] With the demise of *The Unitarian,* Brownson continued his articles to *The Christian Register* which for some time had been attracting the increasing attention of the more distinguished Unitarians in Boston. Already in January of 1833, George Ripley, acting editor, had written Orestes Brownson:

> As acting editor of The Christian Register, for the time being, I take the liberty to say, how much pleasure your valuable communications have given not only to myself, but to our religious public in general — and to beg that you will continue to favor us with them. The Register, as you well know, has been far from doing justice to the great cause, to which it is devoted. We are determined, if possible, to revive and improve it. But we must look to our friends for aid. We wish to give it some point, energy, and actual effect. Nothing can be better than your articles. Permit me to say, what I have often heard, that they are very much approved. Their style is pithy, lucid, and direct — just what is needed for a religious newspaper. Now, let me beg of you to do for us what you can. You have had an uncommon experience — let us be benefitted by the results of it.[33]

Ripley, Channing and other distinguished Unitarians, had of late become alarmed about the increasing drift of the workingmen from the churches. At this time already they had perceived the beginnings of the evil that Pope Pius IX was to lament later when he said: "The great scandal of our time is that the Church has lost the working class."[34] Ripley, Channing and others felt that something had to be done to stem the unhappy tide, and to win back those who had already strayed. And they were in hearty agreement that Orestes Brownson, of all people, was just the man who could do something about it if any man could, provided he were placed in a center of activity. His own association with the Workingmen's party in the past, and his experience with skepticism, rationalism and infidelity, gave him splendid advantages for addressing the workingmen and christianizing their whole movement, if only a program could be rightly managed. And Boston, they felt, was the most strategic theater for launching the experiment.

On March 26, 1834, Ripley wrote Brownson from Boston about the possibility of inaugurating some kind of an apostolate to the disaffected members of the churches and to those already unchurched. The first part of the letter makes plain that there had been previous discussions of the matter between the two, and as Ripley wrote:

> Since I saw you, I have conversed on the subject with a few intelligent gentlemen, who agree with me in thinking that in all probability, such a ministry could have a salutary effect. I have supposed that if a man of talents, judgment and piety, wise as the serpent and harmless as the dove, were to come here, on his own responsibleness, in the true spirit of Christian enterprise, to seek and save them that are lost, his labors will meet with success. I have little doubt that in two or three years a society might be built up, of Christians plucked as brands from the burning — of persons who are disgusted with orthodoxy and insensible to liberal Christianity in any of its modes, in which it is now represented, but who would gladly hear the Gospel of Jesus preached in the spirit of Jesus, in a way to meet their intellectual and moral needs. . . . You have rare advantages from your former relations with scepticism, and it appears to me are designed in Providence to act upon larger and different classes of men from those to whom you now have access. A large city presents the true field of your labors where you would meet with congenial spirits, and infuse your soul into them.[35]

Ripley then speculated on the advisability of connecting a journal of some sort with the proposed project in such wise as to widen and intensify the contemplated appeal. He made plain to Brownson that he was writing merely to inquire whether he would be willing to make the attempt, what he would regard as a sufficient encouragement in the matter, and what plan of operation he would deem the most judicious. Nothing of the affair, he assured Brownson, had been let out to the public, nor would be, until Brownson would make known his own feelings about the venture.

Ripley's letter, however, reached Brownson a little too late to have any immediate effect. During the previous month Brownson had made a tour in and around Boston. He had visited some of the most prominent Unitarians and was apparently in quest of a new location. Canton had engaged his attention to a degree. From Fall River, February 19, 1834, he wrote to Sally telling her of the happenings on his journey and his speculations about the future:

> My Dear, Dear Wife:
> I have received only one letter from you. Whether it be yours or Mr. Whitman's fault I know not; but I hope you are still well and meet with no troubles. I expect now to be in Walpole next week on Saturday for breakfast.
> I was much pleased with Canton. I think probably they will invite me to settle with them; but whether or not I will accept is uncertain. I do not think I should gain anything in accepting except access to the Boston and Cambridge libraries.
> I spent last week in Boston. Tuesday, called on Dr. Channing, found very well, spent a few pleasant hours with him. Wednesday dined with him at his house. Thursday, I preached for Mr. Frothingham; dined with Mr. Ripley, editor of the Christian Register. Like him very much. Friday dined at Mr. Mason's; had for company Mrs. Parkman, Dr. Channing, and Mr. Gasinetta. Pleasant time.
> Mr. Ganneth told me that I was a great favorite with Mr. Mason's family. I

like them much. There is a great ease and simplicity combined with their high style of living. I came here last Saturday. I find mud in great quantities. No snow here — none of any consequence this winter. This place is 50 miles from Boston — nearly south; 17 miles from Providence, 17 miles from Taunton, 15 from New Bedford, about 18 from Newport, Rhode Island, and 12 from Dr. Channing's summer residence. He is anxious that I should come here, but I do not find much to make me wish to come. This place, I have no doubt, is pleasant in the summer. It is rapidly increasing, has about five thousand inhabitants, and six religious congregations. The Unitarian congregation last Sabbath was not over one hundred and twenty. They are building a great overgrown house in which their congregation will lose itself. They invited a minister to reside with them; they have failed as yet to get a minister. They have offered a salary of $1000. Nominally large, but really not better than $600 in Walpole. I do not believe I shall receive a call. I feel in my bones that I shall not suit them. I do not think I should accept should they invite me. They want me to go to Boston, and raise up a new Society — also to New York; but, I shall stay in Walpole if they make out $500, let who will call.

I see no place so pleasant, no people I like so well as Walpole, and my congregation. . . . I am anxious to get home, to kiss my wife and children, and sit down in peace.

Tell Dolly that I salute her with a brother's love; remember me to Catherine, good girl; tell the little boys to be wide awake and good, to love me — each other, Dolly, Catherine, and everybody. Je vous braise. Au revoir.

Yours forever and longer,<br>
O. A. Brownson[36]

Shortly after this letter was written, Orestes Brownson received a call to become the pastor of the First Congregational Church of Canton, Massachusetts. In spite of all his acknowledged fondness for Walpole and its congregation, he decided to accept Canton's offer. It is not unlikely that the proximity of the Boston and Cambridge libraries as well as other cultural advantages exercised a strong influence in his decision. Already by March 10 the church committee of Walpole had drawn up its testimonials of esteem for their pastor which they wished him to carry with him upon his departure. This antedated by some weeks the letter Ripley was to write Brownson the last of March urging him to come to Boston and inaugurate an apostolate to those drifting from the churches, particularly the laboring classes. What Brownson might have done had Ripley's letter reached him some weeks earlier is a matter of idle speculation. The letters of both Brownson and Ripley show, however, that the project had been previously discussed with some earnestness among a number of prominent Unitarians in Boston, and was known to Brownson. Perhaps at this time Brownson may have felt that the venture was of too chimerical a nature to risk a try. The fact that it was to be altogether unconnected with any of the churches only underscored the shaky underpinning of the project.

In the interim it must have been a genuine pleasure for Brownson to carry with him to his new pastorate in Canton the testimonials of good will and esteem his parishioners of Walpole tendered him:

Walpole, N.H., March 10th, 1834

Whereas a separation being about to take place between the Unitarian Church and society at Walpole, N.H., and the Revd. Brownson, their pastor. It is esteemed proper that he carry with him some testimonials of the friendly regard of a people who have for nearly two years past been under his religious instruction.

It may in candor be said, that some differences of opinion have arisen between him and some of his hearers — but nothing which has excited unfriendly feelings (as we believe) on the part of pastor or people.

It seems he is called to a more extensive field of usefulness, where he is likely to be rewarded in a measure much more adequate to the wants of a young family than he could expect from this small society. It is gratifying to us that his own personal interests are thus encouraged, and that this wide and extended field for usefulness is opened to him.

Of his moral character here, it is without blemish, and from whatever has come to our knowledge, previous to his connection with us, nothing has appeared to call it in question.

Whereupon this society unanimously recommends him to the church and society of Canton, as a gentleman of talents, capable of doing much good in his vocation, and may with the divine blessing be a useful ornament in the cause of Christianity.

Thomas Bellows, Chairman

John Bellows, *Clerk pro tem*

The foregoing being read, it was voted that the same be signed by the chairman and the clerk, and presented to the Rev. Mr. Brownson.

John Bellows, Clerk pro tem"

# 7

## THE YEARS AT CANTON

*Brownson's Fourth of July oration at Dedham • The reaction to it from Rev. Samuel C. Allen and Rev. James Walker • Henry David Thoreau lives in Brownson's home, tutors his boys and teaches in the town school • Brownson's influence on Thoreau • Brownson contributes to the* Christian Examiner, *prepares for the publication of his first book,* New Views of Christianity, Society, and the Church, *and is concerned about his Church of the Future • He seeks a new pulpit.*

Orestes A. Brownson was just beginning a significant and influential period of his life when, on Wednesday, May 14, 1834, he was installed as pastor of the First Congregational Church of Canton, Massachusetts. At this notable event a number of Unitarian dignitaries were present. Among them was Adin Ballou, the founder of Hopedale, that most successful of Utopian communities. Ballou has frequently been compared to Brownson. He was "assigned an important part" of the ceremony.[1] The presence of the attending clergymen was their welcome to Brownson. If he could not be brought to Boston at once, as Ripley and a number of his friends had devoutly hoped, it was at least something to have him in Canton, at that time still fifteen miles south of Boston. He was now at close range to those from whom he had been drawing inspiration, and they, in turn, had become increasingly interested in him as sharing a cognate mentality. The logical person to preach the sermon of installation was no other than the man who had been the most active in bringing him toward Boston: the Rev. George Ripley. When invited to do so, he accepted in spite of it being contrary to his "tastes and habits."[2]

Brownson began gradually to increase his influence with the New England literary group. As C. C. Hollis remarks, it has not been sufficiently realized that that group was a closed circle. No outsider, he says, ever gained entrance to that group before 1860.[3] Genius alone was no passport. Poe would not have found acceptance had he come to Boston; even Herman Melville, though living in Boston, did not belong. What then was Brownson's open sesame in the case? He had not grown up around Boston. It is true that he was a full-fledged son of New England, but he had spent the first thirteen years of his life in the most remote and distant part of New England, Vermont, and had then lived eighteen years in New York State before returning to New England in Walpole. His background, therefore, gave him largely the makeup of an outsider, and if so considered, he is the only outsider, as Hollis observes, that ever succeeded in becoming an important figure in the New England literary renaissance.[4] How did it happen? His dynamic personality, the forceful writing and lecturing he had been doing, a certain similarity of thought and aims, had been advertising his growing importance. As Hecker said of him later: "He was one of the few men whose power was great enough to advertise itself. Wherever he was, he was felt. His tread was heavy and he could make room for himself."[5] He had been instinctively drawn toward those who were then stirring up an intellectual ferment in Boston, and they, on their part, had recognized him as a kindred spirit and were welcoming him into their midst.

The installation over, Brownson's participation in New England life became increasingly pronounced. He had now a more ample field for the release of his immense energies. By this time he was becoming well-known as an orator, and was invited to deliver in 1834 the customary Fourth of July oration at Dedham, the adjoining county seat.[6] His oration was replete with bold thought nervously expressed in which he was still fighting his old campaign for the poor and underprivileged members of society. He at once launched the question whether the Founding Fathers had envisaged the full import of their declaration that "all men are created equal"; that is, whether or not they had given it any more meaning than just political equality. He attacked the current forms of inequality wherever extant, particularly the laws that bore the most heavily on the poor, such as imprisonment for debt; he excoriated society's denial of a decent education to the poorer classes of society, an injustice which was keeping them forever helpless underlings of scheming, heartless demagogues. Inequalities existed, he argued, because society had failed to carry out the true spirit of the Revolution. The oppression of the poor would continue until a more effective means of education would be found through which the masses could gradually effect their own elevation. He deprecated the fact that the higher seminaries, not open to the common people, fostered factitious distinctions, and were little concerned with the more common class of citizens. He would have a system of education that would value man, not according to his social rank or accumulated wealth, but according to his intrinsic worth.

He did not indicate precisely the type of schools he had in mind for the special benefit of the lower classes of society, but his son says that his known preference for schools in which the mechanical art should be taught, would indicate what are called manual or industrial schools. This type of school he soon endeavored to promote as best he could.

The address was so well received that his audience requested that it be published in pamphlet form. The author then sent copies of it to a number of the more prominent ministers in the vicinity. The Rev. Samuel C. Allen, pastor of Northfield, Massachusetts, to whom it was sent, found it most stimulating and replied in a long and thoughtful letter. He was at the time the workingmen's candidate for governor and had given a great deal of thought to the theme Brownson had dealt with in his oration. Much of what he said in his letter to Brownson might well have come from the pen of Brownson himself, but it was the approach to the social question that marked the difference between the two men. Allen insisted that the reforms needed in society could only come through a change in social institutions. "I may say," he remarked, "and in this I may perhaps differ from you, I do not think that any extensive and permanent reform can be effected without a change in the economical relations of society."[7] Brownson's approach, on the other hand, like that of Channing and other intellectuals of the day, was still at this time moralistic, that is, reform the individual and you will work the eventual reformation of society.

Allen's letter had many interesting speculations on economic and social questions, but his central concern was with the objection of those who complained that after so many ages Christianity had done so little to benefit the mass of mankind. Allen firmly believed that Christianity "was intended by its divine Founder for the relief and enlightenment of the laboring classes among all nations, and to change the then existing political and economic relations of society." In this matter, he said, it had in fact "done something, and indeed a good deal." But with that acknowledgment, he proceeded to grapple with the question of why it had not done more for the poorer classes of society. Though a clergyman himself, he drew up an indictment on this score against the clergy. He wrote:

> The gospel was good news to the poor, *as a class,* and the poor were the laborers, whether held in actual slavery, as most of them were, or not. I believe that it was intended to have its first effect *in the present world,* and if there is any cause which has contributed more than any other, to defeat its influence, and to render the mission of Jesus frustrate, it is that its ministers, as well as other priesthoods, have attached themselves to the privileged classes, and have lent themselves to uphold an order of things wholly irreconcilable with its principles, its spirit, its aims. The clergy, as a class, have always been ready to come in for a share in the advantages of the privileged classes, and in return for the ease and convenience accorded them by these classes, to spread their broad mantle over them.[8]

Did Brownson draw inspiration for some of the slashing passages in his famous "Essay on the Laboring Classes" in 1840 from this same letter of Allen? Certainly some of his cannonading in that essay against the clergy was only an echo or paraphrase of what Allen had said in this letter.

However this may be, Allen deeply appreciated Brownson's efforts in behalf of the laboring classes, and encouraged him in the concluding words of his letter: "In the meantime I hope you will not relax your exertions in this great work which will go forward, I am sure, to its end and redemption of the laboring class from economical oppression as well as political, by whatever methods it may please Providence to advance it."[9]

The approach of both Brownson and Allen to the social question in that day, bold as it was, was put in the right focus by Henry Brownson when he said:

> These men, who like Allen and Brownson, were so zealous in advocating the rights and interests of the laboring class, were not demagogues seeking to raise themselves up by standing on the shoulders of workingmen; they were not incendiaries; they were not anarchists; but ministers in good standing in a highly respectable denomination, remarkable for the earnestness of their preaching, and their devotedness to the welfare of mankind, and had thought long and seriously on the question which they clearly foresaw was the great question which would press harder and harder for a solution for generations to come.[10]

From the Rev. James Walker, pastor of the Unitarian Church in Charlestown, also then editor of the *Christian Examiner,* and soon to become professor of philosophy at Harvard and eventually president, came also a letter of quite a different type in response to the Dedham oration Brownson had sent him. He thought he smelled sansculottism in the oration, and proceeded to cool Brownson's democratic ardor a bit. "I need not hesitate to say," he remarked, "because you will perceive that my solicitude involves a flattering compliment, that I am extremely anxious that on this subject you will proceed, independently indeed, yet cautiously and circumspectly. Keeping continually before your eyes the example of the great Reformer."[11]

The Dedham oration was only one of many others. During his two years in Canton, Brownson spent himself in a flood of energy looking to the mental and moral elevation of the laboring class which so largely made up the population there. He spent time among the textile workers and fostered manual training or industrial schools; he finished *Charles Elwood; Or The Infidel Converted* which he had begun at Walpole; he began his remarkable contributions to the *Christian Examiner* which George Ripley spoke of as forming "a new era in the history of that able journal."[12] He also organized a lyceum for the general mental and literary improvement of the community at which weekly lectures were delivered, some by himself and some by eminent men from Boston or its vicinity; in addition he started a small library connected with the lyceum for the use of its members.[13] Among the distingushed scholars who were invited to lecture at the lyceum was the Rev. Edward Everett, then governor of Massachusetts. Although Everett found it necessary to decline the invitation because of a multiplicity of prior invitations, he cordially acknowledged kinship with Brownson in the work he was doing for the rank and file of the community in Canton. He wrote in part:

> To cheer as far as I am able, the efforts of this class, has been with me — as with you — an object of which I have never lost sight. . . . Born and bred — as you observe of yourself — in obscurity and straitened circumstance, and owing every thing I have or can hope for, to public institutions and common free schools of the country, I have ever felt a warm sympathy with the friendless young; and ever taken a peculiar interest in all efforts and means devised to equalize the conditions of life, by diffusing the advantages of education.[14]

George Ripley, too, was greatly interested in the humanitarian work Brownson was doing in Canton. Since the two shared so much in common, an aptitude for philosophy, a fondness for foreign literature and social reform, their friendship grew apace during these years. They had already begun to exchange volumes of the French philosophers while Brownson was still at Walpole.[15] C. C. Hollis informs us that many letters passed between the two at this time on social reform through the agency of religion, but that since not all the letters are extant, there is no way to discover whose thought predominated, or who channelled the thought of the other.[16]

Very stimulating, too, for Brownson was another young scholar who came for a visit and stayed with him for a short while: Henry David Thoreau, a junior at Harvard. Taking advantage of a college ruling which allowed him to drop out for a year in order to earn enough money to see himself through college, Thoreau had come to Brownson to be examined on his fitness for teaching school. William Ellery Channing, Jr., informs us that upon Thoreau's arrival "the two sat up until midnight," after which "they stuck heartily to studying German, and getting all they could of the time, like old friends."[17] Brownson informed the school committee of Thoreau's fitness as a pedagogue. The exact time of this visit is somewhat uncertain. Kenneth Cameron, however, believes that it must have occurred in January and February of 1836, which marked also the beginning of Brownson's last five months in Canton (January through May), a period during which he was clarifying his philosophy and planning his move to Boston. During this seminal period Brownson was working on his *New Views of Christianity, Society and the Church* — a work to which Thoreau looked forward and promptly bought.[18]

Thoreau stayed on in the Brownson household for six weeks tutoring his sons and teaching in the town school. Later he acknowledged the perennial inspiration he had drawn from the meeting of his own mind with that of Brownson in a letter he wrote Brownson December 30, 1837. Opening the letter, he wrote:

I have never ceased to look back with interest, not to say satisfaction, on the short six weeks I passed with you. They were an era in my life — the morning of a new *Lebenstag*. They are to me as a dream that is dreamt, but which returns from time to time in all its freshness. Such a one I would dream a second and a third time, and then tell before breakfast.[19]

He wrote this letter to ask Brownson to help him find a job at teaching school, or "what is more desirous, as private tutor in a gentleman's family." But this time Brownson does not seem to have come to his assistance. Perhaps he remembered that Thoreau's former teaching had left something to be desired in the way of discipline and regularity. To say nothing of other evidence in the case, this same letter of Thoreau could imply as much when he wrote: "I have ever been disposed to regard the cowhide as a non-conductor — methinks that, unlike the electric wire, not a single spark of truth is ever transmitted through its agency to the slumbering intellect it would address." Whatever the case, the letter seems to have been the last communication between Brownson and Thoreau. Thoreau faded out of Brownson's life as the influence of Emerson became ascendant, especially after he went to live with Emerson. Henry Seidel Canby, however, remarks that "the influence of Brownson upon the later Thoreau was much greater than has been supposed."[20]

In introducing this letter Thoreau wrote his father, Henry Brownson asserts that the time Thoreau spent in the Brownson household "had an important influence on Thoreau's after-life, for it was Brownson who roused his enthusiasm for external nature."[21] As to Brownson's influence on Thoreau, Theodore Maynard has remarked that he could find little evidence for such a statement. "There is no evidence, however," he asserted, "that it was Brownson 'who roused his enthusiasm for external nature,' or that Brownson had any such enthusiasm himself, to any marked degree."[22] But this statement may not be entirely accurate. There does seem to be considerable evidence to substantiate Henry Brownson's assertion.

In his article, "Thoreau and Orestes Brownson," Kenneth Walter Cameron cites a passage of Amos Perry in which Perry relates the influence of Brownson on Thoreau in turning Thoreau's mind to an enthusiastic love of external nature. Said Amos Perry:

> Thoreau's figure seems to me as distinct as if I had seen him yesterday. He was during more than two years a diligent student, bright and cheerful [at Harvard]. I consulted him more than once about the translations of some of Horace's odes. In his junior year, he went out to Canton to teach school. There he fell into the company of Orestes A. Brownson, then a Transcendentalist. He came back a transformed man. He was no longer interested in the college course of study. While walking to Mt. Auburn with me one afternoon, he gave bent to his spleen. He picked up a spear of grass, saying: "Here is something worth studying; I would give more to understand the growth of this grass than all the Greek and Latin roots in creation." The sight of a squirrel running on the wall at that moment delighted him. "That," he said, "is worth studying." The change he had undergone was thus evinced. At an earlier period he was interested in our studies.[23]

This is interesting testimony in itself. But there exists double testimony from Amos Perry. Cameron seems unaware of another relevant statement of Amos Perry, one that has come down to us from M. J. Harson. Writing in *The Catholic World,* April 1904, Harson, a Rhode Islander himself, and a former graduate of Brown University, made this further disclosure concerning Brownson's influence on Thoreau:

> Hon. Amos Perry, of Rhode Island, who succeeded John Howard Payne as consul at Tunis, was a classmate and intimate friend of Thoreau at Harvard, and he told me that during their college career Thoreau's thought was almost entirely dominated by Brownson, and that he spoke of him with greater admiration than any other writer. Perry asserted, moreover, that Thoreau told him that his profound love of nature was inspired by Brownson, not by Emerson, as is generally supposed.[24]

It is in reference to Henry Brownson's statement that it was his father who roused Thoreau's enthusiasm for external nature that C. C. Hollis has remarked: "Some credence must be put in this statement, for Henry Brownson wrote with complete and sometimes embarrassing honesty." He says further that Henry Brownson wrote when "Thoreau was so little known there could hardly be any temptation to augment his father's reputation by association. It was, in fact, because Thoreau was so little known that Henry Brownson did not bother to substantiate his claim."[25]

Henry Brownson touched more than once on his father's great love of external nature. Speaking of his father's loss of close contact with external nature when he moved from Boston to New York in 1855, he remarked: "No one could have a greater love of external nature, of an unimpeded view of the sky, the fields, the rivers, than had Brownson; and for him to give up the free air and rugged hills of New England for the confined streets of our mercantile metropolis no compensation could be offered."[26] This statement would seem to be much nearer the truth than Per Sveino's representations in the matter,[27] especially since Henry Brownson wrote "with complete and sometimes embarrassing honesty." He had no reason to exaggerate. When Brownson himself reviewed "Wood Notes" in the *Dial* (apparently by Emerson) he rated them "passable," but asserted that they fell "far short of the sweet, wild, sad music, every true lover of nature hears whenever he walks the woods. For ourselves we have no patience with the poetry that babbles of flowers, woods, rivers, and other external objects. The poet rarely reproduces what we have felt when left alone with nature. . . . We love nature too well to read the poet's descriptions, and her wild notes are ringing too distinctly, too sweetly in our ears, to permit us to be pleased with any attempt to imitate them."[28]

Kenneth W. Cameron believes that Thoreau must almost certainly have attended the meetings of Brownson's club for the young men in his parish, and possibly used his library. He observes that it may also well be that Brownson's "idealistic messages" to the young men of this club may have constituted his greatest influence upon the developing mind of the Harvard boy who spent six weeks in his home which became "an era in [his] life — the morning of a new *Lebenstag*." One address in particular to the club, given May 24, 1835, is quite noteworthy. Cameron calls it a "stirring" address.[29] Since it was widely distributed in the Canton area, Cameron surmises that Thoreau may well have seen a copy of it even though it was delivered six or seven months before his arrival there.[30] Whatever the fact, Cameron also feels that the inspiring contents of the address must have entered in no small degree into the conversations of the two during Thoreau's sojourn in the Brownson household. On that score Cameron appended the entire address to his article on "Thoreau and Orestes Brownson" in *The Emerson Society Quarterly*. It is not possible to capture the eloquence of such an address in a condensed form, but the merest framework of it is here attempted. Brownson took for his text: "Seek ye the kingdom of God and his righteousness; and all these things shall be added to you" (Matthew 6:33).

He began by reminding the young men that they would soon be the active generation with duties to church, to country and to God, and urged them with much earnestness to prepare themselves to discharge those duties with fidelity and promptness.

He continued: The first thing I would impress upon your minds is the importance of determining at the outset of your career what shall be the object of your lives. Each one must have a definite object. You must not go through life objectless, floating in the direction of every wind, like the leaf severed by the frost from its parent branch. What then shall this object be? Shall it be mere pleasure? Shall you wrap yourselves up and say: "Let the world take care of itself; let others take care of themselves. I shall look to my own pleasure." Let such selfishness become universal, and you will soon sigh in vain for love and sympathy, for generosity and disinterestedness. Talk not to me of pleasure as an object in life. You were made for something higher. God made you social beings. "He has linked, all over the earth, men with men, society with society, and made the good of each consist in the good of the whole. He has given you faculties which are forever leading you away from yourselves, giving you an abiding interest in others, and enabling you to weep with those who weep and rejoice with those who rejoice. The most miserable beings on earth are those who seek only to please themselves." Surely then you will not want to live and act just in search of your own pleasure.

What then shall be the great object of your lives? Shall it be wealth? Will you live and toil simply to become rich? Many among the young look around and inquire: How may I become rich? But are there no more important inquiries? Is wealth the greatest good to be obtained? Can you conceive of no higher good than the rank and distinction in society given by wealth? What is the value of rank and distinction? How long will it last? Go to the graveyard and read the answer. "The grave is the grand leveller of all distinctions. The small and the great are there." The rich and the poor are there, side by side. A winding-sheet and a small spot of ground is all that you can claim at last. No, no, my friends, rank and distinction must not be made the great object of your lives. What then? The word of God gives the answer: "Seek ye first the kingdom of God and his righteousness, and all these things shall be added to you." Here is the greatest, the supreme good. Here is the real object of your lives. Seek God, seek his righteousness with your whole hearts, with your whole strength.

By "the kingdom of God" is rightly understood the *reign* of God, and Jesus says "the reign of God is within you." By the reign of God is meant the moral attributes or perfections. To seek to have God reign in you, and over all men, is what you are to understand by seeking the reign of God. The reign of God is the reign of love and goodness. When love and goodness reign in you God reigns in you. "To have love, or goodness, reign in you, is the same as to be good yourselves, the same thing as it is to be just in all your actions, pure in all your wishes, benevolent in all your feelings and aspirations. When you are good yourselves you will delight to do good to others. When love reigns in you, you will love all men and labor for their well-being." To seek, then, the reign of God and his righteousness is to seek to be good and to do good. Here, my young friends, is the good to be obtained, infinitely superior to that of merely sensual pleasure, or that which wealth can purchase. If wealth be your object, seek it here. Let it be moral wealth which shall perdure through all eternity. Let it be the pleasure of being good and doing good. It is a pleasure as much superior to the gratification of the appetites and propensities, as the soul is superior to the body, or as God is superior to the animals around us.

"And all these [lesser] things shall be added unto you." We often wrong God in his Providence. It is wrong, my young friends, to think that the path of virtue is obscure and pleasureless. God has not made the road to distinction and pleasure lie through fields of sin. Every good man is a little stone cut from the mountains without hands, has within himself the principle of a growth that will fill the earth with benefits. "He who exemplifies, in its perfection, a single moral virtue, he who discovers and places in the world a single truth in morals, in religion, or in the philosophy of the mind, outdoes the proudest of earth's heroes, exerts a power greater than any king or emperor ever did or can exert. He commences a new creation, forms the nucleus of a new world, round which atom after atom shall gravitate, till it becomes a new heavenly body to revolve forever in a new orbit."

Brownson concluded his address by again earnestly reminding his audience that they would soon be the active generation of the day, replacing those who had gone before them, and of the great importance for them of fixing on the right object in life. Their own weal and happiness as well as that of their fellowmen would depend upon the right choice.[31]

Walter Harding records that "there is no question that Orestes Brownson opened Thoreau's eyes to the tumult of the age as they had never been opened before."[32]

After Thoreau had fulfilled his mission in the Brownson household and had departed, Brownson was perhaps left with greater freedom to plunge more unrestrainedly into his various works of benevolence and into a continuation of his studies. In his assiduous reading of theology, philosophy and social theory he was now in the last period of preparation for the more important work of his life which was fast approaching — though he of course read and studied all his life long. During these two years he gave more thought to the work of Benjamin Constant in five octavo volumes on *Religion, Considered in Its Origin, Its Forms, and Its Developments* which he had read at Walpole in the original French. This elaborate treatise of Constant was the theme of Brownson's first contribution to the *Christian Examiner.*

Constant's theory is, as we have partly noted, that religion has its origin in a sentiment natural to man, the religious sentiment, which finds its natural expression in an act of worship. Man necessarily clothes his religious sentiments or ideas in external forms or institutions. But while his religious sentiment is as permanent as human nature itself, the forms of worship into which it develops are constantly mutable. For with the advance of man's intelligence, his religious sentiments or ideas also become ever more progressive, calling for embodiment in ever loftier forms or institutions as he abandons the outdated. Thus man's dead institutions become so many stepping-stones by which he rises higher and higher in the scale of civilization and the expression of his religious sentiments.

Brownson tells us that he was completely captivated at the time by Constant's theory, for it harmonized with the theory of progress of the human race which he himself had evolved. The theory was so enthralling that it never occurred to him at the time to ask whether or not it had any basis in history, however slight a knowledge of history or philosophy would have sufficed to refute it.[33] But the point of the theory that Brownson fastened on at the time was that man naturally seeks to embody his religious sentiments and ideas in institutions, and that these institutions serve as agencies of progress. What was needed now, he argued, was a new religious institution or church that should embody the advanced intelligence of the age and meet the new wants of the times which the march of civilization had brought with it. All the religions of the past were good and useful in their day insofar as they corresponded to the wants and intelligence of the time, but they had become outdated with the progress of the race, and "the human race has cast them off, as the grown man casts off the garments of childhood." In the Christian order, Catholicity had served mankind nobly in the Middle Ages, was in harmony with the intelligence of the times, commanded respect and met the wants and aspirations of the soul. But it had become fixed and unalterable, and therefore opposed progress, as the Reformation attested. Protestantism itself, he asserted, is no religion, it is a chaos of sects. "Its mission was simply one of destruction, as I wrote in the *Christian Examiner*, in 1834," he said. What was needed now was a new religious institution or church, one that would carry within itself the principle of progress, a principle at once unifying yet expansive enough to meet all the new wants growing out of man's further advance. Such he envisaged must be *The Church of the Future*, the embodiment of the true hopes of mankind for the future.[34]

From this time forward until he was well-nigh on the threshold of the Catholic Church, nearly a decade later, Brownson was full of his idea of the Church of the Future, and he lost no time in communicating his enthusiasm to all who were interested in the progress of the race. This was the stirring theme of the article he contributed to the *Christian Examiner*, September 1834, on Benjamin Constant. Perry Miller says that Brownson used the article as an "opportunity to deliver the most explicit blast yet uttered in Boston against religious institutionalism (no one could mistake that he meant his fellow Unitarians)." Yet it was to these same Unitarians that he looked hopefully for the workmen who were to come forth for the building of the new temple. He spoke enthusiastically about the propsect:

> We think the time has come to clothe the religious sentiment with a new form, and to fix upon some religious institution, which will at once supply our craving for something positive in religion, and not offend the spirituality which Christianity loves, and toward which the human race hastens with increasing celerity. We think, we see indications, that this presents itself to many hearts as desirable. Every religious denomination must run through two phases, the one destructive, the other organic. Unitarianism could commence only by being destructive. It must demolish the old temple, clear away the rubbish, to have a place whereon to erect the new one. But that work is done; that negative character which it was obliged to assume then, may now be abandoned. The time has come to rear the new temple — for a positive work, and, if we are not mistaken, we already see the workmen coming forth with joy to their task. We already see the germ of re-organization, the nucleus, round which already gravitate the atoms of a new moral and religious world."[35]

Having been appointed at this time chairman of a Unitarian committee for the diffusion of Christian truth, Brownson did not overlook his opportunity to blueprint his plan for the Church of the Future to the two other members of the committee, Ezra Styles Gannett, the distinguished pastor of Federal Street Church, Boston, and Joseph Allen, of Northborough, Massachusetts. Writing to them, Brownson deplored the fragmentation of the Church, and urged them to an earnest quest of some principle of organization, some point of Christian union, which would be acceptable to people of all Christian parties. Both these clergymen responded in lengthy, earnest letters. Gannett's letter dealt with a specific plan for the diffusion of Christian truth; Joseph Allen stated the difficulty he saw in the way of arriving at any principle of organization that would unite the various Christian sects. His thoughtful words may have given Brownson pause. Allen wrote:

> Your suggestions are important, and yet I do not see that we are likely to gain anything by looking for some new principle of organization, some new point of union, and which may be the same for all the world. The fact is, as you state, "the church is broken up into fragments"; and one saith he is of Paul and another saith he is of Apollo, and the different sects are so organized and trained that it seems to me a hopeless task to attempt to bring them to act in concert, "to meet in the same temple, devoid of fear, full of love, and to pay their devotions to the same God." Something may be done to soften the asperities of party and to promote good feeling among members of different sects, especially when they live in the same neighborhood, or dwell beneath the same roof. But I fear for the present at least, we shall be compelled — if we do anything *for the spread of Christian truth* — to do it by ourselves, as Unitarian Christians, or else to put our contributions into the hands of our Orthodox brethren to be disposed of as they may think best.

Brownson was of a more optimistic view, since he believed himself quite free from religious prejudice, at least in the sense that he was ever ready to embrace the truth the moment seen, no matter what had been his previous beliefs. He subconsciously felt, perhaps, that others might be expected to do the same. When Brownson further urged his plans at the next meeting of the committee, his two associates began to realize that they were in partnership with a man fully determined to be effective about resolving the religious chaos that so sadly and widely divided and hampered the Christian world. The absence of that Christian unity among his followers for which Christ prayed so devoutly in his last hours was a sign of contradiction for Christian leaders. Yet, fearing that Brownson was only becoming a disturber of the peace, Gannett and Allen suggested to him that he try his experiment on his own, in Boston or elsewhere.[36]

For Brownson everything now pointed unmistakably to Boston. Ripley, Channing and others had been urging him to come there and begin an apostolate to the indifferent and churchless, particularly among the laboring class. But now he had an objective beyond the plans of his Boston sponsors. His recent study of the French philosopher, Victor Cousin, had furnished him with what he believed was a formula effective enough to reunite the scattered fragments of Christ's Church and to weld them into one progressive religious organization. He needed only a useful theater to try his socioreligious experiment. And no place in the nation could be more suitable than Boston, a simmering caldron of new ideas, a center of free thought and bold religious inquiry, the home of philosophy, philanthropy and liberal investigation of every sort. Accordingly, in the winter of 1835-1836 he decided on Boston as the place to launch what he was to call his *Society for Christian Union and Progress*. It was to be the greatest venture of his life, unless one should choose to call his eventual conversion to the Catholic Church a venture. It seems evident that though his society did attain a certain degree of success, it gradually became probably the greatest disappointment of his life. His son Henry felt very deeply about the matter and in twelve pages of his biography argued pro and con why his father's venture was not a greater success. Whatever the truth of the matter, the eventual termination of the bold enterprise was to mark a major turning point in Brownson's life.

Brownson's eagerness to try his experiment cannot be doubted. Yet the precariousness of what he and his sponsors proposed may also have given him second thoughts in his sober reflections. However, there was one matter in particular that may have pushed him to an affirmative decision to go on to Boston. The fact is that he had at this time become financially embarrassed, a point which has recently come to light through the efforts of Kenneth W. Cameron. This information is contained in a letter Brownson wrote the church committee of his parish in Canton on the eve of his departure. Dated May 9, 1836, it is addressed to:

> Messrs French Crane and Tucker,
>
> Gentlemen, I beg you to present to the Congregational parish in Canton, of which you are the committee, my thanks for the favors I have received from them since I have been their pastor, my respect for and attachment to the parish, my prayers for its prosperity, together with my request that the pastoral relation which now exists between them and me, may be dissolved. My reasons are such as imply no reproach upon the society and I trust will not have any influence in interrupting our relations of friendship and Christian communion. It is due to the parish to state that the principal reasons for asking this dismission are my pecuniary embarrassments, and my hope of obtaining a new Society in Boston, where I think my sphere of usefulness will be enlarged.
>
> I am, gentlemen, with Christian love and esteem,
>
> Yours truly,<br>O. A. Brownson[37]

Due to his bold reformatory discourses, Brownson at this time was not quite as popular in the parish as he had been. Cameron informs us that in 1835 the vote of the committeemen had been unanimous for his retention as pastor, while in this year, 1836, the vote had been thirty-seven for his retention and ten against it.[38] Rev. William Henry Knapp, who succeeded Brownson as pastor, touched in his autobiography on the posture of affairs in the Canton parish when he said:

> In this town of Canton my predecessor [Brownson] had been remarkable for his bold reformatory discourses; and as I was deeply interested in all the exciting questions of the time, I followed up the work begun, and was of course allowed greater freedom of expression than I expected. Of course there were in my congregation many persons more or less affected by the old Calvinistic dogmas, who missed the old tone and phraseology of the pulpit — one at least who complained that I did not have enough to say about "a state of nature" and a state of grace; and another who, when told I was a suggestive preacher, and made people think, answered she did not care for that, she wanted Sunday as a day of rest.[39]

In the farewell letter to his parish, just quoted, Brownson spoke of his "pecuniary embarrassments." Although C. C. Hollis does not cite the source of his information, he asserts that Brownson received financial assistance from both Ripley and Dr. Channing as an inducement to try his apostolate in Boston. Certain phrases in Ripley's letter of March 26, 1834, where he speaks of "a guarantee of support, for a limited time," if Brownson were to come to Boston, and his further inquiry to know "what he [Brownson] would regard as a sufficient encouragement" in the case, seem definitely to imply that Brownson's sponsors had in mind to offer him financial assistance in making his change to Boston. This is entirely credible on the score that both Ripley and Channing were probably even more enthusiastic than Brownson himself that the experiment be tried. And their confidence in Brownson's abilities had no doubt been mounting as "his reputation had been growing rapidly from the comparative unknown at Walpole to the popular and powerful preacher of the last months at Canton."[40]

But however dedicated this social reformer was to the causes that look to an improvement of man's lot on earth, he at times sought surcease from the stress and strain of hard work. As he has described himself "a man of the world," he must have mixed socially at least moderately in the world he knew. An occasional fling at chess was also an outlet for him. Late in life his son Orestes, writing to his brother Henry, recalled how when he was a lad his father "was constantly studying; occasionally, however, he would send for me to play chess, and from 8 a.m. to 12 p.m., there was no respite."[41] But whatever relaxation this ultra-serious man allowed himself it was only a means to an end. He was soon back at the anvil with renewed vigor and earnestness.

# 8

## THE SOCIETY FOR
## CHRISTIAN UNION AND PROGRESS

*His removal to Chelsea, adjoining Boston • He launches his new Society from the rostrum of the Masonic Temple in Boston • Certain factors which militated from the beginning against the success and continuance of his new Society • The publication of* New Views of Christianity, Society, and the Church *• He also becomes editor of* The Boston Reformer.

With two more sons, William Ignatius and Henry Francis — besides Orestes, Jr., and John Healy Brownson — Orestes Brownson in May 1836 moved to Mt. Bellingham, Chelsea, a suburb of Boston, separated from Boston proper by the Charles River. During the months of May and June he held services in Lyceum Hall, Hanover Street, Boston. In serving notice of the meetings to be held, the name *The Society of Social Reform* was first used. But this was soon dropped as expressing only one object of the work Brownson had in mind. On the last Sunday of May the title *The Society for Christian Union and Progress* was adopted. By the first Sunday of July the organization of the Society had been fully implemented, and, those attending having increased, the meetings were then held in a larger edifice, the Masonic Temple. Although the Society was to know a considerable interruption after three years, it continued in existence until near the end of 1843.[1]

But Brownson did not appear on the scene in this new field haphazardly. He had prepared, as early as March, for the inauguration of his Society in Boston by a series of addresses under the caption, "Free Lectures on Christianity." Basing his thought on the principle that social and religious feelings are natural to man, he rebutted "in a masterly manner," said a reporter, the pretensions of unbelievers that religion has its origin in imaginary ideas, is the result of the machinations of priests and politicians. The reporter on the lectures continued: "The mode of handling the subject must have been new to most of those who listened to it, and could not fail to suggest a solution of many difficulties, which are perhaps oftener felt than expressed. It is rarely that the philosophy of religion is presented before a popular audience with more clearness of expression, strength of argument, or discrimination of thought, than were exhibited on this occasion."[2]

It was with all the earnestness of a dedicated apostle that Orestes Brownson was to address himself to his task when he arrived in Boston. It had become quite clear to him, however, before his move to Boston, that if Christianity was to become a real force in human affairs and set mankind forward on the path of progress, all its forces would have to be gathered into that vital unity which it had had when the Messiah had first given his saving message to the world. As in unity there is strength, so in division there can be only weakness, frustration and ineffectiveness. His hope was to heal the divisions of the Christian world and bring the total message of Christ as an operative power to the souls of men. The dismemberment of the body of Christ had gone so far that the scattered fragments could scarcely bring any real life or spiritual warmth to the souls of men. Man's soul could not be fed on negations nor find strength in the divisions which the long era of destructive criticism and denial had brought to the Christian world. Here, argued Brownson enthusiastically, was the crying need for his envisioned *Church of the Future*, a religious organization that would harmonize and unite the various sects in one common vital creed. Speaking of the melancholy situation in which he found the Christian world bogged down, he said:

> The work of destruction, commenced by the Reformation, which had introduced an era of destruction and revolution, had, I thought, been carried far enough. All that was dissoluble had been dissolved. All that was destructible had been destroyed, and it was time to begin the work of reconstruction — a work of reconciliation and love.
>
> Irreligious ideas and sentiments are disorganizing and destructive in their nature, and cannot be easily cherished for a single moment after the work of destruction has been completed. When the work to be done is that of construction, of building up, or organizing, of founding something, we must resort to religious ideas and sentiments, for they, having love for their principle, are plastic, organic, constructive, and the only ideas and sentiments that are so. They are necessary to the new organization or institution of the race demanded; and the organization or institution, what I call the church, is necessary to the progress of man and society, or the creation of an earthly paradise. The first thing to be done is to cease our hostility to the past, discontinue the work of destruction; abandon the old war against the papacy, which has no longer any significance, and in a spirit of universal love and conciliation, turn our attention to the work of founding a religious institution, or effecting a new church organization, adapted to our present and future wants.
>
> This we are now, I thought, in a position to attempt. Men are beginning to understand that Protestantism is no-churchism, is no positive religion; and while it serves the purpose of criticism and destruction, it cannot meet the wants of the soul, or erect the temple in which the human race may assemble to worship in concord and peace. Unitarianism has demolished Calvinism, made an end in all thinking minds of every thing like dogmatic Protestantism, and Unitarianism satisfies nobody. It is negative, cold, lifeless, and the advanced minds among Unitarians are dissatisfied with it, and are craving something higher, better, more living and life-giving. They are weary of doubt, uncertainty, disunion, individualism, and are crying out from the bottom of their hearts for faith, for love, for union. They feel that life has well-nigh departed from the world; that religion is an empty name, and morality is mere decorum or worldly prudence; that men neither worship God nor love one another. Society as it is, is a lie, a sham, a charnel-house, a valley of dry bones. O, that the spirit of God would once more pass by, and say unto these dry bones, "live!" So I felt, so others felt; and whoever enjoyed the confidence of the leading Unitarian ministers in Boston and its vicinity from 1830 to 1840, well knows that they were sick at heart with what they had, and were demanding in their interior souls a religious institution of some sort, in which they could find shelter from the storms of this wintry world, some crumbs of the bread of life to keep them from starving. Not only in Boston was this cry heard. It came to us on every wind from all quarters — from France, from Germany, from England even; and Carlyle, in his *Sartor Resartus,* seemed to lay his finger on the plague-spot of the age. Men had reached the centre of indifference; under a broiling sun in the *Rue d'Enter,* had pronounced the everlasting No. Were they never to be able to pronounce the everlasting Yes?[3]

Perry Miller sets great store by the significance of this passage. In this passage, he says, Brownson "looks back on the situation in the vicinity of Boston in the 1830s and says perhaps the most penetrating thing upon it that survives from the literature of that decade. Of course, Brownson was looking down upon the past from the heights of his conversion, but even so, he could remember with tenderness and pity the spiritual drives that had produced the transcendental outbreak."[4] In laboring to set the pattern for the Church of the Future, Brownson was evidently only attempting to articulate and answer the vague spiritual longings of his Transcendentalist contemporaries.

Describing further the situation as it was at the time in the vicinity of Boston, Brownson continued:

> Among them all I was probably the most hopeful, and the most disposed to act. If I lacked faith in God, I had faith in humanity. The criticisms on all subjects sacred and profane, the bold investigations of every department of life, continued unweariedly for three hundred years, by the most intrepid, the most energetic, and the most enlightened portion of mankind, had, I thought, sufficiently developed ideas and sentiments, and obtained for us all the light needed, all the materials wanted for commencing the work of reorganization, and casting broad and deep the foundation of the Church of the Future. All that was wanting was to collect the ideas which these three hundred years of criticism and investigation had developed, mould them into one harmonious and living system, and then to take that system as the principle and law of the new moral and religious organization.[5]

But Brownson had not at this time, as he later acknowledged, thought things through with sufficient care. He had not concerned himself with the knotty problem of just where such a syncretic system was to derive its life, its basic principle of unity and vitality, nor had he inquired into the question of what precise form the external organization of his church was to be given. This oversight is perhaps explained by the fact, as C. C. Hollis suggests,[6] that Brownson was carried swiftly forward in this matter by the romantic wave of the age. His ardent temperament, highly sensitive to ideas, sometimes propelled him to utterances or action without due reflection. This precipitancy spelled a certain impatience and impetuosity in demanding action when something was to be done. He apparently considered it more expeditious to bypass the question of the external organization of the Church of the Future and seek out "the representative man" who would himself lay the foundations of the church and rear its structure.

It may be well to recall here that these same speculations had also occupied the mind of Brownson while he was still in Canton, and it was only after he had failed to discover "the representative man" while there, that, being impatient to wait any longer, he had decided to move to Boston and begin there preparations for the Church of the Future in the hope that "the representative man" would make his appearance. This is what the proclamation of his *Society for Christian Union and Progress* was all about. One man, and one man only, had been privy to all his hopes and plans in this matter, and had helped and encouraged him to transfer to Boston to launch there his daring experiment: "One man, and one man only, shared my entire confidence, and knew my most secret thought. Him, from motives of delicacy, I do not name; but in the formation of my mind, in systematizing my ideas, and in general development and culture, I owe more to him than to any other man among Protestants. We have since taken divergent courses, but I have loved him as I have loved no other man, and I shall so love and esteem him as long as I live. He encouraged me, and through him chiefly I was enabled to remove to Boston and commence operations."[7] By almost common consent reference is here made to George Ripley. Aside from other indications, a letter Ripley wrote Brownson, quite similar in content, December 18, 1842, would seem further confirmation.[8]

In earnestly looking about for the man who would found the new order or new religious organization Brownson naturally took a long and close look at his Unitarian brethren. Among them one man stood out from all the rest:

> There was a time [he wrote] when I looked to Dr. Channing, the foremost among the Unitarians, as the one who was to take the lead in this work of organization. His reputation in 1834 was high, and he loomed up at a distance in my eyes as the great man of the age; but a closer view, an intimate personal acquaintance with him, soon disabused me.[9]

This does not mean that he overlooked in any way the many outstanding qualities that explain Dr. Channing's high reputation. Brownson acknowledged in particular his own indebtedness to Channing who had consoled, encouraged and aided him in various ways; he had ever been his warm, considerate and steady friend to the end, and Brownson could never forget his personal obligations to him. But Channing, to Brownson, was not a great man. He was benevolent, philanthropic and anxious to do all in his power for the benefit of mankind, especially for the relief of the oppressed and the downtrodden. But he was neither a theologian nor a philosopher, and was no match for the more vigorous controversialists of the day. He was an eloquent sermonizer, but lacked vigor and robustness. He owed his reputation somewhat to the felicitous manner in which, when the matter did not lie beyond his depth, he would sum up and state clearly the various points in a question after it had been thoroughly discussed by more vigorous and original, but less polished and graceful minds than his own.[10]

As far as Brownson's own part in the inauguration of the Church of the Future was concerned, he acknowledged, humorously or not, that while the thought had crossed his mind that he himself might be the destined man, he had not seriously entertained it. He saw himself, perhaps, as merely the precursor, another John the Baptist, a voice of one crying in the wilderness, "Behold the Lord cometh; prepare ye to meet him." His mission was not to found the new church, but to proclaim its necessity, and to prepare men's minds and hearts to welcome it. Yet inasmuch as he himself was for the moment leading the way in proclaiming its necessity, "many," he said, "came to ask me if I was not a second Messiah."[11]

Not finding "the representative man," who would "rival or more than rival a Moses, and a greater than Moses," Brownson proceeded hopefully nevertheless with his Society for Christian Union and Progress. The name he gave the Society was clearly indicative of its two great objectives — Christian union and the progress of the race. His first great aim was the unification of worship in America. But how precisely was he to unite the various Christian sects? He had extracted from the French philosopher, Victor Cousin, whom he had begun to study in 1833, the eclectic principle that all systems are true in what they affirm, and false only in what they deny. If this formula be true in philosophy, he had argued at the time, it must be true also in religious systems. All that was needed, then, to arrive at unmixed religious truth would be to examine the creeds of the different churches, search out only the positive or affirmative doctrines of each, weld them into one harmonious creed, and the result would be a broad and universal profession of faith upon which all who bore the Christian name could unite.[12] As he explained it to the public in the *Boston Reformer,* June 1836:

> Though all sects differ from one another, and have their peculiar ideas, yet there is a broad ground of Christian truth common to them all. This is a high table land, elevated far above their differences, and which overlooks them all. On this high table land, it is proposed to erect a Christian temple within whose spacious courts may meet all, of all sects, names, and creeds, in peace and love, and depositing at its entrance all their badges of distinction, prostrate themselves with one heart before one altar of a universal father.[13]

In his comparative study of religion while thus attempting to discover "the broad ground of Christian truth common to all," he was brought for the first time to the study of Catholicity. But it amounted to very little at this time, for he tells us later that prior to his conversion "he had read only two Catholic books, to wit, Milner's *End of Controversy,* and the *Catechism of the Council of Trent,* and these only partially."[14] The fact is Brownson had acquired very little accurate knowledge of Catholic doctrine previous to his conversion. But, as he tells us, he had guessed the Catholic doctrine in many instances from the contrary Protestant teaching.

The other great objective of his Society was the progress of the race, or social reform. As a religious society he would ally it with the modern progressive movement of the day and age. If he drew his eclectic principle for uniting the various sects from the philosophy of Victor Cousin, he drew his notions of reform from the Saint-Simonians, the disciples of the French nobleman, Saint-Simon, the author of *Noveau Christianisme,* or *New Christianity.* What deeply appealed to Brownson at this time was Saint-Simon's interpretation of the Gospel as an evangel of social reform in behalf of the downtrodden classes in society. But while Saint-Simon and his disciples proclaimed a new Christianity, Brownson held that their heavy emphasis on the social message of the Gospel spelled only the old Christianity as it lay in the mind of Jesus, its author. But he agreed with them on the necessity of a new religious organization whose overriding concern would be the speediest and continuous moral, intellectual and physical amelioration of the poorer and more numerous classes of society.[15] He believed also in their motto: *Paradise on earth is before us.*

Thus in the midst of his shifts, or the steps in his intellectual development, he was ever aiming strenuously and unswervingly at the one great goal to which he had pledged himself in 1828: the creation of a paradise on earth for his fellowmen.

It was with this framework of socioreligious thought for its background that Brownson had launched his Society for Christian Union and Progress with his famous sermon on *The Wants of the Time* in Lyceum Hall on the last Sunday of May 1836. To appreciate the situation that here confronted him as an evangelist a slight glance at Boston as it then was will be helpful. Although Brownson seems to have been called into Boston to save primarily those drifting from the churches among the laboring classes, there were many also in all strata of society who were dissatisfied with the churches as they were. Their numbers had swelled into astonishing figures. It was estimated that out of a population of 70,000 in the city of Boston at the time, no less than 20,000 to 30,000 were no longer regular church-goers in any sense.[16] Whether or not this religious indifference had infiltrated from elsewhere, or was an internal development, there seems to have been a spirit of increasing indifference to religion in the country at large at the time. It is of course such a situation that instinctively challenges the fire of a crusading evangelist. Whether or not Brownson matched such an image, he was the man called into Boston to bring his rare talents into play to reclaim if at all possible the drifting multitudes. No doubt both he and his backers had high and fervent hopes from the beginning. The field was ripe for the harvest.

But if Brownson was to address himself intelligently to the work before him, a further bit of preliminary reconnaissance was called for.[17] What were the causes for the dissatisfaction among those who had strayed from the churches? How came it that they no longer frequented the churches where their fathers had worshiped? Many he found had become estranged because they felt the church was unfriendly to free inquiry and would shackle their minds to a frigid orthodoxy. They wished to be untrammelled in their search for an ever fuller and deeper truth. To such people, Brownson could make a special appeal, for he had ever professed himself a fellow inquirer, had advocated free inquiry, and had adopted it as a cardinal principle of his new Society. Only those beyond the Christian pale — *atheists* and Jews, pagans and Muhammadans — were excluded.[18] Indeed, professed atheists fared badly at Brownson's hands. Abner Kneeland, an atheist of the more vulgar sort, who had been creating considerable excitement in Boston by his harangues against the Christian religion, met his match in Brownson. Rufus W. Griswold cites as a proof of the success of Brownson's Society the fact that Kneeland's infidel organization "was broken up, its press stopped, and its leader compelled to find a new home."[19] But to the foundering skeptic Brownson was the kind physician. Had he not been a skeptic himself? Gladly would he be of assistance to any such. The bruised reed he would not break and the smoking flax he would not quench. He was sympathetically disposed and admirably qualified to come to the aid of those lost in doubt and unbelief. As a contemporary editor remarked:

> His [Brownson's] is not, however, the faith of the zealot or bigot. He has experienced the agonies of doubt, and he pities rather than severely condemns the infidel. There is no living writer, perhaps, whose works do more to supply the great want of the times, a philosophical foundation for the Christian faith.[20]

Another class that was a potential part of Brownson's audience were the anti-formalists who had tired of religion drained of its vitality by an excessive attention to mere ritual and dogma. They wanted something more than mere pietism, something pulsating with spiritual vitality caught from the word of God applied to real life. And for them the founder of the Society for Christian Union and Progress had the answer, for few aimed more earnestly at applying religion directly to real life than Orestes Brownson. As the editor of the *Boston Reformer* he forthrightly declared: "The Reformer [Brownson] contends that religion by its spirit should pervade and sanctify all that engages the attention of human beings, and that clergymen have a perfect right to discuss the great principles of social science, and that it is their duty to labor to perfect society."[21] He had laid it down, too, as a guiding principle of his Society that it would aim at a higher and purer morality than that preached in the churches of the day. His whole plan was to go back to the pristine religion of Jesus as the great need of the time.

Again, Brownson found that many of those who had drifted from the churches belonged to the class of reformers. The most numerous of these were those opposed to social inequalities in society, to monopoly and privilege, and who were themselves laboring for an improvement in the condition of the masses. These reformers had become weary of the type of preaching in vogue. It did not seem to them to carry any message relevant to the social and economic life of modern man. There was enough said that seemed a tacit approval of abuses in the reigning order, but these reformers wished to hear something, too, about the Christian virtues of charity and justice in the economic order. Was not the Gospel of Christ full of great concern for the poor and underprivileged members of society? Has his Gospel, then, no message for the disinherited and downtrodden? Hearing none, many of the reformers of the day had turned away in disappointment and discouragement.

To this class of the disaffected perhaps no minister in the country at the time could make a more vibrant appeal than Orestes Brownson, for there was at the time perhaps no minister in the country who laid a heavier emphasis on the social message of the Gospel than did he. A contemporary wrote:

> No author of this age applies himself more devotedly to the interests and well-being of the workingmen, a term synonymous with the multitude, than Mr. Brownson. The ardor of his soul and the energy of his gigantic intellect are poured out on the altar of humanity.[22]

He had adopted as one of the great aims of his Society, as we have noted, the Saint-Simonian principle that religion should look earnestly to the speediest possible moral, intellectual and physical amelioration of the poorer and more numerous classes of society. He believed at the time that Saint-Simon was the sage who had at long last got at the real meaning of the Gospel of Jesus. "He," said Brownson, "has been in our day the truest interpreter of the thought of Jesus, the first since Jesus to comprehend the *social* character of the New Covenant."[23] It was this challenging interpretation of the Gospel that Brownson now proceeded to preach with so much verve and abandon in behalf of the socially and economically disinherited. He was convinced that all that was needed to Christianize the radical social movement of the day was to expound the real meaning of the Gospel of Jesus. It must be made clear, he insisted, that Christianity, like democracy, is all for the people. "The gospel is emphatically the workingmen's religion."

> I say to you [he thundered in the opening discourse on *The Wants of the Times*] that Jesus was emphatically the teacher of the masses . . . the prophet of the workingmen. . . . Were I to repeat his words in this city or elsewhere, with the intimation that I believe that they meant something; were I to say, as he said, "it is easier for a camel to go through the eye of a needle, than for a rich man to enter the kingdom of heaven," and to say it in a tone that indicated that I believed he attached any meaning to what he said, you would call me a "radical," an "agrarian," a "trades-unionist," a "leveller," a "disorganiser," or some other name equally barbarous or horrific.[24]

He was hitting the keynote of the social doctrine at which he was to hammer away continually from the rostrum of his new Society.

Among the audience that had gathered to hear his discourse on *The Wants of the Times* was the gifted Harriet Martineau, sister of the Unitarian theologian, James Martineau. She had brought with her her famous ear trumpet lest she miss anything the exciting new minister in Boston had to say. During her extended visit in America, 1834-1836, she was setting down her recollections of the American people in a book titled *Society in America*. So impressed was she with the discourse on *The Wants of the Times* that she appended the greater part of it to her book, thereby promoting its circulation both here and abroad. The sermon was apparently the only pleasing one she heard in New England. She took up twelve pages in her book excoriating the American clergy in general as "the most backward and timid class in the society in which they live; self-exiled from the great moral ques-

102

tions of the day." Against such a drab background she hailed Brownson with all the greater enthusiasm. "A multitude flocks around him," she wrote, "the earnest spirits of the city and day. . . . The rising up of this new church in Boston is an eloquent sign of the times."[25]

To gather in the straying sheep is never an easy chore, no matter what the method used. No doubt the novelty of Brownson's new Society attracted many people curious of the new. Perhaps on that score the attendance was more numerous in the beginning. His son Henry tells us that the average was something upwards of five hundred, mainly of those under middle age.[26] Isaac Hecker, who attended in later years, gives the average figure at not more than three hundred. After mentioning that Brownson always began the meeting with prayer in the posture and style of a Protestant minister, wearing no gown, and following no ritual as was the Unitarian custom, he said:

> Of course the sermon was the main feature, and he attracted to hear him a class of men and women who were thinkers rather than worshipers — persons with whom religion had run off into pure intellectuality. But it was original thinking. There was more original thinking in that congregation than in all the rest of Boston put together; and that is saying not a little. The profound thinkers were there. Most of the radical minds of Boston sat under Dr. Brownson in those times.[27]

Unhappily, certain factors operated from the very beginning against the growth of the Society or the increase of its membership. Although Brownson had taken Ripley into his full confidence regarding his whole purpose in coming to Boston, his plans for the Church of the Future were at first unknown to Dr. Channing and others.[28] Their great object in working for his removal to Boston had been that he might save the workingmen from drifting into infidelity, and that he might Christianize the whole labor movement. Consequently, these sponsors had urged him to address himself directly to the laboring classes, to confine his apostolic efforts to that particular sector of society. In yielding to these urgings he made a decided mistake. Worse yet, as his son notes, "he began with the most odious part of the workingmen, the Trades Unionists."[29] When he tried to rectify his mistake, continues his son, he only made matters worse. For in addressing himself in turn to the upper classes and trying to show them that he understood and likewise recognized their side of the social question, the laboring classes, so often betrayed by their professed friends, became distrustful of him; and when he turned to address the laboring classes not only did he run the risk of offending the upper classes but also of disappointing the laboring classes whose more radical ideas he never could accept. The results were irritating misunderstandings all around. In opening his apostolate, Henry Brownson insists, he should have disregarded the advice given him, recognized no special class, and let who would come to hear him. After he had made his mistake, it was a compounded mistake to try to correct it.[30]

There were other factors, too, which hurt the prosperity of his Society. He had always been intensely concerned about the deeper economic, social and cultural inequalities in society. And in pointing out the grosser inequalities in society he may well have seemed to deny that class distinctions had any basis at all in Christianity. Creating such an impression would only have tended to exacerbate the problem of financial support for his Society. A few of the wealthier class did perhaps extend some assistance at first, but only a few, for, since Brownson began with the laboring classes, his project soon became suspect among the wealthier citizens of the community. They of course appreciated his attempts to bring under religious influences the unruly spirits in the ranks of labor, but they were also a bit fearful of just how far this man of power might go after all. The result was that what financial support he was to receive would have to come from the laboring classes who attended the meetings. This limited source made financial support the most precarious problem that faced the Society. This fact becomes clearer when we recollect that the Society had to weather the years which were to know the worst social effects of the Great Depression of 1837. Many of the Society's best friends were thrown out of work during those years, and could in consequence be of no financial assistance. But in spite of all, the Society struggled along, and many who began with the Society, continued to believe in its future, and remained loyal.

A further and formidable difficulty was that Brownson received neither the sympathy nor the cooperation of all the clergy of the city, a support he had counted on. Some things said from his pulpit were distorted in subsequent reports, and misunderstanding arose even among some of the clergy of the city. Speaking of these misrepresentations, Brownson later confessed that "they had discouraged him, and it need not be disguised, had soured him toward a portion of the clergy of the city, who had not extended to him the sympathy to which he knew himself entitled, and without which it was impossible for him to succeed in the very delicate undertaking to which he had been invited."[31] It was in particular his extemporaneous sermon of July 10, 1837 ("Happy are ye, who hunger and thirst after righteousness, for ye shall be filled") which had given rise to very disturbing misrepresentations. In the sermon Brownson had pleaded eloquently with his audience to *live* the real life of Christ and thus contribute to the great need of the times. Among those in the audience was Miss Elizabeth Palmer Peabody. When she heard of the disturbing misrepresentations of the sermon, she wrote Brownson, July 14, 1827:

> Sir:
>
> I heard, much to my astonishment, this morning, that a most excellent lady said, that she had heard from several spiritual minded and liberal Christian friends, who heard your sermon last Sunday, that it was blasphemous — that you asserted in it that it was not *necessary* to believe in a God — and that all the clergy were infidels, etc., etc.
>
> It happened that I was present at that sermon — and with those around me, was very much affected and stirred up by the glowing faith in Christ, which so strongly pervaded it; and the first words I heard respecting it, after it was over, were from a lady of most careful religious education and of early piety, who exclaimed — "this is preaching Christ." Moreover, when I came home, I began to write it down in my journal and I wish you would print in your paper my sketches — feeble as they are — for I think even they will be sufficient to show that this report which has gone abroad is widely untrue.[32]

Miss Peabody's five-page sketch contained also the particular passage which had been misrepresented. As she worded it:

> He [Brownson] declared that the doubt of being able to *live* Christ was the fatal scepticism of our times, that people smiled on you as a mad enthusiast when you proposed it as the point to which all the community were to be brought, and this fatal infidelity prevents all progress, for it belonged not only to the vicious, but to the respectable, not merely to the uneducated, but equally to those who occupy the shining places of literature and science, that it pervaded even the clergy in their pulpits. And this want of faith in man, he continued, was the real denial of Christ.[33]

Although Miss Peabody asserted that "the whole exhortation was perfectly thrilling," the sermon was greatly distorted and "very severely denounced as unchristian." Apparently some of the clergy of the city felt they had been besmirched and threw the epithet "infidel" at Brownson. Could it be expected that as great a trailblazer in thought and action as was Brownson that he would not be misunderstood and in part misrepresented? (It is the common lot of all such.) Such misunderstanding was to continue all through his life, though sometimes he himself was at fault in not having made his meaning more clear. No prophet is without honor except in his own country. Often did Brownson observe that the world perversely crucifies its redeemers. It seems the greater the good done, the higher the price that is exacted.

But in spite of a number of unforeseen obstacles which prevented the Society from flourishing in a more spectacular fashion, it did attain to a measured degree of success. Of it Brownson himself said:

> My Society was one time prosperous, but in general I could not pride myself on my success; yet I saw clearly enough, that, with more confidence in myself, a firmer grasp of my own convictions, a stronger attachment to my own opinions because they were mine, and a more dogmatic temper than I possessed, I might easily succeed, not in founding a new Catholic Church indeed, but in founding a new sect, and perhaps a sect not without influence. But a new sect was not in my plan, and I took pains to prevent my movement from growing into one. What I wanted was not sectarianism, of which I had felt we had had quite too much, but unity and Catholicity. I wished to unite men, not to divide them, to put an end to divisions, not to multiply them.[34]

It is quite credible that his refusal to assume a more dogmatic tone had acted as a hindrance to the growth of his Society. To inspire confidence in any cause the leader must speak in the assured tones of one who has settled all things in his own mind. If the trumpet gives an uncertain sound, who shall rally to the cause? But to speak as one who had settled all things in his own mind Brownson could not honestly do. Knowing that he had no infallible criterion of truth, he refused to put forth his mere opinions as dogmas or his private convictions as eternal verities. This honesty is all the more noteworthy, and creditable, in a man who was temperamentally inclined to dogmatism. Speaking again of the matter, he said:

> I never concealed, or affected to conceal, that I regarded myself as still a learner, a seeker after truth, not as one who had found the truth, and has nothing to do but to proclaim it. I always told my congregation that I was looking for more light, and that I could not be sure that my convictions would be tomorrow what they are today. Whether I preached or wrote, I aimed simply at exciting thought and directing it to problems to be solved, not to satisfy the mind or to furnish it with dogmatic solutions of its difficulties. I was often rash in my statements, because I regarded myself not as putting forth doctrines that must be believed, but as throwing out provocations to thought and investigation. . . .
> I was in fact too honest, too consistent, and too distrustful of myself to succeed.[35]

It was only after the Society had been operating for some months that Brownson published his first book in November 1836, entitled *New Views of Christianity, Society, and the Church*. Its purpose was to set forth his views of a new church, to explain the principle upon which it must be founded, and to call attention to the signs of the times favorable to its speedy organization. Although he claimed that the views expressed were original, he acknowledged seminal indebtedness to his old friend Benjamin Constant, to Dr. Follen (author of a book entitled *Religion and the Church*), and especially to Schleiermacher, as well as to the thought of Heinrich Heine, Victor Cousin and the publications of the Saint-Simonians.[36] The book was in fact a manifesto to the public of what the founding of *The Society for Christian Union and Progress* was concerned about. As amusing as it may seem, when he reviewed his own book in 1842, he claimed that the whole plan had been revealed to him in a "flash of veritable inspiration."[37]

The book was entirely too philosophical to become popular. Besides, it abounded in statements that could not but be offensive to Protestants. Though it was no doubt read by some of the intellectuals of the day, it made no great stir in Boston or its environs. Yet when he reviewed Brownson's Works for the *Dial* in 1840, George Ripley pronounced *New Views* "one of the most remarkable [works] that has issued from the American press, although it attracted less attention at the time of its publication than it has since received." Ripley went on to state what in his judgment was the reason why it had not been a greater success: "The ideas which it combats have no general prevalence among us; and their refutation could accordingly call forth no general attention. It is, in fact, an answer to the objections brought against the Christian religion by Henry Heine, and some disciples of the Saint-Simon school, on account of its being, as they suppose, a system of exclusive and exaggerated spiritualism."[38] Ripley may have had this directly from Brownson himself; at least it is what Brownson himself affirmed later in his own comments.[39] This makes the book largely a Christian *apologia* in response to the allegation of the Saint-Simon school that Christianity could not be the social ideal of the future.

Brownson answered the objections of the Saint-Simonians against historical Christianity by repudiating as authentic the two main forms into which Christianity has developed in the Western World: Catholicism and Protestantism. Taking his cue from Heine and the Saint-Simonians, he rejected Catholicism as based on the principle of exclusive spiritualism to the neglect and depression of the material order. "It fitted men to die," he said, "but not to live; for heaven, but not for earth — promising a heaven hereafter, but creating none here."[40] Protestantism, on the contrary, he rejected because it was based on the principle of exclusive materialism to the neglect and denial of the spiritual. It looks well to this world, but neglects to provide for the next. In it "the material predominates over the spiritual. Man labors six days for this world and at most but one for the world to come." Protestantism is in principle a revival of Greek and Roman heathenism, and its real character and logical development may be seen in the French Revolution of 1789. "Properly speaking," he added, "Protestantism finished its work and expired in the French Revolution at the close of the last century."[41]

To Brownson the original sin of the historic Church was that it misconceived the mission of Jesus. He had come as the God-man, as a mediator, a reconciler of spirit and matter. But the Church had exchanged the name "mediator" for that of "Redeemer." With this change there was no middle term to mediate between spirit and matter. Hence the polar exaggerations of Catholicism and Protestantism: Protestantism came as a protest against exaggerated spiritualism. What was needed, he insisted, was the union of the affirmative in both systems on the eclectic principle of Cousin, the union of the spiritual and the material, the heavenly and the earthly, the eternal and the temporal, the divine and the human, symbolized in the God-man: what was needed was a vital synthesis of these elements in a new church for

106

mankind which would be the solvent of the antagonism between the things of body and soul, between the interests of time and eternity.[42] "We of the present century," he said, "must either dispense with all religious instructions, reproduce spiritualism and materialism, or we must build a new church, organize a new institution free from the imperfections of those which have been." We cannot go back either to exclusive spiritualism, or exclusive materialism. "We must go forward, but we cannot take a single step, but on condition of uniting these two hitherto hostile principles. Progress is our law and our first step is Union."[43] This, he was saying at the time, is precisely what the Society was founded to achieve.

But as Per Sveino has correctly observed, Brownson exaggerated in speaking of the exclusive spiritualism of the Catholic Church, charging that it had adopted an idea of the old Asian world with its notion that matter is essentially unholy. Brownson readily acknowledged that the Church had always taught the doctrine of the atonement made by Jesus, but that at the same time it did not comprehend its real meaning. Instead of affirming the essential holiness of both spirit and matter, the Church regarded spirit only as holy. Hence to the Church the mission of Jesus was not to effect a reconciliation and union of spirit and matter, but merely to redeem the spirit from matter. But in the *New Views* of Brownson true "Christianity declares as its great doctrine that there is no essential, no original antithesis between God and man; that neither spirit nor matter is unholy in its nature; that all things, spirit, matter, God, man, soul, body, heaven, earth, time, eternity, with all their duties and interests, are in themselves holy. . . . It writes therefore, *Holiness to God* upon every thing."[44]

In this effort of Brownson to put forth *New Views* of Christianity he really distorted and misrepresented one of the central doctrines of the Catholic Church. For the Church has never declared that matter is "essentially unholy." The word of God is too clear for that when it relates: "And God saw all things that he had made, and they were very good."[45] Nor did the Church ever demur to the dictum of Scholastic philosophy that *"omne ens est bonum"* — "every being is good [including the material]." This, too, is in no way out of line with the antagonism asserted by St. Paul between "the flesh" and "the spirit."[46] For St. Paul was here speaking of a moral antagonism which in no sense implies that the one or the other is unholy in itself. As Per Sveino further observes, the Catholic Church dogmas of the Incarnation and the Resurrection are a sufficient refutation in themselves of the sweeping assertions of Brownson at the time that Catholicity is an exclusively spiritualistic religion.[47]

Indeed, Brownson himself acknowledged later the potpourri of strange errors concerning Catholic doctrine contained in his *New Views*. "The book is remarkable," he said, "for its protest against Protestantism, and its laughable blunders as to the doctrines and tendencies of the Catholic Church, to which I was by no means hostile, but of which I was profoundly ignorant."[48]

Compressing the entire history of Christianity in the Western World into a small compass, the book dealt largely in generalities, and generalities abound in half-truths and inaccuracies. But by far the greater part of the book is an interpretation of modern history. Brownson looked sharply at the nineteenth century, particularly in the light of the movement that was then stirring Boston. In what is perhaps the most glowing passage in the book he linked together the births of the American Republic and the French Republic. "Our Republic sprang into being, and the world leaped for joy that 'a man child was born,' " he exclaimed. But the French Republic, after electrifying the world, was quickly swallowed in the military despotism of Napoleon, "uttered a piercing shriek, and fell prostrate on the grave of its hopes."[49] But what of the American Republic? Would it fulfill its promise, or default? Perry Miller believes that Brownson was here far ahead of his contemporaries, so far indeed that they could not even begin to understand what he was talking about. He wrote:

> Brownson's reading of the Middle Ages was no doubt sketchy; but his interpretation of the eighteenth century and of the French Revolution — and more strikingly, his linking of the American Revolution with that epoch — sprang from a historical sense that could not, in 1836, find many appreciators in this country. (To twentieth-century students it may even sound commonplace.) From his studies in Cousin and the French socialists, particularly the Saint-Simonians, Brownson was able to comprehend that American society, including the society of liberal Boston, was a product of the Enlightenment and was therefore caught in the toils of the failure of the Enlightenment — a realization to which few or no Americans had yet been brought.
>
> To Brownson it seemed rather too clear that the liberal surge of the two revolutions could, in this latter phase, be consolidated only by a progress of social cohesion. He set himself to oppose the atomistic and individualistic legends which the inheritors of the two revolutions persuaded themselves had been the meaning of those events. Indeed, looked at from today, Brownson's pamphlet was nothing less than prophetic — if it was not that in 1840 he was to become even more prophetic — but there is little difficulty in comprehending why, in 1836, his message fell upon ears totally unprepared to understand a syllable of what he was saying. Their owners, already non-plussed by the new metaphysics, could not begin to follow the logic — to us become familiar — through which the romantic philosophy of history became a basis for "union."[50]

Could Brownson's contemporaries have discerned as much in *New Views* as the penetrating insights of Perry Miller reveal to us, they would probably have read the book with greater care and enthusiasm. The writing and publication of the book had marked a special effort on his part to enlist their sympathy and verve in the movement he had initiated for the establishment of the Church of the Future. He had already founded his *Society for Christian Union and Progress* on a preliminary basis, but the real building of the Church of the Future required the genuine interest and cooperation of the public. The rather poor reception the book was given was but one of the disappointments he experienced while vigorously endeavoring to gather into his Society those whom he hoped would form the nucleus of the Church of the Future.

C. C. Hollis thinks it rather puzzling that Brownson should have had "such tremendous conviction and such evident faith in something so anomalous and amorphous" as his Church of the Future.[51] Brownson himself later acknowledged that there was a "mild, visionary, absurd" aspect to his plans for the Church of the Future, but he insisted that it was all only a development from premises held by "the leading Protestant minds of France, Germany, Great Britain, and the United States."[52] But what is perhaps of more interest to us in this ecumenical age is that well-nigh a hundred and fifty years ago there lived a man in Boston who made use of every lever he could get his hands upon to push forward an ecumenical movement in his own day. That the Catholic Church should foster so formally such a movement in our own day is only in harmony with its perennial mission and commensurate with the vast resources both human and divine ever at its disposal. But for a single individual to have essayed such a movement entirely on his own called for great courage indeed. He was moved thereto by a genuine longing to heal the schisms in the religious world that to this day sadly divide the hearts and minds of his fellowmen, that cripple their well-meant efforts at progress and forestall the era of greater peace and concord. Whether or not he was mindful of the earnest prayer of Christ for unity among his followers, he appears to have recognized the all-importance of unity of Christian faith and worship among Christians.

In concluding *New Views,* he wrote:

> I have uttered the words of Union and Progress as the authentic creed of the new church, as designating the whole duty of man. Would that they had been spoken by a clearer, louder and sweeter voice, that a response might be heard from the universal heart of humanity. But I have spoken as I could, and from a motive which I shall not blush to own either to myself or to him to whom all must render an account of all their thoughts, words, and deeds. I once had no faith in him, and I was to myself "a child without a sire." I was alone in the world, and my heart found no companionship, and my affections withered and died. But I have found him, and he is my Father, and mankind are my brothers, and I can love and reverence.
>
> Mankind are my brothers — they are brothers to one another. I would see them no longer mutually estranged. I labor to bring them together, to make them feel and own that they are all made of one blood. Let them feel and own this, and they will love one another; they will be kindly affectioned one to another, and "the groans of this nether world will cease"; the spectacle of wrongs and outrages oppress our sight no more; tears be wiped from all eyes, and humanity pass from death to life, to life eternal, to the life of God, for God is love.
>
> And this result, for which the wise and the good everywhere yearn and labor, will be obtained. I do not misread the age. I have not looked upon the world only out from the window of my closet; I have mingled in its busy scenes; I have rejoiced and wept with it. It craves union.[53] The heart of man is crying out for the heart of man. One and the same spirit is abroad, uttering the same voice in all languages. From all parts of the world voice answers to voice, and man responds to man. There is a universal language already in use. Men are beginning to understand one another, and their mutual understanding will beget mutual sympathy, and mutual sympathy will bind them together and to God.[54]

If his hopes in the matter proved overly optimistic, we should not forget that nothing great is ever accomplished without allowing hopes to soar and expand freely. Whatever the case, the various aspects to Brownson's *Society for Christian Union and Progress* and its backdrop have been explored in this chapter at some length on the score that his attempt to establish the Church of the Future was no doubt the most daring and challenging venture he ever entered upon. It was only gradually that he came to understand that man is "no church builder."[55]

But while busily engaged in pushing forward an ecumenical movement, Brownson also edited an important newspaper in Boston, the *Boston Reformer,* through which he could not only express his religious sentiments, but likewise promote his views on social and political reform.

# 9

## 'THE BOSTON REFORMER'

*His manifesto as editor of the* Reformer • *The trials of an editor* •
*His first brush with the slavery question* • *His friendship with
George Bancroft* • *His appointment as Steward of the Marine Hospital in Chelsea* • *His reaction to the Great Depression of 1837* • *He
decides to publish his own* Quarterly Review.

It was at the same time Brownson had completed the organization of his
*Society for Christian Union and Progress* (July 1, 1836) that he had also
assumed the editorship of the *Boston Reformer*. In making what he called
his "best bow to the public," he specified the objectives he contemplated and
enunciated the principles which were to preside over his editorial direction
of the newspaper. Whatever its merits or demerits in the past, the *Boston
Reformer* was now to be a medium of free discussion of all the topics connected with the great interests of mankind — religion, morality, literature,
politics and cognate subjects — regardless of party or sectarian prejudice.
Inasmuch as justice for all was to be the great aim of the paper, he promised
to advocate fearlessly and zealously the rights and interests of all the industrious classes, refraining from making the workingmen or any other class a
privileged order.[1] To make plain his opposition to all privileged orders or
parties, and his wholehearted dedication to the vital interests of all his
fellowmen, he nailed his motto to the masthead of the *Boston Reformer:*

No Party but Mankind

The editorship of the *Boston Reformer* afforded Brownson a needed
opportunity to provide the public with a right perspective of himself. It was
now fully seven years since he had become an active member of the reform
party of the day. His early religious and social theories had startled many in
the meantime. Not all people had been following his career closely enough to
have noted that his views on the great questions of religion and society had
been undergoing important modifications with the passing years. Now as editor, he felt it was necessary to clarify the direction of those changes since
the radical days of the Genesee *Republican and Herald of Reform.* His
great zeal and devotion to the cause of humanity, particularly to that of the
laboring classes, had not changed; but his views of the nature of needed
reforms and of the means by which they could be effected had, indeed, altered. In a manifesto addressed to all his readers, but perhaps obliquely to
his former associates in the Workingmen's party, he indicated the shift he
had made from the left to something like the vital center:

> When I connected myself with the cause the workingmen profess to have at
> heart, I had no confidence in religion, and concerned myself with it, but to op-
> pose it; now I embrace it as the lever of reform, as the very soul of progress.
> Then I regarded man as passive in the hands of external circumstances; I now
> recognize in him an active principle by which to a certain extent he may rise
> superior to circumstances. I then looked upon the outward for reform; I now,
> without undervaluing the external, look mainly to the inward. Then I was indig-

110

nant at the past, and wished to destroy all memory of it; I wished to destroy all existing society and to create a new society modeled after certain notions of social perfection of which I dreamed. But now I absolve the past, see much in the present to approve, and have no wish to destroy, but to perfect what is already begun. I would not, if I could, blot out the past. I love it too much.

These are important changes of opinion, and in a logical mind must lead to results widely different from those I then contemplated. I was then truly a revolutionist, in principle, and in spirit. I am now much more of a conservative. The age of revolutions has passed by. We live in an epoch, at least in this country, of orderly, legalized progress. . . . Here the conservative and the radical should be combined in the same individual. The ruling idea of the conservative is order, that of the radical is progress. The conservative opposes the radical because he thinks the radical would break up all order, and introduce confusion and anarchy; the radical opposes the conservative because he believes the conservative is opposed to all progress, and is determined to perpetuate all existing abuses. Both may unite and be fellow laborers for humanity, the very moment that the means of obtaining progress without interrupting order, and of preserving order without preventing progress, is discovered. This is the great problem it seems to me our government has solved. In our republican institutions a provision for amendments is inserted; the voice of the people quietly and constitutionally expressed, can make or unmake such laws as seemeth to the people meet and just. There is, then, here no need of the conservatives and radicals.

I am, then, it may be seen neither conservative nor radical, but a combination of both, and the *Reformer* will labor to unite both parties, or rather, to melt both parties into one great party of humanity. In this sense I adopt the motto of the *Reformer,* "No Party but Mankind."[2]

This it would seem is the first formal statement on Brownson's part of his shift from the left, and marks, therefore, in a measured degree, a turning point in his career. Whatever he had been in the past, from now on it will be more difficult to classify him as belonging to one polar group or the other. It is perfectly true that in the years immediately ahead he would at times speak the language of the liberal, if not the radical, in trumpet tones, but it may have been merely to call long-delayed attention to hoary abuses that are clamoring for redress. If his statements and their emphasis are studied closely, it may be seen that his thought from now on, however provocative at times, contains also, by and large, an accompanying strain of conservatism. There may be exceptions to this (the "Laboring Classes" essays), but these are exceptions. Leonard Gilhooley's observation would seem to be accurate: "[Brownson] was as complex a man, perhaps, as nineteenth century America produced, and at any period of his life he cannot be summed up in such slippery terms as 'liberal,' 'radical,' 'ultra,' or even in the converse."[3] His complexity stemmed no doubt in part from the great variety of his intellectual interests, and one is reminded of the statement made by a reviewer in *Queen's Work,* June 1939: "Perhaps Orestes Brownson is so hurtling in mind and emotion, possessed of so many interests, so shrewd in his analysis of the times, so correct in his prophecies that he defies analysis." Anne C. Lynch, an early correspondent and admirer of Brownson, also noted his strangely complex character when she remarked that there were half a dozen persons in Brownson, the man of the world, the preacher, the philosopher, the reformer, etc.[4]

It is this many-faceted quality of Brownson's character, reflected also in his thought, that may help to explain how it came about that he was at this time invited to preach in the Park Street Church of Boston, that citadel of exclusive orthodoxy. He was the only Unitarian that was ever invited to preach there, and the event caused no little wonderment in the city.[5] Nor is it strange that he did not receive a second invitation. The immediate occasion of the invitation extended may well have been, as has been surmised, the high tribute of praise Harriet Martineau had paid him.

In his first editorial for the *Reformer* Brownson expatiated on the great necessity of a wider diffusion of education among the people if they were to be properly qualified to discharge their political duties as citizens. Under the American system the people are the political sovereigns who elect to office whom they will. But if the sovereign people were ill-equipped to discharge their civic duties, "miserably educated," great evil would result. The people would be made the unsuspecting victims of designing demagogues who by unctious flattery would inflate their vanity, set them swaggering as wondrous wise, and finally do with them what they please. These evils Brownson deplored and he was ready to sacrifice his reputation if only he could, as a true patriot, do something to counteract them. "In fact," he said, "politicians are continually making an April-fool of the sovereign people. This, we know, is plain language to the sovereign; he may resent it if he will, dismiss us from court if he will, but we shall never flatter him. So long as we are one of his counsellors we shall tell him the truth and run the risk of his displeasure. We have no ends but honest ones to serve."[6] This gruff, honest Vermonter loved justice and hated iniquity, and he would stand by the cause of the people whether his services were appreciated or not. He received further encouragement in this from Dr. Channing who wrote: "You must *love* your fellow-creatures unaffectedly, love them too much to leave any room for anger towards opponents, and for solicitude for reputation."[7]

Brownson made immediate use of the columns of the *Reformer* to reproclaim himself a doughty champion of social equality. He believed that the social condition of all classes could be made to harmonize with the political equality on which American free institutions are based. By social equality he did not mean, however, that all members of society must be of the same height, the same size, or have the same quality of purse; no harm if some are greater, better, or wealthier. All he asked was that no one because of matters beyond his control should be doomed to stay on the lowest rung of the social ladder. In his *Oration before the Democracy of Worcester,* he said:

> This word equality has a frightful meaning for many good folks. Although I mean much by it, I am far from meaning that all men must become exactly the same size in mind, in body or in possessions. What I oppose is not the natural diversity there may be between man and man, but the artificial inequality that has been introduced. I complain not that another man is taller than I am; but I am by no means willing that another man, short by nature, should contrive to stand with his feet on my shoulders, and then look around at the multitude and exclaim, "See how tall I am."[8]

What he was really contending for was not equality of status, but equality of opportunity for all; that no man should be barred from those sources from which he could gain the moral and educational qualifications to fit him for the best society in the land. That those sources might be made accessible to the laboring classes he stressed again and again the importance of a general diffusion of education among the people. But neither at this time, nor at any other time in his life, did he ascribe any thaumaturgic or magical properties to education, particularly in the way of obliterating differences and rendering all people equal. He wrote:

> There are differences in man's capacities which it is impossible to obliterate. Education may modify, lessen, or exaggerate them, but it has never been able, and I do not think it ever will be able, to obliterate them. No education can make every man a Homer, a Milton, a Locke, a Washington, a Franklin. Perhaps it is well there are differences.[9]

Quite soon after Brownson had become editor of the *Reformer* its old patrons began to complain that the journal had now too much religion. This complaint to Brownson was a strange grievance. There were those who had called him an infidel. If the complaint, replied Brownson, meant that the *Reformer* did not indulge in muckraking, nor publish all the unsavory scandals of the day, then he assured his critics that the set aim of the *Reformer* was the moral and religious regeneration of man and society, not to lash this man, this bank, or that corporation. Other journals could act as scavengers if necessary. If any of his subscribers had dirty work they wished done, they were thereby advised to go elsewhere to have it done. Whether such a course on his part meant loss of subscribers or not, he would not accommodate the lovers of muckraking. "We wish," he said, "to conduct a paper which a judicious parent need not fear to put into the hands of his children."[10]

Brownson's articles did accordingly breathe a distinct moral and religious tone, all the more so since he wished so devoutly to win over to the reform movement of the day the friends of religion and morality. The clergy in particular he wished to have with him to swell the ranks of the grand party of reform. A strong spirit of reform was in the air, he declared, and he counseled the clergy that it was to their own vital interests that they identify themselves with it: "Reform is the order of the day," he cautioned, "and the people will not long sustain a body of men, whom they feel to be inimical to their rights, and who stand between them and the corrections of abuses. . . . The people are going ahead, and ahead they will go; with the clergy, if they choose, without them, if they choose to stay behind." He continued:

> It is desirable that the clergy unite with the reform party. They may sanctify it by their presence, and warm its faith. Disowned by the clergy, the reform party will believe itself infidel, and great harm will come from its so believing itself. . . . It needs the learning, the piety, and the benevolence the clergy might inspire, in a word, the warming, guiding, restraining influence of religion. . . . We would not destroy the church, but save it, and *the salvation of either can come now only from a hearty cooperation with the people to meliorate their condition.*[11]

Much of Brownson's social thought had a prophetic insight. Much of it, revolutionary in ring as it was for his day, would seem to fit better the post-conciliar twentieth century than his own time. In this he seems to have been far ahead of most clergy of the day. He read the times correctly. His warning to his fellow clergymen that their lack of cooperation in the active improvement of social conditions would lose them the people, was prescient. The failure of Christians in the past to give greater attention to the social implications of the Gospel has been used by many of the unchurched as an excuse for turning away from religion.[12]

While Brownson was thus valiantly endeavoring through the *Reformer* to push forward the reform movement, he was also, *pari passu,* advancing his program for Christian Union and Progress. As William L. Gildea has observed, Brownson had convinced himself that, supposing the existence of a divinely instituted church, its task and duty would be to watch over the interests of the poor. On this point he laid great stress in the first issue of the *Reformer,* not indeed as characteristic of the true church, for he had much earlier come to the conclusion that no such divinely instituted church existed, but as the work and office of any religious Christian society which could, with any confidence, claim a hearing with the public.[13] Noticing the zeal with which Brownson was putting forth his efforts for the establishment of the Church of the Future, the Boston *Pilot* (Boston's Catholic newspaper) suggested to him that he study the nature and teachings of the Catholic Church and that he would find there all that he was so laboriously striving to realize outside the church's pale. His reply was respectful: he shared none of the common Protestant hostility to the Catholic Church, but he felt that the Catholic Church had already fulfilled its historic mission, and was dated. Echoing the influence of the French philosopher, Benjamin Constant, he asserted that the Catholic Church had served the race well in its childhood and youth, but that it no longer had the capacity to serve it in its adulthood. The race "asks not now to be treated as a child whose duty is merely to obey, but as a man who is capable of reasoning and of understanding the nature of things."[14]

It was also only shortly after he had assumed the editorship of the *Reformer* that Brownson had his first brush with the slavery question. When on August 3 the Anti-Slavery Society of Boston attempted to celebrate the anniversary of the emancipation of the slaves of what was then known as the British West India Islands, a mob gathered about the building where the Society was to assemble, and had the entrance to the hall closed by the lessee of the building. Wishing to avoid violence, the Society repaired to a private residence, where Brownson, who was to have delivered the oration in the hall, led in a prayer, a hymn was sung, and the Society dispersed. The feelings of indignation on the part of the members of the Society were by no means mollified by the fact that the "mob" which had interfered was made up mainly of very respectable Southern gentlemen and Boston merchants.[15]

Up to this time, Brownson, though decidedly opposed to human slavery on principle and by every instinct of his being, had refrained from joining in any activities aimed at the abolition of slavery where it existed by law, and had said little or nothing on the subject. But the action of the "mob" in their efforts to prevent the assembly of free citizens to commemorate peaceably the emancipation of slaves in the West India Islands he considered an outrage upon the rightful freedom of American citizens. The ugly affair almost drove him into the arms of the abolitionists. His indignation is reflected in the *Reformer* of the next day, August 4. He wrote:

> We have never been able to go with the abolitionists; we have never approved their modes of proceeding; but we have now no liberty left us. As the conductor of a public journal expressly devoted to the melioration of humanity, and owning no party but mankind, we cannot be silent. We must speak, and however much the abolitionists may have been in the wrong, their cause *now* becomes the cause of every freeman, every patriot, every philanthropist, and every Christian. It is a fearful crisis, and woe to the cowardly spirit that would shrink from it! It must be met, and manfully, and it *shall be.* If southerners come here and mob peaceable women, they *shall* be made to know that there is here too much of the spirit of the Pilgrims to bear it in silence. If they can come here in open daylight, and instigate, and in spirit form a mob, we tell them now, that from this time henceforth and forever, that we espouse the

114

cause of the slave, and that we will not cease to importune his owner till he is free.[16]

We will probably appreciate better the role Brownson was playing as the new editor of the *Reformer* if we recall that it had formerly been a political journal, and had supported, by and large, the Jackson administration. Typically, the new editor refused to align the journal with any political party. He still continued, however, to make it a political paper in some respects, reserving to himself the right to discuss as it pleased him first principles in politics as in morals and religion, and to pass judgment on all public measures and views expressed. His impassioned interest in all public affairs was a full guarantee that he would vigorously oppose or promote any political measure accordingly as he understood it to be harmful or beneficial to the public weal.

A highly complimentary notice Brownson gave in the *Reformer* to a Fourth of July oration of George Bancroft, 1836, was the beginning of a friendship between the two. Brownson's notice was all the more appreciated since Bancroft had been subjected to "bitter and long continued assaults." He wrote Brownson, September 21, 1936:

> My Dear Sir:
> Having failed to meet you the other day when I was in Boston, I cannot forbear writing you a line to say how I feel indebted to you for the kind and firm support your criticism of my oration gave me. The views there contained I have defended on various public occasions during the last ten years. Little did I think that the publication of them would have been followed by such bitter and long continued assaults. But these attacks do not annoy me — a clear conviction I dare avow and were I left alone, I would scorn to conceal my thoughts from fear.
> With your newspaper which I often see, I am much charmed. On the principle of the advance of humanity Mr. Van Buren is sincerely with us. . . . The country is Democratic; the people need higher conviction, a clearer consciousness of its democracy. . . . The government cannot be improved except by the advance and improvement of the people.
> If you come upon the Connecticut River, pray let me see you. The Democracy in Franklin and in Hampshire is entirely on the highest and purest system. . . . In this country the tendency is steady towards a firm and vigorous system of truly popular doctrines. The people want light. The instinct is right; they want consciousness. "Know thyself," said Solon to Athens as a commonwealth — our commonwealth wants the consciousness of being an organic whole, and of feeling the corresponding obligation to make progress, as a state.
> Yours truly,
> George Bancroft[17]

The background of these two men was quite different. Bancroft, the future illustrious historian of the nation, enjoyed all the advantages Harvard and the University of Berlin could bestow. But they had much in common in their political philosophy. Both believed strongly that America's special mission was to effect the moral and social elevation of the masses, but Bancroft was a Democrat in a more absolute sense than Brownson. Although Brownson acknowledged at this time that there is much truth in the old saw, *Vox populi vox Dei,* yet it was with only certain reservations. He called himself a humble member of the Democratic party, insofar as he belonged to any party, but he was not satisfied with the party. The party as such was too much disposed to ask, "What is the will of the people?" and when ascertained, to act on it, whatever it might be. But we go a step further, said Brownson, and ask, "Is it right? Is it just?" If it is not, we will not conform to it; we will, so far as in our power, oppose it and endeavor to set the party right. Thus we see that already in this year, 1836, this stern and indomitable reformer, bucking the ultra-Democratic current of the times, was evolving in his own mind a sound political philosophy. Concerning the unlimited sovereignty of the people, he remarked:

> This is our democracy. We admit the sovereignty of the people when the question is of the many or the few; we deny it when we speak absolutely. The people are not sovereign. There is no sovereign, but the infallible, that is, God, that is again, the Right, the Just. We dissent from the Democratic party, therefore, and of course from the popular doctrine of the day, by denying the infallibility of the people, and the absolute sovereignty of their will. We make justice paramount to the popular will, and acknowledge allegiance to the popular will only so far as it is in harmony with our convictions of the Just. The popular doctrine, and of course Van Buren's, we take it, is somewhat short of this.[18]

Brownson was quite pleased with the letter Bancroft had written him on September 21, 1836, and replied to it on September 25, 1836, writing from Mt. Bellingham, Chelsea:

> G. Bancroft, Esq.
> Dear Sir:
> I received today yours of the 1st. inst. I need not say that it was very acceptable indeed. I am glad that my remarks on your Oration were not displeasing to you. I saw in your Oration, aside from its special party aspect, a deep social philosophy. I recognized in it more than the politician. I saw the philosophy of Humanity.
> I was much surprised at your letters a few years ago to the workingmen. I did not expect to find a man occupying your position in society, venturing to proclaim such doctrines. When I read them, I said to one of my friends, we may now take hope. The cause of the people is safe. The reproach that has been cast upon you for publishing your opinions has not surprised me in the least. I could have told you beforehand that you would have received it. I am glad however that it does not annoy you. A little firmness will neutralize all its effects. You are on the right side. You are but following out the direction which modern civilization is to bring. All things tend to democracy. Those who support it are sure of the future.
> Providence is seen in throwing the History of the United States into your hands to be written. That is a triumph of Democracy indeed. Democrats have as yet written no history of the country, and that is the reason there has been as yet no history. Give us the literature of the country and we are safe. You are doing your part to place it on the side of the people.
> I am trying to democratize religion and philosophy. In this work in which I have been laboring in obscurity seven years or more, I have found very few to encourage me, and scarcely one to sympathize with me. Judge then of my pleasure on reading your Oration, and finding in it the words union and progress, as the maxim of democracy. I saw that you have the same thought with myself. And I said, I am not alone. I now begin to find friends. I have a good friend in Rev. George Ripley. He has finally philosophized himself into Democracy. Dr. Channing has democratic instincts, and our Mr. Emerson in his recent publication, Nature, has a presentiment of social progress which is charming. . . .

In a postscript to his letter of September 21, 1836, Bancroft had inquired of Brownson whether he had Vico and the works of Jouffroy. To which Brownson replied in this letter:

> You mention Vico. I have not read him attentively. I do not read Italian [as yet], and the French translation I find dull. Jouffroy's philosophical *Miscellanées,* and *Cours du Droite Naturel,* I have and am reviewing them for the *Christian Examiner.* I like Guizot on modern civilization in Europe and on French civilization. He is with all his *quasi* legitimacy much in advance of the Whigs. . . . I read too the Saint-Simonian works with great interest. . . .
>
> I was disappointed in not seeing you when you were in Boston. I heard you were here, and I wish to become personally acquainted with you. I have just written to Mr. Cousin. I do not know your opinion of his metaphysics, but I do know his works have made many young men among us democrats. I am glad to hear you say Mr. Van Buren is with us in the great doctrine of rights. I have thought differently of him. . . . Perhaps it is my fault.
>
> Forgive my long letter. I shall be most happy to hear from you.
>
> Yours sincerely,
> O. A. Brownson[19]

Bancroft's first letter to Brownson on September 21, 1836, had glowed with dreams of what the Democratic party was on the eve of achieving in Massachusetts. Resident in Springfield, Bancroft was at the time one of the foremost leaders of Democracy in Massachusetts, and had evidently hoped by his enthusiastic letter to bring the fiery Boston minister into line for an all-out backing of the Democratic party. Brownson was in fact a one-man army in energy to any cause he could be brought to champion, and Bancroft clearly recognized his full worth. Arthur Schlesinger, Jr., remarks of Brownson at this time: "His literary skill put him in demand as an author of party manifestoes and resolutions, and he proved himself a good, slashing stump speaker, whose biting phrases could raise roars from the crowd." But Bancroft's efforts to win Brownson's great energies to the support of the party failed. Instead, Brownson tried to steer the *Reformer* through the heated campaign of 1836 "on a non-political tack until angry readers (who remembered the *Reformer* as a backer of the [Democratic] administration) forced his dismissal."[20] This dogged refusal on Brownson's part to align the *Reformer* with any party whatsoever, but to seek rather to promote the rights and interests of all parties is perhaps what drew from Harriest Martineau the comment that under Brownson's guidance the *Reformer* came nearer the "principles of exact justice" than any other similar publication she had ever seen.[21] After Brownson's dismissal, however, the pleas of the proprietors of the *Reformer* to win him back to the editorship became so importunate that he finally consented to take charge again.[22] This position he continued to hold for the most part of the next year, 1837. Upon his return to the editorship, Bancroft wrote him again on July 9, 1837:

> I received my *Reformer* on Friday night with unusual satisfaction. I was glad to see you again in the field as the champion of the rights of humanity. . . . You are (what so few are) rooted and grounded in the true doctrine. You have the central point, from which truth, as applied to our political relations, must radiate; the seminal principle, that has vitality, springs up, and bears abundant harvest. It is the misfortune of many of our most estimable men, that they have reflected but little; that they have not set their minds in order; that they advance measures blindly without knowing the true principle on which their measure rests. Others again are blinded by present personal interests, and therefore weigh men and measures with false weights. I think your writings

give abundant evidence of that deep philosophy which by the unerring standard of human consciousness, tries the merit of every measure and leading influence of every public man. . . .

I am too familiar with your writings, not to know that our principles accord in many essential points: I would fain hope that we might view practical subjects alike also.[23]

Brownson's growing friendship with Bancroft was to turn into a *quasi* bonanza for Brownson. With the election of Van Buren to the presidency in 1836, and his inauguration in 1837, as a reward for his party services in the presidential campaign, Bancroft was selected as Collector of the Port of Boston. The appointment put him in a position to fill subordinate offices in Massachusetts with men who had worked for the success of the party. Most of the friends of Bancroft's own social standing had eliminated themselves from consideration by their former opposition to the Jacksonian movement. But there were two men Bancroft felt were worthy of consideration, Nathaniel Hawthorne and Orestes Brownson, though of course for quite different reasons. Hawthorne, it is true, had not contributed positively to the success of the party, but he had at least remained neutral, and what really counted, he had important political connections, particularly with Franklin Pierce, the congressional representative from New Hampshire. (Hawthorne and Franklin Pierce were old friends from their days together at Bowden College. In 1852 Hawthorne published his *Life of General Pierce,* a stroke designedly intended to help his friend reach the presidency.)[24] Bancroft offered Hawthorne the office of measurer of salt and coal in the Custom House of Boston, which carried with it the yearly salary of fifteen hundred dollars, a rather handsome annual income on the side in those days, particularly in the lean years immediately following the Great Depression of 1837. Although as we have noted, Brownson had stoutly refused to adopt the party line in the presidential campaign, he had nevertheless supported Jacksonian principles with verve and vigor, and immediately after the election Bancroft offered him the stewardship of the United States Marine Hospital in Chelsea, with the yearly salary of sixteen hundred dollars. Such a salary was enormously welcome to Brownson, yet he at first refused to accept the proffered position. His son explains:

One of [Brownson's] objections was that holding office under the government would hamper his freedom of political discussion, which he was determined to maintain in all circumstances. Bancroft assured him that he was.familiar with his views and his manner of discussing political measures, and that there was no objection to the freedom he had always exercised in this direction; that in fact it was rather desirable than otherwise, and that his independent manner of speaking gave additional weight when he supported government measures, as in most cases he did.[25]

Accordingly Brownson accepted the appointment. This office, including a very good house and duties largely nominal in nature, could have come to him at no better time. For there were hard times for the nation. In May the Great Depression of 1837 broke with a paralyzing impact. The economy of the nation slowed almost to a standstill, and as Arthur M. Schlesinger, Jr. — who has given us a superb, if brief analysis of Brownson's economic thought — remarks, "Such a collapse of the nation's economy speedily produced its critics, of whom the most searching was Orestes A. Brownson, a Boston minister and editor."[26] In this same month of May Brownson delivered an address from the rostrum of his Masonic Temple hall titled: "Babylon Is

Falling." Babylon symbolized "the Spirit of Gain"; its collapse was figuratively the massive depression which had engulfed the nation. The real causes of the depression Brownson laid to the privileges enjoyed by the upper classes. All the modern industrial arts and appliances had been made to redound to their especial advantage. He told his audience:

> The result of the progress of civilization thus far, has not been to elevate in any conceivable degree, the producing classes, as such, but merely to increase the number of those the producing classes must feed. The progress of science, the various implements and new inventions in the arts of production and for abridging labor, and of which we hear such loud boasts, have not yet, so far as I can see, in the least lightened the burdens of working men and women, properly so-called; they have merely facilitated the means by which a poor man, a producer, may pass to the class of the non-producers, from one of the ridden to one of the riders.[27]

This statement no doubt contains much truth, but it would be an oversimplification to say that it contains the whole truth. Yet Brownson was quick to show an uncanny ability in unscrambling the factors that bring about depressions in the business world. Arthur M. Schlesinger, Jr., again remarks that although the Great Depression of 1837 had to repeat itself half a dozen times before the professional economists realized that depressions are organic in capitalism as it exists, Brownson's extraordinary penetration traced the roots of depressions to the business cycle itself even before the Great Depression of 1837 had run its course (1843).[28] In acknowledging Brownson's wizardry in getting to the bottom of the shifty factors that operate in the economic order, Schlesinger wrote:

> Brownson made no pretense of being an economist, but of all his writings his economic thought is today the most striking. He reasoned on economic problems, not systematically, but in a series of flashes which momentarily revealed in blazes of white heat ideas later to rule the world. Unhappily, few were looking, and few benefitted.[29]

It was the Great Depression of 1837 which had brought Brownson for the first time into practical politics. During the canvass for the President in 1824, he was in the territory of Michigan, and of course had no voice. His sympathies in the contest, however, had been for John C. Calhoun; but learning that Calhoun was to be a candidate for the vice-presidency, not the presidency, he was for William H. Crawford. Shortly thereafter Brownson entered the Christian ministry and partly forgot politics for a time. By 1828 the political arena engaged his attention again, and he foolishly (as he claimed) voted for the electors in favor of John Quincy Adams. In the years immediately following he was one of those, as we have noted, who originated and pushed forward the Workingmen's party in New York State, but more with moral and social aims in view than political. In 1836 he had come to Boston on a *religious* (as he stressed) rather than a political mission. But the moral shock the mammoth depression brought him had catapulted him headlong into the melee of practical politics. As he explained it:

> The wickedness of the banks in 1837, in refusing to pay their debts, and the moral obtuseness of the community which could tolerate, nay defend, in these moneyed corporations, conduct which would have been severely censured and even punished in the case of private individuals, brought me for the first time fairly into practical politics; for I felt that a system of special legis-

lation had been adopted and fostered, which, if not arrested, would bring us under the absolute control of associated wealth.[30]

The whole force of current factors and circumstances now compelled Brownson to align himself more closely with the Democratic party. For him Jacksonian democracy had neither been sufficiently radical nor earnest to carry out the true principles of what he called social democracy. But with the extra session of Congress then called by President Van Buren, he thought he saw the Democratic party on the eve of adopting, on the one hand, the states' rights doctrines of the South — to which he had become a convert by the famous Senate debate between Webster and Hayne — and of accepting, on the other hand, the Locofoco doctrines of equal rights for all with a corresponding campaign against all privileges and monopolies of banks and banking, and other corporations. This new turn of the Democratic party, as it seemed to him, now determined him to give the party all the support in his power as the one party that gave promise of social reform and progress.[31] His passionate interest in the laboring classes drove him in this direction, and on that score he was to continue with unabated devotion to write on political and economic questions to the end of his life.

Likewise, in the field of education, Brownson continued his lively interest in the people's cause. For two or three years now he had been vitally interested in manual-labor schools as a means of placing the best education within the reach of the poorest. His plan was to connect labor with study in such a way that the student would grow up healthy and vigorous while developing and opening up his mind to the various cultural sources. (His plan here foreshadowed the system to be later adopted at Brook Farm.) But not being entirely satisfied that there might not be aspects to the subject with which he was not sufficiently acquainted, he opened up the columns of the *Reformer* to communications from any of his readers who might be able to enlighten him further on such schools as might already exist in the country, on the manner in which they were conducted, and concerning the principles upon which they were operating. Dr. Channing wrote him an encouraging letter, saying that manual-labor schools "seem to me at present the only means of giving a thorough education to the mass of the people." Governor Edward Everett of Massachusetts, in response to an invitation extended to him to attend a meeting relative to the matter, replied that perhaps the name "Industrial Schools" by which such schools were known in Germany might be a better term.[32] The fuller attention Brownson might have given this project was to be rather abruptly cut short when he soon determined to start his time-consuming *Boston Quarterly Review.*

Brownson at this time was discussing popular education from all angles. In the May 1837 issue of the *Christian Examiner,* he had an article on the "Education of the People." In concerning himself with the question as to who should give direction to popular education he answered unhesitatingly that only one body of men was properly qualified to furnish the directors, namely, the Christian ministry. Yet he would have their influence felt rather in a persuasive than a dictatorial manner. Whatever their influence in the past, it seemed to him inadequate; he would have them put forth greater efforts to see that each member of society was properly educated both as an individual and as a social being, both in relation to time as well as to eternity. Here again he was laying heavy emphasis on the social implications of the Gospel:

Undoubtedly the first concern of Christianity is to perfect the individual, to fit him for that glorious social state into which the good enter after death; but it contemplates also the fitting of him for a more perfect social state here. The angels sang, "On earth, peace and good will to men," as well as "Glory to God in the highest."

To the objection that should the clergy bring out more clearly the social element of the Gospel and labor for the perfection of society, they would soon "loose themselves in a land of shadows and merely amuse the people with dreams," he replied:

> Be it so, then. Even dreams are sometimes from God. Those visions of what is better than what is, which are forever coming to minds and hearts of the gifted and the good, are our pledges of higher destiny. They familiarize us with loftier excellence, enchant us with a beauty superior to that of earth, and quicken within us the power to do and to endure everything to realize them. . . . No one ever attained to eminence who did not see mountains rising far above the highest he could reach.[33]

In midyear 1837 Brownson was settling down in his new position as steward of the Marine Hospital in Chelsea. The salary connected with the office freed him from financial worry and made possible an ambitious project he had been meditating for some time. His movement for the Church of the Future had gathered little momentum. He had begun to wonder about the experiment he had undertaken. Why had it not prospered better? He finally became convinced, he said, "that I had gone too fast for the public, and that there remained a greater preliminary work to be done than I had supposed."[34] He felt, too, that his ideas had been misunderstood, and that he had, in consequence, perhaps awakened religious and social fears in the minds of some. He was becoming conscious, as C. C. Hollis observes, that he was gradually losing the audience he most prized, the new thinkers, the advanced Unitarians.[35] If only he had a proper medium in which to express his ideas more fully, he felt that their truth and justice would be more readily acknowledged.[36] With this one conviction in mind, he decided to establish a quarterly review of his own devoted to religion, philosophy, politics and general literature. Although he was to give it the name *The Boston Quarterly Review*, it was to bear so distinctly the stamp and character of Orestes A. Brownson that it would have been more becomingly called *Brownson's Quarterly Review*. Yet it was clever to call it the *Boston Quarterly Review*, for such a title tended to integrate it more intimately into the community in which he lived. This journal he was to conduct "almost single-handed" for five years.

His friend, George Ripley, set off the extraordinary venture and character of the *Boston Quarterly Review* when he said:

> [This journal] was undertaken by a single individual, without the cooperation of friends, with no external patronage, supported by no sectarian interests, and called for by no motive but the inward promptings of the author's own soul. The variety of subjects it discusses is no less striking, than the vigor and boldness with which they are treated. The best indication of the culture of philosophy in this country, and the application of its speculative results to the theory of religion, the criticisms of literary productions, and the institutions of society, we presume no one will dispute, is to be found in the discussions of this journal.[37]

Brownson's comments on his forthcoming *Boston Quarterly Review* in a letter to his friend, George Bancroft, together with other interesting matter the letter contains, make its insertion here worthwhile. He wrote from Chelsea on November 10, 1837:

George Bancroft
Dear Sir:

I owe you a thousand apologies for having so long neglected to answer your favor of 9th of July last. I trust however that you will forgive me when I tell you I have hardly [had] a breathing spell since I received it. Since I left the *Reformer,* I have been busy preparing the first number of the *Boston Quarterly Review* which I shall have out on the first of January. The *Review* is to be published quarterly, 128 pages each number, three dollars a year, and open to the free and full discussion of all topics of general and permanent interest. My design in publishing it is by means of a higher philosophy of man than Reid's or Locke's to christianize democracy and *democratize* the church. I shall have a long dissertation on Democracy in the first number, founded on the Address adopted by the State Convention at Worcester, September the last, in which I have attempted to give to Democracy a philosophical definition, to state what it is and to legitimate it. I think you will not greatly dislike the article.

I must thank you again and again for the second volume of your History. It is no flattery, and indeed not very high praise, to say that it is the best historical production in our language. What is more to the purpose, I say honestly, that in my opinion it is destined to do more for the cause of free principles, universal liberty, than any other work in the English language. . . .

My dear sir, I will assure you that it is with no ordinary feelings that I see you giving your time, your talents, your learning, genius and reputation to the cause of the masses. I will not say that in doing this you are doing more than your duty, but it is so rare that one can find a man in our country, especially in New England, whom God has richly endowed, and qualified to be a benefactor of his race, daring to side with the industrious classes, that when I see one doing it, I want to take him by the hand and in God's name, in Humanity's name, in the name of the wronged and downtrodden of all ages, to thank him, and bid him Godspeed. I have long been engaged in the cause of the masses. I know what it is to sacrifice ease, property and reputation in their cause. There were few men of learning, few men of standing to side with them when I did, and it is not without emotion, that I see to-day so many of the choicest spirits of the land, not ashamed to be advocates of the many. I now feel this cause is safe.

I say I have sacrificed something in the cause of the people. I mean not to complain, nor to ask praise. I have not given much, but I have given what I had, all that I had, and I love that cause as a man always loves that for which he has suffered somewhat. You love the cause a great deal more than you would had you suffered nothing for it. These slanders and this obloquy you have had to endure have done no harm, and you will work altogether more earnestly in the good cause. Mankind are saved only by crucified redeemers. Go on, dear sir, and be assured there are warm hearts bidding you Godspeed, and noble minds becoming enlightened by your expositions of Democracy. We are in the midst of a revolution, a revolution of minds, and the success of the fight is registered in heaven.

The conversion of thy friend George Ripley to Democracy, is to me a pleasing event. When I first became acquainted with him he was dead set against Democracy, but he is now about right, only in danger like all new converts of becoming a little too enthusiastic. Let me say of Mr. Ripley that I regard him as one of the first men in our country. He has a mind of uncommon purity, clearness and vigor. He is a close student, a fine scholar and a most amiable man. His mind is free and his heart open. Few men if any among us surpass him as a metaphysician. And I may say of him as said Dr. James Walker of Charlestown, that "he has the soundest head in Boston." Several young men of the Divinity school of Cambridge are coming on well, and be assured, that we shall soon have the literature and philosophy and all that belongs to scholarship on the right side.

I shall send you the first number of my *Review,* with the hope that it will so strike you that you will aid it by contributions to its pages. The work is published as a labor of love and I want all who love the cause to which it is devoted to bestow somewhat of their love upon it. I should be glad to see you. I miss[ed] you while you were in Boston in consequence of living out of town. But nothing could give me more pleasure than to see you in my humble cottage on Mount Bellingham, Chelsea.

I am truly,<br>
O. A. Brownson[38]

Brownson was approaching a landmark in his life: the inauguration of his famous *Quarterly Reviews*. The volumes were to continue to flow from his prolific pen until they had reached twenty-nine in all.

# 10

## 'THE BOSTON QUARTERLY REVIEW'

*His indomitable defense of human rights • His sturdy opposition to the centralization of power in government • The commencement of his major book reviews • His doctrine on religious freedom • His forthright pronouncements on the slavery question, which won for him the friendship of John C. Calhoun • The defense of himself against an attack in* The Liberator.

The first issue of the *Boston Quarterly Review* appeared in Boston in December 1837. In his introductory remarks Brownson explained to his readers why he had been left no choice in the establishment of the journal he was now sending out to the public. There were all kinds of thoughts — on the Destiny of Man and Society — germinating in his mind, ideas which, clamoring for utterance, would out at any cost. A journal of a graver sort, such as a quarterly, in which he could give free and full expression of his thoughts, was the only answer in the case. The periodical press of the country, particularly the *Christian Examiner,* "for freedom and freshness unsurpassed in the world," had always been at his service. But writing for a journal not one's own always includes censorship, and, for Orestes Brownson, censorship worked as a brake upon his free flow of thought. Precious to him beyond all price was absolute intellectual independence and freedom to say just what he wanted to say in his own way and time. Nothing would ever set limits to that independence and freedom save the discovery of new truth. In the meantime his mind would range freely over all fields of thought in its earnest and unremitting pursuit of truth. Stressing this spirit of grim independence, he hit off in a few telling sentences the design and character that was to mark so largely his *Quarterly*. He wrote:

> I establish no journal to carry this or that proposed measure, or to give currency to this or that doctrine, to support this or that party, this or that class. I belong to no party under heaven, to no sect on earth, and swear allegiance to no creed, no dogma. I have no wish to build up one party or to tear down another, to aid one sect or to depress another, or to recommend this school in preference to that. I would discourse freely on what seem to me great topics, and state clearly and forcibly what I deem important truths — push inquiry into all subjects of general interest, awaken a love of investigation, and create a habit of looking into even the most delicate and exciting matters, without passion and without fear. . . . This is all.[1]

This plain declaration can only mean that however much he may have reflected, and however passionately he may have sought the truth in the past, his mind was still unsettled in many matters. Yet in spite of his asserted detachment from dogma and sects, it would scarcely be correct to conclude that he had no fairly crystallized religious sentiments or opinions of his own. Brownson was only serving notice that he was not to be a champion of any sect, school or party. In the introductory notice of this first volume of his *Quarterly,* he also wrote:

> I own, however, that I am desirous of contributing something to the power

124

of the great Movement Party of mankind, or rather of showing that I have the will, if not the ability, to aid onward the great Movement commenced by Jesus of Nazareth, and which acquires velocity and momentum in proportion as it passes through successive centuries, and which is manifesting itself now in a manner that makes the timid quake, and the brave leap with joy. With this movement, whether it be effecting a reform in the church, giving us a purer and more rational theology; in philosophy seeking something profounder and more inspiring than the heartless Sensualism of the last century; or whether in society demanding the elevation of labor with the loco-foco, or the freedom of the slave with the abolitionist, I own I sympathize, and thank God that I am able to sympathize.[2]

Henry D. Thoreau was among the first to write Brownson his congratulations on the appearance of the first edition of the *Boston Quarterly Review*. He wrote enthusiastically on December 30, 1837:

> I have perused with pleasure the first number of the *Boston Quarterly*. I like the spirit of independence which distinguishes it. It is high time we know where to look for the expression of *American* thoughts. It is vexatious not to know beforehand whether we shall find our account in the perusal of an article. But the doubt speedily vanishes when we can depend upon having the genuine conclusions of a single reflecting mind.[3]

While the *Quarterly* did, in truth, become the product of "a single reflecting mind," the editor did not originally intend it to be such. He declared its columns open to the discussion of all subjects of general and permanent interest, by anyone who was able to express his thoughts — "providing he has any — with spirit, in good temper, and in good taste."[4] Brownson's own thoughts, remarked O. B. Frothingham, "came in floods."[5] With this invitation extended to the public the editor did receive at times some assistance from his friends in Boston and elsewhere, among whom were George Bancroft, George Ripley, Margaret Fuller, Theodore Parker, Alexander H. Everett, Sarah Whitman, Elizabeth P. Peabody, W. H. Channing, John S. Dwight, Albert Brisbane and others.[6] As articles were unsigned in those days, it is frequently somewhat difficult to establish with certainty the authorship of an article. Sometimes just the initials of the author were given. Brownson's, however, were sometimes signed "The Editor."

Each issue consisted of six essays, usually occasioned by some recently published book, and a series of "Literary Notices." There was no corner reserved for poetry as such, but some poetry occurred in the articles published. The themes of each issue covered such a wide variety of thought that almost anyone, from the common laborer to the accomplished theologian or philosopher, could find something that would appeal to him in particular. C. C. Hollis states that the *Quarterly* had a subscription list of over a thousand, but adds that the correspondence seems to indicate that it was read by many more out of curiosity than spiritual hunger.[7] The fact is that the author himself was an object of immense curiosity to Bostonians of the time. His vibrant personality either attracted or repelled, but could not be ignored. His latest doings and sayings were topical. And his literary genius had a mesmerizing effect. Sarah Helen Whitman, Poe's friend, wrote him from Providence, Rhode Island: "One may form some idea of the popularity of your *Review* by casting an eye on the reading table of our Athenaeum where it is to be seen in a very tattered and dog-eared condition long before the end of the quarter while its sister journals lie around in all their virgin gloss and freshness."[8]

125

A contemporary critic indulged in a comparison between some of these sister journals and the Brownson *Quarterly*. He felt, above all, that the *Boston Quarterly Review* filled an important hiatus in American literature. The common brotherhood — the people — had previously had no organ like this new *Review;* none in which individual man could speak out unrestrainedly in his own stout spirit, and according to his own conceptions of truth. For what was the *North American Review* in this respect? It was "afraid of Humanity; its sympathies, its regards and affinities cluster around the educated, the refined, the aristocratic; its philosophy is circular selfishness, its equality the spirit of caste; its republicanism, a torpid abstraction." The *American Quarterly Review* was not a whit more serviceable to the cause of the people. The *Christian Examiner,* though somewhat freer in tone, and bolder in speculation, "wears the features of a sect, and lacks moral courage. The *United Sates Magazine and Democratic Review,* a monthly journal just started [Washington, D.C.] professes to be imbued with the spirit of liberty, but assumes a party aspect. The object of the *Boston Quarterly Review,* on the contrary, is not to favor any sect or party, as such. It is open to the free discussion of all topics of general and permanent interest by any who are able to write. This is both manly and liberal."[9]

After speaking of the way in which commentators have strained diaries, letters and periodical literature for evaluations on the significance of the *Boston Quarterly Review,* C. C. Hollis has remarked that the reading of a few pages of that journal would afford the best of all tributes to the author and editor.[10] Harold Laski pronounced the *Boston Quarterly Review* "astonishing." It "has," he recognized, "a permanent significance in American intellectual history."[11] Laski's statement that "it is important to realize that his [Brownson's] work of serious stature was done before his conversion [to the Catholic Church in 1844] is effectively rebutted, as Leonard Gilhooley has observed, by nothing more than a mention of Brownson's *The American Republic: Its Constitution, Tendencies and Destiny"* (1865).[12]

That Brownson himself was quite pleased with the immediate success of his *Review* is evident. He wrote his friend Victor Cousin in Paris on September 6, 1839:

> My Review has but a limited circulation, but I think I can say without vanity that it has taken a deep hold on the public mind. It is taken by the first literary men and leading politicians of the country, by men of all political parties and religious sects.[13]

Brownson took up in his *Boston Quarterly* where he had left off in the *Reformer,* which he had left only in time to begin this journal of his own. Nothing will more strikingly impress the reader of the *Boston Quarterly* for the whole year of 1838 as the momentous campaign Brownson at once got under way for the defense of human rights on a sound social and political basis. Whether our own times have a more pronounced consciousness of the dignity of the human person and the inalienable rights that inhere in every human being than obtained in the last century, is a point that might be argued.[14] Whatever the truth of the matter, we have here a man in the nineteenth century who had indeed a lofty perception of the dignity of every human person, the meaning of his rights in a well-ordered society, and was ready to do battle in his defense. When Brownson found James Fenimore Cooper indisposed to allow the terms *gentleman* and *lady* to be applied to footmen and cooks, Brownson had a contrary word to say:

Every human being, in our belief, is of noble, aye, of royal birth, and may stand up and claim to be a king, and demand royal honors. This is the foundation of our democracy, and he, who has yet to learn that no human being is or can be ignoble, is in our judgment a sorry democrat.[15]

When Brownson repeated the phrase (as he often did) that "man measures man the world over," that meant for him the individual, not just man in general. He perceived as clearly as any man could that almost all past governments have tended to curtail in part or in whole the natural rights of the individual citizen, and hence Brownson's arduous efforts to evolve a sound social and political philosophy that would stand as an intellectual bulwark against the ceaseless encroachments on the rights of the individual by selfish economic groups or corrupt political parties. Perhaps at no time of his life was that more conspicuous than during the period of his *Boston Quarterly Review*.

Brownson accordingly led off in the first issue of his *Review* with an elaborate article on Democracy in which for the first time he concerned himself closely with the vexatious question of how to maintain a just balance between freedom and authority, between liberty and order in society — a question he would continue to concern himself with in the decades ahead. Alexis de Tocqueville had just completed the first part of his *Democracy in America* in which he had said concerning the tyranny of the majority in America: "The majority, therefore, in that country [the United States], exercises a prodigious actual authority, and a power of opinion that is nearly as great; no obstacles exist which can impede or even retard its progress, so as to make it heed the complaints of those whom it crushes in its path. This state of affairs is harmful in itself, and dangerous for the future."[16] Brownson, too, was beginning to take alarming views of an unrestrained majority rule. He had flatly denied in the *Reformer* the doctrine of the underived sovereignty of the people, the doctrine of "people king," and "people-god," as he was to call it. If the people taken collectively are sovereign (absolutely), if the majority has the undisputed right to decree what it will, absolutely, then plainly the individual must obey. But absolute subjection to the will of an irresponsible majority would spell slavery for the individual. Only by making justice paramount to the will of the people would the rightful freedom of the individual be safeguarded.

"By bounding the state of justice," affirmed Brownson, "we declare it limited; we deny its absolute sovereignty; and, therefore, save the individual from absolute slavery. . . . Justice is then the sovereign, the absolute sovereign, the King of kings, the Lord of lords, the supreme law of the people, and of the individual."[17]

What he was really opposing here was the tendency to accept the will of the people expressed outside the country's political organism as a guide in government. As long as the will of the people could be made to operate within the established legal forms, the rights of minorities or individuals would be safeguarded. For in the bills of rights which precede many of the several state constitutions is to be found an inventory of the essential rights of man, rights which authority must hold sacred, and which people neither gave nor can in any shape or form alter or abridge. In the Constitution of the United States and that of the various states, boundaries have been set to the powers of the state. Such limitations embedded in the political institutions of the land teach us, said Brownson, that the individual has certain rights which dare not be altered or abridged, which authority dare neither invade nor suffer to be invaded. They teach us that if majorities may go to a certain length, there is a line beyond which they must not pass. "In denying the sovereignty of the people," he explained, "we deny the people can make or unmake rights, bind or unbind; we limit their functions to the discovery and promulgation of the law, as it is in justice, which is anterior and superior to all conventions."[18]

Yet, in whatever political system authority has been constituted, in all ages of the world and under almost all governments, Brownson stressed again, man has been little more than a pawn in the hands of the state. Governments have claimed to own him, and then conferred on him only certain grants according to its own caprices, interests, or necessities. "To put an end to this system of privilege," declared Brownson, "is now the great end of democracy."[19] This calls for great changes in governments throughout the world, whether royal, aristocratic, or popular in nature, changes which perhaps cannot be effected without violence or bloodshed, but he who pleads for justice is never anxious to promote violence, bloodshed or suffering. Still, whatever might be the exigencies of the case in other countries, the situation in our own is quite different, he affirmed. With all his agitation for reform, it is instructive to note that there was a real strain of conservatism in him at this time. He counseled:

> But there can be, in this country, no occasion for any but orderly and peaceful measures, for the acquisition of all that we have supposed. We must not dream of introducing it all at once. We must proceed leisurely. Let the men of thought speculate, and speak boldly what comes to them as truth; but let men of action, men who have more enthusiasm than reflection, greater hearts than minds, and stronger hands than heads, guard against impatience. Practical men, men of action, are, after all, the men who play the most mischief with improvements. Our principle is, no revolution, no destruction, but progress. Progress is always slow, and slow let it be; the slower it is, the more speed it makes. So long as we find thinkers canvassing all matters, discussing all topics of reform, and publishing freely to the world the results of their investigations, we have no fears for the individual, none for society. Truth is omnipotent. Let it be uttered; let it spread from mind to mind, from heart to heart, and in due season be assured that it will make to itself hands, and erect to itself a temple, and institute its worship.[20] Set just ideas afloat in the community, and feel not uneasy about institutions. Bad institutions, before you are aware of it, will crumble away, and new ones and good ones supply their place.
>
> We hold ourselves among the foremost of those who demand reform, and who would live and die for progress; but we wish no haste, no violence in pulling down old institutions or building up new ones. We would innovate boldly in our speculations, but in action we would cling to old usages and keep old lines of policy, till we were fairly forced by inward pressure of opinion to abandon them. *We would think with the radical, but often act with the conservative* [italics mine].[21]

This passage clearly indicates Brownson's increasing conservatism in a time that has been somewhat indiscriminately labeled the "liberal" or "radical" period of his life. So to label it is an oversimplification of the matter. The fact is, most commentators on Brownson's thought seem to have missed a dual sense in his thought of this period. As Leonard Gilhooley has remarked:

> The result is that the Pre-1841 Brownson has been seen as "an American Marxist before Marx" in Schlesinger's unfortunate phrase, chiefly because of the fact that his "Laboring Classes Essays of 1840" tend to become the early paradigm of Brownson's thought. They are not. Hollis admits as much, and

implies that a reappraisal "is demanded by the evidence." And that evidence, it seems, goes beyond a thin but perduring conservatism in religious philosophy, and indeed, serves, though its author seems unaware of it, to strengthen R.W.B. Lewis's more or less original contention that tradition and a sense of continuity are exerting a strong influence upon Brownson in the early 1840s. The point here is that the double sense did not originate after the "Laboring Classes Essays of 1840."[22]

We will perhaps get at a better understanding of Brownson's political thought if we assume — which really seems to be the case — that in much of his radical thought he was really blasting away at the absolutism and oppression that then obtained under European governments. He seemed to fear, however, that such a state of affairs might stealthily creep in here to blight and blast the fair hopes of this new world. It was only one phase of the grim battle he was waging in defense of the individual against any and all encroachments on the part of governments. Reasserting that the design and purpose of all government is to maintain to each individual the full possession and enjoyment of his natural rights, he laid his strictures already at this time on the doctrine of Jean Jacques Rousseau (previously that of Hobbes and Locke also) that the powers of government are made up of rights individuals ceded to it by way of a social contract:

> The powers of government [staunchly declared Brownson] are not made up of the individual rights surrendered to it. The notion that individuals give up any portion of their natural rights to society, in order to secure protection for the remainder, is false. The *Jus Divinum* must be asserted, if there be any government to be maintained. The magistrate is ordained of God. Define the legitimate powers of government, and those rights are sacred, and are derived from God. [Brownson always asserted also that the people are the medial source of political power from God.] But as they are from God they can never be in opposition to individual rights, which are also from God. Whenever the rights of individuals are disregarded, be the end what it may, the rights of every individual and of the whole community are invaded.[23]

When reviewing James Fenimore Cooper's *The American Democrat, or Hints on the Social and Civic Relations of the United States of America,* which C.C. Hollis calls Brownson's "first full scale literary review,"[24] Brownson praised Cooper for his free and independent spirit, his love of country and his forthrightness in avowing himself a Democrat while belonging to the literary class of the country. His book, too, he found "written with ability, in a clear, strong, and manly style, and handles a subject with great freedom and with much justice, on which American citizens — shame to say — needed to be instructed." Brownson was likewise fully aware of the sharp drop in Cooper's popularity between his sojourn in Europe and the period following when he carried his case from court to court against the assaults of newspapers. During his years in Europe, Cooper had heard many unfriendly comments on American ways or the American character. Returning home, he felt the urge to turn social critic in the interests of his countrymen. The newspaper assaults followed. It was a characteristic of Brownson to take up the cudgels in defense of the beleaguered, and he readily felt sympathy for Cooper in the brave fight he was making in the name of literary independence and freedom of speech.

Yet there was much in Cooper's book with which Brownson could not agree. That Brownson's criticism of the book has its merits is vouched for by C. C. Hollis who remarks that there is "little in the review [Brownson's] that later critics would change, and it remains one of the first objective appraisals and tributes to Cooper as a social critic."[25] Brownson began his criticism by noting that Mr. Cooper "thinks he sees two tendencies among us, which are alike dangerous to the stability and beneficial working of our free institutions." The upper classes, the affluent, the fashionable, he thinks somewhat anti-American. They do not heartily accept American institutions, magnify the evils of our system of government, and laud beyond measure the excellences of the aristocratical institutions of the Old World. The lower classes, the mass, by contrast, are pushing American institutions to the opposite dangerous extreme, tending toward disorder, if not revolution. They are idly dreaming of substituting "a fancied perfection for the ills of life. This disorganizing tendency of the mass, he thinks, if not arrested, will check civilization, destroy the arts and refinements of civilization, and reduce us all to the . . . level of barbarism."[26]

Hence Brownson saw in *The American Democrat* "a double battery, charged alike against those who believe too much in the past, and those who believe too much in the future, . . . those who have too much democracy and those who have too little. To be democratic over much, is ungentlemanly, and may lead to a kind of levelling not agreeable to those who are ambitious of being distinguished, and to be democratic not enough, is unwise, not to say absolutely foolish."[27]

Brownson acknowledged that this analysis of American society had a certain validity to it, but he took sharp issue with Cooper over the question of just where human rights and those of the government begin. Cooper had allowed that government may restrict to a certain extent the natural liberty of the citizen for the purpose of maintaining more effectively peace and order in society. This, snapped Brownson, is Hobbism. The only difference he found between the doctrine of Hobbes and that of Cooper was one of degree: Cooper allowed a larger portion of his natural liberty to the citizen; Hobbes thought that "a larger portion of liberty" to the citizen could not be allowed with safety to the state. Brownson repudiated the doctrine of both emphatically:

> Now we contend that the design of government is to maintain to every man all his natural liberty. Liberty, according to our definition of it, is freedom to do whatever one has a natural right to do; and one has a natural right to do whatever is not forbidden by natural justice. . . . The government that restrains or abridges in any sense, in any degree, the natural liberty, that is the natural rights, of any, the meanest or the guiltiest citizen, is tyrannical and unjust.[28]

In checking then the tendency to the two extremes spoken of by Cooper, we should, said Brownson, endeavor to point out the precise limits prescribed by justice. We should deny the justice of all restraints on natural rights, and thus check as effectively as possible the tendency to arbitrary government. This, Cooper's book had failed to do. He had made good and wise observations on the starting points of the two parties, but had only besought them not to go quite so far in their extremes as they had hitherto been disposed to go. For this reason Brownson did not think Cooper's book would succeed in arresting the two extremes. The masses, said Brownson, go where their principles logically lead them. To change their direction one must change their principles, alter or enlarge their premises. "Change the theory, the philosophy of a nation, its ideas, and you change its history."[29]

Whatever his criticism, Brownson was not unfriendly toward Cooper, and gladly acknowledged the good points of his book. All the more so since Cooper like himself was a social critic of some stature. His book, Brownson said, "is full of wise and just observations; is in most cases characterized by good sense, and its views, on all the great political topics it treats, are in the main just and democratic. It corrects many false notions, separates numerous matters which had become confused, and gives us much useful information, for the want of which our citizens have suffered, and our institutions been endangered." He felt, however, that he himself had more faith in the masses and more sympathy with them, as well as an altogether stronger love for progress, than Cooper. Cooper seemed to be a bit sour, "half mad at mankind." But his book in the main breathed a free and independent spirit, and could be looked upon as written in the interests of the people. The type of democracy it preaches was not altogether according to Brownson's taste, since it was reportedly written somewhat out of spite for the Whigs. But Brownson "was thankful that democracy is preached, though it be through spite, through ill-will to the aristocracy."[30]

Although Brownson in this article indicted also the state governments for their tendency to override the personal rights of citizens, his loudest complaints were leveled at the increasing federal centralization of power. This complaint was squarely in the tradition of Jefferson and John C. Calhoun. Apparently, about this time, Brownson began to adopt the states' rights doctrine then so vigorously upheld and defended by Calhoun. The stout sectional individualism in which the editor had grown up in Vermont had inclined him in that direction. In a passage prophetic as well as exhortatory, he called upon the American democrat to stand guard against the danger of the federal government absorbing the powers of the state governments and thus become one top-heavy, unwieldy bureaucracy weighing heavily upon the whole country. He wrote:

> Again, in a more restricted sphere, the American democrat is one who is jealous of power, and always interprets all doubtful questions so as to increase the power of the people, rather than that of the government. In this, his first duty is to watch that the Federal Government do[es] not swallow up the State governments. Power has a perpetual tendency to extend itself.[31] The functionaries of government, whether executive, legislative, or judicial, almost inevitably so exercise their functions as to enlarge the sphere of government. There is a tendency in the Federal Government, from its central character, to engross as much of the public business of the country as possible. The first danger to our liberty is to be apprehended from that quarter. Cooks may be called ladies, and footmen gentlemen,[32] and still our country be tolerably secure; but when the Federal Government has succeeded in getting under its control, directly or indirectly, nearly all the internal affairs of the States, and is able to make its acts, like the frogs of Egypt, reach to our domestic hearths, and to come up into our sleeping chambers and kneading troughs, we may be assured that the first barriers to a consolidated despotism have been leaped.[33]

In this review of Cooper's *The American Democrat,* Brownson was consolidating his embattled stand as the Argus-eyed guardian and champion of the natural rights of man from which he would never retreat, whatever the storms that might engulf him. To him, human rights were truly sacrosanct, even in a sense, divine. After further excoriating the tendency of state governments also to enlarge their powers at the expense of the rights of the individual, he counseled in conclusion:

> We must throw around each individual a bulwark of sanctity, and not per-

mit society to break through it, though it were to do the individual an unspeak-
able good. God leaves man his freedom, and does not control it, though the man
in abusing it brings damnation to his soul. Let the Divine government be a
model of ours. We may not control a man's natural liberty even for the man's
good. So long as the individual trespasses upon none of the rights of others, or
throws no obstacle in the way of their free and full exercise, government, law,
public opinion even, must leave him to take his own course.[34]

Brownson continued his vigorous, unrelenting fight in defense of human
rights when he reviewed the book, *An Inquiry into the Moral and Religious Character of the American Government.* The author, whose
name was not given, claimed that this is a Christian land and that therefore
the government should show preference for Christians. This was discrimination, claimed Brownson, and that by virtue of the doctrine of inalienable
rights every human person in the matter of religious freedom must stand on
a footing of perfect equality — with preference for none and discrimination
againt none. Because of the dignity of every human person the right of the
atheist or that of the deist to hold what opinion he will must be regarded in as
sacred a manner as the right of the Christian to profess what religious faith
he would. This right to be of one opinion or another, or of no opinion, is an inalienable right of every individual. (Especially is this a requirement of a
highly pluralistic society.) There is no possible way, Brownson emphasized,
in which to legitimate the right of any individual to his own form of religion
before the state except that which legitimates the right of every person
before the state to be of what religion he will — or none. Once the state is
allowed to encroach in the least on this matter of religious freedom, and
"there is no stopping place this side of absolute religious despotism." Religion, the rights of conscience, are so intimate, so sacred, that they brook no
interference whatsoever. As Brownson worded it concisely:

> Religion is an individual concernment. It is what is most intimate and holy
> in man. Governments have no right to interfere with it. They must put off their
> shoes when they approach it, and stand in awe before it, as Moses did before
> the Burning Bush. Its place is in the interior sanctuary of the individual heart,
> where it should be screened from all human observation, save as it manifests
> itself through a sweet and gentle, a just and beneficent life.[35]

Unfortunately, his intransigent defense of human rights was to put him
in a paradoxical position on the then burning question of Southern black slavery. It goes without saying that a man of Brownson's temperament was
"wholly and totally opposed to slavery."[36] As editor of the Boston *Reformer*
he had said: "[We] will oppose slavery, whether it be of the white man or the
black, without asking any man's leave."[37] Yet he found it necessary to separate himself from the abolitionists of the day. This necessary action he deeply regretted: "For there is," he said, "something extremely unpleasant in
being, even in appearance, opposed to the advocates of freedom. . . . There
is something in the very idea of freeing two or three millions of slaves,
which, in these mechanical and money-getting times, is quite refreshing and
capable of dazzling many an imagination. . . . There is something almost in-
toxicating in the idea of going forth as a bold knight in the cause of Humanity, to plead for the wronged and outraged, to speak for the dumb, and to do
valiant battle for the weak and defenseless."[38]

But the American Constitution, protested Brownson, made slavery a
question of the states in which it existed. Any meddling with it on the part of

other states or the federal government was clearly an invasion of states' rights. However noble and enkindling, therefore, the great object of the abolitionists, irreparable harm would result if in proceeding to the accomplishment of their object the Constitution was trampled and its inviolability destroyed. What protection or safeguard would then be left for the rights not only of those already free, but even of the slave set free? What if, in liberating one class of individuals, the great bulwark of the personal rights of all were battered down? Here is why he separated from the abolitionists. It was not that he loved freedom less than the abolitionists but rather that, as he saw it, he loved it more wisely in demanding a firm maintenance of the Constitution in all its integrity as paramount to all else. He owned again that he felt all the mighty appeal of the noble aspect of abolitionism, "but self-denial, even in the indulgence of what we call noble impulses, or rather the subordination of our impulses to the clearest and soberest convictions of our understanding, is one of the first laws of morality."[39] However paradoxical the stand he was thus forced to take in the case, he could say as a point of honor:

> We speak on this subject strongly, but we have no fear of being misunderstood. There is not a man or woman living that can accuse us of defending slavery. The whole number of our *Review* is devoted to the defense of the rights of man, not the rights of one man, of a few men, but of every man. We can legitimate our own right to freedom, only by the arguments which prove also the Negro's right to be free. We have all our life-long sympathized with the poor and oppressed, and we yield to no abolitionist in the amount of sacrifices we have made, wisely or unwisely, needlessly or not, in the cause of human freedom. It is not to-day, nor this year, that we have pledged ourselves, for life and for death, to the holy cause of human freedom. But everything, we say, in its time. First, we must settle the bases of individual freedom, settle the principle that man measures man the world over, establish our government upon it, and secure the action of the government in accordance with it, and then we may proceed to make all the details harmonize with it.[40]

In his article in *Abolition Proceedings* he owned that the whole abolitionist movement had filled him with "fearful forebodings." To fear, or to tremble at the prospect of evil in the future, was not in his nature, he explained, but the proceedings of the abolitionists were such that he had begun to tremble for the very safety of his country. He found them "fast adopting the ultra-radical doctrine that all government is founded in usurpation, and is an evil which all Christians must labor to abolish." Their "mobocratic" spirit, he asserted, threatened the disruption of our federal system, the destruction of the relations between the states and the Union and between the states themselves. He begged them, in the name of God and man, to pause, and, if they really loved liberty, to ask themselves what liberty would gain in the long run by the destruction of the system of government inherited from their forefathers. In a passage that breathes the ardent zeal of the genuine patriot he laid down once and for all the political creed he was to live by and for which he was to do valiant battle to the end of his life. He wrote:

> For ourselves we have accepted with our whole heart the political system adopted by our fathers. We regard that system as the most brilliant achievement of Humanity, a system in which centres all past progress, and which combines the last result of civilization. It is the latest birth of time. Humanity has been laboring with it since that morning when the sons of God shouted for joy over the birth of a new world, and we will not willingly see it strangled in its

cradle. We take the American system as our starting-point, as our primitive data, and we repulse whatever is repugnant to its preservation. We take our stand on the Idea of our institutions, and labor with our whole soul to realize it. If we demand the elevation of labor and the laboring classes, we do it only in accordance with our institutions and for the purpose of preserving them by removing all discrepancy between their spirit and the social habits and condition of the people on whom they are to act, and to whose keeping they are entrusted. We demand reform only for the purpose of preserving American institutions in their real character; and we can tolerate no change, no innovations, or alleged improvements not introduced in strict accordance with the relations which do subsist between the States and the Union and between the States themselves. Here is our political creed. . . .

The Constitution then is our touchstone for trying all measures. Not indeed that we have any superstitious reverence for written constitutions or any overweening attachment to things that are; but because we have satisfied ourselves by long, patient, and somewhat extensive inquiry, that the preservation of the Constitution is strictly identified with the highest interests of the race. Its destruction were, so far as human foresight can go, an irreparable loss. We would preserve it then, not because we have a dread of revolutions, but because the safety and progress of liberty demand its preservation.[41]

Believing, therefore, that the preservation of the Constitution was paramount to all mundane considerations, he could not ignore the threats of its overthrow by the abolitionists. He freely allowed there should be a full and honest discussion of the whole question of slavery, but incessant, inflammatory denunciations carried on by thousands and thousands of men, women and children banded together in fifteen hundred anti-slavery societies through the non-slave-holding states, clamoring for the immediate emancipation of the slave, seemed to him more like a pistol pointed at the breast of the Southern slave-holder than a proper and restrained discussion of the subject. His preachments to the abolitionists of restraint in this matter only met with an attempt to blacken his reputation. What better way to denigrate his name than to fasten on it the epithet of being "An Open and Avowed Infidel"? When Brownson read a tirade against him under that caption in Lloyd Garrison's *The Liberator,* he wrote in answer to the charge, apparently directly to the editor:

Sir:

Mr. Brownson was never "an open and avowed infidel." He was never a disbeliever in the existence of God, or the truth of Christianity. Some years since he had serious doubts on the principal points of religious faith, a fact he never sought to conceal, but has frequently published. But Mr. B[rownson] does however contend that he has never changed his opinion in regard to its truth or falsity. The only opinion he has ever entertained respecting it is that it is true and from God. To doubt as he did for a time the correctness of that opinion is not to entertain a contrary opinion, but for the time being to entertain no opinion at all.

Brownson then proceeded to explain what in a large degree had brought him to entertain religious doubts:

Mr. B[rownson] has always entertained substantially his present views of social progress. For this twenty years nearly, it has been his leading object to bring about a state of society in which man shall enjoy all his rights, in which every individual shall have free scope to be all that God and nature have designed for him to be, in which all men shall take rank according to their intrinsic moral and intellectual worth. His doubts as to the truths of Christianity were created in a large measure by finding the clergy and the church indifferent or opposed to this object, and they were shaken by finding that Jesus came to build up his kingdom *on earth,* and that he teaches us to sympathize with the poor, the neglected, the oppressed, the enslaved.

As to his stand on the slavery question, he summed it up in a few sentences:

> Mr. B[rownson] was born in a state that never held a slave, and from his cradle he has abhorred slavery in every possible form. He has ever been an anti-slavery man, always sympathized with the disposition that would abolish it, and he came, perhaps, pretty near being a thorough friend of the Abolitionists, though never agreeing with them any further than that the slave should be free. A thorough examination of the Abolitionist Societies in their bearing on State rights, a question to which certain movements of the Abolitionists forced him, brought him to the conclusion stated in the article on slavery in the *Boston Quarterly Review.*[12]

But if Brownson looked to the Constitution for the surest defense of the rights of man, whether the threats came from the abolitionists or elsewhere, he looked to democracy for the fullest recognition of those rights and for a forward-looking program of reform and social progress. In his article on democracy in the January 1838 issue of his *Review* he had refused to identify himself with the Democratic party as such, as no party is always right or always wrong. He reserved his right to differ according to his honest convictions. But democracy taken in the sense that it designates a great forward-looking social and political doctrine, and the powerful movement of the masses toward a better social condition than had hitherto obtained, he accepted with all his heart. Of that movement his *Review* would ever be a "fearless and untiring advocate."[43] He noted with elation that the *London Quarterly* itself was forced to admit that Alexis de Tocqueville was right in saying that all Western Europe has been for several hundred years hastening toward democratic equality.[44] "All classes, each in turn, have possessed the government; and the time has come for all predominance of class to end; for Man, the people to rule," affirmed our stalwart advocate of the interests of the people.[45] If it be alleged, he added, that the people cannot govern themselves, they will have a hard time of it to show, even with a good share of infernal aid to boot, that they will govern themselves worse than kings, nobilities and hierarchies have governed them in the past. The people may indeed be deceived at times, or led astray for the moment, but they can be counted on to come right in the end, and "prove that 'vox populi,' is, after all, the surest rendering of 'vox Dei.' "[46]

In his article, "Democracy of Christianity," he now reviewed the book, *Principles and Results of the Ministry at Large in Boston* (1838), by the Unitarian minister Dr. Joseph Tuckerman, and two books by the widely known Félicité de Lamennais: *Affairs de Rome* (1837) and *Paroles d'un Croyant.*[47] Catching new democratic fire from the last named work of Lamennais in particular, he now proclaimed the noble birth of democracy from Christianity.[48] He acknowledged that the mission of Jesus had been twofold. One of his objects and "perhaps its most important," was "to make atonement for sin, and raise man to God and heaven in the world to come." But that object in this particular article he would skip. The other object of the mission of Jesus was "to found a new order on earth, to establish a kingdom of righteousness and peace for man while in the flesh." This to him stressed

135

the social and political implications of Christianity. And has not democracy the very same great aim, he inquired? Hence he now saw democracy as simply the social and political application of Christianity to the practical affairs of life.

Yet Christianity had been too seldom considered in its social and political bearings. The church, in both its Catholic and Protestant divisions, had been largely unconscious of its broader mission, and, in that respect, false to Christ, its founder. For Jesus was, under a social and political aspect, the prophet of democracy. His mission was to the poor and afflicted, to the wronged and outraged, to the masses, to the downtrodden millions, to whom he spoke as a brother, in tones of infinite love and compassion, while he thundered his withering anathemas at their oppressors. Hence the mission of his church must be the same. Against this backdrop Brownson arraigned the clergy severely for their indifference in the past to the social and political side of Christianity, and asserted, Lamennais-like, that the whole cause of the church is bound up with its espousal of the cause of the masses. Yet he mollified his indictment of both church and clergy somewhat by saying that the real time for the application of the social and political principles of Christianity had perhaps not come until then. Nor was he insisting on such an emphasis on the social and political principles of the Gospel as would thereby draw men's minds off from the world to come. He had no wish that men would strive less to save their souls and secure a heaven hereafter, but he solemnly charged the clergy with the duty of bringing out and preaching the great democratic principles of the Gospel, of espousing the cause of the downtrodden, and of inspiring in others faith in the possibility of an improvement of man's earthly condition. They must do it, he warned, or the church will die.

He gladly acknowledged the noble work the church had done in the past: how it protected the friendless, fed the orphan, raised up the bowed down, cared for the perishing, tamed the ruthless barbarian, infused into his heart the sentiments of Christian virtue, and filled it with aspirations toward the generous and the humane; how it made kings and potentates who trample without remorse on their brethren, and lord it over God's heritage without scruple, feel that there is a Power above them, and that thrones and diadems would avail nothing in the presence of the King of kings, before whom they would one day be summoned to stand judgment as well as the meanest of their slaves. He acknowledged that the church had done a thousand times more good for the human race than he had space or ability to relate, and eternal blessings on its memory! Eternal gratitude to God for that shining band of saints, martyrs, and heroes that the church has nourished in its bosom, whom it has sent out to teach the world, and to introduce into society a divine-human energy that must needs operate toward the redemption and elevation of the toiling millions.

But he regrettably saw the church of his day as too closely leagued with absolutist governments. Its only safety lay in dissociating itself from all such regimes and lending its support to the great movement now looking to a greater and higher equality among all the inhabitants of the earth. He warned:

> If the Altar is supported on the Throne, and the church joined to the Palace, both must fall together. It is a melancholy thing to reflect on the ruin of that majestic temple which has stood so long, over which so many ages have passed, on which so many storms have beaten, and in which so many human hearts have found shelter, solace, and heaven. It is melancholy to reflect on the

condition of the people deprived of all forms of worship, and with no altar on which to offer the heart's incense to God the Father. Yet assuredly churchless, altarless, with no form or shadow of worship will the people be, if the church continue its league with Absolutism.[49]

Brownson had now come to that period of his life (1838) when he would make all things subservient to democracy. Particularly was this true in regard to literature. American literature must become truly democratic in tone and character if it is to be truly a national literature. On this score he welcomed with delight the *United States Magazine and Democratic Review* when reviewing its first edition. "A literature cannot be a national one," he declared, "unless it be the exponent of national life, *informed* with the national soul. . . . It must be based on the great Idea of the nation, and cemented together by the national instincts. . . . The national soul of America is democracy, the equal rights and worth of every man, as man. This is the American Idea."[50] In his observations on George Ripley's "Specimens of Foreign Literature" he deplored the fact that American writers had remained mere literary vassals of England. Hence the tameness and servility of their writings, wanting freshness, freedom and originality. Americans write as Englishmen, not as Americans. They have studied too much to imitate English literature which can only clip the wings of the American national genius, for it is aristocratic in spirit and tone. Without discounting the excellences of English literature in its own setting, he averred that it would be better for American authors to turn to continental literatures, particularly those of France and Germany, for a freer and more democratic spirit. The writings of the French he thought altogether more democratic than those of American authors themselves. The study of French and German literature, he said, "will break the dominion of England, and, without excluding English literature, furnish us new elements, and a broader and more democratic basis for our own."[51]

With all his zeal for the cause of democracy, Brownson would naturally be sensitive to the appearance on the American scene of any semblance of aristocracy as a foreign excrescence in the land. After residing in America, principally Boston, for the space of ten years, Francis F. Grund, an aristocratic visitor, wrote a book entitled *The Americans in their Moral, Social, and Political Relations* in which he disclosed a certain admiration for democratic institutions and expressed some unfavorable sidelights on a would-be American aristocracy.[52] Although Grund did not equal the penetrating insights of a De Tocqueville, Brownson considered his book noteworthy. C. C. Hollis tells us that "the book had aroused considerable discussion and had been denounced by those who represented the Federalistic or Whig spirit in letters."[53] Which statement also reminds one of the comment of R. W. B. Lewis: "Brownson did have a sharp eye for the significant; in retrospect, it must be said that he talked about the important trends and the right books."[54] In an extended notice of Grund's book, indulging in a vein of keen irony, Brownson attempted to exorcise the aristocratic spirit he thought he saw stalking American society and pervading the American literature of the day. Grund's literary reputation and standing in American "Good Society," will be seriously affected, quipped Brownson, because his book has not been written in the interest of the aristocracy, because, in truth, the author has shown some respect for democratic principles.

> Will it be believed [asked Brownson ironically] in the Saloons, in State Street, in Wall Street, and especially in Old Harvard, that a man capable of

writing a book of unquestionable ability, has spoken of General Jackson in terms of respect, and has even gone so far as to approve of his administration? The fact is even so, incredible as it may seem.[55]

Brownson then drove his barbs a little deeper. He knew that Grund's book was an embarrassment to some of Boston's higher society who had entertained Grund over the years. He now proceeded to explain to them by what strange chance a man of Grund's social position could have written such a book:

> This is probably because Mr. Grund was neither born nor educated in America. Had he been born and educated in this country, it is not likely that he would have been guilty of such high handed *lesse-aristocratie*. The presidents and professors of our colleges take proper care that no democracy infect their halls, which are duly fumigated, and ever and anon, ventilated with fresh currents of good English atmosphere.[56]

To add more color to his irony, Brownson further jabbed that he saw a conspiracy among those who staffed the colleges and universities of the day to keep democracy under the ban. To this they were forced by their very position, since were democracy and democratic literature to become fashionable, gone would be their influence, gone would be their high office. For them to allow the development of democratic literature would be to work their own death warrant:

> A foreigner might naturally think that the literature of a democratic country should be democratic; but we can teach him better. This country is too democratic to tolerate a democratic literature. What would become of our aristocracy, if our literature, by any strange chance, should become democratic? Where would it be, if the "Rabbis of our universities," together with the learned Deans who preside over the *North American*, should, by a singular confusion of ideas, embrace democratic notions, and undertake to train up the young men entrusted to their care, to love the free and democratic institutions of their country? Gone were it, and gone forever. Aristocracy dies in this country the day it loses the aid of our literature. The people of this country will do very much as they have a mind to do; and if they take it into their heads to give the aristocracy the go-by, they will do it, and no power on earth can hinder them. Need is there then that the aristocracy keep in their own hands the control of all the influences which go to form the mind of the people. This is their only means of salvation. Of these influences the most important is literature. The men who come forth from colleges are looked upon as the masters of literature, as its creators rather, and hence the necessity of keeping democracy out of colleges.[57]

With the reign of such an aristocratic tone in high places, continued Brownson, it will be the fashion to praise Washington Irving since he has apparently written nothing not acceptable to the *North American* and the *London Quarterly*. But Cooper, after having been a favorite, has fallen under the ban of all the quarterlies — except his own — for having unfortunately infused some American thought and feeling into his work. William Henry Channing was made out to be a Locofoco, with political ambition, since he has shown some little sympathy with common Humanity. Bancroft, guilty of "the sin of democracy," from which he can be absolved neither in this life nor the one to come, must, however, be endured since no one but a thoroughgoing Democrat can write the history of the United States, and a history of the United States must be had. The Whigs, or their Fathers, have tried to write it, but they can no more write a history of democracy than a Mussulman could write a history of Christianity. Alexander Everett, once acknowledged the accomplished scholar and an able and elegant writer, is now no longer allowed to be the one or the other. Why? Because he has had the extremely bad taste of changing from a Whig to a Democrat. "The truth of the matter is," concluded Brownson, "the democratic writers are the great writers of the age and nation. This is indeed one of their principal sins."[58] Harriet Martineau seems to have been pretty well in agreement with him as she observed that the Democratic party in the United States included the underprivileged, the careerists, the humanitarians and "an accession small in number, but inestimable in power — the men of genius."[59]

Yet Brownson admitted to his readers that he had perhaps made too much of a fuss about the significance of aristocracy in America, a point that had, after all, been raised by Mr. Grund. As for himself, he was entirely confident that whatever the forces pitted against the reign of democracy in this country, they were doomed to wane and die. Wealth, fashion, learning and refinement may conspire as they will, but all in vain. Democracy is at long last to have a home of its own here where it can display its true worth. He summoned every friend of human freedom to rally to its cause, and to make all things subservient to its further advancement. "The policy we recommend," he urged, "would be for every friend of this country, to do his best to enlist literature, philosophy, religion, and refinement on the side of democracy. This has been our policy, and we trust ever will be."[60]

While Brownson had been thus waging his vigorous campaign in the *Boston Reformer* and his *Boston Quarterly Review* in defense of the rights of the individual, whether social, religious, political or economic, a new school of thought had been gradually forming in Boston that came to be known as Transcendentalism. Transcendentalism is a term not easily defined. Perhaps Brownson's own words on Transcendentalism and Transcendentalists afford us as clear notions as any others: "Transcendentalism, in its good sense, . . . means the recognition of an order of existences, which transcend time and space, and are in no sense dependent on them, or affected by them. . . . Transcendentalists recognize a world lying beyond or above the world of the senses, and in man the power of seeing or knowing this transcendental world immediately, by direct cognition, or intuition."[61] What apparently appealed to Brownson initially in Transcendentalism was the emphasis laid on the interior sentiments as opposed to logical deduction in the ascertainment of the truths of religion and morality. To the development of this phase of Transcendentalism Brownson himself had contributed his share. Writing on Benjamin Constant in the September 1834 edition of the *Christian Examiner,* he had said: "Religion and morality rest not on the understanding, not on logical deductions, but on the interior sentiments." To him it seemed at this time that the sentiments were just as trustworthy as guides, if not more so, than the understanding or logical faculty. "To us," he continued, "the sentiments seem to be peculiarly the human faculties. They give to man his distinctive character."[62]

Whether or not he was ever committed to all that went under the name of Transcendentalism is debatable. Although the time was to come when he would speak of it as merely "much ado about nothing," or "a tempest in a teapot,"[63] it was most certainly to be a part of one of the most exciting intellectual periods of his life and was to mark broad stages in the development of his religious and philosophical principles. The historical significance of Transcendentalism is at once seen in the fact that it was the medium with which many of the finest minds in nineteenth-century New England were to handle the fundamental religious and philosophical problems raised by the age. That Brownson expected the role he played in this movement would be well-remembered, cannot be doubted. When writing his criticism of Transcendentalism in 1845, he remarked: "For it cannot be denied that, in the history of American Transcendentalism, the Editor of the *Boston Quarterly Review* should not be forgotten, pronounced as he was by *Blackwood's Magazine* the Coryphaesus of the sect, and by Victor Cousin as one who promised to be 'a philosopher of the first order.' "[64]

# 11

## BROWNSON'S TRANSCENDENTALIST YEARS

*The origin and meetings of the Transcendental Club • Brownson represents the French influence on the Club • His contributions to the* Christian Examiner *• His strictures on Emerson's Divinity School address • The controversy over Andrews Norton's* Evidences *• Brownson makes an elaborate reply to the two articles Andrews Norton had republished from the* Princeton Review *against the Transcendentalists, and makes clear in what sense he is not a Transcendentalist • The various areas in which Brownson differs from the Transcendentalists.*

Clarence L. F. Gohdes remarks in his *Periodicals of American Transcendentalism* that although many of the younger followers of Dr. Channing, such as George Ripley, Frederic Hedge, William H. Furness and Brownson, had already expressed their Transcendental views in print before 1838, it was not until that year that Transcendentalism had really begun to attract public attention — the same year in which Brownson had established his *Quarterly*.[1] Besides the writing these Transcendentalists had been doing, they had also, from being a number of scattered individuals, gathered themselves together into a distinct group or club. The origin of the club or new school indicated that the prime movers in its formation had grown disgusted with what Emerson called "the corpse-cold Unitarianism of Brattle Street and Harvard."[2] They were in deadly earnest in their search for a more soul-satisfying spirituality than could be found in the churches of the day. They craved something that would really fill their souls.[3] In his biography of Margaret Fuller Ossoli, Thomas Wentworth Higginson tells us how this spiritual hunger led to the first meeting of what came to be called the Transcendental Club.

It so happened that Harvard College held its bicentennial celebration in the autumn of 1836, at which many of the Unitarian alumni were in attendance. After the exercises were over, four Unitarian ministers — Ralph Waldo Emerson, Frederic Hedge, George Ripley and George Putnam — got into a lively discussion about the narrow tendencies of thought in the churches of the day. They became so engrossed in the topic that they adjourned their conversation to a room in Willard's Hotel where they could leisurely talk the matter out at length. This meeting ended in the agreement that they would meet again for a renewal of their discussion at George Ripley's in Boston on September 19, 1836. Present at this meeting were Amos B. Alcott, Robert Bartlett, Cyrus Bartol, Orestes A. Brownson, James F. Clarke, Ralph W. Emerson, Convers Francis, Frederic Hedge, Theodore Parker, George Ripley and Charles Stearns Wheeler, joined on the distaff side by Margaret Fuller and Elizabeth P. Peabody. Such was the genesis of the club quite generally called the Transcendental Club. Alcott, however, dubbed it "The Symposium Club," and occasionally it was called "The Hedge Club" by its members because its meetings were arranged to suit the occasional visits of Rev. Frederic H. Hedge of Bangor, Maine, where he had gone to be pastor.[4]

Brownson attended four meetings in all of this Club, including the meeting at his own house in Chelsea, on October 18, 1836, when the theme for discussion was the "Education of Humanity." Listing the meeting on September 8, 1836 in Willard's Hotel as the first meeting, Joel Myerson informs us there were thirty meetings in all of the Club over a four-year period, the last meeting being held on or about September 20, 1840, at which the theme for discussion was the "Organization of the New Church." (Perhaps this subject indicates Brownson's continuing influence on the group although he had attended no meeting since May 29, 1837.) In 1853 Theodore Parker earnestly urged Emerson to attempt a revival of the Club, and again in 1856 he urged James F. Clarke to the same end, but nothing came of these urgings.[5]

The Club being a group of some of the finest minds in New England, just what topics engaged their free and active intellects is a matter of some interest. Octavius B. Frothingham gives us a clue to the general nature of their discussions when he says:

> The topics debated turned on a few central ideas: Law, Truth, Individuality, the Personality of God. The last came up in connection with matters pertaining to theology, Revelation, Inspiration, Providence. An extreme reaction from Puritan conceptions set in, leading some to the verge of pantheism, and to a belief in the sufficiency of the human mind to itself in all emergencies.[6] The conversation was at all times earnest and elevated, though there was warm discussion over some of the views submitted.[7]

In the same year in which the Transcendental Club met at Ripley's (1836), Emerson brought out his book, *Nature*, on September 9, a rhapsodic utterance of his Transcendental beliefs in which he views world phenomena as sort of symbolic of man's inner life and stresses individual freedom and self-reliance.[8] Perry Miller tells us that it was not a smash hit, first off, but that it gradually grew into high favor after the other Transcendentalists had had sufficient time to realize that Emerson had really anticipated every point at issue among them. In the same month also Brownson published an article in the *Christian Examiner* on Victor Cousin "of a more immediate impact." As Perry Miller expresses it: "The motifs of Brownson's essay turn out to be so close to those of *Nature* that many passages of the latter, particularly some of its obscure pages, are wonderfully illuminated by comparison with this contemporary effort."[9] Of *New Views of Christianity, Society, and the Church* which Brownson published this year, as we have already noted, George Ripley said in the *Dial* four years later: "It has already formed a conspicuous era in the mental history of more than one who is seeking the truth of things, in the midst of painted, conventional forms."[10] This sudden flowering of Transcendental thought now appearing impelled Convers Francis, the oldest member of the Club, to note in his journal:

> I find that George Ripley is publishing *Discourses on the Philosophy of Religion*; besides, Brownson is out with *New Views,* and Alcott with *Questions on the Gospels,* for children. Then there is Furness's book, *Remarks on the Gospels,* so that it seems the Unitarians must break into two schools — the one, or English School, belonging to the sensual or empiric philosophy, and the new one, or German School (perhaps it may be called) belonging to the spiritual philosophy.[11]

Writing in 1955 about Brownson's remarkable articles in the *Christian Examiner,* C. C. Hollis expressed the opinion that Brownson's contribution to the Transcendental movement had not yet been properly evaluated, although René Wellek in his "The Minor Transcendentalists and German Philosophy"[12] had shown new insight in naming Brownson the medium of the French and not the German influence on the movement. That this fact has not been duly recognized in the past is partly explained, Hollis thinks, on the score that the simplifications required in intellectual and cultural histories have indisposed their authors to bother about specifying the strong French influence on New England Transcendentalism. That influence was not equal to the German, but it was strongly present, and brought with it a different intellectual culture and flavor.

Another reason why the French influence on the movement has been overlooked, Hollis further notes, is that O. B. Frothingham, whose *Transcendentalism in New England* was for generations the only history of the movement, was himself emphatically of the German school. Past neglect to note that Brownson was the main medium of the French influence on the movement may be again partly explained by the fact that he had become a Catholic before the Transcendental movement had passed its zenith. Whatever the reasons in the case, the French influence was pervasively present, says Hollis, "as any examination of the table of contents of the religious journals of the day would testify. Brownson's contribution is an important one, for something of the elation of discovery attendant on his reading of those books in their native language is communicated in the series of six articles in the *Christian Examiner* through which he introduced to New England the French eclectics, Benjamin Constant, Victor Cousin, Theodore Jouffroy, and others."[13] This interpretation of Hollis is indirectly corroborated by Brownson's own statement in January 1844 that "the German philosophers have afforded me very little satisfaction . . . so far as I know them, I claim no affinity with them" — though he did own "the eminent analytic ability of Kant."[14]

Whatever knowledge of contemporary German philosophy Brownson gained during the 1830s seems to have come to him through his acquaintance with the French philosophers. On November 15, 1836, he wrote his friend Victor Cousin: "In behalf of myself and my friends I wish to thank you for the light you have thrown on German philosophy. You give us the key which unlocks its secret stores. We can now read and understand. We like Germany all the better for being filtered through the brain of France."[15]

So deeply had Brownson become immersed in the French philosophers that he consulted James Walker, editor of the *Christian Examiner* and later president of Harvard, on the advisability of publishing a choice selection from the philosophical writings of Constant, Cousin, Jouffroy and others in an English translation. When Walker, unacquainted with the French philosophers except Constant, expressed some misgivings about whether such a book could be made sufficiently popular to justify the expense of publication, Brownson dropped any further thought of the project.[16] But his interest in the French philosophers continued unabated, and he had his share also in introducing Pierre Leroux and Félicité de Lamennais to New England readers.

But whatever the particular angle from which Brownson made his contribution to American Transcendentalism, his general importance to the movement was variously recognized by contemporaries. Emerson in 1836 was discussing "a question out of Brownson's book." Alcott visited him, and noted in his journal: "Emerson and Hedge promise more than others among us; with Furness, Brownson, and Ripley they furnish the best talent in the liberal church."[17] The *Western Messenger,* a Unitarian journal founded in

143

Cincinnati in 1835, gave Brownson more attention than even Emerson or Dr. Channing, reprinting several of his articles and letters, and defending him at any cost.[18] Besides the superlative tribute Brownson received from *Blackwood's Magazine,* already quoted, a writer in the *New York Review* announced in 1841 that Brownson, Parker and Emerson were to be held as "the new world apostles" of the "New Christianity."[19]

One of the most arresting statements of C. C. Hollis in his study of Brownson is that neither Brownson himself, nor his son Henry, nor either of his recent biographers (Schlesinger and Maynard) seem to have realized that Brownson came as near "taking over" the New England or Boston group in 1836 as he ever would. The statement is entirely true in as far as the chances for doing so were more favorable then than at any time later. But that admitted, the chances were not truly propitious even then. True, Brownson had certain factors in his favor at the time. As Hollis explains at length, he had the backing of the two most prominent men in the budding renaissance, Dr. Channing and Ripley: Channing the diplomatic leader of the earlier period, and Ripley the only representative of the movement at the moment. Theodore Parker, who was to become quite important in the Transcendental movement later, was just being graduated from Harvard in 1836. Emerson, though prominent, was only slowly moving toward the forefront of the movement in the last months of that year. William Henry Channing, nephew of Dr. Channing, had gone to New York. Leadership in the field was open to anyone of outstanding talent and energy. And Brownson was a man of tremendous energy. He was in fact a real leader in the sense that he was addressing himself to all the vital interests of the Boston community in which he had come to reside. "He was intellectually astute, and learned, albeit self-learned; he had caught the democratic upsurge of the era and strained zealously to idealize and Christianize it."

But there were other factors, carefully detailed by Mr. Hollis, which most certinly tended to neutralize any chances that might otherwise have led to Brownson's leadership of the Boston circle. He was a newcomer in the area and had a rather checkered background. All, however, recognized his immense energies and luminous gifts as a writer and lecturer, but the very suddenness with which it had all come about had left some wonderment and instinctive caution in sensitive minds. His intellectual and religious instability in the past also gave them pause. Then, too, upon the advice of Dr. Channing and Ripley, he had addressed himself first to the laboring classes when he founded the Society for Christian Union and Progress. In espousing their cause in particular at the outset, he was naturally driven to play up his own radical background. This aspect of his past tended to draw to him a variety of persons whom some of the upper classes in Boston probably looked upon with disfavor — the leaders of the Workingmen's party, Jacksonian Democrats, Free Enquirers and the like. However praiseworthy his efforts to effect the spiritual and social redemption of these classes, it all did little to ingratiate him with the genteel Bostonians who were forming a new school of thought indigenous to Boston. He was after all something of an outsider to that highly select group. They would all of course benefit from the shock of their minds with his powerful intellect, but it was not in the nature of the case that he should become their acknowledged leader.[20]

Much less did Brownson himself aspire to any such leadership. He was entirely too independent to be obliged to speak always according to the modes of thought, often vague and misty, of the other Transcendentalists. Even as a Transcendentalist he would remain ever a free lance as a thinker.

Knowing that he was not in possession of certified truth, he freely acknowledged it. He would therefore hold himself entirely free to embrace truth when and wherever found, and wished only to stimulate others in their search for it. Speaking in the *Convert* of this precise period in his life, he wrote:

> The public read me more or less, but hardly knew what to make of me. They regarded me as a bold and vigorous writer, but as eccentric, extravagant, paradoxical, and always changing, and not to be counted on; not perceiving that I did not wish to be counted on, in their sense, as a leader whom they could safely follow, and who would save them the labor of thinking for themselves. My aim was to induce, to force others to think for themselves, not to persuade them to permit me to do their thinking. This was proper and just for one who knew he had no authority to teach.[21]

As it was, the leadership of the Boston circle, or the Transcendentalists, was to pass to "that curious half-Yankee," Ralph Waldo Emerson, soon after his publication of *Nature* on September 9, 1838. He was to reign as the acknowledged high priest of American Transcendentalism through its expansion, peak and decline. (Margaret Fuller was the recognized high priestess of the movement.)[22] It was Emerson, too, who first brought the Transcendentalists to public notice, though not at all favorably, with his Divinity School address to the senior class of Harvard in July of 1838. His wide departure in that address from traditional Christian beliefs was the occasion of considerable excitement which brought down "severe censures" on him. After calling the address "the most inspiring strain I ever listened to," Theodore Parker spoke of the great outcry it caused, the one shouting, "The Philistines be upon us!"; another, "We be dead men!"; while the majority called out, "Atheism!" The dean said, "That part of it — as I apprehend — which was not folly was downright atheism."[23] In fact, so revolutionary was Emerson's thought in that address that it led to a prolonged and rather bitter controversy.

Remaining for a time a mere observer of the reaction to the address, Brownson finally published his own formal notice of it in the October issue of his *Review* for that same year. He began with handsome acknowledgments of the vigor and freshness, the freedom and independence, the richness and beauty of the address. But he could not help regarding "its tone as somewhat arrogant, its spirit quite too censorious and desponding, its philosophy as indigested, its reasoning as inconclusive."[24] He recalled that in his address on *The American Scholar* before the Phi Beta Kappa Society, Cambridge, in August 1837, Emerson had much to say about the instincts, and had bidden us "plant ourselves on our instincts, and the huge world will come round to us." In the present address Emerson's ethical rule, "obey thyself," when translated into practice, will only mean, said Brownson, follow thy instincts, follow thy inclinations, live as thou listest. The spiritual man may well indeed follow his higher nature, obey his higher instincts. But what of the sensualist, Brownson wanted to know? What instincts will he follow? And who shall determine which are the higher instincts and which are the lower? He thought Emerson's ethical rule full of moral peril. "Strike out the idea of something above man to which he is accountable, make him accountable only to himself, and why shall he not live as he listest?" The only truly moral man is he, affirmed Brownson, who recognizes his obligation to obey the command of a power out of him, above him, and independent of him. "There may then be," he politely suggested, "some doubts whether the command 'obey thyself' be an improvement on the Christian command, 'deny thyself.' "

Brownson really went into considerable detail in his review of the Divinity School address, finding among other flaws, as it seemed to him, the thought of Emerson resolving itself into a worship of the soul, "another name for self-worship, or worship of self," which is nothing but "a system of Transcendental selfishness. It is pure egotism." He was alarmed to find Emerson, after his masters Carlyle and Goethe, making the soul everything, or rather the center of the universe, for which all exists that does exist. Self is made the end and measure of all things, to which all is subordinate. Always is the *doing,* whatever it is, to terminate in self. But does not true morality propose to us an end separate from our own, above our own, and to which our own good is subordinate? Look at the matter as he would, turn it over as he could, our sharp critic could only conclude that for the present at least, instead of adopting the formula, "obey thyself," or Carlyle's formula, "act out thyself," we must continue to approve the Christian formula, "deny thyself," and "love thy neighbor as thyself."[25]

But what alarmed Brownson most of all was what Emerson had to say against preaching a traditional Christ, against preaching what he called historical Christianity. Inasmuch as Emerson's object in this was to draw men's minds off from an exclusive attention to the "letter" and to fix their minds on the "spirit," and thus the better to induce them to reproduce the Gospel histories in their lives, Brownson found him not only not censurable, but praiseworthy. But if Emerson really wished to dispense with historical Christianity and its historical documents as no longer relevant to the present, he plainly could not go with him. Most emphatically did he protest against dispensing with the historical Christ. "As in philosophy, we demand history as well as psychology, so in theology we ask the historical Christ as well as the psychological Christ."[26] The world needs him, he said, and his character precisely as presented to us by the Gospels:

> His is the only name by which man can be saved. He is the father of the modern world, and his life is the life we now live, so far as we live any life at all. Shall we then crowd him away with the old bards and seers, and regard him and them merely as we do the authors of some old ballads which charmed our forefathers, but which may not be sung in modern drawing-rooms? Has his example lost its power, his life its quickening influence, his doctrine its truth? Have we outgrown him as a teacher?

This review of Emerson's Divinity School address probably revealed to Brownson himself that his own Christian roots were much deeper at the time than even he himself suspected. As liberal as his social philosophy might seem at times, he recoiled with something like mild horror and instinctively fell back on traditional Christianity when confronted with a novel system of thought which he judged calculated to undermine Christian faith altogether. This is all the more striking inasmuch as he professed at the time a great liking for bold speculation, and counted a certain freedom of expression as necessary for progress. But for all that, he still liked to see "a certain sobriety, a certain reserve in all speculation, something like timidity about rushing off into an unknown universe, and some little regret in departing from the faith of our fathers."[27] This reserve and caution he had found wanting in Emerson. Brownson detected at this early date the thoroughgoing anti-Christian tendency of Emerson's thought. After making certain acknowledgments and admitting that it is easy to be unfair to Emerson, Randall Stewart said in his book, *American Literature and Christian Doctrine:*

> These qualifications and extenuations are true enough, and yet the fact remains that Emerson is the arch-heretic of American literature, and Emersonism the greatest heresy. By no dint of sophistry can he be brought within the Christian fold. His doctrine is radically anti-Christian, and has done more than any other doctrine to undermine the Christian faith in America.[28]

As free and frank as Brownson's strictures might be on Emerson's thought — in this instance and later — for the man himself he showed a marked respect, not to say a certain uniform tenderness. He exemplified in this case admirably the rule he enunciated later for judging an author: "In judging him [the author], we must judge him according to his intentions; but in judging his book, we must judge it according to the obvious and natural sense of his language."[29] The tribute he now paid Emerson's character left little to be desired in the way of an encomium. Perhaps the harsh things other critics had already said against Emerson disposed him to speak as gently as he might. Concluding his observations on the Divinity School address he cautioned his readers against interpreting his criticism as implying any reflections on the character of Mr. Emerson himself. Explaining, he wrote:

> Let not the tenor of our remarks be mistaken. Mr. Emerson is the last man in the world we would suspect of conscious hostility to religion and morality. No man can know him or read his productions without feeling a profound respect for the singular purity and uprightness of his character and motives. The great object he is laboring to accomplish is one in which he should receive the hearty cooperation of every American scholar, of every friend of truth, freedom, piety, and virtue. Whatever be the character of his speculations, whatever be the moral, philosophical, or theological system which forms the basis of his speculations, his real object is not the inculcation of any new theory on man, nature, or God; but to induce men to think for themselves on all subjects, and to speak from their own full hearts and earnest convictions. His object is to make men scorn to be slaves to routine, to custom, to established creeds, to public opinion, to the great names of the age, of this country, or any other. He cannot bear the idea that man comes into this world to-day with the field monopolized and foreclosed. To every man lies open the field of truth, in morals, in politics, in theology, in philosophy. The labors of past ages, the revelations of prophets and bards, the discoveries of the scientific and philosophic, are not to be regarded as superseding our own exertions and inquiries, as impediments to the free action of our minds, but merely as helps, as provocations to the freest and fullest spiritual action of which God has made us capable.[30]

Mr. Hollis remarks that this encomium "forms one of the first great tributes to Emerson in American criticism." It stands out "as the first public expression of what we now recognize as Emerson's distinctive merit." Hollis goes on to specify that in the review of Emerson's "Address" Brownson was more concerned with the philosophical and theological implications in Emerson's thought than with the purely literary merit of his writing. This was in no sense peculiar in this case. Brownson generally gave more attention when reviewing a work to the validity or soundness of the ideas it contained than to the literary form. But as Hollis observes, it does not necessarily follow that he thereby removed himself from the field of literary criticism.[31]

Curiously enough, whatever the truth of his strictures on the tendency of

Emerson's thought, Brownson was to regret the freedom of his criticism when he saw "the world" had turned against his friend Emerson. "Heavens! only think," he exclaimed in the July issue of his *Review* of the next year when reviewing Bulwer's novels, "only think of the *Boston Quarterly Review* joining with grave doctors and learned professors to write down a man who has the boldness to speak from his own convictions, from his own soul! It was a great mistake on our part, and one which, alas! we perceived not till it was too late. Honor to every man who speaks from his own mind, whatever his word. He is an Iconoclast, a servant of the true God, even though it be a left-handed one."[32] Emerson was to pay in more ways than one for what the orthodox would call his temerity. F. O. Matthieson tells us that "after the scandal of the Divinity School address, Emerson was not invited to lecture in Harvard again for thirty years. Following the Civil War, when Transcendentalism could no longer be thought dangerous, he was chosen one of the Harvard Board of Overseers."[33]

The sizzling controversy that had been set off by the Divinity School address between the Transcendentalists and the Unitarians was to be followed by an even more fierce hassle between the same two camps over the polemical value of miracles. The Unitarians, led by Andrews Norton, "the hard-headed Unitarian Pope," rested the whole case for Christianity on the value of miracles as vouchers for its truth. After being tutor at Harvard from 1811, Andrews Norton had become Dexter Professor of Sacred Scripture there in 1818, and continued to rule the Divinity School until his resignation in 1830. He then devoted all his time and energy to what he considered a most important work of biblical scholarship: *The Evidences of the Genuineness of the Four Gospels*. This elaborate work he published in 1838. Its appearance at once whipped the gale that had been blowing between the Unitarians and the Transcendentalists into a raging tempest. Norton's book was in substance a defense of "historical Christianity," the very thing Emerson had spurned in his Divinity School address. In its very nature it was an attack on the Transcendentalists in general who would rest the case for Christianity on an inner light or sense by which the truths of Christianity are directly or intuitively recognized as divine. Emerson had no stomach for controversy, and perhaps just as little talent, but few men relished a good resounding battle more than Orestes A. Brownson. (Perry Miller calls him the "bulldog" of the new school.)[34] He was not long in taking notice of Norton's imposing work. He probably felt all the more urgency in the case as his very good friend George Ripley was bearing the brunt of the battle from Norton in the newspapers.

Brownson began his review of Norton's *Evidences* with a tactic that bespoke the master strategist. It must have been very disconcerting to the "Harvard Goliath" to be reminded at the outset that those who live in glass houses should not throw stones. "When we heard that this work was announced as actually published," remarked Brownson, "we trusted that it would wipe out the suspicion of infidelity, which had long been attached to the author in the minds of some of his religious friends, as well as religious enemies; but we are sorry to say, that, to a certain extent at least, we have been disappointed."[35] The full force of this thrust will be understood when it is recalled that Norton himself had been suspected of heretical views in his earlier career, but just the same, had not hesitated in the present instance to attack the Transcendentalists as a pack of downright infidels. This, said Brownson, is very much like the pot calling the kettle black.

Brownson now proceeded to charge on Norton that his method of authenticating Christianity by miracles was something novel in Protestant theology. The reformers, he said, had discarded it, more particularly Luther. He then buttressed the point with lengthy quotations from Jonathan Edwards, "the Father of New England theology," whom he had been lately reading for the first time "since our boyhood, when we read but did not understand him, [and] we have been astonished at the wealth of his intellect, the depth of his philosophy, and delighted with the rational and spiritual character of his theology. . . . His mind stood in the front rank of the master minds of the day."[36] The New England churches, following in this tradition, had rejected the historical method, and had uniformly borne testimony to what they called Experimental Religion, said Brownson; he pointed out that:

> Experimental Religion means an inward perception and love of the truths of religion, and obedience to their commands. All who embrace it contend for another source of evidence than that of ancient, recorded miracles. They contend, they have, from their own experience, a firm persuasion, and well-grounded assurance of the truths of Christianity. The doctrine of Experimental Religion is the prevailing doctrine of the American churches.[37]

This had the added strategy of taunting Norton with the implication that the great work upon which he had spent so many long years was after all scarcely relevant to the times. But the cleverness of Brownson's apologetics is further seen in the way in which he attempted to use the philosopher Locke against the Lockeans, Norton himself being perhaps the most prominent Lockean in America. Asserting that Norton's *Evidences* were based on Locke's philosophy, pure sensism — that there can be nothing in the mind that had not been previously in the senses — Brownson went on to show in considerable detail (at least to his own satisfaction), that it is impossible by such a system of philosophy to rise to the supernal truths of Christianity. "Every disciple must, therefore, conclude with Abner Kneeland and Frances Wright, that as the objects of religion transcend the horizon of human observation, we can decide nothing concerning them; and that the words God, the Soul, and the like, are mere words, to which the mind can affix no positive meaning."[38]

Brownson went still further in his attack on Norton. During the Jacksonian era of the 1830s, he was subjecting all things to the democratic yardstick. If they could not abide it, they were summarily cast into the limbo of the worthless. And on this score, Norton's theology again came short. What chances had the masses to make a long and patient study of the evidences of Christianity such as Norton's system seemed to demand? If such were the requirements of his theology, to Brownson it meant a favoring of the few and a disinheritance of the masses. Such a theology evidently could not be sound.[39] (Brownson was here of course sidestepping the question whether or not Christ had established a church with adequate authority to vouch for the truths of his message to mankind.)

Again, Brownson found Norton's theology in conflict with the real spirit and workings of democracy. Genuine democracy postulates the belief that "there is a spirit in man, and the inspiration of the Almighty giveth him understanding." But if the masses cannot come to a knowledge of the truth by their own power, but must obtain it from teachers possessing inherent and miraculous powers, powers denied to themselves, then is democracy an illusion, a Utopian dream, nay, a mad attempt against nature. The real democrat is one who believes that reason, "the light which shines out from God's throne, shines into the heart of every man, and that truth lights her torch in the inner temple of every man's soul, whether patrician or plebeian, shepherd or philosopher, a Croesus or a beggar. It is only on the reality of this light, and on the fact, that it is universal in man, and in every man, that you can found democracy, which shall have a firm basis, and which shall be able to survive the storms of human passions."[40]

The quarrel between the Unitarians and the Transcendentalists was now approaching something like white heat. Andrews Norton had been so badgered by his Transcendentalist adversaries, particularly Ripley and Theodore Parker, that in desperation he was driven to seek ammunition against them in the camp of his old-time foes, the Presbyterians. He went so far as to have two articles republished which had appeared in the *Princeton Review,* the staunch foe of all the Unitarians stood for, in which Calvinist theologians had excoriated Emerson and the Transcendentalists generally. But he did so at a high price indeed. For the same articles contained the mortifying statement, underscored, as Perry Miller points out, that the Unitarians had no one to blame but themselves for the unfortunate hassle in which they found themselves, since "by becoming Unitarians in the first place [forsaking Calvinism] they had opened Pandora's box."[41] Surely Andrews Norton had almost forgotten his dignity when he had resorted to such a tactic. But such was his desperation that he was willing to pay the price for the ammunition against the Transcendentalists which the two articles contained.

Norton's publication of the two Princeton articles drew from Brownson a rejoinder in the July 1840 issue of his *Quarterly,* running to a ponderous ninety pages. As Perry Miller again notes, Brownson commanded the kind of scholarship in systematic theology that made him a match for the Princeton pundits. Miller also calls Brownson's reply to Norton "the best of the apologies for Transcendentalism that arose in answer to Norton's accusation of infidelity."[42] Brownson proceeded at once to pay his respects to Mr. Norton himself. Again, the clever way in which he dismissed Norton, if a bit flippant, is capital. After an expression of his own liberal views on the whole controversy, he acknowledged that he had read Mr. Norton's publications relative to the debate "with the attention due to the high source from which they emanated." They bear "the marks of a cultivated mind," but do not show a real comprehension of the movement he opposes, as would be necessary, "if he would oppose it effectually." "It is said," he added, "that he usually sits in his room with the shutters drawn, which has the double effect of keeping the light out and the darkness in. This may be a calumny, but his productions, it must be confessed, afford no satisfactory refutation of it."[43]

The rest of the article is devoted to a long discussion of Transcendentalism itself. It was Brownson's proud contention that Transcendentalism in New England was of American origin, and was not a foreign importation, as claimed the Princeton theologians. In a passage that tells us something of the heterogeneous mentality of the Transcendentalists, and their real aim in their novel searchings, he said in reply to Norton's charge of "infidelity":

> They differ widely in their opinions, and agree in little except their common opposition to the old school. . . . Some of them embrace transcendental philosophy, some of them reject it, some *ignore* all philosophy, plant themselves upon their own instincts, and wait for the huge world to come round to them. Some of them read Cousin, some Goethe and Carlyle, and others none at all. Some of them reason, others dream. . . . The movement is really of American origin, and the prominent actors in it were carried away by it before they

ever formed an acquaintance with French or German metaphysicians; their attachment to the literature of France and Germany is the effect of their connection with the movement, not its cause. . . . The real aim of the Transcendentalist is to ascertain a solid ground for faith in the reality of the spiritual world."

In concluding his essay, which Perry Miller calls "magnificent,"[45] Brownson made clear, however, that he was not to be classified as anything like a totally committed Transcendentalist. He was a Transcendentalist, he owned, as far as the term meant man's "capacity of knowing truth intuitively." But when it is understood to place "feeling above reason, dreaming above reflection, and instinctive intimation above scientific exposition; in a word when it means the substitution of lawless fancy for an enlightened understanding, as we apprehend it is understood in this neighborhood, by the majority who use it as a term of reproach, we disown it, and deny we are Transcendentalists."[46] In the introductory remarks to the January 1840 issue of his *Review,* speaking of the Transcendentalists, he had also said: "There are some who pay little attention to the senses, hold reasoning and logic in slight esteem, and treat the demand for proofs of their statements with contempt. With these individuals I do not entirely agree. If I started with them, I could not stop short of exclusive mysticism, and should end by denying the existence of man and the universe."[47]

Perhaps these latter statements were somewhat disappointing to the simon-pure Transcendentalists. If so, they had perhaps disappointed him a bit, too. It had long been the ambition of some Transcendentalists to have a periodical of their own in which they could give unhampered expression to the new school of thought. Already on November 15, 1836, Brownson had written his friend, Victor Cousin, in Paris: "Some of my friends contemplate establishing a review for the purpose of laying before our countrymen the results attained by European scholars in philology, history, theology and philosophy."[48] In the meantime Brownson had established his *Quarterly* in 1838. It may have been a journal of great merit, but the Transcendentalists dreamt of something superior even to that, as Amos Bronson Alcott disclosed in his diary on March 27, 1840: "Brought home with me Brownson's *Quarterly Review* for April. This is the best journal now current on this side of the Atlantic, but it falls far below the idea of the best minds among us." When the project of the new Transcendental journal was being considered, Brownson suggested to Alcott that it might well be combined with his own. Alcott relayed the suggestion to Margaret Fuller, and she in turn relayed it to Emerson. But they rejected it.[49]

There was of course more than one reason for the rejection. For one thing, Brownson was entering more and more into the arena of active politics, and was becoming known as one of the "reform men." As Author I. Ladu observed, Brownson had come to emphasize two ideas which other Transcendentalists did not touch upon, or did not much emphasize. The first concerned the necessity of positive action on the part of the state to secure the best opportunity for individual development; the second concerned the value of a suitable political organization to secure the development.[50] This was out of character with the other leading Transcendentalists. Then, too, they may well have recoiled from the idea of being under Brownson's thumb in any sense. They could never have had things their own way. C. C. Hollis has noted that Brownson's suggestion that the Transcendentalists combine their project with his *Quarterly* may well have been due to his waning health, and that they had reason to fear that his revived health would reawaken "a truculence that would be disastrous to their lilac color plans."[51] Whatever the case, the results was the founding of the *Dial* on the part of the Transcendentalists, the first edition of which appeared in July 1840. In the October 1839 issue of his own *Review*, Brownson had announced its discontinuance. Failing health due to "excessive labors," compelled him "to lie by for a while, and recruit."[52] But in spite of a touching valedictory to friends old and new, his *Review* reappeared bright and early again in January 1840, with gracious apologies to the good-natured public for its appearance after he had announced its discontinuance.

Its reappearance was a great satisfaction to one editor in particular who wrote:

> What had always especially pleased us in that periodical, is its freedom; its independence and vigor of thought. Whether the opinions there expressed be true or false, they have at least been stated boldly and forcibly, and defended by fair and manly argument. The editor is evidently a man who thinks for himself:
> "Nullius addictus jurare in verba magistri."
> He takes nothing on trust; he adopts no opinion on mere authority, but subjects it to a rigid and searching examination, before he will admit it to form a part of his creed, however hallowed it may be by time or the sanction of great names. His writings all bear the impress of thought, and cannot fail to make the reader think also. In this respect, they afford a strong and most refreshing contrast to the solemn cant, the decorous dullness, the tame, lifeless, vapid, commonplace, with which our leading journals are too generally filled.[53]

With Brownson's increasing criticism of Transcendental vagaries, it was becoming ever more clear that although he was an associate of those gifted individuals, and derived much stimulation from his association with them, it would not be accurate to classify him as a full-fledged Transcendentalist. Per Sveino has pointed out in what sense Brownson diverged also in the religious realm from the Transcendentalists when he wrote:

> First, he did not share their dislike of churches and institutions. He maintained that men "must and will embody their ideas of the true, the beautiful, the good — the holy in some institution."[54] Yet this idea, which he later was to develop further and which led him in the direction of the Catholic Church, in 1836 was still in its embryonic state. Second, Brownson's skeptical attitude toward Protestantism as such was not typical of most Transcendentalists. Theirs was in opposition to Calvinist orthodoxy, not to the Protestant emphasis on individual reason and conscience. Nor did they generally share Brownson's positive appraisal of medieval Catholicism; in his own words: the Middle Ages "are deemed . . . to be 'dark ages' only because we do not have light enough to read them.' "[55]

Neither was Brownson a Unitarian in any full sense. When reviewing *Unitarianism Vindicated against the Charge of Skeptical Tendencies*, by James Walker, later president of Harvard, he surprisingly remarked: "Were we obliged to be either Unitarian or Calvinist, with our present views, we should unhesitatingly prefer to be a Calvinist."[56] He said this on the score that Calvinism seemed to him to have more truth, although Unitarianism, too, had elements with which humanity could not dispense. The fact seems to be that it is extremely difficult to classify Brownson during these years with any group at all and say that he belongs there in any real sense. These were the years when he was desperately seeking truth, and when he encountered any tenet in the realm of thought which did not seem to match reality, there was an immediate change or shift. In this sense he tended more and more to become a loner, a *tertium quid,* a party by himself. Commenting on this unclassifiable stance of Brownson during these years, Leonard Gilhooley remarked:

> What is suggested is first, that the terms "liberal" and "conservative," "Party of Hope," "Movement Party," . . . tend to polarize and thus oversimplify any discussion of the movement of thought in the American nineteenth century; and second, that when a possible "third party" is suggested as existing either in the thirties or forties, the name of Orestes Brownson is at least prominent, if it does not, like Abu Ben Adhem's, lead all the rest."[57]

In answer to the question whether Brownson had ever really been a Transcendentalist, or to what extent, Arthur M. Schlesinger, Jr., has well remarked: "The question whether he was ever a Transcendentalist is purely verbal. In later years he confessed and denied it as suited his polemic purposes. He certainly shared many of the Transcendentalist tastes and enthusiasms." That is, this would seem to mean, he denied in later years that he was ever a totally committed Transcendentalist, but there was no denying that he had been a fellow traveler, that he had "shared many of the Transcendentalist tastes and enthusiasms." But almost from the beginning of the movement Brownson had begun to put distance between himself and most of the other Transcendentalists by a disposition to expand Transcendentalism into a wide application to the more practical affairs of life, the social question, government and politics. Emerson's attitude to the state, by contrast, is pretty well summed up in his contention that "the less government we have the better."[58] Commenting on the strange attitude of both Emerson and Thoreau in regard to the state, Duane Smith remarked: "It is this mild and rather bland dismissal of the state which is one of the most amazing aspects of Emerson's and Thoreau's writings. The state for Thoreau is something to be pitied. Emerson informs us that he pays his taxes because the state is 'a poor good beast' which means well, and he simply will not begrudge it its rations."[59] Brownson could not have any sympathy with any such individualistic and anarchistic tendency. To him, as a Transcendentalist, the state held centrality as a great agency for the good of its citizens.

# 12

## NEW DIMENSIONS TO TRANSCENDENTALISM A LA BROWNSON

*Brownson's democratic aesthetic for judging literature during his Transcendentalist years • He continues his campaign for social justice • He joins Calhoun, Silas Wright and Thomas Benton in federal politics against Webster, Clay and John J. Crittenden in opposing ill-advised bills • His friendship with Calhoun • He throws in his lot with the Democratic party • His oration at Brown University, Providence, Rhode Island, on "American Literature" • His absorption in the social question.*

Brownson once wrote: "I sought truth in order to know what I ought to do, and as a means of realizing some moral or practical end. I wanted it that I might use it."[1] And so it was with Transcendentalism for Brownson. He wanted to give the truth it contained a wide application, including social and political reform. During his Transcendentalist years he measured the worth of literary authors according to the degree they promoted social reform, or advanced the cause of democracy. Speaking of the literary critics of the day, C. C. Hollis remarked that "Brownson alone seems to have had the necessary social convictions worked out into a philosophical system broad enough to include a democratic aesthetic. . . . Although never the official or acknowledged spokesman, he [Brownson] remains the only Jacksonian literary critic of impressive stature, or, in current terminology, he may be properly considered the only sociological critic of the age."[2] Accordingly, in his review of Emerson's oration on the "American Scholar" before the Phi Beta Kappa Society at Harvard, Brownson expressed his mild disappointment that he did not find Emerson "more fully warmed with the great social idea of our era — the great idea of brotherhood, of sonship to God."[3] Stressing that man "measures man the world over," Brownson insisted that "the great author is he who embodies in language the spirit of the time. The great American author will be he who lives out the American idea — the Christian idea — the divine idea of *Brotherhood*."[4] Reviewing another address of Emerson before the Literary Societies of Dartmouth College on "Literary Ethics," Brownson sounded a louder and more enthusiastic call for a proletarian literature in this New World (protetarian in the less pejorative sense). He asserted, however, contrary to Emerson and Goethe, that literature is never to be sought as an end in itself, but is to be looked upon as a means to an end. A national literature never comes about by merely willing it. He explained:

> In point of fact, few things are less dependent on mere will or arbitrariness than literature. It is the expression and embodiment of the national life. Its character is not determined by this man or that, but by the national spirit. The time and manner of its creation are determined by as necessary and invariable laws, as the motions of the sun, the revolutions of the earth, the growth of a tree, or the blowing of a flower.[5]

Hence great literature has come about when men have dedicated themselves to some great cause, straining all their literary powers to advance that cause. Great national literature has resulted when men have engaged in some great social, political or religious revolution or great national excitement, being always the spontaneous expression of the national life or idea. The great idea of this nation is democratic freedom, the rights of man, emphasized Brownson. No man who does not entertain this idea, "who does not love it, and struggle to realize it in all our social institutions, in our whole practical life, can be a contributor to American literature." Only "when our educated men acquire faith in our democratic institutions, and a love for the Christian doctrine of the brotherhood of the race, shall we have scholars enough, and a literature which shall disclose to the whole world the superiority of freedom over slavery."

And only he who is democratic enough to make himself a part of the lives of the people, who is able to sympathize with them in their sentiments and passions, their joys and their sorrows, their hopes and their fears, their truths and their prejudices, their weal and their woe, will be able to speak to the heart and mind of the people and contribute to American literature. He had some difficulty in abiding Emerson's notion that the scholar must be a solitary figure, living apart and in himself alone. "It will be because a man has felt with the American people," said Brownson, "espoused their cause, bound himself to it for life or for death, time or eternity, that he becomes able to adorn American literature; not because he has lived apart, refused to 'serve society,' held lone reveries, and looked upon sunsets and sunrise."[6]

It seems that at this time no author could win Brownson's kudos unless he were a champion of social justice, that is, social reform. Only those who looked to progress in the future through reform were writers of true literary merit:

> They, then, who seek to spread a halo around the past, to make men quiet under the existing order of things, ready and staunch to uphold the monstrous injustice which is daily practiced, and strong and bold only in suppressing all efforts to obtain a redress of grievances, are the immoral writers, the really dangerous writers, because they commend only what it is popular to commend, and are sure to be sustained by those who profit by the wrongs which should be righted.[7]

When reviewing the "Poetical Works" of Wordsworth he acknowledged that he "is a kind-hearted man, that he would hurt no living thing," and all that, but "he has no faith in any thing like social justice." Hence his lack of popularity among the people.[8] Byron, on the contrary, in spite of his personal faults and the aspersions of critics, "everybody reads; millions clasp him to their heart, for they recognize him as a poet of Humanity, . . . speaking out for man, for freedom, and declaring his plain, sworn, downright detestation of every despotism in every nation."[9] Although he found the novels of Sir Edward Lytton Bulwer defective on "the moral side of art," he commended him at this time for being on the side of the people, as it appeared to him. "In this fearful but glorious war," said Brownson, "we find Bulwer on the right side, fighting, with what skill and bravery are in him, for the *people*. . . . Every man on the democratic side is our brother in arms, and as such is welcome. His friends we hold to be our friends, and his enemies are our enemies."[10] While owning his "strong love for Carlyle," and acknowledging his transcendent literary gifts, his thought he found by no means unexceptionable. Carlyle may say many fine things, but "he has no faith in efforts to meliorate society, and he sneers at him who would labor for the progress of the species."[11] Walter Scott, too, is deficient from the moralistic standpoint. He is not concerned about social justice. His characters are indeed drawn from actual life, but they are not selected from among the real heroes or seers of humanity who burn with visions of righting grievous wrongs and relieving the oppressed. "There are no Wat Tylers, Jack Cades, Van Arteveldts, Rienzis, Sidneys, Hampdens, Vanes, Miltons, among his off-spring."[12] Something of the same complaint is made against Goethe: "We find in him no pure love of Humanity, no unquenched thirst for a purer and better social order, no throbbing of the heart, no intense longing to stand by the weak, to raise up the lowly, to bring down the high."[13]

This incessant clamoring for social justice for the masses, coming from the very depths of his soul, was for him a valid interpretation of Transcendentalism. For there is, as Clarence L. F. Gohdes has observed, "an undeniable connection between the attempt to uphold the dignity of man [stressed by the Transcendentalists] and the effort to better the conditions of the working classes and to abolish slavery."[14] This relentless campaign for social justice Brownson carried to a high pitch in his article on "The Kingdom of God" in the July 1839 issue of his *Quarterly*. It is perhaps the most radical piece that ever came from his pen prior to his essay on "The Laboring Classes." In it he drew a sharp distinction between what he called the Christianity of Christ and the Christianity of the Church, a distinction he was to underscore heavily in his essay on "The Laboring Classes."[15] His whole thesis in this article was that "the kingdom of God is not meat and drink," as says the Apostle, "but righteousness and peace, and joy in the Holy Spirit"; that is, as he unfolded it scripturally, the kingdom of God on earth is the empire of truth and love. Yet the scandal to him was that so many who claim to be members of God's kingdom on earth are concerned with nothing more than minutiae and pass over "the weightier things of the law," the obligations of truth and love in their social relations. The real Christian to him was the man who "in all revolutionary struggles takes sides with the underprivileged, the great Unwashed, as somebody has called them, and braves the wrath of kings, nobilities, and hierarchies":

> He is such that when the interested few, who fatten on the sweat and blood of their brethren, and ride rough-shod over human rights and human affections, in a moment of panic, cry out "Order," "Rights of Property," he cries out in still louder tones, "Liberty," "Rights of Man!" and in tones, too, which fetch an echo from afar, and ring on the oppressor's heart as a summons from God to judgment, and in the souls of the wronged, the enslaved, the down-trodden, as the jubilee shout of deliverance. The cause of the suffering sons of toil, who, from time immemorial, have been made mere drudges, debarred from all the sweets of existence, and doomed to be brutes . . . is for him the cause of God; and to blaspheme that cause or its friends is to blaspheme the Holy Ghost, to commit the unpardonable sin; and to wish to impede its progress, or to embarrass the operations of its friends, is to wish to impede the progress of the eternal God, and to retain the earth under the accursed dominion of the devil and his angels.[16]

Although this passage has an inflammatory ring to it, Orestes Brownson was a man who believed strongly in authority and abhorred violence. He would often use such exciting language in an attempt to wake others up to the social miseries of the underprivileged, and to induce them to engage in active measures for their redress, but it was never his intention to upset the reigning order of society in a revolutionary manner. As he wrote earlier in his article on "Democracy": "We would think with the radical, but often act with the conservative."[17] Balancing the radical tone of much of his writing during the first two years of his *Boston Quarterly Review* was a hard core of underlying conservatism. Speaking of progress the same year in which he wrote the above paragraph, he also said:

> Progress there may be, and there is; but no one can advance far on his predecessors — never so far that they shall sensibly diminish in the distance. These arrogant reformers with a tithe of an idea, who speak to us as if they had outgrown all the past, and grasped and made present the whole future, are generally persons who, having advanced on their infancy, imagine, therefore, that they have advanced on the whole world. But the more we really advance, the more shall we be struck with the greatness of those who went before us, and the more sincere and deep will be our reverence for antiquity. The darkness we ascribe to remote ages, is often the darkness in our own minds, and the ignorance we complain of in others may be a reflex of our own. Progress we should labor for, progress we should delight in, but we should beware of under-rating those who have placed us in the world. "There were giants in those days."[18]

Differing again from most of the Transcendentalists, though he may have had the backing of Ripley and Dr. Channing, Brownson also engaged actively in the political battles of the decade. As C. C. Hollis has observed: "For better or for worse, Brownson was the only major figure (if one excepts Bancroft) of the New England group to perceive fully the radical social philosophy which Transcendentalism demanded and to carry it into a political program. In so doing he parted company with his fellow Transcendentalists just as completely in 1840 on the political level as he did in 1844 on the religious level."[19] When the exciting fight was on in federal politics over the Sub-Treasury Bill, Brownson entered the fray. The object of the bill was to provide for the withdrawal of federal funds from private banks and the establishment by the federal government of its own banking facilities. To deposit government funds in private banks meant virtually turning them over to the business community. The business community would in turn always favor high taxes, and the accumulation of a surplus, because by having the use of the funds to sustain its credit, it would get back more than it was obliged to pay in taxes. The only answer to the evil, Brownson asserted, called for the withdrawal of federal funds from private banks and the foreclosing of the opportunities of banks to pervert the resources of the government to the further oppression of the people through taxation. The policy of the government, emphasized Brownson, should be to keep taxes as light as possible.[20]

The bill for the withdrawal of the federal funds was opposed by two stalwarts, Daniel Webster and Henry Clay, and had for its principal champion John Caldwell Calhoun. Convinced of the wisdom of the measure, Brownson collaborated with Calhoun in an article in his *Review,* and was in correspondence with him over the matter. To the satisfaction of both, the bill passed into law in 1840.[21] When another bill came up this same year for the distribution of the proceeds from the sales of public lands among the various states, Brownson again entered the lists and vigorously opposed the bill as unconstitutional and ill-advised.[22] He was again collaborating with Calhoun, and with Silas Wright and Thomas Benton against Webster, Clay and John J. Crittenden. When the bill nevertheless passed, Calhoun sent Brownson a copy of the speech he had delivered against it, and Brownson wrote a powerful appeal for a reversal of the bill.[23] Within a year after it had been signed into law by the President, it was repealed.

Robert Barnwell Rhett, United States congressman of South Carolina (Calhoun's lieutenant and successor), also delivered a speech supporting Calhoun, Wright and Benton in their opposition to the bill. When Brownson wrote him a letter of complimentary remarks on his speech, Rhett outdid Brownson's compliments to himself in those he extended to Brownson in reply. In a letter written in June 1841, he stated in part:

> If I needed encouragement to sustain me in the advocacy of the great truths which lie at the basis of our free institutions, and which I have endeavored to elucidate in my speech, it would be the strong voice of cheering and approbation from him, whom the first mind in England has pronounced the greatest genius in America. Yours is not a mind that schools have made, or schools can control; and if it sometimes errs — and what mind is infallible? — it will be from the glare of its own innate light, and not from false beacons which other minds have erected; and though I believe you have erred in your too partial estimation of my late effort, I assure you I would rather have the commendation your letter contains, than those of all the literati and politicians of Boston and Harvard combined.[24]

In the support that Brownson was now giving Calhoun as United States senator through his powerful articles in his *Boston Quarterly Review,* we have the beginnings of a friendship that was to wax ever warmer during the span of that *Quarterly.* Both were political conservatives in the sense that both fought hard, each in his own sphere, to preserve our political institutions essentially as they were bequeathed to us by the Founding Fathers. Calhoun wound up one of his letters to Brownson, saying: "I am moving toward one single end, to bring back the government as far as constitutional measures are concerned, to where it was when it commenced."[25] This was precisely one of the great lifelong aims of Brownson in all his political writings. To what extent "the brooding and clean-cut intelligence of John C. Calhoun" influenced Brownson is an interesting question. Certainly Brownson's admiration of him was truly great. After listening to Brownson discourse to him on Webster, Calhoun and Jackson, on his visit to America, Sir John Acton was so impressed by what Brownson had to say about Calhoun that he wrote back to his preceptor in Munich, Ignaz Döllinger: "If I were a *hero-worshipper* I would surely worship Calhoun above all Americans"[26] — this of the man whom Harriet Martineau described as "the cast-iron man, who looks as if he had never been born and could never be extinguished."[27] Writing in 1873, Brownson was to declare Calhoun "the most sagacious and accomplished statesman our republic has ever produced."[28]

At the end of the year 1839, Brownson was nearing the peak of his democratic fervor. The previous year he had written: "True and holy for us are the instincts of the masses. . . . We stand in awe of them, and apply ourselves to the work of enabling them to march to the glorious destiny God has appointed them, and to which his hand is leading them."[29] The people for him at this time, in some respects, held the place the church was to hold later.[30] He liked hugely his friend Bancroft's definition of democracy: "Democracy is eternal justice reigning through the people."[31] He himself defined democracy to be "the supremacy of man over his accidents," meaning that democracy regards man as supreme over all the trappings of birth, wealth or social position. (For which he got unmercifully ridiculed, but remained unmoved.)[32] In an article on "Democracy and Reform," October 1839, he now actually threw in his lot with the Democratic party itself, and earnestly called upon all reformers, all friends of progress, to do the same. The Whig party he labeled the anti-progress party, concerned mainly, as the true descendants of the Federalists, about the rights of property and the accumulation of wealth. Their great idea is "not *Man,* but *Money,* and the contest between them and democracy was rightly declared by Mr. Benton to be a contest between *Man and Money.*"[33] By contrast, the Democratic party was the party of progress, of freedom, of patriotism — the true people's party. The Democratic party, he cried out, is the Christian party. To him the aims of both were almost identical:

> Christianity values man for his simple Humanity, not for his trappings, the accidents of birth, wealth, or position; so does democracy. Christianity, aside from its high design to fit the individual for communion with the blest after death, seeks to introduce a new order of things on earth, to exalt the humble, to abash the proud, to establish the reign of justice and enable every man "to sit under his own fig-tree, with none to molest or make afraid"; and who does not know that this is the tendency of the democratic party.[34]

The astonishing thing to be noted at this juncture of affairs is that Brownson declared himself a Democrat in a party sense — though it was to be quite short-lived. Except on rare occasions he had never acted with the Democratic party as such, and knew that he could not well be a party man. His joining the party is to be explained mainly by the fact that for the moment he had convinced himself that only by joining a party could one work the most effectively for the people. And the Democratic party was dedicated to the reform of abuses, the elevation of the masses, and the promotion of freedom for all. In response then to these broad principles of freedom to which he had for so long and so ardently devoted his best energies, he now joined the Democratic party itself. After giving his reasons for his decision, he added:

> Sinking now the editor, and speaking in my own name, I may say, here is my view of the democratic party, and here are my reasons for enrolling myself among its members. I have formed this view not hastily, nor without considerable reflection; I have adopted it only as I have been compelled by my general principles of politics, religion, and philosophy. I have never been a partisan. I have it is true, always been a democrat. I sucked in democracy with my mother's milk; I imbibed a feeling and love of freedom, as I roamed a child over the Green Hills, or clambered up the scarped rocks, or plunged in the dark forests of my early home. I could not have been a Green Mountain boy, bred in a mountain home, in what may one day be regarded as the Switzerland of America, without cherishing a free spirit, and becoming the friend of the "largest liberty." I have always been found on the side of freedom in its widest signification. To love of it I have given years of intense study, sacrificed ease, sometimes reputation, pecuniary independence, and professional success. But, except on rare occasions, I have never acted with the democratic party as such. I have had my prejudices against it, and against its prominent members. I have thought it too intent on office, on maintaining itself as a party, and too indifferent to the progress and application of free principles. It may readily be believed, then, that I have not given in my adhesion, so unequivocally, without having been compelled by, what seemed to me, cogent reasons.[35]

In the field of education, too, he looked to democracy for the best results. When reviewing in the October 1839 issue of his *Quarterly,* the *Second Annual Report of the (Massachusetts) Board of Education, together with the Second Annual Report of the Secretary of the Board,* he raised his voice in protest against an apparent attempt to straitjacket the education of the people. The establishment of normal schools (teacher-training schools) proposed by the board, he regarded as an incipient attempt to bring education under the complete control of the state, wiping out the district school in which parents of the locality have control over the kind of education they wish their children to receive. As no one can have more interest in the education of children than their own parents, so experience proves that the more control parents have over the education of their children, the better will be the school in which they are educated. The establishment of normal schools, with state control, he felt would only tend toward the kind of education that is received under the Prussian system and other autocratic governments where the state dictates what will be taught in the schools. When this state of affairs comes about, "adieu then," said Brownson, "to republicanism and progress." He added: "We may as well have a religion established by law as a system of education, and the government educate and appoint the pastors of our churches, as well as the instructors of our children."[36] To hand over the children of a district to the state board of education would be like taking them from their parents and entrusting them to strangers. Once again Brownson was defending the rights and interests of the people which he judged to be more securely safeguarded under local self-government.

In the same elaborate article he also excoriated the American press for defaulting on its role as a faithful educator of the people. What was direly needed was a press free and intelligent enough to instruct and lead the people, not just slavishly follow public opinion. He felt that public opinion or popular prejudice exercised a censorship in this country hardly less paralyzing than that established by Austria or Prussia. The reviews of the day, he asserted, took as great pains to avoid the utterance of any new or leading ideas as might be expected if they were published under the immediate supervision of the Spanish Inquisition, or the Ottoman Porte. Even the reputable *North American Review* closes its columns to the truth should it not be palatable to its learned editor. "The honest and enlightened contributor to its pages must submit to a censorship altogether more humiliating than would be expected by a European despot."[37] As to his own *Review,* insofar as it had been commended, he asserted that it had been commended for those very qualities in which the American press is the most deficient — proof positive that the public wants a free, bold and fearless press. What reputation he had acquired as editor had been secured by reason of the independence, the freedom and boldness which had always characterized his discussions. The fact is that he could not act otherwise, for false to his conscience, false to his God in the matter, he could not be. In a paragraph that many a time-serving editor would find excellent staple for meditation, he wrote:

> Shall I bend to popular prejudice? Shall I be false to my soul — false to all that is true within me, that I may be thought better of, feed on costlier viands, or wear a finer coat? Let me be cast out from the society of men; let me wander the earth in sheep-skins, or goat-skins; let me dwell alone on the mountain, or in caverns; let me beg, let me starve sooner. When God gave me a manly nature, he bid me be true to it; when he gave me reason, he bid me listen to its oracles, when he gave me a social nature, and linked me by ties as sweet as heaven to my kind, he bid me be true to whatever I should honestly be convinced would be for their good, and let me die, nay, let me sink into eternal torture, sooner than be false to the trust committed to me. This, it strikes me, is the only language becoming a man. Talk not to me of my party or my sect, talk

not to me of reputation or wealth; these are nothing; they can follow me only to the tomb. They cannot make amends for having been false to my God. They will not quench the eternal fire, which must scorch the tongue which has uttered falsehood, or refused to utter truth. He, who shrinks from free thought and free speech, is the most abject of slaves, is not a man but a pitiable thing, unworthy of heaven, and too imbecile for hell.[38]

This paragraph might well be considered a luminous commentary on the whole career of Orestes A. Brownson as writer and editor.

In the January issue of his *Review* for 1840, Brownson published an oration he had delivered on "American Literature" before the United Brothers Society of Brown University, Providence, Rhode Island, in September of 1839.[39] The occasion was a rather auspicious one. *The Republican Herald* of Providence took notice of it in its issue of September 7, 1839, in a long commentary, the first part of which read:

> Bancroft, Brownson, and A. H. Everett
> The anniversary celebrations during the present week of the Literary Societies connected with Brown University have been uncommonly interesting, and have furnished intellectual gratification of a high order to all who had the pleasure of attending them. We have frequently listened on former occasions to men of various talents and accomplishments, but never before to three such men in the same week, as those who are named at the head of this article — George Bancroft, of Boston, delivered an oration before the Philomenian Society on Tuesday forenoon; he was followed by Rev. Orestes A. Brownson, of Boston, in the afternoon before the Society of United Brothers; and the literary exercises of the week were concluded on Wednesday afternoon with a discourse before the Phi Kappa Society by Hon. Alexander Everett, of Roxbury, Massachusetts. These three gentlemen are well known as standing in the first rank of the scholars and writers of the country.

Space was then devoted to a detailed account of each oration. Of Brownson's it was said at the outset: "The oration of Mr. Brownson was marked by originality, a high toned vigor of thought, and an earnest spirit of democracy which arrested general attention, and assured to it the reputation of the ablest production of the week."[40]

In the forepart of his oration Brownson expatiated on the causes for the meagerness of American literature to date. One of the foremost reasons he ascribed to the fact that our literary men have been too slow to accept our democratic institutions, and to conform to the order of society set up by the Founding Fathers. Educated in schools modeled after the English, they had imbibed an aristocratic taste, had come to look down on democratic institutions as unfavorable to the development of genius, and consequently could fetch nothing more than a feeble echo from the national heart. The literary men of the country, at least until recently, had neither properly sympathized with the people, nor had they any clear conception of the great doctrine of equal rights and social equality, to which the nation is pledged. In a word, they had not been true democrats in their hearts, and hence there had been a gulf between them and the American people.[41]

Reaching the climax in the stirring crescendo of his thought, Brownson stressed perhaps more strongly than ever before that the great problem facing American society was the class conflict, the struggle between wealth and labor, between the accumulator of wealth and the simple laborer who produces it, between Man and Money. Whatever the political status of the masses in Europe, the question of political equality had long since been settled once and for all here; but what of the boasted advantage of democratic government "if the people are in point of fact cursed with all the evils of social inequality"? Assuming a sterner tone, he said:

> The question has been asked, too: Can a rich man, a man who has accumulated and possesses great wealth, be a good Christian? There are among us those who begin to suspect that Jesus meant something when he said, "it is easier for a camel to go through the eye of a needle, than for a rich man to enter the kingdom of heaven." There are those who ask themselves, when they see the extremes of wealth and poverty which meet us in our cities, bloated luxury and pining want side by side, if this be a Christian order of things, if indeed this order of things is to last forever. As a Christian, am I not bound to love my fellowmen, even the lowest and the most polluted, well enough, if need be, to die for them, as Jesus died on the cross for me? Am I then permitted to avail myself of the labors of others, so as to accumulate an immense estate; am I then permitted to live in luxury, to feast on the rarities of every clime which commerce procures for me, while my brother languishes in poverty, while the poor mother at my next door is watching, pale and emaciated, over her starving boy, and the poor seamstress is prostituting herself so as not to die of starvation?[42]

Questions like these, continued Brownson, are coming up among us, and the attempt to suppress them, to hush them up, cannot succeed. They demand an answer, and in grim terms, too. He ominously warned his audience of the class struggle looming on the horizon, and declared that in that war, on one side or the other, each must take his stand, and do battle as best he can. And in the struggle of these two social elements, true American literature will be born "before which all literature now extant may, perhaps, shrink into insignificance." Here, to him, was a great and noble cause that challenged the abilities and dedication of the best. But he repeated again that literature must always be regarded as a means, not as an end in itself.

As for himself, "the plumed troop, and the big wars" beckoned him on: "I confess, Brothers, that notwithstanding the fearful nature of the social contest coming on, I am not alarmed. I even behold it with the joy with which the war-horse snuffs the battle from afar. I behold it, and feel that I have not been born too early, nor too late; that there is a work for me also, if I have but the skill and the courage to undertake it."[43]

The martial tone of his thought in this oration is to a degree a prelude to his coming essay on "The Laboring Classes," which nevertheless to most of his contemporaries must have come as a thunderclap. It was of this precise period in Brownson's life and thought that Harold Laski wrote when he said: "Orestes Brownson insisted, with a power that becomes the more remarkable the more fully it is known, that the class struggle was already the central fact in the American issue, and that the problems it postulated were insoluble on the plane of political democracy."[44]

Brownson's review of *Chevalier's Letters* in the April 1840 issue of his *Quarterly* (three months before his essay on "The Laboring Classes") shows that he had thought long and hard on the social problem in an effort to get at the heart of the matter. Explaining why the employee is ever so largely at the mercy of the employer, he wrote:

> Everywhere the workman at wages is a sort of a slave, more or less at the mercy of the employer. The capitalist invests his capital not for the purpose of obtaining the means of subsistence, but for the increase of wealth. For this end he purchases labor. But the workman sells his labor that he may obtain not

wealth, but the means of subsistence. Now as the urgency to obtain the means of subsistence must always be greater than the urgency to grow richer, the laborer must always be more desirous of selling his labor than the capitalist can be of purchasing it. Hence the purchaser is in a position to exert more influence on the terms of sale and purchase than can be exerted by the seller. He has much more power over the laborer than the laborer has over him, as the urgency to get something to eat is greater than the urgency to grow rich. How much this is may be inferred from the fact, that long ago one Esau, to obtain a mess of potage to save himself from immediate starvation, resigned to his brother the right, as the eldest born, to the inheritance and patriarchal authority of his father.[45]

Brownson was now on the eve of a deed of valor so audacious in its nature that he probably had not the positive endorsement of a single friend, to say nothing of parties. For some dozen years now he had been a tireless agitator for justice for the laboring classes, straining every nerve to turn the attention of the public to the redress of their age-old grievances. Nothing like signal success had crowned his efforts. Perhaps he felt that his clamorous appeals were growing "flat, stale and unprofitable" through repetition. Was there no possible way to arrest the attention of the public, still so apathetic to the cause he was advocating so ardently? He knew that some of his thought on the subject was regarded as quite radical, but there was more of a somewhat frightening kind in his mind, still undisclosed. He finally decided to make a clean breast of it all, and gave to the world his memorable essay entitled "The Laboring Classes," which was to fall on the public ear with the impact of a bombshell. It appeared in the July 1840 issue of his *Quarterly*, the same issue in which he made his ninety-page reply to Andrews Norton. The echoes of its publication were to be long in dying away.

# 13

## ESSAY ON 'THE LABORING CLASSES'

*He finds no answer to the sorry plight of the laboring classes in Thomas Carlyle's* Chartism • *He indicts the factory system of wages, preferring the system of slave labor in the South to the system of wages in the North • He lays to the charge of the Christian ministry, both Catholic and Protestant, the low condition of the laboring classes • Making his distinction between the Christianity of Christ and the Christianity of the church, he calls for the destruction of the latter and a return to the pristine religion of Jesus as practiced by the early Christians • He insists that the government must repeal all laws bearing against the laboring classes, that the control of the government by banks with their credit system must be destroyed, and that the government root out all privileges and monopolies • He proposes for discussion the hereditary descent of property.*

The key to a right understanding of Brownson's essay on "The Laboring Classes" is to see it against the backdrop of the Great Depression of 1837. In 1840 the people were still suffering intensely from its effects. Samuel Rezneck, who made a close study of its social effects, asserts that the social effects extended over a span of seven years, and that the year 1843 was "one of the gloomiest in our industrial history." The years in between were full of doubt and distress in the business world. A restoration to anything like normalcy was being effected only very slowly. The suffering came from the fact that the country at large was passing through "a national pay day." Prior to 1837 the nation had been drawing heavily on the future through the credit system. But came 1837 and the future refused to honor the draft. When a forcing process was resorted to, widespread panic and ruin engulfed the nation. In New York alone six hundred banks failed, as well as thousands of others throughout the country; everywhere factories were closed, and men by the thousands were thrown out of work who aimlessly wandered through the streets of our cities with starvation stalking them. A long period of economic paralysis ensued.[1] It was when the people were in the midst of these sufferings brought on by this mammoth depression that Brownson made his supreme effort through the publication of his shocking essay on "The Laboring Classes" to draw the attention of the public to the unabating sufferings of the people.

Giving no hint of the roll of thunder that was to follow, Brownson began his essay in low key with a review of Thomas Carlyle's pamphlet on *Chartism*. The pamphlet was a discussion of the deplorable conditions of the laboring classes in England, but as Brownson observed, it had a pointed relevancy to the condition of the working classes throughout the world. It was just the kind of a pamphlet calculated to fan Brownson's fire of indignation into a fighting mood over the hopeless plight of the laboring classes as portrayed by Carlyle's graphic pen. He could see only revolution as the inevitable result if remedial measures were not applied. The two Morrison pills prescribed by Carlyle, however — universal education and general emigration — were to Brownson no better than mere quackeries. What comfort could education be to a people already starving, he would like to know? "For God's sake," he exclaimed, "beware how you kindle in them the intellectual spark . . . if you doom them to the external condition of brutes. . . ." As to general emigration of the proletariat, the proposal was beside the point, he complained — a mere palliative at best. "The evil is not from overpopulation," he insisted, but from the "unequal repartition of the fruits of industry."[2] The evil is that the laborer is robbed of his just share of the fruits of industry. After a close analysis of the class struggle in England, where a powerful middle class was oppressively holding down the laboring classes, he declared the condition of the laboring classes there to be the worst of any country in Europe. If our voice could reach the Chartists, he said, we would bid them be bold and determined, for their cause is the cause of justice, and in fighting for it they will be fighting for the cause of God and man. Still, he had little hope that their movements would effect anything worthwhile. He added: "We have little faith in a John Bull mob. It will bluster, and swagger, and threaten much; but give it plenty of porter and roast-beef, and it will sink back to its kennel, as quiet and as harmless as a lamb." But if the Chartists could effect little, from where would the answer to the plight of the British laboring classes come?

He left it to the British intelligentsia to find the answer, but added ominously:

> It [the answer] will be found only at the end of one of the longest and severest struggles the human race has ever been engaged in, only by that most dreaded of all wars, the war of the poor against the rich, a war which, however long it may be delayed, will come with all its horrors. The day of vengeance is sure; for the world after all is under the dominion of a Just Providence.[3]

To anyone who can read the signs of the times, continued Brownson, the struggle shaping up in modern society is that between the operative and his employer, between wealth and labor. By his very position the employer is the natural enemy of the workingman. Wherever one looks, the same spectacle stares him in the face: the workingman is poor and depressed while those who profit by his labors grow wealthy. Whether in the offices of government or the jobs of industry those who perform the real productive work are largely let off with the most paltry wages. Hence the whole class of simple laborers are poor, and in general unable to procure for themselves anything beyond the bare essentials of life.[4]

He next turned his searching scrutiny on the two systems of labor in the country: slave labor in the South and free labor in the North. Except for the feelings that might be involved in the case of the Southern slave, slave labor to him was decidedly less oppressive. The slave had security, freedom from the nagging cares of how to procure the bare necessities of life which forever haunt the free laborer. As to actual freedom, the one had about as much as the other. The laborer at wages had all the disadvantages of his freedom, and few or none of its blessings, while the slave, if denied its blessings, was free from its disadvantages. Yet he protested most emphatically that he was no apologist of slavery, but if there must be a laboring population distinct from proprietors and employers, he could not but regard the slave system as preferable to the system of wages. "It is no pleasant thing," he added, "to go days without food, to lie idle for weeks, seeking work and finding none, to rise in the morning with a wife and children you love, and to know not where to procure for them a breakfast, and to see constantly before you no brighter prospect than the almshouse."[5]

The factory with its iniquitous system of wages was only augmenting the grievous inequalities in social life. The rich were getting richer and the poor poorer. Men and women in sweatshops, factories and brothels were giving of their all that the few might feed on the rarest dainties of every clime, and ride in gorgeous carriages. And he who was coining the sweat and blood of his fellowmen into wealth for his coffers was accounted a distinguished citizen in his community. As a master of biting sarcasm he said of the employer of operatives:

> The man who employs them, and for whom they are toiling as so many slaves, is one of our city nabobs, reveling in luxury; or he is a member of the legislature, enacting laws to put money into his own pocket; or he is a member of the congress, standing for high tariff to tax the poor for the benefit of the rich; or in these times he is shedding crocodile tears over the deplorable condition of the poor laborer, while he docks his wages twenty-five percent; building miniature log cabins, or shouting Harrison and "hard cider." And this man too would fain pass for a Christian and a Republican. He shouts for liberty, stickles for equality, and is horrified at the Southern planter who keeps slaves.[6]

Seen against the backdrop of the other evils of the factory system, to this mordant social critic "wages [were] a cunning device of the devil, for the benefit of tender consciences, who would retain all the advantages of the slave system, without the expense, the trouble, and the odium of being slaveholders."[7]

He then asked the question: Under such a system of wages, what are the chances that any portion of the current generation of workers could ever attain to sufficient funds that they might operate on their own capital or become independent laborers? He acknowledged that men born poor sometimes become wealthy, and men born to wealth become poor, but that does not necessarily alter the comparative percentage between the rich and the poor in society. One thing for him was certain: no man born poor has ever, by his wages, as a simple operative, risen to the class of the wealthy. Rich he may have become, but not by virtue of the wages received. Only by contriving to tax the labor of others in some way for his own benefit, or by passing from a clerk to a partner in business, or through lucky investments could he have done so. The simple market wages for the ordinary laborer had never made it possible for him to pass from poverty to wealth. This he considered decisive of the whole controversy and damned the system of wages as practiced. Either the system must be supplanted by some other system or else one half of the human race would remain forever the virtual slaves of the other half.[8]

We have no evidence that Brownson had read Alexis de Tocqueville, but his thought is in close agreement with what De Tocqueville had observed in American society, namely, that:

> The manufacturing aristocracy that is growing up under our eyes is one of the harshest which ever existed in the world . . . the friends of democracy should keep their eyes fixed in this direction; for if ever a permanent inequality of conditions and aristocracy penetrate into the world, it may be predicted that this is the channel by which it will enter.[9]

It had accordingly become Brownson's firm conviction that the great work of the age was to raise up the laborer, to realize in new social arrangements and the general condition of all men that equality between man and man as would be a true reflection of the rights of the one and the other as established by God himself. The great work was "to emancipate the proletaries as the past had emancipated the slave." If the system of wages was to be tolerated at all, it should be under such conditions that by the time the individual is of age to settle in life, he shall have accumulated enough to operate as "an independent laborer on his own capital — on his own farm or in his own shop."[10]

Brownson is here caught, it would seem, looking backwards, not forward. His proposal appears to envision a return to an order of things that was rapidly receding into the past. Anything like a revival of the medieval guilds was scarcely any longer practicable. He apparently did not see, or did not want to see that the Industrial Revolution had inaugurated a new system in the economic order that had come to stay. Since technology had made it possible through the factory system to produce vast quantities of goods by virtue of labor-saving machinery, there remained no chance that the industrial juggernaut could possibly be reversed in its course. Perhaps he did see this to a certain extent. In any case, he felt an overmastering compulsion to hurl himself against what he counted the debasing evils of the factory system. To a man of his temperament, brought up in the wild freedom of his Vermont home, the idea of a man chained to a machine day after day was quite revolting. Such a system tended to mechanize him, to deform him as a human being. And the price paid him for such a fate was often barely sufficient to keep body and soul together. Such a system of employment he would tear up root and branch. His proposal in the case, however impractical, was simply an attempt on his part to liberate modern man from what he counted industrial slavery and to restore to him some measure of human dignity and independence.[11]

But how were the sorely needed changes in the economic order to be effected? How set about it? The religious reformer would reply that inner reform was the answer. Make men good and wise, and these evils will gradually disappear, or be sanctified by the spiritual growth of the soul. There will then be no further need to bother about altering the present social arrangements. This religious theory, said Brownson, is sure to be supported by all those who fatten on the toil and blood of their fellows under present conditions, and he had the employer say of his operative: "So far as the salvation of his soul will not interfere with my income, I hold it worthy to be sought; and if a few thousand dollars will aid you, Mr. Priest, in recommending him to God, and making fair weather for him hereafter, they are at your service. I shall not want him to work for me in the world to come, and I can indemnify myself for what your salary costs me, by paying him less wages." A capital theory this, scornfully sneered Brownson, which one may advocate without incurring the reproach of being a disorganizer, a Jacobin, a leveler, or without losing the friendship of the rankest aristocrat. But the theory entailed one slight objection: it had been tried for six thousand years with only sorry results. Under its practical operation, mankind, if totally depraved at the beginning, had only been growing worse and worse ever since.[12]

As for his part, he yielded to none in his reverence for science and religion, but he could not look to priests and pedagogues for the regeneration of the human race. They had had their fair chance, and had only for the most part unhappily leagued with the people's masters in upholding the reigning order. They seek to reform without disturbing the social arrangements which make reforms necessary. "They would change the consequents without changing the antecedents, secure to men the rewards of holiness, while they continue their allegiance to the devil."[13]

While he admitted to a certain extent the importance of what Dr. Channing called "self-culture," he still protested that it cannot abolish inequality, or restore men to their rights. The evils complained of are not individual in character, but are inherent in social arrangements, he stoutly insisted. Evils of a purely individual nature may be corrected through the individual's efforts to perfect himself. But those which inhere in a system cannot be gotten rid of through isolated efforts: "The only way to get rid of its evils is to change the system, not its managers. . . . You must abolish the system or accept its consequences. . . . No man can serve both God and Mammon. If you will serve the devil, you must look to him for your wages; we know no other way."[14]

The gifted British economist, Barbara Ward, told five hundred delegates at the close of a three-day conference on world poverty that present *economic structures* (italics mine) will not prevent the world poor from becoming poorer. Miss Ward, author of *The Rich Nations and the Poor Nations,* said citizens of the emerging nations are "12 times poorer than we are now, and in about twenty years will be 18 times poorer."[15]

We also have something of a reflection of Brownson's thought in this matter in the present-day writings of Archbishop Helder Camara who has written: "What is needed is a reform in depth, a profound and rapid change; what we must achieve — let's not be afraid of the word — is a structural revolution." He even went so far as to say: "I respect those who feel obliged in conscience to opt for violence."[16]

Brownson realized of course that in castigating the clergy of the church for having failed to work the regeneration of mankind over the long haul that he was laying himself open to a confused charge of hostility to Christianity itself. To this he quickly interposed a demurrer which, however, was to be hastily overlooked by most of his readers. He asserted that he in no sense denied the power of Christianity itself to work the needed reforms, that is, if all men would become real Christians. The crux of the matter was that so many were no better than nominal Christians. By contrast, the real Christian is he who begins his career by making war on the mischievous social arrangements which oppress and degrade his brethren. He was making his distinction here between the Christianity of the church and the Christianity of Christ, and added: "One might as well undertake to dip the ocean dry with a clam-shell, as to undertake to cure the evils of the social state by converting men to the Christianity of the Church."[17]

But whence had originated the evils in the social order so glaring and so deplorable? How comes it that all over the world the working classes are depressed, are low and vulgar, and virtually the slaves of the nonworking classes? "For our own part," he said, "we are disposed to seek the cause of the inequality of conditions of which we speak, in religion, and charge it to the priesthood." But how in the world did it ever happen that priests succeeded in gaining such control over the people as to be accountable for their low condition and the continuance of such a state? Sacerdotal corporations, found among every people as they emerge from the savage state, had gained "control of the individual conscience through moral laws, the assertion of the supremacy of the moral order over physical force" — a great truth, said Brownson, when rightly understood — "but which at this epoch can only enslave the mass of the people to its representatives, the priests." Through an instilled awe of the gods, through a fear of their displeasure, and a dread of the punishments such a displeasure might inflict, and by pretending that they possessed the secret of averting it, the priests had been successful in reducing the people to a most wretched subjection, and keeping them there — at least for a time.[18] Such was the genesis of the enormous priestly power which our probing reformer found obstinately obstructing the way to the needed reforms in society. An ingenious theory which he would later only laugh at heartily.

Continuing his distinction between the Christianity of Christ and the Christianity of the church, he indicted the latter for having been associated with the abuses of the reigning order in the past, and for having failed to concern itself properly with the redress of those selfsame abuses. Hence the Christianity of Christ demanded its destruction, that is, the destruction of the priestly type of Christianity. Assuring his readers that "we are Christians," he insisted that it is only by following out the real Christian law, and the example of the early Christians that anything can be effected in the way of the needed reforms. "Christianity," he declared, "is the sublimest protest against the priesthood ever uttered, and a protest uttered by both God and man; for he who uttered it was both God and man." He admitted that a priesthood had been instituted in the name of Jesus, but asserted that the religion of Jesus repudiates it. It recognizes one mediator between God and man, Christ who gave himself once and for all for all mankind on the cross. Hence no priesthood is needed. Although the Christianity of Christ could not prevent the establishment of a hierarchy, it prepared for its ultimate destruction by denying the inequality of blood, by representing all men as equal before God, and by insisting on the law of celibacy for its clergy.[19]

But in speaking against the priesthood he made no distinction between the Catholic priest and the Protestant minister; to him both were on the same plane, and were alike obnoxious. He wanted no longer any professional class of preachers. Each Christian should speak out from his own heart as the Holy Spirit gave him to speak: "But none of your hireling priests, your 'dumb dogs' that will not bark." What have the priests of Christendom amounted to? Nothing but miserable panderers to the prejudices of the age, vehement in denouncing sins no one is guilty of, "but silent as the grave when it concerns the crying sin of the times; bold as can be when there is no danger, but miserable cowards when it is necessary to speak out for God and Humanity. As a body they never preach the truth till there is none whom it indicts. Never do they as a body venture to condemn sin in the concrete, and make each sinner feel, 'thou art the man.' "[20]

After the annihilation of the priestly type of Christianity, the next step looking to the elevation of the laboring classes was to be the resuscitation of the Christianity of Christ. Brownson's blueprints for this restoration he laid down in some detail. According to the Christianity of Christ, he thundered, no man can be a Christian who does not labor with all zeal and diligence to establish the kingdom of God on earth; no man can be a Christian who does not labor to reform society, to mold it according to the will of God and the nature of man so that each individual may grow up into the full stature of the perfect man in Christ. What is really required, Brownson exclaimed in rising tones, is that the genuine Gospel of Christ be preached, not just a pseudo-gospel which lulls the conscience to sleep, and permits men to consider themselves good and honorable Christians, although rich and with eyes standing out with fatness, while the great mass of their brethren are oppressed by mischievous social arrangements, and are pining away for the bare necessities of life. The mischief in the past has been, he continued, that under the influence of the historic church, efforts have not been directed to the reorganization of society, to the introduction of equality between man and man, looking to the removal of the corruptions of the rich, and the misery of the poor. But as to the Christianity of Christ, he acknowledged that we "cannot proceed a single step" in elevating the laboring classes without the exaltation of sentiment, and the generous sympathy and moral courage it inspires and quickens. The mistake of the historic church had been that it perverted those noble elements and rendered them inefficient in producing the good they could have effected: "Here is wherefore it is necessary on the one hand to condemn in the most pointed terms the Christianity of the Church, and bring out on the other hand in all its clearness, brilliancy, and glory the Christianity of Christ."[21]

After the resuscitation of the Christianity of Christ, with its great emphasis on the social message of the Gospel,[22] Brownson's next proposed step was to invoke the power of government to push forward the cause of the laboring classes through remedial legislative enactments. The grievous evils suffered by the vast army of working people had grown up under governments instituted by society. But government is a servant of the people, not its master. Hence the laboring classes have a claim on government to rectify their deep wrongs. What is the duty of government under the circumstances? The first thing must be an *undoing*. He would have the government circumscribe itself within narrower limits: there has been not only too much government in the past, but also the wrong kind of government. If the cause of the laboring classes was to be served, the government must proceed to repeal all laws oppressing the poorer classes, and enact such laws as will enable them to gain and maintain their equality: it must enact such legislation as will free it from all control of banks, whether state or federal. For banks are controlled largely by the business community, and as such hold in subjection the laboring community. By the same token, as long as the government is under the control of the banks, it can be made an instrument for oppressing the underprivileged classes of society. The only answer is the destruction of the power of the banks over the government as they exist, "for such is the subtle influence of credit, and such the power of capital, that a banking system like ours, if sustained, necessarily and inevitably becomes the real and efficient government of the country."[23]

The next step for working the uplift of the laboring classes was to be the rooting out of all privileges and monopolies. And to Brownson the chief of all privileges in the economic order was the hereditary descent of property, by which some are born rich and some poor. As the capstone to all his proposals for the emancipation of the laboring classes he now suggested the abolition of the hereditary descent of property. As the American system had abolished hereditary monarchy, and hereditary nobility, it should now come full circle and abolish the hereditary descent of property which he called "an anomaly in our American system." Under the proposed alteration a man should be allowed to retain as long as he lived all he had honestly acquired. But his power over his property would cease at his death, and would then become the property of the state to be distributed under some equitable law among those of the succeeding generation. Here was a measure of talismanic effect, as he saw it, for the removal of all the major distressing inequalities. But would the measure be easily carried? On that point he had no illusions:

It will cost infinitely more than it cost to abolish hereditary monarchy or hereditary nobility. It is a great measure, and a startling [one].The rich, the business community, will never voluntarily consent to it, and we think we know too much of human nature to believe that it will ever be effected peaceably. It will be effected only by the strong arm of physical force. It will come, if it ever come[s] at all, only at the conclusion of a war, the like of which the world as yet has never witnessed, and from which, however inevitable it may seem to the eye of philosophy, the heart of Humanity recoils with horror.[24]

It is important to note that Brownson stated in his concluding paragraph that he did not feel that the times were ripe for the abolition of the hereditary descent of property, and that he himself would be the last to bring it before the legislature. The time had come, however, for its free and full discussion. Society should canvass it closely. No doubt those who broach it, and particularly those who are ready to support it, will experience their full share of "contumely and abuse." But what of that? No one worthy to be called a man will allow that to disquiet him. Men have, in all ages, for what they accounted the cause of God and man, braved the dungeon, the stake, the scaffold, the cross, and they can do it again. A free and full discussion of the matter must be had, no matter what the fate of those who broach it.[25]

As indicated, Brownson could not but know beforehand the whirlwind of excitement and incrimination his essay would stir up. But he had too much of a sense of honor to allow any of his friends or associates to be implicated in the censures that were sure to fall upon his own hapless head for a bold and reckless venture which was strictly his own. He therefore appended to his proposal concerning the hereditary descent of property an explanatory note:

> I feel bound to say, that my doctrine, on the hereditary descent of property, is put forth by myself alone, and on my own responsibility. . . . Whatever may be the measure of condemnation the community in its wisdom may judge proper to mete out for its promulgation, that condemnation should fall on my head alone. I hold not myself responsible for others' opinions, and I wish not others to be held responsible for mine.[26]

Immediately upon the publication of the essay came a storm of protest and invective from far and near, though not in every instance in the form of a wholesale condemnation. The aging Dr. Channing was shocked. He had long been prepared for the unexpected from Brownson, but this was far and away beyond anything he could have imagined. To Elizabeth P. Peabody, whose bookstore he frequented, he complained that Brownson had painted the lot of the laboring classes much too darkly; that, as a matter of fact, they were much better off than the professional or business classes since they were free from the acute disappointments that often beset those aspiring classes. "To me," he continued, "the matter of complaint is, not that the laboring classes want physical comforts, . . . but that they live only for their physical natures." He lamented that Brownson's remedies "are shocking and absurd. How foolish to talk about abolishing the law of inheritance, and dividing the estates of the dead among the people. . . . No good can come but from the spread of intellectual and moral power among the classes, and the union of all by a spirit of brotherhood."[27]

Dr. Francis Wayland, president of Brown University, became one of Brownson's most vehement denouncers. In arranging the commencement exercises for that year he made it an occasion for launching an attack on him. The speaker's whole address was directed against Brownson's article on "The Laboring Classes." Anne Lynch, a staunch friend of Brownson, wrote him that it was fortunate that he did not show up for the occasion "unless you would have had a chance to reply." She added, "Your views are opposed with so much vehemence that I begin to think they may not be impossible to realize, after all."[28] She also quoted from a book of Dr. Wayland showing that his own thought had been much in the same vein as Brownson's. Sarah Whitman likewise wrote Brownson to tell him of the hypocritical way in which Dr. Wayland had denounced him.[29]

To the Dialists Brownson's article must have been thoroughly disconcerting. The first issue of the *Dial*, which appeared the same month as Brownson's essay, July, carried a high tribute to Brownson's writings. It was something of a panegyric, by George Ripley. But here was matter that gave them solemn pause. Would they incur guilt by association? What the reaction of most of them was, is not recorded. Theodore Parker, however, noted critically in his diary: "Brownson has recently written an article on the laboring classes calculated to call the philosophic to reflection. . . . I like much of the article, though his property notions agree not with mine. Yet the present property scheme entails awful evils upon society, rich no less than the poor. The question, first, of inherited property, and, next, of all private property, is to be handled in the nineteenth century."[30] Emerson, a man of bold speculation himself, was delighted with Brownson's essay, and enthusiastically wrote Margaret Fuller: "The hero wields a sturdy pen which I am very glad to see. I had judged him from some old things and did not know that he was such a Cobbet of a scribe. Let him wash himself and write for the immortal *Dial*."[31]

Brownson was to have his most intrepid and loyal defender in William Henry Channing (nephew of Dr. Channing), editor of the *Western Messenger,* Cincinnati, Ohio. But his bold defense of the harried Brownson in the October edition of the *Messenger* was to cost him dearly. By December a whole avalanche of protest and abuse had descended upon him. After four more issues the *Messenger* folded. Perry Miller calls the episode "an unsung deed of courage in the annals of American journalism."[32] William H. Channing was to remain ever an admirer of Brownson, and Brownson in turn held him in high esteem and affection.[33]

One of the most thoughtful reviews of "The Laboring Classes" appeared in the *Methodist Quarterly Review* in January 1841, under the heading, "The Rich against the Poor."[34] The author of the article had the advantage of having seen Brownson's defense of his essay (October 1840) before he wrote his own review. He found it rather paradoxical that Brownson should have declared in his essay that "this world after all is under a Just Providence." To him such an idea had a jarring relation to Brownson's description of the coming apocalyptic clash between the haves and the have-nots. He remarked: "Though his [Brownson's] patriotic blood boils over with burning charity for the poor, he deliberately throws the rich and the business community into the fiery furnace which is heated seven times hotter than ever furnace was heated before, and looks calmly on while the conflagration is raging around him, though it be such fire as the world has never yet witnessed. And yet this unprecedented war, this unheard-of struggle, this horrid and most sanguinary conflict, is to be invoked in the name of Providence."[35] But he was not quite fair to Brownson in representing him throughout his article as invoking war as the answer. Brownson predicted rather than urged revolution as the inevitable result unless remedial measures were applied in time. He advocated reforms, but did not urge the overthrow of government. Here is where he stood apart from Karl Marx and all his ilk.[36]

Yet the Methodist reviewer's article contained a goodly degree of honest thought. He acknowledged that in pleading the cause of the laboring classes Brownson showed that "he is a full believer in Christianity," and only deplored that Brownson should "so piously, and pathetically, and eloquently invoke the genuis of Christianity" wrongheadedly. He added: "We here take the liberty to remark that we freely award him the virtue of *sincerity*. However enthusiastic he may be, he is not a hypocrite, for no hypocrite can be an enthusiast."[37]

"The Laboring Classes" also evoked many anxious letters from prominent political figures of the day. His friend, John C. Calhoun, who shared his own sentiments concerning northern industrialism, liked much of the article, including its anticlerical thrusts, but admonished him to reexamine his doctrine on the hereditary descent of property.[38] George Bancroft also expressed himself quite similarly. Blamed for still keeping Brownson in office (at the Marine Hospital in Chelsea), he kept his promise to Brownson that he would not interfere with the freedom of his pen, and replied that "the Democracy of Massachusetts is no more responsible for Brownson's notions, than the Whigs for the Mormons."[39] Charles Sumner wrote W. Whewell of Trinity College, Cambridge: "Brownson has recently avowed some strange doctrines, for which he has been sadly badgered, both by politicians and philosophers."[40] Stalwart old John Quincy Adams, though but recently eulogized by Brownson in grand style,[41] pondered the situation pensively, and sneeringly wrote off "Brownson and the Marat Democrats" with other plausible rascalities "of the day such as the transcendentalists, the abolitionists and phrenologists."[42]

But the reverberations of "The Laboring Classes" was loudest of all down in the arena of practical politics. There it created something like pandemonium in the ranks of the Democrats. Martin Van Buren was running for a second term for the presidency, and the Whigs had picked William Henry Harrison, the hero of "Tippecanoe" in the Indian wars, for their presidential candidate. The two parties were just coming to mortal grips in one of the most fiercely fought battles in American presidential campaigns. Any untoward incident might turn the tide disastrously for either party. Gleefully then did the Whigs pounce upon Brownson's essay on "The Laboring Classes" when it appeared. At last they had proof positive of the true colors of the Democrats. They were a subversive party who would bring ruin to the whole country were its destiny entrusted to their hands. They had Brownson's essay reprinted by the thousands and tens of thousands and distributed throughout the country as a socialistic flag hoisted by a prominent Democrat.[43] The Democrats stood aghast at the mischief which had so suddenly befallen them. When the high command of the party attempted to call him off, he turned a deaf ear, and there was nothing left to do but disown him. To what extent he contributed to Van Buren's defeat in the November elections is beyond any accurate calculation, but Brownson himself recorded later that Van Buren had ascribed to him "personally the principal share in his defeat."[44] As this belongs to the area of imponderables one would not expect any mention of it by historians.

It goes without saying that an old warrior like Brownson would not be unduly disturbed by the resounding uproar attendant upon the publication of "The Laboring Classes." In fact, as his son records, "Brownson himself seemed to feel a proud consciousness of the free spirit that dares to say plainly and openly what it believes is true and right, at every peril."[45] The publication of the essay did, however, bring upon him one particular hardship. Those who had been collaborating with him on his *Review* now quietly shied away from him. So far in this year, 1840, contributors had supplied eight of the seventeen articles in his *Review*.[46] The resourceful editor was now reduced to the necessity of filling out the entire issue for October, unassisted. This he adroitly managed by publishing two sermons he had preached two or three years previously.[47] The fact that he was abandoned for the time by his former collaborators may well have momentarily increased his mounting indignation at the harsh manner in which some of his critics had dealt with him. In any case, Hercules now turned to meet his assailants point by point in a powerful ninety-eight-page rejoinder. Speaking of the affair in the *Convert,* he wrote:

> The manner in which I was assailed aroused for a moment my indignation, and made me resolve, contrary to my original intention, to defend myself, and to show that I could more than regain before the public the position I had lost. I defended my essay at length and with vigor in the following number of my *Review,* and silenced the noisy clamors raised against me. I retained and enlarged my audience, and assumed a higher tone and position than I had ever before held, though not without making the greatest intellectual efforts, and using all the arts of popularity I was capable of. I felt in those times, that to be popular or unpopular, is simply a matter of one's own choice.[48]

# 14

## BROWNSON'S DEFENSE OF HIS ESSAY ON 'THE LABORING CLASSES'

*He rebuts the charge of disloyalty to party • He clearly shows the falsity of the confused charge that he had called for the abolition of Christianity • He opts for the absorption of the church by the state • He explains his views on religious worship and his criticism of the Christian ministry, both Catholic and Protestant • He has nothing to recant in the withering indictment he had made of the mercantile and industrial system • He explains what he had said in favor of the system of slave labor • He deals with the remedies proposed for benefiting the conditions of the laboring classes • He discusses the hereditary descent of property • He replies to the female operatives of the textile mills of Lowell • He repeats his dire warning of the consequences should the cause of the laboring classes be ignored • Comments by Arthur M. Schlesinger, Jr., Harold Laski, Charles C. Hollis, Leonard Gilhooley and Brownson himself seventeen years later.*

It would indeed be difficult for anyone to capture the spirit of the powerful rhetoric and force of logic that went into Brownson's essay on "The Laboring Classes" or to furnish an adequate idea of the masterly reply he made to his critics. They must be read to be appreciated for the literary *tour de force* they are, whatever the social heresies mixed in with his thought. There is a reason why he said his reply "silenced the noisy clamors raised against me."[1] Leonard J. McCarthy remarks that " 'The Laboring Classes' is Brownson's most sustained piece of argumentation. In it we have seen that he uses all the proofs of argumentation: induction, deduction, analogy and refutation. And in the second article he uses all the forms of refutation, direct by denial, distinction and retort; the indirect by the *argumentum ad hominem,* and the *reductio ad absurdum.*"[2] All that can be done in this chapter is to touch upon some of the salient points this master logician made in his rejoinder and to furnish a few estimates of his essay on "The Laboring Classes" by knowledgeable commentators.

Brownson began his reply by dealing with the charge that he had been a traitor to the Democratic party. He denied flatly any responsibility to the party. In casting his lot with that party he had made no agreement to be a slave to the party. As a thinking man he had reserved to himself the right to sit in judgment on any and all measures that party might propose, and the right to promote or reject the same at his own discretion. He had made no pledge to refrain from proposing any measure the party might not approve. The party, therefore, had no grounds as a party to chastise him. He reaffirmed his perennial rule for judging any measure: Is it right, is it just? "We approve no measure because it is a measure of this or that party. It is not the party that recommends the measure, but the measure that recommends the party."[3] He was prepared to act with the Democratic party generally only insofar as it was through that party he could hope to realize such legislative reforms as are needed to carry into practice the great doctrine of equality to which the American people stand pledged. He utterly proscribed the rule, "Go with your party whatever the measures it puts forth."[4]

But to the politicians, his essay was above all regrettably ill-timed. To publish it when he did, just when an important national election was pending, was highly injudicious. If he was to publish it at all, it should have been at a time other than on the eve of an exciting election. As it was, its author ran the risk of ruining the chances of the party with which he was associated. After asserting that he had never believed that "anything we could write would have much influence on an election," our stern moralist replied to this that the success of no party could be counted worthwhile that is endangered by the fearless utterance of a salutary truth, even though its application might be still in the distant future. Success bought by the suppression of truth is more disastrous than defeat. The time for proclaiming a truth is when its importance is clearly perceived, when it is pressing on the heart and demanding utterance in clear and earnest tones. "The world is lying in wickedness," he exclaimed, "great social wrongs obtain; man is everywhere suffering by the hand of man; and what are they doing, who should be bold and invincible reformers? . . . In the language of Jesus, we say, 'Lift up your eyes, look on the fields; for behold, they are white already to the harvest.' . . . Always it is the time to war against sin and Satan; always is it the time to proclaim truth, and discomfort error."[5]

All this is ingeniously well said, but a man of Brownson's intelligence could not but recognize also that it was something of a *faux pas* for him to have published his essay when he did. In a postscript to his October edition he stated that he had months previously really intended to close the publication of his *Review* with the October issue. And it was on that score that the appearance of his article on the laboring classes at the precise time of great political excitement was to be explained. For had he intended to continue his *Review* for another year, he might well have postponed his discussion of the laboring classes until the next year and thus have pleased his political associates better. But he had had certain things pressing on him for utterance which he knew he could say in no journal but one of his own, and for that reason he had made sure of his opportunity while his *Review* was still current. Yet, all in all, he could not regret that he had spoken out when he did, for the interests of the workingmen have been everlastingly delayed to accommodate the politicians. The vast army of workers have no medium through which to plead their cause, and whoever can speak for them and will not, is a traitor to God and man. To him the progress of their cause was paramount to the triumph of any political party, and he could value no party triumph except insofar as it aided that cause.[6]

Although Brownson asserts that "the gravamen of my offense [in his essay on 'The Laboring Classes'] was my condemnation of the modern industrial system, especially the system of labor and wages,"[7] he nevertheless began his rejoinder to his critics with a refutation of the grave charge that he had proposed the abolition of Christianity in his essay. Such a charge, he asserted, was an unblushing perversion of his language, unwarranted by anything he had ever written in his *Review*. He reminded his assailants that it was just ten years previous that very autumn that he had publicly announced his conversion to the Christian faith, and that since that time he had neither entertained nor uttered any doubt about the truth of the Christian religion. "No man in this country has preached or written more," he affirmed, "during these last ten years to defend Christianity . . . than the Editor of this *Review*."[8] He had distinguished, it is true, between the Christianity of the church and the Christianity of Christ, the former he held in low esteem, the latter he loved and reverenced, but that was quite another thing. As he conceded the right of others to interpret Christianity for themselves, so he claimed that right just as stoutly for himself. If his version of Christianity was more like the Christianity of the first century than the nineteenth, he could scarcely expect that his views would not appear heretical to a large portion of the Christians of the nineteenth century. Yet whatever the case, Brownson said, let those who bring the charge of infidel against us, look into our writings, and they will find there "distinct avowals of our belief in the inspiration of the Old and New Testament; in the Reality of miracles; the Deity of Christ, and the Holy Ghost; in the Trinity,"[9] and the other fundamental doctrines of the Christian creed.

Far from having called for the abolition of Christianity, he had said distinctly, he emphasized: "We are Christians, and that it is only by following out the Christian law, and the example of the early Christians, that we can hope to effect anything": and he had added, "The second step we propose in the work of elevating the laboring classes is, we say there [in his former article] 'to resuscitate the Christianity of Christ.' "[10] He could then have little respect for the intellectual acumen of readers who from what he had written inferred that he proposed to elevate the proletary by destroying Christianity.

He had always spoken of Christianity as favoring, rather as even demanding, the moral and social elevation of the masses. Democracy he had often defined as nothing but the application of the principles of the Gospel to the social and political affairs of life. His great aim all along had been to Christianize democracy, and to *democratize,* if the word was permissible, the church.[11] It had been a leading doctrine with him that Jesus was a social reformer, that the aim of his mission was to establish the reign of equality on earth, as well as to secure the salvation of the soul hereafter. When entering upon public life, he had found the advocates of social reform at war with religion, and the friends of religion at war with social reformers. If there was anything distinctive about his writings, it was that they sought to reconcile the disciple of Jesus with the social reformer, to bring out Christianity in bold relief as the means of social reform, and to enlist the church on the side of the downtrodden masses. He had long been laboring to do in this country precisely what Abbé de Lamennais had been laboring to do in France. Almost at the very moment that de Lamennais had been writing his *Words of a Believer,* he himself, without knowing there was such a man on earth, was writing his essay on "Christianity and Reform," which advocated in sober prose substantially the same doctrines that glowed in that inspired poem. His essay on "Christianity and Reform" was written in 1833, and published in 1834 in the *Unitarian,* a Unitarian journal. In that essay he had labored "to prove that no salutary reform can be effected by infidelity, and that the spirit of reform is the very spirit of the Gospel."[12] To support his assertions he quoted copiously from that essay.

He acknowledged that he had been contending for years now for truly radical reforms, not in government and politics only, but in society itself, reforms which go far beyond anything as yet dreamt of by the Democratic party itself. But those reforms he had demanded not in his own name, or on his own authority, but in the name and on the authority of God. He surmised that it was precisely that which had offended his conservative brethren. They professed to be Christians, and he had scathingly arraigned them for their type of Christianity which could allow such callous indifference to the unrelieved oppression and pining misery of the underprivileged classes of society. Theirs was not the Christianity of Christ. There was between their Christianity and that of Christ a great gulf indeed, as wide and deep as that which separated the rich man in hell from the poor beggar lodged by angels in Abraham's bosom. "In the name of Christ," he thundered, "we summon the community to answer for its Christianity, to show that it is really Christian, or else to abandon its pretensions to the Christian name. Is this infidelity? Then we are infidels. Is this to prove ourselves hostile to the Christianity of Christ? Then we are hostile to it."[13]

Making again his distinction between the Christianity of Christ and the Christianity of the church, Brownson frankly owned to his critics that he aimed at the replacement of the Christianity of the church with a new organization. This new organization he had already foreshadowed in *New Views* in 1836 when speaking of the church and the state, but he sketched it more clearly in his article on the "Tendency of Modern Civilization."[14] He now called again not only for the union of church and state but for the unity, the identity of the two, or the absorption of the church by the state. The church Christ had come to found, he insisted, was in reality an inward, a spiritual kingdom, but had been mistaken for an outward, visible church. The church, therefore, had developed into a corporate, independent society of its own, distinct from civil society, or the state. Hence the double organization of society — each with its own set of officers, one for the spiritual and the other for the temporal needs of its members. Now to this *double* organization of society he strenuously demurred. He would have a single organization, and this organization should be called not the church, but the state. This would indeed destroy the church as a *separate,* or distinct organization, but it would do so by transferring to the state the moral ideas on which the church had professedly been founded, but which the church had failed to bring to fruition.[15] With the sagacity of the master tactician in argument, he added:

> This [new organization] would realize that idea of a "Christian Commonwealth," after which our Puritan fathers so earnestly and perseveringly struggled. . . . [These views] are nothing but the views of the first settlers of this state, developed and systematized, and freed from the theological phraseology in which they were expressed. We are true to their idea, to their spirit, and are laboring to realize that which they most desired. We therefore remind those who profess to reverence our Puritan ancestors, that they would do well to study the history and opinions of those ancestors, and forbear to censure us, till they are prepared to condemn them.[16]

The further charge that he would dispense with religious worship he met with a glowing passage, well-buttressed with scriptural language, on what to him was true worship of God. He averred that he contended as strongly as any man for religious worship, but to him religious worship was something more than psalm-singing and a little sermonizing, something more than what is called "Sabbath worship of God." He would carry his religious worship into all the highways and byways of life to be interwoven with all the human relationships that make up the complexity of life. It was on this crucial score that he felt so many Christians were only nominal Christians. For their special benefit he quoted the Apostle St. James on true worship of God: " 'Pure worship (for so the original should be rendered),' says St. James, and 'undefiled before God the Father, is to visit the fatherless and widows in their tribulations, and to keep oneself unspotted from the world.' ''[17] This to him was pure and elevated morality. He then spelled out further what he understood by genuine worship of God by enumerating what is known in the Catholic catechism as the Corporal and Spiritual Works of Mercy. In a word, true worship of God means to seek to redress all individual and social wrongs, and to cultivate in the heart the reign of truth, justice and love.

In matters of religion, the assailed editor had still to answer for his temerity in proposing the abolition of the priesthood. By the priest, he indicated again, he meant not only the Catholic priest but the clergymen of all denominations. He knew that the bizarre proposal he had made could raise him up "a numerous and powerful host of foes." He used up twenty solid pages of his essay in discussing the office of the clergy from every possible angle. He explained that he was not opposed to teachers of religion as such, or ministers of the Gospel. He would have more of such, not less; more congregations, not less. His quarry in this case were preachers of religion as members of "an ecclesiastical corporation" in which a numerous class of men derive their revenue. "We believe," he said, "the time has come when the clerical profession, *as a separate profession,* a sort of trade, is no longer needed. . . . We war then not against the preaching of the Gospel, but against the preaching of the Gospel as a trade, a regular business, from which a numerous class are to derive their revenue."[18] It seems his shafts were here directed at the clergy as a privileged class in society, as he saw it. In line with this criticism he thought the best feature of the Catholic Church was its denial to the clergy of the option to marry. It had thus prevented its clergy from ever developing into a priestly caste such as existed in India and Judea. This same idea, namely, that "it was the celibacy of the clergy alone which prevented them from forming a caste like those of India," had also been expressed by the distinguished French statesman and historian, Francois M. Guizot, in his *General History of the Civilization of Europe.*[19] As to the ministry of the word, Brownson preferred the practice which obtains among the Quakers. Each one speaks when a word presses on his heart for utterance.

Although he was indisposed to allow the necessity of the clerical profession, as a separate profession, he was somewhat partial in attesting the utility of the Catholic priest because of that Church's elaborate *cultus.* That Church has an imposing liturgy, he acknowledged, which cannot be carried out without priests. Priests are necessary to administer the sacraments, which are seven. In that Church the sacramental ministrations of the priest are needed from the cradle to the grave if the soul is to know salvation. He owned then some show of propriety in the Catholic Church in having priests, because there is a considerable work for them to do for the worship of God which the individual cannot do for himself. The same he acknowledged to be true to a degree in the Anglican Church.[20]

He had also a deal to say about the impossibility of the clergy measuring up "faithfully and honestly" to the duties customarily expected of them, with the implication that it all argued against the existence of a separate clerical profession. He deplored in particular that subservient status of the Protestant clergyman, pointing out that he is utterly dependent on the congregation which employs him; that he must cautiously tailor his words to the tastes, habits and interests of the various groups in his congregation, whether stockholders, bankers, factory owners, railroad magnates or whatnot, or he will not be paid his salary or be any longer retained in their service. There is then only this alternative before the clergyman: "Either to preach to suit his people, or to be sullied in reputation, and sent supperless to bed. Need we doubt which alternative the majority will take? . . . We believe that most men are disposed to turn an eye to their bread and butter, and few have the courage to look hunger in the face and bid it welcome to them, and especially to a wife and little ones they tenderly love. . . . This is no fancy sketch. Every clergyman knows, or may know, the truth of what we say. We have ourselves been in the ministry, and have had some opportunities of making observations."[21]

Coming to the economic thought in his former essay, Brownson dealt with the charge that his account of the conditions of the working classes was exaggerated and false. He asserted that the objection would have much more weight with him were it not urged exclusively by those who live by availing themselves of the labors of the workingmen, and who, therefore, have a stake in keeping them as they are. He had nothing to recant in his withering indictment of the modern mercantile and industrial system with its enslavement of the laboring classes. He acknowledged that he had read with as much attention and patience as could be expected of him the various arguments with which his thought had been assailed. In response to his assailants he suggested that he himself may well have studied the subject longer and on more sides than they had. Their arguments merely amused him with their simplicity, or grieved him with their ignorance. He claimed a point of vantage over his critics: he had been born and reared in the class of the proletaries, and there was a formidable presumption that he knew precisely whereof he spoke in what he had written. "Our good friends," he counseled, "would do well to brush up their ideas, purge their vision, and look a little deeper into the subject." He noted that those who were loudest in their denunciation of him were the *nouveaux riches, parvenus,* upstarts, who had themselves come up from the ranks of the proletaries, and had then made it a virtue to forget "the rock from whence they were hewn." Standing now on the shoulders of their former associates, they have precious little chance to see what is going on at the bottom of the social organization. To learn that, he tartly suggested, one must interrogate those at the bottom and who feel the pressure. "One does not interrogate the rider in order to ascertain the sensations the horse has in being ridden."[22]

He filled up several pages with his massive thought and incisive rhetoric on the inequalities and hardships that our modern capitalistic society works on the defenseless poor. Utterly scorning as rank blasphemy the allegation that the downtrodden are such by the appointment of God, he punctuated his thought with a citation of the famous passage in which St. James so fiercely indicts those who defraud the laborer of his hire. "A terrible book for you, ye scribes and pharisees, ye rich and great of this world, is this same New Testament," he exclaimed. "Be sure now," he jabbed, "to call him an infidel who reads you this terrible book, just as the thief, when the hue and cry is up, is loudest in calling out 'stop thief,' that he may turn the pursuit from himself."[23]

He dealt in turn with the objection that he had expressed a preference for the slave system of labor in the South over the system of wages in the North. To clarify matters, he explained that he had never pretended that the proletary is not in advance of the slave. His rights are in fact legally recognized, though not yet fully enjoyed; he is nearer his complete enfranchisement, and has a better status in society. It was only on the supposition that if one or the other of the two systems were to become permanent in the country, that he had expressed a preference for the system of slave labor in the South — as securing more advantages to the laborer. But he opposed both systems with all his might. He would have neither. "We would combine labor and capital in the same individual," he emphasized. What he was opposing was the division of society into two classes, of which one class owns the capital, and the other performs all the labor. He stressed that in preferring the slave labor of the South to the free labor of the North he was by no means alone. He had conversed with many intelligent mechanics of the city, and they had all with one voice agreed with him. Why, he asked, are so few of the real workingmen of the North abolitionists? Because they feel that they themselves are virtually slaves, while mocked with the name of freemen, and that movements in behalf of freedom should begin with themselves. They had applauded him just in proportion as the upper classes had condemned him.[24]

He freely acknowledged that the law declares workingmen equal to the other members of society, but what avails such a declaration of the law if those in whose favor it is written cannot take advantage of it? What avails a mere theoretical recognition of their rights if workingmen lack the power to make those rights respected. Nor is the law, after all, so impartial as some would pretend. He furnished damning evidence when he said:

> In the state of New York, laborers have been fined and imprisoned for refusing to work at wages offered them; or rather, for agreeing together, not to sell their labor unless at a higher price than they had hitherto been paid. Yet manufacturers, floor dealers, physicians, and lawyers, may band together on the same principle, for a similar end, form their Trade Unions, and no law is violated.[25]

After showing how the laws of the country bear with peculiar severity on the poor, he assured his readers that it was nevertheless no intention of his to be stirring up the wrath of the laboring classes against other members of society. His forbearance in the case made his conservative brethren his debtors. For if he were so disposed, they would find him speaking in far different tones, and making an appeal "which would be responded to from every section of the country, in no soft, lulling strains, but with one burst of indignation, which should ring, as a summons to the last judgment, on the heart of every man who would lord it over his brother." But he could find no delight in such appeals, nor pleasure in such responses. Looking at society compassionately, he was quite willing to acknowledge whence it had become what it is. It was the growth of ages. No one man, no one class of men was responsible for its vices and corruptions. All classes in society were victims of the systems and organizations which had come down from the past. If he deplored the condition of the laborer, he by no means envied the capitalist. He knew not which to pity the most. The cry of distress comes to us from all classes, he said. All are in a false position; all are out of their true condition, as free, high-minded, virtuous men. He called upon all classes to look at things as they are, and set themselves earnestly to work, and in good faith, to find the proper remedies, and apply them.[26]

He admitted, likewise, that the lot of the laboring classes was still somewhat better in our own country than in other lands. But this Brownson ascribed to accidental factors. The first of these was the original equality that had existed among the first settlers in an exclusive agricultural society. But that situation had vanished. A second factor, and the most important that had operated in favor of the laboring classes, was the former low price of land. An individual with only a small amount of capital had been able in the past to emerge from the class of mere laborers into the class of landowners. He pointed out at this time what Frederick Jackson Turner was to stress more than a century later, namely that the free lands of the country had been operating previously as "a safety valve"[27] for the underprivileged and oppressed classes. But they were now rapidly receding to the West, and their price was rising beyond the reach of all who did not have a certain amount of cash on hand. Moreover, said Brownson, "these new lands are not inexhaustible. Fifty years to come, if emigration go[es] on at the rate it has for fifty years past, will leave very little for the new emigrant."[28] (Turner says that the experiment period ended after four hundred years, 1492-1892. This jibes perfectly with Brownson's statement about "fifty years to come.") The predominance of agriculture in the country in the past had long prevented the stratification of American society, but with the incoming industrial era, the class lines were beginning to harden more and more. As our economic system was becoming ever more similar to that of England, Brownson could see nothing that would prevent a reproduction in this country of that sorry state of affairs in relation to our laboring population "that gangrenes English society."[29]

As to the remedies for improving the condition of the laboring classes, he enumerated those generally relied upon: universal suffrage and free trade as proposed by political reformers, universal education and religious culture as proposed by moral reformers. These remedies he owned to be good and necessary in themselves, but insufficient in their nature to bring about anything truly effective in behalf of the laboring classes unless coupled with something more radical. They would be mere palliatives. They would not go to the roots of the evils in the economic order.

Universal suffrage he could rate little better than a mockery where marked inequality abounds in society. He laid it down as a settled rule that "no matter what party you support, no matter what men you may select, property is always the basis of your governmental action. No policy has ever yet been pursued by our government, state or federal, under one party or the other, notwithstanding our system of universal suffrage, which has had for its aim the elevation of man, independent of his relation as a possessor of property."[30] In no instance do the rights of the proletary prevail over the interests of the proprietor. Our social critic considered it impossible, under the prevailing system, to separate power from property. Always will its interests predominate in the measure of government, though it may be defeated in elections. Even then it will triumph in the legislative halls, and at the tribunal of justice. The votes of the proletary, as he analyzed it, go mostly only to swell the final count for one party or the other. He admitted, of course, that universal suffrage is a right, something in itself, but he protested that it is by no means the sovereign remedy for the evils under which the laboring masses were suffering which shallow theorists seem to think.

Nor was the system of free trade any more efficacious in the case. He approved it, as advocated in the country, as an attempt at social amelioration, and acknowledged that it might possibly effect something that would help the underprivileged, but asserted that it would be fatuous to rely upon it alone as sufficient in the case. Only if competitors started even, with equal chances for success — which was not to be thought of in the present constitution of society — could it amount to anything. Besides, if the system of free trade were to go altogether uncontrolled, it would become a system of universal competition, of unrestrained selfishness and strife. Since the divorce of ethics from economics in the modern world individual selfishness has taken over in which dog eats dog and the devil takes the hindmost. He was disposed to limit the sphere of the government as much as possible, and enlarge that of the individual, but the *laissez-faire* policy would effect little in behalf of the laboring classes. As an organ and agency of society, government has a positive role to play, and cannot be dispensed with in the economic order. No, he could not hope to introduce an improved social order through a system in which selfishness and strife run riot.[31]

As to universal education and religious culture as remedies, he had faith in them indeed, but not as ultimate measures. Their office was to generate the moral force needed, but the generation of that force was not the needed reform itself. All reforms come from within, but they will remain insufficient unless brought out of the interior, and made an active force to remodel the exterior.[32] He emphasized again that he did not hold that these various proposed measures are not essential, indispensable means of social regeneration, but that if relied upon alone, they are sure to prove inadequate. Something more radical was required to eradicate the evils inherent in the present organization of society. His own plan would include these self-same measures, but would go much further. In short, his plan was still the abolition of the hereditary descent of property, a measure, he declared, foreshadowed, at least in his own mind, by almost every article he had written on social reform. He had long since been convinced that it was simply useless to talk about social reform, or to speak in behalf of the laborer, unless resort be had to some such measure. This measure he had contemplated for a long time.

He felt that the creed in general of the American people, which is opposed to all privilege, should favor such a measure. But he recommended it to the attention of the Democratic party in particular. To be consistent as a party, they should stand ready to implement it. In their convention at Worcester, Massachusetts, on September 20, 1837, they had adopted as a motto, "the party of equality against privilege." The hereditary descent of property is either a privilege or it is not a privilege, he argued. If it is not, if it confers no social advantage on him who inherits over him who does not, then it is valueless and to abolish it does harm to no one. If, however, it is a privilege, then the Democratic party should labor to abolish it, or abandon any such motto as "the party of equality against privilege." But the hereditary descent of property, unless the amount inherited by each individual can be rendered equal in some way, is undoubtedly a privilege. For it gives certain members of society an advantage over other members to which no special endowments of intellect or virtue entitle them. Hence his proposal for the abolition of the hereditary descent of property seemed to him merely a logical conclusion from the admitted premises of the American people, and, *a fortiori*, of the Democratic party.[33]

He owned that he had expected to be censured for his proposal of the measure, but confessed his surprise that it had appeared such a novelty to his countrymen. His assailants had reminded him that property is a sacred institution, and that to meddle with it in any way would be to unhinge the present order of society and perhaps set it back into a near savage stage. So claimed, too, he replied, the apologists of monarchy, of hereditary nobility, and of a hereditary priesthood, of primogeniture and entail, in the past. Yet society survives, and has the promise of as long life as ever. In a passage that antedated by a century President Franklin D. Roosevelt's emphasis on the priority of human rights over property rights, he said: "Now for ourselves, we are not quite so squeamish on this subject as some others are. We believe that property should be held subordinate to man, and not men to property: and therefore it is always lawful to make such modifications of its constitution as the good of Humanity requires."[34]

He proceeded to show by copious citations from a galaxy of the most eminent jurists that his proposal to abolish the hereditary descent of property, and to dispose of it by some equitable law to the next generation, is founded firmly in natural right. As he stated later: "Nearly all jurists maintain that the testamentary right, by which a man disposes of his goods after his death, as well as that by which a child inherits from the parent, is a municipal, not a natural right."[35] He made his proposal a bit more palatable to his countrymen, however, when he claimed qualified fellowship in the matter with Thomas Jefferson:

> The proposition of our article, which gave so much offense, is virtually the same with Jefferson's. He says, "the portion occupied by any individual ceases to be his, when he himself ceases to be, and reverts to society." We say, "a man's power over his property must cease with his life, and his property then becomes the property of the state, to be disposed of by some equitable law, for the use of the generation that takes his place." Jefferson merely declares what is the natural law on this subject; and we, that the actual arrangements of society should be conformed to that law. This is all the difference there is between us in principle, although he, in laying down the principle, had one object in view, and we another.[36]

Amid the reckless incrimination heaped upon him, he found it necessary to explain that it was no part of his plan to see to it that each individual would be provided in his lifetime with an equal share of possessions, the indolent and the improvident faring just as well as the industrious and thrifty. He was not contending against inequality of property, but would only contrive that each one be given an equal chance at the start of life. The rest would depend upon the exertions or industry of each individual. He had never been known in his life to contend for equality of possessions, nor against inequality of property. It was not the inequality introduced by difference of character, of talent, or aptitude for the accumulation of property, that he was warring against, but that which is brought about by the laws of society. Let all be treated as equals, and after that, let each one be treated according to his works. But it was not yet so.[37]

Brownson found himself attacked also from what was probably an unexpected quarter. It is not surprising that he should have had something to say in his original essay on "The Laboring Classes" about the conditions under which eight thousand girls were working as operatives in the textile mills of nearby Lowell. That his indictment of conditions there may have been a bit inaccurate may be due to the fact that he had possibly made no personal inspection of the mills, but had judged from exterior impressions and had gone by report. Nevertheless, he was no doubt convinced that he was substantially correct when he wrote:

> We pass through our manufacturing villages, most of them appear neat and flourishing. The operatives are well dressed, and we are told, well paid. They are said to be healthy, contented, and happy. This is the fair side of the picture; the side exhibited to visitors. There is a dark side, moral as well as physical. Of the common operatives few, if any, by their wages acquire a competence. . . . The great mass wear out their health, their spirits, and morals, without becoming one whit better off than when they commenced labor. The bill of mortality in these factory villages is not striking, we admit, for the poor girls when they

can toil no longer go home to die. The average life, the working life we mean, of girls that come to Lowell, for instance, from Maine, New Hampshire, and Vermont, we have been assured is only three years. What becomes of them then? Few of them marry; fewer still ever return to their native places with reputation unimpaired. "She has worked in a factory," is almost enough to damn to infamy the most worthy and virtuous girl. We know no sadder sight on earth than one of our factory villages presents when the bell at break of day, or at the hour of breakfast or dinner, calls out its hundreds, or thousands of operatives. We stand and look at these hard-working men and women hurrying in all directions, and ask ourselves where go the proceeds of their labors?[38]

Although the shafts of this criticism were really aimed at the owners and operators of the Lowell mills, it is quite understandable that at least some of the girls in the mills felt themselves besmirched by what the Boston editor had said. They had their own publication, *The Lowell Offering,* and this was used as a vehicle to get back at him. One of the more gifted girls, Miss Harriet Farley, the editor, took up the cudgels to defend their honor in the December 1840 issue. It is doubtful whether she could take in the larger issues involved in Brownson's whole essay, but the loose charge of immorality among the girls was not to be endured. She apparently did perceive, however, that Brownson's essay was by and large a frontal attack on the factory system itself, for her rejoinder was in large measure an apology for the conditions prevalent in the Lowell mills; as to the charge of immorality, she refuted it in high dudgeon, and called upon Brownson to "prove his words, if he can." Yet she added meekly enough:

> But it may be remarked, "you certainly do not mean to intimate that all factory girls are virtuous, intelligent, etc." No, I do not; and Lowell would be a stranger place than it has been presented, if among 8,000 girls there were none of the ignorant and depraved. Calumniators have asserted, that *all* are vile, because they know some to be.[39]

When Miss Farley spoke of "calumniators" she was evidently not referring to just Brownson. On July 13 of the previous year (1839), an article had appeared in the *Boston Daily Times* on the health and morals of the operatives of the Lowell mills. The writer claimed that the girls there lived in an unhealthy environment, were worn down by long hours, and had only poor and inadequate food, so much so that they soon became "pale, feeble, and finally broken in constitution." He went on to charge that great numbers of loose women came to work in the mills, and that innocent operatives were often seduced. He added: "There has been and there is now growing up in Lowell a manufacturing population whose tendency in the scale of civilization, health, and morals, and intellectually, is manifestly downward."[40] This may well have been the source upon which Brownson partly relied in some of the things he had said. If we remember, too, that the purpose of his whole essay had been to point up the neglected rights of the undefended laborer, we will probably have the explanation of why his picture of the Lowell operatives may possibly have been a bit overdrawn.

The charges of both the *Times* and Brownson regarding the health and morals of the Lowell operatives were not to go unnoticed by those whom they pilloried. No less a person than Dr. Elisha Bartlett, who was the first mayor of Lowell after its incorporation as a city, came to a pious defense of the Lowell mills. He painted a roseate picture of the conditions there, maintaining that the girls were quite well off in every respect. After animadverting on Bartlett's "impressive misuse of the scientific method, considering he was a doctor," Miss Hannah Josephson remarked that "Bartlett's white-wash only stimulated controversy," being followed shortly by an article of "A Citizen of Lowell" in *Vox Populi,* who described Bartlett's reasoning as silly, his figures distorted, and the man himself as a "servant of the aristocracies." The "Citizen" named specific abuses: "Long hours, desperately hurried meals, filth and vermin in the boarding houses."[41]

To a reproving letter Brownson had received from the Lowell operatives, he replied at length. In part only he wrote:

> To the Editors of "The Lowell Offering"
> Ladies:
>
> I have received the first and second numbers of your periodical, for which I beg to thank you to accept my thanks. Your paper is conducted with spirit and ability, and I read it with pleasure. I am particularly interested in it, for I am told it is written entirely by girls employed in the mills. It is highly creditable to their talents and taste, and may turn out to be of no slight advantage to them.
>
> I perceive, ladies, that you labor under a slight mistake in regard to me. You seem to have taken it into your heads that I am hostile to you and have slandered you. If I may be allowed to be my own interpreter, I have had no thought of speaking disrespectfully of you. My sympathies are with the laboring classes, and I have done what I could to ameliorate the condition of both workingmen and workingwomen. I have been an operative myself for no small portion of my life; I have no sympathy with the aristocracy; I have burned with indignation at the injustice done to those who are obliged to support themselves by their own labor; and this indignation I have expressed as best I could; and for expressing it I have fallen under the condemnation of your masters and employers. This alone, it would seem, should be sufficient to satisfy you that I have had no intention of slandering you.
>
> The passage which has offended you I think you must have misinterpreted. I have said nothing against you; I have merely spoken of the injustice the world does you; and I have represented that injustice great enough to "damn to infamy" the most worthy and virtuous girl, if she be a factory girl. Now it may be possible that the feeling I have spoken of is not as strong as I have represented it; but if you will read the article in which my remark appears you will perceive, I think, that my object was to rebuke your employers and the community generally, not to speak ill of you.
>
> My offense consists solely in saying that there is in the community an unjust prejudice against girls employed in factories. . . . That there is a prejudice against you I know, and that it is *unjust* I have not a doubt. . . . I have never charged it to you or your fault, nor have I ever so regarded it. I charge it to the factory system. I am opposed to that system, and opposed to it, among other reasons, because it subjects you to the prejudice of which I have spoken. . . .
>
> I am contending for social reform; I would put "the plough in the owner's hand," and also the spindle and the loom. Your employers do not wish for this change. I wish you, the operatives, to be not only operatives but owners. For this I am laboring. Do you not see then that I am laboring for you against your employers? Do not then be caught in their trap. Do not war for your natural enemies against your friends.[42]

Having met with singular vigor and force the objections of his assailants to the contents of his original essay on "The Laboring Classes," he now concluded his rejoinder by repeating his previous dire warning. The conservatives themselves were driving the masses into revolt by fighting against all reforms, and by their stern repression of all aspirations for a better social order: "The Past has always stood in the gate, and forbid the Future to enter; and it has only been in mortal encounter, that the Future has ever been able to force its entrance." In England, in France and throughout Europe, an armed soldiery was holding down the lid on an explosive order of things. In Asia and Africa, too, there were signs of great unrest and disaffection with the reigning order. While warlike preparations were everywhere going forward, iniquitous speculators were already contriving how they could turn the coming conflict to their own pecuniary advantage. His dire warning he could not repress:

> If a general war should now break out [he cautioned] it will involve all quarters of the globe, and it will be in the end more than a war between nations. It will resolve itself into a social war, a war between the two social elements; between the aristocracy and the democracy, between the people and their masters. It will be a terrible war! Already does it lower on the horizon, and, though the storm be long in gathering, it will roll its massive folds over the whole heavens, and break in fury upon the earth. Stay it, ye who can. For ourselves we merely stand on the watch-tower, and report what we see.[43]

Arthur M. Schlesinger, Jr., calls "The Laboring Classes" an "extraordinary performance." Specifically he said:

> It is clear, direct, compelling and brilliant, written with an intensity of emotion that occasionally burns into genuine eloquence. As analysis or as polemic, it deserves a high place in revolutionary literature. Brownson actually was a revolutionist only in the sense that he thought the class struggle was not to be resolved by prayer and kindliness. . . . Though inferior as a systematic thinker to Marx, Brownson on the whole surpassed him as a pamphleteer. He discriminated between condemnation and invective, and almost never suffered the lapses of taste which have filled Marx's pamphlets with cheap sarcasm and personal abuse.[44]

As Schlesinger observes, Brownson "actually was a revolutionist only in the sense that he thought the class struggle was not to be resolved by prayer and kindliness." His prediction that revolution would come unless the dire grievances of the laboring classes were redressed — though it might be long in coming — was a prophecy, not an expressed wish or intended incitement as has been asserted. His warning words referred evidently more to other lands than to his own, for he had acknowledged that the plight of the masses was worse abroad than at home. If we recall the revolutions that erupted all over Europe in 1848, in France, in Germany, in Hungary and Italy, and those subsequent in that century, culminating eventually in the great revolt of the masses in Russia and other lands in our own century, perhaps Brownson's jeremiad is not wholly without significance. For practically all wars are at bottom economic in origin. Whatever the case, Brownson's savage onslaught on the widespread economic evils of the day led some to label him a "Jacobin," and the "American Robespierre." To which he replied that he liked those names, and asserted that if ever he could find sufficient leisure, he intended to immortalize the *sansculottes* in a novel, to be called "The Jacobin," of which Robespierre shall be the hero.[45] For a man who believed so strongly in authority and order, this retort, as Leonard Gilhooley has suggested, may well be written off as a flippant specimen of *ad hoc journalism.*[46]

Schlesinger also asserts that Brownson was Marx's "nearest forerunner in America."[47] Already two years before the publication of "The Laboring Classes" in 1840, Brownson had penetrated the intricacies of the economic problem. As Schlesinger states the matter: "The analysis that Orestes

Brownson arrived at is perhaps disconcerting to a generation which believes that Marx invented the Marxian theory of history. In 1838, a decade before the Communist Manifesto, Brownson interpreted history in the terms of the inescapable conflict between those who profited by the existing order and those on whom its burden chiefly fell."[48] Harold Laski likewise observed that "Orestes Brownson, in those remarkable papers which preceded his conversion to the Roman Catholic Church, is predicting, on lines not very dissimilar from those of Marx and Engels at the time, the approaching catastrophe through the struggle between the classes in America."[49] He also called Brownson an "intellectual giant"[50] in the field of social analysis. But Professor H. S. Foxwell, in his long introduction to Anton Menger's *The Right to the Whole Produce of Labor,* when referring to Brownson's essay on "The Laboring Classes," is not entirely accurate when he says: "This is socialism of the true Marxian type."[51] Widely different from Brownson's economic philosophy, Marxism is dedicated to the overthrow of all existing governments, world revolution and the abolition of private property. The difference between the two social philosophies is the difference between freedom and slavery: personal freedom is largely an adjunct of private ownership while a propertyless proletariat are the abject slave of an omnipotent state.[52]

Writing seventeen years later, Brownson tells us that he had had his object in publishing his essay on "The Laboring Classes" when he did. At the persuasion of friends, he had thrown in his lot with the Democratic party in the hope that he might use it as an instrument for the realization of his own plans for social reform. But the more prominent he became in the party, the less he found himself disposed to insist upon his own doctrines of social reform, and the less free he felt to follow his own convictions. The highest offices in the state and nation seemed open to him, at least so his vanity suggested, that is, if he wished to make use of all the arts and skills by which such offices are often attained. But to be successful in such a career, he would have to give up his personal freedom and independence, and to follow as well as lead the party. He admitted, too, that he was beginning to feel the workings of political ambition, and scarcely dared to trust himself any longer. Were affairs to go on thus much longer, he would forget all his early dreams, abandon the work to which he had pledged himself, and become so enmeshed in party politics that he could no longer return to his work without compromising his friends, his party and perhaps himself. There was one way out, the shortest and the best: to come out and state in the most startling manner all his ulterior thought without any concealment whatsoever. As to the result, though he spoke of alternatives, he knew beforehand there could be but one reaction:

> If the party accepts my views, which of course it will not, well and good; if not, as will be the case, the party ties will be broken, and I shall be free to publish my honest opinions without fear of compromising anybody but myself. I shall be free to act as I think proper, unshackled by party obligations, or even personal friendships. Such were my reasons, avowed to those who shared my confidence, before the article was written. For my party the act was impolitic; for myself it was necessary and prudent. I look back on it today as the least discreditable act I had hitherto performed; and there was something in it bordering on moral heroism, which has not been without its reward.[53]

Brownson further states that he could not reread his original essay on the laboring classes without feeling shocked, and wondering at his temerity in ever having published it. Yet even now (1857), he affirmed, "Place me outside the Catholic Church, with only Protestant and democratic principles for my guide, and I would today repeat and endorse every paragraph and every word I then wrote." Never had he been truer to himself than when he had made a clean breast of it all in that essay. It had marked a crisis in his mental disease, and from its publication he dated his convalescence. From a heavy load which had been accumulating for years, it had freed him. He had never once calculated what the publication of the essay might cost him, for, as he informs us, "I had one principle, and only one, to which, since throwing up Universalism, I had been faithful, a principle for which I had perhaps made some sacrifice: that of following my honest convictions whithersoever they might lead."[54] This is the sentence which his friend and lifelong associate, Fr. Isaac T. Hecker, said "is so perfect an epitome of the man that it should be put on his monument."[55]

Perhaps nothing in his essay seemed more radical than his reflections on the hereditary descent of property. Yet he insisted, as we have noted, that it had not been thrown out for immediate adoption, but merely for free discussion, as he himself realized there was no question of its ready acceptance. We shall perhaps understand this bold venture better if we keep in mind that he was still embarked on his quixotic enterprise of introducing a paradise on earth for his fellowmen. He had long been under the spell of the French comet, Saint-Simon. In the April edition of his *Review* for this same year, 1840, he had given an exposition of the doctrines of the Saint-Simonians, stating their affirmation of the right of private ownership, but their opposition to the hereditary descent of property.[56] For a full dozen years he had given all his days and all his nights to the one thought of how the economic redemption of the poorer and more numerous classes could be worked. But with only meager results to say the most. Here, however, was a measure capable of introducing a good amount of equality among the members of society, and which, so it seemed to him, was in harmony with the democratic premises so loudly professed by his countrymen. It was a desperate resort, surely, and one that called for great courage even to broach, but Orestes A. Brownson was never known to have lacked courage in what seemed to him a worthy cause. "Every man," he was to say, "who would achieve a noble victory for humanity, must have a sort of resklessness, at which the wise and prudent shake their heads."[57] He had not lacked an astonishing courage in this instance any more than in many another in his lifetime.

C. C. Hollis has suggested that the uproar created by Brownson's bold proposals in his essay of what he considered the needed reforms prevented a proper appreciation of his keen analysis of the whole social fabric of modern society. He asserted that:

> The emphasis on the positive steps (suggested in Brownson's essay) in social reform has led to an unfortunate neglect of his larger analysis of the culture of the day. He saw Carlyle's pamphlet as a correct diagnosis of the evils of Manchester liberalism and its bourgeois culture, but he saw what few in America were capable of seeing that Carlyle's implicit fascism could not provide the answer. . . . Consequently, he announces his rejection of the qualified transcendentalism of his friends (who wanted a radical religious philosophy without its sociological counterpart) by rejecting Carlyle. This is a major step in his own development and a turning point of his career.[58]

This much space has been given to Brownson's writings on the laboring classes inasmuch as they have been more highly thought of by posterity than they were by Brownson's contemporaries. In truth, much of his social thought, with its heavy emphasis on the social message of the Gospel, fits better the temper of our post-conciliar era than it did that of any decade since it was written. When Brownson asserted that "no man can enter the kingdom of God who does not labor with all zeal and diligence to establish the kingdom of God on earth; [that] no man can be a Christian who does not labor to reform society, to mould it according to the will of God and the nature of man, so that free scope shall be given to every man to unfold himself in all beauty and power, and to grow into the stature of a perfect man in Christ Jesus,"[59] he was anticipating language used by Vatican Council II:

> They are mistaken [says the Council] who, knowing that we have here no abiding city but seek one which is to come, think they may therefore shirk their earthly responsibilities. For they are forgetting that by faith itself they are more than ever obliged to measure up to those duties, each according to his proper vocation. . . . The Christian who neglects his temporal duties neglects his duties toward his neighbor and even God, and jeopardizes his eternal salvation.[60]

When all has been said on Brownson's "Laboring Classes" essays, it should still be remembered that they are, as Leonard Gilhooley has observed, typical of only one side of Brownson's many-sided mind. They are out of harmony with much that he had written before and much that he was to write afterwards. They lack that liberal-conservative or conservative-liberal balance of thought which had marked his writings generally from the time of his editorship of the *Boston Reformer,* 1836-1837, and which had been on the increase since the inception of his *Boston Quarterly Review,* 1838. They were, as Gilhooley has expressed it, an extreme assault on an extreme entrenchment of the bourgeoisie and the upper classes of society in favor of the poorer and more numerous classes. However brilliant and prescient in style and content, they cannot therefore be considered a true index to the general caliber of his thought during these years.[61] They are something of an effervescence, though not without its own species of solidity, of his agitated thought over the sorry plight of the poor and the oppressed. Brownson himself did not consider these essays representative of his more general thought. He remarked that they represented only "the last stage"[62] on the journey from which on second sober thought he was quick to turn back. He had reached journey's end in the direction in which he had been traveling. He wasted no time in turning about to address himself with his wonted vigor to the building of a better society according to a more conservative pattern.

# 15

## A GRADUAL TURN TO THE RIGHT

*Brownson's reaction to the national elections of 1840 • His continuing battle for the rights and interests of the people, and his war on absolute democracy • Constitutionalism the only safeguard of the rights of the individual citizen • His veneration for the United States Constitution • His review of his friend Bancroft's* History *on the Colonization of the United States • He sides with John C. Calhoun in an effort to put a check on federal power • His hefty efforts in support of the Locofoco party • The importance of government as an agent of reform • His letters from Calhoun and Alexander H. Everett.*

Orestes Brownson tells us that when he published his essay on "The Laboring Classes" he had supposed that it would end his literary and political career.[1] Whatever the probability of his supposition in regard to his political career, he could scarcely have meant his statement very seriously in speaking of his literary career. The literary career of such a man is not so easily jettisoned. In fact, the effect of the essay was to be just to the contrary. If it did not bring him literary fame, it did bring him a notoriety so extraordinary that it raised him to the status of a national figure almost overnight, which he was to turn to good account. Speaking of the remarkable reply Brownson had made to the assailants of his essay on "The Laboring Classes," George Parsons Lathrop remarked: "The old Adam and the new American rose up in him with the energy of colossal twins. He resisted the attack; formed himself, if one may say so, into a solid square; and bringing all his intellectual forces into play, succeeded, by three years of vigorous and brilliant effort, in regaining through his *Review* perhaps even greater sway over the thinking public than that which he had lost."[2] Yet the violent manner in which his essay had been assailed when published had given Brownson solemn pause. He had more than one occasion to refer to the way in which Whig orators and Whig editors had "shrieked" over his essay on the laboring classes "in such loud and piercing tones of horror from Maine to Georgia, and from the Atlantic to the Rocky Mountains."[3]

Yet why such an uproar? He felt that in what he had said he had only carried to their logical conclusions the democratic principles professed by his countrymen. A writer remarked in the *New York Daily News* that Brownson's "famous Essay on the Laboring Classes [had] brought to a culminating point the vague radicalism which was at the time predominant among many restless minds in New England."[4] But the refusal of those same "restless minds," who had talked so glibly about improving the condition of the masses, to identify with him, taught our incomparably bold reformer a salutary lesson. He began to see clearly that "democracy, socialism, radicalism, and most of the other *isms* usually professed, were simple shams — neither more nor less."[5] This new insight forced him to reexamine closely the democratic principles upon which he had been so vigorously writing and acting. Suppose, he said, we examine these premises, and see if the democratic theory of man and society, to which the world seems tending, is not itself founded in error.[6] Another harrowing event occurring at this time likewise pushed him in the same direction.

Simultaneously with the uproar over his essay on "The Laboring Classes" had come that other event, already mentioned, which was to revolutionize his political thinking — the presidential campaign of 1840, carried on by the Whigs, as he said, "by means utterly corrupt and corrupting."[7] The shock in store for him had been all the more uncushioned on the score that the Democratic party had appeared to have so much in its favor to assure victory in the coming elections. As Brownson noted after the event:

> Well, the canvass for president came on in 1840, and we all went into it, with the precise issue made up that I and my friends had wished; and we went into it, under as favorable circumstances as can ever be looked for in the history of this country, and more favorable than we can in my opinion ever look for again. We had our full share of the scholars and literary men of the country; also, of all that was distinguished for eminent service in practical political life; we had the whole patronage of the federal government, and that of twenty states out of twenty-six. Who when the campaign opened could have doubted our success? But we were defeated, and driven in disorder from the field.[8]

How had it all happened? The Whigs, the party of property and wealth, *quasi* successors of the old Federal party, had been quick to see that if they were to win at the polls they would have to make the people believe that they themselves — all appearances to the contrary — were the people's real party. They proceeded to put on one of the greatest shows in American political history. They regaled the people with endless torchlight processions, humbugged them with flattering speeches in high praise of "log cabins" and "hard cider," mesmerized them with such jingles as "Tippecanoe and Tyler too," and ran the whole gamut of democratic horseplay. Martin Van Buren was pictured as wearing silk underwear and quaffing champagne from a golden goblet while his opponent, William Henry Harrison, would be quite happy with just a log cabin and a jug of hard cider.[9]

If the results of the elections were to depend on playing down to the people, the Whigs were determined that they would teach the Democrats a trick or two. For as Brownson himself told it, they "descended into the forum, took the people by the hand, and, led on by the *Boston Atlas* and the *New York Tribune,* undertook to be more democratic than the Democratic party itself, and succeeded in out-heroding Herod."[10] The whole political circus revolted and disgusted our sedate Boston editor beyond measure with what goes under the name of democracy, as distinguished from constitutional republicanism, undermined his wavering faith in popular elections, and shattered forever his belief in the unassisted virtue and intelligence of the people. The fact that he was still holding office under the Democratic administration (as steward at the Marine Hospital in Chelsea) by no means lessened the sting the defeat of his party brought with it when the final results were tallied. He stared in disbelief at the figures: Harrison 234 electoral votes, Van Buren 60. The traumatic effect upon him of that election was still vivid in his mind when writing on the "Democratic Principle" more than thirty years later. He wrote:

> What I saw served to dispel my democratic illusions, break the idol I had worshipped, and shook to its foundations my belief in the divinity of the people, or in their will as an expression of eternal justice. I saw that they could be easily duped, and carried away by an irresistable passion in the wrong as easily as

in the right. I was forced by the shock my convictions received, to review first my logic, and then to examine the premises which I had taken on trust from my countrymen, and which I had not hitherto thought of questioning.[11]

The impact of this numbing experience now drove him for the first time to a systematic study of government, in its ground, its origin, its forms and its administration. He began at the beginning with Aristotle's *Politics;* then he took up the best treatises on government, both ancient and modern, available to him, including of course the history and political constitutions of ancient Greece and Rome, and the modern states of Europe. As a result of this elaborate study he came to the conclusion that "the condition of liberty is order, and that in this world we must seek, not equality, but justice. . . . Liberty is not the absence of authority, but in being held to obey only just and legitimate authority."[12] Government he no longer looked upon as merely an agency of society itself, as had been dinned into his ears by his political masters, but rather as an authority from on high to govern society, to aid and direct it, as a wise Providence, in fulfilling its destiny. He was thus turning into a political conservative, and, as he tells us, this political conservatism led rapidly in the direction of a religious conservatism.[13] Thus did the burlesque presidential campaign of 1840 and the wide hostile repercussions to his essay on "The Laboring Classes" vie with each other in the roles they played in turning his mind in the direction of general conservatism.

When Brownson tells us that what he saw in the campaign and elections of 1840 "served to dispel my democratic illusions," we must be on our guard lest we give his words a wrong interpretation. In the sense that he strongly believed that all men have equal rights, that government and all its acts should contemplate the good of all citizens impartially, and that the people, under God, are the rightful depositories of political power, Orestes Brownson was still as ardent a Democrat in the best sense of the word as he had ever been — and was to remain staunchly such to the end of his life. What had really happened was that the romantic faith he had once had in the capacity of the people, aside from constitutional or other guidance, to govern themselves wisely under a popular form of government, had been rudely shattered. This was to lead to his acute criticisms of some democratic processes. But in this he was by no means singular. It is interesting to note that his great contemporary, John Henry Newman, once remarked: "No one can dislike the democratic principle more than I do."[14]

In Brownson's case, whatever the change that had come over him, he was to continue to contend as vigorously as ever for the popular form of government, and to battle as fiercely as ever for the rights and interests of the people. But in doing so, he was now to make a distinction between the *form* and the *end* of government.[15] The mere fact that a government was democratic in form did not necessarily mean that it was the sum of all good both politically and socially. It was rather a government that aims assiduously at the freedom and progress of all its citizens, especially those of the poorer and more numerous classes, which spelled for him true democracy. "It is not democracy we want," he said, "but good government, a government which secures to each individual, by effective guarantees, the free and full enjoyment of all his rights."[16] Brownson was becoming more and more convinced that the absolute form of democratic government (unconstitutional) cannot effectively promote such an end — because of the chicanery and corruption of demagogues who are forever misleading and betraying the true interests of the people in order to serve their own immensely selfish ends. As an answer to this evil he began his intense battle for the maintenance of constitutional government as the surest safeguard of the rights and interests of the people.[17]

In taking this course he was by no means forsaking the Democratic cause. Although he could not accept the type of democracy then gaining ascendency in the country, he in no sense abandoned the Democratic party itself, which he considered less radical, less unsound, and more conservative than the victorious Whigs themselves. He labored incessantly, day and night, with voice and pen, especially in his *Boston Quarterly* to make the Democratic party still more conservative, and to bring home to its leaders that the people as a state need governing no less than the people as individuals.[18] In so laboring, he was resisting to the utmost the rising tide of absolute democracy, a form of government in which the people are supreme, and may, if not morally, at least in point of fact, do as they please — unrestrained by any constitutional safeguards. The whole tendency of the American people, not just of one party, he observed, was to sweep away all barriers to absolute democracy (which he often called "Jacobin" democracy), and to make government responsive to every wave of popular opinion, or popular caprice. The evidence of this he saw in the inaugural address of President William H. Harrison in 1841 when he spoke of the government as resting upon the will of the majority "which a breath of the majority has made and can unmake."[19] What wonder, then, that it was reported how the Goddess of Liberty had dropped from her hand the scroll of the Constitution as President Harrison had approached the Capitol for his inauguration.[20]

No doubt there were not a few in the country at the time who were wondering just what Orestes Brownson would have to say in the first article on politics in his *Quarterly* after the Democratic party had gone down in such ignominious defeat at the hands of the Whigs. What he had to say was contained in an article in the January 1841 issue of his *Review*, entitled: "The Policy to be pursued hereafter by the Friends of the Constitution, and of Equal Rights," or "Our Future Policy." It was forty-four pages in length.[21] We may gain some idea of its quality from the estimate put upon it by the editor of the *Boston Times*, when he said:

> We at last find room in our columns to commence one of the ablest, the most profound and philosophical essays from the *Boston Quarterly Review*, that we have ever published or even read. It is the production of one of the most gigantic and original minds that constitute the glory of the present age. . . . That there are paragraphs in "Our Future Policy" (which we commence today) that we do not accord with, we readily admit. . . . They are like spots on the sun, not sufficient indeed to dim its effulgence or mar its beauty, yet they are spots nevertheless. With the extracts we shall make in our paper, we cordially and fully concur; every sentence, word, letter is just what it should be; not a single point of punctuation would we alter; it is the outpouring of the heart of an ardent friend of the toiling millions. . . . That a man of such bold originality, of such deep devotion to the principles of political equality, of such ardent, untiring zeal in the cause of the down-trodden masses, as is Orestes A. Brownson, should be unpopular with the miserable upstart politicians who have crawled into high places, is not surprising; that the degraded parasites who control a large majority of our mis-called democratic papers, should vent their spleen against him, is a matter of course.[22]

Brownson's article itself on "Our Future Policy" contained no desponding note over the recent elections. He acknowledged, however, that the elections had not tended to increase what confidence he had had in the actual virtue and intelligence of the people, but he had great confidence in the capacities of human nature to arrest any parlous tendencies in the government before it was too late. Above all, he believed in an overruling Providence — the same overruling Providence that had selected this country as the chosen land of freedom, that had thus far watched over and protected it, and has prepared it for the work assigned it in the progress of civilization. In utter calm he trusted that the God of our fathers would rescue us from regressive political fallacies, and enable us to complete effectually the temple of freedom in this Western World. He did not feel that the people in the recent elections had really rejected their ancient democratic faith; they had simply voted a change of men, not measures. They had judged the present administration to be low-minded and corrupt, deficient in both capacity and integrity, and had called for a change. The people, however, had been deceived, woefully deceived, but the moment they would become aware of it, they would rectify their mistake. And what was more, if the officials of the incoming administration should undertake to carry out a policy different from the one that had been pursued during the last twelve years (the Jacksonian era), the people would be sure to hurl them from power at the earliest moment permitted by the forms of the Constitution.[23]

But since Brownson had lost faith in the inerrant instincts of the people, saw that they could become the easy prey of unscrupulous demagogues, he had to look elsewhere for a bulwark against the ceaseless attacks and inroads on the rights and interests of the people. He found it in a strict maintenance of the Constitution which had been framed to safeguard impartially the rights and interests of all classes and individuals. Two parties, he said, have always existed in the country, and two parties there will always be: a party in favor of property and the business classes, who endeavor to make government an instrument for facilitating trade; and a party in favor of man, whose leading object will be to secure to the workingman a greater share in the proceeds of labor, and to elevate labor and make it honorable. For his part, he would always be found with the second party, the party of the Constitution and equal rights, whether in power or out of power. He reiterated his claim that the real mission of this country is to emancipate the proletary, to make every man free and independent. He repeated his demand that every man should have at least enough wealth at the start of life that, should he make proper use of it, it will guarantee him an equal rank with any other man in the community. In a word, he demanded a state of society in which the virtues and intelligence of people would be as nearly equal as the diversities of men's natural aptitudes would allow, and then the rank of each should be measured according to the practical operation of the capacities, virtues and intelligence of each. His Utopian blueprint approached a classless society:

> There shall not be a learned class and an unlearned, a cultivated class and an uncultivated, a refined class and a vulgar, a wealthy class and a poor. There shall not be one class owning all the funds, and another performing all the labor of production. There shall be no division of society into workingmen and idlers, employers and operatives. There shall be workingmen but no proletaries; for we would have all men work each on his own capital, associated or unassociated, on equal terms with his brother. This is the end we aim at; this is the mission of this country, and to this should all the measures of government directly or indirectly tend.[24]

He owned that he did not envisage a speedy implementation of this ideal society. It seemed for the present far beyond the dreams of either the people or their leaders. But he insisted that every true Democrat should check the wisdom or unwisdom of every political or legislative measure against its tendency either to promote or retard its realization. Government itself was of no value to him except insofar as it could be used for the fulfillment of this mission of America. Although his faith in government was not unbounded, he made it clear that he by no means agreed with those who regarded it as "at best a necessary evil." Man must act collectively as well as individually, and to act collectively requires government. He regarded government, therefore, not only as a necessity but "as a great good."[25] He would still leave a large margin of freedom to the individual, but would by no means leave him entirely uncircumscribed. He could not go with those politicians who advocate the *laissez-faire* doctrine. Men need to be governed, even coerced in one form or another. In short, the duty of government is twofold: on the one hand, to *protect* the rights of individuals, and on the other, to *force* individuals to perform their duties to one another. While thus limited to these spheres, it must enforce its commands with authority.[26] Only by the aid of such government would the mission of America be promoted and advanced.

For the actual realization of this mission of America he looked more hopefully to the states than to the federal government. As an ardent states' rights man he believed that the true democratic principles are embedded in the states. They alone would allow the freedom necessary to work for the fulfillment of the nation's mission. Hence it was necessary to resist all efforts of the federal government to enlarge its powers, directly or indirectly, at the expense of the states. But as he saw the powerful middle and western states favoring a consolidated federal government that could be dragooned into serving their sectional interests, he called loudly for a new party — a constitutional party that would "stake every thing on one bold effort to save the Constitution, and establish the reign of Justice and Equality."[27] He envisaged three elements in the nation as having a special stake in this new constitutional party: the small states, to which the Constitution was a bulwark against any aggressions of stronger powers; the slave-holding states whose "peculiar institution" would be best protected by the Constitution; and the friends of equal rights and progress. He counseled that if these three elements would unite on the broad platform of the Constitution, they could head off the unlawful enlargement of power and prestige by the federal government; but without the strictest union among the three, the consolidationists would carry the day with disastrous consequences to the whole country, and with a fatal threat to liberty.[28]

Nothing was more important to him politically, then, than the preservation of the Constitution in its purity and integrity as he regarded it as a "miracle of wisdom." He added: "We see clearly in it the hand of Providence, and we have for it a sort of religious veneration."[29] Arguing that the moment the government steps beyond its constitutional bounds its tendency is to favor business at the expense of labor, the capitalist rather than the operative, he insisted that every Democrat *ought* to be a constitutionalist. After appealing to all patriots throughout the nation, of whatever class or creed, to rally to the defense of the Constitution, he proceeded to assure the South that although there was not a Democrat north of the Mason and Dixon line who did not loathe slavery, still he promised that he would do all he could to resist the efforts of the Abolitionists to interfere with slavery through any action of the federal government if the South would in turn unite with Northern Democracy to save the Constitution from the encroachments of capitalists, and the businessmen of the middle and western states. But he warned the South that should they refuse to join the Constitutional Party, there would be nothing left to prevent an onslaught on slavery once the Constitution had been overridden.[30]

Our doughty protagonist for the Constitution now warned its friends that under the incoming administration the consolidationists would aim at three measures: they would seek to establish a national bank, to impose a protective tariff, and to assume the state debts by distributing among the states the proceeds from the sale of public lands. All three measures, he asserted, are unconstitutional. The last measure he saw as an open attempt on the part of the federal government to establish a guardianship over the states. It carried with it the implication that the states were incapable of taking care of themselves, that the federal government must take care of them. This would be to buy off the autonomy of the states and render them some sort of prefectures. How could a state while being a pensioner of the federal government remain disposed to arrest the tendency to consolidation by asserting its own sovereignty? "The moment," he said, "you make the states pensioners on the bounty of the federal government, you destroy the balance between the States and the Union, and give to the centripetal force an overwhelming power."[31] He cautioned that unless the constitutionalists everywhere stood firmly together for the maintenance of the Constitution the consolidationists would disarray our system of government. But Brownson was by no means alone in this battle against federal consolidation. Allen Nevins asserts that nearly all political figures in the country, beginning with Thomas Jefferson down to 1850, were for keeping the federal government as weak as possible.[32] But perhaps none contended more strenuously for that in practice than John C. Calhoun and Orestes Brownson.

Brownson's valiant efforts to rally his countrymen to the support of the Constitution were equalled only by his unflagging efforts to expose and eradicate the evils of majoritarian democracy. In his article on "Social Evils, and their Remedy,"[33] he proceeded to lay bare the dangers of simple majority rule, and further amplified his thought on the matter in his review of his friend Bancroft's *History of the Colonization of the United States*. Although Brownson's review of the *History* was not to be one of wholly unmixed praise, he began by saying that "official relations" with the author of the *History* had previously rendered it indelicate for him to speak of the work in terms worthy of its merits. (He was of course referring to his stewardship of the Marine Hospital in Chelsea which had been awarded him by Bancroft, but which office had now expired.) He had been too desirous to witness the unbounded success of his friend's *History* to be found commending it at a time when all the world was railing against him (because of his essay on "The Laboring Classes"). But now the official relations no longer existed, and clamors against him were subsiding, and as there was no longer any danger that Mr. Bancroft might incur guilt by association because of his own offending heresies, he felt quite free now to speak just as he thought and felt.[34]

Although Brownson rated Bancroft's *History* as among "the very first productions of the age, and an age rich in historical productions . . . with no historical work in our language that can rank above it," he nonetheless regretted to find him favoring absolute democracy. Such a theory of government meant the unlimited freedom of the people as the commonwealth to do as they pleased. In what way would such a type of government be better than absolute monarchy, Brownson wanted to know, if even as good? For Brownson the real end and aim of every sound government is to secure to each individual the full and free enjoyment of all his natural rights. But this could never be achieved under the workings of a pure or absolute democracy. His meaning he made crystal clear:

> In an absolute democracy, such as Mr. Bancroft seems to us to contemplate, where the people are absolutely sovereign, with none but moral limitations to their power, the stronger interest will always command a majority of votes, govern the government, and therefore through government have always the means of strengthening and perpetuating itself. The government will always be made the instrument for protecting special interests, and it is by protecting special interests that government encroaches on the rights of the citizen; because the favor it bestows on one part is always taken from the other parts.[35]

Moreover, it was ridiculous to pretend that the majority can never do wrong. We have, said Brownson, no more faith in the maxim, "the people can do no wrong," than we have in the elder maxim, "the king can do no wrong." To him both maxims were fictions, and far from harmless fictions at that. People taken individually, he could confide in and trust, for there is so much good in every individual. But taken collectively, he had come to question to what lengths they might go. With rare perspicacity he pointed out the mysterious workings of mob psychology, or what is akin to it: "The more attenuated responsibility is by the numbers who share in it, the weaker it is. Unite men into corporations, and they will applaud themselves for doing in their corporate capacity, what they would shrink from with horror as individuals. Enlarge your corporation till it becomes the state, and you have increased the evil, not diminished it."[36]

In this ceaseless war on absolute democracy Brownson acknowledged a *quasi* fellowship with the old Federalists who demanded a limit to democracy, but unlike them, he did so only that the rights of the individual citizen might be the better safeguarded. Bancroft, his friend and benefactor, he esteemed highly for his democratic zeal, his love of the people, and thought him capable of great heroism in what he counted the cause of human freedom, but insofar as he was laboring for an absolute democracy, without check or balance, he could not regard him as an enlightened friend and abettor of true freedom. "Against such a government," he said, "we have ever warred; and we took occasion in the very first number of this journal to utter our loud and indignant protest [his article on 'Democracy,' January 1838]. We are as much opposed to monarchy, to aristocracy, as Mr. Bancroft, and we are also opposed to all unlimited government."[37]

Perhaps no American of the time had a deeper concern for the political safeguarding of human rights than had Orestes A. Brownson. No matter what political question he was discussing, the kernel of his thought almost invariably centered on just how to erect an impregnable barrier around the natural rights of man. The loud call he made at this time for constitutional government was simply a loud call to others to rally to the defense of the rights of the individual citizen. He saw the two, the Constitution and human rights, as inextricably bound up together. No constitutional government, no security for individual freedom. Apart from constitutional government, he no longer believed that any one form of government would guarantee the defense of human rights better than another. He had arrived at the conviction, which was henceforth to be a settled doctrine with him, that no one form of government is *per se* better than another, whether monarchical, aristocratical, democratic, or some modification of one or all. That type of government will fit a people best which best realizes for them the true end of government, namely, the genuine promotion of the common good.[38] He grew somewhat impatient with those who "do little but scream democracy from morning till night, and from night till morning; and those of us who scream the loudest are by no means the truest friends of equality." Acerbly he commented:

> The liberty we should now struggle for, is not, strictly speaking, *democratic liberty*, that is, the liberty of the people, but individual liberty, or securing to each and every citizen the free and full enjoyment of his natural rights. And this is to be done, not by shouting "aristocracy" or "democracy," but by wisely arranging the state, so that it shall have no power to encroach on the individual, but be always able and obliged to protect him. Liberty with us is to be carried out, not by the heavings to and fro of a lawless mob, but by the orderly workings of constitutional government. . . . Our first duty to liberty, to the inalienable rights of man, is to establish and maintain constitutional order. . . . Consequently, every attack on the sacredness of Constitutions is a stab at the very heart of liberty.[39]

He now made a close inquiry into the workings of constitutional government, and published his findings in an article under the same title. Whatever might be the solutions already found to other political problems, the question still remained of just how constitutional government can be so arranged that it not only *will* but *cannot* extend itself beyond its constitutional limits. He knew full well that although constitutions are intended to be a restriction on power, that power "has a perpetual tendency to exceed wholesome limits."[40] Could anything have been more patently unconstitutional than the Distribution Bill so lately passed by the majority of both Houses of Congress at its extra session, and signed into law by the President who had so solemnly sworn to preserve and uphold the Constitution?[41] How then erect a barrier to the wanton extension of power? Such a problem in a democracy is compounded by the fact that the people themselves are allegedly the sovereign power. To frame a constitution and then entrust it to the people on whose will it is intended to operate as a check is, said our political philosopher, very much like "locking up the culprit, and entrusting the key to him."[42] Where then can a device be found that will halt the federal government if and when it should attempt to overleap its bounds?

It is an axiom of political science, affirmed Brownson, that for a wise and just administration there must be in government a division of powers into the positive and the negative, the negative power being so lodged that it can interpose a barrier to any encroachments of the positive power. The prosperity of ancient Rome dated from the establishment of the tribunicial power, a veto on the acts of government; it so continued to operate until the tribunicial power together with all others were finally absorbed into the emperorship, and, Rome becoming a huge centralism, declined and fell. The merits of the old feudal system consisted mainly in the veto the great vassals had on the crown, and on each other. The stability and balance of the English government is due, he said, to the veto, imperfect though it be, the House of Commons has in granting or withholding supplies. Only in Poland, where the power of the veto had been magnified out of all reasonable proportion, did it prove harmful to the Republic. History itself demonstrates that for sound and just government anywhere, there must ever be in the state a positive power called the government, and a negative power, ready to arrest the action of the government should it attempt to play the tyrant. "Almost the sole art, in constituting government," he emphasized, "consists in devising an effective veto, one that shall operate naturally, peaceably, when, and only when required."[43]

In this matter Brownson thought that this country has been singularly favored by Providence. Under the providential constitution of the country the American people at the time of the Revolution set up two divisions of government, the state governments and the federal government. Through congress the majority of the people govern, but according to the Constitution, and hence its rule is not absolute. It can govern only within specified limits. Should it transcend those limits in its acts, those acts are unconstitutional, null and void. Whenever it does so transgress, there is a negative power, the state organization, to act as a veto in arresting it. A state is to the Union what the tribune was to the Roman Senate. When the Union enacts any law that transcends the Constitution, and every law does transcend the Constitution which bears unequally on the different states, the state can interpose a veto, and arrest its action. There is thus in the providential Constitution of the country a political organism back of the written Constitution operating to control and check any unjust extension of federal power.[44]

It is not improbable that some of the political ideas Brownson was now expounding were garnered from conversations with John C. Calhoun, the famed South Carolinian. From the casual way in which he speaks of meeting Calhoun in Washington about this time, we may assume they often met there on Brownson's lecture tours.[45] Calhoun was a firm believer in state sovereignty, together with the doctrine of nullification, and the theory that Brownson was here setting forth chimed in agreeably with Calhoun's tenets.[46] Calhoun, too, would agree with Brownson when he said: "There are constantly occurring and ever will occur cases, in which the state interposition in some form will be necessary to arrest the encroachments of the federal government. Nothing but the fear of this, on the part of that government, can be effectual in keeping it within constitutional limits."[47] Brownson also favored Calhoun's theory of concurring majorities, according to which Calhoun would have each of the different trades or business interests of a people in any section of the country organized into individual majorities which would equal one another in political proceedings irrespective of the numerical strength of each.

These concurring majorities would balance and cancel out the power of each when introduced on a larger scale in the nation, and would thus tend to prevent any numerical majority from getting control of the legislature and plundering the people through the enactment of special legislation favoring their own interest. Insofar as the division of the states in those days marked also in a goodly degree a difference between the business pursuits of the country, sectional interests or trades could be readily organized into concurring majorities.[48] But as Brownson later observed, after the abolition of slavery, the pursuits and interests of the country at large became so homogeneous as to render wholly impractical any thought of introducing a system of concurring majorities.[49] But however looked upon from this distance, both the theory of the veto on unconstitutional acts of the federal government, and the theory of concurring majorities were ingenious measures put forth by Calhoun and Brownson in a desperate effort to put a curb on the predatory instincts of numerical majorities who were using "the government as an instrument for plundering the people to the greatest possible extent."[50]

In his article on the Distribution Bill, Brownson again excoriated the

Whig administration for placing "the welfare doctrine" above the Constitution. It is this policy, he said, that had induced the Whigs to pass the bill in contravention of the Constitution. He frankly owned that there were perhaps few men in the country who would defend in precise terms "the general welfare doctrine," but he found this doctrine lying confusedly in the minds of a large portion of his countrymen, and producing the saddest results. It was this very doctrine that was shaping the policy of the Whig administration and playing hob with the Constitution. The real issue between the Whigs and their opponents was becoming clearer every day: *the Constitution or no Constitution: freedom* of law and order, or the *tyranny* of an irresponsible majority; the rule of the people constituting the state, or the rule of a lawless mob.[51] In the interests of sound government he demanded the utter repudiation of "the general welfare doctrine." He would have no fellowship whatsoever with those who were attempting to bend the Constitution to their own convictions as to what was for the general welfare. Even if it were demonstrated that a measure was of the "highest utility," it would avail nothing with him if it were in its nature unconstitutional. He laid it down that:

> The first and permanent good that can be obtained, or secured, to this country, is the maintenance of the Constitution in its strict inviolability; and in administering the government according to its express provisions, rigidly construed. For without this there is, according to our manner of viewing it, no possible good for us. Show us that your proposition is in itself never so wise, just, or useful, if it be unauthorized by the Constitution, we cannot entertain it for a moment.[52]

Brownson also protested firmly against what he declared a false and mischievous principle laid down by James Madison when President for interpreting the Constitution. Although Mr. Madison had previously opposed the United States Bank on the ground of its unconstitutionality, he finally did sign a bill of incorporation as President, alleging in justification of himself that "a power repeatedly exercised by Congress, and acquiesced in by the people, should be taken as constitutional." This seems to be the only instance on record, observed Brownson, prior to General Jackson, of regarding the will of the majority not constitutionally expressed, as paramount to the Constitution itself. But such a rule, he said, virtually abolishes the Constitution. For if the stress is laid on the *acquiescence* of the people, it leaves the majority the right to pass any law they please that the people will tolerate (which would be precisely the same as the case would be if there were no Constitution at all). If the emphasis is laid on the *repeated* exercise of power, it asserts that wrong by repetition becomes right. And if the emphasis is laid on the repeated exercise by *Congress,* it claims for the simple majority in Congress the right to alter or amend the Constitution as they please, a power which, according to the Constitution itself, can be exercised only by a concurrence of several states, at least three-fourths of them. Yet Brownson was not insensitive to the great perplexity in which President Madison had found himself: "Mr. Madison was a great and good man whose services to his country are not easily measured; but the injury he has occasioned, in this instance, to the cause of constitutional liberty, is one from which we shall be long in recovering. It was indeed one of those mistakes, to which the wisest and best of men are liable in cases of perplexity and emergency; but it is one which the earliest opportunity should be seized of correcting."[53]

We should note well that in turning to a more earnest study of government Brownson was by no means abandoning any of his burning zeal for reform in behalf of the laboring classes. He had for some time been editing a radical journal for the Workingmen's Association of Charlestown, Massachusetts. His relationship to the Association having become quite close, he wrote for them an eighteen-page pamphlet on the eve of the elections, 1840, called: "An Address of the Workingmen of Charlestown, Massachusetts, to their Brethren throughout the Commonwealth and the Union."[54] This address he published in his *Review,* January 1841. In a five-page introduction to it he had much to say about *social* democracy:

If under democracy, aside from suffrage and eligibility, men may be as unequal in their social condition, as under other forms of government, wherein consists, he wanted to know, the boasted advantages of democracy? Is all good summed up in suffrage and eligibility? Yet this is all that political democracy, reduced to its simplest elements, proposes. He felt that the popular mind, having once attained to *political* democracy, should naturally aspire and tend to social democracy, going naturally from equality before the state to equality before society. He claimed that the social equality doctrine was gaining acceptance, that three-fourths of the Democratic party were social democrats. In fact that party had been labeled the Locofoco party by its enemies. He rejoiced in the appellation, for Locofocoism stood for *social* democracy. He appealed, then, to the Workingmen's party that, instead of rallying around the old-time Workingmen's flag of 1829, they should fling to the breeze the Locofoco flag as their symbol and inspiration: "For on this Loco-foco Flag, if we read aright, is inscribed, *Equality before Society, as we already have Equality before the State.* Loco-focoism is social democracy, as distinguished from political; and a Loco-foco is a Jeffersonian Democrat, who having realized political equality, now passes on to another [phase of the revolution], social equality."[55]

In the first and second editions of his *Quarterly* for the year 1841, Brownson also published his impassioned "Conversations with a Radical." The radical was of course his *alter ego.* He again excoriated the method by which ideas favorable to the higher classes in society are inculcated in colleges and seminaries, by churches, and various forms of literature, only a portion of the newspaper press being excepted. For the upper classes, education was a method of "training up their sons to manage the people skillfully, and to ride them gracefully and securely. Our professors are mere riding masters, giving lessons in the noble art of horse-manship."[56] Helen S. Mims has remarked that this metaphor was taken over by Edward Bellamy and made famous.[57]

While the whole course of his "Conversations with a Radical" is sprinkled with acerb remarks on the grievous wrongs done the lower classes of society, Brownson took occasion to declare what he conceived to be his real mission in life, and to disclose why at times his language might seem intemperate. Only through such language could he hope to attract attention. Earnestly he wrote:

> I have a mission. I am called to espouse the cause of the laboring classes. I have studied their condition in this and other countries. My life is devoted to their service; for them I live, and if need be, die. My head is gray with efforts in their behalf. I have grown old, though yet hardly a middle aged man, in seeking to elevate their condition. No matter; I devote myself to their interest without wrath or bitterness. It is not that I hate, or envy, or despise the more favored classes, that I proclaim myself the champion of the less favored; but because with the workingmen today is the cause of Humanity. . . . What Hu-

manity will demand of her servants and friends tomorrow I know not. I hear her voice, which to me is the voice of God, and I dare not hesitate. I must speak. I am full of words, and I must utter myself. But if I speak hot, scalding words, words which go to the quick, it is because none other can do justice to myself, or to the work I am sent to perform.[58]

We will keep things in right focus if we bear in mind that all Brownson's campaigning at this time for good government, which he called "the greatest of all blessings to any people,"[59] and which for him meant constitutional government, was really done in behalf of the poorer classes in society, the wronged and oppressed. With them lay all his sympathies. He knew full well that the upper classes could well manage for themselves and that many of them were ready enough to forage and plunder. The real font of mischief in society for him was not "the unwashed mob," men who live by daily wages, but "the well-clad mob of brokers, stock-jobbers, speculators, and ambitious and intriguing politicians . . . who want government administered for their special benefit. . . . The poor and more numerous classes are with us, the fast friends of law and order; and would endure almost any conceivable wrong, sooner than, violate them."[60] And for the defense of their rights and interests Orestes Brownson was ready to give "the last full measure of devotion."

The work that Brownson was thus tirelessly carrying on in behalf of the laboring classes and the strenuous efforts he was putting forth to eradicate abuses in government were bound to raise him up many enemies. A reformer is one who attacks abuses, and he is sure to trigger a Pavlovian counterattack from those who profit by existing abuses. A reformer such as Brownson, something of "an American Savonarola,"[61] who drove home with such tremendous power in his efforts at reform, could least of all expect to escape the common fate of all reformers. But if his reforming efforts raised him up a goodly number of adversaries, he also had those who stood by him in his brave and righteous battle. The editor of the *Boston Times* wrote of him at this time:

> We have known Mr. Brownson intimately from his first entrance upon the stage of public life; and we have had to make no small drafts upon our philosophy, to restrain our burning indignation, when the ephemeral tribe of editorial insects which buzz about the degraded press, have attempted to shed their impotent malice upon the editor of the *Quarterly Review*. He is as far above the petty venom of such reptiles as the Alps are higher than an ant-hill.[62]

Since Brownson had come to look upon constitutional government as the only hope for working the needed reforms in society, it is quite understandable that he felt little sympathy with those reformers who thought of reforming without the aid of government, or of introducing a state of society in which government would be superfluous — a class of reformers, he remarked, who are becoming somewhat numerous in the community. He called them our no-government friends, referring evidently to the Transcendentalists, whom he personally held in high esteem, and among whom he counted many of his warmest personal friends.[63] Their total reliance on moral, intellectual, religious and physical culture alone to work the needed reforms, he could not share. He himself had once inclined to their views, but further reflection had convinced him that reason and morality alone are feeble barriers to cope with the unruly passions of man ever attempting to leap their bounds, or the selfishness of man ever ready to trample on the rights of others. He assured his no-government friends that far from being an obstacle to reform, or a superfluous machine that should be thrown aside, government is "a great and indispensible agent of reform." Instead of advocating no-government schemes, he counseled them to plunge into the science of politics, acquaint themselves with practical statesmanship, and turn all the energies of their minds and wills to the work of making government what it ought to be. In this he was plainly bidding them follow in his own wake who had come to believe that the great need of the day and hour was a serious study of the proper management of a wise and sound government for securing to society the greatest possible good.[64]

After reminding his readers that he had written his article on "Social Evils, and their Remedy" for the purpose of drawing attention more directly to the importance and precise nature of constitutional government, he proceeded to explain that his new emphasis on government as an agent of reform by no means discounted other vital factors that make for success in schemes of social reform. But for religion and morality to be potent agents of reform, he stressed that they must be organized forces in society, not mere interior sentiments:

> In appealing so directly as we do to government, and making it almost the sole agent through which we are to remedy social evils, we by no means forget religion, morality, or individual intelligence. No man can rate them higher than we do. We hold them absolutely indispensible. But they must not be imprisoned in the bosom of the individual. They must be brought out of the interior of man, and made to disclose the true end of all social institutions, and contribute to their adoption. We would write always as the Christian and the moralist, as well as the statesman. But we would use Christianity and morality in organizing the state and shaping its measures, not less than in our private exhortations to individuals. The end disclosed by true religion, the one enjoined by morality, and that sought by the state, are one and the same: to wit, the freedom and progress in virtue and happiness of every individual. Unless the state maintains freedom for the individual, religion and morality can do little besides solace him in his sufferings, and strengthen him in his trials. This is no doubt a high office, and never to be thought lightly of; but the intelligence, purity, and loftiness of soul, religion and morality are fitted to quicken, should be directed to the establishment of such institutions, and the enactment of such laws, as shall always favor truth, justice, order, and well-being.[65]

If Brownson believed at this time that government is "almost the sole agent" through which social evils can be remedied, he also continued to emphasize that government itself is likewise in constant need of reform if it is to be an effective instrument of reform. In his first article on government after the fall elections of 1840, he had written: "In nearly all ages and countries, the office of government has been to impose burdens on the people, to force from them a larger portion of their earnings, or to keep them quiet under an order of things from which the few alone profit."[66] The Herculean efforts he was now putting forth to bring about a reform of the current evils in government were beginning to attract attention more and more. Alexander H. Everett (brother of Edward), then president of Louisiana State College, wrote him an approving letter on July 9, 1841:

> My dear sir:
> . . . Your remarks on "Social Evils, and their Remedy" are full of highly important meaning. I agree with you entirely in regard to the disposition of our philanthropists to undervalue the influence of government. The truth is, that

nine-tenths of the difference between a New Zealander and the Englishman is the effect of the difference between the political institutions under which they have been respectively educated. Such a man as Dr. Channing ought to know this. The meagerness of our political disquisitions is a fact melancholy enough. We reverse the old rule about writing, and write *multa, non multum*. Even in Mr. Webster's speeches there is no profound or thorough discussion of general principles. It is all syllogizing on a given brief, and I have my doubts whether the "Great Expounder," if suddenly called upon, could tell the meaning of the word Constitution. I intend, the next time I meet him, to try the experiment.[67]

In October of this same year, 1841, Alexander H. Everett attempted in another letter to stimulate Brownson to a further discussion of the principles of political science. Brownson's recent articles he had found intriguing:

My dear sir:
    . . . I have just received the October number. . . . I have read the greater part of the present number with much interest. Your article on Bancroft's History is a generous tribute to real merit. I am rather curious to see the development of your theory of government as indicated in this and another recent article. In general we want nothing so much in this country, in a literary way, as a thorough discussion of the principles of government. Libraries are published every year on men and measures, but almost nothing on principles. . . . In the meantime I am looking to you for a Restoration of Political Science.[68]

Whatever these lines meant to Brownson from a man distinguished in the realm of letters, and later to gain further distinction as an American diplomatist, he probably appreciated even more the words of approbation that came to him from John C. Calhoun — a man who appeared to him ever more like a knight in shining armor in the political arena. From Calhoun's letter to him it would appear that he himself had sought Calhoun's opinion on his article, "Social Evils, and their Remedy." We learn, too, from the letter that there was some probability at the time that Brownson might be a candidate for Congress. The letter of October 31, 1841, reads in part:

Dear Sir:
    I not only read with pleasure the article to which you refer, when the number first appeared, but I have read it again, in order that I might answer your letter from fuller and more recent impressions. It is in the right track, and very able. There is scarcely a view taken, or a sentiment expressed, in which I do not fully concur, and it gives me pleasure to say, I heard several of our friends during the late session speak highly of it. I do hope, it will contribute to give a practical and true direction to the rising spirit of liberal inquiry, which has manifested itself in New England, and especially in Boston, within the last few years. Next to the Staple States, New England has the deepest interests in the views, on which you have successfully touched.
    I am much gratified to learn, that you have a prospect of a seat in the Legislature, both because it indicates the strong hold you have on those around you, and will enlarge the sphere of your usefulness.[69]

It is rather surprising that this prospect of a seat in Congress should have come to him so soon after his essay on "The Laboring Classes." Whatever the prospect amounted to, it may be assumed that he himself had little to do with promoting it. For as Fr. Isaac T. Hecker remarked: "No man can accuse him of political ambition. His personal convictions were too strong ever to allow him to win that kind of average popularity which would enable him to get public office. He was always a powerful man and always made his mark; but his tongue and pen were the servants of a disinterested and impulsive honesty."[70]

If Brownson at this time received no written words of approbation from his friend, George Ripley, for his strenuous efforts to resolve the social problems of the day, it may be partly because Ripley himself had now embarked on a daring sociological experiment of his own, the launching of Brook Farm. Brownson's son Henry tells us that the two (Brownson and Ripley) had often compared their views on social reform, and found them, as on so many other subjects, to be very much akin. To what extent, however, if at all, Ripley was indebted to Brownson in the launching of Brook Farm, seems rather conjectural. All that is certain is that the principles upon which it was founded had been talked over between the two.[71]

# 16

## BROOK FARM

*The founding of Brook Farm • Its constitution and noble aims • Those who figured prominently in its management • Brownson's article on Brook Farm in the* Democratic Review *• His farewell to his former Utopian dreams of world reform as declared in a letter to Ralph Waldo Emerson • A remarkable letter to Brownson from the Hon. Hugh A. Garland, Clerk of the House of Representatives in Washington, D.C. • Brownson's visits to Brook Farm • George Curtis on the friendship of Brownson and Isaac T. Hecker • The change into a phalanx rings the death knell on "The Brook Farm Institute of Agriculture and Education."*

Orestes Brownson described Brook Farm as "an attempt to realize the Christian Ideal, and to do this by establishing truly Christian relations between the members and the community and between member and member."[1]

George Ripley and Orestes Brownson were social reformers who not only speculated, but bravely endeavored to translate their social ideas into actual institutions. In this the one acted and reacted on the other. Brownson, under the influence of Ripley, had come to Boston in 1836 to found there a reform society, and now, gathering inspiration from Brownson, Ripley was ready to launch his Brook Farm project. As a Unitarian minister, he had become quite dissatisfied after fourteen years of service with his type of Christian ministry. He had come to feel that in caring only for the well-to-do of his own Purchase Street Church, he was really neglecting the more important part of a Christian ministry — the care of the "down-trodden and suffering poor." To the elders of his congregation, who apparently had little enough sympathy with his views, he said in a farewell letter: "Blame me for it if you will, but I cannot behold the degradation, the ignorance, the poverty, the vice, the ruin of soul, which is everywhere displayed in the very bosom of Christian society in our own city, while men look on idly, without a shudder."[2] In his sermon at the ordination of John S. Dwight, Northampton, May 20, 1840, he added: "The true work of the evangelist at the present day is to bring the religion of society into accordance with the religion of Christ." Late in this same year, he resigned his Purchase Street pulpit, and sought Dr. Channing's advice with the thought of exploring "whether it were possible to bring cultivated, thoughtful people together, and make a society that deserves the name."[3] What precisely passed between the two men is unknown. Years later, the nephew, William Henry Channing, denied that his celebrated uncle had encouraged Ripley's project, though he allowed he had sympathized with his noble aspirations.[4]

A man of uncommon courage, Ripley lost no time in giving shape and form to the dream that had been haunting his mind. His first move was the purchase of Brook Farm during the winter of the same year. It was a tract of 192 acres in West Roxbury, nine miles west of Boston, marked by country quiet and beauty, enhanced by the undulating sweep of the terrain, and not far from the winding Charles River. It was first occupied by Ripley himself during April of the next year, 1841. After another six months spent in rigging it up — work presumably done by the fifteen pioneer members of the project — it was ready for general occupancy by September, and was given the name "The Brook Farm Institute of Agriculture and Education."[5]

Although Brook Farm was the outcome of the Transcendental quest to find a new and better way of life — some never-never land nestling somewhere between the distracting cares of a competitive business world and solitude — none of the Transcendentalists followed Ripley to Brook Farm at its founding, and "of later members, only Hawthorne and John S. Dwight followed him there."[6] Of all the Transcendentalists, Emerson was perhaps the least sympathetic. When replying to Ripley's letter soliciting an investment in the purchase of the Farm, Emerson said frankly that he considered investments in Concord much safer than in Brook Farm. He simply did not believe in reform movements in any case. He wrote in the *Dial* that young men "who have been vexing society these last years with regenerative methods, have failed to see that the Reform of reforms must be accomplished without means."[7] But whatever he may have thought of the impracticality of the venture, neither he nor anyone else should have been unsympathetic to the noble aims which had guided the Ripleys in launching this daring project, namely:

> . . . to insure a more natural union between intellectual and mental labor than now exists; to combine the thinker and the worker, as far as possible, in the same individual; to guarantee the highest mental freedom, by providing all with labor adapted to their tastes and talents, and securing to them the fruits of the industry; to do away with the necessity of menial services by opening the benefits of education and the profits of labor to all; and thus to prepare a society of liberal, intelligent, and cultivated persons, whose relations with each other would permit a more wholesome and simple life than can be had amidst the pressure of competitive institutions.[8]

In his charming *Brook Farm: Historic and Personal Memoirs,* John T. Codman speaks of "the happy buzz"[9] that prevailed at Brook Farm, prophetic of ever better things to come. Seldom, it would seem, was any movement attended by greater enthusiasm among those who had joined it. Commenting on the school there, O. B. Frothingham remarked: "The teaching was of a high order, not so much by reason of the accomplishments of the instructors, as in consequence of the singular enthusiasm that animated all concerned in it."[10] Hawthorne, before his first bucolic experience with the famous "transcendental heifer," wrote in his first letter from there to his sister: "The whole community eat[s] together, and such a delectable way of life has never been seen on earth since the days of the early Christians."[11] Many other letters from Brook Farm during the first years were to breathe a similar spirit.

This feeling of enthusiasm overflowed, too, into the field of entertainment. Miss Amelia Russell, "a little plump woman, with a pleasant smile, dimpled cheeks, and round laughing eyes," was known as "Mistress of Revels."[12] She showed great skill in arranging various games, dances and theatricals. The dances were frequent, and joined in by young and old, to the lively tunes of accomplished musicians. Literary societies and reading clubs also flourished there. A Miss Cornelia Hall, who boarded at the Farm at periods of varying length, used to give dramatic readings. Father Taylor, the well-known Methodist minister, used to count it a delight to go out to hear her read "The Rime of the Ancient Mariner."[13] There, too, often appeared Margaret Fuller who sometimes conducted her famous Conversations, but not always with the most pleasant results. However, of all those who entertained at the Institute, none approached the variety of Christopher P. Cranch in the histrionic art. "With powers of entertainment almost unlimited, [he] was also possessed of a splendid baritone voice. He could play the piano, guitar, flute, or violin as the occasion might suggest. He read from his own poems or travestries, and his ventriloquism embraced all the sounds of nature and the mechanical devices, from the denizens of the barnyard to the shrieks of the railroad locomotive."[14]

The Brook Farmers also found much social diversion in boating in the summer, frequent picnics in the nearby grove, skating or sleighing in the winter, or long walks over the Farm or into the countryside. Hawthorne had much to relate in his *American Notebooks* about his own strolls over the Farm or into the countryside.[15]

But there was another side to Brook Farm: the hard work on the 192 acres of land, with its substratum of sand and gravel,[16] the cleaning of the stables, the milking of the cows, and the retrenchments which came progressively with the waning of finances. But withal, Brook Farm could not but become an intriguing curiosity to the public, and people came in droves. The record book showed no less than four thousand visitors in a single year.[17] Among the more distinguished visitors were Emerson, A. Bronson Alcott, Margaret Fuller and Orestes Brownson. Brownson's relations to the Brook Farm Institute seem to have been quite similar to his relations to Transcendentalism itself: he went along with it, but only with certain misgivings and reserves. The most practical endorsement he gave it was the sending of his eldest son, Orestes, to live there. A little over a year after it had been in full operation, he also wrote an article on it for publication in the *Democratic Review*, November 1842. After laying his strictures on various systems of world reform, those of Robert Owen and Charles Fourier in particular, he acknowledged that he was more favorably disposed in regard to Brook Farm. It did not interfere with the three great pillars of society (the family, the church and the state), and respected the sacred right of property. The systems of Owen and Fourier aimed at being little worlds in themselves, complete substitutes for the larger associations of church and state. By contrast, Brook Farm made no break with the law of continuity, but was in itself:

> . . . simple, unpretending, and presents itself by no means as a grand scheme of world-reform, or of special organization. Its founder — and I speak from personal knowledge, for it has been my happiness to enjoy for years his friendship and instruction — is a man of rare attainments, one of our best scholars, and as a metaphysician second to no one in the country. No one among us is better acquainted with the various forms of world-reform which have been projected, from Plato's Republic to Fourier's Phalanx; but this establishment seems to be the result, not of his theorizing, but of the simple wants of his soul as a Christian. He felt himself unable, in the existing social organization, to practice always according to his conceptions of Christianity. . . . He sought to create around him the circumstances which would respond to it, enable him to worship God and love his brother, and to live with his brother in a truly Christian manner. [This sounds very much like an echo from the farewell sermon Ripley addressed to his Purchase Street congregation upon his departure, given at the beginning of this chapter.][18]

Yet there was an air of caution in what Brownson said. He remarked to

Sam Larned regarding his article on Brook Farm that he "hoped they would deserve half of it."[19] In other words he had strained hard to speak as favorably as he did, his old friend Ripley having of course a great deal to do with it. It appears that the whole drift of his article on Brook Farm was a sort of farewell to all schemes of world reform. His own experiences had been crystallizing into hard convictions on the matter. Plainly, his former Utopian dreams had burst. If any further confirmation of this fact were needed, we have it in a letter he wrote Emerson in this same month of November. The fact that Emerson himself had little or no faith in schemes of social reform may be one of the reasons why he unburdened himself at this time to him. Emerson had evidently invited him to meet at his home to join in a discussion of the social question with the promoters of Fruitlands, Messrs. Charles Lane, A. Bronson Alcott, and H. G. Wright. In a reply from Chelsea, Massachusetts, dated November 9, 1842, Brownson wrote:

> Dear Sir:
>
>     It grieves me that a previous engagement must prevent me from meeting at your home — to-morrow agreeably to your invitation. I am engaged to address to-morrow evening the good people of Nantucket. Be so obliging as to make my respects to Messrs. Lane, Alcott and Wright, and assure them from me that I should listen with great interest and respect to their exposition, anxious as I always am to be enlightened as to the means of ameliorating man's social condition, though I must say that I have long since ceased to have any faith in any actual or possible schemes of world-reform. The world jogs very much in its own way, and with or without our cooperation. The perfect social state these men seem to be dreaming of, I look upon as perfectly chimerical. A perfect social state is incompatible with the imperfection of individuals; and imperfect individuals must be, till they cease to be finite. All that remains for us, it seems, is to do what our hands find to do, but advancing toward a better state, by trying to make the best of our present.
>
>     Forgive me, I did not intend to philosophize in this way, but simply to acknowledge your note, and my inability to accept your invitation. I have worn out the best part of my life devising schemes of world-reform. And as far as I am concerned to no purpose. I am disposed very much to withdraw into myself, and confine myself to the discovery of possibly the great truths of philosophy and history. But allow me to assure you of my great respect for yourself, and my increasing sympathy every day with views you have put forth, and which I have at times been disposed to combat.
>
> Yours truly,<br>O. A. Brownson
>
> R. W. Emerson[20]

Whatever the evidence in his article on Brook Farm in the *Democratic Review* that Brownson was saying farewell to schemes of world reform, inasmuch as he had exempted Brook Farm from his general strictures, Ripley was pleased with it. But he still expressed his chagrin and disappointment that Brownson should have waited so long before writing any word of encouragement. Ripley apparently had been a trifle remiss in perceiving that Brownson was no longer quite the same man, at least in his social philosophy, that he had known only a short time before. They had frequently communed in times past in close harmony of spirit on the great social problems of the day and their likely solution. The occasion of harking back to those happy communings was furnished by the Hon. Hugh A. Garland, Clerk of the House of Representatives in Washington, D.C. After reading Brownson's article on Brook Farm in the *Democratic Review,* Mr. Garland, anxious to find a fit school for his young daughters, wrote Brownson a letter of inquiry concerning the moral climate of Brook Farm, and expressed great admiration for Brownson himself. He wrote in part:

Petersburg, Va., November 28, 1842

Dear Sir:

I trust you will not be surprised at receiving a letter from me. I have the boldness to write to you as a friend, for you are my friend — unconsciously to yourself the most intimate and precious friend I have. With you have I communed of late more than with any other man — and in you alone have I found a correspondence of thought and sympathy of feeling. You have given voice and utterance to what has been anxiously struggling in my bosom for years — cast a ray of light athwart the dark weltering chaos of the Past, Present, and Future — given shape and distinctness to a wild sea of thought — furnished the lofty, heart-gladdening ideal for which my soul had been longing — in a word, you have led me through the wilderness and placed in my hand the golden bough which serves as a talisman to conduct me into the Elysian Fields. For all this I thank you — with all my heart I thank you — and would take you to my bosom, if I could, as a loving father, and open my inmost thoughts to your kind scrutiny.

There is much yet, very much which I wish to know and have solved by the living voice face to face. This privilege I hope some day to enjoy. I would gladly go all the way to Boston for no other purpose, had I the time and the means. So earnest am I to *know* the truth, and from you alone of living men, who speak the English tongue, have I any hope of being *imbued* with that knowledge.

But it is not on my own account that I write to you now. I wish to know something more about that school you speak of in your last communication to the *Democratic Review*. I have *six* children — the three oldest daughters — fourteen, eleven, and nine years of age — and just such a school I have been long anxiously looking about for, that I might send them to it. It is only in such a place do I think it possible that all the faculties can be developed, moral, intellectual, and physical, and that education imparted which will fit them to discharge justly and magnanimously all the offices and duties of life. Such is my present impression, received from yourself and your lady correspondent. . . . But before I am fully satisfied I wish a word from you whispered into my private ear. Can I with undivided faith, trust the precious jewels of my heart to the keeping of those people with the full assurance that they will be preserved bright and untarnished?[21]

Brownson sent this letter to Mr. Ripley in order that he himself might furnish the desired information to be forwarded to Mr. Garland. After using up considerable space in a reply letter to Brownson himself concerning his son Orestes at the Farm, Ripley harked back to old times. He wrote:

I hope you know me too well to believe that any small thing [there had been a complaint or two at the Farm about Orestes, Jr.] would diminish my great respect for your intellect, or the sincere friendship I have cherished for you from the first in our acquaintance. We have truly sympathized as few men have done; you have always quickened my love for humanity; and for no small share of what mental clearness I may have, am I indebted to the hours of genial, pleasant intercourse I have enjoyed with you. If I had never known you, I should never have been engaged in this enterprize. I consider it as the incarnation of those transcendental truths which we have held in common, and which you have done so much to make me love. . . . With the vivid feeling that the great revolution in my life plan was the inevitable fruit of the ideas for which you most valued me, I will own to something of disappointment that you should have given us so little sympathy or recognition, when a friendly word would have been cheering amidst such a tempest of abuse as fell upon us from the conservative sky.[22]

But whatever the doubts of Brownson about the ultimate success of Brook Farm, he must have enjoyed his visits there. From what has come down to us about his visits, he evidently mixed a considerable amount of religion into his conversations, and, to the offense of some, even indulged in Catholicizing tendencies. This may account for the remark of Marianne Dwight Orvis: "Brownson is expected here next Sunday, in which I do not rejoice, but many are glad."[23] There is no question Brownson was now turning more and more toward Rome. Of the preaching he was doing, Isaac Hecker remarked: "To a very acute observer it was evident that, consciously or unconsciously, he was aiming at Catholicity. It was also evident that his own difficulties were not settled; he was gradually settling them by this very preaching."[24] But the statement Brownson made earlier in October 1842 is even more significant: "For ourselves we are no Protestants. We believe the problem of the age is Catholicism without the Papacy."[25] This trend of thought was bound to show itself also in his conversations at Brook Farm, and not without some effect. After mentioning that some Brook Farmers did pass over to Rome, Lindsay Swift adds: "There is no pretense that this transition ever threatened to assume the importance of a stampede." Yet "the external charms of the historic faith have their fascinations even for those who never embrace it — and it is probable that some effect was produced by the strong arguments of Brownson."[26] But whatever the effects produced by the "strong arguments" of Brownson on the members of Brook Farm, Lindsay Swift thinks that Georgiana Bruce Kirby exaggerated when she said that "rough, wooden crosses and pictures of the Madonna began to appear, and I suspected rosaries rattling under aprons."[27]

But there were probably more than just Mrs. Kirby who resented Brownson's "strong arguments" in favor of the ancient faith. Yet to refute them might have been a trifle difficult. What to do? As Arthur M. Schlesinger, Jr., remarks: "Staggered by his theology, they found consolation in making him the butt of their transcendental humor."[28] Word has come down to us, too, from Mrs. Georgiana Bruce Kirby that fun was had at times badgering Brownson on such sore points in church history as the Spanish Inquisition. "Do you approve," flashed out one of the ladies one day to Brownson with a twinkle in her eye, "of the priests of the Inquisition roasting off the feet of children under fourteen?" He replied, "Certainly I do; it was better for them to have their feet roasted off in this world than their souls to be roasted forever in the next."[29] (Who was having the more fun in this case?)

Brownson's son Henry claimed that his father was "the main instrument" in bringing about the conversion to the Catholic faith of at least three rather prominent persons at Brook Farm: two ministers, Rev. William J. Davis and Rev. George Leach, and the third person was Mrs. Ripley, wife of the founder of Brook Farm. She was a member of the gifted Dana family. Both she and her brother, Charles A. Dana, were founding members of the Brook Farm Institute. After her conversion, Henry Brownson tells us, "she devoted herself almost wholly to spiritual and corporal works of mercy; her labors in New York, especially at the institutions on the islands of the East River, cannot yet be forgotten. [He wrote this in 1899.]"[30] Miss Sarah Stearns of Brook Farm, a niece of Mrs. Ripley, also became a Catholic, and eventually a nun. Charles Sumner's brother and Isaac Hecker, the future founder of the Congregation of the Missionary Priests of St. Paul the Apostle, also became converts. Ripley himself, as is well known, never became a Catholic. Brownson's last effort to convert him was made after Ripley had been for some time one of the editors of the New York *Tribune*. Ripley put off the idea saying that he would ask to be received into the Catholic Church as soon as he had a sufficient amount laid aside to support himself when his job was gone, as it would be, he claimed, when he became a Catholic.[31] When Fr. Isaac Hecker returned from Europe a Redemptorist, he went to see Ripley at the *Tribune* office. Ripley asked the newly ordained: "Can you do all that any Catholic priest can do?" When Fr. Hecker replied "yes," Ripley said: "Then I will send for you when I am drawing near my end." When the end did come, Ripley sent for him, but the message was not delivered. Finally hearing of Ripley's illness, Fr. Hecker hastened to his bedside, but it was too late. Ripley's mind was gone, and he could do little for him.[32]

No religious services were held at Brook Farm at any time unless some minister came who wished to preach. Some of the members went to West Roxbury or elsewhere to church. Insofar as any attempt was ever made to sustain a vital religious life there, it was made by William H. Channing, the Unitarian minister, whom Isaac Hecker called "Catholic at heart, but Protestant in head."[33] After resigning his pulpit in New York City, he wished to join the Brook Farmers with his wife and children, but Mrs. Channing demurred. Doing the next best thing, he remained around them like a hovering spirit. Full of hope and inspiration in Brook Farm as a new Eden, he would invite the members to services in the nearby pine woods, or preach to them in the long parlors of the Pilgrim House.[34] By October 1845 he was planning a separate place of worship in the phalanstery being erected.[35] He was an object of much affection and admiration among the members of the Institute. "His figure was tall and stately, though rather slender. He carried himself finely, and walked with head erect. His features were sharp cut, clean and regular. His hair was dark and curling, and worn a trifle long for those days. His forehead was high and slightly retreating. His eyes were sharp and piercing, deep set, with delicate dark eyebrows. His complexion was warm and brilliant, his beard closely shaven."[36]

The style of life at Brook Farm might well be described as plain living and high thinking. There was much wit, fun and innocent gaiety, but the pattern of life was serious and Christian. The members there, most of them descendants of the New England Puritans, were at a much farther remove from Puritan beliefs than from strict Puritan discipline.[37] A fair sprinkling of ministers among the members guaranteed all the more securely the place that Christ was to hold as the model of their lives. J. Homer Doucet, resident there from the spring of 1844 until the summer of 1846, later remarked: "I never heard loud or boisterous language used; I never heard an oath; I never saw or heard any quarreling; I never knew that any one was accused or suspected of having acted in an ungentlemanly or unlady-like manner anywhere on the place."[38] In response to Brownson's letter in behalf of Hugh A. Garland who had written Brownson inquiring about the moral climate at Brook Farm, Ripley remarked that some of their young members were not "quite free from nonsense." They worshiped Ralph Waldo Emerson with too much infatuation, and, like their master, talked confusedly. But "they are pure, simple souls, apparently without an erring instinct, and their beautiful divine lives would seem to sanction their doctrine."[39] Such testimony left little or nothing to be desired.

Starting with fifteen members, the Brook Farmers had increased to one hundred and twenty. George M. Curtis tells us that they were composed of every type of person: "There were the ripest scholars, men and women of the most aesthetic culture and accomplishment, young farmers, seamstresses, mechanics [and] preachers."[40] Some paid a fee and attended the excellent school there, which had such accomplished instructors as Ripley in philosophy and mathematics; George Bradford in literature; J. S. Dwight, assisted by his two sisters Marianne and Frances, in the department of music; Charles A. Dana in Greek and German; Mrs. Sophie Ripley in history and modern languages; Hannah Ripley in drawing; and Amelia Russell in dancing. Other members were admitted among the group upon the agreement that they would work the full hours of the day, or part-time, using the rest for education. Some could not grow accustomed to work on the Farm. This was especially true of Hawthorne, a city-minded man. He had come there on April 12, 1841, and had even considered the community as a possible home for himself and his betrothed, Sophia Peabody, when they would be married.[41] Ironically he was given care of the cows and the pigs. After a three-week vacation at Salem while there, he complained upon his return of the "cold reception" given him by the cows.[42] Whether that or his disconcerting experience with his "transcendental heifer" had more to do with it, he was gone by the end of the year.

Neither did Brownson's son Orestes stay long. After being there less than a year, a great longing to go to sea was aroused in him by hearing the accomplished Miss Ida Russell, daughter of Jonathen Russell, sing one evening the song, "A Life on the Ocean Wave." Although Ripley would have been happy to "retain" Orestes, Jr., it was summarily decided that he should be allowed to ride the ocean wave. The Sturgis family, wealthy merchants who were members of his father's congregation, took considerable interest in the matter. Besides giving the young Orestes much counsel concerning life at sea, they presented him with a sextant, a copy of Bowditch's *Navigation,* and a few other books, chiefly mathematical. They also selected a good ship for him, the *Dover,* commanded by an excellent master and their friend, Captain Austin. Under these favorable circumstances Orestes, Jr., shipped out for Calcutta.[43]

That Ripley did not have the hearty sympathy of all people in founding Brook Farm is evident from his reference to "such a tempest of abuse as fell upon us from the conservative sky" in his letter to Brownson.[44] Yet he had been much encouraged by the temper of the times. As John Morley expressed the matter: "A great wave of humanity, of benevolence, of desire for improvement — a great wave of social sentiment, in short — poured itself among all who had the faculty of large and disinterested thinking."[45] George Ripley was certainly one of the men of the age who were sensitive to the keen desire for social improvement that was abroad. Although his brave project was to fail eventually with the burning of the uncompleted phalanstery, the memory of Brook Farm remains as a monument to the high and noble aspirations of Ripley and all those who had a part of it. Of it William H. Channing remarked years later: "Never did I feel so calmly humble, devoutly thankful that it had been my privilege to fail in this grandest, sublimest, surest of all movements."[46] Of it Fr. Isaac Hecker also remarked: "It was the greatest, the noblest, the bravest dream of New England. Nothing greater has been produced. No greater sacrifice has been made for humanity than the movement that Brook Farm embodied. It collected the dreams of New England. Brook Farm was the realization of the best dreams these men had of Christianity, it embodied them."[47]

Isaac Hecker came to Brook Farm on the advice of Brownson, who, as

Fr. Walter Elliott tells us, "was the strongest purely human influence, if we except his mother's, which Isaac Hecker ever knew."[48] He arrived there on January 3, 1843. He soon became a general favorite among the members, being "always equable and playful, wholly simple and frank in manner." The community being in need of a baker, Isaac finally consented to fill the role of baker. "I am sure of a livelihood," he remarked one day with evident satisfaction, "for I can make good bread."[49] But he had come to Brook Farm for studies, and he used his opportunities to attend what classes he could. Also while kneading in the dough trough he would be scanning Kant's *Critique of Pure Reason* which he had fastened up on the wall before him.[50] After a couple of months, however, he relinquished the role of baker, and gave himself more completely to studies, mapping out an ambitious program for himself. He became known among the Brook Farmers as "Earnest the Seeker," a name given him by George Curtis, because he seemed to match so well a character in a story published at the time in the *Dial* by William H. Channing — the story of one who was painfully conscious that he did not have the truth, but was earnestly seeking it.[51]

It is a fair guess to assume that on Brownson's visits to the Farm Isaac Hecker was of all persons the one he sought out, since he had directed him there. George Curtis, a close friend of Isaac when there, later gave us his impression of the relationship that was developing between Isaac and Brownson at the time. Speaking directly of Isaac, it had seemed to him that:

> . . . of "all the apostles of the newness," as they were gaily called, whose counsel he sought, Brownson was the most satisfactory to him. I thought then it was due to the authority of Brownson's masterful tone, the definiteness of his views, the force of his "understanding," as the word was then philosophically used in distinction from reason. Brownson's mental vigor and positiveness were very agreeable to a candid mind which was speculatively adrift and experimenting, and, as it seemed to me, which was more emotional than logical. Brownson, after his life of varied theological and controversial activity was drawing toward the Catholic Church, and his virile force fascinated the more delicate temper of the young man, and, I have always supposed, was the chief influence which at that time affected Hecker's views, although he did not then enter the Catholic Church.[52]

Isaac Hecker's sojourn at Brook Farm was not an extended one. On June 19 of this same year he visited Fruitlands, a new type of community founded by Amos Bronson Alcott, having as associates the Englishman, Charles Lane (who largely financed it), and H. G. Wright. Isaac thought he saw a more perfect way of life lived by that community. On the evening of July 11, 1843, he also joined them.[53] With Isaac's departure from Brook Farm, and with Brownson's son Orestes gone from there, Brownson's interest in that romantic venture began to wane more and more.

Isaac Hecker had probably seen Brook Farm at its best. At any rate, Ripley and his associates almost immediately now began to experiment with Fourierism, as interpreted by Albert Brisbane, to meet the exigencies of the American scene. But it was not until May 1, 1845, however, that the Brook Farm Institute of Agriculture and Education was transformed into a phalanx with the adoption of a new constitution.[54] What had influenced Ripley to make the change? An explanation is really called for, as Lindsay Swift indicated when he commented: "The single point of interest is to understand how such a theory [the system of Fourier] could have found even partial acceptance with Horace Greeley, Parke Godwin, Margaret Fuller, George

Ripley — all possessed of sound mind and disposition, to say nothing of lesser known Fourierists."[55] It is not at all improbable — in fact there is good evidence for it — that financial troubles had so preyed upon the mind of Ripley that he was disposed to turn in desperation to anything that promised a way out.[56] But turning to Fourierism was scarcely the way out, for as Brownson observed: "A Phalanx cannot well go into operation without a capital of half a million. A simple establishment like the one of Brook Farm has gone into operation with less than five thousand dollars, and would be able to do well with ten or twenty thousand."[57]

That financial difficulties did multiply is no cause for wonderment. For as John Codman well observed, there were philosophers enough at the Institute, and plenty of sweet, charming characters and amateur workmen, but the hard-fisted toilers and the brave financiers were absent.[58] One thing is certain: the adoption of the Fourierist constitution on May 1, 1845, rang the death knell on what had been the Brook Farm Institute. After that date neither Brownson nor Isaac Hecker could have had much interest in the place. From then on, it was to share at least partly in the odium loosely associated with Fourierism elsewhere. Zoltán Haraszti tells us that with the changeover to a phalanx "a storm of attacks began in the newspapers," and that the number of pupils "rapidly diminished."[59] He says the change was made during the winter of 1843-1844, with William Henry Channing the moving spirit behind it, assisted by Albert Brisbane playing the role of a mesmerist. Haraszti further informs us that some of the residents of the Farm, who had never believed in the phalanstery, only experienced a feeling of relief when it burned down — that they had wished to see it "blown away or burned down."[60] John Van Der Sears even goes so far as to suggest that the phalanstery was set on fire out of hatred by the old Puritans of Roxbury.[61]

In any case at all, the fire that destroyed the phalanstery in March of 1846 seems to have been for Ripley more of a deliverance in disguise than a catastrophe — little as he may have realized it at the time. As for his friend Brownson, Brook Farm seems to have helped to develop further his maturing conviction about the fragility of all such organized effort at world reform as Brook Farm. While he had given it a measured amount of his attention, he had been immensely busy at the same time with efforts of his own to solve questions both social and political. This threw him into closer relationship with Isaac Hecker.

# 17

## THE BEGINNING OF A FRIENDSHIP
## AND THE END OF A QUARTERLY

*Isaac Hecker's first meeting with Brownson apparently occurred when Brownson came to New York City to lecture in March 1841 • The participation of the Hecker brothers in programs of reform had prepared them to appreciate Brownson • Brownson's repeated lecturing in New York City • He accepts hospitality in the Hecker home during the course of four lectures • He differs from Daniel Webster on the basic office or duty of government • Isaac Hecker's description of Brownson • Brownson's vigorous backing of his friend John C. Calhoun for the presidency • He toys with the idea of reviving his* Boston Quarterly *which he had discontinued the previous October • His relation to the Dialists • Tributes to the high quality his* Boston Quarterly *had attained • The offer made him to become a contributor to the* United States Magazine and Democratic Review.

We have already spoken of Orestes Brownson and Isaac Hecker as a part of the scenes of Brook Farm, but we should note that they had probably first met when Brownson came to New York City in March 1841 to lecture.[1] It was the beginning of a friendship which was to be rendered progressively all the more meaningful as the lives of the two commingled ever more deeply in their mutual efforts to solve together the deep problems of life. How many golden hours were they not to spend together exploring the mazes of philosophy or searching for the ultimate answers in the realm of religious truth! Isaac, the younger by more than a decade and a half, had no doubt the fairer chance of being the greater beneficiary intellectually in their growing friendship. Contact with the vigorous and powerful mind of Brownson was bound to stimulate and enlarge his own. It so happened, too, that Isaac was soon to experience considerable anxiety in his endeavor to find his place in life, or in the settlement of his vocation. It was to this stalwart, impressive man he had apparently seen for the first time on the lecture platform in his native New York City that he was to turn so often for guidance. He was to be Isaac's constant adviser and close friend in these years, particularly 1843 and 1844. In March 1844 Isaac wrote his friend Brownson: "I feel and perceive the need of advice and counsel in the present event of my life. This being so, leads me to you for there is no one who I look up to with so much confidence and in whose judgment I put so much trust as in your own."[2]

Whether or not Isaac Hecker was already acquainted with Brownson's long campaign for social justice before he came to New York City to lecture, he has not told us. It appears, however, that he was among the audience for Brownson's first lecture in New York City. A responsive chord must have been struck in his heart as he listened with rapt attention to the lecturer expounding his thoughts on Christian democracy forcefully and eloquently. For he himself had been much interested in social reform, and had plunged into politics as offering the most hopeful lever for reform. He and his brothers had joined the political party called the Locofocos, social democrats, an offshoot of the Tammany Democrats, who proclaimed themselves the defenders of the rights of the underprivileged, the common laborer and the immigrant. The party was organized in 1835 and the next year developed into the State's Equal Rights party. The party aimed its shafts particularly at bank monopolies. Convinced that the issuance of paper money on the part of banks far in excess of the collateral on hand was bound to work financial hardship on the common laborer in the way of depreciated bank notes, they declared "their unqualified and uncompromising hostility to bank notes and paper money as a circulating medium because gold and silver [are] . . . the only safe and constitutional currency."[3]

Into this political party the Hecker brothers (John, George and Isaac) entered enthusiastically. Isaac and his brother George were at the time too young to make themselves felt at the ballot box, so they devised a scheme of their own to register their opposition to the misuse of money. They bought a hand printing press and set it up in the garret of their quarters at 56 Rutgers Street. The bills collected in their thriving bakery business they smoothed out and then printed on them the words: "Of all the contrivances to impoverish the laboring classes of mankind, paper money is the most effective. It fertilizes the rich man's field with the poor man's sweat." As soon as the bankers found out what was going on, they were incensed over the matter, and attempted to invoke the law on these defacers of the currency. Relating the story later, George tartly remarked: "We beat them. We didn't deface it; we only printed something on the back of it."[4]

In the political election of 1837 the Hecker brothers were also very active in the Equal Rights party in New York City. After attending meetings for the choice of candidates, they worked in every possible way for the success of the ticket. George and Isaac made the rounds posting handbills long after the people had retired for the night. Fr. Hecker recalled years later how they had worked at this until three o'clock in the morning, which, he added, "was not so inconvenient for us, for we were bakers." But especially on election day itself had they worked hard, particularly in their own ward, the old Seventh. Referring to this period of life, Fr. Hecker said: "My brothers and I had long been playing men's parts in politics."[5]

With this background, Isaac Hecker, a young man of twenty-one years of age when he became acquainted with Brownson, must have found himself quite sympathetic to Brownson's fiery flow of thought on social reform. His presence in the audience for Brownson's first lecture would argue that he had already known something of this man famous as the Boston Reformer. Apparently, Brownson's first lecture was on "The Democracy of Christ," and was delivered on March 4, 1841, at Stuyvesant Institute to "a numerous and fashionable audience." The second, given the next evening, was on "The Reform Spirit of the Age" in Clinton Hall.[6] Speaking of the first lecture many years later, Fr. Hecker remarked: "Of course the life and teachings of Our Savior Jesus Christ were brought into use, and the upshot of the lecturer's thesis was that Christ was the big Democrat and the Gospel was the true democratic platform."[7] This was no new theme with Brownson at all. It had formed the staple of his preaching for almost a dozen years, and had received additional emphasis in his *Quarterly*. In his article on the "Democracy of Christianity" in the October 1838 issue, he had called Christ "the prophet of Democracy."[8] To Brownson still in this year, 1841, a perfect Christianity spelled a perfect democracy. The actual identification of the two was called "the great heresy of the nineteenth century" by the Cardinal

Archbishop of Paris, as we have noted, which had many a stalwart champion both in Europe and America, both clerical and laic.[9] That fascinating heresy was in fact the doctrine of the whole movement party of the day. This misconception Brownson himself was soon to slough off. But in the meantime he could show with clarity the remarkable similarities between the two that do exist on the social and political levels. He wrote:

> The Christian thought as it existed in the mind of Jesus of Nazareth, was coincident with democracy. His kingdom was to be set up in the world; his mission was to establish the reign of justice and love on earth. He claimed to have come from God, because his mission was to the poor and oppressed. "The Spirit of the Lord," he said, "is upon me, because he has anointed me to preach the glad tidings to the poor, to heal them that are bruised, to bind up the broken-hearted, to set the captive free." To the disciples of St. John the Baptist, sent to ask whether he was the Messiah promised, or whether they were to look for another, he said: "Go tell your master, the poor have the Gospel preached to them." He declared the poor blessed, heirs to his kingdom, and pronounced a woe upon the rich, declaring it "easier for a camel to go through the eye of a needle, than for a rich man to enter the kingdom of heaven." He rebuked all cant, sham, or make-believe goodness, and declared to the Scribes and Pharisees, the saints of his day, that publicans and harlots would enter the kingdom of heaven before them. He discarded all titles and distinctions created by human pride and vanity, recognized no earth-born nobilities, no pomp of rank or earthly majesty, but looked upon simple naked humanity, and accepted and honored man for his real or intrinsic worth. He loved man as man, and died for his redemption. The great law of his religion was love of man, "By this shall all men know that you are my disciples, if you love one another." "We know," said the beloved disciple, "that we have passed from death to life, because we love the brethren." Nor was this love to be confined to one's own family, friends, or nation. We are to love our enemies, and bless them that curse us, do good to them that hate us. We must love our neighbor as ourselves, and count every man our neighbor to whom we can be of service, as was the Samaritan to the Jew who fell among thieves. Jesus proclaimed the worth of man as man, taught the great law of love, and proposed the universal brotherhood of the race — liberty, equality, fraternity: the noble devise of the democratic banner.[10]

Although Brownson's lecture on "The Democracy of Christ" seems no longer extant, the sweep of his thought in that discourse must have included the substance of the above quotation. The New York *Evening Post* characterized the address as "a bold and eloquent discourse on the dignity of Christian and democratic principles," the burden of the message being "that the Christian religion as taught by its Founder and democracy as it exists in every rational mind were the same great and eternal principles regarded in different relations." A large and distinguished audience was in attendance.[11]

Brownson returned to New York City this same year (1841) to deliver a Fourth of July oration. We learn from Fr. Hecker that he and his brothers had secured Brownson's consent for the engagement, and made the necessary arrangements for his coming. The oration was delivered in Washington Hall. In content it was similar to the Fourth of July oration he had delivered at Dedham, Massachusetts, 1835 — immensely given over to a passionate concern for the laboring classes or the underprivileged in society. In thunderous tones he drove home the point that "the great principles involved in the American Revolution, and the mission of this country, was the alleviation of the condition of the laborer, giving to him an equality with the mercantile and feudal lord, so that man should everywhere be recognized as

219

man." Such were his sulfurous outbursts of oratory as he swung into a subject which lay so close to his heart that "he shook the old hotel to its foundations and made the glass in the windows rattle again."[12]

Someone who signed himself, G.W.D., who had the oration put in pamphlet form, remarked in his introductory comments: "We lay before our readers one of the most brilliant orations it has ever been our good fortune to listen to, on the Fourth of July. . . . It is the opinion of Mr. Brownson that all political reform should have its foundation in religion; or, in other words, that true religion is the ground-work of every thing beneficial to the human race. He opened the meeting with prayer; after which the Declaration of Independence was read." On this evidence it would seem that Fr. Hecker was not altogether accurate in his statement that when Brownson came to New York to lecture (at this time), that "religion had sunk down [with him], not out of sight, but out of practical prominence."[13] In the course of his oration Brownson said:

> We often hear people speak of the American Revolution as if it were opposed to Christianity; but had not Jesus lived, and preached, and died for man, there . . . [would have] been no American Revolution: and if there had been one, it would have been like so many other revolutions where men contended which shall have the right to plunder their brethren. It was those great principles which were taught then, that were preached by the humble Nazarene, and for which he was crucified between two thieves, silently working their way, which brought about that Revolution.
>
> We are too much in the habit of taking too low views of the American Revolution, and of considering the question in a light altogether inferior to its real merits. It was not only a question between the colonies and the mother country; it was a question between the past and the future; and when the troops met in battle, as on Bunker's Hill, or Saratoga's plains, it was entire humanity struggling to decide the question whether humanity should continue where she was, or continue her march onward toward freedom and union with God.[14]

After Brownson's delivery of the oration, Isaac and his brothers met with him to discuss the possibility of a future course of lectures in the city. An agreement was reached that the Hecker brothers would make the necessary arrangements. As the lecture season approached they interviewed the president of the New York Lyceum with the intention of having Brownson engaged as a lecturer. But without success, for the sponsors of the lyceum feared that the people might not attend in goodly numbers as they themselves considered some of Brownson's ideas peculiar and unpopular — this being probably a reference to Brownson's essay on "The Laboring Classes" of just the previous year. They feared financial loss, and would take no risks. In a letter to Brownson the Hecker brothers frankly acquainted him with the situation, and, greatly enthusiastic for the reform movement, assured him they would engage a hall for any subject upon which he wished to lecture. They added: "Whatever you make up your mind to do we are always ready to cooperate with hearty cheer as long as it makes a stir, a shaking among the people. In fact if we could think of any other than the ordinary way to pursue so as to excite enthusiasm, we would do it with all our might. We hate the beaten track."[15] In conclusion they suggested the holidays as the best time for the lectures.

The place finally chosen for the lectures was Clinton Hall on the corner of Nassau and Beekman Streets. In January 1842, Brownson returned to New York City to deliver a course of four lectures on civilization and human progress. The *Tribune* gave notice of the coming event in its issue of January 17:

> O. A. BROWNSON, Editor of the *Boston Quarterly Review,* will give a Course of Four Lectures, "On Civilization."
>
> First Lecture — A general Survey of Civilization, and the Law by which it is advanced.
>
> Second Lecture — Modern Civilization: its Elements: Influence of Religion and Philosophy in advancing it.
>
> Third Lecture — Influence of Property on Legislation and Political Institutions.
>
> Fourth Lecture — The part this country has played, and is destined to play in advancing the Civilization of the Race. The First Lecture will be given on MONDAY EVENING, Jan. 17, and the second on WEDNESDAY EVENING, 19, at half past 7 o'clock.
>
> The time and place of the Third and Fourth Lectures will be announced at the close of the Second.

The lectures were in fact delivered on January 17, 18, 25 and February 2.

From Fr. Vincent Holden, C.S.P., we learn that "the New York City papers were generous in their notice of these lectures, especially the *Tribune,* the *Evening Post* and the *New Era.*"[16] The fourth lecture, "The Part this country has played, and is destined to play in advancing the Civilization of the Race," was a pet theme with Brownson, and seems to have left the deepest impression on his audience. The *Evening Post* of February 3, 1842, reported:

> The closing lecture of Mr. Brownson, delivered at Clinton Hall last evening, was the most eloquent and interesting of the whole course. It treated of the part the United States is destined to play in the civilization of the world. He insisted that the mission of this nation was to assert and extend the great principles of individual freedom. Its physical position, no less than its political history and social arrangements, clearly designate that it has been chosen for this purpose by Providence. It was discovered just at the time when the theocratic and political elements of society had reached the majority of their power, and kept down by their pressure, the development of the liberties of the individual. The first effect of the discovery was to afford a field for the free action of the surplus and poorer population of Europe.
>
> The broad theatre thus opened in the western world, for labors of the industrious placed the balance of power in the hands of the industrious classes. Property was more generally diffused; the prejudices of birth and rank broken down; and a strong sense of individual dignity and right sprung up in the hearts of men. "I am as good as you," and "you shall not be my master," was an expression of a spirit, which, silently growing ended in the American Revolution.
>
> Mr. Brownson gave a striking history of the rise and effects of the French Revolution, defended it as a mighty agent in advancing civilization and a glorious example to oppressed nations. From the past, he turned to the future, and showed the principle which must govern American action. This principle he stated to be freedom — freedom of commerce, freedom of industry, freedom of utterance. He spoke with great energy, and was frequently and rapturously cheered by his audience.

Although it seems we no longer have any record of his third lecture on "The Influence of Property on Civilization," we do have a letter he published in the Boston *Times* (March 30, 1842), protesting a misrepresentation of his views on that subject, quite possibly as he had expressed them in that same third lecture. The editor had mistakenly represented his views on the influence of property in relation to government to be the same as those of Daniel Webster. His letter in reply is of special interest on the score that it again exhibits him as the indomitable champion and defender of the natural rights of man above all else. In part his letter reads:

Dear Sir:

You do not represent precisely my doctrine as to the duty of government to protect property. You represent my doctrine concerning the influence of property to be the same as Mr. Webster's. I should deem it no reproach, to be proved to agree with Mr. Webster, for whose talents I have the highest respect: but his doctrine as you state it, is none of mine. Mr. Webster and I agree that the concentration of property in large masses is an evil, and we both contend that government should pursue such a policy as tends naturally to diffuse it as much as possible among all members of the community. But he, as you say, [contends for the diffusion of property] so that every man may have an interest in government; while I contend for the diffusion of property so that every man may be able to maintain his rights. According to your views of Mr. Webster's doctrine, the end of government is to protect property, and therefore only men of property have an interest in its proceedings. Suffrage then should be limited to men of property; and in order to justify you in making it universal, you must render every man a proprietor. This is not my doctrine. I deny that the end of government is the protection of property; its chief end is the maintaining of every individual of the community in the full possession of all his natural rights. But as government follows always the direction of property, it will always be so administered as to dispossess of their liberty all who are destitute of property. Property, then, should not be diffused, in order to give every man an interest in government, but as *the means of enabling government, or of compelling, if you please, government to maintain every man in the free and full possession of his natural liberty.* The difference between Mr. Webster and myself, as you state his doctrine, is simply this: according to him property always rules; therefore, you should found your government on property, and admit to political power only men of property; according to Mr. Webster, property always governs; therefore, again, in order to maintain universal freedom, you must make all men proprietors. Mr. Webster, you see, is intent on providing for government, and for basing it upon the strongest interest in the community; but I am intent only on providing for the maintenance of liberty. The difference between us then, if you state his views correctly is all the difference there is between one who studies to secure the strength and stability of government, and him who would put into the hand of every member of the community the means of maintaining his own freedom, and of compelling the government to maintain the liberty of all.

It was the four lectures Brownson delivered in January and February of 1842, in New York City, that afforded Isaac Hecker an opportunity of becoming better acquainted with him. Listening to him on the platform, Isaac had been "immediately struck by the force of this extraordinary man who was six feet two inches tall, with black hair brushed straight back from his forehead and deep-set eyes of mixed gray and hazel that seemed black when he grew excited."[17] A more intimate acquaintance with this "extraordinary man" now developed. At the invitation of Isaac and his brother John, Brownson accepted the hospitality of the Hecker home at Rutgers Street during the course of his four lectures. Speaking of Brownson's stay with them, Isaac (years later) gave us a glimpse of the man in private life:

In private life he was sociable. Although cheerfulness was not a marked feature of his character — for his temper was grave — yet he was chatty and talkative, and often very much so. His conversation with us was always on those political and social questions in which we were deeply interested. . . . His was a conspicuously philosophical mind, and he was always ready to go off into a metaphysical or other argument to prove his theories. He never knew any time or place inopportune for such a diversion, often during or after breakfast, dinner, or supper launching us off into the region of high philosophical disquisition.[18]

Fr. Hecker also gave us another glimpse of Brownson in private life when speaking of his visit with him for several weeks at Brownson's home in Chelsea just before he himself had left for Brook Farm, the third week of January 1843. All their thought was again about philosophy, not only in the home circle, but, as Fr. Hecker tells it, as they walked the streets of Boston, on down toward the ferry, on the boat as they crossed the harbor, and from the ferry wharf up the hill to Mt. Bellingham. With the evident wish of satisfying the curiosity of any who might wonder what sort of a person this man of giant body and mind was in private conversation, he said:

> Those who knew Brownson only superficially might ask, Was he not peremptory in private intercourse? I answer, Yes, in one way. What occupied his mind at the moment he would crowd upon your attention, and never be content until he had you full of his idea. He would do this without bullying, and yet would encroach upon your independence if you were not careful to maintain it. Has the reader ever met a man who was in earnest who acted otherwise? If you did stand up against him and maintain your independence, it generally ended in a disturbance of the elements; the breeze nearly always freshened into a gale, and the exchange of views was a stormy one. Woe to the man who measured strength with Dr. Brownson and had not the pluck and nerve to withstand him.
> In another way he was not peremptory. He did not want you to take his *ipse dixit*. He wanted you to appreciate his argument for its merits, never to take it on his mere word.[19]

Fortune was again to bring our far-famed Boston editor and Isaac Hecker together in their common backing of the candidacy of John C. Calhoun for the presidency. After their disastrous defeat at the hands of the Whigs in the election of 1840, the leaders of the Democratic party turned quickly to a consideration of who could lead them to victory at the polls in 1844. To many of them Calhoun seemed their brightest hope. In his correspondence with Brownson, Calhoun referred to a rising sentiment in his favor. After assessing the political situation in the country, he wound up his letter to Brownson, dated December 31, 1841, saying:

> If I know myself, I would not, at my time of life, accept the highest office, if proffered, without opposition, but from a sense of duty; but if it should be thought that I am capable of turning to the best account for the country this deeply important juncture, I would not decline the responsibility. You will, of course, understand what I write to be in strict confidence, and intended only for yourself.[20]

Soon after the receipt of this letter Brownson began his exertions to influence the Democratic party in favor of the nomination of Calhoun for the presidency. He had done all he could through the pages of the *Boston Quarterly Review,* and would later do all he could through *Brownson's Quarterly Review,* to convince Democrats North and South that Calhoun would be their best choice.[21] He also opened a correspondence in the forepart of 1842 with Dixon H. Lewis of Alabama, a member of the House of Representatives, who was one of the leaders, if not the chief promoter, of the Calhoun movement. Brownson received two letters from him, one dated June 8 and the other June 16. Earnestly discussing with Brownson the political situation in his first letter, Mr. Lewis urged him to throw an article on Calhoun into one of the leading newspapers of the North, "and I can have the article," he said, "republished here and then have it go through the Union." In his second letter he threw out to Brownson hints of his own, "to be worked up into an article under your hand, which like a thing of life will *speak* to the feelings of Democracy North and South. I know no man so well qualified as yourself saving your want of that *intimate knowledge* of the *temper* of the different sections on this point."[22]

When D. H. Lewis showed one of Brownson's letters to his Southern colleague, R. Barnwell Rhett, Mr. Rhett also took pen in hand to write Brownson. One of the great problems of the pro-Calhoun Democrats was to head off Martin Van Buren from recapturing the nomination for the presidency since they looked upon his possible candidacy as only an encumbrance to the party. The antipathy of Rhett to Van Buren was equalled only by his deep attachment to Calhoun. Rhett was at the time a member of Congress, and later became editor of the *Charleston Mercury*. Both he and Brownson were looking to Calhoun as the only man who could measure up to the qualifications of the stern moralist who would effect the reforms in government so desperately needed. Yet Rhett had his doubts whether even the "cast-iron" Calhoun would be equal to the Herculean task of cleaning the Augean stables of his own political party. In the same letter in which he suggested to Brownson that he could do "immense good" by throwing a series of pro-Calhoun articles into the *Boston Post*, he remarked:

> My desire is not merely to restore the Democratic party to power, but to reform this party as well as bring it to power. It has long needed reformation. The Government is rotten in all its branches, corrupt and perverted in administration as well as in legislation. Mr. V[an] Buren has not the spirit and genius of a reformer. I know but one man in the party who possesses the qualities the occasion requires. You know who I mean. And even he, when he stirs the muckheap, will see worms and snakes in myriads which will crawl up on him, and endeavor to stifle him.[23]

Beyond the Southern states, the strongest pro-Calhoun sentiment was to be found in Boston and New York. Among the most enthusiastic backers of Calhoun were the Hecker brothers, John and Isaac. John being the older by nine years, had got into the swim of politics ahead of Isaac, but Isaac had quickly moved along after him. As a mass meeting was soon to be held in New York City at the time to promote the name of Calhoun for the nomination at the Democratic convention of the next year, 1844, John Hecker wrote to Brownson to inquire whether he would furnish an address for the occasion. What was wanted was an electrifying appeal that would not only fire the New Yorkers with enthusiasm for Calhoun, but would influence as well the local delegates to the state convention at Syracuse. John Hecker was prominent in the pro-Calhoun movement, and spoke for the other backers when he wrote Brownson on August 20, 1843. At the time of writing he expected the convention would be held on September 15, which would have given Brownson three weeks in which to furnish the address. But John was in error regarding the date of the convention: it was to be held, not on the fifteenth, but on the fifth.[24] However, when the mistake was discovered, John was out of town. Isaac accordingly immediately wrote Brownson on August 30, apprising him of the mistake and the correct date, September the fifth. He emphasized to Brownson that a spirited address would be "a matter of great importance as you are fully aware that this being the first demonstration of this character it would be one which will tell the country through, as we all have reason to hope it will in numbers as doubtless it will by the character of the address which will come from your able and powerfully impressive pen."[25] But unfortunately Brownson found it impossible to accommodate. He wrote:

> I regret that it will not be in my power to furnish the address. I did not get my article off to the D[emocratic] R[eview] till yesterday after noon, and I am worn out. It would have given me pleasure to have furnished it, had it been in my power, but it is not.[26]

Henry Brownson did not know of this letter of his father to Isaac Hecker. Thinking that his father had furnished the requested address, he mistakenly stated that Isaac sent a call for another address in another letter of September 6.[27] In this same letter of September 6 Isaac Hecker related to Brownson that at the pro-Calhoun mass meeting in City Hall Park a committee of three had been appointed, one of whom was his brother John, to draft an address to the people of the United States setting forth the reasons for the preference of John C. Calhoun as the Democratic candidate for the presidency. But this was done with the private understanding that Brownson himself would with pleasure provide the address, if circumstances permitted.[28] With this wish Brownson immediately complied.

The address which Brownson sent for use was, however, unsigned, a copy of which was sent also to R. Barnwell Rhett. Immensely pleased with it, he wrote Brownson from Washington:

> Dear Sir:
> I have just received a pamphlet on a "National Convention" from New York, but which the style will not allow me to impute to any one else but yourself. . . . Your pamphlet is excellent, and a few more such will knock the caucus machinery, as it did in the election of Gen. Jackson, into atoms.[29]

Rhett concluded his letter by saying that he was in Washington to give life and vigor to the press set up there, that is, for the promotion of the Calhoun movement. He added: "We want an able press in New York. Cannot Boston and New York put up and sustain one until the fight is over?"[30] Such, too, were the sentiments of those pushing the Calhoun cause in New York City. They wanted a newspaper that would really spark a fiery enthusiasm for the whole movement. And who but Brownson was the man to spearhead such a widespread thrust as editor. Isaac Hecker was again asked to contact him and ascertain under what conditions he would accept the editorship of such a paper. Brownson was highly elated when the letter of September 14 reached him, and he replied at once:

> With regard to the editorship, I need not say that it would please me, for I shall delight in being at the head of a daily paper in your city, devoted to the support of Mr. Calhoun. So much I can say. As to the terms, the persons who have the management of the business must decide themselves what they will do, and make me an offer on such terms as seem to them good; if the terms meet my wishes, I will accept; if not, I shall say so at once. I, of course, can state no conditions. They must come from the party soliciting my services. Let them state:

1. What they expect me to do.
2. What compensation they will offer me.

One condition only I mention, namely, I will have nothing to do with the pecuniary affairs of the paper; my business shall be solely Editorial, with no responsibility but Editorial responsibility.[31]

But Hecker had in no sense urged Brownson in his letter to accept the editorship. Just the previous October (1842), Brownson had brought his *Boston Quarterly Review* to a close. Hecker knew that Brownson was already toying with the idea of reviving it, and that he hoped to get back his old job as steward of the Marine Hospital in Chelsea. In a letter to Isaac, dated September 2, 1843, Brownson remarked: "I am expecting to get back to the hospital; though I have not yet received my appointment."[32] Reappointment there would make the revival of his *Review* much easier. Friend Isaac seems to have been in hearty agreement with these views of Brownson, and said so plainly in his letter about the editorship of the pro-Calhoun paper by inquiring:

> Would it not be more commanding and better suited to your tastes if you should receive the hospital appointment, to start the *B[oston] Q[uarterly]*? Much as I desire your coming here, still I would regret much more the loss of your pen in that higher sphere which the *Review* would be the channel of, and the newspaper not. Still this may present advantages to you that I am not aware of.[33]

As enthusiastic as Brownson had at first been about the editorship of the pro-Calhoun paper, within two weeks he had changed his mind. Whether or not his friend Isaac had influenced his decision to revive his *Quarterly,* is not recorded. In any case, there were other factors that told in the case. For one thing, the ever-increasing conservatism in politics and government Brownson's writings had been showing since the elections of 1840 was little acceptable to the run-of-the-mill politicians in the country, of whatever party. Brownson's son Henry refers to this when giving the reasons why his father gave up the idea of the editorship of the pro-Calhoun newspaper: "It had lately become plain that Brownson's views of the origin, office, and limitation of government were not in accord with the new theory of popular sovereignty which had taken hold of all politicians, Whig and Democratic, north of the Mason and Dixon's line."[34] This meant, as Brownson himself clearly perceived, that he would scarcely be acceptable by and large as the editor of the proposed paper. He turned instead to the idea of reviving his own *Quarterly*. Accordingly he indited a letter to his friend Isaac on October 3, 1843, requesting him to:

> . . . stop all proceedings in my behalf, if any are making. I have altered my plans and do not wish to become editor of the paper. I fear I would not be the choice of all concerned and, moreover, I wish to resume my *Quarterly*.[35]

Just what the reasons were which had induced Brownson to discontinue his *Quarterly* seems largely a matter of surmise. Neither Brownson himself nor his son Henry have given us any clue to the real reasons in the case. The statement made by C. C. Hollis, namely, that "by 1842 the circulation of the *Boston Quarterly Review* had dropped to a dangerous degree,"[36] probably had more to do with Brownson's decision to discontinue than anything else. This, too, probably explains why he had gone off on lecture tours to Philadelphia and New York at this time — in an effort to augment his waning finances. The time immediately following the publication of his essay on "The Laboring Classes" was bound to be a period of uncertainty, and might easily become one of letdown. After the wide notoriety of his essay had worn off, he still had on his hands the problem of retaining the interest among his readers of those who hoped he would go further and those who were of a more conservative stamp. Although he had begun a gradual turn to the right, this may not have been overly perceptible in the social and theological orders, and it is not improbable that some of his patrons may have lost interest and dropped the *Review*. Neither can it be doubted that he was at this time suffering diminution of stature among the Boston circle of intellectuals. He had launched out vigorously into realms, particularly the political, in which the Transcendentalists had little or no interest — and had chided them for their insouciance to affairs of government. Although he had always professed high esteem for them personally, he was becoming more and more estranged to them. For various reasons there does seem to have been a decline in the patronage of the *Review* within the year following the publication of his essay on "The Laboring Classes" — which may well have been the main reason for its discontinuance. Yet this reasoning about the matter is speculation.

Scarcely either shall we find the reason for Brownson's decision to discontinue his *Review* in any competition he was experiencing in the literary field with that other quarterly in Boston, the *Dial* of the Transcendentalists, started in July 1840. The two quarterlies were so dissimilar in nature that they could scarcely encroach on the patronage of each other. The *Dial*, too, had one feature in particular which Brownson's *Quarterly* lacked: a corner or column for poetry. Even at that, Brownson thought some of the *Dial's* prose pieces more poetical than most of its pieces of verse. Yet "The Problem," in the first edition, he owned to be not merely verse, but genuine poetry, unsurpassed, if equalled, by any production of the American muse, with which he was acquainted. "Wood Notes," in the second issue, apparently by the same author (Emerson), he rated passable, but still far below what he himself feels "when he walks the woods" alone. All in all, he felt the *Dial* promised "to exert no inconsiderable influence on the thought and literature of the country."

Although he called the Dialists radicals of the ultra stamp, "who would *radicalize* in kid gloves and satin slippers," he paid them a handsome compliment in concluding his notice of them when he remarked:

> The Dialists belong to the genus *cullotic,* and have no fellowship with your vulgar *sans cullotic.* . . . To our taste they lack robustness, manliness, and practical aims. They are too vague, evanescent, aerial; but nevertheless there is a "sad sincerity" about many of them; and one cannot help feeling that these are after all the men and women who are to shape our future.[37]

The contrast between the *Dial* and the *Boston Quarterly Review* was further expressed by Theodore Parker, who was himself one of the important contributors to the *Dial*, when he remarked:

> Apropos of the *Dial*, to my mind it bears about the same relation to the *Boston Quarterly Review* that Antimachus does to Hercules, Alcott to Brownson, or a band of men and women daintily arrayed in finery, walking in vain show, with kid mitts on their "dandies," to a body of stout men in blue frocks, with great arms and hard hands, and legs like the pillars of Hercules.[38]

There were those of course who regretted much the passing of the *Boston Quarterly Review*. Typical of such was William H. Channing who was greatly interested at the time in social reform and progress. Tersely he remarked: "Take it all in all, it was the best journal this country ever produced, at once the most American, practical and awakening."[39]

In what was the final issue of his *Boston Quarterly Review*, 1842, Brownson brushed aside in a charming note any thought of saying farewell to his old-time readers (he had engaged to write for the *Democratic Review*). They had been with him for five years, had shared with him good report and evil, had become a part of his life, and they were all dear to him. No farewell, then, as he expected to meet them all again in the columns of the *Democratic Review*. As he looked back he felt much satisfaction over the frank manner in which he had spoken, the honesty and truthfulness to himself in all that he had uttered, thereby affording his readers, too, a real opportunity to know him just as he was, as far as worth knowing at all. The five volumes of his *Review*, written largely by himself alone, might well be taken in the light of a private journal. He had spoken as he thought and felt at the time of writing, as unrestrainedly as if he had been writing in a private diary, for no eye but his own. Happy the man who can so speak. The five volumes embodied five years of his life — his thoughts, likes and dislikes, his loves and hates, his aspirations and hopes. Whatever their merits or demerits, they could rightly be looked upon as the outpourings of one who, whatever his shortcomings, had possessed at least the virtue of being "able, in good report and evil, in weakness and in strength, in poverty and disgrace, to be true to the great Idea which had possessed him almost from the cradle — that of man's moral, intellectual, and physical amelioration, on earth."[40]

We have already noted that Harold Laski spoke of the five volumes of the *Boston Quarterly Review* as "astonishing."[41] They contain much of the most vigorous writing Brownson ever did, and have the additional merit of including thoroughgoing discussions of practically every question before the public at the time. Yet they have received little or no recognition in the surveys of American literature. Commenting on this fact Perry Miller observed:

> Only the fact that in 1844 Brownson became a Catholic, and so induced his former friends to erase his name from their memories, explains the otherwise inexplicable negligence with which histories have treated this journal [the *Boston Quarterly Review*], the most vigorous of its day. Between 1838 and 1842 it was the one effective assailant in America of prescription and authority, and it inflicted upon them an infinitely heavier damage than the *Dial* ever dared attempt.[42]

What apparently had finally brought Brownson to a mature decision in his consideration of a discontinuance of his *Review* was the offer made him by John L. O'Sullivan that he become a contributor to the *United States Magazine and Democratic Review*. This monthly magazine, of which O'Sullivan was editor, was started in Washington, D.C., in 1837 by Langtree and O'Sullivan, but was afterwards dated from New York City where it was published by the Langleys.[43] Of this publication Rufus W. Griswold remarked: "It has been the most successful magazine of a political character in the United States, and has been conducted with ability, dignity, and good taste."[44] Such a journal must have appeared fairly inviting to Brownson as an outlet for his writing ability. Speaking of Brownson becoming a contributor to this magazine, Frank Luther Mott noted: "In November, 1842, the *Boston Quarterly Review,* edited and owned by the Jovian journalist, Orestes A. Brownson, was merged into the *Democratic Review,* and with it came Brownson himself on an agreement for two years of freedom as a contributor."[45] The agreement had been reached in October of 1842.

# 18

## A STOUT CHAMPION
## OF POLITICAL CONSERVATISM

*Difficulties over Brownson's terms as contributor to the* Democratic Review *• Editor O'Sullivan is disappointed with his articles • Their extended hassle over the legitimacy of majority rule • Brownson's three massive articles on the "Origin and Ground of Government" • He reaffirms his faith in the sovereignty of the people, under God, when legally expressed through the political organism of the country • He stands by the good old cause, the cause of the people • He continues to fight for democratic forms of government • Similarities between himself and John Randolph of Roanoke • His involvement with the Suffrage party of Rhode Island • His utter rejection of the principle of the underived sovereignty of the people in the political order • He insists on truly Christian principles as the basis of the state, and opts for the church-state relationship that obtained in the Middle Ages which "always [worked] to the restricting of the power of the civil ruler, and to the enlarging of the liberty of the subject" • Proscribing rebellion and revolution, he looks to charismatic statesmen as the great hope for working the needed reforms in government and society • He again denounces demagoguery • Tributes to his articles on the "Origin and Ground of Government."*

Already, on May 4, 1842, John L. O'Sullivan, editor of the *Democratic Review,* a monthly magazine, had written to Brownson suggesting that "your admirable *Review* might be advantageously merged into the *Democratic Review* — I purchasing your list of subscribers at a fair rate, and you continuing a contributor, at a rate of compensation which you would have no reason to complain of, with your name appended to your articles, if you think proper. . . . If you and your publishers are favorably disposed to this suggestion, there will probably be little difficulty between us in relation to details."[1]

Though the suggestion was favorably received by Brownson, the working out of the details in the agreement was to prove a real jinx. In fact, from beginning to end the whole project was involved in vexing difficulties and misunderstanding. This is no doubt the reason why Brownson said not one word in his autobiography about this episode in his life. It would be a trifle unsafe to come to any definite conclusions concerning the responsible source of the difficulties in the working out of the agreement between the two since we do not have Brownson's letters to O'Sullivan, though we do have at least most of the letters of O'Sullivan to Brownson. As O'Sullivan saw the matter, Benjamin H. Greene, Brownson's publisher, was the villain in the piece. In a letter dated July 5, 1842, O'Sullivan complained to Brownson that "your publisher by his suspiciousness and captiousness has succeeded in casting a good deal of a disagreeable entanglement over a very simple and easy matter."[2]

It does seem that O'Sullivan had some reason to complain. If, however, he had been irritated in any degree by Brownson himself it was apparently because Brownson insisted on a strictly businesslike procedure in the whole affair, not being willing to rely on mere verbal assurances. Whatever the case, O'Sullivan expressed himself hugely grateful to Brownson for the fine things he had said about him in his address to his readers in the closing edition of his *Review,* October 1842. Said O'Sullivan: "Laus est a te laudari."[3]

When it came to the articles themselves Brownson was to contribute to the *Democratic Review,* the affair was not one whit less infelicitous, that is, apart from the intrinsic value of the essays themselves. Although the *Democratic Review* purported to address itself to the popular intelligence of the country, those who had some smattering of learning — Arthur M. Schlesinger, Jr., calls it "the liveliest journal of the day"[4] — Brownson led off with a ponderous article on "Schmucher's Psychology" in the October 1842 issue. This was soon followed by a series of equally massive articles setting forth his "Synthetic Philosophy" in depth. Very few readers of O'Sullivan's popular magazine could make anything of such articles, and fewer yet had any relish for articles of that caliber. What they largely wanted was reading matter that would entertain, not what would tax their mental capacity to the breaking point. Whatever high hopes had been entertained that the illustrious name of Orestes A. Brownson would bring new éclat to the *Democratic Review* and promote wider readership, were being hopelessly dashed at the very outset. Great indeed was the disappointment and chagrin of editor O'Sullivan. He feared of course a sizable cancellation of subscriptions at the end of his subscription year, June 1843. Of all this he frankly apprised Brownson in a letter dated February 12, 1843:

> Especially now [he said] for the coming three or four numbers of the year, it is necessary to aim at the object of interesting and satisfying the mass of subscribers — whose continuance for the next [year] is so important. "The greatest entertainment of the greatest number" — to vary the Benthamic formula — becomes at this time in particular the consideration of the highest moment.[5]

There can be no doubt that Brownson shrank from the thought of being a disappointment to O'Sullivan, whom he highly esteemed at this time, and who had been quite generous in the agreement they had reached,[6] but in casting about for a new tack (he had freedom of choice as to topics), he was no luckier than before. In fact, he now really got into hot water. In discussing in his next article, "Democracy and Liberty" (April 1843 issue), the jolting events of the election of 1840 — a catastrophe, he said, that had "wrought a much greater revolution in us than in the government" — he proceeded to express his lack of faith in the wisdom and intelligence *alone* of the people to work good government. Yet this in no sense meant in his mind that popular suffrage was to be abandoned, or that the popular form of government had proved a failure, and least of all that there should be a return to aristocracy or monarchy. Pointedly he said: "We have lost no confidence in nor love for popular institutions."[7] "The struggle for democratic forms of government has, moreover," he continued, "been too long and too severe, has enlisted too many of the wise and good, and been consecrated by too many prayers, sufferings, and sacrifices, to permit us, even if our confidence of ultimate success were altogether less than it is, to think even for one moment of ceasing to continue it."[8] He opted to be foremost among those whose faces were turned toward the promised land, and let the word, he said, be passed along the ranks: Forward, march! He assured his Democratic friends, both in the Old World and in the New, that, whatever he had to say, he had no words of comfort for their enemies. No deserter, no traitor was he to the great cause of human freedom and progress. "We stand by our colors," he stoutly affirmed, "and will live and die, fighting for the good old cause, *the cause of the people.*"[9] He further threw out the *caveat* against misunderstanding: "We would not, we cannot dispense with popular suffrage and intelligence, and we pray our readers to remember this; but they are not alone sufficient, and we must have something in *addition* to them, or we shall fail to secure those results from the practical working of government, which every true-hearted democrat is laboring with all his might to secure."[10]

The "something in *addition*" he demanded to popular suffrage and intelligence was of course constitutional guarantees. For popular suffrage and intelligence to be sufficient in themselves would really mean that "the people can do no wrong." A beautiful theory, he said, but it is still as true as Holy Writ that it simply does not square with the hard facts of history. Deeply did he deplore the way in which unctuous demagogues did not hesitate to keep shouting the blasphemy, *vox populi est vox Dei.* Much that he said in his article had the appearance of pulling the beard of the sovereign people. He even went so far as to say that "if we mean by democracy that form of government that rests for its wisdom and justice on the intelligence and virtue of the people alone, it is a great humbug."[11] This assertion and others similar to it grated harshly on the ultra Democratic ears of the ultra *Democratic Review.* O'Sullivan had trouble on his hands. Foreseeing a storm of protest, he again appended to Brownson's article a five-page note of criticism, but graciously wound up, saying: "The loss of Brownson would indeed be a loss more than Ajax Telamon to the Camp of Democracy. Long distant be the day when we shall have to record and lament that so great a man has fallen in Israel."[12] To any complaints Brownson made to him about the note, O'Sullivan replied that had he not subjoined the disarming note, "I have no doubt I shall have had at least 500 withdrawals of subscriptions."[13]

After Brownson had published an article on "Popular Government" in the May issue of the *Democratic Review,* which plainly showed the widening gulf between his political philosophy and that of O'Sullivan (O'Sullivan again appended an eight-page note), he soon began a series of articles on "The Origin and Ground of Government." These articles were to bring him into ever sharper conflict with editor O'Sullivan. There was one particular political heresy which Brownson had been fighting with all the vigor and determination he could muster, infiltrating more and more into the country through foreign political quackery, namely, the absolute sovereignty of an irresponsible majority. The type of government the advanced liberals of the day were contending for amounted in the main to an absolute or pure democracy in which there were no effectual restraints on the will of that group that happened for the time being to be the majority. (Brownson called it "Jacobinical democracy.") Inasmuch as our government came in time to be called a democracy, Brownson found a strong tide of sentiment setting in at this very time among his countrymen to interpret our political institutions in the European or purely democratic sense.[14] With the zeal of the true patriot, he braced himself once again to do what he could in these elaborate essays to put down this political heresy threatening the gradual erosion of the real nature of our government as set up by the Founding Fathers. He took pains to mark sharply again for his readers the difference between the rule of the majority solemnly expressed through the legal and constitutional forms of the country's political organism and the people as mere population, that is, between the people as a political entity and the people as a mere mob, and uttered his alarm over the growing menace of an irresponsible majority operating outside the political organism. This irked editor O'Sullivan, brilliant but not deep, who went for majority rule in any shape or form:

> If the people [rejoined O'Sullivan], the people of a given territory, or the numerical people — choose to come together, in their own way, whether inside or outside the existing forms of law, and to alter the Constitution, it is to their will and their act, that my loyalty is morally due, provided that I am *bona fide* satisfied of the fact of the majority. By the truest and highest legitimacy of natural right, and the only "divine right" we can know in political affairs, this new constitution subverts the old one, which is left behind like the cast-off skin of the serpent, or the moulted feathers of the bird."[15]

The enunciation of such a doctrine was to place the caucus squarely on a par with the constitutional assembly. Its advocacy by a single individual might be of no great consequence, but Brownson asserted that he found it being "avowed on all hands," and indicted in particular "no small portion of our political friends [the Democrats] as well as Mr. Clay and a large portion of the Whig party."[16] (R. W. B. Lewis has called Brownson "an alert trend-spotter and an able cataloguer of the intellectual forces of the day."[17]) In adverting, then, to O'Sullivan's statement, Brownson was forced to acknowledge that O'Sullivan had put forth no new doctrine of his own. In direct reply to O'Sullivan's statement, Brownson said:

> This is a broad doctrine, and one I do not recollect to have seen so clearly and broadly stated by any other writer; nevertheless it is the new theory which has sprung up within these last few years; and acted upon by Gen. Jackson, proclaimed by Gen. Harrison in his inaugural address as President of the United States, assumed by Mr. Dorr and his friends in the case of the suffrage movement, by the Governor of New Hampshire in his letter to the Governor of Rhode Island, in refusing to surrender Mr. Dorr, and implied in Governor Morton's and ex-President Van Buren's letters to the committee of the great clambake, last fall, at Medbury Grove.[18]

Considering this doctrine so boldly advanced by Mr. O'Sullivan as one of the worst political heresies of the time, Brownson devoted the substance of his second elaborate article on "The Origin and Ground of Government" to its close examination and thorough, systematic refutation. Unrestrained majority rule he found flying in the face of all morality. Majorities change. The minority of yesterday will be the majority of today, and the majority of today will be the minority of tomorrow; consequently, what was wrong yesterday is right today, and will be wrong tomorrow. Is it to this changing morality that obedience is required? "Is it in this nineteenth century, and this Christian land," he gravely inquired, "we are to be taught this doctrine, which would have revolted even a pagan Greek or Roman? . . . Right is right, eternally the same," and cannot be dependent on majorities.[19] As to the sanctity of majorities or minorities, he added: "Truth and justice are, in this world, oftener on the side of the minority than the side of the majority; all progress is effected by the few in opposition to the many; the reformer treads always the winepress alone, and of the people there are none with him. It is then absurd to pretend that the minority alone need governing."[20]

Nor can the right of the majority to rule be grounded on the fact that they are the strongest. This would confound might with right and open the door to the most oppressive enactments that ever issued from the most absolute monarch or the most lawless aristocracy — and all done under the patina of legitimacy.[21] Our unbending defender of constitutional democracy countered O'Sullivan's type of unlimited democracy with the statement: "We believe in the sovereignty of the people, under God, when *legally* assembled in convention; we contend that the will of the people so convened, formally expressed, is the law to the representative, and the only law to which he is in his official conduct amenable. Show us the constitution and the laws, and you show us the authentic will of the people, that we admit to be binding on us; which we cannot disregard without proving ourselves disloyal."[22]

Brownson further pointed out that "our Fathers felt that the Constitution, the ground-work of the commonwealth, should not be altered at the pleasure of the majority, and they uniformly made the assent of more than a majority necessary."[23] Referring again to the doctrine of the absolute sovereignty of the people, expressed outside and independently of the country's political organism as advocated by O'Sullivan, Brownson warned:

> Let it once become the settled doctrine of the country, and it is fast becoming so, and our liberties are gone; constitutional freedom, constitutional government has proved a failure, an illusion; and nothing remains for us but submission to the caprice of an irresponsible majority. Every act will be held to be constitutional that the legislature has the ability to pass and the administration the power to enforce; right will be swallowed up in might, and we shall have a [despotism] worse than an oriental despotism; for the despotism of one man may be glutted with victims, that of the many never, but like the daughters of the horse-leech, will cry always: Give, give.[24]

Brownson was here fighting the same battle that John Randolph of Roanoke had fought so vigorously in his day. Randolph fought it under the title, "King Numbers."[25] Indeed, there are quite a number of similarities between Brownson and Randolph whom Russell Kirk calls "probably the most neglected of our eminent Americans."[26] As Randolph challenged the "divinity of the Demos" and questioned the sufficiency of popular wisdom alone, so did Brownson just as boldly;[27] as Randolph fought for a strict construction of the Constitution, so no less did Brownson;[28] as Randolph waged a ceaseless battle against centralizing tendencies in the federal government, so did Brownson just as unrelentingly;[29] as Randolph contended strongly for a just division of powers in the government, so did Brownson;[30] as Randolph scorned the theories of government advanced by such political philosophers as Locke, Rousseau, Jefferson and Tom Paine, so did Brownson.[31] John Randolph was an ardent disciple of Edmund Burke,[32] and much of Brownson's political thought was in the Burkean tradition.

Brownson likewise deeply deplored the tendency of mere majority rule to undermine the morals of public men. Such a doctrine creates a multitude of demagogues, he said, who flatter the *dear* people with unctuous laudations on their virtue and intelligence with no other intention than to elevate themselves through popular ignorance and credulity. He saw the tendency of playing down to the people as paving the way to gross bribery and corruption, as generating a habit of appealing from truth and justice, from wisdom and virtue, to the mere advantage of numbers, thus destroying all manliness and independence of character in public servants and turning them into time-servers and cowards. When candidates are up for office, the whole tendency would be to ask, not who is the ablest and most honest, but merely who can roll up the most votes for the party. And when it comes to a measure for adoption, the question will not be, is it in the best interest of the public good, but merely, will it be acceptable to the majority? Deeply did he lament the perversion of right principles in politics and the emergence in so large a degree of degrading demagoguery. Brownson felt that it would be rare to find anywhere a statesman who would stand up for what he honestly believes to be right, if he must stand alone. He challenged:

> Go into your halls of legislation, and show the wisdom and justice of the policy you propose, so clearly as to flash general and instantaneous conviction; what then? Will it be adopted? We doubt whether our whole political history affords one instance of the adoption of a measure merely on the ground of its justice, or of its rejection solely on the ground of the general conviction produced by the discussion of its injustice. The history of the proceedings of our legislative bodies is full of sadness, and makes one almost despair of his race. Even a good measure is rarely carried in a straightforward way, by fair and open means. Professing the greatest respect for, and confidence in, the people, few of us dare risk the success of what we honestly believe a good measure on its own merits; we intrigue and manoeuvre to carry it, as much as if it were a piece of consummate villainy. A plain, honest, blunt-spoken man, who speaks always the plain honest truth, would be looked upon in the political world as a simpleton; all parties would regard him as a man not to be trusted, whose imprudence would ruin them.[33]

This continuing imbroglio between editor O'Sullivan and contributor Brownson over the alleged right of the majority to rule even when operating outside constitutional forms, was waxing warmer and warmer, and threatened a speedy termination to the agreement they had entered into, as the notes and letters of O'Sullivan at this point indicate. The contract initially entered into between the two could not but issue all too soon in a fiasco. One wonders how either could have been so naïve as to conclude such an agreement. Brownson later asserted that he had "reluctantly" entered into the agreement, from which he had "never really augured a favorable issue."[34] He should have known full well that his philosophical style of writing would not fit a popular magazine such as the *Democratic Review,* to say nothing about his challenging political doctrines. And O'Sullivan should have known that Brownson's conservative doctrines would only have a raspy sound in his *Democratic Review* — that is, if he had been following Brownson's growing political conservatism during the previous two years. When O'Sullivan appended a note to Brownson's very first political article on "Democracy and Liberty," April 1843, protesting as unexpected Brownson's onslaught on the rule of the majority operating outside the country's political organism, Brownson defended himself by saying most truthfully that he had only set forth again the very doctrine he had uniformly held and for which he had done brave battle since the distant days when he was editor of the *Boston Reformer* in 1836.[35] In fact, Brownson forthwith became fiercely indignant at O'Sullivan — not for disagreeing with his doctrine — but for representing him as undergoing a change of political doctrine. Bitterly said Brownson: "It strengthens the prejudice already too strong against me, of my everlasting fickleness. . . . Some[one] in the New York *Post* speaks of me as in a trasition state. Would to God, before men accuse me of changing, they would ascertain what I am changing from. I am sore on this point. . . . I am in a trasition state, forsooth, when I never preached a different doctrine in my life."[36]

235

From the antecedents in the case, therefore, O'Sullivan should have known what political doctrines to expect from Brownson. He acknowledged his slip in the matter, but asserted, and not without some show of reason, that he had been misled by the support Brownson had given the Suffrage party of Rhode Island.

Over a number of years Brownson had now and then visited Providence, Rhode Island, for the purpose of delivering lectures or orations, some at Brown University. On these occasions he made many friends, among whom was Thomas W. Dorr, a lawyer and a member of the Assembly, and after 1838, a Democrat. Rhode Island was at the time under the charter government which had been granted by Charles II in 1663, the state having neglected to frame a new constitution after the Revolutionary War. The charter government, it was claimed, restricted the elective franchise by reason of a freehold qualification to about one third of the entire male population of the state. A movement called the Suffrage party was initiated to change this. Brownson himself aided in the formation of the party, assuming that its real purpose was to compel the charter government through the force of public sentiment to form and adopt a more liberal constitution. With this understanding, he had accepted an invitation to address the party in Providence in January 1841, in favor of the extension of suffrage. Engrossed in other matters also at the time, his mind had been drawn off from the movement until it had gained wide attention in organizing a government of its own in May 1842, with Thomas Dorr its elected governor. Brownson considered its proceeding illegal and revolutionary, but was disposed to look with indulgence upon the development of events since the current charter supposedly contained no provision for its revision, and therefore no legal way in which to bring about an extension of the elective franchise. Inasmuch as "an immense majority of the people" were satisfied with the newly framed constitution, Brownson rather hoped that the charter government would "suffer the new government to go quietly into operation." Accordingly Brownson wrote a strong letter to Mr. Dorr urging him to firmness in asserting the constitution under which he had been elected, which letter Mr. Dorr had published a day or two before his attack on the arsenal. That this letter could be construed into an approbation of Dorr's revolutionary principle, Brownson did not deny, but he asserted that it was "not intended to express approbation of any thing but his cause," to wit, the extension of suffrage, "for that was all in his proceedings he really approved."

Brownson's only excuse in the case was that he had simply not understood the situation rightly, and had accordingly misjudged. After Dorr's failure in his assault upon the arsenal, it came to light that the restriction of suffrage to the freehold clause was not a *provision of the charter, but an act of the legislature.* This altered the case completely, for it could no longer be pleaded that there was no legal authority in the state competent to extend the elective franchise according to a constitutional method of procedure. Brownson had innocently taken the word of the advocates of the Suffrage party as true that there was no provision in the charter itself to allow a legal extension of suffrage. But when new light came to him from a very able pamphlet on the subject by Mr. Elisha Potter, a representative in congress from Rhode Island, he saw clearly that he could not in any shape or form countenance the proceedings of the Suffrage party without contradicting the sound principles he had always held. He had no apology other than that he should have examined the charter for himself in lieu of relying upon the word of partisans. It was nothing to him that a number of political bigwigs of the day approved of Dorr's rebellion. From this time on, having got the real facts in the case straight, Brownson took occasion to express his dissent from the Suffrage party, even though it had been led by his close friend, Thomas Dorr.[37]

With Brownson's increasing emphasis on sound principles in politics and government, he found an avalanche of misunderstanding and abuse sweeping down upon him. He was not only called a conservative, but an aristocrat, as though he were now abandoning his lifelong, passionate devotion to the great cause of human freedom and social progress. O'Sullivan even intimated that he was attempting to alter the democratic principle of our free institutions by introducing an aristocratic or monarchical element into them. To this Brownson replied that such an accusation was entirely unwarranted by a single word he had ever written or spoken, and was not what he had a right to expect from the "known candor and personal friendship" of the editor of the *Democratic Review*. All he was trying to do was to confine the people to operating within the accepted political organism of the country.[38] He acknowledged that the election of 1840 had indeed shaken his romantic faith in the unassisted virtue and intelligence of the people, but it was for that very reason that he was laboring all the harder to maintain those constitutional safeguards which would save the people from the danger of betraying their own interests. He owned that the ends the people seek to gain are for the most part just and desirable, but affirmed that they are so often misled in regard to the means by which those ends can be attained, being knavishly worked upon by corrupt and designing politicians.[39] He had anticipated the misunderstanding and abuse now coming to him, and had concluded his first political article in the *Democratic Review* by saying: "As we grow older, sadder, and wiser . . . we cease to exclaim: 'Liberty *against* Order,' and substitute the practical formula, '*Liberty only in and through Order.*' The love of liberty loses none of its intensity. In the true manly heart it burns deeper and clearer with age, but it burns to enlighten and warm, not to consume."[40]

Our intense American patriot was extremely sensitive to the charge that he was deserting the banner of popular government and popular freedom. It was like touching the apple of his eye. He reassured the friends of freedom everywhere that he had suffered quite too much through long years for his devotion to the great and glorious cause of human freedom and social progress to have any thought now, as the "snow-flakes" were beginning to fall upon his head, to "slough off" into a cold and heartless conservatism. He repledged that he was bound irrevocably to the *Movement;* for it he had labored and struggled; in good report and evil, in sickness and in health, in poverty and in want; and in and for it, let others do what they would, he would live and die. In adopting a new course he had not forgotten for a moment in his advancing years the iridescent dreams of his youth. It was precisely because he remembered those dreams, because young enthusiasm had matured into firm and settled principle, and youthful hopes into positive convictions, that he had embarked upon a new course. "Man of progress," he exclaimed, "I assure you I am with you heart and soul, for life and death, and ready to serve you in any capacity within my power, and against any enemy, or any odds."[41] He called for a truce to all fears or predictions that there was any possibility of him deserting the great and glorious cause of popular government and human freedom.

At this time he also gave his old friends, the workingmen of the country, his assurances that through all the vicissitudes of the passing years he was still with them heart and soul in their persevering battle for equal rights and equal opportunities for all. Though he did not deem them always wise in choosing the means by which to reach their goal, so often allowing themselves to be basely used by political parties for their own sordid ends, to those same workingmen he repledged without reserve every assistance within his power. Harking back to 1829 when they had first come forth from their carpenter's shops, their blacksmith's forges, and their shoemaker's benches to form their party, and to plead their cause, he exclaimed:

> Noble-minded men! I heard your voice as it rang out from your workshops, and responded to it from the Christian pulpit, where I then stood. It still rings in my ears and in my heart, and, though you have been decried, denounced, and your noble aspirations blasphemed, I yet dare to echo your voice: and, amid all the charges of fickleness, of change, of conservatism, with which I am overloaded, I fear not to say, that never for a moment have I ceased to stand by your cause, and to defend it as the cause of truth, justice, right, patriotism, humanity, religion. Under your flag, which ye flung out to the breeze fourteen years ago this very month, I enlisted; under it I have fought, and in it I will be wrapped, when laid in my grave.[42]

In the vigorous writing Brownson had been doing in the *Democratic Review* his great objective had largely been the same as that of the workingmen's parties (particularly that of the Locofocos), namely, the eradication of all monopolies and privileges in government and society. In his powerful advocacy of constitutional government he had had for his overriding objective to confine government to those measures only which concern the common good, that would benefit all classes of citizens equally, with privileges or favors for none. The Constitution itself favors no one class or group more than another (which explains the reason for all the lobbying everlastingly going on in Washington), and hence Brownson's ceaseless battle to restrict the administration to true constitutional government. Only the Constitution, if rightly construed, can act as a curb on the administration favoring one class or another. "What we must sedulously guard against," cautioned Brownson, "is leaving any class, no matter what class, or which class, even if having possession of the government, the power to make the government an instrument for plundering the other classes for its own profit."[43]

In these three articles in the *Democratic Review* on the "Origin and Ground of Government," our political philosopher made a close inquiry, as the title indicates, into the source of the power or authority in government. He went back to the theory of the native underived sovereignty of the people so strongly contended for by the ultra liberals of the day at home and abroad, and traced the authority of government to its origin in divine right, showing that there can be no authentic government unless it speaks with more than human authority. As he explained it in the *Convert*:

> I never myself held the doctrine of the native underived sovereignty of the people. When I believed in no God, I believed in no government; for I could never understand why the people collectively should not be under the law as well as the people distributively. I always said with St. Paul, *Non est potestas nisi a Deo*. When I renounced my atheism, I derived all power from God, the source of all law and justice. I might, and probably did, even as I do now, derive it from God through the people, as the medial origin of government, and thus accept Mr. Bancroft's definition, that "Democracy is eternal justice ruling through the people"; but the popular doctrine which puts the people in the place of God, and asserts not only people-king, but people-god, I never held, and

it is one of the few errors into which I have never fallen. I had to make too frequent war on popular prejudice and popular errors, to believe that whatever is popular is true, right, and just. I found majorities too often wrong, to believe them either infallible or impeccable."

The notion that man can invest government with authority from themselves alone which they must then obey, to which they owe loyalty, struck him as a gross absurdity. He held that no government of merely human origin (excluding the notion that its power and authority comes from God) is or can be a legitimate government. Man can in nothing dispense with superhuman support, and no government will ever work well, or accomplish its ends unless it has God for its foundation and stay." His son Henry remarked that there is nothing in all his father's writings which he so strenuously and so unrelentingly insisted upon as the denial of the native underived sovereignty of the people in government."

What is truly surprising in the three articles in the *Democratic Review* is that he opted already at this time for the system of government that obtained in the Middle Ages when the Catholic Church was recognized as truly divine, speaking in the name of God, and holding civil rulers accountable to the law of God when they oppressed their subjects." He favored that system of church-state relationship because it was the only theory of government he was acquainted with that could legitimate resistance to the tyrannical civil magistrate without at the same time legitimating rebellion, which he considered incompatible with sound government. To allow the individual to sit in judgment on government in case of alleged oppression in one form or another would be to introduce an extreme individualism into human affairs which cannot safely coexist with government inasmuch as government by its very nature demands cooperation, subordination and subjection. The church, therefore, as he saw it, commands the individual to be subject to the powers that be, never permitting the individual citizen to resist the constituted authorities on his own responsibility. To itself the church reserves the right, when the constituted authorities oppress their subjects, to absolve them from their obligation to obey, and may even authorize them to resist, and by force of arms to depose the tyrant, asserted Brownson. This power the Catholic Church claimed and exercised in the Middle Ages, and, he added, "always to the restricting of the power of the civil ruler, and to the enlarging of the liberty of the subject."" He confessed that the triumph of civil government over the church, and its supremacy as established by Protestantism, did not strike him as a progress, but, in reality, as a return to the paganism of Greece and Rome."

Insofar as Brownson insisted that only a declaration by the church could absolve individuals from their obligation of obedience even to a tyrannical civil ruler, he was perhaps a bit overborne by his own logic. The late Fr. Joseph P. Donovan, C.M., a reputable canon lawyer, remarked that Brownson did not know "that the Catholic Church with all her insistence on obedience to authority was more lenient than he was disposed to be. For she never demands an authoritative declaration on plainly obvious things, including the case of a confirmed tyrant. Her rule is: 'de notoriis non judicatur,' " the self-evident is seen, not pronounced upon."

Brownson acknowledged that he had considerable difficulty in evolving a theory of government that would be acceptable alike to both the Christian and the infidel. Premising that in the bosom of the state both Christian and infidel must be held strictly equal before the law, and saying that he would resist even unto death any prescription of religion by the state since it is beyond the province of the state to inquire into the religion of its subjects, he asserted that only a government founded on Christian principles could ever be acceptable to a Christian. How deeply his only political philosophy was permeated with Christian principles he indicated when he wrote:

> I can accept no theory of government that does not imply as its basis the truth of Christianity, and the truth of Christianity, not as a mere system of philosophy, but as a gracious scheme, devised by infinite love and mercy for the practical redemption and sanctification of mankind. At the bottom of all my thoughts on politics, ethics, art, philosophy, lies ever in my mind, the Gospel of Our Lord and Savior Jesus Christ, and I see not, I cannot understand how it can possibly be otherwise with any consistent, straightforward-minded man, who honestly believes in Christ the Son of God, the Redeemer and Sanctifier of man, through Whom alone we have access to the Father. A Christian people must needs form the state on Christian principles, and administer it for Christian ends. It is therefore I hold, not to the union of church and state, but to the *unity* of church and state, as Samuel the prophet anoints Saul in the name of the Lord to be King of Israel.[51]

Inasmuch as he founded government in divine right, he frowned forbiddingly upon what was called "the glorious right of rebellion and revolution." The right to resist civil government, even to subvert it when necessary for human freedom, he freely admitted and contended for in the most unqualified terms, though he deemed such resistance and subversion rarely, if ever, necessary or expedient. But, as already stated, he favored a decision of the church in cases where government had become corrupt and intolerable. To admit in the people the right on their own of rebellion and revolution would simply destroy the very foundation of civil government, that is, except in the case when they acted under the constituted authorities as was the case with the American colonists. The lawful province of the people would be to labor earnestly for a modification of the existing forms of the civil constitution, but *in obedience to the constitution itself.* He could recollect no instance in his historical reading where the state had been modified to the good by a practical resort to rebellion and revolution. He could think of only three instances in which insurrection, or rebellion, ever does, or ever can succeed: (1) where the people rebelling has been a conquered people, and falls back on its national laws, customs and usages, and under a descendant of one of its national chiefs, or under its national banner, strikes for its old nationality and independence; (2) when colonial populations, acting under the authority of colonial governments, declare themselves independent of the mother country; and (3) where the people act, under the command of their religion, through its, to them, authorized interpreters.[52]

Gravely discounting, therefore, the good effects that can ever accrue from rebellion and revolution properly so-called, he emphasized rather the great importance of enlightened and patriotic statesmen for bringing about the needed reforms in government. Who could estimate the services of a Washington, a Jefferson, a Madison, a Samuel Adams, a Patrick Henry — not to mention Jackson and Calhoun — to their country? It is through the wisdom and virtue, the enlarged intelligence, ardent patriotism, and all-enduring love of country on the part of such leaders that the masses are lifted up, inspired with an enthusiasm for truth and justice, with a true love of country that will lead to their hearty cooperation to make government all that it should be. He blessed God that he does from time to time send us noble and high-minded statesmen to direct our government who, while guiding its action within constitutional limits, work out the needed reform in its administration, and continually enlarge its beneficent action.[53]

These are some of the salient ideas that our American political philosopher expounded in his three massive essays on the "Origin and Ground of Government" in the *Democratic Review*. A great sense of urgency had impelled him to set forth his own thoughts on the theme inasmuch as he could discover no American who had previously treated the great problems relating to the origin and ground of government scientifically and in depth. Specifically he said: "No work on politics, of the slightest scientific value, written by an American citizen, has ever, so far as our knowledge extends, issued from the American press. This all but universal neglect of politics as a science, is deeply to be lamented, and at first view is truly astonishing; but we are so engrossed with questions of practice, that it is rare that we ever dream of recurring to first principles." He could not find that any American had made "a single contribution . . . to political science."[54] So far, Americans had done little more than borrow from Hobbes, Locke, Montesquieu and Rousseau.

Brownson was fully aware that this statement of the case would not be received with favor, that there was nothing in it flattering to national vanity. But he was also fully aware that there could be no advance from an unscientific approach to government to political sophistication without a true knowledge on the part of his countrymen of their present limitations in the matter. That Brownson was knowledgeable in deploring the lack of any notable development in political science on the part of his countrymen seems to be acknowledged by political scientists of a later era. As Robert E. Moffit has pointed out, Professor Charles Merriam in his book, *American Political Ideas: 1865-1917,* concurs generally in Brownson's judgment concerning the lack of any prior development of political science in the United States. At most, Merriam could discover nothing more than minor advances that Americans had made in the systematic development and presentation of political ideas. He wrote: "On the whole, there was little energy expended in the study of politics, in comparison with contemporary English and continental developments in social science, economics and politics, where the rise of a science of society under the inspiration of Auguste Comte, and of Utopian and proletarian socialism, avowed general interest in social problems."[55]

Brownson had pinpointed the dearth of political science among his countrymen because, as he said, he found it to be really true, and because he would prod them into an earnest inquiry into the principles of government as a *science,* into the principles of just legislation and wise administration. But here he found himself confronted by what he called a dangerous tendency — the tendency to defer to "the alleged wisdom and good sense of the mass[es]." He called it a leveling tendency that levels downwards, not upwards. Instead of recognizing their imperious duty to instruct and elevate the masses, so many of the country's political leaders were taking the law from the masses, and bringing thought down to a level with the narrow views, crude notions and blind instinct of the multitude. If this tendency were to continue and be encouraged, it would only spell intellectual decadence for the nation and leave little or nothing worth preserving in the boasted political order of this New World.[56]

What was of special abhorrence to him was that all this was being done in the name of "democracy." He flatly denied that such a tendency is democratic, or that it originates in democracy. He labeled it decidedly antidemocratic. Real democracy obtains when each man is properly qualified to form an enlightened judgment and to speak his own mind without having his voice lost in that of another man. He had the fullest confidence that the people themselves were eager and willing to receive instruction and enlightenment, but found politicians of superficial intellectual ability, as he considered them, standing between them and the light. He wrote:

> The genuine people, if their voice could be really heard, would be loud and earnest in their condemnation of the tendency of which we speak. They feel they want intelligence, want light, and they look eagerly around for it; but between them and the light stand ever the immense body of shallow-pated politicians, who dread nothing so much as popular intelligence, and whose sole chance of success is in shutting out the light, and making the people believe that they, the people, are already masters of political science.[57]

In the name of "outraged democracy" he uttered his stern and solemn protest against this leveling tendency. Servility to the masses is a servility to which no man will submit except for purposes at once base and selfish. Our ardent patriot was ambitious to see his countrymen taking the lead in every department of high and manly thought. He was quite unwilling to be always dependent on foreigners for his intellectual nutriment; he blushed to think that when he would read a profound book of a scientific character, he must order it from France or Germany. Yet so it would remain as long as the tendency persisted to hold it democratic merely to echo the thoughts of the people, even though it be their "sober second thoughts." We must labor for the elevation of the people, he insisted. The real root of the evil was that to defer to the people meant simply to agree with the miserable demagogues and petty politicians who are raised into prominence by the energy with which they scream "Democracy!"[58]

He emphasized that he had as great faith in the capabilities of the people as any of his brethren. Of them he demanded no blind reverence, no passive obedience to the distinguished few. What he wished for them was only a free and full opportunity for the manifestation of all the wisdom and virtue they have, and a chance to acquire all they were capable of acquiring. But he demanded for them wiser and better leaders than the general average as the condition for augmenting the sum of their wisdom and virtue. His censures fell not on the people, but on the mischievous demagogues who lay down the rule that we must echo the opinions of the masses instead of doing our best to form in them just and enlightened opinions. This would require scholars, statesmen and moralists, and of these he sternly demanded that they fulfill their duties as *educators of the people,* that they seek earnestly for the truth, boldly and conscientiously proclaim it, whether it coincide or not with the previous convictions of the people. The wisdom of the people will be equal to the requirements of good government only on the condition that every man, according to the measure of his ability, throws the highest wisdom he can command into the masses to enlarge the general intelligence.[59]

In expressing these thoughts Brownson was only underscoring the reason why he himself had written his profound articles on the "Origin and Ground of Government." He asserted that he had not attempted a regular treatise on government. That could not well have been done in hasty and crude essays in a magazine, prepared amid a multiplicity of other engagements, and while the printer was waiting for copy.[60] Years later, immediately after the Civil War, he was to be favored with circumstances more propitious for writing a regular treatise on our American system of government.

Far from the turmoil of the political arena, he evolved in the quiet of his study his main work on government and politics, *The American Republic*. But so fundamental in nature were his essays in the *Democratic Review* on the origin and ground of government that they were to form the basis of his post-Civil War treatise. His son has pointed out that there is little or no variation of political doctrine and views in the two treatises written a quarter of a century apart other than an enlargement of political theory occasioned by the many questions the Civil War and its aftermath had raised.[61] The thought in both disquisitions is that of a truly ardent patriot whose only wish was to serve his country to his utmost ability by contributing what he could to a right interpretation of the distinctive character of our free American institutions.

To say that the great overriding objective of Brownson's articles on the origin and ground of government was to preserve our free institutions as they were bequeathed to us by the Founding Fathers is only to stress their merit. "I write on government," he said, "as a patriot; and my sole motive in sending forth these essays, is to guard as far as so humble an individual can, against any departure, by my countrymen, from the true nature of the order already established among us."[62] He stoutly maintained that our system of government is a constitutional republic.[63] The formidable threat to constitutional government that had come with the accession of the Whigs to power in 1840 had occasioned him much alarm. He had come forth at once at the time and called in all tones and through all agencies to his Democratic friends to form themselves into a Constitutional party that would act as a bulwark against the revolutionary and mobocratic doctrines preached by Henry Clay and his Whig associates, both in and out of congress. Practically all the political essays he wrote during the three following years, especially those in the *Democratic Review,* had one and the same great objective: to war vigorously and relentlessly on all the forces attempting to scuttle the "constitutionalism a wise and beneficent Providence enabled our Fathers to establish."[64] The loose radicalism he found creeping in among his countrymen, disregarding the established political forms, and striking down constitutional barriers, he fought tooth and nail. Loss of reputation did not mean a thing to him. If the true interests of his country required him to buck wind and tide, he had that in him which transformed him at once into a hero, even into a martyr. Well did Fr. Isaac Hecker, his lifelong friend, say of him: "No man ever loved his country more devotedly."[65]

The merit of Brownson's three essays on the origin and ground of government with their bedrock principles is perhaps augmented all the more when seen against the backdrop of an era of intellectual turmoil and change. It was an era in which little was considered settled. America in particular wanted to proceed with a clean slate. Bold speculations went forward in every department of thought with little respect paid to the wisdom and traditions of the past. Technology and the industrial arts largely drew men's minds off from recurring to a study of the basic principles in the sciences, and no less so in the political realm than in the other disciplines. The welter of ideas that obtained unsettled many minds that were in grave need of a scientific exposition of the fundamental principles that underlie all sound and stable government. Society in general was in a state of flux and fermentation. Charles Merriam has charactered the nineteenth century well when he wrote:

> The Nineteenth Century was full of new political forces and forms. The individualism of the Eighteenth Century type deepened into Nineteenth Century

laissez-faire, and still further developed into unanticipated doctrines of philosophical anarchism. Democracy, the revolutionary ferment of the Seventeenth and Eighteenth Centuries, took the new form of Liberalism, in its varying shades, and at times passed over into the garb of collectivism and socialism.[66]

Those who contended for an ultra democratic interpretation of our American institutions did not of course appreciate overmuch Brownson's political articles in the *Democratic Review*. Of such Brownson himself remarked: "Perhaps the day will come, when the very men, who now testify their displeasure at my speculations, will own, that I have spoken a true word, and spoken it seasonably. At any rate, I have aimed to do my duty, and shall wait cheerfully the result."[67] But there were contemporaries, too, who set a high value on those articles. In a letter to Brownson, dated October 16, 1843, Isaac Hecker stated: "I have understood, not being there, that last Sabbath morning Mr. [William Henry] Channing in speaking of your three last published articles on government which he pronounced as calculated to excite a very great interest, he took the occasion to speak of you as a man, which he did in the very highest terms, and with great warmth and eloquence."[68] Fuller reflections on these political articles are contained in a letter from Joseph W. Lesesne, dated August 16, 1843. He wrote:

> I should leave my conscience with a heavy debt of gratitude undischarged if I did not write this letter to acknowledge how much I owe you for those able essays on the principles of government which have appeared in the *Democratic Review*. I do not know you personally, and you have never heard my name, but I have mistaken much, if that will impair at all the value of my acknowledgment — the voluntary confession unsought of one soul to another, that its improvement, its emancipation has been wrought by truth wisely and boldly expressed. I have long been a diligent reader of all that has come from your pen. I have been near you in mind though far from you in person. I have been so because, out of this vast nation, I saw there was one man who valued the liberty of his own mind above all price, and acknowledged from day to day its continual progress. . . . I trust you will go on with the work you have so well commenced, and that you will not abandon it until you have touched in some degree upon every topic of government which pertains to the practical administration of our own.[69]

As Mr. Lesesne urged, Brownson did continue to write on government and politics the rest of his life, but he did so perhaps a bit more fully with the approach of the Civil War. In the meantime a great variety of interests continued to engage his attention. Perhaps nothing so progressively engrossed his mind as the study of philosophy in which he hoped to find at last the answers to questions which had for so long a time been tormenting and perplexing his mind.

# 19

## BROWNSON THE PHILOSOPHER

*His temporary enchantment with the French philosopher, Victor Cousin • Cousin wishes him appointed to the chair of philosophy at Harvard • Alexander H. Everett's letters to Brownson • After an extended discipleship of Cousin, Brownson lays his grave strictures on his philosophy • The French philosopher, Pierre Leroux, succeeds to Cousin's influence over Brownson • The immense meaning to Brownson of Leroux's doctrine of life by communion and/or his doctrine of providential men • Brownson's remarkable letter to Dr. W. Ellery Channing on "The Mediatorial Life of Jesus" • Brownson's entirely new concept of God and his providence • He explains that belief is normal and unbelief abnormal • His treatise on "The Philosophy of History" • He rejects the subjectivism of the Transcendentalists, and reviews Emerson's* Essays *• R. W. B. Lewis classifies Brownson as belonging to "The Party of Irony" • Although his thought is still somewhat ambivalent, Brownson confesses that a decided change has come over him.*

Those who have read Brownson's writings extensively would probably feel little disposed to quarrel with the statement of Fr. Isaac T. Hecker that Brownson was "a born philosopher."[1] Almost every paragraph he wrote shows the philosophic cast of his mind. Yet it was only slowly that he turned to the study of philosophy as a young man. He had in his youthful years, it is true, come across and read such philosophers as Locke, Reid, Stewart and Thomas Brown in the line of his general reading. But the study of philosophy as a science had for him for many years no attraction. The fact is he had a sort of a contempt for metaphysical studies, apparently regarding them as unrelated to real life, and fit only as a pleasant distraction for the less serious hours of the scholar. When, however, he had entered the Unitarian ministry in 1832 he was quite conscious that he had not yet succeeded in discovering any solution to his former doubts in matters of religion, and that of all places where the answers should be found would be in the realm of philosophy. This scientific solution he wished even more for others than for himself, for he felt that by proclaiming it widely he could do immense good in helping to save the world from infidelity. It was this motive that had driven him as a young man to plunge headlong for the first time into metaphysical studies.[2]

It was with the works of Victor Cousin (1792-1867) that Brownson was to begin his assiduous, if not altogether systematic, study of philosophy. Victor Cousin "exercised a great influence on his contemporaries and founded the spiritualistic or eclectic school in philosophy."[3] As Robert E. Moffit has observed, Cousin was in the forefront of the movement against "sensationalism" or radical empiricism, and for spiritualism.[4] In this respect, he was one of those responsible for the "shift" in French philosophy.[5]

Although in his approach to Cousin's philosophy Brownson soon found himself succumbing to the witchery of his style, "the splendor of his diction, the brilliancy of the generalizations, and the real power of his genius," he made from first to last certain reserves in regard to his philosophy.[6] Yet he now thought he had found in Cousin what he had been looking for in basic human thought, and immediately put to use Cousin's absolute ideas of the true, the good and the beautiful in constructing an argument for the existence of God in a book he wrote partly at Walpole in 1834, and partly at Canton in 1835, but which he published only in 1840 — *Charles Elwood; Or the Infidal Converted,* already mentioned.[7] The reserves, however, that he made at the time in regard to Cousin's philosophy, he indicated in a measure in an article he contributed to the *Christian Examiner* in September 1836.[8] But for all that, Cousin's influence upon him was to remain powerful for a goodly number of years, so much so that he clearly regarded himself as the chief expositor and defender in this country of Cousin's philosophy. He assured Cousin in a letter dated September 6, 1839, that "my ambition is to introduce your philosophy to my countrymen, and to infuse it in their literature."[9] His *Boston Quarterly* for the year 1839 contained three articles on Cousin's philosophy: "The Eclectic Philosophy," an inquiry into Cousin's *Cours de Philosophie;* "Eclecticism — Ontology," a further discussion of the same; and a critique of Cousin's *Fragments Philosophiques.* The first two essays were written by Brownson himself, and the third by an unsigned contributor, to which Brownson added a five-page footnote of criticism. In 1840 Brownson declared: "I am an eclectic and seek to carry the spirit of eclecticism into all departments of life and thought."[10] He was in temporary thrall to this French genius whom he had already pronounced in October 1838 to be "unquestionably, if not the first, one of the first philosophers of the age."[11]

Brownson's personal acquaintance with Victor Cousin dates apparently from a letter he wrote him on November 15, 1836, accompanied by the September 1836 issue of the *Christian Examiner* which contained his article on Cousin's philosophy.[12] When Charles Sumner, during his youthful tour of Europe in 1838, visited Cousin in Paris, he noted in his journal that the French philosopher spoke of Brownson "as a man of great talent, and indeed a most remarkable man — his interest in Brownson seems to be unfeignedly great."[13] A little later in the year Sumner enthusiastically wrote Justice Story, then a member of the Harvard corporation, telling him of "a very remarkable conversation" he had had with Cousin. He reported that the French metaphysician was "very anxious in regard to the professorship at Cambridge," and had suggested that the chair of philosophy there be given to Brownson "whom he thinks one of the most remarkable men of the age, and wished to be placed where he can pursue philosophy calmly, thinking his labors will redound to the advance of science throughout the globe."[14] Cousin gave further notice to the world of his lofty estimate of Brownson's philosophical aptitude when he said in the preface to the third edition of his *Fragments Philosophiques,* published in midyear 1838: "In 1836 and 1837, Mr. Brownson published an apology of my principles wherein is displayed a talent of thought and style, which if properly developed, promises America a philosophical writer of the first order."[15]

A letter Alexander Everett wrote Brownson in July of 1841 clearly implies that Cousin had invited Brownson to come to Paris and live with him for a time. "I have always regretted," said Everett, "that circumstances did not permit you to accept Mr. Cousin's invitation to go and live with him at Paris. A residence in his family for a year or two would have been, on all accounts, both agreeable and useful, and would have given you importance with our wide public, who, in general, can only see American merit through European spectacles. *Au reste,* with your activity and perseverance there is no danger of you not ultimately reaching your level."[16] In another letter, dated April 1, 1842, Everett said: "I have no other motive in seeking and cultivating your acquaintance, but the pleasure I have found in your conversation. I have always cherished the hope, that some lucky chance might throw us into the same circle, and regret that we have not the means at present at this college [Louisiana State] of tempting you to the genial climate of Louisiana by the offer of a chair of philosophy — a permanent situation of that kind would, I think, better enable you to pursue your habitual studies, and present their results, than you can under the pressure of the various avocations in which you are engaged."[17]

The fact that Brownson neither obtained the Harvard chair of philosophy nor went to Paris to live with Cousin probably only argues that there was a divinity shaping his ends. Harvard halls could scarcely have contained his fiery spirits nor afforded an ample outlet at this time to his ebullient energy. He was at that very stage in his career when the trammels of a professorship would probably have grown irksome to him. And there is just as little reason to believe that he could have managed at this time a visit with Cousin in Paris. In any case at all, time was now running out for him when Cousin's philosophy could any longer meet the wants of his mind and heart. In a letter to Cousin, dated November 15, 1836, he had thanked him heartily for the aid he had afforded himself in making the passage from the subjective to the objective: "Your works, sir, found me sunk in a vague sentimentalism, no longer a sceptic, but unable to find any scientific basis for belief. I despaired of passing from the Subjective to the Objective. You have corrected and aided me; you have enabled me to find a scientific basis for my belief in Nature, in God and in Immortality, and I thank you again and again for the service you have done me."[18] But by the time Brownson reviewed his *Charles Elwood; Or the Infidel Converted* in his *Boston Quarterly,* April 1842, he had come to quite different conclusions. He there pointed out, upon a closer examination of Cousin's philosophy, that Cousin had never, after all, really established the objectivity of the true, the good and the beautiful (which he himself had used in *Charles Elwood* in his argument for the existence of God). Cousin did indeed assert their objective existence, but at the same time he contradicted himself, said Brownson, by making them a part of *me.* His failure to establish their objectivity meant that he remained bogged down in the subjectivism of Kant, a system of pure idealism. Hence Cousin's absolute ideas of the true, the good and the beautiful "which he labors to identify with God, were, after all, . . . only abstractions," asserted Brownson, "and could give me only an abstract God, no living God, no real God at all." To this conclusion Brownson acknowledged himself reluctantly forced to come regarding Cousin's philosophy, "for with all his eclecticism he really establishes no distinction between the subject and the object."[19]

Brownson went on to point out, already at this time, that the refutation of Kant and Fichte, and hence of all idealism, egoism and skepticism, whether atheistic or pantheistic, is found in the same fact that *the objective element of thought is always not-me.* The error of Kant, and the error which has led astray his whole school and others, is in the assumption that the *me* can or does develop itself as subject, that is to say, become its own object, and therefore be at once both subject and object. Kant assumes that the *me* develops itself, without an exterior object, in cognition; hence

247

the conclusion that all knowledge is purely subjective, and the impossibility of reason according to his philosophy to carry us out of the sphere of the *me*.[20]

As René Wellek has observed, referring to Brownson's critique of Cousin's philosophy, in "1842 Brownson rejected philosophical idealism as clearly and as forcefully as he did the rest of his life."[21] From this time forward Brownson was to contend valiantly for the objectivity of all knowledge; no object of the mind, no intellection, no real knowledge.

Whatever Brownson's criticism of Cousin's philosophy, he was not the churl who would now pretend that he had not profited greatly from the study of Cousin's writings. He reasserted in eloquent terms his great respect for Cousin as a man, and as a philosopher. If his philosophy, in its entirety, was not all that it had at first appeared to be, to himself at least it still contained nearly all the elements requisite for the construction of a sound philosophy, and Cousin himself deserved, he contended, a high rank among the eminent men who at different epochs have contributed to the advancement of metaphysical studies. Even the very light by which he himself had made his criticism of that philosophy he had borrowed, he acknowledged, from Cousin himself.[22] In his first notice, too, of Pierre Leroux he deplored his "virulent" attack in his *Réfutation de l'Eclecticisme* on Cousin personally, while at the same time owning that Leroux was the sounder philosopher.[23] In contrast to his own acknowledgment of his debt to Cousin, Brownson chided the Italian philosopher, Abbé Gioberti, for refusing to admit his own personal debt to both Cousin and Leroux, two French philosophers the Italian only affected to despise. Of Victor Cousin and his disciple Theodore Jouffroy, Brownson frankly said: "They have served me hardly less by their errors than by their truths."[24]

His erstwhile enthusiasm for Cousin's philosophy he explained by the fact that when he had first made Cousin's acquaintance (1833) he had felt a great need for a profounder, a more religious philosophy for both himself and his countrymen than that taught in American schools. He did not feel able to construct such a philosophy himself, nor did he know any American equal to the task. In fact there seemed to be a great indifference to the whole subject. He had come to feel, as others also had, that of all philosophical writings available, those of Cousin were best adapted to the wants of his countrymen. On September 6, 1839, he had written Cousin: "Your system is perfectly adapted to us because it is eminently Christian and eminently democratic. By giving us the element of the supernatural [your philosophy] gives us a firm basis for our faith as Christians and democrats."[25] He had therefore enthusiastically recommended Cousin's philosophy in the hope that his writings would prepare the way for a sounder philosophy in case they were not found altogether satisfactory. With this view in mind he was at first little disposed to dwell on any defects in Cousin's system of thought, but rather wished to commend it for its merits. He was much pleased to note that Cousin's writings were now being introduced as a textbook at Harvard, inasmuch as he still considered them the best available, all things considered, for those who would become acquainted with metaphysical studies. That Brownson felt he had fulfilled an important role in introducing Cousin more widely to his countrymen may be inferred from his statement that he "had perhaps contributed more than any one man to draw attention of American thinkers to his philosophy."[26] Brownson was not the very first, however, to bring Cousin to the attention of the American public. Per Sveino mentions that Henning G. Linberg's English translation of Cousin's lectures on the history of philosophy appeared in Boston in 1832.[27] As noted, Brownson's acquaintance with Cousin seems to have dated from 1833, though Brownson was not altogether certain about the precise time.[28]

Although Brownson asserted that his later criticisms of Cousin's philosophy had been anticipated by his earlier observations, he did not try to disguise the fact that he had erred in his judgment as to the full merits of Cousin's philosophy. "In the course of [this] article," he said, "we have spared neither ourselves, nor our master in philosophy, Mr. Cousin."[29] To those who would now accuse him of inconsistency, he replied that he was no lover of that consistency which is purchased "at the price of wilfully shutting the eyes to the light, or by obstinately adhering, in spite of convictions, to one's former utterances." It is doubtless best never to err, but the next best thing, if one has erred, is to correct the error. He professed himself an inquiring disciple, ever ready to accept the truth wherever found. And that he might the more readily accept it wherever found, he had resolved never to allow himself to be "the slave of his own shadow."[30] Let others do what they would, this he had made his own charted course. After all, the man who detects and exposes his own errors, is not the one least deserving of confidence. Before closing his article he announced that he had, for the first time in his life, constructed a system of philosophy of his own, though not without some assistance, which he intended to lay before the public at the earliest date possible. He felt confident that it would "be able to reconcile many jarring creeds," though he pretended not to have made any discovery that would "supersede the necessity of Divine Revelation, or a childlike trust in the wisdom and goodness of Providence."[31] (He referred of course to his coming essays on synthetic philosophy to be published in the *Democratic Review*.)

There was one overall defect in Cousin's philosophy, however, of which Brownson now began to complain more and more. In his article on "Reform and Conservatism" in his *Boston Quarterly* he owned that he had for years mistaken "an imbecile eclecticism for a powerful and living synthesis."[32] One of the attractions of eclecticism for Brownson had been no doubt its evident acknowledgment of the wisdom of the past or the traditions of the race. But now in another article on "Leroux and Humanity" his complaint against an "imbecile eclecticism" became even more shrill. He acknowledged that eclecticism could speak with great truth and clearness about the past and the present, but before the future — it was distressingly dumb. It had no message. To the question, what has been, what is, it had a ready answer, but to the question what *ought* to be, for response there was only dead silence. It could propose no ideal, no inspired program of action by which eternal life could be inherited. It was in reality not a doctrine of progress, but of immobility.[33] He confessed that the more he came under the influence of eclecticism the more clearly he saw that he could take part in the affairs of community, church and state "only at the expense of systematic consistency." Under the same influence he found himself growing cold and indifferent, little concerned about how things might come and go, and less concerned yet about how the lot of his fellowmen might be improved.

It was the discovery of this tendency in himself that gave him alarm, and made him feel how inadequate after all was the philosophy he had been professing. He turned from it instinctively as his soul clamored for a philosophy that would disclose to him some mission in life, some work to do — "a philosophy that explains the past only to enlighten and to quicken us in regard to future action, or let us have none. God's curse, and man's curse too, on each and every system of philosophy that is merely retrospective."[34] As Robert E. Moffit has well observed: "Brownson was firmly convinced that philosophy ought not to be a matter of idle speculation, but rather, a guide to action in the practical circumstances of social and political life."[35]

More alarming yet, in his treatise on "The Philosophy of History" in the *Democratic Review*, May and June 1843, he had found Cousin's theory of spontaneous reason resolving itself into the exclusion of human agency from any responsible part in the production of the phenomena of history. Cousin asserted human freedom, it is true, yet only in the sphere of reflection. But according to his theory the whole of human history originates not in the sphere of reflection, but in that of spontaneous reason, which, while it is human, is more than human, being the overriding operations of God himself. This divests individuals and nations of any power to direct and control, or impede the march of events. This was, to Brownson, a reassertion of the doctrine of old pantheistic India. Were we to accept such a theory, said our dynamic protagonist for progress:

> We would fall into absolute indifference, smoke our pipe, and say, "God is great, what is written will be." Cousin as well as Jouffroy, seems to have felt this. He is a man of active temperament, of great energy, and noble sympathies, and yet he has not answered our question, What shall we do? He says, humanity is doing so and so; but pray, Mr. Cousin, tell us what humanity *ought* to do, and we as individual manifestations of humanity? No answer! We have interrogated your writings, we have questioned [them] in all lights, in all moods, and demanded of them in all tones an answer to this question, and we have found only this cold, heartless answer, "Do nothing; fold thy hands and leave thyself to be borne onward by the irresistible current of the spontaneous reason." Suppose we resist, and seek to withstand the current: "Do so if you will, it makes no difference. The current flows on, and you with it, whether willingly or unwillingly."[36]

It now seemed to Brownson that his former adherence to eclecticism, "orienting" his readers so often to the past, had introduced into his train of thought a certain dichotomy, confusing to his readers, if not to himself. No man, he felt, had labored harder through the years for progress, yet as an eclectic he had been simultaneously turning the minds of his readers to the wisdom of the past. Hence those strong passages of both liberalism and conservatism in his former writings, especially prior to 1840. In his own mind he thought he had harmonized the doctrines of liberalism and conservatism, but use what language he would, he felt he had seemed to his readers to be contradicting himself. The moment he awakened them to efforts of progress, they were suddenly thrown aback, nonplussed, when they heard him in almost the same breath cautioning them that they should not run away from the wisdom of the past. His doctrines of progress had offended the conservatives, and his conservative doctrines had offended the protagonists for reform and progress. It seemed to him that in emphasizing that man should capitalize on the wisdom of the past as well as put forth valiant efforts to conquer the future he had failed to find the right language to show how these two elements can be united into one harmonious program. This failure he now laid to the fact that he had mistaken an imbecile eclecticism for a living synthesis, an effective system of thought that would bind together the past and the future into a living unity.[37] What he really wanted was a philosophic system that would "preserve the continuity between the past of humanity, its present, and its future."[38] And this desideratum he confessed to have now found in the philosophy of Pierre Leroux, a contemporary countryman of

Cousin. Leroux's philosophy helped him to understand that "we *are* a synthesis of what has been, and of what is to come." No need for deciphering the monuments of the past. The wisdom of the past has been so incorporated into the race that "Licurgus, Solon, Socrates, Plato, speak in your pettiest village politician, and debate through your least significant disputant in your least significant lyceum."[39]

Pierre Leroux (1797-1871), to whom John B. Bury assigns partial credit for coining the word "socialism" was a "humanitarian communist" who included among his disciples George Sand.[40] It was this French philosopher who now succeeded to Cousin's influence over Brownson. Yet, as in the case of Cousin, Brownson by no means accepted his philosophy in its totality.[41] But what he did prize in Leroux's philosophy, and prize highly, was his doctrine of *life and communion.* It was this doctrine which was to furnish him not only with the true key to progress, but which also started that train of thought in the mind of this great American which was to lead him to the threshold of the Catholic Church.

Cousin had held that thought, "or the fact of consciousness," consists of three elements: the subject, the object and their relation. The subject is always *le moi,* or the thinker; the object is always *le non-moi,* or something standing over against the subject, and independent of it; and the relation between the two is the form of the thought, "or what the subject notes, in the act of thinking, of both subject and object."[42] Developing this teaching further under the tuition of Leroux, Brownson maintained that the subject and object are not only included in every thought, but that they coalesce into a dynamic synthesis. Thought in every instance results from the intershock of these polar elements, subject and object. So essentially interdependent in all thinking are subject and object that the subject can never think without the concurrence of the object and the object can never be thought without the concurrence of the subject as thinker. Since the subject and the object are simultaneously included in one and the same thought, or act, the reality of the one is as certain as the other. In the fact of consciousness, the object affirms itself as distinct from, and independent of, the subject; and the subject recognizes itself as the thinker, distinct from, and opposed to the object. "This," said Brownson, "stripped philosophy of its mystery, divested it of its endless abstractions and vain subtilties, and harmonized it with the common sense of mankind."[43] This train of thought he systematically developed in his treatise, "Synthetic Philosophy," which appeared in the *Democratic Review,* December 1842, and January and March 1843. The treatise is contained in his *Works* (Vol. I, pp. 58-130).

Man, then, cannot live intellectually, that is, think, without an object. He is in every sense a dependent being and can in no sense live in and by himself alone. To live is to manifest oneself, but only God, the self-existing and self-living, is capable of manifesting himself by himself alone, uninfluenced and unaffected by anything distinguished from his own being. Man, for example, has a capacity to love, but man is dependent on an object to love, cannot live and love without an object. An object of love is as essential to the production of an act of love as the subject that loves. Man's life is ever jointly in himself and that which is not himself — in the *me* and the *not-me.* His life is at once subjective and objective. Here Brownson stated the philosophic basis to the law of Christian charity. Since man cannot manifest himself without an object, and since his object in the matter of charity is his brethren, his life exists jointly in them and in himself, so that if he injures them he injures the *objective* part of himself, no less than the subjective part of himself.[44]

From this analysis of the nature of thought our American philosopher proceeded, taking his cue from Leroux, to apply this idea of a vital synthesis to all man's other diverse activities, and drew the conclusion that all human life in its variegated forms is essentially made up of a dynamic coalescence of subject and object, or results from the intercommunion of the two. This basic principle he thus set down:

> Having settled it that man does not suffice for himself in the intellectual order, that he cannot think without thinking what is not himself, or without the concurrence of the object with the subject, I learned from Leroux that the same principle extends to all our acts, that no act of life is possible without the concurrence of the object. Man lives and can live only by communion with what is not himself. In himself alone, cut off from all not himself, he is neither progressive nor a living being. . . . Hence his elevation, his progress as well as his very existence, depend on the object. He cannot lift himself, but must be lifted, by placing him in communion with a higher and elevating object.[45]

Here he enunciated the principle that to elevate the subjective life of man you must elevate his objective life. When man is brought into relation with a higher and nobler object, a higher and nobler life will flow into him from that higher object. To bring a divine element into the life of man he must be brought into relation with the divine. "God, as the divine object of our life, must present himself in a higher order, or we are not elevated above or advanced beyond what we already are."[46] But how can man be brought into communion with the divine, with God? Leroux taught that man communes in a threefold manner: with nature through property, with his fellow creatures through the family and the state, and with God through humanity. Brownson agreed with him in regard to the first two statements, namely, that man communes through property, the family and the state, three institutions, he said, which, however much warred against, are really "as indestructible as human nature itself." But he asserted that Leroux had added nothing at all in his third point, for to commune with God through humanity is simply to commune with our own kind, which is no communion with God at all in an order higher than the natural. This left man with no objective element for his own life above the natural level, the plane common to all men.[47] "Consequently," concluded Brownson, "confined to his natural life, the race must come to a standstill; no more progress, no more advance. Individuals would grow up from infancy to the level of this natural life, and there stop, struck with the curse of eternal immobility, which is eternal death."[48] Rejecting therefore Leroux's doctrine of "communion with God through humanity" as "pantheistic," Brownson affirmed as the real solution to the problem that: "I must recognize God as superior to humanity, independent of nature, and intervening as Providence in human affairs, and giving us, so to speak, more of himself, than he gives in nature."[49]

We will understand better how desperately Brownson was here struggling with the idea of progress if we keep in mind that progress had been the great evangel of his life for the last fourteen years. He was obsessed with the idea of progress. In 1842 he wrote: *Man is progressive, society is progressive, the race is progressive.*"[50] Although Leroux's doctrine of "communion with God through nature" was of no avail to him, Leroux did nevertheless come to his rescue from a slightly different angle, to wit, with his theory of "providential men." Leroux expounded the theory that God at successive periods in history had raised up certain men to supernatural communion with himself so that they shared his divinity in a singular manner, and that the rest of mankind who communed with them shared then in that selfsame divinity communicated to them. Who were these providential men? Brownson mentioned Abraham, Noah, Moses, Zoroaster, Plato, Socrates, Paul and others.[51] Jesus he was scarcely willing to place in the same category, or if so, only as the head and crown of them all, for in him "dwelt the fulness of the Godhead bodily." Other providential men were only the image of him, but "he the very express image of God."[52]

Jesus Christ, then, is the supreme object of man's communing through which a divine, elevating element flows into him. Although Brownson with others had been preaching and writing not long before that Christianity could stand without Christ, that the historical personality called Christ had no essential bearing on the religion called Christianity, he now made Christ utterly central to Christianity and asserted his necessary mediatorship between God and man. In a remarkable letter to Dr. W. Ellery Channing on "The Mediatorial Life of Jesus," June 1842, he affirmed that Christ, the literal person of Christ, *is* Christianity. All begins and ends in him. To reject him historically is to reject Christianity.[53] Christ had now become for him "very God of very God, and very man of very man," able to mediate between God and man because he was both God and man — the bridge between heaven and earth. All who commune with him, according to the principle by which the object becomes a part of the subject, share in his divine-human or supernatural life. "As the living Father sent me, and I live by the Father," said Jesus, "even so he that eateth me shall live by me."[54]

But comparatively few of mankind communed with Jesus while he was on earth. How, then, are the rest of mankind to commune with him? How are we of today to commune with him? Evidently it can be done only through the mediation of others. The Lord's disciples lived in personal communion with him, and therefore communed with him directly as their object. And through this immediate and direct communion his divine-human life was communicated to them. By the law of life by which it was communicated to them, it was communicated virtually to the race. For the disciples became objects with whom others communed, and these in turn communicated this same divine-human life to their descendants. "By the fact that one generation overlaps another, and thus becomes its objective life, the generation in which Christ appeared must necessarily transmit it to its successor, and that successor to its successor, and thus carry it on to generations, as long as the succession of generations should last."[55]

Upon receiving this letter from Brownson, Dr. Channing, whom Brownson saluted as his "spiritual father," spoke of "the pleasure and edification" he had derived from reading it over carefully twice (it was thirty-two large pages in length when printed in his *Works*). He felt, however, and rightly so, that Brownson had not been clear enough in indicating the precise manner in which the divine-human life is communicated to each individual. "If you write more on it," he counseled, "I hope you will state your idea of the mode by which the individual soul wins communion with the divine life of Jesus; for some passages of your letter would lead an incautious reader to think you a thorough-going Universalist and as asserting the actual appropriation of the life of Christ to the whole human race, past and present, will they or nill they." He concluded his letter by congratulating his "spiritual son" on the peace and confidence he had found in the views he had expressed. "You have found new light," he happily assured Brownson, "and I am disposed to look upon your changes, not as fluctuations, but as steps of rational progress, and to wish you joy in your consummation."[56]

Referring to this episode in Brownson's life, Joseph Henry Allen commented many decades later on what this doctrine of life and communion had really meant to Brownson:

> The hard, restless, implacably honest, and domineering temper of Orestes Brownson had just been greatly softened, at the time I first met him, by a sudden flow of religious feeling in channels he had thought dried up. A mere accident, as it were had turned him from a very positive disciple of the French Eclectics to an equally positive and unsparing critic of them in the name of a new teacher [Leroux], whose phrases he recently took for the key to a new rendering of Christian revelation — a reading of it which, with a certain pious and grateful fervor, he detailed in a letter to Dr. Channing on "The Mediatorial Life of Jesus."[57]

Although Brownson in his letter to Dr. Channing had treated this doctrine of apostolic succession in some detail regarding the transmission of the divine-human life of Christ, he gave it a fuller exposition in *The Convert*. This divine-human life must be the same in all who receive it, a real life, and as such, must be organic, molding and forming all who receive it into one body, the body of Christ, expressly so called in the Sacred Scriptures. This divine-human life which flows down from the Incarnation is in a sense a continuation of the Incarnation. Having been received through the Apostles, it has been operative in the Catholic Church at every moment since the Church's very beginning, by virtue of an uninterrupted communion with the Apostles. Each generation transmitted to the next what was received from the Apostles. This is what is known in the Church as the principle of "Tradition," called under another aspect the "Apostolic Succession," and under still another aspect the "Apostolic Tradition." But as the apostolic or ecclesiastical tradition is really the tradition of the divine-human life of Christ, it is authoritative with the authority of Christ himself. No higher authority can exist. Yet it was against this tradition in the Church, said Brownson, that the Protestant principle of private interpretation was asserted:

> The error of Protestantism was in that it broke with tradition, broke with the past, and cut itself off from the body of Christ, and therefore from the channel through which the Christian life is communicated. Protestantism was a schism, a separation from the source and current of the divine-human life which redeems and saves the world.[58]

The case thus stated by Brownson has greatly impressed R. W. B. Lewis. Referring to this quote from Brownson, he said:

> It was a packed statement, linking together in one swift series of clauses the relation of man to the historic past and the relation of man to transcendental being. It was packed the more tightly because there went into it the long interior dialogue and the public and private experiences that had constituted Brownson's life to that moment.[59]

This theological application of Leroux's doctrine of life and communion was original with Brownson. Of the immense meaning to him of that same doctrine in the social order, he said: "I had made the greatest step I had yet made, in this recognition of the fact that the human race is advanced by the aid of providential men."[60] In fact, Leroux's doctrine seems to have turned on a whole flood of new light. He seemed now to be overwhelmed by the evidence of how Providence intervenes in the affairs of men and nations. As he scanned again the Old and New Testaments, he saw now, in a way he had never seen before, all history bristling with prodigies "which are inexplicable to us, save on the hypothesis of the constant intervention, in a *special* manner, of our ever-watchful Father." The deep realization of this reassuring truth was to him a great solace; he had at long last found balm in Gilead. That God, so good and so great a God, should so care for his creature man, gave him fresh courage in his darkest days to take up anew the arduous labors of life. "We had thought differently in our day," he confessed, "but let this confession, written while tears of contrition and joy are falling fast, plead our pardon."[61]

What is more, the doctrine of the Providence of God brought home to him in a way he had never realized before the freedom of God. To him the freedom of God was now only another name for his sovereignty. However he had reasoned or spoken of God in the past, he had regarded him as a *fatum*, an irresistible fate, an iron necessity, creating from necessity, and hedged in by the uniform and inflexible laws of nature which he himself had established — a God therefore necessarily deaf to human prayers, entreaties and contrition. (This erroneous view is more common among philosophers, or so-called freethinkers, he said, than is generally supposed.) But in the doctrine of the Providence of God he now saw in a new light that God is free, is above the laws of nature, is a kind and merciful Father ever ready and able to supply the wants of his children when they cry to him.[62] Providence thus became to him the foundation of piety, for as he had written in his letter to Dr. Channing, protesting against those who would resolve God into the inflexible laws of nature: "Either we must give up all ground for piety, or suffer Providence to intervene in the affairs of the world, and of the human race."[63] In the light of this doctrine of Providence he had come to see that while "God binds nature, nature cannot bind him."[64] God being all-sufficient in himself and for himself, no necessity could have coerced him into creating the world, any more than he could want the freedom or sovereignty to intervene as he would in the works of his own creation. This new concept of the freedom of God seemed to emphasize for him his own freedom and added a new ecstatic dimension to his relationship to God. He said:

> This [reasoning] threw a heavy burden from my shoulders, and in freeing God from his assumed bondage to nature, unshackled my own limbs, and made me feel that in God's freedom I had found a sure pledge of my own. God could, if he chose, be gracious to me; he could hear my prayers. . . . He was free to love me as a child, and to do me all the good his infinite love should prompt. I was no longer chained, like Prometheus, to the Caucasian rock, with my vulture passions devouring my heart; I was no longer fatherless, an orphan to the tender mercies of inexorable general laws, and my heart bounded with joy, and I leaped to embrace the neck of my Father, and to rest my head on his bosom. I shall never forget the exstasy of that moment, when I first realized to myself that God is free.[65]

The Providence of God, his freedom or sovereignty, and his operations through providential men in his gracious governance of his creature man, were now all closely linked together in the restive mind of this American prober of deep truths. It was this doctrine of providential men which aided him greatly in understanding that God can infuse the supernatural into the lives of individuals without the least violence to reason or nature. On the strength of this theory the divine-human life gained by men elevated to close communion with God can quite smoothly flow into others who commune with them. The apprehension of this truth was of the very last importance to a man such as Brownson. Few or none were more set on guarding the rights and dignity of human nature than he. In the process of regaining his Christian faith, he had written to Dr. Channing that he had "disputed the ground inch by inch,"[66] and had yielded only after he no longer had any ground on which to stand. Few or none understood better than he that God must be a God of utter reason, and that therefore anything that runs counter to reason in the least can not possibly be any part of true religion. Calvinism had taught him that nature and grace, reason and revelation are mutually antagonistic, that the one can be asserted only at the expense of the other. But in throwing off Presbyterianism at the age of twenty, he had resolved irrevocably: "Henceforth I will, let come what may, be true to reason, and preserve the rights and dignity of human nature."[67] It was a signal service, therefore, that this doctrine of providential men had rendered this sturdy defender of the rights and dignity of human nature in showing him that nature and grace correspond, "that it is possible for God to afford us supernatural aid without violence to our nature, and without suspending, superseding, or impairing the laws of our natural life."[68]

Later he wrote: "We shall never forget the joy with which we found our objections to the Old Faith of Christendom, one after another, giving way, and began to see that we too might believe, and might enter the communion of Saints, claim kindred with the Saints and martyrs of all climes and ages. Unbelief is an unnatural state, a state of violence, and no man who is a man, is at ease in it. The human mind, as soon as relieved of the pressure of unbelief, springs back to faith, and joys to be once more in its normal state."[69]

Although Brownson had readily foresworn Calvinism in his youth, it seems evident that a fugitive vestige of Calvinistic teaching had nevertheless clung to him, namely, the false teaching of the antagonism between nature and grace, reason and revelation. It is not unlikely that this asserted antagonism was at least partly at the bottom of his wavering faith as a young man. He was unable to resolve it at the time. He says that of those born and reared in Christian countries who reject Christianity, most do so, not because they see no reasons for believing, but rather because they see, or think they see, many and stronger reasons for not believing. This means that the real work of apologetics is to clear away the reasons for not believing, and this is precisely what was now happening in Brownson's own case. When reasons for not believing have been cleared away, the human mind, maintained Brownson, will instinctively embrace the truth presented to it:

> To believe [he said] is normal, to disbelieve is abnormal. When the mind is in its normal state, nothing more is ever needed for belief than the removal of the obstacles interposed to believing; for, if we consider it, the mind was created for truth. Truth is its object, and it seeks it and accepts it instinctively, as the new-born child seeks the mother's breast, and from which it draws its nourishment. Place the mind and truth face to face, with nothing interposed between them, and truth evidences itself to the mind, and the mind accepts it, without seeking or needing any other reason. The assent termed knowledge follows immediately from the joint forces of the intelligible object and the intelligent subject. So in belief. Practically, it is never a reason for believing, but the removal of reasons against believing, that is demanded. Hence, we always believe what a man tells us, when we have no reasons for not believing. . . . I never wanted reasons for believing; what I wanted was, to have the real or imaginary obstacles to believing removed; more than that I never needed,

never sought; and therefore, precisely as were removed my reasons against believing, I believed.[70]

In clearing away the obstacles in his own mind to belief, Brownson was now laying deeper and deeper the rational foundations for a strong religious faith. It was his newfound concept of the freedom of God, or the notion that God dispenses freely his goodness and mercy to mankind through providential men, that had changed, as he has told us, "almost instantaneously not only the tone and temper of my mind, but the direction of my whole order of thought. . . ."[71] His mind was now overflowing more and more with the idea of God's providential intervention in the affairs of men and nation. So strong appeared to him now the evidence in history of the Providence of God that he declared "the works of providence a far better demonstration of the existence of God than the works of creation."[72] He expanded his notions on the Providence of God in a treatise on "The Philosophy of History" which was published in the *Democratic Review,* May and June 1843. This treatise seems to have been unfairly overlooked by most biographers and commentators on Brownson's general thought.[73] It is of decided importance in showing the continuing trend of his mind in the direction of the Catholic Church. He was to amplify his thought further on this subject in an article he wrote in 1852 on "Bancroft's History of the United States."[74]

A sound philosophy of history can be arrived at only in the light of man's appointed destiny. Only in the light of that destiny can it or does it take on meaning. After examining closely and rejecting the war theory of M. Michelet, the humanitarian theory of Theodore Jouffroy, and the rationalistic theory of Victor Cousin for writing history, Brownson affirmed the necessity of adopting the providential theory, or the view that explains the facts and events of history by a constant intervention of Divine Providence in the affairs of men and nation — that is, if history is to receive anything like an objective and true interpretation. This view recognizes both divine and human action intermingling in human history. Brownson was far from contending that the two can always be separated "by a broad and continuous line," but he pointed out that pantheism can be escaped only if we are careful not to confound or identify the two. His central question was therefore: "Where shall we find in the facts of history, not the *separation,* but the *distinction* between the divine action and the human; or where find the force properly and strictly human, and the force properly and strictly divine?"[75] However strong his feeling about the part played by Providence, both special and general, in human history, he did not minimize the part played by human action or volition. "To a great extent," he said, "human history depends upon human volition."[76]

As the representative of the "religious view," or the providential theory of interpreting history, Brownson chose the celebrated Bishop of Meaux, Jacques Bénigne Bossuet, the author of *Discours sure L'Histoire Universelle.* While acknowledging that the work had been written with great power and eloquence, with the force and dignity becoming an eminent prelate of the Catholic Church, he yet regarded it as somewhat defective considering the state of historical knowledge at the time when it was written, and all the more so with the advance of historical science in the later centuries. He thought the originality of Bossuet was more in the execution of his plan of a world history than in its conception, as the pattern for such a work had been rough-sketched already by St. Augustine in his *City of God* and his *City of the World.* But Bossuet was the first, taking the providential theory for his guide, to give a regular and continuous history of the active intervention of Divine Providence in the affairs of this world, including its relations and connections also with the mundane history of states and empires.[77]

Bossuet sketched two empires: the empire of God, the religious, and the empire of man, the political. In the history of the people of God, the Jewish nation, Bossuet finds the history of God's providential intervention in the affairs of man. Brownson of course agrees with this, but finds it necessary to add thereto that God's providence is for all men, an elect people being only his agent or medium of communication to all others. According to the doctrine of life and communion that he had expounded, he affirmed that God used an elect people to communicate to other nations the elements of that higher life which they had themselves received from him. "We are loathe, then," he said, "to believe that the gentile nations were disinherited by their heavenly Father, and left exclusively to the dim and flickering light of nature. Placed as the people of God were in the midst of the empires of the world, the law of human life must have been miraculously changed, if they had not communicated even to the heathen somewhat of their own divine life."[78]

And as with the ancient elect people of God, so with the Catholic Church since the coming of Christ. It is to be regarded not only as the depository of faith, the witness of the truth, but as God's agent and minister for effecting and carrying on his purposes of love and mercy toward all mankind, for he is no respecter of persons, but the God and Father of all: "In explaining what is called profane history, as well as in explaining sacred history, we are to recognize, in its true *religious sense,* the providential intervention, mediate at least, if not immediate."[79]

He used a simile to convey some idea of the manner in which God's providence is intended to work in human affairs:

> The true view of providential intervention in human affairs is that taken by Lessing in his tract on the *Education of the Human Race,* which represents our Heavenly Father intervening as an educator, giving us now one lesson, and now another, according to our wants and proficiency. But the educator does not do all. The pupil must work; and if he exert not his own faculties, the lessons and efforts of assistance of the educator will prove unavailing.[80]

In blazing this new trail for himself among the New England intellectuals, Brownson was now moving farther and farther away from his old associates, the Transcendentalists. Their doctrine of individual improvement and self-culture, founded on the hypothesis that man can be his own object, that his life is all in himself, and therefore wholly subjective, was to him altogether untenable.[81] It was the very negation of his formula for progress. Nor did they go along with him in his theory of providential or supernatural intervention. Where Brownson saw the supernatural intervention of God in the affairs of men and nations, all to them was mere natural development. But if Christianity is to be regarded as a mere natural development, why, Brownson wanted to know, did it not first appear in such intellectual centers of the world as Athens, Rome, or Alexandria, or in the renowned schools of the time, instead of a by-corner of the world, in an obscure hamlet, in the person of an obscure peasant, followed by fishermen and despised publicans? Had the tendencies of the age reached their finest development in the fishermen and boatmen of Lake Genesareth?[82]

Although he called Emerson's poem, *The Problem,* "a most remarkable production," he more than once quoted lines from it only to condemn Transcendental heterodoxy in its denial of the supernatural:

Out from the heart of Nature roll'd
The burdens of the Bible old;
The Litanies of the nations came,
Like the volcano's tongue of flame,
Up from the burning core below —
The canticles of love and woe.[83]

Tell us not, protested this doughty defender of Christian orthodoxy, that nature has produced the Bible. Man today has the same nature, the same senses, the same soul, and yet from out of his heart no Bible rolls its "burdens, its litanies." As to relying on natural development or the powers of reason alone for progress, he deemed the Transcendentalists just as sadly deceived. "Alas," he exclaimed, "we have seen enough of mere individual reason. It is impotent when it has not, for its guide and support, the reason of God, speaking not only to the heart, but through revelations and the traditions of the race."[84] Those who would reduce God to mere nature, and the authority of his word to that of individual reason ever varying with individuals and with every age, are sorry reformers indeed.

But Brownson was always generously disposed to recognize any element of truth inherent in Transcendentalism — or for that matter in any system of thought. When he gave Emerson's *Essays* a full-scale review in July 1841, he praised them as a reflection of the reaction to the materialism of Unitarianism, and a return to spiritualism. In them he saw the author playing the part of a seer, rising into the region of the Transcendental, and reporting what he there saw. "There is a sacredness about them," he said, "a mystic divinity, a voice issuing from them, saying to critics, 'Procul, Procul, este profani.' "[85] But Emerson, he observed, also at times descends from the role of seer, and assumes the role of reason. As such, he cannot but adopt some theory, some system of thought, some sort of philosophy, and on that score Brownson felt that his *Essays* could be examined without impertinence. As already indicated, he found Emerson first speaking from the viewpoint of the Transcendentalist. But is the Transcendental view cosmic in its sweep, or does it take in only a part of the universe?

Insofar as he found Emerson taking his stand in the Transcendental region in his *Essays,* and acknowledging the order of existences lying beyond the world of the senses, Brownson owned his thought to be eminently religious and worthy of all acceptation, as he himself had always asserted in the pages of his journal. But all who enter that region are in danger of losing sight of the world of the senses and of allowing one aspect of the universe to escape them. For there is so much in that supernal region that is "altogether richer, sublimer, more beautiful than this visible world." One may become so enamored of the realities of the Transcendental world that the world of the senses may fade from his horizon and its existence be denied. This would spell a false idealism.[86]

Again, in the Transcendental world one rises to the principle of things. But all principles proceed from and center in the one and same great principle — God. The diversity in creation noted by the senses may then easily seem only phenomenal or illusory to him who has risen to the conception of absolute unity. Diversity in creation once overlooked, the distinction between cause and effect, between God and the universe becomes less intelligible, and may easily seem one and the same. In short, Orestes found Emerson so stressing unity and identity in creation so as to blur the distinction between God and the universe. This to him was inchoate pantheism. "Whoever takes his stand exclusively in the transcendental," he affirmed, "must fall into ideal pantheism. From the transcendental point of view alone, a correct view of the universe cannot be made out, any more than from the point of view of the senses."[87]

He did not accuse Emerson outright of pantheism, but he asserted that the unbalanced spiritualism running through his *Essays* tended in that direction — a tendency sure to be exaggerated by his disciples into downright pantheism. "He [Emerson] brings up one pole of truth, the one which has been too much depressed; but in bringing up that he is not sufficiently heedful not to depress equally the other. We have revolted against exclusive materialism; let us be careful not to fall into exclusive spiritualism."[88]

But whatever Brownson's criticism of the contents of Emerson's *Essays,* his praise of their literary craftsmanship was high. He acknowledged:

> As mere literary productions, these *Essays* must take rank with the best
> in the language. There is now and then an affectation of quaintness, a puerile
> conceit, not precisely to our taste, but it detracts not much from their general
> beauty. In compactness of style, in felicitous choice of words, in variety, in
> aptness, and wealth of illustration, they are unrivalled. They have a freshness,
> a vigor, a freedom from old hackneyed forms of speech, and from the conven-
> tionalism of the schools, worthy of praise, and which cannot fail to exert a salu-
> tary influence on our growing literature. They often remind us of Montaigne,
> especially in the little personal allusions, which the author introduces with in-
> imitable grace, delicacy, and effect.[89]

That Brownson showed a remarkable perspicacity in his analysis of these *Essays* is vouched for by Arthur H. Quinn, editor of *The Literature of American People:* "Mr. Brownson," he said, "showed his ability to a high degree in his review of Emerson's *Essays* in July, 1841. Many of his interpretations of Emerson's position as a seer and as a Transcendentalist have anticipated present day criticisms by almost a century, and the essay is quite as important in the estimate of Emerson's reception in 1841 as in the study of Brownson's writings."[90]

Brownson's recent intellectual journeying had now brought him into a sort of no-man's-land. He surely no longer belonged to any of the recognized parties, schools or groups in New England, or for that matter in the country. His had been an absolutely independent career in the intellectual movement in New England. Of the polar parties, liberal and conservative, he had remarked already in his introductory address as editor of the *Boston Reformer* (1836) that he was neither, but a combination of both.[91] Whatever is to be said of the years before 1840, after that date he had definitely begun a decided turn to the right, though perhaps not an even turn in all areas of thought. C. C. Hollis thinks that the better term to qualify Brownson's stance at this time is "realistic"[92] rather than conservative. Brownson had come to grips realistically with what had appeared to him as a shifting situation R. W. B. Lewis asserts that Brownson had come to belong to a third party he calls the "Party of Irony" in which he classes such other celebrities as Dr. Holmes, Hawthorne, Horace Bushnell, Francis Parkman, and the elder and younger Henry James. What distinguished the "Party of Irony"? Says Lewis: "In all its forms, the preoccupation of the ironic mentality was communion with the common experience and the common reality of the human race." Those of the "Party of Irony" commonly fed on tradition, and found diversified nourishment and enlargement in communion with the race. "Their irony in short," adds Lewis, "was in the great tradition: inclusive and charitable, never restrictive. Their aim was to enlarge. The shared purpose of the Party of Irony was not to destroy the hopes of the hopeful, but to perfect them." On what grounds in particular was Brownson assimilated to this party? "Man's very chances for redemption rested," according to Orestes Brownson, "upon his ability to commune with God by participating in the traditional life initiated by Christ and carried forward through time by the Christian church."[93]

Brownson was now becoming more and more conscious that he was no longer quite the same man he was but a short time previously. Two articles on the theology of Theodore Parker, one in October 1841, the other in October 1842, show how widely he had shifted within a year from liberal Christianity to theological conservatism.[94] His articles on politics and government in the *Democratic Review* had shown a similar shift in the political order. A review of Sir Edward Lytton Bulwer's "Zanoni" in the July 1842 edition of his *Quarterly* revealed a corresponding alteration in his literary, if not social standards. Although he had previously praised Bulwer rather lavishly, he was now ready to "fix the brand of infamy" on his brow for what seemed to him Bulwer's abandonment of the cause of the people, or social progress.[95] Being still fiercely on the side of the people in the French Revolution, he excoriated Edmund Burke for his *Reflections* on that apocalyptic event: "We have never forgiven, and will never forgive, Edmund Burke for his infamous Reflections on the French Revolution. . . . All we can say of him is, let his name be forever execrated by the friends of truth, righteousness, and freedom."[96] He also further castigated Bulwer for belonging to the Satanic, and in part to the sentimental, school. "The truth is," he owned, "we suspect, we should condemn in Bulwer now much which we formerly commended, did not notice, or regarded as venal."[97] This acknowledged change that had come over him, extending to many fronts, he marked well in a striking passage:

> Time and events have changed to no small extent, what was for years the habitual state of our feelings. The world and its contents, life and its concernments are not to us what they once were. Ask us not whence or wherefore. "The wind bloweth where it listeth, and thou hearest the sound thereof, but canst not tell whence it cometh or whither it goeth." Life's mysteries who can explain? or tell whence these new tones of feeling, changing the hues of all on which we gaze? Our convictions, our doctrines, our purposes may remain the same, but suddenly light streams in from an unexpected quarter, or through an unaccustomed medium, and lo, we stand in a world both new and strange. The hues of this world have changed, and we confess that our tastes have been revolutionized. The kind of literature, in which our youth and early manhood had found delight and nourishment, has lost its charm for us, grown distasteful and offensive. There was a time, when we sympathized, like most of our age, with what has been not inaptly called the "Satanic School." We admired the daring self-reliant spirit, that deemed it a derogation from its own manhood to kneel even before High Heaven. We embraced Cain and Lucifer as brother spirits. But we have ceased to discover true courage in daring to blaspheme, or true manhood in refusing to acknowledge a superior. Man never appears more truly heroic than when shrinking from the least dishonest or dishonorable act; than when, with meek and reverent spirit, he bows at the feet of the greatest and the Best. We ask not for the spirit that dares defy heaven and hell, to brave the wrath of the Almighty, sooner than not gratify his own passions, or follow its

own headstrong will; but the spirit which, trembling before all wrong-doing, is able to obey the call of duty, truth, righteousness, love of God and man, though compelled to go through exile and the dungeon, to the scaffold or cross.[98]

This passage indicates the new direction in which Brownson was now being swept along as a result of his wide investigations in many fields. The passage speaks for itself. It plainly marks something like the end of an era in his life. What further turn he is now to make on his journey is of course the remaining question of interest. Although he was beginning to see that his line of thought pointed in the direction of the Catholic Church, such a possibility as ever becoming a Catholic never so much as crossed his mind at this time. For the time being he was simply honestly following the light he was receiving from his earnest philosophical investigations. He needed more time to resolve fully the problems which were pressing ever more heavily on his mind.

# 20

## GLIMPSES OF CATHOLIC TRUTH
## AND A CHANGING SOCIAL PHILOSOPHY

*Brownson assumes the role of an assured teacher • He returns to the pulpit • He explains how he had come to adopt Leroux's doctrine of life by communion • His relationship with Theodore Parker • His critique of Parker's lectures • Brownson's developing thought coincides widely with Catholic doctrine • He revives his Review and calls it* Brownson's Quarterly Review *• A crystal-clear declaration of his religious position • His efforts to promote an ecumenical movement • A change in his social philosophy • He makes the Catholic Church the great agent of social and political improvement • He scourges demagogues • His Church of the Future becomes the historic church of the past • His absorption in the church question • His article on "No Church, No Reform" • His review of Archbishop Hughes' lectures • His strenuous efforts in support of John C. Calhoun for the presidency • His stirring articles in* The Christian World *• The possibility of becoming a Catholic crosses his mind for the first time • His hesitation • The obstacles which gave him pause • His final decision.*

The years 1842 and 1843 are to be looked upon as transition years in the life of Orestes Brownson. He himself evidently regarded the year 1842 as marking the beginning of that transition. In that year he had looked back and reviewed the two most formal statements of his thought to date, namely, his *New Views of Christianity, Society, and the Church,*[1] and *Charles Elwood; Or the Infidel Converted.*[2] In view of the light that had come to him since they were written he had now corrections and additions to make, some of which we have already noted. But no light had come to him in the interim more significant than that revealed to him through the doctrine of life and communion, or the doctrine of "providential men." These new doctrines had not freed his mind from all grievous errors, but the basic principles and facts which underlie them had, he asserted, placed him "on the route to the Catholic Church."[3] In the July 1842 issue of his *Boston Quarterly,* he also reviewed his epochal letter — epochal in his own life — to Dr. Channing on the *Mediatorial Life of Jesus.* In doing so, he carefully pointed out to his readers the essays he had recently written which gave an outline of the entire spectrum of his thought: philosophical, political, social, ethical, religious and theological. He seemed more anxious now than ever before that his thought be rightly understood. Those essays signalized his transition from the mere inquirer to that of the assured teacher. "In these essays," he said, "it will be seen by the reader, that we have spoken as the teacher, not as the inquirer. In them, for the first time, we have really put forth positive doctrine. These doctrines we profess to *know* to be true, and by them we will henceforth live or die."[4] This declaration was like announcing the coming of a springtime in his life. The mists and vapors that hang upon departing darkness were waning and clearing, and a bright sun was just peering over the horizon for Orestes Brownson.

The great and meaningful boon his new doctrine of life by communion had brought him was a mighty upsurge of Christian faith. It was indeed his metaphysical studies which had disclosed to him this doctrine of life by communion, but having brought him that far, that same doctrine of life by communion had become transformed for him from mere thought into warm vital love; what before had been mere abstraction metamorphosed into pulsating life. That same kindling doctrine of life by communion now bound him more closely to his fellowmen, and through providential men he was brought more intimately into communion with God. He now felt, as he said in his letter to Dr. Channing, that he need know nothing but Christ and him crucified, to the Jews a stumbling block, and to the Greeks foolishness, but to them that are called, Christ the power of God, and the wisdom of God. This new doctrine of life by communion inspired him to seek God more earnestly as his Father, Jesus as his very life, and mankind as his brethren. His heart bled to see these same brethren so largely divided, worrying and devouring each other, and he longed to go forth again and preach to them the gospel of peace and love, and to bring them back into unity and fraternity in Jesus Christ. "My early profession I therefore resume," he announced, "with a fervor for it which I never felt before. I resume it because my heart is full, and would burst could it not overflow. I must preach the Gospel. Necessity is laid on me, and woe is me if I do not."[5]

In giving notice in his *Boston Quarterly* in July 1842, of his resumption of his former profession as a preacher of the gospel, he felt that an explanation was in order. He recalled briefly to his readers how it was that he had come to the city of Boston in 1836 at the invitation of friends who had wished him to labor there to bring under religious influences the many who were drifting into infidelity, particularly those among the laboring classes. When, however, in spite of his best efforts, misunderstanding and misrepresentation had eventually replaced the sympathy and encouragement he knew such a difficult type of evangelism deserved, and without which he could not succeed, he had become discouraged, and had brought the venturesome apostolate to a close after a three-year experiment. He was at the time still steward of the Marine Hospital in Chelsea, a political appointment. Ceasing at the time to preach any longer — some of the clergy of the city had been his unsympathetic critics — he had turned his mind more earnestly to the reform of government through vigorous and sustained writing. But had this really taken the place for him of his old profession? He explained:

> I have always loved to preach the Gospel. Theology has from a child been my favorite study. Politics have been but a mere episode in my life, and would not have been even that, had I not seemed to see my country in such a crisis, as to call for the aid of every citizen. I felt that I could do somewhat, at least that I could try to do somewhat for the cause of freedom and good government. I have done what I could. My countrymen will, to say the least, be none the worse for what I have done. Even while most thoroughly engrossed with political discussions, I was carrying on at the same time my religious and theological investigations, and I felt occasionally the wish to resume preaching. . . . I felt I had deserted my post, abandoned the cause to which I was early consecrated, and could not be satisfied with myself. An opportunity offering last April [1842], I returned with joy to the pursuit I should never have forsaken.[6]

In his introductory remarks from the pulpit he reminded his congregation that he had not now come before them as an inquirer any longer but as a preacher of settled doctrines. "I am not here," he told them," to inquire what I ought to believe, but to tell you what I believe. I have positive doctrines to state, a positive faith to preach, and my purpose will not be to speculate, to philosophize, but so far as possible to point every hungry soul to the bread of life, the living bread that came down from heaven and gives life to the world.'"[7]

Brownson makes no mention in *The Convert* of his resumption at this time of his role as a minister, probably because it was of such short duration. He did, however, after giving a thorough exposition of his doctrine of life by communion, relate to us just how it was that he had finally come to a forking of the ways in his life, and his resultant adoption of the doctrine of life by communion. For the new turn he had taken he had Theodore Parker, a fellow Unitarian minister, partly to thank — though the service had been unwittingly rendered. Who was Theodore Parker and what were the relations of these two men?

That Parker was one of Brownson's most ardent admirers at this period of his life cannot be doubted. Henry Steele Commager tells us that Parker "admired Brownson immensely, admired his energy and courage and sympathy for the underdog."[8] Brownson's estimate of Parker was also correspondingly high at this time, but was evidently less lofty when he wrote *The Convert* a decade and a half later where he sketched him:

> Mr. Parker was at the time [he said] one of my highly prized personal friends, a young man, full of life and promise. There was no man of my acquaintance for whom I had a higher regard, or from whom I hoped so much. He had very respectful intellectual ability, was learned, witty, and eloquent. His ideas were perhaps a little crude, and his tastes needed a little chastening, but his fancy was lively, his imagination brilliant, and his rhetorical powers of the first order. He had devoured an immense number of all kinds of books, and could discourse not badly on almost any subject. He was more brilliant than solid, less erudite than he appeared or was thought to be. . . . His powers of sarcasm and declamation were, however, superior to his powers as a reasoner, and his attachment to his own opinions was stronger than his love of truth.[9]

Brownson had first taken notice of his friend Parker's religious thought in a formal way when he reviewed Parker's sermon on "The Transient and the Permanent in Christianity" in the October 1841 issue of his *Boston Quarterly* — a sermon he had preached in the spring of that year.[10] Revealing himself in that sermon as little better than a deist, Parker became an object of wide and vicious attacks. As R. W. B. Lewis remarks: "After his sermon in May, 1841, he was abused as a scorner, a blasphemer, a hypocrite, a second-rater, and a sentimentalist; he was invited (but refused) to withdraw at once from the Unitarian association."[11] Brownson, however, who had a weakness for championing the underdog, endeavored to put the best possible construction upon the wording of Parker's thought, and defended him as best he could. Later, that fall, Parker rounded out his thought into a series of lectures which he delivered in Boston. Among those who came around to listen to his lectures was Orestes Brownson, evidently expecting or hoping for some new light on doctrines of his own which seemed similar to Parker's in some respects. Speaking of these lectures — he attended only two — he said:

> [They] contained nothing but a learned and eloquent statement of the doctrine I had long defended, and which I have called the religion of humanity. But, strange as it may seem, the moment I heard that doctrine from his lips, I

felt an invincible repugnance to it, and saw, or thought I saw, at a glance, that it was unphilosophical and anti-religious. . . . I perceived that, though we apparently held the same doctrine, there was and had been a radical difference between us. We had both, it is true, placed the origin and ground of religion in a religious sentiment natural to man; but while I made that sentiment the point of departure for proving that religion is in accordance with nature and reason, and therefore of removing what had been my chief difficulty in the way of accepting supernatural revelation, he made it a starting point for reducing all religion to mere naturalism, or as Carlyle calls it, "natural-supernaturalism," another name for downright pantheism, or rather, atheism.[12]

But if their religious thought was thus poles apart, how explain there had been a seeming agreement between them? Brownson went into an explanation of the matter when reviewing Parker's lectures after they had been published in book form under the title, *A Discourse on Matters Pertaining to Religion.* This review was a most searching analysis of practically the whole religious thought of the day in New England, and filled the entire October 1842 issue of his *Quarterly,* sixty-three pages in length with a goodly part of it in fine print. The apparent similarity of thought between Parker and himself he explained by the fact that — whatever the similarity of expression — each had attached an entirely different meaning to his phraseology. Brownson saw that as Parker's language had led himself to suppose that Parker had accepted his (Brownson's) supernaturalism, so Brownson's language had led Parker to suppose that Brownson had accepted his naturalism. From the moment that Brownson discovered this confusion, he had at once changed his phraseology. This in turn occasioned some to accuse him of changing his views again. To which he replied that there had been no real change, but only a modification of the manner in which he set them forth. He pointed to the fact that there was a chapter in *Charles Elwood* under the heading, "Supernaturalism." "We have always," he added, "ever since known to this community [1836], in the strictest, in the most orthodox sense of the word, believed in supernaturalism; instead of it being true, as some have supposed, that we were trying to present our naturalism so as to commend it to the supernaturalists, we have been doing exactly the reverse, trying so to present our supernaturalism, as to win the attention, and ultimately the affection and belief of the supporters of naturalism. We shall get no credit for this statement, and yet it is true; and the real key to much we have written offensive to our more orthodox friends."[13] This very same explanation he had given in his letter to Dr. Channing when speaking of why his faith in the supernatural had seemed to some in the past to have been less pronounced than it was in reality.[14] It is also in accordance with this settled belief in the supernatural that he had commended the philosophy of Victor Cousin in a letter to him, dated September 6, 1839, already cited, namely, because it contained "an element of the supernatural."[15]

That Brownson's critique of Parker's book was no ordinary performance is attested by the estimate put on the article by a critic in the *Boston Post,* in October 1842:

> It is needless also to waste time [said the writer] in setting forth the masterly manner in which this article is written. We recommend it to all who interest themselves in the theological and metaphysical questions that are agitating the community; and hazard but little in saying, that it is one of the best — if not the best — of Mr. Brownson's productions. It certainly leaves unfavorable impressions with respect to Mr. Parker's philosophical powers; as the able criticism in the *Christian Examiner* did in respect to his scholarship. According

to these two reviews, Mr. Parker is as little to be depended upon for the correctness of his references as he is for the soundness of his logic.[16]

It was upon detecting the real divergence of theological thought between Mr. Parker and himself that, as Brownson informs us, his "mind was forced to take the direction it did."[17] He was forced to reexamine what had been the basis of his religious faith. And when he did so, he found he could no longer accept mere religious sentiment as the origin and ground of religion. It was here that the doctrine of Pierre Leroux had come to his rescue in opening to him a new way of communion with God, and the infusion into human life of an element called the supernatural, as already set forth. Of Leroux's writings he later said: "They revolutionized our own mind both in regard to philosophy and religion, and by the grace of God became the occasion of our conversion to Catholicity."[18] While still acknowledging at this time the religious sentiment as in a sense natural to man, and indeed in harmony with nature, he now placed the origin and ground of religion in the relation of Creator and creature, of God and man, as made known by God through divine revelation, and in the participation of man in the life of God through communion. It was with his theological thought thus further enlightened and ennobled on these grounds that he had reviewed the volume of Parker's lectures. The manner in which his theological thought progressed further through his reading of these lectures of Parker is quite significant. He said simply:

> In reviewing the volume and refuting its pantheism, naturalism, or infidelity, I found myself advancing step by step toward real Christian belief. I was impressed, as I never was before, with the utter insufficiency, the nothingness, of the system to which I had been more or less attached for nearly twenty years, and which, I must say, had never satisfied my reason. I caught glimpses of Christian truths which were both new and cheering, and I saw, though dimly as yet, that the deeper philosophy was with the orthodox, not with the heterodox. I began to discover that the doctrine of the Church in the Catholic sense was far profounder and truer than the doctrine of no-church asserted by Dr. Channing and my Unitarian friends. I obtained the main conceptions of the Church, and of her principal dogmas, which I have set forth in the foregoing chapter, and went so far as to assert the problem of the age is, "Catholicity without the Papacy."[19]

What were some of those dogmas of the Catholic Church which Brownson had at this time (October 1842) come to recognize and accept? In his criticism of Parker's thought, he had proved, at least to his own satisfaction, that the authority of the Catholic Church must be *supreme* over all individualism, undergirded by the power of the keys given to St. Peter; that the Church in its very nature must be one and universal, not many; that out of the Church there can be no salvation; that the Church is the only authoritative interpreter of the Sacred Scriptures; that heresy and schism are the worst of evils.[20] In another article in July of 1842, he defended strongly (as had his counterpart a hundred years previously, Dr. Samuel Johnson) the Catholic doctrine of purgatory when speaking of the Communion of Saints — a doctrine, said Brownson, "which short-sighted Protestants vainly, not to say rashly, pronounced a popish error." "This doctrine," he affirmed, "also authorizes us to offer prayer for the dead, to make efforts for their salvation [sic] and sanctification, as we would if they were still with us. O, it is not a popish error to pray for the dead, but a blessed privilege, proceeding from a blessed hope, which has its foundation in the everlasting truth of things."[21]

He knew that he was entering more and more on a path of his own. "This much," he remarked, "we have ventured, in opposition to the Protestantism of the country, and the individualism which we have inherited from our fathers, to say in favor of the unity, catholicity, necessity, and authority of the church."[22]

This was two years before Brownson's conversion to the Catholic Church, and shows clearly that his thought was already at this time turning definitely in the direction of that church on a fairly wide front. It indicates to us that his eventual conversion was no fly-by-night affair, but rather the result of mental processes that had long been in operation. It is scarcely to be expected that we could pinpoint all the factors which were turning his mind toward Rome at this time, some of which he himself did not mention even in *The Convert*. For example, he tells us only late in life, seemingly supplying an oversight on his part, that the first writer who had turned his mind in the direction of the Catholic Church was Abbé Maret, later Bishop Maret, by his work on *Le Panthéisme en la Société Moderne*.[23]

Although he spoke much at this time of the Catholic Church in its unity and catholicity, he did not identify it. He thought the Roman Catholic Church was it, in a large measure, down to the time of Pope Leo X, but since then that church was "the church in the wilderness." As none of the sects was it, he looked for a *Church of the Second Advent*.[24] But still incumbent on the ideal church he envisioned was the obligation to preach a strong Saint-Simonian social message, pledged to "unremitting efforts to effect the continued amelioration, in the speediest possible manner, of the moral, intellectual, and physical condition of mankind, especially of the poorest and most numerous classes."[25]

While about to bid adieu to the Saint-Simonians and the Unitarians, he still retained fairly pleasant memories of both. In *The Convert,* he said: "Yet I imbibed no errors from the Saint-Simonians, and I can say of them as of the Unitarians, they did me no harm, but were, in my fallen state, the occasion of much good to me."[26]

During the latter part of 1842 and the greater part of 1843 Brownson had been, as already noted, a contributor to the *Democratic Review*. His articles had been mainly philosophical and political in nature. When, however, he returned to the pulpit in April 1842, his mind had turned back more and more to its preoccupation with the religious question. But now he had no medium of communication for the discussion of the religious or the church question. Yet a multiplicity of thoughts on that question of questions was fairly swirling in his head and clamoring for utterance. For he was just now working his way into daylight; or as he himself expressed it, the fetters that had bound his soul, and against which he had struggled in vain for the last twenty-five years, were being broken, and he could see now more clearly where he stood, and in what direction he should now move.[27] What more natural then than that he should decide on the revival of the *Quarterly* he had owned and edited for five years, and which had served him so well as a vehicle for saying just what he had wanted to say up to the close of 1842 — after which he had written for the *Democratic Review*. But when the time came for him to sever his connections with that publication, O'Sullivan's publishers would not allow him to resume the title of the *Boston Quarterly Review*.[28] Whereupon he called his new journal *Brownson's Quarterly Review,* a more highly significant title, the first issue of which appeared in January 1844.

Never was a journal to bear more distinctly the stamp of its proprietor and editor than was *Brownson's Quarterly Review*. He chose the title, not out of a touch of vanity, as he said, but simply because it matched perfectly what that journal was intended to be — a true photographic reflection of his own mind. In the twenty-eight-page introductory notice to the first issue, he said quite characteristically:

> This is *my* Review [he had known the irksomeness of being connected with publications over which he had no control]; I am its sole proprietor; its editor; and intend to be its principal, if not its sole writer; and to make it the organ of my own views of truth, on all the great and little topics, on which I shall judge it worth my while to discourse. It shall be the journal of my own mind, and, doubtless, reflect all its various and varying moods. It may support, and oppose, first one existing party, sect, or school, and then another. It will be bound by none, but be free to approve, or to criticize, one or all, just when and where its editor judge. proper. . . . All parties, sects, and schools must be free, so far as I am concerned, to accept what they like, and to reject what they dislike; to praise me when they please, and, when they please, to scold me to their heart's content.[29]

This declaration was the keynote that was to characterize his *Quarterly Review* down to the very last edition that was to issue from the press in October 1875. The contents of his introductory notice was a brief and succinct summary of his intellectual odyssey to date, his present state of mind, and the direction his thought could be expected to take in the future on a variety of fronts. He was more conscious at this turn in his career than usual that he would probably be freely badgered for his alleged everlasting changes. That he had shifted his position from time to time there is no denying. Did it argue fickleness or instability? "To live is to change," said John Henry Newman, "and to be perfect, is to have changed often."[30] The great end to which Brownson had directed all his arduous efforts over the last twenty years had never changed, to wit, the amelioration, moral, intellectual and physical of the condition of the poorer and more numerous classes of society. That there had been a change from time to time in the means or method he had adopted in his attempt to promote that great end, suggested by an enlarged experience, was of course true. Speaking of the matter, he said:

> Yes, I deny that I have *changed,* though I own that I seem to myself to have *advanced.* . . . My views have, in general, become more fully developed, and systematized; I seem to myself to understand myself better, to know better what I would effect, and what means I must use to effect it. The young dreamer, the visionary speculator, let me hope, has ripened into the sober, practical man. If this be to change, I doubtless have changed; but in this I have only changed, as all change, who are not incapable of profiting by experience.[31]

He apparently felt that he owed it to the public at this juncture to make a clean breast of precisely where he stood in matters of religion. He had been continually changing, or at least developing his religious views and beliefs over a period of almost twenty years. Where did he stand now? He had come a long way indeed from the low-water mark of mere naturalism or no-religion he had reached in 1829 when consorting with Fanny Wright and Robert D. Owen. It was only by a "long and painful struggle," as he told Dr. Channing — not by a single bound — that he had been able to place himself on the high tableland of Christian faith and hope.[32] He admitted that in the enlargement of his faith there had been a sloughing off of naturalistic and

269

pantheistic tendencies which had fettered his soul. But the clear-cut declaration of faith he could now make to the public should have been amply reassuring to the Christian world, by and large. Forthrightly he said:

> I accept with all my heart, without any prevarication, mystification, or reservation, the Gospel of Jesus Christ, in the ordinary sense of the Christian world; and I hold the [Catholic] Church to be the depository of the sacred Traditions, and the medium through which the Divine Life of Jesus, or the Holy Ghost proceeding from the Father *and the Son,* is transmitted from generation to generation, and communicated to the world, for the redemption and sanctification of sinners. I hold that the Church is a divine institution, an inspired body, founded on the Rock of Ages, and that the gates of hell shall not prevail against it; that it is the ground and pillar of truth; and the authoritative interpreter of the will of God on earth. Moreover, I hold that the Gospel, deposited with the Church, contains the *principles* of all truth, and that the whole future of mankind, dating from its promulgation by Jesus and his Apostles, consists in developing those principles, and reducing them to practice.[33]

That he was now advancing perceptibly toward the Catholic Church was becoming ever more clear. So much so in fact that he felt called upon to state that "there is no truth in the report, that I have joined, or am intending to join, the Roman Catholic Church. I am free to confess, that I accept the general theory of that church, as the true theory of the Church of Christ; but the theory itself prevents me, *in the present state of the religious world,* from seeking to unite myself to the Roman Catholic communion."[34]

His paramount objection to the Catholic Church at this time seems to have been that it was not Catholic enough, that is, according to his own theory. He favored the theory at the time of a continuous development or evolution of truth from Christian principles — something apparently similar to the theory of Newman on which he was later to lay his strictures. He also spoke of a *continuous inspiration* in the church by virtue of the indwelling Holy Spirit. (The more correct term is *divine assistance* of the Holy Spirit. No *new* Christian doctrine can ever be added to the deposit of divine faith.) As he saw it, this continuous evolution of truth from Christian principles, according to the exigencies of time and place, would provide the solution to every emerging problem, theological, political, social and ethical, and prove to be the real elixir of social progress. The theory had a special appeal for him inasmuch as it still allowed ample room for "the largest liberty of thought and speech, which no consideration could induce me," he said, "to surrender, for they are manifestly the indispensable condition of human progress."[35] But the Catholic Church had acted on this theory "only feebly and timidly" in the past. It had remained too much bound to Christian antiquity, and had allowed too much interference from the state with its developing life. The reason why the Church had not succeeded more completely in its mission, he said, was not to be found "in the arrogance of her pretensions, but in the modesty of her claims; not in asserting, but in *not* asserting, her independence in regard to tradition, written and unwritten, and in the face of the civil authority." Protestantism, on the other hand, had failed more completely in asserting the supremacy of the written word, not as to principle, but in a full and perfect code, admitting no further development.[36]

Because the Catholic Church had failed to act more fully on the free development of the Gospel and in asserting its own independence, Brownson felt that in spite of "her unquestionable apostolic descent, externally considered, her high antiquity, and general soundness of faith," the Church must take its stand, very nearly, on the same level with other communions.[37] But where was he to look for the Church of Christ since no Christian communion met his expectations? His answer makes one feel that he is listening to a fervent ecumenist of the post-conciliar twentieth century. He called upon all, in whatever Christian community lodged, to labor earnestly for such a reorganization of Christendom as would lead to a general unity among all Christians, assuring all that he himself would labor assiduously for that great end from the *"very position where God in his providence has placed me."* (Italics mine.) If all will so cooperate, gradually but effectually, a spirit of unity will spring up, which will lead to a unity of faith, which in turn will induce a unity of organization and discipline. The new organization, strictly speaking, will not be new, but the old transformed.

> Here, in brief [he said] is my Catholicism, on which I shall have, in the progress of this work, much to say. To speak technically, I am neither Protestant nor Romanist. I belong to neither the Protestant world, nor to the Roman world. I look upon Protestantism as a blunder, and as having proved a decided failure; on the other hand, I look upon Roman Catholicism as substantially true, under the relation of theory, but upon the Roman Catholic Church, under the relation of practice, as having but imperfectly fulfilled her mission. Theoretically considered, she forms the basis of reunion; practically considered, she herself is more or less Protestant, and schismatic.[38]

Brownson also served notice in the introduction to the January issue of his *Quarterly* that his social philosophy had undergone a considerable change. He had come to realize more than ever before that no practical reforms for the elevation of the laboring classes could be successfully introduced without the cooperation of the educated and more influential classes in society. In this great work he now felt more confidence in appealing to the more favored than the less favored classes, for he had found warmer friends of the laboring classes among the aristocratic classes, in spite of their pretensions, than among the rank and file of mankind. Besides, he asserted, it would be folly to try to introduce reforms in opposition to the wealthy classes of society — they were all too powerful.[39]

But to secure this aid of the wealthy and influential classes, the first great need was to recall the age to a living Christian faith. There must be faith in men's souls that will raise them above the horizon of this world, that will make them treasure eternal values which are purchased only through painful sacrifices. Wealth can be equalized, if at all, only by raising the souls of the wealthy above the love of it, and by teaching the poor to count the wealth of this world as mere dross, as so much dust in the balance, if only they can lay up treasures "where neither moth nor rust doth corrupt, nor thieves break through and steal." Christianity in the past had brought men to count poverty and want the greatest blessings, and so had changed the face of the earth; and this same tremendous power Christianity had in no sense lost. In a striking passage reminiscent of the famous saying of Montesquieu, Brownson asserted that Christianity, and only Christianity, can work the great social improvement so avidly sought but so elusive of human schemes and dreams. Boldly he declared:

> I dare avow, in the very face of this infidel age, in whose infidelity I once shared, my full and firm faith in the truth and power of Christianity to work out, for us, the highest social good here, as well as to secure for us the blessedness of heaven hereafter. The attempt to reform the world, to regain the lost Eden, by human agencies, human philosophies, political economies, work-

houses, and "cash payments," has been made, and failed, and will always fail, repeat we the experiment as often as we may. God leaves men, now and then, as it were to themselves, to their own wisdom and strength, which is but weakness and folly; but he is jealous of his honor, and his glory he will not give to another. Our own devices, our own schemes and systems, wrought out with infinite pains, may appear to ourselves worthy of all praise; but the High and Holy One holds them in derision. The great moral power that overcomes the world, is religious faith. . . . Here is my hope for the world. . . . It is God's will to work out for us a great and abiding social good, in the establishment of his kingdom on earth; but he will do this, only in his own way. . . . The Gospel of the kingdom is the only possible medium of renovation and growth.[40]

This formal statement marks a decided alteration in his convictions concerning the means to be adopted for the promotion of social progress. In the *Boston Reformer* he had labored earnestly to enlist the Church on the side of reform, as a supporter of the cause of the people, and as a condition of both saving itself and rescuing the age from infidelity. The formula he now adopted was quite different: he now accepted the Catholic Church as the body of the Lord, as the divinely commissioned agent for the effectual working out of all social regeneration and progress. This placed all his hopes, both spiritual and material, entirely in the Church. He felt accordingly a great compulsion to labor zealously not only to bring men to the Church for their spiritual salvation, but also as the preliminary condition for the working out of all plans of reform. The Catholic Church had thus moved squarely to the center of the stage in his social as well as his religious thinking. Having arrived at this position, he was not unmindful of the hostile confrontation he must expect to the efforts he would put forth:

> In this [he said] I shall have for enemies the worldly wise, the selfish, and unbelieving, and the indifferent, a formidable host, well marshalled and led on by the great Enemy of all righteousness. But I shall not be alone; for I shall be only one of the still mightier army of the Faithful, and shall be encouraged by the saints and martyrs of all ages, whose prayers I dare invoke, and dare believe will be effectual with the Great Head of the Church, to whose service I have consecrated myself anew, and without reserve.[41]

But if he was now a hard-shelled conservative in his social philosophy, he was no less so in his political thought. He reminded his readers, old and new, that he had fought doggedly on the conservative line in politics since the commencement of the *Boston Quarterly Review* (1838), "the thousand voices of the country, vociferating to the contrary, notwithstanding."[42] He reiterated what he had laid down when introducing himself as editor of the *Boston Reformer* (1836), namely, that the existing political order in this country is to be preserved as it is, and no alteration attempted. "Our fundamental institutions are to the statesman, what the Gospel is to the churchman — the law which he is to develop and apply, but in no case to change, or to set aside. He may seek progress, but only progress through and under existing institutions. This is the law I prescribe to myself, and what I mean by conservatism."[43]

Turning his attention to the actual political scene before him, this Boston reformer flailed away in an article on demagoguism at the skullduggery and corruption becoming ever more rampant in the country.[44] He still expressed "great confidence" in the enlightened voice of the people, but deeply deplored that the voice of the people was so frequently only the voice of corrupt and intriguing politicians who wheedle and cheat the people out of their votes. The real enemies of the people are these selfsame demagogues who "praise the people with their lips and with their hands pick their pockets, or those who act as jackals to dainty chiefs who are too exalted to plunder — except by proxy."[45] Deeply did he lament the perversion on the part of demagogues of the principle of the responsibility of officers in government to the people. A good principle in itself, since the electoral people may eject from office any civil servant who abuses his power or defaults on his duty. But the perversion of this same principle he found had raised up a whole swarm of greedy and unprincipled demagogues who knavishly flatter the people, and ask only, not what is right and conducive to the welfare of the people, but only what will be popular and serve their own base interests and nefarious designs. He sadly warned that the growing perversion of this principle, with its accompanying mad scramble for wealth, place and power, was spreading vice and rottenness all through society which like a cancer was eating into the very vitals of the nation, irrespective of whether or not others perceived and acknowledged the lethal malady.[46]

He lost no time as this election year came around to do all he could to promote further the candidacy of his friend, John C. Calhoun, for the presidency of the United States. The January issue of his *Quarterly* carried a review of *The Life and Speeches of John C. Calhoun* which could scarcely have been surpassed for its eloquent recital of the merits which made Calhoun the logical choice for the presidency. "What," he exclaimed, "is the Presidency of these United States to such a man as Mr. Calhoun? . . . It may be a matter of moment to the country, whether Mr. Calhoun shall or shall not be President of the Union; to him it is none at all. The Presidential chair may receive new dignity and lustre from him; to him it can give none."[47] He admired Calhoun greatly not only as an original thinker and philosophical statesman, but also thought his administrative powers were unsurpassed by anyone in modern times, unless perhaps by Napoleon. In an attempt to head off Van Buren from recapturing the nomination for the presidency — thus favoring Calhoun — he lambasted roundly the ruthless party machine with its "spoils" system, putting devotion to party above devotion to the welfare of the people or the country. He charged Van Buren with being the most conspicuous representative in the country of the "spoils" system, if it had not been actually founded by him.[48] This was good "fence-patching" in favor of Calhoun, but it was to be nothing more than a case of love's labor lost.

But what in the meantime had become of his long-discussed *Church of the Future?* Little or nothing had been heard of it during the last year. He had gradually been coming to see that the Church of the Future was none other than the historic church of the past. He had envisioned his Church of the Future as the great instrument of progress for men and society. But when he came to reflect on the matter deeply, he realized that he needed his new organization beforehand for effecting that very progress without which the new church could never come to be established. He had been wistfully planning a much-desired result without an adequate means to effect it.[49] This forced upon him the conclusion that man is no church-builder, or for that matter, no founder of any institution really capable of elevating and setting mankind forward. This major break in his thought he indicated in the first edition of his new *Quarterly* (1844). When reviewing an oration of Frederic H. Hedge, he rejected Transcendentalism outright, and added that man can in no sense be a church-builder. He said:

We are sorry to discover, here and there, in this Oration, some traces of

273

the miserable Transcendentalism which has of late obtained amongst us, and which spins Truth, Good, Beauty, even God himself, out of the human soul, as the spider spins its web out of its own bowels. We had flattered ourselves that Mr. Hedge had worked himself entirely clear of this false notion. The [Catholic] Church, and all really valuable institutions, by which society is elevated and carried forward, are given to man by his Maker, and not developed by, nor from, the human soul. God alone is able to create without preexisting matter; man can create only by means of a matter foreign to him.[50]

Brownson's most significant article in the January 1844 issue of his *Quarterly* was the one titled "The Church Question." He called the church question "the question of questions for our age."[51] His mind was now full of that question. In the article he introduced the *Tracts for the Times* of the Oxford divines as a text upon which to offer some reflections of his own "on the very important religious movement, of which they are one of the pregnant signs." It was by this time clear to him that there is, and can be, but *one* Catholic Church. To acknowledge *national churches* would be to render Christ's seamless garment. He asserted that the Church of England, on the ground it assumes, had never been able to convince him of the validity of its claims. What then? Should he proceed to unchurch that institution, and say that all in its communion are out of the way of salvation? That was a terrible responsibility from which he at this time shrank. Eschewing all theological argumentation in the case, he set himself the role of a zealous ecumenist. He saw the body of the Lord, though broken into fragments, still living, each fragment quick with *immortal* life. The great question was how to gather these scattered fragments into a healthy reunion, that is, how to bring together the many Christian communions that divide Christendom into a renewed unity and catholicity. Advocating an irenic policy, he earnestly admonished the members of the fragmentary churches to play down their rival claims and doctrinal differences — which could only widen separations — and to labor in all earnestness for a restoration of true unity and catholicity among the entire Christian family of the world.

> Let every one [he pleaded] who has come to believe in, and to long for, the great principles of unity and catholicity, preach them from their own standpoint; the Congregationalist from his Congregational pulpit; the Presbyterian from his Presbyterian pulpit; the Anglican from his episcopal chair, the Roman Catholic from his cathedral; and let it be done here in Boston, in New York, in Baltimore, in Oxford, at Berlin, at Paris, at Rome; and instantly it will be seen, that throughout all Christendom, in the bosom of the most exclusive and hostile communions, there is a real unity of faith as to what the Church, as a body, really is, and as to what are its mission and authority.[52]

He recommended as of prime importance a return to a study of the nature itself of the Church, its rights, its offices, and its authority, as the most effective means to ensure a restoration of its unity and catholicity. He likewise urged the calling of an ecumenical council for adjusting the bases of a renewed communion as to faith, polity and discipline. The council was to be composed of delegates from all Christian communions the world over who "believe in the Holy Catholic Apostolic Church, and are willing to submit to its authority, and to abide its decisions, fairly and formally promulgated." The few who would not submit to the decrees of this ecumenical council would rightly be regarded as heretics and schismatics as they would have no excuse for not hearing the voice of the Church, enlightened by the indwelling light of the Holy Spirit.[53]

His general counsel, therefore, to all who found themselves members of one or the other of the sects, was that they should *stay where they were,* and there pray and labor for a restoration of unity and catholicity among all Christians. And in the adoption of this policy he promised to lead the way.

This article, "The Church Question," was impressive enough to draw from an anonymous reader in Philadelphia a letter, evidently from a learned divine, postmarked January 10. In referring directly to the article on the church question, the reader said in part:

> Sir:
>
> I have been reading the first number of your *Review* with deep attention and admiring interest. You have the power of doing good or evil beyond most men of our age and country, and with it a fearful responsibility. God has blessed you with a fearless heart, and a tongue, as you rightly say, "trumpet-tongued," and what is better, true to your heart's convictions. With those convictions mine harmonize, in many of the great points to which you call attention. But in some, to me, of all-absorbing interest, I believe you wrong, and I think I see *why* you are wrong.
>
> Most truly do you set forth the *rights* and *powers* of the living body of the Son of God. Of its *nature* and *offices* you have yet to learn.
>
> How can *you*, who so powerfully appeal to the "fact of eighteen hundred years," set aside the *historical* view, by which alone you get at the fact. . . . The *organized* life of the one Body has been seen, heard, looked upon, and handled, from the day of the Apostles until now.[54]

This letter Brownson took up for discussion in an article entitled "The Nature and Office of the Church" in the April issue of his *Quarterly.* He replied to his anonymous correspondent that he had not entered largely into the nature and office of the Catholic Church as in that article he was addressing his old friends (the Unitarians) who make little of church authority. His main object in the article had been to move the church question itself by stating that men had broken from the Church simply because they had lost the sense of the true significance of the Church. But he had indicated in the article that only a study of the nature and office of the Catholic Church could show them the necessity of returning to the Church. For from the moment they came to perceive the true nature and office of the Church they must perceive that a church that is not one and catholic is no church at all.[55] The urgency of recognizing the unity and catholicity of the Church was what his article had been all about.

He further assured his correspondent that he had misunderstood him if he implied that he himself had been proposing in the article a reconstruction of the one holy Catholic Church. His inquiry was not, "How may the church itself recover its unity and catholicity?" but, "How may professedly Christian communions find their way back to the one Catholic Church?" Brownson's concept of the unity and catholicity of the Catholic Church was quite orthodox. In our day when there is so much loose talk about extensively reforming the Church, almost carrying with it (at least apparently in the minds of some) the subtle suggestion that the church itself is in need of reformation, it is refreshing to note the clear-cut distinction Brownson made while still a Protestant between the Catholic Church as a divine institution and the human element in the Church. Tersely he said:

> The church has never lost her unity and catholicity, for it cannot lose them without ceasing to be the Church of God. The Church never stands in need of reform. The censures we bestowed, in our remarks, were not bestowed on the

church as an organization, but on the church, in the modern Protestant sense, as an *assemblage of individuals;* that is, upon churchmen. The church was as pure in the days of Luther and Calvin, as it was in the days of the Apostles, though, doubtless, many of its members, and some of its dignitaries, even, were corrupt, and abused their powers and privileges. The reform we demand is never of the institution, but of the individuals.[56]

He likewise explained that he had not fallen back on history in his article on the "Church Question" for the simple reason that the real question was: *What* is the Catholic Church itself, its nature, its rights and duties? Such a question could not be answered by the historical method of the Oxford divines. It relates to philosophy, not history. The historical approach is the proper method when the question is, *which* is the true church, but not when the question is, *what* is the true church? Only after the question — *What* is the true church? — has been settled, can it be identified in history.[57]

Brownson's anonymous critic also demurred to Brownson's statement that each of the fragments of the Lord's broken body, that is the sects, is still "quick with life." He seemed to imply that they were spiritually entirely dead. To this Brownson replied that all sects, not precisely *as sects,* but as professing Christians, do have some portion of Christian life, deriving from an intercommunion, however tenuous, with the Catholic Church from whom they had broken off. This tenet is in harmony with Vatican Council II which affirmed: "The Church recognizes that in many ways she is linked with those who, being baptized, are honored with the name Christian, though they do not profess the faith in its entirety or do not preserve unity of communion with the successor of Peter."[58] But while contending there is a Christian life in every sect, Brownson did not assert that there is a valid and sufficient ministry in each sect, but a ministry, however, that is at least sufficiently valid to authorize it to labor with all zeal and perseverance to bring its own communion into Christian fellowship with the one Catholic Apostolic communion. "If," he said, "you find yourself invested with authority in a revolted province, you have the right to exercise that authority for the maintenance of order and the restoration of the authority of the legitimate sovereign."[59] It was to this statement Fr. Isaac Hecker referred many years later when he said: "He [Brownson] once told me that he was like the general of an army born in rebellion, and it was his duty to carry as many back with him to the true standard as he could. This delusion he soon got rid of, and went alone at last."[60]

While unequivocally acknowledging the one Catholic Apostolic communion, it was Brownson's lament that the power and efficiency of that communion for communicating life to mankind had been sadly crippled by sectarian divisions that so abound in Christendom. Not only those in schism suffer, but the whole body of the Lord suffers in consequence of being impeded by so many divisions from carrying out its mission to mankind with all the requisite energy and vigor. The whole Church suffers from the distracted state of Christendom. It is for that reason he spoke of the torn and bleeding, though still living, body of the Lord. "It is the Church, the Catholic Apostolic Church, the spiritual mother of us all," he said, "but, alas! not the church in full strength, full glory, full operation. This is the ground we take, because it is obviously true, and involves no contradiction of Catholic principles."[61]

In conclusion he assured his critic that on the "Church Question" he was not guessing, but was sure of his ground, and had no wish to innovate. The church of the past was now gleaming before him in ever clearer and lovelier outline as the Church of the Future. We see very clearly, he said, the end to be reached, and the road that leads there. But he did not want anyone to push him in the matter. He insisted instead of being allowed to proceed at his own pace. He had made up his mind to allow neither friend nor foe to turn him aside either to the right hand or to the left, but was determined to proceed unflinchingly on the line where the comely form of Truth was beckoning him forward. Least of all did he intend to allow himself to be drawn into any premature argumentation which would only prove unprofitable to the furtherance of the great cause of unity and catholicity. For the present, he called again for a new ecumenical council for the settlement of differences on Catholic principles.[62] What he had in mind was evidently similar to what we know within comparatively recent times as the meetings of the World Council of Churches, particularly such as the one held at Uppsala, Sweden, in July 1968, with its prime concern about *The Holy Spirit and the Catholicity of the Church, dealing especially with the Theological Basis of Christian Unity.* He of course envisioned at the time the Catholic Church itself as an important member of the World Council of Churches as it was his hope that it would "become the nucleus of reorganization, and ultimately absorb all other communions into herself."[63]

Brownson's overriding interest in the "Church Question" was now increasing in intensity as he perceived with ever sharper clarity that the right solution to the social question depended entirely on the right solution to the "Church Question." It was all as clear to him now as a demonstrated theorem in Euclid that until the Church was reestablished in its rightful authority and influence over mankind no schemes of reform, however cunningly devised, whether individual or social, political or industrial, could carry with them any real promise of success. This is the reason why he called the "Church Question" the first and paramount question of the age and country. But when he now spoke of the Church, of its unity and catholicity, he clearly meant an outward visible body or institution, "through which will be given us one Lord, one faith, one baptism, or, in other words, the unity of faith and discipline."[64] He was at last resolving the great questions of the social and political order which had so agitated his mind during the last two decades into the simple question of the Catholic Church — simple only in the sense that the solution to that one question held the key to the answer to all other questions however perplexing. His elaborate thought on this intricate matter was given to the public in the April 1844 edition of his *Quarterly,* under the forthright title: "No Church, No Reform."

What added a high degree of significance to this article was the fact that he spoke from his own personal, deep-felt experience of some twenty years as one of the most dedicated and persevering reformers of the age. Early in life he had begun to reflect on the wide disparity among the social classes, the general degradation of the great army of operatives, and the immense advantages capital holds in the modern industrial system over labor. He saw that the whole tendency of modern industry is to separate capital from labor, and to create an ever increasing proletarian class that could be coerced by the captains of industry into laboring for a mere minimum of human subsistence, and often for less than that. The lot of the laboring class appeared to him (in his own day) no better than feudal serfdom, or even worse, for the feudal serf knew nothing of the sudden fluctuations of modern industry with its menacing threat to the security of the hard-working operative. Reflecting on this sorry plight of the modern workingman struggling in many instances against baffling odds to wangle enough from the modern industrial Moloch to keep body and soul together, "I was seized," he said, "with a passion for social reform, and solemnly consecrated myself to the work of discovering and applying a remedy to the evils I saw."

In his first frenzied attempt to get to the bottom of the economic question he had assumed that the *causes* of existing evils were due to the vicious *organization* of society. Everything operates on the principle of selfishness. The priest lives by our sin; the lawyer by our quarrels; the doctor by our diseases. All is an unchanging scheme of consuming strife in which only the strong few adequately survive. Every man's hand is against that of his brother. Where can a remedy be found for this unrelieved contention? Evidently since these evils flow from the vicious organization of society, creating everywhere an antagonism of interests, the remedy can be found only in so reorganizing society as to harmonize the interests of each with interests of all. Brownson asserted that he had first solved the problem in his young manhood by the theory of *association* and *attractive industry*. He did not claim that he had drawn out in his own mind a complete system of *association*, nor that he had established all the laws of *attractive labor*, much less that he had worked out all the details of the system. But he did claim that he had grasped all the great principles of the practical part of Fourierism, long before the name of Fourier was heard in this country, and even before he had attracted much, if any, attention in his own country, and that was before the year 1829.

But Brownson's enchantment with these theories was brief. He soon discovered that Fourierism in all its features was a mere jack-o'-lantern. It was impractical; it could not be made to work. It is based on selfishness and excludes entirely all the higher and nobler motives furnished by religion which can be invoked looking to a redress of the many grievances in society. Brownson's problem was: How on the groundwork of selfishness does one get men to cooperate for the introduction of his system of *attractive industry*? He found each person a center of his own interest, selfishly unconcerned about promoting the interests of all. Enlightened self-interest simply made no appeal to the average individual. Brownson soon found that the machine he had constructed with his theory of *association* simply could not be thrown into operation. He needed for the introduction of that system the very union among men which his system was intended to effect. Operating on the principle of selfishness could only produce the fruits of selfishness in society, grievous inequalities, widespread inhuman oppressions, injustices in a myriad of forms — the very evils he had longed so ardently to eradicate. Young man that he was at the time, he saw that he had no answer to his problem.

Further thought and experience brought him to the discovery that for the introduction of remedial measures into society the principle of selfishness must be replaced by a spirit of disinterestedness, benevolence and self-sacrifice. This discovery brought him in turn out of the cold and heartless philosophy of the eighteenth century and into the company of the philanthropic Dr. Channing whose magnetic eloquence and flowing periods had so often touched deep chords in his heart. For a time he was a fellow laborer with him; but the solution to his problem was not to be found there either. The Unitarians taught indeed the necessity of disinterestedness and sacrifice as motives requisite for social reform. But the problem was: Where does one obtain the *power* of disinterestedness and sacrifice so necessary for social reform? Men by nature are selfish, and do not naturally possess these qualities in themselves. Where and how can they be obtained (and obtained they must be if there are to be any successful efforts at social amelioration)?

Pressed hard on the point, his mind turned back to reflecting more deeply on the Gospel which places excellence of character in love, fraternity and sacrifice. Its first and great command is that we love one another as Jesus has loved us, even, therefore, if need be, to die on the cross for our fellowmen. Lo, Christianity would solve his problem. His heart bounded as he thought he had at long last hit upon the talismanic power needed for social reform. Cheered and animated, he went forth and preached the Gospel of love, disinterested affection, brotherhood, and many were the burning words that fell from his lips, and perhaps not altogether in vain. But, alas! his difficulties still remained. Merely to stand up and say to men, "Love one another; be ready to die for one another," would not of itself make them love one another. It was like saying, "Be ye warmed, be ye filled, be ye clothed," while imparting none of those things that were needed.

What the corrupt and selfish who were oppressing their brethren and spreading misery and wretchedness through society most needed, was not to be told their duty, but to be endued with a power enabling them to do it; not just to know they *ought* to love, but to be brought under an influence that would induce them to love. He reflected that he might preach until doomsday, but unless he had some agency to induce the *power* to love, "that power to become the sons of God," into the hearts of men, men would continue to be the plague and oppressor of their own kind. "Men are not redeemed by the teachings of Christ, but by Christ himself, by his being formed in them, the wisdom of God and the power of God, and through his indwelling Spirit constituting them sons of God, and heirs to the heavenly inheritance."

Out of this particular difficulty, therefore, neither Dr. Channing nor any of his Unitarian friends could help him. They said truly that the fruits of the Christian life are love, brotherhood and benevolence, but the means of inducing men to live that life they did not indicate. How was the problem to be solved? Would it be enough to say — as was the common admonition: Come to Christ, and all needed wisdom and power to live that life will be imparted to you? Doubtless Christ is in himself that wisdom and that power, and all who come to him will receive them. But what is meant by *coming* to Christ? Coming to Christ can only mean coming into *moral harmony* with Christ, that is, obeying the divine law, and being at one with God. But he who obeys the divine law is no longer a sinner, but already lives the Christian life. To propose, then, coming to Christ as the means of obtaining the power to live the Christian life, is like telling a man to live that life as the condition of obtaining the ability to live it. His problem remained unresolved.

The great difficulty in the case is that Christ and the sinner stand at opposite poles, the Holy and the unholy. Some ministry, some middle term is needed to connect them, to bring them together so that the Holy may act directly on the unholy, imparting the wisdom and the power of God to live the Christian life. This third term (to be accessible to the individual who is body as well as soul) must be an external institution embodying Christ himself who from that center communicates himself to man with his powers and graces to live the Christian life of love, self-sacrifice and brotherhood. This institution is no other than the Catholic Church founded by Christ, at once as necessary for the regeneration of society as for the individual's moral redemption. Is it not a commonplace preached from the pulpit, continued Brownson, that man, his spiritual powers wasted by sin, is inadequate to work out his own redemption — that he cannot rise from moral death except through the new life given him by the Son of God? Will it, then, be contended that he is equal, unassisted, to the still greater task of the regeneration of society by his own unassisted powers?

Where do social evils come from? Will it be contended that they are the result of the viciously organized society which perverts the minds and corrupts the hearts of its members? But how did that come about? Does man make society, or does society make man? Even granting that the one acts and reacts on the other, yet, with holy men, could you ever have a viciously organized society? Or with ignorant, depraved men, can you have a rightly organized society? Is it not plain, then, that individual reformation and social reform proceed on the same principle and are worked out by the operation of the same powers and virtues? If the Church is essential to individual regeneration, it is no less essential to social regeneration. For only the Church founded by Christ can communicate to the souls of men that spirit of disinterested love and self-sacrifice through which reforms in society are made possible. Hence Brownson's conclusion: "No Church, No Reform."[65]

The fundamental error of almost all modern reformers, complained Brownson, is that they proceed on the assumption that man is sufficient unto himself for his own regeneration on all fronts, and needs not that help which can come only from the divine institution called the Church. But man equals only man. With man only nothing higher than man can be had. "Man cannot lift himself by his own waistband."[66] Progress depends upon the communication of a wisdom and a power higher than man which modern reformers fail to recognize.

> Here [said Brownson] is the terrible sin of modern times. We vote God out of the State; we vote him out of the community; and we concede him only a figurative, a symbolical relation with our churches, denying almost universally the *Real Presence,* and sneering at it as a popish error; we plant ourselves on the all-sufficiency of man, and then wonder that we fail, and that, after three hundred years of efforts at reform, nothing is gained, and a true state of society seems as far off as ever. These three hundred years of experiments and failures ought to suffice, one would think, to teach us, that no reforms, if at all worthy of the name, are possible, save by means of more than human power. Men may cavil at this statement as they will, call us all the hard names for making it they please; but all experience asserts it, all sound philosophy demonstrates it, and all history confirms it.[67]

At this time Brownson's mind was turned further in the direction of the Catholic Church by two lectures delivered by Bishop John Hughes of New York at the Tabernacle in New York City in December 1843: *A Lecture on the Mixture of Civil and Ecclesiastical Power, in the Middle Ages,* and *A Lecture on the Importance of a Christian Basis for the Science of Political Economy, and its Application to the Affairs of Life.*[68] Brownson himself had previously in the winter of 1842-1843 given a series of lectures on the Middle Ages in Philadelphia and New York. In those lectures (no longer extant), his son tells us, though still a Protestant minister with no notion of ever becoming a Catholic, he had proscribed the age-old prejudices of Protestants against the Catholic Church. Those prejudices, in which he had never shared, must be due, he explained, either to a misunderstanding of that Church, or an unwillingness to be fair to it. Such hostile feelings are ungenerous, for say what we will, he insisted, the Catholic Church is the historic Church that has come down from Christ and his Apostles, and to which the Christian world is indebted for nearly all the good there is in Christianity. Whatever of positive teaching Protestantism retains, he asserted, is largely a reminiscence of Catholicism. Humanity at large is indebted to that church for the survival and revival of ancient classical literature, for the preservation of the Sacred Scriptures, the treasures of patristic literature, and for priceless works of religion and piety. Surely, here was enough to mollify any ungenerous or hostile feelings toward that ancient church. "To speak, as some of us do, of the dark ages," he added, "proves nothing but our own ignorance."[69]

This fair-minded Protestant minister also brought out in his lecture how the Catholic Church had served so well the cause of democracy, or the people, during the Middle Ages. As long as there was a united Christendom, with the pope as the great spiritual head revered by all, kings and princes knew that no oppressive or tyrannical government over the people could escape the rebuke of the common father of all, speaking to them in the name of God. They feared his censure would lose to them the loyalty of their subjects, and were therefore restrained from oppression. But the Protestant movement changed all that. In those nations where the august authority of the papacy was no longer recognized, kings and nobles felt there was no longer on earth an organized power strong enough to confront and rebuke them. Their regimes in consequence readily developed into political absolutionism. On this score, Brownson asserted that the Catholic Church had tended more toward democracy in its defense of the people while Protestantism in its tendency had favored the growth of absolute monarchy or aristocracy. For the papal power had really befriended the lower orders in society during those times, but when no longer recognized, the poor, the oppressed, the defenseless had lost an intrepid advocate and defender.[70] Already in 1836 Brownson had written: "Aristocratic Protestantism, which never dared to enforce its discipline on royalty and nobility, may weep over the exercise of such a power [the papal power], but it is to the existence and exercise of such a power, that the *people* owe their existence, and the doctrine of man's equality to man its progress."[71]

But it was with Bishop Hughes' lecture on *The Importance of a Christian Basis for the Science of Political Economy, and its Application to the Affairs of Life* that Brownson concerned himself mainly when reviewing the two lectures in his *Quarterly* (April 1844). The views expressed by Hughes were so similar to those of Brownson himself that John Hecker, who attended Hughes' lecture, wrote him: "I thought sometimes I was listening to you."[72] Brownson himself in commenting on the bishop's lecture referred to his own article on "No Church, No Reform" being published in the same issue of his *Review*. Concerning the relationship of the economic question to the Church, Brownson wrote:

> The conclusions to which we have come may be inferred from the article in the foregoing part of this journal, headed "No Church, No Reform." We have been fully satisfied, for some time, that the present deplorable condition of the laboring classes is due to the rejection, in the sixteenth century, by nearly one half of Europe, of the authority of the Catholic Church. The rejection of that authority left men without the necessary moral restraints on their natural selfishness, free to regulate all individual and social matters according to the dictates of the self-interests of individuals and governments, instead of the dictates of Christian duty and love. During the Middle Ages, and prior to the Reformation, the Catholic Church, by insisting on the Gospel of charity, on the merits of good works, and especially on the merit of voluntary poverty, and self-denial, had confined within some bounds the accumulative propensity of our nature, and compelled it, through considerations drawn from a future life, to make rich

and ample provision for the poor. . . . The Reformation changed all this, and, for the system of Gospel charity, voluntary poverty, good works, and self-denial, substituted self-interest, and sought to neutralize excessive selfishness by pitting the selfishness of one against the selfishness of the other. The result has been precisely what ought to have been expected — the reduction, in the more industrious and enterprising nations, of labor to complete dependence on capital, and the operative to a minimum of human subsistence, and in some cases, below it. The remedy, we are convinced — and we have devoted over twenty years of investigation to the subject — can be found only in a return, if not to the Catholic Church, at least to a system of political economy similar to the one always insisted on, and enforced to a greater or less extent, by that Church.[73]

In this paragraph we have a remarkable anticipation of the widely known studies of Weber, Tawney and others on the relationship between Protestantism and capitalism.[74] Brownson's penetrating analysis of that relationship antedated those studies by more than half a century. His prescience in this area seems to have been largely overlooked by commentators on his thought. Even though there be those who look upon this theory advanced by Brownson and developed by Weber as something of an oversimplification of the matter, still it would probably be difficult to show that there is no real substratum of truth in the theory. It is interesting to note that Perry Miller seemed definitely to favor this theory. He wrote: "There can be no denying that in Puritanism as in all Protestantism there was an economic motive, that the creed had its origin in society as well as in the Augustinian temperament, and that its ethic was adapted to such considerations. Weber and Tawney have shown how far the teaching of "weaned affections, through seemingly a spiritual ideal, also jibed with the disposition of a rising middle class, that it was in effect a fine psychological assistance to the growth of capitalism."[75]

What impressed Brownson so favorably with Bishop Hughes' address was to find an eminent prelate of the Catholic Church speaking with the warmth and vigor of a living and thinking friend of the people on what he considered one of the all-absorbing questions of the day, the relation of capital and labor. Over the years he had held the view that the Catholic Church had done a grand work in the Middle Ages, but that it was something of an anachronism in the modern world. Hughes' championship of the interests of the operative, however, denouncing in eloquent tones the crime of regarding the operative as merely a machine for the production of wealth instead of treating him as a moral, religious and intellectual being with inherent rights to be respected, opened Brownson's eyes and warmed his heart toward that church of which the bishop was so distinguished an ornament. In conclusion, he thanked the bishop for his lecture "in the name of truth and Christian charity; in the name of the poor and oppressed, the starving widows and orphans; in the name of our country and humanity."[76]

Although deeply engrossed at this time in the church question and social reform, to say nothing of philosophy, education, moral systems and literary criticism, Brownson continued to write extensively on government and politics in this same year, 1844. His absorbing interest in who was to become the next President of the United States remained unabated. As the Democrats were to meet in convention the following month, May, at Baltimore, to nominate their candidate for the presidency, Brownson did all he could again to head off Van Buren from recapturing the nomination, thus to clear the way for his political idol, John C. Calhoun, in an article entitled *Calhoun and the Baltimore Convention.* Whether Brownson had been flattered or irritated by Van Buren's statement that he had "personally the principal share in his defeat"[77] in his last run for the presidency — a fact Brownson mentioned — it might be hard to say. But as far as in his power, Brownson was leaving no stone unturned in his last-minute efforts to throw Van Buren out of the race and turn the convention in favor of John C. Calhoun. Besides his elaborate article on the approaching Baltimore convention, he also wrote the leading political articles in six newspapers against Van Buren and staunchly in favor of Calhoun.[78] While the convention was in session the excitement had grown intense. When Brownson's son, as was his custom, brought his father the morning newspaper before breakfast, his father eagerly inquired: "Well, have they made a nomination?" "Yes, sir," replied the son, "James K. Polk has been nominated." "Who is James K. Polk?" exclaimed Brownson in a tone of utter scorn, and indignantly dashed the papers to the floor.[79] Little wonder. In that news he had sustained perhaps one of the greatest disappointments of his whole life. It would have been highly gratifying to him to have had his friend Calhoun the occupant of the White House. He had worked hard to bring it about.

But the great question for Brownson was after all the church question. As noted, he called it "the question of questions for our age."[80] In promoting the ecumenical movement all he could in his *Quarterly,* he was really only continuing the work he had already begun in the *Christian World* in 1843. The *Christian World* was a weekly journal published by George G. Channing, the brother of Dr. Channing. When consenting to become one of its editors, it was Brownson's intention to use its columns to promote further the union of Christendom, not on a new church basis, but on the basis of what had been the Catholic Church from the very beginning of Christianity. In that journal he immediately began a series of essays on "the mission of Jesus" which were so stirring in nature that the well-known Dr. Samuel Seabury, editor of the *New York Churchman* remarked that "a new era" had dawned on the Puritan city of Boston. In these essays Brownson had endeavored to draw attention to the Catholic Church as a living organism through which the Son of God redeems, saves and blesses mankind. As he later related, the first and second essays pleased his Unitarian friends, the third was warmly praised by a Puritan journal, the fourth "threw the Tractarians into ecstasies," the fifth, sixth and seventh were so Catholic in thought and tone that they were copied into a Catholic publication with enthusiastic comments. The eighth, which posed the touchy question as to which is the true church or body of Christ, the publisher refused to accept, and it was not therefore published. It was the concluding essay in the series, and as Brownson had evaded rather than answered the question posed, so he tells us, he was just as pleased that it was not accepted for publication. A Catholic editor offered him the use of his columns, but for the reason mentioned, he was glad to have an excuse for declining the offer.[81]

It was not until he saw his articles copied into a Catholic journal that the possibility of ever becoming a Catholic had so much as crossed his mind. He was indeed fully aware that the principles he had worked out led by an "invincible logic" to the assertion of the Catholic Church as the true Church or living body of Christ. Those principles did not indeed bring him into the Catholic Church, but they required him, as he understood the case, either to renounce his reason, or go further and accept the Catholic Church and its doctrines, in its own sense, not merely in the sense in which he had asserted them in his philosophy. In the enthusiasm of the moment he almost did just that forthwith — and then drew back. And for the first time in his life, he tells us, he refused to follow out his own principles to their logical conclusions. It was to be fully a year before he made up his mind to seek admission into the Catholic Church. Later he was to reproach himself for having betrayed "inexcusable weakness" in having delayed so long.[82]

Perhaps his delay was just sufficient to save him from the charge of undue precipitancy or rashness in a matter so grave. Whatever his hesitation, as a writer in the *Nation* remarked: "The royal road to Rome Brownson travelled was in remarkable contrast to Newman's long-drawn agony. He had ten times as far to go and he went ten times as quickly."[83] We have already seen that Brownson had at first determined to stay *where he was* that he might work the better (as he thought) to carry back with him as many as possible to "the true standard," and he was fearful of disturbing conscience. In this he was similar to Newman who remarked: "I dread shocking, unsettling people." On this score Newman had wished to defer his conversion a full seven years from the time when his conviction about the Catholic Church being the true Church had first begun to fall upon him.[84] He took two years to think the matter over (after once convinced of the truth of Catholicity) at Littlemore.[85]

Humanly speaking, Brownson's hesitation in the matter was quite understandable. He had been reared in his childhood on weird stories which represented the Catholic Church as the "mystery of iniquity" whose history was full of all kinds of abominations. The dark mystery had deepened all the more as he had never so much as seen a Catholic church until he had reached man's estate. As his learning had widened in his adult years, he had shaken off many of the Yankee prejudices which had been instilled into him, but something of it all had surely remained. Like most of his countrymen of the time, he had no doubt come to look upon the Catholic Church as an alien institution in the land, the Church of uneducated and downtrodden foreigners who huddled together in ghettoes or slums of our great cities. It had seemed to him, too, that the Protestant nations were the more moral, the more enlightened portion of mankind. At least so it had been represented to him, and he had not yet come to inquire into the truthfulness of such representations. Only one or the other Catholic book had fallen into his hands, controversial in nature, and the spirit and style of the authors had left on him a poor impression. He had no Catholic friends or acquaintances from whom he might learn something at first hand about the Catholic Church, Yet, a certain Dr. Charles Poysen, who had initiated him and many other New Englanders into animal magnetism, a fallen-away Catholic, had given Him many valuable hints about the Catholic religion and had turned his mind toward Catholic principles.[86] Brownson had found him to be a man of extensive learning, had become his personal friend, and was impressed by the fact that he regretted his defection from the Church, and had often spoken of returning to it. Yet he was only one; of the large body of Catholics in the country he had no acquaintance, and had only a poor opinion.[87] However this may have been in itself, he was nevertheless invincibly drawn toward the Catholic Church in the abstract, by a catholicity in general as indicated by his principles; but his Yankee prejudices were now scolding him for as much as even thinking of throwing in his lot with those who belonged to the Catholic Church. For a man of his background, such thoughts were simply never thought.

There was one stumbling block in particular that had held him back from the thought of becoming a Catholic which he called "the greatest and last obstacle in my mind to be overcome in embracing the Church." He had lived as a man of the world, he tells us, had strayed from the path of virtue, and had felt himself sinking, but was powerless to help himself. What to do? He had heard of the grace of assistance the Catholic Church professes to impart through its sacraments, but could he trust the Church? What about all those bad Catholics, "the vilest and the most abandoned, as Catholic apostates usually are," such as the Achillis and the Gavazzis? What had the grace of the sacraments done to help or save them?[88] His difficulty arose from the fact that, although he had long since abjured Presbyterianism, he had not succeeded over the years in completely rooting out of his mind the Calvinistic notion that grace is irresistible and inamissible. But this difficulty was to vanish the moment the true Catholic doctrine became known to him, namely, that grace is neither irresistible nor inamissible, that the individual remains ever a free moral agent capable of cooperating with grace or rejecting it. The individual is accordingly on his own: he may choose freely to be a saint or a sinner, or something in between. Sacramental grace strengthens the will but does not coerce it.

But the more he thought on the possibility of becoming a Catholic the more he was disturbed by what he thought he saw ahead in the event he decided to make the great venture. To pass from one Protestant sect to another, as he had done in the past, was like passing from one apartment to another in the same house. One really remains in the same world, in the same general order of thought, without the loss of old-time friends and acquaintances. One does not go from the known to the unknown, and may return, if he so chooses, to the sect he left, or try another, without incurring the stigma of being a turncoat, or without any serious disturbance of his social and domestic relations. He wrote:

> But to pass from Protestantism to Catholicity is a very different thing. We break with the whole world in which we have hitherto lived; we enter into what is to us a new and untried region, and we fear the discoveries we may make there, when it is too late to draw back. To the Protestant mind the old Catholic Church is veiled in mystery, and leaves ample room to the imagination to people it with all manner of monsters, chimeras, and hydras dire. We enter it, and leave no bridge over which we may return. It is a committal for life, for eternity. To enter it seemed to me, at first, like taking a leap in the dark; and it is not strange that I recoiled, and set my wits to work to find out, if possible, some compromise, some middle ground on which I could be faithful to my Catholic tendencies without uniting myself with the present Catholic Church.[89]

Every worldly consideration was now pleading with him to forgo the step he was contemplating. Although the long-range view of his life showed quite a checkered career, he had come with the passing of the years to occupy a distinctly prominent and honorable place in the community where he resided. "I was greeted warmly," he said on the eve of his conversion, "in quarters where I had hitherto been denounced or not recognized, and felt that, for the first time in my life, I had the sentiments of the better portion of the community with me."[90] He had carved out for himself in the American literary world quite a respectable niche — had indeed acquired "a philosophical and literary reputation sufficient to make a proud man vain."[91] As far as his worldly success was concerned, it had been a rugged, uphill battle all the way, testing his mettle to the utmost. But it was evidently with some satisfaction he remarked: "[Never had I] stood higher, commanded more of the public attention, or had a more promising career open before me, than at the moment when I avowed my conversion to Catholicity."[92] At the same time he must have foreseen clearly enough what would happen should he take the step he was now mulling over, to wit, that his name would be erased from among those of his distinguished non-Catholic countrymen, as actually happened. Would he then throw away all "in one fell swoop" in his surrender to Rome?[93] His answer was: "It did not cost me a pang to throw all away on becoming a Catholic, and to be regarded henceforth of no account to my non-Catholic countrymen, as I did not doubt I should be. There is something else than reputation worth living for."[94]

With such a man as Orestes A. Brownson, worldly considerations could never weigh a feather in the balance — not really. If John Henry Newman could say that he had never sinned against the light, Orestes Brownson could say the same with no less honesty. Did not his whole career show a consuming thirst for truth and justice? "From our youth up," he said, "we have loved truth, and wooed her as a bride, and we wish to die in her embrace."[95] In the present instance, then, could he be false to the inexorable claims of truth? If he allowed his mind to dwell upon the worldly disadvantages involved, his conscience at once began to talk back to him. Here he was, he had to admit, asserting the necessity of the Catholic Church as the condition of living the life of Christ, and as the medium of salvation, and yet holding himself aloof from it. To follow the example of the weeping Isis, and seek to gather together the fragments of the torn body of the Lord, was all well and good enough, but suppose he was to die before he had effected the reunion of Christendom, while still an alien to the body of the Lord, what would become of his soul? He reflected in his final musings that although it might, in many respects be unpleasant to take the step his principles and logic demanded, "to be eternally damned would, after all, be a great deal unpleasanter."[96]

But however deeply he felt the necessity of being visibly joined to the Catholic Church, he may have overstated his convictions when, on being asked, he "instantly and grimly" told Joseph Henry Allen that he would have gone to hell if he had died the day before he was actually received into the Church on October 20, 1844.[97] Yet John Henry Newman, too, had his fears lest he die before he was actually received into the Church. Interestingly he said: "The simple question is, Can I (it is personal, not whether another, but can I) be saved in the English Church: am *I* in safety, were I to die to-night?"[98] In Brownson's case, the conviction fastening itself upon him ever more firmly that the Catholic Church was the one divinely appointed means of salvation, being the man he was, there was only one decision he could make in the case: to Rome he would go without further delay.

# 21

## CONTINUED INVESTIGATIONS AND HIS CONVERSION TO CATHOLICITY

*His first visit with Bishop Benedict Joseph Fenwick • Troubled over the religious status of his Protestant friends, he hesitates a year • Upon his third interview with the bishop he declares his wish to be prepared for reception into the Catholic Church • Bishop John Bernard Fitzpatrick is appointed his instructor in the faith • His article on Come-outerism • Church unity requisite for social amelioration • A further change in his social philosophy • His slashing attack on Richard Hildreth's "theory of morals" • Three elaborate articles on Emmanuel Kant's* Critic of Pure Reason *• Subjectivism the great defect in Kant's philosophy • Brownson finally makes known to the public that his investigations have left him no choice other than to become a Catholic • He is instructed in the faith by Bishop Fitzpatrick • He is jolted when Bishop Fitzpatrick fails to give his doctrine of life by communion any cognizance • He is received into the Church on the strength of the traditional arguments which show the truth of Catholicity • His great and lifelong gratitude to Bishop Fitzpatrick • Brownson stresses the all-important part grace plays in the process of conversion • He declares that he has brought nothing into the Church but his sins • Archbishop John Hughes speaks eloquently of his humility • The conversion of his brother, Oran • The friendship between himself and Isaac Thomas Hecker grows closer • Fr. Hecker's tribute to Brownson's great love of truth • Arthur M. Schlesinger's admirable paragraph on Brownson's conversion • A letter of Martin John Spalding on the significance of Brownson's conversion.*

During an audience Pope Pius IX had granted Arthur P. Stanley, Anglican dean of Westminster Abbey, His Holiness said to him: "Do you know Pusey? When you meet him, give him this message from me — that I compare him to a bell that is always calling the faithful to church, and itself always remains outside."[1]

Perhaps no two men were more dissimilar than Edward Bouverie Pusey and Orestes Augustus Brownson. The sin of inconsequence was abhorred by Brownson. Not to follow one's principles and honest convictions, no matter where they might lead, was to him almost unforgivable.[2] Accordingly, after quitting his Unitarian pulpit in the spring of 1843, he made straightway for a visit with the Right Rev. Benedict Joseph Fenwick, then the Catholic bishop of Boston. Bishop Fenwick being kept quite busy with calls (it happened to be Holy Week), Brownson and his companion limited their visit to fifteen or twenty minutes, and the real object of the visit was never broached. After Easter, Bishop Fenwick left Boston immediately to attend a provincial council at Baltimore and then to visit relatives in Maryland, his native state, and did not return for quite some time.[3] Mulling in the meantime over the problem he had wished to submit to the bishop, Brownson did not seek another interview for a whole year.

It came home to him now clearer than ever before that he could not join the Catholic Church without saying, by his act, that he believed Protestantism to be an unsafe way of salvation. For if salvation was attainable outside of the Catholic Church, there was then manifestly no reason for joining it; and if salvation was not attainable outside the Catholic Church, what was to be said of the whole Protestant world, and of those eminent Protestants whom he had come to love and revere as the honor and glory of their age and country? To allow that all these living and dying outside the Catholic Church would be lost was more than he was prepared to accept. (And rightly so, for there are qualifications to be added in the teaching of the Catholic Church on the matter.) Could not an alternative be found, he asked? Was there no ground upon which he could accept the Catholic Church without abandoning hope for his Protestant friends? It was his tussling with this problem that had held him back for a whole year from joining the Church after he had become convinced of the truth of Catholicity. In the midst of these reflections his conscience had gravely reminded him that he had no lease on life. Dying where he was, could he see God? He finally concluded that perhaps the best charity to his Protestant friends would be to set an example by following the light of his own conscience. Accordingly he sought another interview with Bishop Fenwick in the last week of May 1844. In the following week he visited him again, made known to him his wish to become a Catholic, and begged the bishop to introduce him to someone who would have the kindness to instruct him and prepare him for his reception into the Church, if judged worthy. Bishop Fenwick immediately introduced him to his coadjutor, who was soon to succeed him, Bishop John Bernard Fitzpatrick, as his instructor in the faith.[4] Precisely when the instructions began we are not told, but apparently it must have been some time in June, at least a letter Brownson wrote his close friend, Isaac Hecker, the day after his second visit with Bishop Fenwick, dated June 6, 1844, would seem to indicate such to be the fact.

Friend Isaac had written Brownson for spiritual advice, and Brownson in reply informed him that he himself had already begun preparations to join the Church, and urged Isaac to do the same. Brownson's letter reveals his tender concept of the Catholic Church as a true mother which was to mark so uniquely his later writings. He wrote in part:

Dear Isaac:

. . . I thank you for your letter, and the frankness with which you speak of your present interior condition. You ask my advice. . . . Do you really believe the Gospel? Do you really believe the Holy Catholic Church? If so, you must put yourself under the direction of the Church. I have commenced my preparations for uniting myself with the Catholic Church. I do not as yet belong to the family of Christ. I feel it. I can be an alien no longer, and without the Church I know, by my past experience, I cannot attain to purity and sanctity of life. I need the counsels, the aids, the chastisements, and the consolations of the Church. It is the appointed means of salvation, and how can we hope for any good except through it? Our first business is to submit to it, that we may receive a maternal blessing. Then we start fair. . . .

I want you to come and see our good bishop. He is an excellent man — learned, polite, easy, affable, affectionate, and exceedingly warm-hearted. I spent two hours with him immediately after parting from you in Washington street, and a couple of hours yesterday. I like him very much.

I have made up my mind, and I shall enter the Church if she will receive me. There is no use in resisting. You cannot be an Anglican, you must be a Catholic or a mystic. If you enter the Church at all, it must be the Catholic. There is nothing else. So let me beg you, my dear Isaac, to begin in owning the Church and receiving her blessing.[5]

We will understand the nuances of Brownson's thought better from here on if we keep in mind that the articles which were to appear in the July issue of his *Quarterly* were written or at least received their final form, after he had begun preparations for his reception into the Catholic Church. In concluding his article in the April edition on "No Church, No Reform," Brownson had assured professional reformers, particularly the Come-outers, that the Church, essential to social as well as individual regeneration, still exists, fully competent to the work of reform, and admonished them to return to its bosom and there receive direction for a program of reform.[6]

In the July issue of his *Review* he now addressed a full-length essay to his readers on "Come-outerism: Or the Radical Tendency of the Day," in which he dealt unsparingly with practically every species of revolutionary dissent of the day. This strange and uncouth name was coined from the Scripture text: "Come ye out, come ye out from the midst of Babylon, and be no longer partakers of her iniquity; drink ye no longer the wine of her abominations." Insofar as Come-outerism was a protest against the distressing abuses and disorders spread so widely through society, and demanding the realization of a higher ideal, Brownson found it worthy of sympathy and support. But that was only one phase of it; in its overall nature it was a subversive movement that found a dynamic outlet particularly in the Abolition frenzy of the day. The great evil as Brownson saw it was that the Come-outers were ready to sweep away both church and state as far as found in the way of the program of reform they would realize.[7] This trend threatened a ruthless and total demolition of the existing order. Robert Carter relates that these extreme Come-outers denounced the churches as "synagogues of Satan," and says that the nature of their attacks on the churches may be gathered from the title of one of their favorite books: *A Brotherhood of Thieves, A True Picture of the American Church and Clergy.* The author of the book, the prominent Stephen S. Foster, associate of William Lloyd Garrison, and one of the foremost Abolition lecturers, was accustomed to preface his discourses by laying down the proposition that it would be better for the people of a town to establish among them a hundred rumshops, fifty gambling houses and ten brothels, rather than one church. And these same extremists assailed the state with equal fury, declaring the Constitution to be "a covenant with death and an agreement with hell."[8]

What wonder that Brownson came to grips with these iconoclastic rebels of the day, naming in particular "Garrison, Rogers, Foster, Abby Folsom, and their immediate friends and associates."[9] He freely admitted that there are times when the old order has become corrupt, and must give way to a new order, but he flatly laid down the principle that no man has the right, *on his own individual authority,* to attempt its destruction. "Have our modern abolitionists a warrant from the Almighty to set aside Church and State?" he gravely inquired.[10] What alarmed him most was to be forced to acknowledge that Come-outerism was already largely the common creed of his countrymen simply pushed to its last logical conclusions. What is individualism in religion and the sacred right of insurrection in politics, professed by the majority of the country, but Come-outerism evolved to its ultimate consequences? Many, however, he observed, who condemn and decry Come-outerism do so with an ill grace, for they are too cowardly to follow out the principles they avow, while the overt Come-outers have at least the grace to be consistent with their doctrines. He appealed to his countrymen to make sure of their principles, and then never to fear the consequences of a sound principle. He wrote:

> Either your principle is sound, or it is not. If it is sound, you have no right to stop short of its legitimate consequences; you have no right to say, "thus far, but no further." If it is not sound, you have no right to act on it at all. . . . There is no such thing as pushing a sound principle too far. If your principle will not bear pushing to its extreme, you may know that it is false, and that the error is, not in pushing it too far, but in adopting it at all.[11]

One cannot but be impressed as we proceed in the career of Brownson by the fact that he stood like an impregnable wall, as far as any individual could, against all the subversive forces of the day both at home and abroad. One might well doubt whether any journalist of the last century did so much for the preservation of law and order in society as he did. It is no doubt on this score that the late Msgr. Matthew Smith, founder and editor of the *Denver Register* and knowledgeable student of Brownson, remarked that Brownson is one of the men who have made the nation what it is, constructively speaking. The revolutionary or subversive principle was to him anathema. In spite of fiery appeals for reform, Brownson abhorred revolutionism in all its shapes and forms. Already when he became the new editor of the *Boston Reformer,* in July 1836, he had firmly laid down his social premise:

> Laws may be bad, unequal, oppressive, but in this country there is a constitutional remedy, and we hold all but constitutional methods of remedying bad laws, unjustifiable; therefore, we say, the laws, while they are laws, whatever their character, are to be obeyed. If they are bad, let them in a constitutional and peaceable manner be made good, but *never disobeyed.* Let those, however, who complain of the growing disrespect witnessed in our country to the laws, exert themselves to have such laws as deserve to be respected.[12]

From the formula he had laid down in the April issue of his *Review,* "No Church, No Reform," he now advanced to the principle, "No Reform under Sectarianism" in his article "Church Unity and Social Amelioration."[13] With the whole Christian world cut up into sects or groups and its efforts at social reform thereby sadly dissipated and crippled for want of unity of action, what chance of success, he wanted to know, had any scheme of reform, however cunningly devised? He pleaded again for the unity and catholicity of the Church founded by Christ. Either God, he said, has established the Catholic Church as the medium of the good, social as well as spiritual, that he designs us to receive or work out, or he has not. If he has not, then there is nothing for us to do but to wait till Providence intervenes in a new way in our behalf; but if the Church is this medium, the divinely appointed instrument of human regeneration, of social as well as of individual progress, then should we be content with it, and confine ourselves to its principles, and proceed according to the modes of action it prescribes.[14]

The worst feature of the age he found to be "a miserable eclecticism" which pretends that each sect has its own truth, but that the whole truth is to be found nowhere. Did not Christ say, "I *am* the way, the *Truth,* and the life"? Must not his Church then contain truth in its unity and universality? To deny it is to give the lie to Christ himself who declared that he would build his Church upon a rock, and that the gates of hell would not prevail against it. If you do admit it exists, he continued, can you conceive of any truth in any sect that it does not contain in its purity and integrity? Here again this master of logic compressed his line of argument into sharp and compelling alternatives as was his wont in his concise reasoning:

> Do, then, take some position; either accept the Son of God, or reject him; either accept the Church as it is, or reject it altogether. For if it has become corrupt, it is a false Church, was always a false Church, and always will be a false Church; and if it be not corrupt, but the true Church, then to refuse to accept it is to refuse to submit to God.[15]

The closer he was now approaching the Catholic Church the more he realized that the acceptance of that church meant a fuller change in his social philosophy. Whether or not he realized at this time to any appreciable degree that the doctrines of the Catholic Church do actually promote the real progress of society (for which he was to contend strenuously in after years), he knew at least that the Catholic Church gives the interests of another world decided priority over those of this. He had labored incessantly for twenty years to create a heaven on earth for his fellowmen, but the Church points above all to a heaven to be gained hereafter, all things in its teaching being subordinated to that one end. This teaching called for a radical change of outlook on Brownson's part which now began to be reflected in his writings. After roundly castigating the Fourierists for attempting to advance their cause under the banner of Christianity while starkly repudiating its moral principles (with what force he argued in such cases can be known only by reading him at firsthand), he lamented that mankind (and he included his own past) should be so slow to believe him who rebuked us for being troubled about many things, and declared that "one thing is needful."[16] Christianity plainly subordinates temporal interests to those which are eternal. On this point he had once been so audacious in his lusty manhood as to give Christ the Lord "a flat denial."[17] His thought now showed a complete about-face. Not by laboring to multiply material riches, and to facilitate their acquisition, would the problem of poverty and human suffering be best met, he asserted, but by teaching men to restrict their bodily wants and to turn their minds in a moral and spiritual direction:

> St. Bernard, living on water in which pulse had been boiled, laboring at the head of his minks, is more to be envied than Apicius at his feast; and far better was it for Lazarus, who begged the crumbs which fell from the rich man's table, than for the rich man who fared sumptuously every day. On wishes, wishes grow; one desire gratified, a stronger is made. The rich man of the world's goods has more wants he cannot satisfy, than has the poorest beggar himself; and to die of starvation is not more terrible, view the matter rightly, than to die of a surfeit. You must once more make voluntary poverty honorable, and canonize anew, not your rich old sinner, gorged with the spoils of the widow and the orphan — whose eyes stand out with fatness, whose heart vaunts itself against the Lord — but the man who voluntarily submits to poverty, that he may lay up riches in heaven, where neither moth nor rust do corrupt, nor thieves break through and steal. You cannot serve God and mammon; and the Fourier attempt to reconcile the service of the one with that of the other will turn out a miserable failure, and will cover with merited disgrace all concerned in making it.[18]

Brownson here briefly turned aside from the church question in its relation to social amelioration to meet what he considered a grave threat to public and private morals which had appeared in the form of a book written by Richard Hildreth, entitled: *The Theory of Morals: An Inquiry Concerning the Law of Moral Distinctions, and the Variations and Contradictions of Ethical Codes.* Inasmuch as Hildreth sneered from the beginning to the end of his book at those who believe "in a personal God," Brownson excoriated the book as striking at the foundation of all morals, robbing morals of all sanction, and setting men loose in a perfect chaos of moral license. He classified Hildreth's system as belonging to sentimental moral systems, that is, Hildreth made the distinction of what is morally good and what is morally bad depend upon whether an action gives pleasure or pain to others. To say nothing about the difficulty often involved in determining such matters, Brownson wanted to know where the binding force of such words as duty or obligation are to derive their meaning if the idea of a personal God be rejected. All morality, he asserted, is necessarily founded in theology, and he who denies the existence of God has left himself no ground upon which he can establish any moral obligation. Moral obligation exists only where there is a binding law, but there can be no binding law where there is no Lawgiver whom the individual is *bound* to obey. How, then, establish a system of morals if no Lawgiver is recognized?[19] (Mere sentiment as a basis of morals would be as mercurial as the shifting sands.)

Under Hildreth's proposed system Brownson saw the whole moral foundation giving way, at least theoretically, and his review of his book was a veritable slashing attack. It did not help matters any with Brownson when he came to see that Hildreth's system was Benthamism all over again with only a slight modification that amounted to practically nothing. For Brownson considered Jeremy Bentham "a humbug," guilty of "intolerable stupidity, ignorance, and dogmatism . . . a man innocent of all philosophical conceptions and of all philosophical tendency, . . . crying out against cant and humbug, and all the time the very prince of canters and humbuggers, and the most egregious dupe of both." He admitted that Bentham had had a heart and good intentions, but that he "had never succeeded in getting even one tolerably clear notion of the science of morals, either in its principle or in its details."[20] This whole matter was further compounded with guilt when Brownson was forced to conclude that Hildreth's book seemed to have been written "for the express purpose of furnishing a moral basis to our Transcendentalists and Come-outers."[21]

Brownson's alarm over the book is quite understandable. It is a truism that social well-being and political prosperity depend upon sound ethical and spiritual principles. It is this truth that the illustrious historian, Arnold Toynbee, has emphasized to the world in his history of the rise and fall of nineteen civilizations. No nation can survive the decay of its ethical and spiritual roots, whatever the resulting form of blight. It was evidently the consciousness of this fact that had roused Brownson into such a flailing mood as was to provoke a rude and abusive rejoinder from Hildreth himself. Leonard Gilhooley has revealed a penetrating insight into what Brownson must have seen in Hildreth's book when he wrote:

> But there is no mistaking here his [Brownson's] abhorrence of the budding pragmatism which, after the Civil War, would ride triumphant over transcendental misgivings, governmental ineptitude, and an American ethic in some ways so devitalized as to become mere etiquette. Perhaps Brownson sensed the trend this early, for his pessimism, a feature usually associated with his later thought, is not absent from his *Review* in 1844.[22]

Among others, Elizabeth P. Peabody, educator and proprietor of the famous Boston Bookshop, wrote Brownson concerning his criticism of Hildreth's book: "I think your review of Hildreth's book is *excellent* — but is it not a little savage to refute a man completely and garnish your refutation with such withering contempt? . . . But I am glad his book is demolished."[23] She might have added a thought expressed by Francis H. Greene who had asked Brownson to review his own book, and added: "A good scolding or even a good whipping from Mr. Brownson would not be without its value, nor, I trust without its uses. Whatever there is of life or truth will and must live; all else will and of right ought to die."[24]

While Brownson had been assiduously pursuing the church question, he had also been investigating the philosophical question; for Brownson always regarded philosophy as a preamble to theology. Only a sound philosophy can furnish the rational certitudes which undergird the Christian faith. Emmanuel Kant was the great name of the day in philosophy, and Brownson turned to a close examination of his works. He began by translating a great part of Kant's *Critique of Pure Reason* in his own hand, and contributed three closely reasoned essays to his *Review* for this year, 1844, on Kant's subjective theory of knowledge. So immersed did he become in the subject at the time that nearly all the talk in the home dining room that year — the rest of the family going along — was on the great theme of Kant. When visitors came to stay for a meal, or as overnight guests, they were introduced to the same topic, and the Brownson household echoed, sometimes into the late hours of the night, to the exciting conversations occasioned by the German metaphysician.[25]

René Wellek has some excellent observations on Brownson's criticism of Kant's philosophy in his article on "The Minor Transcendentalists and German Philosophy" in the *New England Quarterly*. In speaking of Brownson he remarked that he had:

> . . . a stronger philosophical bent than his friends and associates, and a genuine gift for speculation as well as an altogether unusual grasp, in his time and place, of philosophical technicalities. He alone of all the transcendentalists seems to have been seriously disturbed by the problem of knowledge and truth, and he alone made a close examination of Kant's text. [Interestingly Wellek added:] The remarkable consistency and uniformity of his criticism of Kant and Hegel, which extends over a period of some thirty-five years of indefatigable writing, seems to point to a greater coherence and consistency in Brownson's philosophical outlook than is usually allowed by those who see only the shiftings and changes of his religious associations.[26]

Wellek's statement that Brownson was about the only person in the country who concerned himself with the problem of knowledge seems altogether correct. Writing to Victor Cousin in Paris on September 1, 1844, Brownson himself said: "I believe that I am almost alone in my devotion to philosophy; at least I find none who bow with me at her shrine. Nobody seems to be aware of my speculations, or to trouble themselves with the subjects they concern."[27]

Although Brownson expressed great admiration for Kant's "eminent analytical ability," his table of contents, or his analysis of the mind, he could not agree with his epistemological position. Kant's philosophy, for Brownson, resolved itself into sheer phenomenalism. Kant posed the question, Is science possible? To which Brownson replied: "To ask if the human mind is capable of science is absurd; for we have only the human mind with which to answer the question." Kant's fundamental error, affirmed Brownson, was his attempt to find the object in the subject, his failure to distinguish between the *me* and the *not-me*. Emphasizing the polarities of the *me* and the *not-me*, whatever is objective is not and cannot be me, Brownson said: "This simple truism, which is nothing but saying, what *is*, is, completely refutes the whole Critical Philosophy [Kant's]."[28]

Yet Brownson was in complete agreement with Kant that there are certain *a priori* or non-empirical elements in the knowledge situation, but parted company with him when Kant assumes that the forms (categories or ideas) under which objects are mentally apprehended are without any foundation in the objects apprehended. According to Kant: "They (the categories or ideas) are forms under which the object is cognized, not because they are the necessary forms of the object considered as a thing existing objectively *in re*, but because they are the necessary forms of the human mind itself."[29] This assumption is simply an assertion that the operations of the human mind do not make contact with reality as it is. Thus imprisoned in subjectivism, Kant failed to construct a bridge to the outer world, God and his creation, and so undermined the objectivity of knowledge.

Brownson could not but regard Kant as an arch-skeptic, and his philosophy as "the most masterly defense of Hume" that could be written. If Kant is right, continued Brownson, then man is simply incapable of demonstrating the reality of any existence outside the subject, and "so all science vanishes, all certainty disappears, the sun goes out, the bright stars are extinguished, and we are afloat in darkness, on a wild and tempest-tossed ocean of universal Doubt and Nescience."[30]

As previously noted, to redress the balance, Kant also wrote his *Critique of Practical Reason*. Heinrich Heine remarked that he did so partly "through fear of the police," that is, since his *Critique of Pure Reason* led necessarily to atheism. Discounting the *quasi* theism of the *Critique of Practical Reason*, Brownson had concerned himself in his three massive articles with the *Critique of Pure Reason*. The final verdict in the concluding paragraph of his treatise on Kant's philosophy was quite unfavorable to the widely acclaimed philosopher of Königsberg. He wrote:

> We took up his work with a profound reverence for it. We had been accustomed by those whose opinions we most valued, to look upon Kant as the great metaphysician of modern times; we expected much; we have found — nothing. There may be depths in the *Critique* we have not sounded, diamonds we have not discovered; but we have sounded to the depth of our line, and have searched diligently for the gems which might be concealed at the bottom; but, alas! we have found nothing but bald atheism, and cold and heartless scepticism, erected into a system bearing all the imposing forms of science.[31]

In accordance with what Brownson had written Victor Cousin, there seems little or no evidence of any American comment at the time on his treatise of Kant's philosophy. Perhaps because there were few or none competent to pass an enlightened judgment on his criticism. But if Brownson's treatise drew little or no comment in America, it attracted close attention in at least one quarter in Europe. Among Brownson's acquaintances of the day was Joseph Coolidge Shaw (who belonged to the Brahminical caste of Boston). After traveling extensively in Europe as a young man, Shaw had become a convert to the faith in Rome through the instrumentality of "the noble old English Jesuit" there, Fr. Thomas Glover. Shaw declared that Fr. Glover had "the soundest and profoundest mind of any man" he had ever met. When Brownson sent copies of his *Review* with his articles on Kant to Shaw at Rome, he in turn gave them to Fr. Glover. After reading the articles on Kant, as Shaw reported, Fr. Glover (adding dramatic effect to what he had to say) took off his spectacles, and declared with great emphasis:

> This man *astonishes* me; he is clear and strong beyond compare; that is the most masterly refutation of Kant I have ever read. And again, after reading several of the articles a second time, Fr. Glover returned to the attack a second time: He pleases me more and more, he said; I think God has raised him to hunt down and destroy the absurd principles now in vogue in politics, philosophy, and religion; but, he went on solemnly, *but,* his very greatness makes me fear for him; for unless he is solidly grounded in humility, the success which so great power applied to teaching the truth assures him, will turn his head, and make him forget that he has all from God, and none from himself. May he remember there have been Origens and Tertullians as well as Augustines.[32]

In returning to the church question, Brownson took notice of four letters of John Henry Hopkins, Protestant Episcopal bishop of the diocese of Vermont, which he had addressed to the members of the Protestant Episcopal Church under the title: "The Novelties which disturb our Peace." The "Novelties" to which Bishop Hopkins referred were of course the agitations going on in the Christian world, especially the Oxford Movement, in favor of a restoration of church unity and Catholicity. In an article entitled "Bishop Hopkins on Novelties," Brownson traced out the tendencies in the Anglican Church, from which the Protestant Episcopal Church in America had derived, namely, a Catholic tendency and a Protestant tendency. He had been watching with alternate hope and fear the current struggle between the two. For a moment he had indulged the hope that the Catholic tendency would carry the day, and the Anglican Church become again, in very deed, a living branch of the Church Universal, but alas! he had momentarily forgot that the Anglican Church is under the Erastian curse, bound hand and foot by the state. He had yet hoped more from the free Protestant Episcopal Church in this country, and could only grieve to find Bishop Hopkins opposing the Catholic and abetting the Protestant tendency. He acknowledged that the Episcopal Church was professedly the church of his ancestors, speaking his own tongue. To enter it would not be like going among strangers, but rather like sitting down among one's kith and kin, friends and neighbors.[33] But on no ground whatsoever could he find any justification for the separation of the Anglican or Protestant Episcopal Church from Roman communion. As he himself had already begun preparations to enter the Catholic Church, he was only inviting Bishop Hopkins to follow him when he said in conclusion:

> Well, if we must have a Church, and cannot have one without returning to the Roman communion, then, let us go to Rome. Either accept no-churchism and say no more about it, or have the courage to accept and avow principles on which a Church is defensible. . . . We own that we are waiting for our Episcopal friends to show us some ground on which we may defend the Reformation, or rather, the reformers, in separating from the Roman communion; but we must tell Bishop Hopkins, and we do so with all becoming respect, that to Rome we certainly ought to go, if his is the only ground of defense his Church has to offer.[34]

The distinguished editor of *The Churchman,* the Rev. Samuel Seabury, D.D. (1801-1872), Episcopal clergyman of New York City, attempted to meet the objections Brownson had brought against Anglicanism in his review of the letters of Bishop Hopkins on "The Novelties that disturb our Peace," but with little show of success.[35] Dr. Seabury apparently made a slip when he called his church "The Reformed Catholic Church." Such a statement meant to Brownson that Seabury's church was a fallible church, for if it had not been fallible, it could never have been in need of reform; and if fallible, it may be in need of reform again. This was enough for Brownson. He had been forced by his errors of the past, by his frequent changes on almost all subjects, even the most vital, to conclude that reason was no adequate guide at all for the settlement of the great questions that concerned his peace and salvation. "I had felt from my boyhood," he said, "that I had need of an authoritative religion; that a religion which does not and cannot speak with divine authority, is simply no religion at all."[36] Mock us not, then, he said, with a fallible church. He had followed a fallible guide long enough. But fully convinced was he that Christ did establish an infallible church, rendered such by his perpetual presence and divine guardianship. Dr. Seabury's church being on its own admission fallible, Brownson concluded that he was forced to look beyond Anglicanism or the Episcopal Church to find an infallible church.[37]

Whatever he had said previously on the church question, it was not until he wrote his article on "Sparks on Episcopacy," in July 1844, that Brownson made his first plain avowal to the public as to the definitive convictions he had reached on that question. He wrote:

> We have no wish to disguise the fact, nor could we, if we would — that our ecclesiastical, theological, and philosophical studies have brought us to the full conclusion, that, either the Church in communion with the See of Rome is the one holy catholic apostolic church, or the one holy catholic church does not exist. We have tried every possible way to escape this conclusion, but escape it we cannot. We must accept it, or go back to the no-church doctrine we put forth in our somewhat famous or rather, notorious, Essay on the Laboring Classes. Our logic allows us no alternative between Catholicism and Come-outerism. But we have tried Come-outerism to our full satisfaction. We are thoroughly convinced in mind, heart, and soul, that Christ did institute a visible church; that he founded it upon a rock; that the gates of hell have never prevailed against it, and cannot prevail, against it; that it is the duty of all to submit to it, as the representative of the Son of God on earth.
>
> We know not what light may break in upon our mind, but, so far as at present informed, we are compelled, by what seems to us to be the force of truth, to look upon the separation of the reformers from the Roman communion, in the sixteenth century, as irregular, unnecessary, and, we may add, as a serious calamity to Christendom. We deny not that there was a necessity for a thorough reform of manners; but we cannot but think and believe, that, if the reformers had confined themselves to such reforms, and such modes of effecting them, as were authorized or permitted by the canons of the Church, they would have much more successfully corrected the real abuses of which they complained, and done infinitely more service to the cause of religion and social progress. Their separation, if not a terrible sin, was at least a terrible mistake, which sincere lovers of the Lord and his Spouse should deeply lament, and over which no one should permit himself to exult.[38]

These convictions of Brownson had matured before his first visit with Bishop Fenwick, and had received further confirmation in his second interview with the bishop. As already noted, no intellectual obstacles had remained in the way of Brownson's acceptance of the Catholic faith since the beginning of 1843. Only his concern for the religious status of his Protestant brethren had held him back. This difficulty he submitted to Bishop Fenwick for solution in his second interview with him. The account is given in his own words.

He informs us that the bishop received him in a frank and cordial manner, remarked that he read his *Review* with attention, and had noticed that he objected to the pope.

> What can be your objection to the pope, inquired the bishop. I do not object to the pope, he replied. Some time ago I was foolish enough to say that the problem of the age is *Catholicism without the Papacy*; but I no longer entertain that notion. I have no objection to the Church, and the Church without the pope would be no Church at all.
>
> Why, then, are you not a Catholic, came the query. I could be were it not for these Protestants, he replied. I do not like to say that they are all wrong, and out of the way of salvation; and if I could discover some ground on which I could be a Catholic without saying so, I should have no difficulty.
>
> Oh, so that is your difficulty, remarked the bishop. But why should you allow that to bother you? God is just, and never punishes any one unless it is deserved. You may confidently leave your Protestant friends in his hands.
>
> True, replied Brownson, but I am not willing to believe that all who live and die out of the pale of the Roman Catholic Church must be finally lost. I wish to be able to find some justification, at least some excuse, for the Protestant movement; and it is this which has kept me back.
>
> The inquiry is no doubt an interesting one, observed the bishop. But you will find it, probably, somewhat difficult. Have you thus far met with much success? I cannot say that I have, answered Brownson, and I am almost afraid that I shall not succeed, he admitted.
>
> The bishop then added: It is best not to be hasty. The question is a serious one, and you will do well to inquire further and longer. Perhaps you will find some excuse for the Protestant movement. If you do, you will not fail to let me know.[39]

After more conversation on the question, and other topics of the day, and with assurances from the bishop that it would afford him pleasure if he would call again, Brownson took his leave. What struck Brownson on this visit with Bishop Fenwick, and which did much to confirm his convictions about the truth of the Catholic faith, was the firm and uncompromising character of the bishop's Catholicity. He saw plainly what was holding Brownson back, that he was ready to join the Catholic Church if given some assurance in regard to those living and dying out of the pale of the Church, but with all his art — and he tells us he did his best — he could not extract from the bishop the least concession in regard to what appeared the severity of the Catholic doctrine: outside the Church there is no salvation. He later asserted that had the bishop hemmed and hawed over the matter, he would have unceremoniously walked out on him.[40] As it was, he had found a church that was straightforward, that felt no necessity to apologize for any of its doctrines, for it knew it had not invented them — they were from God. No other church would have fit the temperament of Orestes A. Brownson. He craved absolutes in religion.

Bishop John Fitzpatrick, Brownson's instructor in the Catholic faith, was just as uncompromising in another sort of way. Understandably, Brownson had set considerable store by his doctrine of life by communion which had led him to the threshold of the Catholic Church. And it was scarcely to be assumed that Bishop Fitzpatrick himself was not acquainted with that same theory — at least he knew that Bishop Fenwick had been reading his *Review*. Unfortunately there was a jolt in store for Brownson. He soon came to realize that, whether Bishop Fitzpatrick was acquainted with his novel theory or not, he was indisposed to give it any cognizance. Trained in a different theological school than himself, the bishop, he saw, was more likely to oppose than to accept the theory. Not that he himself had any overweening attachment at the time for the doctrine, Brownson tells us, but if rejected, what reason had he any longer for accepting the Church? It was only by its light that he had been led to its door. Here was a great difficulty — a difficulty he could not disclose to the bishop lest he send him back into the world "utterly naked and destitute." "I had made up my mind," he relates, "that the church was the last plank of safety, that it was communion with the church or death."[41] Yet he would not be a Catholic blindly; he had once gone it blindly and had lost all.[42] Never again! Happily, he informs us, Providence did not forsake him, for he soon learned from his instructor another method by which to prove "even in a clearer and more direct manner" the divine authority of the Church and its mission to teach all men and nations all things pertaining to eternal salvation.[43]

It was not, therefore, on the strength of his doctrine of life by communion, but on the strength of the traditional arguments found in all theological manuals and apologetic treatises, that he was ultimately received into the Catholic Church. Those arguments are generally presented under the heading, "Motives of Credibility." "We have found no new way," said Brownson, "we have only found the old way. But this old way, beaten by millions of travelers for these eighteen hundred years, is sufficient for us. It is plain, straightforward, and easy: we do not feel equal to the windings, obscurities, and asperities of a new and unbeaten path."[44]

When informing Victor Cousin in Paris of his conversion to the Catholic faith, he also indicated the intellectual processes by which it had come about. He wrote: "To this change I have been gradually brought by philosophy, aided by some acquaintance with the Scholastics, and a more thorough study of the Fathers. To me this is a change of some magnitude and importance, and more especially as Catholicism is in much less repute here than Unitarianism."[45] Brownson felt that Cousin never forgave him for becoming a Catholic. Forgetting his French politeness, remarked Brownson, he never deigned "to answer a single one of [my] letters."[46]

Although Brownson was disposed at the time to discount the worth of his doctrine of life by communion, by the time he wrote his autobiography (*The Convert*, 1857) he went into a nine-page eulogy on its validity and worth as an argument for the conversion of unbelievers. He then doubted whether the traditional arguments used by Catholics would have brought him to the Church, not because those arguments are not conclusive and convincing in themselves, but because they do not meet the subjective difficulties of the unbeliever. In his own case, he had been already convinced, and those arguments had only to confirm convictions he had arrived at by another process of reasoning. But addressed to him as an unbeliever, they would have failed to remove from his understanding the *a priori* objections he had entertained to a supernatural authoritative revelation. They would have crushed rather than have enlightened, silenced instead of convincing his reason, he asserted. He stated that he had never known anyone who had been converted by those arguments who had not been already disposed to become a Catholic, or who was not already on his way to the Catholic Church. His own method, he felt, might well be used as a preparation to the apologetics of theologians, "especially in this age, when objections are drawn from philosophy rather than history, from feeling rather than logic."[47]

The necessity Brownson was under of suppressing his doctrine of life by communion when he began his instructions under Bishop Fitzpatrick to become a Catholic resulted in the lack of a greater frankness and unreserve on his part toward the bishop, instinctively detected by the bishop himself, and occasioned a month or two of an uneasy relationship between the two.[48] But with the settlement of his difficulty by the presentation on the part of the bishop of another method of arriving at the divine authority of the Catholic Church, a very cordial and happy relationship developed between them sturdy enough to weather the changing fortunes in the years ahead. The bishop gradually became almost all things to him in sundry ways. Particularly in after life was Brownson to prize the theological science Bishop Fitzpatrick had imparted to him. Gratefully he acknowledged:

> He was my instructor, my confessor, my spiritual director, and my personal friend, for eleven years [that is, as long as he remained resident in Boston]; my intercourse with him was intimate, cordial, and affectionate, and I owe him more than it is possible to owe any other man. I have met men of more various erudition and higher scientific attainments; I have met men of bolder fancy and more creative imagination; but I have never met a man of a clearer head, a firmer intellectual grasp, a sounder judgment, or a warmer heart. He taught me my catechism and my theology; and, though I have found men who have made a far greater display of theological erudition, I have never met an abler or sounder theologian. However for a moment I have been attracted by one or another theological school, I have invariably found myself obliged to come back at last to the views he taught me. If my *Review* has any theological merit, if it has earned any reputation as a staunch and uncompromising defender of the Catholic faith, that merit is principally due, under God, to him, and his uniform support. Its faults, its shortcomings, or its demerits, are my own.[49]

Any man who had studied theology as assiduously as had Brownson over a long stretch of years should have been a fairly good judge in bestowing such a high compliment on Bishop Fitzpatrick as a theologian. In 1861 Harvard College granted Bishop Fitzpatrick an honorary degree in sacred theology — the first ever bestowed on a Catholic bishop.[50] Brownson told Sir John Acton on his visit to this country in 1853 that Bishop Fitzpatrick was "the most intellectual bishop in the United States."[51]

But if Brownson's estimate of Bishop Fitzpatrick was truly high, Bishop Fitzpatrick's estimate of Brownson was correspondingly lofty. Acton informs us that Fitzpatrick set Brownson "far above Newman."[52] He must accordingly have felt his very best efforts challenged to prepare such a man properly for reception into the Catholic Church. Brownson relates that his instructor fulfilled his office with "a patience and uniform kindness of which it does not become us to speak."[53] The memory of all that Bishop Fitzpatrick had done for him was to mellow deeply during the long years. What should be noted in particular is that he insisted that his own theology, so often under attack, was simply a reproduction of the theology Bishop Fitzpatrick had taught him (though made truly his own because it contained the most balanced views in the light of reality). Hence those who are disposed to quarrel with Brownson's theology should first quarrel with the shade of Bishop Fitzpatrick. Near the end of his life when his theology was again under attack by a writer in the Boston *Pilot,* Brownson wound up his vigorous reply, saying:

> So much for our Boston theologian, who was not, we apprehend, trained, as

we were, in the school of the late illustrious bishop of Boston, a theologian, whose exactness and soundness we, every day as we advance in life, find confirmed. and whose teachings we but feebly reproduce. May he who was our spiritual father on earth, still remember and watch over his spiritual son with whom he had so much affectionate patience, and whom he took so much pains to instruct in the principles, doctrines, and precepts of our holy religion! Never can we repay his memory, for ever blessed, his labors and pains, his uniform sweetness, his unfailing kindness, and above all, his tender and unaffected piety, and profound and courageous love of truth. God has, we trust, rewarded him.[54]

From such testimony we may well conclude that his weeks of instruction under Bishop Fitzpatrick must have been indeed truly pleasant and edifying as well as profitable in the acquisition of theological science. The time passed quickly with July fading into August, August into September, and September into October. Judging his candidate duly prepared for the reception of the sacraments of the Catholic Church, the bishop heard his confession, received his abjuration, administered conditional baptism, and the sacrament of Confirmation on Sunday, October 20, 1844, shortly after he had reached his forty-first year of age, and just twenty-two years after he had joined the Presbyterians at Ballston Spa, Saratoga County, New York. The next morning at an early Mass the new convert received Holy Communion from the hands of Fr. Nicholas O'Brien, then pastor of the church in East Boston. The great step had been taken.[55]

It is interesting to note that Brownson found his way to the Catholic Church without the aid of any priest or the guiding help of any Catholic. He had sought out Bishop Fenwick entirely on his own when once convinced of the truth of the Catholic faith. Yet as Fr. Hecker remarked: No man knew better "what he was about" when he became a Catholic.[56] Newman also remarked: "Catholics did not make us Catholics; Oxford made us Catholics."[57] But Newman had the advantage of having many collaborators in the great Tractarian movement who were an encouragement to one another. Newman's friend, too, Dr. Charles W. Russel, later president of Maynooth Seminary, Ireland, had also greatly influenced him by his visits and the books he sent him.[58] Our American convert seems to have been a complete loner in blazing a trail to the threshold of the Church.

It is rather remarkable that a man of such intellectual force as Brownson should have laid such *uncommon* emphasis on conversion as the work of grace. "I repeat, again and again," he would say, "that philosophy did not conduct me into the Church, but, just in proportion as I advanced towards a sound philosophy, I did advance toward the Church."[59] "Faith," he would reiterate, "is not of ourselves, it is the gift of God; and conversion is the work of grace, not of argument or logic, though it is always logical, or in accordance with the supreme logic," whether or not it is always so perceived by the convert.[60] "I never sought truth; it came to me, how or whence I could never say; but it came and brought with it the force of conviction, and I believed as the child believes the father or the mother. . . . God showed it to me, and gave me the grace to open my heart, and accept it. The way to learn the truth is to open one's mind and heart to it, as the sunflower opens her bosom to the rays of the sun, and permit it to penetrate the soul and give it light, warmth and life."[61] The office of logic, he would repeat, is simply to remove the intellectual objections that may be in the way of belief, and to show that one *ought* to believe, but it cannot motivate the assent of the will which is involved in the act of divine faith. That is the work of grace, for man is not pure intellect, but a bundle of affections, passions and appetites which may cloud the intellect and influence the will to withhold consent.[62]

In his humility Brownson declared that he had brought nothing into the Church with him except his sins. Archbishop Hughes called that statement "an example of humility that will be an edification to Catholics of future ages as well as the present. . . . Brownson brought much to the Catholic faith, but his humility would permit only the foregoing declaration to be put on record." Such a declaration, continued the archbishop, is "imperishable."[63] Nor could Brownson himself for a moment indulge the thought that he had made any little sacrifice in exchange for the incomparable treasure that was now his in "the faith once delivered to the saints." As Archbishop Robert J. Dwyer has remarked: "Never after, having set his hand to the plough, did he once look back"[64] — and that despite the fierce storms he was to encounter through the long years. He had now a joy that was to know no ending. He had only words of mild censure for those Catholic novelists who make such an ado about the great sacrifices made by their hero-converts. Whatever those sacrifices, to him there were less than dust in the balance over against priceless gain. How could there be any thought of sacrifices!

> For ourselves [he said] we know that with us there was nothing of the sort, and nothing could exceed the joy we felt as the truth flashed more and more clearly on us, and we saw there was deliverance for us from error and sin, the doubt and uncertainty, we had suffered from for more than forty years of a wearisome life. We were the wanderer returning home, the lost child returning to lay his head on his mother's bosom. Every step that brought us nearer to her was a new joy. And when we found ourselves in her embrace, our joy was unspeakable. We could not recall any thing we had lost, or count any thing we might have to endure; we could only sing the *Magnificat,* and have done nothing since but sing in our heart the *Te Deum.*[65]

It has been remarked that the solidarity of affection in the Brownson household may be seen in the fact that the entire family came into the Catholic Church with the father, that is, all except the eldest son, Orestes, Jr., who had put out to sea after a year at Brook Farm and had not yet returned. The family had increased over the years. Besides the births of the four sons we have already noted, that is, Orestes Augustus (Ithaca, New York, April 18, 1828); John Healy (Auburn, New York, April 14, 1829); William Ignatius (Walpole, New Hampshire, January 4, 1834); and Henry Francis (Canton, Massachusetts, August 7, 1835), the further additions to the family were Sarah Nicolena (Chelsea, Massachusetts, June 7, 1839); George (Chelsea, Massachusetts, November 20, 1840), and Edward Patrick on October 16, 1843, in Chelsea, Massachusetts. (Charles Joseph was yet to be born to the family on November 15, 1845 in Chelsea, Massachusetts.) From these dates it is evident that the children were mostly too young to make any decision for themselves and simply entered the Church in the wake of their parents. But it is inaccurate to suggest, as has Arthur M. Schlesinger, Jr., that Mrs. Brownson was overborne in the matter of conversion by her stern husband.[66] It so happens that Brownson himself has informed us that the convictions of his wife preceded his own in his and her conversion.[67] Only one member of the family, still at large, had not entered the Church.

When Orestes Brownson, Jr., had put out to sea in 1843, his father still occupied his Unitarian pulpit, and upon his return in the spring of 1845 he was dumbfounded to find his parents and all the other children members of the Catholic Church. It was too much for his Yankee prejudices. He immediately left the Brownson household and moved to the home of his mother's sister in Ohio, the Goodriches. Trying to find his way out of the mazes of religious doubt, he had there discussed religion with the local minister. When the torment of doubt and confusion remained, Orestes, Jr., turned back to write his father about his perplexities. At the end of a long and ponderous letter his father told him that the real question is simply: Did Christ found a church, and give it authority to teach in his name? And if so, which of the so-called churches is it? In the meantime, as the Goodriches wanted Orestes, Jr., to improve his French for the purpose of teaching in their academy, they sent him to St. Francis Xavier College in Cincinnati, Ohio. There he continued his earnest discussion of religion with the result that he was finally received into the Catholic Church on the feast day of St. Francis Xavier, December 3, 1845. The local bishop, John Baptist Purcell, who had taken much interest in him since his arrival, was the minister of the sacrament of Baptism.[68] Orestes' attendance at the college was the occasion of the exchange of quite a number of letters between his father and the bishop.

Of Brownson's brothers and sisters only one became a Catholic, Oran, and that apparently only through the missionary efforts of Orestes himself. But not before Oran had undergone some religious experiences of his own. The story of his conversion we have from an article by George Parsons Lathrop in the *Atlantic Monthly* of June 1896. Lathrop had obtained much of his information for the article directly from Henry Brownson. The story goes that when Oran, perhaps piqued by curiosity over just why Orestes had become a Catholic, visited him in August 1851, they fell into a long argumentation about the great question of religion. Oran would put a question which Orestes would answer with characteristic terseness and force. Without saying a word, Oran would dart out of the house and walk for a long time in the hot sun thinking it over. Returning again, he would put another question. Then he would go through the same process as before, making no rejoinder at any time to what Orestes had said. Neither was there any summing up at the end. Oran finally took his departure in silence. From Dublin, Ohio, he had gone to Dublin, Ireland, where he was received into the Church, and was afterwards confirmed in the Catholic faith by Archbishop Purcell of Cincinnati, Ohio. Notice of his conversion appeared in the Paris *Univers,* Paris, France.[69]

Brownson's mother, Relief, who corresponded with him as occasion suggested, and who was a frequent recipient of generous donations from him, never became a Catholic. In a typical letter dated November 17, 1845, she wrote: "I feel under great obligation to you my Dear Son for what you had done for me in my old age, poverty and affliction; it is more than I could expect or even think. May the Lord reward you for all your kindness to us."[70] She lived on in Ballston Spa, New York, up into the year 1865. Orestes's twin sister, Daphne, appears to have attempted some kind of a conversion to the Catholic Church, but in any case, she did not remain a Catholic. She is the only one of Orestes's brothers and sisters who kept up a lifelong correspondence with him, beginning in 1836 and continuing right up to the last year before Orestes's death in 1876 — though it was somewhat irregular. She wrote quite affectionate letters, in a good hand, reminding Orestes in one of them in a tone of hurt feelings that it was their common birthday, September 16 — had he forgotten? In another she remarked ironically that she was no "Lady Doctor," and therefore had no right to expect more frequent letters.[71] Many of her letters were pathetic appeals for help in her struggle to rear her family after her husband had turned out to be a ne'er-do-well. In one of her letters she told Orestes she had become a Catholic, but this may have been only an attempt to touch the right chord in his heart for more liberal donations. She frequently received financial help from him. One reason for believing she may have made some kind of a contact with the Catholic Church is the fact that one of her daughters became a Catholic. Daphne, known as Mrs. Ludington, lived on in Bay City, Michigan, and died there in December 1892, apparently outliving all the rest of the family.[72]

One would like to know more about Orestes's eldest brother, the oldest member in the family, Daniel, who became distinguished as an orator.[73] But as far as any records are concerned, he has disappeared into the shadows. In one of her letters Daphne complained that Daniel could do more in the way of contributing to his mother's support since he is now "Squire Brownson."[74] Orestes's other sister, Thorina, apparently lived on at Ballston Spa to the end with her mother. None of these followed Orestes into the Catholic Church.

Brownson's close friend, Isaac Hecker, "perhaps because he was younger and more impulsive,"[75] had preceded him into the Church, having been received on August 2, 1844. After leaving Brook Farm and then Fruitlands, Isaac continued to seek Brownson's counsel. As Brownson had advised him to prepare himself in Greek and Latin for the eventuality of turning to the ministry (in which direction Brownson had also encouraged him), Isaac, after a brief stay at home in New York, had eventually gone to Concord in April 1844, where he began a study of those languages under the tutelage of George Bradford.[76] As he did not at once get the detailed attention from that distinguished classicist he had counted on, he felt at first he would have done better if he had chosen Henry Thoreau for his tutor, all the more so since he was boarding in the home of Thoreau's mother, "a stone's throw from Emerson's Concord."[77] But as it was these gentlemen, Emerson and Thoreau, who were soon to be of some annoyance to him, it was perhaps just as well that he had not chosen Thoreau for his tutor. Thoreau at the time got wind of the fact that Isaac was showing leanings toward the Catholic Church, and he liked it not. In the meantime Isaac interviewed Bishop John Hughes of New York in March, but did not find the bishop as understanding as he had hoped. He wrote friend Brownson, however, that he had narrowed his choice of churches down to one between the Roman Catholic or the Anglican Church, and he felt a growing disposition to opt for the Catholic Church.[78] This trend seemingly became an offense to both Thoreau and Emerson.

According to the story told later by Fr. Hecker, when Thoreau had heard that he (Isaac Hecker) had finally decided to become a Catholic, Thoreau said to him: "What is the use of you joining the Catholic Church? Can't you get along without hanging to her skirts?" Thoreau apparently passed the word to Emerson on Isaac's new turn as he also tried to rid him of such strange notions. He invited Isaac to tea, and kept leading up to the subject of his leanings toward Rome, while Isaac kept leading away from it. The next day Emerson invited him for a ride over to the Shakers where they stayed for the night. All the way over and all the way back Emerson kept fishing for Isaac's reasons for becoming a Catholic, with the evident intention of dissuading him. Then both Emerson and Amos Bronson Alcott contrived to corner him in a sort of interview, with Alcott becoming the more inquisitive about Isaac's new turn. Finally the beleaguered Isaac snapped: "Mr. Alcott, I deny your inquisitorial right in this matter," and so they let the subject drop. One day as Isaac was walking along a road, Emerson joined him, and touching on the subject again, presently remarked: "Mr. Hecker, I suppose it was the art, the architecture, and so on, in the Catholic Church which led you to her." "No," replied Isaac, "but it was what caused all that."[79]

Fr. Isaac Hecker further relates that when he later came to Concord during the Civil War (as a Catholic priest) and wished to find a hall in which to lecture, Emerson refused him help in the matter. Meeting Emerson on the street after one of his lectures they had a little chat. Fr. Hecker noted how Emerson avoided his square look, and actually kept turning to avoid his eyes until he had quite turned around. He added that such men feel exceedingly uncomfortable in the presence of a person who has well-defined and certain convictions.[80]

But these affairs caused no break between Isaac and these two distinguished New England gentlemen. That he continued at this time on very friendly terms with Thoreau is quite evident. With all the zeal and enthusiasm of the new convert, Isaac wrote Brownson the morning of his baptism, August 2, 1844 (administered by Bishop John McCloskey of New York), that he was toying with the idea of a penitential trip to Europe, eventually to Rome, the heart of Christendom. His plan was to work his way overseas, and then work, walk and beg his way the rest of the distance. He could think of no better way to show his gratitude to God for the great gift of faith than such a pilgrimage. "I have my eye," he wrote friend Orestes, "upon one person who can live on bread and water and sleep upon the earth who can walk his share; if he should consent to go, I might go." Henry D. Thoreau was the man who matched the description. As Isaac could not understand why such journeys should not be just as meritorious in our modern day as they were in the Ages of Faith, he decided to propose the journey to Thoreau and then let Brownson know the outcome. By September 2 Isaac informed Brownson that he found Thoreau indisposed to go, and was accordingly abandoning the idea as he did not wish to go alone.[81]

In these days as Isaac and Brownson were entering a new world, they must have been of no little encouragement, not to say solace, to each other. They were leaving old friends and acquaintances behind. As far as Brownson was concerned, his ties with the literary group of Boston were little more than a memory. The chill of loneliness was hovering over him. Not that he had not always experienced a certain amount of loneliness. It had been his lot in childhood (which he had lamented), and had followed him into adulthood. It was partly forced on him by the enormous amount of work to which he felt himself committed, compelling him to live apart.[82] Yet his overflowing heart yearned ever toward his fellows. As M. J. Harson remarked: "Great as he was physically and intellectually, he had a heart big enough to dominate both. He loved God and country with all the intensity of his great soul, and his sympathy for all mankind was as tender as that of a woman."[83] He might be compelled to live largely apart from his fellows, but he frankly owned that at least "a choice circle of friends" was essential to his happiness. Anne C. Lynch, a gifted young woman who wrote for his *Boston Quarterly Review,* had noticed this in a glowing letter dated April 18, 1840, and begged to be admitted to that "choice circle."[84] As a young man Orestes himself had written in his *Notebook of Reflections:*

> O Heaven if ought on earth thou grant, O grant me a friend. There is nothing on earth that can supply the place of a friend. Let me live and in friendship's circle be a part. O let me when adversity presses hard on me, when misfortune overwhelms me, let me find some kindred soul to whom I may reveal the sources of my grief, some affectionate bosom to soothe my affliction with the balm of kindness.[85]

Isaac had now come to occupy a prominent place in that choice circle of friends so essential to Brownson's happiness. The mysterious web of destiny spun by no human finger, had drawn their lives together. If Brownson seems to have had the dominant role in their relationship to date, it is to be remembered that he was far more mature in years. Each was destined to play a unique part in the history of the Catholic Church in America, and each had been of assistance to the other as they groped their way to that church built upon a rock by hands divine. In the years ahead each was to look back often in nostalgic memory as they recalled their heart-to-heart communings while they searched their souls to know God's will and to seek out his true Church. Brownson spoke touchingly of all this years later, in 1855, when he reviewed the first book written by Fr. Isaac Hecker, *Questions of the Soul:*

> We owe personally more than we can say to our long and intimate acquaintance with him [Fr. Hecker]. How often, when neither of us knew or believed in the glorious old Catholic Church, have we talked together by our fireside, on the great questions discussed in this volume before us, and stimulated each other's endeavors after truth and goodness! His modesty and docility made him in those times regard us as his teacher as well as his senior, but in truth we were the scholar. It was in these communings, where each opened his mind and heart to the other, that we were led, the grace of God aiding, to feel the need of the Church, and that we talked, if we may so say, without intending or foreseeing it, each other into the belief and love of catholicity. Each was perhaps of service to the other, but he aided us more than we him, for even then he was the master mind. Years have passed away since those times when we were both groping our way from darkness . . . but always will the recollection of our early intercourse be fresh in our heart.[86]

"Magnanimity," said William G. Ward when speaking of Brownson, "is the finest quality in his character."[87] Whether it was anything Bishop Fitzpatrick had done for his *Review* as censor for a decade, or whether it was a companion who had shared communings on their way to the Catholic Church, Orestes A. Brownson wanted the other person to have the lion's share of credit.

Ever dear to Isaac, too, was to retain his friendship with Brownson. It is interesting to note that near the end of his life Fr. Hecker felt a gentle compulsion to enter a disclaimer to what he considered the extravagant praise in Brownson's tribute to him. In the last article he wrote in the *Catholic World* (November 1887), he begged to be indulged the privilege to quote Brownson's noble tribute to him, which recalls, he remarked, "the affection of so true a heart and so noble a soul." But he prefaced the quotation with the words:

> I know that his error in his estimate of both himself and the present writer is palpable and his praise extravagant. He was the master, I the disciple. God alone knows how much I am indebted to him. To the channels of thought opened to me by Dr. Brownson I owed, more than to anything else, my conversion to the Catholic faith.[88]

It goes without saying that the conversion of Orestes Brownson to the Catholic Church in mid-nineteenth-century America was something of a shock to Puritan New England and liberal United States.[89] That Orestes A. Brownson who in the past had ruthlessly brushed aside all trammels in his daring exercise of the boldest flights of thought and expression should now meekly submit to the shackles of Rome was a phenomenon at which many stood aghast. Some, it is true, such as Dr. Samuel Seabury, editor of *The Churchman,* who had been reading for some time Brownson's *Review* "with delight," had perceived the direction in which he had been heading.[90] Brownson's friend, Theodore Parker, had also clearly perceived his trend, and remarked to an associate that he did not know exactly where Brownson stood at the moment "as I have not heard from him for eight days, when he defined his position in public. He seems tending toward the Catholic Church. God bless him, where ever he is! He has a hard head."[91] His old and steadfast Unitarian friend, Isaac B. Pierce, seeing the direction in which Brownson was rapidly moving, had earnestly called out to him to halt before it was too late.[92] But the public at large were suddenly mystified that a man whom Lord Brougham had pronounced the greatest genius in America should now yield his gigantic intellect to the mental slavery of Rome.[93] One of those so thoroughly mystified by his conversion was his friend, John C. Baldwin, who wrote him on December 31, 1844, to say in part:

> I have observed the course of your mind for a long time, and with a feeling far deeper than any emotion of mere curiosity, and I must say that to me your conversion from the "Church of the Future" to the "Church of Rome," or to the church of the past, as I regard it, is most inexplicable. That you are sincere I feel too deeply to doubt for a moment. But I do not understand this conversion. I cannot explain it; though to say the truth, I have presumed you would yet acknowledge that your mind has submitted to Catholicism as a refuge from the temporary triumph of weariness and despair. . . . I long to understand you, and see the process by which your conversion to Catholicism has been realized.[94]

Baldwin spoke no doubt for not a few who figured that Brownson had thrown himself into the arms of the Catholic Church to escape intellectual despair, or outright infidelity. Others again consoled themselves with the thought that, whatever the explanation of his conversion, he would surely not tarry long within the gates of Rome. "We know an able lawyer and statesman, who at the time offered to wager any amount that Brownson would not remain three years a Catholic," related the distinguished Dr. James A. Corcoran after Brownson's demise.[95] How little those who thus spoke realized the depth of conviction and the sincerity of belief with which Brownson had become a Catholic. Such predictions of his turning back came to Brownson's ears, and he did not refrain from comment. In the third year after his conversion he wrote:

> The time has gone by that was set for our relapse into Protestantism, and as it has done so without our relapsing, we trust that the public will make up their minds to let us live and die a Catholic. We find ourselves very well satisfied with the Church, and with our Catholic friends; we ask nothing but the boon — and it is a very great one — to be permitted to devote what may remain to us of life and strength to the cause of the Church. Would that we had known the Church earlier! From many a pang it would have saved us. The world is too poor to pay the price of one hour of Catholic life.[96]

What Brownson's critics failed to note when harping on his many changes is that he never returned to what he had once come to recognize as error. But for the discovery and possession of new truth he was ever willing to pay any price, and when once laid hold of, he felt an ineluctable obligation to hold on to it though the world tumble about his ears. He would have been the last man in the world to understand any other course. He himself related that when on one of his lecture tours a short time before his conversion, he dropped into a club in Washington, D.C., where James Buchanan was discussing with Calhoun the necessity of the Catholic Church for salvation. When Webster joined them, acquainting him with the subject of conversation, Buchanan said: "We were talking about the Catholic Church, and I, for one, am pretty well convinced that it is necessary to become a Catholic to get to heaven." "Have you just found that out?" replied Webster. "Why, I have known that for years."[97]

Just how seriously these remarks are to be taken would be difficult to determine. Of one thing only can we be certain: Orestes Brownson, of all men, was sure to follow the light when once seen. "They little know me," he wrote, "who think that I love my opinions better than truth."[98] He had long been like a gallant knight in quest of truth; though often foiled, he never abandoned the pursuit. For he was confident that the God who had implanted in his heart such a burning thirst for truth would not deny him the answer. That answer came to him when, through the grace of God, he was led across the threshold of that church called by St. Paul "the pillar and ground of truth."

No one could have known better, and no one has expressed better, Brownson's consuming love of truth than his close friend, Fr. Isaac T. Hecker. Touching on it many years after Brownson's death, he wrote:

> What native trait of Dr. Brownson marks him off from other men? I answer, love of truth, devotion to principle. Oh! how many hours did he spend agonizing for truth! How coolly he touches on it in *The Convert!* How lightly he passes over the great conflicts of his soul! God is now rewarding him for that noble honesty of mind, manly fidelity to reason in the struggle for truth, that sincere humility in his adhesion to it. What Alban Butler says of St. Justin, philosopher and martyr, is true of Brownson: his predominant passion was love of truth. This was all his glory and all his trouble; all his quarrels, friendships, aversions, perplexities, triumphs, labors — all to be traced to his love of truth. . . . He accepted truth with calm and unbroken certitude, yet not in the quiescence of stupidity. Catholicity but emphasized the more that vigorous and frank manliness which was native to him; such a quality, in one always hot on the scent of truth, new truth, more truth, clearer truth, is sufficient to explain minor inconsistencies in Dr. Brownson's writings, and a warmth of expression such as even canonized saints of like temperament have often indulged — St. Jerome, for instance.[99]

Arthur M. Schlesinger, Jr., expresses intelligently in an admirable paragraph why for Orestes Brownson the Catholic Church had come to be the only answer in his long and wearisome search for the truth. Of pilgrim Brownson he wrote:

> The pilgrim inevitably paused before the gates of Rome. To his inexorable honesty and his thirst for certainty, Brownson added a passionate and concrete belief in God and a deep need for a rich and logical theology. Such a man could not long continue within nineteenth-century Protestantism. If his vision for God had been less definite, he might have turned Transcendentalist. If his sense of logic had been less exacting, he might have stayed a Universalist. If he had been less fervently honest, he might have remained a Unitarian, a Presbyterian or a socialist. If he had been content with anything short of absolute certainty, he might have continued forever a Protestant. But he tried Protestantism and found it wanting. Rome proved the only refuge. Entering the gates, he finally found a place to rest. To the end he remained troubled over minor doubts; but he found in the Catholic universe the security he had sought

307

so long, and rested joyously in the Catholic solutions of the central problems of life.[100]

Although the great mass of uneducated Catholics in the country could little appreciate the significance of Brownson's conversion to the Catholic Church, some of the more educated, particularly the clergy, did fairly recognize that a new day had dawned for the Catholic Church in America. Referring to Bishop John Hughes and Bishop John McCloskey of New York, Brownson's friend, Isaac Hecker, wrote him: "I don't hesitate to say that they look to your union with the Christian Church as an era in Catholic America."[101] But of all the ranking officials of the Catholic Church at the time, it seems that only Martin John Spalding (then vicar general of the Louisville diocese and later to be archbishop of Baltimore) took the trouble to write Brownson a fairly long letter. His letter expressed in general his hopes of the great work that Brownson would do in the Church in America. Addressing his letter from Louisville, Kentucky, dated November 21, 1844, he said in part:

Dear Sir:
　　Although personally unacquainted with you, I feel as though I were addressing a friend of long standing, with whom I am already on terms of intimacy. During the present year I have held communion with you through "Brownson's Quarterly Review," and to say that I have been much pleased and instructed by perusing the able papers of this periodical would be but feebly to express the delight I have experienced in reading them. Often have I felt the sentiment: *Talis cum sis, utinam noster esses* [Since you are such, would that you were ours]. You may conjecture how great was my delight on perceiving through the public prints, that the wish had been gratified. From an earlier period of the volume I had no doubt that your mind was taking this direction; & I entertained not a doubt from its strict logical complexion, as to the conclusion it would reach. I fervently unite with you in thanking God for the gift of faith which he has vouchsafed to grant you, after so many years of wandering and doubt. You have found rest where alone it can be found, and from the tenor of your later articles especially, I was pleased to perceive, that you have not only found the priceless jewel of faith, but that, with the divine blessing, you appreciate its full value. I was particularly struck with the theological accuracy of your doctrinal articles, and with the independent fearlessness with which you proclaim the truth.[102] The latter trait is more especially admirable in this time-serving & money cringing age of enlightenment in the matters of dollars & cents.
　　At a time when the very foundations of true philosophy and religion have been torn up, & scattered to the winds by adroit advocates of crude and false systems, it is indeed refreshing to behold able champions stepping forth in defense of outraged truth. May God grant you the entire fullness of that blessed Catholic spirit, the elements of which he has already so abundantly infused into your mind & heart.
　　I feel that you will pardon the freedom I take in thus addressing you. I really view your accession to our ranks as an era in our Church history. I trust to see you an instrument of *immense* good in this country. You understand its genius, its institutions, the character of our people and the source of its errors; I know no one (I speak in all sincerity) better able to disabuse Americans of their errors.
　　The great obstacle to conversion among Protestants of intelligence, I humbly conceive [to be] a certain pride of understanding which is a bar to the grace of God essential to the virtue of faith. This obstacle may give way before the influence of such examples, as are not unfrequent in our day, of men of the

very highest order of intellect, bowing down, becoming as little children, for Christ's sake, "captivating their understanding unto the obedience of faith."

The Catholics of the Union need just such a *Quarterly* as yours has been of late. ... I much fear that now you have taken your stand, you will lose subscribers among the children of the pilgrims. You may also expect to drink somewhat of the cup of bitterness & persecution with Christ [how prophetic!]: "the disciple is not above the master." But I am sure you will not quail.

Thanking you for the kind notice of my first offering to Catholic literature "D'Aubigne Reviewed," and begging that you will pardon the liberty I have taken in opening a correspondence with you.

I have the honor to remain yours truly in Xto.

Martin J. Spalding

Orestes A. Brownson, Esq.[103]

To some it might appear a source of wonderment that Brownson did not find his way to the Catholic Church sooner than he did. Dr. Fairfax McLaughlin recalled that it was only after Brownson got his hands on Abbé Maret's *Le Panthéisme en la Société Moderne* that "the blind giant" began to see and grope his way upward toward the Catholic Church.[104] Perhaps if Brownson could have centered his mind more thoroughly on the historical approach to the Church the way for him might have been simpler and shorter. Newman has somewhere remarked that to be deep in history is to have one's mind turned toward the Catholic Church. It is true that Per Sveino has observed that Brownson's partial enchantment with the Middle Ages did incline him toward the Church, but he was above all a philosopher. And the labyrinthine ways of philosophy are mystifying. To him the philosophical road did in fact become the surer way, if indeed the longer. Chesterton has remarked that the Catholic Church has a thousand gates, and no two converts ever enter it at quite the same angle. But at whatever angle the Church is approached, the way is not always easy and simple for him who starts at a goodly distance. Of the perplexities or puzzlement that may be encountered, St. Augustine, speaking of his own experience, said: "Let those make use of severity who are not acquainted with the difficulties of distinguishing error from truth, and in finding the true way of life amidst the illusions of this world."[105] It is a fair guess to assume that Orestes A. Brownson came to the Church at precisely the time that had been so decreed in the Providence of God. When John Henry Newman took leave of Msgr. Nicholas Wiseman (who later became a cardinal) on the occasion of his visit to Rome as an Anglican minister in 1833, the monsignor courteously expressed to Newman the hope of a return visit to the Eternal City on his part. To which Newman replied with unusual gravity: "We have a work to do in England."[106] Strangely prophetic words! Brownson, too, had a work to do in America.

# PART
# 2

*THE HEALY PORTRAIT*
*OF ORESTES A. BROWNSON*

# 22

## THE CATHOLIC APOLOGIST

*Brownson's concern for his livelihood • Under the influence of Bishop Fitzpatrick he continued his* Review *in exposition and defense of Catholic doctrine • In preparation for his assigned work he is given a systematic course in theology by Bishop Fitzpatrick • His appearance by this time • His advantages and disadvantages as a Catholic apologist • His advantages: his great logical power, and an exceptionally forceful literary style • Tributes to his literary style • The situation he faced as a Catholic apologist • The three-day riots in Philadelphia in 1844 • The aggressive stance of Bishop John Hughes prevents their repetition in New York City • In controversy Brownson adopted the rule: "What is to be avoided is not the severity of reason, but the severity of passion" • The influence of Brownson's Puritan descent upon him • His zeal as an apologist in his writings and other missionary activities • No evidence that Bishop Fitzpatrick made a mistake in directing Brownson to adopt the traditional line in Catholic apologetics • Brownson's belief in his theory of life by communion badly shaken already before he became a Catholic • The weapons of scholastic logic fit well his gifts and temperament • He adopts the new tactic of throwing the assailants of the Catholic Church on the defensive • Brownson's honest endeavor to meet fairly an opponent's argument • His advantage from knowing both sides of the question • The Hoover incident • Brownson lacks a fully adequate library • His great appreciation of the security afforded by papal authority in the Church.*

Although overjoyed with the spiritual treasures that were now his on becoming a Catholic, Orestes Brownson was left with the problem of mapping his future life anew in the altered circumstances. What was now to be his occupation or source of income for the future? This was a crucial question. He was a married man with a large family to support. In the past his *Review* and his frequent lecturing had been his source of income. His *Review* being mainly only for the intellectual elite, contributed only in a measured degree to the support of himself and his family. He could, however, by hard work, make up for what was wanting by his lecturing, and he did so. Anyone who has gone through the Brownson papers will have been astonished at the amount of invitations he continuously received from various quarters to lecture, and at the handsome acknowledgments he received on how well he had met the expectations of his audiences. This accustomed lecturing could of course be still continued as a source of revenue. But what of his *Review*? It had always covered a wide range of subjects: philosophy, government, politics, literature in general, subjects religious and theological. But at the moment of entering the Catholic Church he was largely a stranger to its theology. He had previously read only two Catholic books, Milner's *The End of Controversy,* and *The Catechism of the Council of Trent,* and those not thoroughly.[1] How then was he to discourse on that which he had not studied?

As a solution to the problem, he first toyed with the idea of dropping theology altogether from his *Review.* But what wonder if on second thought it became unacceptable to him. Theology, from his youth up, had been the very breath of his nostrils. As well could he have quit breathing as to leave off theology. As an alternative in the case, he considered turning to the profession of law, for which he had already nearly all the necessary qualifications, and which would likewise provide for him an opportunity, if he so wished, of entering practical politics, and perhaps rising to political eminence.

But when Bishop John Fitzpatrick heard of this turn of mind in his new convert he was decidedly against it. He knew well what he had in Brownson and he was determined to make the most of it. He was eager to put him forth as a stalwart champion on the side of Catholic truth. He saw clearly what might be accomplished by a continuance of *Brownson's Quarterly Review* in the exposition and defense of Catholic doctrine.[2] Nor was he by any means alone in this. It was a dream that had intoxicated Bishop (later Cardinal) John McCloskey of New York, as told by Isaac Hecker. Both bishops there, Bishop John Joseph Hughes and Bishop McCloskey, were anxious that Brownson make New York the headquarters of his *Review.* And Hecker seemed to agree with them when he wrote:

> You will find the heads of the Church more to your mind in New York than in Boston, it seems to me, and more able, and with greater enthusiasm to second your plans. I don't hesitate to say that they look to your union with the Christian Church as an era in Catholic America. They feel much stronger, and are disposed to break the silence which the Church has suffered herself to keep. If you are disposed to restart your *Quarterly* under different auspices I think it would be well for you to see the bishops of this diocese prior to the undertaking. I think it very probable that Bishop Hughes will write to you soon by what Bishop McCloskey said to me.[3]

Bishop Hughes apparently never got around to writing Brownson about the matter, and Brownson stayed on in Boston. It was probably just as well. He had always loved Boston, and it was in that area that he could hope for the widest patronage of his *Review* among Catholics and non-Catholics. After all, he had something to say to all classes of people who had come to know him, whatever their religious beliefs or state of mind. He had always felt a magnetic relationship between himself and his readers, and he was anxious to retain as many of them in the locality as possible. His association with Bishop Fitzpatrick had, too, by this time become confidential and familiar. It is quite credible, then, that the bishop would have been decidedly unwilling to see his protégé leave Boston, for he appreciated fully as keenly as the bishops in New York what Brownson and his *Review* would mean to the Catholic cause.

After Brownson had once acquiesced in Bishop Fitzpatrick's wish to relaunch his *Quarterly* as a Catholic publication, the bishop set about preparing him in that which he most needed and in which he was most wanting — Catholic theology. He selected for this purpose Billuart's *Summa Theologica* of St. Thomas, acting himself as the expounder of the treatise to Brownson. Next came the *Summa Theologica* itself of St. Thomas, and then some of St. Augustine's *Works*. Bishop Fitzpatrick was an admirable master in theology, and could explain it clearly, was calm and authoritative in his exposition, and sound in his views, remarks Brownson's son Henry.[4]

Brownson was now moving along in his forty-second year. His giant, muscular six-feet-two-inch frame, just beginning to put on weight, was becoming even more formidable in appearance. His great shock of hair, brushed straight back from his high sloping forehead, balanced by a full spreading beard, giving him something of the appearance of a biblical prophet, was already streaked with gray. Under shaggy brows his eyes looked out through small gold-rimmed spectacles that rested on a slightly beaked nose. Ruddy of complexion, his whole appearance was leonine. And like the lion he was ready for any battle. The battles he had passed through had only served to prepare him for those ahead, and his greatest battles by far lay in the future. He had fed on battles, and seemed to bid Armageddon welcome. His sword was the pen he held in his long graceful fingers. His countenance wore the mien of a no-nonsense man. And he was utterly without fear. As Arthur M. Schlesinger, Jr., has said: "He was not a man to be intimidated by all the devils in hell when he thought he was right."[5]

What precise advantages and disadvantages did this man bring to his role as a Catholic apologist? That he had not had a more ample opportunity to study Catholic theology at leisure before beginning his career was of course to be a partial drawback. It would have been ideal if he could have been allowed sufficient leisure to become a doctor of divinity in preparation for his work, but the situation did not allow such a delay. As it was, he rushed into, or was pushed into his appointed work without so much, observed Daniel Sargent, as an opportunity to make a spiritual retreat for calmly collecting his thoughts and making plans for the important assignment given him.[6] As to his lack of an opportunity for a more lengthy study of Catholic theology at the time, he simply had to make the best of it, and labored indefatigably day and night from the start to acquire the requisite theological science for his role as a Catholic apologist. As a safeguard against error, however, he accepted Bishop Fitzpatrick as his theological censor for the first decade of his career.

But whatever his disadvantage on this score, on other scores he had great advantages. Not the least of which were his transcendent logical powers. George Parsons Lathrop relates that "a well-known Boston man said of him [Brownson] that the only safe way, in arguing with Brownson, was to deny everything. If you admitted anything, even the most simple and obvious, that he proposed, you were lost: he would proceed logically and prove his point triumphantly."[7] The late Viatorian, Fr. William J. Bergin, professor of philosophy at St. Viator's College, Bourbonnais, Illinois, and later Catholic chaplain at the University of Champlaine, pronounced Brownson "the greatest master of applied logic the English-speaking world has ever produced."[8] Though the statement takes in an immense sweep in time and space, this writer has not the least doubt about its literal accuracy. So famous was he for his logical powers, and his argumentative tendency — sometimes an offense or a humiliation to others — that it is little wonder that James Russell Lowell made them the object of his humorous satire in his *Fable for Critics*. While paying tribute to Brownson's "transparent and forcible prose," he jocosely rhymed away:

> The worst of it is, that his logic is so strong,
> That of two sides he commonly chooses the wrong,

If there *is* only one, why he'll split it in two,
And first pummel this half, and then that, black and blue;
That white's white needs no proof, but it takes a deep fellow,
To prove it jet black, and that jet black is yellow.[9]

Another redoubtable asset Brownson brought to his role as a Catholic apologist was his powerful style of writing. It was Buffon who said: "The style is the man." Brownson gave us a variant of this when he remarked that every writer, "whatever he writes, he always writes himself."[10] Never was this more true of anyone than Brownson himself. His towering personality he crowded into almost every paragraph he wrote. His style, effortless and unadorned, he made an apt vehicle for the great vigor and directness of his thought whatever the theme he touched upon. Daniel Sargent observed "that as a master of forceful English prose, he [Brownson] had scarcely an equal, save centuries before him, Dean Swift."[11] *The Christian Examiner,* a polemical foe of *Brownson's Quarterly Review,* pronounced his style "almost beyond compare, clear and nervous."[12] Comparing Brownson's style with Newman's, Rev. C. H. Leonard, president of Tufts College, Massachusetts, said of Brownson: "I loved to read after him. He was always stimulating to me even when I could not believe. His style was so *strong —* grand idiomatic English — pure as Newman's, with more imagination, perhaps."[13] Brownson himself listed English style as first among the subjects to which he had given his close attention. "The only subjects I have really studied," he said, "are English style, philosophy, the philosophy of history and religion, or theology. Under the head of philosophy I include politics, or the moral law applied to the state."[14]

In his dissertation, *Rhetoric in the Works of Orestes Brownson,* Leonard J. McCarthy, S.J., distinguishes three literary styles used by Brownson: the lyrical or poetic, more marked in his earlier period, in many of his essays on Emerson, and in his orations; the logical style which predominates in his writings generally, and is seen conspicuously in his famous essays on the laboring classes; and the philosophical style which is at its best in his most important book, *The American Republic.* These styles are, however, intermingled variously in his writings. Fr. McCarthy added: "At best, Brownson's style was the style of an apologist who thought like a philosopher, argued like a logician, and who illuminated his expression with the apposite imagery and appropriate emotion of a master rhetorician."[15]

In getting down to the practical work of a Catholic apologist, Brownson apparently found that the views of Bishop Fitzpatrick and those of himself were not entirely coincident. He dreamt wistfully of bringing as many as possible of his New England friends into the Catholic Church after him. Bishop Fitzpatrick, too, was desirous of making converts, but the situation being what it was, he was perhaps equally, if not even more intent on "stopping the anti-Catholic fury of the Protestant journals of the day." And well might he be. Anyone who has read Ray Billington's *The Protestant Crusade* — even though he knew much about it before — will be shocked at the flagitious character of the deep and wide flood of abuse and vilification launched against the Catholic Church in the first half of the nineteenth century. (Billington's book covers the period 1800-1860.)[16] If it was a virtue to heap wanton abuse and slander on Catholics and their Church, then the Lyman Beechers, the Samuel B. Smiths, the Samuel B. Morses, the Nicholas Murrays, the Robert Breckenridges, the Rebecca Reeds, the Maria Monks, the J. J. Slocums, the Arthur Tappans, the Parson Brownlows, *et alii et aliae,* were indeed persons of exalted virtue, and did their work well. As one writer remarked in 1835: "The abuse of Catholics . . . is a regular trade, and the compilation of anti-Catholic books . . . has become a part of the regular industry of the country, as much as the making of nutmegs, or the construction of clocks."[17] Nor was the situation any better in England at the time. So overwhelming was the vast body of anti-Catholic tradition that Newman could only exclaim: "The Maker of all, and only he can shiver in pieces this vast enchanted palace in which our lot is cast; may he do it in his time."[18]

Such anti-Catholic abuse and slander in America could not but erupt into violence and arson. The first major instance was the laying of the Ursuline Convent, Charlestown, Massachusetts, in ashes on the night of August 11, 1834, by a raging mob that was allowed a free hand by the law.[19] Ten years later the No-Popery agitation rose to white heat and disgraced Philadelphia, the City of Brotherly Love, with three days of seething violence and bloodshed in 1844.[20] Flames again consumed two Catholic churches, St. Augustine's and St. Michael's, as terror spread through the city, particularly Kensington, priests and nuns trembling in mortal terror and Catholic home dwellers suddenly fleeing for dear life with their few belongings.[21] As to the safety of Catholic churches, Ray Billington affirms: "In New England, where the people had had a taste of rioting, mob attacks on Catholic churches became so frequent that many congregations posted regular armed guards to patrol and protect their property, and insurance companies refused to place a policy upon Catholic buildings which were not of non-inflammable material!"[22]

But matters fared better in New York City where ruled a prelate of a strong hand, Bishop John Hughes. As soon as the contagious orgy of violence and arson began to invade the city from Philadelphia, he took a firm stand. Forthrightly he declared that "if a single Catholic church were burned in New York, the city would become a second Moscow." He went to Mayor Morris and demanded protection for his churches. The mayor, unwilling to displease a Protestant mob, asked nervously, "So you are afraid for your churches?" "No," replied Hughes, "I am afraid for yours." He had, he explained, plenty of fighting Irishmen in the city on whom he had to exercise considerable restraint in keeping them orderly in the threatening circumstances.[23] Hughes went on to blame Catholics themselves for what had come to pass in Philadelphia. "They should have defended their churches," he complained, "since the authorities could not or would not do it for them. We might forbear from harming the intruder into *our house* until the last, but his first violence to our church should be promptly and decisively repelled." After ascertaining from legal authorities that the law did not require the city to compensate Catholics for any churches destroyed, he promptly stationed 1,000 to 2,000 fully armed men about each church and hurriedly published a statement in a special edition of the *Freeman's Journal* calling upon his stationed men to keep the peace as far as possible, but to protect their churches at any cost.

The rioters, who had already held one meeting in the city on May 7, 1844, took alarm. A second mass meeting had been planned to be held in Central Park, May 9, but after a hasty conference of the mayor with other civic authorities in the city it was concluded that only by a cancellation of the mass meeting could violence and bloodshed be avoided, and the leaders of the riotous party were finally won to that view. On the afternoon of May 9 placards were posted about in the city announcing that the meeting had been postponed. Bellicose as had been Hughes' stand, in all probability nothing less would have been effective — judging from what had happened in Philadelphia. Ray Billington awards much credit to Bishop Hughes for his bold and fearless stand in a dark crisis.[24]

This phase of our history has been briefly mentioned here for the reason that if we are to do justice to Orestes Brownson as a Catholic apologist in his day we must visualize clearly the fiercely anti-Catholic backdrop against which he perforce had to operate in his day. He lived, it must be clearly kept in mind, not in the ecumenical latter half of the twentieth century, but in mid-nineteenth-century America in a social and religious milieu entirely different from our own. He was a man of his times and simply had to take the situation as he found it. It is highly worthy of note that he came to the Catholic Church at that very moment when the Protestant churches were poised for a united frontal attack on Roman Catholics. Ray Billington tells us again that:

> . . . [by] the middle of the 1840s the American Churches were able to present a virtually united front against Catholicism. Swept away by pleas of organized nativists, they had accepted the challenge to make America the scene of a new Reformation in which Popery would be driven from the land and the work of Luther and Calvin brought to a successful end.[25]

To meet the challenge, Brownson on his conversion to the Catholic Church joined battle with the various attacking journals. It may well be that Bishop Fitzpatrick did say to him: "Lay on MacDuff!" But Van Wyck Brooks thinks that there was really no call for it. "As well urge a bull not to be a lamb," he remarked.[26] Whatever the case, it would seem that it was right here that Orestes Brownson came into his own. For it really seems a part of Divine Providence that to the strong Brownson was to fall the special mission of putting down hostility to the Church in America through a vigorous, crystal-clear demonstration of the reasonableness of the Catholic faith and an acceptance of Catholic teaching — that is, to all who were willing to listen to reason. His highest gifts were adapted to that end rather than to the direct winning of converts — though they operated effectively in both directions. The arguments advanced by this "Hercules of American controversy" remain unanswered to this day. Those arguments, when rightly put, are in very truth unanswerable, but if any man was needed to put them in their most forcible form, that man was Orestes A. Brownson. Van Wyck Brooks gives it as his opinion that Brownson never had in this country opponents of a sufficiently formidable caliber to bring "his great powers into full play."[27] But accepting such adversaries as were at hand, no corner escaped his eye in which error might lurk. Though asserting it on a slightly different score, Msgr. Matthew Smith, founder and editor of the *Denver Register,* has said that it is to Brownson that "we owe the peace of the Church in America."

Asserting that falsehood can never be harmless, Brownson now rained down sledgehammer blows in article after article — not on the head of his opponent, but on error's head. Speaking of Brownson as a Catholic apologist, Dr. John W. Nevin remarked: "He deals his blows like a conscious Hercules, sent forth on a divine errand to reform the world."[28] Though always respectful of his opponent personally, Brownson was utterly unsparing and remorseless in his logic. From the truth of his premises, he ruthlessly swept on to legitimate conclusions. He professed "a great horror of the mortal sin of being inconsequent."[29] So intent was he on the defense of truth that the *fortiter in re* counted more with him then the *suaviter in modo.* But however strong and earnest he might be in argument, he was ever disposed to observe the courtesies of gentlemanly debate. With much reason could he say: "We mean never to disfigure our pages with any other severity than that of reason."[30] "What is to be avoided is not the severity of reason, but the severity of passion."[31]

This rigid strain of logic which was part and parcel of Brownson's mental composition is one of his curious attributes. How did he come by it? One thing is certain: he did not imbibe it from the Catholic religion. Theodore Maynard has said that "all in all the most remarkable mind American Catholicism had produced is that of Orestes Brownson."[32] But American Catholicism did not produce the mind of Orestes Brownson. His mind was what it was long before he came to the Catholic Church. The real explanation would seem to be that this particular bent of his mind was a part of his Puritan heritage. And he gloried in his Puritan descent. "I have departed far enough from the stand-point of my Puritan ancestors," he remarked, "and have few traces in my moral constitution of my Puritan descent; but I care not who knows it, I am proud of these stern old men, the Bradfords, the Brewsters, the Hookers, the Davenports, and stout old Miles Standish, who came forth into a new world to battle with the wilderness, the savage, and the devil."[33] Perry Miller tells us that these same Puritans considered logic "a special gift of God," and its authority "divine." "Few logicians," he added, "have ever put so much trust in logic."[34] Brownson was strictly an old-line Puritan in his tremendous belief in the worth of logic. And he had besides probably more of the Puritan in his basic makeup than he ever realized.

That a certain severity of tone also marked some of Brownson's thought in controversy is not to be denied. He himself frankly acknowledged it, saying that no other tones than those of a just severity were in place—because of the outrageous nature of the charges flung at the Church, sometimes by persons of no inconsiderable culture. But whenever it was his pleasure to meet an opponent who exhibited the qualities of a gentleman, if not the Christian, his manner and tone were mild, though his logic in all cases was equally forceful. When reviewing Cardinal Wiseman's *Essays*, he took occasion to express his regrets that he did not always have in this country the cultured and gentlemanly type of persons to address which was the good fortune of His Eminence. He wrote:

> We cannot read these *Essays* on the Oxford controversy without something like envy of their illustrious author — not, of course, for his talents, his genius, his erudition, his courteous manner, and his graceful and dignified style, for these are far above our humble aspirations, but for his public, for the men he had to refute, and bring within the pale of truth. He had a great and important movement setting towards the Church to deal with, conducted by men of mistaken views indeed, advocating, in itself considered an absurd and ridiculous theory, but sincere, honest, and loyal, well-bred, cultivated, eminent for their abilities and learning, who were too much in earnest to be cavillers, numerous enough to make it an object to address especially, and respectable enough to enable one to address them in gentle and hopeful terms. . . . One could so treat these men as to refute their errors and retain their respect, and even secure their affection.[35]

Theodore Maynard, however, opines that Brownson had little or no reason to complain of the type of opponents he encountered in this country as a Catholic apologist.[36] Yet Brownson found even so high-class and respectable

319

a journal as *The Christian Examiner* coming short in courtesy and fair dealing. He had considered that publication "second to no periodical in the country." But he came to regret that such writers as James Freeman Clarke who had attempted a reply to his article on "Church against No-Church" were only downgrading its former high dignity and excellence. Clarke in his reply to Brownson's article had harped largely upon what he considered Brownson's personal foibles as an answer to the elaborate argument framed by Brownson showing why he was forced by the evidence to become a Catholic. To which Brownson in the course of his rejoinder demurred, saying: "Nothing is gained in the long run by seeking to substitute personal detraction or vulgar prejudice for solid argument. In our article against the *Christian Examiner* we made no personal attack; we appealed to no popular prejudice against either it or its doctrine; we reasoned fairly and conscientiously; and it owed it to its character, and to us, as one of its former contributors, to have met us in the same tone and manner. It has not done so; and for its sake, and for the sake of its readers, for the sake of honorable and profitable controversy, we regret it."[37]

When therefore Dr. John W. Nevin, one of the chief founders of the school of Mercersburg Theology, contributed an extensive article to the *Mercersburg Quarterly Review* on Brownson's advocacy of Catholicity, Brownson was especially gratified with the style and tone of his essay. "It is refreshing," he remarked, "to meet such an opponent, and we are sorry to add, he is almost the only direct opponent we have ever had that we did not feel it a sort of a degradation to meet."[38] Dr. Nevin he estimated to be "a man of great abilities and earnestness, and as a scholar, as a logician, and as an original and vigorous writer, inferior to no Protestant divine in the country." Dr. Nevin was a member of the German Reformed Church. Fair and candid, he can be accepted as an unexceptional witness to the contemporary situation which confronted Brownson as a Catholic apologist. Frankly he acknowledged in his article:

> It is just one of the miseries of fashionable pseudo-Protestantism that it legitimates and accepts so readily every sort of polemical assault upon Rome, without proof or examination; as though it were the easiest thing in the world, to fight this battle to purpose; in consequence of which we are flooded here with more insipid trash, in the name of religious argument, than is to be met with probably in any other quarter. It is with a most wretched grace, that such easy literature, whether figuring in the newspaper, the catch-penny book, rostrum, or pulpit allows itself to overlook and despise the vigorous pen of such a man as Dr. Brownson, as though it were a flourish of mere empty words and nothing else. There is nothing gained in the end, and much lost, by such imbecile self-conceit. Over against its blind though proud pretensions, it is no wonder that true learning on the other side should be excited to indignant scorn. Mr. Brownson has full right to retort on this spirit, as he often does with withering scorn, its common charges against Rome. It is not reason; it sets logic at defiance; it shrinks from the light; it goes blindly and dumbly by its own tradition; it substitutes cant for argument; it turns the Bible into a nose of wax, to suit its own taste; it plays the pope as fully as though it were itself the wearer of the triple crown, and held all the thunders of the Vatican in its hand.[39]

It might well then be argued whether withal anything less than the rigid line of argumentation adopted by Brownson would have been effectual in meeting and turning back the venomous attacks being leveled at the Catholic Church in his day. His providential mission is seen precisely in the fact that he was a perfect match for the scene before him. Only a strong man of great controversial powers and learning would have been able to meet the challenge. A writer of the last century seems to express a just view of the matter when he suggests the reasons why Brownson dealt ruthlessly, not with his opponents, but with error or falsehood. He wrote:

> There were, and probably there are still, Catholics who thought that Brownson's style of attack was unnecessarily harsh and severe; but we must not forget that he wrote in the midst of rampant bigotry, when every ignorant fanatic deemed (or feigned to deem) it a sacred duty to vilify the Catholic Church. He knew the value of truth; he had experienced the cost of its attainment; he knew the thorny paths, dark and difficult, that must be trodden by the inquirer; he had, therefore, no mercy for those who held out false lights to lure the wanderer to his destruction. And his manner had the decided advantage of driving from the field of controversy many a garrulous disputant who would have held out far longer under less telling blows.[40]

Whatever the truth of the matter, now that Brownson knew that he had the truth, for which he had searched so long and so painfully, he was all afire with zeal to proclaim it from the housetops of the world that others might share it also. Not only through his writings did he endeavor to share it, but he was no less alert to turn opportunities in his daily social life to the same end and purpose, particularly when traveling, and he traveled much. Especially on the ferryboat that plied between Chelsea and Boston proper did he become a familiar apostolic figure. Rev. C. M. Leonard, president of Tufts College (and who was not a Catholic), recalled almost half a century later how "Dr. Brownson was full of the motive of the Catholic faith, and loved to talk of it to persons — twenty or more — who were sure to gather about him of a summer morning on the deck of the ferryboat." Rev. Leonard also spoke of the conversations on religion Brownson was wont to strike up in the shops of Chelsea, speaking of the "real rest" to mind and heart which the Catholic Church gives — not the rest of "passivity, but the rest of activity." In a letter to Brownson's son Henry, Dr. Leonard expressed his regrets that, being young at the time of Brownson's conversion, he did not have more of an opportunity to become better acquainted with him. "I can only tell us," he said, "how awed I used to be by the 'man of power,' as some of us used to call him, and how I longed to know him."[41]

The hope of conversions was not the only motive behind these missionary activities of this zealous new convert. A further motive is to be found in a wish strongly expressed to him by Bishop Fitzpatrick, to which he was already definitely inclined himself, namely, that he do all he could to elevate the tone of Catholics in the country. The bishop had come to lament the timid and apologetic spirit of the Catholics generally in the country. Largely a class of illiterate immigrants, they were without any standing; even the old-time Catholic families were glad enough to keep their religion out of sight. As a means of counteracting this cringing spirit, Brownson determined to assert his Catholicity everywhere. On the occasion of lecturing in Andover, Lawrence, Haverhill and other places in the vicinity, he made a spectacular display of his aggressive Catholicity. At the hotel in Andover, one Friday morning, after going with all the other guests to a common dining room, he called out to a waiter in a loud voice to send him the landlord. When he came, Brownson asked him in a loud voice that could be heard throughout the dining hall, "Why don't you have something in your house a Christian can eat?" The landlord mentioned that he had beefsteak and other meats that could be served; but Brownson cut him short saying: "Why don't you have fish? No

Christian eats meat on Friday." (This was in a day when the Friday law was sacred to devout Catholics.) Fish was readily procured, and the matter ended there. Brownson's only motive in the affair, his son assures us, was to assert his Catholicity fearlessly in that "hot-bed of Puritanism."[42] The motive was of the very essence of the matter. Were one to forget that, the affair might well be entirely discounted.

In such an exhibition Brownson was simply taking deadly aim to scotch and destroy that three-century-old siege mentality among Catholics in America which Frank Sheed has told us that Hilaire Belloc and Gilbert Keith Chesterton did so much to obliterate in England in the forepart of this century. And here we are readily reminded of an anecdote in the life of Belloc whose temperament was somewhat similar to Brownson's. When Belloc was campaigning as a candidate for Parliament some of the clergy timidly counseled him to keep the religious question out of sight as far as possible lest it undo his chances for election. Brushing aside such pusillanimous advice, he boldly declared as he rose to address a packed audience:

> Gentlemen, I am a Catholic. As far as possible, I go to Mass every day. This (taking a rosary out of his pocket) is a rosary. As far as possible, I kneel down and tell these beads every day. If you reject me on account of my religion, I shall thank God that he has spared me the indignity of being your representative.

His biographer, Robert Speaight, says, "There was a hush of astonishment followed by a thunderclap of applause."[43]

As American Catholics became less apologetic about their religion, Brownson drew less and less attention to his new religion in his travels and social life. His ready compliance with the wish Bishop Fitzpatrick had expressed to him in this matter is only one of the sundry ways in which he showed a marked degree of docility and humility in surrendering himself to the directions of the bishop. This spirit is especially seen in his prompt suppression, at the evident wish of the bishop, of his philosophical doctrine of life by communion which had led him to the door of the Roman Catholic Church, barely mentioned in the previous chapter. To suppress it outright must have meant no little sacrifice on his part in the circumstances, for such compliance was to place him, as he saw it, in a false light in the eyes of his non-Catholic friends. At least so he himself explained it many years later in *The Convert*. Many, he went on to elucidate, who had read him saw clearly whither he was tending, and had no reason to be surprised when he became a Catholic. The doctrine which he had brought out, and which they had followed, seemed to them, as it did to him, to authorize the step he took, and perhaps not a few of them were making up their minds to follow him, but were suddenly thrown aback when they heard him as a Catholic defending his conversion on grounds of which he had previously given no public intimation at all and which were utterly unconnected with those he had previously published. Unable to reconcile the two, some who had been following him, were disposed to look upon his conversion as an act of intellectual despair or willful caprice for which he could in reality offer no good reason. So they refused to trouble themselves any longer about the reasonings of one who had apparently acted in the case without any rational motive for what he did.[44] So Brownson reasoned about the matter as he looked back thirteen years later. That there is some truth in what he said is obvious. Rufus Griswold no doubt spoke for many when he said: "It would be impossible to link his former opinions with the present ones, by any connection, either logical or psychological."[45]

On this matter, Fr. Isaac Hecker, too, felt it was a great mistake for Brownson to have bypassed as a Catholic apologist the philosophical theory which had led him to the Church. By developing it as an apologist, he affirmed, he would have opened an inviting pathway to many of the more cultivated New Englanders to follow him into the Church. After quoting passages from *The Convert* in which Brownson speaks of his abandonment of his special theory of life by communion as an apologist at the wish of Bishop Fitzpatrick, Fr. Hecker remarked:

> These passages reveal plainly how Brownson, by shifting his arguments, shifted his auditory and lost, never to regain, the leadership Providence had designed for him. I always maintained that Dr. Brownson was wrong in thus yielding to the bishop's influence, and that he should have held on to the course Providence had started him in. His convictions were an outgrowth of the best American thought, and, as he plainly proves in *The Convert,* were perfectly coincident with sound Catholic philosophy. Had he held on to the way inside the Church which he had pursued outside the Church in finding her, he would have carried with him some, and might perhaps have carried many, non-Catholic minds of a leading character. . . . But he was switched off the main line of his career by the influence of Bishop Fitzpatrick, who induced him to enter upon the *traditional line of controversy against Protestantism* at a time when the best minds in New England had given up belief in the distinctive errors of that heresy.[46]

But Fr. Hecker overshot the mark somewhat in emphasizing how he had insisted with Brownson that he follow his own line of apologetics when he said:

> I told him at the time that in confining himself to the historical proof, and in pointing out that road alone to truth, he had forgotten the bridge by which he himself had reached it, if, indeed, he had not actually turned about and broken it down. And when, shortly after my conversion, I went to Europe, all the letters I wrote to him were filled with complaints that he had given up his first principles, or at any rate ignored them.[47]

But as Fr. Vincent Holden, C.S.P., has brought out, there are only three letters in the Notre Dame archives of Isaac Hecker to his friend Brownson while abroad, and no one of them has as much as a passing reference to Brownson's new apologetics. This is mentioned as also affording an occasion of pointing out that a few critical remarks that Fr. Hecker made of Bishop Fitzpatrick at the end of his own life when recalling his visit with him as a prospective convert, are of very dubious historical value likewise. All the evidence available, as Fr. Holden has shown, would seem to indicate that Fr. Hecker's failing memory confused the incidents of the conversations he had had with Bishop John Hughes of New York with the conversations he had had with Bishop Fitzpatrick.[48] The critical remarks, the evidence indicates, apply to Bishop Hughes, not to Bishop Fitzpatrick. This is of some historical importance insofar as the critical remarks have misled biographers who have drawn on Fr. Hecker's article, particularly Theodore Maynard who quotes them in a measure. From Fr. Hecker's remarks Maynard concludes that Bishop Fitzpatrick had a "negative rather than a positive mind," and that he influenced Brownson accordingly.[49]

But aside from this, it is by no means certain, with all due respect to the views of both Brownson and Fr. Hecker on the matter, that Bishop Fitzpatrick made a mistake in directing Brownson to follow the traditional line of argument as a Catholic apologist. (After thirteen years it was a flattering view for Brownson himself to take as an explanation of why more of his New England friends had not followed him into the Catholic Church.) But if it was Brownson's special mission to put down hostility to the Church in America in his day through irrefragable argumentation, the old scholastic weapons of rigid logic were most likely the most powerful he could have employed. And the most powerful were called for. He felt justified in throwing back at the assailants of the Church: "They who suppose that reason has anything to do with the opposition to Catholicity are grievously mistaken. Infidels do not reason against us; they declaim, they denounce, invent stories and tell gross falsehoods about us; and when they fail, they burn our convents, our churches, seminaries [and] dwellings."[50] If then Brownson's ironclad reasoning did not always carry conviction in the degree hoped for, it was at least something to silence in the intellectual order those who were viciously attacking the Catholic Church. What would have been accomplished had Brownson followed his own philosophical line of thought is the sheerest speculation. Besides, Brownson recognized as clearly as any man that for the winning of converts something more than reasoning, on whichever line, is required.

> A man convinced against his will
> is of the same opinion still.

As he remarked: "A single prayer offered in secret to Almighty God by some devout soul, unknown to the world, shall effect more than our most elaborate articles or brilliant and stirring editorials."

There is in fact little or nothing on record to indicate that his New England associates were paying much or any attention to the doctrine of life by communion that he had been developing. Quite the contrary. As we have already noted, he wrote his friend Victor Cousin in Paris on September 1, 1844 (the very eve of his conversion): "I believe I am almost alone in my devotion to philosophy; at least I find none who bow with me at her shrine. No one seems to be aware of my speculations, or to trouble themselves with the subjects they concern."[51] The New England literati were not interested in philosophical theories, and apparently left our American philosopher severely to himself in his somewhat mystifying lucubrations. Hugh Marshall has rightly observed that the New England intellectuals were caught up in the romantic movement that dominated that period, and had little or no taste for savoring philosophical speculations, or for being influenced by them.[52] That Brownson could have turned them around to follow in his direction in any numbers, seems, humanly speaking, very unlikely. It may be a nice dream that such would have been the case, but nothing has yet been turned up that would seem to give it any support. In the case of the Oxford movement, the soil there had been cultivated for years for a flow of converts into the Catholic Church. In New England there was nothing whatsoever to parallel that situation.

This is not at all to say that the line of argument which had led Brownson to the Church does not have its own distinctive merits and unique potential appeal to others. The real question is whether or not more was accomplished in following the scholastic line of reasoning. By the time Brownson's work in America was done he had made the Roman Catholic Church, so long calumniated and despised, at least respectable with all who would lay honorable claim to rationality and intelligence in any real degree. That was the first step to the gaining of a fair consideration of the Church in that day, and, humanly speaking, cleared the way for others to find the haven of truth. Whatever the case, Brownson did come to be quite at home in the realm of scholastic logic where he had such ample room for the use of his famous logical powers. On this line he could and did exhibit many qualities of a great apologist. As a reviewer of his *Works* remarked:

> [He was possessed of] a passionate love of truth, unswerving fidelity to principle, fearless honesty of purpose; an inherent love of liberty in its true sense — his powerful mind rigidly logical, one would almost think by necessity; such were the leading features of his character; they are traceable in every page of his writings, and they explain not alone his excellent qualities, but also what some regard as his defects.[53]

It is an intriguing fact that Brownson's faith in his theory of life by communion was considerably shaken already before his reception into the Catholic Church. Brownson has told us, already noted, that it was some weeks before he and Bishop Fitzpatrick could come to a confiding relationship. It was because the bishop feigned ignorance of his theory of life by communion, or because he was indisposed to give it any recognition. Whichever the case, a deal of skepticism about the theory entered Brownson's mind after the publication of the July 1844 issue of his *Review* — the very time he was under the instructions of Bishop Fitzpatrick. He acknowledged only a few months later, in April 1845, his conviction that while the theory had led him to the *door* of the Catholic Church, "it does not do so necessarily, but only accidentally." He would have no one set any value on his philosophical doctrines. With all the indiscriminate zeal of the overly fervent convert, scorning the errors of his past, he now wished to throw overboard all his former writings prior to 1844, unless they were his criticisms of Kant, some political essays, and his articles in his current *Review* on Social Reform and the Anglican Church.[54] Later he was to call this "an excess of self-abnegation" to which he was perhaps "encouraged."[55] As to the theory of life by communion, he would put it on the shelf until he had sufficient leisure to reexamine it in the light of more extensive theological studies. As he said in the *Convert:* "It had served as a scaffolding, but now [that] the temple was completed, it might serve only to obscure its beauty and fair proportions."[56]

Particularly was it an advantage for Brownson to follow the immemorial scholastic method of explaining and defending Catholic doctrine if he was to implement the wish of Bishop Fitzpatrick as an apologist. Long had it been the policy of Catholics in controversy with adversaries of the Church to explain away as far as possible doctrines of the Church offensive to outsiders, to adopt an apologetic tone, and to allow themselves to be thrown on the defensive by being forever kept busy parrying blows or answering objections to the Church. This spelled hopeless defeat at the very outset. As Brownson expressed it: "The party which acts on the defensive only, which suffers itself to be attacked in its lines, and seeks only to prevent them from being broken, in some sense confesses its own weakness. . . . Whatever apparent advantages Protestants have ever gained in their controversies with Catholics, they have gained by acting on the offensive; by throwing out objections, and keeping us busy with refuting them."[57] Bishop Fitzpatrick being of the same mind, he called upon Brownson to reverse all this by throwing the adversaries of the Catholic Church themselves on the defensive, summoning them to the bar to give an account of their own stance and tenets. Few or none were more fitted for this high endeavor by gifts and temperament than

Brownson. Apart from his singular gifts for accomplishing this task, he knew, too, that he had now a body of doctrine that made sense. He knew now the truth of what Daniel Webster had once remarked to him in a Boston bookstore when he happened to be glancing at a book on Catholic doctrines in his non-Catholic day. Peeping at the book and noting its contents, Webster said to him: "Take care how you examine the Catholic Church, unless you are willing to become a Catholic, for Catholic doctrines are logical."[58] Brownson needed nothing more than just that — logical doctrines. He promptly proceeded to erect the great body of Catholic doctrine into a sort of intellectual juggernaut capped with the tenet of papal authority as its supreme piece of weaponry which rolled triumphantly into the assailants' territory. A new day had dawned for the Catholic Church in America. Speaking of Brownson's aggressive prowess in religious controversy, Dr. Nevin acknowledged:

> In this warfare he wields a most active pen; not confining himself by any means, as some of his opponents might wish, to the business of parrying or warding off thrusts from the contrary side, but seeking rather to carry the main brunt of the battle into the very heart of the enemy's country, fiercely assailing Protestantism in its own strongholds, and defying it to mortal combat where it is accustomed to look upon itself as most secure and strong.[59]

After deploring the timid and apologetic defenses of the Catholic Church, so long in vogue, M. J. Harson spoke with almost unbounded enthusiasm of the new tack adopted by Brownson in defending the Church. The great mass of defenses in the past he had found defective, leaving the case undecided or at least creating doubts. In Brownson he had at long last found his man. After reading him, he asserted, he was exposed to the sin of pride in feeling that no man was his equal who was not in possession of the Catholic faith. So deeply had he been made to feel the truth and glory of the Catholic faith after reading Brownson that, far from feeling any reason to apologize for the faith that was his, he could not but feel that an apology was due him from every man who differed from him. This, he affirmed, he owed to Brownson more than to all other Catholic writers combined.[60]

As a lifelong controversialist, Brownson was of course in a number of heated controversies, but to whatever temperature the heat of controversy might rise, he always made it a point of honor as well as of conscience to deal fairly in presenting his opponent's side of the argument. Truth was his quarry at all times. Disingenuousness was almost as distasteful to him as outright falsehood. Speaking of the matter, he said:

> Many a man may find in our pages his objections to our views put in a clearer and stronger light than he had himself put them. We make it a rule to meet an opponent in his strength, not his weakness, and answer his objections in their real meaning, without chicanery, or the substitution of any false or collateral issue. We write never to win a victory, but always to elicit, defend, or recommend the truth, and we cannot understand how a Christian, or even a man who respects himself, can do otherwise, and yet we have rarely met a man who, in arguing against Catholicity, consents to meet the question on its merits. There is less, both of candor and clear, sharp intelligence in popular writers, and even writers of reputation, than is commonly supposed. Some of the criticisms of our own religious friends, as well as enemies, confirm us in this. There are few men who can write without prejudice, fewer still, perhaps, who can go at once to the heart of a question, and seize vividly and firmly the principle on which it hangs.[61]

In his great fairness in presenting his opponents' views in their fullest force, Brownson showed kinship with Thomas Aquinas. In his excellent treatise, entitled *Guide to Thomas Aquinas,* Joseph Piefer remarked: "Thomas expounds the arguments of the opposite camp; if theological matters are under discussion, these arguments may well be heretical; yet the reader will almost be inclined to consider the arguments irrefutable — so entirely without bias does Thomas present them. He himself brings to light their force with a persuasiveness which the opponent himself might well have envied."[62]

One of the distinct advantages Brownson had as a Catholic controversialist was the fact that he could lay claim to a knowledge of both sides of the question relative to Catholicity and Protestantism. "Think you," he remarked in his analysis of Transcendentalism, "that we, who, according to your own story, have tried every form of Protestantism, and disputed every inch of Protestant ground, would ever have left the ranks of Protestantism in which we were born, and under whose banner we fought so long and suffered so much, if there had been any other alternative for us?"[63] In many a case a disputant may say with some truth: "What you say is true enough, but you do not take a broad view of the whole question. You see only your own side of it." This could scarcely be alleged in Brownson's case. He had his answer for James Freeman Clarke when Clarke remarked that there would be no point at all in refuting the arguments Brownson had advanced in favor of Catholicity since "judging by experience. Mr. Brownson would himself be ready to confute [them] in the course of a year or two. No man has ever equalled Mr. Brownson in the ability with which he has refuted his own arguments." If, replied Brownson, your argument is that as Protestant I was in the habit of changing my views "about once every three months," how do you account for the fact that as Catholic I have made no change in these six years? "You cannot say," he added, "that it is owing to our ignorance, either of Protestantism or of Catholicity, for you concede that we have said the best things that can be said in favor of, as well as against each. . . ."[64] That is, on Clarke's own admission, he was thoroughly acquainted with both sides of the question.

And Brownson was by no means without advantages, too, in dealing with the skeptic or infidel scientist in a day when much went under the imposing name of science which was nothing more than unsupported theory or mere conjecture.

In an article on *The Conflict of Science and Religion*, he asked fearlessly and scathingly:

> Well, gentlemen, what truth of science do you allege that the Church prohibits, opposes, or contradicts in her teaching? . . . What fact or truth that you yourselves dare pretend is scientifically certain or unquestionable, that conflicts with her teaching, or which she anathematizes? Can you name one? Suffer me to tell you that you cannot. We take no pride in the fact, but, we belonged to your party before we became a Christian, and we find, in reading your works, nothing . . . we were not familiar with before any of you were heard of, and before some of you, it may be were born. Our youth was fed on the literature from which you pilfer, and our young mind was nourished with the absurd and blasphemous theories and speculations which you are putting forth at present as something new, original, and profound — as science even — but which had become an old story with us long before you reproduced them. And we know, *minus* a few details or variations of phrase, all that you can say in favor of your pretended science, and all you can maintain against the Church. Were we not trained in Boston, "the Hub of the Universe," at a time it

was really the focus of all sorts of modern ideas, good, bad, and indifferent? What has any one of you to teach one who participated in the Boston intellectual movement from 1830 to 1844? We Bostonians were a generation ahead of you. We have the right to speak with confidence, and we tell you beforehand that you have no truth the Church denies, and that you have disproved or demonstrated the falsity of no doctrine the Church teaches.[65]

A man such as Brownson who had brought so much to the Catholic cause when he left Protestantism, was bound to encounter those who would look upon him as more or less a traitor from their ranks. A man named Hoover, somewhat disreputable in character, from Charleston, South Carolina, began abusing Brownson one day to his publisher, Benjamin H. Greene, calling him a traitor to his country, another Benedict Arnold, because he had become a Catholic. When Brownson suddenly appeared in the doorway, Mr. Greene said to the assailant: "There is Mr. Brownson himself, talk to him." Whereupon Hoover turned to Brownson and began abusing him violently for having become a Catholic. Brownson interrupted him at once, saying: "Another word and I will throw you over that stovepipe," which ran from the front of the store to the rear. As Hoover continued his violent invectives, Brownson took hold of his coat-collar with one hand and the seat of his trousers with the other, and forthwith pitched him over the stovepipe. Hoover initiated an action for assault and battery against Brownson, but it came to naught as the local Masonic lodge, looking into Hoover's dossier, advised him to leave town. Henry Brownson tells us that the phrase, to *Hooverize* someone, was added to the language at the time, but gradually fell into desuetude.[66]

Brownson's heart was wholly in the defense of the Catholic Church, which afforded him an ample outlet to his immense energies altogether congenial to his gifts and temperament. During the honeymoon period of his conversion, before the stormy times came, and they came quickly indeed, he enjoyed some good days. When he rapidly gained weight until he tipped the scales at two hundred and fifty pounds (he had previously weighed two hundred), he jocosely attributed it to his newfound peace of conscience. One day he was walking down Washington street in Boston with one of his sons when he was accosted by two doctors of divinity, Slater and Woods, who were as spare as Brownson had formerly been. As they conversed, one of them asked: "How is it, Brother Brownson, that you, who used to be as lean as we are, have grown so big of late? Tell us the secret."

To which Brownson replied: "It is all very simple; all you have to do is to become Catholic, go to confession and get your sins off your conscience and you will grow fat and laugh."[67]

Another instance of pleasant banter, but which, however, Brownson intended to convey a solemn truth, is recorded by his son Henry. The friendly relations between Brownson and his publisher, Benjamin Greene, began when they were both Unitarian ministers, and grew firmer when Greene became the publisher of his *Boston Quarterly Review*. The same friendly relationship continued on after Brownson had become a Catholic and Greene was still retained as the publisher of his Catholic *Review*. Some years after Greene had served Brownson as a Catholic reviewer, he pretended to Brownson that he had a right to a reward in the life to come for having published such a sturdy Catholic *Review,* and asked Brownson if he did not think so, too. To which Brownson replied: "Yes, I believe you will have your reward, and once in a million years will be permitted to rest your foot for a millionth of a second on the coolest spot in Satan's dominions."[68] This is indicative of the uncompromising character of Brownson's apologetics in general; he was fearful all his life, as his writings clearly show, of holding out false hope to anyone where the eternal salvation of the soul was at stake.

It is somewhat astonishing that a man living in the midst of the world, as did Brownson, could write in that deep Catholic spirit which marks his eloquent pages. This we could readily understand of the monk writing in his cell, sheltered from the contagion of the world, but the layman in the world enjoys no such advantage. Perhaps his great love for the writings of the early Fathers and Doctors of the Catholic Church helps to explain it. But apparently the full explanation of his deep Catholic spirit is that it flowed from his own interior spiritual life. He always wrote with the crucifix before him, flanked by a statue of the Blessed Virgin Mary. He wore Our Lady's scapular and recited the rosary daily, usually at sundown. These pious practices were dear to him as aids to meditation on the great mystery of the Incarnation, rendered his faith more lively, and strengthened his charity toward God and his neighbor. His constant meditation on the Blessed Trinity and the Incarnation not only enlightened his mind and guided his pen, but also excited such love and gratitude in his heart as had the power, his son tells us, to save him from any temptation to rebel against ecclesiastical authority (as happened in the case of so many distinguished Catholic leaders of the day), however great the provocation, or of yielding in any degree to a desire for popularity.[69] Orestes Brownson did not wear his religion on his sleeve, but was nonetheless a deeply religious man. As Virgil Michel remarked: [His] piety was of the nature of those whom the Gospel mentions as especially fit for the kingdom of Heaven."[70]

As time wore on, Brownson became more and more aware that he was operating under a decided handicap, namely, the lack of a more resourceful library. Some needed books he had, others he did not have. Looking over Brownson's library when he visited him here in 1853, Lord Acton (then Sir John) estimated its contents at "about 1,500 volumes."[71] (George Bancroft's library of 5,000 volumes Acton supposed to be the largest private library in the country.) Brownson could of course borrow books from the Harvard Library, but even that library Acton found to be "very incomplete by German standards."[72] Brownson acknowledged at the time that he could not lay his hand on books he needed. Acton tells us that during his four-day visit with him at Mt. St. Mary's College, Emmitsburg, Maryland, in 1853, Brownson had remarked that he was thinking of writing on the Council of Constance (1414-1418), but Acton advised against it, telling him he did not have the required sources to draw upon.[73] Whatever the effect of Acton's counsel, Brownson never did write on the theme *ex professo*.

Nothing in the Church did Brownson appreciate more as an individual member and as a Catholic apologist than papal authority. He had at long last found an authority that could give him security against error. He had had much sad experience with error in its multiple forms as he had painstakingly picked his way through various systems of thought both of the ancient and modern world until he was finally led, humanly speaking, along the road of philosophy to the threshold of the Catholic Church. Search as he would, he had long been the sport and victim of many an *ignis fatuus*. A few weeks after his conversion, in an oration in Old Broadway Tabernacle in New York City, he compared himself for the last twenty years to one stepping on cakes of ice, each one of which was barely enough to support his weight until he could reach the next, until at last he had come to solid ground.[74] He expressed the matter slightly differently when he wrote: "[The convert] is conscious of an unfailing support, and no longer fears he is in danger every step he takes of falling through."[75] It was the papacy that provided him that support and that certainty. "The papacy is," he said, "the Church, the pope is the Vicar of Jesus Christ on earth, and, if you war against the pope, it is either because you would war against God, or because you believe God can lie. If you believe God has commissioned the pope, and that God will keep his promise, you must believe his authority is that of God, and can be no more dangerous than would be the authority of Our Lord, were he present to exercise it in person."[76]

Speaking of Brownson as an apologist, we should not overlook the fact that the most formidable argument he ever furnished the American public in favor of the Catholic Church was his own conversion. That a man in whom reason was so powerful, whose sincerity and love of truth was beyond question, who had run the gamut of religious affiliations, who had tried all theories of social and religious progress of the modern world, and had then turned at long last to the Catholic Church as the only answer to all the problems of life — here was a phenomenon that should have given thinking men pause. And the significance of his conversion for Catholics themselves was well noted by a Catholic contemporary:

> At a time when a dark cloud of slander and persecution is overhanging our Church in this country, and when Catholics are bitterly assailed, not only in their religion, but in their very persons and character, it must be consoling that such a man as Mr. Brownson has thought proper, after a long and mature investigation, to embrace our holy religion. The testimony of one such man for us is far more weighty than that of a thousand fierce and unmitigated bigots against us; for *his* testimony is disinterested and founded upon an enlightened judgment; *theirs* is often the result of mere blind passion, and of the grossest ignorance and prejudice.[77]

# 23

## ARGUING THE CASE FOR THE CHURCH

*Brownson explains why he became a Catholic in the article "The Church against No-Church" • His controversy with the Rev. James H. Thornwell, professor of Sacred Scripture and the Evidences of Christianity in the South Carolina College • Letters relative to the controversy • Brownson's significant article on "The Church a Historical Fact" • He defends the Catholic Church in the political order against the unpatriotic charge • He adopts a new and higher tactic in its defense • He stresses heavily the necessity of the Catholic Church to sustain our free popular institutions • His exhaustive examination of Transcendentalism • His review of books by Margaret Fuller • He asserts the equality of the sexes, and pays a grand tribute to womanhood • His important distinction between persons and doctrines • Transcendentalism exalts the inferior soul above man's spiritual nature, and has no answer to the origin and problem of evil • C. C. Hollis's tribute to Brownson's shrewd approach to Transcendentalism • Brownson's reply to Richard Hildreth's counterattack upon him • As a Catholic apologist Brownson gave a full and clear exposition of Catholic doctrine.*

Some there are who count Orestes Brownson second to none as a Catholic apologist in the age in which he lived. A man of vast diversified learning, he defended the Church on all fronts — the theological, the philosophical, the political, the literary, the historical, the scientific, with occasional incursions into other fields. He had the advantage, too, of living at a time before "specialization made it impossible for a man to work with equal facility in a dozen fields," as observed Arthur M. Schlesinger, Jr.[1] Inasmuch, however, as the major part of the nineteenth century was an era of great political turmoil and widespread discussion of forms of government, Brownson had perhaps more frequent occasion to meet the assailants of the Church on political than other grounds.

It was to be expected that a man of Brownson's temperament would make a formal statement to explain frankly to his former coreligionists just why after all he had become a Catholic. This he did in a forty-seven-page article he wrote for the July 1845 issue of his *Review* entitled: "The Church against No-Church." Although he called the article "incomplete" in respect to all that might have been said, it was one of the more massive and closely reasoned articles he had ever written. It was addressed to those Christians who admitted the Catholic Church in name, but denied it in fact — a state of mind toward which so many of the denominations were then tending. Assuming the fact that God has made a divine revelation to mankind, Brownson proceeded to show that Christ really did found a church, that he instituted an apostolic ministry to mediate his message to mankind, and that the true apostolic ministry is to be found in the Catholic Church alone. The article is typical of Brownson's ironclad reasoning. No doubt he felt that each link in his chain of reasoning was equally unbreakable, and that the force of the argument could not be evaded. But he was in for a surprise. Critics, both Unitarian and Episcopalian, objected that the argument was inconclusive and therefore unsatisfactory because he had assumed and not proven the fact of divine revelation made to mankind. The demurrer, as Brownson rightly observed, would have been perfectly valid in the mouth of a pagan or heathen, but without any validity in the mouth of anyone who called himself a Christian. In religious discussion between those who call themselves Christians, the fact of divine revelation is the basic starting point. Brownson had properly, if innocently, assumed it in addressing his former Christian coreligionists.[2]

The conclusion Brownson appended to his argument is not without interest:

> We have been asked, "How in the world have you become a Catholic?" In this essay we have presented an outline, or rather a specimen, of the answer we have to give. It is incomplete, but it will satisfy the attentive reader, that not without some show of reason, at least, have we left our former friends and endearing associations of our past life, and joined ourselves to a Church which excites only the deadly rage of the great mass of our countrymen. The change with us is a great one, and a greater one than the world dreams of, and one which may have cost us some sacrifice. At any rate, it is a change we would not have made, if we could have helped it — a change against which we struggled long, but for which, though it makes us a pilgrim and a sojourner in this life, and permits us no home here below, we can never sufficiently praise and thank God. It is a great gain to lose even earth for heaven. If, however, we be pressed to give the full reason for our change, we must refer it to the grace of God, and the need we felt of saving our soul. We were a sinner, and we wished to be reconciled to God.[3]

To what extent such laborious articles may have been the means of drawing others here or there to the Catholic faith, we cannot know. Bishop Patrick Kenrick of Philadelphia wrote Brownson in January of 1849 to say: "It will encourage you to know that your article, 'The Church against No-Church,' has led a physician (I cannot recall his name) to embrace the faith at Georgetown, as Father Mulledy assures me."[4]

A Mr. J. H. Longborough also wrote Brownson from Salem, Virginia, on January 22, 1846, to say that the article "Church against No-Church" had rescued him from the yawning abyss of infidelity. Although the article had not yet completely converted him, it had definitely faced him in the right direction. In part, he wrote:

> The attentive perusal of the article Church against No-Church has settled for me a difficulty which I have *suffered* for more than twenty years. Your argument has satisfied me that there are "mysteries of the faith" which the human mind cannot reason upon; for therefore I was, whenever I thought upon the subject, and reasoning upon it, but increasing my difficulties the more I reasoned. Thus I was almost settled in infidelity. Certainly, I was not a believer in the truth of the Bible. Your article has shown me the point at which the "natural" stops and the "supernatural" begins — or where the "supernatural" begins, which should, I suppose be placed first. . . . I congratulate you on the success of your argument on the church against no church in my own case — and I thank you. You have almost persuaded me to be a Christian, and entirely satisfied me that the true Church is the Holy Roman. It surely is the faith of ages. As such I at this moment esteem it.[5]

It is not of course possible to take notice of the many, many religious controversies in which Brownson was engaged with the assailants of the Catholic Church, particularly in the years immediately following his conversion. It must suffice to say that he was unwearied in his apostolic efforts to explain the true meaning of any Catholic doctrine he found misunderstood or misrepresented by those outside the Church, whether from ignorance or any other motive. On that score he did not overlook objections to the Catholic Church brought by mere popular writers, though the objections in some cases had been refuted already a hundred times over. They could still be stumbling blocks to sincere inquirers, and he deemed them worthy of his close examination. He was as thoroughgoing in his refutation of the simpler objections to the Church as in the case of those of a more philosophical nature. Whatever the difference he may have had at times with Catholics themselves, they did appreciate the good services he thus rendered in the cause of Catholic truth. A certain J. Elmsley wrote him from Toronto, Canada, seeking advice on the choice of a Catholic college in which to have his four sons educated, and wound up, saying:

> May Almighty God prosper you and your holy undertaking. You are an apostle in these latter days. Your pen is the most powerful weapon of offense and defense in the cause of the faith which has appeared in our own or any other language. The seed is sown, and the Lord will I trust grant an abundant harvest in his own good time.[6]

Most of Brownson's controversies, however, were carried on with adversaries of some culture and attainments in the intellectual world. One such controversy was with Rev. James H. Thornwell, a Presbyterian minister and professor of Sacred Literature and the Evidences of Christianity in the South Carolina College. In 1841 Professor Thornwell published an essay against the divine inspiration of those books of the Old Testament which Catholics accept as part of the canon of Sacred Scripture but which Protestants reject. To this essay the Rev. Patrick Lynch of Charleston, South Carolina, replied in a series of letters to Dr. Thornwell through the columns of the *Catholic Miscellany,* of which he was one of the editors. Thornwell's original essay, with the substance of Dr. Lynch's letters in reply, together with twenty-nine more letters of Dr. Thornwell covering practically the whole ground of controversy between Catholics and Protestants, was then put into book form in 1845 by Thornwell. The controversy on the Presbyterian side was conducted, as Brownson himself acknowledged, with considerable learning and ability. Into this theological fray Brownson himself was to enter at the pressing invitation of others.[7] Two letters will set the stage for his entry, one from a non-Catholic, the other from a convert to the faith.

Both gentlemen wrote Brownson as soon as Thornwell's book was off the press. Both quickly sensed that the situation had grown tense and dramatic. The letter of the non-Catholic came from Henry Sumner. Writing from Newberry, South Carolina, on January 21, 1845, he said in part:

> You . . . are aware that . . . a year has passed since a controversy originated in this state in relation to the Apocryphal Books, between Dr. Lynch and Professor Thornwell of South Carolina College. Thornwell has completed his task and published it in book form, labelled on the back of the volume: *Arguments of Romanists discussed and refuted.* The book is regarded by Presbyterians of this state as a complete overthrow of the whole system of the Catholic doctrine. I have read a portion of the book, and though he is as able as a man can be, yet there is a spirit of bitterness and rancour perhaps which can only be

justified on the supposition that he is fully satisfied that the Catholics are involved in gross and damnable error. I bring your attention to this book — for I am anxious that you should examine it and review it in your *Review*. It would be gratifying to many of your friends, were you to do so; and to me personally. I wrote to Messrs. Little & Brown, of your city, a few days since, to procure and present it to you for me. If you have not one, be so good to call on them and get it, and if you should, after examining it, come to the conclusion, not to notice it, will you write to me privately your opinion of it. But, before you determine, let me insist that you do review the book — for a searching and powerful article on it and the subjects involved would be of essential service to the cause of truth, not only here, but everywhere. You are engaged in the great work of enlightening the mind, and of presenting the truth as you embrace it — let your light *shine* — hide it not — and great may be the good conferred on some mind which, like yours was, is now seeking light.

The January issue of your *Review* is before me. I am highly pleased with its contents. The third and fifth articles I have not yet read, but the others I have, and I must say that "The Literary policy of the Church of Rome," and "Native Americanism" are powerful articles — that on "The British Reformation" is an able paper.

I learned, a few days since, that you delivered a lecture in Boston, the subject of which was to show that the only hope for the perpetuity of the institutions of our country is to be found in the doctrine of the Catholic Church. I see something of this in the article on "Native Americanism" — and though not prepared to agree with every sentiment advanced, I must confess that Protestantism has failed, as Protestantism, to effect much good for the people.

The other letter came from John Bellinger, M.D., who seems to have been quite concerned about the status of the Catholic Church in South Carolina. His letter had the merit of acquainting Brownson with the real posture of affairs in the controversy, in particular Dr. Lynch's inability to attempt any reply to Thornwell in the near future because of his pressing pastoral duties. Writing from Charleston on January 31, 1845, Mr. Bellinger said:

Sir:

I have sent you a copy of Rev. Mr. Thornwell's recently published letters on the Apocrypha, hoping that you will review them. He attacks, at length, our fundamental dogma — infallibility — and should be answered. Our champion, Dr. Lynch, is so engrossed by multifarious duties, that I do not believe that he can possibly reply for a long time to come; although it is his intention to do so when he can prepare a book. In the meantime our doctrine might be fairly stated and maintained; and our Holy Mother vindicated from the gross calumnies that this fresh assailant has endeavored to fix on her. This may be done in your *Review,* without any interference with Dr. L[ynch]'s intention or plans.

Excuse me for remarking that your progress towards Catholicity was watched by my family and self with intense interest — because of the services which we foresaw you would render to religion, and because, being all of us converts, we could conceive and sympathize with the state of mind and feeling through which you were passing. Among your admirers there are none, we are sure, who regard you with warmer sentiments than we do — strangers though we be. Strangers — yet brothers! For we feel, and know, that we are of the same faith and Christian brotherhood with yourself; and that we (however obscure) are combating in the same fight in which you hold such a conspicuous position.

I am, my dear sir, your fellow Catholic and fellow convert,

John Bellinger, M.D.[8]

In response to these importunities, Brownson inserted a brief notice of Thornwell's book at the end of his April *Review,* indicating that he would review it soon. This meant great encouragement to the leaders of the Catholic Church in South Carolina, for Thornwell's bold publication of his book was a gauntlet triumphantly thrown down to the "Romanists." The absence of any reply would most certainly be interpreted as meaning that no reply would possibly be made, that the Catholic side of the controversy had collapsed completely under the impact of Thornwell's swashbuckling onslaught. Thornwell taunted the Catholics, sneering that we are not "prattling babes or silly women," but are "bearded men."[9] Under such a vaunting attack, it is understandable that no one was more anxious than Dr. Lynch himself that Brownson review the book as soon as possible. When Brownson's reply did not appear in the next number of his *Review,* Dr. Lynch wrote him, saying in part: "The announcement contained in your April number, if I mistake not, that you would devote some pages of your excellent *Review* to an examination of Professor Thornwell's book on 'the Aprocrypha' caused us here to look with anxiety for your succeeding numbers. An article from your vigorous pen on that subject would be of great service to our Holy Religion. We trust, and none more earnestly than myself, that you have not changed your intention."[10] This of course removed all feeling of delicacy on Brownson's part restraining him from interfering in the controversy where Dr. Lynch was directly concerned, and he made reply to Thornwell in three separate articles, marked by his usual irrefragable logic. Neither Dr. Lynch nor anyone else felt any need to add anything to Brownson's devastating answer. Though Thornwell had brought a long series of charges against the Catholic faith, Brownson observed in conclusion that "in no instance has he done better than simply assume the point he was to prove."[11]

We may judge how Catholics felt about Brownson's reply from a letter (Rev.) J. J. O'Donnell wrote Brownson from Columbia, South Carolina, on January 1, 1849:

> I congratulate you and our holy faith on the manner in which you have *used up* Thornwell. The *Review* has created an excitement here, and the *Presbyterian bear* finds himself bearded in his den. He is seething and panting and foaming in the well-knit net you have flung around him; and his position in the college makes him feel his degradation tenfold. The Presbyterians want and ask for the *Review,* but once they get out of our hands, there is no tracing their navigation. I wish you would publish all three articles in one pamphlet. . . . The limited circulation of the *Review* is the only evil. This plan would obviate it and I think procure subscribers too.[12]

When Brownson found time to turn aside from refuting calumnious charges hurled at the Catholic Church, he showed a technique in apologetics that was expert and sagacious in presenting the Church affirmatively. This shone forth particularly in his article "The Church a Historical Fact." He repeatedly insisted that it is a fatal mistake for Catholic controversialists to allow themselves to be kept forever busy refuting objections urged by the adversaries of the Church. To him the only questions to be settled in religious controversy between Christians are: did Jesus Christ actually found a church? And if so, is this church the Catholic Church or some other? Once it is established that the Catholic Church is the church Christ founded, all debate on any particular questions is forthwith foreclosed. For all objections or arguments urged against such an authority are and must be quite futile and unavailing.[13]

However, it will not do for the adversaries of the Catholic Church to begin with a simple denial that Christ established a church. For *the simple existence of the Catholic Church,* stretching in unbroken succession from the time of the Apostles to the present moment, asserting itself to be the church of Christ, received as such for fifteen hundred years by nearly all Christendom, and still received as such by the overwhelming majority of all those bearing the Christian name, puts the Church in possession. But possession in law is *prima facie* evidence of title. It will not do then to call upon the Church to produce its titles that it is the true church of Christ; because the question is not, shall the Catholic Church be admitted to be the church of Christ? but, shall it be declared to be *not* the church of Christ? It is not a question of *putting* the Catholic Church in possession, but of *ousting* it from a possession it holds and has held from the beginning, and for the greater part of the time without any serious opposition. It is not a question of admitting the title of the Church, but of impeaching it.

"The *onus probandi* is, therefore, on the shoulders of the party contesting it. It is for them to show good and valid reasons for setting aside the title of the Church, and ejecting her from possession. A government *de facto* is, presumptively, a government *de jure,* and must be respected as such, till it is proved not to be. The Roman Catholic Church is unquestionably the Church of Christ *de facto,* and therefore is to be presumed to be His *de jure,* till evidence be produced to convict her of usurpation."[14]

Nor will it do to attempt to unchurch the Catholic Church by quoting Sacred Scripture, for they are an integral part of the Church in possession. From the very beginning the Church has been their legal keeper and interpreter. Adversaries cannot, therefore, legitimately quote them as the word of God against the Catholic Church, save in the sense it authorizes, unless they succeed in removing the presumption it derives in law from prescription, and getting themselves legal possession of them. The Church admits that the Scriptures, taken in the sense it authorizes, are the word of God. This is the full extent of its admission. But taken in any other sense, it denies them to be the word of God; for the word of God is not the mere letters, but the sense intended by the Holy Spirit. Consequently, before one can go into an inquiry as to their sense, one must, on the one hand, dispossess the Church of its prescriptive right to declare their sense, and establish one's own authority to be their legal interpreter. Till one or the other has been done, the sense of the Scriptures is not an open question, and cannot be opened without assuming the point in dispute.[15] To anyone who might complain that this tight line of reasoning left no chance at all to argue a case against the Catholic Church, Brownson replied:

> I am . . . predisposed to believe the Almighty to be more than a match for the devil, and that, if he should establish a church, he would so constitute it that no attack could be made upon it which should not recoil upon those who made it — no argument be framed against it which should not serve to demonstrate the folly and absurdity of its framers. It is unquestionably a very difficult matter to make an action lie against the Church, or to find a court in which an action can be legally commenced against her; but I have yet to learn that this is her fault.[16]

There are two ways, however, Brownson acknowledged, in which it is possible for the assailants of the Catholic Church to impeach its title. The one is to convict it of having contradicted in its teaching some known principle of reason; the other is to convict it of having contradicted itself in its teaching, that is, of having taught doctrines which mutually contradict one another. For no church could be from God that teaches, as the word of God, any doctrine which contradicts a known principle of reason. But a known *principle* of reason is to be emphasized in the case.

> A doctrine may be repugnant to our feelings, it may run athwart our prejudices, fancies, or caprices, and therefore seem to us very unreasonable, and yet contradict no known *principle* of reason. To be *above* reason is not necessarily to be *against* reason. The Church has unquestionably taught, and continues to teach, doctrines which are above reason, and concerning the truth or falsity of which reason has nothing to say; but no doctrine which contradicts any known *principle* of reason.

Nor can the Catholic Church be convicted of any real instance of a contradiction of itself, or a variation of its doctrine. This is a thing that even the Church's most learned and subtle enemies have never been, and never will be able, to do. The Church varies its *discipline* according to the exigencies of time and place in the course of ages, but it never teaches at one time and place a doctrine as of divine revelation which it does not teach as such in all times and places. Much less does it teach doctrines which are mutually self-contradictory. "Even her [the Catholic Church's] enemies are struck with the systematic consistency of her teaching. The infidel Saint-Simon declared that her catechism and her prayers are the most profoundly systematic works ever written."[17]

As an apologist, Brownson understood full well that it was just as important for him, if not even more so, to refute the Church's assailants on political as well as theological grounds. The unpatriotic charge so often preferred against Catholics is as old as Christianity itself. Said the Pharisees of Christ: "If we let him alone so, all will believe in him; and the Romans will come and take away our place and our nation."[18] This objection to Christ was political. The ancient Romans considered the Christians a menace to the state and rewarded them with ten fierce persecutions. Coming down to the nineteenth century, one of the most popular objections to the Church — in fact ever since 1789 — was that the Church is incompatible with the democratic form of government. In the sixteenth and seventeenth centuries when the age was monarchical, James I of England wrote (1617) his *Remonstrance for the Divine Rights of Kings and the Independency of their Crowns* in reply to a speech of the celebrated Cardinal Duperron in the States-General of France. The king objected to the papacy, and therefore to the Catholic Church, on the ground that it is incompatible with kingly government. The pope claimed to be superior to kings, held them subject to his spiritual authority, and consequently denied the independence of their crowns. But when the spirit of the times changed from the monarchical to the democratic temper, beginning with the French Revolution, then the great objection to the Catholic Church was that it denies popular sovereignty, and is incompatible with democratic or republican government. Numberless anti-papal journals, pamphlets, preachers and lecturers were briskly operative creating the impression — especially among the middle and lower classes of American society — that the predominance of the Catholic Church in this country would destroy our free institutions, and prove the grave of civil and religious freedom. Such an impression could only erect a formidable barrier to the spread of Catholicity in the country, and as an apologist Brownson was anxious to break a lance or two in the interest of truth.

337

Many other apologists of the day also took notice of this unpatriotic charge against Catholics, but what is most worthy of note in Brownson's answer to the charge is the technique he employed. While other apologists assumed only sectarian ground in being content to show merely that Catholicity is in harmony with the American Constitution or Republic — thus unwittingly making the Republic the touchstone of all truth natural and supernatural — Brownson assumed higher ground, stoutly maintaining that religion, if anything at all, is the supreme law of life, and that therefore one must conform his politics to his religion and not his religion to his politics. Religion being ultimate rather than politics, he emphasized, no political theory or form of government is ever to be admitted as a test or standard by which religion is to be tried. He wrote:

> Religion if anything, is for men the supreme law, and must take precedence over everything else; and the very idea of a Church, is that of an institution founded by Almighty God for the purpose of introducing and sustaining the supremacy of law in the government of human affairs. If religion and politics are opposed, politics, not religion, must give way. No man, I care not who he is, whether Catholic or Protestant, pagan or Mahometan [Muhammadan], if he has any conception of religion at all, denies, or can deny, that he should place his religion first, and that all else in life should be subordinated to it. He who denies that his religion should govern his politics, as well as his action, virtually denies morality, denies the divine law, and asserts political atheism. To subject his religion to his politics, or to object to religion because it is incompatible with this or that political theory, is, in principle, to deny the sovereignty of God himself, and to fall below the most degrading form of gentilism.[19]

Without, then, subordinating his religion in any way to his politics, Brownson made formal reply to the unpatriotic charge that the religion of Catholics is incompatible with democratic government in two articles in his *Review* the year after his conversion, 1845, namely, "Catholicity necessary to Democracy,"[20] and "Native Americanism."[21] In these two articles he advanced the theory that the unassisted virtue and intelligence of the people are insufficient to sustain democracy or popular liberty. "A republic can stand only as it rests upon the virtues of the people and these not the mere natural virtues of worldly prudence and social decency, but those loftier virtues which are possible to human nature only as elevated above itself by the infused habit of supernatural grace."[22] To all those optimistic enough to believe that the natural probity of the people alone is sufficient to guarantee sound government, he tartly replied: "It is a beautiful theory, and would work admirably, if it were not for one little difficulty, namely, *the people are fallible, both individually and collectively, and governed by their passions and interests, and produce much mischief.* . . . Who or what is to take care of the people, and to assure us that they will always wield the government so as to promote justice and equality, or maintain order, and the equal rights of all, of all classes and interests? Do you answer by referring to the virtue and intelligence of the people? We are writing seriously, and have no leisure to enjoy a joke, even if it be a good one."[23]

After showing that neither education nor the public press can supply the required augmentation of virtue and intelligence in the case — though they can do something — he proceeded further to demonstrate that religion alone can supply the want, but that it must be a religion which is entirely free and independent of popular control, that is over and *above* the people, speaking from on high, and able to command them — which is the Catholic religion

338

alone. Protestantism, he acknowledged, may indeed originate and establish free institutions, but, as he saw it, lacks the power to sustain them, for it is itself too much subject to popular control, popular passions, interests, prejudices, or caprices, and imparts not the requisite degree of supernatural virtue and intelligence for the people to rise above mere temporal interests and seductions to govern themselves wisely. As to the widespread charge, then, that Catholicity is incompatible with democratic government, he said forthrightly:

> Here is our hope for our republic. We look for our safety to the spread of Catholicism. We render solid and imperishable our free institutions just in proportion as we extend the kingdom of God among the people, and establish in their hearts the reign of justice and charity. Here, then, is our answer to those who tell us that Catholicism is incompatible with free institutions. *We tell them that they cannot maintain free institutions without it.* It is not a free government that makes a free people, but a free people that make a free government.[24]

These must indeed have been novel thoughts not only to the members of the Nativist party of the day, but especially to such prominent men in the nation as Dr. Lyman Beecher, Samuel B. Morse, John Breckenridge and all their ilk who had been giving fiery lectures and writing their flaming letters to convince the American people that the spread of Catholicity in the country would ring the death knell once and for all on the free institutions of the land.[25] What unheard of audacity for this American renegade to be saying such things to his former coreligionists! What impudence! "What gave sting to Brownson's words," remarks Ralph Henry Gabriel, "was the fact that he was not a foreigner, but had been born and reared a Protestant among the granite hills of Vermont."[26] "Protestants themselves," continued Brownson, "have foolishly raised the question of the influence of Catholicity on democracy, and have sought to frighten our countrymen from embracing it by appealing to their democratic prejudices, or, if you will, convictions. We have chosen to meet them on this question, and to prove that democracy without Catholicity cannot be sustained." If any of his countrymen resented what he was saying, he reminded them:

> We are American as well as they, love our country as much, and have as much at stake as any one of them; for, in becoming a Catholic, we did not cease to be a man, a citizen, or a patriot; and we are as well convinced as we are that we are now writing, that the preservation and wholesome working of our democratic institutions depend on the general prevalence among our people of the Catholic religion. We say this not merely as a Catholic convert, but as the citizen who has not wholly neglected political and philosophical studies.[27]

The necessity of the Catholic religion to sustain democracy had become so deep a conviction with Brownson that he was constantly repeating it in these years. When he reviewed Bishop Francis Patrick Kenrick's *The Primacy of the Apostolic See Vindicated,* he reiterated that where the Catholic Church does not predominate to inspire the people with reverence, and to teach and accustom them to obedience to authority, democracy readily becomes a mischievous dream.[28] In his remarkable article on "National Greatness" he lamented that under popular forms of government the people tend to forget the supernatural end for which they were created, lose contact in their aspirations and conduct with things invisible and eternal, and readily come to set their hearts wholly on the acquisition of wealth and worldly dis-

339

tinctions. Yet there is no reason why it should be so, he said, where at least the majority of the people are truly Christian, live by faith, feel that this world is not their true home, and prepare for another and better world. But in the matter of restraining the people from an overweening attachment to the things of this world he counted the influence of the Catholic Church indispensable. Hence "democracy with the Church would be a good form of government, if not indeed the best of all forms of government; without the Church, it is the worst, as our own experience as a people, if we continue as we have been going on, will soon demonstrate to all who have eyes to see or hearts to understand."[29]

With this trend of thought Brownson opened up a new line of apologetics which, as Thomas P. Neil observed in *They lived the Faith,* enabled such eminent churchmen as Cardinal Gibbons and Archbishop John Ireland to develop later the theme that a good Catholic in the United States makes a good American citizen.[30] But it took an incredibly bold and fearless man in Brownson's day to preach such a doctrine as the necessity of the Catholic religion for the maintenance and preservation of the free institutions of the land. The day was yet far, far off when the Catholic Church would be so well appreciated in the country that such a distinguished churchman as Cardinal Gibbons would have in attendance at his Golden Jubilee celebration in 1911, representatives of all faiths, including among other distinguished guests on the roster of speakers President Taft, former President Theodore Roosevelt, Elihu Root and James Bryce.[31]

Immensely interested in the establishment of truth and the overthrow of falsehood, it was inevitable but that Brownson would soon come around to a close examination of Transcendentalism — the form of philosophy he had been associated with for a time before his conversion. As an apologist, he was bound in duty to give it a searching analysis insofar as it now appeared to him that it was under its banner that those unfriendly to the Catholic Church were rallying to make their last stand.[32] And to him Transcendentalism loomed large. He did not suffer the idea that it was a small affair, just "a Yankee notion," thriving in a small corner of New England, but looked upon it as one of the dominant errors of the times, almost as rife in one section of the country as another, manifesting itself, at least in principle, in almost every popular anti-Catholic writer of the day, whether German, French, English, or American.[33] To him Transcendentalism was a fountainhead that was tincturing almost all modern philosophy and literature and bearing poisonous fruit in unsuspected places. He had little hope of influencing the Transcendentalists themselves, but by going into an exhaustive examination of it his aim was to put the unbitten on their guard, and to caution against what he called novel doctrines current in philosophy and literature.[34]

His approach to the subject was gradual. When Margaret Fuller published a memoir of a trip she had made the previous year through the Middle West under the title, *Summer on the Lakes,* Brownson took notice of it in the October 1844 issue of his *Review.*[35] To many, Miss Fuller (once the editor of *The Dial*) was the modern Aspasia of Boston, if not of the country. She was probably not wholly unconscious of her remarkable gifts. Whatever the merits of her famous Conversations, she is perhaps best remembered today for her remark which Emerson repeated to Carlyle, namely, "I accept the world." To which Carlyle replied: "Gad, she'd better."[36] Although Brownson acknowledged that Margaret exhibited certain gifts of a very high order, he plainly could not take her seriously. He mourned the great harm she was doing in substituting art for religion, and in adopting exotic principles for the stern morality of the Gospel. To him her memoir was a sad book he could not commend.

When she soon published another book, *Woman in the Nineteenth Century,* Brownson gave it an eight-page review, entitled "Miss Fuller and the Reformers."[37] A portion of her book aimed at giving the Women's Liberation Movement of her day a boost, if not at asserting the superiority of woman. Brownson had always maintained the equality of the sexes; only each had been allotted a different sphere in life, equally important and equally honorable. While owning exceptions in the matter, he felt that the happiness of society would be best consulted by each operating largely in his or her own respective sphere. He did not like comparisons where none are admissible. As to the superiority of the one, or the superiority of the other, he sagely observed, "Nothing can be said, except that the one is not the other, and would gain or lose nothing by being the other."[38] He agreed with Miss Fuller, of course, that there are evils, and very great evils in society, but he could not agree that they arise so largely from discrimination against women. While laying strictures on many of Miss Fuller's feminist ideas in her thesis, he had no fear of falling into "the common herd of libellers of women," for he had lived too long, and been too fortunate in his acquaintances, ever to think lightly of woman's worth, or woman's virtues. He wrote:

> We remember too vividly the many kind offices we have received from her hand, the firmness with which she clung to us in adversity, when all the world had deserted us, and also the aid which her rapid intuition and far-glancing sense has afforded us in our mental and moral progress, if we have made any, to be in danger of this. It has been our good fortune to have experienced all woman's tenderness, and her sympathy when we were in sorrow and destitution, her joy when the world brightened to us, her generous self-forgetfulness and self-sacrifice for the beloved of her heart, and the sweet and gentle companionship in intellectual pursuits and in moral duties which seem to double man's power and to make virtue thrice more amiable; and we do not feel, that, so long as we retain our memory, we can be in any danger of speaking lightly of woman, or of doing her injustice.[39]

Arlene Swidler gave Brownson's views on the "Woman Question" an exposition in the *American Benedictine Review* in 1968.[40] Perhaps she might have brought out a bit more clearly that he did definitely hold the doctrine of the equality of the sexes. In 1841 he wrote: "We admit her [woman's] equality, but we are as incapable of yielding her the supremacy as we should be of claiming it for ourselves."[41] Yet he was driven a trifle to the masculine side when the promoters of the women's rights movement claimed superiority for woman. In his autobiography he remarked that he had remained generally silent on the subject "till some of the admirers of Harriet Martineau and Margaret Fuller began to scorn equality and claim woman's superiority. Then I became roused, and ventured to assert my masculine dignity."[42] In our day he would no doubt have spurned Betty Friedan's *The Feminine Mystique,* but be in cordial agreement, at least by and large, with the ideas of Mrs. Helen B. Andelin in her book, *Fascinating Womanhood.*[43] He did not believe that society is bettered by women mixing on a large scale in politics. Brownson's son Henry remarks that his father's judgments on the question of women's rights "were not lightly or capriciously formed," and were constantly adhered to through life, "in spite of their unpopularity."[44] In the May 1869 issue of the *Catholic World,* Brownson published an article on the

"Woman Question" which was highly praised by Fr. Isaac Hecker, the editor, and by Archbishop John McCloskey of New York.[45] In the October 1873 issue of his *Quarterly,* he published another article under the same title.[46]

As a Transcendentalist, a goodly part of Miss Fuller's book, *Woman in the Nineteenth Century,* was also given over to the propagation of Transcendental doctrine. Brownson had often rebuked the Transcendentalists for their tenet that nature alone suffices for all man's wants, that nothing more is needed to reintroduce the lost Eden on earth than the free, full and harmonious cultivation of nature alone. While utterly rejecting this doctrine of Miss Fuller and the whole race of modern reformers, he nonetheless defended her and her book against certain animadversions which had appeared as newspaper criticisms. However acute any of his own remarks may have been, in concluding his review of her book he again made the distinction between the person and the doctrine advanced when he wrote:

> We are able, we trust, to distinguish between persons and doctrines. For persons, however far gone in error, or even sin, we trust we have the charity our holy religion commands, and which the recollection of our own errors and sins, equal to any we may have to deplore in others, requires us to exercise. But for erroneous doctrines we have no charity, no tolerance. Error is never harmless, and in no instance to be countenanced.[47]

Brownson's first major criticism of Transcendentalism was made in a fifty-page article in his *Quarterly,* July 1845, entitled: "Transcendentalism, or the latest Form of Infidelity."[48] He had once battled Andrews Norton for so labeling Transcendentalism, but he had now come to agree with him. After a painstaking examination of the real core of this new but pretentious philosophy, he came to the carefully reasoned conclusion that the plain, simple meaning of Transcendental doctrine is that *passion and imagination are superior to reason.* Insofar, it exalts what the schoolmen call the inferior soul, the seat of concupiscence, above man's spiritual nature, the soul. What the Transcendentalists call the impersonal soul of man, to them the higher nature, is simply the "carnal mind," spoken of in the Sacred Scriptures as man's inferior nature, which according to Christian faith, has been disordered by the fall, inclining man to evil. Transcendentalism, asserted Brownson, has revealed no new mystery, no new fact or element of human nature, but has simply called *higher* that which the Gospel calls *lower,* called true and good that which the Gospel calls false and evil, and *vice versa.* It flatly gives the lie to our Blessed Savior; where he says, "Deny thyself," it says, "Obey thyself," thus purporting in effect to liberate man from the restraints of reason, and to deliver him to the license of passion and imagination.[49] And not the least objectionable to Brownson was Transcendentalism's neo-Pelagian doctrine that man is utterly sufficient unto himself, and its total inability to give any explanation of the origin of evil in the world.[50] Evils of various kinds stalk the earth. Where do they come from?

In the critical process leading to these conclusions Brownson showed again his shrewdness in the attempt he made to meet the minds of the Transcendentalists realistically. He dealt at length with the Transcendental aesthetic theory, and pressed home his arguments from that angle, showing that the theory did not match reality. He was quite conscious beforehand of the fact that the Transcendentalists would not condescend to countenance philosophical arguments contravening their pet "faith." Knowingly he said: "Transcendentalists regard this question of proofs as a delicate one, and are apt to look upon a demand for proofs as a decided breach of politeness, a downright piece of impertinence. They do not reason; they affirm, and we should take their simple assertion as sufficient. They are not reasoners, but *seers;* and will we not believe them, when they tell us what they see?"[51] Hence a shrewd tactic was called for on Brownson's part in dealing with Transcendentalism. As C. C. Hollis has so well expressed the matter:

> Whether one accepts Brownson's position or not, this article is the best example of the logical force and dialectical skill for which he was famous. But of more significance to the present study, it also shows Brownson's shrewd awareness of the only approach open to the philosopher who wished to attack the new views. Emerson's famous statement that "a foolish consistency is the hobgoblin of little minds" spoke for a general conviction that lifted Transcendentalism above philosophical argument. Brownson recognized the futility of logical duel with enemies that spurned philosophical weapons, but he also saw one conviction they would defend, transcendental aesthetics. There may have been other passages to the lofty and apparently impregnable transcendental citadel, but if so, no philosopher in the nineteenth century found them.[52]

When the famous Transcendental novel, *Margaret, A Tale of the Real and Ideal, Blight and Bloom, including Sketches of a Place not before described, called Mons Christi,* appeared, Brownson viewed it with considerable alarm. Its appearance was to him positive confirmation that the Transcendental virus was spreading among the people. With this view, he set out to demonstrate that, by virtue of the acknowledged Protestant principle of private judgment, Transcendentalism was only the logical and historical evolution of Protestantism. Indeed, he entitled his article "Protestantism ends in Transcendentalism."[53] Although many Protestants might spurn the idea of passing under the name of Transcendentalists, he could not but regard the acknowledged Transcendentalists as the more respectable Protestants because they were more consistent. However that may be, he found Transcendentalism actually serving the cause of truth inasmuch as it was the last stage on this side of *nowhere.*[54] Once its falsity was perceived, there would be nothing left, he asserted, but to return to Catholicity or plunge on over into the abyss of nihilism. By his attacks on Transcendentalism he was attempting to carry the last fastnesses of what to him were the protean forms of Protestantism. The real question of the age he now regarded as between Catholicity and infidelity. He had been so far only clearing the ground for a discussion of the real question. Anyone, he said, who reads my previous writings against Anglicanism, No-Churchism and Transcendentalism, "will be troubled to find a single stronghold in which he may intrench himself between the Roman religion and infidelity."[55]

In spite of these poignant criticisms of Transcendentalism, it will not, however, do at all to suppose that Brownson was without a sympathetic regard for the Transcendentalists themselves. (Again the distinction between persons and doctrines is in place.) He had by no means forgotten that he himself had once been of their number, although never in any full sense. Whatever the nature or tendency of Transcendentalism, he remembered well the noble sentiments in which the movement had originated, and in which he himself had shared enthusiastically for a time. He and others had deeply lamented the infidelity they had everywhere encountered, and nothing was further from their thoughts than to disseminate doubt themselves. They had wished to get rid of doubt. In a passage that strongly supports Perry Miller's interpretation of Transcendentalism as a "religious demonstration,"[56] he remarked of the early Transcendentalists:

We were generically Protestants; we accepted in good faith the Protestant movement, and we confided in the principle of private judgment; but we deplored the infidelity we everywhere encountered. It was our grief that the temple had been battered down, the altar overthrown, the Holy of Holies profaned, and the worship of the Most High suspended. How often have we and our more intimate friends, in those days when our countrymen were everywhere denouncing us as disorganizers, infidels, seeking to destroy faith and abolish religious worship, mourned together over the desolation of Zion, and given vent to our earnest longings to see the waste places restored, the Church of God rise from its ruins, with more than its pristine beauty, symmetry, and glory, and the world once more be able to say, "I believe!" We felt deeply that doubt is the death of all life, that there is no living without faith; and our earnest desire, and unremitting efforts, were to discover the means of its recovery. We owe this statement in justice to ourselves, and to those of our former friends who have not had the happiness of following us into the Church of God.[57]

As this indicates, the Transcendentalists, Brownson and the others, had in fact been looking for a solid and imperishable basis for a new and more living faith. But, alas, upon close examination of their new "religion," for those who were willing to understand, at least for Brownson, it had turned out that they had not found it. Yet his former associates had been deserving of something better than "the sneers and scoffs they [had] received from an unsympathetic world," as he remarked years later.[58] He concluded his exhaustive treatise on Transcendentalism by assuring his former associates that what they were so earnestly seeking and so ardently craved would be found in the Catholic Church and there alone.[59] As to Transcendentalism, "it is merely 'much ado about nothing,' or 'a tempest in a teapot.' Dressed up in the glittering robes of a tawdry rhetoric, or wrapped in the mystic folds of an unusual and unintelligible dialect, it may impose on the simple and credulous; but to attempt to satisfy one's spiritual wants with it is as vain as to attempt to fill one's self with the east wind, or to warm one's freezing hands on a cold winter's night by holding them up to the moon."[60]

As in the case of Transcendentalism, some of the topics which now engaged Brownson's attention were carry-overs from his pre-conversion days. Such was the case with Richard Hildreth's theory of morals. It was not to be expected that the murderous onslaught Brownson had made on his theory would end there. Hildreth came back furiously in a pamphlet entitled: *A Joint Letter to O. A. Brownson, and the Editor of the North American Review.* (The *North American Review* had also made an attack on his theory.) Hildreth's very title was unfortunate, and gave Brownson an opening for an acute thrust. Always wide awake, as remarks C. C. Hollis, for the detection of any inaccuracies in the use of language or grammar, Brownson reminded Hildreth rather pertly that a joint letter is not a letter addressed by one person to several others in common, but a letter addressed in the joint names of two or more authors, whether to one or many. "As it is not probable [said Brownson with tongue-in-cheek] that Mr. Hildreth wishes to deny his identity, or to intimate that he is, as the respectable Mrs. Malaprop says, 'two gentlemen at once,' he would express himself more correctly, in our judgment, if he would say, *A Letter addressed conjointly,* etc. A philosopher should never disdain to use language correctly."[61]

When it came to the reply itself Hildreth had made to Brownson, he was even more unfortunate than in the title of his pamphlet. Completely losing his temper, he loaded Brownson with such inelegant names as "Gnostic, Sophist, Thwackum," etc. To which Brownson quietly made reply: "Some men will be ridiculous, though you call them by their baptismal names; others cannot be made ridiculous, call them what ridiculous names you will. Moreover, admitting the appropriateness of these names, we cannot perceive how from them Mr. Hildreth can logically conclude the soundness of his Theory of Morals:

"Mr. Brownson objects to my Theory of Morals;

But Mr. Brownson is a Gnostic, a Sophist, a Thwackum;

Therefore, my Theory of Morals is sound.

"The man who could reason in this way would make an admirable professor of logic!"[62]

Brownson assured Mr. Hildreth that he had read his letter with becoming care, but that he could not find that he had vindicated his theory from the very grave objections he himself had brought against it. Mr. Hildreth's restatement of his theory only reassured critic Brownson that he had apprehended him rightly in the first instance, and had in no way misrepresented him. Nor had Hildreth bettered his case by calling him "a Gnostic of the Roman school." Brownson owned that he was now a Catholic, but pointed out that he was not when he wrote his original critique of the book, for his conversion dated only from October of the previous year, and the ethical theory he had opposed to Hildreth's was one which, consistently or inconsistently, he had advanced for years. "A moralist," acerbly observed Brownson, "should be exact even in trifles."[63]

Again Brownson laid down the basic principle that no doctrine except the one which makes morality consist solely and simply in obedience to the will of God can abide the test of reason. On that score atheism leaves just as little foundation for morals as for theology. But how ascertain the will of God? Up to a certain point, it is disclosed by the light of reason, with which a system of natural morality may be constructed. This is good and true as far as it goes, but it is deficient in clearness, extent and power, as may be gathered from the history of all nations destitute of divine revelation. Only divine revelation, authoritatively interpreted, can supply the deficiencies in the case.[64] It was on this score that he found Theodore Jouffrey's ethical system coming short, too. Brownson's clear statement on the elements with which a sound ethical system is constructed is instructive. Of Jouffrey's system in particular, he said:

> His ethical system we reject, because it is constructed from principles derivable solely from natural reason, and natural reason cannot furnish adequate and safe rules for the conduct of life. We do not dispute the reality of the law of nature (droit naturel); we admit that ethics is a science, but a science whose chief fundamental principles must be borrowed from faith, the supernatural revelation God has made to us. We believe that God has made us a revelation of truths pertaining to the supernatural order, and because it was necessary for the conduct of life that we know them. Believing this, we cannot believe in the sufficiency or safety of rules which are deduced from natural reason alone. If natural reason could have sufficed for our guidance, no supernatural revelation would have been needed or made. From the fact, that such a revelation has been made, we infer its necessity; and from its necessity, it is perilous to disregard it.[65]

But to return to Hildreth's slashing attack, Hildreth as well as many others, were puzzled over why Brownson had become a Catholic. Attempting to interject a little mordant spice into his pamphlet, Hildreth had suggested that it was perhaps visions of lawn sleeves, a cardinal's hat, or even perhaps the thought of a Yankee pope that had floated before Orestes's imagination and had captivated him. "What, even, if the Church should have a Yankee pope? Does not Orestes I sound as high and as probable as Gregory VII or Gregory XVI?" To which the new convert quietly replied that it was, after all, too bad for him as there was "a lady in the way." He was a married man, and no dispensable being possible in the case, he simply had to submit. He assured Mr. Hildreth that he estimated him far above his worth in the visions of grandeur he had conjured up for his future. "We are nothing to the Church," he said, "except that we have a soul to be saved. It is not the Church that needed us, but we needed the Church; and we would fain hope that a poor sinner, long beaten about in the world, might fly to her maternal bosom and find peace for his troubled conscience, rest for his weary soul, and helps to a holy life, without dreaming of lawn sleeves, or even a cardinal's hat."[66]

In many of the controversies in which our Catholic apologist was engaged it was his aim not merely to meet and refute the assailants of the Catholic Church, but also to give a full and clear exposition of the Catholic doctrine involved. As examples, his two articles, "Faith not possible without the Church,"[67] and "Liberalism and Catholicity,"[68] give a full, clear and profound exposition of the act of supernatural faith. The dominant notes of his exposition were always clarity and power. Sir John Acton remarked of Brownson in his letter to Ignaz Döllinger: "The bishops regard him very highly. Several believe he can write on dogmatics as well as any Father of the Church."[69] When Theodore Maynard remarked that Brownson's "forthrightness and honesty and courage . . . were united to a power of exposition that has rarely, if ever, been equalled," he only expressed what is readily perceived by any attentive reader of Brownson's writings.[70] For we have in his writings his own profound reflections on the thought of the great fathers and doctors of the Church of all past ages in their interpretation of the great body of Christian doctrine. His was the advantage of being benefited by the light of the masters of past ages, and ours the advantage of sharing in that light that has come to us through the alembic of his own independent and original mind. No man was ever less the copy of another. He was the one and only Orestes A. Brownson, genuinely respectful of the Christian wisdom of past ages, but deeply conscious of a personal mission of so presenting Christian doctrine as to make it understandable to modern man. In all things he was ever eminently contemporary, and ever addressed himself to the scene before him, both at home and abroad. As the famed Quin O'Brien of the Chicago bar said in his address at the meeting of "The Friends of Brownson" in May 1926: "He [Brownson] was one of the greatest minds and souls that ever flourished under the American flag — theologian, essayist, reviewer, historian, controversialist beyond compare."[71]

Inasmuch as Brownson was a reviewer and literary critic by profession, it would seem in place to devote a separate chapter to his principles of literary criticism and their application in his writings.

# 24

## BROWNSON'S PRINCIPLES OF LITERARY CRITICISM

*Standards of literary criticism set by Thomas Stearns Eliot •*
*Brownson's similar basic standards: Catholic faith and morals •*
*The dictum of Gerard Manley Hopkins on this form • Brownson*
*discusses the relative importance of the content and matter of art •*
*His critique of "R. W. Emerson's Poems" • His great praise of*
*Daniel Webster's classical style, and his less flattering estimate of*
*other prominent American authors • His pronouncements on*
*Byron, Wordsworth and other English poets • His estimate of*
*James Fenimore Cooper, Nathaniel Hawthorne and other Ameri-*
*can novelists • He acknowledges the importance and popularity of*
*the modern novel, but feels compelled to utter his protest against its*
*grave blemishes in many respects, especially among the "realists"*
*• His thought on the religious novel • His estimates of George*
*Bancroft and Francis Parkman as historians • He falls into a hassle*
*with John Gilmary Shea over Henry de Courcy's history,* The Catholic
Church in the United States *• Lawrence Sterne's dictum on the offen-*
*sive office of a critic • Brownson reviews his own* The Spirit-Rapper:
An Autobiography.

In an article entitled *Dogma and Literature* in the October 1956 issue of the *Irish Ecclesiastical Record,* the author, Fr. Thomas Halton, remarked that the *ars gratia artis* principle had been operative in literature now for a full three hundred years with the result of the complete secularization of literature, especially the novel. For a slight change in this state of affairs, he gave considerable credit among eminent literary critics to Thomas Stearns Eliot who hammered out a new literary *credo* in two works he published, *The Sacred Wood* (1920) and *Homage to Dryden* (1924). *The Sacred Wood* he subtitled *A Primer of Orthodoxy* to indicate its didactic nature, and its concern with first principles. The central theme put forward in the last-named book is that no literary criticism can be considered fully valid or complete that does not include an evaluation of a work from a definite ethical or theological standpoint, the Christian one. Because of his insistence on this principle, T.S. Eliot, asserted Fr. Halton, must be looked upon as having inaugurated a critical movement in modern times which acknowledges the prior claims of the supernatural in the literary realm, and insists that the greatness of no literary work can ever be judged by mere artistic literary canons.

One almost receives the impression from Fr. Halton's discussion of the matter that the modern world has had to wait on T.S. Eliot to bring forward and formulate these Christian standards of literary criticism as something brand-new in the modern world. But this is scarcely true, for perhaps no eminent literary critic ever insisted more staunchly on bringing all literary works to a definite theological test, namely, that of Christian faith and morals, than did Orestes A. Brownson. That he reached a genuine eminence as a literary critic seems beyond question. After a close analysis of Brownson's theory of aesthetics, Charles Carroll Hollis concluded: "For the theory itself, it must be admitted that Brownson was not always as clear and as logical as one might wish, but in fairness to him, it must be granted that he pioneered in an area which none had mapped before him and which few, with the exception of Maritain, have explored with as full regard to the integrity of art."[1]

We are here concerned with Brownson as a reviewer or literary critic during his Catholic career. Whatever the value of his former literary criticisms, it was only as a Catholic that he began to formulate his principles of literary criticism with assurance and finality. It was not that he ever evolved systematically a set body of principles which he had at hand; it was rather that he formulated and applied his thought-out principles as he went along from year to year according to the nature of the books sent to him for literary notice. In this, as in all else, his standards of judgment were formed in the light of man's ultimate destiny as disclosed by the teachings of divine revelation. "We live under the Gospel," he said, "and we insist upon our right to try all things by the Christian standards."[2] The dictum of Gerard Manley Hopkins on this matter was the same except that he expressed it differently when he said: "The only just judge, the only just literary critic, is Christ, who prizes, is proud of, and admires, more than any man, more than the receiver himself, the gifts of his own making."[3]

Holding inflexibly to Christian standards in the realm of literary criticism, Brownson early acquired the reputation of being a bigoted and narrow-minded critic, unable to see anything beautiful or meritorious in anything that did not square with his theological and philosophical principles. To which he replied:

> This reputation, except as to the bigotry and narrow-mindedness predicated of it, is merited, and the one, so far as we seek reputation at all, we wish to secure. The first thing to be exacted in any literary work is truth, and we know not what other standard of truth a man can have than his philosophical and religious principles. A work faulty as to its principles and in error as to its doctrines cannot be commendable, whatever the genius, talent, or taste of its author. Art simply as art is indifferent to good or evil, and becomes the one or the other according to the thought or sentiment it expresses; and the standard by which to test whether that thought or sentiment be the one or the other is always and everywhere Christian faith and morals.[4]

To prevent misconception, however, he stated that in bringing every literary work to this strict test of Catholic faith and morals, he did not at all wish to exclude from consideration all works not of orthodox and practical Catholics. We find much sound philosophy in Plato and Aristotle, he said; no little beauty in the ancient Greek and Roman classics; and some in the masterpieces of poetry, music and eloquence of modern Protestant and infidel nations. This is because all nations, even the most heretical, are still blessed with some rays from the sun of Catholic truth and goodness shining through the darkness.[5] The fact that a work is written by a Protestant, in itself considered, weighs nothing with us, he said. Before reading a book, we often ask, "Who wrote it?" But in making our judgment of it, we ask simply, "What is it?" We do not, because we conduct a Catholic review, he continued, feel ourselves bound to condemn every book not written by a Catholic. We can name books written by Protestants which contain more principle than some written by Catholics. The fact is, a man may be a Catholic, keep the precepts of the Church, and yet, in all that concerns the application of principles to the various departments of life, have the views and feelings of the heterodox. Leibnitz, a professed Lutheran, was far more Catholic in principle, in the tendency of his philosophy, than Descartes, a professed Catholic.[6] Yet, since the Catholic alone is in full possession of the integral elements that form the basis of true art, Catholic faith and morals, he would, he said, expect the masterpiece only from the Catholic author. But in all that pertains to artistic skill alone — the literary form, the style, the expression — he frankly owned the excellence, even the superiority, at least in the English language, of those outside the Catholic Church, and devoutly wished that Catholic writers were not so far behind them. "They dress better than we do," he said. But when it comes to that which they dress — the important thing — that is quite another matter.[7] When it comes to mere form alone, Brownson held that the ancient classics "are unsurpassed, and not to be surpassed."[8]

From this it is plain that he attached more importance to the content than to the form of art. It is not precisely that he undervalued the form of art, but rather that with him the form exists more for the sake of the content. "We like to see a man well dressed," he explained, "but we cannot value the man for the dress, or the dress without the man." The content is the important thing. Every artist, painter, sculptor, or musician, must, he continued, have an end in what he does, besides the doing, a good end, one that is in the moral order, which is in some way referable to God, the supreme good and ultimate end of all things. The first thing therefore a critic has to do in reviewing a literary production is to inquire into the end or purpose the author has had in mind, and that once ascertained, he may then proceed to consider with what degree of literary taste and beauty the author has succeeded in accomplishing the work he has had in hand. As detached from its end, Brownson thought a work scarcely a worthy object of criticism. Perhaps it was on this score that George N. Shuster remarked of Brownson in a letter dated January 9, 1974 : "His criticism resembles that of Samuel Johnson." Mr. Shuster further stated that in clinging to the literary principles he had adopted, Brownson was pretty much in harmony with "the English Reviews, the Edinburgh for example, which clung to principles pretty much like his. They were somewhat to the right of Dr. Samuel Johnson." Said Brownson:

> To us the end is no less important than the principle, and the philosophy which denies the final cause is as atheistic and absurd as that which denies the first cause. Our theology determines our ethics, and our ethics determine our aesthetics.[9]

But a work once referred to a worthy end, not only the content, but its form, its style, its diction, become very important for the very good reason that we are not merely intellectual beings, and it is not, therefore, sufficient merely that he who writes for us have the truth, and is able to state it in logical form. We have will — imagination, affections, passions, emotions — as well as intellect, a perception of the beautiful as well as the true and good, and can be pleased as well as instructed, and generally refuse instruction if not offered in a form that pleases, or at least does not displease. In the light of this, the form of art becomes no mere matter of indifference: "A correct literary taste, a lively sensibility to the fit and beautiful, the command of an easy and noble style, of appropriate expression, and graceful diction, are matters of importance, which no one who writes at all is at liberty to neglect. Here we prize literary taste and culture as highly as any one can, for they are not for themselves, but for a legitimate purpose beyond themselves, and are prized as a means to an end."[10]

With such a *credo* of literary criticism he could not be otherwise than an exacting critic. If faithful to his principles, he could not always commend, and was often obliged to censure, but he would not have his readers "suppose that to censure is more to our taste than to commend."[11] One of the most interesting essays of his literary criticism in his early years as a Catholic is his critique of "R. W. Emerson's Poems." As Alvin Ryan correctly observed in his *Brownson Reader*, "No American writer engaged Brownson's interest so deeply and so continuously as did Emerson."[12] Not only did Brownson have a great admiration for his lofty gifts, regarding him as "almost the only original writer of distinction we can boast,"[13] but he could speak of him, too, as more than a mere acquaintance; he tells us that he had "enjoyed his hospitality," and "the charms of his conversation," that "as friend and neighbor," he is "one it is not easy to help loving and admiring." Much loath was he, therefore, to say anything severe against him or his works, but "his volume of poems," he sighed, "is the saddest book we have ever read." However high Emerson's artistic sense, the thread of thought running through much of his poetry forbade Brownson to bestow unqualified praise. Of the poems in general he said:

> As artistic productions, then, notwithstanding they indicate, on the part of the author, poetical genius of the highest order, they can claim no elevated rank. The author's genius is cramped, confined, and perverted by a false philosophy and morality, and the best we can say of the poems is, that they indicate the longing of his spirit for a truth, a morality, a freedom, a peace, a repose, which he feels and laments he has not.[14]

Brownson singled out two of Emerson's poems for closer examination, *The Sphinx* and *The Threnody,* quoting copiously from both. He had startling comments indeed on certain passages in these two poems, particularly on passages in *The Threnody* which dwelt upon the death of Emerson's little son Waldo. "There are passages in them (the poems in general)," said Brownson, "which recall all too vividly what we, in our blindness and unbelief, have dreamed, but rarely ventured to utter. We know these poems; we understand them. They are not sacred chants; they are hymns to the devil; not God, but Satan do they praise, and can be relished only by devil-worshippers."[15] While others might be captivated almost entirely by the verbal felicity and imagery of these poems, Brownson, while dealing with poetry or prose, was always more intent on the content of thought, and as a former Transcendentalist he no doubt understood the thought and its implications in Emerson's poems better than many another. Theodore Maynard remarked, in speaking of this very matter, that what makes Brownson's literary criticisms really worthwhile or interesting is the fact that he often said what no one else said, or dared to say.[16]

It is interesting to add that Hawthorne's son-in-law, George Parsons Lathrop, speaking of one of his visits with Brownson tells us that "on another occasion Brownson read aloud to this same caller Emerson's noble and affecting *Threnody* on the death of his little son Waldo; and as he read, his face became wet with tears, which he took no pains to conceal. The incident was a revelation to me. I had heard Dr. Brownson described as a rude, rough man, apparently without feeling. The more I saw of him, the more I saw that behind the somewhat rude manner was beating a warm, kind, tender heart."[17]

Many of Brownson's other literary judgments are included in his review of "The Works of Daniel Webster." The first part of the article is given over to a discussion of the common law as inherited from England. He asserted that in following the common law Webster had done so in every case to his own great advantage, so admirably exemplified in the famous Dartmouth College case, and had only less credit to himself whenever he departed from it.

> Whenever he speaks as a lawyer [said Brownson] according to the principles and maxims of the Common Law, what he says is remarkable for its good sense, its profound truth, and its practical wisdom; but when he leaves that, and attempts to discuss questions which lie further back, he is the disciple of Hampden, Sidney, Locke, and Rousseau, and proceeds from principles he did not learn from the law, and which are utterly repugnant to it. This is not a peculiarity of Mr. Webster; it was equally the case with the elder Adams, and, indeed, with the whole of the old federal party; and it was this that prostrated them, notwithstanding their personal respectability and practical wisdom, before their less scrupulous, but more logical and self-consistent rivals, headed by Thomas Jefferson.[18]

Brownson's highly interesting judgments on so many literary celebrities in this article will plead the length of the quotation here inserted. Even those who may not agree with all his comments will find them far from banal.

Speaking of Webster as a writer of a pure and classical style, he said:

> We shall look in vain in the whole range of American secular literature for works that can rival these six volumes before us. . . . In these times a man is to be commended for the faults he avoids, as well as for the positive excellence to which he attains. Mr. Webster is free from the ordinary faults of even the more distinguished literary men of his country. American literary taste is in general very low and corrupt. Washington Irving and Hawthorne have good taste, are unaffected, natural, simple, easy, and graceful, but deficient in dignity and strength; they are pleasant authors for the boudoir, or to read while resting one's self on the sofa after dinner. No man who has any self-respect will read either in the morning. Prescott is gentlemanly, but monotonous, and occasionally jejune. Bancroft is gorgeous, glowing, but always straining for effect, always on stilts, never at ease, never natural, never composed, never graceful nor dignified. He has intellect, fancy, scholarship, all of a high order, but no taste, no literary good breeding. He gesticulates furiously, and speaks always from the top of his voice. In general we may say of American literature that it is provincial, and its authors are uncertain of themselves, laboring, but laboring in vain, to catch the tone and manner of a distant metropolis. They have tolerable parts, often respectable scholarship, but they lack ease, dignity, repose. They do not speak as masters, but as forward pupils. They take too high a key for their voice, and are obliged in order to get through to sing falsetto.
>
> From faults of this kind Mr. Webster is free. . . . His elocution and diction harmonize admirably with his person and voice, and both strike you at once as fitted to each other. His majestic person, his strong, athletic frame, and his deep, rich, sonorous voice, set off with double effect his massive thoughts, his weighty sentences, his chaste, dignified, and harmonious periods. Whatever we may say of the eloquence, the rhetoric is always equal to it. Mr. Webster is perhaps the best rhetorician in the country. No man better appreciates the choice of words or the construction and collocation of sentences, so as to seize

at once the understanding, soothe the passions, charm the imagination, and captivate the affections. He is always classical. His words are pure English, and the proper words for the occasion, the best in the language. . . . We know in the language no models better fitted than the orations and speeches in these volumes for the assiduous study of the young aspirant who would become a perfect rhetorician, or master a style at once free and natural, instructive and pleasing, pure and correct, graceful and elevated, dignified and noble.

The quiet majesty of his style in the more felicitous moments of the orator, or when the reporter has been more competent to the task of reporting his speeches word for word as delivered, has seldom been surpassed, if equalled, by any American, or even English writer. Burke is the English writer with whom we most naturally compare him. As an orator he is far superior to Burke, as a profound and comprehensive thinker, perhaps, he falls below him; as a writer he is as classical in style, and as refined in his tastes, and simpler and more vigorous in his expression. In many respects Burke has been his model, and it is not difficult to detect in his pages traces of his intimate communion with the great English, or rather Irish statesman, who, perhaps, taken all in all, is the most eminent among the distinguished statesmen who have written or spoken in our language. We have no thought of placing Mr. Webster above him; but he surpasses him in oratory, for Burke was an uninteresting speaker, and in the simple majesty and repose of his style and manner. Burke is full, but his fancy is sometimes too exuberant for his imagination, and his periods are too gorgeous and overloaded. Now and then he all but approaches the inflated, and is simply not bombastic.

The only modern writers, as far as our limited reading extends, who in this respect equal or surpass Mr. Webster are the great Bossuet and the German Goethe, though we must exclude Goethe's earlier writings from the comparison. The simple, natural majesty of Bossuet is perhaps unrivalled in any author, ancient or modern, and in his hands the French language loses its ordinary character, and in dignity, grandeur, and strength becomes able to compete with any of the languages of modern Europe. Goethe is the only German we have ever read who could write German prose with taste, grace, and elegance, and there is in his writings a quiet strength and majestic repose which are surpassed only by the very best of the Greek and Roman classics. Mr. Webster may not surpass, in the respect named, either of these writers, but he belongs to their class.[19]

Another article of Brownson which contains a goodly number of his literary judgments as well as a detailed exposé of his literary principles upon which we have already drawn is his review of (Richard H.) "Dana's Poems and Prose Writings." Brownson had genuine praise for Dana's essays, and expressed the single regret that the writer had not given the American public more like them, a regret he seldom had occasion to acknowledge in the case of contemporary essayists. He found nothing in his poems which "transgress good taste, or ordinary morality, as understood by the better class of our countrymen. They are marked by a certain moral aim, a certain religiousness, and, as far as words go, express a reverence for and a belief in Christianity." Yet he found their thought and sentiments seldom or never rising above the natural order — lost to the truth and beauty of the supernatural."[20]

He considered Dana's elaborate paper on *Hazlitt's Lectures on the English Poets* superior to anything of the sort ever written on this side of the Atlantic. In his judgment, nothing finer, more tasteful, acute, or just had ever appeared in the whole range of literary criticism than Dana's remarks on Alexander Pope and his poetry. He was also delighted to find Dana doing justice to Swift. Brownson acknowledged that Swift had his faults both as a man and as a writer; that he was occasionally coarse, and in his *Tale of a Tub* downright profane; however, "he was taller by head and shoulders than any of his Protestant literary contemporaries, and among all the celebrated writers of Queen Anne's reign the author for whom we have the most esteem and affection. . . . We confess his rare genius, his satirical wit, his strong masculine sense, and have a profound respect for his political sagacity and wisdom. The political policy he advocated, and which the Whig Addison opposed, was wise and profound, and England is the sufferer today, and will be the sufferer hereafter, for having rejected it."[21]

He found Dana rating Wordsworth higher as a poet than he himself had been in the habit of doing. He acknowledged that Wordsworth did not lack the poetic temperament, and that he had written some very good poetry; that he wrote, too, with an honest aim, and such religious thought and feeling as he might without being a Catholic. But he always remains, he said, too near the ground, and never rises above the level of a respectable Greek or Roman gentile, save in words. His philosophy, if higher and broader than that of Locke and Paley, is too low and narrow, and occasionally verges on pantheism. He found himself wearied, half to death, with Wordsworth's interminable descriptions of natural scenery. Descriptions should be introduced, Brownson contended, only insofar as they subserve the action of the piece. "All description, introduced for description's sake, is a blemish." In a letter of April 3, 1974, George N. Shuster remarked that "one person who felt about Wordsworth's 'vernal wood' pretty much as Brownson did was the late Irving Babbit, spokesman for the Humanist Movement, whose greatest book was *Rousseau and Romanticism.*" In short, Wordsworth, in Brownson's estimate, "had the temperament of a poet, but lacked the intellectual strength to be a great poet."[22]

In a separate review of "Wordsworth's Poetical Works" Brownson asserted that no sane man would think of naming him in the same day with Pope and Dryden, far less with Chaucer, Spencer, Milton or Byron. Byron he considered to be without a peer among modern poets in the whole civilized world — though he acknowledged that Byron often abused, and terribly abused, his poetical genius. "He was our Napoleon of poetry,"[23] he said. Goldsmith's *Deserted Village,* he remarked, he would not exchange for all seven volumes of Wordsworth's poems. Though Scott has no separate passages or verses to compare with many that may be selected from Wordsworth, yet what poem of Wordsworth, he inquired, can be read with as much pleasure as Scott's *The Lay of the Last Minstrel,* or even *The Lady of the Lake?* The same might be said regarding Coleridge's *Christabel* or *The Ancient Mariner.* He mixed praise with censure for Wordsworth when he remarked:

> Wordsworth seems to have formed a tolerably just conception of what poetry should be, but to have labored all his life long in the nearly vain attempt to realize it. He made poetry step down from her stilts, and walk on her natural feet and legs, and so far he did good service, but we are afraid he will have to answer for not a few of the sins of the recent school of the Brownings, the Barretts, the Tennysons, the Lowells, and their followers, with which our present youthful generation is so grievously afflicted.[24]

But Wordsworth has grown in popularity since Brownson's day, and seems to qualify admirably as one of the people's poets. Wordsworth was already deceased by the time Brownson archly remarked when speaking of Longfellow: "Cesar Cantu says Longfellow is our best poet, and as he says in the same sentence, we are North America's best prose writer, we are bound to believe he is right, and we are really disposed, as to the poet, not the prose writer, to believe he is right, and we know no poet at present, in England, to place before him.''[25] Brownson did not rate Longfellow a truly great poet any more than he did Wordsworth, but still "there is a melody in his verse that charms us, and recurs to our hearts as the half-forgotten strains we loved in the remote days of childhood and youth. We like him because he always brings back to us our young feelings, mellowed by time and distance, and pleases us in our manhood, as Mother Goose did in our childhood, without demanding too much intellectual labor.''[26]

On James Russell Lowell Brownson bestowed one of his larger literary criticisms. When reviewing his *Vision of Sir Launfal* he found the false ethical system underlying his poem doing much to mar its beauty. In the poem Lowell had discountenanced Sir Launfal's notion of giving to a beggar at the gate from a sense of duty:

> He gives nothing but worthless gold,
> Who gives from a sense of duty.[27]

"The author," said Brownson, "is either a bad psychologist or a bad moralist." To give from a sense of duty is to act from the very highest and noblest motive known to man. It may indeed, he admitted, be for our greater convenience and pleasure that our emotions be always in harmony with our sense of duty, in giving alms, but it is in no sense necessary in order that the deed be meritorious. On the contrary, to act from mere impulse, without a rational motive, is scarcely a thing of genuine human merit. Yet Brownson had his meed of praise for Lowell, the author. With solid training under the direction of religion and philosophy, he could become a great poet. He has no complaint to bring against nature, he remarked. But he has not subjected himself to the necessary discipline, nor devoted himself to that serious and patient labor of thought necessary to bring the potentiality of his poetical genius to fruition. Alas, exclaimed Brownson, we must say this, not alone of Lowell, but of nearly all our contemporaries, in this superficial and frivolous age.

> We love art [he continued] and, of the various species of art, we love poetry the best. But we have too high an appreciation of its character and office, to receive with favour the light and frivolous productions of our modern race of poetasters and versifiers, however beautiful their print and paper, or rich and tasteful the bindings. . . . We have no wish to treat harshly our young aspirants to poetic fame, to wound feelings, or to damp courage; but, for the honor of our age, and the interests of modern civilization, we feel that it is necessary to raise our voice, feeble though it is, against the miserable trash which, under the name of literature, is inundating Europe and America, and threatening the extinction of what little virtue and manliness may yet remain. Would that there were among us a st·ong masculine voice, that could make itself heard amid the din and clatter of the age, and, with mingled kindness and severity, recall our youth to the antique depth of thought, greatness of soul, and energy of will, and impress upon their ductile minds the solemn truth that they must aim higher, submit to longer and more rigid discipline, devote themselves for years to those solid studies which task all their faculties, and call forth all the potentialities of their souls, before venturing to appear before the public either to instruct or to delight.''[28]

This passage gives us some inkling of the high standards and lofty vocation he associated with the true poet.

Among American novelists, James Fenimore Cooper engaged Brownson's attention in a goodly measure. He devoted an eleven-page review to his *Sea-Lions* and a twenty-four-page review to his *The Ways of the Hour.* Of Carlyle Brownson had once said: "Whatever the book he writes, Mr. Carlyle may well adopt from Schiller his motto, *Ernst ist das Leben . . .* he writes always with an earnest spirit, for a high, noble and praiseworthy end."[29] Of Cooper he said:

> Mr. Cooper is an earnest-minded man, and, though a novelist, he is no trifler. Through all his works runs a serious aim. In some of his earlier novels there is, perhaps, a little too much leaning towards the religion of nature, and not so deep a feeling of the importance and necessity of revealed religion as we would wish. . . . But he is never really lacking in morals, never prurient in his fancies; we remember no sentence in all he has written that could raise a blush on the cheek of modesty, and we recall no scene attractive to a libertine taste, or that could sully the chastest imagination. He never scoffs; he is never irreverent; he never forgets that man is a moral being, accountable to his Maker for his thoughts, words, and deeds. This, as the times go, is high praise, and honorably distinguishes him from the herd of popular novelists and romancers.[30]

C. C. Hollis gives us an admirable analysis of Brownson's literary criticism of Cooper and his works. He sees Brownson as a solitary contemporary who succeeded in getting at an understanding of Cooper and his case. In Cooper's early years *The Spy* and *The Pilot* had brought him fame and popularity. Then the media of public opinion in the country, as said Brownson, hailed him as "an American Scott." But later, during his long stay in Europe, Cooper had come to know something of the unflattering notions many Europeans had of Americans. Upon his return home, he yielded to an inner compulsion to turn social critic of American life and manners in the interests of his own countrymen. Then a portion of the American press turned on him in a snarling, libelous outburst. This drove Cooper from court to court in a determined effort to clamp the law on his assailants for libel — in which he succeeded in most cases. The result — with so much of the powerful Fourth Estate up against him — was an unfavorable reversal of judgment on Cooper as a man and as an author. Although Brownson frankly acknowledged that Cooper was not without his shortcomings, he took up the cudgels in his defense as an honest social critic of worthwhile stature, and feelingly deprecated the reversal of judgment that had come about in his case. But "that Brownson was the only contemporary critic to understand the reversal," points out Hollis, "has been overlooked by students of Cooper's career."[31]

Hollis asserts that the most useful treatment of Cooper is Spiller's introduction to the volume, *Representative Sections of James Fenimore Cooper,* and adds: "The view taken there of Cooper's changing reputation is so much that of Brownson (with of course no indebtedness; Brownson does not appear in Spiller's bibliography), that one is tempted to think of Spiller's essay as a current indication of the prophetic quality of so many of Brownson's literary criticisms."[32]

In conclusion Hollis says:

> The revaluation that is almost entirely of this century has placed our first major novelist in a different perspective and has granted him merits his contemporaries, with Brownson as a major exception, were unaware of. His weaknesses Brownson saw as did other critics of the day; Brownson would have enjoyed Twain's "Fenimore Cooper's Literary Offenses" as we do. But that Coo-

per was a serious and important critic of American life and manners is a judgment we make today and Brownson alone of Cooper's contemporaries could make.[33]

So important a novelist as Nathaniel Hawthorne naturally came in for his meed of attention from Brownson. His genius Brownson acknowledged on various occasions, but for his critical notes on Hawthorne he is perhaps best remembered for his review of *The Scarlet Letter*. Speaking of Brownson's review of it, Hollis significantly says: "The notice is brief, and it is more severe than any other comment on a recognized classic. Yet it is also one of Brownson's most provocative criticisms."[34]

Why the severity, and what made his criticism so thought-provoking? Brownson began by observing that "God gave us our faculties to be employed in his service, and in that of our fellow-creatures for his sake, and our only legitimate office as critics is to inquire, when a book is sent us for review, if its author in producing it has so employed them." Brownson owned that according to "the popular standards of morals in this age and this community," Hawthorne can hardly be said to pervert God's gifts, or to exert an immoral influence. Yet there is another standard of morals. He found Hawthorne's story told with great naturalness, ease, grace and delicacy; still it is a story that should not have been told. Such a story of crime, "of an adulteress and her accomplice, a meek and gifted and highly popular Puritan minister in our early colonial days — a story not altogether improbable" — he could not consider a fit subject for popular literature. It constituted a threat to the moral health of the community.

> There is [he said] an unsound state of public morals when a novelist is permitted, without a scorching rebuke, to select such crimes, and to invest them with all the fascinations of genius, and all the charms of a highly polished style. In a moral community such crimes are spoken of as rarely as possible, and when spoken of at all, it is always in terms which render them loathsome, and repel the imagination.[35]

Again, Brownson accused Hawthorne of a number of "mistakes" in his conduct of the story. It is true, observed Brownson, that Hawthorne makes the guilty parties, Hester and Dimmesdale, suffer, and suffer terribly, but their sufferings are not so presented as to inspire his readers with the horror of their crime. There is really no repentance of the sin in the case:

> Neither ever really repent of the criminal deed; nay, neither ever regard it as really criminal, and both seem to hold it to have been laudable, because they *loved* one another — as if the love itself was not criminal. . . . They hug their illicit love; they cherish their sin; and after the lapse of seven years are ready, and actually agree, to depart into a foreign country, where they may indulge it without disguise and without restraint. Even to the last, even when the minister, driven by agony, goes so far as to throw off the mask of hypocrisy, and openly confess his crime, he shows no sign of repentance, or that he regards his deed as criminal.[36]

The adulteress suffers, not from the consciousness of having offended God, but from the disgrace to which the crime exposes her, and the minister suffers not from the sense of his breach of God's law, but because he has failed to maintain "integrity of character." They lowered themselves in their own estimation, and can no longer hold up their heads in society as honest people. It is not their conscience that is wounded, but their pride:

> He cannot bear to think that he wears a disguise, that he cannot be the
> open, frank, stainless character he had from his youth aspired to be, and *she,*
> that she is driven from society, lives a solitary outcast, and has nothing to con-
> sole her but her fidelity to her paramour. There is nothing Christian, nothing
> really moral, here. The very pride itself is a sin; and pride is often a greater sin
> than that which it restrains us from committing.[37]

Brownson evidently detected some Transcendental reminiscenses in
Hawthorne's thought, and regretted that he did not speak more in accordance with Christian concepts. It would surely be unjust to Hawthorne to suppose that he did not recognize the sinfulness of pride in its various manifestations, but, as Mr. Hollis suggests, his concepts of the matter were quite different from those of Brownson. Said Brownson:

> Mr. Hawthorne seems never to have learned that pride is not only a sin, but
> the root of sin, and that humility is not only a virtue, but the root of all virtue.
> No genuine contrition or repentance ever springs from pride, and the sorrow
> for sin because it mortifies our pride, or lessens us in our own eyes, is nothing
> but the effect of pride. All true remorse, all genuine repentance, springs from
> humility, and is sorrow for having offended God, not sorrow for having offend-
> ed ourselves.[38]

There seems no reason to believe that Brownson wished to be more
severe in his strictures than the case appeared to him to warrant. Hawthorne was an old friend of his. Randall Stewart is not correct when he says
that Brownson "led the attack" on the novel.[39] Brownson's review appeared
in October, six months after its publication, and really came at the tail end
of reviews rather than leading the attack. However stern Brownson's views
of morality may seem, he was by no means unmindful of the fact that "compassion for the fallen is a duty which we all owe, in consideration of our own
failings, and especially in consideration of the infinite mercy God has manifested to us erring and sinful children." Yet binding as this duty may be, we
are never to forget that sin is sin, and that forgiveness can be won, through
the great mercy of God, only on condition of the sincere repentance of the
sinner.[40] As C. C. Hollis again suggested, before beginning his critical notice
of *The Scarlet Letter,* Brownson must have realized that his review would
be looked upon as the official Catholic view of the novel. Yet, in the broad
view of his criticism, it is also probably correct to say that it has a touch of
Puritanism in it.

Whatever his strictures on this particular novel of Hawthorne, he
frankly conceded that Hawthorne's craftsmanship was excellent. In his
glowing review of *Twice-Told Tales,* he judged him fitted "to stand at the
head of American literature."[41] And in his review of the *Blithedale Romance,* he acknowledged that Hawthorne had "fully established his reputation as the first writer, in his favorite line, our American literature can
boast."[42]

Jedediah Vincent Huntington was another American novelist to whom
Brownson repeatedly turned his attention. It was of Huntington's *Alban, or
the History of a Young Puritan,* partly biographical, that Brownson took
particular notice. Brownson, as well as several other Catholic reviewers,
found some passages a trifle too daring. Although Brownson acquitted Huntington of any dishonorable intentions, and laid the passages to Huntington's
peculiar theory of art, he nonetheless complained: "We think it repugnant to
the laws of true art for a writer, every time he has occasion to introduce a
woman, to stop and give us a full length portrait of her, the color of her hair,

the form of her eye-brows, the cast of her features, the pouting or not pouting of her lips, the shape of her bust, the size of her waist, with remarks on the flexibility of her limbs, and the working of her toes." In spite of this criticism, Brownson allowed Huntington ability of a high order, and acknowledged that the book contained passages of rare beauty and interest. He added: "If we are to have works of fiction, he is, perhaps, as well fitted to produce them as any author we have."[43]

Still, all was not well even after Huntington had brought out a new and revised edition of *Alban* in which several passages which had been considered offensive were omitted. Brownson felt that the job had not been done satisfactorily, and further remarked:

> The author, we are sure, means well, but he is a little fussy where women are concerned, and is too fond of adjusting their corsages, tying on their slippers, or smoothing the folds of their petticoats, and not content with indulging his fussy disposition, he looks you very innocently in the face, and tells you there is nothing improper in all this, for he means nothing. Perhaps there is not, but he would do better not to challenge us to discuss it.[44]

Brownson has sometimes been spoken of as hostile to the modern novel in general. But this is scarcely the precise truth of the matter. What he was sternly opposed to was the modern trashy novel in all its shapes and forms — the abuse of fiction, not its use. Fiction, he said, adopted as a vehicle of a false philosophy, a false morality, false political or social theories, or amusement or diversion at the expense of innocence, is simply not allowable, not because it is fiction, but because it is an abuse or misapplication of fiction. No one, he continued, who has read *I Promessi Sposi* of Manzoni, can doubt that fiction in the form of the novel or romance can be made to serve good and worthy ends; and the romances of Scott, Bulwer Lytton, James and others, show us what advantage can be derived from the historical novel if properly cultivated by talent and genius. The novel, he averred, may not be, absolutely speaking, the best literary form, but here and now it seems to be the most popular literary vehicle, after the newspaper and the review, and Catholics, faith and morals safeguarded, are as free to conform to the reigning fashion in literature as they are to the cut of a coat or the shape of a bonnet. In fact, it is only by cultivating this particular literary form that Catholics can hope to act immediately in any degree upon their age and country in the world of letters. *Fabiola,* by His Eminence Cardinal Wiseman, he opined, could have a greater popular influence than the *Lectures* of His Eminence on Catholic faith, admirable as those lectures be.[45]

To no class of novelists was Brownson more adamantly opposed than to those who call themselves realists, who take so much credit in professing to paint life as it really is, ignoring for that reason the ideal, or whatever might elevate the soul, and inspire it with noble and lofty aspirations. This so-called realistic school Brownson pronounced as:

> . . . the most corrupting and infamous school of literature that has ever existed. Better a thousand times [he exclaimed] for the morals of the community, the extravagant romances of the fabled knights-errant, so unmercifully ridiculed by Cervantes in his "Don Quixote," than the modern three volume novels copied from the "Police Gazette" or the "Newgate Calendar."[46]

The bane of this school is that it familiarizes the reader with vice and crime, makes him the companion of thieves, robbers, swindlers, cutthroats, social outcasts of either sex, caring never a pin that "evil communications corrupt good manners," little less so in the pages of a highly spiced novel than in actual life. The works of this school serve only to enfeeble the intellect, to corrupt the heart, to debase character and to render youth of both sexes mean, low, groveling and sordid. There is no reading such works, he said, without having all noble, pure and lofty aspirations checked, spiritual life stunted, and the heart rendered unfit to receive and profit by the sacred truths and holy inspirations of the Gospel of Christ.

On this score he singled out for particular censure the disgusting realism of your Dickenses, your Trollopes, your Ainsworthys and others which, pushed to still greater extremes by their feminine imitators, was already in his day destroying the last vestiges of chivalry in the modern world, and obliterating from the minds and hearts of the reading public all traces of Christian morality. He set his face against Charles Dickens, he said, from the very beginning of Dickens' literary career, long before he himself had become a Catholic, and he could not but regard Dickens's popularity as one of the worst symptoms of the age in which he lived. He owned freely that Dickens had wit, humor and a high artistic skill, but no elevation of mind, no noble and lofty aspirations; his nature he regarded as low, groveling and sordid, and his morality a vague and watery philanthropy. He called him "the prince of realists," and remarked that he has perhaps "exerted a more malign influence on English popular literature than any other recent writer than can be named." Never could he succeed, he said, in reading through his *Pickwick Papers*. "None of his characters in any of his works are such," he added, "as one of refined feelings and noble aspirations would choose as his associates." Thackery, on the contrary, though he owned that he, too, had his faults, he could endure, for while he was a realist in his own way, he had at bottom a warm and gushing heart, and aspirations far above the world he too faithfully painted. His idealism redeemed his realism. In fact, Brownson liked Thackery's novels so well that he deemed them worthy of a second reading.[47]

Yet Brownson's inveighing against this class of novelists of his day might easily be misleading. He knew as well as Newman that "you cannot have a sinless literature of sinful man."[48] In point of fact he defended the novelist's perfect right not only to represent characters as he finds them in real life, but to make us love and esteem them, though marked by grave faults, even vices and crimes. It is no objection to modern literature, he said, that it paints vicious and criminal characters, that it makes us acquainted with the shocking depravities and loathsome corruptions of human nature. He thought it might be well if youth sometimes learns how rotten human nature can be so that they are put more on their guard against its depraved appetites and vicious propensities. The fault of modern literature is not here, he said. It is elsewhere; it is in the fact that it enlists our sympathies, our love and esteem for characters as persons because they are vicious and criminal. He wrote:

> What it compels us to approve in them is the moral weakness, the lawless passion, the criminal strength of purpose, the successful vice, the triumphant crime. Read the writings of Goethe, of Byron, Bulwer, Victor Hugo, Balzac, George Sand, Ida Hahn-Hahn, and you will be cheated into sympathizing with the illicit, the vicious, the criminal. Take away from their characters what is contrary to Christian morality, and nothing is left to love or admire. Their very excellence is made to consist in what is condemned by the laws of God and man. Here is the error; here is the fatal poison; here is what makes their writ-

ings so immoral and corrupting. They might have painted the same amount of depravity, uncovered the same festering wounds, and exposed the same abyss of corruption, and yet have exerted a healthful influence, an influence that would have tended to heal, instead of deepening and perpetuating the running sores of individuals and society. All they needed to have done this was to have a correct moral standard for themselves, and to have refrained from sympathizing with the corruption they represented.[49]

Another charge Brownson laid to the account of the so-called realists is that they do not make good their boast that they paint life as it really is. Their pictures of society are as false to real life, he said, as were those of the medieval romances so unmercifully and so justly ridiculed by Boiardo and Cervantes. Society is corrupt, rotten, if you will, but less so than in the pages of a Bulwer or a Trollope. Virtue is still the rule, he insisted, and vice the exception, for if it were not so, society would come apart at the seams. There is corruption enough in high places, he admitted, to make Satan laugh and angels weep, but by no means all, nor anything like a majority of those in public office or connected with government are peculators, swindlers, tricksters, villains intent on the "pickings and stealings" or their own self-aggrandizement. Some lack capacity, and fail to aspire to a heroic sense of duty, but the evil-intentioned bear a small comparison to the whole. In domestic life, too, there are of course unfaithful husbands and unchaste wives, but there are few countries, as is well known, in which this is not the exception. In the business world, likewise, there are rash, fraudulent dealers, swindling bankers, corrupt railroad and corporation presidents, directors, treasurers and the like, he said, but the great majority are, according to the accepted standards of the business world, fair and honest in their dealings. Imperfect virtue in the world there certainly is, but nothing like total depravity. Hence the so-called realists, in introducing into their pages such a monumental amount of corruption and rascality, are not true to life or society as it exists, affirmed Brownson. They give us pictures of just certain aspects of life, but paint for us neither high life nor low life, nor even middle life as it is actually lived.[50]

To Brownson the so-called religious novel in which profane love and theological discussion are mixed was also objectionable under the relationship of art — what is sometimes called the novel of instruction. No two interests could be more diverse, said Brownson, or less capable of coalescing than a love story and theological arguments, and when joined together they are as offensive under the relationship of art "as a picture in which the painter joins the beautiful head of a maiden to the body or tail of a fish."[51] The one interest in the story demands action, movement, and is impatient of delay, while the other calls for quiet, repose, and ample time for the activity of the intellect. Hence the two can be mixed no better than oil and water. Yet novels of a distinctly religious nature may be written in which religion is never mentioned. All that is required is that the author be imbued heart and soul with true faith and piety. Then he will inspire and expire what is in his soul with every breath he takes and every line he writes, and his piece will flow on spontaneously from a full heart and a full mind. His productions will then teach no particular doctrine, inculcate no special moral, but they will breathe a truly religious, a truly Catholic spirit, and unobtrusively unfold the beauty of true Catholic piety to the reader. It was this, he said, which gave such unction and power to the writers of the Middle Ages. They said little of the Catholic Church, spoke little of religion unless treating it professedly, but every word they wrote betrayed the source from which the thought came.[52]

Although Brownson always endeavored to be just in all his literary criticisms, he was not partial to women novelists. Rightly or wrongly, he felt they often over-spiced their novels with sentimentalism. One of the well-known women novelists of his day was Lady Georgiana Fullerton. He first criticized her *Grantley Manor*[53] rather sharply on various scores, then had warm words of approval, with reservations, for her *Lady-Bird,*[54] and some two decades later, he had extremely high praise for her *Mrs. Gerald's Niece.*[55] Another prolific woman writer of the day was Mrs. James Sadlier of Montreal. Patrick Donohue, a Catholic publisher of Boston, agreed with Brownson's standard for Catholic stories and novels, and offered a prize for the best tale that could be offered in accordance with that standard. He appointed Brownson the judge who would award the prize. Although several competitors of distinction entered the lists, Brownson pronounced *Willy Burke* by Mrs. Sadlier an admirable story, and awarded her the prize. Fr. John Roddan, who submitted *John O'Brien,* and George Miles, who submitted *Loretto*, though close friends of Brownson and contributors to his *Review,* came off only second best.[56]

As to reviews of historical works, his longtime friend, George Bancroft, did not come off so well when Brownson reviewed the fourth volume of his *History of the United States.* Brownson took the occasion to lay his strictures on the modern school of so-called philosophical historians, especially in France and Germany, who, prior to all study of history, form to themselves some pet theory — metaphysical, ethical, political or whatnot — about God, man and society, and from which they infer what is and must be found in history. Facts which are needed to explain and establish such theories, if not encountered, are invented; facts which have no apparent bearing on such theories one way or the other are discarded as unimportant and without historical significance. As instances in point he named not only his friend Bancroft, but Herder, Kant, Hegel, Guizot, Cousin, Michelet and even Carlyle and Macauley. It is the common error of this school of historians, said Brownson, to suppose that history may be reduced to the terms of a speculative science, and written, as it were *a priori.* In explaining the matter further, he said:

> Herder finds in all history only his ideas of human progress; Kant finds nothing but his categories; Hegel finds the significance and end of all history, the operations of divine providence, of all mankind, of all nature, to have been the establishment of the Prussian monarchy; Mr. Bancroft finds that the original purpose of creation, of God, and the universe, is fulfilled in the establishment of American Democracy. No doubt history has a transcendent plan. . . . But the science of this plan and of this purpose is God's science, and not man's, and can be shared by us only as he pleases to make it known to us by his revelation. It is not the historian as such who possesses it, and can unroll it before us. It is only a Bossuet, a Christian bishop, in the possession of divine revelation, and speaking from the height of his episcopal chair, that can give to history something of the character of a speculative science, or furnish a philosophy of history; and that philosophy of history is a divine, not a human philosophy.[57]

While including Bancroft in this criticism, he acknowledged gladly that he is "unquestionably one of our most distinguished men. He is an accomplished scholar, a man of a high order of intellect, and a brilliant and fascinating writer."

When noticing the fifth volume of Bancroft's *History,* Brownson was yet more irenic in tone and much friendlier in manner. He found the volume largely free of the faults he had criticized in the previous volumes. "If the remaining volumes," he said, "show an equal improvement on the preceding, we shall have no great fault to find with them, and shall begin to be proud of our countryman."[58]

Brownson was still much more pleased with Bancroft's sixth volume. He rejoiced to see that he had taken a deeper Christian view of history, that he had passed beyond, "far beyond Gibbon, and sees something more in the controversy between the Athanasians and the Arians, which for nearly two centuries convulsed the world, than a simple dispute about a single diphthong," and that Bancroft further recognizes "that the God of consciousness, of humanity, of history, as well as of theology, is triune." He now saw Bancroft's *History* becoming "undeniably the great fact of American literature." When it has received its last revision, Brownson stated, "it will remain, we trust, a noble monument to the genius of the author and the genius of his country."[59]

To another American historian, Francis Parkman, Brownson awarded signal honors when he reviewed his *History of the Conspiracy of Pontiac.* He felt too much praise could not be given him for the fidelity and pains with which he had collected the authentic materials for the work, or the rare felicity with which he had worked them into one of the most truly historical volumes which has ever issued from the American press. His style he found richer, more animated and varied than Prescott's, and less artificial and more flexible than Bancroft's. Parkman's true historical genius had been fostered by his close study of the Indian character, not only in the narratives of the early Puritans of the country, or in the high-wrought romances of Cooper, but more especially in the Indian's village and wigwam. This close-range acquaintance had given him a more just appreciation of the Indian than any other American Brownson was acquainted with. In only one thing did Brownson find that he could not agree with Parkman: his skepticism as to the capabilities of the Indian for civilization, and his doctrine that it is idle to endeavor to convert the Indian from paganism and incorporate him into the Christian family.[60]

Brownson's criticism of the early literary efforts of the distinguished American church historian, John Gilmary Shea, were to bring him into strained relations with him. While praising highly Shea's *History of the Catholic Missions among the Indian Tribes of the United States,* he had also referred in unflattering terms — apparently not without reason — to an essay Shea had written on American Catholic literature.[61] But the main trouble began with Brownson's criticism of Henry de Courcy's *The Catholic Church in the United States,*[62] in which Shea had had a hand and of which he was the translator from the French. Speaking of how the misunderstanding had come about between Mr. Shea and himself, Brownson said:

> We censured severely Mr. De Courcy for certain contributions we had seen of his in the *Univers, apropos* of his and Mr. Shea's "Sketches of Ecclesiastical History of the Church in the United States"; but our censures of those contributions were not intended to apply to the History. It is true the History did not please us; it was not well written; it was marked by a narrow spirit, contained many inaccuracies, and was lamentably defective. It was partial, one-sided, and written apparently for the glorification of France, not in the service of the United States. Yet the fault we found was with Mr. De Courcy, not with Mr. Shea, his translator. Yet Mr. Shea saw in our criticisms hostility to him

personally, and the evidence of a determination to injure his literary reputation.[63]

When a second edition to the *History* had been brought out, Brownson saw himself accused in a paragraph of the introduction written by Mr. Shea of having attacked De Courcy's history "in accents of passion and wrath." To which Brownson replied:

> Our readers ought by this time to know that we seldom make statements against a writer, without having tolerable reasons for so doing. We have never yet written a word in this *Review* from passion, wrath, or revenge, or censured in it a living mortal from a sense of personal wrong, from personal motives, or from any other than public reasons. The manner in which a class of scribblers allow themselves to write of us and our *Review*, has never been adopted by us, and never will be. Time will show that we have suffered wrong, but that as a Reviewer we have wronged no one, unless through a very pardonable error of judgment; and whenever we have discovered such an error, we have always been prompt to acknowledge it, and to make all amends in our power. We claim no credit for this; it was our duty.[64]

Brownson's criticisms of De Courcy's *History* was the occasion of a rupture between himself and Mr. Shea which seems never to have fully healed. These two stalwart Catholic laymen of the day were to stand apart to the end. Writing to J. V. Huntington, Brownson said: "I am willing to be Mr. Shea's friend, but he will never be mine. I can make no advances to him, for I regard myself as the aggrieved party. But I assure you that nothing in the past or the future will affect my notices of any works that may fall under my criticism."[65]

The office of literary critic is a very delicate and difficult one, that is, if the critic is to show a conscientious regard for the promotion and growth of a better and higher literature — and Brownson was to find himself in hot water time after time. As Lawrence Stern remarked: "Of all the cants which are canted in this canting world, though the cant of hypocrites is the worst, the cant of criticism is the most tormenting,"[66] and Brownson paid accordingly. As a conscientious critic, he could not puff works where merit was plainly wanting. But if he did not praise, offense was often taken. By and large, whenever obliged to censure, he mixed praise with censure, and generously. He stated that it was his conviction that "the error that can be laid to our charge is, that our judgments are often too favorable — rarely if ever too severe. We are guided in our judgments by a strong desire to encourage Catholic talent wherever we discover it; but we cannot wholly overlook the demands of good taste, and of a sound and elevated literature."[67]

Yet he was often the target of offended authors, and no less so during his Catholic career. Few or none had the ability to lash back as did Lord Byron in his *English Bards and Scotch Reviewers,* but they not infrequently dipped their pens in gall. As a last resort, the offended party would at times indignantly make a loud demand for the cancellation of his subscription. George Miles explained well how it went when he wrote:

> But let a man stand and lash the age,
> Let reason rule, and truth inspire his page,
> Let folly quake to hear his lordly tread,
> And captive error hang her hydra head —
> Then, just so long as our celestial selves
> Escape a drubbing, *Brownson* tops our shelves;

But once the scourge on our shoulders' laid, —
Stop the Review! — gag the gray renegade![68]

Although Brownson was a man of steel, human nature, after all, can take only so much. Strong men hold high their heads in public no matter how wild the gale, but occasionally the curtain is raised a bit, and we are granted a surprising glimpse. That the beleaguered Brownson had at times his low moments might well be guessed, but we are not left to guesswork. Writing to his old friend, Fr. John Roddan, editor of *The Pilot,* on September 3, 1852, after expressing to him his disappointment that he had not come to visit him, he said:

> I want to see you very much. I am in low spirits, nearly discouraged, and I want to be renewed, and posted up, and I have none but you on whom I can depend. Come and see me, and make a man of me again.[69]

But no one was hurt when Brownson reviewed one of his own works. A curious book that Brownson wrote was *The Spirit-Rapper: An Autobiography.* In the preface to the book he was puzzled just how to categorize it. "It is not a novel," he said, "it is not a romance; it is not a biography of a real individual; it is not a dissertation, an essay, or a regular treatise; and yet it has some elements of them all, thrown together in such a way as best suited my convenience, or my purpose." Whatever its character, the aim of the book was serious, and its statements truthful. In it Brownson maintained the undoubted connection "of spirit-rapping, or spirit-manifestations with modern philanthropy, visionary reforms, socialism, and revolutionism" — a fact asserted, he said, by the spiritists themselves, or spiritualists as they prefer to call themselves, and fully substantiated by their own literature on the subject.[70] His investigations had led him to believe firmly that spirit manifestations, or such phenomena, are, at least in some cases, inexplicable except by the intervention of superhuman power, and since the character of that power is often such in nature that it cannot be assumed as coming from heaven, it must be of Satanic origin. He wrote his book because of the sudden appearance and alarming spread of spiritism at the time, both at home and abroad, counting in its ranks then in our own country nearly a million believers in it. In the course of the book, Brownson said:

> The infection seizes on all classes, ministers of religion, lawyers, physicians, judges, comedians, rich and poor, learned and unlearned. . . . It is making sad havoc with religion, breaking up churches, taking its victims from all denominations, with strict impartiality; and yet the great body of those not under its influence merely deny, laugh, or cry out, "humbug!" "delusion!" Delusion it is. I know it now, but not in their sense.[71]

The occasion of briefly reviewing his book was the receipt of a huge volume, *The Healing of the Nations,* by Charles Linton, sent to him from an unacknowledged source. He refused to review it, asserting that he had previously gone into a thorough investigation of modern spiritualism, "or more properly spiritism, or daemonism," and had embodied the results in *The Spirit-Rapper.* He had nothing to add on the subject. He only emphasized that spiritism is to be carefully eschewed. He asserted that he would not trust himself in a spiritist circle, and that he would not read another spiritist book. He could have no motive for so doing except idle curiosity, and were he to indulge any such curiosity, he could no longer count on the grace of God to protect him.[72] This was many decades before the Catholic Church had laid its strictures on attendance at spiritistic phenomena. Brownson was, however, to return to this theme in 1872 when he reviewed Robert Dale Owen's *The Debatable Land between this World and the next.*[73]

Fr. Herbert Thurston, S.J., in *The Church and Spiritualism*, acknowledged the merits of Brownson's *The Spirit-Rapper* by quoting a sizable passage from it which, he tells us, furnished the cue for the attitude taken in more than one chapter of his book — a paragraph from *The Spirit-Rapper* which cautions against the folly of denying indiscriminately the reality of spiritistic phenomena. Thurston also acknowledged that the term "spiritism" which Brownson had advocated as a more accurate word to describe the new cult, had gained currency among Catholics in this country, but he thought it inadvisable to continue the usage. A body of believers in reincarnation on the Continent had adopted it in the meantime as their designation. Besides, the followers of the new cult of spiritualism had from the beginning called themselves spiritualists. Usage is the arbiter of correct form.[74]

Although Brownson was fully conscious of the mighty influence of the Fourth Estate, and therefore of the great importance of the right quality of literature in general, he was more directly concerned in the years immediately following his conversion with religious or theological issues. It is to that we will now turn our attention again, noting, however, as we go along, in their place, some of his other literary criticisms.

# 25

## CONTROVERSIES OVER CHRISTIAN DOCTRINE: NEWMAN'S THEORY

*John Henry Newman's book,* An Essay on the Development of Christian Doctrine *• What it was meant to explain • Bishop John Baptist Purcell objects to the theory • Brownson is backed by his bishop, John B. Fitzpatrick, in his criticism of the theory • Bishop Martin John Spalding's comment on Newman's book • Archdeacon Edward Manning finds it beyond his powers to reply to Newman's book • Brownson's own statement on why he concerned himself with Newman's theory • Newman's statement of the view upon which his book had been written • Brownson's various articles in criticism of Newman's theory • Newman's side of the case is represented in controversy by William George Ward • Ward and Brownson exchange letters also • Brownson seeks the views of other knowledgeable persons on Newman's theory • An important letter from Fr. T. Glover, S.J., in Rome • The controversy with Ward comes to an end • Newman questions whether or not he had applied his theory too freely • Brownson fears that mischief will result from Newman's terminology • Fr. Edmond D. Benard notes in his book,* A Preface to Newman's Theology, *the corrections Newman made of his terminology in 1878 • Brownson riles Newman by his further strictures on developmentism, and Newman complains in a letter to the* Dublin Tablet, Ireland *• Brownson replies in a long letter to the* Tablet, *explaining his own position and views • In what sense Brownson admitted development of Christian doctrine, and in what sense he did not.*

It would be a great mistake to suppose that the profession of faith Brownson made in Catholic teaching on the occasion of his conversion was to remain quiescent, although made of course with absolute certitude of mind. His mind was immensely inquisitive, and any doctrine at all that came under his observation was sure to be given a minute examination as to its real meaning. And so it was to be with Catholic doctrine also. Belief in Catholic doctrine is one thing, but its interpretation is quite another. Hence the various schools of theology in the Church. It was Brownson's concern about the correct interpretation of Catholic doctrine that was to give him almost as many controversies with those within the Church as he had with those assailing the Church from without. If a martial-tempered man revels in battles and storms, Orestes Brownson was to have a lion's share of all that within the Catholic Church itself. Not that he preferred the tempestuous to the quieter sort of life, but his sincere solicitude for the correct interpretation of Catholic doctrine — the interpretation he felt would render it truly salvific — was necessarily to involve him in almost endless imbroglios during his Catholic career. If we were to speak of the Catholic Church as a mansion with various kinds and sizes of windows, we might say that Brownson did not always look through the same windows as others when contemplating Catholic doctrine in its relation to life and society. And being Brownson, he felt an ineluctable obligation to battle for what he had become convinced was the right and salutary interpretation.

The first controversy he engaged in among Catholics was over the novel book the distinguished English convert, John Henry Newman, published in 1845 detailing the intellectual process of his pathway to the Church, *An Essay on the Development of Christian Doctrine*. Although Newman himself never replied to the strictures Brownson was to lay on his theory as first presented, his defense was taken up by one of his ardent admirers at the time, William George Ward, in the *Dublin Review*. The resultant clash of thought between these two prize converts of the day, Ward representing Newman, was something of a spectacle to the Catholic public.

As an Anglican minister, Newman had read deeply and widely in the early Greek and Latin fathers of the Church.[1] The Church claimed to be the lineal descendant of this same church of the early Greek and Latin fathers who were witnesses to the faith of the primitive Church. But Newman encountered what seemed to him a difficulty. The faith of the Catholic Church in the nineteenth century seemed to contain doctrines he did not find witnessed to in the early fathers of the post-apostolic age. How then explain it if the Catholic Church is to be counted the lineal descendant of the church Christ founded? Anglicans simply asserted that Rome had made "additions" to the original deposit of faith, and called them "Roman corruptions." This of course disqualified the Church utterly in their eyes. The whole purpose of Newman's book was to show that, if there were any new doctrines in the Catholic creed of the nineteenth century, versus the primitive creed, they were simply developments from the original deposit of faith made to the Apostles. This view of the development of Christian doctrine may have been somewhat unconsciously abetted at the time by the theory of evolution in the physical order which was already in the air. Although Newman extended his theory of development to discipline and theology as well as doctrine, Brownson made it a point to confine himself largely in his criticisms merely to the theory of the development of Christian doctrine.[2]

It is proper to note that Brownson was by no means the only one at the time who looked askance at Newman's theory of development. There seems to have been considerable commotion in the country generally over Newman's book. Writing to his friend, Bernard Dalgairns (later a fellow Oratorian), Newman, in Rome at the time, said: "Knox writes me that the whole American Church, all the bishops I think, are up in arms against my book. They say it is half Catholicism, half infidelity. Of course they know nothing of antiquity, or the state of the case."[3] Francis Knox (later another fellow Oratorian of Newman) had just visited in America, and had most probably exaggerated somewhat in what he said. But the reverberations of the commotion in America were to roll across the Atlantic and caused Newman real embarrassment when he reached the Eternal City, as told by his biographer, Wilfrid Ward.

John Baptist Purcell, bishop of Cincinnati, seems to have been the first person in the country of any prominence who came out in print in the *Cincinnati Telegraph* against Newman's theory.[4] But no one approached Brownson in the extended criticism he made of Newman's book. And in this he was backed to the hilt (at least privately) by his bishop, John B. Fitzpatrick. There is a letter in the Notre Dame archives from Boston to Bishop Purcell of Cincinnati, dated September 27, 1847, condemnatory of Newman's theory. The name of the writer has been clipped from the bottom. But it is a certainty that the letter was written by Bishop Fitzpatrick of Boston, for the longhand is identical with that of another letter of Bishop Fitzpatrick to Bishop Purcell. The letter fits well into the center of exchanges between Brownson and William George Ward over Newman's theory. It reads in part:

> You will see by the new number of Brownson's *Review* that the article in the *Dublin Review* has not been allowed to pass unnoticed. [Fitzpatrick was Brownson's theological censor and knew therefore just what was coming.] Mr. Ward, the Oxford convert, is the author of the paper in defense of the developmentists. I think he will have a rather tough job to make out a reply to Brownson. But if he does attempt it B[rownson]'s ammunition and courage are still far from being exhausted, and the developmentists, if they stand their ground, will have many a hard broadside to stand yet. I really think that these gentlemen have not come into the fold by the right and proper door; they appear to me not to have that reverence which every Catholic should have for the living & ever-speaking Church of God. Their faith is an historical one in practice, not based upon the superior and divine authority of the Church which is the same yesterday, today, & forever. They have read the Fathers no doubt; much more perhaps than any of us have done. But in their reading they have followed a wrong principle for guide: the principle of private judgment which is equally dangerous whether applied to the Scriptures or the writings of the Fathers. They have read them as Protestants read the Bible or as Jansenius read them. In the course of their studies they have fancied that a wide distance is discernible between the faith of the present day and that of the Church of the first ages. That in these early times the teachers in the Church were ignorant of many things now ordained to be of Catholic faith or even in some points held as opinions. This discovery, which was of things too abstruse for the acumen of the Catholic intellect but could not escape their superior sagacity, kept them for a long time in the ranks of open heresy. At length the same sagacity enabled them to discover a solution, also unknown to Catholics, and that was the system of developments. By this means they got into the Church imagining that they brought to her many advantages and means of defense of which her doctors had hitherto been ignorant. But in truth their whole difficulty was a phantom with no foundation but their own false conception of the scope of the Holy Fathers, and their solution of it is, we think, a still greater and more dangerous error which they must abandon unless they are prepared to differ with all Catholic theologians.[5]

This line of thought is practically identical with that of a letter Brownson wrote William G. Ward two days after this letter was written (September 29, 1847), particularly pages 55-59, and indicates Bishop Fitzpatrick's agreement with and support of Brownson.[6] After visiting the bishop of Boston in 1853, Sir John Acton reported: "Dr. Fitzpatrick fully approves of Brownson."[7]

Martin John Spalding, bishop of Louisville, Kentucky, was another prelate in the country who commented on Newman's book. In a letter to Bishop Purcell of Cincinnati, Ohio, dated January 30, 1846, he remarked:

> Newman's book is a "vasty deep" of thought and learning. I like it in the main, though it is often loose & inaccurate in doctrine. That "development theory" is a dangerous two-edged tool. It would never do for an unskillful hand to attempt using it. Religion is a fixed *fact* & not a theory of doctrine more or less developed. The work will, however, do much good among the Anglican clergy for whom it is intended.[8]

And over in England, Paul M. Thureau-Dangin tells us, Anglican Archdeacon Edward Manning (later convert and cardinal) was to take up his pen to reply to Newman as soon as the book appeared. But the book proved beyond his powers and he abandoned it. Thureau-Dangin thinks, however, that Manning's concernment with the book was not without effect in widening his spiritual horizon, and in indicating to him questions to which Anglicanism could give him no answers.[9]

There is no doubt, nonetheless, that there were prominent people in the Catholic Church who were silently disposed to let Newman's book pass for what it was worth — an attempt to clear a pathway for Anglicans to enter the Catholic Church — especially since he had written it as a Protestant, not as a Catholic. If it had its imperfections or inaccuracies, they might be outweighed by the good the book could effect. Why then did Brownson launch an attack on it? It may be best to let Brownson himself tell us why. We have his statement on the matter as reported to us by Sir John Acton in his *American Diaries* after he had visited Brownson at his home in Chelsea (Boston) in 1853. Speaking of his conversation with Brownson, Acton said:

> We spoke of his attack on Newman. The book on development was thought dangerous here for reasons connected with the character of the clergy of the country, which were not felt in England. He was requested to refute it, but refused at first out of respect for Newman. At length the book began to do harm. It was taken up by the enemies of the Church. A New York paper printed parallel passages from it and Gibbon, and Newman's were found to be the worst. It became necessary to disclaim all solidarity with his opinions. The bishops, particularly the Bishop of Boston, insisted that he do it, and at length he consented. Ward defended him (Newman), but Brownson said doing him more harm than good, and wrote him a long letter without proving anything. Brownson is very sorry about the hostility it has produced, but quite convinced of Newman's errors, though of course he admits development of another kind.[10]

What we should note carefully here is that, as Acton informs us, Brownson did acknowledge a development of a certain kind, but still objected to the phraseology in which Newman had originally expounded his theory. Fr. Giovanni Perrone, S.J., perhaps the foremost theologian in Rome at the time, found fault, too, with the terminology in the original edition of the work, and Newman did make alterations later. Referring to Newman's *Letter addressed to his Grace the Duke of Norfolk on the Occasion of Gladstone's recent Expostulation,* Brownson remarked in an article (July 1875): "Dr. Newman has added a postscript to a new edition of his Letter, which removes most of the objections we had indicated against it. He has not, indeed, entirely explained away his doctrine of development, but he has so far modified it as to make it mean very little."[11] But Newman, as we shall presently see, made a much more important revision in 1878, two years after Brownson's death. It is possible, if not probable, that with the revision of 1878 Brownson would have considerably modified his objections to the theory. It is upon Newman's *Essay* in its original form, we should keep in mind, that Brownson laid his strictures.

In saying, as Brownson told Acton, that a New York paper had printed parallel passages from Newman's book and Gibbon, Brownson made reference to statements about the doctrine of the Blessed Trinity. Newman had said in his book that "there was no formal acknowledgment of the doctrine of the Trinity till the fourth century."[12] This the Unitarians of the country, to whom Brownson himself had formerly belonged, were quite willing to accept as another proof that the doctrine of the Trinity was no primitive doctrine at all but merely a development of the third century. Here was a blow to the Catholic faith. This in itself for Brownson made a close inspection of Newman's theory a matter of no little importance.

Brownson, now gradually assuming the position of a watchdog of orthodoxy in his sincere pursuit of truth, obtained a copy of Newman's book as soon as possible, and plunged into it with consuming curiosity. He peered sharply through his bow-rimmed gold spectacles when he came to read Newman's statement of the view on which his book had been written:

> That the *increase* and expansion of the Christian *creed* and Ritual, and the *variations* which have attended the process in the case of individuals and churches, are *necessary* attendants on any philosophy or polity which takes possession of the intellect and heart, and has had any wide or extended dominion; that from the nature of the human mind, *time* is necessary for the full comprehension and *perfection* of great ideas; that the highest and most wonderful truths, though communicated once for all to the world by inspired teachers, could not be comprehended all at once by the recipients, but as received by minds not inspired, and through *media* which were human, have required only the longer time and deeper thought for their full elucidation. . . . This may be called the *Theory of Development.* . . . We shall find ourselves unable to fix a historical point at which the *growth of doctrine* ceased . . . [Italics are Brownson's except *Theory of Development*].[13]

This to Brownson sounded at least dangerous in tendency, if not theologically unsound. Growth in theological *science* he of course freely admitted, but that there had been a growth in the sum of truths contained in the original deposit of faith, he was not altogether prepared to accept. New definitions of faith, certainly, but no new dogmas or articles of faith. It was precisely here that Fr. Perrone, too, the eminent Roman theologian, made his criticism. Recognizing his weight as a theologian, Newman was extremely anxious to secure his *imprimatur* for his theory. He went to the trouble of writing a summary of his argument in Latin and sent it to Perrone. Whether or not he found any other flaws, Perrone's main objection was confined to Newman's expression "new dogmas" instead of "new definitions."[14] Newman seems to have satisfied Perrone that though his terminology might be inexact, his meaning was orthodox.

Perhaps the two most prominent persons in Rome who were really opposed to Newman's theory were Carlo Passaglia, S.J., professor of theology at the Gregorian University, and Fr. Thomas Grant, rector of the Scotch College.[15] (Grant later became the first bishop of Southwark, England.) He also acted as theologian to the English bishops at the First Vatican Council, Rome, 1870, and died there during the Council. Bishop Grant had likewise been present in Rome on the occasion of the solemn papal definition of the Immaculate Conception in 1854, and had there apparently spoken against Newman's theory of development. This fact we learn from a letter Fr. Hecker wrote Brownson relating information he had gleaned from a conversation he had had with Bishop Michael O'Connor on a train ride from Pittsburgh to Cincinnati, Ohio. Said Fr. Hecker:

> On the way we talked on several topics; among others when we arrived at Cincinnati was that of Development. You know that Bishop O'[Connor] was at Rome at the declaration of the dogma of the I[mmaculate] Concep[tion] of Our B[lessed] Lady. He told me that at the assembly of the bishops he made some objections to certain words or statements of the Bull as it was read to them on account of its seeming to countenance that view of development which he considered false. This drew out Perrone, who made a speech of half an hour's

length defining what he considered to be the true and false doctrine on this point. Bishop O'[Connor] took notes of P[errone]'s speech and has them at home. Some of the Italian prelates wondered what B[ishop] O'[Connor] was driving at, when Dr. Grant of Southwark rose and said some words about Dr. Newman, and they saw then. The words of the Bull were changed.

Bishop O'Connor says there is a capital statement of the true doctrine of development in the Bull, but as we could not find the document, he was unable to point it out. The Latin Bull and not its translation must be read to find it. He said also that Perrone held precisely the same doctrine as he did on the point. And B[ishop] O'[Connor] expressed his satisfaction of your course in regard to that controversy.[16]

Brownson himself having spotted in his first reading of Newman's book what he considered dangerous terminology, backed by Bishop Fitzpatrick, led off with an attack on it in the July 1846 issue of his *Quarterly*. He took the position that the variations in Catholic doctrine, which Newman seemed to assert, were not real, but only apparent. The only variations in Catholic doctrine that can be conceded, he maintained, come with the greater clearness and distinctness as to what Catholic doctrine is not, which results when the Church defines Catholic doctrine explicitly in condemning novel errors which have arisen. (The doctrine was always there before.) This implies no variation in substance or form of the doctrine itself, only in the mode of opposing it to the insurgent error.

Brownson stressed that the Catholic Church received at the beginning a formal commission to teach all nations all things whatsoever the Lord had commanded his Apostles. And with this was necessarily included the utter competency of the Church to teach truly and infallibly the whole Catholic faith on every point of doctrine (although not necessarily known to every individual pastor). And if so, there could be no difference between the faith of the Church in the early ages and that of the nineteenth century. He could not appreciate Newman's difficulties. And he liked just as little Newman's comparisons between the development of philosophical systems or human institutions and that of the divine Catholic faith of the Church. He forgets, he added, that the Church "is withdrawn from the ordinary laws of human systems and institutions by her supernatural origin, nature, character, and protection. . . . The Church has no natural history, for she is not in the order of nature, but of grace."[17]

When he reviewed half a year later J. Spencer Northcote's *The Fourfold Difficulty of Anglicanism, or the Church of England tested by the Nicene Creed, in a Series of Letters,* and had found the author, a fellow convert and an admirer of Newman, setting forth what he regarded as substantially Newman's theory of development, he concluded that a whole school of developmentists was gathering about Newman, first formed outside the Church, but now operating within the Church. As these Oxford men were men of acknowledged talents, learning and zeal, he could not but assume that they would exert a decided influence on the Catholic literature of the day, and if favoring Newman's theory, do much harm in spreading it abroad. The age, he said, has a strong tendency to theorizing or innovation, from which Catholics themselves are by no means free. (He would have liked Bishop Spalding's statement, unknown to him, that "religion is a *fixed* fact.") Here to him was a new and increasing danger, and he pitched into developmentism in another vigorous article, marshaling a galaxy of eminent theologians on his side, and quoting the great bishop of Meaux, Bossuet, at considerable length.[18]

This drew a long letter from another Oxford convert and admirer of Newman, who had come into the Catholic Church in the same year as Newman himself, 1845, William G. Ward.[19] He had fought alongside of Newman in the stormy days of the Tractarian movement, and had originated the slogan, *Credo in Numannum.*[20] He would have loomed larger in the movement had he not been overshadowed by a greater man, Newman himself. He, too, had written his controversial book in 1844, *The Ideal Christian Church,* and had in consequence lost his university degrees as an Oxford don.[21] He was now tutoring in Old Hall in England, and was soon to be teaching dogmatic theology at St. Edmund's, the oldest Catholic college in England.[22] He was by no means a lightweight. Being a friend of Newman, he was much disturbed by Brownson's attacks on his friend's theory. It is possible that he was not overly concerned about just how sound Newman's theory was, but for a certainty he could ill endure the annoyance Brownson was causing his friend. Figuring that he could do something to soften Brownson toward Newman by a warm personal letter, he addressed him a long letter from Surrey, England, on April 7, 1847. In the letter he attempted to show that from the studies Newman had made of the early fathers of the Church, he had no alternative left but to devise some such theory as he actually had, if he were to become a Catholic. He also took Brownson to task, gently enough though, for what he regarded as inconsiderateness, if not unfairness, toward Newman on a number of counts.

Brownson had acknowledged at the conclusion of his two articles on developmentism that they were marked by a tone of severity, but he asserted he was again making his distinction between "the author and his book," and frequently threw in expressions of the highest regard for Newman himself, his eminent talents and learning, his sincerity and piety. But Ward did not feel that Brownson had succeeded so admirably in maintaining his distinction throughout his articles. Moreover, Brownson had given offense on another score. When reviewing the reasons Henry Major, a Philadelphia convert from Anglicanism, had given for his conversion under the title *Reasons for acknowledging the Authority of the Holy See of Rome,* Brownson had wound up, saying:

> We are pleased to find that Mr. Major is a simple-minded convert, who comes to be taught, and is willing to take the Church as she is, and on the grounds on which she has hitherto been taken. He brings no theory or ingenious hypothesis of his own, and, laying it at her feet, modestly assures her it will give him great pleasure to find his own thoughts on the subject coincident with hers. We like this.[23]

Brownson of course did not mention Newman in connection with this comment, but it did have all the appearance of a good side thrust at Newman, and Ward threw it up to Brownson in his letter. From there Ward went on to complain about what seemed to him to be Brownson's starting point in regard to Newman's formulation of his theory. Said Ward:

> The idea you seem to have formed is that he (Newman) has devised his theory in a wanton sort of way, as a sort of an intellectual exercise, instead of submitting himself humbly to the teachings of the Catholic Church as he found it. I cannot but think that a statement of the facts in the case will induce you, in some degree at least, to modify this opinion.[24]

Ward then proceeded to lay the facts before Brownson as he understood them. He took Brownson through several pages of his long letter along Newman's pathway via Anglican theology and the early fathers of the Church, in both of which Newman had read deeply, with the result that history to him showed doctrines in the Catholic creed of the nineteenth century that were not in that of the primitive Church. How establish the identity of the two as the true Church of Christ? Ward complained feelingly, if not bitterly, that no Catholic at the time had come forward to help Newman solve his difficulty, but had left him to struggle all alone as best he could. Said Ward:

> I cannot but feel it an extreme *injustice and cruelty* that Catholics who were silent when he was searching in their direction for some way of escape, should afterwards, when he had found one for himself and actually brought himself into the Church by help of it, be loud in their objections to the legitimacy of the way. If this be not the right way, why did they not, years ago find for him another?
> This observation, my dear sir, cannot be supposed to reflect upon yourself, because you were not, I believe, at the time a Catholic. But I do think that all who find fault with his theory, should ask themselves the plain question, "Except for this theory, how could he have possibly become a Catholic?" I *do* think that Newman has some right to complain of *your* treatment of him. Here we have a person of ability and thought, who has devoted himself to the studies of the Fathers, and who is most anxious to find in them all possible agreement with the present Catholic Church, and yet cannot for the life of him, read them any other way than as being either discrepant or ignorant, on various points which are now ruled to be points of Catholic faith. If on the one hand it is historically clear that the Catholic Church of the nineteenth century is the lineal heir of the Catholic Church of the fourth century, it is equally clear (so he thinks) that the doctrine of the first named Church is in many particulars an addition on the doctrines of the last named.[25]

Although Brownson told Acton, as we have already noted, that Ward had written him a long letter without proving anything, he of course read this letter at the time carefully and pondered well its contents. After all, he was willing to look at the question from every angle. He had in the meantime not only been canvassing the eminent theologians of the past on the question, but he was also consulting living authorities on the matter. Besides consultations with his own bishop, letters of inquiry went out — among others — to Bishop John McCloskey of New York, and to Bishop Michael O'Connor of Pittsburgh, reputedly one of the ablest theologians in the country. He even got a letter off through his friend, J. Coolidge Shaw, S.J., to Fr. T. Glover, the Jesuit in Rome, to gather what intelligence he could from the center of Christendom. Of all the responses that came back, that from Rome was probably the most satisfactory to him. Referring to Brownson's first article on the question, Fr. Glover said in his letter to Shaw:

> I told you before, and I see no reason to change my opinion, that the greatest part of Brownson's critique on N[ewman]'s Development, is very just and cannot be easily confuted. . . . There can be no doubt that the Apostles were enabled, on the day of Pentecost, to expound, or develop, explicitly, any dogma to its utmost extent, if there had been any need of it, as well as their successors at any subsequent period. But it does not appear they did so, whereas their successors have developed explicitly many truths, which were implicitly contained in the original deposit.[26]

Brownson no doubt took this letter of Fr. Glover as strong confirmation of his own views on the subject. In a reply letter to Ward he told him that

373

the supposed difficulty in the case arose from Newman and his followers assuming that their *own view* of the teaching of the primitive Church was unquestionably the true one, instead of seeking to learn from the Church itself what is the true one. "I complain," he said, "of the assumption of the infallibility of your own private judgment in the matter, and for supposing that a theory of explanation is called for because in your judgment there is a seeming discordance between her present teaching and your *view* of her primitive teaching, as collected from your private interpretation of the early Fathers — the Anglican view." As to the Catholic Church changing from age to age, he observed:

> As a Catholic you cannot distinguish between what the Church teaches in one age and what she teaches in another. For you the Church has no ages. She is *one* and Catholic in *time* as well as space, and, like eternity, she has duration, but no succession. You must go to her, as she is today, to learn what she taught before the Council of Nice, no less than to learn what she teaches now. If you assert the alleged discordance, it must be on her authority; you cannot say she has varied from age to age, taught in one age what she did not teach in another, in one age doctrines repugnant to those she taught in others, unless she tells you so. If she tells you so, that is enough: she has then confessed her fallibility, abdicates her throne as the Church of God, and you need no theory, for none can save her.[27]

In his further eagerness to dissuade Brownson from continuing his attack on Newman's theory, Ward had slipped badly when he cautioned Brownson in his letter, saying: "Should you then (to argue *per impossible*) succeed ever so fully in showing him that his view is irreconcilable with the teachings of the Church, you would only throw him back on his original perplexity and shake his whole Catholic faith to the foundation."[28] To which Brownson replied: "In this I must believe that you do Mr. Newman great injustice; since, if not, he is no Catholic."[29] Brownson was entirely right. Years later Newman was to say: "When I became a Catholic, I sent a message to Dr. Baggs, that, at the word of the bishops, I would put into the fire my then forthcoming book on development of doctrine."[30] It does not appear that Newman had any overweening attachment to his theory, but at the same time, as he remarked to his friend, Bernard Dalgairns, he did not relish the idea of beginning his "Catholic career with a condemnation or retraction."[31]

Ward followed up his letter to Brownson with an article in the *Dublin Review,* July 1847, on "Doctrinal Developments," which Brownson took notice of in a forty-page reply in the October issue of his *Quarterly* of the same year. After thanking Ward for the obliging terms in which he had spoken of him personally, Brownson characterized Ward's article as "singularly deficient" either as a reply to himself, or as a defense of Newman's theory of development. As he saw it, Ward had only given his own ideas on "doctrinal developments," but had not really replied to his objections to Newman's distinctive theory of development, had in fact left all his arguments standing in full force. Moreover, he expressed a regret that the "task of replying to us had not been committed to the hands of some learned Catholic doctor, instead of one, who, however able and well disposed, from the defect of professional training, is not less likely, perhaps, to mistake the sense of the authorities which must be cited than we are."[32] But he freely acknowledged that his friends in England had the right to choose their own champion, and all that remained for him was to conduct the controversy on his side of the Atlantic the best he could with the aid of divine assistance.

In his second reply to Ward in April 1848, "The Dublin Review and Ourselves," he endeavored to pin Ward down to a direct reply to his objections to Newman's theory of development. To show that we are in the wrong, he said, and that he is in the right, or to defend the theory of development in the sense in which we have set it forth and objected to it, he must establish:

> 1. The original revelation committed to the Apostles, and through them to the Church, was imperfect, inchoate, containing gaps to be filled up in the process of time by the uninspired action of the human mind; 2. It is impossible to make a revelation which the uninspired human mind can take in or apprehend, except through a long and laborious process of thought, which can go on only successively, and be completed only after a considerable lapse of time; 3. Christian doctrine, or the object embraced in the act of believing, is not the revealed fact, but the mind's eye of it, always more or less inadequate, or the form which the mind by its own uninspired action imposes upon it; 4. It is no objection to a theory that it degrades Christianity to the level of sects and human philosophy; 5. No provision was made in the apostolic revelation, as originally delivered to the Church, for infant Baptism, or post-baptismal sins; 6. The sacrament of Penance was not an original Apostolic institution, but a development effected after the establishment of the Church; 7. Purgatory was a development effected subsequently to the first ages, as a form of Penance due to sins committed after Baptism; 8. The doctrine of the Trinity was only imperfectly understood by the Ante-Nicene Fathers, and not fully *formed* till the sixth century; 9. Excepting some of the elements of the principal mysteries, nothing is formally of faith till controverted, and judicially defined and declared by the Church.[33]

It was in regard to these specific points that he had opposed Newman's theory, Brownson insisted, and he told Ward that in ignoring these objections he had made no reply to him at all. It was not against just any type of development of Christian doctrine that he was arguing, but against Newman's distinctive type. Brownson also noted that Ward had complained that he himself had expressed a wish that the task of replying to him had not been committed to the hands of some learned Catholic doctor, and had added: "Surely, what a layman and a recent convert is at liberty to write, a layman and a recent convert is at liberty to answer." Unquestionably true, said Brownson, but the real question is not one of liberty, but one of competency. It was not at all that he felt himself entitled to an opponent of a higher grade than Ward himself, but he had so wished because a learned Catholic Doctor would have understood more clearly the authorities cited, would have addressed himself precisely to the points upon which the controversy turns, and would thus have brought the discussion to a speedy and satisfactory termination — "because it was error, not defeat, we dreaded — truth, not victory, we desired." The reviewer's second article, "we are sorry to say," added Brownson, "has served only to justify and increase the regret we expressed."[34]

Ward's January 1848 article in the *Dublin Review* had purported to be the first half of a rejoinder to Brownson's article in the October 1847 issue of his *Review*. When the promised second half of Ward's reply to Brownson did not appear in the next edition of the *Dublin Review*, Brownson assumed that Ward was silently disposed to drop the controversy, and he did a little summing up of the discussion in the October 1848 issue of his *Quarterly*. There the theological swordplay came to an end. Both had endeavored to show knightly courtesy in the encounter, and both had suffered lapses in the knightly code. Both had been more gracious in their letters than on the field of encounter. Ward had courteously wound up his letter inviting Brownson to visit him in England, should occasion offer, and added the pleasant news: "Your name is well known to the students (here), and they have lately ordered your *Review* to come regularly to them."[35]

Newman himself was gradually coming to realize that perhaps the statement of his theory was not after all entirely without some flaws. In a letter to his friend, Robert Isaac Wilberforce, dated December 11, 1853, he wrote:

> It is long since I read my "Developments," and I dare say, did I read it, there are things which would startle me in it. I did not know at the time the Catholic doctrine in detail, and I *applied* the theory to details in which it ought not to be applied. Indeed I was conscious when writing it that I was making a very bold and needless application of it in reference to the *facts* in the case — but I said, well, it is all *a priori*. If facts are more clearly in the first age in favor of the received Catholic faith than I have said, then we need not apply the theory so *fully* as we might; that is all.[36]

One thing that should not be overlooked in this matter is that Brownson's judgment in the whole affair may well have been somewhat colored by the fact that he himself had been requested to abandon his own philosophical theory which had led him to the threshold of the Catholic Church. He himself had entered the Church, profound philosopher that he was, in the greatest simplicity of mind and heart, bowing low, and "bringing into captivity his understanding unto obedience of Christ." This, he must have felt at the time, was the only way for anyone to come. He himself had had his full share of theorizing and speculation over the long years, even unto nausea, and would gladly have done with all theories. They could do no good, and might do much harm. It was on the strong meat of fixed doctrine that he would feed. He admitted it was natural for one to concoct theories when out of the Catholic Church, but they were no offering to bring to the Church. He wrote:

> The more empty-handed we come to the Church, the more affectionately she will embrace us, and the more freely and liberally will she dispense to us her graces. She needs nothing, and the greatest and best of us can offer her nothing but our sins and uncleanness. Naked, and all defiled with filth in which we wallowed while away from her maternal care, must we come, and implore her to be our mother, to cleanse us in the laver of regeneration, and to cover our nakedness with the white robe of her charity. So must we come, if we come at all; and when we so come, when we have reposed our weary head on our *Mother's* bosom, we feel she is our true, our own blessed *Mother,* and all we ask is to believe, and obey.[37]

Prophetic in one respect Brownson certainly was when touching upon one particular aspect of Newman's book, namely, some of its terminology. He objected to certain forms of expression as rash, if not erroneous. Words are things, he said, and when used by persons of eminence with inexactitude will easily become the occasion of errors and heresy in others. Many of the errors which have afflicted the Catholic Church have slipped in under the shelter of loose and inexact expressions, expressions which even saintly men have sometimes allowed to escape them. The proud and restless seize upon them, ascribe to them a sense they may bear, but not intended by their authors, and thus lay the foundation of "sects of perdition."[38] Fr. Edmond D. Benard, M.A., S.T.D., in his book, *A Preface to Newman's Theology,* has brought out that the Modernists, particularly their chief spokesmen, Alfred Loisy and George Tyrell, frequently quoted Newman in support of their heresy.[39] Not at all that they could claim him in any sense, but they so interpreted his language as favoring their heresy, one of the deadliest that ever threatened the Catholic Church. Which reminds one of the remark of the scientist, Thomas Huxley, that he could compile "a primer of infidelity from Newman's writings,"[40] again, of course, misinterpreting his language.

There is no question but that some of Newman's terminology in his essay on development as first published was inexact. We have already noted the objections of the eminent Roman theologian, Fr. Giovanni Perrone, S.J., to certain expressions of Newman. Indeed, Newman himself eventually, in 1878, corrected some of his ambiguous phraseology. Referring to Newman's notion of the development of Christian doctrine, or to the section of the book on the "power of assimilation," Fr. Benard observed:

> Orestes Brownson may to a large extent be excused for having reached the conclusion he did regarding this third note, because in the first edition of the *Essay,* the section is somewhat ambiguous, and it is, to our mind, only with the preface and additions to the later edition that Newman's meaning becomes quite clear. . . . In the reprint of 1878 we are quoting, pages 380-382 contain several paragraphs that did not appear in the first edition.[41]

Whether or not Brownson would have agreed more fully with Newman had he revised his book earlier, is something we do not know — though there is some indication he might well have done so. The revision was made after Brownson's death in 1876. In a sense, it is regrettable that Newman did not make it earlier. Meriol Trevor tells us that his friends wanted him "to answer Brownson, but he scorned to do so," calling him a "half-converted Yankee."[42] In his controversy with Ward, Brownson had asked to be told frankly whether what he took to be Newman's real meaning was correct or not.[43] Again he called for an unequivocal statement of Newman's meaning when four years later, 1852, he reviewed Fr. Brande Morris's work on the *Incarnation.*[44] Morris was another Oxford convert. Finding him to be a developmentist, after correcting some of his faulty theology, Brownson turned his attention in the latter part of the article to some further reflections on Newman's theory of development. Although he again acknowledged Newman's lofty intellectual gifts, he ventured the opinion that such was the caliber of his mind that his views at times were less broad and comprehensive than might be wished. He wrote:

> To use a form of expression borrowed from himself (Newman), he takes in an idea, not as a whole, but by viewing it successively under a variety of separate aspects — by walking all around it, and viewing it successively under all its aspects. He thus attains to particular views, never to unity of view, or to the comprehension of the idea as a whole. No man has, within the range of these particular views, a clearer or keener sight than he, and no man can more clearly, vividly, distinctly, accurately, or forcibly express what he thus apprehends. But nevertheless, whenever he attempts to mould his particular views into a systematic whole, he becomes confused, obscure, vague, and vacillating.[45]

All this quite understandably irritated Newman, and he complained in a letter to the *Dublin Tablet,* Dublin, Ireland, which had taken notice of Brownson's article, that he had been subject to a personal attack — and that by a layman! This drew from Brownson a sedate and well thought-out reply to the *Dublin Tablet.* As the letter is a bird's-eye view of the whole controversy from Brownson's standpoint, it may be well to include it here in its entirety. He wrote:

To the Editor of the *Dublin Tablet*

Boston, October 15, 1852

Dear Sir:

A friend of mine has called my attention to a note in your paper of the 18 of September last, from the Very Rev. Dr. Newman, to which I beg you to permit me to offer a brief reply, as it has been called forth by some remarks in my *Review* which you were so obliging as to copy into your excellent journal.

Of the tone and temper of Dr. Newman's note, and the severe charge it brings in its closing paragraph against me personally, I have nothing to say, for he is a priest, and I am only a layman, and if the charge against me is untrue, it is nothing severer than I deserve to have said against me. Yet I regret that the illustrious writer should have broken his silence for the first time against me in defense of his personal character, which I have never attacked, instead of his doctoral tendencies, which I have attacked, and labored to prove, are subversive of the Catholic religion; for I had supposed it to be always characteristic of the Catholic doctor to be more sensitive to charges against his doctrine than to charges against his person.

If Dr. Newman had done me the honor to read what I have written in regard to him and his school, he would have seen that I have from first to last been careful to distinguish between the man and the author. I have never doubted his Catholic intentions; I have never entertained the least doubt of the sincerity of his faith, or that of his disciples. I have uniformly expressed my full confidence in the purity of their motives, and professed warm love and reverence for their personal virtues. But he and they do themselves great injustice when they construe what I have said into attacks on their characters, or fancy that I am moved in what I write by personal hostility to them. I am not their judge, and in no instance have presumed to judge them, at least unfavorably. They have entirely misapprehended the state of my feelings towards them, and if I have not been as eulogistic in my remarks on them as others have been, it is because I have not dared to express the admiration and esteem I felt, lest I should give countenance to doctrinal tendencies which I regard as likely to prove dangerous to the purity and integrity of Faith.

I have freely and frankly pointed out the errors of the development school, or what appeared to me to be errors, as I have the right to do. Dr. Newman, when he wrote his Essay on Development, was not a Catholic, and when I first wrote against it he was only a layman like myself. He had, indeed, been a Protestant minister, and so had I, and there was nothing in our relative positions that made it improper for me to review his book. I could not dream that by doing so I should touch his personal feelings, or incur the charge of being personally hostile to him. I supposed that he, like myself, had no wish but to know and obey the truth, and it is with no less surprise than pain that I have found myself regarded as his personal enemy.

I am, I very well know, a layman, and write on religious and theological subjects, which no layman has of himself the right to do.[16] But I do so at the request of the ecclesiastical authorities of my country, and I never publish an article, written by myself, on theological questions, without first submitting it to my own Bishop, or a competent theologian approved by him. I do not presume of myself to teach, for I well know that I have no authority to teach.

Dr. Newman's doctrine of development was submitted here to a close and rigid examination, not by me only but by Bishops and professional theologians. I have only censured what they bid me censure, and I am responsible only for the manner in which I have done what they instructed me to do. Under these well-known circumstances Dr. Newman can scarcely excuse himself for not replying to the charges I have preferred against his doctrine, either on the

378

ground that the charges are not preferred by a theologian, or that they are charges against his person.

The only thing that operates here to Dr. Newman's disadvantage is his refusal to explain himself publicly with regard to his doctrine which has been publicly controverted, and his apparent disposition to regard attacks on his doctrines as attacks on his person. His silence in this respect is not edifying, and if continued, will lead to suspicion of his motives. What is asked of him is, to tell us whether we have rightly apprehended his meaning; and if we have not, to set us right; if we have, to tell us how that meaning can be compatible with Catholic Faith. There is no Catholic who wishes to quarrel with him, and all, I can assert, that I aim at is, to be at once just to him and to Catholic truth. I have no theory of my own that he interferes with, and I seek only to defend the tradition of Faith as it has come down to us from the beginning.

I have written at greater length than I intended. I have simply wished to prevent a false issue from being made up before the public. I have had no fair play before the British public, for very few Catholics on your side of the water have seen what I have written; and in every instance which has fallen under my notice in which your journals have attempted to reproduce my views, they have misrepresented. Even you yourself, in your notice of my review of Mr. Morris's book, did not deal fairly with me; you reproduce passages which bore against Dr. Newman and the converted Puseyites, but you did not reproduce even one of the many passages which prove at a glance that I bring no such charges as you and Dr. Newman imagine. Is it that we deceive ourselves when we imagine that we speak a common language? Is it you do not understand American, and that I do not understand English? I am half inclined to suspect that there is something of the sort, for I have full confidence in your personal kindness towards me, and your disposition to be just to every man. However this may be, allow me to subscribe myself,

Your sincere friend and obedient servant,

O.A. Brownson
Editor of Brownson's Quarterly Review[47]

There may have been something to what Brownson said about he himself and his English friends deceiving themselves into believing that they spoke and wrote one common language.[48] However that may be, Fr. Edmond Benard gives it as his opinion that Newman meant nothing more by his theory of the development of Christian doctrine than the formulation of what had been merely implicit in Christian doctrine into explicit teaching. Nevertheless, even conceding that Newman, when speaking of the development of Christian doctrine, meant not the revealed truth itself, but the mind's eye of it, Brownson still strenuously objected to the theory on the ground that Newman designated the human, not the divine mind, as the formative power in the process. He, observed Brownson, "undoubtedly transports human activity into the first cycle, the peculiar province of God, and makes man joint Creator with the Holy Ghost of Christian doctrine."[49] Whatever development or explication of Christian doctrine there has been, affirmed Brownson, has been effected through the agency of the Holy Spirit, not through the mental or moral action of the faithful.

Although Brownson had softened toward Newman after he had read Newman's book, *Loss and Gain*,[50] and had received Newman's invitation to become Lecturer Extraordinary at the proposed Catholic University of Ireland, he was to continue his opposition to Newman's theory to the end as Newman had first presented it.[51] Yet certain events at this time did operate to mollify further the opposition he had shown in the matter. The notorious Dr. Achilli, an unfrocked priest, was then lecturing against the Catholic

Church in England and Ireland. In his fifth lecture on the *Present Position of Catholics in England,* delivered on the Corn Exchange of Birmingham, 1851, Newman had exposed and scathingly denounced him. Achilli sued for libel. The charges Newman had preferred against him were entirely true, but as some of the documents necessary to substantiate the charges were not produced in time to forestall the trial, the judgment went against Newman in the trial that followed. Even the London *Times* complained of the miscarriage of justice.[52] Great sympathy was felt for Newman by all his coreligionists, and Brownson, too, was sensibly touched. He expressed his sympathy, saying:

> Our last article on Development, which seems to have given some offense, was written and printed before Dr. Newman had had his trial; otherwise, we may say, it would have been written somewhat differently, for it is not, we hope, in our disposition even to appear hard on those whom an unjust world oppresses. . . . At any rate, we feel we have done all that can reasonably be expected of a lay journalist, and that, should the theory be reasserted, we are under no obligation to take further notice of it. We shall therefore leave it in the hands of the pastors of the Church to take such action or no-action on the subject as they judge necessary or expedient.[53]

In concluding this chapter it might be well to do a little summing up. We should recall that Brownson was not opposed to every kind of development of Christian doctrine, but did object to certain features of the theory of development as Newman had first presented it in his book. Said Brownson:

> Development of a certain sort we concede, indeed, maintain. That some things in the beginning were only implicitly revealed, not explicitly, we are loath to deny; but implicitly and explicitly may, according to Suárez, be understood in two different senses. Implicit may mean what is not clear and distinct; or it may mean what is revealed only as the effect in the cause, or the property in the essence. As opposed to the latter sense, we maintain that the whole revelation was explicitly revealed from the beginning; but as opposed to the former sense, we do not maintain that the whole revelation was explicitly revealed from the beginning: and therefore we admit, with St. Vincent of Lerins, that faith, as time goes on, may acquire light, evidence, and distinctness.[54]

Again, in 1875, Brownson remarked that Newman in a postscript to a new edition of his *Letter to the Duke of Norfolk* had so modified his theory of development "as to make it mean very little."[55] Had Brownson lived long enough to learn of Newman's important revision of his theory in 1878, it is quite possible he would no longer have seen latent scares in Newman's famous essay which he considered "an ingenious work, indicating severe intellectual labor, rare speculative powers, extensive erudition, and much honest endeavor."[56]

# 26

## BROWNSON'S DOCTRINE ON THE CHURCH AND SALVATION

*A statement of what Brownson uniformly held concerning the Catholic Church and salvation • Why he stressed the strict construction of the Church's doctrine, "Outside the Church there is no salvation" • His article on "The Great Question" • He enunciates the theological distinctions on the question in his article on "Civil and Religious Toleration" • He demonstrates that belonging merely to the "soul" of the Church is not sufficient in the case • His contention has been upheld in our day by the encyclical letter of Pope Pius XII, Mystici Corporis • A statement of the qualifications of soul that will join anyone to the Church invisibly who is not actually a member of the Church • A discussion of the meaning and limiting worth of invincible ignorance • Brownson's arguments showing that there can be no exception to this dogma of the Church • A mention of those who have misrepresented Brownson's doctrine of this question.*

Perhaps no Catholic doctrine was to be the occasion of such prolonged controversy for Brownson as the doctrine, "Outside the Church there is no salvation." There seems to have been considerable misunderstanding and confusion in the minds of biographers and contributors to periodical literature in the past as to the precise doctrine Brownson set forth in his elaborate exposition of this solemn dogma of the Catholic Church. But this misunderstanding and confusion need not to have existed if he had been read chronologically on this theological theme. No one will ever rightly understand his approach to, and his interpretation of, this dogma who has not first read carefully his article "Recent Publications" with its illuminating remarks introductory to what was to follow so soon.[1] This article is the key to his whole subsequent formal treatment of the matter. This particular article appeared in the April 1847 issue of his *Quarterly,* and was the harbinger of his first *ex professo* treatment of the dogma in the very next edition of his *Review* under the heading, "The Great Question."[2] Although he recurs briefly time and again throughout his career as a Catholic publicist to this dogma — it seems to have been a sore point with him inasmuch as he had been badly badgered because of the stand he had taken — his other main discussions of this solemn definition of the Church occur in the articles: "Civil and Religious Toleration,"[3] "Extra Ecclesiam nulla Salus,"[4] and his lengthy rejoinder to his critics of the last article.[5] Briefly stated, the doctrine that he uniformly set forth and defended in this matter was that in order to be saved one must in some real sense belong to the *body* of the Catholic Church even though one be not necessarily a member of the visible communion of the Church actually.

Some there are who seem to have dismissed Brownson's interpretation of this dogma as highly individualistic. What Brownson's critics in this matter seem to have missed — at least no reference has been made to this particular point — is that Brownson's theology of this doctrine is not just a crotchety interpretation of his own, for his original exposition of this solemn definition of the Church was written in 1847 at the "command" of Bishop Fitzpatrick of Boston, and was "revised and approved by him before it was published."[6] Brownson rated Fitzpatrick to be "the soundest theologian, and one of the ablest we have ever met . . . whose teachings we but feebly reproduce."[7] He could say in reference to his exposition of this Catholic doctrine as well as any other:

> We have not wished to put forth any crotchets of our own, or to *improve* the doctrines taught us. The Catholic Church, faith, and worship, as they are, always have been, and always will be till the end of time, is what we have embraced, what we love, and what we seek to defend — not relying on our own private judgment, but receiving the truth in humility from those Almighty God has commissioned to teach us, and who he has commanded us to obey.[8]

In approaching his first exposition of the Catholic Church's exclusive claim of salvation, he deeply deplored in his article (entitled "Recent Publications") latitudinarianism, the increasing tendency among authors of current popular literature to soften or explain away altogether the qualifications or restrictions which theologians attach to the dogma. (This sort of literature seems to have reached its apex in A. J. Cronin's *Keys of the Kingdom.*) Such a tendency was only aiding and abetting a fatal latitudinarianism already rampant and widespread. Against this tendency in popular literature Brownson entered his vigorous protest. In doing so, he was anticipating by more than a century the solemn protest of Pope Pius XII uttered in his encyclical, *Humani Generis,* against those who were reducing this dogma to "a meaningless formula." (Brownson, too, used the identical word used by His Holiness, "meaningless."[9]) Such loose and brief explanations of this dogma as appear in novels, periodicals, newspapers and even *manuals,* continued Brownson, and which from these are caught up hastily by careless, half-educated, and unreflecting readers, already under the influence of a wide latitudinarianism, are sure to be given a latitudinarian turn or twist in such wise as to become false in doctrine and harmful in effect. He asserted that not only had he himself been so led to understand these qualifications of theologians when still a Protestant, but also that although he had never doubted, after the age of twenty, that if Christ had established any church at all, it was the Roman Catholic Church, he had been repelled for years — he was forty-two years of age when he became a Catholic — from investigating the claims of that church by finding Catholics themselves apparently conceding that it was not necessary for one to be joined to the Catholic Church in order to be saved.[10] Concerning the qualifications of theologians touching this dogma and the popular mind, he had this to say:

> Theologians may restrict the language of the dogma, they may qualify its apparent sense, and their qualifications, as they themselves understand them, and as they stand in their scientific treatises for theological students, may be just and detract nothing from faith; but any qualifications or explanations made in popular works, as the general reader will understand them, especially when the tendency is to latitudinarianism, will be virtually against faith; because he does not and cannot take them in the sense of the theologians, and with the distinctions and restrictions with which they always accompany them in their own minds. We never yet heard a layman contend for what he supposed

to be the theological qualifications of this article of faith, without contending for what is, in fact, *contra fidem*.[11]

(Here we should carefully note that Brownson did not at all deny these qualifications or restrictions of theologians — of which he has been accused — he only regretted that as reproduced in popular literature, they are either not properly stated, or are incorrectly understood by the reader. Here no doubt is the reason, at least partly, why he did not include them in his first exposition of this dogma.)

To Brownson's mind, then, the paramount question was: how to head off and roll back this ever rising tide of latitudinarianism? The only answer he could find was to stress the strict construction of this dogma, *Extra Ecclesiasm nulla Salus*. To this he was already inclined on other grounds. He had learned his lesson about liberal theology long before he had become a Catholic. Moreover, he had been roundly abused by some of his countrymen for having become a Catholic, was even looked upon as a traitor.[12] The stricter construction he gave this Catholic doctrine, the plainer he was making it to those outside the Church that as far as he himself was concerned he had been left no choice in the matter.

In his original proclamation, then, of this solemn dogma of the Catholic Church, writing in the capacity of a magazine editor, he took a practical rather than a theoretical course in the matter, and it will not be amiss to recall that this tactic was endorsed by Bishop Fitzpatrick. In writing his first treatise on the subject, entitled "The Great Question," he feared that any but an undistinguished proclamation of the dogma might do more harm than good. With him, rightly or wrongly, it was a matter of *polemical* policy. He was greatly fearful of giving those outside the Catholic Church false hopes, and thought there was always less to be apprehended from saying anything that might offend them than from failing to arrest their attention and engage them seriously in the work of investigation. He was already thoroughly convinced of what he was to write some years later:

> We must preach in all its rigor the naked dogma. Give them the slightest peg, or what appears so, not to you, but to them — give them the slightest peg, on which to hang a hope of salvation without being in or actually reconciled to the Church by the Sacrament of Penance — and all the arguments you address to them on the necessity of being in the Church in order to be saved, will have no more effect on them than rain on a duck's back.[13]

It seems proper to interject at this point that although Brownson did not go into the theological distinctions connected with this dogma in his first exposition in 1847, "The Great Question," he did so just two years later, 1849, in the article, "Civil and Religious Toleration,"[14] and in later discussions of the theme. Those who have misrepresented him in the matter have failed to recognize that he did enunciate the theological distinctions in his later discussions. His first article was written more from the standpoint of the apostolic missionary than the professional theologian.

Perhaps the most popular theory resorted to by the latitudinarians to explain away the necessity of being a member of the Catholic Church in some real sense was the theory which purports to guarantee salvation by asserting the sufficiency of belonging to the so-called soul of the Church though an alien to the body. As the late Fr. Joseph Fenton said in an article in the *American Ecclesiastical Review,* this false theory crept stealthily into Catholic thought and literature and gained considerable currency through the misinterpretation and misapplication on the part of certain eighteenth-century theologians of the terms *soul and body* of the Catholic Church as used by St. Robert Bellarmine in his treatise *De Ecclesia Militante,* but which he himself used merely as metaphors in elucidating various portions of his teaching on the nature and component parts of the Church.[15] But Brownson was theologian enough not to be misled by such a specious theory. The soul and body of the Church, he affirmed, are distinguishable but not separable:

> She [the Catholic Church] is not a disembodied spirit, nor a corpse. The separation of the soul and the body of the Church is as much her death, as the separation of the soul and body of man is his. She is the Church, the living Church only by the mutual commerce of soul and body. . . . If as all theologians teach . . . the life of the Church is in the mutual commerce of the exterior and the interior, the body and the soul, no individual not joined to her body can live her life. Indeed, to suppose that communion with the body alone will suffice, is to fall into mere formalism, to mistake the corpse for the living man; and, on the other hand, to suppose that communion with the soul out of the body and independent of it is practicable is to fall into pure spiritualism, simple Quakerism, which tapers off into transcendentalism or mere sentimentalism.[16]

Hence, as Brownson further explained, whenever the Holy Scriptures, the fathers, the popes and the councils speak of the Catholic Church, in connection with salvation, they always speak of the visible Church, or the Church in the concrete, not of an invisible Church, or the Church as a disembodied spirit. He related that in a letter he had addressed through a theologian to the Prefect of Propaganda, Cardinal Alessandro Barnabò, mindful of the qualifications which some theologians give the dogma, and of some articles he had read in the *Civiltà Cattolica,* he said: "I shall never leave the Church, for I am certain there is no salvation out of her communion, *at least for me.*" The cardinal noticed the apparent limitation, and in the name of the Holy See, rebuked it, and asked: "Does not il Signore Brownson believe that there is salvation for any one else out of the Church?"[17]

In consonance with this interpretation of the dogma, he hit out vigorously at the fiction of an invisible Church which the reformers fell back upon when hard pressed for an explanation of where then was the Church before Luther and Calvin had appeared. "The Church," asserted Brownson, "which Catholics believe in is a visible kingdom, as much so as the kingdom of France or Great Britain, and when faith assures us that out of the Church there is no salvation, the plain, obvious, natural sense of the dogma is, that those living and dying out of that visible kingdom cannot be saved."[18] To yield the necessity of membership in the visible Church, in order to be saved, would be, he said, to leave "the dogma no meaning that even a Socinian or a Transcendentalist has any urgent reason to reject."[19] And he cited the fact that St. Robert Bellarmine holds, as do most theologians, on the authority of St. Ambrose, that catechumens, dying before they receive the visible sacrament of baptism in fact, may be saved; but that St. Robert Bellarmine still felt a difficulty in the case, and "labored hard" to prove that "catechumens are after all, in the Church, not actually and properly, but only potentially, as a man conceived, but not yet formed and born, is called man potentially." And he further cited St. Augustine and Billuart to underscore the point that these theologians understood clearly that if they were to count as saved catechumens who died before actually receiving the sacrament of baptism, they were under the necessity of proving that they were members in some real sense of the body of the Church — either in fact or in desire.[20]

Brownson's contention of the inadequacy of belonging merely to the so-called "soul" of the Church, or of belonging to some sort of an invisible church or society, was sustained once and for all in the encyclical letter of Pope Pius XII, *Mystici Corporis*:

> We deplore and condemn [said the Sovereign Pontiff] the pernicious error of those who conjure up from their fancies an imaginary Church, a kind of society which finds its origin and growth in charity, to which they somewhat contemptuously oppose another, which they call juridical. But this distinction, which they introduce, is baseless.

It is important to note, however, that this interpretation of the dogma in no way excludes the possibility of salvation for any who have the desire of belonging to the Catholic Church, provided the desire be animated by the requisite dispositions of soul. For Pope Pius XII in this same encyclical, *Mystici Corporis,* spoke of those possessed of an implicit desire of belonging to the Church as "unsuspectingly related to the Mystical Body of the Redeemer." Explaining the dispositions of soul required for efficacy unto salvation in the desire of belonging to the Church, whether explicit or implicit, the Holy Office said in a letter dated August 8, 1949:

> However, this desire need not always be explicit, as in the case of catechumens; but when a person is involved in invincible ignorance, God accepts also the *implicit desire,* so called because it is included in that good disposition of soul whereby a person wishes his will to be conformed to the will of God. . . . But it must not be thought that [merely] any kind of a desire of entering the Church suffices for one to be saved. It is necessary that the desire by which one is related to the Church be animated by perfect charity. Nor can an implicit desire produce its effect, unless a person has supernatural faith. "For he that cometh to God must believe that God exists and that He is the rewarder of those who seek Him" (Hebrews 11:6).

The whole case, therefore, for the possibility of salvation for those who live and die outside the Catholic Church would seem to turn on whether they attain to these dispositions of soul, perfect charity and supernatural faith, in cases where a desire, at least implicit, is had, that is, when there is invincible ignorance of the true Church. Into these practical aspects of the question Brownson entered in no small detail. He did not seem to think that these qualities of soul are to be so easily presumed in those of his countrymen who live outside the visible communion of the Church. All that can be done here is to present a few of his salient thoughts or reasonings on the subject.

As to the perfect charity required in the case: in his original exposition of the dogma, Brownson asserted that while there may be many persons in heretical sects who are guiltless of the formal sin of heresy, yet such, he said, may be judged and condemned "for sins not remissible without true faith, and for want of virtues impracticable out of the communion of the Church." He quoted St. Augustine as authority for the statement that *charity cannot be kept out of the unity of the Church.*[21] This statement of St. Augustine seems to find some support in the encyclical letter *Mystici Corporis* of Pope Pius XII wherein the Sovereign Pontiff while speaking of those who, though not actual members, yet have the implicit desire of belonging to the Church, said: "Even though they are unsuspectingly related to the Mystical Body of the Redeemer in desire and resolution, they still remain deprived of so many precious gifts and helps from heaven which one can enjoy only in the Catholic Church."

When we come to the question of supernatural faith so necessary for salvation, as stipulated by the Holy Office, we encounter no small difficulty for those outside the Church. True supernatural faith implies absolute conviction of the truth of divine revelation made by God and proposed by his Church. For the Catholic the Church is the infallible witness in the case. But where is the competent witness for what is really God's word for those outside the Church? Infallibility being disclaimed by all the sects, and the members of each being left to interpret the Bible according to the principle of private interpretation, what is there to guarantee security against error, or to assure the individual that he has anything more than probable opinion? Hence Brownson always maintained that those outside the Catholic Church have nothing more than mere opinions in matters of religion. "Even the Protestant laggards or old fogies," he said, "who adhere to the old Protestant confessions or formulas, adhere to them as opinions not as dogmas of faith. They, as well as the more advanced Protestants, speak of differences among the sects, and between them and Catholics, as differences of opinions. This is the established phraseology of the journals, the best exponents, not indeed of truth, but of the spirit, the views, the tendencies of their time and country."[22] Archbishop Patrick Kenrick, one of the foremost theologians our country has produced, also seems to have shared Brownson's view as to the lack of the proper conditions for true supernatural faith outside the Catholic Church. He wrote:

> We may be pardoned, then, for doubting whether in any instance the persuasion of sectaries can fairly be called faith. Their sincere attachment to the leading doctrines of Christianity we need not question; their pious dispositions and tendencies we do not doubt; but we fear they have not that deep and unshaken conviction which constitutes divine faith, and which is the result of the recognition of an infallible authority.[23]

We are still to note that the letter of the Holy Office, August 1849, further indicates that the implicit desire of belonging to the Church is of such a nature that it presupposes "a person involved in invincible ignorance." While those who have been Catholics from infancy generally make the most liberal concessions regarding the good faith of those outside the Church, Brownson plainly did not agree with those unreserved concessions, though he always protested he had no disposition to judge anyone individually. We only record here his convictions, whatever their worth. That there is much ignorance of the Catholic Church among those outside of the Church in our country, Brownson of course knew as well as anyone, but that it is to be dismissed in wholesale fashion as *invincible* ignorance (ignorance that could not ordinarily be overcome), he plainly did not believe. Speaking of the matter near the end of his life, he said:

> We do not believe that in our times there is much, if any, invincible ignorance among Protestant sects, or many instances of what is called good faith. . . . The Church is a city set upon a hill, and her light shines out through all the region round, even to those in the valley. Her missionaries are in all nations, and there is not one in a Protestant nation that need remain ignorant of the Church or her titles, if he cares to know them, or is earnest to save his soul. The fact that persons from all ranks and conditions, learned and unlearned, freemen and slaves, have been converted, St. John Chrysostom urges, in one of his homilies, as a proof that all might, if they would.[24]

It is also quite important to note that, as Brownson pointed out, even should ignorance be genuinely invincible, it is in itself no passport to beatitude. Invincible ignorance is sometimes spoken of as if it were a positive virtue, whereas it is entirely negative, and though it excuses from sin in that whereof one is invincibly ignorant, it has no positive virtue, and advances one not a single step toward the kingdom of God. Being negative in nature, it has no power to elevate the soul to the supernatural order, or to place it on the plane of its supernatural destiny. This is why theologians tell us that unbaptized infants dying in infancy can never see God in the beatific vision. Not even the absence of all personal sin, to say nothing of invincible ignorance, suffices to establish one in the supernatural order. For that, an act of supernatural power is required. The reason for that is that the two orders, the natural and the supernatural, lie in radically different planes, and the supernatural can never be developed or evolved from the natural by any law of natural progress. "We are not placed by our birth from Adam on the plane of our beatitude," said Brownson, "but to reach it [we] must be born again, created anew in Christ Jesus; a newer and higher life must be begotten in us, the life which flows out of the Incarnation, a life of which the Lord made flesh is the author and fountain."[25]

Neither could Brownson believe that the order of grace established and revealed by God allows one to suppose that he leaves those who are invincibly ignorant of the Catholic Church to be saved just where they are. He always emphasized, following St. Augustine, that the graces received by those outside the Church are given them by God not only to live godly lives but also to draw them into unity with the Church. Bishop Hay, another convert, likewise strong in his belief that salvation is to be found only in the Catholic Church, expressed the like conviction that when God by his grace enlightens and moves persons out of communion with the Church, if they are responsive to his graces, they will be finally drawn within the Church's pale.[26] That God ever saves men by extraordinary means or without the *medium ordinarium* (the Catholic Church), is, "as far as our knowledge goes," affirmed Brownson, "authorized by no decision of the Church, by no *consensus theologorum,* by no analogy of faith, by no *ratio theologica,* and is expressly contradicted by the Fourth Council of the Lateran." Speaking of the matter at greater length, he wrote:

> [That there are persons invincibly ignorant of the Catholic Church] who so perfectly correspond to the graces received, that Almighty God will by *extraordinary means* bring them to the Church, is believable and perfectly compatible with the known order of grace, as is evinced in the case of the eunuch of Queen Candace, that of Cornelius, the captain of the Italian band, and hundreds of others recorded by our missionaries, especially the missionaries of the Society of Jesus. In all cases of extraordinary or miraculous intervention by Almighty God, whether in the order of nature, or the order of grace, known to us, he has intervened *ad ecclesiam* [that is, drawing to the Church], and there is not a shadow of authority for supposing that he ever has miraculously intervened or ever will intervene otherwise.[27]

This completes substantially Brownson's exposition of the dogma, "Outside the Church there is no salvation." Believing ever strongly in the power of truth, when clearly proclaimed, he had little patience with namby-pamby Catholics who were too timid to assert this dogma in all its rigor. "If there is any thing we detest," he remarked, "it is the attempt on the part of Catholics to modify Catholic dogmas to suit the prejudices of their hearers or readers. Catholicity can stand being stated truly; if not, let us away with it at once, and have nothing more to say about it.''[28] The real lack of charity is not in asserting this dogma in all its truth, he emphasized, but in not crying danger to those who are not in the safe way of salvation. "The weakness of many Catholics, or their false liberality which makes them refrain from asserting the plain truth [of this dogma], is most deplorable, dishonorable to God, and fatal to immortal souls redeemed with the precious blood of our Lord.''[29] In the final sentence of his discussion of this dogma, stretching well-nigh over thirty years, he said:

> There is no more fatal mistake than to soften, liberalize, or to latitudinize this terrible dogma, "Out[side] . . . the Church there is no salvation," or to give a man an opportunity to persuade him that he belongs to the soul of the Church, though an alien from the body.[30]

Just the same, some Catholics were shocked, or affected to be shocked when they heard Brownson proclaiming forthrightly to his countrymen that there is no salvation outside the Catholic Church. They said it was harsh, illiberal, and uncharitable to say so.[31] And some of them read the sturdy old reviewer's lectures on the wisdom of a more studied effort at presenting Catholic truth in a more inoffensive mien. In this they held up St. Francis de Sales as a model of sweetness and light. To which Brownson replied:

> We are often reminded when we insist upon this, that St. Francis de Sales, whose labors restored over seventy thousand Protestants to the Church, was wont to say that "more flies can be caught with honey than with vinegar." This is unquestionably true, but they who are familiar with the saint's works do not need to be told that in his own practice he gave considerable latitude to the word *honey*. Certainly we ask no more severe and bold mode of presenting Catholic truth, or stronger or severer language against Protestants, than he was in the habit of adopting. Even the editor of his controversial works did not deem it advisable to publish them without softening some of their expressions. In fact, much of the honey of the saints generally, especially such saints as St. Athanasius, St. Hilary of Poitiers, and St. Jerome, would taste very much like vinegar, we suspect, to some of our modern delicate palates.[32]

Whatever is to be said of Brownson's polemical policy in this matter, there can be no doubt that in all he had to say about the Catholic Church's claim of exclusive salvation, he was motivated by a truly ardent charity toward his countrymen.[33] The Church, he said, does not propose itself as just the best religion among others, but as the *only* religion whereby men can be saved. "It is for this reason that we urge upon all to become Catholics; it is this which fires our zeal for conversions, and makes us willing to suffer any torture, if we can win but one soul to Christ.''[34] "There is no sacrifice in my power," he assured, "that I would not make to bring 'my kinsmen after the flesh' to Christ.''[35]

In his exposition of this particular dogma Brownson wrote with an absolutely assured pen, for he had gone behind the dogma to find the principle which underlies it. Every Catholic dogma, he affirmed, is but the infallible expression of some great underlying principle which it is the business of the cultivators of the profounder theological science to find out and evaluate. The principle underlying the dogma, *Extra Ecclesiam nulla Salus*, is the great truth that "the *Man* Jesus Christ is the one Mediator between God and man," and that the Church is, as it were, his visible extension in society. St. Paul calls the Church the "body of Christ." To be saved, then, one must belong in some sense to the *body* of the Catholic Church, in reality, or in desire and intention. To assert salvation through the disembodied spirit of the Church would be meaningless, since the Holy Spirit did not become incarnate, is not the one Mediator between God and man, and would leave the *flesh assumed* in the womb of the Blessed Mary by the Word no office or representative in the economy of salvation. There can be no exception to this, or any other Catholic dogma, for all the dogmas of the Church are *Catholic,* universal, and admit of no exception; an exception in regard to this dogma or any other would negate or destroy Christianity as the teleological order established by God. It was when following this line of reasoning that he pointed up the little word *omnino* ("no one at all") which appears in the original solemn definition of the Fourth Council of the Lateran: "Una vero fidelium universalis Ecclesia, extra quam nullus omnino salvatur."[36]

That Brownson, for the reasons already stated, adopted a strict construction of this dogma, is obvious. Some, not looking closely at his wording, have misapprehended his interpretation. One of the offenders in the matter was a writer in the *Boston Pilot,* in 1874, who accused him of maintaining that "whoever is not *actually* a member of the visible *body* of the Church cannot belong to the soul of the Church." This is not what we wrote, and is not what we hold, replied Brownson. The error, he indicated, is in the surreptitious insertion of the little word *actually.* "We said and we say that whoever is not a member, at least an inchoate member, of the body of the Church cannot belong to the soul of the Church, and therefore cannot be saved," if the dogma means anything.[37] Even the acute and erudite Jesuit, the late Fr. Wilfrid Parsons, also thought he was making a point against Brownson when he charged him with holding "the extraordinary view that only those who are in visible communion [with the Catholic Church] can be saved."[38] Brownson held no such thing. In an article on "Orestes Brownson, Montalembert, and Modern Civilization," Leon Bernard, Ph.D., also charged Brownson with an undistinguished proclamation of this dogma.[39] It is quite possible that Leon Bernard as well as others have drawn for information on commentators in what they take to be Brownson's interpretation instead of investigating the matter personally. (Bernard drew freely on Theodore Maynard's biography of Brownson in his article.) However this may be, Brownson's son Henry put his father's interpretation correctly when he wrote: "In the question as to exclusive salvation, he never denied or questioned the qualifications of the dogma suggested by many eminent theologians, but insisted on the necessity of regeneration to put man on the plane of the supernatural destiny."[40] The statement of Maynard that Brownson "rejected [the ordinary theological distinctions in the case] against the weight of accepted theological opinion," is simply false.[41]

In 1864 Brownson wrote: "We by no means hold that we are to consign to perdition all who are not visibly in her [the Catholic Church's] communion."[42] Maynard implies that this was a change of doctrine on Brownson's part, and that he later came to look upon the statement as a "weak and shameful concession."[43] In this there was no change of doctrine on Brownson's part, for he had never denied that people may be saved without belonging visibly to the Church, that is, if the requisite qualities of soul are present. When writing as an apostle in his first exposition of the dogma, 1847, he did not include the theological distinctions, as we have already noted, but two years later in his article on "Civil and Religious Toleration" he did enunciate the qualities of soul which join one invisibly to the Church — perfect charity, and supernatural faith when one is invincibly ignorant of the true Church." (This is repeated here for emphasis.) He cannot therefore be rightly accused of ever having held that one must be visibly united to the Catholic Church in order to be saved. He most unequivocally acknowledged the theological distinctions connected with this dogma already in his article "Recent Publications,"[45] written before his first formal treatise on this solemn definition of the Church under the heading, "The Great Question."[46]

Nor was Maynard less unfortunate in criticizing Brownson for what he interpreted as an expression of "contempt" for the theologians "who open wide the door of salvation."[47] This is again to misinterpret Brownson. In winding up his long discussion of "The Great Question" as a Catholic apologist, Brownson said: "We have not presumed to question the explanations modern theologians give the dogma; we say not *exceptions,* for every dogma is Catholic, and what is Catholic, as we have said, admits of no exception. We have only endeavored to fix after theological reasoning and the greater theologians the limits of these explanations, and thus check the latitudinarianism which the popular understanding deduces from them."[48] After showing that a single exception to this dogma would destroy the whole teleological order as established by God, Brownson observed that *as a consequence* of this, even those theologians "who by their explanations open wide the door of salvation, labor with all their might to prove that those who apparently die outside the Church, and whose salvation, they tell us, is not to be despaired of, do not really die out of her communion, but, in fact, in it, and as Catholics. That is, men may be in the communion of the Church while apparently out of it, and adhering to sects hostile to it, being excused through invincible ignorance."[49] There is no "contempt" expressed here on Brownson's part for the theologians. He was simply asserting again the simple, solemn truth, "Outside the Church there is no salvation," rightly understood.

Nor was Hugh Marshall any less incorrect when he asserted that Brownson took the "extreme" position that "outside corporate membership in the visible Roman Catholic Church no one could avoid damnation."[50]

Orestes Augustus Brownson never wasted any time in his day fighting windmills or strawmen. He always attacked the real enemy that held the field or was moving onto the field. The latitudinarianism or religious indifference he found devouring men's souls in his day, and which is devouring them with a tenfold greater voracity in our day, he attacked with every weapon he could bring into play from his gigantic intellectual armory. If he slew not this voracious dragon, it was no fault of his own. His was a most valiant fight for what he considered the real significance of the Catholic Church's claim of exclusive salvation, because he could not bring himself to believe that it is a small matter whether one belongs to the true Church or not, whether one gains or loses heaven forever.

# 27

## A VALIANT ONSLAUGHT
## ON POLITICAL RADICALISM

*Brownson finds Count de Maistre's* Essay on the Generative Principle of Political Constitutions *in harmony with his own political views • De Maistre's seminal principle: political constitutions are not made but develop, or are generated • Brownson excoriates the idea of "paper" constitutions arbitrarily imposed • Acknowledgment of the generative principle makes for stability of government • Brownson's heavy onslaughts on the revolutionary principle • A revolution, strictly so-called, never works an improvement • The American Revolution not such in the true sense • Tyranny and oppression can never be legal • Brownson agrees, "Resistance to tyrants is obedience to God" • His attack on "Jacobin" democracy • His significant article, "The Republic of the United States" • Our political system is rightly called a republic, a federal republic • Brownson censures President Polk for usurping congressional powers in personally declaring war on Mexico • He is abused by Catholics for his efforts to put down revolutionism • He tells revolutionaries that religion is the very matrix of liberty • His searching analysis and proscription of socialism • Brownson and Daniel Webster in accord on the slavery question and the Fugitive Slave Law • Senator William Henry Seward appeals to the "Higher Law" • Brownson's exhaustive discussion of the Fugitive Slave Law • His denunciation of the piratical invasions of Cuba • He censures Daniel Webster for the sympathy and support he extended, as Secretary of State, to Louis Kossuth and the other Hungarian Rebels.*

For the first three or four years after his conversion, Brownson addressed himself rather exclusively to arguing the case for the Catholic Church directly, or in making a defense of what he considered sound Christian doctrine. But after having expended his best efforts in vigorously combating liberalism and latitudinarianism in the theological order, he turned again to make war on destructive revolutionism or radicalism which was becoming ever more rife at home and abroad in the political order. Not that considerable political thought had not also been mixed in at times with his theological thought in many of his previous essays as a Catholic publicist, but he had not to any considerable extent treated political topics *ex professo* in his first years as a Catholic. As the only effectual antidote to the increasing political radicalism would be the inculcation of sound political doctrine, he felt the time had come to open the pages of his *Quarterly* to a discussion of the great political and social questions of the day which were agitating the public mind at home and abroad. He considered it of great importance that these questions be freely and boldly discussed in the light of Catholic faith and morals. Believing firmly that the political principles enunciated by the Church spell true order and freedom for society, he felt that Catholics had (and still have) an imperious obligation to proclaim those principles and make them tell upon the public sentiment of the country.[1] He had found Catholics in the past, in common with many of their countrymen, borrowing their political notions from the school of Hobbes, Locke, Jean Jacques Rousseau and Tom Paine, forgetting, or tending to forget that Divine Providence plays a part, an all-important part, in the political order also.[2] Catholics must learn the Church's true philosophy in the matter, he counseled, and no longer shirk the duty incumbent upon them to proclaim to their fellow countrymen those sound moral and political doctrines which flow from the teachings of their Church and which they should know are required for the permanence and stability of society.

As a sound basis for the political doctrines he wished to set forth and defend, Brownson drew at the time largely on Count de Maistre's *Essay on the Generative Principle of Political Constitutions* which he reviewed in the October 1847 issue of his *Quarterly*. De Maistre's seminal principle asserts that political constitutions are not made but rather grow, develop, or are generated. Whatever the real constitution of a people, it is something that has grown and developed through the agency of Divine Providence, God using men and circumstances as they are, and is never something that has come about by being arbitrarily framed and imposed on a people that are to live under it. It is ever the work of Divine Providence. Said Brownson:

> The written constitution may sometimes be a memorandum of the real constitution, but it is never that constitution itself; and is always a mere cobweb, save so far as it is written on the hearts of the people, and in the habits, the manners and customs of the people, as daily experience proves. The constitution is the living soul of the nation, that by virtue of which it is a nation, and is able to live a national life, and perform national functions. You can no more write it out on parchment, and put it into your pocket, than you can the soul of a man.[3]

Being ever the work of Providence, imposed by God himself (indirectly), each constitution is an expression of the divine will for each particular people, and is therefore sacred and inviolable as well as the best suited form of government for each respective nation.

This is the political doctrine Brownson was to oppose so vigorously to all those — some regarded as profound political philosophers and statesmen — who contend that a political constitution is something that may be made "as one makes a handcart or a wheelbarrow, or drawn up beforehand as one draws up a note of hand." Such a constitution he denounced as a destructive delusion, and after referring to the fact that even Carlyle had ridiculed it unmercifully, called upon his readers to bear witness that he had himself argued and declaimed against this selfsame delusion with all his might ever since he had begun to address the public on political themes.[4]

The great merit of De Maistre's political doctrine, one with his own for Brownson, was that it makes so strongly for the stability of government — the very doctrine so direly needed by an age stricken with a mania for revolutionary changes in government. It forbids the subjects of a monarchy to throw off monarchy and attempt to create another form of government without just cause, and it forbids the subjects of a republican form of government to throw off republicanism and found another form of government without just cause. If we wish to preserve our republican institutions, counseled Brownson, in all their vigor and vitality, we should as true Americans embrace earnestly the generative principle of political constitutions as enunciated by De Maistre, acknowledging therewith the Providence of God in the form of government that has come down to us.[5] In this he was harking back to the sentiments expressed by the immortal Washington in his inaugural address in 1789 when he said: "No nation can be bound to acknowledge and adore the Invisible Hand that conducts the affairs of men more than those of the United States. Every step by which they have advanced to the character of an independent nation seems to have been distinguished by some token of providential agency."

In the light of the generative principle, it was not therefore the foresight of the people nor the wisdom of statesmen that gave the American people their distinctive republican institutions. It was rather Divine Providence which controlled and determined the basic historical facts in the case. It is to be noted that royalty and nobility did not emigrate to America, but only the common people. Royalty and nobility not being here, they furnished no element in the formation of the original political constitution of America. (This in contrast to the case in South America.) Hence when the foreign authority was thrown off, we were left with our own basic political constitution, to wit, representative democracy, or an elective aristocracy, if the term may be used, which had emigrated here from England. Brownson at this time looked upon our government as simply the British House of Commons, without the king and House of Lords, divided for the sake of convenience into an upper and lower chamber, and with such changes and modifications as were necessary to provide for an executive authority.[6] But he was to take a somewhat different view of this matter when he wrote *The American Republic* in 1865.[7]

Although he was to stress the point elsewhere, he also emphasized in this article that a political constitution can never be essentially changed by the respective people or nation, deliberately or otherwise, without the destruction of the nation itself. If we are to credit the lessons of history, he cautioned, any such change is always and inevitably the destruction of the state itself. (He drew heavily on history to establish his assertion.) It would be just as easy to extract the soul from the body, and give to the body another soul, without causing death, as to take from a state its original constitution and give it a new one, and still retain the life of the nation. But if the original constitution has died out, the nation of course is dead, and is no more capable of receiving a new soul and of being restored to life than a dead body is capable of receiving a new soul and being made a living body. A new constitution must mean a new political people, which replaces the old, as is clearly seen in the case of the downfall of the old Roman Empire, and the rise of the modern states of Europe. Even religion could not prevent the downfall when the old constitution had decayed from within; it might have delayed the catastrophe, but it had not the power to avert it. Constantine, Theodosius, Justinian — none of these could prevent the doom of Rome, old or new.[8]

As much as Brownson admired De Maistre for his conservative political philosophy, he did not refrain from saying how widely he differed from his monarchical views. De Maistre was a staunch monarchist, and counted monarchy, tempered with a due mixture of aristocracy and democracy, the best of all possible forms of government. Such a preference was unintelligible to so staunch a republican as Brownson who believed that no one form of government is *per se* preferable to another.[9] Perhaps De Maistre's greatest service to Brownson was serving as a vehicle to him of Edmund Burke's political philosophy. It is rather surprising that Brownson did not discuss

Burke's political philosophy. This may be partly explained by the fact that some of his *obiter dicta* on Burke in his early writings were extremely acute.[10] Yet he fully recognized Burke's transcendent endowments as a political philosopher. In 1852 he spoke of Burke as "the great English, or rather Irish statesman, who, perhaps, taken all in all, is the most eminent among the distinguished statesmen who have written and spoken in our language."[11] And in a letter to his Munich preceptor, Ignaz Döllinger, Lord Acton remarked that Brownson "sets Burke and De Maistre above all other political writers."[12] Brownson's political philosophy is in remarkable harmony with Burke's in more than one respect. His incessant war on radicalism was on a par with Burke's eloquent advocacy of the constitutional principle and his championship of the established order in opposition to atheistical Jacobinism in his *Reflections on the French Revolution.*

In his article on "Conservatism and Radicalism" Brownson now launched out into a full-scale attack on the political radicalism of the day at home and abroad. The article was largely a defense of himself against the charge that he had really become hostile to liberty and favorable to despotism. He proceeded to show that he had lately only re-enunciated the same conservative principles he had so strongly emphasized in the massive article he had written in 1837 on "Democracy" and had published in the January issue of his *Boston Quarterly Review* in 1838.[13] He owned that it was true that he may have had more in mind in that article the defense of the rights of the citizen, while more recently he may have been more intent on the rights of authority. But a change had come about — revolutionism was now on the march. And he would have it understood that in coming lately more to the defense of rightful authority he had done so simply out of a genuine love for true freedom, for liberty is impossible without order, order impossible without government, and government impossible without the loyalty and obedience of subjects. Significantly he said:

> Versatile as we may have been, we have always had certain fixed principles, and what they were may be known by noting what we have cast off in our advance towards manhood, and what we have retained and still retain. The conservative principle is evidently one of these, and as we undeniably held it when no one dreamed of charging us with hostility to liberty, we cannot see why our holding it now should be construed in proof that we are on the side of despotism.[14]

Reasserting the divine origin and right of government, he again prescribed in good set terms the revolutionary spirit of the day, what Lafayette called "the sacred right of insurrection." Any attempt to subvert the constitution of the state, that is, the constitution which God in his providence had given a particular people, and which is to be looked upon as the legitimate, the legal constitution, must be condemned. Such a constitution is sacred and inviolable, and any changes or innovations, under the name of progress or reform, that would essentially alter it, or seriously impede its free operation, are not to be tolerated. But a government that has been arbitrarily imposed on a people, or which betrays its trust, or usurps powers to the grave injury of its subjects, is an illegitimate government. Such a government may be lawfully resisted, and sometimes the gravity of matters may become such as to impose an imperious duty upon citizens to resist it. But this lends no sanction to the revolutionary principle as such which asserts the indefeasible right of a people to conspire and rebel against a legally established government in utter disregard of public law or historical rights.[15]

The increasing popularity of the revolutionary principle that was fast gaining ground at home and abroad alarmed Brownson, and he fought it tooth and nail as a journalist. Revolutions, he averred, only throw society back into barbarism and savagery. Yet it was asserted by radicals — those who called themselves progressives — that existing institutions are swept aside only in order to make way for a new and better organization of the state. It is all done for the sake of progress. To which Brownson replied in rising tones:

> When you have shown us an instance, in the whole history of the world, in which the destruction of an existing constitution of the state has been followed by the introduction and adoption of a new and better one — better for the particular nation, we mean — we will give up the point, acknowledge that we have been in this whole matter consummate fools, and become as mad revolutionists as the best of you. But such an instance cannot be found. How often must we tell you that a constitution cannot be made as one makes a wheelbarrow or a steam-engine — that of the constitution we must say, as we say of the poet, "nascitur, non fit"?[16]

Again the revolutionists cited the American Revolution as their justification for subverting a constitution in the hope of getting what they dreamt would be a better form of government. To which our political philosopher replied that he did not contest the right of the Anglo-American colonies to separate from the mother country, and cheerfully conceded the prosperity that has followed from that separation.[17] But the American Revolution was no revolution at all in the sense in which he condemned revolution, for there was no subversion of the state, no destruction of the basic existing constitution of the colonies, and the assertion of no right to destroy that constitution. It was merely a resistance to what the colonists considered the tyranny of King George III. After the war of liberation the American states retained substantially the same constitutions which they had as colonists. The action of the colonial governments in separating from the mother country, and in setting up for themselves, was totally different from the action of a mob against an existing constitution, destroying it and attempting to replace it with one they dream will be better. "We [reasoned Brownson] were children of our majority, leaving our father's house to become heads of establishments of our own; the revolutionists are parricides, who knock their aged parent in the head or cut his throat in order to possess themselves of the homestead."[18]

Brownson was careful to emphasize that the conservative principle which he was inculcating is in no sense hostile to such social ameliorations and administrative changes which time and its vicissitudes may render necessary or expedient in the name of progress. The true reformer, he underscored, is the state physician, and proceeds in precisely the same manner as does the medical doctor in regard to the human body. A medical doctor seeks to heal and restore to life, and such is the office of the state physician. "What would we think of a physician [he inquired] who would undertake to restore a man to health, or to increase his soundness and vigor, by destroying his constitution? What we should think of him is precisely what we ought to think of the statesman who seeks to advance civilization by subverting the constitution of the state."[19] Should affairs, however, come to such a pass that there is no longer a government, then the people may of course set about reconstructing a form of government that is the most acceptable to them.[20]

But with all Brownson's intransigent insistence on the doctrine of legitimacy in government, he by no means interpreted it to mean — as did many European legitimists of the day — passive obedience, nonresistance. Tyranny and oppression, he stoutly affirmed, can never be legal. Hence while the doctrine of legitimacy "smites the rebel or the revolutionist, it must equally smite the tyrant or usurper. . . . Tyranny, oppression is never legal, and therefore no tyrant or oppressor is or can be a legitimate sovereign. To resist him is not to resist legitimate authority, and therefore demands for its justification no assertion of the revolutionary principle." Hence "the doctrine of legitimacy gives a legal right to resist whatever is illegal, and therefore lays a solid foundation for liberty."[21] In other words, he firmly held with Jefferson that "resistance to tyrants is obedience to God."

In his political disquisitions Brownson labored at times under the dual handicap of advocating unpopular doctrines and of having his real meaning misunderstood. This in spite of the fact that he took "unwearied pains" to make his meaning unmistakable. The difficulty arose partly from the fact that he attached a meaning to some of his political terms different from that entertained by the popular mind. This was particularly the case in regard to the word *democracy*. After defining the term according to what he considered should be its true significance, he eventually found that his readers had not taken notice of his definition, or had forgotten all about it. Using the word in a more philosophical sense, he wrote in 1837: "The word *Democracy* . . . may be taken as the name of a great social and political doctrine, which is gaining much in popularity, and of a powerful movement of the masses towards a better social condition than has heretofore existed."[22] Restricting the word to this meaning was only inviting misunderstanding. When he so unsparingly rebuked the excesses of lawless democracy, often only in reference to the European scene, some seemed to gather that he was really lashing out at democracy in every form. This was indeed a touchy matter, for to Americans generally the word democracy was one of the untouchables. Fr. John H. McCaffery, president of Mt. St. Mary's College, Emmitsburg, Maryland, who often wrote Brownson very interesting letters, gave him a bit of sage advice when he said:

> Apropos of democracy, when you execrate it, you must explain a little more. Do not tire of repeating definitions. I agree with you that democracy, as it stands in the popular mind — as it is understood by at least four-fifths of us and by nearly all Europe — means among other things, rebellion — resistance to authority; but as it does not technically mean that, nor necessarily — and as the people never define their ideas, you would at least do well to define them for us — and moreover a definition repeated and learned by heart is often the whole argument; I do not wish that you should try to rescue the term, for that would be labor lost. Yet, as it is a name of power and a name dear to many, touch it prudently.[23]

The pregnant sentence in Fr. McCaffery's letter was of course: "Do not tire of repeating definitions." Exploring the many facets of democracy in its historical contexts, both past and present, there was vital need for Brownson to make quite clear in *each case* just what kind of democracy he was speaking about when he excoriated the evils variously appearing under that form of government as well as under any other kind. In 1849 he wrote: "In fact, the democratic government is expressly devised, not to restrain the people in their collective or public conduct, but to relieve them of all restraint, and to give them free scope to do whatever they please, to follow without let or hindrance whatever is the dominant passion or sentiment for the time being."[24] From the context it is plain enough that he was talking about pure or unlimited democracy, but it would have been wise to have made it more plain. The distinction he most frequently made was between a pure democracy, what he often called "Jacobin democracy," and constitutional democracy. The first type was abhorrent to him, the second — though he preferred the term republic — he truly loved and cherished as the form of government bequeathed to us by the Founding Fathers, whatever the evils inseparable from any form of government. But however acute his criticisms of the practical workings of democratic institutions, no man was a more ardent democrat than Brownson himself in the sense of being a militant protagonist for all that makes for the rights and interests of the people. Again, with him the form of government was not the all-important thing, but rather the end and aim every government should have in constant view, namely, the freedom and commonweal of the people. As he succinctly expressed it, "Democracy and liberty are not necessarily coincident. . . . What we want, whatever the form of government, are safeguards for liberty in the shape of checks on power. Absolute governments are always evil, and the wisdom of the statesman consists in the adoption of methods for their limitation."[25]

One thing is certain: Fr. McCaffery's advice in no way restrained Brownson from dealing as forthrightly as ever in his onslaughts on lawless democracy. With the rapid increase of radicalism abroad circa 1848, having erupted into one revolution after another on the continent of Europe, in France, Germany, Hungary and Italy, shaking the Old World to its foundations, Brownson now turned hurriedly to combat the encouragement those revolutions abroad were giving to the ultra democratic tendencies among his own countrymen. Allen Nevins remarks that those revolutionary outbreaks delighted the radicals in America,[26] and even won the support of the majority in the North. To them they were happy omens that the cause of human freedom was really on the march. But to Brownson they were omens that boded great harm to society, and he valiantly endeavored to roll back the revolutionary tide from American shores in another article significantly entitled: "The Republic of the United States." The whole design of the article was to expose and refute the purely democratic interpretation the radicals of the day were giving to American institutions. He repeated that the name democrat was unknown to any political party in the earlier decades of the Republic, that it finally began to be used in the administration of John Quincy Adams, and came into general use only in the second administration of Andrew Jackson, 1832-1836. That party, previously called the Republican party, had scorned the name democrat. He asserted that the popularity of democracy could be traced, in a great measure, to the influx of English and Scotch radicals, headed by his old-time allies, Frances Wright, Robert D. Owen and Robert L. Jennings — to the writings of Amos Kendall, William Legget and George Bancroft — to the administrations of Andrew Jackson and Martin Van Buren — to the declamations, cant and sentimentality of the abolitionists and philanthropists. An ultra democratic fever had so spread in the latter years that he found the leaders of the two great political parties now *out-democrating* each other in their reckless bid for the votes of the people.[27]

In analyzing this whole tendency, Brownson further held President Jackson, as already noted, subject to the charge of having placed the political caucus on a par to no small extent with the legal convention, that is, for collecting the will of the people. Insofar he had confounded the people as population with the people as the state. Not that President Jackson gave such informal expressions of the will of the people official recognition, but that he made it his defense against his enemies and acted upon it. In so doing he had allowed, unconsciously, the rise and progress of a wild and lawless democracy in the country to the injury of the original character of American institutions. To the objection — What difference does it make how the will of the people is collected just so it is ascertained? — he replied:

> None in the world, if the will, whatever the form in which it is collected, is always the same. But the presumption always is, that the popular will expressed through legal and constitutional forms will be the popular will regulated by reason, while that expressed irrespective of such forms will be the popular will subjected to popular passion — the voice of corrupt nature, of faction, of demagogues, disorderly passion, and selfish interests, to which it is always fatal to listen.[28]

It would be a great mistake to suppose that Brownson did not recognize the great native abilities of President Jackson, the eminent services he had rendered his country in his gallant defense of New Orleans, and the many beneficent measures of his administration, especially his opposition to the United States Bank. But he felt that having placed the political caucus on a par with the legal convention, he had "unchained that very spirit of wild and lawless democracy that the Constitution was avowedly intended to repress." In this one thing he faulted President Jackson. In criticizing him on this head, Brownson not only gives us a general estimate of President Jackson that is not without interest, but also makes an interesting, if not original, point about the American Constitution:

> General Jackson was a great man; the American people idolize his memory, and we have no wish to detract from his merits; but he was, in the higher sense of the word, no statesman. He was a man of heroic impulses, of strong mind, and an iron will; but a man who had made no profound study of political science. No one doubts his integrity, or his devotion to what he believed for the best good of the Republic; but like all strong-minded men, men of great natural parts and little science, he had a tendency to cut rather than untie the Gordian knot of statesmanship. He appears never to have understood that our government is a government *sui generis* — not any one of the simple forms of government, but a peculiar combination of them all. Instead of seeking to preserve them all as nicely adjusted by the Convention of 1787, he sought to simplify the machine, and gave an undue prominence to the monarchical element on the one hand, and to the democratic on the other. He did more, perhaps, than any other President we have had for the external splendor of the republic; but we are obliged to add, more also for the destruction of the Constitution and the corruption of public morals.[29]

Brownson by no means denied that the democratic element enters largely into our system of government, but he protested against giving it exclusive sway. "Under any just interpretation of our system," he said, "the democratic element must be recognized, and the labor of the statesman must not be to exclude or suppress it, but to prevent it, as it is constantly striving to become, from becoming exclusive."[30] He asserted that our political system is more properly called a republic, a federal republic, and that to turn it into a pure democracy or any other form of government is to destroy its original providential character. He again cited the Convention of 1787 as having been called for the very purpose of erecting barriers against an irresponsible democracy. The reports of Mr. Madison on the debates in the Convention clearly establish that such was the purpose of the Convention. "The evils we experience," said Mr. Garry, "flow from excessive democracy."[31] Mr. Randolph also observed that "the general object [of the Convention] was to provide a cure for the evils under which the United States labored; that, tracing these evils to their origin, every man found it in the turbulence and follies of democracy; that some check, therefore, was to be sought for against the tendency of our government."[32] Other distinguished members of the assembly expressed themselves to the same effect. Brownson asserted that the members of the Convention had not provided as strong checks against excessive democracy as they had wished, for fear, if they did, they would be unable to get their amendments adopted when submitted to the people.[33] He also observed elsewhere that the members of the Convention did not at that time have before them the ominous warnings of the horrible excesses to which an irresponsible democracy may go as was to be provided by the French Revolution of 1789.

> They had no experience [he pointed out] of the Jacobinical revolutions which followed the establishment of our Republic, and consequently could not anticipate the facility with which their principles could be perverted to serve as the basis of a system with which they had no affinity. They did not see that the *Social Contract* was already in Locke's Essay on Government, and that the French Revolution and all its horrors were in the *Social Contract,* and that all modern red-republicanism, socialism, and communism were in the French Revolution. They had no suspicion of the poison contained in the phrase *sovereignty of the people* — a phrase in their sense so innocent and so just. Hence they did not take the precautions which were requisite against the perversion of the institutions they founded to a pure democracy, or which they would have taken if they had had our experience.[34]

Inasmuch, then, as the Convention of 1787 had failed to provide more trusty checks against the dangers of excessive democracy, Brownson thought it was the part of wisdom for the American statesman to strengthen those checks as far as he could constitutionally, and to repress the tendency of democracy to become exclusive. He asserted that such had been the policy pursued by the administration of Washington, as well as that of his immediate successor, the elder Adams. It was due, he affirmed, to the high-toned conservative principles upon which those administrations had been conducted, and to the little or no heed paid to the demagogues and radicals of the day, that the Republic of the United States had escaped being numbered among the things that are no more. "The merit of the Federalists," he said, "was in their just appreciation of the un-American character of the Jacobinism favored by Mr. Jefferson and his party."[35] It would only be by a sincere and hearty return to that selfsame policy pursued by Washington and Adams, he counseled, that the country could be saved "from the curse of lawless and shameless democracy — a democracy that could, if left to itself, develop into anarchy, which must be the precursor of military despotism."[36]

The steady war Brownson was now waging against radicalism was but the reverse side of the shield in his relentless campaign for constitutional government. Any violation of the Constitution, by whomsoever or in whatsoever manner was sure to call forth his emphatic protest. On this score he took to task no less a person than President Polk for having prosecuted the Mexican War without ever having obtained from Congress an official declaration that war existed between the two countries. When Mexican troops crossed the Rio Grande and engaged American forces, President Polk declared that a state of war existed between the two countries by an act of

Mexico herself, and merely requested of Congress the means to prosecute the war to a successful issue. In so proceeding, Brownson contended, President Polk had usurped congressional powers, for the only war-making power known to our laws is Congress. All that President Polk, or any other President in similar circumstances, was authorized to do, was to present to Congress the grievances of his country against the respective foreign power, and recommend a declaration of war on the part of Congress. There his functions as a constitutional President would end. But in making war without the intervention of Congress, President Polk had in effect, said Brownson:

> . . . trampled the Constitution under his feet, set a dangerous precedent, and, by the official publication of a palpable falsehood, sullied the national honor. It is no pleasure that we speak thus of the chief magistrate of the Union, for whose elevation to his high and responsible office we ourselves voted. But whatever be our attachment to party, or the respect we hold to be due from all good citizens to the chief magistrate, we cannot see the Constitution violated, or the national honor sacrificed, whether by friend or foe, from good motives or bad, without entering feeble though it be, our stern and indignant protest.[37]

Brownson at this time was continually alternating in the heavy artillery he was directing at radicalism or revolutionism between that at home and that abroad. It was a foregone conclusion that his voice would be raised in loud protest when the Jesuits were driven out of Rome and other Italian states in the revolution of 1848. All the more so was he disposed to protest since his relations with the Jesuits were so friendly and cordial. To their college, Holy Cross, Worcester, Massachusetts, he sent his four eldest sons, and he himself was a visitor there whenever opportunity permitted. His esteem of the Jesuits both as men and as religious was the very highest. He had already written two powerful articles in their defense against the current calumnies of their enemies, "The Dangers of Jesuit Instruction,"[38] in reply to a certain Dr. Potts, a Presbyterian minister, and "The Jesuits," in refutation of the infamous slanders of M. M. Michelet and Quinet, professors in the College of France.[39] Interestingly enough, he had a theory that the utility of an institution or person may be accurately measured by the amount of opposition encountered. This theory he applied in particular to the papacy and the Jesuits. And as he himself met with much persistent, not to say vehement, opposition, it was a theory he might lay as a flattering unction to his own heart. Whatever the truth of the theory, the July 1848 edition of his *Quarterly* carried a scorching denunciation on the expulsion of the Jesuits from Italy. In part it read:

> We cannot close this number of our *Review*, without expressing our indignation at the expulsion of the Jesuits from Rome and other Italian states, by the pretended friends of liberty and popular institutions. . . . Those Italian liberals show us, by their persecutions of the Jesuits, what sort of men they are, the nature of the liberty they are contending for, and what humanity has to expect from their movements. Their conduct admits of no defense, of no palliation, and justly excites the indignation of every honest friend of religion and true freedom; we were born and bred in a free country; we understand and love freedom; and we scorn to recognize these infidel madcaps for our brethren. *They*, the friends of liberty! *They*, the men to regenerate Italy! Vain braggarts! Base cowards! Do they imagine there is a freeman on earth that does not despise them, and hold them in unspeakable contempt? Who are they? Who gave them the right to make war on peaceable men, devoted to religion? What right have they to freedom, which the Jesuit has not also? Are

they such fools as to be ignorant that there is and can be no freedom, where any class of our fellowmen, however large or however small, are not free; that freedom is for our neighbors as well as for us; that no man is secure, where every man, unless convicted of crime before the competent tribunal, is not secure in his person, his possessions, and his conscience? . . . Need they be told that liberty may be outraged in the person of a Jesuit as much as in the person of an Italian incendiary?[40]

This drew from Fr. Augustine Thébaud, S.J., president of St. John's College, Fordham, a letter of deep appreciation. He wrote:

St. John's College, July 7, 1848

Dear Sir and Dearest Friend:
    I have just received the July number of your *Review,* and I hope you will allow me to thank you warmly for the short article "On the Expulsion of the Jesuits from Italy." Thank God! There are men yet who feel and dare speak. We cannot but pray for our enemies; but we rejoice to see the mask taken from the face of enemies of the Church, of those who attack her through us.
    We have men among us — men passing for Catholics — who do not see what you see and express so warmly; may they open their eyes before it is too late.
    In the name of all my brethren, of the Italian Fathers and Brethren chiefly, I tender to you my most heartfelt gratitude. We have nothing to give you in return but our prayers. God never turns from the afflicted who turn to Him. Yet, may God bless and preserve you yet a long time to defend his Church.
Yours sincerely devoted in Christ,
Aug. J. Thébaud, S.J.[41]

As. Fr. Thébaud hinted in his letter — using a phrase from Brownson's own article — there were not a few in Catholic ranks quite thoroughly infected with the virus of the false liberalism of the day, and some of no little prominence. One of the hardest battles Brownson engaged in during the years immediately following his conversion — which cost him much indeed — was to put down the increasing tendency to radicalism or revolutionism among Catholics themselves whether at home or abroad. It was in no light vein he remarked: "Many *liberal* Catholics have been liberal in their abuse of us, and we have not had the rare fortune to escape being wounded in the house of our friends."[42] And he had also some taunting words for those outside the Catholic Church who had been haunting him with predictions that he would soon somersault back into Protestantism. To them he said: "We enter now on the fifth year of our Catholic life; we have, through the grace of God, falsified the predictions of our friends that we should turn back to Protestantism in six months, and rendered it idle for people to repeat their old nonsense about 'changing with every moon.' Since we left Protestantism, we have escaped the lunar influences to which we were formerly subjected, and come under those of the Sun of Justice, which are not liable to vary."[43]

Perhaps in no country among other nations did Brownson follow political events more closely than in France. Long before the Revolution of February 1848, he had found Count de Montalembert and the Catholic party cooperating there frequently with the so-called liberals, whose principles were subversive of all order, of society itself. This ominous trend on the part of the Catholic party Brownson rebuked and traced back to Abbé de Lamennais and his associates who had attempted to engineer some sort of an alliance between Catholicity and the radicalism of the day. Although the false move had been promptly condemned at Rome by Pope Gregory XVI in his encyclical *Mirari vos,* and all evidently implicated had submitted except the unhappy

Lamennais, the subtle poison of the revolutionary spirit kept on spreading through the Catholic body.[44] Montalembert, who had been the leader of the party at the time, gradually came to see his mistake, and in a letter to Brownson, dated January 28, 1850, confessed his guilt and asked absolution. He wrote:

> I am completely and wholly of your opinion. I have loved and still love liberty; but I recognize, with you, that I too often confounded its cause with that of the Revolution. I am now occupied in repairing the damage to which I very unintentionally contributed. . . . After having battled twenty years against the idol of Gallicanism, which confounded the altar with the throne, I will battle twenty more years, if necessary, against the more revolting idolatry which seeks to have us adore democracy as the consequence of Christianity.[45]

Even more pointedly yet did Brownson lay his strictures on what he considered a subtle manifestation of the revolutionary spirit in the famous funeral oration over Daniel O'Connell in the Eternal City, June 1847, by the distinguished Theatine, Padre Ventura, who had apparently attempted (so said Brownson) to pass off to the world his views as those of Pope Pius IX himself. Liberal Catholics of the day seemed entirely innocent of the baleful consequences of the revolutionary spirit which was sweeping them along, but to Brownson it was only too painfully patent that it could lead finally only to the demolition of church and state, if unchecked, and he labored unweariedly to instruct his fellow Catholics in the principles of a sound social and political science.

Although Brownson had foreseen and warned his fellow Catholics before 1848 that a hurricane of revolutions was about to sweep through Europe, he gave no credit to himself on that score when all had come about. He was quite conscious that he had all the advantage in the matter from having been a liberal, a radical himself, and knew perhaps as well as any man living the treacherous nature and ruthless course of the revolutionary spirit. Well did Fr. John McCaffery of Mt. St. Mary's College remark in a letter to him touching on the social and political heresies of the day: "We all need instruction you can give us. The ablest opponents of pagan errors and apologists of Christianity were often converted pagans. St. Augustine as a theologian derived profit from his early wanderings among the mazes of heresy."[46]

Knowing, therefore, the revolutionary spirit so intimately, that it is the very antithesis of Catholic teaching, the enthusiastic plaudits so widely tendered Pope Pius IX prior to 1848 when he had opted for an out-and-out liberal policy, were a shock to Brownson. He confessed that he was forced to draw on his Catholic faith for relief when he heard the whole Protestant, infidel and socialistic world applauding Pius IX to the echo. He even breathed easier when the mob took possession of the Eternal City and the Holy Father was forced in 1848 to flee for asylum to Gaeta. He averred that those shouts, "Long live Pius IX," from infidel throats would have, if anything could have, shaken his faith in Christ's promises to Peter. To him the sincere applause of the age is always worse than a dubious compliment. Whenever we are commended by any of the popular organs of the day, he cautioned, we should retire and make our examen of conscience, and ask, with fear and trembling, "O, Lord, what iniquity hath thy servant committed that the wicked should praise him?"[47] Instead of trusting to the hopes and promises of a false liberalism, if a better order is to be reconstructed in society, it must always be sought through orderly processes, emphasized Brownson, never by attempting the overthrow of government and the consequent in-

402

troduction of chaos. The heinous nature of revolutionism he painted in dark colors:

> The rebel against the established and legal order is guilty of the blackest crime of which man can be guilty against society. He is even a rebel against the Church, for she enjoins obedience to such government — a rebel against God, for all legitimate power is from God, and whoever resists it resists God and incurs damnation.[48]

In the great turmoil of the times, our American political philosopher had news for the radicals who were turning governments topsy-turvy in one country after another on the continent of Europe. Their loud cry was *Liberty!* as they swept ruthlessly forward. Certainly to large numbers of them the one formidable obstacle in their pathway was the Catholic Church with its conservative principles. To them it stood in the way of their idol, Liberty. But to them Brownson flatly laid it down that religion, believe it or not, is the very matrix of true liberty. How far awry they were on this point Brownson trenchantly set forth in his strictures on Padre Ventura's funeral oration over Daniel O'Connell in the Eternal City wherein the Padre had suggested (at least so Brownson interpreted his language in the English translation) that the Catholic Church form an *alliance* with liberty, that is, join the popular movements of the day. This proposal Brownson could not distinguish from the policy contended for with such ardent zeal and eloquence by Felicité de Lamennais and his associates, after the revolution of July 1830, in the erudite columns of the *Avenir*, and which was so promptly proscribed by the Church. He acknowledged that Ventura's phraseology might be interpreted by his Roman hearers as acceptably in harmony with Catholic teaching, but that it would not be so understood by the people of France, England and those of his own country. For to call for an *alliance* between the Church and liberty seemed to imply, which was wholly false, that religion had hitherto been divorced from liberty, and stood apart, or had formed an adulterous union with tyranny and oppression. Moreover, an alliance plainly presupposes that the allies are separate and independent powers; but how suppose such a power as liberty as standing alone, separate and independent of religion? Acerbly he remarked:

> Religion is the origin, ground, and condition of liberty. Where religion is, there is liberty; where religion is not, whatever license there may be, there is not liberty, and cannot be. The two are in their nature inseparable, and undistinguishable even, save as the effect is distinguishable from the cause, the property from the essence, the stream from the fountain. How, then form an alliance between them, since they are already in their very nature so intimately united? How form an alliance between the sun and its rays, the rainbow and its tints?[49]

Although Brownson bestowed considerable thought in his writings on politics and government in France during the years 1848-1851, it was particularly his expertise on the French political scene in the article "The Licentiousness of the Press" that was to impress Count de Montalembert so deeply. In his analysis of the French scene, Brownson came up with the statement that there were really only two elements in French society, the Catholic and the socialistic. Hence no government in France could live, and perform its functions, that does not make a final choice between these two elements, and strictly conform to the one of its choice. But the great majority of the French nation is Catholic, he asserted, and no government except one administered in accordance with Catholic principles, could hope to restore peace, or retain any hold on the affections of the people. With government so administered, in harmony with the sound convictions of the vast majority of the nation, the defects of the current constitution could be easily corrected, and the blessings of liberty and internal peace satisfactorily secured. The men of the De Tocqueville stamp, whose policy it was to hold a balance between Catholics and socialists, seemed to him only to threaten the destruction of the republic inasmuch as they could never rally a party sufficiently strong to sustain the government. "It is the policy," he remarked, "to madden the socialists and disgust the Catholics, without whose cordial support no government in France can stand."[50]

Montalembert was so impressed at what seemed to him a display of veritable wizardry on the part of Brownson in cutting through the complexity of French politics that he took pen in hand on Easter Sunday, 1850, to write Brownson a second time. In the excess of his admiration he said:

> My satisfaction and my *edification* have been so great that I cannot better employ some moments of this Holy Day than in thanking you *ex imo corde* for the good you have done me. I am happy to state that I am in perfect unison with you. Nothing could exceed nor indeed equal, in my opinion, your most judicious, because most righteous, appreciation of men and things in Europe. I can but admire how the light of *Faith* and *Prayer* can illuminate, at so many miles distance the events and characters of our hemisphere.[51]

Continuing his gallant attack on the radicalism of the day, Brownson was bound to meet it head on in due season in its most compact form, Socialism. He made his direct attacks on it at the time in three articles, "Socialism and the Church,"[52] and two other articles, "Channing on the Church and Social Reform,"[53] and "Channing on Christendom and Socialism."[54] In reply to those little disposed to take socialism seriously, some quite grave men at that, he underscored that "in one form or another it has already taken possession of the age, has armed itself for battle, made the streets of Paris, Berlin, Frankfort, Vienna and other cities, run with blood, and convulsed nearly the whole civilized world."[55] In his first article alone, "Socialism and the Church," to say nothing of the other two, he gave the subject a most searching analysis. Its secret appeal he found to be largely veiled in the fact that "it steals the livery of the court of heaven to serve the devil in." It presents itself in a Christian garb, and seeks to speak the language of the Gospel. Men whom the age delights to honor hesitate not to call Christ "the first Socialist." He asserted that Dr. Channing, the elder, had taken the lead in our own country in reducing the Gospel to socialism, and that the fallen priest, Abbé de Lamennais, was the first in France, as he recollected, who labored to identify socialism with Christianity — whom he himself had at the time warmly commended. To illustrate his assertion he quoted several fiery passages from his *Boston Quarterly Review,* and reminded his readers of "the zeal and perseverance with which he himself had preached, in the name of the Gospel, the most damnable radicalism."[56] He was only giving his readers notice, one and all, that in now castigating socialism in unsparing terms, he was not speaking as a novice, but as one who knew whereof he spoke. As Russell Kirk has remarked: "Brownson was a socialist long before the name of Marx was known, and in several respects anticipated Marx's thought — which made him the more formidable as an opponent of socialism in his maturity."[57]

Brownson characterized socialism as a masterpiece of deception. He wrote:

> Veiling itself under Christian forms, attempting to distinguish between Christianity and the [Catholic] Church, claiming for itself the authority and immense popularity of the Gospel, denouncing Christianity in the name of Christianity, discarding the Bible in the name of the Bible, defying God in the name of God, Socialism conceals from the undiscriminating multitude its true character, and appealing to the dominant sentiment of the age and to some of the strongest natural inclinations and passions, it asserts itself with terrific power, and rolls on in its career of devastation and death with a force that human beings, in themselves, are impotent to resist. Men are assimilated to it with all the power of their nature, and by all their reverence for religion. Their very faith and charity are perverted, and their noblest instincts and their sublimest hopes are made subservient to their basest passions and their most grovelling propensities. Here is the secret of the strength of Socialism, and here, too, is the principal source of its danger.[58]

Inasmuch as socialism feigns to be Christian, but really denies the Christian faith, it is a heresy. While speaking in the name of Christian doctrine, it eviscerates the Catholic system of its entire meaning, making itself the *résumé* of all particular heresies which ever have been or can be. The iniquity of man in its heretical vagaries can go no further. Never was heresy more subtle, nor more fitted for success. "Surely," said Brownson, "Satan has here, in Socialism, done his best, almost outdone himself, and would, if it were possible, deceive the very elect, so that no flesh should be saved."[59] And in paragraph after paragraph, in a long succession, he dramatically opposed the real teaching of Christ to the heresies of the Socialists. His friend, Fr. McCaffery, wrote him again his appreciation, saying:

> As to Socialism, all good men must thank you for dragging it into the light and giving it so many mortal thrusts. Your experimental knowledge of it enables you to pierce through its disguises and to trace the one monster evil in its various workings and manifestations.[60]

Russell Kirk who has a just appreciation of Brownson's importance in the intellectual history of the nation recently underlined Brownson's prescience in having been the first to mark the heretical derivation of socialism from Christianity. Said Kirk: "He [Brownson] seems to have been the first to describe Marxism as a heresy from Christianity, a concept recently affirmed by Christopher Dawson, Arnold Toynbee, Father D'Arcy and other scholars."[61]

Certain events now transpiring on the home front were presently pinning down Brownson's attention more and more to the domestic scene. The slavery question, like Banquo's ghost, would not down. It made its ominous reappearance in the Compromise Measures, including the Fugitive Slave Law, passed in 1850, which guaranteed the slave owner the right to recover his runaway slave wherever found, forbidding to the slave free soil anywhere. This enactment brought the slavery question violently before the whole country once again. Brownson, as we have seen, as a Christian and as a man, was decidedly against the moral implications of slavery as it existed in the South as he had set forth once and for all in his article on "Slavery — Abolitionism" in his *Boston Quarterly Review,* April 1838. Regarding it as an odious evil, he was greatly desirous of getting rid of it, but he still maintained that it was one of those social evils which it is allowable to remove only in accordance with fidelity to the Constitution and the Federal Union. Great as the evil of slavery was, the evil of disunion, or the disruption of the union of the states, he stoutly maintained, would be incalculably greater. Hence the patriotic duty of every citizen to uphold and obey the Constitution overrides every other consideration in the case.

This doctrine was entirely in harmony with the social philosophy he had always held. Even in his most radical days he had always held that it is never permitted to break up a social or political order for the sake of removing an evil existing under it.[62] It was for that reason he had opposed the abolitionists with all his might who were moving in that direction. As to the Fugitive Slave Law, which they abominated, he felt that the South had really blundered in bringing pressure for its enactment (as provided for by the Constitution), for it was sure to stir up a bitter controversy with little advantage to the slave owner in the way of reclaiming his runaway slave. But, the enactment once made, Brownson adamantly maintained that it must be observed in the interest of public law and order lest society resolve itself into lawlessness and anarchy to which it seemed rapidly enough hastening. The South was becoming more and more incensed over Northern abolitionism interfering with their "peculiar" domestic institution.

In these matters there was close agreement between Brownson's views and those of Daniel Webster. Webster always held that where slavery existed by local laws, it was untouchable, that the federal government and the non-slave-holding states were denied any and all rights by the Constitution to interfere with it, and were bound to carry out all stipulations imposed by the Constitution. But Webster also steadily opposed with every legal and constitutional means available the extension of slavery into new territory where it did not exist. This stance of Webster on the slave question, together with his stout defense of the Fugitive Slave Law, Brownson found to be in conformity with his own views, and he warmly commended Webster's speech on the floor of the United States Senate in reply to Clay's resolutions. He said:

> His speech itself in our judgment, does the distinguished senator more credit as a man and as a statesman than any other he has ever made. It is worthy of his station and the occasion, and, in the circumstances in which it was delivered, rises above mere intellectual greatness, and approaches the morally sublime. The orator rises to the full dignity of the American senator, above all sectional prejudices, and all party interests and personal ambition, to those high moral and constitutional principles which so many lose sight of, but which should ever animate and guide the American statesman.[63]

But there were many prominent persons in the nation who did not agree with the views of Brownson and Webster on the question of slavery or the Fugitive Slave Law. When the Fugitive Slave Law had first come to the floor of the United States Senate for discussion, one of the senators from New York State, William Henry Seward (later the famed Secretary of State in President Lincoln's cabinet), refused to vote for the measure, though it was necessary to carry out an express provision of the Constitution, precisely on the ground that it was, as he alleged, contrary to the law of God. But when he thus appealed to the "higher law" of God in the case, he was told by those who had sponsored the bill that, having taken an oath to support the Constitution, he had thereby debarred himself from the right, as long as he retained his seat in the senate, to appeal to any such "higher law" of God that might require him to act in contravention of the Constitution. The abolitionists and the Free-Soilers at once took this assertion by their opponents to be tantamount to a denial of the existence of any such "higher law," and their papers and periodicals teemed with sulfurous articles to prove the supremacy of the law of God over all mere human enactments.

Brownson at once perceived that here was a question of no little gravity, not to say complexity, and he devoted several massive articles in his *Review* to a thoroughgoing exploration of the whole affair.

He agreed entirely, of course, with Mr. Seward and his abolitionist and Free-Soil friends as to the fact that there is a higher law than the Constitution. The law of God is patently supreme and must of its very nature override all mere human enactments. Any human enactment incompatible with it is necessarily null and void from the beginning, for, as said the Apostle, "We must obey God rather than man." Wrote Brownson:

> This is a truth the temporal order not seldom practically denies, and on which the Church never fails to insist. This truth is so frequently denied, so frequently outraged, that we are glad to see it asserted by Mr. Seward and his friends, though they assert it in a case and for a purpose in which we do not and cannot sympathize.[64]

But the concession that there is a higher law than the Constitution does not of itself, Brownson argued, justify an appeal to it against the Constitution by Mr. Seward and the opponents of the Fugitive Slave Law. How, in fact, could Mr. Seward appeal to such a higher law against the Constitution — as incompatible with it — after he had taken an oath to uphold the Constitution? Could he, in the first instance, conscientiously take an oath to uphold the Constitution? If he could, he could not then afterwards refuse to carry out any of its express provisions by merely asserting that any such were contrary to the higher law of God. For in swearing to uphold the Constitution he had declared in the most solemn manner possible his conviction that the Constitution imposed on him no duty contrary to the law of God. If, however, after having taken his oath he discovered its incompatibility with the law of God, he was bound from that moment to resign his seat. The same principle, therefore, by which he appealed to the higher law against the Constitution would also nullify the authority by which he held his senatorial seat, since the federal government has no existence independent of the Constitution, or powers not created by it. Evidently, in any view of the case, Mr. Seward could not justify an appeal to a law above the Constitution while retaining his seat in the senate and bound by oath to uphold it. Concluded Brownson:

> It is then perfectly easy to condemn the appeal of the senator, without, as the abolitionists and free-soilers pretend, falling into the monstrous error of denying the supremacy of the divine law, and maintaining that there is no law above the Constitution.[65]

This line of argument, while conclusive against the honorable senator from New York, Mr. Seward, did not precisely apply to those who resisted the Fugitive Slave Law after it had once been passed. These people, according to Brownson, took the view that the law of God is higher than any human enactment, and that therefore we can never in any case be bound to obey any mere human enactment that is in contravention of it. Such enactments, he continued, are violences rather than laws, as said already St. Augustine, and we are commanded by God himself to resist them, at least passively. To this every Christian is bound to hold even to death. But who is to decide whether a special civil enactment is or is not repugnant to the law of God? "Here,"

407

said Brownson, "is a grave and perplexing question for those who have no divinely authorized interpreter of the divine law."

The abolitionists and Free-Soilers, adopting the principle of private judgment, claimed the right for each one to decide for himself. But this places the individual at once above the state, private judgment above the law, and renders wholly incompatible the simplest concept of sound and durable government. What becomes of government if each individual can interpret the law as he pleases, or if there is nothing to restrain him from disobeying the law if it does not happen to square with his notions of what is the law of God? Clearly, this would be to abolish civil government in any real sense, and to open the door to anarchy and license — everybody left to be his own boss. Clearly, again, if government is to be retained, if it is to govern, the right to decide when a civil enactment does or does not conflict with the law of God cannot be lodged with the individual subject. Should it then be lodged with just the state? Then you make the state supreme and absolute, and bind yourself to absolute obedience to every and any law the state may make. This is to deny the principle of the higher law, with no appeal from the state, no relief for conscience left in the case, which is tantamount to pure civil despotism. Here, said Brownson, is a sad dilemma.[66]

But Brownson would not on that account allow those caught in this dilemma to evade the consequences or to withdraw themselves from the obligation of obedience to the law. Government itself, he said, is a divine institution, is ordained of God. "Let every creature be subject to the higher powers, for there is no power but from God; and the powers that be are ordained of God. Therefore he that resisteth the power resisteth the ordinance of God. And they that resist purchase to themselves damnation."[67] Brownson did not, of course, claim that all the acts of government are ordained of God. That would exclude the possibility of asserting a higher law than that of the state and would force us to regard every enactment as a part of the divine law. In affairs of government, God does not enjoin obedience to each and every act of government, but only to those which come within the bounds of his own divine law. For he did not make civil government the supreme and infallible organ of his will on earth, and hence it may err and go contrary to his declared will. Whenever it does so, its acts are null and void. Yet, as Brownson pointed out:

> Government itself, as civil authority, is a divine ordinance, and, within the law of God, clothed with the right to command and enforce obedience. No appeal, therefore, from any act of government which in principle denies the divine right of government, or which is incompatible with the assertion and maintenance of civil authority, can be entertained. Since government, as civil authority, is an ordinance of God and as such the divine law, any course of action or assertion of any principle of action, incompatible with its existence as government, is necessarily forbidden by the law of God. The law of God is always equal to the law of God, and can never be in conflict with itself. Consequently, no appeal against the government as civil authority to the law of God is admissible, because the law of God is as supreme in any one of its enactments as in another.[68]

It is now clear, continued Brownson, that Mr. Seward and his friends, the abolitionists and Free-Soilers, have nothing to which they can appeal from the action of the government in the Fugitive Slave Law but their own private interpretation of the law of God as individuals. But to appeal from the government to mere private opinion, that is, to allow the individual to sit in judgment on public authority, is, as has been shown, incompatible with the very existence of government, and, therefore (since government is a divine ordinance), absolutely forbidden by divine law. Here, said Brownson is matter for solemn pause, which condemns on the authority of God himself the pretended right of the individual citizen to set aside civil enactments merely on the strength of his own private judgment. To attempt to do so brings one at once athwart not only the human law but the divine ordinance of God as well. Hence, no one can ever be justified in resisting a civil enactment as repugnant to the law of God when he has nothing more than his own private opinion to assure him what the law of God is, for the principle upon which he would be acting in such a case is destructive of the very notion of government, and is therefore in contravention of the divine ordinance, government being ordained of God himself. But how necessary government is to society he made plain when he said:

> Man's prime necessity is society, and the prime necessity of society is government. The question, whether government shall or shall not be sustained, is at bottom only the question, whether the human race shall continue to exist or not. Man is essentially a social being, and cannot live without society, and society is inconceivable without government. Extinguish government, and you extinguish society; extinguish society, and you extinguish man. Inasmuch as God has created and ordained the existence of the human race, he has founded and ordained government, and has made it obligatory on us to sustain it, and refrain in principle and action from whatever would tend to destroy it, or to render its existence insecure. . . . In no case can any man be justified in setting aside or resisting civil government, save on an authority higher than his own and that of the government.[69]

Although Brownson had battled as heroically as any man could through long years as a journalist in the cause of rational freedom, he was here battling just as heroically in the defense of sound and durable government. The abolitionists and Free-Soilers had taken it into their heads, in Boston in particular, that the Fugitive Slave Law was not to be carried out, and proceeded to offer stout resistance. In the midst of their indifferent success against the officers of the law, Theodore Parker, on April 10, 1851, delivered a sermon at the Boston Melodeon on "The Chief Sins of the People," the chief sins of which were their suffering the Fugitive Slave Law to be carried out. This address of Parker drew from Brownson a second powerful article on the disputed law in which he reviewed Parker's address. Brownson at once disclaimed all sympathy with any and every species of slavery, as he always had, and professed a deep and true devotion to the cause of human freedom. Hence he had no quarrel at all with the Free-Soilers on being hostile to slavery. He opposes them he makes crystal clear, not for being hostile to slavery, but because of the principles and methods by which they oppose it. Mr. Parker, he pointed out, "plainly counsels resistance to the laws, downright treason, and civil war — only not just yet. The hour has not yet come, and armed resistance might be premature, because just now it might be unsuccessful. . . . The traitorous intention, the traitorous resolution, is manifest, is avowed, is even gloried in, and nothing is wanting to the overt attempt to carry it into execution but a fair prospect of success. And, what is of more serious consequence, the party of which this fierce declaimer is an accredited organ is in power in this state and has the Governor and the majority of the representatives of both houses of Congress."[70]

Brownson went on to point out that this same party, "absorbing into its bosom all the separate fanaticisms in the free states," was fast gaining the upper hand in several of the great states of the East, and, half unknown to itself, was burgeoning into opposition to all law. Against Parker he proves that the Fugitive Slave Law was not unjust, but constitutional, so declared by Judges Woodbury and Nelson of the United States Circuit Court, and by the supreme judiciary authority of the Commonwealth of Massachusetts. Chief Justice Shaw, "than whom it would be difficult to find a higher legal authority," in giving the unanimous opinion of the court said the law was not only constitutional, but necessary, and that Congress was bound to pass it. The new enactment did not differ in principle from the original law of 1793, but differed only in devolving on the officers of the federal government duties which the original law made incumbent on officers of the separate state governments. But as no one could pretend that the original law of 1793 was unconstitutional, so must the federal enactment of 1850 be regarded as constitutional. Therefore, averred Brownson, no man can ever have the right to set that law aside save on an authority higher than his own or that of the state.[71] When reviewing, in a third article, the speeches of the Hon. Charles Sumner "On the Memorial for the Repeal of the Fugitive Slave Law," delivered on the floor of the United States Senate, on June 26 and 28, Brownson gave his reasons in one forceful sentence for opposing with all his might the Free-Soil party:

> As a friend of social order, as the advocate of wise and practicable government, as the defender, according to the measure of our poor ability, of genuine republicanism, we are obliged to oppose with all our might the anarchical and despotic doctrines it [the Free-Soil party] holds and seeks to propagate, because those doctrines cannot prevail in this country without involving the subversion of constitutional government, the disruption of society, and the destruction of all possible guarantees of freedom, whether for white or black men.[72]

The dilemma, however, in which the Free-Soilers and the abolitionists were caught by asserting either destructive individualism on the one hand, or state absolutism on the other, does not exist for the Catholic, affirmed Brownson. For he has a public authority higher than his own and that of the state to guide and direct him, namely, the living teaching voice of his Church, which, since it is inerrant in matters of morals can never be oppressive in its moral decisions. To Catholics, therefore, the Fugitive Slave Law could present no difficulty at all. As the law was necessary to effect the fulfillment of an obligation imposed by the Constitution, and as the Catholic Church had never decided that to restore a fugitive slave was necessarily contrary to the law of God, a Catholic was bound to obey the law, and could not — without resisting the ordinance and purchasing damnation to himself — disobey the law. St. Paul did even more, for it appears he sent back Onesimus to his owner, Philemon, before he had asked him to do so.

It is in such reasonings in the political order that Brownson saw the duties and freedom of Catholics as citizens admirably harmonized. On the one hand, the Catholic Church enjoins upon them strict obedience to the state in all things except where the law of the state contravenes justice or the law of God. The vital point in the matter being that the Church is inerrant in declaring a case where the law of the state comes in conflict with the law of God, leaving no loophole for the destructive individualism of private judgment to creep in and disrupt society. On the other hand, the just freedom of the subject is likewise safeguarded, for should the state make iniquitous or unjust laws that oppress its subjects, the Catholic Church opposes to them the higher law of God and wages an unceasing spiritual warfare for the freedom of the citizen as we see the Church doing today in so many lands under communistic domination. It is this that gives to the Church the aspect of a great balance wheel in society, defending on the one hand the just authority of the state, and, on the other, the just freedom of the citizens, an office which the Church alóne in the whole structure of society has been designed to fulfill. As Brownson remarked:

> He [God] has not seen proper so to constitute society and endow government that they can get on without the Church. She is an integral, an essential element in the constitution of society, and it is madness and folly to think of managing it and securing its well-being without her. She is the solution of all problems, and without her none are solvable.[73]

It is highly important to understand that the inviolability of justly enacted law was not the only reason that steeled the courage of both Brownson and Webster in defending the unpopular Fugitive Slave Law. They clearly perceived that the preservation of the Union was involved in the whole affair. Southerners were becoming increasingly restive over the activities of the Northern abolitionists, and were threatening to break up the Union if interference with their "peculiar institution" did not stop. Both Brownson and Webster were doing all in their power to wipe out sectional animosities and establish in their place a broad-based nationalism throughout the country. Nonobservance of the Fugitive Slave Law would have been regarded by the South as a *casus belli,* and war was something no one wanted.

Somewhat connected with the slavery question were the piratical expeditions from our shores against Cuba at mid-century, which went under the name of filibusterism. The doctrine of "manifest destiny" that was in the air at the time seems to have fostered the idea that the territories close to the United States should be annexed in the interest of rounding out the Republic. This appealed in particular to Southerners inasmuch as it carried with it the prospect of the further extension of slavery. Likewise mixed in with this notion was a feeling of hostility toward monarchical government, and as Cuba was a colony of Spain, the filibusters volunteered to rescue it from monarchical Spain. This whole sentiment and movement received considerable impetus under the administration of President Franklin Pierce who had given it countenance in his inaugural address. There was a persistent effort made to acquire Cuba by one method or another.[74]

The chief conspirator in the revolutionary movement against Cuba was Narciso López, Venezuelan born, who had entered Cuba in 1841, identified with the revolutionaries there, and in 1849 had fled back to the United States where he rallied about him a considerable band of so-called liberators for the invasion of the isle. The first invasion of Cuba in 1850 having proved abortive, a second invasion was made in 1851. But after several engagements with the Spanish troops, López and his associates were defeated, and to a man killed or captured. Colonel Crittenden and his party of fifty men were captured in their attempt to escape from the island, and having confessed their piratical acts of invasion, were executed by reason of an order the Spanish government had issued already before the expedition had left New Orleans. A portion of the American public had sympathized with López and his buccaneers, and when the news of overwhelming defeat reached American shores, a most humiliating vengeance was wreaked upon unoffending Spanish resi-

411

dents in New Orleans and Key West by wild mobs that had collected there, and upon shipwrecked Spaniards (sixty-seven in number) who had sought refuge in the port of Mobile.

Perhaps no man in America raised his voice louder at the time in denunciation of these piratical expeditions than did Orestes Brownson. As a part of his protest he refused to vote for Franklin Pierce in the 1852 elections as he informed Fr. John Roddan beforehand — because of his expansionist stance. Brownson saw only in piratical expeditions from American shores the practical application of the destructive doctrines with which the American people had been indoctrinated by the American demagogues of the day, and by nearly the whole American newspaper press of the time against which he himself had been inveighing with all his might for many a long year. Once lay it down, he said, that the will of the people outside the political organism, that is, the will of the mob, may rebel against the sovereign authority of the state whenever they judge proper, and it becomes impossible to visit any censure on López and his associates in their mad attempt to get possession of Cuba by rebellion, murder and robbery. Such conduct is only the revolutionary principle which "strikes at all legality, all legitimacy, abrogates all laws, municipal and international, renders loyalty an unmeaning word, and leaves the people, theoretically at least, in a state of pure anarchy and lawlessness."[75] He reminded the politicians of the day that people cannot hold and act upon principles which would justify such piratical expeditions without "placing themselves out of the pale of civilized nations, and authorizing the civilized world to treat them as a nest of pirates and to make war on them as the common foe of mankind." He appealed to the American people to abandon once and for all the pernicious principles of the old French Jacobins "which have convulsed the nations of the Old World, consecrated rebellion, and instituted the worship of the dagger,"[76] and to return to the legal and sound republicanism bequeathed the nation by the Founding Fathers, remembering that "justice exalteth a nation," but sin is a reproach to any people.

Brownson's first article on the invasion of Cuba brought him to the attention of the Spanish minister at Washington, D.C., A. Calderón De La Barca. After expressing great satisfaction with Brownson's article, Calderón earnestly urged upon him the writing of a second article on the same subject, giving him much authentic information relative to the subject which had come to him in the dispatches to the Spanish Legation. This information was contained mainly in Calderón's second and longer letter. He expressed a great desire to go to Boston and make Brownson's personal acquaintance, but he gave his pressing duties at the exciting time as the reason which made the journey impossible. When Calderón received word that Brownson had consented to write a second essay, "being more than usually occupied," he expressed a wish to his wife, Mrs. Fanny Calderón De La Barca, that she write Brownson in his name, laying as many facts bearing on the subject before him as might prove useful for the contemplated article. After dealing for some pages in her letter with points of consequence, she indicated the great importance her husband attached to the forthcoming essay when she said:

> He is convinced that this article will be reprinted throughout the world, and everywhere read with interest; that it is one that will greatly serve the cause of morality, which will console more than one good man now afflicted by the actual state of society, and which may, perhaps, rescue from the path of perdition some young Americans led astray by bad example and false principles,

and that by it the world will see that there are men in America who value virtue more than gold or conquest, and above all have the courage to confess it.

If you could point out any other way in which Mr. Calderón might be useful to you in regard to this article, it would give him the greatest pleasure. Ever since he has become acquainted with your *Review,* he has looked forward with impatience to each number, and always calls you the *Balmes* of America. Will you allow me, dear sir, to express my own pleasure in being permitted to make acquaintance with you, even though through the medium of correspondence. . . .

But I shall not trespass longer upon your time, and begging you to remember me respectfully to your Bishop, I remain with Mr. Calderón's regards,

Yours truly and respectfully,
Fanny Calderón De La Barca[77]

Although Brownson's first article on the invasion of Cuba appeared in the October 1850 issue of his *Review,* his second appeared only with the January edition of 1852 as Calderón's second letter, dated September 4, 1851, had reached him too late for the article's appearance in the October issue of that year. Brownson's response to Calderón's letter was also somewhat delayed by reason of domestic affliction. Brownson's youngest son, Charles Joseph Maria, the only child born to him after he had become a Catholic, was taken from him in death on September 7, 1851, at the age of eight, a victim of scarlet fever. The boy's loss was deeply lamented by the family, and caused an unavoidable interruption in the father's work.[78]

One receives the impression that one of the genuine pleasures of Brownson's life was the personal acquaintance he made of the Calderón family when he visited them in Washington, D.C., soon after their correspondence had begun. Brownson came to regard Mr. Calderón as a high-minded man of unusual ability, and a mutual friendship and esteem between the two was fostered by a similarity of views on diverse subjects.

At about the time Brownson was leveling his barrage of acute criticism at the filibustering invasions of Cuba, he also took Daniel Webster to task for the moral support he had extended as American Secretary of State to the Hungarians in their rebellion against the Emperor of Austria. Here he re-enunciated the doctrine that *rebellion* merely for the purpose of changing from one form of government to another, whether from a monarchy to a republic or from an aristocracy to a democracy, whether from a democracy to an aristocracy or from a republic to a monarchy, is never justifiable. For no form of government is *per se* more legitimate than another, as the true ends of government may be as adequately secured under one form of government as under another. The only justifying cause the Hungarian insurgents could have had in the case would have been tyranny or oppression on the part of the Emperor of Austria, a fact, Brownson affirmed, they neither had nor could make out.[79] The Austrian minister, Chevalier Hülsemann, complained to Mr. Webster therefore, because of the official sympathy he had extended to the Hungarian rebels, and Mr. Webster grounded his reply on the assumption of the legitimacy of rebellion everywhere against monarchy in favor of popular institutions. Although Brownson acknowledged that he did not feel competent to enter into the intrinsic merits of the controversy between the two governments, the ground assumed by Mr. Webster, he said, "strikes us as extraordinary, indefensible, and extremely dangerous"[80] — an aggravation in fact of the offense already complained of and a moral descent in the political order tending to place us outside the pale of civilized nations. There could be no justification of the Hungarian rebellion except on the destructive principle of the exclusive legality everywhere of the principles of popular government — a doctrine as subversive as it is anti-American. Turning to American history Brownson underscored the point:

> The American Congress of 1776 did not set forth that King George III was a king, and they wanted a republican government; they did not declare the colonies absolved from their allegiance to the Crown of Great Britain on the ground that republicanism is the natural right of every people, and that no people can ever owe allegiance to a monarchy. The moral sense of the colonies and the whole world would have been outraged by such a declaration. Even Mr. Jefferson adopted the motto, not "Resistance to Kings," but "Resistance to Tyrants, is obedience to God."[81]

The increasing tendency of his countrymen to sympathize with rebellion wheresoever rampant, Brownson attributed largely to a misapprehension in their minds of the principles upon which our own government was founded and rests. Not on revolutionary principles, he emphasized repeatedly, but on legal principles, is our separation from the Crown of Great Britain to be defended — on the ground that George III had, by his tyranny, after our repeated remonstrances and protests, absolved us from any further duty of allegiance. Whether or not there was on our part any error in the application of the principle, the principle itself is a sound one; and if error there was, the defect was supplied the moment the British Crown acknowledged our independence. In proceeding thus to our independence as a nation, we placed ourselves in harmony with the civilized world, and could accordingly deal with other nations on terms of mutual esteem and respect, whatever their forms of government. And, there being no real change in the original groundwork of the colonies, there was no revolution in the ordinary sense of that term.[82]

Webster in his letter to Mr. Hülsemann had failed to mark this distinction between the establishment of our government and the various rebellious movements of the day, whether in Hungary or elsewhere. Brownson consequently charged him with identifying the subversive principles of the European revolutionaries with the principles upon which our own government had been founded, so that it would no longer be possible to denounce rebels anywhere without the necessity of involving the United States and their forms of government in the same proscription. Webster was thus giving encouragement to the American people in their sympathy with rebels everywhere, and their growing readiness to extend an ovation "to every popular miscreant, who, having lighted the flames of rebellion and civil war in his own country, flies hither to save his neck from the halter he so richly deserves."[83] Such sympathy he considered incompatible with the safety of our own institutions as well as disgraceful to our honor as a nation. "We have no solid support for our own institutions," he warned, "till our people know that treason is a crime against the state and a sin against God, and that every one who rebels against legal authority, and conspires by force of arms to overthrow it, is a traitor."[84]

Seeing in Louis Kossuth, the Hungarian leader, only the destructive principles of rebellion, Brownson could not of course look upon his visit to our shores with an approving eye. Brought here by the government from England, Kossuth was greeted on his arrival with great salvos of artillery, was cordially welcomed by the President, Cabinet and Congress, was feasted and toasted by members of the Senate and the House of Representatives, by state governors and legislators, by cities, towns and committees. Being an orator of no small magnetism, he became for the moment a sort of national sensation. But Brownson foresaw that it was all a frothy affair. He concluded his notice of it all in the January 1852 issue of his *Review* with the words: "As for Kossuth, we care not for him. He is not the man, unless we are greatly mistaken, to make any lasting impression upon Yankees. We shall have a good time with him, feast ourselves, have our own jollification, let him laugh a little at us in his sleeve while we laugh a good deal at him in ours, and then — cast him off."[85] In the October issue of his *Review* he quoted those words to show that he had correctly taken in the passing scene accorded the Magyar. After a few months, leaving the bill to his landlady unpaid, Louis Kossuth crept stealthily on board a steamer in June at New York, bound for England, and departed amidst the perfect indifference of the American people. Brownson was gratified that grass-roots America itself had given him such scant attention.

Perhaps Brownson's greatest regret in the whole affair was over the part his friend Daniel Webster had played in it all.[86] Before the immense ovation given Kossuth after landing on our shores, Brownson had written off to his friend in Paris, Count de Montalembert: "We are to give Kossuth an ovation here, and show to the world what fools we are."[87]

While laying his strictures on what he could not but regard as an indefensible course of our government in supporting Hungary against Austria, Brownson protested that he did so as the truehearted patriot, sensitive to the honor of his native land, professing to yield "to no man in his love of country, and attachment to her form of government." For Mr. Webster himself, in consideration of his public services and what he had seen of him in social intercourse, he "entertained a very great, indeed a profound respect"; to him in particular he had looked as the natural leader of that true American party which he had fondly hoped would be formed out of the conservative principles of the two great parties which divide the country. It was therefore "with great disappointment as well as unfeigned sorrow," that he deplored Mr. Webster's lapse in this one instance, and, referring to Mr. Webster's reply to Chevalier Hülsemann, he concluded by saying:

> In it Mr. Webster leaves the statesman for the demagogue, the conservative for the radical, and instead of availing himself of his position and the occasion to announce sound and salutary principles, he has assumed the *bonnet rouge* of the French Jacobin, and descended to pander to the worst principles, the basest passions, and the most dangerous tendencies of his countrymen. Little did we think that he who some years since applauded, and induced not a few others to applaud, our own indignant denunciation of these principles, passions, and tendencies, would himself one day need to be remonstrated with for proclaiming them, and proclaiming them as American, and inseparable from the American character, condition, and destiny. We hope this lapse will prove but momentary, that he will hasten to take back his defense of rebels everywhere, and assume his rightful and natural position once more on the side of authority, in defense of historical rights, and liberty through law.[88]

This gallant stand of Brownson for sound principles in government, as presented in this chapter, reflects his stalwart figure against the skyline of the nineteenth century as a lone American knight battling heroically the titanic forces that were bent on the destruction of law and order, and the freedom and security that go therewith. Fr. C. J. Osthoff, C.M., of De Paul University, Chicago, one of the organizers of "The Friends of Brownson" in Chicago in 1926, named Brownson's "moral courage" as one of the three reasons for accounting him a genius.[89]

# 28

## BROWNSON RESORTS TO THE LECTURE CIRCUIT AS THE 'REVIEW' WANES

*His pecuniary embarrassment due in no small measure to the defalcation of the agents for his* Review *and other related causes • He lectures in Montreal and Quebec, Canada • The proceeds from his lectures make it possible for him to afford his sons an excellent education • The American bishops give his* Review *their formal endorsement in their seventh provincial council in Baltimore, 1849 • Brownson's lectures in 1852 in St. Louis on Catholicity and civilization • The reaction of the St. Louis newspapers • Excerpts from the lectures • Citizens of St. Louis engage Hugh A. Garland, Esq., to present another view of civilization in a course of lectures, but he refrains from any appearance to be replying to his friend, Brownson • On his return journey from St. Louis, Brownson lectures in Baltimore and Cincinnati • In May of this same year, 1852, he gives another course of lectures in Montreal • After lecturing in many of the major cities of the nation in 1853, he returns to St. Louis for another course of lectures in 1854 • Pen-portraits of him as he appeared on the lecture platform • A challenge is delivered to him from the Protestant clergy of St. Louis • His reply • Many conversions result from his lectures • His lectures in New Orleans and Mobile in 1855.*

Deeply concerned as we have been with Brownson's recent writings, we have almost neglected to point out that lecturing had also long been the other outlet to his astonishing energies. During the years immediately following his conversion, however, he did not engage in much lecturing. At most, he made a trip a year to New York City at the invitation of Bishop John McCloskey or Fr. Jeremiah Cummings for a course of lectures. There was good reason for little lecturing at the time. As a convert now conducting a sedate *Catholic Quarterly Review* he was under the necessity of acquiring a thoroughgoing knowledge of Catholic theology, Catholic tastes and habits of thought. As he himself expressed it: "We had much to unlearn, and everything to learn. . . . We had Catholic faith, Catholic fervor, and Catholic docility, and scarcely anything else to qualify us for our post. . . . We had to study day and night, and to task our physical and mental powers to the utmost."[1] On the systematic course in fundamental theology he had taken on the occasion of his conversion, he had therefore continued to build assiduously in the following years — still directed no doubt in some measure by Bishop Fitzpatrick. On this score it seems correct to say that there were two particular times in his lifetime when he went to school, as it were: during his two years at Walpole, New Hampshire (as we have already noted), and during the years immediately following his conversion. How much longer this special time of study might otherwise have extended in this instance, had not the fluctuating fortunes of his *Review* pulled him out again on the lecture circuit, it is hard to guess.

At the outset Brownson's Catholic *Quarterly* had a sparkling success. The extensive noise made by his conversion, and the efforts made by his Catholic friends, soon procured for it a wide circulation. But after 1845 its fortunes began to dip, and continued a downward spiral till in the spring of 1849 they reached a low register. The editor tells us that it was only through the goodly offices of his friends in Canada that his *Review* was saved from failure.[2] They invited him to give a course of lectures at Montreal and Quebec. It would appear that James Sadlier, the publisher, had the main hand in arranging the invitations. In replying to Brownson's acceptance of his invitation, Mr. Sadlier counseled, not a change of the topics of the lectures, but a slightly more irenic heading of one topic in particular — "lest you scare off Protestant attendance." He added: "Every person to whom I have spoken, Protestant and Catholic, seems pleased with your coming. The New-Englanders particularly, notwithstanding your 'embracing the errors of Popery,' are somewhat proud of you, and you will find a large number of them among your audience."[3]

His first course of lectures at Montreal was delivered in April 1850, but there is no record of just what the topics of the lectures were. The last lecture of the course was given on April 16, to which an extra lecture was added by special request on the eighteenth. Immediately thereafter Brownson took a boat for Quebec where Abbé Taschereau, the future archbishop of Quebec, and some of Brownson's friends, had previously arranged for a repetition of Brownson's Montreal lectures. Among the treasured friendships Brownson formed while in Montreal was that with the popular novelist, Mrs. James Sadlier,[4] and that with George Edward Clerk. During Brownson's stay in Montreal the proposition of starting a journal in the English language was seriously discussed — Mr. Clerk leading the way. A few months later the idea was put into execution, and Clerk became the first editor of *The True Witness*. On July 3, 1850, Clerk wrote Brownson to acquaint him with the actual establishment of the proposed journal, and said:

> His Lordship of Montreal, knowing your zeal for everything connected with our Holy Religion, held out to me the hope that, perhaps, you also would from time to time be induced to favor us with your support, perhaps occasionally a few lines from your pen. For you may be assured that your chaff will be of more use to us than other men's wheat. . . . [You] as an old soldier, I a recent recruit, ask instruction as to the mode of carrying on the spiritual warfare in which I am about to be engaged — to be allowed to have the honor of reckoning you among our correspondents, with or without, the sanction of your name, as to you may seem the more appropriate.[5]

In the fall of the same year (September 1850), publisher James Sadlier again wrote Brownson to say that his Lordship, Msgr. Bourget, bishop of Montreal, had expressed a wish that he give another course of lectures that fall or winter. To encourage Brownson's coming, Sadlier remarked: "I am sure you would attract much larger audiences than you did on your former visit. Many persons have spoken to me on the subject and all are of the same opinion. If you can come without great inconvenience to yourself, do so. Your lectures last winter have done a great deal of good to Catholics as well as set a number of Protestants inquiring." The sturdy old lecturer again responded to this invitation, and, during the latter part of October and the forepart of November, delivered another series of addresses at Montreal to larger audiences. Again there is no extant record of the precise topics of the lectures. In one of them, however, while condemning divorce, he asserted that there is no real agreement between parties to a marriage if they merely agree to live together only until one or the other asks for a divorce. Such a marriage is no real marriage, he stated, but rather legalized concubinage. At the next session of the Canadian legislature a divorce bill was introduced, and in the discussion of the subject the Protestant newspapers of the city greatly distorted Brownson's statement into the assertion that "Protestant marriages are null, and, at bottom, nothing but concubinage." There was a great hubbub over the matter, and the editor of *The True Witness,* George Clerk, hurriedly got a letter off to Brownson to acquaint him with the state of affairs, and to obtain from him a flat denial of the outrageous distortion.[6] We have no record of a statement from Brownson, but there can be no reasonable doubt that he sent one.

As Brownson himself asserted, it was the proceeds from these lectures that had saved his *Review* from failure at the time. His list of subscribers had been dwindling, but this was by no means the exclusive source of his financial embarrassment. The agents which he had accepted and appointed to look after the interests of his *Review* in various parts of the country had in some cases either neglected their duties or had swindled him out of considerable sums. At this time in particular he had lost through his agent in Philadelphia three hundred dollars. Worse yet, when *The Catholic Observer,* edited by Fr. Nicholas O'Brien, failed, Brownson became liable for the financial loss entailed. Fr. O'Brien was pastor of the parish in East Boston at the time of Brownson's conversion, and Brownson and his family often attended church there in his early years as a Catholic. It was at that church that his wife and four youngest children were baptized. A close friendship between Fr. O'Brien and Brownson had grown up, and when Fr. O'Brien was transferred to the cathedral, he made known his wish to found and edit a Catholic newspaper, and appealed to Brownson for financial help. Brownson, the father of a large family, never had any money to spare. But he did what he could for him — he secured a sum of money for his venture. Unfortunately, Fr. O'Brien soon showed his incompetence through negligence, both as manager and editor, and the project collapsed, involving Brownson in indebtedness to the amount of five hundred dollars.[7]

These sums were of no little meaning in days when money had an entirely different value. They were enough to drive the honest old editor to the wall financially as he made plain in a letter to his friend, Fr. Jeremiah Cummings, June 23, 1849.[8] How he struggled through the year 1849 we are not told. Bishop Francis P. Kenrick of Philadelphia, well-known for his diffusive charities, sent him an unspecified sum, saying: "The loss you have suffered by your agent induces me to beg your acceptance of the inclosed contribution to your indemnification. It is too bad to be swindled out of subscriptions."[9]

Fr. Jeremiah Cummings now begins to figure more prominently in Brownson's correspondence. He was a Roman doctor, and, while pastor of St. Stephen's Church in New York City, frequently contributed to Brownson's *Review.* Always sound in doctrine, and vigorous in expression, he sometimes got Brownson into hot water by the unpalatable way in which he set forth his unpopular ideas. (Articles in Brownson's *Quarterly* were unsigned.) He wrote Brownson to tell him of "an article done into Italian with editorial remarks laudatory in the highest degree of said *Boston Quarterly* and Signor Brownson," and assured Brownson that the authorities in the Eternal City would "have no objection to present you with a cap of a Doctor of Philosophy, a thing you would only care about as going to show that your sincerity and earnestness are approved of there."[10] Brownson in response told Cummings: "I wish, very quietly, to make my *Review Roman Catholic*, and must rely on the *Romans* for instruction. The *Review* is a sort of joint-stock concern, you know, and its purpose is to get as far as possible the whole policy here on the *Roman* track.[11]

Few had a greater interest in Brownson's *Review* than Fr. Cummings. When he visited Washington he found the interests of the *Review* "woefully unattended to," and he did everything he could to improve matters. "I am more and more convinced," he wrote the editor, "that your *Review* does not receive half the support it would receive had it a proper corps of agents."[12] Brownson's son Henry was of the opinion that had his father on becoming a Catholic continued to send his *Review* to those who had previously distributed it, and had selected established houses where more agents were in demand, he would have had a better circulation among non-Catholics. As for Catholics, those really interested in the *Review* would have taken it without agents to drum up interest. As it turned out, the unlucky editor suffered through the agents of his employ. Said his son Henry: "The pecuniary loss from defalcation of agents, first, and later, of his New York publishers, and then the London publisher of the English edition of his *Review*, was large, and to one who could ill afford it, very serious."[13] Appleton's *Cyclopedia of American Biography* says that Brownson's *Review* "was the first American periodical reprinted in England, where it had a large circulation."[14] This meant that the failure of his publisher, Charles Dolman, involved him in considerable financial loss. But Appleton's *Cyclopedia* is not quite accurate when it says that Brownson's *Review* "was the first American periodical reprinted in England." Frank Luther Mott informs us that Brownson's *Review* "was not the first American review to be republished in England, since Walsh's *American Review* had had that distinction."[15]

However unfortunate with his publicity agents, it must be acknowledged, as was acknowledged by his son Henry, that his father was at times somewhat negligent in business matters. This was almost inevitable with a man so deeply buried in studying and writing.

Another factor that operated against his *Review* ever attaining a wider circulation was Brownson's dogged refusal, to put it negatively, to play to the gallery in any sense whatsoever. His journal was for the earnest few with scholarly tastes. He indicated the character his *Review* had assumed from the beginning when he remarked:

> We have spoken freely, frankly, boldly, we hope not rashly, on all subjects which have come up; and our aim has been to encourage a free, bold, and manly tone in our Catholic literature, to make Catholics feel they are at home in this country, and need but courage in avowing and fidelity in practicing their religion to make the country Catholic. That we have sometimes erred in our judgment as to the proper topic to be treated, as well as the manner of treating the topic selected, is very probable; that we have disturbed many prejudices, trodden on a good many corns, and vexed not a few good souls, who would never have Catholicity speak above her breath or in any but apologetic tones, is very likely; but we have aimed well, and done the best we could. The character of the *Review* is now well established, and such as it has been it will continue to be. We could easily make it more popular, and double our list of subscribers; but we have a conscience, and we can do nothing for the sake of popularity or the gaining of friends. . . . Our *Review* is devoted to the cause of Catholic truth

and morals, and we seek to please God, not man. We would sooner beg, sooner
starve, than shape a single sentence to win the applause of the multitude, although that applause is as sweet in our ears as in those of any man. As long as
we can secure the approbation, and lose not the confidence of the pastors of the
Church, we are content.[16]

And that approbation and encouragement of the pastors of the Catholic
Church did come to him just when he most needed it. The bishops of the
country had just met in their seventh provincial council in Baltimore, May
1849, and, at the suggestion of his "very dear friend," Bishop Francis Patrick Kenrick of Philadelphia, all the bishops in attendance affixed their
names to a statement acknowledging the high merits of his "literary labors
in defense of the faith," of which he had proved himself "an able and intrepid advocate."[17] This high endorsement helped to bring up the waning subscription list of his *Quarterly*. Being assured it was so intended, the apostolic editor placed the letter of approbation with the bishops' names on the
cover of his sedate *Quarterly*. He could not of course have foreseen the distressing imbroglio in which this was to involve him so soon.

In response to this gracious gesture of approbation and confidence on the
part of the American hierarchy in his regard, he wrote in part:

> We cannot resist the temptation to publish the following letter, designed to
> approve and encourage our humble labors in the cause of Catholic literature.
> The letter was as unexpected as it is kind and cheering, and we are utterly at a
> loss to express our deep sense of the high testimony it bears to our *Review*. No
> higher authority could be asked, and no higher authority, out of Rome, could be
> given; and to say that we are grateful is to say nothing. We thank the eminent
> prelate who drew up the letter, and each and all of the illustrious Archbishops
> and Bishops who generously signed it, and gave us their approbation and a
> pledge of their support. It was more than we deserved, more than we can
> deserve, more than any other editor can deserve; but we shall do our best not
> to make them regret their generous act.[18]

However great the hazards he had to surmount in the year 1849, we know
from a letter his wife wrote her sister Betsy, that Brownson's fortunes had
mended by 1850. In her letter of March 13, 1850, after mentioning that the
subscriptions to her husband's *Review* were about fourteen hundred, she
said: "This with Mr. B[rownson]'s lectures has given us a comfortable living
and has enabled us to educate our children pretty well." Orestes, Jr., who
had recently married, was teaching school at Evansville, Indiana, and William had gone there to live with him; Henry, fourteen years of age, was in
the Jesuit Novitiate at Frederick, Maryland, after three and a half years at
their Holy Cross College, Worcester, Massachusetts. His mother Sally remarked: "I rejoice that he is willing to forsake father and mother and all
things for Christ's sake. May God strengthen him in so holy a vocation."
John was now at the Sulpician Seminary in Montreal, Canada. The child
Sally (or Sarah) was just ten, and is, said her mother, "a great deal of company for us." Edward, only six, was going to school and appeared to be "a
pretty good scholar." Charles Joseph was just four, and was "more like
John." George had lately died of scarlet fever.[19]

Of the four Brownson boys who went to Holy Cross College, John seems
to have fared more prominently than the others. It is evident that Henry was
somewhat handicapped during his youth by poor health. Albert S. Foley,
S.J., tells us that John battled on equal terms with James Healy, a student
who was eventually to become bishop of Portland, Maine, for many of the

EDWARD P. BROWNSON

HENRY F. BROWNSON

ORESTES A. BROWNSON, SR., IN LATER LIFE

ORESTES A. BROWNSON, JR.

SARAH M. BROWNSON

honors of the college. Already on July 29, 1846, John had delivered an oration on the "Vision of Liberty" after his friend James Healy had declaimed his story of "Cyrus the Mede." At the first commencement of the college, on July 26, 1849, "old Brownson was there to hear and see son John declaim an oration on Liberty." (He was entitled to be there, for he was one of the prominent Catholic laymen of Boston who had appeared before the educational committee in the statehouse to plead for a charter for Holy Cross College — because of reluctance to grant it.)[20] Later, on July 24, 1851, John and his friend James Healy were awarded together the degree of Master of Arts at the college.[21]

James Augustine Healy was a black student from Macon, Georgia, who had been baptized together with two of Brownson's sons at the college. Apparently some of the students there made James Healy and his brothers, Michael, Hugh and Patrick, quite conscious of their color. But Albert Foley tells us:

> It was among the Yankees, who composed more than sixty percent of the boys of the [Holy] Cross [College] that James found his warmest friends. John Brownson and his brothers William and Henry proved to be constant in their friendship for James, bound as these latter were to James by the special tie of baptism on the same day. Fifty years later James was still sending anniversary greetings and presents to Henry in remembrance of that day. . . . James was a frequent visitor at the Brownson home in Chelsea. There he listened as the shaggy philosopher, Orestes Brownson, dispensed wit and wisdom at his hospitable table. Brownson's *Review* (together with other journals) became a formative influence in developing young Healy's social and political maturity. He devoured the *Review* as soon as it came out, and reacted to its opinions intelligently if independently.[22]

In the year 1851 we find William Brownson at a seminary in Quebec, Canada, and we learn from a letter of Fr. Isaac Hecker, dated September 5, 1851, that Brownson's two sons Henry and John had just embarked from New York for Europe. They were en route to the Semenaire de St. Sulpice, Paris. Before embarking they had visited the Redemptorist Monastery in New York, and Fr. Hecker assured their father that he had done what he could to make their visit agreeable. On the previous Sunday they had gone to pay the bishop a visit, and on the last Sunday they took their dinner with Fr. Hecker and the Community. Fr. Hecker also mentioned in his letter that he had learned from Henry and John that their father intended to make a spiritual retreat in Baltimore in the fall.[23]

Henry and John having reached their destination, John gave his father some idea of how things were moving at the Semenaire de St. Sulpice in a letter dated October 20, 1851. He wrote in part:

> Our retreat finished last night, & this morning the classes begin. Henry commences his theology; I am to follow the course of Canon Law & the theology of the grand course. M. Icard is professor of the former, & M. Gally, as his name indicates, [is] a Gallican, and one, I am assured, of the first (or if you like, of the muddiest) water. Questions from the treatises de Fide & de Ecclesia are to be treated this year. Henry has for director one Mr. Beaudry, who, in my opinion, is pursuing an injudicious course with him, that is, he wants to crowd too much upon him.
>
> I am not going to study Hebrew, unless the bishop insists upon it, for I think I can employ my time much more advantageously. Henry is to study it, however, his director says. My director is M. Detual, & I like him very much. I guess there is no fear of his interdicting Billuart to me, nor the *Review*, of which I

suppose you will send one copy to us. Billuart I will probably get tomorrow and all St. Anselm for you, which I shall immediately forward. I desire also to get some one of the Greek Fathers, & I intend to see what editions I can find in order to have some Greek reading as soon as convenient.

I shall also go to see Montalembert (if he is returned to Paris, & M. Carrieres will permit). France is a great country undoubtedly, and Paris a great city, and if the devil does not have some rare pickings here, appearances are deceitful. Here is some piety, and *some* impiety. Gallican liberties have been carried to perfection in some particulars; and Love brought or helped to bring the laws of the Church into contempt. Sunday is very much like any other day as far as servile labor is concerned. No wonder heretics are scandalized, & that all sorts of bad things are said of Catholics. A revolution, as I have written before, seems expected. Troops are coming and going, and while I write the drums are rolling & a body of the National Guards are marching past.

John excused himself for a postscript on the margin, but pleaded that he had more worthwhile news: the textbook in canon law that had been taught in the seminary there had just been put on the Index in Rome because of its Gallican propositions, it was said. This news came on the eve of his father bringing his heavy artillery to bear on the monstrous (at least to him) evil called Gallicanism.[24]

Extra money was needed if Brownson was to continue these splendid educational opportunities for his sons. The lecture circuit was highly agreeable to him and could pretty well be depended upon to provide the extra money needed. In reporting his lectures, some, remembering that he had formerly been a Protestant minister, referred to him as Rev. O. A. Brownson; others as Professor Brownson; and others still did not fail to put LL.D. behind his name. This title had been bestowed on him in 1846 by Norwich University, Vermont.[25] In a letter written in July 1850, Fr. Augustine J. Thébaud, S.J., president, had conferred on him the honors of St. John's College, Fordham, New York, he being the first person to be so honored by the college.[26] But what were such titles to such a man as Orestes Brownson? As his old friend, Isaac B. Pierce, remarked in a letter to him: "There are men to whom titles can add nothing. You, my friend, are such a man; and you owe nothing to titles or diplomas in your gigantic march through metaphysics and polemics."[27]

Only in such centers as New York and Baltimore did Brownson lecture in 1851, but in 1852 he engaged in much wider lecturing, traveling as far west as St. Louis. His course of lectures was on the general subject of Catholicity and civilization, in which his aim was to show that all true civilization is of Catholic origin, that all nations in the ancient world in proportion as they departed from the patriarchal religion, and all nations of the Christian era in proportion as they recede from the Catholic Church, necessarily tend more and more to barbarism. He did not maintain this precisely as an argument for the Catholic Church, since the *direct* object of the Church is spiritual, not the advancement of civilization, but the promotion of the glory of God in the salvation of souls. He maintained it because he found it to be historically true, and because it rebuffs the "carnal Judaism" into which the world has lapsed, and which proposes little more than material civilization and temporal well-being as its sole end and purpose. In short, his lectures were a running commentary on the sacred text, "Seek ye first the kingdom of God and its justice, and all these things shall be added to you." It was Brownson's good fortune that the lectures were listened to by large numbers of the most respectable and influential classes of St. Louis with deep interest, almost enthusiasm. Nowhere, he tells us, had he ever found a more intelligent audience, or been listened to with more respect and sympathy.[28]

His first invitation to lecture came to him from the archbishop of St. Louis, Peter Richard Kenrick, October 27, 1851, seconded by a letter the next day from the Committee on Lectures, headed by Alex J. Garesche. Having accepted the invitation, Brownson delivered a course of four lectures before the Catholic Institute of the city, to which a fifth was added on socialism by special request of both the Catholic and the Protestant citizens of St. Louis.[29]

Brownson delivered his first lecture in Wyman's Hall on January 21, 1852. The St. Louis *Intelligencer* gave notice on January 21 that a lecture was to be delivered that evening at the Odd Fellows Hall "by Rev. O. A. Brownson. Whatever difference of opinion may exist between Mr. Brownson and any portion of his audience on some subjects, we do not doubt that his theme will be handled in a manner worthy of his reputation and ability." But in reporting his lecture of the evening the *Intelligencer* badly mangled and misrepresented his thought. The *Morning Signal* of St. Louis sinned even more deeply on this score. The writer who signed himself *Americus* betrayed extreme unfairness and bitterness. The *Western Watchman* was less obnoxious. As Brownson himself wrote after the lectures: "The secular and sectarian press, with one or two honorable exceptions, kept up during the delivery of the lectures a continual fire against the lecturer and his assertions, and even sought to crush him beneath the weight of his own shameful writings prior to his conversion, and which he had long since retracted."[30]

About the only newspaper in the city that dealt with entire fairness in reporting the lectures was *The Shepherd of the Valley,* a Catholic journal edited by Robert A. Bakewell, a convert. In reporting Brownson's lecture of January 21 on January 24, the editor remarked that "the room [Wyman's Hall] was crowded to excess, notwithstanding the severity of the weather," and added: "The lecturer was evidently laboring under the effects of a cold, and on rising to address his audience, remarked that he was not in good voice; that he feared that his tones would remind them of Milton's gates of hell, which, 'on brazen hinges turning, grated harsh thunder.' "

In this first lecture Brownson dealt with the objection: "Protestantism promotes material or worldly prosperity, but Catholicity does not." In no sense would he admit the validity of such an objection to Catholicity. Such an objection was only the modern version of "carnal Judaism":

> The very objection was brought against Jesus Christ by those who crucified him between two thieves. If Christianity be true, it was certainly given, not for this world, but for the world to come. It teaches us that this world is not our home. We are called pilgrims on earth, and our destiny is not to be realized on this globe. God did not create us for a temporal end, not to gain a temporal good. He created us for eternity. Our true good is not to be attained here, but hereafter, when this world is done with, and has passed away with all its follies. . . . The adverse judgments passed on Religion by those who think that its peculiar office is to make a Heaven on earth are worthless, and the objections based upon such a supposition fall to the ground. . . . The world is but an inn, and I am a guest for one day. What care I if it is better or worse. The moment you say man's good is eternal, all the pomp of this world vanishes; all its goods sink into trifles; all its boasts become empty and nothing is good or evil, except as it assists or embarrasses me in gaining the eternal destiny for which I was made.

Brownson's second and third lectures, "delivered to very full audiences on Friday and Monday evenings," January 23 and 26, were reported conjointly by *The Shepherd* on January 31. Of the two lectures, editor Bakewell remarked:

> The lecturer was enthusiastically applauded at the conclusion of his discourses, and was frequently interrupted by applause during their course. Much was due to Mr. Brownson, who says what he has to say much better than any man we have ever had the good fortune to hear, but was also due to the truths which he uttered, and which are uttered by every Catholic heart, and will be uttered by Catholic lips and acted upon by Catholics, we are sure, however much our politicians may be scandalized at the proposition that the principles of Religion have a bearing upon politics, upon society, and upon every day life.

The theme of Brownson's second lecture was: "All true civilization is of Catholic origin." After expounding at length the political principles that must go into the formation of a civilized state if it is to allow the citizen his true measure of freedom, he asserted that:

> The civilization of the modern world is of Catholic origin. The old civilized world that existed when our Savior came on earth, had passed away. No one of the old dynasties of the East stands. The Old World was swallowed up by barbarians. Your great modern States, France, England, Germany, Spain, had no existence, and those countries were the homes of savage tribes, when the Prince of the Apostles went from Jerusalem by Antioch to erect his Chair in Rome. Those nations are now civilized, and to whom do they owe their civilization, but to the Catholic Church? They were all rescued from barbarism at a period when no Religion but that of the Catholic Church was regarded as Christian.
>
> . . . In our Western World, the Cross was planted and the Gospel first preached by Catholic priests; all the aborigines who have embraced Christianity have been converted by the Church; and there is no portion of our western continent not consecrated by the tears and blood of the Catholic missionary.

His third lecture was on the theme: "Nations advance toward Barbarism just in proportion as they recede from the Catholic Church." Defining barbarism as the supremacy and reign of passion, he asserted that only the true religion, that is, the Catholic religion, can control and subdue the passions. In the course of his lecture, he said:

> Why did the barbarians of the West become converted and civilized, whilst in the East, the barbarians remained the same and those nations there had no power to convert them? The Castilian drove out the Moor from Spain; the barbarians of the West were absorbed by the Church; but, in the East, where the remains of original civilization afforded means as great, or greater, than those of Europe, the Saracen remained a Saracen, and was supplanted only by the Turk, who lived on the edge of Europe for eight hundred years, and remains as much a barbarian as when he first approached its borders. The North of Africa was once highly civilized; the African church numbered eight hundred bishops; it was one of the fairest branches of the fruitful vine which stretches into every land; but Northern Africa was over-run by the Goth, the Vandal, the Hun; the followers of the imposter Mahomet established their superstition where once had flourished the Church of Christ, and these nations have ever since remained barbarians and have shown no signs of recuperative energy. The answer to the question is this: the West adhered to the centre of Unity, the Chair of Peter; whilst, in the East, the nations were always infected with heresy through the subtle minded Greek; they broke from the Church, and when the barbarians came like a flood, they fell, and fell to rise no more.

The theme of Brownson's fourth lecture was: "Civil and Religious Liberty." It was delivered on January 28 before the Catholic Institute in Odd Fellows Hall, "the committee having been unable to procure a more commodious room for the purpose. The hall was crowded to excess, and many who came for the purpose of hearing the distinguished lecturer, were unable to find standing room within the doors." So reported *The Shepherd* on February 7. In the course of his lecture, Brownson said:

> Liberty, true liberty is not possible without Religion. You cannot have a State without submission and obedience, for mere physical force is not sufficient to compel the obedience of law. You may, for a time, hold the people together by force; check their excesses by your troops, but such an expedient as this, can only be temporary; for, after all, the State can be sustained only by the consent of those who are governed. A free people make free institutions; and no form of government can confer freedom upon a people. You cannot enforce laws unless there is a loyal disposition on the part of those for whom they are enacted. You must have law reigning in the individual heart and conscience; you must have virtue; and in proportion as the people are virtuous, you have free government. That which makes men virtuous and gives them control over themselves, is what founds and sustains the State; but this is Religion, and not any false system. We must always have Religion to give us order. The man who is governed by his passions is really a slave; he alone is free who can subdue his passions and act in accordance with reason and judgment. Religion, true Religion alone enables us to do so; and therefore Catholicity alone, which is the true Religion, can make us free.

Among the distinguished guests in the audiences attendant on these lectures were William Tecumseh Sherman and his wife Ellen, daughter of Thomas Ewing, United States senator from Ohio. Listening intently to the forceful lecturer, Ellen "was delighted with the fearless way he defended and exalted the Church." When Ellen visited her father in St. Louis in later years, and heard he was interested in the Catholic faith, she said she would send him "some of Brownson's articles. He has a brain like yours and he had to think his way into the Church just the way you will have to do."[31] Mr. Ewing became a Catholic in 1869.

In his lecture on socialism, delivered in Wyman's Hall on Monday evening, February 2, and reported by *The Shepherd* on February 14, Brownson inveighed against the danger of the socialistic movement eroding and overthrowing our free institutions through its meretricious promises of something better in their stead. After speaking of the nature and historic course of socialism, the alert observer of the times warned:

> The men engaged in this movement are generally ignorant and conceited. They are men of many words, having what is called the gift of gab. They can use high-sounding words and lofty phrases, but they have no practical wisdom except in destroying. The devil is great at destroying, and they resemble him in this, as well as in many other respects. It is only divinity that gives men the capacity to build, and sanctions their efforts, thereby giving to the work permanency. But they endeavor to induce you to overthrow what is good by telling you that they will give you what is better, but you will find that they are always lacking, like the lady who used to eat vegetable oysters, and said as she was about to eat them, "it always *seems* just as if I was about to taste an oyster, but I don't taste it." So, it is with the socialists, they are just going to give you something better, but they don't quite establish it.
>
> . . . What do we want better than our present institutions, and I would ask you to preserve those institutions. Let us labor with all our might in season and

out of season to preserve them in their purity, in the full force in which they were given us by the Providence of God, through our patriotic fathers, and by laboring for their preservation, we shall do good. We must plant ourselves on these institutions, and regard every one who labors to destroy them an enemy, a traitor to his country; whilst he who would labor in perpetuating them is the only true American, the only friend of his country.

The secular press of the city gave little or no notice at all to Brownson's lecture on socialism. The more is the pity, for here the scribes could have been free from the distorting medium of religious bias. It must be acknowledged that Brownson's St. Louis lectures were decidedly aggressive in character, and it is not surprising that a number of citizens of the city got busy and arranged a course of lectures intended to favor Protestantism. On this score they picked Hugh A. Garland, Esq., as lecturer. Garland was a warm friend and admirer of Brownson — the same who had written him an incredibly flattering letter when he was Clerk of the House of Representatives in Washington, inquiring whether Brook Farm was a suitable place to send his daughters for schooling.[32] Brownson's visits with Garland while he was in St. Louis were very cordial. In the course of the lectures that Garland gave he made no pretense to be *replying* to Brownson, and made only one reference to him before opening his lectures, when he said as reported by the *Intelligencer* on February 11, 1852:

> Ladies and Gentlemen: Many people of St. Louis have recently enjoyed what does not often fall to the lot of any community. They have enjoyed the privilege of hearing a great man on great and vital subjects — a man who came thoroughly furnished with all the information on those subjects, and with a mind capable of grasping the great principles involved. This gentleman I have known long, and the cast of his mind I was well acquainted with. I knew him to be one who fearlessly pursues principles to their consequences, and to hear such a man discourse, I say, is a privilege to any people.

As Brownson had received invitations before going to St. Louis from Archbishop Francis Patrick Kenrick, and his two friends, George Miles and T. Parkin Scott, to lecture in Baltimore also, he responded to those invitations by giving a series of lectures there on his way back from St. Louis. The lectures given were similar in nature to those delivered in St. Louis, to which was added by request, one on the Hungarian revolutionist, Louis Kossuth, who at the moment, as already noted, was almost a national sensation. Perhaps in no year of his life did Brownson lecture more widely than in this year, 1852. There was mention in *The Shepherd* on March 6, 1852, that Brownson had given his tenth lecture on "Non-Intervention" before the Young Men's Mercantile Association of Cincinnati, Ohio. His lectures in Montreal, however, seem to rank next in importance to those delivered in St. Louis.

Soon after Brownson's return from St. Louis via Baltimore, James Sadlier, the publisher, being in Boston at the time, spoke to him again about another series of lectures in Montreal during the month of April. After returning to Montreal, Sadlier wrote Brownson on March 26, 1852. The letter is of interest as indicating the militant style of Brownson's apologetics. Never did Chesterton's dictum, "In apologetics I am just the opposite of apologetic," apply more aptly to anyone more than to Brownson. Sadlier wrote:

Dear Sir:
    I received your note in reply to mine some days since. I am rejoiced, as

well as all your friends I have seen, that you have consented to deliver another course of lectures to us. . . . I need not say how happy Mrs. S[adlier] and myself will be to have you and your daughter make your home with us during the stay.

Mrs. Donohue [wife of Patrick Donohue of Boston, publisher of the *Pilot*] has written to say she intends coming on with you. We will advertize your first lecture for the 15. Perhaps the secretary of the Institute will write you, if he has anything to communicate after the meeting. I do not know whether it will be necessary or not until it takes place. The Protestants begin to grumble a little at your coming. They have never forgiven you for your last course of lectures. I tell them that you intend finishing them now completely.

Madam wishes to be kindly remembered to Mrs. B[rownson].

I am yours respectfully,
James Sadlier[33]

Before opening his course of lectures in Montreal, Brownson received a bit of discouraging news in a letter dated April 13, 1852, and signed, "A Bible Reader." After considerable abusive language, the writer finally cautioned:

But I must tell you, Sir, that if you and Bishop Hughes and Mr. Clark [George Clerk], Dr. Newman and Cardinal Wiseman with paper hat and red stockings, and all the Jesuits from Rome to Montreal would do all you could, you cannot stop the onward march of Christian Protestant truth. Babylon is falling, is falling, and the present Pope knows it.[34]

It is said that Brownson carried this letter about with him for some time, having much fun reading it to others.

Brownson's first lecture in Montreal was on the theme: "Why are you a Catholic?" *The Shepherd* gave a transcript of it on May 22, 1852, as it had appeared in the *True Witness* of Montreal. It read in part:

On the evening of Thursday the 18th instant, Dr. Brownson delivered his first lecture in Odd Fellows Hall. In spite of the inclemency of the weather, the room was crowded, and the only regret was, that, unfortunately, the Hall was too small to accommodate the numbers eager for admittance to hear this celebrated champion of the Catholic religion.

[As reported, Brownson stressed the strictly objective character of the reasons which had brought him to the Catholic Church.]

The lecturer commenced by stating, that he had been invited by the Catholic Institute to answer these two questions — "Why I am not a Protestant?" and "Why I am a Catholic?" It was the first of these two questions he intended to answer that evening. He did not intend to hold up his conduct for imitation, or give his *experiences* as reasons, to others for following his conduct, as was the habit of those who considered religion as a mere matter of feeling, in which there were no dogmas propounded to man's acceptance, and to which obedience was claimed. He would, however, endeavor to lay before them the reasons which had chiefly contributed to his conversion — reasons which, from the importance of the subject, ought to weigh with every mind.

*The Shepherd,* issue of May 23, 1852, gave another transcript from the *True Witness* of Brownson's second lecture in which he resumed the theme of the first lecture. It opened with the notice:

On Tuesday evening, Dr. Brownson resumed the question, "Why I am not a Protestant?" The attendance was . . . fully as numerous as on the first evening of the lecture.

The learned gentleman commenced his discourse by remarking that some people are hard to please, and had complained that, in his first lecture, though professing to explain why he was *not* a Protestant, he assigned no reason why he *was* a Catholic. He had professed to give *some only,* out of many, of the reasons why he was *not* a Protestant, but not all the reasons. The objection therefore was unfounded, for had he given all the reasons why he was not a Protestant, he would in the case, have given the reasons why he *was* a Catholic, for every man must be either the one or the other.

*The Shepherd,* May 24, gave another transcript from the *True Witness* of Brownson's third lecture — "Why I am a Catholic?" In the conclusion of his discourse Brownson stressed the miraculous character of the Catholic Church. The Church is a standing miracle:

> The simple historical existence of the Church — the fact that she exists today, in all her loveliness and strength, notwithstanding all the opposition she has encountered, is conclusive proof that she is God's Church. Had she been human, she would have fallen long ago, and disappeared from the earth. Her continued existence is the most stupendous miracle ever recorded. She is a standing miracle — then she is God's Church — if God's Church she is what she professes to be, for God cannot sanction or miraculously sustain an imposter — if what she professes to be, she has authority to teach what God requires us to believe and do — and then, what she teaches is infallibly true, for God cannot authorize the teaching of errors. Then, to know the way of salvation, and to secure salvation, I must enter her communion, believe what she teaches, and do what she commands. I must become a Catholic.

Having finished this series of lectures, Brownson stayed on in Montreal to meet the request of the Catholic Institute that he deliver a lecture on Louis Napoleon. As Louis Napoleon had just executed a coup d'etat on December 2, 1851, declaring himself emperor of France, he had become a very exciting topic for discussion, and Brownson willingly remained to give his views on a subject so engaging at the moment. He was quite disposed to look favorably upon Louis Napoleon at this time, and concluded his discourse, saying: "Let us accept the good he has done, suspend our judgment for the future; and applaud him in so far as he has pursued, and continues to pursue, the path of truth and justice, law and order."[35]

No matter how much lecturing Brownson did, it does not seem to have created any extra difficulties for him in regard to the work he had to do on the *Review.* His son relates that "once he returned home from lecturing after the first of March, with nothing for the next number, and without assistance he wrote the whole April number in time to have it printed and sent out several days before the end of March, and the number was more than usually praised by the journals." Neither the manual labor of writing nor the mental exercise of composing seemed ever to tire him. And inasmuch as it was his practice to have his *Review* in the hands of subscribers on this side of the Atlantic by the first of each quarter, he was a model of promptness to all editors. This meant that he had to have what is called "copy" in the hands of his publisher a fortnight beforehand. In writing, many of his articles were begun over again, in some cases after a few pages, in others after quite a number of pages. He seldom attempted to patch.[36]

In the autumn of 1852, besides his invitations to lecture in Mobile and Chicago, he also lectured in Philadelphia and New York. During the year 1853 he received invitations to lecture in Hartford, Baltimore, Washington, Buffalo, Cleveland and Louisville.[37] He was the recipient of an almost uninterrupted flow of invitations to lecture, some couched in the most flattering terms. As the year 1854 approached, arrangements were made again for

429

another series of addresses by him in St. Louis. A letter of Alex Garesche (chairman of the Committee on Lectures), dated December 1, 1853, informs us that these arrangements were made in conjunction with the advice of the archbishop of St. Louis, Peter Richard Kenrick.

The archbishop had a very lofty opinion of Brownson. Writing to Brownson on February 13, 1852, George Leach, referring to an interview he had had with the archbishop of St. Louis, told him: "The Archbishop holds you in the highest admiration. Said I to him: 'We have probably hardly his equal in the country.' I said this rather timidly in his presence. What think you was his reply: 'Where will you find his equal in any country?' " Leach added: "Indeed, Sir, your praise is in all the churches. The clergy universally speak of you in the highest terms. Three admitted in my presence that they did not think there has been your superior since St. Augustine."[38]

We learn from a letter Brownson wrote his wife Sally on January 3, 1854, that he had had something of a narrow escape on his journey to St. Louis at this time. The letter ran:

Planters House, St. Louis
My Dear Wife:

I arrived through the protection of the Blessed Virgin and St. John, at this place, on Sunday between eleven and twelve o'clock. I had no serious accident until within eight miles of the city (I travelled all the way, except six miles, at Lake [name not legible], by RR to Alton, twenty miles from St. Louis), when our boat, Altona, ran on a sandbar. In getting off the sandbar, she struck upon a chain of rocks; from these she struck her bow upon a [word not legible] which knocked a hole in her bottom, and swung round and struck her stern upon another which broke six pins of her timbers.

She came across the channel, with a rapid current, and ice drifting against her with awful force. By means of pumps and buckets at which passengers as well as the crew worked for some eighteen or twenty hours, till completely exhausted, we kept her afloat for a time; but the frigate sank to her guards. Sunday morning, about eight o'clock, the Ben West could not move; but after two hours' detention, the Brunetta came along and took us off.

No lives were lost, and no passenger suffered otherwise than from apprehension, which the general disregard for life in these parts fully justified. For twenty hours, she was twice in imminent danger; for navigation is nearly closed, and the ice could have knocked us to pieces before a boat could save us. And we had no way of getting ashore; yesterday was mild; and today is as warm as a mild day in April.

I give my first lecture tomorrow evening, and my last in this city on Wednesday of next week. I hope to be in Louisville the week following. My friends received me cordially here, and have provided me with rooms in the Planters Hotel, the best in the city. Yesterday, I was out all day, making calls and paying the compliments of the season. I drank my quantity of egg nog, which with a cold bath last night has more than half cured the cold. I am a little hoarse; but not any more ill; and am as comfortable as I can be away from my home, my dear wife and children. I shall not expose myself on the river again, if the water remains as low as it is now. So do not suffer any apprehension. Let Father [name not legible] say a Mass of Thanksgiving for my preservation, and another for my protection.

I hope you are well, and that all goes well. Give my love to the boys, to Sarah, and believe me,

Your own affectionate husband,
O. A. Brownson

Mrs. O. A. Brownson, Chelsea, Mass.[39]

Before reporting Brownson's first lecture delivered on January 4, *The Shepherd* in its issue of January 7, 1854, made reference to his lucky escape on his journey. It said: "Mr. Brownson arrived in St. Louis on Monday last; he was on the ill-fated Altona, and, in company with all the passengers, had something of an escape. God has work for Mr. Brownson yet, and we Catholics of America cannot well afford to lose him."

Heretofore we have had only one pen-portrait of Brownson as he appeared on the lecture platform, that left us by Fr. Hecker. There must be others scattered here or there in newspaper files that were penned by reporters who listened to his lectures. What is perhaps one of the best is the one left us by Robert Bakewell, editor of *The Shepherd*. He had listened to and reported Brownson's lectures in St. Louis in 1852, and had had ample opportunity to size him up from every angle. After praising him as a model of English style in *The Shepherd* (December 31, 1853), he pointed out that:

> As a lecturer, Mr. Brownson is no less distinguished than as a writer. His style of lecturing is the very perfection of the lecturing style. Calm, massive, unimpassioned, he begins by telling you what he will prove, and he ends by proving it. He looks his audience in the face, and learns from their eyes when they have caught his sense, and whether they are following his chain of reasoning; now he goes back to pull the last link to show that it is strong; now he proceeds rapidly, adding strand after strand to his cord, till no Titan can make it crack; occasionally he rises with his subject to the highest eloquence. From first to last he impresses you with the idea of power; you may not like the goal to which he would take you, but place yourself once in his hands, and you feel it is in vain to resist.[40]

Brownson's first lecture was on "Civil and Religious Liberty," and was delivered at the Mercantile Library Hall. "The immense Hall was well filled, only one or two seats at the lower end of the room were left unoccupied." As further reported by *The Shepherd,* the lecturer proceeded to say:

> Civil and Religious Liberty is a big word in our day. Don't misunderstand me. I do not appear here as an opponent of either Civil or Religious Liberty. I have always loved liberty; I have sacrificed something for it; I have always been its advocate. My hair is now gray and my blood thinner, than it has been, but I am still ready to fight for liberty in word, and in deed if need there were. But I fight for *Liberty,* and not *License.* I love liberty in its strictest sense; in this sense I have always advocated it, in action and in words; but whether I advocate it or not, I shall exercise it tonight in the freest way.
>
> Whoever has watched the tendencies of these things knows that, though there is no law against liberty of speech, there is in reality no place where there is so little freedom of thought and speech as in the United States. (Here the speaker was interrupted by a storm of hisses and groans, mingled with determined applause; the noise lasted for a minute or two, during which Brownson crossed his arms and very calmly looked his audience in the face. When order was partially restored, he continued.) If proof of my assertion were needed, I would ask no better than that hiss. (Loud applause.)

The editor of *The Shepherd* remarked: "He concluded [his address] amidst loud and prolonged applause."

The St. Louis *Intelligencer* of January 6, true to itself, after remarking that "on Wednesday the Mercantile Hall was crowded to its utmost capacity to hear Prof. Brownson on the important and interesting subject of Civil and Religious Liberty," gave only a travesty of his thought. The writer wasted many words in ridiculing Brownson's statement that, while sincerely seeking to correct his country's faults, he had a deep, patriotic attachment to its institutions.

Brownson's second lecture was on "The Mission of the United States," and was delivered on January 6. It was largely a protest against the notion that America's destiny is to export a radical type of democracy to the rest of the world. Said the lecturer as reported by *The Shepherd* on January 14:

> The mission of the American people was to subdue this new world, to cover it with a new civilization, and new institutions, with as much freedom for the individual and communities as is compatible with the frailty of our nature; and to act thus on other nations. Such was our mission which we might have fulfilled. But instead of this, we have conceived it to be our mission to propagate to other States, Democracy as a creed. Republicanism in its honest sense has lost ground, and is daily losing ground, amongst us. The man who would be popular — and popularity with us is the only avenue to success — must be prepared to shout Democracy at the top of his lungs, to speak smooth things to the "dear people" and to encourage all the lawless tendencies of the age.

A writer in the *Evening News* (January 7), after giving Brownson's thought on the country's tendency toward absolute democracy, noted the conclusion to his lecture:

> The hope of America is not in the intelligence, or even in the virtue of the people, but in the Church of God. To the conservative influence of Catholicity, are we to look for a check on the rampant spirit of democracy, the tendency to the absolute will of the majority.

The theme of Brownson's third lecture was "Protestant Liberality," and dealt with the claim that Protestantism gave liberty and progress to the modern world. Reporting the discourse on January 21, *The Shepherd* remarked that it "was delivered on Monday evening the tenth instant to a large audience." Although the editor devoted several columns to the address, he subjoined a note, saying:

> We regret that the latter part of our report of this splendid lecture — the most popular certainly of the whole course — should be so imperfect. The fact is, that we forget the Reporter in the listener, and we were so carried away by the interest we took in the eloquent conclusion, in which Mr. Brownson surpassed himself, that we could do no more for our readers than we have done. On the whole, the last part of the lecture would have lost so much in passing through our hands that we hardly regret it.

The *Evening News* of the city, which did show a certain willingness to be fair in reporting Brownson's lectures, quoted him on January 10 as saying in this same lecture:

> The greater wealth of Protestant countries, so often cited as an argument against the Catholic Church, arises from that worldly spirit which attaches greater importance to the temporal than to the spiritual. Because the Church does not take care of the physical well-being of her children, provide for their bodily wants, and incite them to the pursuit of riches and lucre, she is said, not to favor human progress and happiness. Government, institutions, and politics may claim the attention of mankind; but when we meet to discuss questions relating to our eternal welfare, your mammoth sheet, *The Republican,*[41] tells us there is no necessity for it, and no benefit to be derived from it. Catholicity acknowledges the force of the divine command: "Seek ye the kingdom of

Heaven, and its justice," and says to her children, "be not solicitous of what ye shall eat, nor of what ye shall drink," thus drawing their minds from worldly calculations, and directing them to higher and better objects of thought.

Brownson's fourth lecture was on the theme, "The Church a Miraculous Fact in History." *The Shepherd* remarked on February 4: "The Mercantile Hall was crowded on the evening of Friday, 13, ultimo. A larger audience could not have been accommodated there. A more splendid effort of genuine oratory, we never had the pleasure to hear." Said the lecturer:

> The [Catholic] Church has struggled with enemies from the first. At her birth, she found wealth, genius, and talent arraigned against her; her enemies have not been poor or ignorant. She had to fight the Jews, the Romans, the proud emperors of the Middle Ages, the States of modern times. She finds arraigned against her, the wealth and influence of England, the industry of the United States. . . . But she comes forth from the fiery ordeal to which she is exposed as young, as beautiful, as fresh, as vigorous, as when she came first from the catacombs, and bound her brow with the diadem of Caesar.

Again, by special request, Brownson added an extra lecture to his course on the Russo-Turkish question. In reporting the lecture, the *Evening News* of January 17 said by way of introduction:

> Owing to the inclemency of the weather, there was not so large an audience assembled at Library Hall, to hear Prof. Brownson, last night, as usual; nevertheless the room was about two-thirds filled, and those present were well compensated for their trouble, by the luminous and comprehensive manner in which the lecturer handled the absorbing subject.

Brownson's coming to St. Louis for this second series of lectures was the occasion of a slight display of pyrotechnics. In the December 31, 1853, issue of his journal, Robert Bakewell had had a somewhat glowing eulogy on Brownson prior to his arrival in the city. During the course of his eulogy Bakewell said:

> Like another St. Augustine, he has been permitted, though late, to see the ancient Truth and the ancient Beauty, in the unsuccessful search of which he spent so many years. His conversion is an epoch in the History of the American [Catholic] Church, and American Catholic journalism has taken a new turn from him. He has brought to the controversy a mind in all the vigor of its maturity, a profound personal knowledge of the errors of his age and country, a nerve and skill for combat braced and perfected by years of incessant conflict. When he had truth on his side he was invincible; and who, since that time, has — we do not say gained over him a temporary advantage, however slight — but who has dared to meet the sturdy warrior face to face and have a stand up fight with him? Not one. For years and years, like old Entellus, he has gone round and round the ring, poising his brawny arm and seeking with his practiced eye an opponent in the crowd, but no one *Dares* to put on Caestus and brave the fight. It is to be regretted that there is not on this continent a man who has the courage, the skill, or honesty, to meet him in honorable combat and show something like a contest.

Although this was written by Robert Bakewell, the Protestant clergy of the city seemed to think that it was a cartel delivered to them by Brownson himself. The chairman of a committee they formed, Rev. E. Thompson Baird, handed Brownson a challenge to meet in debate the champion they were ready to put forward, one Dr. N. I. Rice. Bakewell published the letter

433

of challenge to Brownson under the heading, "Parsons in an Uproar," after which he published also Brownson's reply to the challenge. It ran as follows:

Dear Sir:

I have received and considered your letter signed by some thirty Protestant ministers of St. Louis, which as chairman of a committee formed by them, you did me the honor to hand me yesterday. This letter, I presume, professes to be an acceptance of a challenge which it is pretended that I have thrown out to the Protestant world, and to discuss in public the matters in difference between Catholics and Protestants, and informs me that the aforesaid ministers have chosen one Dr. N. I. Rice as their champion.

Allow me to say, my dear sir, that the Protestant ministers of St. Louis labor under a gross mistake, and their assumed acceptance, is the acceptance of a challenge never given or even dreamed of. The article in *The Shepherd of the Valley* on which they rely, contains no challenge of the sort, and if it were not so, I am not responsible for it, for it was written and published without my knowledge, authorization or consent. I am ready, according to the best of my ability, in my *Review* and in my public lectures, in my own way and time, to defend my Religion, and to expose the fallacies and vain pretensions of yours, but I have never sought to do it in the way proposed, for I am no gladiator, and no friend to oral public discussions, from which I have never seen any good results.

I could not, permit me to say, consent to meet your champion in the way you propose, without, in some measure, compromising the rights of my Religion, conceding that the question between Catholics and Protestants is a debatable question, and granting that Catholicity and Protestantism, in some measure, stand on the same level, a concession to heresy and error and an indignity to truth, of which, I trust to God, I shall never be guilty.

Moreover, during the last nine or ten years, I have published in my *Quarterly Review* a series of elaborate articles in defense of my Religion and in refutation of yours. These articles remain unanswered, and, so far as I am aware, no Protestant has seriously attempted to answer them. I would respectfully suggest, that it would be well for the Protestant clergy of St. Louis, to make at least an attempt to answer them before asking me to engage in public debate, and also it will be time enough for me to consider whether I will meet their champion or not when they have done so.

I have the honor to be,

Your obedient servant,
O. A. Brownson

Rev. E. T. Baird,
Chairman of Committee[42]

Brownson's son Henry tells us that the excitement his father's lectures in St. Louis created resulted in a closer examination of Catholic doctrine on the part of Protestants, and led to numerous conversions. *The Intelligencer* of the city, issued on January 7, 1854, acknowledged the wide stir caused by the lectures when it said: "The distinguished gentleman who is now lecturing before the Catholic Institute of this city, is not likely to escape a very searching and severe criticism, in enunciating the principles and expounding the sentiments he does, before the large and intellectual classes of St. Louis — already the propositions he has advanced are undergoing a general discussion in the private circles of our city as well as in the columns of newspapers." The very purpose of the lectures was to make converts, and they were not without results. Henry Brownson states: "Garland's own daughter's conversion has been told in one of Garesche's letters,[43] and from time to time his letters announced the reception into the Church of some one whom Brownson had met in St. Louis. Thus, a few months after Brownson's visit, he [Garesche] writes, under date of April 15, 1854: 'It may afford you pleasure to know that Miss Hull (whom you met at Dr. Van Studdeford's) has, in the face of bitter opposition from her family, become a Catholic. She showed her appreciation of the importance of her step by entering the Convent of the Visitation for a retreat of nine days. On the last day (Saturday), she was baptized, and the next morning received Holy Communion.' "[44]

In the autumn of 1852 Brownson gave a series of lectures in Chicago and Milwaukee, and single lectures in a number of other cities on his journey between those two major cities. His lecture tour during 1855 wound southward, to New Orleans and Mobile. This afforded him an opportunity to become somewhat acquainted with the Southern people in those regions, their habits, their convictions and sentiments. During the intervals between his lectures he visited in the homes of many of the Southerners. The acquaintances and information gained on such occasions were to prove valuable to him in later understanding better some of the issues of the Civil War.

As early as February 1852, the diocesan newspaper of New Orleans, *La Propagateur Catholique,* had urged that Brownson be invited to deliver a course of lectures in New Orleans. It is not improbable that this resulted from seeing notices in the Catholic press of the country on the lectures Brownson had just delivered in St. Louis. However, it was not until February 5, 1855, that Brownson actually received an invitation from Thomas J. Semmes, secretary of the Catholic Institute there, to lecture in the city. After receiving Brownson's acceptance of the invitation, Semmes attempted in his letter of March 5 to apprise Brownson of the complexion of the people he might expect to make up his audience. "The city tho' Catholic in name," he said, "is in reality not so. The men among the native population are generally infidels, tho' the women are pious Catholics. The Catholics themselves are what may be called liberals, and a vast number of them are Catholics in sentiment, tho' not, I am sorry to say, in practice. The fact is, there is a great laxity on the subject of religion among them. I give you these hints that you may know our people who are to constitute your audience. There is also a very large Protestant population, entirely indifferent on the subject of religion."[45]

In a letter of February 26, 1855, Brownson's friend, Fr. J. W. Cummings, remarked: "I am very much pleased that you are going to lecture in New Orleans. You will find a set of people there who are American to the backbone, and although they are negligent in attending to their duties [that is, in receiving the sacraments], they are able to stand good, old-fashioned, high-toned principles. I think, too, and I know the locality pretty well, that you will find the press free from the bigotry of the New England papers, and the mean, drivelling, sneering mediocrity of the venal dailies of New York."[46] (Fr. Cummings scarcely proved accurate in speaking of the New Orleans press.)

To reach New Orleans, Brownson took a steamboat at Pittsburgh down the Ohio and Mississippi rivers. He arrived there on Thursday, April 12, and took up quarters in the St. Charles Hotel. The *Daily Orleans* of the same day tells us that among the first to visit him was Dr. Theodore Clapp, whose *Autobiographical Sketches and Recollections during thirty-five Years' Residence in New Orleans* Brownson was soon to review in his *Quarterly.*[47] Other newspapers of the city that were to take notice of Brownson's series of lectures were: *La Propagateur Catholique,* the

*Creole,* the *Delta,* the *Picayune,* the *Daily True Delta* and the *Courier.* The dates and themes of Brownson's lectures were: April 12, "The Mission of America"; April 15, "Protestantism and Liberty"; April 18, "The Papacy and Liberty"; and April 22, "The Infallibility of the Church." On April 25, Brownson journeyed to Mobile for a lecture, but returned, by request, to New Orleans to deliver a fifth lecture on April 29, entitled: "The Spirit of the Age." The first three lectures were delivered in Odd Fellows Hall, the last two at the Armory Hall.

D. R. LeBreton wrote an article for *American Literature* in May of 1944 on these addresses Brownson gave in New Orleans. He tells us that "controversy flared about Brownson's discourses, and ran from the opinion of the sympathetic *Courier* to that of the antagonistic *Creole.*" The *Daily True Delta* of April 13, though utterly dissenting from some of Brownson's views, nonetheless entertained "a great respect for his wonderful talents, powerful logic, and great erudition." The *Daily True Delta* (April 19) remarked that Dr. Brownson's lectures were exciting a great deal of interest. The *Courier* of April 19 spoke of the lecturer's audience "as of more than ordinary intelligence." Even the bellicose *Creole,* which had brought the apostate Achilli to lecture in the city, remarked on April 24 on the "immense crowds" attending Brownson's lectures as compared with the straggling few who had gone to hear Achilli. The *Creole* had sympathized on April 14 with Achilli as the "gentleman twice immured in the dungeons of the Inquisition at Rome in the cause of Truth and Liberty." The April 28 edition of the *Daily Orleans* observed that "large crowds of our most intelligent citizens" are attending Brownson's lectures.

Whether for or against him, the newspapers of the city were in agreement as to the originality and boldness of his thought, and the eloquence of his style of controversy. Nor did they overlook his striking appearance and vibrant personality. He was described as "a good-looking gentleman with a strong, clear enunciation and possessing a pleasing voice," and again, as having "a fine manly form, a noble head and a strong and clear enunciation." From D. R. LeBreton we learn that it was on the afternoon of April 30 that the famous lecturer embarked on the steamer *New Latona* for the North, "leaving a trail of vivid memories behind."

Special attention has been given Brownson's lecturing during the years 1852-1855 as Brownson himself seems to have attached more importance to those lectures, especially the ones delivered at St. Louis in 1852 and 1854. Henry Brownson remarked: "In no place did Brownson find such interest in the questions he was discussing in his lectures as in St. Louis."[48] Yet it might be unfair to make much of a comparison between any of Brownson's lectures. They were always of a high quality. A man of uncommon versatility, he was also, during these same years of lecturing, the main actor in a high drama of the intellectual order. To that we must now turn our attention.

# 29

## GALLICANISM AND
## THE PAPAL PREROGATIVES

*Brownson charges Gallicanism with having enthroned political atheism as the religion of the modern state • A statement of Brownson's papal doctrine relative to Gallicanism • Particular exception is taken to his doctrine that it was by the power of the keys that popes deposed tyrannical rulers in the Middle Ages • Brownson replies that he had discussed the power of the keys only as an incidental question, that the real question was the superiority of the spiritual order over the temporal — the assertion of which is the only possible way in which political atheism could ever be put down • Bishop Michael O'Connor of Pittsburgh enters the lists against him • Their passage at arms and the resultant letters • Bishop John Baptist Purcell of Cincinnati also attacks him through the columns of the* Catholic Telegraph *• Archbishop Anthony Blanc of New Orleans counsels mildness and conciliation • Bishop Purcell invites Brownson to attend a provincial council dinner in Cincinnati • Brownson finds support for his papal doctrine in Abbé Rohrbacker's* The Universal History of the Catholic Church, *as approved at Rome • Remarkable letters in further support of his doctrine • The advocacy of his papal doctrine commented on by Lord Acton and Cardinal Manning.*

No matter how well-seasoned as a warrior Orestes Brownson had become from the sturdy battles he had passed through over long years, he was now heading into one lusty donnybrook after another that would try his mettle to the utmost. Some might be disposed to assert that the wild storms he was about to encounter were of his own making, and set him down as the stormy petrel of the Catholic press in nineteenth-century America. But that would scarcely be fair to him. His troubles stemmed largely from the fact that his deep sense of duty as a Catholic publicist demanded of him the earnest espousal of unpopular truths, or unpopular causes. As he himself explained, he had always believed it the first duty of every publicist to defend the outraged truth, the truth the least popular for the time being, the most offensive to public opinion, and therefore the most needed to be set forth and defended in the general interest of all. The popular truth, the truth assailed by no one, is in no need of special defense. Rather: "It is the unpopular truth, as the unpopular cause, attacked by all the armies of error, and deserted by all its timid and time-serving friends, that calls for defenders, and that the Christian hero or really brave man will make it his first duty to defend."[1] This is in no small degree the explanation of Brownson's ceaseless battles: he was chivalrous enough to champion with all his might the unpopular truth, the unpopular cause. Particularly was this the case in the battle he waged for a recognition and acceptance of the papal prerogatives of primacy and infallibility in their bearing on society.

437

It has been said that Brownson's philosophy of history has never been surpassed. In his philosophy of modern history he brings a heavy indictment against Gallicanism, which he held answerable in a large degree for the spread and growth of political atheism in the modern world, particularly among the old Catholic nations. For, as Brownson understood it, the essential principle of Gallicanism, as given formal and final expression in 1682 by the French clergy under the headship of Bossuet, was not its denial of the pope's infallibility, but rather the denial of his spiritual independence and supremacy as the respresentative of the spiritual order. Gallicanism subjected the pope to both the episcopacy and to the temporal order. It asserted the moral independence of secular governments in the face of the Roman Catholic Church, and denied that the Sovereign Pontiff, as the divinely appointed guardian and expounder of the law of God, had any authority to declare that law judicially as it applies to secular courts and governments. This was in principle to emancipate the state from the dominion of the law of God, leaving the secular prince to rule as he listed, a law unto himself. Thus it securely enthroned political atheism as the religion of the modern state, encouraging universal and unmitigated despotism. "Never," said Brownson, "was conceived a doctrine more favorable to despots, or more hostile to civil and religious freedom, than that of the Four Articles of the Assembly of the French clergy in 1682."[2] The denial of the infallibility of the pope was, according to Brownson, a mere smoke screen. For papal infallibility once admitted, the Gallican principle denying the pope's supreme spiritual authority, could not be defended, since the popes had repeatedly condemned it.

Such being largely the genesis of political atheism in the modern world — which Brownson called the plague spot of modern society and the gangrene of modern politics — the most effectual way to attack it would be to attack the source from which it flowed: Gallicanism. The attack demanded the positive assertion of the spiritual supremacy and infallibility of the pope. But in bringing out these meaningful truths at the time, not yet explicitly and formally defined by the Catholic Church, Brownson encountered some embarrassment. In 1851 a Jesuit priest, president of a college in Dublin, Ireland, asked him to reply to a specious article in the *Edinburgh Review* entitled: "Ultramontane Doubts." The reply would have been easy and simple if Gallicanism could have been rejected and the answer grounded on truly Catholic principles, but that could not be done at the time. Gallicanism was still at the time a tolerated opinion in the Catholic Church — a *sententia in ecclesia* though not a *sententia ecclesiae*. "I regret," said the bishop whom he consulted at the time, "that we cannot treat Gallicanism as a heresy, but we are not free to do that; you must make the best reply you can without condemning the Gallian doctrine."[3] The reply which Brownson made was masterly, but not satisfactory to himself.[4] A few years later, in 1853, he endeavored to complete his teaching on the subject in a series of articles by demonstrating and elaborating on the superiority of the spiritual order over the temporal *by its own nature,* encompassing therewith the spiritual supremacy of the Sovereign Pontiff as the representative of that order and the divinely appointed guardian and interpreter of the law of God. From this angle he aimed a deathblow at Gallicanism and political atheism.[5]

Since he was proceeding to ground his arguments largely on the natural superiority of the spiritual order over the temporal, he laid it down as axiomatic that:

The supremacy of the spiritual order is a dictate of the most vulgar common sense — a universal conviction of mankind. It is in the nature of things, and was recognized by all gentile antiquity, however it may have been disregarded in practice. It runs through all the Old Testament, and no one can deny that under the old law, in the Synagogue, the kingly power was subordinated to the sacerdotal. The Church, as continuing in itself the whole priesthood, and all the spiritual authority instituted under the primitive law, and as succeeding to the Synagogue and continuing it in all not of a local or temporary nature, necessarily inherits and possesses this supremacy in its plentitude.[6]

The immediate occasion which led Brownson to his championship of the superiority of the spiritual order over the temporal seems to have been the publication by the excellent and learned M. Gosselin, director of the Seminary of St. Sulpice, Paris, of a number of volumes on the popes of the Middle Ages. In these volumes the author expounds the theory, adopted from the famous Fenelon, archbishop of Cambrai, that the power exercised by Sovereign Pontiffs over temporal princes in the Middle Ages was not inherent in the papacy by divine right, nor was it held from the inherent and univeral supremacy of the spiritual order, but was a power granted the popes by the concession of secular sovereigns, and consent of the people — what was called the public law, the *jus publicum* of Christendom. In advancing this theory, M. Gosselin had had the laudable motive of exculpating from the charge of usurpation the Sovereign Pontiffs who had exercised the power of deposing tyrannical princes in the Middle Ages. This theory, however, unfortunately gave a mere human origin to this power exercised by the popes, asserted that they had held and exercised it *jure humano,* not *jure divino.* As convenient and popular as this theory might be, Brownson could not accept it. He did not indeed deny that the popes held the power they claimed in the way and by the title alleged. But he objected to the Gosselin theory, in brief, not in what it asserted, but in what it denied.[7] He could not but regard Gosselin's theory as a sturdy prop to Gallicanism that would further foster the spread and growth of political atheism. The best interests of religion and society made a mighty appeal to him to put forth his most gallant efforts to discredit both Gallicanism and Gosselinism, and to exalt the papal prerogatives to the highest point of orthodoxy as a means of curing the manifold ills of a society already so largely emancipated from the checks and restraints of the law of God.

Yet this power he claimed the popes possess by virtue of the power of the keys, it is important to understand, is only an indirect (spiritual) power in the temporal order inasmuch as the secular order itself has an ultimate spiritual end or purpose. It is an indirect spiritual power *in* the temporal order. No civil authority whatsoever was claimed for the pope outside his (at that time) own Ecclesiastical States. As Brownson explained it:

> What he [the pope] does is to declare and apply the law of God to a particular case, and what he decides is the spiritual question involved, and therefore in doing it he transcends not the limits of his spiritual functions. The power of the pope in regard to princes is limited by the law of God, but of that law he is the guardian and judge of its infractions by princes as well as subjects, and both are bound by his judgement, and *ought* to give practical effect to the sentence; but if they refuse, the pope uses only spiritual arms to compel them, for he has no other. He can pronounce the sentence of forfeiture, and declare subjects absolved, but practically there his power ordinarily ends.[8]

What we are here to bear well in mind is that Brownson's primary purpose in discussing this matter was to defend the action of the medieval

Supreme Pontiffs who had deposed outrageously tyrannical princes, and to show that they did so by divine right, by the power of the keys. It was a right exercised only against grossly transgressing Catholic princes with Catholic subjects. He clearly recognized that the concrete conditions required for its exercise do not exist in the modern world, rendering its exercise "impracticable."[9] Moreover, it was an ecclesiastical censure most rarely resorted to even in the "Ages of Faith," as has ever been the tradition of the Church in relation to any such affairs of the state.[10]

But that the pope has the *right*, as vicar of Christ on earth, to judge the morality of all human acts whether of princes or ordinary individuals, is not, said Brownson, to be questioned. So much at least Pope Innocent III asserted in his letter to Philip Augustus, King of France. "We do not," affirmed the Pontiff, "intend to judge of the fee; that belongs to the King of France. But we do have the right to judge of the sin, and it is our duty to exercise it against the offender, be he who he may."[11]

Such was Brownson's papal doctrine. But when he opened up his vigorous bombardment on Gallicanism, it at once stirred up a raging gale of controversy. Particular exception was taken to the assertion that the popes in the Middle Ages used the power of the keys in deposing Catholic sovereigns who had violated their oaths of fidelity. Even bishops and priests told him that he was defending not Catholic doctrine but "ultramontane views" of Catholic doctrine, that he was only reviving a medieval concept of society of little or no relevancy. The controversy that had resulted, they charged, was likely to expose the Catholic Church in this country to unnecessary odium. The sooner a quietus was put on the whole affair, the better for all concerned.

To this charge Brownson replied that he had not discussed the deposing power of the popes in the Middle Ages as an isolated, but only as an incidental question. The real question he had set out to discuss concerned the mutual relations between the two orders, the spiritual and the temporal.[12] This question he could not ignore, for every controversy between church and state, every controversy between the Catholic Church and any one of the sects or any individual, is at bottom a controversy between the two orders, and resolves itself into the question: which of the two orders is supreme? On the solution to that question turn the great controversies of the age. How, he asked, can one refute political atheism and defend the rightful dominion of God over the political order if one cannot assert and maintain the supremacy of the spiritual order, and therefore that of the pope as its representative and guardian in his spiritual guidance or direction of men and nations? There is no possible way, he affirmed and protested, of putting down the great heresy of the age, political atheism, other than drawing on the highest-toned ultramontanism. "Is there any effectual way of refuting an error, but by opposing to it and defending against it the truth it contradicts?" he inquired.[13]

Again, without exposing Gallicanism and its pernicious effects in the history of nations, how, he asked, is the Catholic Church to be cleared of having been an accomplice of the absolutism of the state in the past centuries — at least by the Church's reprehensible silence? His articles aimed to show the great injustice of charging on the Church, as its enemies do, the tyranny and oppression, the social and political degradation so glaring among the populations in old Catholic nations since the rise of Gallicanism. Why should the Church be blamed in the case? Had not the Gallicans and their sympathizers protested that the Church had no right to proclaim the law of

God as it applies to secular courts and governments — leaving no shield to be interposed as a barrier between the tyranny of the secular prince and his hapless subjects? How can the Church be held responsible for the temporal conditions of the people after the rise and triumphant reign of Gallicanism — muting the voice of the Church as the great defender of the moral order?

> We deplore [he said] as much as any man can the moral and social degradation of the people of Europe during the eighteenth century; but we cannot forget that the generations so immoral and so degraded were formed under the despotism of Caesar and the prevalence of Gallicanism, or the doctrine that separates the two orders, denies the Church all authority over temporals, and proclaims the emancipation of civil rulers in their public capacity from the law of God as interpreted by the Church, and we find no cause to blame her, but only most powerful reasons for asserting the necessity and the utility of maintaining her supremacy in all things, and of condemning in the strongest terms of which the language is capable the folly and impiety of those sovereigns, statesmen, lawyers, courtiers, and demagogues who seek to restrict her freedom, to restrain her discipline, and to deprive her of her right to pronounce on the morality of the acts of secular authority.[14]

He also protested firmly against the thought of degrading the Sovereign Pontiff to the level of a mere temporal prince. For to suppose that his authority over temporal princes rests only on a merely human basis, is held *ex jure humano,* is to degrade him "to the rank of a temporal prince, who may be opposed as any other prince without prejudice to Catholicity, and indirectly favor the error of the human and popular origin of power, against which every friend to religion and society has now to wage an unrelenting war."[15]

To the charge in particular that he was advocating an "ultra Catholicity," he replied that there could be no such thing as "an ultra Catholicity." The charge was patently absurd: "Catholicity is a definite system of truth, and to be more or less Catholic is not to be Catholic at all. Catholicity, as long as it continues to be Catholicity, cannot be carried to excess. . . . It is simply the truth, the whole truth, and nothing but the truth."[16] He asserted that not one of his opponents could cite a single papal pronouncement that contravenes the doctrine he was defending. The popes in every instance professed to exercise their power *jure divino,* by the power of the keys. Much less was any author ever put on the Index for maintaining the indirect power of the pope in the case. His own doctrine, then, was moderate enough, it seemed to him, in view of the fact that Pope Sixtus V placed even Robert Bellarmine, the classical protagonist of the papal prerogatives, on the Index for denying the *direct,* and maintaining *only* the indirect, temporal authority of the Sovereign Pontiffs.[17]

It may be interesting to state that although Bellarmine's papal doctrine was placed on the Index, it remained there only eight days as Pope Sixtus V was dead after that time. His successor, Pope Urban VII, who reigned only a dozen days, immediately removed Bellarmine from the strange company in which he had been placed. As history records, Sixtus V was one of the more fiery Pontiffs that ever occupied the papal chair. The cardinals of the Congregation of the Index had been afraid to tell him that Bellarmine's teaching had really been drawn from the teachings of the saints lest he give them an exhibition of his brusque manner, and "perhaps put all the Saints on the Index."[18]

But whatever good and sufficient reasons Brownson might give for his championship of the indirect power of the pope in temporals, he did not succeed in allaying the storm that was fast gathering and which was to break with such fury over his hapless head. His friend, Robert Bakewell, editor of *The Shepherd of the Valley* in St. Louis, wrote to warn him of what was impending. After mentioning to him that Bishop Miege had suggested that his articles on the papal power "should be translated into French and presented to the Holy Father," Bakewell continued:

> There is a storm brewing against you, I am sure, and I believe that the *Metropolitan* will be the organ from which it will burst. The archbishop [Peter Richard Kenrick of St. Louis] thinks that Bishop O'Connor wrote the article against you in the last number [February], and is the author of one with which you are threatened. The archbishop will stick by you, I am sure; but except for him and Bishop Miege, all the clergy, the Jesuits, and others with whom I have spoken, are unanimous in saying, "you go too far." I never heard any one take your part so gallantly as did Bishop Miege today, and he is quite indignant at your opponents and especially at the premonitory squib of Bishop O'Connor in the *Metropolitan*.[19]

Sure enough, Bakewell was quite right. Bishop O'Connor of Pittsburgh seems to have taken the view that Brownson was only stirring up useless trouble in his discussion of the relation of the two orders, the spiritual and the temporal. He wanted the discussion stopped, and apparently set out with the dogged determination that he was going to make Brownson bite the dust.[20] Brownson's son Henry says that "forgetting his great friendship for Brownson, he turned violently against him" — and this in spite of the fact that he had recently begged Brownson for help after he had got himself in "a regular scrape."[21] Bishop O'Connor objected especially to Brownson's ultramontane doctrine on the score that it seemed to cast a slur on the bishops of his native land, Ireland, who took an oath of fealty to the British Crown apparently inconsistent with Brownson's doctrine.[22] As Bakewell had forewarned, O'Connor exploded his attack from the columns of the *Metropolitan Magazine* in its March issue. He set forth what he represented to be Brownson's doctrine, and then proceeded to argue against it with warmth and vigor.

Previous to this, it so happened that while Brownson had been lecturing in Buffalo in February of this same year, 1854, he had met Bishop O'Connor on the occasion. They discussed at some length what Brownson had made the burning question of the hour with the result that Bishop O'Connor seemed disposed to discontinue any further discussion of the matter, and Brownson "pretty clearly intimated that he would not press his doctrine." But O'Connor's article was to come forth anyway in the *Metropolitan Magazine* in the March edition. When Brownson reached home, Chelsea, apparently in the forepart of March, he found a note from his bishop, Fitzpatrick, requesting him to reply to O'Connor's article in the *Metroplitan*. (Here we see again that Brownson was not advocating a crotchety theology of his own. He had Bishop Fitzpatrick behind him again.) Bishop Fitzpatrick had already set off on a journey to Rome when Brownson had reached Chelsea, and could not be reached for consultation. This left Brownson with no choice but to reply to O'Connor, which he did in the April issue of his *Quarterly*.[23]

Bishop O'Connor began his criticism of Brownson's papal doctrine in the March issue of the *Metropolitan* by remarking that "we do not intend to enter deeply into the intrinsic merits of the question."[24] In reply to Brownson's theory on the deposing power, he adopted that of Gosselin, which was simply the Gallican theory, namely, that the power by which the popes in the Middle Ages deposed tyrannical princes was an *acquired* right. [Italics O'Connor's.] They had exercised it only in medieval times after they had obtained a certain temporal preeminence, he asserted. Being simply a constituent element of medieval society, purely adventitious, it had no other foundation or validity.[25] He labeled the doctrine that the popes had ever deposed tyrants by divine right as simply "untenable."[26] He added: "They [the popes] did not directly teach that the power they exercised was inherent in their offices."[27] This Brownson was to show as being incorrect.

Refusing to enter into "the intrinsic merits of the question," Bishop O'Connor proceeded to demonstrate to his own satisfaction that his own theory regarding the deposing power was the one widely accepted in the Catholic Church, especially in the United States, the British Empire, Germany and elsewhere.[28] He complained that Brownson was only reviving an old exploded theory, by no means accepted by those esteemed for calm judgment and correct views, or by persons whose opinions carry weight. There might be an individual here or there who delighted in extreme views who held it, but their views, grating on the sentiments of the age, only neutralized the effect of the many other good things they said, and, after having made a big noise in the world for a time, were soon forgotten. He cited Lamennais as a melancholy example of such.[29] And he made a great ado about the entrenched silence of Rome on the question, which, "considering that this power [deposition of divine right] was always denied," was all the more significant.[30]

In reply Brownson asserted that he felt deeply that the *Metropolitan's* rejoinder had been ill-advised, for in attacking his defense of the rights and authority of the spiritual order, it had the appearance, at least in the popular mind, of taking the side of the temporal against the spiritual, of the state against the church, and of Caesar against Peter. The temper of the times and the true interests of society were far from needing any such encouragement. He endeavored to set the question in its right perspective by affirming that it pertained not to the province of faith, but to that of opinion. Hence, for good and sufficient reasons, either opinion could be adopted. But as for himself, he had believed that Catholic dogma required him to maintain at least the *indirect* temporal authority of the pope, or to forswear his logic; by which he meant, "not that it is a Catholic dogma, but a strict logical deduction from it. This may be the case, and yet one who denies it not be a heretic; for the Church does not hold a man to be a heretic because he happens to be a poor logician."[31]

He reminded the *Metropolitan* that Rome had "never uttered a word favorable to the opinion espoused" by itself, and regretted that it had not seen proper to discuss the subject, if at all, on its own intrinsic merits. The extrinsic considerations it had urged in the case — that is, that its opinion was widespread and popular — were effectual enough in bringing the weight of popular prejudice to bear against him, but really settled nothing at all in the case. Its opinion had always been the doctrine of temporal princes, jurisconsults, bureaucrats, courtiers, demagogues and those whose personal interests inclined them to side with Caesar against Peter. By contrast, he said: "The opinions assailed we hold in common with the greatest and most approved Catholic doctors [elsewhere he mentioned Thomas Aquinas, Robert Bellarmine, Suárez and others], and they are undeniably such as we may hold without any impeachment of our orthodoxy [which did seem to have been impeached]." He used up a whole paragraph citing eminent names of his own day who favored the doctrine he held on the question, and ended by saying: "Indeed, we had supposed that there was throughout the whole Catholic world a decided reaction, since the disastrous effects of the old French Revolution, against Gallicanism, and in favor of ultramontanism, and we had supposed that we were ourselves only obeying the common tendency of the Catholic *renaissance* of the nineteenth century."[32]

Bishop O'Connor replied again to Brownson in the July edition of the *Metropolitan*. The nub of his criticism amounted to a detailed accusation that Brownson in advocating his doctrine of the indirect authority of the pope destroyed the distinction between the two orders, the spiritual and the temporal. This in spite of the fact that Brownson had said in his April article: "We have never confounded the two orders, never merged the one in the other, or denied the substantive existence of either; we have simply asserted that the temporal order exists not for its own sake, but for the spiritual, and that the spiritual order is by its own nature supreme over the temporal."[33] O'Connor also made the strange statement that "It [the teaching authority of the Catholic Church] has never been understood to imply the right to pronounce on the merits or demerits of an individual."[34] He even went so far as to make Brownson's doctrine on the deposing power to mean that the pope could have the right to depose a secular prince "even when no crime had been committed," but the measure was merely "required by the good of the spiritual order."[35] This seems a clear perversion of Brownson's doctrine. This, too, in spite of the fact that on the very next page he quoted Brownson as saying: "The Church has no right to depose a legitimate prince . . . for she has no right to do wrong." He ended up his essay with a sort of flourish by quoting the famous statement of Pope Gelasius on the distinction between the two orders, the spiritual and the temporal — as if Brownson was badly in need of instruction on the point.[36]

Brownson did not respond in his *Review* to this July article of Bishop O'Connor in the *Metropolitan*. But its tone and tenor were highly offensive to him, and he unburdened himself to the bishop in a personal letter. He wrote in part:

> When we parted last February at Buffalo, I fully intended not to reply to your previous article, but on reaching home I found directions left for me which I was not at liberty to disregard, and which made a reply on my part a duty. I replied as I thought, as I certainly intended, in a perfectly respectful manner, and in a way I thought would not provoke a rejoinder. I hoped the controversy would be suffered to drop. I did not believe you would take offense at what I had done, and I intended to avoid all future provocation. I have therefore to find you disposed to continue the controversy. I have been pained also at the tone of your reply, which strikes me as harsh, and not as such as I had a right to expect. Your article seems intended to make an end of me, and to rouse up the indignation of the whole Catholic world against me, rather than elucidate the question. It strikes me as unfair and unkind, and to assail me with passion rather than argument. . . .
>
> In your article you do not give me fair play before your readers. You charge me with doctrines and consequences which I disavow, and which in my article I reason against, and use your great ability to hold me up now to the ridicule and . . . to the indignation of the public.
>
> Permit me to ask, what am I to do: my character, my reputation, my means of subsistence are threatened. Of this I would not complain if I had broached a novelty, far less a heresy. The doctrine I have defended, if not precisely of faith, is one which I am at liberty to hold, and can hold without reproach. What then am I to do? I can hardly believe that you could have ex-

444

pected when writing your article against me that I would suffer it to go unanswered. . . .

You are opposed to the discussion of the question. There is a simple and easy way to get what you wish without ruining me and mine. Convince me, you will not. If Rome decides against me, of course, I shall know I am wrong, and shall take pride in retracting. For though err I may, a heretic I will not be. You have only to write to my bishop, and tell him what doctrines you do not wish to have broached or discussed in my *Review,* and I assure you I will be governed entirely by his orders, or known wish. I naturally look to him, and have never knowingly gone contrary to any suggestions of his. The articles to which you take exception were read and approved by him before they were printed, and I have his positive assurance that he wished them published. When bishops disagree, what is a poor layman to do? Do nothing, you say? Why not follow the advice of his own bishop rather, especially when that bishop is both his bishop and director. Why am I to be governed by the Bishop of Pittsburgh rather than the Bishop of Boston? Shall I follow simply my own judgment? I had enough of that as a Protestant, and moreover, I have a very mean opinion of my own judgment. What better can I do than submit myself to the direction of my own bishop? And when I do, ought I to be assailed by another bishop?[37]

But matters were not to improve. It is really something to see a strong man in tears. Bishop O'Connor now returned to the columns of his own *Pittsburgh Catholic* to reply to Brownson's letter, and to express his dissatisfaction with his doctrine on this and other matters. This drew from Brownson the following letter to the *Pittsburgh Catholic,* dated August 1, 1854. He wrote in part:

To the Editor of the *Pittsburgh Catholic*
Dear Sir:

I just read your article devoted to me, in your paper of the last week. For the kind and considerate tone in which you speak of me personally — the tone of a Christian gentleman, and which I have seldom been greeted with in any one who differs from me — you must permit me to thank you with tears of gratitude in my eyes. I do not know why it is that my brethren, who differ from me, usually express their difference in a harsh, sneering, contemptuous tone, or why they almost always make it a personal affair, and refuse me the ordinary courtesy due from one gentleman to another. In the present storm of indignation which I have unwittingly excited, I am happy to acknowledge the *Metropolitan Magazine,* the *Catholic Herald,* and the *Pittsburgh Catholic,* honorable exceptions to the general rule of a portion of the Catholic press of the country, in my regard, when they do not agree with me.

I beg you to permit me an observation or two on some of your remarks. I think I can bear admonition and rebuke without anger towards him who administers it, and if I know myself, which is very doubtful, I am better pleased with it than with praise, of which I have had more than I desire. I believe that I was myself in my own *Review* the first to rebuke the praise bestowed on me by the Catholic press on the occasion of my conversion. . . . I did not dream of holding in the Catholic world the place so much above my merits which has been assigned me. Requested to continue my *Review* by several of the American bishops I consented to do so, and have continued it up to this time, not so well as I could wish, but as well as I could, being what I am.

I have worked hard, I have studied diligently, and I have always acted under advice, and never published an article written by myself, without first submitting it to my bishop, or a theologian appointed by him to examine my articles, except now and then a literary criticism or my literary notices. In almost all instances I have consulted him, or in his absence the theologian appointed, as to the propriety of discussing the topic, before proceeding to write.

This was especially the case with regard to the topics of exclusive salvation, religious liberty, developmentism, and the power of the popes in regard to temporals. . . . I have never refused to make an alteration required, or to suppress an article which the authority consulted suggested it would be better not to publish.

I do not say this, Sir, to throw any responsibility from my shoulders to those of another, but to show you that I do not arrogate to myself quite so much as I am accused of doing. The Bishop of Boston, in whose diocese I live, is the Church to me, at least in the first instance, and I am not aware there is any higher voice through which the Church speaks to me, except that of the Holy Father; and the Bishop of Boston, except where his authority is in question, is to me the legitimate interpreter of the voice of the Holy Father himself. Now I am not so ignorant as to pretend that this gives the stamp of authority to what I publish, or that it would screen me in the least from having my opinions called into question, but it should, I think, screen me from having my Catholic loyalty impugned, and save me from the charge of setting myself up as a preceptor of Catholics here or elsewhere. If I have ever assumed the airs of a preceptor or placed myself in opposition to the pastors of the Church, I unquestionably deserve rebuke; but if I have done so, it is unwittingly. If the pastors, however, themselves disagree, I suppose all that can be asked of me is to follow my own. With regard to the unpleasant controversies in which I am involved, I wish to make a remark or two. If those who oppose me will permit me to do so, I will drop the controversy on the power of the pope in regard to temporals after offering, indirectly, a reply to the article in the Metropolitan for last July. This I cannot in justice to myself and my readers avoid doing, because that periodical charges on me doctrines which I am not conscious of maintaining, and makes me responsible for inferences which I deny, and I do not think the writer of the article against me would wish me to remain under the stigma of maintaining views which I do not. He has either misunderstood me, or I do not understand myself, for I certainly do not understand the doctrine I defend as he does, and would not defend it if I did. . . .

Whatever Catholics may have to complain of me, they shall never have that of a schismatic or heretical disposition, or of a disposition to persist in error. I cannot promise that I shall never err, for I am human, but I can promise that I will retract, reprobate, and condemn as heartily as any one can wish any error into which I may have fallen, the moment authority bids me. Let any one formulate my errors and transmit them with the decisions they contravene to my bishop, and let him present the list to me, and nothing more will be needed, whatever the subject to which they relate.[38]

But Orestes Brownson's explanations gained little enough credit with Bishop O'Connor. In disclosing to him that he submitted all his articles to Bishop Fitzpatrick, or a theologian appointed by him, to act as censor before publication, Brownson's purpose was to give O'Connor absolute assurance of his good intentions as a Catholic publicist, and that therefore his Catholic loyalty should neither be questioned nor impugned. But O'Connor saw in this only a sly maneuver to hide behind his bishop's crosier, and admonished him for the future "not to shrink from bearing the whole responsibility alone."[39]

Bishop O'Connor, as we have seen, had taken Brownson to task in the *Metropolitan* in particular for asserting that the popes in the Middle Ages had deposed tyrannical princes by the power of the keys, that is, by divine right. In answer to that complaint Brownson stated further that he so held because he had found in the history of the Catholic Church that such illustrious Sovereign Pontiffs as St. Gregory VII, Alexander III, Innocent III, Innocent IV, Boniface VIII, St. Pius V and Sixtus V had claimed and exercised that power by divine right, as representatives of the spiritual order. In every instance the Sovereign Pontiffs professed to hold and exercise that same power by virtue of their apostolic authority, as vicars of Christ on earth.[40] And that they do so hold this power was actually defined to be of Catholic faith by Boniface VIII in the papal bull *Unam Sanctam,* which has never been and never can be abrogated. Pope Clement VIII, when Philip the Fair demanded its recall, answered that he could not recall it, because it contains a dogmatic definition.[41] No Catholic, therefore, is at liberty to suppose that the Sovereign Pontiffs were ignorant of the title by which they claimed to hold and exercise that power or that they misstated it, for the office, the powers, and the prerogatives of the papacy are as much a matter of definable faith as the Mystery of the Blessed Trinity or the Incarnation.

It is by having drawn this great truth out of the history of the Catholic Church that the late Fr. Joseph P. Donovan, C.M., erstwhile rector of Kenrick Seminary, opined that Brownson established one of his claims to greatness. Speaking of the matter, he said:

> Cardinal Gasquet referred to Lord Acton as the most erudite man of his age: but this historian could not discover the obvious in the history of the Church. Nor could the great Newman. Brownson was the opportunist because his Catholic instincts were deep and sure. The gifts of the Holy Ghost working within his mind made him more than the greatest of mere human historians, when it came to reading aright the footprints of the Milk White Hind adown the centuries.[42]

Bishop O'Connor was not the only prelate in the country who threw down the gauntlet to Brownson over his articles on the papal power. Although Archbishop John Baptist Purcell of Cincinnati had assured Brownson beforehand that he could not go too far in his assertion of the papal powers, as far as he himself was concerned, he afterwards turned against him and denounced his papal doctrines as "vagaries" in the *Catholic Telegraph,* warning him that he might yet fall like Origen, Tertullian, Lamennais, etc., if he were thwarted in his peculiar theories.[43] Like Bishop O'Connor, he had chided him for trying to hide behind his bishop in what he was advocating in his *Review.* In a letter of some length, similar to his letters to Bishop O'Connor, Brownson endeavored again to set the matter straight. Though addressed to the editors of the *Catholic Telegraph,* it was meant for Archbishop Purcell who was the author of the writings against him. To quote only in part, he said:

Boston, August 20, 1854

To the Editor of the *Catholic Telegraph*
Messrs. Editors:

In your paper of the 19th Inst., you make some statements, or express some fears, with regard to me, on which, as they affect not only myself but also my relations to the Bishop of Boston, I trust you will permit me to offer through your columns a few brief remarks. . . .

If you had done me the honor to read my letter to the *Pittsburgh Catholic,* I think you would have perceived that I allude to the fact that I always, with insignificant exceptions, submit my articles to the revision of the bishop, or of a theologian designated by him, before publishing — not to throw the responsibility on the shoulders of another, nor to prove that they contain no errors, but to show that I am not justly charged with bringing out "vagaries" of my own, or with a want of docility or submissiveness to authority — in a word, to prove my Catholic intentions, which you and others have impugned. This is all the fact proves. It leaves you free to criticize my writings as you please, but it does not leave you free to impugn my Catholic loyalty, or to charge me with an heretical or even arrogant disposition.

You intimate that I express a determination, in the conduct of my *Review,* to abide by the decision of my own bishop, regardless of the other bishops of the country. In this again you misapprehend me. The Bishop of Boston, under the Holy Father, is the Catholic Church to me, for he is my pastor. If I have fallen into any errors which require public retraction, I expect the requirement to be made to me by him, or through him, as the legitimate authority in the case, as long as I live in his diocese. But to attribute to me a determination to disregard the wishes of the other bishops in conducting a *Review* which circulates in their dioceses, is to make me somewhat a greater fool and less a Catholic than anybody who knows me is likely to believe.

Your fears that I shall array one portion of the hierarchy against another, I think are entirely groundless. The Bishop of Boston would by no means suffer me to do so, were I able and disposed to do it; and I assure you that I would not do so if he would permit me. I may be involved in a controversy without intending it, but I shall never persist in a controversy offensive to the pastors of the Church.

I have been unexpectedly engaged in a controversy with the *Metropolitan* on the papal power, but that controversy will not be continued on my part. In my October number will appear a conversation between "Uncle Jack and his Nephew," in which the subject comes in incidentally, and what I wish to be understood as holding on the subject is stated as clearly as I am able to state it, but I think not in a form or temper to provoke a rejoinder. But with that conversation I shall drop the discussion, whatever may be said against me, or however the doctrine may be distorted, and I held up to the derision or horror of the Catholic public. I am willing at all times to sacrifice my right of self-defense for the sake of religion. . . .

I have no wish to continue my *Review* a moment after it ceases to be useful to the cause of religion. I can beg, I can starve, but I cannot consent to be the cause of division among brethren. Whenever my own observation convinces me, or the pastors of the Church hint to me, that the continuance of my *Review* will be a disservice to the cause of Catholicity in this country, it will cease to appear, and in such case I am sure the Bishop of Boston would require me to stop it.

I shall not claim the insertion of these remarks in your journal as an act of justice to me; yet I shall feel much obliged to you if you will insert them. I do not suppose you are governed by any other motives than zeal for religion. You believe me untrustworthy and dangerous to the Church, and therefore believe it your duty to denounce me. I have nothing to say to this, except that I pray God that you may find that you have judged me harshly, and treated me with unmerited severity, and also that I may have the grace to bear the castigations I receive as a Catholic should bear them. I have the honor to be, Messrs. Editors, your obedient servant."

Archbishop Purcell had used his minatory finger a bit too freely when, referring to Origen, Tertullian, Lemannais and others, he warned Brownson so publicly that his might be a similar fate. There were those who little appreciated and relished less what he had said. In the midst of all the excitement attendant on the current controversy there was one eminent prelate in the country who seems to have kept his cool remarkably well — Archbishop Anthony Blanc of New Orleans. In a fairly long letter to Archbishop Purcell in July of 1854 — apparently in reply to one from him — he said in part:

I have noticed the two articles in Brownson's *Review,* and I predicted, at the time, the tempest that was to fall on him, on that account. However, I wish our religious editors who do not approve of the course he has adopted should be more moderate in their remarks about him. . . . To be candid, I cannot approve what I have just read in the *Catholic Telegraph.* He may soon be found to be what he was once before, neither Catholic nor Protestant. One may feel, and be justified in *thinking* so, but saying it aloud in a public press is out of place, altogether; this at least, I believe, for my part. Such a kind of rebuke is not, in my opinion, calculated to redeem him to a right course, if he is out of it; it is on the contrary, throwing oil on the fire.[45]

Archbishop Blanc's handwriting is not overly legible, and he apparently mixed in a French expression here and there. But it is decipherable enough to see that he further deplored a number of things said in the *Telegraph* against Brownson and Robert Bakewell, editor of *The Shepherd of the Valley* (another convert), and spoke of the prejudices that had been excited in certain quarters against the *Telegraph* because of its critical attitude toward Brownson and his *Review*. He counseled mildness and kindness in dealing with Brownson.

Of a similar mind was Bishop John Timon, C.M., the first bishop of Buffalo. In a letter, dated August 3, 1854, to Archbishop Purcell, he spoke of what Brownson had said on naturalization (of foreign citizens) and in his article on the papal prerogatives, "You go too far," as "objectionable," but he wished as little said publicly about such matters as at all possible.[46]

There is no little irony in the position Brownson found himself in during this raging controversy over the papal prerogatives. Really, it was enough to make angels weep and devils howl with glee. While zealously proclaiming truths he considered of vast importance for the good of society, he was also doing everything in the world he could to avoid collisions with the authorities of the Catholic Church. In this respect his efforts were truly admirable. The fact is his reverence for ecclesiastical authority was extraordinary. A critic who reviewed the *Middle Life* of Brownson in the *Dublin Review,* 1900, said of him: "Never has there been a man whose character and upbringing tended more to independent judgment. Yet rarely has there been a man more docile to ecclesiastical authority."[47] Nothing more true could be said. Yet fierce attacks were being launched on him from within the Catholic Church while those outside the Church showed only scorn and contempt for the docility and respect he professed for ecclesiastical authority. One such specimen of the latter we have from the pen of a contemporary:

> Professor Brownson has been regarded not only as a man of capacious intellect, but of a bold and fearless heart, of American instincts, and beyond all individual control. It has been a mystery with those who knew him, who admired his genius, how a mind vigorous by nature, and so highly cultivated, of such broad scope, and of such a philosophic character, could embrace these vagrant and degenerating theories, and advocate them with such earnestness. But the mystery is solved by this unblushing declaration of a blind subserviency to the Roman Bishop [Bishop Fitzpatrick] to be his master. When he left the faith of his fathers, and took upon him the yoke of Rome, he surrendered the free spirit with which he was imbued, and voluntarily placed the stamp of bondage upon the divinity that stirred within him. He gave up to Rome what was meant for mankind, and instead of thinking, or writing, or acting as a free man, as one who was endowed with transcendent intellectual power, he became a slave of a Jesuit, the servile instrument of a propagandism at war with the religious freedom of his countrymen, at war with republican institutions, and opposed to progress in all that relates to popular advancement, or the elevation of the millions.
>
> This declaration of Mr. Brownson is the more deplorable because in intellectual power and attainments he is infinitely superior to the bishop or his "CENSOR," of a grasp of mind altogether beyond either. His voluntary sub-

mission to their dictation would be reconcilable with the peculiarities of human character were their positions reversed. Were theirs the vigorous intellect, the diligent inquiry, the sleepless industry, the indomitable will, and his, the medium capacity, the inert intellectual action, the fondness for indulgence, and love of ease, in that case we could charge to natural weakness what is now attributable to voluntary degradation, to a just consciousness of inferiority what can only be induced by a servile submission of a slavish though powerful spirit.[48]

It will not do, however, to impugn in the least the motives of the prelates who were opposing him in this imbroglio. Brownson himself said he could not suppose they were "governed by any other motives than a zeal for religion." Whatever Archbishop Purcell's criticism of him, he was ready to give Brownson the glad hand and willingly acknowledge, too, the purity of his motives. This he did in a letter or friendly note he sent him when he stopped at Cincinnati, Ohio, on his way back from New Orleans. The bishops of the province were just meeting for a synod, and Purcell invited him on May 12, 1855, to join them at the provincial council dinner. He wrote:

> Orestes A. Brownson, Esq.
> Dear Sir:
>
> It will gratify the bishops of this province, including myself, very much to enjoy your company to-morrow at dinner. Engaged with us in the ministry of teaching the truths of faith in that sphere which Providence has allotted to you, we one and all acknowledge the purity of your intentions and the powers of your mind, even when honestly constrained to differ from you in some of your views. But "Hanc veniam petimus damusque vicissim," and it should never lead to an alienation of Catholic hearts.
>
> Hoping to see you among us to-morrow, I remain very truly yours in our Lord,
>
> > J. B. Purcell,
> > Archp., Cin.[49]

A bit of encouragement in his gallant fight on Gallicanism came to Brownson at this time from his son Henry who was studying at the University of Munich. After describing the daily pattern of university life there, the posture of European politics, the exact prices of various books published at the University, etc., he went on to say in his letter of December 30, 1853:

> I like Germany, the country, the language, the people, the literature, and everything else, better than France, unless perhaps I except the wine. Sr. John [Acton] has sent you another book of Radowitz. Dr. Döllinger has sent you his work on *Hippolytus und Kallistus.* . . . I asked Dr. Döllinger whether he had read the work of Muzzarelli, *De Authoritate Summi Pontificis,* and he said there was no such work. So you may know that he has not read everything that has been written on our side of the question. He is a better historian than a theologian. There is little danger of his making one a Gallican. The Archbishop requested me to lend him the *reviews* containing the articles against Newman. He has read them all and all the other articles in the numbers I had, and is quite delighted with the *Review.* He condemned Newman as heartily as you can wish, and is also very much pleased with what you say against Gallicanism and the Universalists. He cannot endure Gallicanism.[50]

Brownson needed every particle of encouragement in the hard battle he had on his hands. Yet, although he was accused by many in the Catholic Church as arrogating to himself quite too much as a Catholic publicist, and sneered at by those outside the Church for what they looked upon as his slavish subserviency to ecclesiastical authority, his only real concern in the controversy was where precisely lay truth in the matter. In the midst of the uproar, it was a bracing satisfaction to him to be able to point out now that he had further illustrious company in the papal doctrines he had been so zealously advocating and so valiantly defending. The same staunch papal doctrines he now found set forth in the learned and highly esteemed *Theologie Dogmatique* of the illustrious Cardinal Archbishop Gousset of Rheims, as well as in the *Universal History of the Catholic Church* by the learned Abbé Rohrbacker, Doctor of Divinity in the University of Louvain. The Abbé made the papal prerogatives the central theme of his Church history, and hence it appears prominently in each of the twenty-nine volumes. In the midst of the storm that the publication of the Abbé's work had also stirred up, it was a reassurance and an encouragement to him to learn through Cardinal Mai, prefect of the Congregation of the Index, that his history was looked upon at Rome with distinct favor.[51] In this reassurance given Abbé Rohrbacker, Brownson himself saw an approbation of his own stand, and he took pen in hand to write his encouragement to the Abbé:

> Allow me to say that what I most admire in your work is its papistical tone, and its constant effort to make Catholics understand that Our Lord founded his Church on Peter, and has never admitted the state to Holy Orders. Your vindication of the Sovereign Pontiffs, and refutation of the Four Articles of the Assembly of 1682, are alone an invaluable service to the Catholic public, although I fear we shall never find any considerable number of statesmen who will not be political atheists.[52]

Perhaps the greatest encouragement Brownson received from any prelate when he was in the thick of the fight was that from Bishop Charles E. Baillargeon, later archbishop of Quebec, Canada. Writing from Rome where he was sojourning at the time, he reassured Brownson in regard to the charge on so many lips that he "went too far," saying:

> You do *not* go too far, I tell you. Your writings are useful for all — to good Catholics, whom they enlighten and confirm; to tepid and lax Catholics, whom they stimulate and put to shame; and to Protestants themselves, whom they confound and frighten. Then I tell you again that you do *not* go too far. *Tales ambio defensores veritatis.* Therefore I never cease to pray God to preserve you, and to continue to assist you in your labors.[53]

Brownson must have felt that this encomium was a fair offset to Bishop O'Connor's unsparing attacks upon him.

Scarcely any letter could have shown better the salutary effects of the papal doctrine Brownson had been preaching than the one he received from Fr. William Cumming, Rothsay (Isle of Bute), in which he wrote:

> I have been on the point of writing you many a time these three or four years last, were it only to thank you for having completely changed in the right direction my own and many of my companions' views on certain facts of history — for having shown us the *necessity* and I will add the *happiness* of holding fast to the thread that alone can guide us in the mazes of history, *Ubi Petrus, ibi Ecclesia.* I was a great Gallican once — God help me — but if I had been asked why, it would have been found that political prejudice and not *reason* was at the root of it all. Your works gave my mind another bent, which a good papist professor of theology and as good a professor of history served to strengthen and confirm. I will add, that the professor (in the Grand Seminaire of Cambrai) in the beginning looked at the facts of history through the untrue mirror of the respected M. Gosselin's theory; but after a good hard fight in

451

class for some weeks, sustained I admit mainly by your *arguments,* he was induced to study things more carefully, and the result was that he *revint sur lui-meme,* studied the original documents *himself,* and finished by giving us a course which many will remember to the end of their lives, on this idea, that we must take the Church's *own interpretation* of her own acts. You have the glory before God of having sowed the good seed deep in the souls of a hundred or two young priests, who will not have received it in vain.[54]

As anxious as this great protagonist of the papal powers had been to clear the Sovereign Pontiffs in the Middle Ages of any appearance of usurpation of power in their dealings with secular princes, he was perhaps even more anxious to inspire in the hearts of the faithful a becoming esteem, reverence and love for the persons of the vicars of Christ on earth. But this he reaffirmed could never be done by claiming for the Sovereign Pontiffs nothing more than a mere human right based on the concessions of kings and the assent of the people in their dealings with tyrannical rulers. Only the assertion that they are endowed with a divine right directly from on high could inspire that love and affection in the hearts of the faithful for their sacred office. Only this could contribute to a strengthening of the papacy in the face of the temporal order, so necessary if civil freedom was to be maintained and the blessings of true liberty secured. He was therefore far less concerned about vindicating the papacy from the charges preferred by infidels, heretics and schismatics, than he was about securing it the deep love and veneration of the faithful, alienated to such a fearful extent by the prevalence of an ultra-Gallicanism. "We hold," he affirmed, "that all society, properly so called, rests on the Church, and the Church on Peter, and that both are endangered just in proportion as we weaken the power or diminish the splendor of the papacy in the minds and hearts of the faithful."[55]

The end of the year 1854 marked a partial cessation of the mighty campaign he had been waging for a recognition in Catholic society of the papal prerogatives of primacy and infallibility. It was not that the battle had got too hot for him — he had become inured to the heat of battle — but rather that he could not endure to be the occasion of disunity of feeling in the Catholic Church. As he had written to Archbishop Purcell: "I can beg, I can starve, but I cannot consent to be the cause of division among brethren."[56] Yielding, therefore, to the persuasion of friends, as he explained years later, he withdrew from the fight, but with convictions utterly unchanged.[57] And thus it was that only Vatican Council I, held in 1870, finally came to his rescue in solemnly defining the papal prerogatives of supremacy and infallibility in the successor of St. Peter in the See of Rome. With what joy and gratitude the old battle-scarred veteran hailed those solemn Vatican decrees can be guessed only by those who have read the story of the bitter gale he had weathered when years previously he had asserted and defended so gallantly those same high papal prerogatives.

What he considered of the most vital importance as bearing on the controversies of the day was the Council's utter condemnation of the first three Gallican articles, which controverted the supremacy of the vicar of Christ, both in relation to the civil power and in relation to a general council, and the assertion of the primacy of jurisdiction of the successor of Peter in relation to both. The Vatican proclamation of the papal prerogatives leveled, he said, "a death-blow at the wretched Gallicanism and political atheism which enfeebles and kills the life of every modern nation."[58] He felt free now for the first time in his life to defend the Catholic Church unhampered by a mutilated orthodoxy. He could now bring out and insist on the very truths needed to combat the dominant heresies of the age. And with renewed energy and assurance he returned once more to a promulgation of his high-toned ultramontanism as the only medicament that could heal the wounds of a well-nigh moribund society.

It was with rare satisfaction that he noted, too, that Vatican Council I was the first of the ecumenical councils, as far as he could discover, that had ever treated the primacy of Peter as the first part of *De Ecclesia,* or the foundation, before treating the body of the Church. All previous councils, and all theologians with whom he was acquainted, whether Thomists, Augustinians, Jesuits, Gallicans or ultramontanists, those who recognized the primacy at all, had universally treated the body of the Church before treating its head. Even the theologians designated to prepared the *Schema de Ecclesia* for consideration of Vatican Council I, undoubted defenders of the papal prerogatives as they were, did the same. This struck him as very unscientific, for to him an acephalous church is no church at all. His *Review* had steadily maintained that Christ founded his Church on Peter, and that without Peter it has no foundation. A church without a foundation is founded on nothing — a mere castle in the air. Without Peter, Brownson contended, you have no church.[59]

Ever mindful that the Sovereign Pontiff as head of the Catholic Church is the vicar of Christ on earth, Brownson deplored any lack of reverence and loyalty shown him on the part of Catholics — as might be in the case of mere nominal Catholics. He disliked cordially the manner in which authors of our popular histories, whether Catholic or non-Catholic, especially in this country and England, uniformly deal with the historic quarrels between Peter and Caesar. He affirmed that he had read history both as Protestant and Catholic, with at least ordinary diligence, and "we venture to assert," he said, "that in no instance in the contests between the two powers have the secular authorities been in the right and the Sovereign Pontiffs in the wrong. Whatever may or may not be said of their titles, the Sovereign Pontiffs have invariably used their power on the side of justice, and never have they deposed a prince who did not for his tyranny, his oppression, his frightful iniquities, deserve to be deposed."[60] "All history proves that the pope is ever too slow to arrest the tyranny, oppression, the wickedness of crowned monsters, such as Henry IV of Germany, the Hofenstaufen, Henry of Luxemburg, and Louis of Bavaria, to name no others. The papal forbearance to strike, to liberate the Church from oppression and society from wicked and lawless rulers, is one of the marvels of history."[61]

Herculean and relentless were the efforts of Orestes Brownson to crush Gallicanism in his day and to exalt the chair of Peter. Writing in the *Irish Ecclesiastical Record,* Fr. John Healy, professor of theology in Maynooth Seminary, and later Archbishop of Tuam, asserted that Brownson "seems to have gone quite as far, if not further, than Bellarmine" in defending the medieval popes who "pronounced the deposition of outrageously tyrannical kings, who [had] violated their coronation oaths, broke the constitutional pact, and raged like lions against the Church."[62] Lord Acton, speaking of Brownson's papal doctrine, remarked in his letter to Ignaz Döllinger: "Neither Bellarmine nor Orsi nor De Maistre was a more eager Papalist [than Brownson]. . . . For this reason he hates Fleury, Lingard, Gerson, even Bossuet." He added: "He received this [doctrine] from Bishop Fitzpatrick, to whom he is completely devoted, and cannot independently defend his viewpoint historically." Yes, Brownson's papal doctrine was the same as that of Bishop Fitzpatrick, but Acton was altogether wide of the mark when he added that Brownson could not defend his "viewpoint historically."[63] Brownson was the very man who could and who did show its truth historically as has been so eloquently stated by Fr. Joseph P. Donovan. (Refer to note 42, page 447 of this chapter.)

It would, in fact, probably be impossible to find anyone who ever used the English language as the medium of his thought and expression who was ever such a staunch and able vindicator of the authority of the Holy See, or of the immense significance to society at large of the papacy, as was Orestes Brownson. It is in no sense surprising that Cardinal Manning, another great protagonist of the papal powers, especially at Vatican Council I in 1870, wrote Brownson in 1873 to say:

> You see as I see, and your discernment confirms mine. You have so long and so powerfully maintained the authority of the Holy See in the midst of indifference, liberalism, and half-truths that we all owe you a debt of gratitude; and the Church in America will bear the marks of your testimony to the highest conviction of Catholic Truth. We have one point in common. You, I believe, have always had a special devotion to the Holy Ghost. It was this that brought me out of darkness into light. And it is this that has made the prerogatives of the Vicar of Christ the first axiom of my faith.[64]

# 30

## BROWNSON AND THE IRISH

*The Native American party and its hostility to Catholics • Brownson deals with the subject in two articles on "Native Americanism" • His second article a real blockbuster • He adopts a sagacious plan to batter down the religious bigotry and intolerance in the Native American party, but lets slip, or deliberately sets down, certain remarks which offend the Irish deeply • An immense uproar follows • While rightly defending the native American sentiment in the Native American party, Brownson utterly repudiated the party as mainly led by foreign demagogues without any American patriotism • He gives further offense to the Irish by suggesting that they would render the country a real service by their willingness to forgo the privilege of American citizenship and thus at the same time block the chance of foreign radicals to become American citizens • The attacks on Brownson from various Catholic journals • A remarkable letter on the matter from his friend and admirer, George Edward Clerk • His own letter to the editors of* The United States Catholic Miscellany *• Two decades later Brownson frankly acknowledges that he had made mistakes in his campaign against the Native American party: he had made an ill-advised display of his Americanism and he had just as ill-advisedly called upon the Irish to Americanize • A succinct and objective comment on Brownson's relation to the Irish.*

Brownson had not yet emerged from the storm occasioned by his courageous championship of the supremacy of the spiritual order over the temporal before he found himself engulfed in another terrific gale lashing from another direction — his brave discussion of the ominous movement called Native Americanism in an article in his *Review* of July 1854. It was this discussion that was to bring him eventually into violent collision with the Irish. That this collision was to flare up intermittently during the rest of his life we have from Brownson himself. In the valedictory edition of his *Review* (October 1875) he wrote:

> That there has been more or less of antagonism between the *Review* and a portion of the Irish Catholic press published in this country, it were idle to attempt to deny; . . . but no antagonism of this sort has any thing to do with the discontinuance of the *Review*. The warmest and most esteemed friends of its editor, and its firmest and most generous supporters, have been among Catholics of Irish birth or Irish descent, as is the great body of our English speaking Catholics.[1]

As delicate and difficult as the matter is, an attempt will be here made to give a fair picture of Brownson's relations to the Irish. Even the three-volume biography of Brownson by his own son Henry, though admirably objective on a large scale, does not convey an entirely correct impression regarding his father's general attitude to, and estimation of, the Irish people.[2] Arthur M. Schlesinger, Jr., quotes only one-sidedly some of Brownson's animadversions on the Irish.[3] Theodore Maynard followed suit in this.[4] Doran Whalen skirts the question altogether.[5] Inasmuch as the Irish were the dominant racial element in the Catholic Church in America at the time, the question takes on dimensions.

It was Brownson's July 1854 article on "Native Americanism" that gave such dire offense to the Irish. With an article on that same subject, written by Brownson in 1845, no fault had been found by the Irish. In that article he had set the Native American party down as opposed only to *Catholic* foreigners, particularly to Irish Catholics, and defended the Irish all he could against the hereditary dislike of them on the part of his Anglo-American countrymen. He pointed out to them that it was in the very nature of things that Catholic Irish immigrants could not so readily identify with the American way of life in all things, however desirable that might be. If they were Protestants it would be much easier and natural for them to mingle more freely with the native population of the country and flow more readily into the great stream of the national life. But they were Catholics, and had brought with them a faith for which their fathers had "suffered these three hundred years more than any other people on earth." There was nothing more natural, then, than that they should seek to settle together in some neighborhood of their own, with the Catholic Church in their midst, where they might have the consolations of their religion ministered to them. But in so doing they could not avoid the appearance of being a foreign colony, their habits and way of life differing from that of their Protestant countrymen, with the consequence that they naturally did not fraternize with them as completely socially and politically as might otherwise be. In this first article Brownson glossed over the unfavorable aspects to his countrymen of Irish Catholic immigrants and was willing to leave the eventual settlement of racial problems to the "melting pot" process.[6]

But in his second article on Native Americanism, nine years later, in July 1854 — which was to prove a real blockbuster — he took a somewhat different tack, and made crucial distinctions which he had previously failed to perceive or which he glided over in his first article. He stressed again that while the Native American party was ostensibly against foreigners as such, it was really at bottom decidedly against Catholic foreigners, and chiefly against Irish Catholic immigrants who during the previous decades had been the preponderant class of Catholic immigrants.[7] He proceeded to point out, however, that it was somewhat by accident that the Native American party had become anti-Catholic, for there had been in the country from the earliest times a Native American party in contradistinction to foreigners. The first newspaper started as a special organ of the Native American party had been conducted by Catholics themselves, descended on the one side at least from an old American Catholic family.[8] Underlying this same Native American party, therefore, was a certain native American feeling, a spirit or sentiment of nationality, proper to every nation, and shared in to some extent by all natives. If then the party in time had assumed a decidedly anti-Catholic character, it was due, Brownson asserted, to the craft and influence of no-popery lecturers, political demagogues, wild radicals from the continent of Europe, and also to some extent to the imprudences of the foreign-born population of the country themselves, naturalized or resident.

Brownson admitted that he himself had previously made the mistake of confounding the native American feeling of the party with the anti-Catholic feeling, but in this second article on the matter, he got his bearings rightly, separated the two sentiments in the party — the native American sentiment from the anti-Catholic feeling — and adopted the plan of waging an all-out war against the anti-Catholic sentiment as distinctly anti-American in its nature, utterly opposed to the acknowledged principle of religious freedom as embedded in the American Constitution by the Founding Fathers. With this platform from which to launch the counterattack, this keen strategist tried to bring home to his fellow Catholics in the country that any show of hostility on their part to the Native American party as such, without making the aforesaid distinction, would only throw around the whole body of Catholics in the country, native and foreign-born, the appearance of a foreign colony, carrying with it the unfortunate implication that their religion itself was foreign in nature, and therefore incompatible with American institutions. These very appearances their enemies were industriously and nefariously endeavoring to create and maintain. To meet the real situation, then, Brownson counseled that, while waging an all-out war on the anti-Catholic sentiment of the party on the grounds of religious freedom, nothing could be wiser for Catholics than to show a becoming respect for the native American sentiment wrapped up in the movement. But with the bigotry and intolerance toward foreigners so rampant, especially toward Irish Catholic immigrants, the plan laid down was no easy matter to carry through. The plan itself, however, was expertly sagacious and was the real level upon which the battle was fought and won, though Brownson himself was to encounter much misunderstanding and bitterness in his heroic efforts to carry it through.

Pursuant to his strategy, therefore, Brownson proceeded to make crystal clear in the first part of this second article on Native Americanism, in July of 1854, that he stood ready to defend the sentiment of nationality in the Native American party, but gave over the latter part of it to a vigorous denunciation of the bigotry and intolerance of the party as un-American. However, in speaking in the tones of a natural-born American citizen — and somewhat loftily, too, at times — he set down, or let slip, a number of remarks that must have grated terribly upon the sensibilities of the foreign-born population of the country. He reminded them in strong terms that there was in the country such a thing as an American nationality, mainly of English origin or descent, and that it was to this selfsame Anglo-American type of nationality that all foreigners were called upon to conform. He addressed himself in particular to the Irish Catholic immigrants, and called in question their unyielding attachment to their national habits, customs and traditions. For them to attempt to keep up their own foreign nationalism on American soil would be both unavailing and unwise, he asserted, for it was to be counted a certainty that the distinctive American nationality that would claim the future would be determined by the Anglo-Saxon population, and that this same Anglo-Saxon population had the right to say to foreigners: "It is for you to conform to us, and not for us to conform to you. We did not ask you to come here; we do not force you to remain. If you do not like us as we are, you may return whence you came."[9]

It would be unfair, however, not to add that Brownson took broad and liberal views of the whole problem of Americanization on the part of foreigners. While strongly counseling the Irish and other nationalities to drop their distinctive national habits, customs and traditions, he called upon his own countrymen to recognize that it would be unreasonable for them to expect foreigners to be transformed at once into Americans; that nationality is a stubborn thing, and is not to be worn out in a day, or even in a single generation; that nationality, the usages, manners and customs, which are sometimes the immigrant's offense, are in themselves just as respectable as their own, and that much must be pardoned a poor people who for ages had been oppressed by tyrannical and incapable governments.[10]

Yet Brownson's dour insistence on conformity to the Anglo-American style of life may well have had the offensive appearance (to foreigners) of asserting the superiority of that type of civilization to all others. Worst of all, he attributed the growing radicalism of the country, flaring ominously here and there, to the great influx of foreigners into the land. The basic Anglo-American population in the country, he went on to say, had always been marked by a certain integrity and sobriety of conduct, while among the foreigners pouring into the country for so long, there had been many an anarchist or revolutionary demagogue who, having done his iniquitous work abroad, had fled hither to bedevil the American scene with European politics, making "the merits of candidates depend on the views of O'Connell, Kossuth, Smith, O'Brien, Kinkel, Mazzini, Ledru-Rollin, Louis Napoleon or Francis Joseph, Nicholas of Russia or the Sultan of Turkey."[11] Did not those revolutionary demagogues so rig the last national elections that practically the whole country was at the mercy of those who controlled the "foreign vote"?

Catholic foreigners reading the article thus far probably seethed with disgust and indignation, and may have thrown it down in wrath. But had they read on to the end they would have seen that although Brownson had already said something against Irish Catholic immigrants as aiders and abettors in a minor degree of the growing radicalism in the country, he was only leading up gradually to a major indictment not of the Catholic, but of the non-Catholic immigrants. The great body of German Catholics he had found to be quiet, peaceable and industrious, but a portion of the non-Catholic Germans he rated as among the worst radicals in the country. Some of their journals were the vilest imaginable, and some of their associations' avowed doctrines the most horrible. Not from Catholic but from non-Catholic immigrants come the principal danger to American institutions. "Who," he inquired, "got up the Bedini riots in our principal cities, which last winter disgraced our country at home and abroad, and which the secular press dared not oppose, lest it lose for its candidates the foreign vote? They were foreigners, principally German infidels and Italian patriots."[12]

Among the Irish, it was mainly Protestant Irishmen from the North of Ireland that he indicted, who having caught their unholy inspiration from French Jacobinism, and unable to fasten it on their own country, had fled hither in the early days "to blast with its sirocco breath the rich promise of our young Republic."[13] The real Catholic portion of the foreign population in the country he pronounced the most conservative body in the land, and declared again that it was upon them that the country must rely for neutralizing the rising radicalism of the day. Yet he by no means held the whole body of Irish Catholic immigrants to be without blemish. He wrote:

> The great majority of them are quiet, modest, peaceful, and loyal citizens, adorning religion by their faith and piety, and enriching the country by their successful trade or their productive industry. But it cannot be denied that hanging loosely on their skirts is a miserable rabble, unlike any thing the country has ever known of native growth — a noisy, drinking, and brawling rabble, who have, after all, a great deal of influence with their countrymen, and who are

usually taken to represent the whole Irish Catholic body, and who actually do compromise it to an extent much greater than good Catholics, attentive to their own business, commonly suspect, or can easily be made to believe.[14]

Discussing further the radicalism of the day, Brownson deplored the fact that Irish immigrants suffer themselves to be influenced and guided so easily, not by the sound principles of their religion, but too often by their demagogic and revolutionary countrymen. He here lashed out at what he called "that ribald sheet, *The Irish American*," with its twenty thousand subscribers, and *The Citizen* with its forty-five thousand subscribers, conducted by "that Protestant radical, John Mitchel" — both papers widely supported by Irishmen who were nominally Catholic. The case of the so-called *Catholic Standard,* published in San Francisco, was far worse — so radical and vile that he would not even take it from the post office. Still, he acknowledged that it was the non-Catholic or merely nominal Catholic foreigners who were the real pets of the revolutionary demagogues, and who on that score were the major threat to the peace and order of the country. While reasserting his stand on the side of the sentiment of American nationality in the face of all this, he utterly repudiated the Native American party as such:

> . . . for its real leaders are foreigners, mostly apostate or renegade Catholics of the Padre Gavazzi stamp. Those vile European vagabonds have seized upon the honest native American and republican sentiment of the country, and have sought to pervert it to a mere anti-Popery sentiment. . . . These men, the veritable chieftains of the present native American party, care not a straw for American interests, for genuine American sentiment, any further than they can use them for their own base and malignant purposes. It is really a foreign party, and therefore, as Americans as well as Catholics, we disavow it.[15]

In considering ways and means of defeating this native American party, Brownson unfortunately again gave offense — particularly to the Irish — in throwing out the suggestion whether or not it might be wiser for Catholic immigrants to be willing to have the naturalization laws repealed and to forgo the opportunity of political citizenship for the time being if they could thereby debar from the rights of citizenship that radical class of immigrants, Brownson said, who have come here imbued with the infidel and anarchical principles of the mad European revolutionists, carrying on in the country their machinations against legitimate authority and social order in a language which very few citizens of the country understand. By willingly cooperating with such a design to deny the power of the ballot to this corrupt mass of non-Catholic foreigners who were doing their best to ruin the country, Brownson could not but feel that Catholic immigrants would be rendering an invaluable service to the country of their adoption.[16] He emphasized that the elective franchise is a municipal grant, not an indefeasible political right, and therefore may be withheld for good reasons. In any case, he did not want foreigners of any ilk mixing noisily in American politics. At best "they may be voters, but not canvassers. A certain moderation, a prudent reserve, in the exercise of their franchises is expected of them, and they cannot go the lengths they might if natural-born citizens, without giving serious offense."[17] The very suggestion that the elective franchise be denied them must have been highly offensive to Irish Catholic immigrants who for long centuries had been treated as much less than second-class citizens in their own native land. Must it continue here, too? Had they not come to America with the comforting idea that this is the land of freedom and equal opportunity for all?

When the article in which Brownson had expressed these views was published in the July 1854 issue of his *Quarterly,* it created a tremendous uproar. Arthur M. Schlesinger, Jr., says that "in July and August nine Catholic journals censured Brownson."[18] Irish and Catholic editors rushed to reply to what they considered a broadside from a Yankee convert. First in the assault came James Alphonse McMaster, editor of the *Freeman's Journal,* who traced his ancestry to North Ireland, and who evidently took offense at what he considered Brownson's aspersions on the radicals of North Ireland. His comments were copied and published in the *Catholic Mirror* of Baltimore by its editor together with an abusive article by an anonymous correspondent who accused Brownson of venting his malice on the Irish. This drew from Brownson a long letter quoted here only in part:

Boston, July 11, 1854

To the Editors of the *Catholic Mirror*
Gentlemen:

I regret that you should have inserted in your paper of the 8th inst., the article headed "Dr. Brownson and Native Americanism," for I cannot but think that on cool reflection, you will see that it was uncalled for, and unjust to me.

I am surprised that you should not have seen the impolicy, to say nothing more, of denouncing an American Catholic publicist for expressing himself as a loyal American citizen, for that is really the purport of your article, certainly as the non-Catholic public will understand it. An impudent fellow, when I first became a Catholic, called me, because I had become a Catholic, a traitor to my country, and I knocked him down for the insult. The standing charge against us is that our religion is anti-American, and what have you done but confirm that charge, which you and I both know to be false, in the minds of those who bring it? Do you not see that you give them occasion to say, "It is as we said. Dr. Brownson has had the audacity to speak as an American citizen, and here are the Catholics out upon him in full cry." The fact that a native American Catholic deals the blow only makes the matter worse, because they will say, "What but his Catholicity could have induced him to denounce his brother Catholic for his American sympathies?"

I think, gentlemen, here is an aspect of this question you did not consider. If it was imprudent for me to write as an American, it was somewhat imprudent for you to denounce me in no measured terms for so doing.

The temper displayed by your correspondent is not precisely to my taste. It is not that of a gentleman, much less that of a Catholic. . . . [He] speaks of my venting my spleen against the Irish. How does he know that I have any spleen against the Irish? I have addressed them as Catholics, and I shall not be driven to do otherwise hereafter. I have seen the warm susceptibilities of the Irish heart played upon by foreign and native-born demagogues, till my blood has boiled with indignation; and I shall never, for the sake of any base or selfish purposes, imitate those demagogues. My acts must speak for themselves. If ever I let an opportunity pass of rendering them a service, either at home or abroad, when in my power, then let me be called their enemy, but not till then. I may err in my judgment as to what is for their service, but that I am their enemy is as false as hell. Why should I be their enemy? Have I ever received any injury from them? Have I ever received from the great body of them in this country or elsewhere anything but benefits? Does your correspondent suppose me incapable of gratitude?

. . . I have shown in my article, for which I am so unmercifully handled by your correspondent, who, if he has not the merit of charity, seems to have, in a large measure, that of its opposite, that I have no spleen against the Irish or any other class of foreign-born Catholics. I except the great body of Irish and

German Catholics from the charges I bring against foreigners, and I place them in the front rank of American citizens. If your correspondent had succeeded in understanding my article, he would have seen that the foreigners I complain of are the foreign radicals, chiefly Protestant Irish, and the non-Catholics of the continent of Europe. Nobody with whom your paper has any sympathy is attacked by me, or whom the *Catholic Mirror* can defend consistently with its title. I have attacked no Catholic foreign-born citizen or resident. I have charged the growing radicalism of the country to foreigners and foreign influence, but I have said that Catholic foreigners are precisely those on whom we must depend to neutralize that radicalism. Why has your correspondent, and why have you yourself, taken no notice of this fact, but attacked me as if I had attacked with good set purpose all foreigners indiscriminately? If you think the case at best is bad against me, why try to make it worse than it is?

. . . I cannot persuade myself that there is any thing that anybody save radicals and red-republicans need be angry at in what I had said, and certainly said with very different views and feelings from what you have supposed. I had a motive which I supposed would be patent to every Catholic; but it seems that in this I overrated their sagacity, and of course must suffer for my mistake. The end I had in view was, I am sure, such as every Catholic who is, and every foreigner who wishes to become, a citizen of the Union, would have heartily approved; and believing that I enjoyed the confidence of the Catholic public, I felt very sure of accomplishing it. But I was mistaken; and by the hastiness and passion of my Catholic friends it has been defeated.[19]

He spoke here of course of the strategy he had adopted to put down the bigotry and intolerance of the Native American party, and of the line of remarks and arguments in his article he had deemed well adapted to render that strategy effective and successful. But, all things considered, could he really have expected his fellow Catholics to see through his sagacious plan, he being a Yankee convert?

Perhaps no statement Brownson made in regard to the charge that he was anti-Irish sets the matter in a clearer light than the one he made three years later: "We had and have no interests and affections but such as are bound up with the Catholic body of which we are an insignificant member, and as the portion of that body from which we have the most to hope for Catholicity are Irish or of Irish descent, it is ridiculous to suppose that we were anti-Irish in our feelings, or were disposed to join the Know-Nothings in a war against Irish Catholics, which could be only a war against ourselves."[20] When he wrote this the battle had been fought and won, the hurly-burly was mostly over and done, but the last echoes even at that time had by no means died away. That was the reason for his repeated denials that he was anti-Irish. He had even been accused of being something of a clandestine Know-Nothing.

Inasmuch as this July 1854 article of Brownson on Native Americanism had such long and loud reverberations — even international in dimension as we shall see — it merits perhaps a closer evaluation of its contents and the "whirlwind of wrath" it stirred up than it has received in the past. Brownson at the time expressed himself utterly dumbfounded at the violent reaction to it among the Irish in particular. Since the strategy he had adopted for putting down the anti-Catholic movement of the day was beyond all cavil the wisest, must it therefore be said that there was really no reason for the outcry that was heard far and wide upon its publication? Is the violent reaction to be set down just to Irish touchiness? Or are there other factors to be noted? It is in the interest of historical truth to see if the matter can be unraveled.

Upon reflection, in the midst of the uproar, Brownson, rereading his article closely, did finally come upon what was at least a partial explanation of the frothy denunciations which had assailed him. In the article he had played a dual role, giving sometimes his own views on foreigners, and giving at other times the views of his own countrymen, particularly in regard to Irish Catholics. He had not distinguished in the case as clearly as he might have, and hasty readers might easily enough have mistaken the one for the other. And as Brownson had a real edge on more than one of his paragraphs, the offense taken is quite understandable. In a letter to his friend Judge Hilton of Cincinnati, Ohio, written in Boston on July 26, 1854, he acknowledged:

> In reading over last evening my article I perceived that I possibly may not have been in all cases careful to distinguish in describing what the country generally exacts of foreigners and what I myself contend it has a right to exact, and what it regards as an offense in them and what I myself so regard; but I think still that a candid reader would have found me sufficiently clear, and would not have laid to my account what I give as the views of my non-Catholic countrymen. The only excuse I can find for those who bring these charges is perhaps in one or two passages of some little obscurity on this point.[21]

This may well throw some light on a letter Brownson received, dated August 28, 1856, from his friend in Montreal, Canada, George Edward Clerk, one of his most ardent admirers. Of all comments pro and con on Brownson's article on Native Americanism, this letter — eight pages in length — may well have been the most impartial and objective. The distinctions made show an honest attempt to get at the truth. Clerk had animadverted on Brownson's July article in *The True Witness,* of which he was editor, and Brownson had complained to him of having been handled "unjustly and harshly." In reply Clerk really went down into the historical roots in some of his analysis of the matter to be explained, but only the more relevant paragraphs of his long letter are here quoted. In part he wrote:

My dear Dr. Brownson:

I received your letter of the 18th inst. some days ago, but owing to my own sickness . . . I have not been able to find time to answer you before. Believe me, I am not one of those who judge you unfairly, and that I am not one of those who join in the outcry that, in certain quarters, has been raised against you. At the same time, it would have been better, and would have fully expressed my meaning, if in the notice of your July *Review* — which I wrote for *The True Witness* of the 1st inst. — I had said you *seemed* to take pleasure in giving offense to the Irish and in coming rudely into contact in their tender places. I know you do not mean to do it; but it is also true, that exposed to hostile criticism, your writings *are* susceptible of an interpretation offensive to Irishmen, and that interpretation is often put upon them.

It is this I regret: because you thereby lose your influence for good over so many of our people. I do not wish to flatter you, but you know that no one, at one time, exerted a more salutary influence over, or did more to check the exuberance of, our Irish Catholics on this continent, than the editor of Brownson's *Review.* I regret that this influence should in aught be diminished. I regret that your writings are not in the hands of all our people; I regret that any thing should have occurred to lessen the hold that you, but a short time ago, had over them. This is why I *seem* to you to be severe and unfair. I dread that, taking advantage of your apparent (I do not say *real*) hostility to Irish Catholics, they be led astray by noisy demagogues; and of that I entertain the same salutary horror as yourself. Mind you — the Irish must have leaders; they must have some one to look up to; it is a necessity of their very being, but if they have not good leaders, if they lose confidence in those whose influence would tend to keep them in the right path, they give themselves up, too often, to the first noisy demogague who will condescend to blarney them.

Now, it is true, that you do not discriminate betwixt the sound portion of the Irish race in America, and the noisy turbulent rowdies with whom I doubt not, your large cities are infected. [This statement is not entirely true; Brownson did make some distinctions.] I, of course, do not pretend to know as well as you do, how the Irish behave themselves in the States. I judge them here, by what I see. And it is but justice to them to say, that, they are in Canada as a body, quiet, orderly, and attached to their religion. Good practical Catholics. Leaders in all good works. Now these men naturally feel sore at seeing their countrymen . . . in the States roughly handled. The consequence is they attribute to you the same anti-Irish prejudices as are generally supposed to actuate our "Know-Nothing" acquaintances on your side of the lines.

That the Irish have their faults, no one will deny, for they are human. But that they have many virtues is evident from their tried fidelity to the Church; and I cannot but think, that, in spite of their faults, it is because of their virtues — because of their Catholicity, that they are looked upon with so unfavorable an eye by a large body of American Protestants. It is certainly so in England and Scotland.

It may be true, and you are a far better judge of the matter than I am, that the Irish immigrants have been too often disposed, in the exercise of their acquired rights, to postpone American interests to Irish interests. In opposing this, you have done no more than what as an American you were bound to do. And God forbid that I, or any one, should presume to take offense at you for so doing. All that I, and many of your sincere friends and admirers here, complain of is this — that you have been too sweeping in your denunciation, and that you have seemed to justify by your pen, the brutal acts of violence against Irish Catholics of which your countrymen have been guilty, and in the perpetuation of which they show themselves thorough adepts as the Protestants of England and Scotland whom I have the honor to acknowledge my own countrymen.

. . . I have trespassed too much on your valuable time already, but I have done so, because I believe I am writing to one who will credit me when I assure him that I am still, and that I shall ever be, not only a sincere admirer of his writings, but a warm and affectionate friend. Differences [there may] be upon purely secular questions, but God forbid these should in aught alter my feelings to you personally; or make me forget for one instant, that we are children of the same Mother, heirs of the same promises, and nourished with the same spiritual food.

Goodbye. Remember me in your prayers, and, believe me my dear Dr. Brownson ever sincerely and affectionately yours,

George Edward Clerk[22]

Although Brownson knew well in his heart of hearts that he was not anti-Irish, this letter must have given him some slight pause. It was from a warm personal friend who had set down sincerely the impression his July article had made on him and on many of Brownson's other sincere friends and admirers. But a still greater surprise was in store for him when this same anti-Irish charge was made by the more sedate *United States Catholic Miscellany*, published at Charleston, South Carolina. During the latter part of 1854, articles had appeared in that journal accusing Brownson of having vented his malice on the Irish. The distinguished Dr. James Andrew Corcoran, and Dr. Patrick Neeson Lynch, who soon afterwards became the bishop of Charleston, were the editors at the time. Whether Dr. Corcoran or Dr. Lynch was the author of the articles is uncertain. But Henry Brownson thinks it more probably it was Dr. Corcoran inasmuch as it was to him that his father had expostulated over the matter. Brownson had a great respect indeed for Dr. Corcoran, and devoutly wished to disabuse his mind of the notion that he was in any way anti-Irish. In his letter to Dr. Corcoran he assured him that being a plainspoken man, saying what he had to say and getting it over with, that it was not therefore in his nature to be a malicious person, nursing hard pent-up feeling against anyone. In the latter part of his letter he said:

I think the Irish a little touchy, and I think it very bad policy for them, in a country like ours, to be always throwing their nationality in our faces if we happen not to be Irish. I think they are as much bound to respect my nationality as I am to respect theirs. I do not like their claiming the right in their organs to run down all nationalities but their own, and then cry out as if a great wrong were done, if the calumniated nationalities remind them gently that they who live in glass houses, etc. . . . These things are wrong, and which I find no Irish prelate or priest rebuking, do, I confess, occasionally grieve me. They may insult my nationality as much as they please, but if I but open my lips to give utterance to the Catholic doctrine of the unity of the race, then I am accused of stirring up national animosities and disturbing the peace of Catholics.

You will think that these remarks but ill sustain my assertion that I have no spleen against the Irish, and yet what I say is true. I do not like the Irish as editors, as politicians, or as critics; but I do like them as men, as friends, as companions, associates, as Catholics. In all the private relations of life, I love them, and taken as a people, I know no people I could place above them, or that I could place so high. They have done with scanty means an immense deal for religion in this country, and the hope of the Church in this country is under God chiefly in them and their children. I need not tell you these are my honest sentiments, for you will not suspect me of writing to you what I do not honestly feel. But with all this the Irish have their faults, and precisely the faults most offensive to Americans. They are not greater than ours, they are not so great even, but they are different, for the most part faults from which we are free, and all men are most offended by faults of a different kind from their own. I do not like their habit of crying out against a man who happens to displease them, of vituperating instead of reasoning. But I have much worse things to put up with from my own countrymen, and whether you believe me or not, I like the Irish and French far better than I do the English and Germans, although I prefer the political order which is represented by England, and which I call the Germanic order, better than I do the Romanic, which prevails in most Catholic countries.

In reading my *Review*, it will always be well to bear in mind that I sometimes deal in grave pleasantry, in good-natured raillery, which some, many indeed, take to be bitter sarcasm. I am not aware of a single sentence in the whole series that has been written in anger, in bitterness, or in a sarcastic spirit. But enough. I have opened my heart to you, because I am anxious to have your good opinion, and to retain your friendship, and because I know your paper has done me injustice, and I believe unintentionally. Forgive me for the freedom and frankness with which I have written, and believe me very truly your obedient servant,

O. A. Brownson[23]

With the charge of anti-Irishism pelting him from so many directions, Brownson again professed himself utterly unable to get at the bottom of the matter, that is, how in the world it was that his July article on Native Americanism should have exploded such a widespread uproar. Long years were to pass away before he was to perceive and admit with that candor that always marked the man that he had after all made some mistakes in his gallant fight on that bitterly anti-Catholic movement of the day called Native Americanism. He had overplayed his Americanism, and he had called upon the Irish to Americanize. It was precisely these two things which had so rasped the sensibilities of the Irish.

In playing up his Americanism at the time Brownson had had the noblest of motives. He saw clearly that the members of the Native American party based all their hopes for success on claiming for themselves alone the real spirit of American nationality, and in charging Catholics with hostility to that sentiment. Nothing could be more important, then, than to bring out in the most crystal-clear light that there was no incompatibility whatsoever between Catholicity and the honest sentiment of American nationality, that whatever of foreignism attached to Catholics in the country attached to them in their quality as foreigners, and not in their quality as Catholics, and was in no sense a part of their religion. He stressed that the Catholic religion is over and above all nationalities, and is able to coexist, without collision, with any. Brownson felt called upon to emphasize this inasmuch as large classes of his countrymen looked upon the Catholic Church as the *Irish* religion, and would regard becoming a Catholic in about the same light as becoming an Irishman. This was extremely unfortunate since many of the Anglo-Americans were about as prejudiced against the Irish as they were against the Church. To meet this dual objection to the Church, Brownson, as an American convert to the faith, played up his Americanism to the hilt as the most effective answer to these false notions.[24] The Irish sensed the overplay in the case, and took offense. Years later when Brownson revived his defunct *Review*, in 1873, he had come to a slightly different view in regard to playing up his Americanism. He wrote:

> Time was when I paraded my Americanism, in order to repel the charge, that an American cannot be a convert to the Church without ceasing to feel and act as an American patriot, but I have lived long enough to snap my fingers at all charges of that sort. . . . Though my interest in my country and my countrymen is as great as ever, I do not consider it a high compliment to be credited with an intense Americanism.[25]

Brownson's preachments to the Irish that they must forget their distinctive Irish manners, customs, habits and usages, and Americanize, had perhaps an even greater irritating effect than playing up his Americanism. To some of the Irish, especially to those who did not bother about following his thought closely, this must have seemed very much like calling upon them to apostatize or Protestantize. For to them the Catholic religion was part and parcel of their nationality, for which their fathers had lived and died, the one being almost indistinguishable from the other. Could they, then, really denationalize themselves without at the same time casting off Catholicity? Moreover, when Brownson emphasized to them so strongly that the distinctive American nationality is basically Anglo-Saxon, having derived its language, literature, laws, customs, social and political institutions from England, he was emphasizing that which was most unpalatable to them.[26] Was it, then, to this selfsame Anglo-American nationality that they must now conform? Was it for this that as a people they had endured long centuries of persecution and spoliation at the hands of this same Anglo-Saxon people who now boasted this selfsame civilization? Was it not only a quarter of a century previously that those dreadful, barbarous penal laws had been repealed which had been part and parcel of that selfsame boasted civilization? All this was burning deep in the memory of the immigrant Irish. What wonder that they insisted on having their say in the face of those galling preachments from a Yankee convert, and they had little patience to make nice distinctions. They ridiculed and sneered at the whole bigoted and intolerant anti-Catholic movement of the day, calling it "Natyvism," and labeling it correctly "undemocratic and anti-republican."[27] Passions continued to flare wildly on all sides. Yet Brownson at the time seems never to have wavered in his firm conviction that it was altogether the part of wisdom for the Irish to Americanize and submerge their distinctive nationality in the great widening stream of the burgeoning American nation.

However, by the time two decades had rolled away, Brownson had done a complete about-face on this prickly question. When in 1873 he wrote for the October edition of his *Quarterly* his remarkable commentary on Fr. Augustine G. Thébaud's *The Irish Race in the Past and Present,* he frankly acknowledged that he had made a mistake in calling upon the Irish to Americanize. He wrote:

> What they [the Catholic Irish] have now to do, is to guard against becoming Americanized. . . . The moment they exchange their original Irish characteristics for those of the country, they lose the principal part of their power. Some neo-Americans complained, some years ago, that Irish Catholics conducted themselves as a foreign colony in the country; and we ourselves regarded it as a hindrance to the spread of Catholicity; but we have lived long enough to see that it is desirable that they should continue so to conduct themselves. If they were to adopt, faith excepted, American modes of thought, manners, and customs, and become absorbed in the Anglo-American community, they would lose all their influence in softening the hardness, and in relaxing the rigidity of Puritan manners, so hostile to all real virtue, and the power of infusing into our national life a freer, a more hospitable, genial, and cheerful tone and spirit. It is doubtful, if completely Americanized and severed from their traditional relations, they would retain even their faith beyond the second generation.[28]

If there was anything wanting in the peace offering Brownson was now making to the Irish, it was handsomely completed in the flattering encomiums he made in this same article on the Irish type of civilization, which he called Noachic. If his former demand that the Irish conform to the Anglo-American type of civilization had roughly jarred their sensibilities, his encomiums now on the Irish type of civilization must have been quite soothing. He looked upon the Irish race as having been detached from the parent stock before the patriarchal religion had become to any extent corrupt, while the religion and traditions of Noah were still retained in great force and comparative purity. With this religious patrimony, said Brownson, they were directed by Divine Providence to the western isle which they still inhabit. Being there separated to some extent from the rest of the world, they preserved in comparative purity and vigor the primitive religion, the primitive civilization, institutions, manners and customs, as transmitted through Noah and his sons. "They were never," continued Brownson, "an uncivilized, a barbarous, or an idolatrous people; only they were civilized after the Noachic pattern, not after that of Nimrod, and perhaps that of Cain, which alone, in the estimation of the modern world, is civilization." This explains the joy and ease with which the Irish accepted the Gospel when first preached to them, unexampled elsewhere, and also explains the antagonism of the Irish and Anglo-Normans, which was as great when both professed the same religion as it has been since the English nation apostatized:

> The antagonism is not due precisely to difference of race, but to the difference of civilization. To the Anglo-Normans, the Irish, representing the oldest civilization in the world . . . were not civilized at all, but barbarians, sav-

ages of little more account than wild beasts, whom, as it is said to-day of our Indian tribes, the interests of civilization required to be exterminated; while to the Irish mind, the Anglo-Normans were robbers, ruffians, unmitigated savages, cruel, heartless, without any sense of justice or humanity, worthy descendants of the pirates of the North, veneered by a thin covering derived through France — of Graeco-Roman or Italo-Greek civilization, itself of barbaric origin. The two civilizations were essentially antagonistic, and by no possibility could coexist on the same territory in harmony.[29]

This line of thought may be looked upon as representing Brownson's more mature reflections on the Irish people and their national traditions. Although he was at no time anti-Irish, a letter he wrote Fr. Isaac Hecker in 1869 would seem to have marked a slight turning point even more favorable in his attitude to, and estimation of, the Irish people. He remarked:

> I think I am turning Paddy. . . . I am very Irish, when I do not listen to their defenses for themselves. They are remarkable people, the mainstay under God of the Church with us.[30]

When one recalls some of Brownson's remarks in his July 1854 article, and the uproar on the part of the Irish that followed, it is in no way surprising that some set him down as unfriendly, to say the least, to the Irish. Apart from matters already touched upon in this general survey, this writer thinks that one of his pen-pictures of the Irish in the 1854 article was definitely unjust and truly offensive — but no doubt unintentionally.[31] And that the impression stuck that he was unfriendly to the Irish, especially with those who read his *Review* only irregularly, is just as little surprising.[32] But after time has allowed passions to cool and temporary excitement to abate, Brownson is seen in the overall picture to have been a man loftily above all national prejudices or unfriendly national distinctions. He was no more anti-Irish than he was anti-Jesuit, a charge that was also made against him, though he had on occasion criticisms as well as eulogies for both. The whole question of Brownson's relation to the Irish is so justly and so well stated by a reviewer of *Brownson's Latter Life* in the *Irish Ecclesiastical Record,* 1900, that it is worthy of quotation as a succinct summation of the matter. He said:

> Perhaps the most interesting feature of the book to Irish readers, though certainly not the most pleasant, will be the lofty patronage with which the author of the work [Henry Brownson] is pleased to speak of Irish Catholics in America. This tone is also noticeable in the letters of many of Brownson's friends, who speak of themselves as native Americans, and the Irish as foreigners or immigrants. The letters of Father Hecker quoted in this volume are by no means exempt from this blemish. Brownson, the elder, was far superior to any of these men. He had, like Cardinal Manning, a genuine love for the Irish people, and whilst he sometimes reminded them of their defects, he never minimized their good qualities, or spared the self-sufficiency of their critics.[33]

# 31

## BROWNSON AND THE KNOW-NOTHING PARTY

*Brownson writes four articles on the Know-Nothing party • In his first article he defends point by point what he had said in his second article on "Native Americanism" • He stresses there can be no incompatibility between Catholicity and the true American spirit, and calls for conformity to the Anglo-American nationality of the country • Know-Nothingism is no "Yankee Invention," but an imported combination of the worst elements from other lands • He discusses citizenship again in relation to foreigners • Brownson and his friend, Robert Bakewell, are blamed for all the uproar in the country against Catholics • A letter Brownson receives induces him to be a trifle more cautious in his second article on Know-Nothingism when dealing with national susceptibilities • He speaks touchingly of the trying experiences of foreigners • He stresses the starkly anti-American character of the Know-Nothing party • His third article on Know-Nothingism is a review of the Massachusetts Know-Nothing legislature, and its "Nunnery Committee" • A scathing attack on Brownson by John Mitchel • A hot debate on the floor of the United States House of Representatives • Brownson answers an attack by Dr. John M'Clintock • In his fourth article on Know-Nothingism he also replies to charges preferred by the Massachusetts state council • His explanation to a group of sincere gentlemen of his doctrine on the superiority of the spiritual order over the temporal.*

Brownson now followed up his article on the Native American party with four articles on the Know-Nothing party, a party substantially the same in spirit and character as the Native American party, but fitted out with a new name and new organization. In the first article on this party he defended staunchly point by point what he had said in his second article on Native Americanism regarding the necessity of recognizing fairly the native sentiment in the party. He reaffirmed the paramount importance of distinguishing between Catholicity as Catholicity and Catholicity as identified with the Irish or any other nationality. For if the war raging against the Catholic Church was to be quelled, it must be brought home to his countrymen, he emphasized, that there is no incompatibility or antagonism between Catholicity and the honest sentiment of American nationality, that whatever of foreignism attaches for the moment to Catholic immigrants attaches to them in their quality as foreigners, not in their quality as Catholics.[1]

He again summoned all foreigners in the country to conform to the Anglo-American nationality of the land, and somewhat contemptuously rejected the "puerile boasts of foreigners" that the future nationality of the country would be "an amalgam" of all the nationalities which had flowed into the great bloodstream of the nation. Such pratings were only the silly notions with which foreigners attempt to relieve the tedium of their exile, but which should never be suffered to drive a great people from their sobriety. That the future nationality would be Anglo-American he considered a "fixed fact." He repeated his appeal to Catholic parents to Americanize, and to allow their children to Americanize, without ceasing to be Catholic. The fact is, he emphasized the primacy and rights of Anglo-Americanism in decidedly stronger terms in this article than he had done in his second article on Native Americanism.

Much that he said in this first article on the Know-Nothings was really only a restatement of what he had already said in private letters to editors who had attacked him. He deplored deeply that some of his friends, mistaking his purpose and wholly misconceiving the drift of his arguments in his second article on Native Americanism in his July article, had construed his remarks into an attack on the foreign population of the country, and particularly as an insult to Irish Catholics. That, as an American Catholic publicist, he could ever have dreamt of insulting Irish Catholics, no one, he was sure, would ever believe, unless he were willing to count him a fool or a madman, either of which suppositions was not likely to find credence among either his Catholic or non-Catholic countrymen. That charge he repelled "with all the indignation and scorn compatible with Catholic meekness and humility. For the ten years since we became a Catholic we have labored as a writer and a lecturer with the honest intention, and with what ability God gave us, to serve the great body of Irish Catholics, in the only way in which we believed we could serve them."[2]

He could only further deeply regret that the wide and fierce denunciations which had assailed him for having spoken as an American were only furnishing the Know-Nothings with ammunition with which to blast the Catholic Church. Those same denunciations were to them proof positive that no American could become a Catholic, a good Catholic, "without virtually renouncing his nationality, ceasing to feel and act as an American, and making himself a foreigner in the land of his birth. We fear," he continued, "the denunciations of us, under the circumstances, by the larger portion of the Catholic press in the English tongue, will hereafter, when it is no longer an object with them to excite Catholics against us personally, be used by the Know-Nothings with terrible effect against the Catholic population of the country." He hoped, however, that the more honest and candid of his non-Catholic countrymen — and he trusted that their number was not small — would not fail to perceive that the loud outcry against him was made by Catholics merely in their character as foreigners, not in their character as Catholics. Trying to analyze why his strategy had backfired on him in so many different ways, he said:

> The misapprehension of our article, as it seems to us, has been extreme, and we can explain it only on the ground that Almighty God has suffered it to remind us that he has his own method of defending his cause and protecting his children, and to impress upon our heart, what we in our pride were perhaps in danger of forgetting, that his Church does not stand in human policy, human wisdom, human sagacity, or human virtue; that he will prosper no policy, however wise or just it would otherwise be, which might in him who devises or urges it rob God of his glory, or render his supernatural providence less visible and striking. He has permitted a momentary delusion to blind and mislead the judgments of our friends, for his greater glory and our spiritual good. We bow therefore in humble submission, and cheerfully kiss the rod that chastises us. . . . Had our friends understood us, we feel sure they would have stood by us,

and seconded our efforts. If they had done us, we think Know-Nothingism would have received a deadly wound. But God has ordered otherwise, and we submit.[3]

In the meantime Brownson had been accused of contradicting himself in his two articles on Native Americans, the one of 1845 and the other of 1854, in regard to his views on the naturalization laws: in the first his views had been quite liberal, in the second somewhat illiberal. It was up to him to show that it all made sense. He explained that from the years 1820-1845 the flow of immigration into the country had been principally Catholic, and hence sufficiently conservative in character to exert a wholesome moral and religious influence on the country. But since 1845, and especially since 1849, the character of the immigration had been entirely different. The reaction to the revolutionary movement on the continent of Europe that began in 1849 had poured a still larger immigration onto our shores in which an infidel and anarchical element predominated, and which currently seemed likely to predominate. He confessed that he was opposed, not to the coming of such to our shores, but rather to their ready admission into the bosom of American political society. He feared that the support such an element would bring to the current filibustering, ultra-democratic, fanatical tendencies of some of his own countrymen would only tend to undermine genuine republicanism as it was conceived in the minds of the Founding Fathers. He simply did not believe that such immigrants were entitled to political citizenship since they were "to a fearful extent banded together in secret societies, affiliated to the terrible secret societies of Europe, and directed by foreign demagogues and revolutionists, such as Kossuth and Mazzini." Such immigrants showed no intention of becoming quiet, orderly and loyal American citizens. Hence Brownson concluded:

> As an American citizen and as an American republican, we cannot but be opposed to their naturalization, and *a fortiori* as a Catholic; for they are the worst enemies of the Church in this country, are hand and glove with the Know-Nothings taken generally, and may be regarded as the real instigators and the most effective supporters of the Know-Nothing movement. Know-Nothingism is no Yankee invention, no American production, but an imported combination of Irish Orangeism, German radicalism, French socialism, and Italian astuteness and hate.[4]

In speaking of "Italian astuteness and hate," Brownson was of course referring particularly to the notorious apostate priest Alessandro Gavazzi who with the dregs of Italian and German revolutionists fomented the "Bedini riots" through the country on the occasion of the visit of Archbishop Bedini to the United States in 1853. When, on his tour, he reached Cincinnati, an organized attempt was made to attack and hang him and destroy the cathedral. But as John Gilmary Shea tells us: "The authorities acted with energy; they surprised and captured the conspirators, with their arms, gallows, and banner." It is to be said to the credit of our government that Lewis Cass, with eight others, censured on the floor of the United States Senate in the plainest terms the foreign refugees who had brought so much disgrace on the country by such shameless rioting.[5]

The suggestion that Brownson had made that it might be well for foreign-born Catholics to forgo their chance to become adopted citizens if they would thereby debar from political citizenship so large an element of wild foreign revolutionaries, had evidently given much offense. He now used up several paragraphs defending himself. He stated that he had not advocated it, but had only thrown it out for discussion. He emphasized again that naturalized citizenship is a *boon* or a *grant,* not a natural or indefeasible right. As it is the inherent right of every sovereign society to open and to close to whom it will, so is it the right of every nation to close its political citizenship, if it sees proper, to all foreign-born immigrants that might prove a danger, or that would bring no advantage to it. He felt that, as a general rule, the true policy of a nation is to reserve its political — not necessarily its civil — citizenship to persons born on its territory, and to foreign-born individuals who had rendered the country eminent services. To render political citizenship too easy would cheapen it and lead perhaps to a neglect of its duties. However, he owned exceptions to this. In the early history of the country, settlers and laborers were needed for its vast uncultivated territory. Liberal naturalization laws had been framed. And as long as Catholics predominated in the immigration that swept our shores, those liberal laws proved a great boon to the country. For the Catholic population increased and spread through the Union during the earlier decades of the republic and had added to the conservative element in the nation. He explained:

> We need not say that we regard this as an immense gain in a national as well as religious point of view, for as our readers know, our sole reliance for the preservation of American liberty and American institutions, and therefore for the success of what is called the American experiment in self-government, is on the Catholic Church. Catholicity, so far from being opposed to republicanism, as so many of our countrymen believe or pretend, is absolutely essential to its wholesome working and successful maintenance. Hence, identifying genuine republicanism with genuine Americanism, we regard real Catholics as by far the truest Americans amongst us.[6]

But even should the foreign-born in the country continue to be admitted to political citizenship and stand as to title on equal terms with natural-born citizens, he felt a reminder or two were in place. He stated that anyone acquainted with the prevailing sentiments in the country could not be unaware that many things could be done by natural-born citizens that would not be tolerated or suffered if done by foreign-born citizens. The same things done by foreign-born citizens would be an offense, and they could only expect to have their foreign birth thrown in their faces. He was careful to state that he did not say that this was right, nor did he have any wish to justify it. But a fact it was. "In reality," he said, "the country, not by her laws, but by her sentiments, always regards even naturalized citizens in the light of guests enjoying her hospitality, and exacts of them the modesty and reserve expected in well-bred guests."[7]

Perhaps the loudest howl set off by his article on Native Americans in 1854 had been over the parading of his Anglo-Americanism — which some apparently took to mean simply Anglo-Saxonism. To which he replied in this article on Know-Nothingism that his readers were fully aware that he had never been known to boast the superiority of one race over another, to treat any race with pride or contempt, or to discount any man on account of his birth or nation. Hence what he had said had evidently been misinterpreted and misunderstood. "There is not a man in the country," he averred, "who has given stronger proofs of freedom from national and sectional prejudices than we have." Moreover, it was a well-known fact that he had always spoken out "in the severest terms" against his own country whenever the interests of truth or justice demanded it. In so doing as a Catholic — with the

471

same freedom with which he had spoken as a Protestant — he had gone so far as to create a suspicion of his patriotism. Here he gave his readers an additional reason why he had played up his Anglo-Americanism in the style in which he had:

> In point of fact, the freedom of our strictures upon our own country, though made with an American heart, had excited a suspicion of our patriotism, and was beginning to be used as a proof of the anti-American character of Catholicity. We owed it to our brethren and to the cause to which our *Review* is devoted to remove this unfounded suspicion, and to show that we can be sufficiently American, whenever the hour comes for the assertion of Americanism.[8]

What could be regarded as an artful smear was the accusation now made by some Catholics that Brownson himself and his convert friend Robert Bakewell (editor of *The Shepherd of the Valley*) had by their indiscreet zeal brought about all the continuing uproar in the country against Catholics. The doctrines they had been proclaiming had been so ultra and offensive to the American people, particularly the preachments about the papal prerogatives and the Catholic doctrine of exclusive salvation. To which Brownson replied: "We feel quite certain that, had it not been for the fears and complaints of Catholics themselves, our much harped-upon virulence, harshness, and ultraism which they were the first to proclaim, would never have been detected, certainly never complained of, by our non-Catholic countrymen." He opined that the raging hurricane of excitement in the country against Catholics was in no small degree the result of his own war to the knife on the wild radicalism that had long been germinating in the country. Here was what had made him "the best abused man" in all America. He had begun his war on that ominous evil in 1841 in the *Boston Quarterly Review,* had continued it more decidedly in the *Democratic Review,* and had renewed it on higher ground, with clearer and more comprehensive views, during the eleven years of his Catholic career both in his *Review* and in his orations, lectures, letters and conversations. This, together with certain things he had mentioned in his second article on Native Americanism, he counted the real origin of the extraordinary excitement raging in the country against Catholics, an excitement fanned and kept at high temperature by wild radicals, not the least by Irish radicals, mere nominal Catholics, to whom he owed nearly all the abuse he had received since his conversion, and whose policy it was to rob him of any influence he may have gained with Catholics, especially Irish Catholics.[9]

A couple of months after Brownson had published this first thirty-eight-page article on the Know-Nothings, he received a letter that must have staggered him a bit at the apparently sincere impression his July 1854 article on "Native Americanism" had made on a reader. It was from P. F. Ryder of St. Louis, addressed to his publisher, Mr. Benjamin Greene, but intended of course for himself. It was dated December 3, 1854, and ran in part:

> Respected Sir:
> I respectfully return you thanks for having forwarded to me the October number of Brownson's *Review* for 1853 which closed the volume for that year and is paid to Mr. Brownson. In consequence of my absence part of the year from this place, I received no number of this year. I was here in October, but there came no number to my address. Hence there is no charge against me for this year, and you will please to remove my name from your list of subscribers.
> I received from you with the number for October 1853 the July number for 1854 unsolicited which I return to you for your benefit. As I had before read that

number and am sorry to say that its contents has made an impression on my mind which I really never expected to be made by what [sic] I consider the good Catholic, Mr. Brownson. However, until the law of the Constitution is changed I presume the Celtic race will enjoy the same freedom as hitherto granted under its protection, and will not be dependent on the so called toleration and mercy which Mr. Brownson thinks the individuals composing the elements of the Anglo-Saxon race grants them. It is true it appears the motto of the Anglo-Saxon race is persecution in Church and state. And it appears strange that the justice of Catholic principles would not have removed those obstinate, innate feelings from Mr. Brownson at least. However, I hope that the individuals composing the Anglo-Saxon element for whom and in whose behalf Mr. Brownson displays his powerful talents at the present time will treat him with the same affection and respect which the poor downtrodden Catholic Celtic race have [treated him] for the last ten years.

A gentleman professing the great ability of Mr. Brownson ought to know that the great number of Irish in this country cannot be proscribed by a Know-Nothing clique. The Know-Nothing clique will succeed in nothing but the distraction of the peace of the country. After they have triumphed for a time in grasping the loaves and fishes they will quarrel among themselves. They are truly the descendants of a degenerate race in principle with the Tories of the revolution. Mr. Brownson should consider that we do not look for mercy in a pitiful manner from such persons. He should consider that Irishmen, and Irish Catholics particularly, justly venerate the American Constitution and its laws. So likewise will be their firm and unswerving determination to defend their rights granted to them to the last extreme without shrinking in the least to the dictation of the descendants of the Anglo-Saxon race. . . .

I hope you will excuse me for troubling you with these remarks, but it is well for Mr. Brownson to know that we cannot consider his otherwise so respectable Catholic *Review* a proper medium for the diffusion of Know-Nothing doctrine to dictate the terms for us as it pleases. He has mistaken the Irish character as adopted citizens when he undertook to dictate for them secondary measures in his July number. It is a great pity that he should have in this one number displaced the great confidence which his *Review* deserved for the last ten years. Other adopted citizens may think as much and say less.[10]

It is the second last sentence, if nothing else — "it is a great pity that he [Brownson] should have in this one number displaced the great confidence which his *Review* deserved for the last ten years" — that must have given him some truly sober thoughts. He was deeply conscious that he had a mission in life to accomplish, and he realized that the one thing that could imperil its fulfillment would be to have his influence undercut and destroyed. This his enemies, he well knew, were nefariously endeavoring to bring about.[11] And he began to see more clearly, now that his article on Native Americans had really played into their hands to their glee. His warm friend, George Edward Clerk, had also moaned over the huge amount of influence he had thrown away with that one article. However firmly he may have been convinced in his own mind that he had really given no just cause for offense, and labored hard to prove it in this first article on Know-Nothingism, he evidently decided at this juncture to be a trifle more cautious in dealing with national susceptibilities, for his second article on Know-Nothingism strikes a new and milder tone when speaking of foreigners.

In his July 1854 article on Native Americanism, he had complained in a serious tone about the immigrant Irish forming a party of their own in American politics, having their own military companies, maintaining a press clannishly their own, discussing with little or no restraint all questions concerning the internal and external policy of the country, and boasting that they

473

could throw in or out any candidate for the presidency as he pleased or did not please them.[12] As the two great political parties in the country were in many regions almost equally balanced, this was no entirely idle boast. The party that succeeded in bidding the most successfully for "the foreign vote" was sure in many regions to grasp the reins of government. This meant that the "foreign vote," at least in certain sections, was ruling the country. This was verified on a national scale in the election of 1852 when General Winfield Scott, the Whig candidate for the presidency, was defeated, and the Democrat Franklin Pierce was elected.[13] Such a state of affairs could not but be revolting to the natives of the country. What wonder that they saw more grim truth than humor in the joke current at the time concerning the schoolboy who had been asked to parse "America." "America," he said, "is a very common noun, singular in number, masculine in gender, critical case, and ruled by the Irish."[14] What wonder that Orestes Brownson, who had drunk in an intense patriotism from the Green Mountains, the rivers and valleys of his native Vermont, should have felt a dislike for all this, and that it had shown like forked lightning in some of the paragraphs of his July 1854 article.

But in this second article on "Know-Nothingism, or Satan warring against Christ," he now adopted a milder and more conciliatory tone when speaking of foreigners. He softened his indictment of Irish clannishness, modified definitely many of his statements which had given offense, and was more generous on the question of allowing foreigners ready citizenship, though he did not recall his former observations on the subject. He asserted again that foreigners had not always conducted themselves without offense, but that after adoption, "what is lawful for us is lawful for them, and we turn the equal rights we accord them into a bitter mockery, if we practically deny it." This was a broad grant he had not before allowed. And from there he went on to point out (though he had done so before also) with a more effusive generosity of sentiment the great material advantages which had come to the country with the influx of some six million immigrants. Without them the nation could never have developed into a great manufacturing people, nor could the many commerce-laden canals, particularly Erie and Champlain, have been dug, nor the great railroads built as they had been. Nor without them would the various territories of the country have developed into great and flourishing states in the Union, such as Michigan, Wisconsin, Iowa, perhaps Illinois, to say nothing of Texas and California, but would have remained "mere hunting-grounds for the native Indians."[15]

And Brownson's words must now have touched the heart of many a foreigner as he spoke of how his own great heart went out in deep sympathy to poor immigrants in the discouragement and trials they encounter on reaching our shores. Landing on our wharves flushed with hope, "they are crowded into immigrant cars, and hurried away as so many cattle to the place of their destination, with not a sympathizing look, not a kind tone to greet them." He spoke pathetically of "the poor woman from Ireland or Germany seated on the wharf or in the station house, with one or two children nestled around her, waiting for a steamboat or car to carry her further on," and of the flushed hopes with which "she had left the old country," and of "how wearied, disappointed, and desolate she must feel." "The heedlessness, cruelty, and contempt" with which such were treated made "his blood boil with indignation at his own countrymen." Foreigners were callously referred to by the press of the country as mere *immigrants*. "A man is run over. 'O, he is only an Irishman.' A man has fallen from a house and broken his neck. He is a foreigner, and we 'pass to the order of the day.' " He reminded his countrymen that "justice compels us to say, that their account against us more than offsets ours against them, and whatever we may think of the naturalization laws as they stand, we have much to reproach ourselves with in our manner of treating them, and have no right to raise an outcry against them as a body, or on the ground of being foreign-born.[16]

The substance of this article was of course directed with his usual force and skill against the false pretenses of the Know-Nothings who claimed to be "the American party" in the country. Far from being *the* American party he showed that they were in fact anti-American, for in making war on the Catholic Church they were flying in the very face of one of the fundamental principles of true Americanism, religious freedom, guaranteed by the Constitution. To say further that the Catholic religion is a foreign religion, as alleged the Know-Nothings, and that it thereby renders all its adherents foreigners, is of all pretenses, said Brownson, the idlest. As if a man could not be a good Catholic and a true American at the same time. He had a word to say to the Know-Nothings on this point:

> We are ourselves Catholic, unworthy of the name if you will, yet Catholic we are, and as much so as any man in the country. Nevertheless, we are American, and have proved it, as all must confess, in our articles last year on "Native Americanism" and "Know-Nothingism." In them we have proved that we are American in feeling and affection, and prepared to risk all our worldly interest in defending true Americanism against every species of foreignism. . . . We love our country, and no man in the Know-Nothing ranks has dared as much or made as heavy sacrifices for it as we have, whether wisely and needfully or not. We can show as long a line of American ancestry as any man in New England. We are American by descent, by birth, by residence, by education, by habits and manners, by sentiments and affections, and by the Constitution and the laws.[17]

He deplored the deep disgrace the Know-Nothings were bringing upon American institutions, how they were playing into the hands of foreign despots, as he alleged. The proud boast of America had always been that our institutions are based on natural as distinguished from historical right, on the rights of man as distinguished from the rights of castes, orders, or classes, and that they recognize and guarantee the equal rights of all. This had always been its noble boast in the face of despotisms, aristocracies, distinctions, and privileges of the Old World. And what were the Know-Nothings doing in their mad war on religious freedom but robbing America of her time-honored proud boast. To disfranchise Catholics would be a barefaced denial of the doctrine of equal rights which lie at the basis of our American institutions, and would violate the essential principle of true Americanism. That would be recognizing in one class of men rights which are denied to another, and creating in non-Catholics a privileged class, a political aristocracy. Such a course could only bring comfort to the enemies of our republic in Europe, seeking every opportunity to bring our institutions into disrepute and to cover the American character with odium and contempt. Yet this was the glorious work of "*the* American party."[18]

He ended this article by utterly repudiating the Know-Nothing party as "a secret, subterranean organization" totally alien to the free institutions of the land which demand open avowals and free public discussion.[19]

In his third article on the Know-Nothing party Brownson acidly observed that the party was appropriately named as long as it kept to that title. But there was only mockery in the title when the party attempted to pass itself off as the American party, for it owed its very conception, its plan, its organization, and its rules to foreign nations, and did but copy the Orange Lodges of Ireland and the Carbonari of Italy. Every charge, he said, it brings against Catholics and Catholicity "is of British manufacture, and glutted the English market before [being] thrown on our own. . . ."[20] But the bulk of his article was given over to a partial review of the Massachusetts Know-Nothing legislature. It is pertinent to note here that Brownson had a ringside seat in his opportunity to observe the workings of Know-Nothingism at first hand since Massachusetts was one of the hotbeds of Know-Nothingism. As Ray Billington points out: "Massachusetts was the scene of the party's greatest victories; there the governor and all the state officers were Know-Nothings, the state Senate was made up entirely of representatives of the party, and the state House of Representatives was composed of one Whig, one Free-Soiler and 376 Know-Nothings."[21]

Such a Know-Nothing legislature was bound to betray its hand. Besides passing a bill that required the daily reading of the Bible in the schools "in the common English version" (the King James version unacceptable to Catholics), it also appointed a "Nunnery Committee" to report on Catholic convents in the Commonwealth.[22] It being discovered, however, that there were no convents in the state, the commission was further authorized to visit "such theological seminaries, boarding-schools, academies, nunneries, convents, and other institutions of like character as they deem it necessary," and report its findings to the legislature. So empowered, the committee began its inquisitorial tour in March 1855, stopping at educational institutions in Worcester, Roxbury and Lowell. Their conduct from first to last was such as could only bring dishonor to the whole committee, and particular disgrace to Mr. Joseph Hiss, the chairman of the committee. At Roxbury, where a simple and unoffending Catholic school was picked for investigation, twenty inquisitors barged in, although the appointed committee numbered only seven. The whole enlarged party tramped through the school, showing little respect for the nuns, frightening the children by their brusque manners, and poking into closets and corners for incriminating evidence of "popery" which anti-Catholic propagandists had assured them would be found there. After leaving the school in disarray, the party adjourned to a lavish dinner where champagne flowed freely — although its sale was prohibited in the state. At Lowell not only did the enlarged party partake freely of local liquors at state expense, but also charged to the state expenses accruing from their relations with a woman answering to the name "Mrs. Paterson," who was "notorious for her easy virtue."[23]

In commenting on the proceedings of this committee, Brownson thoroughly exposed their dishonorable conduct, and saddled their guilt squarely on the shoulders of the state legislature. In short, he said: "The Committee [members] . . . proved by their conduct that they were ignorant or disrespectful of all the proprieties and decencies of civilized life. They seem to have been wholly under the influence of their lecherous tastes and prurient fancies, and to have imagined they were sent to visit a brothel, and not the residence of reputable and highly esteemed ladies." In a desperate effort to escape implication in the affair, the state legislature decided to sacrifice Mr. Hiss, the chairman. He was expelled from the assembly by a vote of 137 to 15, though 150 members absented themselves rather than vote against him. Feeling the pulse of the public, the legislature was really driven to this measure. For not only Catholics, but all fair-minded people of the state resented the unseemly conduct of which the committee had been guilty. Some satirist gave fit expression to public sentiment when he wrote:

476

One after one the honored Bay-leaves fade,
And ancient glories wither in the shade.
The glorious solons of the state, at duty's call,
Have *hissed* a *loving* member from the Hall.
Take courage, Joseph, in thy great ado;
The world has hissed the legislature too.[24]

Although there was little in Brownson's article on the Massachusetts'
Know-Nothing legislature that Catholics themselves could take exception to,
things had gone so far that there was now little Brownson could do or say to
allay the storm that had been set raging. Some no longer had ears to hear nor
hearts to understand. Like any other storm, it would just have to blow itself
out, its course and direction depending largely on fortuitous factors. In spite
of all his good intentions and heroic endeavors, Brownson found himself at
this juncture in a very unenviable position, acceptable neither to his countrymen nor to his coreligionists. The course he had embarked upon had backfired from both sides. As Van Wyck Brooks has correctly remarked: "Having been too Catholic for the Yankees, he was too Yankee for the Catholics."[25] Or as Brownson himself expressed his plight: "The poor American
Catholic, rejected by his countrymen as a Catholic [convert], and by his
Catholic brethren as an American asserting the right of American nationality on American soil, runs but a narrow chance for his life. Happily, however, if his motives are pure, he has an unfailing resource in God."[26]

The charge from among non-Catholics that Brownson himself was the
cause of the whole wild uproar was scathingly fulminated by John Mitchel.
He of course spoke for the Irish. He had only recently escaped from Van
Dieman's land, to which he had been deported by the British government for
agitating for Irish freedom in his native Ireland. As an Irish patriot, having
suffered much for his homeland, he at once became an idol of the Irish in
America on his arrival here. Moreover, he was the wielder of a gifted, not to
say vitriolic, pen, and started at once a weekly journal called *The Citizen.*
Though not a Catholic, the great anti-Catholic excitement in the country —
aimed mainly at Irish Catholics — at once engaged his attention, and he
quickly took it upon himself to explain to Dr. Orestes Brownson that he was
himself the cause of the whole distressful affair. Referring to the anti-
Catholic furor, he addressed a long communication to Brownson in *The Citizen,* only a part of which is here set down:

> It is a bad world, Doctor, and the time is out of joint. A Native American
> party you approve; but *the* Native American party is all wrong. In respect it
> hates foreigners, you like it very well; but in respect it especially hates Catho-
> lic foreigners, it goes much against your stomach. In respect it knocks men
> down, look you, it fits your humor well; but in respect it knocks the wrong man
> down, it is tedious. Why will it set fire to the churches of its best friends? Why
> will it be hand in glove with German and Hungarian Revolutionists? Why hoot
> Bedini, and cheer Gavazzi, and hearken to the trump of the angel Gabriel? Why
> will it not come to *you,* and clothe itself in a soutane, and get a small tonsure
> on the top of its head, and comport itself like an Anglo-American penitent
> before its confessor?
> It will cost you much pains, I apprehend, to set all this right; especially as
> you, Doctor Orestes, *you* more than any one living man, have aroused and
> kindled this strong anti-Catholic, and therefore anti-Irish spirit in America, by
> your ultra-Catholic and anti-republican teachings and writings. Innumerable
> and disgusting *Shepherds of the Valley* and *Freeman's Journals* have
> been a brood of your begetting; and on the part of my Irish fellow-countrymen,

477

I accuse you of so misrepresenting them and their church before the American people, that any republican nation could not but look on them and all their ways with suspicion and abhorrence.

How easy it would be to turn you inside out now — and to point out in the pages of your own *Review* the very doctrines which have alarmed the genuine republican spirit of this country, and have given to the native party whatever genuine vigor it possesses! Since '48, you have regularly enlisted yourself on the side of the tyrants of Europe, regularly exerted yourself to cry down all attempts of the downtrodden people everywhere to throw off royal and imperial yokes, and become as American republicans.

And all your miserable echoes at the Press, from the Mississippi to Boston Bay, vied with you in adulation of Austria, and in heaping infamous names on the gallant republicans of Italy and France — nay, they improved on your doctrine of intolerance (for you could not restrain the fools within the bounds of your prudent example), until the land reverberated with anathemas on liberty; and men might almost fancy they heard the thunders of the Vatican bursting on the Alleghanies, and saw the tide of the Mississippi reddened by the fire of the Inquisition.

This, I say, has been your work, Doctor Orestes; *hence* has come whatever of bitterness and ferocity is to be found in the Native American party; this outrageous caricature of Catholicity, held up to America by you (after you had tired of all other religions) has been the principal spring, and is the only excuse for the furious anti-Irish spirit which is now raging.

One leading idea of the Native American party is alone sufficient to prove this. They say there must be drawn a distinction between "Citizens of America," and "subjects of the Pope." They have got the idea — it was from you and your echoes they caught it — that a Catholic must be a bad citizen. And if you and your echoes were true exponents of Catholicity, they would be right. In that case I would make no scruple to avow that no Catholic is fit to be a citizen of any country; and, not content with disfranchising, I would exterminate them.[27]

Whether or not Mitchel had dipped his pen in gall, this shows plainly that his notion of Brownson's doctrine on the supremacy of the spiritual order over the temporal was nothing more than a ridiculous caricature of its real meaning. But he was by no means the only one who had misunderstood or willfully misrepresented that doctrine. Nor is this surprising when we remember that distinguished persons in the Catholic Church either misunderstood or misrepresented his doctrine on this head, as we have already well noted. Brownson was at this time receiving letters from many persons throughout the country, containing garbled quotations from his *Review* occurring in local newspapers, inquiring whether he really maintained "the civil authority of the pope in this country," or whether he really held that Catholics owe "civil allegiance to the pope." Although Brownson had explained clearly in his articles on the subject that he plainly recognized the authority of the state as supreme in its own order, and asserted for the pope only a spiritual or indirect authority in temporals as the divinely appointed interpreter of the law of God for Catholics, both princes and people, certain phrases taken alone, such as "the temporal power of the Pope," might, either through ignorance or malice, be turned into the assertion of civil authority for the pope. Such apparently was done on the floor of the United States House of Representatives.

In the closing months of 1854, William S. Barry, a representative from Mississippi, tiring of the attacks of the Know-Nothings on the Catholic Church, launched a counterattack from the floor of the House. During the course of his vigorous denunciation, he asserted that the pope has no temporal power, and that consequently Catholicity poses no threat to the United States or any other civil government. Nathaniel P. Banks, a Know-Nothing member from Massachusetts, immediately took the floor, charging Catholics with holding the doctrine defended by Brownson of the supremacy of the spiritual order over the temporal, and protesting that such a doctrine is incompatible with the loyalty of the subject and the independence of the state. The main rejoinder to this came from Joseph R. Chandler, a representative from Pennsylvania. In replying, Chandler evaded the real point altogether by merely asserting that the pope claims no civil authority by divine right out of the Ecclesiastical States, and from that he pretended to conclude the complete moral independence of the temporal order.[28] (The hypothetical abuse of the pope in which Chandler indulged so eloquently in his speech must have turned the stomach of Brownson.)[29] This Gallicanism of Chandler was replied to by an able and learned Protestant divine, the Rev. John M'Clintock, D.D., editor of the *Methodist Quarterly Review*, in a publication entitled: *The Temporal Power of the Pope; containing the Speech of the Hon. R. Chandler, delivered in the House of Representatives of the United States, January 11, 1855. With Nine Letters, stating the prevailing Roman Catholic Theory in the Language of Papal Writers.*[30]

M'Clintock had shown in his treatise that it is perfectly idle to attempt to meet the objection of non-Catholics to the doctrine of the papal power on the ground assumed by Chandler, that is, that it is just a question of whether or not the Supreme Pontiff claims civil authority over states. Making copious extracts from Brownson's *Quarterly* he showed that the power claimed for the pope is spiritual, not temporal, or only an indirect power in temporals insofar as the Supreme Pontiff is the representative of the spiritual order on earth. He put the matter correctly when he said: "Every one knows that the pope never claimed any civil or political authority out of his dominions. The question is, whether he has 'an indirect temporal authority over kings and people in virtue of his spiritual authority'?"[31] In so stating the case he was accurately posing the question as Brownson had discussed it in the elaborate essays of his *Review*. From there M'Clintock went on to answer Chandler out of the mouths of a galaxy of weighty theologians Brownson had cited in support of his doctrine.

Not long after Chandler's speech in the House of Representatives, Brownson received a letter dated February 17, 1855, from a distinguished American Catholic layman, Richard H. Clarke, LL.D., in which he said in part:

> I cannot let this opportunity pass without returning my thanks to you for the pleasure and instruction I derived from your articles on Native Americanism and Know-Nothingism. They gratified me exceedingly. The outcry against you has been discreditable to the parties and very injudicious. I would have written to you at the time had I not felt that my feeble voice could add nothing to the testimonies of encouragement you were then receiving from the Catholic American public.
>
> But it seems to me, Doctor, there is a weak point on the Catholic side of the recent discussion of the Temporal Power of the Pope. I read in the "American Organ" (the Know-Nothing paper in Washington, D.C.) a complete refutation of Mr. Chandler's speech in Congress by a writer who simply quoted from your *Review*. Also a Methodist preacher answered Father Maguire's Lecture by quotations from Papal Bulls and Ultramontane Catholic writers. You will see at once that the weak point lies in the unfortunate fact that there are two oppos-

ing views on the Temporal Power prevailing among Catholics themselves. Our enemies cannot be silenced as long as they can answer Catholics out of the mouths of Catholics. Mr. Chandler and Father Maguire can never refute Know-Nothingism as long as they deny the indirect Temporal Power of the Pope. I think there is no practical advantage in discussing the question of the Temporal Power, but our enemies have forced us into the controversy, and we ought to maintain the Catholic side, not the Protestant side. Now the theory of the indirect Temporal Power properly explained and illustrated, can by no means offend against American nationality or any other nationality. This is the only answer that Catholics can consistently make against our accusers, and the only one we can successfully maintain. So far from being inconsistent with allegiance to the Constitution, the belief in the indirect Temporal Power properly understood but adds to the vigor of temporal allegiance to the state. Excuse this intrusion on your valuable time. I know of no one so suited for the task of proving that the opinion of the indirect Temporal Power is entirely without danger to the loyalty of Catholics [as yourself].

With great respect and esteem I remain as ever yours truly,

Richard H. Clarke[32]

There were, however, probably not a few who preferred that Brownson would not enter the fray set off by the speeches on the floor of the House of Representatives and just let the controversy die as noiselessly as possible. The great uproar against the Catholic Church was already alarmingly loud enough. What they wanted was peace and quiet. Perhaps some felt that there was really no one who, in the midst of so much confusion, could in fact make a good, effective reply in the case. At this time Fr. Isaac Hecker wrote Brownson a letter in which he said: "It was generally rumored that you would make an onslaught in this number [of your *Review*], but nothing of the kind being found in it, gave general satisfaction."[33] But Orestes Brownson was not the man to stand idly by and allow the Catholic Church to be smeared by its adversaries. He answered Dr. M'Clintock in a powerful article in the October 1855 issue of his *Review*.

He began by saying that M'Clintock's publication was one which he could not, with his sense of duty as a Catholic reviewer, pass over in silence. The authority of the pope in relation to temporal princes and governments is the great question of the day, he said, and cannot be blinked out of sight, if we would. We must meet it fairly and fearlessly, let it offend whom it may. Regarding Chandler's speech he remarked that it would have pleased him better, and, in his judgment, would have served the cause of Catholicity much better, had he in his place in the House repelled the charge brought by Mr. Banks against Catholics, by showing that even on the highest-toned Ultramontanism, so called, there is nothing in Catholicity incompatible with the loyalty of the subject, or the autonomy and independence of the state in its own order. In so speaking, Brownson had merely wished that Chandler had brought out clearly the great truth set forth by Vatican Council I when touching on the relations of "Church and State" it said in Chapter XIII:

God being the Author of the two societies, the Church and the State, it follows by the very nature of things that there can be no conflict or opposition between them. The Church by sanctifying men makes them better citizens, and confirms the authority of rulers by making obedience to them a matter of conscience.[34]

In replying directly to Dr. M'Clintock, Brownson complimented him for having quoted him correctly in the large extracts he had made from his

*Review,* and for having presented his views in a fair and objective manner. This is more, said Brownson, than some of our friends have done. But all this fairness, all this apparent honesty on the part of M'Clintock, observed Brownson, has a purpose. He fancies that in proving that Catholics do hold the doctrine which he himself had so recently and so valiantly defended would be to seal their condemnation in the estimation of the American people. Dr. M'Clintock had not tried to refute the doctrine, but had simply labeled it an "abominable doctrine," and felt sure nothing more was necessary to render the Catholic Church forever odious in the country than to convict it of holding that doctrine. While offering no argument against the doctrine itself, he seemed to regard it, like vice, as:

A monster of such frightful mien,

That to be hated needs but to be seen.

But we are disposed, said Orestes Brownson, to argue this point with the learned Doctor. We are inclined to believe that he has overshot the mark, and that when the excitement of the moment has subsided, his hate will serve powerfully the cause it was intended to ruin. The real question before the public is the supremacy of the spiritual order. Now, if there is anything which is a settled conviction with the American people, said Brownson, it is the incompetency of the state in spirituals, that there is a higher law than any civil constitution, which binds the prince no less than the subject, the state no less than the individual. That same principle of the supremacy of the spiritual order became embedded in American society already in our earliest colonial times with the founding of the Massachusetts Colony of the Puritans. The Puritans had been members of the Anglican Establishment, but had left England in protest against the Established Church because it had allowed the state jurisdiction in ecclesiastical affairs. They were ready to brave the hardships of exile, all the dangers and uncertainties of a bleak and inhospitable coast if only they could set up here an ecclesiastical establishment in which the independence and supremacy of the spiritual order in the face of the state would be recognized. (In this they only fell back on an old Catholic principle. For the Church had always stoutly insisted that the state has no right to meddle in ecclesiastical matters.)

This same principle of the supremacy of the spiritual order is presupposed, too, by all our free institutions. The American people, with one accord, subscribe to the doctrine which forms the principle of the argument in the Declaration of Independence, that the tyranny of the prince absolves the subject from his allegiance, and that there is a spiritual, a moral order above the civil, to which the temporal order is subject. They solemnly asserted that power is a trust, not an indefeasible right, when they declared the Colonies absolved from the allegiance to the British Crown, for no other reason than that George III had proved himself a tyrant, and the reassertion is made with the reading of the Declaration of Independence every Fourth of July celebration. They also asserted the moral order, over and above the civil, and independent of it, in their doctrine of the rights of man, when they prefixed the Bill of Rights to their constitutions.[35]

Dr. M'Clintock is a Protestant divine, said Brownson, of what particular denomination it does not matter, and evidently a man of intelligence, learning and ability. Is it necessary to tell him, he continued, that every Protestant sect in this country asserts, in principle, the very doctrine that we maintain. Every man who has any religion at all, be he Catholic, Protestant, Jew or Gentile, holds his religion to be the law of conscience, and hence the highest law, *lex suprema,* in short, the law of laws. Every man claims before the state to worship God according to the dictates of his conscience, or according to the regulations of the religious authority he acknowledges; and when the state comes into conflict with the solemn obligations of his religion, he replies in the words of the Apostles, "It is necessary to obey God rather than man." Whenever the civil law comes into conflict with the religious law, the civil, not the religious, must give way. No Protestant, no Muhammadan, nor Gentile even, dare deny this. The American people have declared it once and for all in declaring, not religious toleration, but religious freedom. Should the state ordain anything against any one of the sects, would it not tell the state, "You have transcended your province, and meddle with that which is above your power, and independent of it"? Most assuredly. Then every Protestant sect asserts the spiritual order above the temporal, religion as superior to politics, and therefore a law higher than the civil law, and to which, in case of conflict, the civil law must yield. Here in principle, asserted Brownson, is the whole doctrine which Dr. M'Clintock and those who cry out against us call "abominable."[36]

Although there is a great deal more to Brownson's reply to Dr. M'Clintock than is being given here, he summed up his thoughts fairly well in this particular section of his article by asking:

> Who then will dare to maintain that the assertion of the independence and supremacy of the spiritual order, and the subordination of the temporal, is the assertion of an abominable doctrine in the estimation of the American people? Have the American people become a body of atheists, denying God as King of kings and Lord of lords, denying moral justice, and the supremacy of right? Has not Dr. M'Clintock in his insane hostility to the Catholic Church forgotten himself and unwittingly branded as abominable the very principle he asserts, and must assert, in every sermon he preaches, or else shock all the moral convictions of his hearers? Has he, or any other who cries out against the doctrine we in our humble way have defended, the audacity to maintain before his class as professor, or an assembly of Americans as citizens, the contrary doctrine, that is, the independence and supremacy of the temporal, and the subordination of the spiritual — that political law overrides the religious, and that conscience must be subjected to the civil magistrate? No man not in need of physic and good regimen has the effrontery to do it. He who would do it would be hissed as a fool, abhorred as a moral monster, or confined as a lunatic. The native instincts of the human heart, the simplest common sense, would pronounce him a demon rather than a man. . . . Wherein then do we, in asserting the independence and supremacy [in the spiritual order] of the Pope as representative of Christ in the face of the secular authority, assert anything that is not asserted in principle by the American people? What right has Dr. M'Clintock to assume that our doctrine, when they understand it, will be regarded by them as "fearful," or as in any sense "objectionable"?[37]

In the same October 1855 issue of his *Quarterly,* in which he had pulverized Dr. M'Clintock's charges, he also replied to a different charge in a fourth article on the Know-Nothingism of the Massachusetts state council, held on August 7, 1855. In the platform they had adopted, they said: "We repudiate in indignant terms such sentiments as these, put forth by the representatives of the papal power: that Protestantism has no rights in the presence of Catholicism.' " To which Brownson made reply in characteristic frankness:

> "Protestantism has no rights in the presence of Catholicity." This sentence is, we believe, from our *Review,* and was written by its editor. We do

not deny, and are prepared to stand by it. But we have never said, "Protestants have no rights in the presence of Catholics." Between the two assertions there is a distance. We speak as a Catholic, and as a Catholic we hold of course Catholicity to be the true and only true religion. We do not concede that Protestantism is or possibly can be true. In the mind of a Catholic there can be no room for doubt, and on this point there is nothing left to be settled. Catholicity is true, and Protestantism, as its contradictory, is and cannot but be false. We do not admit the possibility of our being wrong in this, or of Protestantism being right. We are as certain we are right as we are that we exist, or that it is impossible for God to lie; and as certain as we are that we are right, so certain we are that Protestantism is a huge error, a Satanic delusion. Now, as error can never have any rights in the presence of truth, Protestantism can have none in the presence of Catholicity. This is what we do and must say as a Catholic, for we are not seeking for the true religion. We have found it.[38]

After further noting such outrageous Know-Nothing charges against Catholics as "religious liberty is only to be endured until the opposite can be established with safety to the Catholic world," and that "Catholics in America are bound to abide by the interpretation put upon the Constitution by the Pope of Rome," he lamented as one of the most painful things, in controversy with anti-Catholics, to be always obliged to complain of the gross perversions and misrepresentations of their writers. It was in sorrow, not anger, that he was compelled to say that since he had become a Catholic, he had not found the least approach to loyalty and good faith in a no-popery opponent. Perversions and forgeries were the stock in trade. And he added a significant point that may well have had more meaning than he at the time fully realized: "Can it be wondered at, that, when a party [the Know-Nothings] professing to be in a special sense American, publishes such foul calumnies, foreign-born Catholics should manifest an unwillingness to Americanize and fraternize with the natives?"[39]

Brownson had by this time become a special target for the Know-Nothings in the land. While it is true that his writings were not the cause of the present excitement, it would be foolish to deny that his advocacy of the indirect power of the pope (spiritual) in civil matters was not being used to fan the widespread excitement into a greater turbulence — that is, as its meaning could so easily be twisted and misrepresented by the enemies of the Catholic Church. He received at this time a letter, dated October 1, 1855, from a group of sincere and honorable Protestant gentlemen of Poolsville, Montgomery County, Maryland, inquiring as to precisely what was his doctrine on the power of the pope concerning the duties of Catholics in the United States. As an attempt was being made with the approach of elections to introduce the contents of a witch's caldron into American politics through garbled quotations from his *Review*, these sincere gentlemen had become alarmed. They were Democrats, members of the so-called Catholic party at the time, and they were having trouble repelling the foul calumnies hurled at the party because of its large Catholic constituency. In their letter they said in part:

To Orestes A. Brownson
Sir:
    The period of our elections draws near, political discussions run high, parties are bitterly arrayed against each other, and public meetings, and political speeches have become the order of the day. We are democrats, and consequently opposed to the destructive party called *Know-Nothings.*
    In all public meetings of the K.N. [Know-Nothings] their text from begin-

ning to end of the address, is the pope — Brownson (yourself) and Catholicity. Now, Sir, we wish to be just to our adopted citizens. You are accused of writing derogatory to our principles as Americans, and to our institutions. These charges we do not believe, and in order that we may be able effectually to contradict such charges, we beg that you will enable us, by some means, written or printed, to put our accusers to shame, and brand them with the lies for which K. N. [Know-Nothingism] is so prolific. We beg also, that you will, if possible, send us your *Review* containing allegiance to the pope and your strictures on the speech of Mr. Chandler of Pa. delivered in defense of Catholic principles during the last session of Congress, etc, etc.

We therefore submit the following questions, hoping they will at once receive a cordial and sincere reply, to be forwarded to our post-master.

1. Are you the acknowledged organ of the Catholic Church in the United States?

2. Do the Catholic Bishops of the United States acknowledge your *Review* as the propounder of Catholic faith?

3. Do you believe, or did you ever assert in your *Review*, that the Catholics of the United States owed temporal allegiance to the pope — of Rome?

4. Do you believe, or did you ever assert in your *Review*, that the principles contained in the speech of [The] Hon. Mr. Chandler were not the principles of the Catholic Church?

Assuring Brownson that their intentions were honest and sincere, as he must recognize, they subscribed themselves, "Respectfully, your fellow-citizens, T. Randolph Hall; Benjamin F. Reid; George W. Chriswell; William A. Chriswell; C. N. Mossburg; Howard Griffith."

In his letter of reply, dated October 8, 1855, Brownson informed these gentlemen that he could not send them the edition of his *Review* in which he had asserted allegiance, if they meant *civil* allegiance, to the pope, because he had never published any such issue. He had never asserted, out of the Papal State, any civil authority or jurisdiction for the pope, or any other than spiritual allegiance to him as the duty of Catholics. Those who had accused him, whether Catholics or non-Catholics, of maintaining that Catholics owe civil allegiance to the visible head of their Church, had grossly misrepresented him. He went on to say in his letter:

The accusation that I have published writings derogatory to our institutions and the principles of Americans, is false. I have uniformly, on all occasions, defended the institutions of our country, and contended that every American citizen is bound in conscience to defend them against every attack upon them, let the attack come from what quarter it may. I am not a revolutionary or a radical. I am a conservative, and believe it my duty to lay down my life, if need be, in defense of American institutions and liberties bequeathed us by our American ancestors. I am bound to do this as a patriot and a Catholic.

Allow me to say, gentlemen, that there never was, and never can be a more ridiculously false charge than that brought against us Catholics of hostility to American liberty and disloyalty to republican institutions. We are men and Americans as well as you, and yield to none of you in our love of liberty or of country. Our religion condemns every species of tyranny, because all tyranny is a violation of the law of God, and it makes it our duty to be peaceable citizens and loyal subjects. We cannot be disloyal to the republican constitution of this country without violating our duty as Catholics. In countries where despotism reigns, men may lawfully by lawful means seek to change the government, and establish institutions which guaranty the rights of man; but in this country we have those institutions, and our duty, whether Catholics or non-Catholics, is to preserve them, and to secure their free development and wise and just application. This, gentlemen, has always been and always will be, the uniform tenor of my writings.

To your first question: "Are you the acknowledged organ of the Catholic Church in the United States?" I answer, no, I am not. The only acknowledged organ of the Catholic Church in the United States, as elsewhere, if we speak strictly, is the Pope, and in common with him the bishops, each in his own diocese.

To your second question: "Do the bishops of the United States acknowledge your *Review* as the propounder of the Catholic faith?" I answer, as an authoritative propounder of the faith, no; as generally conforming in its doctrine to the Catholic faith, yes, otherwise they would censure it as heretical.

You ask in your third question: "Do you believe, or did you ever assert in your *Review* that Catholics in the United States owed (owe) temporal allegiance to the Pope of Rome?" I answer, *Never.* I owe obedience to the Pope only as the spiritual head of my Church, and I assert for him as such only a spiritual authority. Nevertheless, I have maintained and maintain that this spiritual authority extends to the morality of temporal things, that is, to temporal things, in so far, and only in so far, as they are spiritually related or have a spiritual character; that is, so far as to have the right to pronounce for the Catholic conscience, whether they do or do not conform to the law of God; for the Pope as head of the Church is the interpreter and judge for Catholics of the divine law, natural or revealed. To explain myself. The people of this country had on their gaining their independence the right to adopt such a form or constitution of government, not repugnant to natural justice or the law of God, as seemed to them good; this constitution, when adopted, is obligatory upon me as a Catholic citizen, and not being repugnant to the divine law, is obligatory on the Pope in his relations with us as upon me. Then every law made in conformity to it is obligatory on my conscience, and consequently on the conscience of the Pope; for what binds the conscience of the simple believer binds alike the conscience of bishop and of Pope. The Pope has recognized the American constitution as compatible with the law of God. Suppose the supreme court decided the fugitive-slave law to be constitutional, then I am bound in conscience to obey that law, and the Pope cannot dispense me from my obligation to obey. Suppose, however, the constitution or a law passed under it should command me to be an idolater, a Mormon, a Mahometan [Muhammadan], or a Presbyterian, the Pope would have the right to forbid me to obey it, and to declare the law, and the constitution in so far as it authorizes such a law, null and void for the Catholic conscience, because [it is] repugnant to the law of God. But in either case, you will perceive, gentlemen, that I assert no civil or temporal jurisdiction for the Supreme Pontiff, for I extend his authority only to the decision of the spiritual question involved in the temporal.

You ask, finally, if I believe or have asserted in my *Review* that the principles contained in the speech of the Hon. Mr. Chandler are not the principles of the Catholic Church? This question will be best answered by the first article of my last *Review* [his reply to Dr. M'Clintock] a copy of which I send you. I have never asserted and do not maintain that Mr. Chandler's principles are incompatible with Catholic faith; I only maintain that in the sense in which the public will understand him and in which not unlikely he understands himself, he sets forth, not Catholic doctrine, but the opinion of some Catholics, which as a Catholic he *may* hold, but is not obliged to hold. I regard his speech as evasive, and as not meeting the question fairly and frankly. The real question is not whether the Pope claims civil or temporal jurisdiction over Catholics in the United States, for that cannot be pretended; but whether the spiritual authority of the Pope is incompatible with the freedom and independence of the state in its own order. Conceding that when the temporal and spiritual come in conflict, the temporal, not the spiritual must give way, or when religion and politics come in conflict, politics, not religion, must yield, I say, and say fearlessly, that it is not, and all Catholics without exception agree that it is not. Every

Catholic does and must maintain the freedom and independence of the secular authority in its own order.

Thus, gentlemen, I have endeavored to answer your questions frankly and without evasion or reserve, because I am bound to declare my faith when it is necessary, and I have no opinion which I wish to conceal or to explain away. I know that the charges brought both against my Church and even against myself are false. I am an American by birth and education, and I yield to no man in my love of my country or in my loyalty as a citizen. I know that my religion is favorable to liberty, and commands me to be loyal to American republicanism. Personally, I belong to and support the same political party as you do. But I claim the divine, the natural, and the civil right to be a member of the Catholic Church, to worship God by believing what she teaches, and doing what she commands. This right may be denied me. I may be persecuted unto death for daring to exercise it, but I shall never surrender it. I recognize your undoubted right as American citizens to be Protestants, and I demand of you to recognize equally my right as an American citizen to be a Catholic, uncensured and unquestioned. This right is the basis of all true freedom, and he is no true American, no true man, who will not, if need by, die in its defense.

I have the honor to be, gentlemen, your most obedient servant,

O. A. Brownson[40]

The gentlemen to whom this communication was addressed gave it immediately to the public press as an effective answer to the attacking Know-Nothings.

While this high drama was being played out on the open stage of the public, a much less public drama was being enacted behind these public scenes, of which Brownson himself could have had little knowledge, though he may possibly have in the meantime heard some distant rumblings of what was going on. In any case at all, the great anxiety of the leading American bishops over the stormy course his *Review* had embarked upon was in due time to come to his attention. The chief source of anxiety to the bishops was, however, their names on the cover of his *Review*.

# 32

## THE AMERICAN BISHOPS IN A DITHER AND BROWNSON'S PAPAL DOCTRINE

*The mischievous use the Know-Nothings were making of Brownson's* Review • *Bishop Martin John Spalding of Louisville leads a campaign to have those episcopal names removed from the cover of Brownson's* Review. *He writes to Archbishop John Baptist Purcell of Cincinnati • He is joined in his campaign by Bishop Michael O'Connor of Pittsburgh • Purcell writes to Archbishop Francis Patrick Kenrick of Baltimore, urging him to take the matter in hand with Brownson • Kenrick is disposed to temporize • Purcell repeats his plea to Kenrick • Kenrick informs Purcell that he has written to Bishop John Bernard Fitzpatrick of Boston about the matter (Brownson's bishop), and expresses the hope that Brownson will of his own volition drop their names from the cover of his* Review *with the January issue of the next year • Kenrick finally does write Brownson a diplomatic letter in February of 1855 urging him to indicate distinctly in the next edition of his* Review *that the bishops' names by no means imply an endorsement of his every view or opinion • With this Brownson complies at once • But Brownson thinks it more advisable to wait until January of the next year before dropping the bishops' names altogether • In September he receives a letter from Bishop O'Connor calling upon him to drop his name altogether • Bishop O'Connor had referred obliquely in his letter to Brownson's papal doctrine, and this gave Brownson a welcome chance to unburden himself to the bishop in a long letter on what he considered unfair treatment at the hands of O'Connor in their controversy over the papal power • Bishop John Hughes of New York considers Brownson's articles on the papal power impolitic, and charges him with a change of doctrine • Brownson's letter of protest • Letters of Bishop Spalding and Archbishop Kenrick showing the wild violence threatening Catholics • Letters between Brownson and the novelist, Jedediah V. Huntington • Brownson receives a bracing letter from his good friend, Judge G. H. Hinton of Cincinnati.*

It is in no sense surprising that the bishops of the country had now for some time been gravely questioning the advisability of any longer allowing their names to appear on the cover of Brownson's *Review*. He had for the last two or three years kept some of the more prominent prelates of the country continually in hot water, and they had been feverishly writing back and forth to each other on what must be done in the perplexing circumstances. Brownson's great ability as an intrepid champion (even confessor) of the faith they did not of course question, but his persistent public discussion of Catholic doctrines so obnoxious to his non-Catholic countrymen — that was quite another thing. And their names shining there on the cover of his *Review* seemed to imply that they were with him hand in glove in every word he wrote. Among the prelates, no one campaigned more industriously, in letters especially to Archbishop Purcell of Cincinnati, to get those episcopal names off the cover of Brownson's *Review* than did Martin John Spalding of Louisville, Kentucky. And not without reason, for Kentucky, and apparently Louisville in particular, was, like Massachusetts, a veritable hotbed of the Know-Nothings — as was also Maryland, the state in which Archbishop Francis Patrick Kenrick presided. As Ray Billington observed, in the election of 1854, "among border states Maryland and Kentucky went solidly Know-Nothing."[1]

It is interesting to note that although Bishop Fitzpatrick would not come out publicly and defend him, in spite of all the furor, he stood firmly by Brownson in the doctrines he had been advocating. And it is further interesting to note that of those bishops who were in a dither over the continuance of their names on the cover of Brownson's *Review,* no one of them, feeling a great delicacy in the matter, seemed willing to take the affair in hand and write Brownson. Perhaps part of the difficulty was that they sensed that Brownson had Bishop Fitzpatrick behind him.

Bishop Spalding first complained of Brownson in a letter to Archbishop Purcell of Cincinnati, on July 12, 1853. After censuring the indiscreet zeal of converts, he said:

> The article of Brownson on Nativism is most ill timed & badly advised; as much so as were his lucubrations on the power of the Popes. Why could he not have judgment enough to confine himself to the points of real importance, & opportune to our circumstances? Bishop Fitzpatrick is his chief adviser, & I would figure that if you would write a letter to this prelate, strongly stating our view of Mr. Brownson's course, it would do good.[2]

But in his letter of three weeks later to Purcell on August 2, Spalding quickly came to the matter of those episcopal names emblazoning the cover of Brownson's *Review*. Keeping in mind that Louisville was an active nest of Know-Nothings, his agitation is understandable. He said:

> Brownson is doing a world of mischief in Louisville. The Know-Nothings are availing themselves of his articles on the Temporal Power of the Popes & on Nativism; particularly the former, to prove that we are in fact hypocrites & traitors. They triumphantly refer to what they call the endorsement of the Bishops on the cover of the *Review*. Why is that permitted to remain? I would cheerfully unite with any number of Prelates in giving him a hint (not a Paddy's hint), to have that recommendation, cautiously worded though it be, omitted in the future. We are likely to have a warm time yet, before many months will elapse. But God is stronger than the devil; and persecution will in the long run do us good. [The last two sentences could well have been purloined from Brownson's writings.][3]

Following this up with another letter in the same month to Archbishop Purcell (August 20), Spalding wrote:

> Bishop O'Connor (of Pittsburgh) is anxious to have the names of the Bishops omitted by Brownson in the future, and writes to me to request that I . . . give Brownson a hint in the matter. But I think Archbishop Kenrick of Bal-

timore who drew up the recommendation, would be the proper person to act in the premises.[4]

Under pressure from these two prelates, Purcell, who no doubt at all felt the same as they did about the affair, did write to Archbishop Kenrick to urge him to take the matter in hand with Brownson, he being the incumbent, too, of what was then considered the primatial see. (Unfortunately we do not have letters from the archives of the archdiocese of Baltimore.) Others, too, may have been working on Kenrick in the meantime. Whatever the case, Kenrick's letter to Purcell, dated August 25, 1854, is evidently a reply to one written to him by Purcell. After saying that we should all be prepared for martyrdom in these exciting times, he showed that he was disposed to temporize regarding a request to Brownson for a removal of the bishops' names from the cover of his *Review*. He said:

> I am sorry Mr. Brownson has written so unwisely; but I do not fear for his faith. [We have seen before that Purcell did have misgivings about Brownson's faith.] His honesty prompted him to say without disguise what thousands whisper among their friends, without venturing to proclaim it in our teeth. I should be sorry to have to request the omission of my letter from his cover. It was written at the request of the Bishop of Boston, and without any forethought of its being made to serve as an endorsement of all his future views. To withdraw it would be painful, but in all probability he will commence a new series in January, and drop the recommendation. In the meantime the protests of the various Catholic papers will neutralize its effects.
>
> Your br. in C.,
> Francis Patrick Kenrick, A.B.[5]

Purcell apparently replied to this letter rather promptly, urging him again to write Brownson about the matter. To which Kenrick replied in another letter, written in September 1854, saying:

> I feel a great delicacy in suggesting to Brownson to drop the cover. I have written to the Bishop of Boston expressing my dissent from his positions. His trip to Ireland will probably lead to an entire change in reference to the *Review*. Our dissent [evidently referring to that expressed through some Catholic publications] has been so strongly expressed in various quarters that I do not suppose he will claim us as supporters for the new volume. The October number will probably appear with the same cover.
>
> Your devoted s. in Xt.,
> Francis Patrick Kenrick[6]

How devoutly Kenrick wished to absolve himself of any obligation in the affair! But in spite of his hesitations and hopes in the matter, he was soon now to write Brownson about the matter. We do not have any evidence of just what brought him to this decision. But we should not forget that Maryland was one of the border states that had gone "solidly Know-Nothing" in the elections of 1854. And Kenrick may well have been treated to quite a spectacle of their menacing carryings-on in Baltimore itself. He had hoped that Brownson would drop those episcopal names from his *Review* with the January 1855 issue. But he had not. And that fiery debate on the floor of the United States House of Representatives between Nathaniel Banks and Joseph Chandler over Brownson's papal doctrine had broken out in the last months of 1854. Did Kenrick feel that things were getting quite too hot for the tranquillity and safety of Catholics? Whatever the case, some weeks after that debate had flared up on the floor of the House of Representatives,

Kenrick took pen in hand on February 12, 1855, to write Brownson. He showed the master's touch in diplomacy in the two letters he wrote. The first read:

> Dear Sir:
> So much use is made of our endorsement of your *Review* by our enemies, that I think it advisable for you to state distinctly in your next number that it was not intended or employed as a sanction of every opinion or view, which you had advanced even at that time, much less of those which you might at any time afterwards advance.
> Your zeal and ability are commended, and still deserve commendation, but as we do not desire to abridge your liberty in matters not defined by the Church, so we cannot be fairly held accountable for the expression of your sentiments. Some explanation seems required at the present time since your essays on the temporal power are brought forward to prove that we profess principles at variance with our civil duties. By dropping the endorsement you will be more at liberty to state your views, without rendering us responsible, and I trust you will lose nothing, as your *Review* is able to stand on its own merits. You know too well my personal attachment to ascribe this letter to any but friendly feelings.
>
> > Your faithful friend,
> > Francis Patrick Kenrick,
> > Arch'p, Balt.[7]

Having begun the year 1855 with the names of the bishops on the cover of his *Review*, Brownson felt that to drop them now during this same year might seem to imply some sudden change of feelings between the bishops and himself. He considered it much more advisable to make the change with the first edition of the next year. To this suggestion Kenrick replied in the following letter, February 24, 1855:

> Dear Sir:
> I should be sorry to urge you to any measure likely to prove prejudicial to the interests of your *Review,* or to counsel you to do anything without the advice of the bishop, not as superior or director, so much as a friend and earnest well-wisher. Your own prudence will dictate the best course to be adopted to meet the effort which is made to convert our letter of endorsement into an approval of every sentiment or view which you may express. I earnestly desire that your *Review* may be supported, as I am fully convinced of your zeal in supporting the cause of truth. I leave, then, the matter entirely in your own hands, and renew the expression of my unfeigned regard.
>
> > Your constant friend,
> > Francis Patrick Kenrick, A.B.[8]

It is a pleasure to note that Archbishop Kenrick signed himself, "Your constant friend," and so he was indeed. Whatever the trouble Brownson had with other bishops or archbishops, here was a great prelate who never had any misunderstandings with Brownson in any way. This in spite of the fact that Brownson freely criticized his literary productions, though with becoming reverence, pointing out what he considered less meritorious.[9] Archbishop Francis Patrick Kenrick, it need scarcely be said, was perhaps the most brilliant ornament of the American hierarchy of the day in his vast and varied ecclesiastical erudition. His brother Peter, archbishop of St. Louis, was also a good and faithful friend of Brownson. Referring apparently to fulminations against Brownson from some episcopal organs of the day, he said in a letter dated October 7, 1855: "I believe that Brownson & the *Shep-*

*herd of the Valley* have been hardly treated, although I have no idea of discussing their merits or demerits as the case may be."[10]

Brownson lost no time in complying with the wish of Archbishop Kenrick. The next issue of his *Review,* April 1855, carried the following statement:

> We notice with pain a disposition among our Know-Nothing writers to hold the bishops whose names are on the cover of our *Review* responsible for whatever sentiment or doctrine is found in our pages. This is wrong. The bishops have kindly encouraged the publication of our *Review,* having confidence in our loyal intentions, and believing it, upon the whole, useful to the cause of truth; but they endorse no sentiment or doctrine we advance. The whole responsibility rests upon the editor alone, and no bishop is responsible for anything that appears in our pages, and every one is just as free to controvert or condemn anything in our pages as he would be were his name not on our cover. We beg our opponents to bear this in mind, and to remember that our *Review* does not, in any sense whatever, speak by authority of the American hierarchy, and has no other endorser than its lay editor, who is free to write and publish, simply holding himself responsible to the proper authorities, what he pleases. The merit or blame, if either, in all cases belongs to him, and the public cannot justly hold anybody else in any respect responsible. We commend this especially to the notice of Professor M'Clintock and Dr. Edward Beecher.[11]

That Brownson saw the reasonableness, not to say the necessity in the circumstances, of dropping from the cover of his *Review* the names of the bishops, can scarcely be doubted. Yet he seemingly felt some chagrin in the matter. In a letter to his close friend, Dr. Jeremiah W. Cummings, dated February 21, 1855, he wrote:

> Rev. and Dear Doctor:
> At present, my *Review* is doing well as ever. The native discussion has not hurt it, but how it will be affected by the papal question I cannot say. I learn that I am to be sacrificed as a peace offering to the politicians. But perhaps it will not be so bad as I fear. I shall be obliged, only do not mention it, to leave off the names of the archbishops and bishops, and to publish the *Review* solely on my own responsibility, so as to save the hierarchy from the charge of endorsing me. Whether this will ruin me or not remains to be seen. It is hinted from a high quarter that I had better do this, and do it of my own accord. I shall do so without communicating with a single bishop. It seems it is necessary for the peace of the Church that I should make way for the Chandlers to defend Catholicity on Gallican principles.[12]

After the definitive notice he had given freeing the bishops from any responsibility for the contents of his *Review,* Brownson had intended, as he had indicated to Kenrick, to wait until the new year before dropping the bishops' names from his *Review.* But well before 1856 rolled in, he received a letter, dated September 4, 1855, from Michael O'Connor, bishop of Pittsburgh, requesting him to remove his name from the cover of his *Review.* After all, the question of the papal power was still a raging issue in Brownson's pages, and he was still stoutly upholding the doctrine O'Connor had professed to controvert. This was scarcely very palatable to O'Connor. He referred to it in the letter he addressed to Brownson, in which he wrote:

> Dear Sir:
> I am sorry that a sense of duty compels me to request you to withdraw my name from the letter printed on your cover containing a certain approbation of

your *Review.* I do not think that that letter made any of your signers fairly responsible for anything you wrote, and hence though I occasionally found doctrines advanced from which I widely differed, I did not feel called upon to record my disapprobation or to withdraw my name. But since you have adopted as a leading principle of your *Review* a theory which I believe to be itself untrue and the advocacy of which I consider likely to do much mischief, especially if it were considered to be encouraged by any number of the bishops of the country, I feel myself called upon to withdraw any connection with the publication that would seem to imply any kind of approbation.

Yours faithfully in Christ,<br>
M. O'Connor, B'p Pittsb.[13]

Bishop O'Connor referred obliquely to the controversy he had had with Brownson over the papal power, and this gave Brownson a chance in the course of his letter to say some things that must have been weighing heavily on his chest for quite some time. His letter turned out to be mainly a defense of his ultramontane doctrine and himself. He wrote in part:

Rt. Rev. and Dear Sir:

I regret that you have judged it necessary to make the request, but of course it will be complied with.

It has been from last May my intention to leave out altogether the letter with the signatures at the commencement of the new volume. Had I followed my judgment, that letter would never have appeared in my *Review,* but I was assured that it was intended to be inserted. I felt it would cause me some embarrassment and involve me in some trouble. I did not like to leave it out after a volume had commenced (for this year), and when such an outcry was raised, because I was sure for myself that to do so would be impolitic. But with the next number it will be quietly omitted, and the *Review* henceforth be published on my own responsibility, so as to compromise nobody but myself. Most likely I shall remove from Boston and publish my *Review* in another city, as the approval of my bishop does not appear to be any protection to me in the minds of his Episcopal brethren. I shall not publish without the *permission* of my Diocesan, for I am a Catholic — but shall endeavor to let the *Review* stand on its own merits, so that any bishop or any Catholic can say, O! that is one of Brownson's ultraisms, nobody is responsible for what he says.

The Bishop of Pittsburgh will permit me to say that I feel that in his articles against me he has treated me neither generously nor fairly. I do not hold, never have held, and never have set forth or defended the doctrine he persists in laying to my charge, if I may be the judge of my own language and meaning. I think he was bound to give me the benefit of my own explanations and qualifications. I think I have received hard treatment at his hands, and that he has excited an uncalled for prejudice against me. He denounced me, held me up to execration, instead of discussing the question with me. Even he does not accuse me of heterodoxy, and must admit that I have the right to hold even the opinion he ascribed to me, for it has never been condemned, which is more than can be said of some of the opinions he opposed to me. He opposed to me, if I understand him, opinions, or an opinion, condemned by John XXII and Pius VI. If I understand him he denies the right of the Pope to visit the political acts of a secular prince with ecclesiastical censures, which I think is unsustainable.

I think I had a right to hold the doctrine I set forth. I might have been imprudent to publish it. Some three or four bishops have told me that they thought differently, that it was not. I myself believed it prudent, and still believe so, and furthermore I think but for your articles against me that no great outcry would have been raised against us on account of its publication. I know something of the American people, and I am confident that you will never make them believe that my doctrine on the subject is not the true Catholic doctrine. All the bishops in the universe may disclaim it, and they will still believe it. You may silence me, but you will gain no credit with them, and only lose a portion of their respect, both for yourselves and for Catholicity.

Permit me to say that the clamor raised against us does not frighten me, and that the best way to disarm it is to show that we do not fear it. I think there has been some lack of firmness on our part. This is, indeed, the opinion of a layman, but a layman even may sometimes have a sound opinion.

I intended not to reply to your first article, as I told you, but on arriving home I found an order requiring me to do it. I intended to close with my indirect reply to your second article, and should have said no more, if the other side had remained silent. Indeed, I have done nothing since but offer some explanations of my doctrine. . . . Of course, I do not abandon my doctrine. You must either convince my reason that it is wrong, or bring me a judgment from Rome condemning it, before I can do that. I have a profound respect for your judgment, but you cannot expect me to take it as the judgment of the Supreme Pontiff, who is your judge as well as mine.

I have written frankly, perhaps too frankly, but be assured that in my own heart not disrespectfully. I have expressed my grievances, but for your many acts of paternal kindness, and your frequent forbearance towards me, be assured I am deeply grateful, and shall be as long as I live. I owe you much, and I would that I were able to pay you much. But after all, my position is a difficult one, and I, too, have had some things to bear from those whom I counted on to sustain me. I am denounced by the whole non-Catholic world, and there is hardly a Catholic voice raised publicly in my defense. The disposition of many Catholics appears to be to recognize as little solidarity with me as possible. These are not pleasant things. But God knows what is best; I will not murmur. Forgive what is wrong in my letter, and believe me truly your obedient servant in Xt.

O. A. Brownson

Rt. Rev. M. O'Connor
Bishop of Pittsburgh[14]

Archbishop Hughes of New York was another prelate that expressed to Brownson his anxiety over the articles he had published on the power of the pope. He considered them inopportunely published, and thought that Brownson had really changed his doctrine on the subject. To which Brownson replied that the opportuneness of proclaiming a truth may well be gauged by the opposition it arouses. As to having changed his doctrine on the subject, he stoutly denied it. "In what respect you think I have changed," he wrote, "you do not specify, but you say I have abandoned my former ground. Is it not as likely that you have misapprehended my real meaning as it is that I have changed without knowing it? I am the best judge of my own meaning, and I tell you that I have in no respect changed or modified the doctrine of my *Review* on the papal question, and I deny the right of any man, be he who he may, to say that I have. What you really mean to accuse me of, I do not know."[15]

In reply the archbishop wrote from New York on July 7, 1854:

My Dear Mr. Brownson:

I do not think that I should have written to you, if I could have foreseen that my remarks would have afflicted you as much as your letter would seem to indicate. I fear that not much can be gained by private correspondence on the subject, for experience teaches us, that written language is oftentimes liable to be misapprehended by the reader, whereas, if the writer were present to explain, the misunderstanding might easily be removed. I fear very much that the two articles alluded to will give occasion to much injurious speculation, and prove detrimental to the *Review,* which I was amongst the first to encourage, and shall be amongst the last to give up. You may be sure I never doubted the purity of your intentions or the uprightness of your motives in publishing them. Still, whilst all things are lawful some things are inexpedient, and among them I cannot help numbering these two articles. To recall them now, is, as you remark, impossible — to discuss them would be making bad worse. And if they should ever be alluded to by me, or any other Catholic writer, I should wish it done in a style and manner so remote as not to seem to have any direct bearing on the topics discussed. I am sorry to say that more than one of your subscribers have spoken to me on the subject, and with feelings of regret, kindred to those which the perusal of them awakened in me. For my own part, I am decidedly opposed to any notice being taken of them in our Catholic papers. But I feel the enemy will not allow them to escape. I would wish the subject to be dropped, and as far as depends on me, it shall not be alluded to either in writing or in conversation. I am exceedingly sorry that I have caused you pain — that would be far from my intention. And even though I may be myself mistaken, I would have you not to be in the least discouraged by what I have said. I regret that it is not convenient for you to spend a week or ten days with me; but I hope I shall have the pleasure of seeing you in the course of a little time. So far as I am concerned, the matter is now at an end, and I have only to assure you of the continued friendship and good wishes, with which I subscribe myself your devoted friend and servant in Christ.

John, Abp. of N. York

Orestes A. Brownson, Esq., Boston[16]

It cannot be emphasized too much that this whole drama of excitement was set against a backdrop of wild and desperate times. It was not at all that the bishops did not appreciate Brownson for the extraordinary man he was, but they could not but be alarmed at the menacing turn events were taking. How bad things had got in Louisville Bishop Spalding indicated in a letter to Archbishop Purcell, dated September 6, 1855, when he said:

> Brownson and the editor of the *Shepherd [of the Valley]* have done us great harm. Their names have been paraded from every stand in the South, particularly Kentucky. . . . Had they been sworn enemies of the Church, they could not have done as much harm. I think we ought to take some steps to repudiate them *publicly*.
>
> [In a postscript he added:] Many Catholics have left Louisville and many others will leave. Some of my congregations have been diminished over one half.[17]

And how bad matters were growing in Baltimore is indicated in another letter of Archbishop Kenrick to Archbishop Purcell. He wrote on January 20, 1857:

> The assassination of the Archbishop of Paris is a sad event. Some time ago you were in danger [during the Bedini riots], and I could not be considered secure. We must be ready at all times. Some rowdies from Ohio broke [one of] my windows between two and three o'clock at night. They came as a deputation from Ohio to congratulate Maryland on her singular felicity in the late election, and after speeches and a good dinner, some of the Company during the night shouted and threw stones.
>
> [He added a postscript:] I was pleased to see the generous plea of the *Telegraph* for Brownson. His subscribers are reduced to a small number. I hope they will rapidly increase, and that he will avoid obnoxious topics.[18]

Another prominent individual who had misunderstood Brownson's papal doctrine was Jedediah V. Huntington. He had been editor of the *Metropolitan* when Bishop O'Connor had made his attack on what he made out to be Brownson's doctrine, but had in the meantime exchanged editorship of that journal for the editorship of *The Leader,* a Catholic weekly in St. Louis. Having gathered his false notions of Brownson's papal doctrine from the misrepresentations of Bishop O'Connor, he thought Brownson had altered his doctrine when he read his reply to Dr. M'Clintock and his letter to the Maryland gentlemen when it appeared in the press. He could now approve Brownson's doctrine and said so, in spite of the fact that he was still somewhat irate over some former criticisms Brownson had made of his novels.[19] This change of mind and heart toward him, showing at least a disposition now to be fair, pleased Brownson and it was the occasion of an exchange of letters between the two. Brownson's first letter was a concerted effort to show Huntington that he had never changed his papal doctrine in any sense whatsoever. His second letter dealt entirely with the attacks which Huntington and others had made on him for holding that doctrine. Huntington had acknowledged that he had joined in the outcry against Brownson as it gave him an easy opportunity to even scores with him because of some observations Brownson had made on his novels. In his reply from Boston on August 25, 1855, Brownson wrote in part:

J. V. Huntington, Esq.
My Dear Sir:
    I thank you for your very kind letter, but deeply regret to learn that you were obliged to write in bed. I knew you were unwell, but I thought you had recovered. I hope you will soon find yourself in health, and that our good God will long spare you to us.
    Your reason for occasionally attacking me in your columns is frankly stated. I can understand it, but it would not serve my purpose. I can, I think, if need be, die for the truth, but I cannot deny it, or attack my friend for defending it, however fierce may be the popular cry against him. When we find our friends doing what we ourselves are doing and wish to have done, the more honorable course is, it seems to me, to back them, not to turn against them because they happen to be unpopular. Your explanation is what I expected, only you appear to do from friendship what I supposed no man would do except from personal hostility.
    You say you praise me in banter, because otherwise you would not praise me at all. It may be so; but your bantering praise happens to be less useful to me, and more offensive, than no praise at all. I am not so greedy of praise as to be pleased with it even in banter. If a man wishes to speak well of me, and judges it imprudent to say what he feels except in jest, I would rather he should not speak of me at all.
    I find no fault with a journal for disagreeing with me, and expressing in as clear and as distinct and as decided tones as it can its disagreement. I am not thin-skinned on that point, but I think my age and my well-known honest intentions should secure me in my Catholic opponents that courtesy due from one gentleman to another. I am and always have been, and always shall be unpopular, and the usual practice is for those that differ with me to refute me with squibs and sneers. Catholic editors have adopted towards me a manner which they would adopt towards no other man in my position. Personally I care nothing for this, but it diminishes my influence, and takes from me my ability to serve the cause which we ought all to have at heart. Differ from me as much as you please; oppose me when you think I am wrong; but do it fairly and honestly, without discourtesy, without seeking by quibbles, quirks, and verbal subtilties to render me odious and contemptible to the Catholic public. I have never attacked any man personally in my *Review,* when the personal attack was not necessary, at least in my judgment, to the vindication of some public cause. I have never written a line in malice, from personal pique, or to gratify a personal resentment, and I never will knowingly or consciously. I will never

publicly redress my private wrongs except [when] a public cause seems to me to demand it.

I have been most grossly misunderstood, misinterpreted, and even abused, where I had the right to expect better things. None of you seem to be at all aware of my real position or of my actual character. You yourself mistake them almost entirely. You are a man who have and always have had a social position. I have never had one. I have lived all my life alone, and I have not any personal influence, and consequently I am less able to bear the loss of public character than many persons far less known. But a hint is enough. It has been no light task to sustain my *Review* for eleven or twelve years single-handed against the tide of personal unpopularity.

I regret to learn by your letter that no notice was taken of the "Pretty Plate." I wrote a very favorable notice of it, which I supposed till receiving your letter had been inserted. It must have been crowded out, and forgotten. The same thing, I recollect now, occurred with a book of Mr. Shea. I am willing to be his friend, but he will never be mine. I can make no advances to him, for I regard myself as the aggrieved party. But I assure you that nothing in the past or the future will affect my notices of any works that may fall under my criticism.

. . . The course which some Catholic prelates who approved my doctrine to myself personally, have taken, has not given me so high an opinion of their Catholic honor as of their policy. I have dared, at the risk of my reputation and means of subsistence, of all I hold dear except the truth and the approbation of Heaven, to bring out the only doctrine that can save society from ruin, and they who *agree* with me, misrepresent, banter, or denounce me, or remain silent. Is this what Catholic faith and honor demand?

Thank God, I never yet truckled to public opinion, and I think I shall never oppose any man for doing what I wish done, whatever may be the popular outcry against him. The Catholic can die for the truth, but he cannot disown it or its friends. Forgive me, if I speak warmly; for you must be aware that your reason for the attacks upon me by *The Leader* is the one of all others likely to arouse a high-minded and honorable man. It is very soothing to be told: True, you have been and are doing what I wish done, and am myself doing; but then, you are so unpopular that I cannot do it without casting you off, or joining in the popular cry against you. But do not take it ill, for I mean it not in hostility, but in friendship. Sir, I am ready to back my friend to the death. But enough of this.

I have never been able to discover any difference between you and myself on the nativist question, except that I am *not* opposed in my feelings to foreigners, and *not* proud of my New England ancestors. I want precisely what you do, and I wish to bring as far as possible Catholic influence to bear on politics; but that influence must be Catholic, not foreign, because otherwise it will do harm instead of good. The whirlwind that is excited against us has been occasioned, not by the cause or persons your St. Louis friends imagine, but by a premature attempt to organize the Catholic or Irish influence. I could, if I were with you, tell you what has been done, and show you that the Know-Nothing movement is nothing but a punishment upon us for our imprudence. . . . I foresaw and foretold it during the late presidential canvass. I have only been trying to recover the ground we have lost, and nobody except Know-Nothings seems to understand me.

I have never changed in the slightest my doctrine on the papal power. I never held the doctrine which Bishop O'Connor represents me as holding.

But enough of all this. I have unburdened my mind with the frankness and bluntness of my nature, and conclude by thanking you for the spirit in which you accept my advances. I assure you that you will ultimately find that I am a bear only skin-deep, or at least am a tame bear. I would gladly send you the article you ask for, but time and health will not permit.

Very truly and respectfully your friend,
O. A. Brownson[20]

Besides the deeper insights it affords into Brownson's character, this letter is especially interesting because of the reasons Brownson assigns for the rise and progress of the Nativist and Know-Nothing movements in the country, namely, they were really political dating from the elections of 1852 in which the Democrat Franklin Pierce triumphed over the Whig Winfield Scott, and in which the Irish "foreign vote" had played such an important role. Interesting, too, is his statement that in all his laborious efforts he had only been trying to recover for Catholics the ground they had lost since those elections, and that nobody seemed to understand what he had been trying to do except the Know-Nothings. In a letter to his friend, Fr. John Roddan, editor of *The Pilot*, he gives some other sidelights on the tangled fray of which he had been so much the center. He would like to suppose that there was not a Catholic in the country who did not understand perfectly well that the Know-Nothing attacks on him had no other purpose than to get Catholics to distrust and disown him. Have we any Catholics, he asked, who are silly enough to fall into the Know-Nothing trap? He utterly repudiated as "so much moonshine" the idea that his articles on the papal prerogatives had been the chief cause of the current excitement. The present uproar would have come, he asserted, perhaps with greater fury, had he never written a line, nay, had he never so much as lived. And he regretted that some had yet to learn the lesson of standing by a friend when the pressure is on. Yet he added:

> Much must be pardoned to men's fears, and who is not prepared to be denounced by friend as well as foe is not prepared to do a knight's service in the cause of Catholicity.
>
> I have experienced only what every man experiences who seeks to follow truth rather than public opinion, and after all it is glorious to suffer for a good cause.
>
> The storm raging against us will soon subside, the sun will break through the clouds, the sea will be hushed, and men will smile to think that they ever mistook me for Jonah. You, Sir, know very well how false are the notions which a few persons who have nothing better to do, try to induce the Catholic public to entertain of me. But all will be cleared up at last, and each will receive according to his merits.[21]

Brownson was entirely right about the ready cessation of the storm. Soon after this letter was written, Know-Nothingism reached its peak in the latter part of 1855, and readily declined thereafter. As Ray Billington remarks: "The almost complete failure of the Know-Nothings to carry into effect the doctrines of the anti-Catholic and anti-foreign propagandists contributed to the rapid decline of this nativistic party."[22] Neither of the two great political parties of the country would risk cooperation with them, to say nothing of alliance, for they knew full well that it could cost them the votes of uncounted thousands of Catholics and foreigners. After repeated attempts to galvanize themselves into new life by introducing into legislatures discriminatory laws on naturalization, on pauper and criminal immigration, the Know-Nothing party split down the center over the slavery question, and eventually disintegrated completely. In this matter, however, let us not forget the four powerful articles of Orestes A. Brownson in which he turned the Know-Nothings inside out and exposed them to the country for what they were.

But in so doing he had to fend off savage attacks from both the Know-Nothings and Catholics. With so much unsparing abuse from both sides, one wonders how he had the heart to carry on. As a matter of fact, he did waver a bit. In a letter to Lord Acton in January 1855, his son Henry stated that his father, with such a howl all over the land accusing him of being a Know-Nothing, had decided to discontinue his *Review*, but that his friends had coaxed him to change his mind again.[23] As so often happened in such critical times, he received about this time a letter from his friend in Cincinnati, Judge G. H. Hinton, dated February 13, 1856, that must have been of great encouragement to him. It read in part:

> My dear Brownson:
> You have a great mission before you: for this age and country — and in some respects I may say for all ages. No man can touch you. I speak not this in flattery, for I know you are above that — but as friend to friend. As one who owes you a deep debt of gratitude for some of the noblest and best tendencies of his life. And you deserve encouragement; for it has been attempted to put you down, but the great God has use for you. And his work is not to be balked by the cunning and deceit of men. And this too by men in many respects good — yes very good, but who have their weaknesses.[24]

Even those who honestly criticized Brownson for his proclamation of the superiority of the spiritual order over the temporal as the only effective means of putting down Gallicanism, and as the only possible avenue for attacking political atheism so rife in the modern world, never did themselves come forward with any prescription for the cure of those cancerous ills eating so voraciously into the vitals of modern political society. Brownson was certainly on the right track. Should he have been supported by those who should have stood by him, great good might have been accomplished by a restoration, at least in some degree, of ethics to modern politics and government. His doctrine of the superiority of the spiritual over the temporal order could be no reasonable offense to the American people when rightly explained. He had effectually closed the mouth of the learned and able Dr. M'Clintock who had so confidently assailed him by showing that the doctrine he himself had defended was part of the basic religious beliefs of the American people as embedded in American society from earliest colonial times. Even the power of the popes exercised in the Middle Ages in deposing outrageously tyrannical princes could not well be objected to since it was only similar to the right the American colonists themselves had claimed when, in their own way, they declared themselves absolved from allegiance to George III because of tyrannical acts perpetrated against them. Nor did anyone, inside or outside the Catholic Church, ever controvert his doctrine with any show of success. It was first misrepresented, and then assailed as untenable.

# 33

## THE CATHOLIC UNIVERSITY
## OF IRELAND BECKONS

*John Henry Newman invites Brownson on December 15, 1853, to become lecturer extraordinary at the Catholic University of Ireland, and suggests "Geography" as his theme • The subject is not to Brownson's liking, and he hesitated • Hearing of his hesitation, Sir John Acton writes him a remarkable letter in an effort to prevail upon him to accept • After a delay of five months, Brownson informs Newman that the suggested theme does not exactly suit him, and declines the invitation • Newman changes the theme to the "Philosophy of Religion," and Brownson accepts provisionally • But Brownson's article on "Native Americanism" had deeply offended the Irish, and bishops in America reportedly protest his appointment • In much embarrassment, Newman acquaints Brownson with the situation, and suggests that he hold his appointment in abeyance • Some letters unfavorable to Brownson's appointment • Brownson himself decides that it will be best if his name is in no way connected with the university • But Newman is still reluctant to consider his appointment beyond the possibility of fulfillment • The reasons why Newman sought Brownson's appointment as lecturer extraordinary • Brownson seeks to promote attendance at Newman's university • Brownson receives a letter from Professor Thomas Arnold, son of the far-famed Dr. Arnold of Rugby • Brownson remains in America, much to Sir John Acton's disappointment.*

The scorching fire Brownson had drawn upon himself from both Catholics and the Know-Nothings in the uproar over nativism and his doctrines on the papal prerogatives was one of the greatest trials of his stormy life. There had been, as we have seen, some wild and reckless discharges at him from the Catholic camp as well as from that of the Know-Nothings. In a letter to F. X. Weninger, an Austrian Jesuit missionary laboring in this country, he wrote: "I own that I have lost some of my first fervor with regard to a portion of the American Catholic body. They have so misrepresented and denounced me, and are so ready to seize every opportunity to blacken my character, that I do not feel that lively confidence in them that I did. They have wronged me, and brought all manner of contradictory objections against me, and I am only a poor, frail, mortal man. But if I know my heart, I have lost nothing of my Catholicity. I love the Church more and more every day."[1] However that was, many a cloud has a silver lining. In the midst of so much trial and disappointment, came an event that must have been at least a temporary balm to his heart. John Henry Newman was just organizing at the time the teaching staff of the proposed Catholic University of Ireland, and the first invitation he issued to be a member of the staff was directed to Orestes A. Brownson. This was indeed a handsome recognition of his position among all the scholars in the Catholic world, particularly in the English-speaking world. Newman's letter ran:

Egbaston, Birmingham, December 15, 1853

Sir:

You will not be surprised that the persons engaged in the task of starting the new Catholic University of Ireland, should betake themselves to the United States for aid in doing so, or that they should direct their eyes towards a writer so well known and so highly endowed as yourself.

Of course we feel it impossible to offer you any inducement sufficient to lead you to connect yourself personally with the institution, nor indeed are we ourselves yet in a position to make such an offer to any one. But we have thought we might still avail ourselves of the name and assistance of various eminent Catholics, in a way which it is possible both for them and for us to contemplate.

What we take the liberty of asking you, is, whether you could consent to accept the office of Lecturer Extraordinary for (we will say) a year. I am asking the same favor of Dr. Döllinger of Munich, and others of similar literary distinction. The office would not involve residence, but only the delivery of one or two courses of lectures, as might be convenient to the lecturer. And the year proposed would be that running from the autumn of 1854 to the autumn of 1855.

The subject which I should propose to your acceptance would be one of such surpassing interest and breadth that I am often surprised that it is not put more prominently forward in Collegiate establishments. We never omit a professorship of astronomy, but how much more fertile a subject of thought is the province of geography! Viewed under its different heads, as physical, moral, and political, it gives scope to a variety of profound philosophical speculations, which will at once suggest themselves to your mind. It treats of the very stage and field of all history; of the relations of that field to the character of nations, to social institutions, and to forms of religion, of the migration of tribes, the direction and course of conquests and empires, the revolutions and extension of commerce, and the future destinies of the human race. This is the subject I offer to your acceptance.

Should it fall into your views to offer us your aid in the way I propose, I am sure a course of lectures on any such subjects as those I have set down, from so brilliant a writer, would be thronged by the educated classes of Dublin, classes at once numerous and highly intelligent, and would be of great moment and effect in the commencement of a great, an anxious, and a most religious undertaking.

You are the first person to whom I have applied, and hoping I may succeed in my object, I am, Sir, your faithful servant,

John H. Newman,<br>of the Oratory[2]

Brownson's son Henry tells us that geography did not have the same significance for his father that it seemed to have for Newman. He did not believe that it had that influence on religion and morals which many speculators on the subject were ready to advance, and which some of the expressions in Newman's letter seemed to imply.[3] The subject, therefore, did not appeal to Brownson overly much. To lecture in a university on a theme that was not to his taste would not guarantee the happiest results. What to do? Here Sir John (later Lord) Acton intervened with a facile plan of his own for inducing Brownson to come to the new Catholic University of Dublin anyway, namely, that he come and lecture on just anything at all which appealed to him. Shortly after Newman had written Brownson, Sir John was sojourning in England and learned from Newman's friends of Brownson's hesitation in the matter. (He delayed for months in replying to Newman's invitation.) On crossing again to Munich, however, Acton learned from Brownson's son Henry, who was studying at the university there, that Brownson would not refuse the invitation if the theme offered to him would be more to his taste. Dating his letter, Munich, May 13, 1854, Acton wrote Brownson what was one of the most remarkable letters he ever received. After referring to the good news he had just heard from his son Henry, namely, that he would not refuse the invitation if the subject were the right one, Acton wrote in part:

I cannot say how glad I am that there is a prospect of thus bringing you over for a time at least, and I cannot help adding the particle of influence I may possess as being more intimate with you than anybody else in England, and as being most profoundly convinced that you would find this a most happy opening. I will undertake in the first place to remove your difficulty about the subject-matter of your lectures, for I am quite certain that they would be too happy to let you lecture on opposums if you chose to communicate your good things in that way. The vast field of philosophy will be yours, and you will have an opportunity of making philosophical questions familiar to a nation hitherto barely acquainted with them, and I thank God for the good fortune of my countrymen in being initiated in that magnificent science by you of all men living. I am sure you will see how much may here be done for the glory of God, and I do most sincerely hope that nothing will prevent its being done. I can speak with perfect confidence of the facilities which will be given you to choose your own subject, for I am intimately acquainted with Newman's closest friends, and I know the immense price they attach to the prospect of an alliance with you in this work.

I will write at once to them on this point, and this obstacle, if not already removed, as I know not what communications you have had with Newman, will at once disappear. It is very probable that this University may be exceedingly effective in promoting learning and Catholic literature in England and Ireland. Nobody can give it such an impulse as you. Assuredly the part you take in this work will not be the least meritorious of your actions, nor the smallest claim on our gratitude. I only regret that we have nobody to do for history what you can do for philosophy. Let me remind you how deficient the Irish and even the English Catholics are in sound moral principles of politics, and what the country and the cause will gain if you imbue them with such treasures as are contained in your articles on Rights and Duties, for an instance out of many, and in those last admirable discourses of an old fogie.[4] We have no such old fogies in England. Alas! you are well aware that the only students of philosophy in England (of course I always include Ireland), are those disciples of the Germans who maintain and read the *Westminster Review*. They are not wanting in numbers, they are not deficient in men of character like Carlyle. They are numerically always increasing, and their doctrines are developing themselves and deteriorating by sure degrees. Who can resist their progress? All the world knows that Protestantism is no match for infidelity, and offers no weapons to refute it. We Catholics have no philosophy; no philosophical writers exist among us. Indeed, it is pretty certain that they would not be worth much if we had them. I know not how they could have grown up.

You alone can prepare us for the great controversies by founding among us a school and arming it with the principles of a sound philosophy. I believe that the historical proof ought to accompany the philosophical proof, and that we can well use both the History of Philosophy and the Philosophy of History. In choosing history for my occupation through life I am actuated by a hope of following your example in another field, and I hope that according to the measure of my powers I may be of some service in my time by promoting the knowledge of the great truths that are taught in the History of the World. Independently of your lectures, I am sure it will be an excellent thing if you come over to Europe. Your intercourse will be as an infusion of new blood in many societies, in Dublin, in London, in Paris, and other places. There are many who will be very glad to know you, and very many who will be all the better for it. Neither do I think you will have any reason to regret it for yourself. I think you will find it a great satisfaction to know several persons in Europe. You will be able to make yourself more accurately acquainted with much recent literature than it is possible to do at a distance.

I believe you will find that there are many persons who have deserved a great local reputation, but whose books do not get beyond a certain limit, for books travel very slowly, with a few exceptions, from nation to nation; and there are many good things which wise men keep to themselves and that do not find their way into books, and that one gathers in conversation. I am confident, for instance, that in the matter of political philosophy I could make you acquainted with German writers whose fame has never crossed the Atlantic, but who would please you as much as Radowitz. Long before Newman wrote to you, when I used often to recall the happy hours I spent with you at Emmitsburg and at Boston, and to reflect on the excellent things you told me, and on your great kindness, and to read your essays, the idea came constantly into my mind that it would be a great thing if you came over to Europe, and particularly to Germany, for that you could here collect much that you could afterwards use to the great advantage of the Church. It seems to me there is no science nobler than the one that has no name in literature, than the science of Burke and Maistre, and Donoso Cortes.

I believe that a system of laws for those that govern and for those that are governed, a system of political philosophy, if there is no better expression, that such a system remains to be drawn up by a philosopher who should know all truths that those great writers have discovered, and who should reconcile all the scattered fragments with each other by theories derived from the certain doctrines of the Church; such a system as Montalembert speaks of in his life of Donoso Cortes as being a medium between the theories of Gioberti and those of Bonald. Is not such a work a fit undertaking for you who have contributed so much to it in your Essays? I sincerely wish a speedy birth and a long life to the philosophical letters which you told me were in preparation. They will be a proof that your *Review* does not prevent you from carrying on a large work at the same time. Then I venture to hope that when you have crowned your studies in one line with that book you will also set the crown to your Essays in political philosophy by such a work as I speak of.

A writer may influence and instruct both his contemporaries and posterity. By means of a review he can exercise a much more constant and prolonged influence on his own time than by sending forth a single book. But a journal cannot live as a book. It is too voluminous, much of the interest is temporary, much is merely local. Even such a collection of Essays as you have published, and will I hope publish several more, must become after a time a literary curiosity to a certain degree, and cannot continue to have the same effect as a book which is one whole, both in matter and in form as a work of art. Therefore, although any essay you write on the principles of politics deserves to be preserved in a collective edition, no quantity of them will be as good as a single work exhausting the subject and complete in its parts. I believe that besides your fame as an historical personage in America, your most desirable and deserving reputation in literature would be founded on such a task as this.

This thought has often crossed my mind since we parted, and I am sure you are of all men the most fitted for the undertaking. I have often wished to send you some German books on these subjects, and I have given Dolman one or two for you. But you must first of all come to Europe and make acquaintance with the books and the writers here. To inspect the action of the European forms of government would itself probably interest you. I have spoken on these subjects perfectly freely and openly, mindful of our conversations and trusting that you will not think my confidence presumptuous or my friendship intrusive. Your writings, your conversation, and your individuality have afforded me matter for long meditations, and this thought has always appeared to me so natural that I have ventured to communicate it to you. Many good books have owed their origin to the solicitations of persons hardly better fitted to appreciate them and hardly more intimate with the author than is the case with me, and I am encouraged by the promise you have already made me of writing on the Mormons. One satisfactory result at least I looked forward to, namely, a letter from you. If I do not provoke you to write a book or an article, I hope at least I shall provoke you to write a letter.

I hope you have not forgotten your promise of collecting for me a complete set of your *Review*, and of keeping your eye on materials for Professor Döllinger's work on the Reformation. I shall be very glad to know whether I can execute any commissions for you, and whether you would like more works on Radowitz or others of the same kind. If you have not seen Gratry's work *De la Connaisance de Dieu,* you should order it from Paris. More volumes are to appear on Logic and Psychology. It is far superior to many works you notice. Indeed, I have sometimes regretted that you devote so much attention to writers of so little general importance, but I explain it by circumstances connected with the teaching of philosophy in American schools. I hope you will divide your cloak among your sons and friends, and letting them deal with the *Civiltà Cattolica* and the *Ami de la Religion,* will turn your face toward Europe and your attention to the achievement of a great work. I might fill sheet after sheet with matter of little importance but that I would be glad to talk to you about, but I will add nothing incongruous to the seriousness and tediousness (I fear) of my letter, and will only renew my assurances of deep gratitude towards you and I need not say what profound admiration.

Trusting that you will sometimes think of me with kindness and that you will not forget me in your prayers, I remain, my dear Dr. Brownson, most affectionately and sincerely,

John Dalberg Acton[5]

Unbeknown to Sir John Acton, just five days before he wrote Brownson this letter, Brownson himself had finally replied, on May 8, 1854, to Newman's letter with its invitation. He had delayed almost five months in deliberating what answer should be returned. The subject for his lectures which Newman had suggested had no doubt increased the difficulty in making a decision, but there were other difficulties as well. The continuance of his *Review* at the same high standards posed a problem of its own. How could it be managed? Even a temporary suspension, said one writer, would be "little less than a literary calamity."[6] His misgivings about these matters he made known in a letter he now sent Newman. It ran:

Boston, May 8, 1854

Very Rev. Sir:

I have delayed answering your letter of Dec. last, which I received some weeks since through the Rev. Dr. Forbes of New York, because I have been really unable in my own mind what answer to return.

I am deeply sensible of the high honor you have done me by inviting me to be a lecturer extraordinary in the new Irish University, and I am most anxious to visit England and Ireland, and to do everything in my power to aid in the really important enterprise. But I feel my own utter disqualification for the duty you would assign me. I have neither the manners nor the learning you have a right to demand in a University lecturer. I am a plain, untutored backwoodsman, wholly overrated both as to my talents and as to my acquisitions in both your country and my own. I say not this from humility, but from pride rather. I could not acquit myself creditably, and I am sure you have hundreds of men in England and Ireland any one of whom could be of infinitely more service to the University than I could be.

On a few topics I could possibly give a popular course of lectures. But I am by no means well versed in Geography, and have no time to prepare myself to treat it even in the wide sense you allow us it should be treated. The subject I am the most familiar with after theology, and politics, which you do not want, is philosophy, and the only course of lectures I should dare undertake to give in connection with any university would be on philosophy, or the philosophy of history, embracing the questions of Gentile and Christian civilizations. But I could not give them under the head of Geography.

Add to these [reasons] the necessity of devoting nearly all my time to my *Review*, on which I depend almost entirely for my support and that of a large and expensive family, I have reluctantly come to the conclusion that I must therefore decline accepting the post you generously offer me.

Permit me, Very Rev. Sir, to avail myself of this occasion to express the hope that nothing unpleasant may ever hereafter occur to affect our personal relations. To yourself personally I have never had any feelings but such as you would approve, and whatever I may have written in connection with your name or that of your friends, it was only in relation to a theory, which rightly or wrongly, I deemed it my duty to oppose. Circumstances have changed since 1845, and I am most anxious that the bonds between English and American Catholics should be drawn as close as possible.

With deep respect, I have the honor to be your obedient servant,

O. A. Brownson[7]

No doubt Newman was glad to have this reply in hand, for he had waited for it a long time. At least he knew now the lay of the land, and must have considered carefully what he could offer him that would be a sufficient inducement to bring him over. With his usual dispatch regarding all things connected with the proposed university, he got off a reply to Brownson within weeks. Written at 16 Harcourt Street, Dublin, on June 6, 1854, it ran:

My Dear Sir:

I thank you very much for your kind letter, which I received a few days ago. As to what you say about myself, I deeply feel that this is a day above all others in which the children of the Holy Church need to be united, and bear upon their enemies with their entire and concurrent force. Much more should those be one, who have been so wonderfully brought out, each in his own way, according to the will of Sovereign Love and Power, from darkness to light. If there is one misery greater than another, it is division among Catholics, when their walls are beleaguered by the united powers of darkness. If we have traitors among us, of course let them be duly dealt with, but in cases where treason is not suspected, let us interpret each other's words in *meliorem partem,* and aim at cultivating that charity which "thinketh no evil." As for me, these are the sentiments which I have ever felt towards you, and it is a great satisfaction to me, and I feel grateful to you, to find that you reciprocate those sentiments towards me.

Of course it disappointed me that you did not see your way to assist us in the University in the way I pointed out. Theology and metaphysics will, I suppose, be given by the Bishops to Ecclesiastics. The Philosophy of History is already in the hands of a man of ability and name. It struck me that you would not be disinclined to take the chair of the Philosophy of *Religion,* or the Evidences of Xtianity, or of the Notes of the Church, especially as viewed in reference to the needs of this age. This would open upon you the fields of *logic* and *history,* in both of which you are so well practised. Would not the subject you mention of *Civilization* come into it, without going into the subjects of theology and metaphysics, which, as I have said, the

Bishops will reserve for Ecclesiastics? Again, the mythical theory and its attendant errors are now making their way into these islands — are we Catholics secure from the infection? — any logical or historical attack upon them would be of the greatest service to us. As to politics of the *day*, I suppose it will be our prudence to abstain from so exciting a subject.

Excuse this short and unceremonious letter, and believe me, my dear Sir, with true esteem, very sincerely your in Xt,

John H. Newman,<br>of the Oratory[8]

In this letter Brownson was now offered a subject that lay close to his heart — the philosophy of *religion*. He bounded to the offer as far as the theme was concerned. Besides what he was now to say in his letter to Newman on the vast importance of such a chair, he was to emphasize later that "what is most needed in these times [is] — what we trust we may be permitted to call the philosophy of religion, or supernatural philosophy." It was the very thing in which he had found so many eminent Catholic laymen of the age markedly deficient, such as Chateaubriand, Count Montalembert, Louis Veuillot and others.[9] Perceiving clearly how important such a chair would be in supplying the very element missing in modern university education, he wrote back to Newman on July 11, 1854:

Very Rev. and Dear Sir:

I have received your obliging letter of the 6th., ultimo, for which I beg you to accept my thanks. I hope and trust that as regards our personal feelings one to another all is well and will continue to be right.

I feel honored by your renewed request. The chair of philosophy of religion would suit me very well, and would enable me to consider the evidences of Christianity in relation to the peculiar wants, tendencies, and errors of the age, and to bring in what I wish to say of history and civilization without teaching party politics or encroaching upon the peculiar province either of the theologian or the metaphysician. Indeed, I consider the proposed chair as peculiarly adapted to supply what I conceive to be a deficiency in modern university education.

I shall be most happy to comply with your flattering invitation, if I possibly can, but I dare not make any acceptance positive, till I have consulted my bishop and obtained his advice. He has been to Rome and is now I presume on his way back.

I am obliged to say that I am a poor man with a large family, and that I could not comply with your invitation at my own cost, as it would be my pleasure to do if able to do so. I may not be able to leave my family, or to make satisfactory arrangements for the editing of my *Review* during my absence. I have in view of the latter recalled one of my sons from Munich, and if I find him as I hope to find him on his return, this latter difficulty will be overcome.

Subject to these conditions and such unforeseen events as are always to be excepted, I will do myself the honor to accept the chair offered, and will endeavor to give at least one course of lectures commencing in the early part of 1855.

My general preparation for such a course as I propose to give is already made; the particular and immediate preparation I should make after my arrival in Dublin and under the eye of the Rector of the university, so that nothing not meeting his approbation would be inserted. This in times of so great excitement, and in a country where I am a stranger would be necessary prudence on your part and mine.

With the sincerest respect, your obedient servant,

O. A. Brownson[10]

Newman was of course quite pleased that Brownson had finally accepted, and when planning for the leasehold of a house for himself, included in it rooms for Brownson too, and contemplated a table in common with himself and two or three guests.[11] And then came the thunderclap. Newman wrote to Brownson in no little embarrassment to acquaint him with the strange turn of events. He wrote:

> Oratory, Birmingham, August 23, 1854
>
> Dear Sir:
>
> My delay in answering your letter of July 11 is not owing to me. I sent it to Ireland at once, and had it back only yesterday evening. By the same post, I received letters from different places which have perplexed me very much, as well as surprised me — so that now that I write to you, I write, to my great disappointment and concern, with considerable difficulty. But I will neither delay my answer, nor be otherwise than open and straightforward in what I have to say.
>
> I am urged then, for the first time, in quarters to which I cannot but listen, to ask you whether it would be inconvenient to you to postpone your visit here, on the ground of some offense which happens to have been taken *just now*, in America, and, I believe in Ireland, at something you have lately written.
>
> It will be a serious loss to us, if you cannot take part in our undertaking; and I know I have no right to suppose that you will come at all, if I take a liberty so great as to ask you to postpone your coming. But still I must take things as I find them; and, since it rests with me to do what is at once unpalatable to me in itself and apparently discourteous to you, I think it best to state the case as it really stands, trusting that I may not, besides my own disappointment and inconvenience, have the additional misfortune of disobliging you.
>
> I might offer some mere excuse for proposing a postponement, but I think you will be better pleased that I should speak the plain and entire truth. I earnestly trust that this change of purpose on our part may not put you to inconvenience. I am very sorry to see, on looking again at your letter, that you have recalled your son from Munich apropos of your coming to Europe.
>
> I am, dear Sir, with much respect,
>
> John Henry Newman,
> of the Oratory[12]

What precisely had happened? Biographers of Brownson have in the past been quite largely in the dark as to just what went on backstage. But we now have some light on the matter since Fergal McGrath, S.J., drew on the Dublin diocesan archives in writing his book, *Newman's University, Idea and Reality*. It now appears that from the very beginning certain factors in one quarter or another began to operate against Brownson ever becoming a part of the university project. McGrath speaks of a letter Dr. Walsh, bishop of Halifax, Nova Scotia, wrote Archbishop Cullen of Dublin, already on November 12, 1852, as expressing both Walsh's dissatisfaction and that of Archbishop Hughes of New York with some observations Brownson had just made on Newman's mental powers in his article "Morris on the Incarnation." In his letter to Dr. Cullen Dr. Walsh wrote:

> When I came to Boston, I had an interview with Dr. Brownson himself, and I represented to him as strongly and as delicately as I could, the useless, if not the pernicious nature of these attacks, at a time when all the bigotry and power of England were arrayed against Dr. Newman, and when anything disparaging against him would recoil upon the Irish University, of which, it was well known, he was the appointed Rector. Abstracting from his general remarks upon Dr. Newman's writings, I complained particularly of the analysis which

was given of Dr. Newman's mental powers, and the un-called for, if not unjust estimate of his talents. Here Dr. B[rownson] was forced to acknowledge that these passages had better been omitted.[13]

The article to which Bishop Walsh referred, "Morris on the Incarnation," Brownson had published in his *Review* the previous July 1852, as we have already noted. Although dealing in particular with Morris's volumes, Morris being one of the Oxford converts, the article was in general a prolonged criticism of the developmentist school of the Oxford and Puseyite converts. Their style of writing riled him. He acknowledged that they had much in them that he liked, but logically considered, they failed to command his respect. They were loose thinkers and loose writers. "They are nice men," he said, "but shockingly bad logicians."[14] This settled their hash with Brownson. As Fr. Isaac Hecker once said of him: "The thing he detests most is bad logic. It makes him peevish and often riles his temper."[15] As Brownson went along in his article on the developmentist school he finally got around to Newman himself and renewed some of his former observations on Newman's theory of the development of Christian doctrine as he had presented it. It was when expanding on the loose style of writing found among Oxford converts that he was led to etch Newman's mental powers. He did not of course include him among the loose thinkers and writers, but still:

> [Dr. Newman] is a man of sharp rather than a broad and comprehensive intellect. He has little faculty of grasping a subject in its unity and integrity, and he never masters a subject by first viewing it in its central principle, and thus descending to its several details. To use a form of expression borrowed from himself, he takes in an idea, not as a whole, but by viewing it successively under a variety of separate aspects — by walking around it, and viewing it successively under all its aspects. He thus attains to only particular views, never to unity of view, or to the comprehension of the idea as a whole.[16]

This is the particular passage to which Bishop Walsh referred as serving no good purpose. However, Walsh's letter to Archbishop Cullen of Dublin does not seem to have marred Brownson's fortunes seriously, for the archbishop was later to agree to Brownson being invited as lecturer extraordinary. Perhaps Cullen still remembered another letter he had received from Bishop Edward Barron on Brownson, postmarked St. Louis, July 27, 1846, inquiring: "Do you get any numbers of Brownson's *Review*? It is the most thorough Catholic periodical I know of. You would like it. This gentleman is a most extraordinary instance of the wonderful ways of God."[17] Yet Walsh's letter to Archbishop Cullen in 1852 could not have done Brownson any good. But what had happened after Newman had written his second letter to Brownson on June 6, 1854, and Brownson had accepted his offer to be lecturer extraordinary?

McGrath tells us that a correspondent in America wrote Dr. Taylor, one of the secretaries of the university committee, on August 4, 1854, to say, among other things, that "it will be bad business to bring Brownson to the University. He is a man long regarded with distrust by some and [with] dislike by many; but the last number of his *Review* [the July edition] has evoked a perfect tempest of odium and indignation against him."[18] Here we have a crystal-clear reference to that fatal July 1854 article on "Native Americanism" — the very article about which so much has already been said, and which had given the Irish in America such mortal offense.[19] The reverberations of their piercing howl were so mighty as to roll across the

Atlantic and cancel to all effects Brownson's invitation to be lecturer extraordinary at the new Catholic University of Ireland.

Brownson was fairly prompt this time in replying to Newman's letter of August 23 with its news of the strange turn of events. In a letter of September 12, 1854, he wrote:

> My honest opinion is that it will be best all round, that I should not be in any way or manner connected with the University. Your position is one of great delicacy and difficulty, and to succeed in carrying your University through, you have to make many concessions to national prejudices. Here, and unless I am misinformed, also in Ireland, there is a large party by no means pleased to see an Englishman the Rector of an *Irish* University. This party was able for a time to use me against you and your friends, and now that they find I will no longer be their tool, they would break me in pieces. . . . My connection with the University will only give occasion to the party to pretend that its design is to Anglo-Saxonize the Irish. . . .
>
> Allow me, in changing the subject, to say that I have just read for the first time *Loss and Gain*. If I had seen that work at an earlier date, many things which I have written concerning you and your friends, the Oxford converts, would never have been written. I have taken occasion in my *Review* for October to say as much, and to do what I could to repair the injustice I had unwittingly done to men whom I love and reverence, and with whom I wish in my heart to co-operate in the defense of our holy religion.[20]

Newman commented in the postscript of a letter to his friend Hope Scott: "After all old Brownson's coming is suspended. He has been treading on the toes of the great Irish nation — and advocating something like mixed education."[21] Mixed education had little or nothing to do with the "perfect tempest of odium and indignation" raging against Brownson at just this time.

That there was a strong anti-English party in America at the time, as Brownson asserted in his letter, cannot be doubted. Great numbers of Irish immigrants in the country had been driven out of their homeland because of the wide death-dealing famine of 1846-1847, or had been the sorry victims of evictions. Their memories of English rule were most unhappy. And they had probably heard that the great John McHale, archbishop of Tuam, was standing out firmly against the appointment of those numerous English professors at the university.[22] These Irish immigrants in America were painfully concerned about the English "taking over" the university of their homeland. All this is clearly brought out in a letter Fr. Alexander Peyton, one of the priests sent to America to collect money for the university, wrote the university committee. His letter from Baltimore on May 17, 1852, to Dr. Murphy, bishop of Cloyne, reads:

> There is a report here among the priests that the Committee [members] in Dublin have disagreed as to the appointment of professors, the majority, headed by Cullen, wishing to leave the sole arrangement of the University and the selection of professors to Dr. Newman, thus virtually handing over the establishment to English domination. If such be the case . . . the collections in this country may be considered at an end. Both priests and people here think that the Irish prelates and people are too favorably disposed to English rule, and that until they act more independently of English rule, all attempts at improvement must prove abortive. . . . While they give Dr. Cullen credit for patriotism and sincerity, they are beginning to fear from the English appointments that he will be only an instrument in the hands of Dr. Wiseman, and that

508

the Irish Church will be virtually under the control and jurisdiction of Dr. Wiseman.[23]

Only three days later another priest, Robert Mullen, of the diocese of Meath, wrote another letter from Baltimore, Maryland, of a similar nature:

> The great difficulty with us now is that we are unable to point to the Committee as doing anything in Ireland. Hundreds ask us where and when it [the university] will be opened. Many intimate to us their fears that it will be like other Irish projects — a failure. Whilst others say again that Dr. MacHale has despaired of it, since he does not attend the meetings [of the bishops], and even a rumor has reached us that there was a great dissension in the Committee, that the Primate was influenced by Dr. Wiseman! and was about appointing the President [an Englishman] with full powers to appoint all the professors, English, of course. This latter rumor is confirmed this day by a paragraph in the Boston *Pilot* stating that Cardinal Wiseman is going to meet *you all* at Maynooth.[24]

All this seems to lend color to Brownson's statement to Newman that his connection with the university would be looked upon as only further evidence that there was a design to Anglo-Saxonize the Irish, especially in view of his own strong preachments to the Irish on their obligation to conform to Anglo-Americanism in his article on "Native Americanism." Yet Newman was quite reluctant to abandon the idea of bringing Brownson over to the university. Writing from a watering place in Ireland, Mount Salus, Dalkey, on September 27, 1854, he said:

> My Dear Sir:
>     I cannot prevail upon myself to give the coup de grace to an arrangement, which I still hope to come into effect, by putting the notice in the newspapers as you propose. There are many changes in men's minds, and public affairs are at present in that uncertain state, that it is not at all improbable that our present difficulty may blow over, and when it had done so, I should be vexed to have committed myself. I shall not fill up the professorship which I offered you, and we shall see what turn things take. At the same time, I do not mean to say a word to inconvenience you, or oblige you to consider it a suspended engagement, or to hinder your entertaining a renewal of my proposition as a really de novo affair.[25]

It is quite understandable that Newman was loath to give up the idea of Brownson's connection with the university — on several scores. Doran Whalen asserts (on what authority I do not know) that on visiting Newman, Martin John Spalding, archbishop of Baltimore, asked Newman what he thought of Brownson. Replied Newman: "I thought there is only one opinion on the matter. He is by far the greatest thinker America has ever produced."[26] That could be true even to this day. William J. Haggerty, Jr., who did a dissertation on *Realism in the Philosophy of Orestes A. Brownson* at the University of Boston in 1960 (and at this writing is professor of philosophy there), asserted in a letter to this author on October 4, 1967: "It is my conviction that Brownson was the intellectual giant of his age in America, and, moreover, that he has not been surpassed or even equalled in America to this day." C. C. Hollis informs us that "Newman read everything Brownson wrote and had unusual admiration for him," and correctly adds, "was indeed somewhat fearful of him."[27] This explains why Newman very cautiously set about considering the idea of inviting Brownson in the first place, as we now know for the first time.

509

Another letter long gathering dust in the diocesan archives of Dublin throws new light on this matter. In this letter to his close friend, Henry Wilberforce, Newman gives two weighty reasons for seeking to connect Brownson with the university. Writing from Egbaston on November 23, 1853 (three weeks before he first wrote Brownson), Newman said in the letter to Henry Wilberforce:

> Now here you can do me a service. Go to Dr. Moriarity [Bishop of Kerry] and ask him, in confidence, what his cool judgment is about asking Brownson to give a course of lectures. Tell him, in the first place, I am not sanguine at all that he should come, but if he came, he would come as "Lecturer Extraordinary," which is simply that he would give a course of lectures; that my object would be in engaging him, 1. to give éclat in Dublin and in Ireland to the University, 2. to interest Americans in it. Tell him, the only objection I see is, what some people have urged on me, that he would be sure to lecture against me. But I think this is impossible. He would but advance truths, which he fancied I did not hold, or which, as he fancied, would tell against me. Moreover he would be limited by the subject of his lectureship. Lastly, which is the most important question for Dr. Moriarity to have before him, viz., the subject of the lectures. What would he think of logic? Or Ethnology? Or Antiquities? Or Geography might be a great subject.[28]

Although McGrath does not seem to think so,[29] Newman, for the reasons he himself just stated, showed excellent judgment in inviting Brownson to be a part of the university, and gave shining evidence thereby that he had a thoroughly realistic grasp of the whole situation, even though the invitation to Brownson was to prove abortive. As Acton, too, had so strongly emphasized, Brownson's coming to the university would have given it additional éclat, and Newman was fully conscious of how "desirable [it was] to make a show."[30] Dwight Culler has thus commented on the matter: "Initially, Newman's idea of a professor was that he would be pretty much for show. He would be a person eminent in his own field and would attract students by the brilliance of his name to a university which was otherwise unknown. W. G. Ward, Döllinger in Germany, and Brownson in America are examples of persons whose services he attempted to secure."[31]

The second reason Newman gave for his invitation to Brownson was that he might thereby the better gain the interest of Americans in the university. Newman must have perceived from the very beginning that one of the most acute problems to plague the university was the problem of from just where the students were to come. Ireland (poverty-stricken) could furnish comparatively few. When Newman conferred on the matter with Fr. John Curtis, provincial of the Jesuits in Ireland, whom he called "a man of great character and experience," Fr. Curtis told him that the class of youths who would come to the university simply *did not exist* in Ireland. Fr. Curtis ended his general comments by saying summarily to Newman: "My advice to you is this, to go to the Archbishop and say, 'Don't attempt the University; give up the idea.' "[32] The prospect of students in Ireland being so meager, Newman was forced to turn his eyes to England and America. And here we have at least a partial reason why Newman was so strong on bringing in a goodly number of English professors — in the hope of drawing a fair number of English students in their wake. Perhaps his greatest hopes lay in America. He had definitely contemplated making a visit here in the hope of advancing the great cause of the university the more effectively.[33] The visit, however, never materialized. But his persevering efforts — and we have noticed how earnestly he had endeavored — to add Brownson's name to the university staff was a capital stroke in the way of enlisting the interest of Catholic America in the great project and starting a flow of students from our own country. As the case appears, Newman was decidedly farsighted and shrewd in his calculations as to just what was required if the fledgling university was ever to get off the ground.

As an appropriate number of students was to continue to be one of the most vexing problems of the university, Brownson endeavored (long after the lapse of his invitation) when occasion offered to boost attendance from America. When he reviewed *The Atlantis: A Register of Literature and Science,* the university's publication, he wrote:

> This periodical is highly creditable to the University, and proves, if proof were wanting, that this new University has all that is required in the way of scholarship and science, to place itself on a level with the oldest and most renowned Universities in Europe. Till we get a University of our own, we think it would be well for Catholics, who have the means, to send their sons, after graduating at our colleges, there to attend the University course. In fact, we claim a share in it, for we contributed liberally of our means to establish it, and one of the first provisional professors named by its distinguished Rector was an American; and it is the only Catholic University in the world in which our mother tongue is the language of the houses and of the lectures; we think we might do it a service and benefit ourselves by sending it our sons. We doubt if any University in the world can surpass the present corps of Professors, and its Rector, Dr. Newman, is a man whose greatness and worth, rich native endowments, profound and varied attainments, will be admired and esteemed the more in proportion as he is known.[34]

One of the professors at the university there was especially pleased with this notice of Brownson, and, though a total stranger, thought it worthwhile to write him. He was Thomas Arnold, Jr., son of the famed Dr. Thomas Arnold of Rugby. His letter ran:

> Sir:
> I read with pleasure in the *Tablet* a short time since, a passage extracted from your *Review*, in which after commenting favorably on the *Atlantis,* you proceed to urge on your Catholic countrymen the expediency of giving practical support to the Catholic University, by sending their sons to study here. Emboldened by the friendly tenor of your remarks, I venture, though unknown to you, to address you these lines, and to enclose a printed circular which will sufficiently explain itself. I am one of those — and there are many in the three kingdoms — who have a true admiration for your character and genius, and who would value a few approving words from you immeasurably more than a thousand hollow puffs from persons or parties incompetent to give an opinion worth having. I thought, when I read what you said in favor of American Catholics sending their sons to Dublin, that greater practical effect might be given to your words, could it be known, that there was at present a house opened in Dublin for the reception of boarders, offering something like a guarantee that their education — taking the word in its widest sense — would be well and prudentially cared for.
> I therefore determined that I would send my circular to you, and that I would ask you to be so kind as to inform me in what way I could give it the necessary publicity in America, and what practical steps I should take for that purpose.
> I am the son of a man whom you certainly know by name, if not by his writings — Dr. Arnold of Rugby; I am Professor of English Literature in our Catholic University here. I cannot say that the institution is making as rapid

progress as its friends would desire — and this for various causes; still the Irish Bishops are unanimous in their resolution of supporting it, and if they would only appoint an active, sensible man as rector [this was in 1859], I am sure things would soon wear an altered face. It is the headless state in which we have been for so long which has brought us a world of harm. Dr. Newman, as you are perhaps aware, ceased to reside in Dublin and to take an active part in the administration of the University for more than a year before he formally resigned.

Trusting that, for the sake of the cause, you will pardon the liberty I have taken, I remain,

Very faithfully yours,
T. Arnold[35]

How great a disappointment it was to Brownson that his invitation to the Catholic University of Ireland had come to nothing, it would be hard to surmise. Perhaps the loss to the university was greater than the loss to himself.[36] His going there would have entailed considerable difficulty as was indicated by his forthwith recall of his son from Munich. It would not have been easy to keep his *Review* going and to maintain its high literary quality as the distinctive *Brownson's Quarterly Review*. The cancellation of the invitation solved all this. But as Newman indicated in his last letter to Brownson, he himself was quite reluctant to reconcile himself to the idea that Brownson might not be coming after all. But his disappointment in this was probably less than that of Sir John Acton. No man in Europe knew Brownson as well as did Acton. He had had long conversations with him stretching over several days,[37] had come to know him to a degree and to admire him hugely. Besides the lengthy letter he had written Brownson on May 13, 1854,[38] using all the arts of persuasion at his command to bring him over to Dublin and Europe, he had also written another longish letter a couple of weeks later to Edward L. Badeley, the noted London lawyer and close friend of Newman, urging that Brownson be invited to lecture at the university, not on geography, but "on philosophy or the philosophy of history."[39] But his disappointment — and it was probably greater than that of any other man — was all that he was to have for his pains in the project. As things were to turn out, Brownson was destined never to see the shores of Ireland nor those of any other European country. Apparently, as a consequence, Acton's enthusiasm toward the proposed university cooled a bit, but he did allow Newman to put his name down on the university books as an endorsement of the ambitious venture.[40]

# 34

## NEW YORK AND A NEW OUTLOOK

*Attracted to New York City by a coterie of congenial friends and the
more free and open spirit of the metropolis, Brownson moves there
with his family • His article on "Liberalism and Socialism" indicates a more liberal outlook • His support of Count Montalembert
and the liberal Catholic party in France against the political absolutism of Louis Veuillot, editor of the* Univers *• He exchanges letters
with Veuillot • Brownson's lecture on "The Church and the Republic" in the Tabernacle on Broadway, New York City • His controversy with the* Universalist Quarterly Review *• He recognizes a new
technique in apologetics • He rejects the current scholastic terminology, and pleads for forms of expression more understandable to
modern man • His refutation of Earl H. Derby's book,* Letters to a
Kinsman *• He now meets the assailants of the Catholic Church on the
grounds of medieval civilization • His dissatisfaction with the method of defense adopted by Kenelm Digby in his* Mores Catholici, or Ages
of Faith *• He exonerates the Roman Catholic Church from the charge
of an alleged alliance with political absolutism • His autobiography,*
The Convert, *exhibits a new turn in apologetics • It is dedicated to his
instructor in the faith, Bishop John B. Fitzpatrick • Passages of testimony from it to the credibility of the Catholic Church • He receives a conciliatory letter from Bishop Michael O'Connor.*

Although the great editor, called by one critic "the first of writers on
this continent,"[1] was not to travel abroad, he was soon to do some traveling
in his own country. For some time now he had been turning his eyes in the direction of New York City with the thought of making his home there. Boston
had become for him almost too much of a storm center. Perhaps a change of
residence would help to ease the blasts which had been sweeping over him.
And in New York City, too, was Fr. Isaac Hecker and others whose mentality and outlook were now more congenial to his own. Endeavoring to put
behind him the disturbing memories of the violent explosion over his article
on American Nativism, the bilateral uproar attendant on his war on Know-
Nothingism, and the debacle regarding his invitation to the Catholic University of Ireland, he now determined to make the change from Boston to New
York City. His son Henry tells us that as soon as his father's *Quarterly
Review* for October 1855 has been printed, "the Editor, Orestes A. Brownson, putting all things in readiness, carried his family, his household effects,
and his *Review* to New York."[2] The move was to be for him far more
consequential than he perhaps at the time suspected.

Brownson was by this time prepared to enter upon an era of a little more
personal freedom in regard to what he wrote for his *Review.* He had already finished a ten-year novitiate of direction under Bishop Fitzpatrick.
When the bishop went to Europe in 1854, Brownson's friend, Fr. John Rod-

dan, had acted as the theological censor of his articles in lieu of the bishop.[3] During this period Brownson had come to know a new convenience: Fr. Roddan had come to his home in Chelsea to have the articles read to him. After the bishop's return, the thought of toting his articles to the bishop's residence in Boston for theological inspection had perhaps become a bit tedious to him, especially since there was no longer much of a reason for doing so. He had studied Catholic theology assiduously now for a full decade, and felt fully competent concerning the theological aspects of any theme he might wish to discuss. Besides, the assurances he had given his assailants in the past that he had previously submitted his articles to theological revision before publication, had proved to be no shield at all against their unsparing assaults. Beginning, therefore, with the year 1855 he had quietly dropped the practice of submitting his articles to Bishop Fitzpatrick, and wrote and published according to his own taste and judgment.

That Brownson appreciated a little more personal freedom in this matter is not to be doubted. But neither Mr. Schlesinger nor Mr. Maynard have correctly represented Brownson's leave-taking of Bishop Fitzpatrick. Both speak as though affairs had come to some sort of a breaking point between the two. There is nothing to support such representations. It is true, as Mr. Schlesinger observed, that Bishop Fitzpatrick had on several occasions encouraged him to enter the line of fire, and had then left him to himself in the midst of withering barrages. And even when a priest, Jeremiah O'Callaghan, published a slanderous book entitled, *The Atheism of Brownson's Review,* in which he had collected heretical propositions which Brownson had cited in his *Review* only to condemn, and had palmed them off as Brownson's doctrines, Bishop Fitzpatrick had failed to come to his defense. He only told Brownson that a critic must expect criticism.[4] But in spite of this, Brownson knew full well that Bishop Fitzpatrick, whatever may have been his policy, was his true and fast friend. He never complained that the bishop had neglected to give him any public support.[5] And there is no reason for not believing that Brownson was perfectly sincere when he gave as his only regret in leaving Boston the fact that he was parting company with Bishop Fitzpatrick. In a letter to Fr. Hecker, dated August 29, 1855, he wrote:

> I think I should be with you more in the midst of friends, and I could exert far more personal influence than here. I have more and warmer friends in New York than in Boston, and I could leave all here except the bishop without regret. This diocese is becoming more and more Irish. I think I could now get along with his Grace the Archbishop without serious difficulty, and I think I could better breast the storm still raging and likely to rage for some time against me in New York under his patronage than here. So upon the whole, if any way can be prepared, I really do wish to remove to your city. . . . I shall be very grateful to you and such friends in New York as may aid in preparing the way.
>
> [Further on in his letter, he added:] The bishop here is as warm a friend as ever . . . but for myself I have here none but him to sympathize with me, no literary or cultural friends or associates, for Fr. Roddan fritters himself away.[6]

Orestes Brownson was not the man to set down things he did not mean. Arthur M. Schlesinger, Jr., is scarcely correct, therefore, when he says that Brownson had come by this time to find all supervision "galling, especially Fitzpatrick's, and that he had lost all hope of working with him.'"[7] Nor will all that Theodore Maynard had to say about Brownson's eager "escape" from the supervision of Bishop Fitzpatrick stand up any better. Both see Brownson at this time as decidedly impatient of any censorship. Maynard infers that "some coolness" between the editor and the bishop had sprung up, "for soon afterwards Brownson decided to move to New York where, he hoped, there would be no question of any censorship."[8] But a flat denial to both Maynard and Schlesinger in this matter is the fact that in coming to New York Brownson had again asked Archbishop Hughes to act as censor of his articles just as had Fitzpatrick. The archbishop, however, declined the offer. This we know more definitely from a letter recently unearthed in the Vatican's Archives of the Sacred Congregation of the Propaganda Fide, which Archbishop Hughes wrote on September 30, 1861, of which we shall hear more later.[9] But this same fact Brownson also stated in 1862 in his article, "The Church not a Despotism."[10] These evidences provide proof for a more sound judgment in the matter. It is scarcely fair to Brownson or to Bishop Fitzpatrick to have their relationship misrepresented. The late Thomas T. McAvoy, a careful historian, speaking of the relationship that existed between Brownson and Bishop Fitzpatrick when Brownson removed his editorial offices from Boston to New York, remarked that in making the change "there does not seem [to have been] any objection by Brownson to Bishop John Fitzpatrick."[11]

The lure which New York City held for Brownson at this time went beyond the fact that he had a greater number of warm friends there and could hope to exert a wider personal influence in that area. There was also something in the atmosphere of the metropolis that promised to match better the current temper of his mind. A definite change of viewpoint had been gradually coming over him during his last year in Boston — a change that biographers do not seem to have noted distinctly enough, including his son Henry. The change has been loosely spoken of as having come about only after he had become domiciled in New York City. But the change is clearly discernible in an article he published on "Liberalism and Socialism" in April 1855. That article could be looked upon as a sort of watershed in his developing thought, though the change is more apparent than real in the overall view.

In the article on "Liberalism and Socialism" he acknowledged that the anarchic revolutionary movements of 1848 had forced him at the time to throw all his moral weight against the evils of liberalism and socialism without making any distinctions — lest the undiscerning masses be misled. But now that the threat to society was coming from another direction, the excesses of authority, he felt free to distinguish and to acknowledge the truths or half-truths those systems do contain but which are unfortunately misapprehended and misapplied by their sponsors and advocates. He pointed out that liberalism and socialism, like all false systems, end at last in gentilism, yet those same systems could have originated in their modern form only in a society which had once been Christian, and still retained a tradition of the doctrine of Christian charity. There is no denying that, although many errors are mixed up with liberalism and socialism, those selfsame systems or movements look earnestly and benevolently to a redress of the people's grievous wrongs. A real change in the temper of his mind is seen when Brownson adds that there is a sense in which it cannot be denied that "the voice of the people is the voice of God." In recent years he had scorned the saying. In harmony with all this he had definitely come by this time, April 1855, to have little patience with the shallow and indiscriminate outcries of conservatives against revolutionary movements. The only conservatism he could respect is that which frankly acknowledges wrongs, and earnestly seeks to redress them wherever found.

> It is, after all [he said] less against revolutions that we would direct the virtuous indignation of our conservative friends, now that the reaction has become strong, than against the misgovernment, the tyranny, the vices and crimes, the heartlessness, the cruelty, the neglect of the poor by those who should love and succor them, which provoke revolutions, and which give Satan an opportunity to possess the multitude, and pervert their purest instincts and their most generous enthusiasm to evil. . . . Let not the friends of religion and order have censures only for those who sought madly to remove them [abuses] by revolutions, lest they render religion and order odious to all men of human hearts.[12]

In this article Brownson reviewed his early life as a liberal, and concluded by saying that what he had aimed at before his conversion was still dear to him, that he was still in some sense "a man of our age." As said, the article marks a sharp turn in his social philosophy, or perhaps more correctly expressed, a definite shift of emphasis. He changed front, not principles. In politics, however, he had always been a liberal in the sense that he was adamantly opposed to all centralization of power in government, and had been growing much more so with the galloping increase of political absolutism on the continent of Europe. He had quite naturally yearned for a more congenial milieu in which to follow his present leanings, and had thought he saw it in the nation's commercial capital, free and open New York City. After arriving there, he wrote his friend, Count Montalembert: "I think I shall be here more free to advocate our old constitutional doctrines, and I am nearer friends on whom I have chiefly to depend."[13]

Commenting on Brownson's article on "Liberalism and Socialism," the Count remarked: "Your judgment on Donoso Cortes is perfect and nothing could be more useful than to sift and extract, as you do, what is true and just out of Liberalism and Socialism instead of consigning the invincible spirit of modern Humanity to a blind and sweeping proscription."[14] And for this Brownson was exceptionally qualified, for as he himself said, "We . . . happen to know both sides [of the question] by our own experience," having been a "Christian" socialist in his early years.[15]

Although we will take the matter up more fully when we speak of *The Convert,* or Brownson's autobiography near the end of this chapter, it should be noted briefly here that in his article on "Liberalism and Socialism" he had also given further evidence of his veering orientation in 1855 inasmuch as he there affirmed at length his confident belief in his theory of Life by Communion which he had put in abeyance when Bishop Fitzpatrick had shown no disposition to recognize it. Reviewing the theory in his own mind in the light of a diligent study of Catholic theology for ten years, he was now confident of its validity, with certain modifications. The new discussion of his theory had come quite naturally into his article on "Liberalism and Socialism" when he touched upon the doctrine of the solidarity and intercommunion of the race as advanced by Pierre Leroux whom he called "the great man of the modern socialistic school," and who had been his former philosophical mentor.[16]

But who were those friends of Brownson in New York City to whom he had referred in his letter to Fr. Hecker? They were perhaps best represented by Dr. Jeremiah Cummings and Dr. Ambrose Manahan. A group of quite articulate Catholics had banded themselves together who wished to act on their non-Catholic countrymen, and they saw in battle-scarred Brownson their natural leader and inspiration. They wanted him to be in their midst in New York City. Although Fr. Hecker had enthusiastically urged him to New York City in a letter dated August 23, 1853, he did not at first favor the idea of his transfer at this particular time, but he soon came around to be of the same opinion with Brownson's other friends. Even though Archbishop Hughes had been anxious at the time of Brownson's conversion that he come to New York City and establish his *Review* there, it was now a matter of propriety and policy to seek his formal consent, and it was Brownson's intention to do so. But it became unnecessary when he received a letter from Fr. Hecker, dated October 1, 1855, in which he said: "This afternoon I called upon the Archbishop. In the course of the conversation he mentioned that he had heard that it was your desire to come to New York. I told him it was, with his approbation. He replied that he 'would be quite pleased at your coming, and that if I wrote to you I should tell you so.' These were his words."[17]

This New York group with whom Brownson was to become closely associated were liberals in their outlook. But what is more, Brownson was now coming into close association with, not only the liberal group in New York, but also with Catholic liberals in France, and England, if not with those throughout the Catholic world. Even before his transfer to New York, he was already — his *Review* was read by many of the foremost Catholic intellectuals in France — throwing all the moral support he could to Count Montalembert in his gallant fight against the increasing political absolutism in France under Napoleon III. A deep feud had developed there between Louis Veuillot, editor of the *Univers* — perhaps the foremost influential Catholic journal in Europe — and the directors of *Le Correspondant,* the most eminent of whom was Montalembert. The Count and his party objected strenuously that Louis Veuillot and his associates had brushed aside in their indiscriminate allegiance to Napoleon any concern for constitutional safeguards of civil and religious freedom, and, in addition, were identifying the Church with the growing Caesarism of the imperial regime. No one could be more aggrieved at such a policy than Orestes Brownson, and he raised his voice loudly in protest with Montalembert and his valiant associates in an article on "Rome and the Peace," July 1855. The charge against Catholics, said Brownson, is that they are friends of despotism, and the policy of coupling the Church to the imperial car of Napoleon III will only confirm it: "To identify the Catholic cause with Louis Napoleon, or any other Caesar, and to make the Church in any degree responsible for his government, were to alienate the affections of every lover of constitutional government or political freedom."[18] However, were he a citizen of France, he would demean himself as a loyal subject, but as an American citizen he utterly repudiated the Caesarism the imperial parvenu was endeavoring to fasten on his country. If Frenchmen like it, and choose to defend it, Brownson stated, let them do so as Frenchmen, but let them not do it in the name of Catholicity. He himself would take his stand firmly on the side of constitutional government, and demand as a right both political and religious freedom.

How correct Brownson was at this time about Napoleon III and his use of the Catholic Church to serve his own purposes was to be verified all too soon. When the emperor eventually showed his true colors, Brownson was to remind his readers that for seven long years he had stood alone in his own country, and almost in the whole Catholic world, warning French Catholics against "the new-fangled Caesarism introduced by Louis Napoleon, defend-

517

ed by Louis Veuillot, and endorsed apparently by the French Episcopacy."
Yet he could find no gratification in the fact that events had justified his
warnings, for "it was with real pain," he said, "we heard a noble-hearted
bishop say to us, a few days since, 'you were right, and we were wrong.' We
could enjoy no personal triumph which had been gained only by events deeply injurious to the Catholic cause, dearer to us than our reputation, far
dearer to us than our own life."[19]

In the first edition of his *Review* published in New York (January 1856),
Brownson turned his guns on those in the English-speaking world who were
following the lead of Louis Veuillot and his associates in tying the Catholic
Church in with despotism in France. He had seen in England, Ireland, and
even in his own country, with deep regret, a tendency among a portion of the
Catholic press to identify the Church with the rife imperialism in France.
This he attributed to the fact that the Red Republican revolutions of the late
past had so scared some Catholics out of their wits that they had come to
believe that they must accept religion coupled with despotism, or not have it
at all, thus making religion the ally and instrument of political and social
degradation. He warned against the baleful danger of allowing religion to be
associated with absolutism, and liberty with infidelity. Such a state of affairs, he cautioned, if not checked and corrected, would rouse up the whole
modern world with all that is good and all that is bad in it against the
Church.[20] Against this whole trend, Montalembert and his associates in
France were waging a deadly and unremitting war, while Louis Veuillot and
his collaborators in the *Univers* were only unwittingly aiding and abetting
it.

Brownson deeply deplored the division of the Catholic party in France
which the *Univers,* he said, had brought about by its violence, its onslaughts
on liberty everywhere, and its defense of despotism, all in the name of the
Church — the very worst disservice it could render religion in France. By
speaking in the name of the Catholic Church, the *Univers* was fast bringing
the Church in France into subjection to journalism, "the worst species of
Gallicanism we are acquainted with," said Brownson.[21] "We have no ill-will
to the *Univers,*" he assured its directors, "and we find no fault with it when
it does not belie our country, and does not put forth its Caesarism in the
name of Catholicity. . . . [Only] let the *Univers* improve its temper, study to
be just as well as smart . . . and it will find us a friend and collaborator, not
an enemy."[22]

When Count de Falloux published an essay on "La Parti Catholique" in
the April and May 1856 issues of *Le Correspondant,* telling the story of the
unhappy division among the leading Catholics of France, and laying the
blame in no small degree at the door of the directors of the *Univers,* Louis
Veuillot hurriedly replied with a book of the same title. Apparently in an effort to win Brownson over to his side, Veuillot sent him a copy of the book accompanied by a letter written in a kind and conciliatory spirit. As Brownson
said, he had never been able to repel the overtures to peace from any man,
even those of a bitter enemy. Accordingly he read Veuillot's reply to Count
de Falloux with softened feelings, and with every disposition to find the estimate he had formed of Veuillot unjust. But in this he was disappointed. He
found his reply in no small measure irrelevant, violent and unjust, and its perusal left on his mind the painful impression that justice and candor towards
opponents were virtues Veuillot had never acquired. His reply displayed the
temper and breeding of a fanatic, and seemed to indicate that its author
acted on the principle that anyone who differed from him on any important

question in history, politics, or philosophy, must needs be a bad Catholic, or none at all. Brownson did not question the sincerity of Veuillot and his associates, or impeach their good intentions, but he did question the wisdom of the policy they were pursuing.[23]

As these two stalwart Catholic journalists of the nineteenth century were never able to come together in any workable harmony in the interests of the Catholic cause, it may be well to give here a portion of Brownson's letter to Veuillot stating his grievances in the case. Beginning with expressions of disarming sentiments, he then told Veuillot frankly why he was unalterably opposed to his identifying the Catholic cause with political absolutism. He wrote:

> This is very embarrassing to us who live under republican and constitutional governments, and are daily and hourly called upon to defend the Church against the charge of being hostile to civil and religious liberty, especially embarrassing is it after having had in 1848 and 1849 to defend authority against the licentious democracy of your Socialists and Red-Republicans, which threatened the very existence of society. As the conductor of the most influential Catholic journal in the world, you should be on your guard against compromising the Catholic cause out of your own country as well as in it, especially as you profess to place the Catholic question above every other question.
>
> I do not complain of the party you represent for supporting the Empire, but you must pardon me for thinking that it did not do what might and should have been done to obtain a constitutional recognition of the freedom of the Church before proclaiming the Empire. The Church has no legal freedom in your country, and holds her rights at the mercy of the Emperor. You have only his personal will as the guaranty of either civil or religious freedom. The Emperor has not repealed, but has resolutely refused to repeal the Organic Laws annexed by his Uncle to the Concordat of 1801. What security have you that on the first occasion they will not be enforced? I love civil and political freedom, but I have no fear for that when the Church is free, and no hope for it when it is not free. The glory of the constitution of our country is that it recognizes and guarantees the entire freedom of the Church.
>
> These, sir, are my principal complaints against the *Univers* and its party. I state them frankly, not unkindly. I love France and honor the French clergy, but I should feel still more respect for the latter, if they were a little more independent in the face of the Prince, and if they sometimes recollected that Catholic France is not the whole Catholic world. Nevertheless I should be happy to see your journal and my own good friends. You have many enemies, both among Catholics, and non-Catholics, and I can make great allowances for provocation as well as for human imperfection. I too have my enemies, and a severe contest to maintain, against greater odds than you have to encounter, and to maintain it singlehanded. Perhaps I need sympathy more than you and that sneers at me in the *Univers* are not over and above Catholic.
>
> With you personally I have much in common. We have both come to the Church through infidelity, and have both been obliged to gain our respective positions by our personal exertions. We ought to be friends, and can be so far as depends on me, for I ask nothing of any man to be his friend but simple justice. Before receiving your letter I had inserted a note in my *Review* defining my position towards your journal. I belong to no clique in my own country or in any other. I have but one object in view, that of serving Catholic interests to the best of my ability.
>
> With every wish for your health and happiness, I subscribe myself with all sincerity, your obedient servant,
>
> O. A. Brownson[24]

As Brownson's son Henry observed in this matter, the temperament of these two men being quite dissimilar, and their views on freedom and despotism being so different, the one giving his blessing to the latter and the other being a dogged battler for the former, no peace between the two seemed possible, and they were soon at loggerheads again.

It was in the midst of this spirited collaboration with Montalembert and his party in France that Brownson had taken up his residence in New York City. His arrival there was no ordinary event in Catholic circles. It was something for New York Catholics to have this peerless and fearless expositor of the Catholic faith in their midst. They were not slow in manifesting their appreciation. After allowing him a short span to get settled, they at once (a few months after his arrival) drew him forth to the lecture platform in the Tabernacle on Broadway. There was scarcely a prominent Catholic in the city, cleric or lay, whose name was not on the list of petitioners asking that they be favored with his lectures.[25] Wishing to bring home to his countrymen the necessity of the Catholic Church for the support of the American Republic, he chose for his opening theme "The Church and the Republic," the first lecture on the subject being given in February, and the second in April 1856. The precise nature of the treatise is better indicated by the fuller title he gave it: "The Church and the Republic; Or, the Church necessary to the Republic, and the Republic compatible with the Church."[26] Such were the crowds that flocked to hear him that the spacious Tabernacle was too small to accommodate them. The theme of his lectures he knew to be of great significance for his countrymen, and he evidently put forth his very best efforts — much to the gratification of his friends. The two lectures seem to have reached a high-water mark in his lectures. Among others, Judge Hilton of Cincinnati wrote him enthusiastically:

Dear Doctor:

I have read your lectures on "The Church and the Republic" delivered in the Tabernacle, N.Y., as published in the *Pilot* with delight . . . I would be glad to see this lecture published in cheap pamphlet form, for universal distribution throughout the country. Every leading mind and man of thought in the Republic should have a copy of it. You have, ever since I have known or heard you, written many things on the subject. . . . But nothing that you have ever written on that subject has been so clear, consistent, and logical as this. It is perfect in itself and brought to the comprehension of the most ordinary intellect. The difficulties you state and their solution was the great problem of Calhoun, of Kent, of Story, and all great writers on constitutional law and civil polity in all ages.

And here you have given the most satisfactory conclusion. The elements are brought together and so arranged as ultimately by their harmonious action and reciprocal cooperation creating such a society as God wishes. His Church, the great arbiter of the sacred rights of humanity, constituting its peace and joy, creates the moral and social order under God intended for man.

As you say, here is to be developed the highest and most worthy position man has ever gained as a social being, if those constituent elements of government are recognized, heard, and submitted to. . . .

If this lecture is printed as I have suggested, I would like you to send me 100 copies, and I will settle with you for them.

Hoping that you may ever retain good health and strength, and the choicest blessings of God, I remain ever truly yours,

G. H. Hilton[27]

At the request of friends, Brownson also republished the two lectures in the form of an article in the July 1856 issue of his *Review*. The footnote appended to the title of the article is both characteristic and interesting. Referring to the contents of the two lectures, Brownson said in part:

They are adapted to the times, and meet, in a popular manner, the principal objections just now urged with the most vehemence against the Church. We may, perhaps, be pardoned for thinking them not undeserving of the serious attention of our honest and patriotic statesmen, if such we have left. The author is a Catholic, and glories in his religion, but he is also an American, by birth, by education, by feeling, and by interest, and yields to no man living in his love of his country. He has not been wholly unknown to the political world, and has had the honor of the intimate acquaintance and friendship of some of the most eminent and distinguished statesmen our country has produced. No man doubts his honesty and sincerity, and he claims that what he writes seriously on questions of the nature discussed in these lectures, is entitled to the respectful consideration of his countrymen. They are questions he has studied — questions which his antecedents and his present position enable him to understand, perhaps, better than many who are his superiors in learning and ability.[28]

In this treatise on the Catholic Church and the Republic he showed from a review of European history that society when left to itself is exposed to two dangers: on the one hand, to a tendency to the absolutism of the state, and on the other hand, to a tendency to the absolutism of the individual; that is, to a tendency to social despotism, and a tendency to pure individualism or anarchy. To save society from these twin dangers a third element is needed to mediate between the two, and that saving element is religion. But only that religion will answer the purpose which rests on a basis entirely independent of the state and the individual, and is higher than either, an *organic* power which neither the national authority nor the individual authority can control, but is strong enough to restrain either from encroaching on the rights of the other. Only the Catholic religion, he asserted, can answer to the purpose.

A writer in the *Universalist Quarterly Review* of Boston attempted to refute Brownson's arguments in a treatise on the subject and to show that his line of reasoning in favor of the Catholic Church was after all inconclusive. To this Brownson responded under the title, "Brownson on *The Church and the Republic.*"[29] This in turn drew a rejoinder from the *Universalist.* The *Universalist* agreed with Brownson that a third element is required to mediate between the state and the individual, but he denied that the religion required must be a *power,* organized religion, or an organism. To admit so much, he owned, would be to "put himself hopelessly in the power of his opponent." It only remained for Brownson to demonstrate that the Catholic Church is an *organism,* a substantive existence or objective power, not a mere abstraction or subjective idea within the mind of the individual. This he did in his final article, "The Church an Organism."[30]

In his opening article his *Universalist* disputant paid Brownson a tribute it may be well not to pass over in silence. Brownson has sometimes been spoken of as a voice "crying in the wilderness." That his conversion to the Catholic Church did work for him a certain amount of ostracism is scarcely to be denied. Yet there were those, too, who found his thought and literary style a bit too fascinating to be resisted. Speaking of these qualities, the *Universalist* said:

> Few American readers need be told who or what is O.A. Brownson. Perhaps no man in this country has, by the simple effort of the pen, made himself more conspicuous, or has more distinctly impressed the peculiarities of his mind. Other writers may have a larger number of readers, but no writer has readers of such various character. He has the attention of all sects and parties — men who read him without peculiar regard to the themes on which he ex-

pends his energies, or the sectarian or partisan position of which he may avow himself the champion. The extraordinary ingenuity of his logic, the vigor of his thought, and the clearness of his style, will attract attention, regardless of the particular opinions which prove the occasion of bringing out these fascinating qualities.[31]

It will be in place here to note that Brownson's coming to New York marked for him a turning point on more scores than one. Like Newman,[32] in his first years as a convert, Brownson had looked to the edification (the building up) of the faith of those within the household of the faith.[33] He had accordingly spent his earlier years in repelling attacks on the Catholic Church from whatever quarter they had come. In grappling with the many slanders and distortions brought against the Church so widely in his day, as a master of applied logic, he left little to be desired in the way of effectively attacking and demolishing error. So many of the books or articles he had reviewed were little more than a tissue of falsehoods or slanders leveled at the Church. In refuting these, logic was his connatural weapon. But the office of logic is to convince — not necessarily to persuade. Brownson was perhaps well aware of this all along, but was nevertheless somewhat satisfied with the use of his powerful logic in the work he had set out to do — the hurling back of attacks on the Catholic Church. However, he now turned his thoughts more directly to the problem of how he might win his countrymen to the Church. He readily acknowledged that for the direct winning of outsiders to the Church mere logic was by no means the best method to be employed.

In a letter dated March 17, 1856, to Fr. Augustine F. Hewit, then on a Redemptorist mission with Frs. Isaac Hecker and Clarence Walworth, he remarked on the matter.

> My own conviction is that our true policy in dealing with the American mind is to study first to ascertain, not its errors, but the truth it still maintains, and to show it that that truth can find its unity and integrity only in the Catholic Church. We must find our *point d'appui* in the sound principles it still holds, and lead it by arguments, drawn from those principles, of the justness of which they can judge without going out of themselves, and to the conclusion to which we wish them to come.
>
> Prayer, meditation, and reflection are better means than reading to prepare us to do this. The American people are a reasoning people, but not a learned people, and they want not old arguments but new ones, and such as they can appreciate offhand. I think Father Hecker has the right view on this subject, and after his, the next best is Father Walworth's, that of direct appeal to conscience. My own method, I believe, is the worst of all, that of logic. . . .
>
> Forgive me for the liberty I have taken, and regard what I say as only my own thoughts which, after all, may not be worth considering.[34]

All well and good as far as it goes, but, as we shall see in a later chapter, when Brownson, changing his style and method, endeavored to show those outside the Church how much we Catholics have in common with them, and thus tried to coax them into the Church, the results were conspicuously barren. He came to look upon the policy as an unquestionable mistake.

If Brownson needed any reassurances at this time that he himself understood the American mind (of which he was speaking in his letter to Fr. Hewit) and had a high mission to address it in the interest of Catholic truth, he received them in a letter Fr. Hecker wrote him from Richmond, Virginia, on April 12, 1856. He said:

It delights me that you will deliver the lecture on the subject you mention. Let me remind you of what you know, that if your second lecture tells as well as the first, the future is yours. You can talk to the American people mind to mind, heart to heart. . . . You stand before our people as an American and the champion of Catholicity. The reconciliation which has taken place in your own heart between these is to take place also in the nation. Never before had you such a task. The nation's destiny and the interests of God's Church are at stake. Let recollection, prayer, Our Lady, enter into your preparation.[35]

At this time Brownson also made a plea for the adoption of a more intelligible medium of expression when seeking to reach the minds of those outside the Catholic Church. In the past, under the direction of Bishop Fitzpatrick, he had consented to express his thought in scholastic molds, however much it may have cramped his style at the time. Now, when commenting on the English Catholic monthly, *The Rambler,* he took occasion to say that anyone who comprehends the wants and movements of the times knows that new modes of thought and activity prevail in the modern world, and that it is impossible to meet them if encumbered by the obsolete forms of the Middle Ages. "We cannot fight," he complained, "in the armor of the schoolmen any more than we can fight in that of the mediaeval knights." The various intellectual, scholastic, or philosophical forms that grew up with the Middle Ages were indigenous to those ages, but are little intelligible to men of the modern world. The Catholic of modern times must be just as free in his intellectual movements as were the old schoolmen themselves, and be allowed to do for his age what they did for theirs. Catholicity is as fully able to meet the new forms of thought of the modern world, and its errors, as it was to meet those of the Middle Ages. But to do so, the Catholic must be allowed full liberty to cast his thought in modern molds, or to present it in forms more intelligible and viable to his contemporaries. It will not do, he asserted, to suppose that Catholic dogma is identified with obsolete forms of thought, and that its forms of expression cannot be changed without modifying the faith itself, or innovating in that which is of divine revelation or divine institution. "Dogma saved, the Church allows us in this respect all necessary freedom. It is that freedom which she allows us that we should now learn to use, not rashly, not wantonly, but wisely, prudently, reverently." He expressed some impatience with those good souls who cannot understand that there have been some changes in the world since the time of good King Arthur and his Knights of the Round Table.[36]

In this matter Brownson seems again to have been ahead of his times. We are readily reminded here of the call of Pope John XXIII in his opening address in 1962 to the Second Vatican Council for a reaffirmation of Christian doctrine in forms or expressions more intelligible to modern man. "The substance," he said, "of the ancient doctrine of the deposit of faith is one thing, and the way in which it is presented is another. And it is the latter that must be taken into great consideration, with patience if necessary, everything being measured in the forms and propositions of a magisterium that is predominantly pastoral."

Yet little or no alteration in Brownson's style of meeting attacks on the Catholic Church is to be noted at this time. His usual vigorous logic coupled with powerful rhetoric continued to mount the counterattack. Shortly before he left Boston, when he happened one day to be in the law office of his friend, John Healy, Mr. E. H. Derby, a Boston lawyer, entered, and throwing down a book before Brownson, exclaimed: "There, refute that if you can!" The book was a series of letters which Derby had addressed to his son whom he wished to deter from becoming a Catholic. Brownson did refute the book in a series of articles in his *Review* in 1856 and 1857, and Derby's son continued, under the grace of God, on his way to the Church.[37] That Brownson's reply was masterly in character — and of great importance — we learn from a letter he received from a friend in Philadelphia, dated December 11, 1857, who signed himself simply J.B. After commiserating with Brownson on the opposition he was meeting with from Catholics in certain quarters, he continued:

> I consider that Catholics owe you a debt of gratitude for the great ability and learning you have exhibited on many occasions in defending our Holy Religion against those from without, especially for the masterly manner in which you have refuted the arguments and false statements contained in Mr. Derby's late dangerous book. It is just such books as this of Mr. Derby that Protestants consider unanswerable and therefore of the utmost importance that they be answered, and I know of no person who can do so better than yourself. I hope you will continue to do good in that way as occasion may require. It would be well if your answer to Mr. Derby could be printed in a separate book. It richly deserves to be.[38]

Brownson's coming to New York also marked a recognition on his part of a new type of objections being brought against the Catholic Church. He had spent his first ten years as a convert not only in repelling attacks on Catholicity, but also in setting forth a vigorous exposition of practically the whole body of Catholic doctrine. In his clear and vigorous exposition he endeavored to bring into focus every article of Catholic faith, for, as he maintained, nothing at all, however obscure or neglected of God's revelation to mankind, can be without its importance for the weal of human society. If he seemed to exalt orthodoxy to the highest point, it will not do to dismiss it as just the result of the immature zeal of the new convert. His mind did indeed revel and expand in the satisfying fullness of the great body of Catholic truth, but it is to be noted that he never did recede one iota from any article of the unmutilated orthodoxy of which he had made himself the intrepid champion in his first years as a convert. He was, without a break, a staunch ultramontane from the beginning to the end of his life. In this he also had counterparts among the converts of his day in England, particularly William George Ward, Edward Manning (later a cardinal), and Fr. Frederick W. Faber.[39] It was with William G. Ward that he had several traits in common. Both were honored with the title "gladiator." As to ultramontanism, Ward carried it to such heights that he expressed a wish to have a papal bull each morning at his breakfast table together with a copy of the London *Times*. If Brownson was ultra in any way, Manning — who was to wield such telling influence in the First Vatican Council in promoting the solemn definitions of the papal prerogatives — was referred to by his old friend, William E. Gladstone, as "an ultra of ultras."[40] And if these apostolic converts prized so highly the sovereign authority of the Catholic Church over doctrinal matters, it was no doubt because of their former unhappiness over such doctrinal chaos outside the Church. In any case, Brownson had by this time covered the whole theological field in his writings, and insofar, was ready for a fresh start on other fronts. The assailants of the Church were now to be met on more modern grounds.

When reviewing the works of Antoine Frederic Ozanam — the French genius who probably had a greater influence on Brownson than has been recognized — Brownson took occasion to point out that for the advanced minds of the nineteenth century the battleground between the Catholic Church and its adversaries was no longer that of dogma and ritual, but rather that of civilization.[41] The Church's adversaries had come to see clearly enough that medieval civilization, sometimes called Catholic civilization, was far from perfect, that in those ages when the Church is supposed to have been supreme, and the popes the arbiters of Europe, much barbarism, violence, rapine and war were widely rampant — as much or even more so than among some modern nations. Therefore it was concluded that this is all that can be expected of the Church. Kenelm Digby endeavored to evade this objection in his massive *Mores Catholici, or Ages of Faith* by collecting a great heap of data from the Middle Ages highly creditable to the Church while passing lightly over the barbarous elements which were also a conspicuous part of that civilization. This, said Brownson, is no adequate answer at all.

Brownson had also previously dealt at some length with this same objection in his article on "The Church in the Dark Ages."[42] He had pointed out there that there was no truth in the assumption which Digby seemed willing to allow, and which his Unitarian adversary of the moment (in the *Christian Examiner*) asserted, namely, that "the Church had a thousand years of almost triumphant ascendancy for the full trial of experiments" in the Middle Ages.[43] The Catholic Church in this world, stressed Brownson, is never the Church triumphant, only and always the Church militant. Never in those ages did the Church have a fair field and a fitting opportunity to realize its ideal in a Catholic social order of society: "It is all a delusion, the notion which some seem to cherish, that emperors, kings, princes and nobles demeaned themselves as her [the Catholic Church's] obedient sons. Their submission was the exception, not the rule, and their protection of the Church seldom any thing but a pretext for enslaving her."[44] Much true piety, burning charity and heroic sanctity marked those ages, of which the modern world is heir in its own degree, but there was also, alas, much, too, in those ages which did not proceed from the Church, which the Church did not sanction, and which it never ceased to oppose, which defied all its supernatural efforts, and continued to exist in spite of it.[45] Hence the Church's adversaries cannot frame an argument against it by citing the barbarism that existed alongside the Church in those ages. It all existed in spite of the Church. Brownson lauded Ozanam warmly for his noble and persevering efforts to bring this out in the magnificent volumes he left behind at the time of his death, unhappily so premature.

Brownson felt called upon also as an apologist to deal with the claim, another matter in the social order, that the choice of religion is largely a matter of ethnology. Dr. John M'Elheran of Boston had put forth the theory that Catholicity is Celtic, and Protestantism is Germanic — a theory Brownson found being widely defended at the time by Protestant Germans, Englishmen and Americans, and sometimes by Irish and French Catholics. For a Catholic apologist to pass over this claim in silence would be a plain dereliction of duty, said Brownson in his article on "Romantic and Germanic Orders," for such a claim would only confirm Protestants by all the prejudices of race in their Protestantism, and prevent Catholics of the country from making the proper efforts for the conversion of their non-Catholic countrymen.[46] He pointed out that neither the Catholic nor the Protestant seemed to perceive the harmful implications of such a theory. The Catholic failed to see that for religion to be Catholic means that it is for all nations and races, equally necessary for the Celt and the Teuton, the Greek and the barbarian, alike adapted to the nature, the condition and the wants of all men. And for the Protestant to assert that religion goes by race, is to reduce his religion to gentilism, for the essential principle of gentilism is that each nation should have its own religion — be national in character. Brownson wrote his long and elaborate article to show that the theory then gaining currency simply did not fit the historical facts in the case. If the Irish had in the past adhered to the Catholic Church, the German nations were all, for ages, the leading Catholic nations of the world. Even at that very time about one half of the Germans in Germany were still faithful members of the Catholic Church.[47] From there he went into minute historical details with a rather astonishing show of erudition.

Nor would this well-nigh peerless and fighting apologist of the Catholic Church by any means let the claim pass that liberty is Germanic and despotism Celtic, whence it is concluded that Protestantism is the religion of liberty and Catholicity a religion of despotism[48] — another branch of this same ethnological theory. Now, if there was one false charge more than another that was an abomination to Brownson, it was this same charge that the Catholic Church favors despotism. He knew full well that liberty is a magical word with the modern world, and that such a charge could only create an invincible prejudice against the Church. He understood this charge all the better inasmuch as he himself had such a passionate love of just or rational freedom both for himself as well as for others. He once wrote: "There are two things against which, as a Catholic, we declare eternal hostility, the despot and the mob, despotism and anarchy."[49] He would not abide this abusive charge against the Church. He pointed out again that the theory simply does not fit the historical facts in the case. It rested on an assumption, namely, that the southern European nations (Catholic), that is, the Italians, the French, the Spaniards, the Portuguese, are really, properly speaking, Celtic — among whom there has been a long tradition of Caesarism. He proceeded to show that these nations cannot be called Celtic. But even conceding them to be such, the civil or political order among them is not Catholic. It has been Greco-Roman, and the Greco-Roman civilization was itself a form of a consolidated imperialism which the Romans themselves borrowed from the East — of Chamitic, not of Japhetic or Celtic origin. Of this huge system of centralized despotism, brought to perfection under the emperor Diocletian, there is not a trace among any truly Celtic nation. "Nowhere," he affirmed, "have we found the Celts, wherever un-Romanized, the friends of despotism; we have always found them fighting bravely, heroically, if unsuccessfully, for independence and personal liberty."[50]

This great lover of rational liberty, who had become a Catholic, was uncommonly disturbed by the widespread notion that Catholicity has a natural association with despotism. Its discussion runs through a large section of his writings. He did not indeed deny that certain historical facts do seem to lend color to such a claim, but he denied their validity. In an article he wrote on "Religious Liberty in France" he expressed his regrets that since the coup d'etat of 1852, Catholics in France had opted to go hand in glove with the absolutism of Napoleon III, for it placed the Catholic Church in a false position in the eyes of the non-Catholic world. It only confirmed the false appearances of past ages, since for three hundred years the Catholic religion had apparently been associated with absolute monarchy, or civil despotism. It had appeared so in the sixteenth century under its imperial defenders Charles V and Philip II; it had appeared so again under Louis XIV of France, the destroyer of the last vestiges of freedom in France, who proclaimed himself in person the state; it had appeared so again under the unfortunate

Stuarts of England, Scotland and Ireland, who labored to concentrate all power in the crown, and detested the parliamentary freedom of the English nation. "So long, and apparently so strictly, have Catholicity and absolutism been associated," said Brownson, "that a strong conviction has been produced in the minds of non-Catholics and even some Catholics, that Catholicity has a natural inclination for despotism, and that the Church is incompatible with liberty."[51] He pronounced it the grand objection of the age to the Catholic religion, and, though totally unfounded in fact, seemed to be supported by the whole history of the last three hundred years.

All this was a great embarrassment to him as a Catholic apologist. The political attitude so many Catholics in France had assumed, including eminent prelates, in indiscriminately backing the absolutism of Napoleon III was doing more at the moment to revive that objection of the Church than anything else. In vain, he said, do we repel the objection and write elaborate essays, or deliver eloquent lectures to prove that our religion is the grand support of civil freedom. All that adversaries have to do is to cite against us the conduct of the French clergy during the last five years and the columns of the *Univers* as a practical refutation of our essays and lectures. He freely admitted that this attitude of so many French Catholics, and the appearances of the last three hundred years, do seem to justify the notion that Catholicity flirts with despotism and that Protestantism favors liberty. But he stoutly maintained that all such associations are merely accidental, and all such appearances entirely fallacious. The tendency of Catholics in many nations, coming down from Roman times, to associate their religion with the Greco-Roman civilization, itself characterized by Caesarism, had placed the Catholic Church, he explained, in a false and unnatural position, so that the Catholic had often found himself with no choice but either to accept the despotism his soul loathed, or to make common cause with the enemies of his religion and his country. This unnatural alliance, pleaded Brownson, must be broken. He called upon Catholics everywhere who have a free choice, and are free to act, to prove themselves in word and deed, true, firm and enlightened friends of liberty as well as of order, of the rights of the subject as well as the rights of the sovereign. Then the war going on between liberty and despotism, however long it may continue, will cease to be directed against the Catholic Church, and the party of liberty will at least respect the Church, and will count the Church's freedom and independence among the rights they are striving to secure. For collaboration in this battle he looked mainly, not to the Catholic nations on the continent of Europe, but to parliamentary England. However much he regretted England's heresy and schism, he counted that nation the best friend and most energetic supporter in the Old World of that civil and political order which as a citizen he wished for himself and his Church — and which he had as an American citizen.[52]

Perhaps nowhere did Brownson indicate more clearly the new turn in his apologetics after coming to New York City than in *The Convert,* his autobiography. In it he went back and picked up the thread of thought which had led him to the Catholic Church — his doctrine of Life by Communion. That doctrine he had, as already mentioned, put in cold storage at the suggestion of Bishop Fitzpatrick. But the more he now became convinced of its validity in the light of Catholic theology, the greater became his regret that he had suppressed it at the time of becoming a Catholic and had left the public, at least many of his old friends, mystified about his conversion. His purpose in writing *The Convert* was, therefore, to give the public at large, both Catholic and non-Catholic an opportunity to discover the connecting link between his past and his present intellectual life. He wished to state in terms as clear as possible the link in his own thought, as far as he had forged it, between nature and grace, between the natural and the supernatural, so as to demonstrate to all who might have any interest in the matter that in becoming a Catholic he had had no occasion to divest himself of his nature, or to forgo the exercise of his reason.[53] In showing this he gave his doctrine of Life by Communion an expansive exposition which has already been drawn upon in a previous chapter when recording the intellectual process of his conversion.

Although Brownson had by this time come to have an estimate of his doctrine of Life by Communion which apparently had not been shared by Bishop Fitzpatrick, he nevertheless affectionately dedicated *The Convert* to his spiritual father and mentor of many a year in the words:

To the
Right Reverend John Bernard Fitzpatrick, D.D.,
Bishop of Boston,
This unpretending volume
is most respectfully dedicated
as a
Feeble mark of the veneration for his virtues
and the
Deep Gratitude for his services
To The Convert
Cherished by His Spiritual Son.

Brownson's argument in *The Convert* is closely reasoned, and coming from one in whom reason and logic were so powerful, it gives us a very strong piece of apologetics indeed. Commenting on *The Convert,* Fr. Isaac Hecker said:

> It was a new path he struck; he followed it faithfully to his reception into the Church and gave us in *The Convert* what, to my knowledge, no one else has ever done before or since — the philosopher's road to the Church. . . . What great man before Brownson has ever written a book leading step by step, through the very processes of his own actual experiences, in a road from reason to revelation entirely apart from the historical? That the supernatural can be reached by logical processes from premises seemingly natural is what no one to my knowledge, has ever shown can be done, before Brownson.[54]

This is true in regard to the content of *The Convert.* But whether Brownson reasoned himself toward the Catholic Church entirely apart from the historical argument is an interesting question. Per Sveino, as we have noted, argues that just as Newman was drawn toward the Church by his study of the post-apostolic centuries, so Brownson was fascinated by medieval Catholicism, and was thus drawn toward the Church. Yet, while it is true that he was enamored of the church-state relationship in the Middle Ages, in which the pope was recognized as the common father of all and the guardian of human rights, it is no less true that he, as we have seen, laid strong strictures on the defects of medieval civilization — in spite of all the Church could do.[55] In any case at all, Brownson was always careful to emphasize that his philosophy did not conduct him into the Church, but that just in proportion as he advanced in a sound philosophy he found himself advancing toward the Catholic Church.[56] He always stressed that divine grace is the efficient cause of conversion in every case.

Archbishop Martin John Spalding complained that Brownson's autobiography contained no *peccavi*. But Brownson pointed out that it contained no *peccavi* because his special design in writing it was to show the various mental changes he had passed through on his way to the Church.[57] In his pre-Catholic life he had fallen short of Catholicity, but in no instance where he had faithfully followed reason, had he run counter to it. The change he underwent in becoming a Catholic was in taking on, rather than casting off.

> My Catholic life was [he said] under the grace of God, the slow and gradual accumulation of twenty-five years of intense mental activity and incessant struggles for the light and a religion I could rely upon.[58]

One of Brownson's most significant testimonies to the credibility of the Catholic faith is contained in the last paragraph of his philosophical argument. It is a testimony which increases in force when we recollect that it comes from a man of Brownson's intellectual caliber. He wrote:

> I have been, during the thirteen years of my Catholic life, constantly engaged in the study of the Church and her doctrines, and especially in their relation to philosophy, or natural reason. I have had occasion to examine and defend Catholicity precisely under those points of view which are the most odious to my non-Catholic countrymen and to the Protestant mind generally; but I have never in a single instance, found an article, dogma, or definition of faith, which embarrassed me as a logician, or which I would, so far as my reason was concerned, have changed, or modified, or in any respect altered from what I found it, even if I had been free to do so. I have never found my reason struggling against the teachings of the Church, or felt it restrained, or myself reduced to a state of mental slavery. I have, as a Catholic, felt and enjoyed a mental freedom, which I never conceived possible while I was a non-Catholic. This is my experience; and, though not worth much, yet in this matter, whereof I have personal knowledge, it is worth something.[59]

Inasmuch as Brownson was concerned exclusively with his intellectual progress in the narrative of his past, there is little or nothing in *The Convert* on the social side of his life. He speaks little of his childhood (he claimed he scarcely had any at all), and he never even mentioned his marriage or any family affairs. A reviewer of *The Convert* in the *Catholic Mirror* lamented this lack of information about the man Brownson generally, especially about his childhood. This reviewer's thoughts are doubly interesting on the score that he also touches on Brownson as a lecturer. He wrote:

> We regret, we say, that these details are not fuller. The day will come when every incident in Dr. Brownson's life will be valuable, not only to Catholics but to the world: he is one of the few men whom the world will not let die. We are indifferent to the diaries of living men, because we are apt to measure them with ourselves and reduce their stature to our own — because they meet and mingle with us in our play and labors — because when the mere man has passed away and the great name remains we would give much to know more of the brief pilgrimage the great soul has performed among us. We felt this when Dr. Brownson last lectured here [Baltimore], as we glanced along the half-filled benches, as we gazed upon the strong man before us, as we listened to his deep-thought, earnest sentences. We felt we were in the presence of a man in advance of his generation — of one too true to be popular — of one too sincerely the world's friend to be the world's favorite. We felt with something of a pang, that Edward Everett could collect his thousands to hear him, while the abler man and the equal orator scarcely numbered his hundreds.[60]

Whatever the fact about attendance at this particular lecture, we have already seen ample evidence that Brownson regularly drew large and enthusiastic crowds to hear him lecture. During the last year or two, 1856-1857, he had lectured in such centers as St. Louis, Charleston, South Carolina, Chicago, Baltimore, and had given single lectures in a number of populous places on his way to and from these centers. Hearing in the latter part of 1857 that Brownson was to lecture in Louisville, Bishop O'Connor of Pittsburgh thought he might be induced to lecture also in Pittsburgh, and instructed the St. Vincent de Paul Society to send him an invitation to that effect. He himself backed up the invitation with a letter of his own, dated December 7, 1857, in which he endeavored to set things right between Brownson and himself, and to which he subjoined an interesting reference to *The Convert*. He wrote:

> As to the past, you must allow me to say that you would wrong me or yourself if you ever supposed me to be hostile to your person or to your *Review*. I doubted the propriety of some things that were published in the latter and thought them doubly dangerous while the *Review* was supposed to hold a representative character, but I am far from expecting or even desiring that one holding your position should try to please every one, and there was no time that I did not feel an interest in the *Review* with a sincere desire to encourage its circulation as much as possible. With regard to yourself I have never entertained a doubt about your sterling honesty as well as of your talents and power. I hope you will have the kindness to make our house your home while you are in Pittsburgh.
>
> Hoping to see you soon, I remain yours faithfully in Xt,
>
> M. O'Connor,<br>Bp. Pittsburgh
>
> O. A. Brownson, Esq.
>
> P.S. I must disclaim the authorship of the article in the *Pittsburgh Catholic* [i.e., on *The Convert*], but I do so only for the purpose of adding that had I written one as I intended to do and would have done had I not been unwell, I would have expressed my admiration of the book and my respect for the author even more strongly than the editor.[61]

Although Brownson must have been quite happy in having his strained relationship with any member of the venerable hierarchy of the country thus smoothed out, a thing of particular consequence to him was to be on friendly terms with the bishop of the diocese in which he now resided. On this score he was to realize all too soon that his coming to New York City was not to be for him too happy an event. While in Boston, even though Bishop Fitzpatrick had not come to his defense in the fierce battles he had encountered in the theological field, he could at least always count on him as a sympathetic and understanding friend. But he was to find in Archbishop John Hughes of New York quite a different type of churchman. Yet it is gratifyingly obvious that both he and Archbishop Hughes had endeavored earnestly after Brownson's coming to New York to work amicably together for the great cause which both had so deeply at heart. But their initial harmonious relations were soon to deteriorate progressively with the years until Hughes' death in 1864.

# 35

## BROWNSON AND ARCHBISHOP HUGHES

*On coming to New York City Brownson attempts to curry favor with Archbishop Hughes • Hughes' unfavorable comments to the audience after Brownson's commencement address at St. John's College in 1856 • Thomas D. McGee gleefully plays up this collision between Brownson and Hughes in his* **The American Celt** *• Hughes affirms in a letter to Brownson that he had meant nothing disrespectful or offensive to him in his remarks • Brownson responds that McGee had a perfect right to represent the affair as he had • A letter of Louis B. Binsse to Cardinal Barnabò, Prefect of the Propaganda Fide, Rome, on the matter • Brownson is suspected of being a member, if not the unacknowledged leader, of an Americanizing club rising in Hughes' diocese • Brownson's increasing interest in convert work at this time • His dissatisfaction with the current approach to convert work • His article on the "Mission of America" is disturbing to Archbishop Hughes • Hughes' treatise: "Reflections and Suggestions in regard to what is called the Catholic Press in the United States" • Some comments on it in Brownson's article, "Archbishop Hughes and the Catholic Press" • Brownson reviews Fr. Hecker's books:* **Questions of the Soul** *and* **Aspirations of Nature** *• The reasons why he could not or did not give* **Aspirations of Nature** *a more favorable review • Fr. Hecker's mission to Rome • Reassuring letters Brownson received in his hour of dark discouragement • He is also cheered up by letters from converts through his writings • His nostalgic letter to his spiritual father, Bishop John B. Fitzpatrick.*

There are certain persons so constituted temperamentally, however sterling their qualities otherwise, who are ill-fitted to work closely together in any cause. Such seems to have been the case with Orestes Brownson and Archbishop John J. Hughes. They were both immensely aggressive in character, and Brownson certainly not less so than Hughes. They were both tremendous fighters in any good cause. Hughes' life had been, almost from the day of his ordination, one long series of battles, stretching through his protracted public debates with the Presbyterian minister, John Breckenridge, his hard-fought struggle to put down trusteeism, his valiant fight for the right quality of religious instruction in the public schools, and his militant resistance to nativistic attacks on his people, to mention no others. His talents and skills had been thoroughly tested and matured by these long-drawn battles, and he had emerged from them a fearless battler. Moreover, he was well-connected in the political world. He was on very friendly terms with William H. Seward, former governor of the state, currently a United States senator, and later to become the famed secretary of state in President Lincoln's Cabinet. The big newspapermen of New York City, with whom he had had dealings, knew well, too, that he was a power to be reckoned with. As a prelate he was tireless and fearless in his efforts to advance what he had come to understand in his advancing years to be for the best interests of the Catholic cause. Of the role he played in the history of the Church in the United States Brownson himself was to say later: "[His life is] a very complete history of the Church in New York, we might almost say in the United States, from 1838 to 1864."[1] And with his wide experience of so many years in the episcopate, Hughes had come by this time to have great confidence in his own judgment. *The New Catholic Encyclopedia* says of him:

> Archbishop Hughes was a born leader and fighter. Prompt and vigorous in action and unyielding in conflict, he believed he had the duty and the obligation to lead and defend his people, and prove that American Catholics are not second-class citizens. . . . If he was autocratic and at times fought harder than was necessary, he merely displayed the defects of his virtues. . . . Although Hughes became increasingly intolerant of disagreement, he rendered valuable services to both Church and country.[2]

There is no call to recount here the rugged factors that had built Orestes Brownson into the stalwart man that he was. Suffice it to say that his mind had been sharpened and toughened by endless controversies with some of the finest minds of the times. But it is pertinent to note that Brownson, as much as he admired Hughes, seems to have been fully aware on coming to New York City that there might be some little difficulty in working amicably with him. It may not be so easy to unscramble all the subtle factors that may have contributed to the trouble that ensued so soon between the two, but Theodore Maynard is wide of the mark when he remarks that "the sorest point of all may well have been Hughes' expectation of playing the role that had been played by Fitzpatrick, and his chagrin at learning that Brownson intended to act on his own responsibility."[3] Brownson did ask Hughes to act as censor for him. Apart from the evidence in Hughes' letter to the Sacred Congregation of the Propaganda Fide in Rome, to be cited in full later, in his article on "The Church not a Despotism," Brownson told his readers that when he came to New York, "the most reverend Archbishop refused to supervise our articles, and assured us that he wished them to emanate from our own mind, and that we should be perfectly free, in conducting our *Review,* to follow our own judgment and convictions."[4] This can only be regarded as a gracious gesture to Hughes on the part of Brownson. For we have already seen that he no longer felt the need of any such censorship, and preferred to be rid of the extra rigmarole it involved. The suggested censorship could only have meant that Brownson was making every effort to get off to a good start with the archbishop of New York. The favorable results were to be short-lived indeed.

Brownson had been in the city only a short time when the first clash with Hughes occurred. The occasion was the commencement address which Brownson gave in the summer of 1856 at St. John's College, later Fordham University (1907), in response to the invitation of the faculty. Brownson has left no record of his address, but his son Henry says that some of the thought in the address was similar to that in his father's previous address on "The Church and the Republic." As it did not please Hughes, who presided on the occasion, he whispered to Brownson at the conclusion of the address that while his address was entirely in harmony with Catholic teaching, it contained sentiments with which he was not wholly in sympathy. This may not have surprised Brownson overly much, but a real surprise was in store for him. When the commencement exercises were over, Hughes took the floor and made a final address in which he subjected Brownson's address to ironical and hostile remarks, understood as such by all present, says Henry Brownson. Thomas D. McGee, editor of *The American Celt,* and unfriendly to both the archbishop and Brownson, played up the affair gleefully in his journal.[5] When this came to the knowledge of Hughes, he wrote Brownson a fairly long letter, the first paragraphs of which are the most relevant here. He wrote on August 29, 1856:

> My dear Dr. Brownson:
>
> During my stay at Watertown, I saw by chance a number of the "American Celt" in which a malicious construction was placed upon my remarks at the last commencement of St. John's College.
>
> I intended at the time to notice the article. But I have not since been able to find the number in which it was contained. I think it due to myself, not less than to you, to state briefly that in my remarks on that occasion it was farthest from my thoughts to make use of a single phrase or a single word that should in the least be disrespectful to yourself. There was nothing intended as ironical — nothing as censorious, at least as far as you are personally concerned. You are aware that I did not agree with some of the sentiments contained in your address. But that right of difference of opinion is what is mutually acknowledged wherever essential principles of faith and morals are not immediately involved.[6]

Never did Orestes Brownson answer a letter quicker than he did this one. Writing back to Hughes on September 1, he said:

> I never for one moment entertained the thought that you intended in your remarks [at St. John's] anything unkind or disrespectful to me personally. But I was surprised to hear you make those objections in public to my address, after having assured me they were only for my private ear. I regretted that, as I had said nothing against faith or morals of which I had not as a Catholic and an American citizen a perfect right to say, you should have felt it your duty to oppose me thus strenuously in public. It was taking an unfair advantage of me. It was opposing to me, a layman, the opinions of an archbishop and that archbishop, of New York. There was no equality in the case. It was crushing me with the weight of authority, in a matter of simple opinion. You must not blame me, if I did feel that I was harshly treated, and an unfair advantage given my enemies over me. You and I cannot debate a question on equal terms before the public, for you cannot address the public in your own name against me without opposing to me the mitre. Your remarks, however intended by you, were an episcopal censure on me, and I can see no reason why the "American Celt" had not the right so to consider them.[7]

Just the same Hughes insisted on standing on his original statement. A little more than two weeks later (September 17, 1856) he wrote to Brownson again:

> Dear Mr. Brownson:
>
> I repudiate the malicious construction which one of our weekly papers has put upon my observations at the commencement of St. John's College. There was nothing in my remarks or in my mind that was intended to be either ironical or disrespectful to yourself. You must be aware that on not a few points I have differed from you in regard to questions connected with your *Review.* This will not surprise you whose very profession it is as a public writer to differ from others. I may say, however, that no substantial change, in regard to your *Review,* has come over my mind since the publication of the

first number, and I hope you may be spared many years to preside over its pages with increasing patronage and, if possible, with increasing utility to religion.

Very respectfully your obedient servant in Christ,

John, Archbishop of New York[8]

The strange thing about this episode is that Hughes should have returned such a flat denial that his remarks contained anything ironical or disrespectful to Brownson. Certainly neither Brownson nor anyone else had any reason to see anything unfriendly to Brownson in the remarks if it was not there — whatever personal motives McGee had for playing up the affair. The most plausible explanation would seem to be that Hughes may have been carried away a bit after taking the floor without realizing it. In any case at all, it was the opening gun in a drawn battle between Orestes Brownson and the archbishop of New York.

It will be of interest to add here an account of this affair which Louis B. Binsse sent to Cardinal Alessandro Barnabò, Prefect of the Propaganda Fide, Rome. Binsse was a pontifical consul general in this country for the Congregation of the Propaganda Fide from 1850 to 1870. He wrote his letter, however, on October 16, 1856, only after Brownson's article on the "Mission of America" had appeared in the October edition of his *Quarterly*. Binsse wrote:

> I have entrusted to E. Neuss of Aix la Chapelle the forwarding . . . of the last number of Brownson's *Review* to your Eminence. It contains an article, "Mission of America," which has produced a certain sensation because it is not in harmony with the ideas of a certain portion of the population here, namely, that the Church in the United States should not take on a special Irish character, and that the Church can only win by nationalizing itself (if I can be permitted to use that expression) as soon as possible. The article in question has also attracted attention because it has been preceded by a declaration of opposition to these ideas which the archbishop made publicly with much fanfare on the following occasion. The Jesuits had invited Brownson to speak at their commencement for the conferring of the degrees of Bachelor of Arts before a great assembly in mid-June [at St. John's]. Brownson in said address in a succinct manner expressed the same ideas as those of the article in question. Hardly had he sat down when the archbishop got up and, after having declared that it did not seem to him proper that such ideas should be aired without contradiction, harangued the graduates with completely opposing views, denying the existence of the advantages the laws of the country are said to offer Catholics, and which Brownson had taken pains to emphasize; asserting further that liberty for Catholics existed only on paper, and not in fact, and exhorting them to prepare for days of oppression and persecution in the future. This event created a great commotion among Catholics and I have not yet met any one who thought that the sortie of the archbishop had been properly motivated or that it had done any good, rather the contrary.[9]

Some of the real trouble between Hughes and Brownson seems to have stemmed from the notion on Hughes' part that Brownson belonged to an Americanizing party rising in his diocese. There was at the time a small club in New York City which had some such object, composed of priests and laymen, mostly the sons of foreign-born parents. What the purpose of the club was Brownson never fully knew, and met with the club only once as an invited guest, as he has assured us. He was never a member of it, but certainly his recent writings might easily have created the suspicion that he intended to make his *Review* the organ of some such party among Catholics.

He protested, however, that he never so much as dreamt of forming any such party, and never gave any countenance to those who were demanding a native-born clergy, for it was always a matter of indifference to him of what nationality any clergyman might be so long as he understood the duties of his mission and could fulfill them.[10] This is all in perfect harmony with Brownson's antecedents in the case, for if there was any one thing more than another he had been combating in his writings, it was any spirit of nationalism in the Catholic Church. Whatever the facts, Brownson seems to have incurred guilt in this matter by suppositive association, as has often happened in similar cases.

What may have easily misled Hughes in the case is that Brownson was by no means devoid of all sympathy with the general spirit of the club mentioned, while not a member. That is, insofar as he had already been battling furiously to prove that an American citizen on his conversion to the Catholic Church was not required to renounce his American nationality — the very supposition that had been such incriminating grist for the mill of the Know-Nothings — and that other nationalities, domiciled on American soil, should treat his own nationality with respect, and not contempt, as, he claimed, was sometimes done. Who precisely were members of this club in New York City is a trifle uncertain. Dr. Jeremiah Cummings and Dr. Ambrose Manahan were its moving spirits. Dr. Charles C. Pise, Dr. John Forbes, Fr. Isaac Hecker, Fr. Sylvester Malone and Fr. George McCloskey may perhaps be spoken of as at least hanging closely on its fringes. So also Fr. Bernard McQuaid, living in New Jersey, and later to become the bishop of Rochester,[11] New York. There was some talk among the group of adopting a milder tone in apologetics to win over those outside the Catholic Church, and this may possibly have been an additional offense to Hughes, who, as Brownson said, was as uncompromising in regard to Catholic doctrine as his own *Review* had ever been.[12]

Unfortunately, Brownson was soon to lend further coloring to the appearance that he belonged to this Americanizing party in the Catholic Church. To understand this matter, we must keep in mind that Brownson was at this time, as noted in the last chapter, grappling with the problem of just how to present the Church to his non-Catholic countrymen so as to win them to the one true fold. As he said at the time: "As an American convert we have our mind and heart set on the conversion of our non-Catholic countrymen, and we are in the habit of looking upon Catholic questions and proceedings in their bearing on these countrymen of ours, whom we so ardently desire to see converted, but" — he cautiously added — "never with feelings of hostility or indifference to our Catholic brethren of foreign birth."[13] He knew the American mind, and he was thoroughly convinced that the current method of presenting the Catholic Church to those outside left something to be desired. Over in England Newman too lamented the maladroit approach to his non-Catholic countrymen, when he said: "It is so ordered on high that in our day the Church should present just that aspect to my countrymen which is the most consonant with their ingrained prejudices against her, most unpromising for their conversion."[14]

An additional coloring to the appearance that Brownson belonged to an Americanizing party, if not its unacknowledged leader, came with the publication of his article entitled "Mission of America." The article was written and published only two or three months after that commencement spectacle at St. John's College. That unpleasant affair must have been very much on Brownson's mind when he was composing the article. He made Bishop Mar-

535

tin John Spalding's volume of *Miscellanies* the peg upon which to hang his whole article. We may readily see an oblique reference to Hughes, a foreign-born prelate, when he said of Spalding's volume:

> It is the production of a distinguished American prelate, who feels that this is his own, his native land; and who identifies himself with the American people, and consults their interests as his own. He speaks to us from an American heart; and what he says is hardly less valuable under the point of patriotism than under that of religion. . . . The author is not one of those Americans who have no sympathy with the institutions of their own country, and are really foreigners in their sentiments and affections. . . . There is, as far as we know, nothing in the American self-reliance, activity, energy, hurry, and bustle, however repugnant to our old-world notions, that a Catholic may not reconcile with Catholic faith and morals.[15]

The message of Brownson's article was that America is destined to develop here a higher order of Christian civilization than had ever existed before. This it is enabled to do through a combination of favorable circumstances, providentially arranged, which had never existed in any nation in the past nor in any nation of the present. But he was careful to point out that it was not a new development of Christianity he was speaking of, but a new development of Christian civilization by or through the Catholic Church. And he called upon Catholics to throw themselves into the great national stream of the country and be a part of it all. He cautioned, however — in words scarcely palatable to Archbishop Hughes:

> If Catholics choose to separate themselves from the great current of American nationality, and assume the position in political and social life of an inferior, distinct, or alien colony planted in the midst of a people with whom they have no sympathies, they will be permitted to do so, and will be treated by the country at large according to their estimate of themselves.[16]

Brownson was here lashing out again at the ghetto spirit or foreignism. His motive was praiseworthy enough, for he was laboring to remove from the Catholic Church that foreign aspect it wore to his countrymen — masking the Church's fair and lovely non-national features. Could they ever be won to give the Church a second thought as long as it actually appeared to be a foreigner in the land? But was it wise for Brownson to be pushing Americanization so vehemently? He was philosopher enough to have realized that the Americanization process is subject to the inexorable law of a normal evolution. It can scarcely be pushed, but will inevitably come in a generation or two. This he had himself repeatedly asserted in his writings. Impatient though of the seemingly slow process, he gave offense by pushing it with too much ardor. His pleas for Americanization were, however, entirely justified as directed against those demagogues or base politicians who were endeavoring to keep foreigners a ghetto people to be manipulated for their own selfish purposes. And it would seem that it was at these that his shafts were mainly directed.

Hughes was later to cite a paragraph with disapprobation from the article on the "Mission of America" in which Brownson had made a plea in behalf of the Catholic youth of the land. Brownson had always had a lively interest in youth and youth in him. Instead of being snubbed for their inexperience, he pleaded, they — to whom the future belongs — should be encouraged with confidence and sympathy, and cheered on to ever newer and nobler efforts:

O, for the love of God and man [he exclaimed] do not discourage them, force them to be mute and inactive, or suffer them, in the name of Catholicity, to separate themselves in their affections from the country and its glorious mission. Let them feel and act as American citizens; let them feel that this country is their country, its institutions their institutions, its mission, their mission, its glory their glory. Bear with them, tread lightly upon their involuntary errors, forgive the ebullitions of a zeal not always according to knowledge and they will not refuse to listen to the counsels of age and experience.[17]

After reading Brownson's article on the "Mission of America," Archbishop Hughes came to the conclusion that it was time to say something about a matter so influential as the Catholic press. After all, if he was to keep a tight rein on his diocese he had to keep a tight rein on the Catholic press in his diocese. Accordingly he wrote a treatise entitled: "Reflections and Suggestions in regard to what is called the Catholic Press in the United States," published at first in the *Metropolitan Record,* the organ of the diocese, and then put into pamphlet form. But as it concerned itself mainly with Brownson's *Review* and Thomas D'Arcy McGee's *The American Celt,* Hughes sought an occasion to read to Brownson beforehand the parts which concerned himself. This came about on the occasion of the archbishop's administration of the sacrament of confirmation at St. Anne's parish in the city, Brownson having been designedly invited to be present on the occasion. The archbishop had written in the manuscript that it was known to Brownson at least that "several paragraphs" in his *Review* had not met with his approbation. But as published in the weekly, the *Metropolitan Record,* the expression in the treatise was changed to "many articles," which was not true. In the pamphlet the phrase "several paragraphs" was restored. Which paragraphs they were, Brownson was never able to learn.[18] Near the end of his treatise as it had appeared in the *Metropolitan* the archbishop did not refrain from adding an admonition on the implied comparison between himself, a foreign-born prelate, and Bishop Martin John Spalding, a prelate of native growth, in "Mission of America." The archbishop wrote:

We advise that Catholic periodicals abstain from everything having even a tendency to infringe on the regular ecclesiastical authority by which God has been pleased to appoint that His Church should be governed; that they shall not presume to draw odious comparisons, and publish them, between the clergy of one section of the country and those of another; that they shall not arrogate to themselves the position of oracles or umpires to decide where is merit, or where is demerit; that they shall not single out a clergyman for premature panegyric, simply because he is a patron of this or that journal, whilst they pass over in silence other clergymen, oftentimes of more than equal worth.

All in all, however, Hughes was extremely laudatory of Brownson's transcendent gifts as a journalist. The particular faults he charged him with were, first, that he had made an uncalled for appeal to youth; second, that he seemed to think that the Catholic Church would make greater progress in the country after Catholic immigration had ceased, or had slacked off; and, third, that he was too optimistic about the conversion of his non-Catholic countrymen.[19]

As to the plea he had made in behalf of the Catholic youth of the land, Brownson replied that, if uncalled for, the worst that could be said was that he had needlessly thrown away his eloquence. But he assured the archbishop that if he suspected in it a personal application, he was doing him great injustice, and that "if it had given him a moment of pain, we deeply regret it."

He further assured His Grace that when he wrote that paragraph he "had in mind certain facts totally unconnected with the Archbishop of New York. We are laymen, and do not regard it as within our province either to rebuke or to advise the authorities of the Church in what is their own affair. We allow ourselves no liberty of the sort, and would tolerate it in no journalist."[20] As to the charge that he seemed to underestimate the role of immigrants in the progress of the Church in the country, or thought that there would be greater progress after immigration had waned, he showed by ample quotations from his *Review* that the charge was simply not true.[21] It is really a strange fact, as may be remarked by the way, that Brownson's real meaning was so often missed by his readers, by friend and foe alike, which continued to be a source of mystification to him. Newman, too, moaned, "I cannot explain myself to friend or foe intelligibly."[22]

The charge that Brownson was too sanguine about the conversion of his countrymen, opens up a wider discussion. Although Henry Brownson suggested that what had displeased Hughes in his father's address at St. John's College, in the summer of 1856, had been some thoughts Brownson had expressed similar to those in his previous address on "The Church and the Republic," Hughes himself had brought up quite another matter about that address in a sizable letter he wrote Brownson shortly thereafter on August 22, 1856.[23] In it he said: "The drift of your remarks at the 'commencement' at St. John's was to the effect [that] if the Catholic religion had been or could be presented to the American people through mediums or under auspices more congenial with their national feelings and habits, the progress of the Church and the conversion of Protestants would have been greater. This of course is pure speculation. But it is a view in which I cannot concur."[24] Furthermore, when Brownson had reviewed Fr. Isaac Hecker's book, *Questions of the Soul,* in April 1855, he had praised it as a real groundbreaker in convert technique. Other books on convert work had been written for a state of things which had passed or was passing away in the country. "There has been no real medium of communication," continued Brownson, "between Catholic and non-Catholic Americans, and if our Catholic writers have understood the non-Catholic American, he had not understood them. They had not spoken to the comprehension of the real American mind and heart, or penetrated to what we could call the inner American life."[25] Judging from the words of Hughes' letter just quoted, he appears to have grown a trifle weary of all this talk about a new technique to be adopted which would be sure to guarantee a sudden flow of converts into the Catholic Church similar, perhaps, to the Oxford flow on the occasion of Newman's conversion.

It is not surprising, therefore, that this same matter came up for remarks in Hughes' treatise on the Catholic press. In response to what Hughes had said on the subject in his treatise on the Catholic press Brownson showed again that Hughes had expressed himself just as optimistically in his thoughts on the matter as he had ever done himself, for, from the first year after his conversion he had never been confident about the ready conversion of the American people. Yet he had been intensely interested in their conversion and had wished to keep up hope and enthusiasm. And in a work of such kind, he observed, hope tends to fulfill its prophecy. Hopelessness and indifference can effect nothing. Does not God want the country converted? He asserted that the archbishop had seemed "as hopeful as ourselves, and if he thinks to the contrary, he must permit us to believe that it is because he has been led to believe that we have expressed ourselves in stronger terms than we really have."[26] The sum total of Brownson's response was, therefore, that he and the archbishop were in surprising agreement in regard to convert prospects.

This whole problem of the convert apostolate was to loom up much larger in Brownson's review of Fr. Isaac Hecker's book, *Aspirations of Nature,* in October of 1857. As Brownson was to come into closer contact with Fr. Hecker at this very critical time in Fr. Hecker's life, we might well recall here that when Fr. Hecker returned in early 1851 from Europe, where he had gone to make his studies for the priesthood, he was very anxious to visit again his old friend of Brook Farm days — none other than Orestes Brownson. After reaching American shores, he wrote Brownson immediately on March 22, 1851:

> Dearest Friend:
> It is with the greatest pleasure that I announce to you my arrival at New York after a boisterous passage of 52 days via France. It would be a great pleasure to me to speak with you. I hope some arrangement will be made in such a way that I shall have the opportunity of visiting you at your residence.[27]

Fr. Hecker, however, was now a Redemptorist and could not go and come at will as formerly. As a result, he apparently did not manage the visit until the summer of that year. He and Brownson, after a separation of so many years, had so much to talk about, and must have often talked themselves into the late hours of the night. Their talks were of course mainly about what concerned the Catholic Church or about the spiritual life. Brownson must have found his friend Isaac all the more interesting now that he had to his advantage the spiritual training of a Redemptorist. Fr. Hecker presented his friend Orestes on the occasion with a discipline, that is, an instrument of knotted cords for penitential use, and also promised him a hairshirt as soon as he could find time to make one.[28] The discipline, we are told, remained ever unbloodied. From this time on Fr. Hecker was in frequent correspondence with his friend Brownson, and they met now and then on their travels.

Fr. Hecker was soon quite busy giving Redemptorist missions. He often had as his co-workers in the field other Redemptorists who like himself were American converts — Fr. Clarence Walworth, Fr. Augustine Hewit, Fr. George Deshon and Fr. Francis Baker. After laboring a number of years giving missions throughout the country to Catholic congregations, they felt a strong missionary urge to broaden their apostolate and evangelize also the non-Catholics among their countrymen. But as the Redemptorist Congregation was at that time largely German, they wished to establish an American House in the congregation as more in harmony with the work they contemplated. As this permission might not be so easy to obtain, Fr. Hecker was finally chosen to go to Rome to explain there the work they had in mind for the conversion of the American people. But as Fr. Hecker, with great confidence in the apostolic nature of his mission, went without the customary permission of his superiors, his mission to Rome was a somewhat uncertain and delicate one. This Brownson perceived clearly enough, and in a letter of great encouragement to him, spoke also of misunderstandings he might unfortunately encounter. When affairs did take an unfortunate turn in Rome, Fr. Hecker wrote back to Brownson:

> Dear Friend:
> Almost every word of your letter was a prediction. And what has not yet proved to be, may yet become so.

I was condemned and dismissed without a hearing. I demanded a full hearing, but the contrary was decided and my vows were relaxed and I was dismissed. . . . But I am fully convinced that had a full hearing been granted it would not have helped our affairs in the least. These good men from their education political and religious are led with bona fide intentions to misconstrue our motives, misinterpret our language, and misunderstand our actions. Why wait and see the interests of God and country suffer? . . .

If you give my book [he referred to *Aspirations of Nature*] a notice, please send me a half dozen copies as soon as printed. If the proof sheets could be sent, a copy of them earlier, it might serve greatly. A stone shall not be left unturned to accomplish what we believe to be the cause of God and His Holy Church in our own dear country.

Now that my hands are free, I shall act more largely, and shall endeavor to have translated into Italian and published in a pamphlet form or some other way your article "Mission of America." I shall see a book publisher with whom I am already acquainted tomorrow, about the translation and publication of "Mission of America." If you have any suggestions on this or any other points regarding these matters, do write, and speedily.

Allow me to suggest that if you notice my book to mention the dissolution of Protestantism in America in the shape of Calvinism. . . . Make mention that now is the time to prepare for the conversion of the American people.

This article may also be published along with the other. If the latter comes too late, and you find it necessary to delay some days in the publication of your *Review* to accomplish this, I beg you to do it. Now is the time to strike the blow. For God's sake and the love of our country and its free institutions do not let it pass.[29]

Brownson was of course much grieved at the summary dismissal of his friend by the superior general of the Congregation of the Most Holy Redeemer. After expressing his sentiments on the matter in a long letter to Fr. Hecker on September 29, 1857, he also explained to him why he had felt constrained to give his review of *Aspirations of Nature* the precise turn it had received for the forthcoming issue of his *Quarterly,* and further stated his own feelings concerning the conversion of the country. He wrote in part:

My review of your book is long, elaborate, and not unfriendly. It had been in print several weeks before your letter arrived. The *animus* of the review is not unkind, but I have aimed to write as an impartial critic, and on two or three points, which are mere matters of opinion, I have ventured to differ from you, and on other points to guard your statements from being misapprehended. My article has been written as you will see, with the intention of refuting the unfounded suspicion that there is found among us an American party or an American clique. . . . I have disclaimed anything of the sort, so far as my knowledge extends. I have disclaimed every thing of the kind for myself and for you, and all my friends among the laity, as you know I could with strict truth and justice. You know we none of us want a native party, or entertain any other than true fraternal feelings towards our Catholic brethren of European birth. . . .

I have aimed to show that there is no American clique, and to allay the suspicions to the contrary entertained as you and I both know in certain quarters, as also the suspicion of an intention to raise up a lay party through the press against the hierarchy. I say something of the conversion of the country. On this point I confess that I am less sanguine of *immediate* success than you are. I am devoted heartily, in my own sphere, to the work as you are, and I am confident of its ultimate success, but I think, as you know, the difficulty of the work is greater than you consider, greater on the part of non-Catholics, and greater on the part of Catholics. . . .

If you publish Mission [of America], put such an introduction to it as you judge proper. . . . The article was inspired by you and you stand its godfather.[30] My family are all well, except myself, and I am well enough in body. Write when you can, and believe that, if there is any thing so feeble and uninfluential a person as I can do to serve your cause I shall always be happy to do it. Forgive the length of this letter, which I have not had the time to shorten, and believe me more truly than ever,

Your friend in X,

O. A. Brownson[31]

Here we have a plain statement of the urgent and cogent reasons why Brownson did give *Aspirations of Nature* the impartial and objective review that it did receive. The reasons are stated even more fully in the review of the book itself. His review was above all his answer to Archbishop Hughes, who had been harassing him for fostering an American party in the Catholic Church, if not its leader. (Speaking of the alleged American party, Brownson later said: "We ourselves were made to suffer not a little for our supposed connection with it, and the presumed intention of making the *Review* the organ of an American party among Catholics."[32]) In his pamphlet on the Catholic press in the United States, Archbishop Hughes had also complained of this same supposed American party which assumed, as he said that:

> . . . if the Catholic faith were rightly understood, its principles are in close harmony with those of our constitution and laws — that it requires only a skillful architect to dove-tail the one into the other, and to show how the Catholic religion and the American constitution fit each other as a key fits a lock; that without any change in regard to faith and morals, the doctrines of the Catholic Church may be, so to speak, Americanized — that is, represented in such a manner as to attract the attention and win the admiration of the American people.[33]

This Hughes wrote only to proscribe. The archbishop was out to scotch any such ideas of an American party, whether a figment of his own mind or having body and substance. And Brownson was just as determined to give His Grace of New York solemn assurances once and for all in his review of *Aspirations of Nature* that he had no part or lot in any such Americanizing party — as an American party in the Catholic Church, whether out for the conversion of the country or whatever its objective might be. In his review of *Aspirations* Brownson said again for the benefit of Archbishop Hughes:

> There has been much said and written of late on the conversion of Americans, and no man among us is more devoted to the work of effecting it, or more hopeful of its being effected, than our author. He does all by word and by writing in his power for it, and has quickened the zeal of many to do the same, among whom we count ourselves. But from the much we say and write in reference to this subject, and the frequency with which we speak of the American mind, the American people, American institutions, and the appeals we make to American patriotism, some Catholics not of American birth, or not having very lively sympathy with the American character as they see it manifested, are led to suspect us of a design to Americanize Catholicity, and of a desire to induce the American people to embrace our religion through appeals to their American prejudices, passions, habits, or patriotism. This suspicion, so far as we are concerned, is wholly unfounded, although we as well as others may have used expressions which would seem at first sight to warrant it. Unhappily this is a country in which no good thing can be proposed, but there stand ready a large

number of unemployed individuals to convert it at once into a hobby, to mount it, and to ride it to death. Certainly no such thought or design exists as is suspected, but with unreasoning opposition on the one side and unreasoning enthusiasm on the other, we cannot say what may come in the end, if no pains are taken to guard against extremes, and if there is not on the part of those who are so earnest for the conversion of the country a proper respect for our prelates whom the Holy Ghost has placed over us, and a full recognition of their authority and obedience to it.

Every movement intended to advance religious or Catholic interests, initiated by Catholic laymen, and supported by them against the wishes, or without the approval of authority, is to be distrusted, and abandoned by every one whose attachment to his Church is stronger than his attachment to his own private opinion. . . . The bishops and the clergy know at least as well what it is necessary to do, in order to convert non-Catholics, as the laity do, and we are not disposed to run in advance of them.[34]

Now if these assurances did not tranquilize the mind of Archbishop Hughes on the matter, then nothing could, coming as they did from Orestes Brownson, a man of unimpeachable honesty. Brownson may well have felt it necessary precisely at this time to make use of such strong and clear language in making his disavowals, for he may well have feared that even Fr. Hecker's going to Rome with the mission he had, noble as was his motive, might easily be construed by Hughes as further evidence that an American party was ominously rising in his diocese. Brownson was very conscious by this time that he had a running battle on his hands with Hughes. In ending up his response to Hughes' pamphlet on the Catholic press, he had indicated that matters had come to a grave pass indeed between Hughes and himself when he wrote:

We are free within our legitimate sphere as a Catholic journalist, and authority cannot censure us, though the father may counsel us, unless we step beyond that sphere and offend against faith, morals, or discipline. . . . If the bishop or archbishop who judges in the first instance does us wrong, our remedy is not in disobedience, resistance, or public discussion but in appeal to Rome, to the highest tribunal of the Church. The law that governs journalists is, we take it, the same law that governs Catholics in all lawful secular pursuits.[35]

To be entirely fair to Hughes, however, it must be pointed out that in fighting what he took to be a rising American party in his diocese he was trying to head off the possibility of a split of his flock into warring racial factions. In that letter to Brownson, dated August 29, 1856,[36] Hughes had spoken of the happy unity among the people of his diocese not only in faith, but in Catholic charity and mutual kindness, and expressed a dread lest that felicitous harmony be disrupted by irresponsible journalists, such as Thomas D'Arcy McGee. Such an unhappy calamity had already befallen the Catholics of France, England and Ireland. That happened in countries which are largely homogeneous ethnically, and Hughes was doubly apprehensive of what might come about in his own diocese which was so pluralistic racially. We have already noted the split among Catholics in France when recording how Brownson entered the lists on the side of Montalembert and his associates against Louis Veuillot and his collaborators. And now at this very time Brownson wrote an article on "Present Catholic Dangers" in which he dealt at length with the split between the cisalpine school of old-time Catholics in England and the new school there, led on in no small degree by recent converts, some of whom were decidedly ultramontane.[37] On the surface of things, one could scarcely say that Hughes' fears were without any rhyme or reason.

Henry Brownson stated that although Fr. Hecker's letter to his father seeking a favorable review of *Aspirations of Nature* reached him only after the article was already in print, his father nevertheless added "to the article some remarks that seemed to him reasonable and likely to assist Fr. Hecker in the accomplishment of the purpose for which he was at Rome."[38] But Fr. Vincent Holden, C.S.P., Fr. Hecker's biographer, cites a letter to show that any change Brownson finally agreed to was wrung from him by Fr. George Deshon, one of the group associated with Fr. Hecker, and a former West Pointer. Brownson had dropped a remark to his friend, Dr. Henry Hewit of New York City, a brother of Fr. Augustine Hewit, that his review of *Aspirations* would be a candid one and not too favorable. When Dr. Hewit relayed this information to Fr. Hewit it caused some little alarm. As Fr. Hewit did not care to interfere with Brownson as an editor, Fr. Deshon volunteered to visit him and see what could be done about the matter — lest the article embarrass Fr. Hecker's mission at Rome. "After battling back and forth for three hours" on the part of Fr. Deshon with Brownson, Brownson finally consented to make some changes — although the article was scheduled to go to the printer the very next day — Brownson protesting at the same time that Fr. Deshon "had made him strike every thing in the article that had any point to it."[39] It is to be assumed that it was only because of a very warm personal regard for Fr. Hecker that Brownson could be prevailed upon to make any changes at all. He had always maintained the utmost independence as an editor.

The body of Brownson's article contained his criticism of Fr. Hecker's book. To state the matter briefly, his theological criticism stemmed from the fact that his theology did not agree entirely with Fr. Hecker's. He held that the effects of the fall were more pronounced than *Aspirations of Nature* seemed to imply. As Brownson's son Henry put the matter: "Brownson had as much horror of Calvinism and Jansenism as the Jesuits, or Hecker or Hewit; but he was equally averse to Pelagianism, and never found it necessary to exalt nature and reason at the expense of grace and revelation, or these to the detriment of the former."[40] When writing to Fr. John McMullen of Chicago, a Roman doctor and later bishop of Davenport, Iowa, Brownson remarked: "I have labored hard to draw accurately the line between the natural and the supernatural, and to guard against Pelagianism on the one hand and Jansenism on the other, and as good theologians as yourself have assured me that I have done it successfully."[41]

A missionary priest in the state of Georgia, Fr. James Hasson, was greatly pleased with Brownson's critique of *Aspirations*. Writing to Brownson on October 16, 1857, for information on the best apologetic books with which to stock his library, he wound up saying: "If I were asked for a short epitome of my faith I would say, 'Credo in Papa et Brownson.' Among the various articles of your 'Review' to which I am indebted for much information, permit me to thank you for your critique on 'Aspirations of Nature.' It was a revision of the teachings of my dear and disinterested professors on the fall of Adam and its consequences."[42]

Fr. Hecker was of course considerably disappointed with Brownson's review of his book. This he expressed in a letter to him from Rome, dated October 24, 1857:

Dear Friend:

Your welcome letter and also your notice of "Asp. of Nat." [Aspirations of Nature] arrived here on the 19th inst. . . . The article on "Asp. of Nat." I have read again and again, and surely it is a source of great regret that men who have the same noble, and let me add divine, work at heart, should find so many differences between them. This seems to be the usual accompaniment of all really good undertakings. It is, however, most unfortunate that these were put in print and made public at this juncture. The article will increase the unfounded suspicion of the General here and the Provincial in the U.S., and I fear that the latter will use it with terrible effect against the American Fathers. What you say to exculpate me, however sufficient and true, will not be regarded by minds filled with suspicions. Parts of your letter which touch on these points, I will have translated to counteract this influence if the article is used that way.[43]

Apparently it was not so much with any of Brownson's mild theological reflections on the thought in his book that Fr. Hecker was mainly disappointed, but rather with the less optimistic hopes Brownson had expressed about the immediate conversion of the American people on a wide scale. It is true, as Fr. Holden has pointed out, that Brownson spoke a more enthusiastic language in his previous letters to Fr. Hecker on the subject. This was apparently because he was entirely in sympathy with the project Fr. Hecker had entered upon, and wanted to encourage him personally all he could.[44] The thought his article contained, however, was only his long-standing views on the subject. For as we have just noted, he reminded Archbishop Hughes that after the first year following his conversion, he had never been sanguine about any wide conversion of the American people. In his review of *Aspirations,* Brownson said again: "The conversion of a whole Protestant people, like the American, is a work of magnitude, and not to be effected in a day. . . . There is no trait in the American character as practically developed that is not more or less hostile to Catholicity. Our people are imbued with a spirit of independence, an aversion to authority, a pride, an overweening conceit, as well as prejudice, that makes them revolt at the bare mention of the Church."[45] He thought that the conversion of Great Britain at the time would be an easier task, humanly speaking, than that of the United States. One readily recalls here the remark of Newman in response to the enthusiastic Philipps de Lisle and his associates who were at the time dreaming of suddenly bringing the whole Anglican fold into Catholic unity, namely, that such an event would be to him (Newman) "a miracle as great as if the Thames were to change its course."[46]

Fr. Hecker himself admitted at the time that he was presenting one side of the picture in Rome when speaking of the prospects of wide conversions among the American people. He never did get around to having Brownson's "Mission of America" translated and published, although Brownson had told him that "the article was inspired by you and you stand its godfather."[47] Fr. Hecker considered it more strategic to his purpose to publish two articles in the *Civiltà Cattolica* on the American people and the prospects of their conversion. In a letter to Brownson, dated November 27, 1857, speaking of the two articles, he said: "I am aware I have presented the fair side of our country: this was done by design, to attract attention, and interest the rulers of the Church in behalf of our country. The reverse side and in the darkest colors has too long occupied the minds of men this side of the Atlantic. Intentionally therefore I left out obstacles in the way of the conversion of our countrymen, and but slightly hinted at the means to be adopted to accomplish this."[48] Not only Brownson saw the obstacles in the way of a ready

544

conversion of the American people, but no less a personage than His Holiness, Pope Pius IX, pointed them out to Fr. Hecker in an audience he had with him, when he said: "The American people are so engrossed in worldly things and in the pursuit of wealth and these things are not favorable to the spread of the Gospel. It is not I who say so but Our Lord." Then His Holiness showed his just appreciation of the American people when he said: "They [the American people] are willing to give when they possess riches; the bishops tell me they are generous in aiding the building of churches. . . . You see I know the bright as well as the dark side of Americans."[49]

One truly sympathizes with Fr. Hecker that Brownson did not see his way to give *Aspirations of Nature* a more enthusiastic review. A candid and objective review was anything but a help to him at such a critical moment. But if we are to balance up things fairly, neither should we forget that Brownson himself was at the moment passing through a twofold ordeal. There is no need to reemphasize here that Archbishop Hughes was hotly on his trail as the unacknowledged leader of an American party perilously rising in his diocese. Brownson simply could delay no longer a defense of himself, and the review of Fr. Hecker's book was a godsend of an opportunity to do so. And there was also another matter that must be mentioned. Near the end of his review of the book, Brownson said: "With him [Fr. Hecker] hope is constant, ever-living, and active [in regard to convert prospects]; with us it is spasmodic, and is kept up only by effort. . . . But it is always better to take counsel of our hopes than of our fears, and we will not dwell on our gloomy forebodings, which, after all, may spring from ill-health, under the depression of which we are forced to write."[50] In a long letter to Fr. Hecker, dated September 29, 1857, he confessed: "My own affairs are gloomy enough owing to the commercial collapse and money pressure. . . . I can but starve at worst and perhaps my friends will prevent that. I think it doubtful whether I shall be able to keep up the *Review.* I have been out of health and am more profoundly discouraged than ever before in my life."[51] Out of this financial morass Brownson was again to extricate himself by a course of vigorous lecturing through such populous centers as New York, Boston, Baltimore, Cincinnati, Louisville, Chicago, Cleveland, Zanesville and other places.[52]

But what was the source of Brownson's being "more profoundly discouraged than ever before" in his life? Henry Brownson mentions of course Hughes' attitude to his father and the *Review,* and a consequent falling off of subscriptions as one of the serious causes in the case. But whatever mental strain Hughes may have exerted, there seems to have been a physical cause as well. Henry Brownson tells us that after the coming of his father to New York his health was good, at least such as required little medical attention. His friend, Fr. Hecker, however, had come to have great faith in a certain Doctor Watson who had joined the Catholic Church, and whose treatment consisted in bleeding his patients every other day or so, and administering whiskey. The treatment was extremely lucrative: the fee was from fifty to a hundred dollars for each treatment, and was to be paid in advance. After Watson had made a good haul, at least as much as he could hope to get, he quietly skipped town. Whether through Fr. Hecker's influence or not, Brownson, among many others, tried the treatments. The result was, his son states, that his health suffered for a while.[53]

As so often happened, Brownson again in these depressing times received letters which should have helped to keep him going. Although Fr. Hecker and Fr. Deshon were disappointed with Brownson's review of *Aspirations,* another American priest, Fr. Clarence Walworth, took no exception to it. Quite the contrary. Noticing the discouragement Brownson had expressed near the end of his article, he wrote him a bracing letter. Addressing his letter (dated October 20, 1857) from Poughkeepsie, where he was laboring as a missionary, he wrote in part:

Dear Mr. Brownson:

As I said at the outset, I thought I perceived some signs of despondency in the last number, more even than was fairly couched in words. If so, I am sorry. To be sure, I have never counted myself among the most sanguine of those who look for a speedy triumph of the good cause in America. But I do look for that triumph, and feel as earnest as ever in the little part I take in the conflict. And permit me to say that there never was a time when I listened more earnestly to hear the sledge-hammer blows of the 'Review' or felt more confidence in its power to do execution than in the present crisis of affairs. I have never been much tempted to wish to make you suggestions, either as to choice of topics, or the manner of treating them, being always satisfied to hear from you on any subject of common interest, and always liking best those articles which seemed the most characteristic. Go on then, in the name of God, with a light heart, for the sake of many and holy interests, and also for the sake of many young men who, like myself, have learned much from you already, and rely on you for much in the future. While I rank myself among those in general, I would be glad to have you look upon me as one bound to you not only by common principles and religious interests, but by the attachment of a warm personal friendship.

In the sacred hearts of Jesus and Mary I remain ever your faithful friend and brother,

C. A. Walworth[54]

In this same month, Brownson also received a letter (dated October 6, 1857) from Fr. William Cumming, Rothsay (Isle of Bute), that must have been salve for his wounds and balm to his spirit. After expressing great admiration for Brownson's papal doctrine, Fr. Cumming continued:

How can I and my companions thank you also for the high and manly tone which you have taught us to use in speaking of Our Mother the Church? How can I thank you for the many hours of pleasure and instruction with which you supply us quarter after quarter? I see nothing but enthusiasm for you here among my brother clergymen with the exception of the *Irish* fellow laborers. They for the most part are incompetent to judge, having never read you except in garbled extracts. Those of them whom I have persuaded to go to the fountainhead, are even more enthusiastic than myself. One of them the other day to my great amusement, got up of a sudden from a perusal of your article on the worship of Mary and cried out loud, "by this and by that, this man is inspired!" Now you see I have told you the good your works have done for me and others whom I know, with all sincerity. I do not wish to flatter you. I think it below me as a priest of the Church. But amidst so much abuse from open and secret enemies, I want to tell you what some of your friends, even so far away as this, think of your labors.[55]

Brownson was also considerably cheered up at this time by a number of letters he received from various persons sincerely inquiring about the Catholic faith, or seeking instruction. Many of the letters spoke, too, of the happy event of the conversion of the respective writer. Hiram McCullum, renewing his subscription for 1857, wrote from Lockport, January 1857: "I am now 19 years a subscriber of your *Review*. It is to you as the instrument in the providence of God to whom I owe the inestimable grace of faith. Two others who were members of the Congregational Society owe their conversion to the same instrumentality. One of these named Wilbur was 'Superintendent of the Congregational Sunday School.' "[56] Brownson could scarcely have known that he had also been exerting a very salutary influence on a young grocery clerk in New Orleans who in later years was to cut a wide swath indeed in the history of the Catholic Church in the United States — James Gibbons. Having fallen somewhat ill, "as he was regaining his strength, the devout young grocery clerk in New Orleans began to read the powerful religious writings of Orestes Brownson. Earnestly he pondered his future."[57] The grocery chrysalis was to evolve into the great Cardinal Gibbons in the history of the Catholic Church in America.

After a sojourn in New York City of from two to three years, Brownson had come to find living under Archbishop Hughes' jurisdiction too uncomfortable. The archbishop once remarked to him: "I will suffer no man in my diocese that I cannot control. I will either put him down or he shall put me down."[58] Hughes had apparently come to consider Brownson a threat to himself, and was prepared to take strong measures against what might happen. There are those who at times seem disposed to act on the principle of the New England deacon who called up his sons one Sunday morning and gave them a good flogging not because they had done any wrong, but because he foresaw that they might break the Sabbath. If Hughes had any doubts about Brownson's docility to his authority, he judged him unjustly. Brownson could never have brought himself to resist authority, nor to countenance any movement which might be troublesome to the authorities of the Catholic Church. In spite of many unpleasant dealings with a number of prelates of his day, no one can accuse him of the least disrespect for authority, much less of any incipient spirit of insubordination. Before authority he had the docility of a child. One of the disadvantages he experienced at the hands of Archbishop Hughes — if we are to credit the word of his son Henry — was that Hughes always disclaimed to Brownson privately any hostility, but wrote and acted differently in public, and the public was accordingly influenced.[59] Brownson tried to solve the whole difficulty by moving his household across the river to Elizabeth, New Jersey, into another diocese, although he retained his publication office in New York City.

After speaking of the estrangement that had come about between Brownson and Archbishop Hughes before he left New York City, the well-known Virgil Michel, O.S.B., said: "This regrettable condition lasted until the death of the latter, whose conduct throughout this period appears more blameworthy than that of the layman."[60]

About the time Brownson quit the New York diocese, in a letter to Bishop Fitzpatrick of Boston, dated May 12, 1857 — which really concerned a third person — Brownson concluded by remarking nostalgically:

> I take this occasion to renew my assurance of my grateful recollection of all your kindness to me, the invaluable service you have rendered, your steady friendship and support for years, and in confidence, my regret that I am no longer under your spiritual direction and that I ever removed from my only home. Think of me as well and kindly as you can and believe me with all my faults your grateful friend and,
>
> Your dutiful and affectionate son in Christ,
> O. A. Brownson[61]

547

# 36

## A LIVELY DISCUSSION
## OF CATHOLIC EDUCATION

*Bishop Martin J. Spalding gives what is supposedly the views of the American hierarchy on primary Catholic education • Brownson is invited by an illustrious archbishop to give his views on parochial schools and does so • His discussion of the subject raises an "immense outcry" against him • He defends himself and assigns reasons for the attack upon him • He insists that the whole affair must be left respectfully to the decision of the American bishops • He loudly raises his voice in defense of his convicted friend in France, Count Montalembert • A significant letter from Fr. Charles Gresselin on the perennial value of his* Review *• Offensive articles in his* Review *on education in Catholic colleges, academies and seminaries • Brownson's own views • His portrait as etched by Fr. John Boyce in his novel,* Mary Lee, or the Yankee in Ireland *• Fr. William J. Barry's mortifying strictures in an article in Brownson's* Review *on Catholic colleges and academies • Brownson himself is held responsible by Archbishop Hughes in his commencement address at St. John's College (Fordham University) on July 12, 1860 • Fr. Jeremiah W. Cummings' disturbing article on education in Catholic seminaries.*

Although Brownson moved out from under the jurisdiction of Archbishop Hughes, the simmering imbroglio between the two was by no means over; it was only to worsen with time. As matters were developing, the battle between these two stalwarts was becoming more and more one over Irish Catholicism and American Catholicism. Brownson continued during these years to lash out time and again at Irish foreignism in the Catholic Church to the extent that it came close to being his main whipping boy. And Irish domination in the Church had become a sort of *bête noire* to him. Added to this, he now got into the thick of the fight over another sizzling question: Where or in what schools were Catholic children of the land to be educated? The question at that date had not yet been settled, and much heat as well as light was emitted in its discussion. Again in this case, like Newman in England,[1] Brownson was to stub his toe badly in his well-meant efforts to improve education among Catholics. It was to lead to another collision with Archbishop Hughes.

Martin J. Spalding, bishop of Louisville, contributed an article on the "Common Schools" to the January 1858 issue of Brownson's *Review*, giving what was supposedly the general views of the American bishops on the subject. He stressed parental rights in regard to the kind of education they wished their children to receive, the right of Catholics to establish schools of their own in harmony with the standards set by the state, and the claim Catholics have to a pro rata share in school funds, such as obtained in Lower Canada and most European countries.[2] In the October 1858 issue of his *Review,* Brownson took up a discussion of the question in Chapter IX of his "Conversations of Our Club" as to whether Catholics should, and whether they could, establish parochial schools, or whether they should send their children to the public schools. As this was a delicate question at the time, it should be noted that Brownson did not wantonly intrude himself into the discussion, as some commentators on the subject have failed to recognize. As he related later, he had been urged by one of the illustrious archbishops of the country to give his views on the question. When he protested that it did not belong to his province to do so, the archbishop still insisted that it would be advantageous to have all possible views on a subject so important and affording such a wide spectrum of views.[3] Brownson accordingly discussed the question with some thoroughness in "Conversations of Our Club." The members of this fictitious club expressed a great variety of views on the theme, but Brownson's own views among the members are reputedly represented by an interlocutor known as "Father John." The gist of his views were that where good Catholic schools could be separately established, they should by all means be established, but where they were not practicable, or where nothing better than schools definitely inferior to the public schools were possible, Catholic children might well be sent to the public schools — though he censured the sectarianism sometimes taught in them. While bowing most respectfully to the American hierarchy as the judges who must settle the question, he ended his discussion of the question by saying: "In my own view of the matter, I think the public schools, sectarian as they frequently are, [are] preferable to very poor [Catholic] schools, under the charge of wholly incompetent teachers, dragging out a painful, lingering, half-dying existence."[4] He insisted, however, that in such cases religious instruction and moral training must be provided by the parents in the home and the pastor in the Sunday School or wherever it could be properly imparted.

These views on the subject raised an "immense outcry" against him from a number of Catholic journals of the day. To this he replied with an article on "The Public and Parochial Schools" in which he spoke in a strong tone and a touch of acerbity. He made the pastoral letter of Archbishop Purcell of Cincinnati (touching on the same subject) the occasion of correcting the misapprehensions and misrepresentations of his own views on the subject. He said: "[Our *Review* has been accused of] assuming a position on this question of education in opposition to that taken by the venerable and illustrious American Hierarchy." It has been represented as being no longer "a Catholic Review," and we have been denounced as a non-Catholic because we have expressed the view that Catholic children (with the permission of the hierarchy) might be sent to the public schools when and where we cannot have good separate schools of our own. Now, how stands the question, he inquired? Have the prelates of the country interdicted those schools? No one can say they had. Wherein then had he placed himself in opposition to the American hierarchy? Why then the "immense outcry" against him?[5] In his judgment it was patently an oblique attack on him for other reasons:

> It comes not from any opposition we have offered to our prelates, to Catholic education, or to Catholic schools; but it comes, if the truth must be told, from the source whence has come the greater part of opposition to us for the last five years — that is, from our steady and determined opposition to any and every movement the direct tendency of which is to denationalize the American Catholic, and to keep Catholics a foreign colony in the United States, or Catholic-

ity here in this New World linked with that old effete Europeanism which has always, wherever it has existed, been a drag on it, and which all that is true, good, generous, and noble in our American political and social order repudiates.[6]

He assured his Catholic readers that he was, and always had been, decidedly in favor of schools in which our children are taught, and taught well, their religion, and that he could not understand how any Catholic worthy of the name could be of any other sentiments, but he wanted such schools to be truly *Catholic* schools. He had not favored, and, until further advised, he could not favor a system of schools in which our Catholic children would be brought up to be foreigners in the land of their birth, for such schools cannot fail, in the long run, to do more injury than good to the interests of religion. He had no unfriendly or unbrotherly feelings toward any class of foreigners, but he did not want that "miserable Europeanism, by which we mean despotism, in some or all of its ramifications, which oppresses the people, trammels the freedom of the Church, and cripples the energy of the clergy in Continental Europe, brought here to eviscerate Catholics of their manhood, and keep up a perpetual war, in which faith has no interest, between them and the great body of the American people." Leave out the Europeanism, he pleaded, and let the movement be really for Catholic schools and Catholic education, as was no doubt the intention of the American prelates, and he was "for it heart and soul."[7]

Another reason for the fierce opposition he was encountering in this matter was, as he saw it, his refusal to join in the "wholesale condemnation" of the public schools, "or concede that, even faulty as they undoubtedly are, they are corrupt and corrupting as some of our over-zealous friends represent them." He admitted that immorality and irreligion were on the increase in the Union, but thought it not right to charge it all just to the common school system. Even Catholic schools have not always been effectual in preventing immorality and irreligion in Catholic nations. Education is not omnipotent, and can never be a substitute for the sacraments. No system of schools can ever be completely successful in making and keeping a people moral, and religious. Too much should not be expected of the public schools. Individual cases of immorality were, after all, only exceptions to the rule. Did he know whereof he spoke? He reminded his readers that he had been connected as teacher or committeeman with the common schools in New York, Michigan, New Hampshire, Vermont and Massachusetts for over twenty-five years of his life; that eight of his children had been partially educated in them, and he claimed therefore to have some personal knowledge of them. Although he did not by any means consider them faultless, he was very far from recognizing as just the description of them oftentimes met with in Catholic journals.[8]

His thought in this matter had probably been influenced considerably by his long residence in Boston where, he said, Catholic children went to "the public schools with the permission of the bishop, and with no harm to their faith or piety, as I am assured by those best able to judge."[9] He asserted that practically the same situation prevailed in the city in which he was then residing, Elizabeth, New Jersey.

Reaffirming that the whole question should be quietly left to the decision of the American hierarchy, he disclosed the real reason why he had written the article. It was to counsel his fellow Catholics to cease their attacks on the public school system: "The District School is an American pet; it is the pride of the American people, their boast, and really their glory. It is dear to their hearts, and we cannot strike them in a tenderer point than in striking this system, or do any thing more effectual in stirring up their wrath against us, or in confirming their prejudices against our religion." It was only common prudence to cease "exaggerating its defects, and shutting our eyes to its good points." He had been driven, he said, to acknowledge certain good points in the public schools of the land inasmuch as some Catholic journalists had "assailed them unjustly, with a zeal, a vehemence, and a bitterness alike impolitic and unwarranted, and we have wished to say something to neutralize their undue severity, and by frankly acknowledging the merits of the system to allay the wrath unnecessarily excited against us and our Church."[10]

He asserted again that all he had said on the subject was respectfully submitted to the proper authorities of the Catholic Church. Should they tell him that any of his views would be a detriment to the true interests of religion, of which they were the judges and not he, he would forbear to urge them. More could not be asked of him as a loyal Catholic, since if he had exceeded his freedom as a Catholic publicist, it had been done ignorantly, not wantonly. If Catholic journalists did not agree with his views, let them refute them, but cease to cry out that he was anti-Irish or that he was anti-Catholic. With that he dismissed the question from any further discussion in the columns of his *Review*. He ended by thanking *The Pittsburgh Catholic* for the candor with which it had expressed its conviction that, after the explanations of Father John in the last number of his *Review* ("Conversations of Our Club"), he had not placed himself on the school question in opposition to the American hierarchy. If other Catholic journalists had been equally as candid and just, there would have been no call for the article he had written.[11]

The adverse backlash he was now experiencing in the exercise of his right to express his honest opinion on an open question, could only dispose him to sympathize all the more deeply with his friend in France, Count Montalembert, who had so recently been subjected to a trial and imprisonment for expressing his own honest opinions. As Brownson understood the case, Montalembert had committed no offense, not even a technical one, against the laws of the country. He was simply the victim of an ironclad censorship which Napoleon III was then clamping tighter and tighter on the country against anyone who attempted to breathe the air of freedom. His trial and imprisonment was the price he had to pay for speaking as the champion of civil and religious freedom. Brownson joined the voices of those in France and throughout the civilized world who uttered their indignant protest against such an assault upon freedom and intelligence. He wrote:

> The condemnation of Montalembert is a condemnation of freedom, a condemnation of thought, a condemnation of intelligence in France, and the man whose soul does not swell with indignation at the outrage offered by that condemnation to our common manhood, is a slave. . . . The Catholic party, led on by Louis Veuillot, are digging their own graves, and preparing for Catholics in France, when the day of reaction comes, a persecution. . . . The policy of Louis Napoleon is to give the friends of religion and order no alternative but Despotism and Revolutionism. Are Catholics fools enough to aid him in that policy, and to regard him as the champion of Catholic interests? What will be the condition of the Church in France when he falls, as fall he will? . . . He comes too late to extinguish intelligence in France, and to compel the noble French people to submit to his miserable system of enslaving the soul as well as the body. When he falls, when the Socialists with envenomed fury against the Church oc-

cupy the throne, the Catholic defenders of despotism will perhaps remember the words of the noblest Catholic statesman and orator of the age. Let them then build monuments with the bones of slaughtered priests and nuns to Louis Veuillot and his dupes. We ask not that Catholics conspire against Louis Napoleon, but we do ask them to exercise a little common sense and common prudence, to acquire a little understanding of the age, and not deserve by their mole-eyed policy the judgments hanging over them.[12]

Brownson also got off a letter of deep sympathy to the Count in his hour of trial. How deeply it was appreciated is evident from the letter the Count wrote from La Roche en Breny, Cote D'Or, on February 16, 1859:

My dear Mr. Brownson:
I hope I need not tell you that I have been most highly gratified by your affectionate sympathy, with regard to my late trials, as expressed in your interesting letter of December 27, and in the energetic article contained in the last number of your *Review,* which safely reached me. I felt very anxious to know what your opinion would be, as I was somewhat afraid that your anti-English feelings would have precluded you from perceiving the *whole* extent of the cause. But quite the contrary has taken place, and I think I may say that amongst the many hundred letters I have received on this occasion, few or none have given me greater satisfaction than yours. I have directed the Brussels Editor, December 9, to forward to you the full and authentic account of the *two trials,* which has been published there and which, although wretchedly printed, is well worth your perusal. The splendid orations of Fufaure and Berryer contain an immense deal of information on past and present events, besides their eloquence; but all this is quite unknown to France, as the publication of debates before the Courts of Law, in all political cases, is strictly prohibited and severely punished. So that except the happy few who were present, not a soul in France is allowed to know what the *first* lawyers and orators of the country have said on so vital a question! This is what Catholic prelates and writers have dared to call *the restoration of Christian Society — in the world. . . .*
I trust that *Brownson's Review,* which has the privilege of being published in a land of liberty, will more and more say *the truth,* and unveil the base and miserable foundations of the present alliance between Caesarism and and Veuillotism. No lesson can be more striking than the present appearance of war, a war to be undertaken *against Rome* by the man whom the French Bishops called *a second St. Louis,* and which is till now only prevented by the resistance of Protestant parliamentary England.
I have read with pleasure a very good article on your *Review* in the *Ami de la Religion* of the 14th, and hope soon to hear from you (always direct to Paris). I remain your obliged and faithful friend,

Ch. De Montalembert[13]

If Brownson was not unmindful of his friends in their hour of trial, neither did his own friends forget him when beleaguered. In the midst of the extensive abuse he had been taking over his discussion of the school question, he received a letter from a very estimable source which should have helped to save him from slipping into the slough of despondency. It was a letter from Fr. Charles Gresselin, S.J., professor of philosophy at St. John's College (later Fordham University), written on September 16, 1859. (Brownson was later to characterize him as "really one of the most learned and accomplished theologians in the country." Fr. Gresselin wrote:

Perhaps it is owing to my ignorance or want of information, but I see no work either in America or Europe so useful, of so high a standard as your

*Review*. I suppose the *Civiltá Cattolica* is too a masterpiece of the same kind, but I do not know it. Your *Review* will last long after those who criticize you are entirely forgotten; it will pass to posterity among the few works which each century sends to the future and endless generations. Believe me on that point. I am a solitary, perfectly disengaged from the bustle of the world, and therefore I am better posted up to judge many things because of the calmness and peace in which I live.[14]

Fr. Gresselin also proposed to Brownson in the letter that he bring out a second edition of his *Review*, and volunteered to proofread it beforehand so as to have a literary production just as flawless in every way as possible for its final form. He knew of course that Brownson often wrote under the pressure of a deadline, and had not therefore the leisure to go over everything as carefully as desirable before going to press. Discussing the artistic form of Brownson's essays, Alvin Ryan observed that "the form of the book review too often determined the structure of his own essay, and he lacked either the capacity or the leisure to give most of his work the finish, the form and stamp of personal utterance that makes the work of far less penetrating thinkers live as literature."[15]

Brownson was now to get into more hot water for strictures in his *Review* on education in the higher Catholic schools, colleges, academies and seminaries. Not all the animadversions in his *Review* came by any means from Brownson himself, but he was to be held accountable for them as editor, particularly by Archbishop Hughes. It is true that Brownson was entirely in sympathy with the efforts being made to improve education among Catholics. But he did not agree with all that was being said in the articles of other critics who appeared in his columns. For this reason he sometimes appended the initials of the authors of the articles, or would at times add a footnote of dissent. The authors of these articles were mainly Fr. George McCloskey of New York, Fr. William Barry, professor at St. Mary's Seminary, Cincinnati, Ohio, and Fr. Jeremiah W. Cummings of New York City. Brownson himself had of course more than a little to say on the same theme. His more general indictment was that Catholic institutions do not turn out thinking, reasoning Christians, well panoplied, spiritually and intellectually, to grapple with the doubts and corrosive cynicism of a skeptical age. To meet the current temper of the age he asserted that:

> More attention [in our Catholic colleges] should be devoted to the development, to the encouragement of free, bold, vigorous thought, and to individuality, and even originality of character. We must give scope to the reason of the scholar, and not be afraid now and then of a little intellectual eccentricity. Better in our age sometimes to err, providing it is not from an heretical spirit or inclination, than never to think. Nothing is worse for the mind than mere routine, nothing more fatal to all true greatness and intellectual progress than to attempt to mould all minds after one and the same model, and to maintain a certain dead level of intelligence. There is nothing in our religion itself that demands it. Catholicity does not fear, nay, she challenges free thought, and gives to reason full and entire freedom, all the freedom it can have without ceasing to be reason.[16]

In Chapter X of "Conversations of Our Club," he laid a kindred stricture on Catholic female academies. He wrote:

> Our conventual schools for girls are too superficial, run over a great number of studies, but teach nothing thoroughly, unless a few light and showy

553

accomplishments. They seem to forget that girls have intellects, and that intellect in wives and daughters is not a superfluity. . . . I have no patience with your "strong-minded women," but I have great respect for the female mind, and I measure the civilization of a country by the cultivation and intelligence of its women. There are branches in which I do not expect them to equal men, but there is no reason in the world why young ladies who graduate from our conventual schools, should not, with modesty, reserve, and the lighter accomplishments always indispensable, come forth thinking, reasoning beings, and be prepared to give to the society in which they enter, a high moral and intellectual tone.

I do not think, as a general thing, our professors and teachers are absolutely afraid of stimulating and cultivating the intellect, or of making their pupils thinking men and women, [yet they] have more or less fear of stimulating thought in their pupils, and in forming them to habits of self-reliance, and free and spontaneous action. They think they must repress as well as encourage, and therefore confine themselves chiefly to loading the memory, without stimulating real intellectual activity.[17]

Another defect he found in the Catholic educational system of the day was a lack of a preparatory school between the primary school and the college. The result was that mere boys were sent off to college unprepared for the step, and the college was put to the disadvantage of trying to frame a government and discipline to fit alike boys and young men, but which fit in reality neither the one nor the other. The boy, having finished his grammar course, for which he had come, would often then leave to mix again with the world at too early an age. "[After having been nursed in a close spiritual guardianship during his brief stay at the college,] then, when he needs more than ever the spiritual aids and counsels he had been accustomed to, they send him out into society, weak, ignorant, without any habits of self-reliance, self-government, or self-help, exposed to all its seductions and temptations, so much the more to be dreaded, as they have for him the charm of novelty, and leave him, wholly unprepared, to battle with the world, the flesh, and the devil, as best he can. The majority, I believe, succumb, as we might expect, in the struggle."[18]

In a seven-page commentary in the April 1860 issue of his *Review,* on the "American College at Rome" just established for the education of American seminarians for the priesthood, Brownson seemed to show again how restive he was growing under the dominant Irish element in the Catholic Church in America. He preferred the education of the future priests of the country there at the capital of Christendom, for Rome is more cosmopolitan, that is, free from all national peculiarities, and therefore, in the better sense, more truly American. In American seminaries there was too much rivalry between the Irish, the Spanish, French, English, or German for predominance, with the result that the "American element counts for nothing, and is crushed down by foreign nationalities." He made himself more specific:

What we want [in the Catholic Church] is no peculiar nationality. . . . All nationality that attempts to control or direct the Church is evil. To it we owe the Greek Schism, to it we owe the Great Western Schism, to it we owe the rise, progress and continuance of Protestantism. . . . The great body of our English speaking Catholics are of Irish birth or descent — but no intelligent Irishman, priest or layman, supposes for one moment that the Church here is always to be an Irish Church. The Irish readily amalgamate with the natives — and in the second, at farthest, third generation, are more American than we who boast our descent from the Pilgrim Fathers. We know no fiercer Know-Nothings in the country than sons and grandsons of Irishmen. To keep the Church here Irish is simply impossible, whether it be desirable or not.[19]

Yet in all fairness we should note that he added near the end of his comments: "We do not want the Church here national, either in a native or foreign sense. We have not, and never have had, any sympathy with those who insist the clergy of a nation should be born and educated in it. That has been the spirit of the Church. Native nationalism is as much to be guarded against as foreign nationalism."[20]

Some of the Irish were getting mighty tired by this time of the way in which Brownson had been jabbing them from various angles, as they saw it, and felt they had some old scores to square off with him. And out from their midst stepped their champion: Fr. John Boyce. Fr. Boyce was from Maynooth Seminary, Ireland, and was at this particular time pastor of the only Catholic church in Worcester, Massachusetts. He had also become a novelist. Brownson had already taken notice of his two novels, *Shandy M'Guire* and the *Spaewife*. When Fr. Boyce published his latest novel, *Mary Lee or the Yankee in Ireland,* Brownson had a special reason for not overlooking it. In the novel as first published in the *Metropolitan Record,* Brownson was satirized in the person of a certain Dr. Horseman, one of the main characters in the book. He was castigated for his indiscreet zeal as a convert, especially for his interpretation of the dogma that there is no salvation outside the Catholic Church, and the author, as Brownson said, "warned his countrymen [the Irish] against one whom he regarded as their enemy." It is true that the author did not mention Brownson by name, but there could be no doubt in the mind of the public who was meant. For all knowledgeable readers saw at once certain humorous resemblances between Brownson and Dr. Horseman — Dr. Horseman chewed tobacco, and so did Brownson chew "the weed"; Dr. Horseman wore gold-bowed spectacles, so did he; Dr. Horseman spoke in a gruff, harsh voice, and Brownson's voice was deep base, and not very musical. To clinch the identity, Dr. Horseman was given as a Yankee Catholic reviewer, and, as Brownson pointed out, there was only one such in the whole wide world, himself.[21] It was Michael Earls, S.J., who expalined more recently in the *Commonweal* that it was Bishop Fitzpatrick of Boston who prevailed upon Fr. Boyce to tone down the severities attaching to Dr. Horseman's character, and when the novel came out in book form, Dr. Horseman had been metamorphosed into the banal Dr. Henshaw, a Scotch reviewer.[22] While acknowledging the implied apology, Brownson did not appreciate this, saying that the change had really marred the artistic merits of the book. Admirably pachydermatous in the matter, he assured Fr. Boyce that he had not been offended by the personalities indulged in his regard, and that he loved a joke as much as any of his Irish friends. "So here is our hand, Father John," he said, "only give us back our friend Dr. Horseman, and remember for the future that Jonathan can bear with good humor a joke, even at his own expense, if it lack not the seasoning of genuine wit.[23]

But not all the Irish were to believe that Brownson was their adversary; he was far from being anything of the kind. They were ready to stick to him through thick and thin, and turned a deaf ear to the senseless clamors made that they should drop his *Review.* This enabled him to remark with a note of triumph in the following issue of his *Review,* 1860: "It will gratify our friends to learn that the outcry raised from time to time against the *Review* has made little or no impression on its subscription list. We feel confident that the *Review* never had more, warmer, or more determined friends than at the present moment, and without respect to nationality. We wish no better or zealous friends than we have among Catholics of Irish or French birth or descent, and the call upon such, inconsiderately made, to drop the *Review* has not been responded to, and will not be."[24]

But greater drama yet was in store for this indomitable editor. It was really Fr. W. J. Barry, professor at St. Mary's Seminary, Cincinnati, Ohio, who set off the pyrotechnics with a discussion of Catholic education in the higher Catholic schools of the land with his article on "Dr. Arnold and Catholic Education" in the July 1860 issue of *Brownson's Review,* harrowing the sensibilities of Archbishop Hughes with his biting remarks. The thought was really little more than an echo of what Brownson himself had been saying on the subject, but expressed in language which had more of an intentional edge on it. It was not unlike some of the criticism made in our own day of Catholic education, particularly that of Msgr. John Tracy Ellis. After lauding Dr. Arnold and his English system of education, Fr. Barry moaned over the melancholy state of Catholic education in his own native land when he said:

> Our colleges and academies are failures. God forbid that we should slight the good, the very great good that they have done, but they are failures, inasmuch as they have not accomplished more. Let us not mince matters and disclaim the existence of evils because we persistently shut our eyes to them.
>
> The evil of which we complain, in which all minor evils come to a head, is a want in our colleges of activity, of intellectual life. The students, as a body, are not fond of study when they enter college; and they do not acquire a taste for it when there; and they go out into the world with the merest superficial smattering of letters. The causes of this stagnation are three: 1, a want of appreciation by the community of intellectual pursuits; 2, inefficient teachers; 3, a defective system.[25]

Fr. William Barry used his scalpel quite freely in dealing with these tumors on the Catholic educational body. But not all concerned were sure he used it wisely. In dealing with the third point, he lamented that Catholic education in the higher schools of the land was based on the old European system of the post-Reformation period, inaugurated by the Jesuits. It may have been the right answer in those times, he remarked, but it does not meet American needs. Our country, he pointed out, has been modeled after the English system, and we should imitate the English pattern. "An American," he said, "does not think or speak like a Frenchman or an Italian, but like an Anglo-Saxon."[26]

Whether or not Archbishop Hughes read every edition of Brownson's *Review,* he could not possibly escape a knowledge of its contents, for the Catholic press in the country usually was full, pro and con, of what had been said in each issue. Brownson himself spoke of "the denunciation of our views which we expect to receive regularly once every three months from a portion of so-called Catholic press."[27] Hughes of course knew all about those disturbing articles in Brownson's *Quarterly* on Catholic education which had evoked acrimonious repercussions far and wide. Barry's praise of Anglo-Saxon education was especially a very humiliating disparagement of the valiant efforts Catholics had been making in the same field in the face of wellnigh insurmountable odds. The criticisms were a bitter pill to swallow. All this must have been weighing on the mind of Archbishop Hughes as he moved thoughtfully toward St. John's College commencement hall on July 12, 1860, and spied Orestes Brownson sitting there in the audience.

After congratulating the graduates, and acknowledging the merits of the program, he directed some fire at those writers who had been making "invidious comparisons between Catholic and Protestant colleges, and, indeed, education in general, very much to the depreciation of Catholic efforts." Looking out over the audience, and making recognition of Brownson, the New York *Tablet* reported that:

> He [Archbishop Hughes] was now speaking in the presence of the great reviewer, Dr. Brownson, a man who, if not the best and ablest, is one of the strongest thinkers we have among us, and one of the best writers in the English language (applause). He knew that Dr. Brownson was not the author of all the articles in his *Review,* but he was the editor of it, and consequently sanctioned all that appeared in it. He knew that the principal editor of the *Review* has no other object in view but the good of Catholicity. He knew that he never flattered us (laughter) when he told us our faults in argument.

The archbishop continued his remarks by reminding his audience that all the great universities of Europe were Catholic in origin and had based their greatness on fidelity to their Catholic foundations. This he added was not true of Trinity College, Dublin, which had been founded "for the purpose of extinguishing popery." He rejoiced that the Irish clergy had enough courage to stand up against "the pretended boon offered them by that two-penny statesman, Lord Russell." Then turning again to Brownson, he counseled his audience that despite what he had said, all should be subscribers to his *Review.*[28]

It is not uncommon when a man is hit that his friends spring to his defense in one way or another. Brownson was to be the beneficiary of this trait in human nature. The archbishop's attack on him put two hundred dollars in his pocket. Writing to wife Sally and daughter, July 17, 1860, he said:

> I was in the city nearly all last week, and am going to Faunthill — the Sisters of Charity. At St. John's, the Archbishop made an onslaught on me publicly for Barry's articles; but, in revenge, my friends among the clergy have made me up a purse of $200.00. . . .[29]

The archbishop's remarks were meant of course not only for Brownson, but also for all those who had been humiliating Catholics before the public by speaking so disparagingly of their system of education. But those at whom the remarks were directed evidently seemed to consider them rather pointless. It is clear they did not influence them in the least. Fr. G. B. McCloskey had already said all he had to say in his two articles, and said no more. Although Brownson himself had already closed the discussion in his *Review,* as far as he personally was concerned, he was later to let it be known that he stood by Barry's searching article on "Dr. Arnold and Catholic Education," and he had some caustic remarks to make on any high-handed attempt to put a quietus on a fair discussion of the shortcomings of the Catholic educational system.[30] But Fr. Barry did return to the fray in another article in Brownson's *Review* the following January in which he defended his previous strictures and expanded his thought on the subject. He referred to Archbishop Hughes' remarks in his commencement address as "censorial lightnings that flashed in the July sky." He ridiculed the idea that Catholics could or should rest supinely content with the *status quo* of their educational system, and put his sarcasm into rhyme:

557

Like little Jack Horner,
We squat in a corner,
And, jollily winking, agree,
that each Catholic college
is a fountain of knowledge,
And cry, "what a great people are we."[31]

And Fr. Jeremiah W. Cummings now entered the list against the Establishment with an article on "Vocations to the Priesthood" which was to rile the tempers of not a few to something like white heat. Cummings was on good ground in pushing for a native clergy, but the question was a very prickly one in a country served so largely by foreign-born clergymen. All such felt little flattered when he wrote:

> A foreign priesthood will undoubtedly have influence on the American Protestant population of the country. Every good priest knows this from his own experience, no matter what country he may come from. Every good missionary has received into the Church one or more, or many sincere inquirers after Catholic truth. Still it requires a great effort and unusual grace on the part of an American to feel at home with a clergyman different from him not only in religion, but in his feelings, interests, manners and even speech. . . . No telling impression in favor of the Church can be made on the American people, unless by an American priesthood.[32]

In advancing reasons for the increase of a native clergy, he further cast slurs and suspicions on the whole body of foreign-born clergy serving in the country when he pleaded the urgency of the matter on the score that:

> . . . the first-rate men whom the French revolution and the Irish troubles forced out of their country and drove to our shores, will come to us no longer. That class of glorious old priests have made this country what it is, but we cannot hope to see many more of them. Men of that stamp can stay at home and will do so. There are indeed many such men among the ranks of the Irish clergy and the French clergy, but they are watched over with a jealous eye even in their youth, by their bishops, who learn their merit and take good care not to let them come out to America.[33]

Cummings further spoke of "cheap priest factories" on the continent of Europe grinding out their clerical product which, while not suitable for home service, will make "a good enough priest for America."[34] Such slurs on the foreign-born clergy in the country were enough to turn the stomach of more than one ecclesiastic on the home front. William H. Elder, bishop of Natchez, Mississippi, whose diocese was made up almost exclusively of foreign-born priests, sprang to their defense in a sizable letter he published in the *New Orleans Standard* on November 10, 1860. He deplored, in a gentlemanly manner, the too indiscriminate and "contemptuous language" in which Cummings had spoken of the foreign-born clergy in the country, and spoke a high testimonial to those laboring in his diocese.[35] A copy of this letter was sent to Cummings. He defended himself as best he could in another article on "Seminaries and Seminarians." His response was largely a repudiation of the charge that he had referred to All Hallows College, Dublin, Ireland (a missionary college or seminary), as a "cheap priest factory." He pointed out that he had referred to such on "the Continent of Europe."[36]

Nevertheless, he had coupled All Hallows with a slurring remark he had made on the type of priests who come from there to America,[37] and there was a kickback to it in the *Metropolitan Record* from Archbishop Hughes.

The sixth paragraph of a letter Bishop Eugene O'Connell of San Francisco wrote Dr. Woodlock, president of All Hallows, dated April 30, 1861, referred to the article in the *Metropolitan*. O'Connell, who had taught at All Hallows, remarked:

> Did you hear of the severe strictures on Dr. Cummings' abusive article in Brownson's *Review*? They are attributed to Archbishop Hughes, who in the *Metropolitan Record* recommended the critic who dared call All Hallows priests asses, to study more closely the properties of that useful animal, and learn a lesson from him. "The ass," says the Archbishop, "is humble, laborious, and content with hard fare, even with thistles, and perhaps the writer of the article would do well 'to go and do likewise.' "[38]

Fr. Charles Gresselin, S.J., commented parenthetically on this same debate in a letter he wrote Brownson about his article on "Rights of the Temporal." He wrote: "I glanced at your contributor's article on vocations. Next, I hope, he will expatiate on the necessity of holiness, zeal, prayer, disinterestedness, life according to the apostolic standard — all this, indeed, is yet more needed and lacked, than the quality and merit of being a native, and the transcendental fitness thereof, for furthering the knowledge and love of God in this country."[39]

Over in England an acrimonius and humorous discussion was raging in the pages of the *Rambler* and the *Tablet* over this same theme at the time, H. N. Oxenham having led off with an attack on the current training of candidates for the priesthood over the signature, X.W.Z. In a sharp reply under the intitials H.O., Newman laid down as central directives in the training of candidates for the priesthood that "the more a man is educated, whether in theology or secular science, the holier he needs to be if he would be saved"; and "that devotion and self-rule are worth all the intellectual cultivation in the world."[40]

Perhaps the deepest offense Fr. Cummings had given the prelates of the country in his original article on "Vocations to the Priesthood" was the publication with that article of the Decrees of the Council of Trent and the Letters of Pope Benedict XIV on the establishment and maintenance of seminaries in each diocese for the training of candidates for the priesthood.[41] In a struggling missionary country like the United States at the time, the ideals of the Catholic Church in the matter could come to fruition only slowly, and many of the bishops were caught in arrears in the affair. Was this done designedly to badger Archbishop Hughes in particular? What wonder that Brownson wrote his son regarding Cummings' published lucubrations on seminaries and seminarians: "The greatest wrath [Archbishop Hughes'] is manifested to the Dr. [Cummings]."[42]

It was fortunate that Brownson himself had already had his full say in a formal way, that is, *ex professo,* on the theme of Catholic education before Archbishop Hughes had dressed him down during those commencement ceremonies at St. John's College, or Fordham as it is known today, for he was now to get embroiled in a still hotter issue: the temporal principality of the pope. The columns of his *Review* in the ensuing issues were to be replete with sizzling thoughts on the subject.

# 37

## THE TEMPORAL PRINCIPALITY OF THE POPE

*Extreme views of Catholic leaders in regard to the spoliation of the Papal States and the military-political movement for the unification of Italy • Cardinal Manning and William G. Ward take extreme views and Brownson and Newman assume middle ground • Brownson stoutly asserts the rightful jurisdiction of the pope in the Papal States, and condemns rebellion, but is disposed to recognize the aspirations of the Italian people for a united Italy, if the matter could be amicably settled with the Holy Father • His disturbing article on the "Rights of the Temporal" • Some thoughts on the importance of the laity in the Catholic Church • Brownson's reverence for the declaration of the bishops on the Italian question • His embarrassment if required to defend political absolutism at Rome • As a part of the "Rights of the Temporal" Brownson claims an important place and office for the Catholic laity in the field of education • He makes a crystal-clear statement on why he had written the article, "Rights of the Temporal" • He adds a sizable postscript in the hope of forestalling misunderstanding.*

In these years, 1859-1860, the feelings of Catholics throughout the world were being outraged by the manner in which King Victor Emmanuel of Sardinia, aided by the French emperor, Napoleon III, was stripping the Holy Father, Pope Pius IX, of the Papal States, piece by piece. Discontented with the unhappy divisions of his homeland, Victor Emmanuel — and his premier, Count Cavour — had determined on driving out the Austrians and uniting the entire Italian peninsula under one central government. In his effort to carry out this plan Victor Emmanuel was forcibly integrating the Papal States into his general plan of unification. While severely condemning this sacrilegious seizure, some Catholics of the day were not unwilling to understand the patriotic aspirations of the Italian people for a united and independent country of their own under a common government. But tensions ran so high that anyone who made distinctions or added qualifications of any kind to his siding with the Holy Father in the affair, were thereby rendered suspect in the eyes of many. All such were really looked upon as persons of divided loyalty, Catholics of no better than "low views," if not heterodox.

In England Archbishop Manning and William G. Ward assumed extreme rightist views, while Newman considered the question as one of considerable complexity. It was to bring him to much grief. He had already been delated to Rome for his article in the *Rambler* entitled "On Consulting the Faithful in Matters of Doctrine." And now another black mark was to be checked against him, especially after it had been spread abroad that he "had preached in favor of Garibaldi, and had subscribed to the Garibaldi fund."[1] Speaking of Newman's unfortunate experience in dealing with the question of the temporal power of the pope, Wilfrid Ward remarked: "The Temporal Power question completed what the delation [to Rome] of his *Rambler* article had begun. He came to be, to use his own phrase 'under a cloud,' a man suspected in many quarters as not thoroughly orthodox.''[2] This same question was to bring Brownson, too, into a peck of trouble. Dealing with it realistically, as was his wont in such cases, he had some distinctions to make which seemed offensive to pious ears, and the thunder began to roll.

In an article on the "Roman Question" Brownson stressed the fact that the Papal States were the patrimony of the Holy See, and that the pope, as the incumbent of that see, governs them by sacred and divine right. To attack his right to govern them would, therefore, be to attack the rights of the Catholic Church, and incur the guilt of sacrilege. But with this acknowledgment made, he pointed out that since the rights of the pope as sovereign of the Papal States do not derive from his spiritual sovereignty, and are hence precisely what they would be if he were not chief of the spiritual society, the rights of his subjects in the Papal States are precisely what they would be, neither more nor less, in case their sovereign had no spiritual jurisdiction.[3] On that score he was definitely in favor of meeting the aspirations of the Italian people in the Papal States to have a voice in the affairs of government through the grant of a liberal constitution, monarchical and democratic in nature rather than aristocratic and oligarchical as would match their temperament. "Of course," he said, "such a government cannot be extorted from him [the Holy Father] by force, for that would be sacrilege, and to be legal it must be a concession made, as the papal documents say, *motu proprio*."[4] In fact he looked upon the social and political regeneration of all Italy in some such way as a pressing political desideratum. Italy, he sagely remarked, is "the lost pleiad of the constellation of European states. She [Italy] has been struck from the political firmament, and she and all the world have suffered in consequence."[5] Only Italy's restoration to the rank of a great power would answer that nation's own deep aspirations and help maintain a proper balance among the family of European states. These needs and aspirations he declared to be at the bottom of all the current commotion among the Italian people.

Brownson touched again upon this question in his article on "Ventura on Christian Politics." After proudly beating the drum over the fine spirit of loyalty the Catholic bishops throughout the world had shown the Holy Father in the current crisis, he scornfully spurned the hypocritical claim of maladministration in the Papal States, and trenchantly excoriated the swarm of out-and-out revolutionists who were stirring up all the trouble in the pope's territories. He again condemned the so-called right of rebellion. A people, he emphasized, may indeed alter their form of government through an orderly and legal process, but never through out-and-out rebellion. He stressed that this very principle had been asserted by the Supreme Court of the United States in the Rhode Island case, growing out of the Dorr rebellion, and was again reasserted in a way not to be forgotten in the case of John Brown and his associates in their attack on Harper's Ferry. In words that should have made the matter more understandable to his American readers, he said: "Those emissaries of Sardinia and other States that stirred up the revolt in the Romagna were John Browns, and Virginia would have hung them by the neck till they were dead, dead, dead. A great outcry has been raised against the Pope about the Perugia affair; but the Pope only exercised the same right the authorities of Virginia and the United States marines exercised in firing upon John Brown and his companions in possession of the arsenal at Harper's Ferry."[6]

Again, in his article on the papal power he asserted that as a mere statesman, governed by political reasons alone, he would not hesitate for a moment to adopt what is apparently the policy of Count Cavour, and favor annexation of the whole of Italy to Piedmont, under a constitutional monarchy, if the thing were possible, without a violation of vested rights. But he was quick to add: "The Sardinian government has no more right to annex the Papal States, or any portion of them, to Piedmont, without papal consent, than I have to appropriate my neighbor's purse without his permission.'" He owned that he did not see how any Catholic could have any other opinion in regard to the Papal States except that expressed by the Holy Father himself. Yet he did not feel bound by all the arguments and reasonings he had found in some of the recent pastoral letters of the bishops whether at home or abroad. In short, the arguments framed to show how the Papal States are necessary to the spiritual independence of the head of the Catholic Church, and therefore to the very existence of the Catholic religion itself, left him wholly unconvinced. There are different ways, he observed, in which the pope can show his independence; if in no other, by taking refuge in the catacombs, as did his predecessors for three hundred years, from St. Peter down to St. Sylvester. "The renewal of the martyr ages," he continued, "would, perhaps, not be very injurious to the Church and the salvation of souls. The Church has lost by being too much mixed up with a worldly policy, by her children relying too much on the friendship of princes and states, and not depending enough on the naked truth to sustain them."[8]

It was, however, his comments on this question in his article on the "Rights of the Temporal," in the October 1860 edition of his *Review,* which were to brew a wild tempest. That issue of his *Review* was the one immediately following the address of Archbishop Hughes at the Fordham (or St. John's as it was then known) commencement in July of 1860, in which the archbishop had directed his barbs at the critics of Catholic education. In his article on the "Rights of the Temporal" Brownson swung out at his critics on almost all fronts, and the whole edition was in content a veritable time bomb, including Dr. Cummings' article on "Vocations to the Priesthood," which set off rage and indignation in many quarters, as we have already partly noted. To what extent these articles were bombshells to many may be gathered from a letter Brownson wrote his son Henry on October 18, 1860, in which he said:

> My October number has kicked up a bobbery, and made the Archbishop, they say, perfectly frantic. My article on the "Rights of the Temporal," and Dr. Cummings' on "Vocations to the Priesthood" have done the work. The greatest wrath seems to be manifested to the Dr. [Cummings]. A trial has been threatened, and lawyers consulted and retained; but I think it will blow over. The number is one of the best I have ever sent out. You will see that I by no means abandon any of my former positions on the Papal Power, and by no means endorse the conduct of the Emperor, or Count Cavour, but have merely attempted to place the temporal principality of the Pope on its true basis, and to say a word or two in apology for the Italian people. I do not believe the temporal principality of the Pope necessary to the exercise of his spiritual sovereignty, and I do believe that the political and even the religious interests of Europe require the Union of Italy and her elevation to the rank of a great power, either as a Federal State or as a Unitarian Monarchical State. This is the sum of my heresy, but I recognize no one's right against his consent [that is, the Pope's]. . . .
>
> I have rejoiced over the Pastorals of the bishops, for they prove their attachment to the papacy, but they contain many things as to the temporal principality of the Pope I do not think warranted either by history or theology.[9]

He began his article on the "Rights of the Temporal" by assuming responsibility for the views on Catholic education expressed by Fr. William J.
Barry in the last issue of his *Review,* and then proceeded to a defense of his
own right as a Catholic publicist to criticize what he deemed to be defective
in Catholic education, or in need of improvement. He wrote:

> There are persons, very excellent persons too, placed in positions of trust
> and influence, who think a Catholic publicist should resolutely defend every-
> thing Catholic, and especially everything said, done, or approved by spiritual
> persons, direct all his attacks against outside barbarians, and studiously avoid
> agitating any question on which Catholics differ among themselves, or which
> may lead to discussions offensive or disagreeable to any portion of the Catholic
> community. . . .
> The evils which from time to time befall the Church, and often so great
> and deplorable, are in most cases, if not all, far more attributable to the faults,
> errors, and the blunders of Catholics themselves, than to the craftiness or
> wickedness of non-Catholics.[10]

He further insisted on making a distinction between the traditions of
Catholics and Catholic Tradition — a distinction that he was to emphasize
more and more during what is called his "liberal period." He looked upon it
as injurious to regard certain traditions of Catholics as any part of Catholic
Tradition itself. In particular, he deplored the fact that greater care had not
been taken to guard the faithful against a superstitious belief in the power of
sacramentals, such as the Miraculous Medal, the wearing of Our Lady's
Scapular, and the like, wherein a sacramental power is attributed to them
which belongs to the sacraments alone. He asserted that such superstitious
beliefs tend to enervate Catholic faith and piety by drawing off the mind
from a contemplation of the great fundamental truths of Catholic faith which
make for a robust and manly piety. To allow the sacramentals to become
mere amulets, as though they had some intrinsic power of their own, could
not, he said, be without spiritual harm.[11] Newman, too, seems to have felt
there was reason to complain on a similar line: "A people's religion," he
said, "is ever a corrupt religion in spite of the provisions of Holy Church."[12]

In what Brownson said he did not wish to breathe a syllable against the
devout use of Our Lady's Scapular or any other sacramental or devotion in
the Catholic Church. He himself wore piously Our Lady's Scapular[13] and
carried about with him a relic of the true Cross.[14] But he saw a dead routine
in these practices (in some cases) as tending to rob Christians of that spiritual and intellectual dynamism guaranteed them as Christians through a deep
and understanding grasp of the sublime and soul-stirring truths of the Catholic faith. Added to this spiritual enfeeblement, he said, is the safeguard system now so prevalent in all Catholic countries, fearfully shielding the faithful in the midst of dangers, but also necessarily preventing to a degree the
free growth of intelligence and the formation of manliness of character. Unfortunately, the net result is: "We become timid, weak, and imbecile; we
lack energy and courage, we lack self-reliance and feel that we cannot move
without the assistance of a dry-nurse. We have the characteristics of a conquered people, a people who once held and exercised the empire of the
world, but are reduced to slavery, and what is worst of all, are becoming
resigned to their condition."[15]

A few years later Newman in England unburdened himself in language
strikingly similar, when he wrote: "Instead of aiming at being a world-wide
power, we are shrinking into ourselves, narrowing our lines of com-

munication, trembling at freedom of thought, and using the language of dismay and despair at the prospects before us, instead of, with the high spirit of the warrior, going out conquering and to conquer."[16]

Brownson proceeded in his article on the "Rights of the Temporal" to defend his role as a Catholic publicist. He hit out on a line of thought that chimes in much better with post-Vatican Council II theology than thought in his own day on the apostolate of the laity. He wrote:

> Indeed, we cannot accept the assumption which not the clergy, but some laymen in their name make, that laymen, in matters of religion, can neither know nor say anything, that they are wherever the interests of religion are involved, to be counted interlopers or nullities. The Church in the broad sense we now regard it includes the laity as well as the clergy. The clergy and the laity make one Church and are equally members of Christ's mystical body. To the clergy Christ has given a distinct mission in the Church, given them for the discharge of this mission, certain rights, with which the laity have no right to interfere; but this does not mean that the laity are a nullity, and that God has left them nothing to do but passively submit to what they are told. . . . No doubt they must work under the spiritual chiefs, but that is not saying that they may not work at all, nor that it is not lawful for them to work with intelligence of their own, and with free will, as free moral agents. We know of no law of the Church which exempts us, as laymen, from our obligation to labor for the promotion of the interests of religion; that imposes on the clergy alone the duty of loving our neighbor and seeking his salvation; or by which we can discharge our moral and religious duties vicariously. . . .
>
> In our age, when education and intelligence are not confined to the clergy, and are often possessed in as eminent a degree by the laity as by them, when the most notable defenses of Catholic history have been made by laymen, sometimes by non-Catholics, and when the controversy between us and our enemies is removed from the sphere of theology, and made in the main a lay question, to be decided by the reason common to all men, rather than by authority, the fullest liberty must be given to laymen, compatible with the supremacy of the spiritual order and the discipline of the Church. . . .
>
> The modern world is to a great extent laic, and if the laity are not frankly recognized, and freely permitted to do whatever laymen can do, we shall find that they shall undertake — the rise and continuance of Protestantism prove it — to do more than they have a right to do, and will usurp the special functions of the clergy themselves. . . .
>
> We go as far as man does or can go in asserting the rights and prerogatives of the spiritual society as representing the spiritual order; indeed, it has been a grave charge against us that we go too far; but the supremacy of the spiritual order, as we understand it, does not absorb the state in the Church, or deprive the temporal of its autonomy in its own order. We are not pantheists.[17]

In dealing with the Italian or Roman question in this same article he pointed out to the extreme rightists that it was entirely fallacious to assert that the temporal principality of the pope was in any absolute sense necessary to the proper functioning of the papacy since the papal patrimony did not exist until 752 A.D.[18] Yet, with his customary reverence for authority, he disavowed sufficient confidence in his own judgment and personal knowledge to differ from the declarations of bishops throughout the world who had asserted that the temporal sovereignty of the Holy Father was necessary, at least relatively speaking, to his freedom and independence in his spiritual government. "We respect that declaration," he said, "and therefore hesitate to assert what in its absence we should not for a moment hesitate to assert." But inasmuch as he could not regard that declaration of the bishops as dogmatic in character and binding in conscience on the faith of Catholics, he could not condemn as without faith, or as lacking in loyalty, those who were disposed to dispute that declaration, or who thought, from their personal knowledge of history and the current state of the world, that the temporal sovereignty of the pope is not necessary to his freedom and independence in the government of the Catholic Church.[19]

Again he made no effort at all to conceal his sympathy with the aspirations of the Italian people for the unification of their country under some form of a liberal constitution. It was only natural that they should want a voice in the affairs of government, and a career as a nation such as other nations have. The whole temper and tendency of the times counseled a recognition of these aspirations. Even the Chosen People of old were allowed to have a kingly government like other nations when they desired it, though God was displeased with them on that account. As the alert Catholic apologist, always keeping in mind also how the question might look to those outside the Catholic Church, he confessed, moreover, that he should find it embarrassing to defend the Church against the charge of hostility to free government and republican institutions, urged vehemently by the Church's enemies, if obliged to defend absolutism at Rome, which would be the case if obliged to defend the papal government as essential to the freedom and independence of the Sovereign Pontiff. Some were to take umbrage at the pithy statement: "We do not believe that the law of God, or the interests of religion, are opposed to the resurrection and autonomy of Italy, or doom the temporal subjects of the Pope to hopeless slavery or perpetual nonage."[20] But while recognizing what he considered the legitimate civil and political aspirations of the Italian people, and excoriating the war of Napoleon III against Austria, the annexation of the Duchies and Amelia to the Kingdom of Sardinia, and the filibuster operations of Garibaldi in Sicily and Naples, he protested loudly against any unification program of the Italian patriots without the consent of the Holy Father and adequate indemnification.[21]

The great principle Brownson was contending for in his article on the "Rights of the Temporal" was that the supremacy of the spiritual does not absorb the temporal, or imply the supremacy of spiritual persons in all things. He extended the principle further to such themes as Church property and marriage, but its application to the question of education detained him longest. The welkin was still ringing with the echoes of the recent hot wrangle over the status of Catholic education. Education, said the battling editor, is a mixed question, partly spiritual, partly secular. The Catholic Church has the unquestionable right of founding, sustaining and managing in its own way, schools for the education and training of candidates who are to fill offices in the spiritual society. "But beyond this, education is secular."[22] In the bitter debate over Catholic education great emphasis had been laid on the claim that the education of the child is the right of the parent. If so, then parents have a right to inquire into the quality of schools and colleges, and to have some voice in the schools and colleges to which they are required by the spiritual society to send their children.[23] Why then the tremendous uproar over the late discussion of the status of education in Catholic schools and colleges? He added what was apparently an unmistakable thrust at Archbishop Hughes:

> We Catholics, notwithstanding certain appearances to the contrary, do not form a Mutual Admiration Society, bound to laud everything said or done by Catholics, and maintain through thick and thin that it is always just and holy.

565

We yield to no man in our reverence for the clergy, in our veneration for spiritual persons, or our admiration for the various orders and congregations of religious, who are doing so much for the Catholic cause; but we deny that everything done by priests or religious, even under the patronage of the Ordinary, is sacred and privileged, and in no case, and in no circumstances, to be made the subject of public criticism. Our colleges for general learning and science, by whomsoever founded, managed, or patronized, are secular, not ecclesiastical institutions, and as open as any other secular institutions to the remarks of the publicist; and the saddest thing for them that could happen would be to have it understood that they oppose the public discussion of their merits.[24]

Both Brownson and Newman, showing remarkable prescience in the matter, insisted in their day on allowing the Catholic laity their proper place in the management of colleges and universities. Brownson maintained that the college and university, though they should work in subordination and subserviency to the spiritual interests of which the Church is the guardian, are secular institutions. Hence, in all save spiritual matters, they should be under the control of the secular society. Or, if under the control of priests and religious, then under their control as agents of the secular society, not of the ecclesiastical. For the primary object of the college and university, save the faculty of theology, should be to meet the secular wants of a secular society, whether the professors be priests, religious, or seculars.[25] "The Catholic lay society is not a monastery," he said.[26] Newman's views were fairly similar. When rector of the Catholic University of Ireland, his attempt to establish a finance committee composed of the laity was effectively thwarted. Even when he endeavored later to appoint a layman as vice-rector, though it was within his jurisdiction according to the constitutional rules of the university, it was stymied.[27] Later still he was to make a plea when touching on a pastoral of the English bishops, at a highly critical moment, for a greater consideration of lay opinion in matters concerning Catholic education.[28]

What marked Brownson off from many another critic of Catholic education, both of his own day and of more recent times, was his frank and generous acknowledgment of the great handicaps under which the teacher or faculties of Catholic schools labored, both as to the quality of pupils sent to them and as to the monetary means at their disposal for effectively fulfilling the educational process. His was the role of the constructive critic. If Catholic colleges had not accomplished more, the unfortunate drawbacks in the case must be acknowledged; he said:

We must be just to the learned and noble-minded men who devote themselves to the important, but often irksome and thankless task of education, and we must consider the circumstances in which they have been placed, and the means and materials they have had to work with. . . . Most of our colleges are of recent origin, none of them are endowed, all of them are poor, and we have asked them to be Primary Schools, Grammar Schools, High Schools, Colleges, Universities, and to send out their pupils with a finished University education at the average age of eighteen. Having demanded the impossible, we turn round and berate them because they have not done it! This will not do. It is not fair, it is not honorable, it is not just. . . . The mass of Catholic parents, in this country, have had no thorough education themselves. . . . Their children, to a great extent, are sent to the college unformed, or in need of being reformed. Here is the first great difficulty our colleges have had to encounter and overcome.[29]

Near the end of his life Brownson remarked that "one half to two thirds of the boys committed to their care should never be sent to college or high school, for God never intended them to be scholars."[30]

Since this article on the "Rights of the Temporal" was to set off such an immense hubbub, it is pivotal in the case to note closely Brownson's statement on precisely why he wrote the article. Hoping to forestall misunderstanding, he explained:

> We have aimed to show that the high-level papal doctrines, the strong assertions of the supremacy of the Church as representing the spiritual order, which they [the readers] find in our pages, and which we trust they will always find in our pages, do not absorb the temporal in the spiritual, and deny all rights to the secular, or assert the exclusive right of spiritual persons in all things. We have heretofore vindicated the rights of the spiritual order. We have wished, in this article, to vindicate the rights of the lay society and laymen, and to set an example of their free use and application. . . . We have for years fought the battles of authority. . . . We have this once done the same for liberty, for the temporal order . . . [for] we would not have it supposed that we forget the rights of the temporal.[31]

This seems a fair and objective statement of the case. But because of the whirlwind of excitement over the temporal principality of the pope there was little chance it would be given any credit by those who were already lying in wait to waylay the editor of Brownson's *Review*.

Among the book reviews in this same October edition of his *Quarterly*, Brownson's review of the *History of the Protestant Reformation* by Martin J. Spalding, D.D., bishop of Louisville, Kentucky, was his most significant. He praised the work highly as a popular history, but felt that it did not give us the deeper philosophy of the movement, and therefore did not explain it, as the interest of truth and religion required. He asserted that he could not help thinking that the inner psychology of that movement had been treated by both Catholic and Protestant historians, with the exception of some German authors, quite too loosely and superficially. The old Catholic explanations of the movement, giving as efficient causes of that event what were really only the occasions, were not to him at all satisfactory. The thing to be explained is the phenomenon of how a very large portion of the faithful in all Europe, except Ireland and the Spanish peninsula, simultaneously rose in insurrection against the Catholic Church in which their fathers had died, and they themselves had been reared, and were ready to accept the doctrine of the gospelers, and aid the political and civil power in nearly one third of Europe in putting down the old religion by penal laws, fire and sword, fines, imprisonment, exile and the gibbet.

It was a principle of his philosophy, he said, that no new movement could ever acquire enough force to carry away large bodies of the people that is wholly unreal, or wholly founded in falsehood, even though sustained by depravity. All effective power is in truth, in reality, and the devil is powerful only by virtue of the truth and goodness he misinterprets, misapplies and perverts. Falsehood derives all its strength from truth, for pure falsehood it is pure negation, has no bottom, is nothing. No movement is explained by merely setting forth that it is false and evil; a movement is not explained till we have shown that it also contains something that is good and true. He insisted that there must be an aspect under which the Protestant movement can be considered in relation to the evils then existing that is both true and good; that without showing it under that aspect, it is not explained. There is no reason for the Catholic to fear to do it, for the Church includes all good in the natural order, and teaches all truth in the supernatural or Christian order, and therefore he may always examine any movement with the coolness of the philosopher, with the charity of the Christian, and without the misgivings of the sectarian, or the heat of the partisan. This cannot, of course, be done in the case of the Protestant movement without more or less censure of the Catholic party at the time, which must be distinguished from the Catholic Church itself, for it was the capital mistake of both parties (the Catholic and the Protestant party of the time) to confound the question or the state of affairs with the divine institution of the Catholic Church itself.[32]

Brownson then made reference in this review of Spalding's history to Dr. John M. Forbes, a convert from Episcopalianism who had been ordained by Archbishop Hughes, but who after functioning for some years as a Catholic priest, had returned to the Episcopalian ministry. In a brief letter to the public Dr. Forbes gave his reasons for renouncing his obedience to the Catholic Church. In his comments on the matter Brownson hinted at what he thought to be the salient reason for Forbes' defection as well as a reason which makes many intelligent Catholics no better than nominal members of the Church and which prevents intelligent Protestants from giving serious thought to the Catholic Church.

He wrote:

There were, perhaps, many good reasons for not replying personally to Dr. Forbes, but there can be none for not meeting and refuting his objections; for if the truth must be told, they operate not only in keeping those outside from coming into the Church, but in preventing a large class brought up in her communion from practically adhering to it. Look over this city, and you will find that almost all the sons of Catholic parents, who have received a liberal education even in Catholic colleges, and who have become distinguished for their intelligence, ability, and success in law, medicine, or politics, are little more than nominal Catholics, are practically nearly as much in schism as Dr. Forbes and substantially for the same reasons. They believe, or feel, or imagine, that the Church is in her practical administration a spiritual despotism, and that a man cannot be practically a Catholic without surrendering his manhood, and denying his natural sense of right and wrong. . . . There is the fact, and that fact we must meet and explain before we can, in the ordinary course of things, either keep our own, or gather in those who are avowedly without. . . . This work, which has been fearfully neglected, can be effectually done only by meeting and disposing of the objection we have indicated. We must meet it, not by denouncing those who bring it; not by opposing all liberty as license, and all progress insisted on by the modern world as diabolical; but by showing both dogmatically and historically that it is founded in error, that the Church, both theoretically and practically, leaves to her members their manhood, and all reasonable freedom of thought and action, all that reason itself leaves them, and is in no sense despotic. We must recognize and state the facts which have led to the contrary conclusion, that the Church is a spiritual despotism, keeps the souls and bodies of her children in bandages and swathing clothes, and permits no free thought, free speech, or free action. Such facts there are, for it is only in the misconception and misinterpretation, or misapplication of real facts the false notion could have originated.

We must show that those facts do not warrant the conclusion drawn from them, or that at most they warrant conclusions unfavorable only to some churchmen, who forget that they are not to "lord it over God's heritage," and now and then govern those committed to their care as despots, perhaps as capricious tyrants, never any conclusions unfavorable to the Church herself, who condemns the conduct of these churchmen, and does what is possible to correct it.[33]

Brownson's line of thought on a new philosophy of history as applied to Bishop Spalding's *History of the Protestant Reformation* fits in better with trends in historical science in our own ecumenical times, but Bishop Spalding liked not Brownson's criticism. He met it with a rejoinder in the *Louisville Guardian,* which Brownson reprinted in its entirety in the January 1861 issue of his *Quarterly,* asking his readers to procure the bishop's two volumes and to judge in the case for themselves. In his last two paragraphs Bishop Spalding had cast some aspersions on Brownson personally, which, said Brownson, "is not precisely in our style nor to our own taste."[34] Right at the end of this same January issue, Brownson significantly remarked: "With this number we enter upon the seventeenth year of our *Review* as a Catholic *Review.* We have been long enough before the public as a Catholic editor to have an established character."[35]

But Bishop Spalding was by no means the only American prelate who felt a strong compulsion to take pen in hand and write Orestes Brownson about that October edition of his *Review,* particularly regarding his article on the "Rights of the Temporal," and on what he had to say about the Roman or Italian question. It is more than a trifle strange that those who were to complain rather bitterly did not get at a better understanding of the article on the "Rights of the Temporal" and its general drift. For Brownson had not only stated in the article itself, as just noted, the laudable reason why he had written it, but he had further purposely endeavored to forestall misunderstanding by appending an extended postscript to that same October issue. In it he reminded his readers that in conducting such a periodical as his *Review* it was requisite, if it was to be kept up with the times, to vary the aspect under which it treated questions accordingly as those questions vary in the actual world. It was always his unswerving aim to attack the danger to religion and society wherever it threatened. In 1848 he had warred on radicalism, and energetically asserted authority in spirituals and temporals; in 1851 it had been equally necessary for him to oppose despotism, and to defend liberty. And at the present time he was carrying on a war on the one hand against absolutism, and on the other against license, and while asserting the just prerogatives of power, he saw the need to recognize and vindicate the rights of the people. While thus maintaining his stand on middle ground, he feared he would not succeed in avoiding offense to persons of mere one-sided views. There will be readers, he correctly predicted, who will take what we say in defense of the pope's temporal principality as a denial of the just rights and interests of the Italian people; what we say in sympathy with this noble and much-abused people will, by others, be taken as an attack on the pope's temporal sovereignty. To guard against misapprehension, the reader, he cautioned, must take *all* the articles on a subject together, and interpret what in one seems to him to go too far on one side, by what in another may seem to go too far on the other side. The later article always presupposes the earlier, unless expressly stated.[36]

He requested his readers to bear well in mind that his *Review* was a continuous work, and never to be regarded as complete on any subject as long as that subject is before the public for discussion. To get his rounded views on any theme, it is necessary to keep well in mind all that he had said on the subject in past years with what he was saying in the present. Thus, those who had thought his essays in the early fifties on the supremacy of the spiritual had denied the rights of the temporal, would find in the article on the "Rights of the Temporal" the qualifications in favor of the rights of the temporal which he had always had in mind, and had even expressed, though he had not at the time developed them at length. Only by taking in the totality of his views could misapprehension be avoided. Readers should understand that when circumstances make it proper to treat a subject under a different aspect from that under which he had previously treated it, he was simply changing his point of view, not his doctrine.

# 38

## BROWNSON REPLIES TO HIS CRITICS AND RECEIVES ENCOURAGING LETTERS

*Brownson receives a brash letter from John McMullen, a Roman doctor of divinity, on his article on the "Rights of the Temporal"* • *Brownson's long reply* • *A letter from Bishop John W. Luers* • *A complaining letter from Bishop William H. Elder* • *A lengthy letter from Brownson in reply* • *Various reactions in the Catholic press to the October edition of Brownson's* Review, *1860* • *The article in the* Metropolitan Record • *Brownson's name is coupled with that of Dr. John Forbes as restless converts* • *Dr. Jeremiah W. Cummings' vigorous support of Brownson* • *Bishop Elder criticizes Brownson's article on* Catholic Polemics • *Brownson reaches a low-water mark in spirits* • *He finds a measured degree of relaxation in social life and gardening* • *He receives encouraging letters.*

Brownson's words of caution lest his discussion of the Roman question be misinterpreted were largely lost on a number of his readers. Among such was Fr. John McMullen, a Roman doctor of divinity, who years later became bishop of Davenport, Iowa. McMullen was greatly agitated over Brownson's article on the "Rights of the Temporal." His complaining and menacing letter to Brownson is inserted here only in part. It was one of the most astonishing letters Brownson had ever received. McMullen wrote Brownson at the episcopal residence in Chicago on October 11, 1860:

> Doctor:
> I have just received the last number of your *Review* and I am anxious to tell you what I think about it.
> I dislike it very much and it is the only number that I have not read with pleasure and perhaps profit. Your change is undoubtedly for the worst. You have altered your position to carry yourself on the other side. The great trouble in this country and this age is that too much is claimed for the natural order. Natural rights are unduly extended and are no longer the faculty of acting according to reason but are as unbounded as individual caprice. Nature is exalted to embrace or exclude the supernatural. Why then appear as the champion of natural rights at present and put your patrons on their guard against the encroachments of the supernatural, at present more prudential: or how can it be accepted as an apology for want of *Catholic Spirit* and sound theology? I do think your explanation does no more than show a good intention, concerning which there is no question, for certainly if I thought your intentions were as faulty as your late productions I would be praying for you in place of writing to you.
> I would write publicly against your late articles but I prefer to unite with those who attack the common enemy, rather than wrangle in the camp with those who may deserve correction. If you think the expression of my views severe, remember you may yet meet them under a more *formidable* aspect, and if you do they certainly shall be triumphant. If apology be required the only

one I give is the sincerity of one who wishes you every good and who has received much pleasure and instruction from your writings.

J. Mullen, D.D.

O.A. Brownson, LL.D.
P.S. I expect no answer, J.M.[1]

Brownson was of course quite distressed at having received such a brash letter, and felt a compulsion to set the Reverend Doctor straight on more than one salient point. His reply is one of his longer and more remarkable letters and is an excellent commentary on his article, "Rights of the Temporal," to which McMullen had taken so much exception. From Elizabeth, New Jersey, he wrote in part on October 20, 1860:

Rev. Doctor John McMullen
Dear Sir:

I have this moment received a letter dated "Episcopal Residence, Chicago, October 11, 1860," and signed by your name, but of so singular a character that I am unwilling to believe that you are actually the writer. Some mutual enemy must have written me in your name. You are a Christian and a priest, a scholar and a gentleman, and I am sure, if you had found anything wrong in my *Review,* you would have calmly and courteously pointed out the wrong, stated distinctly wherein I had erred, and given me an opportunity to correct my error, and atone for my offense. The letter does no such thing, and deals in severe, but vague censure and threats.

The writer accuses me of lacking the Catholic spirit, of being unorthodox in my argument, and unsound in my theology, but specifies no particulars. He says I am on the wrong side, but I am on the side I have always been on since I became a Catholic, and he cites no proof to the contrary. He complains that I defend "the rights of the temporal" in the face of my repeated declarations that the temporal has no rights against the spiritual, and that it has only the rights defined by the spiritual. Have I claimed any right for it beyond the definition of the supreme Catholic authority? If so, the writer should in charity, if not justice, have told me what right, yet he does not do so. . . .

The writer tells me that I give too much to the natural order. If so, can he tell me wherein? I certainly mean to do no such thing. He intimates that I raise the natural to the supernatural, or bring the supernatural down to the natural, and says some good things about the danger of doing it, as if I could be less sensible of the danger than he is, or as if my *Review* had not said far stronger things of the same sort than he says, or perhaps, can say. It would have been more to the purpose to show me wherein I raise the natural to the supernatural or bring down the supernatural, for he cannot suppose that I would do either knowingly. . . . You know, sir, as a reader of my *Review,* that I have labored long and hard to vindicate and illustrate the theological maxim: *Gratia supponit naturam,* and to draw accurately the line of demarcation between the natural and the supernatural. . . .

The writer likes the article signed J.W.C. and says it is the only redeeming feature of the number. I am glad of this, for the article was written at my solicitation. My own article on the rights of the temporal he condemns without benefit of clergy. Yet the views of that article have a clerical origin, and the article itself was submitted, before being sent to the printer, to the examination, revision, and approbation of an eminent theologian, a Doctor of Divinity, and a Propagandist, like yourself. He told me it was the best article I had ever written for my *Review,* and he commended especially its truly Catholic spirit and tone. This much I know, that while writing it I sought light and guidance from above, and offered my communions to be preserved from all error.

Now if you were the writer [of the letter he had received], I would ask you, my dear Doctor, what a poor devil of a layman like me is to do? You are a

572

priest, a Roman Doctor, and if you are the writer, you denounce me rudely, in terms of unmeasured severity for an article which was suggested, revised, and approved before publication by another priest, another Roman Doctor, your senior in years, your superior in reputation, your equal at least in position, in attainments, and perhaps in natural talents, and a Propagandist as well as you, and really one of the first divines and ablest men in the country. What in this case am I to think? . . .

I have labored long and hard to draw accurately the line between the natural and the supernatural, and to guard against Pelagianism on the one hand and Jansenism on the other, and as good theologians as yourself have assured me that I have done it successfully. I had said nothing on this point in my last *Review* that I had not said perhaps fifty times before. You should remember that I am not a boy just learning my A.B.C. and that it is possible that I have devoted as many years as you have months to the study of this question, the vital question between the rationalist and the Catholic. A young man [McMullen had been ordained only two years], even if a Doctor of Divinity, should point out to me my specific error, if I have fallen into any, and not even in a private letter deal in vague censure, as though I was ignorant of the importance of the question.

You think, if you are the writer, the danger is just now in giving too much to nature and extending the natural rights too far, for that is the error of the age. All error, as all exaggeration, is at times and in all places dangerous. But perhaps the writer has not reflected that one extreme begets another, or paid attention to the fact that the standing objection to the Church in the minds of non-Catholics is that she denies the natural or absorbs it in the supernatural. A few years ago, out of nine bishops and archbishops at Milwaukee, there was only one who did not accuse me, in the vindication of the supernatural, of falling into this very fault, and I had to defend myself against no less a person than Bishop O'Connor. I did not admit the justice of the charge, but I was satisfied that I had not placed in a sufficiently prominent light the rights of the temporal. . . . It will never do to dwell forever on one aspect of the question, and I believed when I wrote the last number, the time had come to bring up the other aspect of the case, and answer the objections of non-Catholics, and to answer it so that they could understand my answer.

I believe the fault of Catholics here and in Europe is that they leave natural rights to be asserted by their enemies, instead of taking their assertion into their own hands. We are looked upon by those outside as leagued with despotism. The writer would forbid me to set them right, and have me continue asserting authority, cramming it down the throats of our opponents against the stomach of their sense. I believe it is my duty, without lowering the claims of authority, to bring up in harmony with them the rights of liberty.

The writer objects to my note as unsatisfactory [at the end of the October 1860 issue of his *Review*], and no wonder; for he took it as an apology, and failed to recognize its meaning. The note was added to remind just such readers as the writer of the letter, that in order to do me justice, they must take what I say of the rights of the temporal with what I had previously said in vindication of the rights of the spiritual, and not to take it by itself alone. I am sure, if you had been the writer, unless you had written hastily and without taking time for reflection, you would have interpreted the later article by the earlier, as well as the earlier by the later. You would not have supposed me such a blockhead as to contradict in October what I had published in April and in July, and at the same time to pretend I had done no such thing. I trust I have too much sense and too much honesty for that, and it would have been perhaps more modest and even more reasonable for the writer to have supposed that he had missed my meaning than to have supposed I could change sides without knowing it, or knowing it, could deny it. . . .

The writer winds up his letter with a threat which I do not understand. Is my *Review* to be denounced at Rome? Let it be denounced. I shall not be found defending anything in it Rome shall declare to be an error in faith or morals. I am a Catholic; a Catholic I am determined to live and die. Err I may; a heretic I will not be, as a *formal* heretic I never was. It will cost me nothing to retract any error authority may point out in any of my writings. . . . They little know me who think I love my own opinions better than truth. . . .

The writer said he expected no answer. I have seen proper to give an answer, and a long though hasty one. I have some reason to complain of unfair treatment. No doubt, some look upon me as a turbulent innovator. Many declaim and exclaim against me, no man reasons against me, nor does more than get off a Philippic against me. No man grapples with my argument. I am treated as a boy, a child, an ignoramus. What is the reason why Catholics in this country cannot be candid and just to one from whom they differ? Why is it that they must always misrepresent and vituperate? In my case this has been the rule, with scarcely an exception. But enough. I remember with lively gratitude the pleasant evenings I spent at the Bishop's, and believe me with profound respect, yours truly,

O. A. Brownson[2]

Brownson's article on the "Rights of the Temporal" also drew from John H. Luers, bishop of Fort Wayne, Indiana, a letter only of a kind and benevolent sort. Writing on November 29, 1860, Bishop Luers said in part:

Dear Sir:
I have taken your *Review* ever since its first appearance, and read it not without great pleasure and delight, but also with no little advantage to myself, and hope to do so for the time to come.

I think, however, that it might do still more good if, at times you were not so unnecessarily severe, more guarded in your expressions, and intent not only upon *what* you say, but also the *manner* in which you express it. The age is blind, weak, and full of self-love; it can neither bear the rod, nor digest strong food. Hence in making it perceive and appreciate the truth, we must make use of as mild and gentle means as possible. Light is indispensible, but when the eyes are weak, to expose them to the sun, will only inflame them more and close them up entirely. Too strong a dose of the best of medicines will only prove injurious, and food, although necessary for the body, must when the constitution is not strong and robust, be prepared with the greatest care; otherwise it will become pernicious and indigestible. So it is with other things. Hence in advancing a question we must not only ask: Is it *true*? but also, is it *expedient*? Are those to whom it is addressed in a proper condition to receive and appreciate it, will it be of beneficial results?

For the last six months and more, I have spoken with several bishops, priests, and others, *your real friends and well-wishers,* and they all desire and are extremely anxious to see you drop, for the present, all those irritating questions which have been the source of so much calumny and personal abuse against you; the more so, since just now, the land is cursed with . . . unscrupulous and mercenary demagogues who wish to render themselves popular, and to thrive and make money by distorting and vilifying your *Review.*[3]

Bishop Luers went on in his letter to counsel Brownson to confine himself in his writings to themes of a more academic nature, whether theology, philosophy, geology, literature, history, politics or whatnot. Little chance was there that his advice might be heeded in any goodly degree. Orestes Brownson wanted to be where the action was: his martial temperament fed on battles. He would no more have shied away from battle than would have the legendary El Cid. Besides, were not the interests of the Catholic Church involved vitally in the burning questions of the day — more than in any other questions? How could he ignore those questions and prattle away about things of little or no practical consequence? To him it would have been a base dereliction of duty as a Catholic apologist. Even Brownson's son Henry says it was a mistake for his father to have treated the Roman or Italian question in his writings.⁴ But it is simply unthinkable that such a wide-sweeping Catholic apologist should have or could have refrained from discussing such an all-absorbing question of the day.

Another prelate, who sent him a letter of frank, if not acute criticism of his recent articles, particularly the one on the "Rights of the Temporal," was William Henry Elder, bishop of Natchez, Mississippi, a former acquaintance of Brownson. He wrote Brownson on December 18, 1860:

Dear Sir:
[After referring to a copy he had sent Brownson of the article he had published in the *New Orleans Catholic Standard* in criticism of Dr. Cummings' article on "Vocations to the Priesthood," he continued:]

I remember that, some years ago, when we had you for a few pleasant days at the Mountain [St. Mary's College and Seminary, Emmitsburg, Maryland] you were *great* on "Discrimination," and I am sure you have enough of that rare virtue to discriminate between a carper who feels happy in finding a fault to bark at, and a friend who desires to see a valuable work as free as possible from blemishes. My desire is to be among the latter. It was partly for that reason and partly as an act of justice to my own meritorious clergy, that I published the letter [in reply to Dr. Cummings]. . . .

I presume you advocate "the right of petition." And you will not be offended if I petition you, in the name of those interests to which you have generously sacrificed your abilities — to consider carefully and conscientiously and to study profoundly some of those more important points which have been found fault with. *Etiam ab hoste fas est doceri,* and even in the angry declamations against you, you will find sometimes a valuable truth. Remember your own great principle, that men never uphold an error for the sake of the error, but for the sake of a truth which is bound up with it, or which they think is bound up with it. They do not discriminate between the two — sometimes because they will not know how, sometimes because they will not take the trouble. But you know how — and you have all your life been taking trouble to do things well.

And as it may be with some of your most unfriendly critics, so it is with some of the things you criticize. Even routine is not absolutely bad. [Elder was here referring to what Brownson had remarked about the routine use of sacramentals.] There are good routines as well as bad. For a man to say his morning prayers, it is not necessary to go over again every day all the reasons for this duty, nor to discuss in his own mind every day why the Blessed Virgin is called the Mother of God. He has been taught to say them — he has adopted that good practice — he has satisfied himself already that it is right — and so he continues. . . .

But there is one matter in which I must enter not a petition but a protest. In regard to your expression that the Italian patriot "feels his wrath burn against the sovereign [the pope]." Aside from all other questions in that connection, this expression is wanting in that respect which a great Catholic publicist owes to the head of the Church, and such a head as Pius IX. Whatever be the sentiments of men about the papal government, no one, so far as I have heard, charges the present Pontiff with any crime which could make "the wrath burn" of any reasonable man. You not only use the expression, but in such a connection as to give the impression that they have *reason* to burn with wrath.

Again I recur to your most wise and generous views. There is a great deal of work to be done in our country, and there is room for all. Let us work spiritedly, each in his own way; each trying to cooperate and support all the others in all that is good; each tender about discouraging others by criticisms too severe or biting; and each trying to practice fortitude if some around are not tender enough towards ourselves. But fortitude is not enough. We must be ready to learn from their censures. And then we ought to try as far as possible not to call forth censures unnecessarily, because they cause divisions, and divisions cause weakness. Accustomed as I am to meet things in your writings which first appear paradoxical, and which you afterwards explain in a satisfactory sense, yet I must say I do not see how to reconcile your remarks on Italy with your former solid refutations of "the right of revolution" in the popular and radical sense of the expression, and your supposition that the Pope judging "in his capacity as a *Sovereign Pontiff*" might have been biased, and might have "used his spirituality to sustain his temporality," seems to me to be substantially the same supposition made by Philip the Fair, and Henry IV of Germany, and all the others against whom the Popes maintained the supremacy of justice over might — even in temporal affairs. You must not wonder if people get alarmed at finding what appears to be a contradiction of your old teachings — and just at this moment when revolution and "universal suffrage" are doing the work of the socialists — and when we need more than ever the maintenance of God's law and the law of nations.

Forgive me, if I have written too much. May God prosper you and your labors for His Holy Truth; and make them every day more fruitful of the only good, His Glory. A Happy Christmas. Your humble servt. in Xt.

William Henry Elder, Bishop of Natchez[5]

Brownson responded to this letter on December 26, 1860:

Right Reverend and Dear Sir:

. . . Your suggestions and advice to me I take in the spirit they were offered. Some of your censures I do not accept as just. The passage you cite as irreverent to the Holy Father, does not express my feelings, but those of the Italian patriots. I am only stating the fact as it exists in their mind. I am not aware of having fallen into any contradiction of myself. I maintain that the subjects of the Pope as a temporal sovereign, have the same right of revolution they would have in case that their prince were not a spiritual person; but what I hold that right to be, you must gather from previous numbers of my *Review*. I have never said, I have never believed, and I do not believe that the subjects of the Pope have any right to revolutionize their government, unless the Pope should become an intolerant tyrant, and such I by no means regard him. I am as far as you or any other man from justifying them, or Sardinia. I wrote to have an influence on those who imagine that the unity and independence of Italy cannot be effected without making war on the Papacy. I wish to show that it necessarily involved no war on any but the temporal rights of the Holy See — rights which cannot indeed be wrested from her without crime, but which she, if she judges proper, may surrender without surrendering any spiritual right, which I presume you will not dispute.

My purpose in the article was not to set up the temporal against the spiritual, for I claimed for the spiritual the right to define her own powers and those of the temporal; but to maintain that not every right of a spiritual person is a spiritual right. There were strong reasons for maintaining this, reasons which, could you know the real state of things in the Diocese of New York, you would not treat as trivial. The real question is: Can I as a good Catholic and as a Doctor of Canon Law maintain this thesis?

I have, with your permission, in no instance talked like Philip the Fair. In administration I believe the Church is to be obeyed; I believe her generally right; but I have never supposed that I was required to believe her infallible save in matters of faith, morals, and dogmatic facts. I believe the Pope is the divinely appointed judge in cases of dispute between temporal sovereigns, and temporal sovereigns and their subjects; but I have never believed his judgment based merely on human testimony could be infallible. I am not aware that in deciding such cases either he or even a General Council has the promise of the infallible assistance of the Holy Ghost. I do not say that in deciding the question between him and his own subjects that I should suspect him of abusing his spiritual power to support his temporal. I am all along giving reasonings and feelings of the Italian patriots [he probably should have made that clear beyond possible misunderstanding], not my own; for it is in their reasons I reason. But you will get a fuller view of the writer's intention from the article, Separation of Church and State, in the number for January.

You make an injurious application of my own principle against me. I shall not say the application is unjust; but I will say that the clamor against me is founded in misapprehension, although very likely the reason why I am misapprehended is in some measure my fault.

I am discussing questions from a point of view and with ulterior purposes not generally considered by my Catholic friends. My own conviction is that the ordinary method of presenting and defending Catholic truth, does not really present that truth to the non-Catholic mind, and the chief cause of the misapprehension of my meaning by Catholics is in the fact that I adopt an unusual method, and use language which, while it conveys a Catholic sense to non-Catholic minds, has a non-Catholic sense to the ordinary Catholic mind. I can easily write so that Catholics will not misapprehend me, but then I should only so write as to give a false impression to the minds of non-Catholics. Here is my difficulty. I know of no way of avoiding it, if I am to do any good by writing.

Bishop Spalding had recently laid to Brownson's charge that while he held himself perfectly free to criticize others he was unwilling to be made the object of criticism.[6] Was this really the explanation of his difficulties with a portion of the Catholic press? Were his complaints about assaults upon himself without rhyme or reason? No man of course is perfect, nor is all the fault usually on just one side. But in this same letter to Bishop Elder, Brownson laid down in as clear language as possible precisely what it was he objected to in a portion of the Catholic press, when he said:

Let me say, I do not complain that Catholics oppose me. I complain that I am unfairly opposed, on some collateral issue, or for some accidental reason, never on the real issue, or on the merits of the question itself. Your official organs do not reason with me, or against me. They denounce me, or combat me by opposing to me popular opinion, or popular prejudice, sometimes false philosophy, false theology, and false history. Yet I do not find the bishops rebuking them, or interfering in my defense when I am manifestly in the right. They seem to lay everything on my shoulders, not only my own faults, but the faults and scandals of the Catholic press. They may lie about me, distort my meaning as much as they please; but it is all my fault; for as Archbishop Hughes tells me, I am responsible not only for my own meaning, but for the meaning others without warrant deduce from my language. I think I have a right to complain of gross injustice on the part of the Catholic press and on the part of a considerable number of Catholic bishops. You all know that I take not and will not take any newspaper article as the voice of authority. I recognize authority only when it speaks to me in its own name. Yet no bishop condescends to write me to tell me wherein he thinks I am wrong, or to inform me of his wishes, or to offer me his advice. You and the Bishop of Fort Wayne are the only two who have done it since I have been a Catholic editor. The first communication I have is, Stop my *Review*. I have wished to conduct it in a manner acceptable to them, and have always held myself amenable to their censures and open to their advice. I am no heretic, I am no schismatic, but an obedient son of the Church, and no word from any bishop addressed in his own name to me but will receive from me due respect. All I say is, you may kill my *Review*, but you cannot manage me through newspapers. I love my religion and wish to serve it not in my own way, but in the way the bishops point out. I wish to act in subordination to them, and under their advice. I am all docility, if they will only themselves speak to me, and tell me their wishes.

Even you yourself seem to misapprehend me, and write as if I was one of the most proud and touchy men in the world. I know not whence this impression with regard to me has got abroad. I do not regard myself as perfect; I have not a very remarkably high opinion of myself, and I seldom do any thing that satisfies myself. But the one thing I can say is, that I am not a proud man; at least, I have no pride of opinion, and can when shown a reason for so doing, abandon without the slightest internal struggle any opinion I hold.

I have been ever since I became a Catholic, in the habit of submitting my articles to theological revision before they are printed, and to the best theological revision within reach. The article on the Rights of the Temporal was inspired, to some extent dictated, and revised and approved by a dignitary of the Church. Numerous alterations were made at his suggestion. Moreover I presented the main points in confession to my confessor, a Jesuit, a professor of theology, and one of the ablest theologians I ever met. I made the subject a matter of prayer, and offered up my communion four times while writing it, for light and guidance. I say not this to excuse the article, but to show you that I am not unwilling to receive instruction.

If the prelates of the Church would deign to communicate to me from time to time their objections, or make such suggestions as occur to them, they would find the *Review* would in its humble way respond to their wishes. The main difficulty lies in the fact that they seem to rely on the weekly press to set me right; but for that press I have in general no respect, for its conductors are men who understand little of the wants of the age and speak only to a narrow circle, while my *Review* speaks to the whole Catholic world. I cannot take my cue from them.

But let a bishop or a priest speak to me privately, and he will find me ready to listen and to correct any errors he convicts me of and to pursue the course he convinces me is the one the Church requires.

I have been threatened with being denounced to the Congregation of the Index. Perhaps I have been. If the Holy See finds aught in what I have written to mark with a note of censure, or that she requires me to retract, I do not think it will cost me a moment's struggle to obey her, and to accept her decision *ex animo*.

That the article on the "Rights of the Temporal" was simply another reply to Archbishop Hughes is evident from the paragraph with which Brownson ended this letter to Bishop Elder:

I have written to you as to an old friend, and have shown you my heart. I will only say that while in Boston, I followed the direction of the Bishop of Boston. I cannot accept the Archbishop of New York as my consultor. His advice I cannot respect, and I am not under his jurisdiction. But for him there would have been but little of the difficulty that has occurred, and it is his conduct and the state of things in his diocese that create the grief and dissatisfaction I feel. Forgive me if I have said any thing wrong, and pardon me for inflicting on you so long a letter, and believe me affectionately and reverently your obedient servant,

O.A. Brownson[7]

There were various reactions in the Catholic press to Brownson's October issue, of which we have been speaking. Some important criticisms were reprinted in the *Metropolitan Record* on November 2, 10 and 17. The *Herald and Visitor* of Philadelphia grappled with Brownson's review of

Bishop Spalding's *History of the Protestant Reformation,* while the *Pittsburgh Catholic* had words of praise for the October edition. Not surprisingly, those who were hostile to Brownson could see nothing in his article on the "Rights of the Temporal" but an attempt to set up the rights of the temporal against those of the spiritual. The definitive commentary came in the December 22 issue of the *Metropolitan Record.* The writer, the archbishop or another, asserted that he had purposely waited until the other Catholic papers and bishops had expressed themselves on the matter so that he could not be held obnoxious to the charge of having tried to influence the jury. Referring to the articles, "Rationalism and Traditionalism" and the "Rights of the Temporal," the writer asserted that "the whole [of the two articles] amounts to the rights of the laity versus the rights of the priesthood from the Pope down." After touching on the general contents of Brownson's October issue, the writer finally came to a close scrutiny of Brownson's review of Bishop Spalding's *History of the Protestant Reformation* in which he indignantly resented the reasons Brownson had given accounting for Dr. Forbes' defection. Dilating on the matter at some length, in which he coupled Brownson's name with that of Forbes as restless converts, the writer referred to Dr. Forbes' fall, saying:

> God forbid that Dr. Brownson should ever follow his example! But his *Review* betrays, especially in its last issue, a certain vague discontent, disappointment, and whatnot, without giving clear and frank expression to any inward grievance, all of which it is painful to read and reflect upon. . . . Having thus spoken of Dr. Brownson and Dr. Forbes, we must make the greatest distinction between the position occupied by the one and that chosen by the other. Of Dr. Brownson's orthodoxy we have not the slightest doubt.

Writing under the letterhead of "College of Physicians and Surgeons, New York," a certain Patrick Pendergast addressed a letter to Brownson, dated November 27, 1860, deploring the base nature of an article in the *Metropolitan Record* on Brownson's two articles in the October edition of his *Review,* "Rationalism and Traditionalism" and the "Rights of the Temporal." Referring to what had been said on the "Rights of the Temporal," he commented:

> The attempted reply to the article on the Rights of the Temporal contains a base unqualified lie in the first paragraph. The readers of the *Record* are led to infer that in the article — Rights of the Temporal — an attempt is made to establish and proclaim those rights against the spiritual. If the *Record* writer had supposed that a tittle [a very small number] of his readers had read the article referred to, he would not have had the audacity to utter a *lie* so baseless. His waiting until the next number of the *Review* is most probably in print only sustains the rule that all *liars* are sneaks. And the prodigious fear which he professes to have entertained of forestalling public opinion will hardly go down with intelligent readers.
>
> Five years have elapsed since I first saw your *Review*. During that time I have had every reason to admire your ability, your disinterestedness, and your indomitable firmness, and last but not least when coupled with so much talent, your humility. I believe and every Catholic with whom I am acquainted believes that your *Review* will be read when the *Record* will be numbered with the Atlantic cable and other things that were.
>
> Resp'y,<br>Patrick Pendergast[8]

The attacks on Brownson fulminating from the *Record* and the archbishop's journal could not but increase the difficulty of keeping his *Review* a going concern. But he had fast friends, too, who were willing to work hard for his cause. One of these old-timers was Fr. Jeremiah Cummings. On the first of January 1861 he sent Brownson an order for twenty-five copies of his *Review* for as many new subscribers. On the fifteenth of the month, Cummings (who was evidently smarting under the treatment Brownson was receiving) wrote Fr. Joseph M. Finotti a letter in which his characteristic spunk flared out:

> As to that melancholy article in the "Record," it was the production of Archbishop Hughes in person. Of this you can be certain. Brownson's *Review* is doing well in spite of many efforts to stop the bread and butter of its Editor. Many of the old fogies have given up taking it, and many underhanded efforts were made to break it down, but he began the new year with more subscribers than he had in 1860 on January 1st. Me they cannot hurt, and when it is time to speak they shall find that I am not to be dragooned into silence. I hate despotism and brutality whether it be practiced in the name of the civil power or of the Church, by Austrian soldiers or American churchmen, I mean to fight it — prudently and prayerfully — but to fight it until I see it die or I die myself. Some of the magnates here have tried to get Propaganda to denounce Brownson, but Roman wisdom is not as easy to entrap as they think.
> My crime is not that I am an enemy of the Irish — they knew that I am not — but that I have dared to publish the Decrees of Trent, and the letters of Pope Benedict giving fits to the Bishops! I have done this and I live. It is the first instance, since episcopal despotism was inaugurated here. They have done all they could to crush me, but I am as good a Catholic and as jolly a fellow as ever.[9]

When Brownson published his thought-provoking article on "Catholic Polemics" in the July 1861 issue of his *Quarterly,* Bishop Elder replied to the letter he had received from Brownson, dated December 26, 1860. It is significant that Bishop Elder wrote Brownson two long letters, this second letter being an extensive analysis of Brownson's article on "Catholic Polemics." He was "a prodigious letter writer."[10] In this instance, he was greatly disturbed over portions of Brownson's article on "Catholic Polemics." Though his letter was truly paternal in spirit, some of his complaints were expressed in a tone somewhat acerb. Brownson had lamented in his article the too little appreciation among Catholics of the advanced culture of the age in different fields, and of the consequent unwillingness on their part to allow the Catholic apologist a free hand in meeting the problems of the age intelligently with a more modern approach and technique. The only active men who could remain in good graces with the Catholic public, he complained, and escape having their orthodoxy and their zeal questioned, were the *oscurantisti,* the *laudatores temporis acti,* "who stoutly maintained all antiquated formulas, hold fast to old abuses, repress all generous aspirations, and anathematize all efforts for progress." It seemed to him that there had never been an epoch in the history of the Catholic Church in which the directors of the Catholic world had had so great a dread of intellect.[11]

Whether or not Brownson definitely intended to include the clergy in this biting indictment, Bishop Elder evidently thought he did. In a paragraph of his long letter he replied pointedly to these animadversions of Brownson. He wrote:

> Certainly it is desirable that all our Catholic Clergy should acquire as much science as possible, and use it in behalf of religion. We have to regret that

many circumstances hinder us from getting all that is desirable. Perhaps we are too slow and indolent about remedying the defect — a good stimulus may be of great service to us. But remember your own maxim, "We must take men as they are." A rebuke, to produce a good effect, must be administered "in a proper spirit, with loyal intentions." Grumbling and abuse are not apt to do good to others, any more than to yourself. If there is *not sufficient zeal for science,* tell us so respectfully, earnestly, warmly, if you please, but don't charge us with *fearing* science and *shunning* argument. If you see something in the spirit of the age which does not strike our attention, point it out plainly — but do not first write an article in strange terms for people to misunderstand, and then accuse us of wilfully ignoring the spirit of the age. [Elder acknowledged that "feeling may have betrayed me into saying some things too sharply."][12]

In an effort to meet the minds of those outside the Catholic Church, Brownson had also raised a few brief questions in this same article on "Catholic Polemics" about the nature of eternal punishment hereafter, that is, concerning what it is precisely that the Church has defined in the matter.[13] Elder thought this liable to give scandal. Together with this, probably none of Elder's criticisms had greater validity than his comments on Brownson's new style or method in apologetics. Brownson had asserted in his letter of December 26, 1860, that the ordinary way of presenting and defending Catholic truth does not present that truth to the non-Catholic mind, that the chief cause of his misapprehension by Catholics was in the fact that he had adopted an unusual method which, while it conveys a Catholic sense to the non-Catholic mind, has a non-Catholic sense to the ordinary Catholic mind. He added: "I can easily write so that Catholics will not misapprehend me, but then I should only so write as to give a false impression to the minds of non-Catholics. Here is my difficulty. I know no way of avoiding it, if I am to do any good by writing."[14] To which Bishop Elder replied regarding his brief speculations on the nature of eternal punishment and his new method in apologetics:

> It is true you only *ask* questions. But you are not so inexperienced in Rhetoric and Human Nature as not to know that interrogations convey statements as clearly as direct assertions — and even often have more power of carrying the assent of the reader. And in this case whatever may have been your intention — such is certainly the impression your words will naturally convey to the popular mind. If you find it necessary to suit your language to the comprehension of non-Catholic readers you ought not to be less tender of the understanding and salvation of Catholics — nor less careful of scandalizing them.[15]

Thick as the fight had now become for him, the sturdy old warrior and editor did not spend utterly all his time on the battlefield. He found respite from the pressures of life in a measured degree in social life. He was often invited out to dinner by lay and clerical friends. And he loved to play whist with his old cronies. A humorous story has come down to us from one of those cronies of New York City. On one occasion when Brownson had visited him, he and his guest, ignoring a capacious cuspidor, moved their card table nearer to the fireplace. They thought they were doing well enough; but the hostess, with apparent good reason, wedged in between the two and the fireplace and placed a silver spittoon at a closer and more convenient angle for them. The host, perhaps bugged by a bad play he had made, mischievously spat past it. Whereupon Brownson, acknowledging the well-meant courtesy, remarked: "If you are not careful, young lady, somebody'll spit in that thing."

Another relaxation the hard-working editor enjoyed after moving to Elizabeth, New Jersey, was a return to his long-accustomed gardening. He had always found it a tonic for good health. In New York City, however, his grounds did not allow an outlet for that profitable exercise.[16] But his Elizabeth residence included ample space in the rear for a garden of considerable variety, including his customary roses. In season he proudly displayed them.

It was also a pleasure for him to make new acquaintances and gain new friends on his lecture tours. And that he could be a charming conversationalist we learn from a letter of Henry S. Randall of Cortland Village, New York, dated May 6, 1862. He wrote:

> Dear Sir:
> I often think of the delightful half day I spent with you. Wouldn't it be nice if one could choose his neighbors — and have an assortment to fit all moods of the mind: If you and I were neighbors you would often find me a looker-in, for though no great craeker of metaphysical Mts., I love now and then to *think* and to talk to a *thinker*. And you sugar-coat over your philosophy with so much amenity and geniality — you are so confounded good natured and engaging — that I verily believe I have thought of you every day since you were here — and every time I have thought of you, I have wished you were my neighbor.[17]

But whatever surcease the old warrior could wangle from the grim cares of life, the heavy bombardment to which he had been subjected during the last years could not but have its telling effect upon his health and happiness. A letter he wrote Fr. Joseph Finnetti on July 1, 1860, tells us that his health had been "very poor" for some months, and that wife Sally and daughter Sarah, too, had been "very ill for the last six months." He had just taken them to Ballston Spa, New York, for a visit with his aging mother and sister Thorina "in the hope that a change of air will aid their recovery." He himself was in low spirits, but remarked, "I still trust in the good God to carry me through."[18] Courage had always been one of the most remarkable traits of his character. Forward he moved, working on his *Review*, lecturing, or attending some public event. Soon he got off a letter to daughter Sarah, followed quickly by a longer one to wife Sally, dated July 17, 1860. He wrote:

> We are all well and get along well, except myself. I am about as fidgety when you are gone as they say you are when I am gone, and though my health is well enough, I shall not be worth much till your return. I really did not know before, how necessary you are to me, and that I really am nothing without you. Yet I wish you to stay where you are as long as you continue to improve, or you and Sarah find it agreeable. Edward will go after you some time next week, and you can regulate his stay. He must be at St. John's [Fordham University] the first week in September, and I suppose you will want a little time to get his things in order. But you must take your own time.
> Margaret [the cook] is quite well, and does so-so; though like myself a little lonesome.

His warm solicitude for his own then prompted him to chart their homeward journey.

> In coming home come by Troy. The boats are not quite as elegant as the Albany boats; but you will have no shifting of cars or baggage. Take your tickets at Ballston, and checks for baggage to New York. Take the last train from the

Springs, about 7 p.m. The boat waits for it, and arrives in New York in season for the 8 o'clock, or at the latest the 9 o'clock train to Elizabeth. You may be coming so late as not to get so good a stateroom as you might wish, but you must run your chance like other folk.

Patrick has done nothing yet to keep out the water, and I presume will not. Even my refusal to pay rent does not stir him up. The garden prospers. I have had two roses from my bush; and Sarah's pinks blossomed finely. . . .

I hope mother is getting better. I am sure you will find her a dear old lady, and Thorina a dear good sister. My love to both of them, and to my own dear daughter. Take all the comfort you can, and get some flesh on your bones, and let me see you hale and hearty when you get home. . . . Write to me, and believe me your

Savage but affectionate husband,
Orestes A. Brownson[19]

While there can be no doubt at all that his valiant wife Sally was his redoubtable mainstay in the great battles he was fighting (behind every great man stands a good woman), encouragement kept coming to him continually from other sources. John W. Condon, editor of the *Commercial Bulletin,* New Orleans, wrote to him in February of 1860:

I think I could make a good fight against your assailants had I the leisure to prepare myself. And it grieves me that I have not. Now I despise to see a noble spirit run to death by the sleuth-hounds of the press, whether in politics, literature, or any other fields of intellectual activity.[20]

Before the year 1860 was out, his true friend, Fr. Charles Gresselin, S.J., also wrote him, dating his letter December 10:

In this house all sympathize with you, and the deeper in proportion as you are treated with less charity and justice. In spite of the few words you have written or admitted in your *Review,* and which, between us, are objectionable, you remain in this country most unquestionably the brilliant and efficacious champion and promoter of Catholicity. So far nothing, in the least degree, is sufficient or calculated to make any just mind forget what you have done for the sake of J.C. [Jesus Christ]. It would be a great consolation for us all to receive some information about your own disposition, if you are not discouraged, if you will turn all the clamorous contradictions to the good of your soul, if you will put them, as an humble and earnest follower of J.C. at the foot of the cross. Perhaps in your next issue a little note, such a note as you can shape so well, would do much to bate down all this irritation; perhaps it is better simply to leave all cares about self in the hands of the One who sees the inmost of your heart, the purity of your motives, and your zeal for his glory. Nothing, you well know, is perfect here below; let us forbear a little more easily what we cannot set right. In fact, when you complain of something, there is something to complain of; and this I own openly; but the inconvenience is you strike too hard. Your aim is to quicken people into life; but at times you quicken them into fever. But, I repeat, these excesses, if so they are to be termed, are naught when compared with the substantial and unequalled merit of your *Review.*[21]

From England also at this time came good testimony for Brownson in support of his orthodoxy. In October 1860, Brownson wrote a review of William G. Ward's two volumes on *Nature and Grace.* Ward was his old opponent in the *Dublin Review* on doctrinal developments. Brownson's name had come into the treatise repeatedly. To Brownson it did not seem that Ward understood his philosophy correctly, and he was at pains to explain it to him. The article was really a long disquisition in which he dealt with the problems of certitude, skepticism, subjectivism, and what he considered the capital blunder of modern philosophers, namely, "placing the question of method before that of principles, as if principles were found or obtained, instead of being *given*."[22] Ward's volumes had been in turn the occasion for Fr. Robert Guy, O.S.B., president of St. Gregory's College, Downside, near Bath, England, of writing to Brownson on August 9, 1860, for counsel regarding a book on philosophy which he wished to compose. He sent Brownson an elaborate outline of the book he had in mind, and wound up assuring him:

> In conclusion let me assure you of the gratification your note at the end of your *Review* for April afforded some at least of your numerous English admirers and friends. Yes, sir, you have many such in England. One bishop told me that the whole hierarchy regard you as a sound and staunch supporter of the doctrines of Holy Church; another, one of the most learned men I have ever met, Dr. Hendren, . . . has long been thinking of writing to urge you to continue your labors in the cause of truth.[23]

But passions in his own native land had already been stirred to such a high pitch, especially over his articles on the Roman question, that the exciting drama in which Brownson found himself involved was now moving rapidly to a climax. The stage was completely set for the play-off. Certain *personnae dramatis* were about to make their clandestine move to bring down their marked man — Orestes A. Brownson. We may not yet know all the details of the affair, and probably never will, but due to recent research, we now know considerably more about it than was known before.

# 39

## AN UNSUCCESSFUL INDICTMENT
## IN THE ROMAN COURT

*Brownson explains why ecclesiastical governments (political) are unpopular • He asserts that no government is a good government that fails to meet the wants and aspirations of the people who live under it, and that a change in the form of government, which is allowable in itself, should not be resisted when generally desired • His article on "Separation of Church and State" adds to the increasing furor • He decides to end his discussion of the Roman question • He counsels that it is useless to defend the* ancien regime *against the incoming republican order • Complaints are lodged at Rome against Brownson's articles on the temporal principality of the pope • His letter of explanations to Cardinal Barnabò, Prefect of the Propaganda Fide, Rome, is entirely satisfactory • Complaints continue to bombard Rome regarding Brownson, and Cardinal Barnabò writes Dr. Cummings another letter of inquiry • Brownson submits a formal statement on his tenets regarding the Roman question which proves gratifying to the Roman authorities • Archbishop Hughes' long letter to Rome on Brownson • Brownson replies to the aspersions of the* Herald and Visitor *of Philadelphia.*

As already hinted, the charges lodged at Rome against Brownson stemmed mainly from his articles on the temporal principality of the Holy Father. Added thereto were also the complaints about some questions he had hastily thrown out on the nature of eternal punishment in his article on "Catholic Polemics" — which will be discussed at length in the chapter on Brownson's liberalism.[1] To have one's orthodoxy impugned is never on the face of it anything in one's favor, but neither is it in itself any stigma. For there are false as well as well-founded charges in such matters. Without explaining the affair, reference was made in a previous chapter to the trouble Newman had brought upon himself through his article in the *Rambler* "On Consulting the Faithful in Matters of Doctrine" after he had briefly assumed editorship of that periodical in 1859. In his article, speaking of the prevalence of the Arian heresy, Newman had asserted that the faithful of the time and their pastors had kept the true faith while bishops had proved faithless — during a period of sixty years. He used the phrase "there was a temporary suspension of the functions of the *ecclesia docens*," that is, after the Council of Nicaea. This expression was censured by theologians in England, and was, by Dr. Brown, bishop of Newport, formally delated to Rome as heretical. Although Newman promptly wrote Cardinal Wiseman, then at Rome, a letter offering to explain his meaning to the Roman authorities, it was mislaid, or at least never reached them. In consequence his name was in disfavor in Rome for seven long years.[2] Brownson was much more fortunate. When charges were lodged against him at Rome his case was handled briskly and his name at once cleared.

The article of the greatest immediate interest in Brownson's *Review* for January 1861 was by far his lengthy article on "Separation of Church and State." The article dealt elaborately in the history of the subject, and treated again somewhat incidentally the Roman question. Explaining why ecclesiastical governments easily become unpopular, he observed:

> ... that the clergy, as a body, have a strong tendency to introduce into civil society the fixedness and unalterability of the Church, is no doubt a fact; and in this fact we may find the reason why sacerdotal governments are generally regarded with disfavor by both statesmen and the people. Dealing in their own order with fixed and unalterable principles, with the absolute and inflexible, often softened in the administration by kindness and charity, they are apt, from their special education and habits of mind, to look upon change as evil, and to seek to prevent it in the civil administration, and to compress all civil and political action and thought within certain fixed and unalterable rules, which permit the people no free spontaneous motion.[3]

He protested vigorously against those — he called them *oscurantisti* — who were trying to identify the Catholic Church with the old order of society with which modern peoples by and large have little or no sympathy, and which he himself considered as already moribund. He advocated the American system of government, and laid down the principle that no government is a good government, does or can answer the end of its institution, if it generally and permanently fails to meet the sentiments and convictions, the wants and aspirations of the people who live under it; that when a people are generally and permanently bent upon a change within limits where change is allowable, the change should not be resisted. For three centuries Italy had been little more than a political football between Spain and France, and France and Austria, keeping it nothing more than "a geographical expression" to serve their own base purposes. The Italian people were now utterly dissatisfied with being kept a people of petty kingdoms, and wished to become united under one strong independent government, ranking as a first-class power among the great nations of the earth. Inasmuch as the Roman question itself lay in the temporal order, Brownson pointed out, changes were allowable when the genuine interests of religion and society required them. Such changes therefore may be introduced, though never through violence, except in case of abuse, which was not to be pretended in the case. He summed up the matter, saying:

> We assert the principle, it is not for us to apply it. All we wish to establish here is, though mixed up with the practical administration of ecclesiastical affairs, the Pope's temporal government, in its origin and character, is neither a spiritual nor a *quasi*-spiritual government, and therefore with the consent of the Pope may be suppressed.... All we say is, that we hold him free to consent to a total severing of all political bonds between Church and State, and we see no other way, with the tendencies of the modern world such as they evidently are, of arriving at a passable solution of the terrible problems pressing every day more and more for a solution.[4]

Although complaints were to be lodged at the Sacred Congregation of the Propaganda Fide, Rome, against Brownson because of this article, his friend, Fr. Charles Gresselin, S.J., had sufficient acumen to appreciate its high merits, and wrote him on January 3, 1861:

> I read with good care your article on Separation of Church and State. I deem it one of the best papers that ever issued from your pen. The *Status*

*questionis* is put forth so clearly that no mistake is possible. The reasoning is so closely and so strongly chained that no link could be broken, and the tone is grave and majestic. The opinion can yet be differed from, but not a word in it can give offense. Our poor mind is so constructed that not unfrequently words prove more offensive than the very opinions clothed with them, but this time such is not the case, in the least degree. Now, for my part, viewing and weighing all the *data* of the problem, all the elements of the question, I admit fully your solution. I have found not a jot exceptionable: and I have admired the stream of manly thought, the power of that eloquence, and the depth of the statesman in it. I wish to see what reception you will meet with from the *so-called* Catholic press.[5]

But this does not mean that Brownson's fortunes were about to mend. Far from it. Many members of the press, like a pack of wolves, were out upon him, bellowing far and wide. And they were holding him responsible for everything that appeared in his *Review*, whether he wrote it or not. Their ire had been so aroused that they were calling for their "pound of flesh," and the nearer the heart the better. On January 25, Fr. Jeremiah Cummings wrote him:

Dear Doctor:
   . . . You have no doubt read the eight columns of abuse in the "Metropolitan Record." Poor Barry is the scapegoat for this number, and is catching it from all quarters. . . . I hope you will keep up your courage. Were your *Review* to suffer no persecution you could scarcely hope any good to be done by it. Personally you are less likely to suffer from persecution than flattery. Were those who oppose you to caress you it would be for no good.
   I am, Dear Doctor, faithfully yours,

J.W. Cummings[6]

Things were getting hotter and hotter, and Brownson decided on allowing a cooling spell. (This may have been partly his response to the admonition of Bishop Luers.) He therefore served notice at the end of the January edition of his *Review* that further discussion was at an end on the Roman or Italian question in his columns, that is, at least until new and unforeseen events should reopen it. He also announced that his son Henry, who had been studying in France for some time, had returned and would assist him with the *Review*.[7]

In his article on the "Pope and the Emperor" in the April issue of his *Review* he stressed the fact that the papacy in no sense depends on the pope's principality, and would continue to exist just the same in its nature were the temporal sovereignty lost. To deprive the Holy Father of his temporal dominion would indeed be a great and grievous wrong, but it would not deprive him of one particle of his legitimate authority as the Vicar of Christ, or the Vicegerent of God on earth. While asserting that such a deprivation of temporal sovereignty could not affect the pope's authority as Vicar of Christ on earth, he admitted nonetheless that such a loss could indeed affect the Sovereign Pontiff's freedom and independence in the exercise of his authority. He also expressed the fear that papal freedom and independence were actually being then threatened as they had never before been menaced since the conversion of the Roman Empire.[8]

In his article entitled "Sardinia and Rome," which was really a review of a letter his friend Count Montalembert had written Count Cavour, he treated the Roman question *ex professo*. He made his basic stance clear when he laid it down that if the success of the Napoleon-Cavour campaign would deprive the Sovereign Pontiff in any way of his spiritual freedom and independence, he would consider it "the greatest possible calamity not only to Italy, but to the whole Christian world."[9] But with that said, he expressed the belief that it was useless to resist the new order that was setting in, the republican movement that was sweeping over Europe and crushing out the *ancien regime.* Yet he emphasized again that it would be the "grossest injustice" were the Sovereign Pontiff deprived of his temporal sovereignty against his will, for "the Pope is the oldest sovereign in Europe, and no sovereign holds his states by a better title, or one so good, so sacred, or so inviolable in its nature."[10] He reminded his readers that there was no incompatibility between the Catholic Church and the new republican order that was emerging ever more victorious in Europe, and thought it a mistake for the friends of the *ancien regime* to be prolonging the struggle against the incoming new order of civilization that was leaving behind forever the outmoded system of the Middle Ages. In this he differed from his friend Count Montalembert who still cherished the hope that the Napoleon-Cavour policy could be defeated, and the Sovereign Pontiff be reestablished in the full possession of his temporal rights. He himself felt that things had gone too far to hope for a restoration of what had been. Yet he would be happy to find that he had taken as *un fait accompli* what not only was not effected, but not likely to be effected.[11]

Whatever might be considered objectionable in these last two articles, the head and front of his offending, that is, in the eyes of his adversaries, was contained mainly in the first articles he had written on the pope's temporal principality. Henry Brownson says that all his father's articles on the subject were denounced to the Roman authorities.[12] But it was the October article on the "Rights of the Temporal" in particular which brought things to a climax and set off the furor.

When the charges against Brownson reached Cardinal Barnabò, Prefect of the Propaganda Fide, Rome, shrewd prelate that he was, knowing full well that not all charges are by any means true, he sought some information on the side concerning the matter. He could think of no one in the United States better fitted to be consulted in the case than Dr. Jeremiah W. Cummings, whose learning and judgment he held in high esteem — the very same who was Brownson's close friend and who was the theologian who had acted as theological censor of his article on the "Rights of the Temporal."[13] As soon as the cardinal's letter of inquiry reached Cummings he immediately notified Brownson of the charges lodged against him at the Propaganda. Brownson in turn wrote back to Cummings on January 11, 1861, a letter of explanations which Cummings translated into French and sent to the cardinal. Apparently the complaints or inquiries of the cardinal's letter had reference to the October 1860 issue of Brownson's *Review*, with the article on the "Rights of the Temporal." Responding to it, Brownson stated:

> Rev. and Dear Doctor:
> As I do not know what particular assertions of mine touching the temporal mission of the Supreme Pontiff His Eminence refers to, I am unable to explain or retract them. I can only say that I have never knowingly made any assertion "deeply offensive to the sincere Catholic heart," or "in open opposition to the sentiments of the Episcopate or the vows of Catholics throughout the world." No bishop of this country with a single exception has complained to me of anything I said in that number of my *Review* of the temporal dominion of the Holy Father and he only complained of single phrases as irreverent. I hold the right of the Holy Father to his temporal dominion to be sacred and inviolable, and as

CARDINAL ALESSANDRO BARNABÒ

such I have always defended it in my *Review*. I have never knowingly justified any invasion of that right in any sense or from any quarter. What I said in my *Review* for October on the subject was said in reference to what seemed to me likely in the near future to be *un fait accompli,* and suggesting what in my judgment would be the best manner in dealing with it, as will be evident from the article on Separation of Church and State in the subsequent number for January, 1861.

Unwilling to continue a discussion which I found unacceptable to many, I gave notice in my *Review* for January, p. 136, that it would be discontinued. I submitted both articles before publication to the best theological revision, and did my best to be correct. If I have erred, I deeply regret it, and am ready to make any explanation, modification, or retraction, required by the Holy See.

If my *Review* has "gone astray," I am anxious that it should at the earliest moment return to the true path, and I can assure His Eminence that I have no pride of opinion to gratify, and that the Holy See will always find me a docile and obedient subject.

Very truly your obedient servant,
O.A. Brownson, LL.D.
Editor of Brownson's Quarterly Review
Elizabeth, N.J.

Rev. J.W. Cummings, D.D.[14]

Cardinal Barnabò was to receive also at this time some interesting information on the man Brownson from Dr. William McClosky, then rector of the North American College in Rome, and later to become bishop of Louisville, Kentucky. Writing to his brother Fr. George McCloskey of New York City, Dr. McCloskey commented:

> As regards Brownson, I do not think his articles [in the October issue] were prudent. I think he was not in humor when he wrote them, but I defended him and told the Cardinal that he was a good man and an able one but not likely to surrender when his foes were battering at the door. I think there was a strong effort made to condemn him, and but for the Cardinal's good sense and sympathy for such an old hero as Brownson, I believe the object of the others, whatever it was, would have been effected. He asked me to write to B[rownson] and advise him in a friendly way, but not being very well acquainted with the old gentleman, and as the next number would have been published before he would get my letter. I did not write. What a pity people can't bear without anger the views of an old man who happens to think differently from them![15]

When Henry Brownson was writing the biography of his father at the turn of the century, he wrote this same Dr. William G. McCloskey, then bishop of Louisville, to inquire what he remembered of his father's writings "having been complained of to the Roman authorities" when he was rector of the North American College, Rome. In reply he received the following letter:

Louisville, 12 January, 1900

H. F. Brownson, Esq.

Dear Sir:

> Of your father's writings "having been complained of to the Roman authorities" during my residence in Rome, I have absolutely no recollection. It was my custom when I had business with Cardinal Barnabò, at that time Prefect of the Propaganda, to call on him in the evening, knowing that he rarely went out after dinner, and that he was more at leisure in the evening than during the busy hours of the day. During one of these visits — perhaps in '63 — His Eminence alluded incidentally to rude criticism that had been levelled

at certain principles broached by your father, presumably in his *Review*. What precisely the subject was to which the Cardinal referred, I have not now, well nigh forty years afterwards, any very clear and definite recollection; especially as it was rather of the *rough manner* in which these critics had dealt with what they regarded as Brownson's shortcomings, than of the *merits of the case* itself that His Eminence spoke; but, unless my memory plays me false, it was in some way linked with the matter of eternal punishment. But be that as it may, I do distinctly remember how strongly the straightforward Cardinal deprecated the fierceness of the attack which had been made on a man whose lofty spirit and fearless character was not unlike his own. Plainly it annoyed him.

What serves to fix the visit in my memory, was the dramatic manner in which His Eminence showed how an old dreadnaught like Dr. Brownson would act, if threatened with the fire of a whole fleet of popular pamphleteers. But that the Cardinal was a very small man, and your father a man of Daniel Webster's build, but taller by some inches, I would have fancied that the Doctor stood before me. Rising from his chair and dropping his scarlet biretta on the floor, His Eminence put himself in an attitude of defense, as if to say: Come one; come all! intimating, for that I remember well, that if his critics had dealt gently with him, and pointed out his error, if error there was, no man was more ready humbly to acknowledge it, than that great champion of the faith, who for us was what Newman was for England.

Each in his own day put Catholicity fifty years ahead in their respective countries; and it is now, when people see there are none to take the place of those two intellectual giants, that they are beginning to appreciate both the one and the other.

I am yours faithfully,
W. G. McCloskey[16]

But even after the initial denunciations of Brownson to Rome had been handled, the storm occasioned by his recent articles had by no means blown itself out in certain quarters. His enemies were not going to give up so easily. After a momentary lull in the affair, Brownson must have been a trifle startled on receiving a letter again from Dr. Cummings, dated July 19, 1861, concerning further charges. He wrote:

Dear Doctor:

There are parties at work to injure you with the authorities at Rome, the complaint being now against the re-opening of the papal question in your last no. but one. I wish you would come to see me this week and I will tell you some particulars. I know that the authorities of the Propaganda are favorably disposed towards your person. They are somewhat puzzled as to your position in the *Review* on the question of the Temporal Power. I may add that in seeking an interview with you I do so with their knowledge and consent. I am sure that I need not add that it is also my earnest desire to serve you and your *Review*.

I am, Dear Doctor, very truly yours,

J. W. Cummings[17]

The result of the subsequent conference between the two was Brownson's letter to Dr. Cummings, dated July 24, 1861, accompanied by a formal statement which he wished Cummings to forward to Cardinal Barnabò. It seems Brownson had expected Cummings to translate the statement, and improve it if necessary, but Cummings decided on sending the statement just as Brownson had drawn it up. After being received at Rome, it was later filed in the Archives of the Propaganda Fide. It ran as follows (the H.E. stands for His Eminence):

I was honored and consoled by the generous and friendly terms in which H.E. speaks of me in his letter of 25 ult. and I hope he will never have any occasion to regret his confidence.

The expression in regard to the temporal power of the Supreme Pontiff, of which H.E. says complaints have been made, must, I think, be found in the article on *Separation of Church and State* in the *Review* of last January and published prior to the date of my letter the reception of which H.E. acknowledges, for since then I have written nothing touching the subject that would have been known in Rome on the 25th of last June. In the number for July there is indeed an article on *Sardinia and Rome* in which I refer to the subject, not to discuss it, but to define the position which I wish to be regarded as occupying in relation to it. I take the liberty of sending to H.E. the number which contains that article, which is submitted to the judgment of the Holy See.

In the same number of the *Review* will be found an article on *Catholic Polemics,* in which, when treating the subject of the punishment of the wicked, I regret to find, owing to the inability to use my eyes in revising the proofs, some expressions escaped me which are inexact and susceptible of a meaning I did not intend. They will be corrected in my *Review* for October next.

I wish to assure H.E. that in nothing I have written on the temporal Principality of the Supreme Pontiff have I had any intention of opposing that Principality or of siding with its enemies. My design has been simply to guard against the erroneous and injurious inference which might be drawn from the statements of many Catholic journals, that the retention of the Principality is *essential* to the maintenance of the Church and to show that its loss, which I regard as possible, and even probable, would still leave the spiritual power of the Pope untouched and by no means involve the downfall of the Catholic Church.

My language has been on this subject the less guarded because having been so long and so well known for my devotion to the Holy See and for my uncompromising defense of the rights and prerogatives of the Chair of Peter, having so earnestly and so repeatedly battled against Gallicanism and for what is here called Ultramontanism, I thought I was free from all danger of being misapprehended or misconstrued, and H.E. will permit me to say that I do not think I should have been seriously complained of had it not been for political and national susceptibilities which my course as a Reviewer had offended and armed against me.

Though the staunch advocate of all legitimate authority however constituted, I am an American citizen and, for my own country, a Republican accustomed from my youth up to free thought and free speech; but the Prelates of the Church in the United States have only to signify to me under their own name the questions which they wish me not to discuss, or to give me frankly the directions they wish me to follow, to find me avoiding everything that could be offensive or disagreeable to them or inconsistent with their views of Catholic interests. I am and will be docile to authority, but I do not and cannot recognize the voice of authority in anonymous newspaper articles.

I wish to say in conclusion that all the articles in my *Review* written by myself which have been complained of, excepting the last number, have been submitted to Episcopal or theological revision and approval before being printed; and the very articles touching the temporal power of the Supreme Pontiff were revised and approved by a theologian designated by Episcopal authority. This indeed excused not my errors and relieved me from no personal responsibility, but is perhaps an evidence of my Catholic aims and docility. My wish is in all things to conform strictly to the teachings and wishes of the Church, and I am and always will be ready and even anxious to correct and avoid any and every error which the Holy See may point out to me. Err I may, but a heretic I am not and never will be. I wish to save my soul, and I believe that, for me at least, there is no salvation out of the Catholic Church.[18]

But before this statement could reach Rome, new charges against Brownson had been lodged there, and action had been taken by Cardinal Barnabò with a letter to Archbishop Hughes. On October 9, Cummings wrote Brownson that his letter of explanations had been "read with pleasure at the Propaganda," and that had it been received sooner the Prefect of the Propganda would not have sent his letter to Archbishop Hughes, which he now wishes considered as not having been sent. Cummings wound up, saying: "I am, in fine, exhorted to comfort the Reviewer especially under various afflictions which God has permitted to befall him at this time."[19]

In the meantime, however, Archbishop Hughes had received Cardinal Barnabò's letter of complaint or inquiry on August 31, and notified Brownson of it on October 3. "The objections are," he told Brownson, "that you oppose, or profess to refute, certain opinions that are sacred in the Catholic Church — that you calumniate the Church by maintaining, either directly or indirectly, that she crushes intellect down to the level of the belief of simple Catholics — that your disquisition on hell is unsound in itself and dangerous to your readers."[20] Hughes added that he had written to Rome that he had no doubts of his personal orthodoxy and that he considered it inexpedient for the Sacred Congregation or himself to make any statement. The following is the letter, dated September 30, 1861, and translated into French, which Hughes had sent to Cardinal Barnabò on Brownson's case:

> The report that was given you concerning the July issue of "Brownson Review," is in every respect in conformity with the truth.
>
> In the October issue, which has just come out, Mr. Brownson makes a kind of a retraction, however much he might try to justify what he has already said. His words were given presumably a sense that he never had in mind. At least that is what he claims. Nevertheless, the article of which I am speaking is almost as unfortunate as the first one. His false speculations were assailed by the "Catholic Mirror" of Baltimore and by the "Pittsburgh Catholic." Brownson refutes or at least he himself thinks he refutes their objections. I don't think it would be very useful to open up a dispute with Mr. Brownson. He likes to argue. I myself have been forced to combat in writing his ideas, which he had proposed on several important questions, and particularly on the rights of the temporal power of the Supreme Pontiff. The articles which I have published have appeared in the Catholic newspaper of the city, the "Metropolitan Record." Brownson has made no attempt to reply to these articles. I have not taken up for discussion out of his article the point of the eternity of the pains of hell or the so-called despotism of the Church that rests so heavily on free-thinkers like himself, and which, if they were allowed to speak freely in independent and daring publications, might according to what he believes present the Catholic Church to Protestants of this country from a point of view that would arouse their admiration and win them over to the faith.
>
> I have not thought it necessary either to warn the clergy and the faithful of this diocese to be on their guard against the erroneous articles that have appeared in the July issue of his *Review.*
>
> First — because the *Review* is on the decline, for lack of financial resources.
>
> Second — because there are in my diocese very few Catholics who subscribe to it or even read it. In fact I myself am in this class and have been so for the past two years.
>
> Third — Doctor Brownson has no more influence, even among Catholics who read his *Review,* than if he were still a Protestant; and never does he have less influence than when he is writing on what touches on matters of dogma or the discipline of the Church.
>
> Considering these circumstances, I did not think it advisable to call the at-

tention of the public to his bad writings. To do so would only give him the opportunity to cause more trouble, and to call the attention of Catholics to what he might say to justify himself. And that is precisely what Brownson would like. For that would serve to give his "Review" which is dying, a new lease on life, and it would also give him some importance in the eyes of the public, which, in the actual state of affairs, shows little enthusiasm either for Brownson or his writings. I have already pointed out to your Eminence that, apart from the personal spiritual good of Dr. Brownson, the Catholic Church has never drawn much profit from his conversion. From the first minute of his submission to the church, the Boston clergy has admitted him to too great familiarity. He was almost always at the Bishop's table, where he laid down the law and taught philosophy as if he were an oracle.

When he came to live in New York, he wanted to submit to me manuscripts of all articles that were going to appear in his "Review," so that I might change, correct, approve or disapprove them as I saw fit. I excused myself for several very good and excellent reasons. I treated him with a lot of consideration, not allowing him either too much intimacy or too much familiarity, but leaving him a little bit off to one side in his aloofness. However he made the acquaintance of several of my priests, particularly of a class of young priests who had the advantage of studying theology in Europe and who had literary and philosophical pretensions. Of this number, four had studied in Europe and two or three others, although priests, were converts. They kept up the practice of meeting just to make conversation — and everything that pertained to the Church all the way from the general administration of affairs by the Supreme Pontiff down to the way of acting of one of our insignificant sacristans, all this was then discussed, criticized, approved or disapproved according to the wise and discreet views of Dr. Brownson and his associates. They were impatient for the moment when they could illuminate the Church of this country with a new light and communicate to it the spirit of the century in which we live. I was the first and principal obstacle to the execution of their plans. They knew very well that if they did or said anything that was contrary to religion or that displeased the archbishop of New York, they would draw down upon themselves the contempt of the faithful. They only attacked me twice and that by means of anonymous letters in the newspapers. I answered one of these letters in such a way that they never forgot it. But if they could not attack me successfully in this town where we were both so well known, they could at least blacken my good name by means of anonymous letters sent to my fellow-bishops through the world and even to Rome.

All this no longer exists. It is a faithful imitation of the Lammenais' school in Paris. But while I knew these things were going on, I never used my episcopal authority against these disloyal priests. Intestinal strife has finished by scattering the group. Two members, both converts, have since apostatized and each has gone his way. Among the priests of this diocese, there is not a one who admits Dr. Brownson to what is called familiarity, except Dr. Cummings. I cannot say for sure whether he has been consulted about the articles that cause us all so much horror. In any case your Eminence will allow me to point out that the faithful of this diocese and of the whole country are, as far as I can judge, too well versed in the principles of Christian and Catholic teachings to let themselves be impressed by anything that Dr. Brownson might write and I would be so bold as to add that even the slightest importance that the Sacred Congregation or myself might seem to attach to him at this moment, would be harmful and would not do any good at all to the interests of the Church.[21]

The archbishop's statement that "apart from the personal spiritual good of Dr. Brownson, the Catholic Church has never drawn much profit from his conversion," would seem to render the objective value of some of his other judgments somewhat suspect. We have just seen the high estimate

Bishop W. McCloskey set upon the services of Brownson to the Catholic cause. Writing in 1927, the late Fr. Virgil Michel, O.S.B., said of Brownson: "Certainly his services to Catholicity were well-nigh invaluable."[22] Many other such quotes might be made. But in the firm assurances that Hughes had given the Holy See of Brownson's personal orthodoxy he had done him good service. This was generous at a time when many Catholic journals were disposed to haggle over his orthodoxy. Particularly was this true of the *Herald and Visitor* of Philadelphia. It put forth the claim that even after Rome had censured Brownson's opinions as *erroneous* he had refused to modify or retract them publicly. This drew from Brownson a letter of denial in which he defined clearly for the public his stance on the Roman question. He wrote from Elizabeth, New York, on April 15, 1862:

To the Philadelphia Herald and Visitor
Mr. Editor:
    You intimate in a brief notice of my *Review,* in your columns of the 12th inst. that Rome has indicated to me some erroneous opinions advanced in my *Review,* and yet, though knowing she regards them as erroneous, I have not publicly modified or retracted them. Permit me to say, in this you labor under a mistake. Rome has indicated to me no opinion published in my *Review* which is *erroneous* and which she requires me to retract or modify. When she indicates any such opinion to me, it will be modified or retracted publicly according to her requisition.
    Your inference is not necessary. Rome could be displeased with some remarks I made on the temporal power of the Sovereign Pontiff, and yet not require me to retract them. In those remarks there was nothing against Catholic faith or morals; and the most that could be said against them is, that they recommend a policy with regard to the Pope's temporal principality, which Rome does not approve, or judges it inexpedient to adopt. For such an offense as this, if it be an offense, the promise of silence on my part, is all that can be reasonably demanded. This promise I had publicly given in my *Review* without its being exacted and before I knew any complaint had been lodged against me at Rome. The Propaganda has asked nothing more of me; and with the general promise to make any retractions or modifications of any views I may have published or may hereafter publish, they expressed themselves satisfied.
    Besides, I have never opposed the temporal sovereignty of the Pope in the Ecclesiastical States nor urged its surrender, save on the hypothesis that it is already virtually gone and cannot be effectively sustained. Its loss when I wrote I looked upon as an accomplished fact, or likely to be so, in a near future. Assuming this, I suggested, argued, if you will, that the voluntary surrender by the Holy Father of his temporal principality, on the best terms then practicable would contribute more to the political and social interests of the Peninsula, and to the interests of Catholicity, both in Italy and elsewhere, than a prolonged and unavailing struggle to maintain it against the almost universal popular sentiment. I may or may not have been wrong in this opinion but you will not pretend that it is not an opinion which a good Catholic may hold.
    You will bear in mind that I never questioned the right of the Holy Father to his temporal principality and never recognized the right of anybody, king or kaiser, prince or people, to dispossess him. I proposed nothing that was to be done without the judgment and consent of the Holy Father himself. He, if he believes it for the interests of religion and society to give up his temporal principality, has the indisputable right to do so. But he is the judge in the case, and in his judgment I and all other Catholics must acquiesce, whatever may be our private opinions. I never went any farther, and so far I had a right to go; for the temporal principality is not a Catholic dogma or an essential element in the Divine Constitution of the Church. The Church does not stand or fall with that principality. The Holy Father judges, it appears, that it is in the existing cir-

cumstances necessary to the interests of religion and society to retain it. My private opinion may remain unchanged; but I must, in my action, yield to his judgment not as infallible, but as that of the supreme court in the case.

You are mistaken in saying that the doctrine with regard to the temporal power of the Pope over sovereigns I formerly defended is erroneous and disapproved at Rome. I happen never to have asserted any temporal authority for the Pope, save over the temporalities of the Church, out of the Roman States. I simply asserted the supremacy of the spiritual and moral order and the *spiritual* supremacy of the Pope as the supreme representative of that order. You will hardly deny this, or pretend that it is disapproved at Rome. It is easy to attribute to a man views he does not hold and get up a clamor against him. But a Catholic editor should seek to be just and truthful.

In conclusion permit me to say that you and many others are quite mistaken in your notions, inferences, and calculations about me, and show as little discernment as charity in your criticism on my lucubrations. Neither you nor your *confrères* will ever succeed in driving me into heresy or schism. You may not always understand me, but have patience and be slow to commit yourself against me, or to create in the minds of an indiscriminating and unreasoning public a distrust of my good faith or my orthodoxy. Never was I more worthy of the confidence and support of Catholics than I am now; never was my Catholic faith firmer, or my filial devotion to the Church warmer or more unreserved. Wait till you understand better what I am aiming at and see more clearly and distinctly the real character of my proceedings. I know very well what I am about and shall not swerve from the line of Catholic duty marked out for me, whatever the misapprehension, misrepresentation or unjust criticism of which I may be the subject.

Very truly your obedient servant,
O.A. Brownson[23]

But whatever the storms that were now swirling about him in his homeland, it must have been a great consolation to the beleaguered editor to know that his name remained untarnished in the Eternal City. In referring to the first judgment of Cardinal Barnabò on his case, he was happy to remark: "I am honored and consoled by the generous and friendly terms in which H[is] E[minence] speaks of me in his letter. . . ." And Dr. Cummings had also written him: "I am, in fine, exhorted [by the Sacred Congregation of the Propaganda] to comfort the Reviewer especially under the various afflictions which God has permitted to befall him at this time." In the midst of so much misunderstanding and acrimony those words must have been balm to his spirit. He no doubt understood quite well that hasty editors, if not some churchmen, might be easily led to misunderstand and misjudge him, but he knew that at Rome, far away from angry passions and local interests, he could expect better things, and he was not disappointed. The sly attempt to get him condemned in the capital of Christendom went awry. Moreover, in handling his case, Cardinal Barnabò had become one of his greatest admirers. It was all enough to brace him again for what he considered the good fight. But we have still to explain more fully what it was that had brought him under suspicion with some at the time and had rendered his orthodoxy somewhat suspect.

# 40

## BROWNSON'S ASSOCIATION WITH LIBERALS AND HIS OWN BRAND OF LIBERALISM

*The change that had come over Brownson's* Review • *The nature of religious liberalism • A coterie of Catholic liberals in New York City • To what degree Brownson never showed any symptoms of being a liberal • His liberalism more apparent than real • His increasing interest in convert work induces him to adopt a more liberal policy • Scholastic terminology no adequate medium of communication • He is influenced by Catholic liberals in England and France, especially Count Montalembert and Abbé Gioberti • He writes an elaborate article to demonstrate that the Catholic Church is not "a despotism" • His statement that he will no longer submit his articles to supervision is grossly misunderstood • The bishop of Philadelphia, James Frederick Wood, declares his* Review *no longer a Catholic* Review • *Brownson's letter of remonstrance • His formal statement on the adamantine nature of his Catholic faith • He explains some questions he had raised regarding the future punishment of the unrepentant • He decides to drop theology from his* Review • *He does not consider himself among those proscribed by the encyclical* Quanta Cura, *though he does beat his breast over the liberal policy he had adopted for a time.*

Archbishop Hughes was of course right in indicating in his letter to Rome that some sort of a change had come over Brownson's *Review,* puzzling to himself as well to a number of others. Even Brownson's good friend, Fr. Charles Gresselin, S.J., whom he rated so highly, wrote him a long letter of specified complaints in which he said: "Now your *Review* is no longer the same as before. I do not know why. I cannot account for the change. But change there is, and a striking one. Assuredly, you still have admirable passages. But you have taken the habit of mixing up with them passages of quite a different nature, which grate terribly on the ears of your friends." Nevertheless Gresselin wound up his letter, saying: "Nothing can ever make me forget the good you have done the Catholic cause, and till the end I will remain your most affectionate and devoted friend."[1]

What was the change, really? It concerns what has been called the "liberal period" in Brownson's Catholic career. Brownson himself afterwards dated it from 1860-1864. However, as previously noted, his article on "Liberalism and Socialism" in the April 1855 edition of his *Review,* and his critical notice of the *Rambler* magazine, July 1856, furnish a definite syndrome pointing to a creeping liberalism of some sort in his mentality from the middle of the 1850s. But by 1860 it had crystallized more definitely, whatever his unique type of liberalism. As there is a sound liberalism as well as a spurious, and various types of liberalism in such departments as economics, politics and government as well as religion, the term liberalism is not easy to define. Nor is its origin to be traced to a single source. We are here concerned mainly, however, though not exclusively, with the term in its ecclesiastical sense, liberalism in matters of religion and things closely related thereto. And in this sense liberalism may be spoken of as a tendency to so water down or interpret the doctrines of the Church as to make them quite acceptable to the spirit of the world or the age. Its whole tendency, therefore, is to play down the supremacy of religion, or to subordinate the interests of religion to the things or interests of this world. As Brownson himself afterwards put it: "While Catholicity makes God and heaven, the interests of eternity, supreme, liberalism makes the world and its interests supreme, not knowing or believing that the goods even of this world can be secured only by turning one's back on them, and living for God and heaven according to the divine order."[2] And because such is the general *animus* of liberalism, it carries with it almost inevitably the lack of a becoming respect for ecclesiastical authority, as was so plainly exemplified by the directors of the *Rambler,* as well as a disregard in many instances of the disciplinary and doctrinal decrees of the Roman Congregations and the teachings of time-honored theologians as was so glaringly evinced in the Congress of Munich, held in September of 1863, only a year before the publication of the *Syllabus of Errors* condemning the false liberalism of the day.

Insofar as a spirit of disrespect for authority is generally manifested by the workings of liberalism, it can be said that Orestes Brownson was in no sense chargeable with that particular symptom of liberalism — ever. In fact, if there was one trait that stood out in his life and character as truly remarkable, it was his respect for, and ready obedience to all lawfully constituted authority. Like St. Augustine, his many and wearisome wanderings before he came to the Catholic Church had taught him the harsh necessity of some sure authority in religion to save the individual both from moral aberrations and the "suicidal excesses" to which the human mind unassisted is so prone. Certain it is that, having once laid firmly hold of the great principle that underlies all obedience to authority as enunciated by St. Paul in his letter to the Romans,[3] he held fast to it through thick and thin to the very end. Writing during the stormiest period of his life, 1862, he could say without any fear of contradiction: "Whatever else may be said of us, it cannot be said of us that we have ever yet refused to demean ourselves before authority, in the first and last instance, as a humble and docile Catholic."[4] That statement stands for all time in Brownson's case, and reminds one of that other statement made by Fr. John Henry Newman in a great crisis in his own life: "I have never resisted, and never can, the voice of a superior, speaking in his own province."[5] Both men were all docility and submission when the mind of authority was once known.

But it is true that Brownson was betrayed for a brief period into some apparent symptoms of liberalism as a Catholic apologist. Those who are acquainted with the real character of Orestes Brownson will have little difficulty in accepting the statement he made in 1873, to wit: "A liberal Catholic I am not, never was, save in appearance for a brief moment, and never can be. I have no element of liberal Catholicity in my nature or in my convictions."[6] In 1954 Karl E. Krummel came up with a truly penetrating article in the spring issue of *The American Quarterly Review* on "Catholicism, Americanism, Democracy, and Orestes Brownson," which goes far to support that statement. After pointing out that biographers of Brownson have divided his Catholic career into three parts — (1) his initial ten years or more of solid orthodoxy; (2) the middle liberal period comprising the Civil

War and the years immediately preceding it; and (3) his last twelve years of intransigent Catholicity — he put forth the claim to the contrary that "a study of Brownson's conception of Catholicism, Americanism, and democracy suggests a unifying strain underlying all of his three decades in the Roman [Catholic] Church: a constant devotion to conservatism and Catholicism, each of which is necessary to the survival of the other."[7] This thesis is carefully and amply documented from Brownson's various writings, and validates the conclusion drawn at the end, namely, that: "Conservatism and Catholicism were the twin ideals which animated Brownson's thought throughout his three decades in the Church. What appears like liberalism is in reality an attempt to strengthen Catholicism by rendering the Church less objectionable to Protestant America."[8] This put the whole matter correctly and succinctly.

A letter Brownson wrote his friend Montalembert in April of 1862 supports this thesis of Krummel. In part he said:

> My Dear Count:
> ... My own position is uncertain, & so far as my Catholic friends are concerned I am under a cloud. I could easily dissipate that cloud, but not without abandoning the work to what remains to me of life & strength is devoted. I am attempting to gain what I lost when I became a Catholic, the ears of my own countrymen. I have heretofore had few but Catholic readers, & they mostly Irishmen or Irishized Americans, between whom and Americans proper there is very little in common. They have praised me, but have seldom understood me. I have availed myself of the present [state] of national affairs [the Civil War period] to address the American public at large, & get the honest, intelligent and liberal non-Catholics to read something on Catholicity. To succeed in this it is necessary to recognize the modern spirit, and accept it as far as possible.[9]

Brownson then did adopt a line of thought and policy which had the appearance of a certain species of liberalism. How did it come about? Although there were various liberalistic influences playing on him at home and abroad during the latter years of the 1850s, as we have noted, Brownson's son Henry says that when his father moved from Boston to New York in October 1855, a number of clerical friends there, with Fr. Isaac Hecker at their head, urged on him that the best way to win converts in this country is to present only so much of Catholic doctrine to those outside the Catholic Church as was absolutely necessary for them to enter the Church; that those outside the Church would be repelled rather than attracted by doctrines and practices which were contrary to their own belief and conduct. Inasmuch as Brownson had often been belabored for being too uncompromising in his exposition of Catholic doctrine and things Catholic, "too Catholic or too orthodox for the times," as it was expressed, Brownson eventually, if gradually, gave in to this new policy.[10] It was all in the interest of a convert movement in which he had in recent years become more hopefully interested.

In particular, then, from 1860-1864, Brownson tried to coax his non-Catholic countrymen into the Church by presenting Catholic truth to them in as inoffensive a light as possible, playing down all that was not strictly of divine faith. It was a time when the body of Catholics in the Church was made up largely of immigrants who had brought to this country with their faith many national traditions or customs which they closely associated with their faith but which at the same time gave their religion a foreign aspect. Lest it appear that to become a Catholic meant necessarily to embrace these foreign customs or traditions, Brownson stressed to his non-Catholic countrymen only the essentials in his advocacy of the Catholic faith, and tried to show them how much they already had in common with the teaching of the Catholic Church. Pursuing this policy, he insisted on the distinction between Catholic Tradition and the traditions of Catholics, and emphasized the danger of confusing "what is of religion and what pertains only to the social life, nationality, or secular habits, customs, and usages of Catholics."[11] He found many Catholics "not up to the level of the Church," but "merely men of routine, creatures of traditions and associations inherited from their ancestors, and which they seldom ever dream of distinguishing from their religion."[12] He was endeavoring in his convert-making efforts to strip the Catholic religion of all anomalies and national incrustations.

But perhaps in no article did the new tack Brownson had adopted in apologetics become more apparent than in his article on "Catholic Apologetics." Although briefly referred to in the last chapter, its full significance belongs to this chapter. Brownson began the article by expressing the conviction in rather trenchant language that neither could the non-Catholic mind be successfully met nor the intellectual problems of the day be effectually resolved by merely pursuing the traditional methods so long in vogue among Catholics. Rightly or wrongly, he was firmly convinced that the modern non-Catholic intellect, by and large, simply does not understand the scholastic molds and forms of thought in which the Catholic faith has been permanently cast and with which Catholics themselves have become so familiar. "Hundreds and thousands of men," he wrote, "read Catholic works of theology where the very questions they wanted treated are discussed with great learning and ability, with clearness, depth, and sincerity, without finding in them any thing but meaningless words, dry technicalities, or antiquated formulas. Why is this so? Is it not because our Catholic writers fail to address themselves to the forms of modern thought, to the idiosyncracies, so to speak, of the age? . . . Truth never varies. . . . But its expression may vary, and must in some degree vary, in order to meet the peculiar wants of time and place."[13] Such sentiments are no doubt much more in harmony with our own times than they were with his. In article 62 of *The Pastoral Constitution on the Church in the Modern World,* Vatican Council II encouraged theologians both clerical and lay, "to seek continually for new and more subtle ways of communicating doctrine to men of our times." Pope Paul VI also counseled more recently in his *Credo:* "The Church has always the duty to carry on the effort to study more deeply and to present in a manner ever better adapted to successive generations the unfathomable mysteries of God." Newman, too, like Brownson was looking for a *Novum Organum* in apologetics in his day. He wrote: "Your cut and dried answers out of dogmatic treatises are no weapons with which Catholic reason can hope to vanquish the infidels of the day."[14]

Brownson went on to say, as already noted, that he had found no epoch in the history of the Catholic Church in which there had been "so great a dread of intellect" in Catholic circles, and grieved over the increasing dichotomy between the Church and the world of modern learning. During the last hundred years, he said, "the most successful cultivators of science, history, literature, and art, have not been Catholics, or, if nominally Catholic, with little understanding of the teaching, or devotion to the practice, of the Church." Are Catholics to be supinely satisfied with this abnormal state of affairs? He surmised that their dread of intellect stemmed at least partly from the fact that the world of learning was running away from them, and they were withdrawing farther from those in the vanguard of learning. "The true policy," he insisted, "would not be to yield up thought and intelligence to Satan, but to redouble our efforts to bring them back to the side of the Church, so as to restore to . . . [the Catholic Church] her rightful spiritual and intellectual supremacy."[15] Again Vatican Council II in the same article 62 admonished Catholics to "live in close union with the men of their times . . . to strive to understand perfectly their way of thinking and feeling . . . to blend modern science and its theories, and the understanding of the most recent discoveries, with Christian morality and doctrine."

But how, Brownson anxiously inquired, are we to reach the leading intellect outside the Catholic Church if tied down to old forms and old methods found in superannuated works? The early fathers of the Church did a great work for their age, but the Scholastics differed from them in method and style for they had a work to do peculiar to their own age, and Brownson pleaded for freedom to address himself to the problems peculiar to his own age in a method and style that could be understood by modern man. He made this distinction between faith and theology: faith is divine, invariable, the same in all ages, but theology is a human science, the human form in which divine faith is expressed, and being a mere human creation, it may vary and is susceptible of progress or development.[16] Vatican Council II also repeated Pope John's distinction between the "truths of faith, and the manner in which they are formulated." But Brownson feared that any attempt on his part to reach the non-Catholic intellect by modifying the forms or molds of scholastic theology and philosophy would only bring down upon him the unsparing denunciations of those who really did not understand the intellectual temper and tendencies of the times, and who were "sure to open fire on him in the rear while he is engaged in doing battle with his and their enemies in the front."[17] Newman, who was likewise clamoring for greater freedom to meet head on the objections of the day to the faith, expressed similar fears when he said: "What influence should I have with Protestants and infidels, if a pack of Catholic critics opened at my back fiercely, saying that this remark was illogical, that unheard of, a third realistic, a fourth idealistic, a fifth sceptical, and a sixth temerarious, or shocking to pious ears?"[18] As to new forms of expression, Newman said: "There is no greater mistake surely than to suppose that revealed truth precludes originality in the treatment of it."[19]

But not all readers took kindly to some of Brownson's acutely critical remarks in his article on "Catholic Polemics." In particular, nothing was to cause him so much trouble as some few questions he had posed regarding the real teaching of the Catholic Church on the eternal punishment of the unrepentant. When speaking of a book — which he had placed at the head of his article — in which the author found the Church's doctrine of eternal punishment a stumbling block as he understood it, Brownson began a close inquiry into the Church's real definitions on the nature of eternal punishment in the hope that such explanations could be given as would "remove many of the most serious objections urged by thinking men against the Church." He wanted to fix what was *de fide* in the matter in contradistinction to popular notions current on the subject.[20] But because he posed some rather novel questions in the case, his brief but incidental discussion — not more than three paragraphs in length — stirred up something more than a flurry of excitement, as previously indicated. In this, as in other matters, he was endeavoring to "sell" the Catholic Church to those outside on the most essential terms only. From having been a prince of "maximizers," defending what some infelicitously labeled a "superlative orthodoxy,"[21] he had become a "minimizer" in the eyes of some — that is, actually in policy only.[22] Let us understand things rightly. Not one jot or tittle of the great body of Catholic teaching would he sacrifice to this new policy, and wrote in deep sincerity in October 1862: "We love our religion, we love the Church, and we would not explain away or compromise any thing really Catholic to gain to our ranks the whole non-Catholic world."[23] Here was the conservatism in his "liberalism" spoken of by Karl Krummel.

But there were other liberalistic influences playing upon Brownson at this time besides the clerical coterie in New York City with whose convert movement he was cooperating. He was also to a degree in hearty sympathy with a set of Catholic liberals in England who were the directors of the *Rambler,* and later of the *Home and Foreign Review,* foremost of whom were Richard Simpson, a convert, and Lord Acton. Simpson had been editor of the *Rambler* and was co-founder with Acton of the *Home and Foreign Review.* Acton was a decided liberal and Simpson was of the same stripe. Pius IX coupled Acton's name with those who were endeavoring to bring in "a semi-Catholicism."[24] Simpson was continually badgering the English bishops by the manner in which he dealt with Catholic doctrine and matters in Church history. The outpourings of both were simon-pure liberalism. After Acton had become editor of the *Rambler* in 1859, succeeding Newman, he applied to Brownson for contributions from him. He wrote on March 7, 1860: "Turning my thoughts to America, it is impossible for me not to think of you in the first place, both as the greatest Catholic authority and as my best friend in the United States."[25]

Brownson had been a regular reader of the *Rambler* since the middle of the 1850s. When he complained that he had received no civilities from the directors of that journal to be reciprocated by himself, the *Rambler* replied:

> We assure Dr. Brownson that we have always assumed him to be the most able and scientific of all our philosophical writers, and his *Review* to be the deepest, most solid, and most consistent periodical in our language. . . . There is enough in one of its numbers to dilute into half a hundred reviews. We gladly own that we ourselves are under great obligations to him; and if it were dependent upon our voice, his *Review* would be found on the study-table of every educated Catholic in the kingdom.[26]

Brownson spoke of the *Rambler* as a periodical "more after my own heart," and it is not to be supposed that it did not have its share of influence on him.[27] In a letter Brownson wrote Simpson, dated May 21, 1863, in response to an invitation Simpson had extended to him to write for the *Home and Foreign Review* which he was just founding, Brownson indicated that it was quite uncertain whether he would be able to continue his own *Review* beyond the current year, and that should he discontinue it, he would then consider being a contributor to the *Home and Foreign Review.* His letter then showed the interplay of influence between the Catholic liberals in England and himself. He wrote:

> You have been fighting a hard battle in Great Britain, & have shown both learning and skill. I trust you will win it, though you have as obstinate *oscurantisti* to contend with as I have. I started as one of the *oscurantisti,* because I thought I must, & very much against my nature. After I saw the battle must come, I for a long time shrank from it, and you yourself have had a good deal to do with nerving me up to the fight. I am in it now, for life or for death, and will do such battle as a poor old, infirm, blind, & halt soldier may do.

Unless we can have manliness & freedom within the Church, it is idle to hope for any considerable extension without. We must get rid of French narrowness, angularity, sentimentality, & Caesarism, & effect a separation of Church and State. We must have reform at Rome & by Rome. That old machine which has driven nearly the whole world into schism, heresy, or infidelity, must be broken up. I mean not the Papacy, but the machinery through which it operates. We cannot have the interests of religion and society sacrificed for the sake of maintaining an imbecile & tyrannical temporal government for the Pope, a government that only secures his dependence, renders his independence impossible, & is itself in hostility to all the ideas & wants of the age. We must have done with the Middle Ages & not leave its putrid carcass above ground at Rome to infest the atmosphere. But the struggle must be long & arduous, & must be conducted with wisdom as well as with boldness and energy.

Forgive me these remarks, & believe me,

Yours truly,
O. A. Brownson[28]

This last paragraph sounds like a man who has been so badly badgered on some question that he finally gives way to an outburst now and then. Perhaps that is why he felt constrained to conclude by saying: "Forgive me these remarks." The paragraph lacks a certain sobriety of thought and expression usual with Brownson. Yet in calling for a dismantling of that "old machine" at Rome, he was only calling for what was finally initiated by Vatican Council II. He did not charge any abuse in his temporal government to the Supreme Pontiff directly, but he did speak of the "imbecile and tyrannical" temporal government "for the Pope." In his articles on the subject he had spurned the claim of maladministration in the Papal States. His whole letter, however, does breathe the spirit of the liberal. But it is too iconoclastic to be considered representative of his general thought.[29]

Simpson had reserved a special section in his *Home and Foreign Review* for articles on foreign politics, and he tried to interest Brownson in furnishing articles on American politics. He wrote: "It is chiefly for this foreign department that we wish to secure your invaluable assistance. No man can give so philosophical a view of American politics and history, expressed in so brilliant a style, as you."[30]

Whatever the influence of these English liberals on Brownson, he was in closer touch with a brilliant galaxy of scholars in France who belonged in varying degrees to the liberal camp: Count Montalembert, Bishop Dupanloup, Père Lacordaire, Père Gratry, Falloux, Augustin Cochin, Prince de Broglie, and others, with a number of whom he corresponded. *Le Correspondant* was the journal in which they endeavored to make their program articulate. None had greater influence on him than Montalembert, their correspondence stretching over a long period of years. In most things they saw eye to eye, but they differed somewhat on the Italian question. Montalembert seemed to think that Brownson had half justified the Italian revolutionists in his article on the "Rights of the Temporal."[31] In his article on "Sardinia and Rome" Brownson made plain that he had misunderstood him.[32] When Brownson had criticized rather sharply the Count in his article "Montalembert on England,"[33] the Count replied in hurt dignity in a long letter in French (he otherwise wrote in English).[34] But they were soon fast friends again after Brownson had made some mollifying explanations.[35] The bond of sympathy which really united the two, however, was a mutual passionate love of constitutional freedom. Born and bred in a republic, Brownson was a liberal in politics, and moving to New York City, the Paris of the New World, at the very time his friend the Count was fighting the new-fangled Caesarism of Napoleon III with its encroachments on the Catholic Church, his sympathies were easily enlisted all the more strongly on the side of liberalism as represented at the time rather generally in the person of the distinguished Count. Both men were opposed to centralism in the state, and this opposition inclined in their case to extend itself to what to them seemed centralism in some of the disciplinary matters of the Catholic Church. Brownson, for instance, was insisting in the 1860s that the accepted philosophy in the Church must be reconstructed if it is to meet the intellectual problems of the age. But whether in this matter, or calling for a reform of the Index, or whatnot, he was ever the humble and docile son of the Church, saying: "It is better to wait, wait patiently and submissively, till the Church gets ready to effect such reforms as are needed. In due time she will effect them, if permitted to count on the loyalty of her children."[36]

But there was another European liberal of some pretensions who also had considerable influence on Brownson, the Piedmontese philosopher, who had finally come from his homeland, Italy, to reside in his later years in Paris — Abbé Gioberti. There can be no doubt that, in a measured degree, Brownson fell for a time under his spell. The work of Gioberti which probably influenced him most was his *Il primato morale e civile degli Italiane* which advocated an Italian confederacy with the pope at its head. In this work Gioberti expounds the theory that there is no necessary antagonism between the Church and the world, that it is only a narrow and one-sided view of Christianity that prevents the establishment of a permanent peace between the two. This called for a program of progress to conciliate the Catholic Church to the world, especially in the domain of politics. As it seemed to Brownson that almost half the world of learning was being alienated from the Church by the current repressive policy of the *oscurantisti*, the *laudatores temporis acti,* as he called them, he insisted for himself in mingling in the progressive movement of the age in an effort, as he said again, "to enlist the intelligence, science, and learning on the side of the Church, and to recover for her the direction of the intellectual movements of the age." Although Henry Brownson says that his father had studied St. Augustine's *City of God* too carefully, and had been taught the principles of Catholicity too correctly by Bishop Fitzpatrick for his better judgment to go with Vincenzo Gioberti in asserting that the Catholic Church ought to accept the spirit of the age, nonetheless some fugitive traces of Gioberti's influence seem discernible in Brownson's writings of this period.[37]

In attempting to unravel the delicate threads of Brownson's alleged liberalism, we should not forget the assertion that "he was rather driven off by the excesses of authority" than attracted by the schemes of ecclesiastical reform.[38] Encountering, too, ceaseless denunciations from those who showed no wish to comprehend his thought, and no willingness to argue fairly with him, he naturally found more sympathy among liberals than among other classes. It is not strange that during this time he was hammering away incessantly for that just freedom which he insisted the Catholic Church allows its members. On the occasion of Dr. Forbes's defection from the Church, he had expressed, as we have seen, a regret that the letter Forbes gave to the public had not been answered with the design to show that the Church is not a despotism. In the April 1862 issue of his *Review,* Brownson took it upon himself to do that very thing in the article we have been discussing, "The Church not a Despotism." The forepart of the article is a reply to various scurrilous attacks made upon himself, but he declared the real design of the article when he wrote:

We have undertaken to prove to our non-Catholic countrymen, both by word and by example, that they wrong the Church when they pronounce her a despotism, and her communion the grave of thought and freedom. Because we have expressed ourselves with more freedom and independence than they suppose she allows, they are inferring that we are shaking in our faith, and some of their journals are representing us as dissatisfied with the Church, and not unlikely to follow the example of Dr. Forbes. Now, we wish to disabuse them. We wish them to regard us as a staunch, uncompromising Catholic, for we should be ashamed to be anything else; and we wish to convince them, that the freedom and independence we manifest, and which they approve, are not anti-Catholic, are not uncatholic, but really and truly Catholic, and in strict accordance with the free and large spirit of our holy religion.[39]

He expatiated on the fact that the Catholic Church is a government of law, not of arbitrary or capricious rule, that those who hold office in it are not the law themselves but are divinely appointed to administer the law. To assume to be the living law is simply to attempt to play the role of Caesar — and that in the very face of the spirit of Christ and his Church. As Brownson understood the matter: "The pope is a pastor, not a dominator; the bishops are pastors, not dominators; the servants, not the lords of God's people. 'The Son of Man came to serve, not to be served.' Hence the pope, the chief pastor, calls himself 'servant of the servants of God, servus servorum.' "[40]

In this same article he raised his voice again in manly defense of the right of free discussion in all matters outside the domain of the Catholic Church's teaching on divine faith and morals. The spirit of repression then in vogue was especially galling to a man of his intellectual independence. He lamented that it stunted free thought and was a dead weight on all intellectual progress. Worst of all, it was no part at all of the Catholic religion. He pensively remarked:

There is nothing that strikes the student of ecclesiastical history more forcibly, than the contrast between the liberty of thought and expression, practically asserted by Catholics in the early and Middle Ages, and that which has been allowed for the last two centuries. In these last two centuries orthodoxy has grown meticulous and the repression of error is far more studied than the evolution and application of truth. The political absolutism of the sixteenth and seventeenth centuries seems to have passed into ecclesiastical discipline. The consequence is that the Church during these centuries has hardly made any progress except in centralization, and in the transfer of obedience to law, to submission to persons.[41]

Neither could Brownson's repeated pleas for a recognition of the rightful role of the laity in the mission of the Church have been very palatable in that day in certain quarters. He wrote:

There is a mission of genius, of intelligence in the Church . . . not necessarily restricted to the clergy, and may be committed to laymen. . . . In discussion, the layman, under responsibility, we hold, may take the initiative, and not await it from authority. . . . This is no more than princes and nobles have always been allowed, or assumed unrebuked the right to do, and princes and nobles are only laymen. What a crowned or titled layman may do, a free American citizen, though uncrowned and untitled, may also do. I have as much right to make my suggestions, and offer my advice to the bishops or to the Supreme Pontiff as had Charlemagne and St. Louis, or as has Louis Napoleon or Francis Joseph to offer theirs. Before the Church, if not before the state, all laymen are equal. [Was he thinking of the Roman question and the solution he had suggested?][42]

Although in all this Brownson's language was strikingly similar to what Newman was saying in England, he was nonetheless harping perhaps a bit too much at this time for his own good on personal freedom and independence. At least his steadfast friend, Fr. Charles Gresselin, S.J., took it upon himself to write him a long letter cautioning him against too great a show of independence.[43] Fr. Gresselin knew (he was his Father Confessor) that Brownson was making a special effort during these years to regain a hearing with his non-Catholic countrymen, and he gave him some sound advice when he observed: "As to Protestants, do not rely upon them; you are far too bad for them; they have given you up long ago. You cannot win over again their confidence. . . . Continue your old golden *Brownson's Quarterly Review*. . . . Avoid what is calculated to irritate without any compensating good. And subscribers will come round again."[44]

In the January 1862 issue of his *Review,* Brownson gave notice that for the future he would write and publish his articles entirely on his own (formerly he had submitted them to revision before publication), simply holding himself responsible, after publication, to "the proper authorities for any abuse we may make of the freedom of the press guaranteed us by the constitution and laws of the country."[45] By "proper authorities" he afterwards explained that he meant the bishops of the country. But his wording could be understood as a new declaration of independence, and James Frederick Wood, bishop of Philadelphia, liked it not. In an official communication to the editor of the *Catholic Herald and Visitor* he declared Brownson's *Quarterly* to be no longer "a Catholic *Review.*" This drew from Brownson a letter of protest dated May 2, 1862:

> Rt. Rev. and Dear Sir:
> As to the request or order addressed to your editor in regard to the course he is hereafter to pursue toward my *Review,* I have nothing to say, for that is a matter between him and you alone; but you must believe that I could not read without deep surprise your "official" declarations with regard to my *Review* itself, especially as you had failed to give me any previous information of your displeasure. You had made no complaint, and given me no opportunity, before publicly denouncing me, to correct any errors I might have fallen into, or to remove the features you in your official capacity held to be offensive. I regret this very much, and it has surprised me very much, after the conversation we had touching the future conduct of the *Review,* at your house, a little over one year ago.
> You say, according to my programme last January, my *Review* is no longer to rank as a Catholic *Review.* Permit me to say that this is by no means in accordance with my own understanding of that programme. In that programme I stated directly to the contrary. I assume the sole responsibility of the *Review,* not for the sake of relieving myself from responsibility as a Catholic editor, but solely for the sake of relieving you and all other Catholic prelates from any responsibility for what I might write or publish. I avow myself a Catholic, submit my *Review* to the judgment of the Holy See, and promise to make any corrections of any sort the Holy See may require or suggest; for I recognize . . . [the Holy See's] full right to teach and to govern the Church. Will you be so good as to tell me what there is in this or in any other part of my programme that withdraws my *Review* from the category of Catholic publications, for I assure you I certainly had no intention of the sort?
> You say you have been constrained, for some time past, to consider the tone and matter of the *Review* as often *wantonly* offensive. That the tone and

matter of the *Review* may have been offensive to you and many others I am not disposed to dispute, but will you tell me by what right you say they have been *wantonly* offensive? The term *wanton,* as you here use it, necessarily implies a moral reproach, and in using it you assume to judge my heart, my intentions, and to condemn them. Allow me to say with all deference and due respect, this is more than you have any right to do. What I have written, I have written deliberately, conscientiously, with pure and just motives. I may have erred, but whatever error I may have fallen into, it has been only an error of judgment.

In a word, Right Reverend and dear Sir, I complain of your denunciation of my *Review* without specifying in what respects it has offended against Catholic faith, Catholic morals, or Catholic discipline. Your wholesale "official" denunciation may have the effect to crush my *Review,* and to do me a most serious personal injury; but it gives me no information as to what are my errors, in what particulars I have offended, or what I am required to retract, to correct, or modify. You seem throughout to proceed on the assumption that I am a proud, obstinate, headstrong man, incapable of submitting to discipline, and holding myself amenable to no correction. In this you do me great injustice, or else I am most woefully mistaken as to my own character. If I write or publish anything uncatholic, you have but to show me that it is uncatholic, and I am ready at any time to make the correction required. If at any time, in my conduct as a publicist, I violate any canon of the Church, commit any canonical offense whatever, I am and always shall be ready when that offense is made manifest to me, to make the best atonement in my power for its commission. But you must be aware that vague assertions, vague charges, where nothing particular is specified, and so shaped that it is impossible to meet them either by confession or a denial, are fitted only to offend my natural sense of justice, without enlightening or correcting my judgment.

I pray you, therefore, Rt. Rev. Sir, either to withdraw your official denunciation, or to favor me with a specification of my offenses. Let me know precisely wherein I have offended, what canons I have violated, what laws I have broken, what specific things I have done, which a Catholic publicist is forbidden to do. I only wish to know my duty and to do it. In open questions I claim the right of holding and expressing my own opinions: beyond, I bow cheerfully to the authority of the Church, as expressed by her pastors. Show me that I have in any respect gone beyond allowable liberty of opinion or expression, and you need apprehend no pride or indocility, on my part, will prevent me from making the called-for corrections and the most ample atonement in my power.

Perhaps what I ask of you will require some pains, but you owe me amends for your official denunciation of me, before giving me a hearing. Your denunciation may be sport to you, but it is beggary and starvation to me, and mine. You have a right, of course, to protect the rights and interests of religion without regard to me, but not by an act of cruelty and injustice to me, for we may never do evil that good may come. The wrong you have done me is great and irreparable; but I ask you to do what is reasonable and just to prevent it from being greater.

Forgive me the freedom with which I have spoken, and believe me, notwithstanding, a humble son of the Church, and your most obedient servant,

O.A. Brownson[46]

To this letter Bishop Wood sent a laconic reply:

Cathedral, Philadelphia, May 5th, 1852

O.A. Brownson, Esq.
Dear Sir:

The publication of the *notice* complained of in your letter of 2nd inst. was simply a discharge of pastoral duty to the faithful of my Diocese.

For yourself personally I cherish the kindest sentiments; but I could not pass by in silence the publication of your letter [about the Roman question] in

607

the *Herald and Visitor*. I could not of course anticipate your approbation and am sorry that a necessity existed for a measure so painful to my feelings.

I am very respectfully your obedient servant,

James Wood, Bishop of Philadelphia[47]

There can scarcely be any doubt that Brownson was at this time fighting what he considered despotism in some of the local officialdom of the Catholic Church. In one thing Brownson never changed: in his ceaseless efforts to maintain an equipoise between authority and just freedom, ever shifting his efforts of support from one side to the other as each in turn was in jeopardy. He was just as adamantine in his defense of just freedom as he was in his support of rightful authority. What he said of Donoso Cortes, Marquis of Valdegamas, was eminently true of himself, namely: "No man ever lived who held despotism in greater detestation, or who was prepared to make greater sacrifices for genuine liberty."[48] But if at times he was disappointed with some of the local authorities in the Catholic Church, he was ever confident that fair dealing could be had at Rome, and assured his readers that "the humblest Christian, when his case is fairly represented at Rome, may be sure of having substantial justice done him. Rome is less hidebound than some of our meticulous Catholics."[49]

Brownson also gave offense in these critical times by some of his remarks on the Scholastics and modern theologians. Like Newman, he had a greater love for the early fathers and doctors of the Catholic Church than for the Scholastics. As great thinkers and writers, the Scholastics, with him, came second to the early fathers and doctors of the Church. Though he said fine things about the Scholastics, he also saw defects in the Scholastic system. Just at this time an incidental passage on the Scholastics and modern theologians in his article on the "Reading and Study of the Scriptures," October 1861, riled some tempers, particularly that of Archbishop Hughes to whom it probably appeared haughty and disrespectful. After saying that faith has languished in the modern world, and piety has grown weak and sentimental in character because of the comparative neglect of the study of the Sacred Scriptures, Brownson added:

> The Fathers studied and expounded the Scriptures, and they were strong men, the great men, the heroes of the times: the great mediaeval doctors studied, systematized, and epitomized the Fathers, and, though still great, fell below those who were formed by the study of the Scriptures themselves; the theologians followed, gave compendiums of the doctors, and fell still lower; modern professors content themselves with giving compendiums of compendiums by the theologians, and have fallen as low as possible without falling into nothing and disappearing in the inane. In devotional and ascetical literature there has been the same process, the same downward tendency.[50]

Père Jean Baptiste Lacordaire, O.P., once compared modern theology to a Swiss tour in which everyone follows a guide who follows a beaten path.[51] Yet Brownson's dictum on modern theologians may have been a bit more uncomplimentary than he really intended. For he had a genuine respect for such theologians as Suárez, Robert Bellarmine, Bossuet, Fenelon and others whom he often quoted.

But what led above all to Brownson being tarred at this time with the brush of a disquieting liberalism in the minds of some was the new conciliatory tone he assumed in speaking to Protestants. This was all the more glaring in his case when it was seen against the backdrop of his former uncompromising orthodoxy. He now remarked that he suspected that the articles in the earlier volumes of the *Quarterly* against Protestants and unbelievers had little or no effect on those who held errors he was laboring to refute for the simple reason that he had not distinguished their truth from their error, and had not properly endeavored to show them that Catholics hold the very truth they have, and hold it in its unity and integrity free from their error. Catholics, he opined, were apt to imagine that whatever truth we concede to those outside the Catholic Church is so much substracted from their own stock of truth. But the concession implies no deficiency at all on our part, "or that the truth we concede them to hold is sufficient for their intellectual and moral life and fecundity. The Catholic Church embraces the whole truth and nothing but the truth; in that Church alone is truth to be found in its unity and universality as a complete and living whole.[52] He frankly admitted that his new policy had made him more tolerant and friendly with those separated from the Catholic communion, but he was careful to add that he was not less intolerant of error itself. Yet he said a number of things quite displeasing to Catholics, and fairly agreeable to Protestants, so much so that some Protestants were mistakenly beginning to look upon him as almost ready to fight their own battles.

In his encyclical *Ecclesiam Suam* (meaning in English, *His Church,* i.e., Christ's), Pope Paul, speaking of the current ecumenical movement for Christian unity, advocated an emphasis on "what we have in common rather than what divides us" from those outside the Catholic Church. Was not this what Brownson was aiming at in these years? But it was out of step with the temper of the times, was greatly misinterpreted and he himself roundly denounced. He came to be looked upon as "shaky" in the faith, and was treated in certain quarters, where once a welcome guest, with the coldness and reserve hardly to be expected by an apostate.[53] The non-Catholic press was on the point of welcoming him back into the ranks of Protestants, and some priests even, as Brownson had heard, were expecting him to backslide into Protestantism, infidelity, or something of the sort. It was even knavishly circulated that he ate meat on Fridays in hotels, or public places, accompanied by pert remarks.[54] As to losing his faith, he replied to the charge with banging emphasis:

> As to our renouncing the faith, we consider the talk there has been about that [as being] ridiculous and absurd, for never was our faith firmer, our love for the Church stronger, or our devotion to the Holy See deeper or more unreserved, than at the present moment. No hostility from without, no hostility from within, no misrepresentation or abuse, no persecution or neglect, come it from what quarter it may, can shake our faith, ruffle our temper, dampen our zeal, or cool our ardor for the religion which we embraced in the maturity of our faculties and the full strength of our manhood. Catholic we are, Catholic we will be, whatever the wrath of men or the rage of devils. So let that matter be put to rest now and for ever.[55]

Here we see again the astounding parallel between the fortunes of Brownson and Newman in the early 1860s. Both reached their low-water mark at the very same time. It was openly stated in the *Stamford Morning Advertizer,* and was reproduced in *The Globe* "that Newman had left the 'Brompton Oratory' and was going to return to the Church of England." This called forth from Newman an indignant denial in which he forgot for once his urbanity.[56] (He asserted that such rumors had been started by the "silly and mischievous statements" of Catholics themselves about him.) Moreover, his reputation had reached such a low by March 13, 1863, that he wrote out a formal profession of Catholic faith as indubitable evidence in case of sudden death that he had really died in the true faith of "the One Holy Roman

Catholic and Apostolic Church." As Meriol Trevor explains: "Newman knew that if he died then, it would be said that he regretted his conversion and had no real faith in Christianity at all. It was said in 1862, and it would be said now. The witness to the truth of the Catholic faith, which had cost him so much, would go for nothing. This was his dying manifesto."[57]

Who really started the maligning rumors in Brownson's case that his faith had become "shaky" he probably never learned, nor do we know to this day who precisely were the persons who lodged complaints against him (aside from the letter of Archbishop Hughes) at the Propaganda in Rome, of which we have spoken. Brownson himself referred to an eminent western prelate — which could well have pointed to Archbishop Purcell of Cincinnati, Ohio — who is said "to have lodged with the Propaganda six charges against us, professing to be deduced from a single article of ours, every one of which was a false charge."[58] Rome, as we have noted, found nothing in his writings to censure when examined. It seems that the only thing that had any semblance of impugning his orthodoxy consisted of some speculations or questions he had thrown out in his article on "Catholic Polemics" on the nature of the punishment of the lost, that is, whether we must regard their punishment as vindictive, or whether we are allowed to regard it as expiatory. He asked specifically: "May we not hope that the sins of this life, may, in some sense, be expiated, and that the reprobate may attain to that degree of good as is foreshadowed in the state of pure nature, or to that sort of imperfect good which is called natural beatitude?" That sentence, he afterwards claimed, had escaped him before his article went to the printer due to his inability to use his eyes in correcting the proofs. But even as that sentence stood, he thought he had sufficiently guarded against any erroneous interpretation as to what he really meant by that other sentence in the same article, namely, that "though they [the lost] may never receive any part or lot in the palingenesia [heaven], [they] may yet find their suffering *attaining*, not *attain*, to the sort of good in question."[59] He admitted at the same time that he should have been more cautious and exact in his phraseology, or should not have touched the subject at all. He reminded his critics, however, that he had not dogmatized on the theme, and therefore there could be no question of anything against orthodoxy. The novel questions he had raised might possibly do discredit to his understanding, but not to his faith. He had laid down no doctrine.[60]

Perhaps little would have been made of this affair had it not come at a time when Brownson seemed to be claiming a greater degree of intellectual independence for himself in pursuing the policy he had adopted. Certainly there were those who passed the matter off as of no consequence. When the July 1861 issue of his *Review*, which carried the respective article with his thought on the punishment of the lost, was sent to Dr. William McCloskey, then rector of the North American College in Rome, to be laid before the Sacred Congregation of the Propaganda, Dr. McCloskey gave it to the Jesuit, Fr. Cardella, for examination. After reading it, Cardella returned it saying that he found nothing in it to be objected to, and expressed the highest admiration for the writer. Interesting to relate, one of the students of the North American College, chancing to see Cardella reading the article, remarked that he had a slight acquaintance with the author. "A slight acquaintance!" exclaimed Cardella. "I would be glad to cross the Atlantic and come straight back for a slight acquaintance with this writer."[61]

As Brownson advanced through the year 1863, he realized more and more that his published reflections on the Roman question, his novel speculations on the nature of the punishment of the lost, his progressive ideas on Catholic education, his militant defense of the role of the laity in the mission of the Church, and other matters, had brought him into stormy waters indeed. To say nothing about the wide attacks on him from Catholic lay editors, his *Review* had been "interdicted by the Bishop of Richmond, denounced by the Bishop of Wheeling, and officially declared by the Bishop of Philadelphia and the Archbishop of Cincinnati to be no longer a Catholic *Review*."[62] The response of its indomitable editor was to head all the more courageously into the storm, grappling heroically with each new peril that threatened to sink him. At the end of 1863 he decided to drop theology from his *Review*. The truth Newman uttered a little later, wrung from him by his own melancholy experience, may have been coming home to Brownson, too. Newman wrote: "Recollect, to write theology is like dancing on the tight rope some hundred feet above ground. It is hard to keep from falling, and the fall is great. . . . The questions are so subtle, the distinctions so fine, and critical, jealous eyes so many. Such critics would be worth nothing, if they had not the power of writing to Rome now that communication is made so easy — and you get into hot water before you know where you are."[63] In any case, Brownson now wished to allay the continuing excitement over theological questions and discussions of reform. And thus came to a fruitless end the well-meant attempt of a zealous coterie of individuals to make Brownson's *Review* "the organ of a movement for the conversion of the country to the Church by converting the Church to the country."

Brownson later asserted that it was against his better judgment and his Catholic instincts that he had yielded to the advice of friends to adopt a more conciliatory tone in apologetics and to hide "the stronger and more offensive features of the Catholic faith." "There is a prudence," he said, "that overshoots itself and becomes the greatest imprudence."[64] Subsequent to the publication of Pope Pius IX's encyclical *Quanta Cura* accompanied by the *Syllabus of Errors* on December 8, 1864, he gradually came to see that his ostensible liberal policy had after all been a mistake for him, for it had not produced the hoped-for results and had only brought him under a cloud of distrust and suspicion with a portion of the Catholic public. Moreover, number 80, the last of the condemned propositions in the *Syllabus* reads: "The Roman Pontiff can and should reconcile and harmonize himself with progress, with liberalism, and with recent civilization." In July 1862 Brownson had written: "We are in our labors . . . only asserting ourselves a man of the nineteenth century, and do our best to show the ground of real harmony between the Catholic Church and modern civilization."[65]

In this he had no doubt taken his cue mainly from, not only his close friend Montalembert, but also from that other prominent liberal of the day in France, Père Jean Baptiste Lacordaire. After praising the persevering efforts of both in his article "Lacordaire and Catholic Progress" to bring about a Catholic *renaissance* in France, he concluded by saying: "Our own country presents a fair and open field for this *renaissance,* for the union of religion and civilization, and that new Catholic development which will restore to the Church the nations she has lost, give her back the leadership of human intelligence, and secure her the willing obedience and love of mankind."[66]

Brownson evidently did not consider himself as having come directly under the condemnation of the *Syllabus* and the encyclical *Quanta Cura* of Pope Pius IX, the publication of which our journalist called "that great act of our century."[67] Speaking of the encyclical of Pius IX in his treatise on

611

*Saint-Worship,* he remarked: "Some honest people have supposed that I am myself among those who have incurred the censures of the encyclical, but I have wished to show them that in my own opinion I am not."[68]

But he certainly did hold himself culpable of having given in too much to a tendency toward liberalism. Nowhere did he say so more unequivocally than in his article on "Religious Orders." His son says that his frank confession in this instance to a fault in the matter "indicates more nobility of soul and real heroism than any thing else in these [Brownson's] volumes."[69] But however that may be, it does seem that Brownson did indulge in an excessive amount of breast-beating over his embryonic liberalism. Would his "liberalism" of the early 1860s be labeled such in our own ecumenical times? Certainly there are those today who are ready, and rightly so, to praise his efforts to harmonize Catholicity with our American order of civilization, as Per Sveino has well noted. Henry F. Browne recently stressed Brownson's role in trying to combine American democracy with Catholicity,[70] and John Courtney Murray has given expression to ideas similar to those of Brownson on the relations between American ideals and Catholic thought.[71] Prominent non-Catholics, too, such as Charles and Mary Beard, have commented favorably on Brownson's attempts to harmonize Catholicity with the American order of society.[72] Robert Ludlow also expressed his regrets that after the publication of the *Syllabus* Brownson too hastily concluded that it condemned his "American position."[73]

Whatever distinctions are to be made in the matter, Brownson's writings during his "liberal" period have the merit of bringing out the other side of many a question and many a problem, Duns Scotus-like, which we would otherwise never have had from him, and of showing those outside the Catholic Church something of the wide margin of intellectual freedom the Church really leaves its members — though he had to do it in the very teeth of fierce opposition. Perhaps this is partly what his son means when he says that to this period belongs some of his father's "profoundest and sublimest writings."[74] But as to liberalism, "a liberal Catholic is a contradiction to himself: for so far as he is a liberal he is not a Catholic; and so far as he is a Catholic he is not a liberal." In this sense Brownson was never a liberal, for he would never for the world have explained away any part of Catholic faith or morals. His unique brand of "liberalism" consisted merely in the conciliatory tone he adopted for a brief period as a *strategic policy* in apologetics. His wish, however, to restore that full, old-time confidence of Catholics in himself may be looked upon as the real explanation of his unsparing words on his former liberalistic symptoms. If he was ever again to do any good among Catholics, that is, have an influence with them, he had to dispel that cloud of distrust which still shadowed him, and nothing could have accomplished that better than those frank, if exaggerated avowals, of the mistaken policy that had cost him the full confidence of a portion of the Catholic public. But whether or not he exaggerated in the matter, there is a noble ring to what he wrote in June of 1872: "I am content with the Church as she is. I came to the Church in 1844 in order to be liberated from my bondage to Satan, and to save my soul. It was not so much my intellectual wants as the need of moral helps, of the spiritual assistance of supernatural grace, in recovering moral purity and integrity of life, that led me to her door to beg admission into her communion. I came not to reform her, but that she might reform me. If I have even for a moment seemed to forget this, it has been unconsciously, and I beg pardon of God and man."[75]

# 41

## THE CIVIL WAR AND A GALLANT STAND

*The state of national affairs at the outbreak of the Civil War •
Brownson is opposed to slavery heart and soul, but insists that the
federal government has no jurisdiction over it in the Southern states
• He differs from the decision handed down by Roger B. Taney in
the Dred Scott case • He is severely handled by Archbishop Hughes
at the commencement exercises of St. John's College (now Fordham
University), June 1861 • Brownson's powerful lectures during the
Civil War, whipping up sentiment for the Union cause • His excoria-
tion of the Peace men in the North as a crippling menace to the cause
• His early advocacy of the emancipation of blacks in the slave
states as a war measure • Another encounter with Archbishop
Hughes • Brownson's article on "Slavery and the War" is mispre-
sented and then attacked • It has international repercussions • The
Trent affair • Brownson is nominated for Congress • Bishop James
F. Wood lifts his interdict from Brownson's Review.*

While Brownson had been battling within the Church for what he believed to be the best methods by which to advance the Catholic cause, the nation had finally stumbled into what in American history is called the Civil
War, with the fall of Fort Sumter on April 14, 1861.[1] With other clear-sighted
men of the times, Brownson had foreseen the apparent inevitability of an
eventual fratricidal clash between the North and the South over the slavery
question. What William H. Seward later called an "irrepressible conflict"
between the North and the South over slavery, Brownson had labeled already
in 1847 "the question of questions" which must be met and disposed of or it
will dispose of the Union itself.[2]

In his article on "Slavery and the Incoming Administration" (Buchanan's), Brownson had endeavored on the one hand to fend off the dangers
threatening the Union from the abolition party and those on the other hand
threatening it from the party bent on the extension of the slave power. He
saw in the slave-holding bloc of the nation and their Northern allies an insidi-
ous attempt so to extend and consolidate the slave power through the Kansas-Nebraska Bill as to get control of the federal government and dictate to
the rest of the nation. He denounced as unconstitutional the clause in that bill
authorizing the people of a territory to decide whether or not they wished to
introduce slavery. He stoutly maintained the Congress itself has no authority
to delegate any such power to a territorial people, and that the people themselves have no underived right of their own in the matter. For under our system, Brownson asserted, slavery is strictly a state institution and can have
no legal existence where no state exists. He acknowledged, however, that
should a territorial people erect themselves into a state with slavery as part
of their constitution, it would be within the jurisdiction of Congress to admit
such a state into the Union.[3]

Brownson dealt vigorously with this same question two years later
(1859) when the Buchanan administration backed the pro-slavery Lecompton

Constitution of Kansas as that territory sought admission into the Union. Two constitutions had been drawn up by opposing forces in the Kansas Territory framed on fraud and expressing in no true sense the legally manifested desires of the people of the territory. Brownson utterly rejected Stephen A. Douglas's doctrine of "squatter sovereignty," or the legislative capacity of a territorial people. Only after a territorial people had erected themselves into a state (in a legal convention), he emphasized, could they incorporate slavery into their constitution and so present it to Congress for approval. The Lecompton Constitution which had come before Congress was presented "neither under an enabling act, nor as a petition voted by a majority of the electors, and it was notoriously not the act of the people of Kansas. It should, therefore, have been rejected by Congress, and not entertained for a moment."[4] To Brownson, the President's attempt to force the constitution on the people of Kansas was a manifest usurpation of federal power not granted by the United States Constitution, and a clear invasion of the internal affairs of the states. In this case, as in that of the Kansas-Nebraska Bill, he was doing all in his power to keep the growth and expansion of slavery within legal limits, for he looked upon its increasing entrance into federal politics as a source of incalculable mischief.

But his views opposing the extension of slavery met with angry opposition, and he found himself "denounced in a Virginia Journal of note and influence as on the verge of Black Republicanism."[5] He reminded his Southern critics that he had given his definite views on the slavery question in his article on the same subject in April of 1838, and that those views were such as to have won for him the friendship of the great South Carolinian, John C. Calhoun, and several other eminent statesmen of the South. The record showed that he had uniformly expressed himself as opposed in slavery, wherever it was an open question, whether it should or should not exist. In January 1841 he had said to the South: "Slavery we cannot advocate, for we see no affinity between slavery and democracy. We shall undoubtedly speak out unquestioned, and unobstructed, in favor of universal freedom for universal man." He added:

> There is not a Democrat north of the Mason and Dixon's line that does not loathe it, and believe it a crime against humanity. We refrain from meddling with it, simply because it is a matter which concerns states of which we are not citizens, and because we can reach it by no constitutional action, and because we believe Liberty is more interested at present in preserving the Constitution, in maintaining State Rights, than in attempting the doubtful good of emancipating the slave without making any provision for him after his fetters have been knocked off.[6]

These quotations give what were Brownson's unchanging views on the question of slavery. It is well to reiterate that he was opposed to slavery heart and soul, as a man, as a social philosopher and as a Christian. The salient point he stressed throughout all his writings on the subject is that slavery can exist only under municipal law, can have no existence outside it, for under the law of nature all men are free, and man by natural law can have no *jus dominii* over man, as all Christian morality teaches, as was declared by the American Congress of 1776, as is implied in our whole system of jurisprudence, and is assumed as unquestioned by nearly the whole modern world.[7] In short, Brownson was as adamantly anti-slavery as he was anti-abolitionist.

He differed, therefore, from the decision handed down by Chief Justice

Roger B. Taney of the Supreme Court of the United States in the Dred Scott case in which it was declared that blacks were a politically and legally degraded race everywhere in the Union. After observing that this may be the case in some states, but that it is not so in all the states, Brownson continued:

> We regret that in giving the opinion of the court the learned judge did not recollect what he is taught by his religion, namely, the unity of the human race, that all men by the natural law are equal, and that negroes are men, and therefore as to their rights must be regarded as standing on the same footing with white men, where there is no positive or municipal law that degrades them. Here is what we dare maintain is the error of the court. We admit that negroes, but not negroes any more than white men, may be reduced by positive law to slavery, but planting ourselves on the Constitution, and natural right as expounded by the church and the common law, we maintain, and will maintain in the face of all civil courts, that where no such law reduces the negro to slavery, he is a free man, and in the absence of all municipal regulations to the contrary has equal rights with the white man. Neither race nor complexion disables a man under our federal system.[8]

In short, he protested that the decision of the court in this matter placed blacks not only out of the pale of the Republic, but out of the pale of humanity itself. The opinion of the court really belonged to an era prior to the introduction of Christianity, and was more in accordance with Aristotle than the Gospel. If such an estimate of blacks actually existed in the United States, then it was the business of the court to brand it with disapprobation, and not elevate it to the status of law. It would have aptly comported with the dignity and duty of the court to have leaned to the side of the weak, and set its face against oppression. The black race, added Brownson, might well be inferior to the white race, but that was no reason why they should be enslaved, or why the court should throw its weight on the side of the strong against the weak.

He acknowledged, however, that there was no appeal from the decision of the Supreme Court, that its opinion must stand as law till set aside. "Though we take exception to it, and believe it in several respects erroneous, we trust," he assured, "that we shall not forget our duty as a loyal citizen." But he deeply regretted the decision inasmuch as he foresaw that it would add much new fuel to the fiery anti-slavery agitation being carried on, and with much more peril now than ever before to the preservation of the Union. The decision was sure to be regarded as an extreme Southern opinion, and the fact that the ablest judges from the free states had dissented from the majority opinion, was bound to rob it of all moral force outside the slave states. The Dred Scott decision, as Brownson seems to have perceived at the time, was a distant trumpet announcing the coming of the Civil War, occasioning, as he expressed it, "the most dangerous [crisis] that has ever occurred in our history."[9]

But however just and wise the views of Brownson on the question of slavery, he was running athwart the prejudices not only of the South, but also of many Northerners who were to an extent pro-slavery. The Democratic party in the North, made up in no small degree of Catholics, was pro-slavery in its leanings. Certainly during the Civil War Brownson was to find himself in sharp conflict with a section of Catholics in the North over the question of slavery. Whether or not it was the main factor that contributed to a renewal of the feud between Archbishop Hughes and himself, it seems to have been the backdrop of some of their clashes. The old feud flared up again and again during the war years. A very dramatic scene occurred between the two just after the outbreak of the war. The Jesuits of St. John's College (changed to Fordham University in 1907), apparently oblivious of the startling scene that had occurred at their commencement in 1856, had again invited Brownson to give the annual commencement address to their graduates in June 1861. In his address Brownson stressed the great obligation of loyalty and patriotism in the great crisis of the nation. As what followed never got into the newspapers of the day, we can only draw on what Brownson's son Henry tells us about the matter, to wit:

> At the close of the exercises Hughes, as customary, made a short address, and, as one of the most venerable and venerated bishops of this country writes: "wound up with some remarks very severe on Dr. Brownson and his school." It was a bolt out of a clear sky. There was consternation on every side. The Jesuits were greatly alarmed lest the affair should find its way into the newspapers. Through the help of some friendly reporters it was kept out. A letter was, however, published in a New York daily paper, signed "a Catholic priest," and purporting to come from Boston, which was very severe on the archbishop, and also attacking his administration, etc. The archbishop threatened a libel suit, and demanded the name of the writer. The paper gave the name of Father McElroy of Boston. Of course Father McElroy's name was a shameless forgery. . . . Suspicion rested on Cummings and Manahan. It may have been Roddan of Boston, who belonged to the party; his name was also mentioned.

Henry Brownson also adds:

> When Hughes spoke so severely against Brownson and the Americanizing Club, of which he insisted on making Brownson out a member, the latter rose to speak in his own defense, but the archbishop commanded him to sit down, and Brownson obeyed. The Jesuits then conducted the archbishop and the other invited guests, except the orator of the day, to the banquet. Not one of them came near Brownson again, but he was left the solitary occupant of the hall till the departure of his train for New York.

Brownson apparently never complained of the conduct of the Jesuits in siding so completely with the archbishop in this dramatic encounter, allowing him to wander off dinnerless to board his train. After all, it was necessary for them to stay on good terms with the archbishop, and, after what had happened any attention given him would probably have been taken amiss by the archbishop. Moreover, Hughes had given them St. John's College and its grounds which plainly carried with it an obligation of gratitude on their part. Nor was Hughes himself without a sense of gratitude on this occasion. When he had first given the Jesuits the college he kept back one of the buildings with the grounds on which it stood. This was needed to round out the college; shortly after the incident related, the building and its grounds were given to the Jesuits.[10]

But if Brownson carried no grudge against the Jesuits because of their conduct on this occasion, another incident soon followed in this same year, 1861, which was to affect him deeply, though, as he asserted, not on any personal considerations. It relates to the refusal of admittance he met with when he called at the Jesuit House in Boston to see his Father Confessor. Whether or not there was any connection between the St. John's College drama and the refusal of admittance to the Jesuit House, Brownson himself was unwilling to believe. A Philadelphia journal, however, did assign the St.

John's drama as the cause of his strained relations with the Jesuits. In commenting on this statement later, Brownson gave a concrete setting to what had happened when he said:

> . . . that, as the same journal alleges, we were forbidden one of their [the Jesuits'] houses, which we had entered to seek our confessor [Fr. Greeselin], is true; but he who did it was one of the warmest and truest of our personal friends, and whom, ever since we have known him, we have loved and revered. We never blamed him; he only did what he felt was expected of him by his superiors. We had just given a lecture before the Emancipation League of Boston, and as the Jesuits hold property in the seceded states, it was feared, if they entertained us at one of their houses, the rebel government might take offense and confiscate it. They wished to give Mr. Davis of the confederacy no occasion to charge them with misprison of treason or hostility to his government. The Rector [Fr. Bapst] who excluded us, though personally sympathizing with us, felt that, under the circumstances, he was bound to exclude us, and did so with tears in his eyes. That the incident affected us unpleasantly, we do not deny, but not in the way assumed, nor because we were the party excluded. As a personal matter we could never have given it a second thought, and the unpleasantness it occasioned was the regret that simple, worldly prudence or property considerations had more influence with the Jesuit body than we expected from a mendicant order, and that the education of the Catholic youth of the nation should be intrusted to a society so destitute of loyalty that it could look on with indifference and see the nation rent asunder and destroyed by a rebellion which every principle of our religion, as we have learned it, condemns.[11]

Brownson went on to say that patriotism is a Catholic virtue, and loyalty a Christian duty, and that in a national crisis when the integrity and even the very existence of the nation is threatened, members of a religious order or community have no more right to remain neutral or indifferent than any other class of citizens. Unquestionably, they should not be required to serve the nation in any capacity incompatible with their clerical profession, but aside from that, they stand as to patriotism and loyalty on the same footing with other citizens. Entrance into a religious order does not, at least in this country, work civil death; and as members of a religious order retain all their civil rights, they remain under all their civil obligations as citizens. Civil rights and duties are correlative.

Brownson's lecture before the Emancipation League of Boston was only one in an extended series of fiery lectures he began to deliver at the outbreak of the Civil War, whipping up loyal sentiments far and wide through the North for the Union cause. His son Henry, who has never been accused of filial partiality, says that without doubt both by his lectures and writings, his father "greatly contributed to the strengthening of the loyal sentiments of the Northern people," aiding in every way he could the general war effort and determination called for if the rebellion was to be put down. "The demand for his lectures was greater than it had ever before been, and never did he appear more powerful as a speaker."[12] It has been asserted, though I have been unable to discover any report of it at the time, that President Lincoln and his Cabinet went to hear him when on one occasion he was lecturing in Washington.[13]

But whatever his patriotic efforts achieved through his lectures, there can scarcely be any doubt that he reached a much wider audience through the pages of his powerful *Quarterly*. To him one of the most disturbing elements in the great national crisis was the Peace men or rebel sympathizers

617

in the North, nicknamed Copperheads. He was incensed over the great harm they were doing the war effort and loudly denounced them. In his second great article on the Civil War, "Slavery and the War," October 1861, he singled out and excoriated in particular John C. Breckenridge of Kentucky, Bright of Indiana, and Clement Vallandigham of Ohio as well as the senators of the border slave states in general not in open rebellion, for the aid and comfort they were giving the enemy in opposing the war and calling upon the government to make peace with the rebels. He treated as the idlest fiction in the world the pretense or belief that the differences in the case could be settled by a convention, or compromise, or any concessions short of absolute submission to the demands of the rebels. All that had been already tried, and had failed.[14]

It is relevant to note how wide and effective the influence of these Peace men had become in the Northern states according to Brownson's son Henry. Writing in 1898, he argued that although only one third of the states were in open rebellion, their allies were numerous in many of the other states, and that when they put forth their full strength, they "proved a majority in the great states of New York, Ohio, and Indiana, and in Connecticut and other important states." As late as 1863, he asserted, "they came near getting control of both Houses of Congress."[15] *Harper's Weekly* spoke of "the secret traitors that swarm in our midst,"[16] and President Lincoln himself remarked that "the enemy behind us is more dangerous than the enemy in front of us."[17] To support his claim of the wide and ominous influence of the Peace men, Henry Brownson cited a letter to his father from Congressman William D. Kelley of Pennsylvania, disclosing the plan of the Peace men to get control of both Houses. The letter, dated June 7, 1863, stated:

> "Are you aware," wrote the Congressman, "that the Peace men are urging on the Southern leaders to encourage the election to our Congress of members enough to give them the organization of the House — and in the event of the loss of Port Hudson and Vicksburg, to ask an armistice during which they may elect Senators and members from all the states? This, they tell us, 'will give them the House so thoroughly as to enable them to prevent appropriations for the interest, etc., until Northern capitalists will force the government to assume their debt and give them the guarantees they need.' Emerson Etheridge's infamous letter to the *Herald* is conclusive evidence that he, who makes up the role of the House for organization, and who hopes for re-election, has faith in the execution of the plan. Against these dangers your counsels would have protected us."[18]

Brownson had long been engaged in the work Congressman Kelley was now urging upon him. He had been decidedly critical of the administration because of its lack of greater vigor and determination in its effort to put down the rebellion. Although in his first article on the Civil War, "The Great Rebellion," he had exulted over the "unprecedented" response of the North in rapidly bringing all into line for an all-out war effort, in his second article three months later, "The War and Slavery," October 1861, he felt forced to lament the apparent procrastination, the hesitancy and indecision of the government which was losing to it the chance to strike against the secessionists with all its might from the very beginning.[19] Yet he saw an extenuating circumstance in the crippling burden of political confusion and apathy the Lincoln administration had inherited from its predecessor, Buchanan's — a bankrupt treasury, the federal arms and ships widely scattered, the government itself honeycombed with disloyal officeholders, if not out and out traitors and conspirators. President Buchanan's failure to dismiss these traitors from office at an early period, and to replace them by men truly loyal to the Union, as well as his failure to discern the coming catastrophe, and to guard against it with all the powers of his august office, made him, said Brownson, more responsible for the ensuing titanic embroilment than any man living. Because he failed to snuff out the conspiracy in its infancy, or at least to crush the erupting rebellion, "his name must go down in our annals branded with infamy, or with imbecility."[20]

Later he asserted that had the nation had at the time a dynamic President like Andrew Jackson there would have been no rebellion or civil war.[21] After a close survey of the leading political figures in the nation at the approach of the Civil War, Allan Nevins, however, seems to think there was no single individual among them with the requisite leadership to have headed off the Civil War.[22]

What strikes one most when reading Brownson's great articles on the Civil War in the pages of his *Quarterly* is the deadly earnestness of the man in the face of the massive organized attempt to tear the Union asunder. It appears to have affected him as something tearing at the very fibers of his heart. And he reacted to it as a man who saw that his all was at stake. He could suffer no indifference in anyone as he looked upon the terrific struggle of the nation for life. All his energy was put forth to galvanize the apathetic or indifferent into life and action. To him it appeared that the people of the North were not at all sufficiently alive to the immense issue involved in the raging conflict. Even those who showed some awareness of the great crisis, still seemed to think the war could be prosecuted to a successful issue without allowing it to interfere in any way with their ordinary avocations and pleasures, each pursuing the even tenor of his way. In his article on "Slavery and the War" he kept hammering away at the awful reality of the war, trying to get through the heads of the people the immense issue at stake. He called loudly for a battle cry that would rouse up the people and fire them with a patriotism and energy that would rally them gallantly to the Union cause and ring the death knell on wavering loyalty and patriotism.[23] General W. T. Sherman was also greatly disappointed with the apathy of the people of the North. As late as August 1863, he wrote: "I sometimes think that our people do not deserve to succeed in the war; they are so apathetic."[24]

Brownson kept ringing the changes, too, on the only true police for the administration in dealing with the rebels: that is, be prompt, strike quickly and strike hard. Hesitation and delay would only be set down to weakness, would only imperil the great cause of the Union by emboldening the enemy and discouraging the true friends of the Union. In a passage that was in part prophetic as well as hortatory, he said all he could say tactfully to goad President Lincoln into a riddance of all in his employ who were only crippling the war effort, and appealed to him to step boldly forward and courageously lead the loyal people on to victory in the appalling crisis of the nation. He wrote:

> The President is worthy of all confidence for his honesty, integrity, and patriotism, and if he will rid himself of the embarrassment of political jobbers and tricksters, dismiss and visit with adequate punishment all secessionists, traitors, or lukewarm patriots in the employment of the government, and put honest and capable men in their place, men who know their duty, and have the courage to perform it, he may yet stand in American history second only to Washington, if indeed second even to Washington himself. Never had a President of the United States so glorious an opportunity to prove himself a man, a statesman, a true civil hero. He has, we are sure, the disposition; let him prove

that he has the courage and ability not merely to follow public opinion, not merely to follow the people, but to go before them, and, by kindling up a resistless enthusiasm, lead them on to victory.[25]

What some might well consider Brownson's greatest contribution to the winning of the war was his early advocacy of the emancipation of the slaves in the South as a strategic war measure. Already in his first flaming article on the war, "The Great Rebellion," July 1861, he recalled that the war had not at all been entered upon with the intention of putting an immediate end to slavery, but solely for the purpose of vindicating the Constitution, enforcing the prevailing laws and preserving the Union. If, however, he continued, the war should turn into a protracted and bitter struggle, "slavery must go, and the war will be in effect a war of liberation."[26] But it was in his second article on the war, "Slavery and the War," October 1861, that he came out forthrightly for emancipation. "Events march," he said, "and men who want to be successful, or not be left behind, must march with them." The disaster of Bull Run and that of Wilson's Creek had convinced him that the rebellion was becoming too formidable to be easily put down, and that the Commander in Chief (the President) would perforce have to choose between the preservation of slavery and the preservation of the Union. Writing his article as early as August of 1861, for the October edition of his *Quarterly,* he remarked that perhaps at that moment the majority of the people of the loyal states would not only shrink from the very idea of the liberation of the Southern slaves, but would be shocked and enraged at the idea; nonetheless, he asserted, it required no extraordinary foresight or sagacity to perceive that if the war was to be continued, and the integrity of the nation preserved, the war could scarcely fail to become a war of liberation in which the North would demand for its expenditure of blood and treasure the emancipation of the slave and the universal adoption of the free-labor system as a measure of indemnification. Whether or not the time had come for the adoption of that important measure, it was for the Commander in Chief to decide. "But in our judgment," he affirmed, "no single measure could be adopted by the government that would more effectually aid military operations, do more to weaken the rebel forces, and to strengthen our own."[27]

Brownson was to plume himself ever afterwards as being the first, or among the first, not an abolitionist, to advocate the emancipation of black slaves as a war measure. "We are proud of it," he said. "It is a legacy we leave to our children."[28] And he also stressed at this early time another extremely important matter, namely, that the adoption of such a measure would bring to the aid of the federal arms, not only the cooperation of the whole black race, but would also secure to the Union cause, what it then lacked, the genuine sympathy and moral support of the entire civilized world, preempting especially any excuse on the part of France and England for siding with the Confederacy.[29]

Brownson's early pressing of this military strategy on the administration was bound by its exciting novelty to have some loud repercussions. Perhaps the loudest of all came with the attack on him from the columns of the New York *Herald.* A report was abroad that it was written by Archbishop Hughes, his old adversary now appearing again on the lists against him. The nature of the *Herald* article is sufficiently indicated in a letter Brownson received from Dr. M. L. Linton of St. Louis, Missouri, dated October 16, 1861. He wrote:

I have just read in *The Herald* what purports to be a review of your article by Archbishop Hughes. I do not believe the Archbishop wrote the review. It falsely states the issue, by accusing you of advocating the war as a *means* of abolishing slavery, whereas you advocate the abolition of slavery as a means of conquering the rebels *and thus* ending the war. . . . In short, it is a miserable article, and a disgrace to its author. If the Archbishop wrote it, "how the mighty are fallen!" . . . Your article has been republished in St. Louis in pamphlet form and will do good.[30]

With Brownson it was a settled fact that the archbishop had written the *Herald* article. Not only that, but the archbishop published also another elaborate review of Brownson's same article on "Slavery and the War" in the *Metropolitan Record,* the official organ of his diocese since 1859. It was Brownson's rule not to take notice of criticism in weekly newspapers, but here was a churchman of great eminence, and he saw good reasons for departing from his custom. He was unwilling to accept the sympathy of those who called the archbishop's article a "brutal attack" on his *Review.*[31] Hughes, he said, had only attacked a strawman by twisting and distorting the principles and doctrines he himself had set forth in the article on "Slavery and the War." Hughes had written: "Dr. Brownson maintains that the end and purpose of the war is not, or at least ought not to be, merely to sustain the constitution, government, and laws of the country, but to abolish slavery in the country." Retorted Brownson: "This proposition he undoubtedly controverts; but his assertion that it is ours must be regarded as made in his character of a newspaper writer, and be taken in a newspaper, or 'Pickwickian,' sense for he knows very well that we had maintained nothing of the sort." Brownson then reiterated distinctly what he had said in his article:

> The liberation of the slave is *not* the purpose and end of the war in which we are engaged. The war is a war against rebellion, an unprovoked and wicked rebellion, engaged in by the rebels for the purpose of making this a great slave-holding republic, in which the labor of the country shall be performed by slaves, either black or white, and if to defeat the rebellion, the destruction of slavery is necessary, and be actually effected, *it will change nothing* of the character of the war.[32]

John R.G. Hassard, the archbishop's biographer, acknowledges that Hughes, writing his essay for the *Record* in the haste and excitement of the moment, said more on the slave question than he really meant, and which he was later to regret. Much he said had the appearance of an apology not only of slavery but even of the slave trade itself. His worse slip came when he wrote: "Under the circumstances, it is difficult to discover in the purchasers [of slaves] any moral transgression of the law of God, or of the law of man where that traffic is authorized."[33]

This gave Brownson a real chance to charge home. Such a statement was in the very face of what Pope Gregory XVI had forbidden and interdicted in his remarkable Bull against the slave trade, *In supremo apostolatus fastigio,* November 1839. Therefore, the writer of the article in the *Record,* the archbishop or another, said Brownson, "has unquestionably incurred the interdict pronounced by the Church, for she not only excommunicates all who are actually engaged in the traffic, as he alleges, but 'absolutely prohibits and interdicts all ecclesiastics and laymen from maintaining that this traffic in blacks is permitted, on any pretext or color whatsoever; or to preach or teach in public or private, in any way whatsoever' in its favor or extenuation."[34]

Homer had culpably nodded. A few days after Brownson's article had appeared, Archbishop Hughes said when meeting him: "I will never write any thing against you again."[35]

Still, Hughes must have felt he had neutralized an enormous amount of mischief in his onslaught on Brownson's article on "Slavery and the War." To his old friend William H. Seward, secretary of state, he wrote:

> Dear Governor:
> You may have seen in the *Metropolitan Record,* a criticism of mine on what I regard as an untimely article in *Brownson's Quarterly Review,* entitled *Slavery and the War.* If you have seen or have had time to read it, it has explained itself. It contains my sincere convictions on the subject. If I had not corrected the reviewer's position he would have done vast mischief, without, I think, intending it, to the struggle in which the country is now engaged.[36]

Hughes' article was to have even international repercussions as well. The times were full of excitement. The "Trent affair" now engrossed all minds when intelligence reached the North that the Confederate commissioners, Mason and Slidell, had escaped the Union blockade, and had taken passage from Havana for Europe where they were to plead the Confederate cause at London and Paris. They were, however, surprised and seized on November 6, 1861, on board the British mail ship *Trent* by Union captain Charles Wilkes of the United States steamer *San Jacinto.* When war with England threatened in consequence of the seizure, the captives were released to the protection of the British flag. They were then free on their mission to the courts of England and France where they would do the Union cause no good. To head off the possibility of those nations recognizing the Southern Confederacy, some person or persons of national stature were needed to represent persuasively the Union cause at those courts. Perhaps mainly through the offices of his long-time friend, William H. Seward, the archbishop of New York received an appointment from the State Department to the court of France, its sovereign, Napoleon III, being a Catholic.

In the meantime the archbishop's article had been translated into French and published in the *Univers,* Paris, the journal of Louis Veuillot.[37] When Hughes arrived there on his mission to the court of Napoleon III, he may have been a bit surprised to find that there were some anti-slavery gentlemen in Paris who were a trifle anxious to learn what precisely were his views on slavery. Among those gentlemen no one perhaps was more concerned than Augustin Cochin, mayor of the Tenth Arrondissement of Paris, whose volumes on *L'Abolition de l'Esclavage* Brownson had used as a peg on which to hang his article "Slavery and the War." Concerning the impression Hughes' article had made in Paris, his biographer, Hassard, says:

> While he was in Paris, in 1861-'62, this article was quoted to his disadvantage by the French journals, and Mr. Cochin suggested to him the propriety of making some explanation. It has been said, in a letter to the editor of the *Journal des Debates,* he [Archbishop Hughes] denied the authorship of the article. This is a mistake; what he did write to the periodical was that, as the article in question appeared editorially in the *Metropolitan Record,* the editor of the *Record* was the proper person to make responsible for it. At the same time, he declared that, although opposed to abolitionism, he was not, and never had been, never could be an advocate of slavery. Among his friends he made no secret of being the writer of the article in the *Record.*[38]

In a letter written in French on January 25, 1862, Cochin thanked Brownson for the laudatory notice he had taken of his two volumes on *The Aboli-tion of Slavery,* which Brownson had pronounced a "work of rare merit." He then reported that Archbishop Hughes had asserted simply that he "had neither signed any article nor given any one authority to translate the pages of the *Record* as attributed to him." As for the rest, the archbishop had explained himself on the question of slavery entirely to the satisfaction of Cochin.[39]

Hughes' statement to Cochin that he had not signed any article, evading the real question, carried no conviction with Brownson. Brownson comment-ed on this in a letter to his friend, Montalembert. On April 11, 1862, he wrote:

> I find by a letter from your friend, M. Augustin Cochin, that he has had an interview with the Archbishop of New York, and that the Archbishop has left on his mind the impression that he was not the author of the article against me, translated for *Le Monde,* and that he is a decided anti-slavery man. The Arch-bishop wrote, that is, dictated the article in question. Of that there is no doubt, and it was written for the purpose of checking the anti-slavery sentiment of the country, and to bring the pro-slavery sentiment prejudices almost universal among Irish Catholics of this country to bear in crushing me and my *Review.* The Archbishop is a man whose word cannot be relied on, and he remembers to speak the truth only when the truth best serves his purpose. I know him well. But he is old, broken in body, and enfeebled in mind, and though he is deter-mined to ruin me, I pray God to keep me from harboring any uncharitable or vindictive thoughts towards him. It will take half-a-century to repair the evils he has done and is doing the cause of Catholicity in this country.[40]

However faulty Hughes had found Brownson's article on "Slavery and the War," it was highly eulogized by Horace Greeley, proprietor and editor of the New York *Daily Tribune.* He republished almost the entire article in the October 9, 1861, issue of his paper, and recommended it to the close study of "thinking men of every persuasion." In his introduction to the article, he said:

> We devoted a large portion of our pages this morning to the reproduction of a remarkable article from *Brownson's Review* upon the mutual relations of Slavery and the War. It is, of course, from the pen of Dr. Brownson himself; and, like everything which proceeds from this ablest of all Catholic writers who use the English language, considers the subject from the standpoint of a Catholic philosopher and theologian. Dr. Brownson discusses his theme in its varied aspects with a sincerity of conviction, an elevation of mind, and a force of logic which must command the attention and respect even of those who are unwilling to admit his conclusions. He contends that emancipation is the only means by which the pestilent cause of the war can be reached and cured, and by which alone the republic can be surely rendered homogeneous and perma-nent. While this argument is presented in a manner more particularly intended for readers of the Catholic Church, it is at the same time so broad and so imbued with earnest patriotism that thinking men of every persuasion and still more, statesmen of all parties, will do well not to overlook it.[41]

But whether required by urgent considerations to reply to attacks on his article on "Slavery and the War" by Archbishop Hughes or from whatever quarter, Brownson wanted no time lost wrangling in the camp at a moment that called loudly for a patriotic convergence of all persons and forces into one mighty effort to put down the raging rebellion and save the life of the na-tion. He was quite willing that each one concerned should be allowed to have his own opinion as to the worth of emancipation as a military strategem. All he really wanted was that each one should wheel into line and put forth all his strength to crush out the rebellion. Referring directly to Hughes' article, he said:

> The writer differs from us in regard to the policy of calling to our aid in suppressing this wicked rebellion the slave population of the South, and so do many others. We think them wrong, very gravely mistaken in their policy, if they are really in earnest to put down the rebellion, and save the integrity of the nation. . . . But we can believe that these people are as honest in opposing as we are in advocating the liberation of the slaves, and, in as far as they will engage in downright earnest to defend the Union, and crush out the rebellion, we are ready to accept them as loyal citizens, and work heartily with them. The life of the nation is at stake, and the salvation of that is now our supreme law. We must, in the forcible language of Cromwell "secure the *being* of the commonweal, before proceeding to discuss its *well-being.*"[42]

Bishop Wood of Philadelphia had by this time withdrawn his interdict of Brownson's *Review,* and his "official organ," the *Herald and Visitor,* took notice of Brownson's October edition with its article on "Slavery and the War" in a sizable commentary on October 19 which was quite eulogistic. In giving the comments of various editors of the time, whether Catholic or non-Catholic, it remarked: "The best notice of this number, as far as we have read, is that of the *Pittsburgh Catholic*. It is brief, manly, and kind. It is a summary of objections and approvals, well and clearly stated; and concludes by urging us all to take and *pay* for the *Review*. Unfortunately, the *pay* has not been what it should have been; what it would have been had talents and learning such as Brownson's been devoted to any cause less than Catholicity."[43]

One of the results of the belligerent stand Brownson was making for the Union cause through his dynamic writings and lecturing was his nomination for Congress by the Republican party of the district of New Jersey in which he lived. His friend, Senator Charles Sumner, wrote him enthusiastically on October 12, 1862: "It seems almost too good to be true that you should be nominated. Pray, get elected. Don't fail."[44] But he did not get elected. The strategy counted on did not work. It was calculated that Brownson being a Catholic would tend to pull over a sufficient number of Catholics from the Democratic party, which was in the majority in the district, to secure his election as a Union man. But the strategy cut the other way. Many Republicans refused to vote for him just because he was a Catholic. Brownson claimed afterwards that from the very beginning he had not taken to the idea of being nominated, and asserted that he had only gone along with Ned and Sarah (his son and daughter). He felt that to have been in the race at all, and then to have been defeated, only did him "great harm."[45] Yet he was assured that he might just as well have been elected. Following the election, as he was traveling between New York and Elizabeth, New Jersey, a prominent politician of New Jersey, who was also a high-degree Freemason, sat next to him on the train. During the course of their conversation Brownson mentioned that he had once been a Mason. Whereupon the other replied: "Had we known that, we should have elected you." "But," said Brownson, "it is more than thirty years since I have been in a lodge, or had any connection with the order." "That makes no difference," was the reply; "if we had known it, you would have been elected."[46]

Whatever Brownson's personal disappointment over his defeat at the polls, it was probably quickly swallowed up by his acute anxiety over the wavering fortunes of the war. To his son at the front, he wrote: "My anxiety for my country keeps me ill, and it is so great that I can hardly be civil. . . . It is hard and you need not wonder if sometimes the gout gets into my temper."[47] One of his greatest anxieties at the moment was to get his proposal of a presidential proclamation freeing the Southern slaves adopted as a military strategem.

# 42

## THE EMANCIPATION PROCLAMATION
## AND THE RECONSTRUCTION OF THE SOUTH

*Why Brownson now felt so pressing an urgency for an emancipation proclamation • He is for immediate emancipation • He urges the measure on President Lincoln in an interview with him • He is not satisfied with Lincoln's proclamation • The famous artist, G.P.A. Healy, requests Brownson to sit for his portrait • The anti-draft riots of July 1-3, 1863 • Brownson lauds Archbishop Hughes for his vigorous support of the Union cause • The fortunes of his Review founder a bit • His "Essays on the Reformation" • Senator Charles Sumner congratulates Brownson on his "powerful" article on "State Rebellion, State Suicide" • Brownson's discussion of where political sovereignty lies in our American system • He cannot agree with Lincoln's plan for reorganizing the lapsed states • Joseph Medill, editor of the Chicago Tribune, strongly endorses Brownson's plan • Brownson's article in support of complete religious freedom • His unfortunate backing of John Charles Fremont for President • The wounding of one son, and the death of two other sons during the Civil War • He decides to discontinue his Review and writes his "Explanations to Catholics."*

Orestes Brownson was all the more anxious to promote a presidential proclamation freeing the Southern slaves inasmuch as he had come to believe that Divine Providence had now at long last given the general government in the Southern rebellion the needed opportunity and right to abolish slavery and to do justice to the enslaved blacks without the assumption of any unconstitutional powers. And he feared greatly that should the government let slip the opportunity thus granted of doing justice to the black race, and of placing the American Republic in harmony with modern civilization, God, who is especially the God of the poor and oppressed, would never give victory to the federal arms, or suffer the North to succeed in putting down the rebellion and restoring peace and integrity to the Union. He pleaded that a deaf ear had been already too long turned to the cry of the enslaved, and that if the proffered opportunity to break their chains and set them free were neglected, it might well be that a God of Justice would no longer suffer the nation to exist. If an all-wise Providence had so proffered this opportunity, "most fearful will be his judgment on us," he asserted, "if we neglect the opportunity, and fail to avail ourselves of the right."[1]

Yet he did not write any article exclusively on emancipation subsequent to his treatise on "Slavery and the War," but he kept recurring to the theme in his general political writings in a spirit of deadly earnestness. He could not agree with the President's scheme of gradual and/or compensated emancipation as a war measure. He freely owned, however, that if the slave states had not rebelled and made emancipation a military necessity he would never have advocated an immediate and unprepared emancipation of the Southern slaves. Barring emancipation as a war measure, he would have begun, he said, by converting them into *adscripti gleboe,* capable of being bought and sold with the land, and from there he would have worked their gradual elevation "to the full civil freedom of the free peasantry of Europe, with full recognition of their moral rights and obligations as men and Christians."[2] But emancipation as a *war measure* was quite another thing altogether. To be truly effective, in the sense of creating chaos and consternation in the enemy's rear, it would have to be sudden, full and complete. "The instant and immediate emancipation of the slaves in the United States, as a war measure, immediately after the first Battle of Bull Run, with assurances of reasonable compensation to loyal owners, would have been effectual, and speedily ended the war,"[3] he asserted. He admitted that he had great difficulty in not losing his patience when he heard people talking about gradual emancipation. Later he was to lament the hundred days' delay between the President's preliminary proclamation of September 22, 1862, and the definitive proclamation of January 1, 1863. He felt that such an intervening period of delay could only hobble and cripple the effectiveness of the proclamation as a war measure.

With such strong convictions on emancipation as a war measure, it is not surprising that he also visited President Lincoln to urge on him his personal views in a matter so crucial. Speaking of his father's visit with the President, his son says:

> Over and over again Brownson urged him in private conversation to proclaim the immediate emancipation of the slaves belonging to the rebels, as a military necessity, to deprive them of the labor which enabled them to draft the whole able-bodied free white population into their army; and all in vain, until finally he was frightened into it, as he told Brownson, by the threatened intervention of France and England in our domestic quarrel.[4]
>
> In August, 1862, when Brownson urged him to give orders to his generals commanding departments in the South to proclaim, each in his own department, the emancipation of the slaves, Lincoln ridiculed the idea, said it would do no good, would only lose him fifty thousand bayonets, and weaken instead of strengthening the Union cause. Brownson replied that it would do good, but not so much as it would have done if he had given the orders nearly a year and a half before, when the nation was startled by the fall of Sumter, and before there was time for an anti-war party to reorganize and oppose him at the North.[5]

The third volume of *Lincoln Day by Day: A Chronicle, 1800-1865,* prepared under the auspices of the Lincoln Sesquicentenial Commission, contains the following notice of Brownson's visit for the date of August 24, 1862: "Dr. Orestes A. Brownson, editor of 'Brownson's Review,' discusses questions of emancipation and colonization with President. Lincoln selects Sen. Pomeroy (Kans.) for commissioner for African Colonization, N.Y. *Tribune,* August 25."

Carl Sandburg represents President Lincoln as only slowly coming to the conclusion that he should issue an emancipation proclamation as a war measure.[6] Brownson had arrived at the same conclusion about the necessity of such a proclamation as a war measure already in August of 1861, that the President arrived at some time shortly before his Cabinet meeting on July 22, 1862.[7] James Garfield Randall in his history of *Lincoln the President* relates that on July 13, 1862, Lincoln took a carriage ride with Welles (Gideon Welles, secretary of the navy) and Seward, and that they were the first to whom (as he said) he had ever spoken about the intended proclamation of emancipation. Randall also records further that Welles noted in his diary that "this was a new departure for the President, for until this time . . . whenever emancipation had been . . . alluded to, he had been prompt and emphatic in denouncing any interference by the General Government with the subject."[8]

Not only was Brownson disappointed with Lincoln's long delay in bringing out the emancipation proclamation, but he was particularly disappointed with the exceptions President Lincoln made in the sweep of the final proclamation of January 1, 1863. Thirteen parishes in Louisiana and counties in Virginia around Norfolk were excepted. These territories were in "the very heart and back of slavery," so that, as Brownson complained, the slaves proclaimed free were surrounded by a broad ban of slave territory through which they would have to pass to become practically free.[9] When Montgomery Blair, postmaster general, and William Seward, secretary of state, spoke against these exceptions in a Cabinet meeting, Lincoln explained himself: after he had made the preliminary proclamation of September 22, one John Bouligny, a representative of a New Orleans district (the only representative of a seceding state who did not leave his seat in Congress), came to Lincoln and wanted to know whether or not, if those parishes in Louisiana should hold elections and elect Union men, they would in that case be excepted from the scope of the proclamation. Lincoln had given a quasi-promise that they would be so excepted. Such representatives having been so elected, Lincoln had felt bound by his quasi-promise. But the representatives had not yet been seated, nor had the opposition to their being seated yet subsided. When Salmon P. Chase, secretary of the treasury, still held out against the exceptions — assuming that opposition would probably prevent them from ever being seated — President Lincoln, on one of these rare occasions, lost his temper a bit and the discussion came to a speedy end.[10]

Clearly, then, Brownson was not the only one who objected definitely to the exceptions made — he considered them "nest-eggs for Slavery."[11] And deeply did he deprecate this particular sentence in the proclamation: "And I hereby enjoin upon the people so declared free to abstain from all violence, unless in necessary self-defense; and I recommend to them that, in all cases where allowable, they labor faithfully for reasonable wages."[12] This, to Brownson, was to cripple the heavy blow emancipation was meant to deal the Southern Confederacy — the total disruption of their labor system, worth more to them "than an army of one hundred thousand well-appointed and well-disciplined troops."[13] Brownson from the very beginning had been fiercely for total war and he had wanted an emancipation proclamation in accord with total war — no shilly-shallying, no dilly-dallying. Not to prosecute the war with the utmost earnestness, he insisted time and again, could only mean an unfortunate prolongation of the struggle with an immense additional expenditure of blood and treasure which would otherwise have been avoided. Total war, if war must be, he considered the greatest wisdom and mercy for all concerned. "It is not true," said Napoleon, apropos of the 18th Brumaire, "that troops fired blank cartridges on the people. It would have been inhuman to do so."[14]

Although Brownson felt that Lincoln had been unduly restrained in his views on the slavery question by too tender a concern for the slave owners in the border states, especially "ole Kentuck," he and the President were in perfect agreement on the great objective of the war, namely, that it was being fought for the preservation of the Union and the integrity of the national territory. Never did Lincoln make that more clear for all concerned than in his reply to the "Prayer of Twenty Millions" addressed to him by Horace Greeley (New York *Tribune*, August 19, 1862) in which Greeley insinuated that a large proportion of the regular officers and volunteers in the army were more solicitous about upholding slavery than the putting down of the rebellion. In reply Lincoln wrote in part:

> Hon. Horace Greeley
> Dear Sir:
>     If there are those who would not save the Union unless they could at the same time save slavery, I do not agree with them. If there are those who would not save the Union unless they at the same time destroy slavery, I do not agree with them. *My paramount object in the struggle is to save the Union, and is not either to save or destroy slavery.* . . . . What I do about slavery and the colored race, I do because I believe it helps to save the Union.[15]

It was in the midst of the war drama while lecturing in Chicago during the winter of 1862-1863 that Brownson sat next to the well-known artist, George Peter Alexander Healy, for his portrait — at Healy's request. Although Healy had painted many portraits, he said "his ambition was to go down to posterity tacked on to Brownson's skirts."[16] Besides painting more portraits of our Presidents than any other artist, Healy spent most of his mature years in Paris and Rome working on commissions he had received from the titled heads of Europe. Marie de Mare, Healy's granddaughter, has given us the setting of the Brownson portrait in her biography of her grandfather. After speaking of how the fortunes of the war were rising and falling at the time, and of the agonies of the nation in its death struggle, she remarked:

> In this exalted atmosphere, civilian portraits might seem tame, yet one model inspired Healy: Orestes Brownson, lecturer, writer, editor, a man to conjure with — big in body and intellect — fearless, ardent, in his denunciation of slavery and his Christian teachings. A convert to Catholicism, he had belonged to the Transcendentalists at one time, but even Brook Farm could not follow his progressive pace and many bishops cavilled at his interpretation of Catholicism, although Bishop Duggan, Healy's friend, fully approved of Orestes Brownson.
>     Healy asked the latter to give him a few settings. They became so animated in conversation that Healy had time to make two three-quarter length portraits, one of which he gave Miss Brownson. Later, in Paris, he again painted this man he so admired.[17]

In a letter to Brownson, dated February 11, 1863, Healy referred to their conversation when he said: "Your words linger in my mind like a strain of music, and your acquaintance has been one of the greatest pleasures of my life. The bishop has been to see your portrait, and is pleased."[18]

We catch another glimpse of Healy's great admiration for Brownson in a letter Eliza Starr wrote to a friend: "You heard that Mr. Brownson was here this winter. . . . Mr. Healy's portrait I consider a little less than a miracle, which was replied to by Mr. Healy in this wise: 'Then it is a likeness, for Mr. Brownson is only less than a miracle.' You must see the portrait. It has been sent, together with those of the dear Archbishop and Mr. Longfellow to the New York exhibit."[19]

It was at this very time, too, that Brownson was calling in rising tones to peoples far and wide "to stand by the Government" in the midst of no little disaffection. Nor is there any blinking the fact that he took to task on the score of enlightened patriotism a portion of the Catholic population of the country whether individuals, groups or journalists. It was part of his general pattern of scourging all in the North who were not heart and soul for the Union in the great crisis of the nation — lest "the hopes of liberty in this New World set in a night of blackness and despair." He even wrote an article entitled, "Are Catholics Pro-Slavery and Disloyal?" On the merits of the article his friend in Paris, Augustin Cochin, who had been knighted by the pope as a reward for his splendid volumes on *The Abolition of Slavery,* sent him warm congratulations, calling the article "remarkable and courageous."[20] Yet Brownson pleaded in defense of pro-slavery Catholics that they were only accidentally such inasmuch as they were largely attached to the Democratic party, the pro-slavery party. Too many of them mistook fidelity to the party for loyalty to the nation.[21] He was also happy to be able to assert that "no loyal Protestant can ever forget that in the nation's struggle for life Catholics have sent to the field both in officers and men far more than their proportion. The proportion of Catholics in the army is probably more than double the proportion which Catholics bear to the whole population of the country."[22]

Likewise did he defend in a grand manner the Irish and Irish Catholics who made up a goodly part of the wild mobs that looted and burned wide sectors of New York City on those terrible days of the anti-draft riots, July 1, 2 and 3, 1863. Not they, simple folk as they were, said Brownson, were to be held accountable, but the disloyal and traitorous demagogues in the Democratic party, Governor Horatio Seymour, Fernando Wood, James Brooks, Clement L. Vallandingham and others, who by their incendiary speeches and leading articles had worked them up to an "uncontrollable fury" against the government, against conscription and against the war.[23] These were the nefarious culprits in the case:

> The mob was literally a Democratic mob — a simple pro-slavery mob. Not a Catholic nor an Irishman, not a German nor an American, who was not a partisan of the Seymours, the Woods, and the Vallandighams, not even a Democrat not hostile to the war, and to negro emancipation, had any part in it, either as agitator or actor. . . . We beseech the public to have some compassion on them, and reserve their indignation for the men who abused their confidence, who deceived them by lies and false hopes, and stirred them up to madness.[24]

However divergent, too, his views might be from those of Archbishop Hughes in matters not of faith, he now expressed himself deeply grateful to the archbishop for "throwing the whole weight of his character and position in favor of conscription."[25] Again when Hughes returned from his mission to the court of Napoleon III, he praised him lavishly for the firm stand he had taken in a sermon he preached in St. Patrick's Cathedral before an immense crowd urging a vigorous and unrelenting prosecution of the war. "That sermon," said Brownson, "more than atoned for all we had personally suffered from him."[26] To the skies, too, he praised Fr. Edward Purcell, editor of the Cincinnati *Telegraph and Advocate,* and vicar general of the diocese — brother of the archbishop himself — for the strong stand he had taken against slavery. "We can forgive him and the Archbishop himself," he said, "for having publicly and officially declared our *Review* to be no longer a Catholic *Review.* . . . We can fully co-operate with our most bitter enemies for truth, freedom, and justice."[27]

By the middle of the Civil War years Brownson had run into some of the hottest times of his life. His militant views on slavery and the war had made him a sort of a storm center among Catholic journalists. And his insistence at the time on the need of a reform in philosophy made things hotter for him. The reform he had in mind would heal, he said, the fatal schism between the Catholic Church and society, religion and civilization, and bring back the modern world to the unity it had lost:

> We must . . . endeavor to find a philosophy that conforms to the system of the universe, as it lies in the mind and decree of the Creator, made known to us by reason and revelation, not to an artificial and unreal system spun from our own brains. This done, we shall have brought the whole world of intellect into harmony with itself and with God. All objections against religion will be removed; all *a priori* objections to supernatural revelation will be precluded, and the positive evidences for it be allowed to have their due weight. Faith will revive, and with it piety and holiness, science and virtue, and civilization and religion will embrace each other and advance together.[28]

To compound his trouble during these war years, Brownson was also writing elaborate monographs on the philosophy of the Piedmontese metaphysician, Vincenzo Gioberti.[29] His admiration for Gioberti at the time was truly great; as to philosophical genius, he ranked him with Plato and Aristotle of the ancient world, and St. Augustine and St. Thomas Aquinas of the Christian era.[30] But the special trouble in the case was that Gioberti's orthodoxy was suspect, and a report was abroad that his works were on the Index. It did not help matters much that Brownson made a distinction between works of Gioberti reportedly on the Index and a work written later, or that while he acknowledged what he considered rich contributions to modern thought by Gioberti, he also unsparingly criticized defects in both his thought and his character.[31] Gioberti was regarded with suspicion and distrust in many quarters, and any qualified admiration Brownson expressed for his genius only tended to tar himself with the same brush of suspicion and distrust. Observing this, we can more readily understand the note he appended at the end of his *Review* for January 1863 when he wrote:

> The times have injured the *Review* a good deal, and the course it has taken for the last two or three years, while it has gained, it has lost friends. The friends we have lost, we of course regret, for not a few of them we love and reverence; but they have turned their backs on us, mainly through misunderstanding and the apprehension of what they feared we might do, rather than for any thing we have done. We have lost them only for a time, for their hearts are in the right place, and their fears were always unfounded. We have reason and conscience, neither of which pride or passion is likely to blind. We are what we have been, what we always shall be — a bold, rough, independent man, but a sincere, earnest, and devoted Catholic, who believes that he can save his soul only in the Church, and has no wish to lose it. The Church is our Mother, and never, knowingly, will we grieve her maternal heart, or, knowingly, have we done so. We have not sought our personal interest or glory. We have remained poor when we could easily have made ourselves rich, and received censure when we could with more ease have gained applause. We may have erred in our judgment; when we are shown or are convinced that we have, we shall confess and make restitution. The best thing is never to err, and the next best thing is to own and correct the error. We claim not the former, but we shall not shrink from the latter. With this assurance to our friends and un-friends, and at peace in our heart with both, we wish them both a Happy New Year![32]

This sincere and warm interchange of feelings with his readers deeply touched the heart of his friend Count Montalembert who wrote him from France on February 5, 1863:

My Dear Mr. Brownson:

I cannot read the concluding words of your January number, without holding out my hand to grasp yours, and requesting you to look upon me as one of those friends you have not *lost*. On the contrary, I feel more and more attached to you, not only because you have always stood by me and held me up, against undeserved obloquy, but also and still more so because I deeply sympathize with your character. I love *bold, rough,* and *independent* men, as you say, and I bitterly regret to find so few men of that stamp among Catholics. You may be right or wrong in your private views on different subjects, temporal and spiritual, but of one thing I feel assured, that you are an excellent Catholic and an *honest* man, besides being a writer of superior talent. Now being turned fifty and having begun public life in the Catholic camp when hardly twenty, my *sad* experience has convinced me that *good* Catholics or so-called people are not always *honest,* and care very little for honesty, still less for honor, which is the flower and fragrance of honesty. Finding therefore all I most esteem and desire united in your own self, I beg once more to take your hand in mine and to claim my place amongst your true and faithful friends.[33]

It was also during these war years that Brownson wrote his "Essays on the Reformation" in which he set forth the guidelines for writing history on a truly objective and impartial basis. The treatise was really an exposition of the ideas he had had in mind when he reviewed Bishop M. J. Spalding's *History of the Reformation.* The profound nature of Brownson's thought may be readily gathered from a letter he received from Fr. A. F. Hewit, dated September 12, 1862, after Hewit had read the first and second essay:

New York
My dear Sir:

I have been thinking repeatedly of late, that I ought to write to you, to express the great pleasure I have found in the speculations on the Trinity and the Incarnation in your recent numbers. I was too languid in mind to give my full attention to them when they first appeared. But while at Bridgeport [he was moving about on the mission field] I took them up, with a brain invigorated by exercise and recreation, and I have never yet found any thing more profound and sublime in the whole range of my reading. Dr. Osgood, whose acquaintance I made at Fairfield, was equally delighted with them, and he appreciates the *Review* generally, very highly. I trust that whatever changes you make in your *Review,* you will not discontinue that series of articles.[34]

Some of the thought in these essays is much more in harmony with the ecumenical spirit of our times than it was with the temper of his own time. He asserted, for example, that without impeaching in the least the sanctity and infallibility of the Catholic Church, Catholics can readily understand how it could happen that the ecclesiastical authorities of the sixteenth century could fail to appreciate the motives of the reformers, "and by an unwise resistance drive them into heresy and schism." It is quite compatible with "a deep and burning love for the Church," he said, "to recognize a good motive and Catholic thought in the outset at the bottom of the Protestant movement, for in the outset it was not Protestant. It was a movement in the Church, by Catholics, and it became Protestant only subsequently, after it had been expelled by the Church."[35]

But to whatever subject this great patriot turned his mind briefly during the Civil War, he readily turned it back again to the war itself. It was to him the one absorbing theme. Later he was to write: "No man took a deeper interest in the struggle, or watched more closely its varying phases, than we did."[36] In 1863 he spoke — scarcely seriously — of applying for a commission of major general, but distrusting his neglected horsemanship at his age and being overweight, he gave up the idea. Having two sons in the U.S. Army who could represent him, he felt he could be permitted to remain at home.[37] He must have known full well that he was doing vastly more for the Union cause through pen and voice than he could do on the battle front.

Not only did Brownson watch closely every movement on the battle fronts, but he was also searching for the deeper meaning of the war for the nation. Of this he spoke in a letter to his friend Montalembert. On April 11, 1862, he wrote:

> My Dear Count:
> I owe you a return for two most kind and interesting letters, which I have neglected to answer, partly because my eyes prevented me from doing so with my own hand, and partly because I had no heart to do so till I could find some assurance of the preservation of free institutions in my own, my dear mother country. Fighting with us is not yet over, but I think I can assure you that the life and integrity of the nation will be secured, and that liberty will come out from the conflict triumphant, purified, and strengthened by the trial.
> The trial has come none too soon, and Providence has sent it in mercy. A few years, as we were going on and it would have been too late. There would not have been virtue enough, public or private, to save us. As it is, we have but barely escaped defeat. The struggle is not yet over, and it will be some years before things will settle down into a normal state. Yet two things you can count on as determined, the utter extinction of negro-slavery at no distant day, and an effectual check for a long time to come, of revolutionism and ultra-democracy. We shall be a more sober, and less extravagant, a wiser, and I trust a more amiable people than we have heretofore been. I may be deceived, but I have hope of my country, and that I shall not have hereafter to blush for her before you Europeans.[38]

Intensely interested in every developing phase of the war, Brownson was quick to see the great importance attaching to the question as to how the states that had seceded from the Union were eventually to be legally reconstructed. Although the suppression of the rebellion was still far from being effected by October 1863, as politicians of different parties were already discussing the modes and conditions of a return of the rebellious states to the Union, Brownson, too, came forward with an article entitled, "The Return of the Rebellious States." Even though the question had been prematurely raised, said Brownson, it should be clear to all "that much of the future strength and prosperity of the republic would depend on the solution the administration would give it." He saw at the very outset that the question would severely tax American statesmanship — more severely indeed than the military suppression of the rebellion had so far taxed American generalship, "for it is always easier to win victories than to secure their fruits."[39]

The correct solution to the question, asserted Brownson, depended upon judging rightly in the first instance what had happened to the states that had rebelled: were they still states in the Union, though in rebellion, or had they lapsed from statehood into mere population and territory under the Union. As Brownson said, his readers were well aware that he had from the outset maintained that "the rebel by his rebellion had forfeited his rights to property, liberty, and even life, and that states by rebellion are dissolved, or cease to have any laws or usages that any body is bound to respect."[40] When therefore Senator Charles Sumner put forth his formula that "State Rebellion is State Suicide," Brownson at once adopted it as expressing tersely his own doctrine on the matter. To give Sumner's formula as wide publicity as possible, he published a massive article in the April 1862 issue of his *Review,* showing why, according to his own reasoning on the matter, state rebellion must necessarily spell state suicide. This drew from Senator Sumner one of his many letters to Brownson during the Civil War years, thanking him for his collaboration in a matter so controversial yet so consequential. He wrote: "I feel proud of your good opinion. The distinction, which I elaborated in my speech, seems to me to save us from all those constitutional scruples by which people have been disturbed. It is in vain to resort to war, if we have not the right of war. . . . I cannot thank you enough for your powerful article on State Suicide."[41]

Brownson held that it was the secession ordinances passed by the seceding states themselves that carried the state out of the Union and effected state suicide in each case: "They were passed by the highest authority in the state, and have been recognized, and acted on, and enforced by all the authorities in the state, legislative, judicial, executive and military."[42] Hence the rebel states seceded in the truest sense of the word, and in seceding ceased to be states in the Union.

He reemphasized his stance on the status of the rebellious states when he said: "The two most important measures ever introduced into the American Congress are, first, the resolutions of Mr. Sumner, in the senate, declaring that a state by rebellion commits suicide, and, second, General Ashley's bill providing for the government of the rebellious states as territories. . . . They are wise and noble measures, almost the only measures introduced into the present congress that belong to high and comprehensive statesmanship."[43] In his view those two measures laid the ground floor clearly for the work to be done in the reconstruction of the rebel states.

An allied question, and more ultimate still, was whether the political sovereignty under our American system resides in the states severally or in the states united. Prior to the outbreak of the Civil War Brownson had not studied the origin of the American Constitution in its historical sense, and had inclined to the view of his friend, John C. Calhoun, who held that the United States are a confederation of sovereign or independent states. Webster likewise maintained that the states were severally sovereign before the adoption of the Constitution, but that after its adoption, losing their sovereignty, they coalesced into one consolidated nation — a conviction he expressed rather colorfully in the concluding words of his celebrated debate with Hayne: "The Union One and Inseparable!" This contention Brownson denied, affirming that if sovereign before the adoption of the Constitution, the states remained so afterwards, though, as he held, not severally, but united or collectively. The whole question, Brownson maintained, once he had turned his mind to it, is to be settled by the simple historical facts in the case. The colonies which preceded the states were never independent and sovereign states or nations; although autonomous and independent in the face of each other, they lacked the complement of sovereignty which vested in the British Crown and parliament. But upon acknowledgment of American independence, subsequent to the Revolutionary War, the sovereignty which had originally inhered in the British Crown and parliament, inured to the political people of the United States, not to the states or people of the states severally.[44] After fighting the war as one people, no state had ever had its own flag or exercised the supreme political authority of a sovereign nation; nor had any one of them ever been recognized as such by any other independent sovereign nation — any more so than when a mere colony of Great Britain. The written Constitution reads: "We the people of the United States."

"The political rights," therefore, "of the states hold from and continue the political rights of the colonies, while the Union inherits and continues the political sovereignty of the British Crown, prior to independence."[45]

It was this reasoning of Brownson that rang for him the death knell on the theory of separate state sovereignty, and gave a philosophic and historic basis for the Civil War cry: "Secession is Rebellion." "The state follows the organization,"[46] and the state organizations of the seceded states had gone out of the Union. As to the *status,* then, of the rebellious states, he could not agree with what William H. Seward, secretary of state, proclaimed as the theory of the administration, namely, that the rebel states were still in the Union. Carl Sandburg represents President Lincoln as "holding that no state could secede and therefore none had seceded, while Sumner and [Thaddeus] Stevens held that in seceding each state had committed suicide and would again have to be admitted to the Union in order to be a state."[47]

It was apparently on this theory — that no state could secede — that Lincoln built his executive plan for reorganizing the rebellious states as states in the Union in his "Message and Proclamation" to both Houses of Congress, December 1863. Brownson objected to the plan primarily as a distinctively executive plan. He felt it had been so presented to Congress that it was "next to impossible for Congress to refuse sanction."[48] In no case, he maintained, did it come within the jurisdiction of the President of the United States to institute either military or civil governments in the conquered states or territories. That was the right and appointed work of Congress, and he looked upon the President's plan of reorganization as a dangerous and revolutionary assumption of power contrary to our Constitution and republican form of government. He exposed sharply the equally discrediting alternatives involved in the President's executive plan:

> If the states are still in the Union, the President violates their constitutions, and wars against the essential principle of every state constitution [no right to interfere]; if they are not states in the Union, but, as we maintain, population and territory belonging to the Union, then he transcends his province as the executive of the government, and attempts to do on executive authority what only Congress can do.[49]

If the states are still in the Union, as the administration claims, by what right, Brownson wanted to know, had the President appointed Andrew Johnson governor of Tennessee, Colonel Hamilton governor of Texas, Mr. Phelps governor of Arkansas, Eli Thayer governor of Florida, Edward Stanley governor of North Carolina, and Colonel Shepley governor of Louisiana. If these respective territories are *states* in the Union, then these so-called governors are intruders, without any legal or constitutional authority, for under the American Constitution the right to choose its own officers is reserved to the state, "and there is no authority in the President or Congress to appoint a single state officer, not even a constable."[50] The error of the administration, said Brownson, is in denying that a state can secede.

But he of course acquitted the President of all revolutionary intentions, or of any design to seize unconstitutional powers. He felt nonetheless that an infinite amount of trouble would have been avoided had Congress adopted General Ashley's bill declaring the states to have lapsed, and directing that their population and territory be erected into territories under the federal government. The government should have appointed military governors over the conquered territories where states had lapsed, bringing them for the time being *under* the Union, not in it. But as was done, he considered the procedure irregular, unconstitutional and revolutionary, for the seceded states existed neither *de jure* nor *de facto* as states in the Union. Part of the difficulty he thought due to the apparent identification in the mind of the President of the war power and the military power — the war power interpreted as almost unlimited power for the President. He admitted that he himself had written his article on "Slavery and the War" under the same wrong impression, but that he had been set right by the able speech Judge Lyman Trumbull, Senator from Illinois, had made in the regular session of 1861-1862 in which he demonstrated that the war power is vested in Congress, and in Congress alone. The President is merely the military or executive arm of the government in time of war, the Commander in Chief of the U.S. Army and the U.S. Navy.[51] To Congress belongs such matters as the reconstruction of defunct states.

This strict constitutionalist stoutly maintained that the federal government had no right to intermeddle with the population of a defunct state with the intention of erecting its territory into a state in the Union. The organization of a lapsed state belongs to the population of the respective territory. He could not therefore accept the President's plan to admit to the Union any territory in which a loyal one-tenth percent of the entire voting population would "reestablish a State Government, which shall be republican." Brownson complained that with nine-tenths of its population disloyal and excluded from any political participation such a state organization would simply be unworkable. It would have to be held up and nursed by the federal government, and this would open the door to political intrigue and corruption. Its representatives in Congress would be virtually nominees of the administration, and congressional districts would be little better than "rotten burroughs owned by the government."[52] "Why," exclaimed Brownson, "the President could easily, by the distribution of Federal offices and patronage in any seceded state . . . grasp for himself the whole power of the Union, reign as an absolute prince . . . and reduce the functions of Congress to that of registering his edicts."[53] Brownson's own plan for reorganization was clear and simple: have Congress establish in each of the seceded states a territorial government, and then as soon as any one of them gives satisfactory evidence of its ability to maintain itself as a loyal state in the Union, let Congress enable it to form a state government and enter the Union with a federal representation and electoral vote, determined by its population.

Brownson objected again that the President's plan directing a loyal nucleus in a seceded state to reestablish a state government lacked consistency on the part of the administration. It had put forth the theory that the seceded states were still in the Union. The administration was attempting to "ride astride both" theories, said Brownson.[54] Mr. Lincoln, continued Brownson, knows that they are not states in the Union, "for this very scheme, while it presumes they are, denies it."[55] It was the same with national sovereignty and state sovereignty. The administration did not seem to adopt either theory outright, but appeared to suppose a *tertium guid* in the case by virtue of which either theory could be favored in prosecuting the war as would best suit the immediate purpose. Yet, as Brownson repeated so often, only on the assertion that political sovereignty resides in the federal government could the war being waged against the seceded states by justified. The theory of state sovereignty would justify the seceders.[56]

In his dissertation on *The Catholicism of Orestes Brownson,* James W. McGrath remarks that "it would be, indeed, difficult to discover a more humane, fair, and calm set of ideas for binding up the nation's wounds, or a less vindictive attitude" than is found in the writings of Brownson. "For that matter, one would also search far to find thoughts on the war more in conformity with the views of the President. Yet, Brownson opposed Lincoln's methods in reconstructing the South, on a technicality as it were."[57] Yes, but Brownson regarded that technicality as an extremely important one. As he saw it at the time, he was fighting a most consequential battle for constitutional government and the survival of guaranteed civil freedom — the same battle that was being fiercely waged by Henry Winter in the House and by Benjamin Wade in the Senate.[58] Concerning what was at stake, he said in a letter to Senator Sumner:

> I agree with you fully as to the importance of obtaining for Congress the management of the lapsed states. . . . This whole matter must be looked into and set right, or we will lose our republican institutions. I fear more the bungling statesmanship of the President and his Cabinet than I do Davis and his armies. You must do all you can with your brother senators. Our only hope is in Congress.[59]

Brownson was becoming more and more fearful that the assumption of congressional powers on the part of the President was setting a precedent that might progressively convert our constitutional republic into a centralized republic, and thus put "an end to the republic of Washington, Jefferson and Madison." "We insist," he wrote, "perhaps to wearisomeness, on the importance of proceeding constitutionally, and of each branch of the government confining itself to its own department and to its strictly constitutional functions. We are and always have been a constitutionalist of the strictest constitutional school, and believe the constitutional way the best and the safest."[60]

The Chicago *Tribune* was one of the principal newspapers in the country that enthusiastically endorsed Brownson's views on the correct way of reconstructing the defunct states of the South, particularly those views contained in his two articles in the January 1864 issue of his *Quarterly*, on "The Federal Constitution" and "The President's Message and Proclamation." Its editor, Joseph Medill, wrote Brownson enthusiastically:

> Sir:
> Your January number of the *Quarterly Review* ought to be placed in the hands of every member of Congress, and in the hands of the President and his Cabinet. Your article on the amnesty, if read by them, will prevent a fatal step from being made. It will cause the errors already committed to be retracted and healed by timely legislation. You are entitled to the thanks of thinking men for your masterly exposure of the dangers in which the amnesty involves the country. Cannot your publisher devise some means of furnishing the republican members each a copy of the January number? An editorial in Forney's Washington *Chronicle* perhaps would cause members of Congress to purchase it. Some person in Washington should be charged with the duty of getting a copy into the hands of all the administration members of Congress. I have written to several Western members advising them to purchase and read this issue of your *Review*.[61]

It is interesting to note that whatever the criticisms at times of this great patriot on the practical workings of our system of government, what he saw during the Civil War "incalculably" increased his faith in the latent strength and efficiency of our free institutions. The great show of strength, energy and bravery in the armed forces had "astonished" him, and made him proud of his countrymen. The foreign-born, too, who constituted one third of the armed forces in the North were also included in his enthusiastic praise. He acknowledged that our liberal naturalization laws, and our open hospitality to foreigners, which he with others had feared might prove dangerous to our order of civilization, had been amply justified, and that Know-Nothingism itself had lost its last advocate. He freely admitted, however, that there had been some blunders, arising from inexperience, and some inefficiency and narrow-mindedness, but "after all," he added, "we have shown an aptitude, an energy, and strength, unsurpassed by any people in the history of the world." For him the war, no matter how long it were to last, had "forever settled the question in favor of free government, and rendered the old arguments against it obsolete."[62] In a high spirit of euphoria he declared: "We love our country with all her faults for she is *our* country; but we love her institutions because we have studied them, and believe them to be the wisest and the best the world has ever seen."[63]

As the struggle of the nation for its life moved forward toward its ultimate climax, Brownson decided at the end of 1863, as already noted, to drop theological topics from his *Review* with the intention of avoiding such controversies as might only divide and distract the nation in its hour of supreme trial. In the January 1864 issue of his *Quarterly,* he announced the commencement of what he wished to be called the *National Series.* He was not of course abating one jot or tittle of his zeal for the religious communion to which, as he said, he had been warmly attached for the last twenty years, but merely adopting a new policy which seemed to him the wisest according to the exigencies of the time.[64] His theological articles had brought increasing storms about his head, and he may well have grown a bit dubious about their overall salutary effect. In no case was he under any obligation to carry on a special evangelism as a Catholic publicist. Mrs. Dahlgren, wife of Admiral John Dahlgren, had written him the previous December 15 from Washington: "I am impatient for the coming number [of the *Review*]. . . . You have been treated so badly by so many of our clergy — it would be a fitting punishment for these ingrates were you to rest from your mighty labors — a penance, however, which would too severely punish the innocent as well as the guilty."[65]

Of Brownson's articles during the year 1864 the one which most concerned the Catholic Church was his lengthy treatise on "Civil and Religious Freedom." It was an article which was to bring him a badge of high distinction a hundred years later. The eloquent addresses of his friend, Count Montalembert, were the peg upon which he hung the article, and was a reply to the Jesuit publication at Rome, *La Civiltà Cattolica,* which had objected to the principles of religious freedom in the civil order as enunciated by the Count for a pluralistic society of the modern world. *La Civilità Cattolica* represented the Catholic Church as willing to acknowledge religious freedom civilly as a *concession* in certain times and localities, but not as an out-and-out right. The *Dublin Review,* the organ of Archbishop Wiseman, seemed to incline to the same view. Even the illustrious Count himself, Montalembert, seemed to be arguing for little more than a concession in the case, not a strict right, as was also the learned and liberal Bishop Dupanloup. Archbishop F. P. Kenrick, too, in his *Primacy of the Apostolic See* had adopted the same view.

But Brownson was great enough to see that this could not be sound doctrine on the subject, and stoutly demanded religious freedom in the civil order as a natural and inalienable right of every person who has reached his majority — applicable in all times and places. His article covers every phase and angle of the subject, but the substance of the principle he contended for he thus stated: "As before the state all citizens are equal in their rights, so all religions, not *contra bonos mores,* or incompatible with the public peace, embraced by its citizens, are equal before it, and entitled to equal and full protection. Hence a free church in a free state implies the liberty of false religions no less than the true one, the freedom of error no less than the freedom of truth — the precise order which obtains in the United States."[66]

Francis E. McMahon, author of *A Catholic Looks at the World* (at this writing, lecturer in philosophy at Roosevelt University, Chicago, Illinois), recently drew attention to the pioneer work Brownson did already in his day preparatory to the formulation of the doctrine on religious freedom by Vatican Council II. A statement of Mr. McMahon, to the New York *Times* on the matter was published on November 22, 1965:

> To the Editor:
> In his dispatch from Rome [October 26] John Cogley accurately describes the Vatican Council's draft on religious liberty under consideration as the "American Schema," and rightly gives credit to Rev. John Courtney Murray, S.J., for zealously defending the thesis.
> For the record it should be noted that the first prominent American thinker to advance the proposal that the individual conscience in religious matters was inviolable by the temporal power was Orestes A. Brownson [1803-1876].
> My article, "Orestes A. Brownson on Church and State," which appeared in the June issue of *Theological Studies,* 1954, demonstrated the remarkable parallel existing between the views of Father Murray and those of Dr. Brownson. . . .
> The forthcoming Vatican Council decree on religious liberty should be known as the Brownson-Murray formulation. Both men deserve enormous credit.
>
> Francis E. McMahon[67]

Scattered all through Brownson's writings during the Civil War are a variety of judgments on military men and matters. All in all, it may well be doubted whether one could find in any journal of the time a more consistent or creditable body of thought on that protracted drama than is to be found in Brownson's *Quarterly.* In the early part of 1863, Count Gurowski wrote in his diary: "Brownson, in his *Review,* almost alone upholds the dignity of the American mind."[68] Yet no journalist of the time could be sure he had gotten all the facts straight on the campaigns and generals from the hurly-burly of reports in the press. In one instance in particular Brownson was to eat the words he had too hastily written — in the case of General William H. Rosecrans, familiarly known as "Old Rosie."

When Brownson reviewed *General Halleck's Report,* January 1864, he made some unfavorable remarks about General Rosecrans who had been relieved of command of the Army of the Cumberland.[69] He acknowledged that he was a truehearted patriot, and a man of great ability, but he likened him to McClellan whom Lincoln had also previously removed because, as Lincoln had said, he had "the slows." This drew from Rosecrans a letter of expostulation, pointing out to Brownson that he had not had all the facts in hand in what he had written.[70] Brownson acknowledged the justice of the complaint, but underscored the fact that he had had an ulterior design in what he had set down: he had found Catholics complaining that Rosecrans had been relieved of his command because he was a Catholic. He had wished to batter down that false charge. The government, he underlined, had been more than fair to Catholic officers and men. He made this acknowledgment all the more readily, he said, since he had been unsparing enough in his criticism of the administration. He further admitted that he had in reality done Rosecrans some injustice. "The terms we used would have been softened if a dangerous illness had not prevented us from correcting the proof of our remarks. But we retract them. . . ."[71]

One of the most unfortunate mistakes Brownson made during these war years was his injudicious backing of John Charles Fremont for the presidency in the national elections of 1864. The Republican convention of that year met at Baltimore and nominated Lincoln on May 31. A division of radical Republicans, those who were opposed to Lincoln, then also met with some war Democrats at Cleveland and nominated Fremont. Some of the leaders of this opposition movement had kept in touch with Brownson, particularly Judge James W. White, judge of the Superior Court of New York, in the hope of winning his influence to their cause. Partly under their influence, Brownson now came out with an article in the July issue of his *Review* entitled, "Lincoln or Fremont?"[72] It was a panegyric on Fremont that lost touch with reality in much that was said. One does not like to think that Brownson really wrote it. And the whole mischief was compounded when suddenly Fremont backed out of the race. Brownson's enthusiastic endorsement is all the more strange inasmuch as he had previously taken Fremont's true measurement. Writing to his son Henry in October 1862, he had said: "Fremont has visited me. I like him personally, but I fear he is not a great general after all."[73] How then explain his seemingly enthusiastic backing of Fremont for the presidency? He had apparently been mesmerized into writing what he did. Mrs. Jessie Benton Fremont, the wife of John Charles, so intensely interested in the career of her husband, had turned the trick on her visit to Brownson. Brownson's son Henry asserts as much, and this is corroborated by what is known of the female eloquence of Mrs. Fremont. Albert D. Richardson of the New York *Tribune* wrote of her: "In a lifetime one meets not more than four or five great conversationalists. Jessie Benton Fremont is among the felicitous few, if not the queen of them all."[74] Brownson's later acknowledgment that the whole affair was a blunder on his part is contained in a letter to Senator Sumner where he gave the Fremont fiasco as the reason why he had discontinued his *Review* in 1864.[75] The wonderful balance of his mental powers had for once been upset. It is interesting to add that in spite of all this he voted for Lincoln anyhow in the elections.[76]

The first Civil War news that brought shock and grief to the Brownson household came hot on the heels of the battle of Chancellorsville where "Fighting Joe" Hooker faced Lee. Henry had gone off to the war in a flare of patriotism caught from his father, and Edward, familiarly called Ned, had joined up as soon as he was old enough to enlist. Both participated actively in the engagement at Chancellorsville in May of 1863, but were under different generals. Henry, though wounded in the engagement, might still have escaped capture, but remained on the spot giving aid to others.[77] However, it was reported to Ned that Henry had been cremated in the roaring fire which had swept the woods that was part of the battleground at Chancellorsville, and Ned had so relayed the story home. The news at once electrified the father into action to ascertain precisely what was what. Inquiries and messages flashed back and forth, and soon the father learned that his son still lived, though a captive at City Point. He proceeded at once to the Commissary General of Prisoners at Washington who promised that he would have his son, Captain Brownson, released in a day or two. Brownson went to Fort

Monroe, where his friend, General Dix, was in command, who detained the boat coming down from City Point until he had put the father aboard to join his son. Encountering what he considered too much red tape in the release of his son when the boat had arrived at the "Pardle Camp" at Annapolis, Brownson at once telegraphed Secretary of War Edwin McMasters Stanton for an immediate release. No prompt reply being sent, he took his son home who was in danger of the necessity of an amputation. An hour or so later, the secretary of war's dispatch of release arrived. From his home Brownson wrote Stanton explaining why he had so proceeded. Stanton's reply, dated May 28, 1863, assured him that his procedure in the case had been proper and in accordance with his own wishes.[78]

But greater shock and grief awaited the family when the news of the death of Ned, Edward P. Brownson, reached them. Ned had been previously wounded in battle, had returned home to recuperate, but had returned to the army against the advice of his physician when his wounds were only half healed. He was killed in the very flower of his youth in the battle at Reams' Station, Virginia, on August 25, 1864, while gallantly rallying the broken forces of the Union troops in the face of the advancing columns of the enemy. His death was much lamented by his comrades in arms. Of all the Brownson children he seems to have been the favorite of people generally. Possessed of ingratiating ways, his sparkling dark eyes and dark hair set off to good effect his regular, comely features. The students of St. John's College (now Fordham University), where he had graduated three years previously, gave him a military funeral. The officers of the staff with whom he had served addressed the following letter of condolence to his father and family:

Head Quarters 2nd. Army Corps<br>August 29, 1864

Dear Sir:

The undersigned officers of the staff of Major General Hancock, and comrades of your lamented son, who fell in the battle of Reams' Station on the 25 inst., feel that some expression of their appreciation of his many admirable qualities will be neither inappropriate in itself nor unacceptable to you.

Long and intimately associated with him as we were we had learned to love and esteem him in no ordinary degree.

He was a brave and faithful soldier, who fell in the very act of rallying our broken ranks. He was as pure-minded and modest as a girl. He was a scholarly gentleman. He was a model of method as to his business. He was a genial companion, a devoted friend, a true patriot, a sincere Christian, a fond brother, a filial son.

These are certainly ample claims to the regard friends greatly felt for him, and, now that he is gone forever, are eager to acknowledge.

The loss of such a son and brother is indeed an inconsolable affliction. Allow us in our measure to share your sacred grief. At the same time, may we all find some alleviation in the reflection that he had died with so many more noble and gallant men in the holy cause of our country, whose approaching rehabilitation and regeneration his precious blood will have helped to secure.

His is one more name inscribed on the long roll of our martyrs. You, his family, and we, his comrades, have a right to be proud of it, to value it as a precious legacy which Time, "edax rerum," can only enhance.

"How sleep the brave who sink to rest<br>By all their country's wishes blest!"

We have the honor to be, dear Sir, cordially and respectfully your friends,

Officers of the staff of Major General Hancock[79]

The year 1864 was to be the darkest in Brownson's checkered life. The death of Ned had only deepened the pall of mourning that had hung over the family since the death of his brother, William I. Brownson, who had met death just the previous month, July 11, near Virginia City, Nevada Territory, when attempting to leap to safety from a runaway stagecoach. He was on his way to join the army. Brownson himself may well have begun to doubt, too, by this time the wisdom of the policy he had been pursuing in the early 1860s in the teeth of so much thorny opposition. Had all his well-intentioned pains and sacrifices been to no good? Who could assure him? Darkness seemed to be closing about him; he was like an old lion at bay. As his son says, "He was certainly discouraged; and it seemed he never again could have the strength to combat opponents as before. He was only sixty-one years of age; but he looked and felt a score older, and believed it was time to rest, and as said, in the Irish expression, to 'make his soul.' "[80]

Although there were other telling factors in the case, it would appear that it was mainly domestic affliction that now prevailed upon him to discontinue his *Review*. He had had a hard struggle to keep it going during the latter years. The defection of his London publisher, Charles Dolman, in 1860 had worked a hardship on him. The war had practically halved his subscription list with the loss of subscriptions in the South. But even at that, there was no real difficulty in making the *Review* a financial success if subscribers in the North had paid their subscriptions, but so many had failed to do so. As already noted, at the end of 1861 he had announced that he had lost seventeen thousand dollars through the failure of agents or the neglect of subscribers to pay their subscriptions, and was therefore forced to put the matter on a cash-in-advance basis.[81] His letters indicate clearly that it was a real question with him from year to year whether or not he should or could continue his *Review*.[82] During the latter years he had been working against the grain, gout crippling his feet, blinding his eyes, and gnarling the fingers that held his pen. Never before had such a variety of reasons seemed to dictate to him to bring *Brownson's Quarterly Review* to a close as in the year 1864. Staunch and intensely loyal Catholic that he had always been, he had a special message for Catholics in the last issue of his *Review*. He spoke to them under the heading, "An Explanation to Catholics," in which he reviewed the different objections which had been brought against various views he had expressed during the last few years, and without attempting to explain away anything, he simply recapitulated them as they honestly stood with the addition of his comments.

> Wrong [he said] they may be, uncatholic in intention we know they were not. We have never, since we became a Catholic, written a line we regard as unorthodox, and not intended to serve the cause of Catholic faith and civilization. From our youth up, we have loved Truth, and wooed her as a bride, and we wish to die in her embrace. We have never adhered from pride or obstinacy to any opinion we have once entertained, and have always been ready — some would say too ready — to abandon any opinion once held the moment we were satisfied of its unsoundness. We repeat, in conclusion, what we have said over and over again in our pages, and to the supreme authority at Rome, that we submit all our writings to the judgment of the Church. Any doctrine or proposition in them that the Holy See will point out as contrary to sound faith, sound doctrine, or to the spirit of obedience that should animate every Catholic, we will modify, alter, or retract, in such way and manner as she shall prescribe. More we cannot say, and less no Catholic ought to say.[83]

His announcement that he would discontinue his *Review* occasioned of course many regrets. One of the most pronounced was that expressed by Count Montalembert in a letter dated December 17, 1864:

> My Dear Mr. Brownson:
> I cannot tell you how grieved I have been to read in the October number of your admirable *Review* that *that* number was to be the *last*, and also to hear of the terrible domestic calamity which has been inflicted on you by the loss of two noble sons. . . . The only *human* consolation I can offer you is to congratulate you on the cause for which your sons have fought and given their lives. . . .
> Except for the Jesuits, about whom you *generalize* too much [see Matignon's and others' excellent contributions to the *Etudes Religieuses*], except on this one point, I agree with *every thing* you say in your *Explanations to Catholics,* and above all on the extreme danger of that centralism [p. 473] which is now exposing the Church to the same dangers which have destroyed monarchy throughout the world. But my sympathy for your opinions and doctrines, though so deep and full, is still beneath my admiration for your manly truthfulness. You are a *man,* and thanks to the prevailing spirit, Catholics in these days are *not men.* [84]

*Brownson's Quarterly Review* had come to an end, and with it the end of an era in the Catholic literary annals of the Catholic Church in America. Neither he nor anyone else could at the time have dreamt that eight years hence would see a rebirth of his *Review.* Count Montalembert was mistaken; the *last* number of that "matchless" *Review* had not yet come forth.

Typical of those who were to miss his *Review* in the interim were the sentiments expressed by William Clay who wrote him from Detroit on March 14, 1865:

> Doc' Brownson:
> Reverend Sir, will you permit me to intrude on your time for a moment to ask if you are at present writing for any publication; and if so, will you be so kind as to name it.
> I have been in the enjoyment of the production of your pen since 1838 — and so accustomed is my mind to the pleasing perusal of your majestic thoughts, that I am almost miserable without them.
> With very great respect, I am your servant,
>
> William Clay[85]

# 43

## 'THE AMERICAN REPUBLIC'

*An annuity affords Brownson leisure for writing* The American Republic • *The specific nature of the book* • The American Republic *has no prototype in history, in what consists its originality* • *Brownson's discussion of the origin and ground of government* • *He rejects the "contractarian theory," and asserts the providential origin of the state* • *The evils that flow from asserting a mere human origin and authority for the state* • *He explains the American Republic in the terms of a "territorial democracy," and attributes to the state the qualities of an organism* • *Definitions of civilization and barbarism* • *He indulges in political prophecy* • *He labels the American Republic "the model republic"* • *His plea for clemency for the defeated South* • *The reception of his book* • *His deep disappointment at the unconstitutional manner in which the post-Civil War amendments were added to the Constitution* • *Signs of a growing interest in his book,* The American Republic.

Before discussing Brownson's *The American Republic,* mention should be made of an important event which helped to provide the leisure necessary for his composition of that work, namely, an annuity given him. When he discontinued his *Review* he was naturally faced with the acute problem of just what was to be a source of income for him in the future. The handsome sums he had spent on the education of his children had kept him chronically short of money, if not at times poor. But even at that, had all his subscribers properly paid their dues, he might have set aside a nest egg in the meantime, but, as just noted, they had not done so. His lectures, too, had been a goodly source of income in the past, but in his debilitated state now he could no longer endure the rigors of the lecture tour, though he was still to lecture a bit now and then. Just what was to be his source of income in these altered circumstances? Happily Divine Providence came to his rescue. As soon as he suspended his *Review,* his friends in New York quickly got busy arranging an annuity for him. Three persons were prominent in making the arrangements: his old friend, Fr. Jeremiah Cummings, Fr. Isaac Hecker and Louis B. Binsse. In a letter Binsse wrote Henry Brownson in June 1889, concerning the American Catholic Congress that was to be held in Baltimore on November 11-12, 1889, he said:

> Well, I knew your deceased father very well, and now one of my very pleasing recollections is to have suggested to Father Hecker the idea of getting up a fund to purchase for him the annuity he so eminently deserved and to have contributed to it myself.
>
> Nor can I ever forget my first acquaintance with his writings in an able article contributed, before he became a Catholic, to the *Democratic Review.* I was perfectly astonished at the vigor, logic and fearlessness of the article!
>
> Yours respectfully,
> L. B. Binsse[1]

Fr. Cummings seems to have been the leading spirit in the project after the movement had gotten afoot. But there was at first some thought among these friends of Brownson whether or not they should attempt to continue *Brownson's Quarterly Review* under the same name with him merely as one of the contributors — using the subscription list Brownson had on hand. But they soon backed away from such an uncertain undertaking. This Fr. Cummings reported to Brownson in a letter, dated November 5, 1864, and then dimly hinted that they were turning to the idea of some such gift as an annuity. He wrote:

> We are now engaged as your friends in maturing an offer which we hope to make to you in a few days. It would if successful, leave you free and untrammelled, be consistent with your dignity, and make you feel that you are as safely provided for as you would have been had our project of a Quarterly been carried on to completion at once.
>
> As we are not yet perfectly certain of succeeding I must beg you to wait a few days for fuller explanations.
>
> The Archbishop [John McCloskey, successor to Hughes] has spent several hours with us in discussing the Quarterly, and has come pretty much to our own conclusions. He is also acting with us in our undertaking as your friends, and no one is more kind, generous, and honorable towards you and your interests than himself.
>
> Father Hecker left town this morning for a mission.
>
> With kindest wishes for your health and happiness, I remain, Dear Doctor, most sincerely yours,
>
> J. W. Cummings[2]

This matter was concluded when these friends made the purchase of an annuity from the Manhattan Life Insurance Company of New York for the sum of $8,050.78, guaranteeing to Brownson the payment semiannually of $1,000.00 per annum for life. It was not until September 1865, however, that this gift was presented to him at the residence of Fr. Cummings where Brownson's friends of the Testimonial Committee and others had gathered for the occasion. In his address of presentation Fr. Cummings said: "On behalf of several bishops, many friends and distinguished laymen, and even some Protestants who had joined in the purchase, that they did not intend by this testimonial to approve all that Brownson had spoken or written, that his best friends were compelled to condemn some of his utterances. But that what they wished to honor was the perfect honesty which they had observed in him for so many years, the fearless and open defense of what he held to be for the interests of religion, the unselfishness that would sacrifice everything rather than the truth, the free and manly use of tongue and pen which should never be denied any honorable Catholic if they could prevent it. . . . They hoped he might enjoy their gift for many years, and continue with all the fire and strength of former days to give the public the thoughts and feelings of his manly nature."

In replying Brownson said, among other things, that calmly reviewing his career as a Catholic publicist he was satisfied that he might have served the cause of truth and justice just as effectively without giving offense, which at times had been occasioned. A little more prudence, skill and dexterity, would have served his purpose just as well. Upon mature reflection, "he thought some views he had expressed should be so modified as to sever his connection with a tendency to which he was wrong in yielding."[3]

As Brownson here hinted, he had already by this time come to question the wisdom of the policy he has pursued during the early 1860s in addressing himself more directly to those outside the Catholic Church. The futility of such a policy now seemed plain to him. Of this he spoke in a letter to his friend, Count Montalembert. On June 25, 1865, he wrote:

> I can tell you nothing about the prospect of religion in my own country, but I am satisfied that whoever would serve it in this country must work with and through the existing population. We cannot address ourselves directly to the non-Catholic mind, because in doing so we lose the confidence of the Catholic public, and our credit with non-Catholics for orthodoxy. Our bishops, clergy, and people have their own way of acting, and they will tolerate no other.[4]

The old warrior of many a decade for truth and justice was now reduced to the status of something like a general without an army. From the year 1838 onward he had spoken regularly through his *Quarterlies* to a wide public on all the burning questions of the day in a style pulsating with unwonted vigor and clarity — many, too, hearing of him through quotations in other publications. He had always been very conscious of his audience as he wrote. But now he had them no more. Muted was his voice for the nonce, and he felt it deeply. Of this he spoke again in that same letter of June 25, 1865, to his old friend Montalembert. He said:

> Partly, perhaps, through my own fault or infirmity, I am now nobody, and live in the most perfect retirement & obscurity, completely forgotten by all my countrymen, except a small number of personal friends, & without the slightest influence on public affairs, or on thought or literature. I am almost amused to find how perfectly dead I have become while I still live. However, it neither frets my spirit nor sours my temper. My health is much improved, my appetite is good, and I enjoy myself very well.[5]

He also complained to his friend E. Oakes Smith that he now had "no personal or political influence." To which his friend replied: "O, my noble great-hearted friend, had you been a century in your grave you would still have influence — 'though dead, he yet speaketh.' Do not feel this way — the country needs the utterance of your wisdom and your experience."[6]

And he was deeply anxious to give his countrymen the benefit of his wisdom and experience. He had remarked in his letter to Montalembert that he was now living "in the most perfect retirement and obscurity," apart from all public affairs. More than he realized at the time this was the most congenial of all atmospheres for the writing of a book which he now took earnestly in hand, namely, *The American Republic: Its Constitution, Tendencies and Destiny*. It was to be by far his greatest book. It was a book that called for philosophical calm and concentration. As Leonard J. McCarthy, S.J., has observed: It was written "comparatively remote from the alarums and excursions of journalism. He wrote it with the calmness and objectivity of a student of the Constitution, diagnosing a disease and prescribing a remedy. It is, in short, written in the philosophical style which we have defined: 'A style which calmly and dispassionately presents the truth for the leisurely contemplation of his readers and hearers. It is a style not involved in partisan strife, not with the reaction of a specific audience, but presents the rhetorician as the expositor of practical wisdom.' "[7]

The book is then a philosophical inquiry into "the nature, necessity, extent, authority, origin, ground, and constitution of government, and the unity, nationality, constitution, tendencies, and destiny of the American Republic." It runs to 222 pages as published in the *Works*, and contains fifteen chapters. The first chapter is an introduction, the next five deal with the origin of government in general, the next two with the constitution of government in general, the next three with the origin and constitution of the government of the United States, the next two with the great problems then facing the nation, secession and reconstruction; one chapter is added on political tendencies, and a final chapter on the destiny of the nation, political and religious. The book bears an inscription to his old political ally of the Jacksonian era, and reads: "To the Hon. George Bancroft, the Erudite, Philosophical, and Eloquent Historian of the United States, this feeble attempt to set forth the principles of government, and to explain and defend the constitution of the American Republic, is respectfully dedicated, in memory of old friendship, and as a slight homage to genius, ability, patriotism, private worth, and public service, by the Author."

Peter J. Stanlis has recently spoken of the all-embracing sweep of Brownson's mind in this work, indicating the broad backdrop of the whole treatise and the interest it should hold for the student of political science. In his review of a new edition of *The American Republic,* he said:

> It is always a great intellectual experience to examine the operations of a powerful, intuitive, and penetrating mind at work upon the perennial public concerns of civilized humanity. The experience takes on significant additional dimensions when such a mind brings to bear upon basic social problems an encyclopedic knowledge of history, political philosophy, and religion of Western civilization, from ancient to modern times. Orestes Brownson had such a mind and such breadth of knowledge. Nowhere is his political genius more evident than in *The American Republic,* in which he examined the origins, nature, development, and destiny of American society and its constitutional system of government, against the whole religious tradition of Christianity and the political philosophy of European civilization.[8]

It is interesting to note that Brownson asserted in 1873 that *The American Republic* was for the most part written in 1864-1865, before the conclusion of the Civil War, only the chapter on reconstruction, as originally written was canceled, under the impression that reconstruction would be completed before the work could issue from the press, and another more general, and less practical was substituted.[9] It was the Civil War that drove him to write the book. He maintained that "neither the administration nor Congress ever took, distinctly and decisively, a ground on which the war was defensible. . . . For neither party understood where, under our system, the sovereign power is lodged."[10] His design then in writing the book was to lay before his countrymen, as far as he could reach them, what he believed to be the true interpretation of our system of government and thus obviate the false theories confusing the public mind. He indicated the need of this when he wrote:

> Among nations, no one has more need of full knowledge of itself than the United States, and no one has hitherto had less. It has hardly had a distinct consciousness of its own national existence, and has lived the irreflective life of the child, with no severe trial, till the recent rebellion, to throw it back on itself and compel it to reflect on its own constitution, its own separate existence, individuality, tendencies, and end. . . . Its vision is still obscured by floating mists of its earlier morning, and its judgment rendered indistinct and indecisive by the wild theories and fancies of its childhood. The national mind has been quickened, the national heart has been opened, the national disposition prepared, but there remains the important work of dissipating the mists that still linger, of brushing away these wild theories and fancies, and of ena-

bling it to form a clear and intelligent judgment of itself, and a true and just appreciation of its constitution, tendency and destiny.[11]

Although Brownson drew upon his past political writings in working out this disquisition, including in particular his articles on the origin and constitution of government in the *Democratic Review*, 1843, he wrote as freely and as independently as though he had never committed himself to any political views or doctrines. The past was of value to him only insofar as coincident with its present views and convictions. "I have never," he said, "been the slave of my own past, and truth has always been dearer to me than my own opinions."[12] But the past was carefully canvassed, for the body of political doctrine he was now setting forth he wished to be regarded as his "political testament," as he wrote Senator Sumner.[13] In the preface of his book, he said: "This book is not only my latest, but will be my last on politics and government, and must be taken as authentic, and the only authentic statement of my political views and convictions, and whatever in any of my previous writings conflicts with the principles defended in its pages, must be regarded as retracted or rejected."[14]

He frankly acknowledged any assistance he had received from other political philosophers in writing his treatise. He owned that he was principally indebted for his view of American nationality and the federal constitution to hints and suggestions contained in the two-volume work of John C. Hurd on *The Law of Freedom and Bondage in the United States*. Scarcely less was he indebted to the aid he had obtained from Plato, Aristotle, St. Augustine, St. Thomas Aquinas, Suárez, Pierre Leroux, and Vincenzo Gioberti. Although his treatise is of course of a strictly political nature, he asserted that he could never have written it without the knowledge he had as a Catholic of Catholic theology and the acquaintance he had with the writings of the great fathers and doctors of the Catholic Church.[15] No man was ever more honest in making acknowledgment of any loans he might make from the thoughts of others.

Brownson indicated the angle from which he approached his disquisition on the American Republic when he wrote:

> Every living nation has an idea given it by Providence to realize, and whose realization is its special work, mission, or destiny. Every nation is, in some sense, a chosen people of God. . . . The American people has a mission and is chosen of God for the realization of a great idea. It has been chosen of God not only to continue the work assigned to Greece and Rome, but to accomplish a greater work than was assigned to either. Its idea is liberty, indeed, but liberty with law, and law with liberty.
>
> Yet its mission is not so much the realization of liberty as the realization of the true idea of the state, which secures at once the authority of the public and the freedom of the individual — the sovereignty of the people without social despotism, and individual freedom without anarchy. In other words, its mission is to bring out in its life the dialectic union of authority and liberty, of the natural rights of man and those of society. The Greek and Roman republics asserted the state to the detriment of individual freedom; modern republics either do the same, or assert individual freedom to the detriment of the state. The American republic has been instituted by Providence to realize the freedom of each with advantage to the other.[16]

He likewise approached his theme in a truly philosophical spirit. Although, as Leonard J. McCarthy, S.J., observes, qualities of his philosophical style run through his *Collected Works*, *"The American Republic* remains the only work of Brownson's written with that style as the predominant one."[17] Brownson himself felt that a treatise written in just such a style was a real desideratum at that precise juncture in our national affairs. As he expressed it: "A work written without temper, without passion or sectional prejudice, in a philosophical spirit, explaining to the American people their own national constitution, and the mutual relations of the general government and the state governments, cannot, at this important crisis in our affairs, be inopportune, and, if properly executed, can scarcely fail to be of service."[18]

To Brownson the American Republic or Constitution offered a special challenge as a study inasmuch as it is entirely unique in its kind. He asserted that it has no prototype in any prior constitution. It can be classed with no one of the forms of government described by Aristotle, or later authorities — whether monarchy, aristocracy, democracy, or mixed governments. It is none of these, nor any combination of them. To attempt to bring it under any of the simple or mixed forms of government would be to attempt "to clothe the future with the cast-off garments of the past."[19] As late as April of 1863, he had asserted that the British constitution is the prototype of the American.[20] This he now denied, saying that the British consitution is "essentially antagonistic to the American, not its type."[21] The British constitution, as he saw it, substitutes estates for the state, in which elements of monarchy, aristocracy and democracy temper, check and balance each other. It operates through an antagonism of estates, classes or interests, counting on such a system to preserve the government from an oppressive centralism. Hence the task of the British statesman is so to manage the diverse antagonistic parties and interests that he can balance the one off against the other in his efforts to keep the government operative.[22]

"The American method demands no such antagonism, no neutralizing of one social force by another, but avails itself of all the forces of society, organizes them dialectically, not antagonistically, and thus protects with equal efficiency both public authority and private rights."[23] Accordingly, Brownson found the originality of the American system — "with Mr. Madison, our most philosophical statesman[24] — to be in the division of power between a general government having sole charge of general and foreign affairs, and particular or state governments having, within their respective territories, sole charge of particular relations and interests of the people. All proceeds in coordinate harmony. Neither the general nor the state governments are superior the one to the other. Each has its own sphere in which to operate without colliding with the other. Each is independent and complete in relation to its own work, but incomplete and dependent on the other for the complete work of government.[25] He thought, therefore, that "nothing could be more hurtful than to attempt to explain or work it [the American system] on the principles of British constitutionalism." Indeed, he felt that the great majority of American statesmen had failed to recognize the originality of the American Constitution and had attempted to explain it by analogies drawn from the constitutions of other states rather than by a profound study of its principles. "They have taken too low a view of it," he said, "and have rarely, if ever, appreciated its distinctive and peculiar merits."[26]

But whatever the inner superior merit of the American Constitution, its interpretation is quite another thing altogether. If the slave states had not held the states to be severally sovereign, and maintained that the United States are only an agreement or compact, they would never have seceded; and had not the free states confounded the Union with the general government, and manifested a tendency to make it the whole national government, the South would have had no occasion or excuse for secession. The great problem to be solved by American statesmen had been from the beginning, as he understood it, how to assert union without consolidation, and states' rights without disintegration.[27] Whatever the precise contribution Brownson made to the solution of this problem, Woodrow Wilson is reported to have remarked that Orestes Brownson's *The American Republic* is the "greatest treatment ever written" on the American Constitution.[28]

Needless to say, *The American Republic* bears the earmarks of Brownson's very best efforts. It is the only book in which he took sufficient time and pains to round out his ideas. It was for him a labor of love. "I am ambitious," he said, "even in my old age, and I wish to exert an influence on the future of my country, for which I have made, or, rather my family have made, some sacrifices, and which I tenderly love."[29]

At the very outset of his treatise we have a statement of his lofty concept of the nature and office of government. It contains in itself the *raison d'être* of why he should engage at all in a discussion of government. Of government he said:

> Next to religion, it is man's greatest good; and even religion without it can do only a small part of her work. They wrong it who call it a necessary evil; it is a great good, and, instead of being distrusted, hated, or resisted, except in its abuses, it should be loved, respected, obeyed, and, if need be, defended at the cost of all earthly goods, even life itself.[30]

Brownson's second chapter on the origin of government is given over to a microscopic examination of the theory of government advanced by Hobbes, Locke and Rousseau, namely, that government originates in a social contract. The theory, as advanced by Rousseau, posits a raw "state of nature" in which men lived antecedently to forming themselves into civil society, without government or any civil laws whatsoever. In this state each individual was independent and sovereign in himself, and these independent and sovereign individuals met, or are supposed to have met in convention, and entered into a compact among themselves, each with all, and all with each, that they would institute government, and would each submit to the decisions and authority of the majority, that is, to the fluctuating will of an irresponsible majority. Civil society, government, the state, thus originated in a compact, declared Rousseau, and government accordingly, as asserted Jefferson in his Declaration of Independence "derives its just powers from the consent of the governed."[31]

No doubt the main reason why Brownson gave this theory such a searching analysis, as modified by the assertion that individuals delegate rather than surrender their rights to civil society, was that this theory had been adopted by the American people in the previous century, and was still prevalent "with those who happen to have any theory or opinion on the subject. It [was] the political tradition of the country."[32] This made his refutation of the theory — to him a major political heresy — of no little practical importance, and it is not surprising that with it he gave us one of the finest specimens of his effective use of logic. As Ross Hoffman has observed when speaking of the matter, "Seldom has the conventional or social contract theory of the formation of political society — which is and ever must be the fundamental dogma of revolutionary democracy — been more effectively refuted."[33] There is no intention here of rehearsing Brownson's extended thought on the theme beyond indicating one or the other of his initial arguments.

To begin, that there ever existed the alleged "state of nature" in which human beings lived seemed to Brownson quite questionable. Certainly history furnishes no proof that such a state ever existed. As Cicero remarked, "Every man is born in society, and remains there." Brownson was careful, however, to make clear that in so saying he was not denying the existence of a law of nature or the natural law. All in philosophy, morals, politics and jurisprudence affirm it; the very basis of the state is founded on it as well as universal jurisprudence; courts acknowledge and administer it. Civil laws are based on it, it being the reason and ground of their existence. It enters into the warp and woof of civil society which develops, applies and protects it. Man in civil society is not out of nature but in it, as the state most natural to him. But the alleged "state of nature" under the natural law was never to Brownson an actual state — nothing more than an abstraction. "But as abstractions have no existence out of the mind that forms them, the 'state of nature' has no actual existence in the world of reality as a separate state."[34]

But for one even to suppose that such a "state of nature" ever existed, said Brownson, would only mean getting bogged down in considerable difficulties. How did man ever extricate himself from such a state? The historian Niebuhr states that history records no instance of a savage tribe or people ever elevating itself from the uncivilized into the civilized state by its own spontaneous or indigenous efforts. But the primitive man, as described by Horace in his *Satires,* and posited by Hobbs, Locke, Rousseau and others, is far below the savage. How did he ever emerge from such a degraded state? In the "state of nature" so described there is no germ of development. A transition from such a state to civilized society would not be a development, but a complete rupture with the past, a new creation in fact. The difficulty involved is seen all the more clearly when it is recollected that it is only with the greatest efforts that reforms are ever introduced even into old and highly civilized nations, oftentimes with terrible social convulsions and political upheavals. How then does one suppose that men without the aid of civil society, without the habits of obedience and command, are capable of initiating, establishing and sustaining government? To suppose it, said our political philosopher, would be to suppose men in "a state of nature," without culture, without science, without any of the arts and sciences, even the most rudimentary, are vastly superior to men formed under the most advanced civilization. "Was Rousseau right," he gravely inquired, "in asserting civilization as a fall, as a deterioration of the race?"[35]

Unable to discover anything to support such a theory and developing further multifarious arguments to demonstrate its unsoundness, Brownson rejected it outright. Following the illustrious Count de Maistre (and John C. Calhoun and Edmund Burke for that matter),[36] Brownson laid it down that no people have ever been made a nation by a mere paper or written constitution, but must have been one before any constitutional convention through the natural or unwritten constitution given it by Divine Providence. Providence gives to each nation, not by direct intervention, but by a combination of fortuitous events and circumstances, its distinctive, unwritten constitution. "Out of war, conquest, migration, leadership, and the multifarious good and evil acts of men, God weaves among men psychic bonds which are stabilized within a defined territory. And so a civil society exists as a result of Divine Causality."[37] As Ross Hoffman adds, "This is not political mysticism. It does not mean that we cannot see our first beginnings and early development in historical daylight. We can investigate our national embryo and that of many other nations, but when we look closely at these historical phenomena

651

we learn that successive generations build a community without consciousness of what they are doing, or of what history will later discover that they have done."[38]

All that competent statesmen can do, then, is to give the people a written document of government in harmony with this unwritten constitution. "Men make governments, but the Lord of history makes nations."[39] Accordingly, said Brownson, "the American people were not made one by the written constitution, as Mr. Jefferson, Mr. Madison, Mr. Webster, and so many others suppose, but were made one by the unwritten constitution, born with them and inherent in them."[40] Hence no government or written constitution will ever work well that is not in harmony with the unwritten or providential constitution of the people. That is why the old Articles of Confederation, based on the theory of separate state sovereignty, were a failure. They were contrary to the internal unity of the American people. "The instinct of unity rejected state sovereignty in 1787 as it did in 1861."[41]

Brownson passed lightly over the fact that some of the Founding Fathers favored the "contractarian theory" of government, but was much more interested in their practical achievement in eventually setting up a government in harmony with the unwritten, providential constitution of the American people. If their theory was unsound, their practical doctrine was not. "The merit of the statesmen of 1787, is," he emphasized, "that they did not destroy or deface the work of Providence, but accepted it, and organized the government in harmony with the real order, the real elements given them. They suffered themselves in all their positive substantial work to be governed by reality, not by theories or speculations. In this they proved themselves statesmen, and their work survives."[42]

Holding, together with St. Augustine, St. Gregory Magnus, St. Thomas, Bellarmine, Suárez, and the theologians generally, that civil government shares a sovereignty that comes from God — *non est potestas nisi a Deo*[43] — Brownson never ceased to lament and deplore the many evils that flow from asserting for government nothing more than a purely human origin and authority (loosely implied in the "contractarian theory"). For nearly two centuries now, he said, the most popular and influential writers on government have rejected the divine origin and ground of civil authority, and have exiled God from the state. They have not only separated the state from the church as an external organization, but have excluded God from it as its internal law-giver, and have thus robbed the state of its sacredness, its inviolability, its hold on conscience. They have mocked at loyalty as a superstition, and consecrated, not civil authority, but "the sacred right of insurrection." Under their influence the age has tended to sympathize with lawless insurgents, rebels and revolutionists, and to cry out against the fair and honest attempts of rightful civil government to sustain itself and protect society. Such, said Brownson, must be the inevitable result of the attempt to found the state on atheistic principles. Unless the state is founded on divine sovereignty, authority can sustain itself only by force, for political atheism recognizes no right but might. With the popularity of the theory that gives a mere human origin and ground to government, Brownson counted it only a natural consequence that there was scarcely a government on the continent of Europe that could sustain itself without an armed force sufficient to overawe or crush the party or parties plotting its destruction.[44]

As to the importance of religion to the foundation of the state, Brownson further stressed the invaluable contribution Christianity had made to the American state with its adoption of the Church's doctrine of the natural rights of man as its basis. "Christianity in the secular order," said Brownson, "is republican."[45] The grand defect of the ancient Greek and Roman republics was that, while they asserted with sufficient energy the public authority, they failed to make any recognition of any such thing as the natural rights of man — allowing at best only what they were pleased to regard as certain privileges or concessions. They had no concept of the natural rights of man held independently of society, chartered into the human personality by the Creator, and held anterior to society. Not until the Christian era, pointed out Brownson, is any trace of them to be found, and that at the dawn of Christianity. He wrote:

> The doctrine of individual freedom before the state is due to the Christian religion which asserts the dignity and worth of every human soul, the accountability to God of each man for himself, and lays it down as a law for every one that God is to be obeyed rather than men. The Church practically denied the absolutism of the state, and asserted for every man rights not held from the state, in converting the empire to Christianity, in defiance of state authority and the imperial edicts punishing with death the profession of the Christian faith.
> In this she practically, as well as theoretically, overthrew state absolutism, and infused into modern society the doctrine that every individual, even the lowest and meanest, has rights which the state neither confers nor can abrogate; and it will be only by extinguishing in modern society the Christian faith, and obliterating all traces of Christian civilization, that state absolutism can be revived with more than a partial and temporary success.[46]

The illustrious historian, Dr. Arnold J. Toynbee, has given us in more recent times some parallel thoughts on this thesis. When lecturing here in 1955 he stressed that religion, particularly the Judeo-Christian tradition, is the one and only basis of freedom. But Western man began late in the seventeenth century to shift the emphasis of his thinking from theology to science and technology. Today, he continued, he is in a position of practicing a technological way of life and still believing in freedom without believing in its religious foundation. History teaches that this paradox can not long continue. He warned: "We must choose, and choose soon, between losing our freedom or re-establishing its religious foundation."[47]

Perhaps Brownson's most original contribution to American political science is his doctrine that our American system of government is a "territorial democracy," that is, that all the political rights, powers and franchises of the American people are theirs only as fixed to the American soil.[48] This doctrine underscores in turn his concept of the state as an organism. He put forth the doctrine that the state is not a mere collection of individuals, an amorphous mass of people, but is organic in its nature, living a life of its own, and functioning through its own internal vitality. To him: "Society . . . is an organism, and individuals live in its life as well as in theirs. There is a real living solidarity, which makes individuals members of the social body, and members one of another. There is no society without individuals, and there are no individuals without society; but in society there is that which is not individual, and is more than all individuals."[49] (He obviously drew here to a degree on the doctrine of the solidarity of the human race put forth by Pierre Leroux, the French philosopher.) This organic nature of the state derives from the basic unwritten constitution of the state, and is in stark contrast to the "contractarian theory" of the state, whether represented by Hobbes, Locke, or Rousseau — implying nothing more than an artificial concept of the state. That Brownson set considerable store by this organismic concept of the state is evident. Francis G. Wilson has remarked: "In the years following the Confederate War, the organismic theory of the State was an idea that writer after writer picked up and used to explain the principles of national existence in the United States. In general, however, we must say that Brownson stands alone in the peculiar emphasis of his thought."[50]

When pronouncing our system of government a "territorial democracy," Brownson noted that the phrase had been previously used by the British statesman, Benjamin Disraeli, "with more propriety perhaps," he remarked, "than he thinks."[51] Opposed to territorial democracy, in Brownson's analysis of the Civil War era, stood two other types of democracy: personal or egotistical democracy, and socialistic or humanitarian democracy. Personal or egotistical democracy, which had become strongest in the slave-holding states, was the closest North American approximation to the feudal nobility of medieval Europe, where each and every landed master was largely a law to himself. This personal democracy was further fostered by the Southern doctrine of state sovereignty which was fiercely opposed to that other erroneous type of democracy: socialistic or humanitarian democracy. This type of democracy, rampant in the North, was represented mainly by the abolitionists who saw their cause as transcending all laws or constitutions of state, and had its counterpart in European Jacobinism or red republicanism. The personal or egotistical democracy of the South, said Brownson, had been scotched in the Civil War, but humanitarian democracy he saw as still on the march.[52] It was the "humanitarian" doctrine of Wendel Phillips, William Lloyd Garrison and the abolitionists generally, who were, as Ross Hoffman remarks, a reflection of the Mazzinian revolutionary sects of the day and the easily recognized ancestors of the "anti-fascist" democrats of more recent times.[53] This "humanitarian" party, whether at home or abroad, said Brownson, "loses men in humanity, sacrifices the rights of men in a vain endeavor to secure the rights of man, as your Calvinist or brother Jensenist sacrifices the rights of nature in order to secure the freedom of grace."[54] This party boasted in 1865 that the victory of the North in the Civil War was exclusively its own. Throughout the world, noted Brownson, they were in ecstasies over it. "The European socialists and red republicans applaud it, and the Mazzinis and Garibaldis inflict upon us the deep humiliation of their congratulations."[55] But with Brownson it was a certainty that they had miscalculated the meaning of the victory: "In spite of all that had been done by theorists, radicals, and revolutionists . . . to corrupt the American people in mind, heart and body, the native vigor of their national constitution has enabled them to come forth triumphant from the trial." "When the smoke of battle has cleared away," he affirmed, "the victory, it will be seen, has been won by the republic [that is, territorial democracy], and that that alone has triumphed."[56]

Referring to Brownson's discussion of these three types of democracy, Professors Thomas I. Cook and Arnaud B. Leavelle said in their erudite study of *The American Republic*:

> Brownson's tripartite analysis of democracy, and his attempt to achieve a balance between extremes in his concept of territorial democracy, is probably the most original and most fruitful aspect of his theory. He deals with the same material or classical political theory that had been explored by such thinkers as Adams, Madison, Wilson, and Calhoun, but gives it an entirely new synthesis. He draws upon and is consistent with Catholic dogma, yet reaches a conclusion capable of application to secular society.[57]

Scarcely less original with Brownson is his doctrine on where political sovereignty resides in our American political system, and his definition of barbarism. From 1828 to 1861, following Calhoun again, as already noted, he had held the doctrine of separate state sovereignty, but changed when the Civil War had jolted him into a study of the real historical facts lying back of the written Constitution. Thereafter he still held that the states are sovereign, not severally, however, but unitedly, as political entities in the federal Union, still governing autonomously in their respective territories and sharing in the powers and functions of the federal or general government. This division of powers between the general and state governments provides effective safeguards against the centralization of power on the one hand and its distintegration on the other.[58] Fr. J. P. Donovan, C.M., J.C.D., stressed Brownson's contribution here when he wrote: "He went beyond other builders of the science of public law because he was dealing with a new element in the evolution of civil society. That element is the civic polity peculiar to America, a polity which first through the natural and then the written constitution of the United States effectively guards against the twin evils of all previously existing forms of government: local autonomy to the point of disintegration and strong central government to the point of Caesarism."[59]

The unique mark of barbarism consists, Brownson held, in the annexation of power to private property or domain; whereas civilization annexes power to public domain, or the state, the population being fixed to the soil. All civilized governments are, therefore, territorial or republican, founded on *res publica*.[60] On December 26, 1865, in a letter to his friend, Fr. Edward F. Sorin, founder of Notre Dame University, he remarked that the first two points enumerated in his letter, namely, his definition of territorial democracy, and his assertion, against the consolidationists, that political sovereignty resides in the states, but in the states united, not severally, against the secessionists, were new doctrines in political science, and had been made, as far as his knowledge extended, by no writer before him. He felt that perhaps, too, his definition of barbarism versus civilization was original with him. He mentioned that the first and third points came to mind while he was writing his book.[61]

Merle Curti has noted that the impact of the Civil War on social thought brought forth a wide variety of interpretations of that gigantic struggle. Among those contributing was Orestes A. Brownson who speculated "with no less feeling than learning on the meaning of the war. His *American Republic,* indebted to St. Thomas, Suárez, and other Catholic lights, rejected the doctrine of the state of nature, natural rights, undiluted individualism, and democratic theory. But if Brownson seemed to be out of line with the majority of his fellow citizens in these particulars, he was with the incoming tide in his attribution of the national sovereignty not to the several states, but to the states united as integral and organic parts of the nation."[62]

No doubt Brownson did reject the natural "rights" of man as asserted by the liberal "contractarians," but not the inalienable rights of man as God-given and anterior to society. It is not entirely clear in what sense Merle Curti asserts that Brownson rejected "democratic theory." Brownson had always accepted democratic theory when expressed through the country's political organism, the rule of the majority, but rejected it when expressed by a mere inorganic mob. And nowhere does he appear more decidedly the democrat than in his book, *The American Republic.* He labeled our form of government, as we have just seen, "a territorial democracy," and awarded to the people themselves the credit for the winning of the Civil War.

"Nothing," he said, "is more certain than that the people have saved the national unity and integrity almost in spite of the government. The general government either was not disposed or was afraid to take a decided stand against secession, till forced to do so by the people themselves. No wise American can henceforth distrust American democracy. The people must be trusted. So much is settled.[63] But it is decidedly true that no American ever lambasted more unsparingly the excesses of ill-regulated democracy, or the foibles of the American people in the political order. It was always done, however, in mercy and hope for the betterment of the country he loved so dearly. As Russell Kirk has remarked: "No man ever was bolder than Brownson in his criticism of American smugness and cant; no man ever loved this country more."[64]

But there is more to Brownson's *The American Republic* than just his philosophy of our political system. He indulged also rather freely, if a bit perilously, in political prophecy. His forecast that the United States would have a strong hand in the settling of European affairs has taken on a novel significance since World War II. He clearly foresaw that "the hegemony of the New World belongs to the United States, and she will have a potent voice in adjusting the balance of power even in Europe."[65] In short, he predicted for the United States "a continental destiny"[66] . . . as foreshadowed by the so-called Monroe Doctrine:

> Of all the states or colonies on this continent, the American republic alone has a destiny, or the ability to add any thing to the civilization of the race. Canada and the other British provinces, Mexico and Central America, Colombia and Brazil, and the rest of the South American states, might be absorbed into the United States without being missed by the civilized world. They represent no idea, and the work of civilization could go on without them as well as with them.[67]

He envisioned these states as being eventually annexed to the American Union. But there was no jingoism in it all. There was no notion that it would be through subjugation or conquest. These various states, he was inclined to believe, would be drawn within the orbit of the United States in due course as naturally as the magnet draws its object — through the compelling force of the highest type of civilized government on this Western continent. They would be freely drawn on terms of perfect equality, sharing "alike the power and the protection of the republic — alike its authority, its freedom, its grandeur, its glory, as one free, independent, self-governing people. They can gain much, but lose nothing by annexation."[68]

Ross Hoffman has spoken of these predictions of Brownson as slightly marring his book. They appeared to him as "extravangances" which seemed out of touch with historical realism. He saw in them the ideologist rather than the pragmatist. But apart from them, he rated Brownson's book "a masterpiece of American political wisdom."[69] It is fair to note, however, that Brownson did not forecast the absorption of these states as a certainty, but only regarded it as the natural "destiny of the American people, which nothing but their own fault could prevent them from realizing in its own good time."[70] Moreover, it should not be forgotten that Brownson wrote *The American Republic* at a time when some vague notion of the doctrine of "Manifest Destiny," possibly extending beyond the nation's boundaries, was still in the air. As Professors Cook and Leavelle note, the only instances of peaceful annexation in the history of the country since Brownson's time have been Alaska, the Hawaiian Islands and the Canal Zone.[71] They also mention the Philippines, but that nation was granted its independence as the Republic of the Philippines on July 4, 1946.

A cardinal defect vitiating the constitutions of these states on the periphery of the American Republic Brownson found to be the abnormal relationship between church and state, religion and politics. "It may be safely asserted," he affirmed, "that, except in the United States, the church is either held by the civil power in subjection, or treated as an enemy. The relation is not that of union and harmony, but that of antagonism, to the grave detriment of both religion and civilization."[72] But under the American constitution church and state have been placed permanently in their normal relations, with the right of neither to absorb or encroach upon the other. Inasmuch as the relation of church and state has ever been a burning question in every age, and inasmuch as there has been much dialogue in our own times and country on whether a Catholic President could be trusted to keep church and state apart, it will be interesting to listen to our American Catholic political philosopher on the relation of these two powers. He wrote:

> The religious mission of the United States is not . . . to establish the [Catholic] church by external law, or to protect her by legal disabilities, pains, or penalties against the sects, however, uncatholic they may be; but to maintain Catholic freedom, neither absorbing the state in the church nor the church in the state, but leaving each to move freely, according to its own nature, in the sphere assigned it in the eternal order of things. Their mission separates church and state as external governing bodies, but unites them in the interior principles from which each derives its vitality and force. . . . The effect of this mission of our country fully realized, would be to harmonize church and state, religion and politics, not by absorbing either in the other, but by conforming both to the real or divine order, which is supreme and immutable.[73]

That Brownson avoided extremes and hit a fair balance in his general views expressed in *The American Republic,* thus imparting perennial value to his thought, is vouched for by Professors Cook and Leavelle: "It is precisely that balance between a moderate conservatism and a constructive liberalism that gives Brownson's thought its significance and its appositeness today. By avoiding a static conservatism, on the one hand, and a radicalism unrelated to social and moral realities on the other, he demonstrated that true conservatism and true liberalism are not necessarily opposed, but simply two sides of the same shield."[74]

The reception given *The American Republic* on its first appearance was not flattering to Brownson. Trying to explain the matter later, he wrote: "It was condemned at the North as southern, and at the South as northern; it was abused at both North and South because it was dedicated to my old friend George Bancroft, by Protestants because written by a Catholic, and by Catholics because it did not favor their political prejudices."[75]

More can now be added on this head. To begin, obviously, *The American Republic* is not an easy book to read and master. One readily understands that Woodrow Wilson would appreciate its high intellectual quality, as well as Ross Hoffman, who remarked that the book "is packed with a kind of political wisdom that is very scarce but almost desperately needed today."[76] But not all people are Woodrow Wilsons or Ross Hoffmans. Not only is the book profoundly philosophical, but it is also conspicuously laced with Catholic theology. In bestowing his encomium on the book, Woodrow Wilson did not overlook to mention that Brownson was a Catholic.[77] Brownson himself, when speaking of his writing the book, remarked: "I am a Catholic by God's grace and great goodness, and I must write as I am."[78] In a letter to Fr. Edward Sorin, he also remarked: "The book can be duly appreciated only by a Catholic theologian." The fact is that in writing the treatise he was still the vigorous Catholic apologist as well as the ardent American patriot. In the same letter to Fr. Sorin, he added: "The book perhaps has more in it than every one will discover, but it at any rate, is an honest book, patriotic, but in my belief, profoundly Catholic, and really the best argument for Catholicity that I have published. I can write nothing better."[79]

Here we have reasons which militated from the beginning against the book's popular reception and wide circulation. Brownson went too unreservedly to theology, and Catholic theology at that, for a sturdy underpinning of his political doctrines or philosophy to suit the popular taste.[80] Robert Emmet Moffit has shown good insight into this matter when he wrote:

> Perhaps one major objection to Brownson's thought stems from his theological intrusions into his general political theory. . . . The concept that the state has its origins in God, that it is the earthly handmaid of the Lord in this world, bringing men to greater perfection is a recurrent theme in political theory [Augustine, Aquinas, Locke and Burke are prime examples]. However, the most provocative aspect of this theme in Brownson is in his unabashed appeals to the truth of God in a visible, historical institution, the Roman Catholic Church.

> It is certainly understandable, at least in historical retrospect, why so many Americans would have been hostile to Brownson's interpretation of political theory. His declarations that there exists no real separation between the natural and the supernatural, and that the state must look to the Roman Catholic Church for moral guidance, were hard, and to many, unpalatable assertions. Such appeals, unquestionably, militate against the traditional American principle of separation between Church and State, a principle well established and so religiously guarded by our judicial institutions. Moreover, such a stringent appeal to the moral authority of any religious institution would be of dubious value in an age in which secular trends have been advancing steadily.[81]

One may well doubt whether Brownson himself ever expected his book to receive wide acclaim in his own day. And it can be just as readily believed that he wrote in his mind's eye for the ages, that he firmly believed that an exposition of the right order in government and politics, as intended by the Creator, would alone provide the right answers and would alone stand the test of time. And in that sense and on that score future generations may yet appreciate his book more fully than it has been appreciated to date. He remarked that Catholics as a class are better fitted than others to understand the American Constitution when they study it in the light of their theology,[82] and it is well known that he never gave up hope that this great nation would one day be Catholic, through a gradual process.

Although Brownson called our American government "the model republic,"[83] and remarked that "I cannot conceive a more profoundly philosophic, or more admirably devised constitution, than that of our American government, as I have endeavored truthfully to present in my *American Republic*,"[84] he knew as well as any man that nothing human is ever perfect. No government intrusted to men can secure all good, and avoid all evils. From imperfect man you can never get perfection. But he considered the American Constitution, taken as a whole, in all its parts, the least imperfect that has ever existed, and felt that under it individual rights, personal freedom and independence, as well as public authority, are better secured than under any other form of government. The few barbaric elements which linger from feudal society would be progressively eliminated as the whole population is molded to the American political ideal.[85]

Not therefore was he caught in any mania to export our type of government to other nations. Holding that every nation has a natural or providential constitution of its own given it, he set his face sternly against all political propagandism whether practiced by the British or his own countrymen in their febrile attempts to transplant their forms of government to other nations. "Forms of government," he said, "are like shoes — that is the best form which best fits the feet that are to wear them."[86] Hence shoes are to be fitted to feet, not feet to shoes, for feet vary in size and shape. To impose another form of government on a people different from the one given them by Providence Brownson considered a mad and disastrous policy. "The doctor," he said, "might as well attempt to give an individual a new constitution, or the constitution of another man, as the statesman to give a nation another constitution than that which it has, and with which it was born."[87]

Nor should we overlook the noble plea Brownson made for clemency for the Southern people of the states that had been defeated. In his chapter on reconstruction in *The American Republic* he expressed deep regrets over President Andrew Johnson's proclamation of May 29, 1865, disfranchising the *pars sanior* of the whole white Southern society. Of that proclamation he said: "It exceeded any thing ever issued in any age by the most barbarous chieftain. It virtually disfranchised and outlawed nearly the whole southern people, certainly every man who could render any efficient service in reorganizing southern society, and in repairing the disasters of the war."[88] This he proscribed as a wholly calamitous policy. What was most needed was to bring about a speedy restoration of the Southern people to citizenship, and thus bring North and South together in friendly and loyal cooperation in binding up the nation's wounds. To inflict on the Southern people unnecessary and ill-timed pains and penalties would only be to disgrace the whole American character and people before the world since the Southern people were a product of the American soil, and a part of the free growth of the American Republic. "The wise Romans," he reminded the Northern victors, "never allowed a triumph to a Roman general for victories, however brilliant, won over Romans."[89] Clemency was called for, too, on the score that the secessionists could not well be charged with the moral crime of treason. For they had held with the majority of Americans the doctrine of state sovereignty, and on that doctrine they were justified in seceding, although the government had the right and the duty, when attacked, to use force to preserve the national unity and integrity of the national domain.

In his protest against President Johnson's proclamation disfranchising practically the whole Southern white population, this strict constitutionalist again laid down what he considered the only correct procedure in the reconstruction of the seceded states:

The general government may concede or withhold permission to the disorganized state to reorganize, as it judges advisable, but it cannot itself reorganize it. If it concedes permission, it must leave the whole electoral people under the pre-existing electoral law free to take part in the work of reorganization, and to vote according to their judgment. It has no authority to purge the electoral people, and to say who may and who may not vote, for the whole question of suffrage and qualifications of electors is left to the state, and can be settled neither by an act of congress nor by an executive proclamation.[90]

In the light of this, he held that the whole series of Republican congressional legislation, bearing on the Negro question, including the Thirteenth, Fourteenth and Fifteenth Amendments, to have been unconstitutionally adopted, even though demanded by the governing majority, "and enforced by the federal courts and bayonets wherever resisted."[91] Touching on the Thirteenth Amendment in particular (abolishing slavery), he affirmed that if the ratification of any of the states that had seceded was necessary for its validity, it was never ratified by the requisite number of states, for the ratification of such states was obtained under coercion, was not free, and hence counted for nothing. The Fourteenth and Fifteenth Amendments (dealing with suffrage and eligibility) he held to be unconstitutional on the ground that they war against the most sacred and fundamental principle of the Constitution, which leaves the whole question to the states themselves.[92] All three, then, he held to have been imposed by arbitrary power, and as such to be unconstitutional, "unless the free acquiescence of, at least, three-fourths of the states have given them, which we doubt, a *quasi*-legality."[93] The double-dealing policy that had characterized the federal government's handling of the states that had seceded, he again indicted sharply.

> To treat the quondam states as simply territory under the jurisdiction of the Union was for the government to stultify itself, and to deny the ground it had taken throughout the war. So it held that of contradictories both may be true, and treated them as states and no-states, as it suited its purposes. When it wanted their votes for amending the Constitution, it held them to be sovereign states; when it wanted to govern them and compel them to vote according to its wishes, it held them to be no-states, but simply unorganized population and territory.[94]

Curiously enough, the late Fr. J. P. Donovan, ventured the opinion that *The American Republic* lacks only one perfection of treatment. He noted that while Brownson included a chapter on secession and reconstruction, he has no specific chapter on amendments to the Constitution. He observed, however, that Elihu Root and Dr. Nicholas Murray Butler were later to stress the basic essentials in the matter, namely, that two thirds of Congress and three fourths of the states can add nothing to the Constitution but germane amendments, and that nothing less than unamimous consent is required for revolutionary amendments.[95]

Inasmuch as Brownson did not add a chapter on amendments in *The American Republic,* it may be assumed that the omission was made by design. Paul Conroy has remarked: "Brownson . . . did not regard the Constitution as a sacred fetish, but held that it should be changed from time to time to bring it into line with the providential growth of the nation."[96] On this score Brownson would of course have favored amendments truly germane to the genius of the American Constitution. But the fact remains that he does not seem to have believed in amendments overly much. He wrote: "We have little or no respect for written constitutions, and still less for constitutional amendments. Every people receives from Providence at its birth an unwritten constitution with which national life and prosperity are indissolubly linked, and any alteration of it or tampering with it, tends only to impair its vigor, and to enfeeble the nation."[97] He saw many of the amendments to the Constitution only fostering a "tendency to centralized democracy, to make the Federal government the supreme and only government, and the States mere prefectures."[98] The fear that seems to have haunted him here was well expressed by Robert E. Moffit: "What he [Brownson] dreaded was the evolution of a Leviathan state, a vast national centralization of authority . . . a politically consolidated empire."[99] Perhaps Brownson felt that a chapter on amendments in his book would have given the theme a greater dignity than it deserves, or that it might have unduly encouraged amendments.

Whatever the merits or demerits of Brownson's *The American Republic,* it is an intensely patriotic book which all American patriots should gladly see preserved for posterity. There are signs, too, that it is making its way into a more general appreciation. Professors Cook and Leavelle speak of the "happy fate of Orestes A. Brownson's *The American Republic* which has found its way into textbook discussions of American political ideals."[100] Notable, too, is the new edition of the book lately brought out by the Augustus D. Kelley publishers.[101] A popular edition in paperback has also been added by Fr. Americo D. Lapati. In his introduction to this new edition Fr. Lapati remarked: "If the *Federalist Papers* of Madison, Hamilton, and Jay can be considered among the best as philosophical explanations on the formation of the American form of government, Brownson's *The American Republic* ought to enjoy a similar evaluation as a philosophical exposition of the Union restored after the Civil War."[102] Writing in the *Atlantic Monthly,* June 1896, George Parsons Lathrop said of Brownson's *The American Republic:*

> Never has the genius of our country and our nationhood been so grandly, so luminously interpreted, from so lofty a point of view, as in this masterly book, published when he was 62. Milford's The Nation, which I have already mentioned, was brought out five years later. One may note the remarkable correspondences and the greater depth and broader sweep of Brownson's exposition.[103]

# 44

## MORE ON BROWNSON'S PHILOSOPHY AND THE CHARGE OF ONTOLOGISM

*The nature of Brownson's philosophical treatise,* An Essay in Refutation of Atheism • *After an intermission covering 1844-1849, he begins again his philosophical investigations • He borrows from Vincenzo Gioberti the formula,* Ens creat existentias • *His defense of the formula creates for him a peck of trouble • The more prominent Catholic critics who accused him of ontologism • Testimony of persons knowledgeable in the field of philosophy that he was not an ontologist • He insists that philosophy is strictly a rational science, and is not served by the unquestioned authority of great names • The reason why he took such deep interest in philosophy.*

While writing *The American Republic,* Brownson discussed its nature and content with his friend, Senator Charles Sumner, and then added that if Divine Providence spared his health and life, it would be only one in a series of books he contemplated writing — on philosophy, theology, and the Catholic Church.[1] Later he specified that the first of these works "will refute Atheism, and demonstrate Theism; the second will prove the supernatural and the Christian revelation against Deism, Materialism, Naturalism, etc. The fourth — the Church; the fifth, ethics; the American Republic concluding the series."[2] From the time of his letter to Senator Sumner in 1865, he had toyed off and on with the idea of completing these ambitious works, but the first one proposed, namely, the one on philosophy, is the only one he ever realized besides *The American Republic.* He had originally intended to publish it in book form, but as he finished it only a short time before he revived his *Review* in 1873, he decided to publish it serially in the *Review.* In it he dealt more fully with the epistemological problem than he had done in the synthetic philosophy he had formulated in 1843 and 1844. Concerning this *Essay in Refutation of Atheism,* Fr. Joseph P. Donovan, C.M., has remarked:

> Brownson, at his entrance of the Church, in 1843 and early 1844, was toiling for data to build a science of epistemology, a science that Noel contends is not yet formulated. Then, thirty-two years later, in his formal attempt to refute atheism, Brownson endeavored to achieve what Maritain maintains is a problem yet unsolved by New Scholasticism, namely, to carry back the principles of St. Thomas, on knowledge, far enough to meet scientifically (and not merely popularly), the objection raised by Kant and all modern subjectivism.
>
> After first stating, like a prophet of common sense of all the ages, that the existence of God is in possession and that the atheist can never oust that presumption, because the truth of God's existence is so interwoven with the valid processes of human reason that its denial logically resolves itself into a negation of a negation, or an affirmation, is equivalent to a contradiction, or an assertation that evidences itself, Brownson proceeds to demonstrate the existence of God from an analysis of the elements of thought, drawing out their implications explicatively, not illatively, until he reaches the triumphant con-

clusion that Real Being at once Personal and Necessary exists, and is the Creator of the Universe and Founder of the moral order.

Such a vital question as that of certainty is disposed of as an incident. Nor does the forward sweep of reasoning ever lose sight of such concrete realities as the human soul and its Maker linked by the inescapable fact of thought. The miracle we have spoken of Brownson seeing in every article of St. Thomas is truly renewed in this remarkable essay in refutation of atheism. Brownson thus showed in his old age the same acumen to deal with the alpha and omega of philosophy that in his young manhood he had exhibited in mastering the thought systems of the ancient and modern world and at times re-stating them with more persuasiveness than their authors had first attained.[3]

The kernel of this argument for the existence of God, as Fr. Donovan indicated, is carefully built on his analysis of thought. Of the process of this analysis of thought Brownson spoke in a letter to his son Henry. He explained that thought is composed of three elements: subject, object and their relation simultaneously given. He then proceeded to the analysis of the object, which is also composed of three elements, simultaneously given: the ideal, the empirical and their relation. The ideal is given in intuition, which must be distinguished from perception or distinct cognition. The ideal is the activity of the object; in cognition or empirical intuition, the cognition *a posteriori* of Kant, both the subject as well as the object act. The ideal intuition answers to the phantasmata or intelligible species of the Schoolmen. It presents, they say represents, the object. In the sensibles the *intellectus agens,* or reflection, takes the object presented immediately from the presentation; the ideal, though presented, can only be taken as represented in language, the sensible representation of the ideal.

He went on to say that he had identified the ideas with the Categories, and reduced their number to three: being, existences and their relation. The necessary or apodictic ideas he integrated into being, and their correlatives into existences. He then showed that the relation (between being and existences) is the creative act of being, whence he proves that being is God, personal because he has intelligence and free will. To this he added four more chapters: one on existences; another on God as Final Cause, in which he arrived at the moral law, which proceeds from God as Final Cause, in distinction from physical laws which proceed from him as first cause; in the next chapter he showed that the moral law commands us to worship God in the way and manner he prescribes, whether naturally or supernaturally; the last chapter is on the place and office of tradition.

He remarked to his son in conclusion that this skeletal outline could really tell him little of what his work really is, but that it would at least give him some idea of the nature of the argument, which had not been constructed without hard thinking.[4]

However clear-cut in Brownson's own mind the meaning of his philosophical terms, they were not always equally clear to all his readers. Like so many other philosophers of the nineteenth century, he used unusual terminology to express his philosophical ideas. The term "intuition" is in itself somewhat baffling. In some instances Brownson explained his terms, but in other instances he seems to have taken it for granted that his readers remembered his former explanations, and did not elaborate. This at times left his meaning open to question. Some of his enemies, it would appear, who could not grapple with him successfully on other heads, more than welcomed this as an opportunity to get back at him by twisting his real meaning or at least so construing it to make him out an ontologist. Not all have been as conscientiously disposed to get at a right understanding of his philosophy as was Joseph Henning, C.SS.R., a theological student, who, writing to Brownson for a further elucidation of some points of his philosophy, ended, saying: "I would not, for all the treasures of earth, misunderstand or misrepresent your meaning."[5] Some, too, however, because of Brownson's unusual terminology, may well have misunderstood his philosophy in all innocence.

Since the charge that Brownson was an ontologist will be dealt with rather fully in the course of this chapter, a word on the meaning of the term is called for. The essential tenet of ontologism is that the human mind has a direct and immediate perception of the existence of God, bypassing the necessity of any rational process in the case. Notice will be taken, in the proper place, of some of the more prominent persons who have brought this charge against our American philosopher.

There is no intention here to review in detail Brownson's many, many massive philosophical articles stretching over a quarter of a century during his Catholic career. Such a project could well be expanded into a volume or two. But some notice must be taken of his philosophical writings for he remarked near the end of his life that philosophy had been his "chief study for half a century."[6] And not without success. His philosophical erudition is truly astonishing. A journal published at Rome, entitled *Correspondance de Rome,* after referring to some of Brownson's philosophical writings in its issue of February 24, 1852, remarked: "The writer shows that he is a perfect master as well of the different ancient as of the modern philosophical systems, and possesses an intelligent appreciation of facts and doctrines."[7] This encomium was matched on this side of the Atlantic by a tribute from a polemical adversary of Brownson in *The Christian Register* when he said of him: "He has analyzed and thoroughly possessed himself of more systems of philosophy than other reputed scholars have even looked at."[8] The truth of this will become at once evident to anyone who delves into Brownson's philosophical writings.

For the first four or five years after his conversion, Brownson shelved his philosophical investigations. Being under the compulsion as a Catholic apologist to give a close study to Catholic theology, only such philosophy as was a part of the theological treatises which engaged his attention came under his notice. This apparently was enough, however, to keep his mind working in the way of revising his own philosophical tenets, though he did no writing on philosophy as such during these years. His last piece of philosophical writing had been his refutation of Kant's philosophy in 1844. In the development of his philosophical thought, he acknowledged, as we have previously observed, his indebtedness to Victor Cousin and Pierre Leroux. Though he imbibed much from Leroux that was unsound (he had the questionable honor of being the first to introduce him to the American public), it was Leroux who had taught him to substitute the ontological for the psychological method in philosophizing. But in the years following 1844, reexamining his philosophical principles, Brownson found that the ontological method taken alone leads to pantheism, and the psychological method taken alone leads to egoism or atheism. Each by itself is sophistical. It is the combination or synthesis of the two, and their essential relation, united by the creative act, that is the key to basic reality. This truth he expressed by the formula: Being creates all that exists.

While thus revising mentally his philosophical system, he was at length recalled to philosophical writing in 1849 when William B. Greene, a Unitarian minister and former associate, sent him for review a copy of his book,

*Remarks on the Science of History; followed by an a priori Autobiography.* To this book Brownson gave a thirty-eight page review in the January 1850 issue of his *Quarterly,* in which he tilted full force at exclusive psychologism in philosophy, which, stemming from Descartes, has vitiated all modern philosophy. In a letter to his friend, Fr. J. W. Cummings, he explained briefly his own philosophy as embodied in the article he had written. He had come to the conclusion many years previously, he said, that it is impossible to think without the presence of the intelligible. Hence the intelligible cannot be sought and found by the intellect, but must present and reveal itself.

From this conclusion follows either no intellection, no knowledge, no philosophy, or the intelligible reveals and affirms itself to us, or that the principles of philosophy are furnished us only as they are revealed to us in direct and immediate intuition. At the same time he came to the conclusion that from the simple conception of being, *ens reale est,* it is impossible to deduce the conception of existences, and that therefore either dead pantheism or autotheism, or direct and immediate intuition of existences, that is of the formula, *Ens reale creator est.* This formula contained for him all the necessary principles of philosophy, and inasmuch as what is intuitively known is a genuine revelation of the intelligible by itself, it was clear to him that the principles of philosophy are and must be divinely revealed or given. To pretend that we ourselves seek and find them is to deny the possibility of philosophy, and to place it on the route to skepticism and nihilism, or nullism. For the intellect does not exist, or at least cannot operate, until it is activated by the presence of the intelligible.

It was this philosophy — which he called the philosophy of realism — that he pitted against "the dead abstractions of modern psychologism." In this same letter to Fr. Cummings, he remarked: "I have struck at the whole fabric of modern philosophy, and have endeavored to revive the philosophy of St. Augustine and the great doctors of the Church. It is possible I shall disturb a hornet's net, but my bishop has given me his imprimatur."[9]

It is at this point in Brownson's career that we encounter a factor that was to stack the cards in the minds of some against a right interpretation of his philosophy, namely, his relationship to Abbé Gioberti, the Piedmontese philosopher, tenuous though it was. In a letter to Fr. Isaac Hecker in September of 1871, he remarked: "I own, however, that I have not been explicit enough to avoid being misunderstood by those who hate Gioberti."[10] Greatly as he admired Gioberti's philosophical genius, he really took nothing more from him than the formula, *Ens creat existentias,* which only gave expression to the philosophical principles he had himself worked out before he had ever heard of Gioberti. What he gave Gioberti credit for was supplying him with a more exact terminology, and thus aiding him to guard against pantheism.[11] Already in his article on "Schools of Philosophy," January 1854, he declared that he had felt from the beginning, long before Gioberti's works were prohibited by the Index, "that he was a dangerous man, whom it would never do to take as a master, and certainly we cannot bind ourselves to any defense of his philosophy."[12]

Although he questioned in this same article Gioberti's interpretation of the formula, *Ens creat existentias,* he set great store by that formula itself, even asserting later "that prior to the perfection of the Giobertian formula, philosophy was not, and could not be a science."[13] The whole matter was further bedeviled by the fact that Gioberti was the author of a terrible work against the Society of Jesus, the *Jesuita Moderno,* in five octavo volumes.

After the publication of that work, as Brownson said, "it was more than any Catholic's reputation with his brethren was worth to venture to speak well of him as a philosopher."[14] This was particularly true after Rome's condemnation of ontologism in 1861, shedding a dark light over Gioberti. Yet it was an admirable trait in Orestes Brownson to give credit where he honestly believed credit was due, no matter how loud the howl that might be put up. "We undertake no defense of Gioberti as a man, as a politician, or as an Italian patriot," he said, "but we will never suffer our dislike of the person to prejudice us against the truth he asserts."[15] He honestly believed that the Giobertian formula, *Ens creat existentias,* was a highly important contribution to philosophical science, and he dared to say so to the end, *ruat coelum.*[16] But he paid dearly for his audacity. As Arthur M. Schlesinger, Jr., has observed: "Gioberti's disgrace became a club which Brownson's enemies in the Church used energetically against him."[17]

But to return to his article on "An A Priori Autobiography." Brownson stressed in that article in 1850 the crucial distinction between intuition and reflection,[18] but stated it perhaps more formally in his article on "The Existence of God," April 1852. His own philosophical proofs for the existence of God he confirmed with copious extracts from St. Augustine who affirmed that in all our intellectual operations, as a necessary condition, we have intuition of the unchangeable, the necessary, the eternal. As the unchangeable, the necessary, the eternal is God, Brownson concluded that we have intuition of God. But lest he be misunderstood to imply direct and immediate intuition of God, he asserted that we must distinguish between the intuition of that which is God, and the intuition of God, as God. This he did in unmistakable terms when he said: "This intuition is like all intuitions, indistinct, indefinite, and we do not from it alone ever know or become able to affirm that its object is God. To know this it is necessary to reflect on the object of intuition as represented to us in language, or sensible signs."[19]

It was also in his article on "An A Priori Autobiography" that Brownson first acknowledged his indebtedness to the Italian philosopher, Vincenzo Gioberti. Before writing his article, he had read the first four chapters of the Abbé's *Introduzione allo studio della Filosofia.* The reading had constantly cleared up his own views, so much so that "without it," he said, "I certainly should not have, and perhaps could not, have written it."[20] He added a footnote to that article making all suitable acknowledgments to Gioberti, at least as far as prudence at the moment would allow, for he knew full well that Gioberti was in "bad odor." Besides, he had not yet mastered his thought, and did not know to what extent he agreed with him. Some were disposed to see only pantheism in the formula, *Ens creat existentias.*[21]

What laid both Gioberti and also Brownson open to easy charges of heterodoxy in philosophy was the somewhat mystifying term, *intuition.* Commenting on this the late Fr. Joseph P. Donovan, C.M., said:

> The term used by Gioberti and also Brownson was unfortunate. I mean *intuition;* because by common use that connotes direct and immediate knowledge of self-evident things, and God and creatures are not known directly and immediately but are discovered by a long process of reasoning. But a little experience leads us to the notion of dependency; and from that we infer independence indirectly. In fact, as Brownson always contended, as soon as we arrive at the notion of dependence, we have already reached by indirection the notion of independence. In other words, God in creating the human intellect gives these two principles in their relation, the relation being the same creative act; and by long reasoning we discover that the very operative principles of reasoning when translated into knowledge spells the synthesis: *Ens creat existentias.*[22]

It was precisely the word "intuition" or "objective intuition" that created all the difficulty for William G. Ward, the Oxford convert, who, as we have noted, indulged in some swordplay with Brownson over Newman's theory of the development of Christian doctrine. Ward had been professor of dogmatic theology at Old Hall in England from 1852 to 1858. As a result of his dogmatic studies he published in 1860 a work entitled *Nature and Grace* with a lengthy introduction in which Brownson is given considerable notice. This volume Ward sent to Brownson for a review. Though he spoke in very courteous terms, Brownson subjected Ward's philosophy to a severe criticism, sternly rejecting what he understood to be Ward's psychologism.[23] He was also at some pains to explain the basic principles of his own philosophy to Ward, which, as he saw it, Ward had misunderstood.

Brownson and Ward did not exchange correspondence over this matter. But there was in England at the time an accomplished young Benedictine priest, Fr. Robert E. Guy, spoken of already. His Benedictine name was Brother Ephrem, and he was at the time prefect of studies at St. Gregory's College, Downside, in England. He was truly a great admirer of Brownson as a philosopher, and counted himself his disciple. He was preparing a textbook on philosophy, and sent Brownson an extended outline of the book for criticism and suggestions. He posed to Brownson a number of queries, and added: "You can scarcely imagine the eagerness with which I — and there are many others in a similar case — look for enlightenment on these fundamental points. Indeed I feel it almost impossible to proceed with my studies unless I am satisfied with respect to them. May I earnestly beg of you, dear sir, to favor me frequently with the results of your study of these all important points."[24] It was this Benedictine scholar who at this time acted as a go-between in the case of Brownson and Ward. Already a few months before Brownson's criticism of Ward's book, Fr. Guy had reported to Brownson in a letter, dated August 9, 1860, that Ward had remarked of his (Brownson's) philosophy:

> My own opinion about Brownson's philosophy is this: Those whom you call the psychologists are quite wrong; their philosophy is nothing better than contemptible. On the other hand, Brownson's formula *deserves* to be true; it makes such an admirable foundation for philosophy and is all-sufficient. But I have never been able (to my great regret) to see a *particle* of evidence for its truth.[25]

Several months after Brownson's review of Ward's work on *Nature and Grace* had appeared, in January 1861, Fr. Guy wrote Brownson another letter on August 17, 1861, in which he referred to a note Ward had written him on Brownson's criticism of his work, and which Fr. Guy wished to send Brownson, but could not at the moment lay his hand on it. He added:

> He begged me to thank you for the very kind way in which you had spoken of him personally and to assure you how much esteem he had for you as a good Catholic and a powerfully philosophical writer. . . . I have just ended a criticism of what he deemed to be the pith of your philosophic doctrines. He drew it up soon after your article on his book appeared — and I need hardly say that in some important points he (to my mind) misunderstood you.[26]

But it was in his article, "A Few Words on Dr. Brownson's Philosophy," in the *Dublin Review* quite some years later that Ward had his say on Brownson's philosophy. He acknowledged that he could follow Brownson's philosophy up to a certain point, but beyond that he found himself involved in obscurity and darkness. "Try as we may," he said, "to get a precise notion of Brownson's meaning, we fail. His words resolve themselves into ontologism, but he solemnly asserverates that he is no ontologist. We can only affirm that he is oracular and sibylline, and that we have no gift of interpreting the gods. He will say to us *'Favete linguis'* and we, not a whit displeased, are ready to depart." Before closing his article, Ward added: "The sooner ontologism is cleared out of the field the better it will be for the right and dispassionate examination of the Scholastic philosophy. And it is the efforts of such men as Dr. Brownson which most impedes this happy consummation."[27]

It is just possible that Ward was human enough to give Brownson tit for tat in saying that his philosophy was unintelligible. Brownson had previously said the very same thing of Ward himself in his article on "Catholic Popular Literature." Speaking of the *Dublin Review,* Brownson wrote:

> Dr. Ward, its editor, is an able man, and, we are told, is held by Englishmen to be a great writer and a profound philosopher. We acknowledge his ability and his learning, we love and honor the man; but, somehow or other, we can hardly read a page of his writings, no matter on what subject, without having our patience tried, or our irascibility excited, we would say, our pugnacity aroused, and we want to fight him, metaphorically, not literally. He writes good English, we suppose, but he is often well-nigh unintelligible to us. His philosophical articles are to us as unintelligible as Dr. Newman's "Essay at a Grammar of Assent," of which we can make neither head nor tail. It is our fault, we suppose. . . . In short, we are not of Dr. Ward's school of philosophy; and we believe the human reason, as far as it goes, sees things as they are, and as they are seen by superior intelligences.[28]

Another European scholar who accused Brownson of ontologism was Fr. John Healy, at the time professor at Maynooth Seminary, Ireland, and later archbishop of Tuam. Writing in the *Irish Ecclesiastical Record* in January 1884, he remarked: "In his philosophy, and Brownson was above all a man of philosophic mind, he was an ontologist. It is not easy to ascertain what phase of ontology he adopted, for he censures Malebranche, openly attacks Gioberti, sneers at the Rosminian *Ens in genere,* and pronounces the Germans to be, as they no doubt are, altogether heterodox ontologists. Yet we think the differences, at least in the first three cases, are only accidental, and that the ontologism of Brownson is radically as untenable and dangerous in its consequences as any of the systems he reprehends."[29] To support the accusation that Brownson was an ontologist, Healy quoted from Brownson's article on "The Existence of God." He said, "Brownson asserts that as a matter of fact every man in every act of intelligence, in every exercise of understanding, in every thought, apprehends and asserts *that which is God,* though he himself may not be distinctly conscious that such is the fact. His whole argument in favor of the existence of God is founded on the fact that the 'mind of man has immediate and direct intuition of being,' that this being is 'real being,' " and he adds, "it is equally certain that this real being is necessary and eternal being, and therefore God."[30]

But Healy unfortunately overlooked to note that Brownston in *this very same article* on the existence of God stressed definitely the crucial distinction between direct and immediate intuition of God, and the office of reflection, asserting that "this intuition is like all intuition, indistinct, indefinite, and we do not from it alone know or become able to affirm that its object is God. To know this, it is necessary to reflect on the object of intuition as represented to us in language, or sensible signs."[31] Is Healy's accusation in this case typical of those who have brought the charges of ontologism against Brownson, seizing on only one phase of his integral thought? In bringing his accusation Healy drew, too, on only one article, "The Existence of God," out of all Brownson's philosophical articles which fill three ponderous volumes. He frankly admitted he had not examined all of Brownson's philosophical essays.

Yet Brownson's son Henry freely admits that in his father's first articles on metaphysics as a Catholic there are some expressions — at least when standing alone — which would seem to indicate that he asserted direct and immediate intuition of God, but that he never intended to teach direct and immediate intuition of God, as God.[32] He further asserts that his father's essay on the Principle of Causality, in which he reviewed Hume's philosophical works in October 1855, marks an epoch in Brownson's philosophical life. Up to that time he had been steadily advancing toward the doctrine he then held, but that with the truth he was trying to bring out and establish, there had been "mingled some obscurity in his thought, and even some inaccuracy of expression."[33] It is on some expressions in the articles prior to 1855 that Brownson's critics have mainly seized, and turned them against the author, says Henry. Such in fact would fit the case of Healy perfectly who quoted only from Brownson's article on the existence of God in 1852.

Whatever the case, Brownson has been accused of ontologism, and it is a grave charge that should be further investigated. We are here dealing with a charge as it concerns his Catholic career. Henry Brownson says that from 1842 to 1844 his father should be classed as an ontologist, but holds that as a Catholic he was never an ontologist.[34] Brownson himself denied over and over again that he had ever been an ontologist after he had embraced the Catholic faith. What is the truth of the matter?

The first thrust to rebut this charge was made back in 1931 when Fr. Sidney Raemers, M.A., Ph.D., did a doctoral thesis at Notre Dame University on Brownson's philosophy under the title, "America's Foremost Philosopher." It appears that Fr. Joseph P. Donovan, C.M., already spoken of, had a great deal to do with this doctoral thesis, if he did not actually promote it in the first instance. It should be readily admitted at the outset, however, that because of Brownson's unusual terminology, at least in some instances, there is a question of getting at Brownson's real meaning. And Fr. Donovan, who coached Fr. Raemers on the thesis, claimed that he had a special advantage here. Besides writing the foreword to the thesis, Fr. Donovan had this to say to the present writer in a letter dated September 12, 1947:

> You will find what I call the authentic interpretation of Brownson's philosophy in Father Sidney Raemer's *America's Foremost Philosopher*. I was appointed by the Notre Dame Faculty to pass upon the thesis and I did. Before the final copy was made I spent fifteen hours here in the seminary [Kenrick] going over the book with the author with time out only for meals. I think I have the authentic meaning of Brownson because the priest I studied philosophy under was a disciple of Brownson as a young priest (the late Father P. V. Byrne, C.M.); and Father Byrne in turn was a disciple of Father Koop, C.M., an older man, who wrote in one of the last numbers of Brownson's Review an article entitled "The Possible Nothing in Itself." [Father Byrne used to quote Brownson as saying that Father Koop had the keenest mind he ever met with.][35]

In another letter, dated August 7, 1941, Fr. Donovan said of Fr.

Raemers' thesis: "Father Raemers gave a very closely documented study of Brownson's philosophy and concluded that if Brownson was not a pioneer in epistemology, he was surely not an ontologist. In fact no man in the language has given stronger refutations of ontologism."[36]

A great deal might be said about Fr. Raemers' thesis, but it must suffice to say that he seems to put his finger on the mistake of Brownson's critics when he states: "These critics of his have made the mistake of confounding intuition of God *by* the mind, with intuition of God *to* the mind, that is with God creating, conserving, and pre-moving the mind and concurring with it in its action."[37]

Another doctoral dissertation on Brownson's philosophy was done by Fr. Bertin Farrell, C.P., S.T.D., at the Catholic University of America, in 1950, under the title, *Orestes Brownson's Approach to the Problem of God.* Fr. Farrell goes into a review of Brownson's observations on the different arguments for the existence of God, and seems to contend that his thought is at least tinged with ontologism, if it is not actually obnoxious to the charge of ontologism. In his summary he says: "There are elements in Brownson's speculation on the existence of God which bear unmistakable resemblances to ontologism." And again, "There are times when he speaks of the *lumen rationis,* the *intellectus agens,* in such wise that he cannot possibly be absolved from ontologism."[38] We note here that he only asserts that "there are certain times" when he so speaks, which definitely brings up the question again as to what is the correct interpretation of what he really meant — in the light of all else that he wrote. It is only fair to interpret each part of his philosophy in the light of the whole. Brownson himself freely admitted, as we have noted in his letter to Fr. Isaac Hecker, that he had not at times been sufficiently cautious in his terminology to exclude the possibility of being *misinterpreted.*

Whatever else is to be said, Fr. Farrell's dissertation is gravely marred by the fact that he does not so much as refer to the very important letter Brownson wrote Fr. H. S. McMurdie, professor at Mt. St. Mary's College, Emmitsburg, Maryland. Fr. McMurdie had written Brownson making inquiries concerning the seven propositions censured by the Sacred Congregation of the Inquisition on September 18, 1861, and condemned as ontologism. Writing from Elizabeth, New Jersey, on May 9, 1862, Brownson said in reply:

Rev. and Dear Sir:

The propositions negatived by the S[acred] Congregation had been through the kindness of a friend previously sent me. On first glancing over them I thought some poor blunderhead has been trying to caricature & get condemned the doctrine defended in my *Review.* But a second reading satisfied me that the one who drew up the propositions could have had no reference to the ideal or synthetic philosophy either as held by me or taught by Gioberti. I suspect they are aimed at the French and Belgian ontologists, and perhaps, at the school of Ruthenflue or more properly, Pere Martin among the Jesuits.

I have never met any of the prohibited [propositions] *totidem verbis* in any author I have read, but I have heard something like them in conversation. But I am sure that neither you nor I, nor any one else who could claim to be even a tyro in philosophy, ever maintained the first proposition — *Immediata Dei Cognitio, saltem habitualis.* Pray, what is habitual cognition? Cognition is always an act, never a *habitus,* for habitus can be affirmed only of the cognitive faculty, never of cognition.

From there Brownson went into a brief examination of each of the condemned propositions, contrasting each with his own philosophy, and then added:

> These, Rev. & Dear Sir, are a few of the remarks that occur to me in answer to your inquiries. . . . There is not one of them that I should not myself, as I understand them, condemn. They seem to me to have been drawn up by some Cartesian or psychologist, who endeavored to give what he supposed to be a fair statement of the fundamental teachings of the ontologists, who can escape pantheism only at the expense of their logic. I am no more an ontologist than I am a psychologist. My philosophy is synthetic, & starts from the original synthesis of things.[39]

Nor does Fr. Farrell make any mention of other important letters in which Brownson stated and defended his philosophy. Brownson's son Henry says that "sometimes, in private correspondence, Brownson's views were set forth in language which to some is plainer and more easily understood than in his elaborate essays," and that this applied to his philosophical views.[40] He referred to a letter his father wrote to Joseph Henning, a theological student "showing philosophical ability of a high order." But a much more important letter, bearing on Brownson's philosophy, is one which Brownson wrote on December 1, 1870, in reply to an article in *The Star of Bethlehem* by Fr. Thomas Lagan of St. Francis Seminary, Milwaukee, in which he had innocently misrepresented Brownson's philosophy. In that letter Brownson gave what is perhaps his most concise statement of the Giobertian formula:

> When I say, the ideal formula, *Ens creat existentias,* is intuitive, I do not mean that the proposition, *Deus creat vel Deus creavit existentias,* is intuitive. Doubtless *Ens* is *Deus,* but this is not intuitively affirmed, and can be ascertained only by discursion or by revelation. When I say *Ens creat existentias* is the *primum philosophicum,* I do not mean that the understanding commences its development with an explicit intuition of that formula. But it expresses the formula to which the principles of all the real and all the knowable are reducible, and therefore that it is the basis of all real intelligence, all real science.

Referring in this same letter to ontologism, he remarked:

> Let me say that the philosophy I defend has no relation with the ontologism of the Louvain professors, which I had condemned and refuted before it was condemned by the Holy See. The seven propositions censured I have never entertained, and always have regarded as pantheistic. I am not an ontologist any more than I am a psychologist: my *primum philosophicum* is the synthesis of being and existences, or being and existences in their real relation, by their nexus, the creative act of being.[41]

Brownson here referred evidently to his article on the "Primitive Elements of Thought," published in 1859 in his *Review,* in which he criticized the writing of certain professors. Reviewing two pretentious volumes of L'Abbé Hugonin, entitled *Etudes Philosophiques, Ontologie ou Etude des Lois de La Pensée,* he remarked of the author: "In the classification of schools, the Abbé Hugonin is a decided ontologist, and like all ontologists of his country we are acquainted with, too much under the influence of Père Malebranche to suit either our taste or our judgment."[42] This was written two years before the proscription by the Holy See of the ontologism of certain Louvain professors in September 1861.

Brownson's first repudiation of ontologism is found, however, in his article in his *Quarterly* on "Schools of Philosophy," January 1854. In it he criticized a modern work of the psychological school, *L'Autocrazia dell' Ente,* allowing it to be "a very successful attempt to turn the shafts of wit and ridicule against those who have the temerity to defend the principles and methods of the onotological school," and admitted that "as a *jew d'esprit* we can read and enjoy it, but as an argument we cannot respect it as highly as we could wish, for it confounds the bastard ontology of the heterodox with the views of the so-called ontologists among Catholics, and concludes against the truth of the latter from the absurdity of the former. . . . We are ourselves as strongly opposed to the bastard ontology as the writer of *L'Autocrazia dell' Ente,* and it is most unpleasant to be held up to the public as embracing it, because we do not happen to embrace the psychological school."[43]

Who, it may well be asked, that has done some work in the field of philosophy, and is therefore entitled to speak with some authority, has ever called Brownson an ontologist? To speak with authority in any field of thought calls for expertise in that same field. For that reason I have consulted living authorities who have made a special study of Brownson's philosophy. Among these is William J. Haggerty, Jr., for some years now professor of philosophy at the University of Boston, who also wrote a doctoral thesis on Brownson's philosophy. To a letter of inquiry about Brownson's philosophy, Mr. Haggerty replied on September 13, 1967, saying in part: "I wrote a Ph.D. thesis on Brownson's philosophy at Boston University in 1960, and as a result I am familiar with several of the works you mentioned in your letter. I agree with your contention that Brownson was not an ontologist, at least, in the traditional sense."

Another living authority on Brownson's philosophical thought is Armand A. Maurer, C.S.B. He is professor of philosophy at the Pontifical Institute of Studies, Toronto, Canada, and coauthor with Etienne Gilson and Thomas Langan of the splendid volume, *Recent Philosophy.*[44] In this volume Fr. Maurer is author of Part Three and Part Four, embracing the history of English and American philosophy. He of course deals with the philosophy of Brownson. To me he seemed to skirt the question concerning the charge that Brownson was an ontologist, that is, he made no reference to the charge at all. In a letter to him I made mention of this fact, and also made the statement:

For a number of extrinsic reasons alone, I cannot but be convinced that Brownson was not an ontologist. His honesty is absolutely unimpeachable, and he denied to the end that he was an ontologist. It would be stretching the matter a little too far to contend that his philosophical gifts were so meagre that he could never really grasp what ontologism is. His whole life shows that he had no pride of opinion, and that he was ever ready and willing to abandon any tenet the moment he discovered or was shown its falsity.

In reply to this letter, April 1, 1970, Fr. Maurer said in part:

Dear Father Ryan:
Thank you for your letter and kind remarks about *Recent Philosophy.* I did not mean to avoid or skirt the problem of Brownson's ontologism. I simply let him defend himself against the charge on p. 583, and I think his defense is adequate. He is no more open to the charge than, say, St. Augustine or St. Anselm. So I think you are correct in your estimate of Brownson.[45]

It may be well to give the particular paragraph, page 583, in which Fr. Maurer lets Brownson defend himself against the charge of ontologism. It runs:

> Brownson strenuously defends himself and his Italian master against this charge. He points out that intuition, as they understand it, is not perception, or vision. These latter are acts of the intellect, whereas intuition is an act of the object presenting itself to the intellect. It is true that God offers himself to the mind in every act of knowing; without him the mind is not intelligent nor is any object intelligible. But we do not immediately perceive or know the divine presence. Reflection and analysis are needed before we grasp the stupendous fact that the being involved in every act of knowledge is creative being, and that this is God himself.[46] Brownson insists that the formula, which is the beginning of philosophy, is "Being creates existences," not God creates existences, because at this stage of the analysis being is not yet seen to be identical with God. Further reflective analysis is needed before this identity is grasped. "We know by intuition that which is God, but not that it is God."[47]

Brownson laid great stress on the fact that philosophy is a rational science — does not go by the authority of great names. On that score he thought the order of the General of the Jesuits in his day directing that the professors of philosophy in the colleges of the Society to teach the philosophy of Aristotle and Fonseca, the latter a Portuguese Jesuit of the sixteenth century, was ill-advised and unscientific.[48] Philosophy being a rational science, it should never be shackled in its free exercise by an absolute commitment to any one man or school. The only authority Brownson recognized in the field of philosophy, aside from sound reason, was the firm voice of the Catholic Church. And for that voice he had great reverence indeed. Dr. Fairfax McLaughlin, a contemporary of Brownson, spoke of that great reverence when he said, contrasting Brownson with some who had less reverence for that voice:

> Döllinger and Hyacinthe might plunge over the abyss into chaos; the eloquent Lacordaire and the noble Montalembert might anon press the bosses of the buckler too far, but touch the pope and, like the needle to the pole, Brownson reverently quivered into place; in the most daring speculation, with his metaphysical zeal aglow at white heat, he would pause to proclaim his unshakable allegiance to the voice of the Church and his readiness to cast aside and retract any opinion which she might pronounce error.[49]

Although he had great respect also for great names in the realm of philosophy, such as Aristotle, Plato, St. Augustine, St. Anselm, St. Thomas Aquinas, Suárez and many others, he insisted on his right to canvass the reasoning of each in every instance, and to differ when good and sufficient reasons justified him in doing so. Of St. Thomas himself he said: "There is no name in philosophy that we respect more than we do that of St. Thomas, but in philosophy we swear by the words of no human master."[50] He explained his attitude further when he added: "St. Thomas, when he uses natural reason in face of the dogma, seldom if ever, errs, but when he leaves theology, and speaks *ex professo,* as an independent philosopher, he is a peripatetic, and can by no means always be followed with perfect security."[51]

Nor could there be, he insisted — since philosophy is a rational science — any such thing as a *Christian* philosophy, strictly so-called. To speak in such a fashion may have a pious and orthodox ring, but such terminology is as much out of place as speaking of *Christian* coats and pantaloons, *Chris-*

*tian* hats and shoes.[52] Yet he stoutly maintained that no sound philosophy can ever be constructed without the assisting or guiding light that comes from divine revelation.[53] While he generally called his own philosophy synthetic philosophy, he emphatically disclaimed having originated any system of philosophy. He defended no system of philosophy, he asserted, and was opposed to all attempts at constructing such systems as were current. Why? Because he had found all such systems abstract in nature, lacking in reality. They were at best only logical representations, not of reality, or of things as they are, but of mental conceptions of things.[54] When his close friend, Fr. Charles Gresselin, S.J., expressed some misgivings about his formula, *Ens creat existentias,* as the *primum philosophicum,* he gave another clear-cut exposition of what he meant by that formula and specified the nature of his philosophy. As it is an important statement it merits a verbatim quote:

> Our philosophy, so far as philosophy we have, is realism, that is, deals with things as they really are, and not as they exist in abstract conceptions. When we assert *Ens creat existentias* as the ideal formula embracing all truth, we assert the real order; and we assert real being and real existences in their real relation. Our reverend friend must concede to us, that in the beginning God created the heavens and the earth, all things visible and invisible; he must also concede, that what is not God, and yet exists, is creature; that what is not creature, and yet exists, is God, and that the relation between God and creature, or between Being and existences, is expressed by the creative act; therefore, he must concede that all truth, whether truth of being, truth of existences, or truth of relation, is embraced in the ideal formula. Furthermore, as *Ens,* or God, is real and necessary being, and includes in himself all real and necessary being, he must concede that, whatever is contingent, depends upon the creative act, and exists only by virtue of that act. How, then, can he object to our formula as the *primum philosophicum?*[55]

From all this it is all the more clear that Brownson, a sort of a philosophical maverick (he said that in opposing false systems of philosophy he was denounced as "an Ishmaelite"[56]), refused to admit discipleship in any school or to shelter under any philosophical master. Fr. Armand Maurer is not quite accurate when he speaks of Vincenzo Gioberti as Brownson's "Italian master" as a philosopher.[57] Brownson was for a time under the spell of many philosophers, beginning with Victor Cousin and Pierre Leroux, but in time he freed himself from them all, including Gioberti, and was his own stout philosophical self. In spite of the singular credit he gave Gioberti for the philosophical formula he had adopted from him as expressing his own thought, he remarked in 1861, still "neither in philosophy nor in theology are we disposed to take him for our master or our guide."[58] Again, on April 13, 1867, when writing his son about his article on "An Old Quarrel," he said: "I think I have defended the Scholastic philosophy and showed the ground of reconciliation between it and my own, or Gioberti's. There is less originality in Gioberti than I once supposed, and while I regret nothing I ever took from him, I do not rate him as high as I at one time did."[59]

How are we to explain Brownson's former fascination for Gioberti? In recording how he had fallen under the spell of Victor Cousin in his early manhood, Brownson spoke of the "witchery of his style, the splendor of his diction, the brilliancy of his generalizations, and the real power of his genius."[60] Something of this sort must have occurred in regard to Gioberti. Apparently it was not only what he regarded as Gioberti's transcendent philosophical aptitude that had captivated him, but the appeal of his literary style as well. Of him he wrote: "As a writer, Gioberti, for classic purity, elegance, clearness, force, and dignity, has no superior, if any equal, in the Italian language. . . . Yet he is never dry, stiff, or stilted; he moves on with an easy, natural grace, and passes on through the most difficult and abstruse problems of theology and metaphysics without relaxing his gait, without the slightest apparent effort, or consciousness that he is not dealing in the ordinary way with the most ordinary topics. He has never to stop and take breath, is never labored, involved, obscure, or difficult. His march is even, easy, unrestrained. . . ."[61] Yet despite his encomiums on Gioberti, his vast and varied erudition, Brownson spoke also of the "very grave errors" into which he had fallen.[62] In fact, Brownson's writings on Gioberti, from first to last, are full of adverse criticisms of the man and his philosophical productions.

Speaking of Brownson himself as a philosopher, it is interesting to note that the only part of philosophy he set much store by was logic. All the philosophy he wanted taught in Catholic schools might be included, he asserted, under the head of logic, both as an art and as a science. But he maintained that the Aristotelian logic taught in schools, regarded not as an art, but as a science, is essentially defective, whether taken directly from Aristotle, or from the medieval or modern scholastics. It is essentially defective because it omits the creative act, as does all gentile philosophy, and does not therefore conform to the real order of things. In dealing with conceptions instead of the real order, it interposes a gulf between the *mundus logicus* and the *mundus physicus,* or the real world, which no art, skill, or labor, can bridge over.[63] For him only a perfect system of logic would match the complete system of the universe: "The universe, if we may so speak, is the logic of the Creator, and a perfect system of logic would be a key to all its mysteries, and enable us to comprehend as thoroughly the operations of the material universe, as the operations of the human mind itself."[64]

To Brownson philosophy was extremely important as a preamble to Catholic faith. The sole aim of his philosophical essays was to show that between true philosophy and Catholic theology there can be no real discrepancy; that it is only a false or defective philosophy that can ever come into conflict with the principles of Catholic theology.[65] He knew well, too, the truth of what Pope Leo XIII had occasion later to emphasize, namely, that nearly every religious error takes its rise in a philosophical error. Hence his great concern for a sound philosophy to be taught in Catholic schools. The lack of it he deemed one of the prolific sources of apostasy among not a few of our Catholic youth after leaving our colleges and universities.

# 45

## THE CONTINUED APOSTOLATE OF THE PEN

*Brownson becomes a contributor to the* Ave Maria, *and then to the* Catholic World *in 1866 • He also contributes to the New York* Tablet, *and becomes its editor • Differences in theology and philosophy between the editors of the* Catholic World *and himself become the occasion of Brownson's severing his connections with the* Catholic World *in January 1872 • His growing correspondence • The origin of the epithet,* Ursa Major, *the Big Bear • The death of his wife Sally, and his long-considered decision to revive his* Brownson's Quarterly Review *in January 1873.*

Of all the works, then, that Brownson had speculated on writing after the suspension of his *Review, The American Republic* and his *Essay in Refutation of Atheism* are the only ones he ever completed. This is largely explained by the fact that other projects intervened in the meantime to claim his attention more immediately. His friend, Fr. Isaac Hecker, founded a monthly magazine in 1865, *The Catholic World,* and Fr. Edward Sorin, founder of Notre Dame University, also inaugurated in 1865 the *Ave Maria,* a weekly periodical dedicated to the promotion of devotion to the Blessed Virgin Mary. To both of these journals Brownson made significant contributions well-nigh up to the revival of his own *Review* in 1873. In 1867 he likewise began his contributions to the New York *Tablet* of which he was also editor.

Brownson's first contribution to the *Ave Maria,* beginning in 1865, was a series on the veneration Catholics pay the saints, especially the Queen of them all, the Blessed Virgin Mary, and on the veneration of relics and images. This ran for nearly half a year, and was followed by another series of articles on the moral and social influence of devotion to Mary, the Mother of God, in 1866. Fr. Sorin was ever endeavoring to prevail upon Brownson to write more for his magazine, and two truly elaborate articles, serially installed, were added later, one on "Heresy and the Incarnation," 1867-1868, and the other on "Religious Orders," 1871.

When Fr. Sorin first appealed to Brownson to enrich the pages of the *Ave Maria* with some of his thought on devotion to the Blessed Virgin Mary and the saints, Brownson was hesitant. He did not wear his deeper religious feelings on his sleeve, and "felt a little awkward about writing on the subject for the public, and he always preferred to be silent in his writings as to sentimental devotions and private feeling and practices of an emotional nature."[1] But Fr. P.P. Cooney of Notre Dame, in a personal interview, assured him that he would not be expected to confine himself to mere sentiments on the subject, but that what would be looked for from him would be a philosophical explanation of the principle which underlies devotion to the Mother of God and the saints. It was with this understanding that Brownson accepted the invitation to become a contributor. In his treatment of the subject, therefore, Brownson seldom or never gave way to emotionalism or sentimentality, but wrote rather as the philosopher who wished to show that the honor Catholics pay the Blessed Virgin Mary and the saints is warranted, and indeed called for, on the ground of the strictest theological reasoning. Speaking of his treatise, he said:

> In the whole series of saint-worship, if I have written indeed as a believer, I have aimed to write with all the sobriety and reason of the philosopher, I have rarely given way to emotional impulses of my own, or appealed to the devotional sentiments of my readers. I have no doubt appeared to most readers cold and insensible, a bold speculator to some, and a soulless logic-grinder to all. My aim has been to state and defend the naked truth to the unsympathizing understanding, and to show to the coolest and most exacting reason that the whole system and practice of saint-worship among Catholics is defensible on the most rigid theological reason, and must be accepted or Christianity itself be rejected as a delusion.[2]

Although Brownson wrote his treatise largely to clear Catholics of any species of idolatry or superstition in their veneration of the saints, the title he used, saint-worship, might almost seem to confirm such a charge. He used the word "worship" in the case because it is the only word in the English language that fully expresses what is meant by the word *cultus,* the Latin word used by the Catholic Church in referring to the honor paid to the saints. The word "worship" is from the Anglo-Saxon *weorthscipe* which in general designates the honor paid to God, to a magistrate, or to any man because of his office, his acquirements, his possessions, or his virtues. Idolatry is not in rendering worship to men, but in rendering to them the worship that is due to God alone. That Protestants should regard Catholics as idolaters in their saint-worship, and rashly "brand the worship paid the Mother of God idolatry," Brownson did not find overly strange or surprising. "They seem not to be aware," he said, "that the supreme and distinctive act of worship to God is sacrifice, and that we offer never to a saint, never but to God alone. . . . Having rejected the sacrifice of the Mass, they have no sacrifice to offer, and therefore really no supreme distinctive worship of God, and their worship is of the same kind, and very little, if any, higher than that which we offer to the saints themselves. They see us give to the saints as high a worship as they render to God, and why, then, should they not regard us as idolaters?"[3] His whole treatise was written of course to remove this false impression.

Although Brownson had in the previous years treated many of the most abstruse problems in the whole range of philosophy and Catholic theology, it is quite understandable to anyone who has read his treatise on saint-worship, that his son should tell us that nothing his father ever wrote gave him more labor, or required more thought, than this same extended treatise on saint-worship. But it was labor that turned out to be very rewarding to Brownson himself since he could say in conclusion: "If my articles have been profitable to no others, their preparation has been profitable to me, and have given me peace and serenity, quickened my love to Mary and the saints of our Lord, and rendered dearer both Catholic faith and worship."[4]

Brownson's treatise, however, had almost been broken off before it really got started. In his second installment he had used the phrase, "as God is, in his essence, triune," and this led to disturbing trouble. The organ of "a latterly promoted archbishop" pronounced it "formal heresy." Fr. Sorin was considerably disturbed and said in a footnote to his letter to Brownson: "You gave me a distraction at High Mass this morning when I came to sing: 'et in essentia unitas.' "[5] In a letter to Mother Angela Gillespie, foundress of the Congregation of the Sisters of the Holy Cross, and St. Mary's College, Notre Dame, Indiana — who had apparently already written him about the matter — Brownson remarked that he had consulted all the authorities on the point from St. Augustine down, and added: "For the life of me I cannot discover wherein my language is either unorthodox or inexact."[6] To relieve his own mind about the matter, Fr. Sorin sent the respective article in which the phrase occurred to Cardinal Barnabò, Prefect of the Propaganda, Rome, who in turn submitted the matter for judgment to a group of Roman theologians. They declared the phrase was unusual, but that there was nothing in it not strictly orthodox.[7]

While Brownson took the question raised over the orthodoxy of his phrase quite meekly, letters show that he was also quite upset over the affair. When Mother Angela learned of this, she took alarm as she was closely associated with the *Ave Maria,* and wrote to him an encouraging letter, dated December 3, 1865, in which she said in part:

> One of my strongest convictions is, that Our Blessed Mother needs you, has special work for you to do in her journal, and out of it also — and that in performing these works, as no other person in the United States can perform them, you have the greatest need of her assistance! Because you stand preeminent in the possession of rare intellectual gifts, and a great, generous, warm heart.[8]

Mother Angela became the "unofficial editor" of the *Ave Maria* in 1866.[9] She may have felt indebted to Brownson inasmuch as he had given her *Metropolitan Readers* a good boost in an article in 1862.[10] This happy relationship between Brownson and Mother Angela explains the interest the late Sister Mary Rose Gertrude, a member of the same sisterhood, took in Brownson. She wrote an undocumented biography of him, *Granite for God's House, The Life of Orestes Augustus Brownson* (New York: Sheed and Ward, 1941). She used the pen name, Doran Whalen, the name of her father.[11]

Although Fr. Sorin had innocently shied at the phrase Brownson had used touching on the Blessed Trinity, there can be no doubt about his great appreciation of Brownson's contributions to the *Ave Maria.* In a letter to Brownson in January 1867, he wrote:

> With regard to your course in the *Ave Maria,* of which by the bye, the Most Reverend Archbishop of St. Louis was good enough to say that he considered it the best paper in the United States, I wish to say that you must consider yourself the representative of the American Catholics, speaking to his own people of the Mother of God, as you think they should be talked to. . . . It seems to me that no one better than yourself could tell the American people what our country has to gain by spreading such a devotion. . . . You have given us excellent articles, of which a number of persons have spoken in high terms, even the editor of the National Quarterly Review, Mr. Sears.[12]

At practically the same time that Brownson began to write for the *Ave Maria,* he also began to write for the *Catholic World.* For a brief period he served as translator for that journal, and first appeared as the author of an article in the July 1866 issue. During the next half year, he contributed three more articles, and thereafter, until 1872, he generally had one or two articles in each issue.[13] In his *History of American Magazines,* Frank Luther Mott remarked that during the first half century of the *Catholic World* Fr. Augustine Hewit, C.S.P., was the largest single contributor, and that "the leonine Orestes A. Brownson came next with seventy articles."[14] Brownson's contributions, however, were confined to six years only, during which time he was also writing for the *Ave Maria,* and the New York *Tablet.* Most of his articles in the *Catholic World* have been incorporated into his collected *Works.*

Some of Brownson's articles were on such themes as "The Independence of the Church," "Union of Church and State," "Rome and the World," "The School Question," "The Future of Protestantism and Catholicity," or themes of a similar genre. The political philosophy embodied in these treatises he summed up and presented rather pithily in an article on "Church and State" in 1870. To these particular essays were added progressively others of a wide variety — philosophical, controversial and scientific. His son remarks that they are of such high merit as to be ranked "among his most valuable writings, as they were by the Author and the Editor."[15] The article on the church and state relationship appealed in particular to Fr. Augustine Hewit, who wrote in December 1870: "Your statement that the rights of man declared in our Declaration of Independence are the rights of God, is one of the pregnant principles that sum up a whole philosophy in a sentence and will live forever as an axiom. I borrowed some of your ideas for a lecture at St. Stephen's Church."[16]

It was the most natural thing in the world that Brownson should have become a contributor to the *Catholic World,* newly founded by his old friend, Fr. Isaac Hecker — that is, after he had suspended his own *Review.* But it soon became apparent that all was not to go as smoothly as desirable between himself as contributor and the editors of the *Catholic World.* To set the stage a bit for what follows, a few points should be touched upon. Although Brownson had experimented with a liberal policy for a few years, as we have seen, he soon turned back, after the suspension of his *Review,* though gradually, into a rock-ribbed conservatism. And by contrast, the *Catholic World* seemed to him to become a trifle too liberal and conciliatory. He once wrote Fr. Hecker: "I protest against the *Catholic World* being put on the defensive."[17] Nor could he agree with Fr. Hecker and Fr. Hewit on the best method for making converts. But worst of all, a goodly portion of the *odium theologicum* and the *odium philosophicum* was to bedevil the honest efforts of these three excellent men to understand each other and to work harmoniously, and each tried heroically. Brownson considered Fr. Hewit's views on original sin as set forth in his *Problems of the Age* as "unsound," and said so in the *Tablet.* When complaints were made, Brownson told Fr. Hecker in a letter, dated January 28, 1868, that his only objection in the matter was that Fr. Hewit gave what was only his theological opinion "as Catholic doctrine."[18] The philosophical quarrel over ontologism was perhaps even more pronounced, not to say bitter. A part, too, of the difficulties was the fact that Brownson had a long career of editorship behind him, and quite naturally found it irksome to work under other editors. It is of course entirely understandable that a man of Brownson's international renown as a writer would be a little sensitive about how manuscripts would be handled which had been sent up to the editor.

There is an undated letter of complaint from Brownson to Fr. Hecker which no one apparently has ever attempted to date, even approximately, not even the preparer of the Brownson papers. But since Brownson mentioned at the end of the letter that he intended to address himself to a review of Professor J. W. Draper's works as soon as his eyes would permit, the letter must belong to the latter part of the year 1867 or the first part of 1868. For

Brownson's review of Draper's works appeared in the May 1868 issue of the *Catholic World*. It is in this letter that Brownson expressed himself quite aggrieved over the mutilation of one of his manuscripts. He wrote in part:

> Very Rev. and Dear Father Hecker:
>
> . . . Hereafter I pray you to return my articles, when they do not suit you, with objectionable passages marked. I can bear the rejection of an article, but I find I cannot bear its mutilation by any hand but my own. I am too old a writer and too old an editor to be treated as a school boy writing his theme for his master.
>
> I think you have injured the article, but let that pass. . . . If you want me to write for the magazine you must allow me a reasonable freedom, and also try & not make me feel that my articles are accepted only as a favor to me. I think I have helped the magazine as much as it has helped me.
>
> With your purposes and general views I heartily sympathize, and I wish to cooperate with you to the best of my ability, but I can no more sink my individuality in another's than you can yours. I would not knowingly interfere with any of your plans, nor come in conflict with the Paulists, published or unpublished, but if you wish me to aid, you must let me feel that I am at home in the C.W. [Catholic World], and welcomed. I must feel that I am free to work in my own way or I cannot work at all. I say this simply, and in no ill humor.[19]

It must have been in reference to this matter that Brownson wrote his son in February 1868, apparently after he and Fr. Hecker had had a visit together:

> Father Hecker and I have had a fight, but it is over now. It grew out of his rejecting one article, and mutilating another, because my views conflicted with some views on original sin by Father Hewit in the Problems of the Age. In the first instance, I did it ignorantly; in the second instance, I thought I had avoided the main objection, as I expressed my view in the words of the Council of Trent, I trusted it would pass. But no, Father Hewit might contradict the council, but nobody in the Catholic World must contradict Father Hewit, whose orthodoxy on more than one point is more than suspected. But after firing off several letters at Father Hecker I feel better. Father Hecker was sick for a week from the scolding I gave him, but we are good friends again. I shall not be surprised if Father Hewit, who is really a holy man, modifies at least the expression of his doctrine, which you will find in Vol. IV, pp. 528-530.[20]

Whether or not there is any distinction to be made between mutilating a manuscript and correcting or revising it, Brownson did as a matter of fact acknowledge the right of the editor of the *Catholic World* to correct and revise as he saw fit the manuscripts he submitted. On January 29, 1868, he wrote Fr. Hecker:

> An editor is and always should be an autocrat. The whole responsibility is on you and your power should be absolute. Yet having been myself an autocrat for thirty years, I have some difficulty in making my mind work freely, if while I am writing, I am in doubt whether what I write will be accepted or not. I always write with the public before my eyes, & when you veil that public from my sight, I lose both my freedom & power of thinking and expression. It may be a weakness, but the habits of thirty years are too strong to overcome.[21]

The great difficulty for Brownson, as indicated, was that his fear of running athwart the views of either Fr. Hecker or Fr. Hewit tended to paralyze his energy and verve and make it impossible for him to do his best writing. In a letter to Fr. Hecker on March 10, 1868, he said: "The harsh word Fr.

Hewit said to me on the article that was rejected disturbed me, and feeling that I must meet his views as well as yours, I lack that confidence that enables me to put my whole soul into what I write."[22]

It is evident that Brownson was striving earnestly for a harmonious working relationship between himself and Fr. Hecker, and it is just as evident that Fr. Hecker was equally concerned to achieve that same harmony. On March 19, Fr. Hecker replied to Brownson's letter, saying:

> It gives me great pleasure that your health is better and of your visiting us soon. I shall be glad to have the opportunity of settling the difficulties which have recently sprung up. Our opinions on the effects of the fall, and what is the best policy [in convert work], do undoubtedly differ, but not to the extent that we cannot work together. This I think can be made evident when we talk it over together. I shall expect to see you at your earliest convenience.[23]

No doubt these visits — there is no knowing how frequent they were over the years — did much to preserve a working relationship between the two. Results were more felicitous, however, when Brownson wrote on themes wherein Catholic doctrine was not so directly involved and a clash of views was less likely. Speaking of an article Brownson had written on the "Woman Question," Fr. Hecker said on March 8, 1869:

> Your article on the subject is most welcome, and your treatment of it most satisfactory to my judgment. If you wrote the article under any restraint, Dear Doctor, in my opinion you never wrote better in your life. I say this in all sincerity. [And again, on June 7, 1869, he wrote Brownson:] You never wrote more finished articles than those on the Woman Question and Spiritism. The first took me quite by surprise — its gentle tone and polish did not at all abate your usual strength. The Archbishop of New York [McCloskey] expressed his complete satisfaction with those articles, and said you had never written better. He is not alone in this opinion.[24]

But his relations with the *Catholic World* were not to continue smoothly overly long. On February 1, 1870, Fr. Hewit wrote Brownson complaining about some remarks Brownson had made in the *Tablet* concerning the *Catholic World,* and on his own doctrines in particular. He wrote:

> We have all of us in this house frequently felt ourselves very much aggrieved by various remarks made in the Tablet which we could not doubt proceeded from your pen, although officially you were not their acknowledged author. For myself, I have always thought it best to make no reply but that of silence. But, as the Catholic World has been twice associated with "Liberals" & "Liberalism" in the Tablet, I think it well to let you know that I consider this as likely to injure the character of the magazine and those connected with it, and to remonstrate with you on the subject. It may be useless, perhaps, to do so, and I have no wish to involve myself in a controversy. I beg you to consider the evil which ensues to the cause of God and his church from every word proceeding from a Catholic writer which lessens the reputation for soundness and loyalty to the church of those who are engaged in its defense. . . . If you think, nevertheless, that it is your duty to censure my doctrines or opinions as unsound, there is no recourse that I am aware of that is open to me, & I must submit to it patiently.
>
> I remain with great respect, your obedient servant in J.C.,
>
> Aug. F. Hewit[25]

Brownson replied immediately on February 3, and said in part:

> I have written an article for the Tablet since receiving your letter in which

I make as far as possible that *Amende honorable*. I hope what I have said will be satisfactory, if not, send to the Tablet what you object, signed, editor of the Catholic World, and any apologies we owe shall be made, and no controversy opened. [Fair enough.]

[Brownson continued:] Will write the article on Education you have requested, if my eyes get better, and you do not in your wrath countermand it. Father Hecker and I have had some doctrinal quarrels, and he has insisted that I should, in writing for the Tablet accord with the Catholic World. I have not considered that he has any right to control not only what I write for the Catholic World, but also what I write for the Tablet. I differ from you on the question of realism and nominalism, on original sin, and probably on the dogma of exclusive salvation. You follow the Jesuit theologians; I follow rather the Augustinians. But however that may be, whenever you feel aggrieved by anything I do or say, I shall always listen with profoundest respect to your remonstrances and as far as possible remove the grievance. I will simply add now, that I will henceforth refrain from all adverse criticisms of the C.W. [Catholic World] and will never allude to it in the Tablet save to commend. Do not run away with the notion that remonstrances are lost on me, especially if they come from yourself, whom I have so much reason to love as a friend and respect as a teacher. There is little, except abandoning principle, that you cannot make me do, if you try, for the truth you tell me even in wrath I will accept as if it was told in love.[26]

In a letter of a few days later, dated February 9, Fr. Hewit articulated what had been his real grievance in the matter. He wrote in part:

I do not complain of you for differing from me in theology. I admit that the Augustinian school tenets have not been censured. I have no objection to your defending your own opinions, and I have no right to complain of you for controverting mine or criticizing my arguments. My sole complaint is that you have applied the epithet "unsound," and other such terms to my writings which reflect upon my orthodoxy, and that you have also reflected on the Catholic World as tainted or suspected in the matter of Liberalism. For a priest, these suspicions are like doubts thrown on the virtue of a nun.[27]

It must have been about this time that Fr. Hewit himself became editor of the *Catholic World*. Fr. Hecker had been invited to attend the First Vatican Council (December 8, 1869 through July 7, 1870), as procurator of the bishop of Columbus, Ohio, Sylvester H. Rosecrans. According to a letter of Fr. Hecker's to Brownson, dated January 12, 1870, it would seem that he did not set off for Rome until after that date, leaving Fr. Hewit editor in his absence. On February 4, 1870, Fr. Hecker wrote Brownson from Rome:

I send you by mail Cantu's article on "Chiesa a Stato," which may serve if you wish as a basis for an article on Church and State, which I suggested for your pen. Cesare Cantu stands high in the esteem of the Pope and all sound Catholics of all parties. I formed his acquaintance here; he resides in Milan, and has returned home.[28]

In a letter to his son, Brownson wrote:

Father Hewit wanted me to write an article on the School Question, and Father Hecker wrote me from Rome the outline of an article on Church and State for me to fill up for the Catholic World. These, with an article on Emerson, and the concluding one on the Abbé Martin, with my article for the Tablet, kept me so perplexed and busy that I have had hardly a moment in which to write you. I beg you to excuse me as well as you can, especially as my eyes are so bad that I ought not to write at all. . . . You may be sure I did not fill our Father H[ecker]'s outlines. I have written the article in my own way. I expressed my own views, which I think agree well enough with Father H[ecker]'s, if he only knew his own mind and could express it. And yet I am not sure it will be accepted or printed as I wrote it, as I have given *carte blanche* to Father Hewit, the editor at present.[29]

In a letter to Fr. Hewit, dated February 22, 1870, Brownson remarked:

> Father Hecker suggested to me some time ago an article on Church and State, but I cannot recall his particular suggestions. He has written me from Rome requesting me to write the article. My doubt is, whether I have not anticipated it in the other article on Abbé Martin, and that just sent him on the School Question.

Brownson must have felt he might have been overdoing the subject to have another article on the church and state *ex professo*. And he asked Fr. Hewit's opinion on the matter. Fr. Hewit having overlooked to answer his question in a letter on February 24, Brownson replied immediately on February 25, saying: "I have, however, after reading Il Signor Cantu's article on the question, which Father Hecker sent me, begun the article," and he added with characteristic candor:

> My articles are of course subject, even when accepted, to your editorial revision and correction; but I am rather particular in my choice of terms, and a little sensitive to verbal changes, for the change of a single term is not unlikely to change my whole sense, and upset my logic. From what I have read of your writing, I think I am more nice and exact in the use of terms than you are yourself, and that you do not always attach the same value to single words that I do. I would more willingly submit to your doctrinal corrections than to your verbal chai.ges, unless in cases where I have been careless and have obviously used an incorrect term.
>
> The Catholic World wants an editor, and an editor that has ample leisure to attend to it. Yet it suffers less than I should suppose it would. There is danger, however, of its becoming too heavy for a magazine, and it has too many feminine writers, whether they wear skirts or breeches. It wants as a whole, robustness, true manliness, which it might have without being less courteous or conciliatory. I do not dare put forth my strength in writing for it, and feel nothing of the freedom that I do in writing for the Tablet. I feel that in writing for the C.W. I am only half a man, and that I must suppress the rough vigor of thought and expression that is natural to me. Father Hecker restrains me, and my mind does not, and will not work freely under his eye. He patronizes me, but treats me as an inferior. I can face-to-face converse more at ease with him than with you, but I can work more freely under you than under him. You do not disarrange my working gear, nor wound my *armour-propre*. But I have done my best things, and am only fit to be laid on the shelf. Have the charity to remember me in your prayers.[30]

Father Hewit replied to this letter on March 3, 1870, saying in part:

> It is undoubtedly a great humiliation for you to be in any respect subject to one so much inferior to yourself in intellect and in most departments of knowledge. The only consolation I can give you under this trial is, that you have the opportunity of gaining great merit and making a sacrifice of the most difficult kind to God, and thus gaining an eternal crown of much greater value than any worldly glory. The powers which I must necessarily have and exercise, I always use with scrupulous respect toward every author who is master of his

art, and to you especially, and never meddle with a word unless conscience or an evident reason of propriety requires it. If there is a difference of any sort, I have to act like Susan Nipper's conscientious goblin in the garret, and fulfill "the painful duty of my position."[31]

After whipping the article on the church and state question into fair shape, Brownson wrote Fr. Hewit on March 8, 1870, to say: "I have written the article on Church and State, and shall finish and send it this week. It will take from 14 to 15 pages. I have modified the original plan in accordance with Father Hecker's suggestions. I have written my own views rather than his, but I do not think I have run athwart them."[32]

This article on the church and state appeared in the May issue of the *Catholic World*. The general thought evolved by Brownson on the problem of church-state relationships is truly of remarkable prescience for the time in which he wrote. Speaking of Brownson's thought on this theme, the late Fr. J. P. Donovan, C.M., J. C. D., said: "His treatise on the nature of the civil power is in remarkable accord with the doctrine put forth fifty years later by the great authority appointed by Pope Leo to the first chair of public law in Rome, Cardinal Cavagnis. With a few changes in terminology Brownson would be in literal agreement with Cavagnis; yet Cavagnis was a specialist laboring at leisure and Brownson the general controversialist crowded with work."[33]

Fr. Hewit had expressed his amazement in one of his letters at this time at the amount of work Brownson was doing. And it was truly remarkable in the face of his bodily infirmities. Gout had so crippled him that he could scarcely get a shoe on his foot, and he ventured out into his yard only now and then with the aid of crutches. Unable to go to church for the last two or three years, he received Holy Communion only when the parish priest brought the sacrament to his home. His eye trouble was critical, and the gout had also gnarled the fingers which held his pen — which helps to explain his almost illegible handwriting at this time. Already on April 12, 1867, he had written his son Henry: "I am still a cripple confined to the house. . . . Write me as often as you can, for my life is very lonely, & I cannot get out to see anybody. Besides, if I work too hard, it brings on the gout."[34] To the surprise Fr. Hewit had expressed at the amount of work he was doing in spite of his infirmities, he replied in a letter of March 8, 1870:

> But you overrate what I have done. I say unaffectedly that to me it seems I have done nothing, and that my life has been frittered away. I have not fulfilled my early promise, nor used the opportunities that I have had given me, and my only sadness is in the thought that it is now too late to redeem the time or to do anything now. Of all my mighty plans not one of them has been executed, and I cannot persuade myself that I have done or can do anything worth remembering. This is said as sincerely as in the confessional.
>
> [He added:] There is no humiliation in being obliged to work under you and Fr. H[ecker]. The difficulty is that under Fr. H[ecker] my mind is restrained, and my faculties will not work freely. It is not that I cannot express freely my views, but that I cannot express them with the ease, *abandon,* or *verve* I wish.[35]

Back in 1838 Brownson had written: "The oracle within will not utter his responses, when it depends on the good will of another whether they shall to the public ear or not."[36]

Brownson's article on the school question, previously requested by Fr. Hewit, appeared in the May 1870 issue of the *Catholic World.* This article together with several others on the same theme in the *Tablet* were greatly appreciated at the time by Catholics generally. The bishop of St. Paul, Thomas L. Grace, took pen in hand to write his appreciation to the publishers of the *Tablet*, Messrs. Sadlier & Company, on March 23, 1870:

> I was greatly disappointed with the lecture of the Rev. Mr. Preston. It was a very feeble statement of the Catholic view of the School Question, and in my opinion will injure rather than benefit the cause. A poor defense is worse than no defense. There is a writer in the Tablet that manifests a thorough knowledge and grasp of the subject in all its strongest points. He could do the subject perfect justice, and he would render a great and most needed service at this moment if he would present the Catholic view and grounds upon the School Question to take the place of Rev. Mr. Preston's pamphlet for general circulation.
>
> Respectfully and sincerely yours,<br>Thomas L. Grace, Bp. of St. Paul[37]

We have seen that Brownson's writing of the church-state article was attended by some friction, and it seems that the danger of clashing with the views of Fr. Hecker or Fr. Hewit, or both, was now becoming more and more the *bête noire* of his relations with the *Catholic World*. There is a letter of Brownson to Fr. Hecker, dated August 25, 1870, in which he laid all his cards on the table and called upon his old friend, Fr. Hecker, to decide whether or not there was any longer any use of trying to carry on together. He had by this time gone over completely to the conservative camp. After delineating at considerable length the views which really did divide them, particularly regarding democracy, he wrote:

> You see, dear Father, where I stand. Can we work together or can we not? If not, it is useless to try; if you think we can, I will do the best I can for the Catholic World, and cease to grumble. Pray let me know your view of the matter.
>
> I wish . . . you would write me expressly in answer to my question, or what is better, come & see me. I want if possible to identify myself with the C.W. & give it my best thoughts & my best labors, but if that is impossible, I wish to know it; but I trust, even in that case an old friendship will remain undiminished.[38]

With the answer Fr. Hecker wrote him on August 30, 1870, Brownson expressed himself satisfied that "there is a deeper and more perfect sympathy between us than I have felt there was for years."[39] Just the same, his letter of August 25, 1870, is plain evidence that he was beginning to despair at this time of working harmoniously with the *Catholic World*. What transpired during the visits between the two we do not of course know. But, in any case, it comes scarcely as a big surprise that a few months later Brownson seems on the point of discontinuing his contributions to the *Catholic World*. Brownson's son Henry says his father at this juncture wrote Fr. Hecker a note signifying his intention to discontinue,[40] but I have been unable to find the note. However, Fr. Hecker's letter of January 30, 1871, with its solemn appeal to Brownson not to quit his contributions carries an evidence of its own that Brownson was on the point of discontinuing his contributions. His letter ran:

> Dear Dr.:
>
> . . . It seems to me that if you would continue to write such articles as you have done the last two years or more in refutation of the calumnies of the

enemies of the church, in applying Catholic principles to the social and political questions of the day, in directing the young Catholic mind how to judge and act in the midst of existing difficulties, which were never greater or more threatening, and in boldly confronting and silencing the leading advocates of heresy and error, you would promote to the greatest degree Catholic interests, give the highest satisfaction to the hierarchy, and interest most readers of the magazine.

Believe me, Dear Dr., you have no idea of the great good which you have done by your pen employed in this direction. I, who am in more direct contact with the readers of the *Catholic World,* hear the satisfaction expressed on all sides and by all classes for articles of this nature, all rejoicing that in you they had found a champion of their faith and a master who teaches them how to harmonize their duties as Catholics with the best interests of society and the state.

Whatever value you attach to my judgment or sincerity to my friendship for you, believe me, that this is a matter of most serious consideration in the presence of God, before you leave this great field of doing good, and give up the privilege of leading and directing the Catholic mind of our country.

I have never known you to falter in what you considered to be your duty, and whatever may be your deliberate conclusion in this matter, the high esteem and sincere friendship which I have borne for you now nearly forty years, will be none the less, or in any way affected.

Ever yours faithfully and affectionately,

I. T. Hecker[41]

By the time, however, that Fr. Hecker had written this letter, Brownson had decided to stay on anyhow with the *Catholic World,* for on this very date, January 30, he was already writing Fr. Hecker and proposing future articles. But he was apparently by no means at his ease. A little later, on March 25, 1871, he wrote his son:

The only trouble I have grows out of the fact that Father Hewit is not sound on the question of original sin, and does not believe that it is necessary to be in communion with the Church in order to be saved. He holds that Protestants may be saved by invincible ignorance, and that original sin was no sin at all except the individual sin of Adam, and that our nature was not wounded at all by it. Father Hecker agrees with him on these points, and is in fact a semi-pelagian without knowing it. So I am obliged to abstain from bringing out what I regard as the orthodox doctrine of original sin and of exclusive salvation. But in all other respects I am unrestrained.[42]

Brownson had been chafing for some time now under the fact that he had to suppress his views on original sin when writing for the *Catholic World.* In a long letter to Fr. Hecker, dated January 24, 1868, he had argued against Fr. Hewit's views on original sin (with which Fr. Hecker seems to have agreed), and added: "Neither my opinion nor yours has been condemned, and neither can assert his own opinion as of Catholic faith. I believe mine [the Augustinian view] is the sounder opinion, and you believe yours the better opinion. The only fault I find on this point is that he [Fr. Hewit] gives the opinion of the school he follows as Catholic doctrine, which I humbly submit it is not."[43]

However that may have been, Brownson was soon to utter a much deeper complaint. To an article he had submitted on Dr. James McCosh's "Christianity and Positivism" (Dr. McCosh was president of Princeton), Brownson had appended a footnote explaining that it has been "erroneously supposed that Gioberti and himself maintained that the ideal intuition was formal intuition of Being."[44] His footnote apparently contained his real doctrine on the point. This footnote was for him of great importance, for it was intended to set straight those who had misunderstood his philosophy. And all the more so since in those days articles in the *Catholic World* were unsigned. Fr. Hewit, however, did not see eye to eye with him in this matter. On August 2, 1871, he wrote Brownson:

My Dear Dr.:

Your two articles have been received. The first will go into the October number, as the September number was already full, and Fr. Hecker had left the list of contents here before his departure for Lake George, where he now is. I am very well satisfied with it, and think it a very able and thorough exposition of the topics handled. The note on Gioberti I think unnecessary and unadvisable. The real point is sufficiently brought out in the text, and will be understood by those capable of understanding a longer explanation. The rest may be left to their own forgetfulness. I have preserved the note, in case you may want to use it elsewhere.

The other article I have not yet read, and will take it up to Fr. Hecker. I have no doubt it is all right, as it must agree with your other articles in whose principles and doctrines I fully concur.

I wish you good health and the blessing of God, and remain yours very truly,

Aug. F. Hewit[45]

To which Brownson replied at once on August 3, saying in part:

My dear Father Hewit:

I am not quite sure I like the omission of my note. I like to go to confession and get absolution, and never go on maintaining views as if I had never held the contrary. Others may forget, but I cannot. I have no doubt that in omitting the note you have done what was best for yourself, for you really had maintained a proposition which the Holy See had censured — immediate intuition of God, which I had never done, though accused of doing it.[46] If I recollect aright, the ideal formula, in the sense ascribed to Gioberti and Dr. Brownson, is modified or rejected in the text, which leaves me in a false position without the explanation given in the note. I am apparently censured, or suffered in the text to lie under a false charge, for I never held any different view of ideal intuition from that given in the article with which you express yourself satisfied. If you strike out the note, it strikes me that you should strike out all allusion to Gioberti and to me in the text. I have never fallen, since a Catholic, on the point in question, into any error the Holy See has censured. My *Review* will show you that I was never an ontologist, and always held that true philosophy is a synthesis of the ontological and the psychological. But I will own to you that I had not sufficiently explained what I meant by *ideal intuition*. Perhaps I did not clearly understand myself, though I think I did, only I thought any further explanation unnecessary.

I have read carefully the propositions of the Louvain professors, M. Branchereau, and now Mgr. Hugonin. My *Review* censured them, as unsound, long before the Holy See censured them, but principally for their pantheistic tendencies. Fathers Ramière and Kleutgen show that ontologism is censured because it asserts immediate intuition or cognition of God, a point I did not hold, but on which I did not dwell. These Fathers are right in their assertion that ontologism is censured, but are we thence to conclude that ontology is no part of philosophy, and that philosophy is reduced, as Sir William Hamilton maintains, to psychology and logic, or with Cousin, that the ontological is logically deducible from the psychological? Because ontologism is censured, must we hold, with these good Fathers, that psychologism is approved and must be held? I wish to speak respectfully of them, but neither of them has any *ingegno filosofico*, or the slightest conception of the question to be solved, and in refuting McCosh I have virtually refuted them and their whole school. . . .

Yet you surprise me by approving my article on McCosh after having disapproved my article on Ontologists and Psychologists, for if I understand myself, both articles maintain one and the same philosophy, which is substantially that of St. Anselm in his *Proslogium*. I can really see no reason why you have approved the one, and reject the other, unless it be in the article on McCosh I have succeeded better in explaining what I mean by ideal intuition, and showing that it is simply intuition of the ideal or ideas, which reflection identifies and verifies as *ens necessarium et reale*.

With great respect and many good wishes for your health, I am,

Yours truly,
O. A. Brownson[47]

In saying that Fr. Hewit had maintained immediate intuition of God, censured by the Holy See, Brownson referred to Fr. Hewit's *Problems of the Age*. In the course of a letter to Fr. Hecker, in September 1871, Brownson said:

The propositions condemned [i.e., by the Holy See] are of two classes. The one censured as pantheistic, & the other as asserting ontologism, or direct & immediate cognition of God, an objection you will remember I made to Fr. H[ewit]'s first article on the Problems of the Age at the time of its publication. [That letter of remonstrance to Fr. Hecker was written on April 28, 1866.][48]

[In this same letter of September, 1871, Brownson went on to say of Fr. Hewitt:] . . . who I am sure has misapprehended both Gioberti and me, & supposed we agree with him when we did not. The censures of the Holy See strike him, but not me.[49]

With the rest of the articles Brownson sent in for the last months of the year, both Fr. Hecker and Fr. Hewit expressed themselves well satisfied; if not enthusiastic in one or the other case. The year 1872, however, was to bring changed relations with the *Catholic World*. Both his articles, the one on "Ontologism and Ontology," and the other on "Reason and Revelation," were rejected. Fr. Hecker wrote him on January 8, 1872, to say that the article on the "Necessity of Revelation" clashed with the views held by both Fr. Hewit and himself. He added: "In my judgment it would seriously impair the influence of the C.W. to bring out in its pages conflicting views on such important subjects."[50]

Brownson saw now more clearly than ever that the rift between his own theological and philosphical views and those represented by the *Catholic World* was too wide to be bridged over in any way. He sat down at once and wrote Fr. Hecker:

Dear Father Hecker:
You are the judge, not I, of what is suitable to your pages, and I regret that my philosophy and theology are under the ban of the *Catholic World*. I will be greatly obliged if you will return to me the two rejected articles. I have had Fr. Hewit's criticism [of the] Ontology article, and though it has surprised me, . . . I beg you to give him my thanks for it.[51]

On the seventeenth of this same month he also wrote his son concerning this matter:

I have been prevented from writing sooner, by bad eyes, a lame foot, and an unusual press of work. I find I had undertaken more work than I could accomplish, that I could not write for the *Catholic World* and the *Tablet*, and have any time left to prepare the series of works I have, as you know, in contemplation. Consequently I have broken off my connection with the C.W.

The immediate occasion of my doing it was the rejection of my article on Ontologism and Ontology, and another on Reason and Revelation. Both my theology and philosophy being under the ban of the C.W., I thought it best to have nothing to do with it, and leave the Paulists to themselves. I shall hereafter devote my time to the *Tablet* and the preparation of my contemplated works.[52]

The rejection of the two articles was, then, the occasion, not the cause of his withdrawal from the *Catholic World*. This, too, is what he emphasized in two other letters to Fr. Hecker, dated January 12 and January 31. He was also quite anxious lest "their long continued friendship" should in any way be interrupted or grow cool as he was not withdrawing "in a pet," as he said. Yet one wonders whether the relationship remained quite the same. There was apparently never any further correspondence between them. On the occasion of Brownson's demise (April 17, 1876), Fr. Hecker wrote his son Henry a very appropriate, if short, note. But more worthy of mention is the fine funeral service Fr. Hecker gave his old friend. Speaking of the memorial service given their father at the Paulist Church in New York, Sarah Brownson (Mrs. Tenney) wrote her brother Henry and said in a letter, dated April 27, 1876: "Yesterday at the Paulists it was done up in a style beyond anything the other churches could attempt. Printed invitations, the church heavily draped, solemn High Mass with innumerable ceremonies, priests beyond counting, and a funeral sermon by Fr. Hewit."[53]

Despite doctrinal clashes, Brownson had remained quite affectionately disposed toward his old friend, Fr. Hecker, while a contributor to the *Catholic World*. He had favored him personally with such frequent mention in the *Tablet* that the publisher, James Sadlier, wrote him on June 3, 1868, to say that a continuance of such a practice would be poor policy.[54] It is also to Brownson's credit that when contemplating a revival of his own *Review* and a consequent withdrawal from the *Catholic World*, he remarked to his son: "My only unwillingness to do it, is the injury Father Hecker may suffer from my withdrawal."[55] Fr. Walter Elliott, C.S.P., in his "Personal Recollections" spoke, too, of the comradely visits Brownson used to make to the Paulist Convent, Fifty-ninth Street, New York, while he was a contributor to the *Catholic World*. On such occasions he would sometimes stay a day and a night, and there were long arguments lasting into the late hours of the night with the priests "about the more unknowable things of God." After which Brownson would seek out the novice-master of the Paulist Community, Fr. George Deshon, "to make his humble confession." Then as Fr. Elliott adds: "Next morning the noble-hearted, great-minded Champion of Holy Church would kneel among us novices and receive Holy Communion with us, as if glad to be one of us."[56]

Brownson must have felt a real wrench in his severance from the *Catholic World*. But whatever the course of events, he turned ever with renewed vigor to the next project at hand. Fortunately, too, he was always receiving letters of reassurance to cheer him on his way. He received at this time, in March 1872, such a letter from William Seton, grandson of Mother Seton, who was studying in Munich, Bavaria. After deploring the political apathy and imbecility of Catholics generally in his letter, Mr. Seton wound up, saying:

I will only add one thing more — but I do it with hesitation, for I hate flattery myself & never wish to flatter — and it is, if Catholics in my own country hold the position they now do, it serves them right. When years ago you were battling for the cause, they deliberately spiked your guns & turned you out to rust; they left you, like an old warhorse that had gone through the fights, to pasture in a stony lot, when they knew what you had sacrificed by leaving the company of Emerson, Holmes, Whittier & all those whose names the American people cherish as household words.

You will still be remembered — you will — and long years hence when people go wandering through Elizabeth they will point their fingers to a house and say: "There is where Brownson lived." Perhaps when the Jesuits have their headquarters in America instead of Rome, some future Father Becx will say: "Well, there was something in Brownson after all — but as we did not understand English, we did not find it out."[57]

This is but one of quite a number of very interesting letters he received from William Seton and his sisters while they were studying abroad. Unfortunately we do not have his replies. It is but a part of the wide correspondence he continued to carry on during the years following the suspension of his *Review*. Not to mention his many letters to journals of the day on government and politics, especially those to the New York *Times*, he carried on a large personal correspondence with persons he had mostly never met, but who had written him for advice on one score or another. Such letters generally received close attention and were answered with care. Sometimes in the case of prospective converts, such as William G. Dix, the questions proposed in his many letters before becoming a Catholic called for replies well-nigh as extended as elaborate articles. But no labor was too great for Brownson where the cause of God and truth were at stake. In one of his letters, dated April 25, 1870, Mr. Dix assured Brownson that his writings were gradually working the destruction of Calvinism in New England. He wrote:

Certainly, all Christians owe to you a great debt, which will be more acknowledged years hence than now, for aiding in that New England reaction, which in God's good time will make all this region as earnest for Catholicity, as it has been earnest for Calvinism, and for the earnest rebellion against Calvinism. I see many tokens the New England thinkers are getting tired of the sea of intellectual chaos, and are struggling back to dry land.[58]

Another correspondent whose numerous letters to Brownson stretched over many years of this period was Mrs. Madeleine Dahlgren, wife of Rear Admiral J.A.B. Dahlgren. She was an accomplished lady living in Washington, D.C., a gifted translator and author, who felt great esteem and admiration for Brownson himself and his wife Sally. She made them godparents by proxy of her twin babies, a boy and a girl. She did so, she said, to express to them both "more than words can do my admiration, profound regard and real affection for you both. . . . May our boy emulate your long struggle for right and truth — and may our girl read as her mother has in the dove-like eyes of your dear wife the fairest womanly virtues which can adorn her sex."[59]

Another brief but interesting correspondence Brownson had during these years was with Fr. Eugene M. O'Callaghan of Youngstown, Ohio, then in the Cleveland diocese. Fr. O'Callaghan's rectory was a perennial rendezvous for a numerous group of priests in the diocese who ran the full gamut in their discussions of diocesan and clerical matters. When a theological dispute arose which could not be resolved, it was to Brownson that Fr. O'Callaghan wrote as to a sort of a theological oracle. The question which divided the disputants concerned was whether or not it was repugnant to the sanctity of God to suppose an order of things in which it is possible for him to forgive a man one mortal sin upon the performance of certain prescribed acts of virtue accompanied by attrition, and at the same time to retain other mortal sins of which the man is guilty. In other words, is it possible to suppose a gradual return of the mortal sinner to God by a partial remission of his guilt?

To a second letter Fr. O'Callaghan had written him, Brownson replied on October 4, 1866, saying in part:

> Rev. and dear Sir:
> I have almost entirely forgotten what I wrote in reply to the question submitted for decision, but so far as I remember, I supposed the question to be substantially as you interpret it, viz: "Can there be a gradual return of a mortal sinner to God by a partial remission of guilt?" Is it compatible with the sanctity of God to forgive on attrition, confession, etc., a sinner guilty of a number of mortal sins, one of his mortal sins, while he retains the rest?
> I think I answered the question, as you state it, and I repeat, in the negative. What I mean to say is this, that though the sinner's guilt undoubtedly augments in proportion to the number of his mortal sins, yet God cannot forgive one of the number without forgiving the whole; therefore the remission must be complete, or no remission at all. Did I not in my former letter so reply?
> My reasons are that forgiveness on the part of God is not forensic or external justification, as Calvinists teach, but intrinsic, remitting not simply the penalty, but removing the sin, and receiving the sinner into Divine friendship, which is not possible so long as one or more mortal sins remain unforgiven and unremitted. With this view of remission I cannot understand in what would consist the remission of A.B.'s *fifth* sin while the *four* were retained. He is just as far from being grateful to God as ever. He who is guilty of one point is guilty of all. Not *as* guilty as if he had broken every point of the law, but just as far from justification. He may deserve less punishment, but he is just as far from the friendship of God, which is as effectually broken by one mortal sin as by a hundred. The man guilty of one mortal sin is just as effectually out of the state of grace as he who is guilty of the five you suppose; and as remission places the sinner in a state of grace, and restores the lost friendship of God, there can, in the nature of the case, be no remission for the other four. This seems to me to be conclusive.[60]

This correspondence of Brownson with Fr. O'Callaghan takes on more interest now inasmuch as a biography of Fr. O'Callaghan has just been published. In many ways Fr. O'Callaghan seems to have been ahead of his times. His biographer, Fr. Nelson J. Callahan, tells us that he was truly a prophet of the Church in America in the last third of the nineteenth century in working tirelessly for more humane procedures in the Church, in appealing for more dialogue between bishops and priests, in pleading that "due process" be established, so that a person accused would have the right to know the accusations, to face his accusers, to have a fair trial, and be given the right to appeal an unfavorable decision. In a day when canon law was in abeyance in missionary America, Fr. O'Callaghan believed there was too much arbitrariness in the exercise of authority on the part of American bishops, including those under whom he served. In his well-meant efforts to bring about a change, he published a series of letters (twelve in all) in the *New York Freeman's Journal* under the title, "The Status of the Clergy." He remained anonymous by signing simply as "Jus." His biographer says:

The "Jus Letters," as they were called, attracted immediate, and wide attention. They said with vigor and eloquence what many American priests felt regarding the relationship existing between priests and bishops, and about episcopal exercise of authority. . . . It was as Jus that Eugene O'Callaghan made a great contribution to the American Church in 1868-1870. The astonishing thing is that what he wrote then seems just as relevant and perhaps even more urgent today.[61]

Whether or not Brownson knew anything about Fr. O'Callaghan's benevolent campaign for "due process," he most certainly would have been cordially in favor of it. He too deplored much arbitrariness in the exercise of authority in the Catholic Church, consequent on the fact that canon law did not apply to missionary America in his day. It was especially in the early 1860s that he was pleading for a reign of law rather than men. It is scarcely to be doubted that Fr. O'Callaghan took at least some of his ideas in his "Letters" from Brownson's *Review*.

Among Brownson's frequent correspondents, Sister Eulalia is also to be mentioned, who belonged to the Visitation nuns, and who founded the Academy of Mt. de Chantal, near Wheeling, West Virginia. She sought his advice on many matters, such as what textbook of philosophy to use in the academy, and often wrote words of encouragement to him through the years when he was in the thick of the fight for truth and justice.[62] Some of the most revealing letters, however, which Brownson himself wrote, were addressed to his son Henry during the years 1860-1875 — seventy-five in all. They are of particular interest insofar as he frequently consulted Henry on various topics. They bear the marks of genuine warmth and affection, but are not of course sentimental.[63]

During the years he contributed to the *Catholic World,* the *Ave Maria* and the *Tablet,* Brownson also lectured now and then, but most notably at Seton Hall College, South Orange, New Jersey. Msgr. Michael A. Corrigan, vicar general of the Newark diocese, and president of the college, engaged him to come for the lectures. The preparation of the lectures cost him little time or energy, but the connections between Elizabeth and the college were extremely inconvenient. Msgr. Corrigan endeavored to settle the difficulty by getting Brownson a suitable residence in South Orange, but the price proving prohibitive, Brownson finally decided to discontinue the lectures.[64]

It must have been a pleasure for Brownson to do such work in the diocese of Newark as the bishop there, James Roosevelt Bayley, was very well disposed toward him, though he professed himself a trifle chary of persons much given to philosophizing. It was he who dubbed Orestes Brownson, *Ursa Major,* the Big Bear. Commenting on this, Archbishop Robert J. Dwyer wrote:

And for once the point of episcopal wit was not altogether wide of the mark. Big and bearish he was, towering over his contemporaries both in physical and intellectual stature, disposing of their trivialities with vast sweeping gestures and settling their hash with Johnsonian downrightness. His eyes burned below their bushy crags, calculated to strike terror in the hearts of friend and foe alike. . . .

Even now, almost a century and a quarter since he trumpeted over the roofs of the world his conversion to the Catholic Church, we are just a little timid of his ghost, as though the Big Bear might suddenly rear up and maul us to death. Which is undoubtedly as good a reason as any why America's greatest convert is sedulously ignored.[65]

Within three months of the time of his withdrawal from *the Catholic World*, Brownson had definitely decided to revive his defunct *Review*. It was in no sense at all a new idea to him. He had been, quite understandably, toying with the idea almost from the time he had suspended it. Already in June 1866 he had written to his son Henry (then in the armed forces) about the possibility of reviving *Brownson's Quarterly Review*, with Henry as proprietor and editor, and himself as a contributor.[66] (This proposed arrangement was of course for reasons of policy.) A suggestion of this kind he again made to Henry in a letter written in March 1870, after he had published his booklet *Conversations on Liberalism and the Church*. He said he had put it out to the public as a "feeler."[67] After all, he was still remembered by many as an apparent liberal of the early 1860s. But he had struck a new tack in this booklet, showing beyond doubt that he was one of the stalwarts in the conservative camp. He received many highly complimentary letters from various quarters on this treatise of the relation of the Catholic Church to liberalism. In his enthusiastic letter, Fr. Luke Wimmer, O.S.B., said: "I should like to point out this book to every sensible thinking man out of the Church, and say: 'Take and read.' "[68] In a letter of April 20, 1870, Fr. Hecker told Brownson that Fr. Hewit had suggested that he send a copy of the booklet to the pope.[69] The *Dublin Review* hailed him "as our great old athlete of the faith,"[70] on this appearance before the public under his own name. Brownson had intended that the "Conversations" be published in the *Catholic World*, but Fr. Hecker decided against it. It was much more felicitous for Brownson that the treatise eventually appeared under his own name.

The response to *Liberalism and the Church* was a decided encouragement to him at the time to revive his *Review*. It convinced him that the public would now again adequately support it. But it was of course the intervening events of the following years which led to his final decision. On March 25, 1872, he wrote his son Henry:

> I have finally resolved to revive my *Review*, Brownson's Quarterly Review, Last Series, Vol. I, beginning the year 1873. . . . There are looming up any number of questions on which I wish to have my say. . . . I want also to place myself *rectus in curia* before I die, for the sake of the cause, for the sake of my children and grandchildren, which I could not do in the C.W. [*Catholic World*], and cannot do in the Tablet. Do not try to discourage me, but speak encouragingly.[71]

There was one event in particular which had helped Brownson to come to this decision after having resolved "the matter for a long time" in his mind, and that was the dying wish of his wife Sally. She was a woman of deep piety, and in spite of increasing feebleness, she kept up her practice of attending Holy Mass daily, though the distance for her to walk was considerable. In a swirling January snowstorm she caught a cold that settled on her lungs, from which she never recovered. She died on April 19, 1872.[72] One of the last wishes she expressed to her husband was that he revive his *Review*, "if only for a year, and prove to the world," as Brownson related later, "that my faith has never wavered; that I am still an humble but devoted son of the Church; that I am, as I always professed to be, an uncompromising Catholic and a thorough-going Papist."[73] This wish of his dying wife became sacred to him, and he felt he could not do otherwise than comply with it. Never in this world did anyone ever receive sounder advice, and never did any man do a wiser thing than did Orestes Brownson in reviving his own *Review*. Only by so doing could the cloud which had hung over him in 1864 ever have been effectually dissipated.[74]

The revival of his *Review* was for him a rather staggering undertaking. At his age it would have been so even under ordinary circumstances, but how much more so when we recall that he was still battling his old enemy, gout in the foot, gout in his eyes, and gout crippling the fingers which held the pen. Perhaps he was encouraged a trifle in the matter by the thought that his resurrected *Review* would mean more revenue for him. The fact is he had been living in varying degrees of poverty since the suspension of his *Review*. It was not at all that sufficient money had come to his hand, but that he was continually giving it away in goodly sums to those in need, mostly to relatives, often to indigent in-laws. This largehearted charity kept him rather permanently impoverished. For decades he had been frequently sending generous sums of money to his mother and to his sister Daphne for their support. But letters show that this period of his life was marked by more diffusive charities than ever. The result was that at times he did not have "decent clothes" to go about in. In a letter to his old friend George Bancroft, he remarked that he would like to visit him, "but my coat is too old and seedy for me to do so."[75] Similar letters were written to his son Henry. In one he rejoices at the prospect that he shall get "a new hat & clothes, & appear once more like a gentleman."[76] An increase in income would have been very convenient for him. Still, if such a thought ever crossed his mind, it could have had little influence in the matter of reviving his *Review*. The overshadowing reason that mattered was the cause he had embraced when he had become a Catholic, which remained ever dearer to him "than life itself."

# 46

## A GALLANT WARRIOR RETURNS
## TO FIGHT ON UNDER HIS OWN BANNER

*The enthusiastic acclaim that greeted the announced revival of his* Review • *His vigorous and prolonged attack on the* anti-Christian *or pseudoscience of the day* • *The general nature of the articles in the last series of his* Review • *His elucidation of the true genesis of freedom* • *His review of Fr. Augustine Thébaud's* The Irish Race in the Past and Present • *His discussion of Fr. Hill's* Elements of Philosophy • *His comments on women novelists* • *The special importance of the volumes of his last series.*

After Brownson had definitely decided on reviving his own *Review,* he began to prepare for the issuance of its first edition in January 1873. To apprize the public of his decision, he served notice in the New York *Tablet* that *Brownson's Quarterly Review* would make its reappearance at the beginning of the New Year. This notice was copied into many other newspapers and magazines of the day. The response in the way of enthusiastic congratulations from many, both in this country and Canada, was much more reassuring than Brownson had anticipated. Michael A. Corrigan had just succeeded to the diocese of Newark as bishop, in which Brownson lived, replacing James R. Bayley who had been promoted to the metropolitan see of Baltimore. Although Brownson had not applied to Bishop Corrigan for permission to reissue his *Review,* the bishop wrote him: "As to the Review, I shall be most happy to see it succeed, and increase in circulation. The articles which you have given to the world will long continue to be read with interest and profit, and I trust that God will spare you many years to carry on the good work. Hoping to see you soon in Elizabeth, I remain very truly yours, M. A. Corrigan, Bp."

Neither did Brownson apply to the archbishop of New York, John Mc-Closkey, for permission to publish, in whose diocese his *Review* was again to be printed. Hearing after some time that the archbishop thought it rather strange that he had not sought his approbation, Brownson wrote to explain that he simply did not wish to implicate the bishops of the country this time in any way with his *Review.* After reading the reasons Brownson had set forth in his letter to him, the archbishop replied:

> I knew them to be as you now represent them entirely free from any discourtesy or disrespect. I wish you to continue as you have begun, and I rejoice to see that your intellectual powers still retain the force and vigor of earlier years. As to your orthodoxy and especially your *Romanism,* both, I think, are established beyond peradventure.
>
> I remain, dear sir, very truly yr. fd., and servant in Xt.
>
> John, Abp. of New York[1]

Bishop William H. Elder of Natchez, Mississippi (later archbishop of Cincinnati, Ohio), a former correspondent, sent encouraging words when he wrote on December 3, 1872:

It is indeed invigorating to see our brave and venerable champion again buckling on his armor — to discomfort the foes of truth and the destroyers of society and to encourage the younger combatants by his example and by his solid blows. Was it not our lamented George Miles [who] gave you the felicitous appellation of "the logical sledgehammer"?[2]

As we have already noted, the voluminous writing Brownson had been doing since the suspension of his *Review* was unsigned in both the *Catholic World* and the New York *Tablet,* and his continuing apostolate of the pen during that period was generally unknown to the public at large. The wording of a letter of congratulations Brownson received from the bishop of Antigonish, Canada, Colin A. MacKinnon, on the announced revival of his *Review* seems to indicate a lack of knowledge on his part of the apologetic writing Brownson had been unintermittently doing. He wrote on December 19, 1872: "The times require the powerful aid of your pen and the Catholic public will rejoice at the news that Dr. Brownson after a long silence, like a giant refreshed with sleep, now rises *ad proeliandum proelia Domini* ['for fighting the battles of the Lord']."[3]

Brownson also received a very good letter of encouragement, among so many others, from Fr. Edward Hipelious, O.S.B., on October 11, 1872:

> I have been requested by a number of priests of this diocese to congratulate you upon the blessed thought of resuming the publication of your peerless "Review." We think it was a thought inspired from above; for, ever since the time when unhappy circumstances necessitated your retirement from the "Review," and the consequent suspension of its publication, there was a vacuum in the English Catholic literature, on both sides of the ocean, and the attempt of filling it was, indeed, not devoid of the merit of a fair intention, but beyond that it did not reach.
> You are, and you will be, entitled to the gratitude of every true Catholic who places his religion above nationalism.[4]

In the introduction to the last series of his *Review,* Brownson indicated the niche it was intended to fill in the literary world of the day and its general aim, when he said:

> The Review . . . will have a character of its own, which will be borne by no other periodical, though others may be far abler, more important and more popular. It will not have a large circulation, for it will not be addressed to the numerous public. It will be addressed only to the cultivated and thoughtful few, the reverend clergy and educated laymen; and will be confined almost exclusively to the discussion of philosophy, theology, ethics, and civil polity. Its aim will be to oppose Catholic principles to the false principles and errors of the proud and arrogant non-Catholic world, which flatters itself that it is on the eve of triumphing over the invincible Church of God. I shall find, I trust "a fit audience, though few."[5]

In this prospectus of the precise character of his *Review* he did not pinpoint the fact that one of his heaviest attacks during these last years was to be launched on the *anti-Christian* or pseudoscience of the day. Here was an enemy that had more recently moved onto the field and was mounting an attack on the Christian faith. The publication of Darwin's *The Origin of Species* (1859) had shocked the faith of thousands, if not of millions, throughout the Christian world. Brownson had boldly confronted this new enemy already in the early 1860s in his own *Review* for its lack of true scientific principles,[6] and then again in the *Catholic World*.[7] But he was now to follow this up with an increasing hammering attack in the last series of his *Review* — that is, on the *anti-Christian* or pseudoscience of the day. He deeply lamented that in his day "science, or what passes for science, is, and for a long time has been *extra ecclesiam,* and in its spirit *contra ecclesiam.* The opinion of the scientific world is against us, and carries away not a few of our own children, and prevents those not in the Church from ever listening to our arguments in her favor."[8] He upbraided Catholics of the day for resorting to the ostrich trick instead of getting into the laboratories themselves and correcting the sorry state of affairs. As for Orestes A. Brownson, he was the last man in the world who would suffer unchallenged an increasing attack on the Christian faith through a long series of unproved theories and conjectures. He saw that all this was being done under the imposing name of science, and he took deadly aim at this monstrous enemy of the Christian faith.

In his biography of Brownson, *A Pilgrim's Progress*, Arthur M. Schlesinger, Jr., remarks on Brownson's "sharp perception of the limitations of science as being rare in a day which tended to confound Newton with God."[9] In taking notice of the reputed antagonism between faith and science, Brownson repudiated at once the naïve argument that science is at once false the moment it comes into conflict with religion. He presented the quarrel not as between faith and science, but as between the opinions and conjectures of scientists and theologians. But only the Catholic divine, Brownson pointed out, has a sure footing in the controversy, for he alone has the infallible teaching authority of the Catholic Church wherewith to test all theories, hypotheses and conjectures of scientists. Brownson further observed when reviewing (1874) a series of lectures by Joseph LeConte, professor of geology and natural history in the University of California, that the non-Catholic or Protestant divine has no such criterion of truth to bring as a touchstone to the domain of science. For the Protestant divine has no such infallible means of determining the sense of divine revelation since he rejects in the church the very idea of an infallible teaching authority. He is thereby shorn of all hope or ability to determine what is false and unscientific in science when it comes in apparent conflict with religion — the very thing Professor LeConte had so unsuccessfully attempted to do in his lectures.[10]

Brownson thought that this inability on the part of the Protestant divine to oppose anything more than mere opinion in matters of religion to the false pretensions of pseudoscience brought religion into disrepute with scientists and tended to emancipate science from theology:

> In the general quarrel of the scientists and Protestant theologians the scientists have carried the day, have for the most part emancipated themselves from theology, and proceeded without attempting to reckon with theologians. They even make it a point to ignore them, and treat their reclamations with silent contempt. The Protestant theologians, having no infallible authority for theology, and unable to help themselves, gradually fall in with the scientists, adopt their theories, and try to explain the Scriptures so as to make them accord with their theories.[11]

When reviewing in 1875 Professor Tyndall's "Inaugural Address before the British Association" on the progress of science, Brownson complained in particular of James McCosh, D.D., president of Princeton — the Presbyterians' outstanding man of the day — that in replying to Tyndall he "concedes so much to the atheistic school, that he reserves nothing worth defending against it."[12] He had also previously complained of Dr. McCosh on a slightly different score when taking notice of McCosh's lectures in defense of Christianity against Positivism:

> We complain of the author of the indignity he offers Christianity by suffering the Positivists to put it on the defensive, and in attempting to prove it against Positivism. Christianity is in possession, and she is not called upon to defend her titles till strong reasons are adduced for ousting her. Consequently, it is for those who would oust her to prove their case, and make good their claim. The Christian controversialist at this late date does not begin with an apology or defense of Christianity, but attacks those who assail her, and puts them on their defense. It is for the scientists, or Positivists, who oppose the Christian religion, to prove their Positivism or science. It is enough for the Christian to show that Positivism or alleged science is not itself proved, or, if proven, that it proves nothing against Christ and his Church.[13]

Though doing so in a reverential tone and manner, Brownson also differed on this matter from Cardinal Wiseman when reviewing the cardinal's *Lectures on the Connection between Science and Religion.* His Eminence was more condescending to scientists than Brownson, and attempted to prove to them that the objections whch they brought against religion from pseudoscience were not scientific. Brownson, on the contrary, planted himself stoutly on the principle that those who bring objections against religion from science must prove, first of all, that what they allege is genuine science, not merely an induction, a theory, a hypothesis, or a conjecture. "We hold," he affirmed, "that Christians should plant themselves on the rights of religion, and yield in these times, even by way of argument, no advantage which they may justly claim. . . . History and science must plead before her [the Catholic Church], not she before them."[14]

He wound up his article on "True and False Science" in the July 1873 issue of his *Review* with the warning:

> We, in our efforts to conciliate the professional scientists, are likely to be successful only in weakening the cause of truth, of obscuring the very truth we would have them adopt. If we are Catholics let us be Catholics, and be careful to make no compromises, and seek no alien alliances. The spirit as the tendency of the age is at enmity with God, and must be fought, not coaxed. No concord between Christ and Belial [wickedness or worthlessness] is possible.[15]

The impression might loosely be got from what has been said that Brownson was not merely illiberal but positively hostile in his attitude toward the scientist. Nothing could be farther from the truth. While he had "a profound reverence for the sciences, and all really scientific men,"[16] he was decidedly hostile toward the whole class of modern *anti-Christian* scientists and arraigned them scathingly before the bar of moral accountability. No man, he maintained, has the moral right to publish any theory or hypothesis which assails or contradicts the Christian faith unless he has infallible authority for the truth of what he alleges in opposition to it — a thing no scientist can have. He attempted to use the branding iron when he wrote:

> From the point of view of morals or tried by the rigidly ethical standard, such scientists as Darwin, Sir Charles Lyell, Sir John Lubbock, Taine, Bucher, Professor Huxley, Herbert Spencer, and others of the same genus, who publish opinions, theories, hypotheses, which are at best only plausible conjectures under the imposing name of science, and which unsettle men's minds, bewilder

the half-learned, mislead the ignorant, undermine the very basis of society, and assail the whole moral order of the universe, are fearfully guilty, and a thousand times more dangerous to society and are greater criminals even than your most noted thieves, robbers, burglars, swindlers, murderers, or midnight assassins. Instead of being held up in honor, feted, and lauded as the great men of their age and country, and held up as the benefactors of the race, they richly deserve that public opinion should brand them with infamy as the enemies of God and man, of religion and society, of truth and justice, of science and civilization.[17]

During his long career as a journalist two themes in particular had always engaged his attention: church and state. Already in 1839 he had written: "Religion and politics do, in fact, embrace all the interests and concernments of human beings, in all their multiplied relations. Nothing can concern me as a man, as an individual, or as a member of society, which cannot be arranged under one or the other."[18] Hence it is not surprising that his more numerous articles during this last period likewise dealt with one or the other of these two subjects — such as "The Papacy and the Republic"; "The Döllingerites, the Nationalists, and the Papacy"; "Bismarck and the Church"; "Papal Infallibility and Civil Allegiance"; "Newman's Reply to Gladstone"; "Gallicanism and Ultramontanism"; and "The Church and the Civil Power."[19] While his principles of treatment remained perennially the same, he added some new thought in these treatises accordingly as world events brought shifting attacks on these two great pillars of society.

Anyone who reads these massive essays will sense at once the presence of majestic thought and the roll of powerful rhetoric. As Archbishop McCloskey had observed, "his intellectual powers still retain[ed] the force and vigor of earlier years." He was now lunging as a giant, happily and entirely unrestrained again, at the enemies of God and society. He claimed an additional advantage in these last years: "I have grown more detached from the world, more independent of it, and less sensitive alike to its censures and its applause. . . . I count on the prayers of my old and new friends to strengthen me for the battle."[20] Like Newman, he saw clearly that the great question of the day was becoming more and more, God or no God. He accordingly brought up all his heavy artillery in successive articles for the counterattack. In his *Essay in Refutation of Atheism* he indicted Emerson and his disciples, the pseudoscientists, the Positivists and worshipers of humanity, the members of the Internationals, and "the majority of the medical profession" as propagators of atheism, open or disguised.[21] And he turned on them with all the intellectual power and might he could muster. His friend, William Seton, wrote him from Bozen, Tyrol, Austria, on October 21, 1874, that he "had felt like a warhorse"[22] while reading his *Review*.

Those who have read Brownson's writings shall have been well convinced that few or no persons were ever more passionately concerned with the principles and conditions which make for the permanent establishment and maintenance of true and well-ordered liberty in society than was he. It was his lifelong concern. His last and most mature thought on this theme is contained in a review of the career of his old friend, Count Montalembert, in July of 1874. The Count — as well as such others as Louis Veuillot, Gioberti, Padre Ventura, Père Gratry and Père Hyacinthe, Döllinger and Lacordaire — had taken the view that liberty and religion are two different forces, the one originating in nature, and the other in grace, needing to be harmonized in order that they may mutually assist each other. This is the classical or Greco-Roman concept of liberty, celebrated in English literature, regarded as coming from without and independent of religion. Brownson himself at an earlier period in his life seemed to adopt this view, but in later years he repudiated the tenet that liberty can or does originate independently of religion. He laid down the principle that true liberty in every case originates from within, depends on the operation of religion in the soul of the individual, and through the individual on the interior life of the nation. This he regarded as the profounder philosophy of the origin of freedom:

> The Church initiates and sustains liberty by regenerating the soul, through the operations of the Holy Ghost, elevating it to the plane of its supernatural destiny, restraining its inordinate passions, moderating its lusts, and warming the heart with the love of truth and justice. She freed society by first freeing the soul from the chains of Satan, its bondage to sin, its slavery to the lusts of the flesh. She can do it in no other way.
>
> It is not a free government that makes a free people, but a free people that makes a free government. You may knock the manacles from the hands, and the fetters from the feet of a people, but they are none the less slaves, unless at the same time you free their souls, and make them freemen in Christ. This is because the source of freedom and of slavery is within, and neither operates from without, in the external, or in man's surroundings. No institutions or external arrangements can make or keep a people free that are as individuals in bondage to their lusts, and no efforts of tyrants or despots can reduce to slavery a people whose souls are free. The English conquerors of Ireland have left nothing undone that malice could suggest or power effect to enslave the Catholic Irish, and yet the Catholic Irish, with their free souls and trust in God, have never been interiorly enslaved, or ceased to feel as freemen.[23]

Although the great body of Brownson's thought over the years is marked more by development rather than change, there is perhaps no area in which he ever did a more notable somersault than in regard to the Irish and their type of civilization. This matter has been touched upon in a previous chapter, but in no full sense. In a letter to James A. McMaster, dated March 13, 1849, Brownson had deplored what he considered the inferior type of civilization Irish immigrants were bringing into the country, even calling it "semibarbarism."[24] But when he read Fr. Augustine Thébaud's *The Irish Race in the Past and Present,* and reviewed it for the October 1873 issue of his *Quarterly,* he frankly acknowledged that Fr. Thébaud had furnished him with a "key to Irish history" which he had heretofore lacked. He now asserted that the Irish type of civilization is based on truer, deeper and more universal principles than the Anglo-Norman, the modern French, or the ancient Romantic order. This he attributed to the fact that the Irish type preserves the primitive traditions of mankind (coming down from the patriarchs), reinforced by the Catholic faith, while all other civilizations have originated since the lapse of nations into barbarism and idolatry, and are repugnant to, or at least a departure from, the normal order of society, or to the Christian order of civilization. In short, he said:

> We have always heretofore regarded the Graeco-Roman type of civilization, as developed in our American Constitution, the highest type of civilization the world has known since the great gentile apostasy, and supposed that it needed only the Catholic faith and worship to be as perfect as any civilized order can be; but Father Thébaud, in giving us a clew to Irish history, which we before had lacked, has enabled us to perceive a higher as well as an older type, which we call the Irish type, and which is not only higher and older, but stronger and more persistent, through what we believe have been and still are

the designs of Providence with regard to the Irish race. Were we writing our "American Republic" now, after having read Father Thébaud — from whom we seldom differ, except in drawing conclusions from his premises different from those he himself draws — we should so far modify it as to place the Irish type above the Roman, and to correct, in some respects our definition of barbarism. We had not studied with proper care the patriarchal civilization, nor did we then understand that the Irish race had preserved it in greater purity and vigor than any orther people, except the Hebrew people, until the coming of Christ.[25]

As indicated in his prospectus, Brownson continued his keen interest in the same wide variety of themes in this last series of his *Review* that had always engaged his attention, philosophy by no means ranking least of them all. Besides publishing his *Essay in Refutation of Atheism* serially during these last years, he time and again turned his attention to matters philosophical, the appearance of Fr. Walter Hill's *Elements of Philosophy* drawing his immediate and special attention. In a succinct notice he gave it in his department of literary notices and criticisms, July 1873, he did not find the textbook in all respects unexceptional, but still "it is the only manual in our language at all fit to be introduced into our higher schools and academies, in which a suitable text-book in English has long been a desideratum." But he begged leave to doubt whether persons not familiar with St. Thomas, Suárez and their Latin commentators could either successfully teach or understand Fr. Hill's *Elements*. The Jesuit author, too, "when thinking philosophy," observed Brownson, "appears to think in Latin." Finally he noted what appeared to be a thrust at his own philosophy, and felt called upon to set down once again his fundamental philosophical principle: "We have no direct intuition of God, but we have intuition of what is real and necessary being in the intuition of the intelligible object."[26]

In the last year of his *Review,* 1875, Brownson gave Fr. Hill's *Elements* two full-length reviews in his *Quarterly,* in the April and October issues, the latter being a reply to a slashing attack upon himself by an anonymous critic in the Boston *Pilot*. In his first review of *Elements*, he acknowledged that Fr. Hill's system contained much that is true and important, but he asserted that the system, as far as he did not misapprehend it, interposes between the intellect and the object (intelligible), or the mind and objective reality, a *mundus logicus*, and nowhere teaches that the mind and the real object existing *a parte rei* are brought into immediate contact. This opened the door wide to subjectivism, or mere abstractions. How, then, Brownson wanted to know, does one cross the *pons asinorum* (asses' bridge) of the psychologists, and prove that there is any reality at all, or that our science is not purely subjective? He went on to say that Fr. Hill's system was "in substance only Kantian subjectivism."[27] But this charge he brought not only against Fr. Hill, but against the whole peripatetic school of the day: Cursi, Liberatore, Tongiorgi, San Severino, Kleutgen, Dr. Ward,[28] and others. But let us not misunderstand Brownson's strictures in this matter: it was not at all that he had an itch for criticizing the philosophical efforts of his Catholic contemporaries, but simply that he was in deadly earnest about getting adopted a philosophical system that would truly arm Catholic youth against "the false science and miserable sophistry" of "a shallow but pretentious age."

Fr. Hill had long been Brownson's friend, and it is to his credit that he took Brownson's criticisms in a truly Christian spirit, at least concerning what Brownson had said in his first notice of *Elements*. In a letter dated

October 14, 1874, after beseeching Brownson to make up a textbook from his writings on ethics which he could use in his classes, Fr. Hill said:

> Let me add, Mr. Brownson, that I do not take your criticisms of my little work written at the suggestion of my superior, in an unkindly spirit; on the contrary, I thank you for your remarks which I can but suppose to have been well intended. The book has met with unexpected success, has reached the third edition, a copy of which I hereby transmit to you. I am surely thankful to you for what you have done towards bringing my book before the learned world; you are harsh in your manner, but I believe you to be upright in your intention. I pen this in cordial and Christian love for you, but it is not for publication. I surely have no right to think hard of you because you differ with me in some matters of opinion.[29]

At the end of the first article on *Elements* in the April 1875 issue of his *Review,* Brownson had assured Fr. Hill that if he felt he had misapprehended him in any respect or had done his system of philosophy any injustice, his *Review* was as open to him for a reply as it was to himself. This invitation Fr. Hill did not accept, but an anonymous writer of an article in the Boston *Pilot* "assail[ed] him with great bitterness and some personal abuse, both of which are very unphilosophical, and neither of which is of any logical value,"[30] said Brownson. In his original notice of *Elements* Brownson had complained about Fr. Hill's English terminology, though acknowledging that it was about as good as that found in similar textbooks on philosophy. The *Pilot* critic now tried to give Brownson tit for tat by making out — a charge endorsed, Brownson was assured, by Fr. Hill himself, if it did not originate with him — that he himself was too ignorant of Latin to understand the technicalities of scholastic philosophy. The assailant had "led with his chin," and Brownson saw the opening for a little playful fun. After assuring his critic that he was by no means without a sufficient knowledge of the Latin of the medieval scholastics to understand their technicalities, he said with tongue in cheek:

> But suppose we have not [such a knowledge]. Does not Fr. Hill write his philosophy for students whose mother-tongue is English, and will it be alleged that we are too ignorant of Latin to understand English? And is it necessary to charge us with ignorance of Latin in order to prove that we misunderstand or cannot understand Fr. Hill's English? This would only confirm the criticism made in our first notice of the work, that his English is unintelligible to a reader who is ignorant of scholastic philosophy and of Latin. Indeed it is a grave charge to the work, as an English work, that it is not intelligible to a simple English reader who knows no language but his own. The attempt to make out that our criticism must be unfounded because we are ignorant of Latin, only justifies our criticism.[31]
>
> We must say . . . that, though we find no difficulty in understanding the author when he explains his meaning in Latin, which we are said to be ignorant of, we have no little difficulty in getting at his meaning when he expresses it in English — a language of which we have been thought to know something. Indeed, Fr. Hill's English is far less intelligible to us than any scholastic Latin we have ever encountered and his terminology would be absolutely unintelligible to us but for the little acquaintance we have with the scholastic Latin. We hope the professor will not take it ill, if, while we do not doubt his proficiency either as an English or Latin scholar, we do not find him very happy in his rendering of the Latin, in which he studied his philosophy, into English. When we translate the scholastic technical terms into English, and conform them to the genius of our mother-tongue, we suspect he and his defenders fail to recognize

them. The author's terminology is un-English, "done out of Latin," if you will, but "into no language."[32]

Brownson never ceased to insist that the principles of science and the principles of things are identical, that science must follow the order of being, for only that which is, or the real, is intelligible, thinkable, or knowable. But as far as Fr. Hill asserted that the unreal or the mere possible is knowable, an object of the mind, he rendered philosophy an unreal science, and therefore no science at all, only nescience or nihilism.[33] Brownson reminded his readers that Professor J. H. Koop, C.M., had contributed two articles to his *Review,* proving that the possible is nothing in itself, or is cognizable or thinkable only in the power or ability of the real. He added: "Fr. Hill and his defender in the Boston *Pilot* would do well to read Professor Koop's discussion of possibilities and the *mundus logicus* — a priest who cannot be accused of being too ignorant of Latin either to understand a work written in English, or to be familiar with the technicalities of St. Thomas and other scholastics."[34]

Who was the author of the slashing attack on him in the *Pilot* relative to Fr. Hill's philosophy? Brownson's daughter Sarah reported that Mrs. L. St. John Echel claimed it was John Boyle O'Reilly, editor at the time.[35] And a similar article appeared in the *Tablet.* Just at this time, too, Brownson had lectured in Boston, and, while there, had visited his friend, Mr. H.L. Richard and family. Mr. Richard wrote him on April 29, 1875, to tell him how hugely he and his family had enjoyed his visit. He then lamented the "scandalous notice" of Brownson's *Review* in the *Pilot,* and deplored "the atrocious attack" on him in the *Tablet.* In the course of his sympathetic letter, he remarked:

> If those cruel, thoughtless men knew you as I know you, if they but imagined half the tenderness, charity, and true mobility of soul that dwelt in that great heart of yours, they would, I'm sure, sooner cut off their right hand than willfully wound you even in the smallest matter. . . . God bless you, dear Doctor Brownson, and give you grace to bear your trial and great will be your reward in heaven. Will you, Dear Doctor, pardon the freedom with which I have written? . . . I could not help speaking a word of encouragement and sympathy even at the risk of seeming somewhat officious.
>
> I am, dear Doctor, most truly and sincerely yours in a common faith,
>
> H. L. Richard[36]

In these last years Brownson was gravely admonished "to follow the tradition of Catholic philosophy." To which he replied: "with all my heart . . . only please tell me what it is and where I can find a statement of it." He added: "Said to us one of the ablest and profoundest prelates of the United States, 'the philosophy taught in our Catholic colleges consists of some fragments of Catholic theology badly taught.' [When Newman visited Rome after his conversion, he found no philosophy in vogue there at all, neither that of Aristotle, St. Thomas Aquinas nor any other.]"[37] To the admonition that he should follow St. Thomas, Brownson replied: "It is a little too much like the Protestant direction: 'Follow the Bible.' "[38] He insisted that no one had the right to impose his interpretation of the Angelic Doctor on him any more than he had the right to impose his interpretation on others. If others differed from him, Brownson pointed out that "our *Review* is as open to them as to ourselves, and we see no good reason why, if confident they are right, they should refuse to meet the question on its merits. We have no opinions we love better than truth, and our whole life proves that we have no reluctance to abandon any views we entertain, when once shown they are untenable."[39]

To his department of literary notices and criticism, Brownson continued to add occasional full-length essays on some phase of modern literature, mainly the novel, and particularly women's novels. As he had a keen perception of the vast influence of literature, he had always been deeply concerned about the creation of a sound and healthy body of popular Catholic literature. "The press," he wrote, "is not merely 'a fourth estate,' as it has been called, but an estate which has well-nigh usurped the function of all the others, and has taken the sole direction of the intellectual and moral destinies of the civilized world."[40] But with all his persevering efforts through the decades for the promotion and growth of a sound body of Catholic literature among his Catholic countrymen, he could only sigh in his last years that American Catholic literature was no better than at "the tail end of the Catholic world."[41] But he did not relax his study efforts as long as he had a pen in his hand to purify and elevate the literature that was pouring daily from the press. Yet he continued to pay a heavy price for his independent and fearless criticism. Not all could abide "the stern masculinity of [his] Review."[42]

In his first essay of literary criticism in the last series of his *Review,* on "Religious Novels, and Woman versus Woman," he ran headlong into trouble in his review of Sister Mary Frances Clare's *Hornehurst Rectory.* He asknowledged that Sister Mary Frances Clare (known as the "Nun of Kenmare") possessed considerable intellectual powers, that she wrote with vivacity and vigor, with earnestness and power, but added: "In those of her writings which we have read, we miss that meek and subdued spirit, that sweetness and unction, that we naturally expect in a daughter of St. Clare. We miss in them the spiritual refinement and ascetic culture we look for in a religious, and their tone strikes us as somewhat harsh and bitter, sarcastic and exaggerated."[43] This was unfortunate.

Although the "Nun of Kenmare" had written Brownson when he had revived his *Review,* "I congratulate you, or rather America, on the reappearance of your admirable *Review,*" she was to be heard now in a different key. The fact that Brownson had included in the same edition of his *Review* a three-page eulogy of his daughter Sarah's *The Life of Demetrius Augustine Gallitzin, Prince and Priest*[44] — which he called a "model biography, a work of sterling merit, which is a valuable contribution to our rising Catholic literature" — only gave the "Nun of Kenmare" a chance to compound her complaint. "I am grieved," she wrote, "that you should allow any article to appear in your *Review,* which has descended to personalities. I know it requires care to avoid the insertion of what an editor may regret, but I am quite sure that you must be above anything so very petty. To attack any lady's private character, is bad enough, but it is surely worse to attack a nun's. . . . It is not Christian to charge a religious with not being true to her vocation; neither does such a matter come at all within the reviewer's province." She concluded by saying: "It will, of course lessen the value of any criticism, when it is observed that the work written by your daughter is the only one selected for enthusiastic and unlimited praise. I have thought it right to say this much. I fear your feeling against any woman (except one) who holds a pen will hardly allow you to receive this as it is meant, but however I may regret this, should it be the case, I must remain, yours sincerely, S.M. Frances Clare."[45]

It would appear that the "Nun of Kenmare" was justified in complaining about reflections on her as a religious, and in saying that such did not come within the province of the reviewer. Yet what Brownson had said had undoubtedly expressed so naturally what he felt regarding the literary production of Sister M. Frances Clare that he was perhaps not really aware at the moment of the full implications of what he was saying. Brownson's literary criticisms were generally penetrating and just, but having the strength of a giant, what to him was only a wee tap of the shillelagh could in some cases be a crushing blow to the recipient. His friend, Anne C. Lynch, wrote him in his earlier years that Mr. Osgood had remarked of his review of Edward Lytton Bulwer's *Zanoni* that it was like "bringing a battle-axe to crush a butterfly."[46] Henry Brownson attempted to defend his father in this matter of the "Nun of Kenmare," but apparently missed the real point at issue. Brownson's sturdy friend, Sister Eulalia Pearce, appears to state the case fairly when she wrote him: "Hornehurst Rectory, as a tale of fiction, is a miserable failure. I am sorry, however, that in your strictures you did not confine yourself strictly to her *Works*, for the personal allusion, exposing a lamentable weakness, appears to me (pardon me for saying it) contrary to Christian charity and beyond the province of the purely literary critic."[47] It is to be feared that what Brownson had innocently enough remarked had a share in starting the "Nun of Kenmare" on that melancholy odyssey that was so long in coming to an end, and which had so sad an ending, as related in her autobiography.[48]

His critical reflections in the same essay on *The House of York* brought a hornet's nest about his head. Of this he spoke when reviewing *Grapes and Thorns* by the same author where he remarked: "In noticing *Grapes and Thorns*, we feel that we must summon up all that remains of our youthful gallantry, and not forget for a moment that the work is written by a sensitive lady. We forgot it when we reviewed her *House of York*, and spoke of it in our natural voice, without softening our tones, according to our honest judgment of its merits, as if the author had been a hard-headed man; and the lady's friends set us down as a bear, and duly berated us."[49] Although Brownson owned that the author possesses many fine gifts as a novelist, he regretted to find her heroine after all a heartless sort of person. He refined his indictment when he said that the tendency of the *House of York* is to lessen the respect of the reader for womanhood, as there was not one true, noble-minded woman to be found within its pages — such as one could love and honor.[50]

Here we encounter one of Brownson's salient objections to women's novels — their tendency to lower respect for womankind. He himself had a huge respect for womanhood, that is, for the true woman (not the mannish type) as he expressed it, whom "we honor, and all but worship."[51] On that score, the tendency of so many women's novels to destroy respect for womankind was all the greater offense to him. In this article of January 1873, he repeated what he had written when he reviewed *Mrs. Gerald's Niece* in 1871:

> Women's novels are very damaging to our respect for woman by the recklessness with which they reveal the mysteries of the sex, expose all her little feminine art and tricks, lay bare her most private thoughts and interior sentiments, and rend from her the last shred of mystery, and expose her unveiled and unrobed to the gaze of the profane world, and leave nothing to the imagination. They divest her of the mystic veil with which man's chivalry covers her. There are passages in *Jane Eyre*, for instance, which show that woman can

enter into and describe with minute accuracy the grossest passions of man's nature, and which men could not describe to their own sex without a blush. To every young man not yet corrupted by the sex, there is something mystic, almost divine, in womanhood, something that fills him with awe of woman, and makes him shrink from the bare thought of abusing her as a sacrilege. This awe is both his protection and hers. Your feminine novelists dispel the illusion, and prove to him that there is nothing more mystic in woman's nature than in man's, that her supposed divinity is only the projection of his chivalric imagination, and that, after all, she is only ordinary flesh and blood, kneaded of no finer clay than himself. It is a sad day for her as well as for him when that illusion is dispelled, and man is, as the French say, désillusioné.[52]

The moral mischief these feminine novelists do to individuals and society is incalculable. "The age of chivalry," exclaimed Burke, when Marie Antoinette was conducted to the guillotine, "is gone"; and that it is gone, women have chiefly themselves to blame.[53]

If there were those who bristled at the expression of such views, there were also those who applauded the courageous statement of such honest convictions. A lady in Cincinnati, Ohio, Mary E. Walsh, who appears to have kept fairly abreast of the feminist literature of the day, wrote Brownson on February 13, 1873:

I am not very old, but I have lived long enough to wish there were more men like you in America — long enough to see talent so perverted among women as almost to be ashamed of being a woman.

I admire your fearless spirit — your independent attitude — your uncompromising position, so clearly defined — your wholesouled Catholicism, most of all.

I think you are a grand old man; I should like to kiss your hand.

Very truly yours,
Mary E. Walsh[54]

Inasmuch as Brownson seems to have expected antecedently to find what he considered faults of the modern novel in their more pronounced form in women's novels, he probably did in that sense have some sort of prejudice against women novelists. But only insofar as they did not come up to his criterion of the good novel — not because they were women novelists. His son says that "his works prove that he oftener commended women's books than men's, in proportion to their number."[55] He was without prejudice in the sense that he was ever ready to acknowledge true merit wherever found and to whomsoever it should be awarded. The high praise he bestowed on Lady Georgiana Fullerton when reviewing her *Mrs. Gerald's Niece* is sufficient evidence of this. He asserted that "for rare ability, rich and chaste imagination, high culture, and varied knowledge, elevation and delicacy of sentiment, purity, strength, and gracefulness of style, and the moral and religious tendency of her writings, she stands at the head of contemporary female writers." Indeed he added high praise to high praise when he went on to say that although she did not perfectly realize his ideal of a novel writer, yet she "comes closer to it than any other writer with whose works we are acquainted."[56]

This chapter has touched briefly upon various phases of Brownson's thought during the last three years of his *Review*. As such it is important. For in writing during this period he had had the advantage of the wisdom he had garnered from previous years and the benefit of his intellectual powers still in their full force and vigor. As a student of Brownson has remarked:

The volumes of the last series reveal Brownson at his best. Not a page can afford to be overlooked by the student of Brownson. Father Augustine Hewit of the *Catholic World* once said of him that he was *sui generis* and his works like him.[57] He is not, therefore, subject to comparison, and it is hard to convey to others an idea of the strength, and power, and force of logic behind his thought. One must read Brownson to know him.[58]

# 47

## DR. BROWNSON'S SUNSET YEARS

*Brief dossiers on the three children still left to Brownson in his old age • The school of Orestes, Jr., encounters opposition from the local bishop • A newly found letter of advice his father wrote him • Of all his children, Henry Francis Brownson was the very apple of his father's eye • After the death of Mrs. Brownson, daughter Sarah and her father set up housekeeping together • It does not turn out very happily • Sarah's marriage to Judge William J. Tenney • After issuing the last edition of* Brownson's Quarterly Review *in October 1875, the famous journalist goes to Detroit to live with his son Henry and family • He contributes an article to* The American Catholic Quarterly Review, *and then falls into a state of lethargy • His death on April 17, 1876.*

In his obituary notice of Brownson, Fr. Augustine Hewit speaks of "the desolation and loneliness which is usually the cloud in which the setting sun of genius goes down."[1] This desolation and loneliness, as we shall see, was to be further accentuated in Brownson's case by a lack of domestic felicity in his last years. At about the same time that he had set about reviving his *Review,* he was under the necessity of considering just how he could continue the management of his household, Mrs. Brownson having died on April 9, 1872, as already noted. There were now only three children left to the father out of a family of eight: Orestes, Jr., now living in Dubuque, Iowa, with a large family, and teaching school there; his son Henry who had become a lawyer, and was now living in Detroit where his father had seen a Catholic church for the first time as a young man half a century previously; and his only daughter, Sarah, who had been making her home with her parents up to the death of her mother, being now thirty-three years of age.

Children, though long adults, often turn back to their parents when they get into disturbing trouble. And so it happened that after long years of seemingly comparative silence, Orestes Brownson heard in the year 1867 from his son Orestes, Jr., who was doing well enough financially, but who had run into trouble with the local bishop who would not allow his children to the sacraments as long as they attended a public school, their father's. The content of the letter he wrote his father about the matter (no longer extant) may be gauged pretty well from the letter of reply his father wrote him on October 9, 1869. This letter has just surfaced after having been in the private possession of the descendants of Orestes Brownson, Jr., more than one hundred years. The letter shows that the father was indeed very deliberate in the advice he gave his son. He wrote on October 9, 1869, from Elizabeth, New Jersey:

> My Dear Son:
>     You are too apt to draw general conclusions from particulars. Your major must always be a universal principle or truth. You would reason better if you would habituate yourself to consider questions in the light of the general princi-

ples involved, and less frequently bring your general principles down to the test of particular facts.

When I tell you that education is a function of the Church, I tell you only what is implied in the Sacrament of Orders. Yet what I mean by this is, not that none but priests and religious must teach, but that the schools should be under the control of the Church. It is necessary so that she may have the disciplining, training, & forming of the mind & character of the young. This is a general principle, though owing to accidental causes, its operation may not in every single instance work happily.

You concede that the Church has the right to take charge of the religious education of children, but you forget, my son, that all the education of children should be religious, and that the precise evil to be guarded against is the separation of physical & mental from religious education. The great danger to religion & society in our own day comes from the secular spirit which is dominant in the non-Catholic world, and invades to a fearful extent even the Catholic world. Even our bishops and priests are not wholly uninfluenced by it. This spirit subjects the Church, which has the authority to teach and govern all men and nations in all things pertaining to faith and morals, to the state, the spiritual to the temporal, the world to come to this present world.

Now this evil which in its operation is the emancipation of the world from the hand of God, can be effectually resisted and rolled back only by placing schools primary and secondary under the control of the Church. The Holy Father sees this, and therefore requires the bishops to withdraw their children [from] secular schools, & provide for them as far as possible schools in which they shall receive a thoroughly Catholic education. The law on this point, always the law of the Church, is revived with greater vigor than in Bishop Smyth's time, or even when your present bishop was consecrated [Bishop John Hennessy]. In the case of your school, and others like it, there may not be any reason for enforcing the law, except that the law is necessarily general, & allowing it particular exceptions, renders its enforcement more difficult. If you look beyond your school, or your state even, to the evil of secularism the Church is doing all in her power to resist, you will see though the state can teach arithmetic as well as the Church, that the bishops are only doing their duty, & that your opposition to their policy is indefensible, and your position against them is untenable. Your offense is not in teaching a public school, nor in taking your children to your school, but in denying the right of the bishop or the Church to control the education of the young. Here you place yourself in conflict with her authority, & set up a claim of a right against her she cannot concede.

I deny not that the temporal has rights, but as the temporal exists only for the eternal, its rights are interpreted and declared by the Church. The passage you quote from the prayerbook, misleads you. If a priest commands you in matters in which the Church has defined to be out of her jurisdiction, you are, indeed, not bound to obey him; but in the present case she has defined that she has jurisdiction. You must remember that the spiritual is superior to the secular, & that the Church defines both her own powers and those of the temporal. You have unconsciously adopted a loose Gallican way of thinking, which has given occasion to the very evil the Church is warring against, & which no doubt the coming Ecumenical Council [Vatican I] will brand as anti-Catholic. There is more involved in the question than you appear to have considered.

I defended the public school system of this country as long as I could as being in fact as I considered it lawful for me to do so, for I know the system, and believe its anti-Catholic influence is greatly exaggerated; but I never defended the system on the ground that the Church had not the right to forbid Catholics to send their children to public schools if she chose to exercise it. She has chosen to exercise it, and in this diocese, as well as yours, the Catholic parent who sends his children to the public schools is debarred from the Sacra-

709

ments & they too, as is so, I presume in most of the diocese, in all indeed, where the Ordinary is able to provide Catholic schools for his children.

I do not quite like the way you allude to the luxury & pomp of your bishop. As a rule our bishops are poor enough and live plain enough. The bishops are princes of the Church, and obliged as they are to exercise a liberal hospitality they ought to be able to support the decencies of their rank. I have full confidence in your judgment where there is nothing to warp it, but like all your family you are subject to fits of morbidity, & under your morbid feelings I am disposed to regard your judgments of the conduct of your bishop & clergy as exaggerated. They may have mismanaged, but you ought to consider that your free criticisms of them, which very likely have been exaggerated as reported to them, may have led them to regard you & treat you as more hostile to them than you really are. There are no more subtle mischief makers in the world than the Irish who can rarely report a conversation or a fact without embellishing or perverting it.

I think, if you can make up your mind, as I think you should, to concede the right of the Church in this case, or of the bishop to prohibit Catholics from sending their children to the public schools, & show him that you do not dispute his authority, that he will make an exception in your case, so far as to allow you to have your children go to your school, without debarring you or them from the Sacraments. In a conflict with your bishop you will come off second best, & you will in the end find yourself deserted by all Catholics who value their religion, whatever assurances they may give you of standing by you. Try your hand at conciliation. Do what is right and proper on your part, and if he refuses, write me, & I will write him.

I hope you have not committed the mistake of publishing your dramas at your own expense; for if you have you may be sure of no sales. Booksellers take no pains to sell a book published at the author's expense. If you cannot find a publisher, which you are not likely to do, at his own risk, you had better not publish at all. You will only have bills of expense to pay, double the amount you were led to expect, and have your book fall dead from the press. If not too late, recall your ms [manuscript].

You have told me nothing about how dear Maggie does. I am glad to learn that the baby is baptized. Give a grandfather's love to all the children. I am glad to learn that Johnny is so good a scholar. I hope he has got over his trick of running away. If it was not so late in the season I would try to pay you a visit. But I must postpone it till spring, when if health is good enough, I will try & visit you & Henry. Your mother sends love to all.[2]

It does not appear that Orestes, Jr., followed his father's advice to try conciliation with the Church authorities. Nor do we have evidence that he wrote his father again until November 7, 1873. His letter shows that the school situation had only grown worse for him. He wrote:

In temporals we are making a comfortable living, in spirituals, receding further & further from the Catholic Church. It seems morally impossible that anything but a miracle can return any of us to the Church, for which you have so long, and so eloquently been a conspicuous advocate. . . . The last hope died within me when I found you did not approve my plan of trying for a foreign consulship. There seems absolutely no other way for me to support my large family than by pursuing my present avocation, which in spite of all I can do, leads me every day further from the Church.

Have you any counsel or advice to give me? What do you recommend? I have no one here to consult. Is it better to attend some Protestant church rather than none at all; and if I do, which one? I suppose I have no faith, certainly I have none in the clerical management of things in Dubuque, which seems entirely devoid of anything but sordid money-making. Not that I complain, except [that] . . . a continual warring upon my interests exists, such as depriving my school of many pupils by perhaps questionable means. That is nothing. The question is where and how shall my children be religiously educated? Or is all religion a human fraud? There is so much good in religion that I would for me and mine profit by it.

From this and other letters it would appear that he had considerable affection and admiration for his father. He wound up this letter, saying:

After all this egotism, I excuse it by saying that I still see you, busily writing at your long-accustomed table! That can drown all your sad memories, unpleasant letters [like this one] and troubles of every kind in the ink you are ceaselessly transforming to words that shall glow long after the Brownson face & form shall have passed from the memory of men.

With ever ardent love and much respect, I am your affectionate son,

Orestes[3]

We do not have all the letters that passed between father and son, particularly those of the father. It would appear, however, from a letter Orestes, Jr., wrote his father on February 23, 1874, that his father had proposed to him the possibility of falling back on farming should he lose his school through opposition from the Church authorities, and had also promised him assistance in such a project. In this same letter of February 23, Orestes, Jr., wrote: "I cannot find words to express our gratitude to you for your kind offer of assistance." He also added: "I shall do my best to get myself back and for all the others to return to the practice of their religion. I cannot be a Protestant and there is no comfort in infidelity." He likewise reported that wife Margaret and the children were ready to start on a journey to her father's in Macon County, Missouri, where she was to look about regarding the possibility of finding a farm on which to locate while he himself continued in his teaching profession. In a letter of March 13, 1874, he tells his father that Margaret and children had arrived safely at their destination, and remarked: "I am enjoying the peace and quiet of a bachelor & it is very agreeable, though I must needs be continually thinking of the absent." But his "bachelorhood" was to be quite short-lived. By May 3 Margaret and the children had returned and the farm project was at an end. He was now in debt and Margaret had announced that another member of the family was on the way.[4]

Orestes, Jr., never did turn to farming, as has been asserted by more than one, although he did later move onto a two-and-a-half-acre plot of ground on the outskirts of Dubuque where the family could have an ample garden. He stayed steadily with the teaching profession. He was principal of the First Ward School which became known in time as the Franklin School, and he taught there for twenty-two years, from 1860-1882. The school had for its motto: "Dare to do right." He also conducted summer sessions at Mt. St. Clair Academy, Sinsinawa, Wisconsin. His daughter Louise used to accompany him when he went for these summer sessions and enjoyed living with the nuns. He had a family of eight children, three boys and five girls.[5]

That Orestes, Jr., left his footprints at Franklin School is scarcely to be doubted. In 1906, marking half a century, a nostalgic "Reunion of the Former Pupils and Teachers of Franklin School" was held on Tuesday evening, February 27. There were various musical renditions by the Grand Opera House Orchestra, and by a number of soloists and violinists. There were three addresses given, the main one by Judge D.G. Lenehan on "Pro-

711

fessor Orestes Augustus Brownson." After "remarks" by J.J. Brownson, M.D., the program was concluded with the singing of "Auld Lang Syne" by the audience.[6]

These are a few facts concerning the family of Orestes A. Brownson, Jr., who came to Dubuque, the oldest son of the original Orestes A. Brownson. Having a large family, he apparently had difficulty at times in meeting all expenses on a teacher's salary alone. Perhaps it was in an effort to garner a little on the side that he became the editor of a chess review and a writer of burlesque melodramas. When his father heard of it, he remarked to son Henry: "Orestes has become a dramatic author. I fear his mind is disordered."[7] All in all, Orestes, Jr., may have been some little anxiety to his father.[8]

Of all Brownson's grown children, Henry alone met his hopes in a goodly measure, or, if he had disappointed him a bit, it was on the score that he had not gone on to the priesthood. He had been with the Jesuits at Frederick, Maryland, when he was fourteen,[9] and had again been in the seminary at Issy, France. If Henry did not continue in the way of a priestly vocation, his father could scarcely have foreseen how kind Providence was being to him personally. Later as a lawyer Henry was to have sufficient leisure to give the world the twenty-volume set of his father's writings, and leave behind also the three-volume biography of his father which is still by all odds the best source of the undoctored facts in Brownson's life. With the passing years Henry was to become the apple of his father's eye. On July 9, 1863, the father wrote him: "I have always loved you as a son, & I am sorry to say, you are the only child I have whose absence I grieve."

In the same letter he complained of Ned and Sarah always putting their heads together without consulting him. He continued to Henry: "Should you survive me, I wish you to understand that my library goes to you, and all my papers are to pass into your hands. I charge you with my honor and my fame."[10] Henry, too, was highly gifted. After leaving Issy, France, he had studied also at the University of Munich. According to a letter the father wrote Fr. Isaac Hecker on January 23, 1869, Henry knew "all the languages of Europe except the Slavonic and Turkish."[11] He made use of his gifts for such works as the "excellent" translation of *Balmes Fundamental Philosophy* (two volumes), and Tarducci's *Life of Columbus,* and the *Lives of John and Sebastian Cabot.* He often contributed to his father's *Review,* and published likewise a book entitled *Faith and Science,*[12] which is mostly a reproduction of his father's philosophical thought. Fr. Hecker dubbed him "cub of the Old Bear in crossness and brightness."[13] In 1897 he was awarded the Laetare Medal by the University of Notre Dame. On that occasion he delivered an impressive address on "Equality and Democracy." It was put in pamphlet form and is still extant.

The story of Brownson's only daughter, Sarah, is somewhat different. She, too, displayed certain talents, being the author of a novel, *Marian Elwood; or How Girls Live,*[14] and the author of *The Life of Demetrius Augustine Gallitzin, Prince and Priest,* as already noted. Being the only daughter in the family, there is some evidence that she may have been petted a bit too much. One biographer of Brownson says that "he (the father) knew he had spoiled her badly."[15] Certainly there are letters which indicate she showed considerable emotional instability on occasions. At different times she had left the parental roof. On June 13, 1861, she wrote from Newburgh, Ohio, asking that books be sent her for teaching school. A couple of months later, on September 15, she wrote her family again that she had given up the idea of teaching and was coming straight home. She added: "I shall be forlorn enough, so I want you all to pet me to the extent of your ability until I get sufficiently recruited to go about something else."[16]

In 1865 she ran away from home to her brother Orestes and family in Dubuque, Iowa, where she stayed three months. In a letter her father wrote her in August 1865, marked by deep paternal affection, he reasoned with her about her faults, such as "tyrannizing" over her mother by "your knack of falling sick when you cannot have your own way."[17] It seems evident, too, that she and her brother Henry were estranged at this time. Inviting Henry on November 28, 1865, to spend Thanksgiving Day with the family (he was in the army), the father urged: "Do not let the fact that Sarah has returned keep you away. Poor girl, the western trip has taught her some things, & I think cured her of some follies."[18]

Whatever the faults of daughter Sarah, her father's letters show clearly that he loved her dearly. While on a lecture tour he had ended a letter to wife Sally, dated January 25, 1863, saying: "Tell Sarah to keep up her spirits, and give her my love and blessing. I shall one of these days have something for her."[19] The reference here is presumably to the Healy portrait of himself which is still in the possession of Sarah's granddaughter, Miss Helene Odiorne. The father wanted daughter Sarah to have something real by which to remember him.

In the same month in which Mrs. Brownson had passed away, April 1872, Brownson said in a letter to Henry: "We do not, to my great joy, break up housekeeping. I shall not be separated from my dear daughter, now doubly dear to me."[20] He added that Sarah had resolved on this arrangement on her own accord. And when Fr. Sorin sent him his sympathy on the demise of Mrs. Brownson, and had invited him to make his home at Notre Dame, Brownson in replying declined the invitation on the score that he wished to provide a home for his daughter.[21]

In a letter to Henry at this time (April 18, 1872), Sarah had said of her father: "He is very kind and accepts the poor fare my incompetent housekeeping sets before him, without a murmur, and keeps up his spirits. He desires to have a director and devote himself to the care of his soul, and this inclines him to St. John's College."[22] (After Mrs. Brownson's death, there was some question whether Brownson would make his home at Seton Hall, St. John's College [now Fordham] or Notre Dame. Apparently he had invitations from all three.)

But things were not to work out as happily as might have been in making his home with Sarah. What follows in the next couple of years, some petty complaints that father and daughter expressed about each other, could be woven into a very gossipy tale by anyone disposed to sensationalize. Yet when all is summed up there is little or nothing of consequence in the whole affair. But since this matter has been dwelt upon by biographers, it is necessary to include it here. Let us not, however, attach too much importance to it. It has been said that there is trouble in all families; in some cases it becomes known, in others it does not. What we should keep in mind is that we are here concerned with two persons quite unwell,[23] who were understandably indisposed to sympathize with the ills and discomfiture of the other, and readily felt disappointment in the other. (Both were to pass away in 1876.) The key to the hurt feelings involved is to be found largely in the fact that each was jealous of the affections of the other going out to someone else. This is so evident in some letters of Sarah that one can scarcely suppress a laugh at times. There is a considerable element of comedy in it all, if one has an eye for comedy — or one might say that the whole affair has the semblance of a game of teasing. We have also a clue to a right evaluation of the factors involved in a letter Mrs. Thomas Odiorne, Sarah's daughter, wrote on July 27, 1839, the custodian of the *Brownson Papers* at Notre Dame University. In the letter Mrs. Odiorne suggested that her mother (Sarah Brownson) had overstated the case in her complaining letters to her brother Henry in the hope of getting Henry to shoulder his own responsibility in regard to their infirm and aging father.[24]

It soon became quite clear to Brownson that he was not to have with daughter Sarah what could be truly called a home. On the same day he wrote Fr. Sorin, May 23, 1872, declining his invitation to make Notre Dame his home, he also wrote his son Henry. The letter was mainly about Sarah. He felt she would become a very able housekeeper, but that she was "as imperious as any old maid in the land," and would not allow him to make a suggestion, or even to ask a question. (Perhaps she feared encroachments.) He continued: "While she keeps my house, and secures a home for herself, I am to have no companionship with her, and to remain in my solitude. No young wife could be more jealous of her husband's speaking to a servant than she is of her old father."

What precisely was the trouble? In the forepart of this letter, the father had mentioned that a certain Theresa (who had been there in Mrs. Brownson's last illness), presumably the servant the father had just referred to, had been away three or four weeks, and Sarah had no choice but to do all the work herself. "I understand," said the father to Henry, "that she [Sarah] had sent her off, but she has come back today to stay, which is a great relief to me, for I could not call upon Sarah, hardly able to be about, to wait on me."

Evidently the father had talked to Theresa more than suited Sarah, and out she went. (In later letters she was to call this "flirting" with the domestic help.) But the work proving too much for Sarah, she finally relented and let Theresa back in. This is the explanation of what the father had said about Sarah's jealousy — worse than that of a young wife just married. But Brownson seldom or never complained about the faults of anyone without saying something good about the same person. So he added in his letter to Henry: "Yet she is high-principled & honest, but oldmaidish. She is uncommonly gifted and firmly attached to her religion, but has many impractical notions. With all her faults I love her dearly, and though my life with her must be all but complete solitude, it would well-nigh break my heart to be separated from her."[25]

He subjoined a note to this letter saying that Judge Tenney's wife had just died and was buried from St. Mary's Church. Little did he dream that that event was the entering wedge that would work a separation between himself and daughter Sarah.

During the next year there were only a few scattered letters to Henry who had been made the confidant of both father and daughter. In a letter of November 22, 1872, the father remarked: "We are getting along pretty well."[26] Besides remarking about the way her father went around shabbily dressed and smelling of tobacco, Sarah's only registered complaint against him as of this time was that he was dosing himself too much with medicines, thereby making himself more difficult. That he used medicines quite freely to alleviate the aches and pains which had been plaguing him now for ten long years is quite possible. But there is no evidence that he used them excessively. Indeed, it is to be feared that Sarah exaggerated in many things, as has been suggested by her daughter, Mrs. Odiorne — and even grossly. The explanation may be found partly in what she wrote Henry in December 1872: "You know I am of a doleful nature."[27] After saying, too, on one occasion that her father broke the promises he had made the day before, she checked the exaggeration, and added: "That is a little too strong, please consider it a little modified."[28] After tearing her father to pieces in page after page in a letter dated November 10, 1874, Sarah still added: "We have no difficulties, nor disturbances. I have no conversation with him. . . . I do not talk to him for three reasons. . . ."[29] And in her next letter (December 10, 1874), piqued by qualms of conscience, she confessed: "I was sorry afterwards I wrote you so much about the government," meaning her father.[30] Indeed, one does not like to think that any child would ever write such letters about an infirm and aging parent.

In a letter to Henry on July 21, 1873, the father mentioned that Sarah had taken another house, more convenient, at the corner of Fifth Avenue and Tenth Street. It was the second time they had moved since they had set up housekeeping together. The father was still in the dark as to just what it was all about, for Sarah apparently had an eye on her approaching marriage. Of this event her father spoke in a letter to Henry, dated November 7, 1873: "I have had no heart to write you for a long time. Sarah has or will I suppose let you know that she is on the point of marrying that old codger Judge Tenney." He went on to say that she had made all the arrangements without his knowledge or suspicion. She and the judge, and the judge's little daughter Jessie, planned to move in with him after the marriage, and he was to bear "the chief expenses of their support." Sarah "insists she will never leave me," but if he himself were to leave she protested he dare not take any furniture. Since their engagement, he added, "the judge does not treat me with ordinary civility." He probably just had a guilt complex, feeling like the cat that ate the canary.

But the dictation of terms to an old independent stalwart like Brownson by a daughter could scarcely be acceptable. He protested in his letter that he would take a house of his own and get himself servants. "This," he said, "will be a terrible blow to Sarah, for her position will be much affected, for she has alienated all her friends and is tolerated out of respect for me."[31] Although he could not help disliking the secret way in which all had been arranged, he gradually became reconciled to the marriage to a degree. However, Sarah remarked that her father "seems to consider every congratulation offered me as an affront to himself." The marriage was solemnized by Bishop Michael Corrigan in St. Michael's Church, Elizabeth, on November 26, 1873.[32]

The married couple did not after all make their home with Sarah's father, but went to live in one of the judge's houses at 85 Elizabeth Avenue. In a letter to Henry, dated February 6, 1874, the father said: "Sarah seems to be very contented and happy. I remain where I was when you were here. Dolly is my housekeeper and cook. A terribly pious girl from Ireland . . . serves me as secretary, chambermaid, nurse and seamstress. And we have peace and quiet in the family, for they are very obliging, and I am master."[33] The Irish girl went by the name of Agnes; she was a person of some education, and all agreed that she was quite pretty — even Sarah acknowledged these qualities, though in time she was to say some quite unlovely things about her. Every evening promptly at nine, the old man, Agnes and Dolly (the black cook), would recite the rosary, and then pious Agnes would retire for the night.

Various letters Sarah wrote Henry indicate that her marriage to the judge was a very happy one. She must have learned that her father, too, was enjoying a stretch of peace and quiet with his obliging servants. She was evidently not altogether unconcerned about what was going on in her father's household. At this time, July 1874, she fired off a letter to Henry in which she said that "whiskey flowed like water" in her father's house, but she added she had heard so "by report." The basis of the gossip was that "the policemen on the beat told some one that the Doctor kept good whiskey," and that one of her father's servants was seen one night giving a glass of it to the policemen. Although Sarah, as already noted, may be suspected of exaggeration in many things she said, she did not, however, charge her father with any personal abuse in this matter. But she did prate in this same letter again about his very hearty eating, and his enormous meat bills, and remarked that she "had heard" that in the beer saloons and kindred places it was said: "If you want a good square meal, old Brownson's is the place to go for it."[34] It may well be that the whiskey the father was taking to kill the dull ache in his bones did put a sharp edge on the huge old man's appetite and that he did eat more heartily in these last years. But to set him down as having "always been a famous trencherman,"[35] as does Theodore Maynard, will in no sense square with the facts. Speaking of the general pattern of his life — aside from the last year or two — his son Henry said: "His diet was sparing, his abstinence from wine and spirits total, though he drank strong coffee morning and night."[36] Reporting his visit with Brownson while in America in 1853, Sir John Acton wrote: "Often, he told me, he went three days without food."[37] As Sister M. Rose Gertrude (Doran Whalen) said of Maynard when she reviewed his biography of Brownson in *Books on Trial,* "he must have got Brownson mixed up with Dante's Ciacco."[38]

In regard to the enormous meat bills Brownson ran up while living with Agnes and Dolly, about which Sarah made such a fuss, Brownson himself blamed it on the extravagance of the cook, Dolly. He said nothing of a roast ever appeared on the table again after it had once been served. He also claimed that Dolly, too, had her share in the disappearance of the whiskey in one way or another.

It might be a trifle hard to guess why Sarah ever took it into her head to move back in with her father again unless it was with the idea of cutting down expenses all around, although her father was the first who proposed it. Extravagant expenses no doubt drove him in that direction. Taking her cue from remarks her father made that he would be glad to be free from the necessity of continuing his *Review* as a means of supplementing his pension, Sarah drew up a memorandum, dated simply "Friday" (1874), in which she carefully calculated the expenses that would be involved on both sides should she, the judge and his daughter Jessie, move in with him. Her letter indicated clearly enough that there was one condition she was counting on — Agnes must go. One can hardly suppress a laugh at how naïvely she showed her colors when she wrote: "I merely send you these figures as an explanation of my remark to Dolly that if you kept Agnes, I did not see how we could come. I am glad she serves you so well, and hope you will live a thousand years in the house you occupy now, as happy as a monarch of all you survey."[39]

The big green-eyed monster was certainly peeping out from behind those lines. The fact is that Sarah simply detested Agnes as her letters plainly show, saying in a letter dated July 9, 1874, in which she had complained so extremely much about her father, that her "character would never be patched up this side of the grave," though her father regarded her as "an angel, or at least a saint."

Although the father seems at first to have balked at the terms of Sarah's proposition, it was not very long before the trio moved in with him. Reporting in a letter to Henry on August 12, 1874, on how all was going, the father said:

> Sarah has been ill all summer, but is getting better. She does admirably for *her* family, of which I am not a member. She means, I presume, to treat her old father well, and does so, as far as is in her nature. Yet I feel I am a stranger, without a family, minus a home. She never comes into my room, never speaks to me, and is careful when at table to carry on a conversation with others present in so low a tone that I can neither take part in it nor catch a word that is said. Yet after all this is a small affair. The best of the trio is Jessie, who is growing up a fine girl. [Sarah on the contrary complained to Henry of her father trying to dominate the table conversation, never allowing a remark to be made between others at the table, and as he is very deaf], she said, "you can imagine how disagreeable he can make it."[40]

There is little wonder there was so little understanding in the home between Sarah and her father. They were both living in worlds apart with no bridge spanning the two. Sarah and the judge, now only a few months from their late marriage, were still doting on the sweets of connubial bliss (as Sarah described it all so profusely in her letters to Henry). They naturally wanted to be just for and by themselves. Yet the father, an infirm old man, was hungering for affection. In a letter to Henry, dated April 24, 1867, he had urged Henry to take to himself a companion for life, for "no one ever more needed to love and be loved," than one of the Brownson nature.[41] The Brownson nature was now an extra cross to the old man, sinking as he now was into old age, infirm and lonely, his life's companion gone, and with no one to speak kind words to him or to comfort him. Ostracism in his own house was a hard lot, intended or not. The worst of it was that Sarah could not even endure that he have a little friendly conversation with the servants. In one of her letters to Henry she remarked: "He is now talking and laughing with the Irish woman who cleans his rooms."[42] It was wormwood to her.

On September 25, 1874, the father wrote Henry to thank him for his good wishes and remembrance of him on his birthday, September 16. Then he added: "The day passed in unbroken silence, and in great suffering for I was very ill. I was thankful, however, that I was let alone, & no virago entered my room to scold and abuse me."[43]

He would occasionally, whenever his infirmities and the press of work on his *Review* allowed, go out for drives through the city, and although Agnes seems to have been no longer in his employ in any capacity, he would sometimes stop to visit with her. Sarah soon spied that out, and quickly wrote off to Henry that he should be prepared for any catastrophe. The father knew she was spying on him, and so he talked a lot about marrying again, trying to have a few secret chuckles to himself, knowing her nature so well. She pretended to enjoy it all "though every word," she said, "was a sword thrust [at herself]." He capped his remarks with the statement to Sarah, facetious or not, that the six months Agnes was in his service were "the happiest ever passed in his life."[44]

In a letter to Henry on January 9, 1875, the father wrote: "Sarah keeps a close watch on me lest I marry again & disgrace the family. This is very kind of her. Do not be uneasy should her vigilance relax, for no woman will ever take the place of your mother. Although every day I miss her more and more." (Then he broke the good news.) "Mrs. Tenney will give me very soon a grand child. . . . Of your brother-in-law, Tenney, I have nothing to say, but that he is very much spruced up. He is to me inscrutable."[45]

Sarah's baby was born on February 7, 1875, a bouncing eleven-pounder, and was christened Mary Elizabeth Ruth. Closely inspecting the child after birth, the shaggy old grandfather pronounced it "a true Brownson." A letter to Henry, dated May 25, 1875, shows the father's deep solicitude for his daughter Sarah in spite of whatever annoyances on either side. After speaking of the baby, he said: "Poor Sarah finds her hands full in taking care of her. I want her to get a nurse, and I offer to pay the expenses, but she is afraid a nurse will spoil her temper. She is afraid to trust her with any one but herself, and is well-nigh worn out taking care of her. The nurse *must* come."[46]

As the Babe of babes brought peace to the world, so many a child has brought peace to many a circle of humans. From this time on tensions seem to have eased off considerably. Complaining letters came to an end, and the weary old giant was to know some surcease of heartburning and isolation. After all, his daughter Sarah had given him a grandchild, even though, as he told Henry, it was not to go through life under his name. Every morning, as the judge wrote Henry, Mary Elizabeth Ruth was brought to her grandfather's room after breakfast at his request, and with the Brownson bundle in his arms, he would walk up and down the room humming some sort of a lullaby.

After the arrival of Mary Elizabeth Ruth on the scene in the Brownson household, the spring and summer months seem to have passed away quite rapidly. The increasing attention a growing child required made it practically impossible for the mother, her own health declining more and more, to look also to the needs of an infirm and aging father. Henry arrived from Detroit to look the situation over, and it was decided that it would be better if the father would move to Detroit and live with Henry and his family. After the far-famed journalist had got out the October edition of his *Review*, Henry returned from Detroit to help him transfer his library and other effects to his new home. When the moment of departure came, he pressed a note into the hand of daughter Sarah which read:

> I am sorry, my dear Sarah, that I showed so much reluctance to the arrangement you & Henry thought best. I am now perfectly satisfied that you were right, & I want you to feel that I am perfectly convinced of it, & am perfectly reconciled to the arrangement.
> You need, and must have, a change of scene, and a change of air; and the sooner the better. This is absolutely necessary, and must not be delayed many days. I am anxious only for you. I shall do well enough, and shall not be unhappy. You need feel no uneasiness on my account.[47]

In the October issue of his *Review* he had also scrawled out his valedictory to the readers of his *Review*. To him they had always been very real. He had always lived a secluded life, much apart from the social world, deeply engrossed in study and writing. But his readers had been his bosom companions with whom he had conversed after the manner of fireside chats, adding great personal charm to much that he wrote. But the time for parting had come at last. Because of his crippling infirmities, he had been forced during the last three years — but only one or the other time — to reprint an article from a former edition of his *Review*. And during much of the last year he had been unable even to hold a pen in his hand. No man, he said, willingly gives up what had been his life's vocation, and he had loved his vocation as a reviewer, but many things admonished him to retire, and leave the field to younger and more vigorous laborers, to men who have hands, eyes and memory unimpaired. He expressed deep gratitude to the Catholic community in particular, both clergy and laity, whom for thirty-one years he had served as a Catholic publicist, yet less efficiently than he had wished. He was deeply grateful for the generous support they had given him, and for the measure of confidence they had reposed in him, and it was not without a pang at parting with friends old and new that he took leave of them. But it had to be. *"Valete,* dear friends, and the blessing of God rest on you and your labors."[48]

Writing to him from Bozen, Tyrol, Austria, on October 1, 1874, his friend Willian Seton had remarked: "When you exchange worlds, pray take the *Review* with you. Don't leave it behind to be published by some boob."[49] There was no danger of that whatsoever. As the unique editor had said in his valedictory, the *Review* bore so much his personal character, was so much the product of his individualistic mind, that no one could possibly continue it after him. Others might publish a quarterly far more valuable than his, but no other man could publish *Brownson's Quarterly Review.* It had originated with him and must die with him. Yet he was conscious of its limitations in the past as he had never been able to realize his ideal of what a Catholic quarterly should be. Nevertheless, "none will be found more sincerely Catholic, though, no doubt, many may be found with more prudence, and with a far better understanding of [Catholic] interests, as well as ability to advance them."[50]

Brownson also mentioned in his valedictory that he had recently received a letter from "A Catholic" urging him to open correspondence with Dr. Döllinger and turn his *Review* to the defense of the "old Catholics." By so doing, the letter writer assured him he would "become immensely popular, and gain for the *Review* an almost unlimited circulation," and, it might have added, said Brownson, "belie all my convictions and the whole Catholic faith, and damn my soul."

> If suggestions such as this could have moved me [Brownson pointed out], I should never have become a Catholic. I did not seek admission into the Catholic Church for the sake of wealth, honors, or popularity. . . . If I am, as I know I am, measurably unpopular even with Catholics, I can truly say then I have never sought popularity, but rather despised it. Yet I have received more marks of confidence from our venerable bishops and clergy than I have deserved, more honors than I have desired, and have been even more popular with Catholics than I have ever expected to be. Speak of wealth! Why, what could I do with it, if I had it, standing, as I do, on the brink of the grave? The generosity of Catholics, in an annuity reasonably secure, has provided for my personal wants. She, who, for nearly half a century, was my faithful companion and devoted wife, is, I devoutly trust, safe with the saints; my children, three out of eight, all that are left to me, are able to take care of themselves, and no one depends on me but an aged sister. What do I want with wealth? What do I care for popularity, which I never sought, and on which I turned my back when not yet of age?
>
> I have, and desire to have, no home out of the Catholic Church, with which I am more than satisfied, and which I love as the dearest, tenderest, and most affectionate mother ["beautiful words," exclaimed William G. Ward, "on the lips of a man whose intellect is so masculine and powerful"].[51] My only ambition is to live and die in her communion.[52]

Although Henry had a house full of children in Detroit, his father was to find a real home there when he arrived in October. He was given a suite of rooms on the second floor, spacious and cheerful, to which his library and other paraphernalia for writing were transferred. What helped greatly to make his days there pleasant was the kindly attention of his daughter-in-law, Henry's wife. On January 8, 1868, Henry had married Josephine Van Dyke — familiarly called Fifine by all. She was beyond compare Brownson's favorite daughter-in-law. Not only had it been a treat for him in the past to visit Henry and Fifine and their family whenever he could manage it, but in his letters to Henry he was always anxiously inquiring about Fifine and speaking of her in endearing terms. In their children, too, he had shown a deep interest, prizing their photos sent him and venturing prophesies about their future.[53] He could not but have won the heart of Fifine, and now it was to his advantage. The children, too, once he had come, used to climb the stairs to the second floor to prattle to him and play about in his rooms.

After reaching Henry's home in Detroit, the father immediately wrote Sarah of his safe arrival. Thereafter there was an exchange of a number of affectionate letters between the two. But the most interesting letter is the one Sarah wrote on December 24, 1875, after receiving a big Christmas box the father had sent from Detroit. It ran:

> My dear Father:
>     We were all taken by surprise the night before last by a box from Detroit. We were equally delighted. Ruthie had one of the quails yesterday, and smacked her lips over the first taste, and cried for more. She evidently knows good things. We expect to celebrate the big turkey in fine style when I have no doubt its principal sauce will be regrets at your absence. Frs. Hennessey and Thebau[d] were here the other day, and expressed the greatest regret that you should have left. Fr. Hennessey told me to tell you that, in the language of the Irish poet, "the nights were long until you returned," and that if you did return they would come to see you much oftener. They both send kind regards and good wishes, as do all whom we see.[54]

Frs. Thébaud and Hennessey had been among Brownson's most frequent visitors during his last years in Elizabeth, as had also been Judge Tenney before he had married Sarah. He had been a regular Sunday visitor.

In the valedictory to the readers of his *Review,* Brownson had also expressed the hope that, though forced to close his *Review,* he would be able to continue to labor in some other way for "the cause so dear to me." After he had got settled in his new quarters, he took up his pen again to treat a theme that was the very breath of his nostrils, the *philosophy of the supernatural* — philosophy and theology having always been his favorite subjects. The article he wrote on the theme appeared in the January 1876 issue of the *American Catholic Quarterly Review,* edited by his warm friend and ardent admirer, Dr. James A. Corcoran. It was only the first of a series of such articles he intended to write, designed to show the relation of each particular doctrine of the Catholic Church to the Incarnation. In this first article he concerned himself with the establishment or identification of the supernatural. He proceeded to show that the natural and the supernatural are intimately and integrally linked together in the one creative act of God. The act that creates the natural is the identical act which creates the Hypostatic Union, and founds the supernatural order. The Hypostatic Union is itself in the initial order, the first cycle, or the order of the procession of existences from God as the first cause by way of creation. It completes that order by carrying the creative act to its highest pinnacle, and initiates and founds the teleological order, or the order of the return of existences to God, their final cause and end, without absorption in him. This is the order spoken of by St. Paul as the "new creation," commonly called the supernatural order, which is therefore founded on and flows from the Hypostatic Union or the Incarnation.[55]

Daughter Sarah in a letter to her father remarked concerning this article: "Father Thébaud says the author of that Italian work you reviewed in the [American] Catholic Quarterly desires permission from you to translate it for some Italian periodical. He is delighted with your article, The Philosophy of the Supernatural, and says that a famous Italian theologian about a year ago took the same view."[56]

Free now from editorial cares, Brownson began to assemble notes with the intention of completing his autobiography from the year 1857. But the continuation of the autobiography of Orestes Augustus Brownson was never really begun, much less completed. Neither did he do anything more than begin the heading of what was intended to be his second essay for the *American Catholic Quarterly Review*. In January of the New Year, 1876, a disinclination to work overcame him, and at long last the war-weary old General yielded to the urge to rest a bit. This feeling of weariness increased from day to day and from week to week, so that by April it was only by an effort that he could arouse himself sufficiently even to converse. Brownson was no longer Brownson.

It was in no sense incongruous that Orestes Brownson was to near his end on an argument. From the day when as a mere lad of only nine years he had accompanied an older boy "to the middle of the town" to witness a muster of the local militia, and had actually wedged his way into the discussion of two old men about free will and election, and had stoutly maintained against Jonathan Edwards the freedom of the will,[57] he had been arguing strenuously all his life through — always of course on the side of truth and justice as he saw it. And so it happened that on Good Friday he and son Henry fell into an argument after lunch about the precise nature of the unforgivable sin (the sin against the Holy Spirit). So engrossed in the subject did they become that the discussion dragged into the afternoon hours. Finally the old philosopher felt that he had had enough. Henry seemed strangely obtuse, and did not grasp the point he was making. Rising suddenly from his chair, he shuffled across the room, and with the aid of his cane and the supporting balustrade, he pulled his huge bulk up the stairs and into his room. Hours later when Fifine knocked at his door, carrying the evening tray, he called out: "If that is Henry, I'm too tired to make it plainer tonight." He was sinking into his last illness. By midnight he was critically ill.[58]

The next day, Holy Saturday, the vicar general of the diocese, Father Hennaert, known for his learning and virtue, who was also his Father Confessor, heard his confession. On Easter Sunday he was brought Holy Communion and was given the Last Anointing, or Anointing of the Sick as it is now called. Shortly before dawn on Easter Monday morning, the soul of Orestes Brownson went forth to meet the God of all Truth and Goodness. It is recorded that at the moment of death he heaved a great sigh. It was a fit signal that a life of enormous labors had come to an end. On April 17, 1876, word went forth that Orestes A. Brownson had passed from the scenes of this life, leaving all who would build a better world much in his debt.

His funeral obsequies were held in St. Ann's Church in Detroit, where he had come half a century earlier as a young man looking for a teaching job.

"An eloquent eulogy was delivered by the Vicar-General of Mobile, Mc-Donough," and the mortal remains of the peerless American Catholic apologist were buried in the city's Mt. Elliot Cemetery. There they were to rest until removed to a crypt in the Sacred Heart Chapel of Notre Dame University ten years later.[59]

*The Evening News* of Detroit, issue of April 17, 1876, noted well his passing and indicated its appreciation of his historic significance when it said in part:

> Dr. Orestes Augustus Brownson, the famous theologian and philosopher, died this morning at four o'clock at the residence of his son, Major Henry F. Brownson on the corner of 2nd. Avenue and High Street, in his 73rd. year. . . . For some years Dr. Brownson had dropped into comparative obscurity in America, although there are few readers of more than 25 years of age who do not remember his name as one often most prominent in the country in the literature of philosophy and theology, and in the higher walks of political discussion. The American encyclopedias give him little more than a dozen lines, but his fame in Europe, particularly in France, grew greater year after year, and possibly when the noisy names and persons of the present pass away, a future generation of Americans, calmly surveying the past, will place the name of Dr. Brownson where it properly belongs, among those of the greatest thinkers and teachers of his country.

George N. Shuster has remarked: "No thinker between the days of Jonathan Edwards and Professor George Santayana is more deserving of careful study."[60]

# 48

## BROWNSON'S NICHE AND LEGACY

*Knowledgeable estimates of the value of Brownson's writings • The transferral of Brownson's remains from Mt. Elliot Cemetery, Detroit, in 1886, to the Brownson Memorial Chapel, Notre Dame University • A movement for the erection of a monument to Brownson's memory • Its unveiling in Sherman Park, New York City, 1910 • An address by the Hon. W. Bourke Cockrane • The Brownson bust is toppled from its base and ends up at Fordham University • A monument is erected to Brownson's memory at his birthplace, Stockbridge, Vermont, in 1913.*

The object of this chapter is not an attempt to fix precisely Brownson's niche in the Hall of Fame, but rather to present a few of the many estimates of the man and his work together with a brief account of some of the attention given him since his demise. The farther any figure retreats into the past, the more accurately can his place and importance in history be gauged. Although it is a hundred years since Orestes Brownson ended his mighty labors on this earth, it is by no means certain that his full historic importance has yet been clearly discerned, either by Americans in general or by American Catholics in particular. It may well be that the man and his works are too much of a challenge to a permissive society to gain wide popularity. As Arthur M. Schlesinger, Jr., has sagely observed: "Perhaps an age more sympathetic with men who would not compromise and would not retreat will accord him his rightful place."[1] Whatever the case, Brownson himself did foresee the possibility that his writings "may one day be allowed a place in the literature of our country."[2] For the benefit, then, of those who have little or no acquaintance with those writings, it may be well to quote the considered judgment of at least a few critics who were well acquainted with the productions of his mind. They are not eulogies, but candid estimates.

Perhaps one of the best appraisals of the man and his work was given on the occasion of Brownson's review of *The Life of the Most Rev. M. J. Spalding, D.D., Archbishop of Baltimore,* written by his nephew, Bishop John Lancaster Spalding, S.T.L. In his review of the *Life* of the archbishop, Brownson acknowledged that he had sometimes thought him too conciliatory in his controversy with Protestants, but "yet," he said, "if he was timid, it was only on the surface of his character. In his nature he was manly, bold, and fearless, and no one contributed more than he to the marked change in regard to the manliness and courage that has come over the Catholic publication of this country within the last thirty or forty years, or to abolish from Catholic controversy that apologetic and deprecatory tone which so disgusted us, while we were still outside the church, and made us look upon Catholics as spineless, mean, crouching, and cowardly, who hardly dared to say, in the face of their enemies, that their souls were their own."[3]

A writer in *The Catholic Advocate,* the official organ of the diocese of Louisville, Kentucky, established by the archbishop himself when he had been bishop of the Louisville diocese, thought that the lion's share of credit for the more manly tone which had come over the Catholic publication of the country should be awarded Brownson, whatever the credit due the archbishop. The critic in the *Advocate* wrote:

> Whilst we also appreciate the services of the late Most Rev. Dr. Spalding in lifting the countenances of Catholics from their time-out-of-mind cringingness to brute force, we are disposed to assign, as the chief instrument in God's hand, not His Grace of Baltimore, but Dr. Brownson himself. It is meet that this should be hidden from the Hercules of American controversy, but it is not meet that we who are benefitted by this more healthy tone should be forgetful of him to whom, under God, it is mainly attributable. Thirty years back dates the commencement of this revival, and thirty years back O. A. Brownson began his career as the chief of Catholic journalists in America. The coincidence in dates alone points to the cause. . . . Born of Catholic and Irish parents, on Irish and Catholic soil, we experience no feeling of impropriety in saying to our coreligionists that which a convert may well hesitate to say.
>
> [The writer continued:] We again assert that in the cause of what may be termed the higher education of the best Catholic intellect in the land, in the true relations of Catholics with non-Catholics, of the Church to the current State questions, Brownson has labored more than all these (England, Kenrick, Spalding, and others). At his feet, more than at those of any other man that taught in America, have the Catholic Bishops sat to hear words of wisdom on the relative position of things divine and things human in this country. To him, more than to any colleges or theological treatises whatever, are the priests indebted for those principles of action which have enabled them to steer with rare prudence between the often sunken rocks of religious politics. And to him is due the honor of creating a line of Catholic political literature in this country which was absolutely necessary for the education of our clergy and intelligent laity, and which has no ante-type in any other country. In his "Autobiography of a Convert," Brownson says: "I brought nothing to the Church but my sins." That is true of everybody, but posterity will recognize that at his death he will have left something more in the church than the soiled water in the baptismal font. Brownson's vocation has been to teach the teachers — to pioneer before the scouts of the Church in America. Brownson has been an eminently providential man.[4]

This is of course quite an eloquent tribute. But it does not necessarily imply, nor should it, that there are not some blemishes of one kind or another here or there in Brownson's voluminous writings. Nothing human is ever perfect. Even the Angelic Doctor came short on some points of Catholic teaching, such as on the doctrine of the Immaculate Conception. St. Augustine, too, late in life, wrote his *Retractatus*. What is to be noted in Brownson's case is that although his enemies preferred charges against his orthodoxy to the Holy See, no fault was found with his writings, and his case was tossed out of the Roman court with the gentle admonition that he might be a little more guarded in some of his terminology.[5]

Another writer, Thomas J. Bergen, M.D., greatly appreciated Brownson's writings precisely on the score that they present so well "the Truth as it is in Christ Jesus." When subscribing to Brownson's *Review* in January of 1873, he wrote him:

> I can never, as long as my poor heart pulsates, forget the great thinker, the philosopher, Dr. Brownson. To his writings I owe most of what I know about what is *really*, and *truly*, *Catholic faith*. You have proven by your writings and lectures that real Catholic truth is the thing for our glorious country. I have studied your writings and appreciated them as far as my limited intellectual

capacity admitted of. I have always told your friends, and your enemies too, that you are the greatest thinker of our age, or, perhaps, of any age. Thousands in this country, and in Europe, are indebted to you for valuable information on the most important of all subjects — the knowledge of the "Truth as it is in Christ Jesus." Years after God shall have called you to receive your reward, you will be appreciated, and your name held in benediction and your memory embalmed in the hearts of countless generations.[6]

Another high merit of Brownson's voluminous writings is the deep and wide culture they reflect. He wrote upon almost every theme under the sun, and whatever he touched, the resultant thought sparkled with freshness and originality from having passed through the alembic of his great mind. His writings, like the man himself, are, as Fr. Augustine Hewit, C.S.P., remarked, *sui generis*.[7] On that score we must go to Brownson, for he has treasures that can be found nowhere else, the productions of his genius being as individualistic as the man himself. To the student, then, who has an interest in all phases of thought, Brownson's writings will prove richly rewarding. A writer in the New York *Daily Tribune* (presumably George Ripley), when commenting on April 22, 1876, on Brownson's *Works* on the occasion of his passing, spoke of the deep and wide culture of his thought. He wrote: "His intimate knowledge of the history of thought in all the lights and shadows of its significance was probably not surpassed by any living writer, and was only equalled by the acuteness of his analysis and his fertility and aptness of expression in the elucidation of abstract ideas. . . . No author of the day exceeded him in readiness or fertility. . . . His essays and reviews afford the material for a library in themselves."

The main obituary notice of Brownson was the one written by Fr. Augustine F. Hewit in the *Catholic World* for June 1876. It is a long article, but the paragraphs bearing more directly on the significance of Brownson's writings may well be quoted. Fr. Hewit wrote:

> Some portions of Brownson's writings deserve to remain as a portion of our standard Catholic literature and to be studied while the English language endures. We are disposed to consider the various essays on subjects belonging to the department of political ethics, the articles on controversy with Protestants and various kinds of free-thinkers, those on transcendentalism, *The Convert, The American Republic,* as the most consummate productions of the great publicist. . . . Such competent judges as Lord Brougham, Cardinal Wiseman, Mr. Webster, Mr. Ripley, and the editors of the principal reviews of England, France, and Germany have pronounced the highest encomiums upon the masterpieces of Dr. Brownson's pen, either in respect to the power of thought and beauty of style which are their characteristics, or the intrinsic value of their argument as an exposition or defense of great truths and principles. The terse logic of Tertullian, the polemic crash of St. Jerome, the sublime eloquence of Bossuet, are all to be found there in combination, or alteration, with many sweet strains of tenderness and playful flashes of humor. There are numerous passages in his writings not to be surpassed by the finest portions of the works of the great masters of thought and style, whether in English or any other language, in the present or any past age. They render certain and immortal the just and hard-earned fame of their author, who labored not, however, for fame and honor; but for the love of truth, the welfare of mankind, and the approbation of Heaven.[8]

For a Catholic, Brownson's career is of extraordinary significance. Before his conversion he had been "all things by turn, and nothing long." As

O.B. Frothingham remarked, "he was an experimenter in systems, a taster of speculations."[9] He had canvassed all social theories, had examined all systems of philosophy, has probed deeply into all forms of religion, had tried everything outside the Catholic Church. He had claimed and enjoyed hugely the freedom to roam at will, and there was necessarily much change in it all, albeit it did not exclude a genuine species of progress. But when he became a Catholic, all this roaming and changing came to an end, that is, as far as the truths and principles of the Catholic faith are concerned. Never so much as a thought against the truth of the Catholic faith ever crossed his mind. And all that in spite of the fact that after the brief honeymoon period of his conversion had ended, he was to run into one fierce storm after another that were to rage on to the very end of his life. To say that his faith was sorely tried would seem to be an understatement. (Whether his or Newman's trials were the more severe would be very difficult to judge.) William G. Ward, the brilliant editor of the *Dublin Review,* when speaking of Brownson's career in the January 1876 issue of the *Review,* wrote:

It is a career that may well deserve to lessen our despondency as we look out upon the world of the nineteenth century. We are sometimes asked if the Catholic Church is not powerless over the minds that have known intellectual freedom, that have ranged abroad, and been enlightened by the philosophy of Liberalism and Socialism. The answer is here. So wonderful is the power of truth that it is able to subdue the charms of licence, to take from so-called liberty its fascination, and from the thirst after knowledge its danger. The same truth which, more than thirty years ago, won to the Church this cultured and energetic nature, has kept it in humble submission to authority which did not appeal to the private judgment of the individual but to faith. Is Christianity unable to bear investigation?

Must it of necessity dissolve under the test of modern thought and severe logic? Here, again, is one more instance of the correct answer. Not, indeed, that Catholicity is in need of the approbation of any human being; but in an age that professes to see a necessary antagonism between intellect and faith, we may lawfully be proud of the men who are conspicuous in their obedience to the Church of God, whilst in intellect they are second to none. And this testimony becomes only the more impressive, when, as may happen anywhere, there arises difficulties after conversion, and the mind has received a bias in some erroneous direction.

Then is it beautiful to see the victory of faith, and to learn how moral discipline avails much more than philosophy. Faith, like every other virtue, has its trials: when false enlightenment abounds, it will be still more exposed to them; and happy is the man who knows where to look for peace — happy if he understands that it is a small thing to possess the liberty of cleaving to his own opinion, and a signal grace from God to be childlike and docile.

Dr. Brownson might have chosen to believe in his own powers of reasoning, in spite of the Church's evident wishes; but with a magnanimity that is the finest trait in his character he preferred to divest himself of many advantages rather than, in any way, to endanger his own or his neighbor's faith. There are men who, under slighter temptations than his, have forgotten to obey. His has been the rare privilege of showing to the world, by a constant and frank submission that humility is the guide and safeguard of wisdom.[10]

But his humble and docile submission in all things was evidently bought at no small price. When he wrote his autobiography in 1857, he drew two letters from the Rev. Reuben Smith who had been the Presbyterian pastor at Ballston Spa, New York, at the time Brownson had joined the congregation. Rev. Smith repudiated, as we have noted, Brownson's description of the

Ballston Presbyterians, and what Brownson had said about the vote taken in the Presbyterian Assembly. In a second letter to the editor of the *Princeton Review,* the Rev. Charles Hodge, D.D., Rev. Smith stated that he had met Brownson when a Catholic in a steamboat cabin on Lake Champlain, and that during the ensuing conversation Brownson had told him that he had concluded that "the truth was not to be found out by private individuals, and [had] thought he should go to the Catholic Church." When asked on the occasion "whether he had been happy during all these changes — '[Have you been] lying on a bed of roses?' " was the way it was put — his energetic reply was, " '[On a bed of] spikes, sir, spikes.' "[11]

This bears further testimony to the depth of his Catholic faith, and his invincible attachment to it.

Another interesting estimate or thumbnail sketch of Brownson was given by J. Fairfax McLaughlin, LL.D., in 1903, the centennial year of Brownson's birth. Its implications may not be entirely accurate in every detail, but its racy style is refreshing, and it hits off much truth. Dr. McLaughlin wrote:

> For years Brownson's *Review,* like a beacon light set upon a hill, was the standard of philosophical literature in this country; its editor was the oracle of logics and metaphysics; prelates recognized him, clergymen hearkened to him, and the laity were justly proud of him. Indeed, they all spoiled him a little, and he became something of a Samuel Johnson. If the trigger missed, he was apt to knock you down with the butt end of the gun. In some other respects he was quite like that schoolmaster of Congress, John Randolph of Roanoke, and shook his locks and frowned, as schoolmaster-general to churchmen and laymen, both in Europe and America, even at the highest — now at Dr. Newman, again at the Jesuits since Aquaviva; once in awhile Father Hewit and Archbishop Hughes were his quarry, and even at rare intervals his life-long, devoted friend Father Isaac Hecker, the beloved Founder of the Paulists. But he never stayed mad long; he emitted a spark or two, and it was all over.[12]

That Brownson was apt to knock his opponent down with the butt end of his gun may be regarded as a mere rhetorical flourish. *The Month,* the English Jesuit publication, remarked when Brownson closed his *Review,* in October 1875, that "Dr. Brownson passes from the field of polemical literature with a stainless and honorable name, and the hearty gratitude of his brother-Catholics in both hemispheres."[13] Writing of Brownson in the *Irish Ecclesiastical Record* in 1888, John Murphy observed that "his faults have been considerably exaggerated, and due allowance has not been made for the circumstances in which he wrote: his faults, such as they were, dwindle into nothing before his great virtues, and his splendid services in the cause of truth."[14]

An explanation of the exaggeration of his faults may be found at least partly in the fact that when adversaries, whether Catholic or non-Catholic, found that they could not grapple with his arguments, they sometimes endeavored to save face by magnifying and then ridiculing some characteristic of the man. Fr. Augustine Hewit, C.S.P., alluded to this in an obituary notice of Brownson when he remarked: "Dr. Brownson's demonstration of the Divine institution of the church is unanswered and unanswerable. It is childish trifling, unworthy of rational men, to ignore his arguments and escape from his logic by petty criticisms of his person. Reason is objective and real; the subjective qualities of the reasoner have nothing to do with its authority."[15]

Of all literary figures, Brownson has perhaps more in common with Dr. Samuel Johnson than any other, as Dr. McLaughlin seemed to suggest. Both were huge in size; both were autocrats; the conversation of both often turned into "voluble monologues"; both were marked by a rugged independence and rigid honesty; both wore a rough exterior that concealed "a nature of infinite tenderness"; both were noted for temper; both grew somewhat slovenly in dress in their later years; both were little disposed to suffer fools gladly. Although both were autocrats, their style of conversation was not quite similar as Boswell's *Life* of his famous idol would seem to indicate. Dr. Bledsoe, the only American editor of his time in any sense comparable to Brownson (so says Frank Luther Mott), irascibly remarked in his *Southern Review* that Brownson thought himself the "autocrat of the intellectual universe."[16] Consciousness of one's gifts may sometimes incline a man all the more to act the autocrat. An English critic wrote of Brownson in the *British Quarterly Review* that he was "intellectually without a peer among Romish [*sic*] editors."[17]

Père Gratry at the Sorbonne, Paris, said of Brownson: "I firmly believe that America is not proud enough of her Brownson. He is the keenest critic of the nineteenth century, an indomitable logician, a disinterested lover of the truth, more than a philosopher, a sage, as sharp as Aristotle, as lofty as Plato, the Newman of America."[18]

Although Archbishop Hughes of New York had many disagreements with Brownson, he paid him a truly meaningful tribute when he said: "We are told by astronomers that there are spots on the sun. And if he [Brownson] has written and published some things that might be offensive, he has written many others that are to perish never. When he and all of us shall have been consigned to the dust, writers among those who are to succeed us will go forth among the pages of his Catholic Review 'prospecting,' as they say in California, for the 'best diggings.' Nor will they be disappointed, if they have tact and talent for profound philosophical, literary and religious 'mining.' But they will not give him credit."[19]

These are but a few of the many estimates of the famous journalist and author who passed from the scenes of this life on April 17, 1876. After the various obituary notices had appeared, the main ones being that of Fr. Augustine Hewit in the *Catholic World*[20] and that of Dr. James A. Corcoran in the *American Catholic Quarterly Review*,[21] Orestes Brownson slipped quickly from widespread fame into comparative obscurity. There is little evidence that many turned back to him in memory during the following decade. In 1882, six years after his death, Joseph Henry Allen complained that "the strong, stormful, rude, yet tender-hearted man passes away, leaving hardly a ripple in our memory to remind us of what his influence had been."[22] But there was to be a gradual revival of interest in the man and his work. One event which no doubt helped to promote a return of interest in him was the transferral of his mortal remains from Mt. Elliot Cemetery, Detroit, to a crypt which had been prepared for his body underneath the chapel at Notre Dame University. The crypt is now known as the Brownson Memorial Chapel. A dispatch from Detroit, Michigan, dated June 10, 1886, recorded the transferral of his remains:

> A delegation of Roman Catholic clergy is in Detroit today for the purpose of removing the remains of the great theological writer, Orestes A. Brownson, to the chapel of the theological College of Notre Dame, South Bend, Ind., which has been called after him and dedicated to his memory. Dr. Brownson died April 17, 1876, and was interred in Mount Elliot Cemetery. The body was ex-

humed at two o'clock this afternoon and was found in fair condition of preservation. It was placed in a metallic case and enclosed in a red oak box. The delegation having the remains in charge left on the Michigan Central train this evening. At Niles they will be met by the entire faculty of Notre Dame College, who will accompany the remains to South Bend. The remains will be deposited in the vault beneath the altar of the Brownson Chapel with impressive ceremonies.[23]

The deposition was accompanied by a Solemn Requiem Mass during which the Rev. Stanislaus Fitte, professor of philosophy in the college, preached an eloquent sermon on the life and character of the great defender of the faith. After the Mass, Fr. Sorin, founder of Notre Dame, spoke briefly of his long and intimate acquaintance with the distinguished dead and of the satisfaction it afforded him that his own Notre Dame was privileged to give a fit resting place to the remains of one who had left all Americans, particularly American Catholics, forever in his debt.[24]

Inscribed on the slab of marble marking his reinternment are the words:

HIC JACET
ORESTES A. BROWNSON
QUI VERAM FIDEM HUMILITER AGNOVIT
INTEGRAM VIXIT VITAM
CALAMO LINGUAQUE
ECCLESIAM AC PATRIAM
FORTITER DEFENDIT
AC LICET MORTI CORPUS ABIERIT
MENTIS OPERA SUPERSUNT IMMORTALIA
INGENII MONUMENTA

In this same year, 1886, a movement got afoot for the erection of a suitable monument to the memory of Brownson, the great American apologist and patriot. No man had more to do with its promotion than M.J. Harson of Providence, Rhode Island, a former attendant at Brown University. M.F. Thomas is not quite accurate, however, in his article on the "National Brownson Memorial" in *Historical Records and Studies* when he says that Harson initiated the movement.[25] The initiator of the movement was Bishop Richard Gilmour of Cleveland, Ohio. Bishop Gilmour may have been flattered a bit by the warm approbation Brownson had given an extensive quotation from one of his pastorals in his *Review* of July 1873, in the article, "The Church above the State."[26] Whatever the fact, Bishop Gilmour clearly perceived the high propriety of setting up some enduring memorial to the memory of one who had contributed so mightily to the Catholic cause in America. Accordingly, he published an editorial in the *Catholic Universe* (April 1886), urging that Catholics of America ought to erect a suitable monument to the memory of Orestes A. Brownson, either in Boston or New York, the main scenes of his labors. The immediate response to this appeal was a contribution of one hundred dollars each from Archbishop John J. Williams of Boston and Archbishop Michael A. Corrigan of New York, and lesser contributions from others.[27]

At a convocation of the Catholic Young Men's National Union of America, held in Philadelphia on May 19 and 20, 1886, of which M.J. Harson was the national secretary, attention was again directed to the Brownson Memorial, and a committee of five was appointed to promote the movement in accordance with the wishes of Bishop Gilmour. The committee formulated a plan which they hoped would enlist the generous support of Catholics throughout the entire country. The plan was cordially approved by Cardinal Gibbons, Archbishop Williams, Bishop Gilmour, Bishop Bernard J. McQuaid and Monsignor Doane, who consented to act as a board of trustees of the memorial fund. Among the distinguished Catholic laymen of the day, besides Mr. Harson himself, none did more to promote the cause than Richard H. Clarke, LL.D., Patrick Farrelly and John A. Sullivan. Although the plans for the memorial were advertised through numerous articles, the financial response was not what it was hoped it would be. While it was expected that the bulk of the contributions would come from the laity, it was, on the contrary, from the bishops and the clergy that the most generous contributions came. At a meeting of the Young Men's National Union held in Boston on September 1, 1897, it was suggested that the fund, then approximately five thousand dollars, be appropriated for the founding of a Brownson scholarship at the Catholic University, on the ground that it would probably be impossible to get a monument erected to him in New York City. But the suggestion was turned down by the chairman of the committee on the score that the donors had contributed with the specific understanding that a monument would be erected to Brownson's memory. However, as six hundred dollars had been subscribed with no strings attached, it was figured that no objection would be made by the contributors if one thousand dollars should be appropriated to the Catholic University, and this sum was presented to the University in October 1898, "for the purpose of furnishing books for a Brownson Alcove in the University Library."[28]

Although the Memorial Movement had not caught fire as had at first been hoped, a commission was given the notable sculptor Samuel J. Kitson of Boston early in 1899 to cast a bronze bust of Brownson. Having once settled on an acceptable image of Brownson, aided by Henry Brownson, Kitson cast what was then the largest bust portrait in the United States. On November 14 of this same year the Kitson bust was exhibited at the Catholic Club in New York City and won favorable commendation from the Municipal Art Commission. It seems there was a long drawn-out discussion with city authorities as to the proper site for the bust. With the resultant delay, interest waned, so much so that it was not until 1910 that, with a new spurt of interest, the Park Department of the city consented to have the bust placed in Sherman Park at Tenth Street and Riverside Drive.

The dedication of the huge bronze bust took place with impressive ceremonies on November 14, 1910. Archbishop John M. Farley of New York presided on the occasion. Among those present was Mrs. Thomas M. Odiorne, granddaughter of Brownson, who unveiled the bust during the ceremonies.[29] The renowned American orator of the day, the Hon. W. Bourke Cockran, U.S. Congressman of New York, made the dedicatory address. The illustrious orator developed the theme that the practical workings of Catholicity evolve inevitably into democratic institutions and a freeman's status for the individual. Echoing some of the thought of the great man whom the occasion was honoring, he said in part:

> The essential principles of democracy were not first formulated in our Constitution, nor in our Declaration of Independence, nor in the English Bill of Rights, nor in the Magna Charta, nor in the Institutes of King Alfred, nor in any monument of human wisdom, evolved from human experience. They were first revealed by the Divine Author of Christianity when he taught that all men are brothers, children of the same Father, equal heirs to the same immortal herit-

*THE BROWNSON MEMORIAL BUST BY SAMUEL J. KITSON*

age beyond the grave. As the political institutions under which men live always reflect the religious beliefs they cherish, a government built upon the principle that all men are equal in the eye of the law resulted inevitably from general acceptance of the religious doctrine that all men are equal in the sight of God.

While democracy was the inevitable, it was not the immediate fruit of Christianity. But this only shows that men find it easier to accept a truth than to regulate their lives by it. It took less than four centuries to convert pagan temples into Christian churches, but it took eighteen centuries for the religious beliefs of Christians to bear fruit in political institutions of freedom. Still from the first hour when the tongues of fire descended upon the heads of the Apostles, it was inevitable that if civilization became Christian two results must follow: the substitution of free labor for slave labor in industry, and the erection of free institutions on the ruins of despotic institutions of government. Here on this soil Christianity has finally borne these, its capital and inevitable fruits. Here the spirit of equality of all men taught by Jesus Christ on Lake Galilee is embodied in a government based upon the political equality of all men. Here labor is not a degrading task reluctantly performed under fear of the scourge by a wretched slave who is chattel, but a voluntary enterprise cheerfully undertaken and loyally discharged by the free man who is sovereign. Never was a system vindicated by results so beneficent — peace, abundance, happiness have blessed the nation which acknowledges no sovereign but the citizen and tolerates no slave but the felon.[30]

The dedicatory ceremonies over, the memorial bust of Brownson was left to its lonely vigil above the Hudson. Nothing more was heard of it until almost three decades later, when a gang of adolescent vandals, out for a thrill, toppled it from its pedestal in 1937. So completely had the man been forgotten that no one at all had the least idea of who the original was, neither the older residents in the neighborhood nor anyone else. The inscription on the bust, "Brownson, Publicist, Philosopher, Patriot," was of little help, but it did send newspaper reporters scurrying to encyclopedias to find out what they could. The New York *Times* published an article headed: "Riverside Statue Stumps Historians." It reported that "the police of 100th station, in opening an investigation of the statue, listed the subject as a 'well-known patriot.' But a casual canvass of historians, literary minds, and young men fresh from study at college showed that Brownson was unknown to modern minds." What wonder that the memorable Paulist columnist and lecturer, Fr. James M. Gillis, came out at the time with reflections on the matter which began: "Alas, alas, that a man once so famous should be forgotten so soon!"[31]

No one apparently laying claim to the Brownson bust, it was soon carted off to the municipal storage yard. There it remained until the former "ever practical and indefatigable" president of Fordham, the Very Rev. Robert I. Gannon, befriended the great American philosopher and publicist. Having asked Mayor LaGuardia if he would authorize the transfer of the memorial to the campus of Fordham University, he received the laconic reply: "You may have Orestes." Accordingly, in 1941, the transfer was made in cooperation with the Catholic Club of New York City and with appropriate ceremonies.[32] There it has since stood in the vicinity of another bust of a former archbishop of New York, no stranger to Brownson, John Hughes.

To this writer the Kitson bust seems to reflect better the real character of Orestes Brownson than any other likeness of him left to posterity. The sculptor seems to have caught (with Henry Brownson's aid) something of the inner spirit of the man together with his mighty works and to have imprisoned it all in his creation. Sally Brownson, Brownson's wife, who was not satisfied with the Healy portrait,[33] would probably have called the Kitson bust a true image of her husband. There is a granite quality in it (from the granite hills of Vermont) that other likenesses lack. Yet it is an image one does not often see. The only place I have ever come across it (apart from the Fordham campus) is in Fr. William H. Sheran's *Text Book of English Literature.*

And in Vermont, his native state, a monument has been erected also to his memory by the Knights of Columbus. It stands at the village of his birth, Stockbridge. The inscription on it reads:

Orestes Augustus Brownson, LL.D.,
Patriot, Philosopher, Publicist.
He loved God, country and truth.
Born at Stockbride, Vermont,
September 16, 1803.
Died at Detroit, Michigan,
April 17, 1876.
This monument erected by
the Knights of Columbus.

One hazards nothing in saying that the once partly forgotten Brownson is destined to come more and more into his own. Perhaps nothing has done more to initiate a revival of interest in Brownson than Arthur M. Schlesinger's *Life of Brownson* which appeared in 1939. Although only a few doctoral theses on Brownson's thought had appeared prior to that date, they have continued to multiply in a goodly degree during the succeeding decades. Two other biographies followed Schlesinger's, that of Doran Whalen and that of Theodore Maynard, from which quotations have been made in the course of this narrative.

New Brownson clubs have sprung up, such as those at the University of Notre Dame and the University of Michigan. In 1965 Americo D. Lapati brought out his *Orestes A. Brownson,* which he modestly calls "A Brownson Primer."[34] In 1970, the Norwegian, Per Sveino, published his "intellectual" biography of Brownson, *Orestes A. Brownson's Road to Catholicism,*[35] and in 1971 Hugh Marshall brought out another book on Brownson entitled, *The American Republic.*[36] To this growing interest in Brownson, Leonard Gilhooley, professor in the English Department of Fordham University, has added still another book, *Contradiction and Dilemma, Orestes A. Brownson and the American Idea.*[37] Daniel Barnes of the English Department in the Ohio State University has announced a forthcoming volume of Brownson's early letters. William Gilmore has completed his treatise, "Religion, Communication and Reform: The Life and Thought of Orestes Brownson, 1803-1844," at the University of Virginia. Robert E. Moffitt is doing extensive work on Brownson's political thought at the University of Arizona. All of which seems to support the statement Russell Kirk made in 1953, namely, that "in the latter half of the twentieth century more attention will be paid to Brownson than he has received in the past hundred years."[38]

Most of the work done on Brownson has been done by Catholics, but by no means all, for as Arthur M. Schlesinger, Jr., has well observed: "He belongs to all Americans, not simply Catholics. . . . He is a part of the national heritage."[39]

# CHAPTER NOTES

## INTRODUCTION

Abbreviations used in the sources:

APF — Archives of the Paulist Fathers (generally referring to Fr. Isaac Hecker's papers).

AUND — Archives of the University of Notre Dame (generally referring to the microfilms of Brownson's papers).

BQR — *Boston Quarterly Review.*

BrQR — *Brownson's Quarterly Review.*

1. *Transcendentalism in New England* (New York: G. P. Putnam's Sons, 1876), p. 359.

2. Henry F. Brownson, *Orestes A. Brownson's Middle Life* (Detroit: H. F. Brownson, Publisher, 1899), p. 476.

3. *Nation* (January 30, 1873), XVI, p. 74.

4. *Orestes A. Brownson: A Pilgrim's Progress* (Boston: Little, Brown and Co., 1939), p. 296.

5. *The American Transcendentalists, Their Prose and Poetry* (Garden City, New York: Doubleday Anchor Books, 1957), p. 39.

6. Henry Tristram, *John Henry Newman, Autobiographical Writings* (New York: Sheed and Ward, 1956), p. 18.

7. *The Literary Criticism of Orestes Brownson* (Ann Arbor: University of Michigan, 1954), p. 350.

## CHAPTER 1

1. Brownson's *Works* (hereafter cited as *Works*), ed. by Henry Brownson (Detroit, 1882-1887), XVIII, p. 398.

2. Orestes Brownson, review of *The History of Waterbury*, by Dr. Henry Bronson, *Brownson's Quarterly Review* (hereafter cited as *BrQR*) (October 1860), pp. 530-532.

3. *The Convert* (Brownson's autobiography), p. 5. (This work will hereafter be cited as incorporated in the *Works*, Vol. V. The pagination will be as it is in that volume. The title *The Convert* and the word "autobiography" may be used interchangeably.)

4. *BrQR* (October 1860), p. 530. In his review of Dr. Henry Bronson's *The History of Waterbury*, Orestes Brownson acknowledged that the Bronson branch was the more distinguished among the descendants of John Brownson. But none was more distinguished than this same Dr. Henry Bronson, a physician. In 1842 "he was elected professor of *materia medica* in the medical department of Yale College," and left there a resplendent record. He was highly regarded by his colleagues. Rev. Joseph Anderson, D.D., *The City and Town of Waterbury, Connecticut, from the Original Period to 1895* (New Haven: The Price and Lee Co., 1896), III, pp. 855-857.

Nor should Silas Bronson (1788-1867) be overlooked. He was a very successful businessman who, among other public benefactions, bequeathed two hundred thousand dollars to Waterbury for the foundation of a public library, known as the Silas Bronson Library. *Ibid.*, III, p. 1007.

5. Published at Dallas, Oregon, 1929. Mrs. Sibley obtained much of her information from George Brownson, J.P. of Devonshire, England, who visited America in 1928, and who had been interested in genealogical and historical research for thirty years. It is due, she said, "to his painstaking efforts and careful preservation of old family records that the American family of Brownson, Bronson, and Brunsun are enabled to trace back their ancestry for 65 years before the landing of their first Puritan forefathers in New England" (p. 4).

Orestes Brownson himself seems to have had some inkling that the Brownsons may well have been of Scottish ancestry. He once remarked: "We take pleasure in tracing our own lineage back to some brave 'cut-throat' of the dark ages; to some border chieftain of Scottish minstrelsy." "The Laboring Classes," *The Boston Quarterly Review* (October 1840), p. 503. (This work will hereafter be cited as *BQR.*)

6. Daniel Stiles, *Town of Waterbury, Connecticut* (Concord, New Hampshire: The Sugar Ball Press, first ed. 1959), p. 55.

7. Letter dated February 14, 1966.

8. *The Catholic World,* LXXVII (June 1903), p. 310.

9. William Cothren, *The History of Ancient Woodbury, Connecticut, 1659-1871* (Waterbury, Connecticut: William R. Seeley, 2nd ed., 1871) I, p. 414.

10. Henry F. Brownson, *Orestes A. Brownson's Early Life, 1803-1844,* Detroit: H. F. Brownson, publisher, 1898), pp. 3-4. (This work will hereafter be cited as *Early Life.*) Quite recently Colonel Herbert Bronson Enderton has made a rather exhaustive genealogical study of the Bronsons, Brownsons and Brunsuns in his work, *Bronson, Brownson and Brunsun Families, Some Descendants of John, Richard and Mary Bronson of Hartford,* published in 1969. For reasons already evident, the Colonel is scarcely accurate in figuring that the original spelling of the name was Bronson. Although he misspells the name, he gives us some information on Sylvester Brownson: "Sylvester Bronson, b. ca [circa] 1768. . . ." 18-11-25, p. 367. That would mean that he died at the premature age of thirty-five. Enderton also states that the Brownsons came over from England on the ship *Defense* in 1635.

11 *Works,* IV. p. 141.

12. *Orestes A. Brownson's Road to Catholicism* (New York: The Humanities Press, 1970), p. 307. Per Sveino's book contains an excellent analysis of Brownson's thought in his progress toward the Catholic Church. In preparation for writing the book he attended Harvard, Notre Dame University and the Sorbonne in Paris. Per Sveino is Norwegian, and at this writing is teaching at Aselund, Norway. He also devotes considerable time to writing.

13. *Early Life,* p. 4. This left Mrs. Brownson with the care of three children: Daniel, who in adult life became somewhat of an orator (*The Catholic World,* LXXIX [April 1904], p. 2.); Orinn (according to the Bible records) or Oran, and Thorina. Thorina was in time adopted by the Dean family, Bernard, Vermont. *The Convert,* p. 31.

14. *The Convert,* p. 4. Brownson was extremely reticent about family matters, and never revealed the names of the elderly couple with whom he went to live. A. F. Hewit, a longtime associate of Brownson, remarked that the elderly couple were "distant relatives of the family." *The Catholic World,* XXIII (June 1876), p. 367. This seems probable on other scores.

15. *Early Life,* p. 5.

16. *The Convert,* p. 6. That Brownson observed the last point most conscientiously throughout life is vouched for by Rev. J. Murphy. When reviewing "Dr. Brownson and His Works" in *The Irish Ecclesiastical Record,* IX (September 1888), Murphy wrote: "No man was ever more ready to atone for a fault once he had become conscious of its commission" (p. 813).

17. *Ibid.,* p. 4.

18. *Early Life,* pp. 6-7; *The Convert,* p. 4.

19. *Early Life,* p. 7.

20. *The Convert,* p. 5.

21. *The Catholic World,* XXIII (June 1876), p. 367.

22. *Works,* XX, p. 183. Writing in his *Review* (October 1859), p. 542, he put the case even stronger for the literary excellences of the King James translation: "In a literary point of view," he said, "it cannot be surpassed or even equalled, and it is hardly possible for one who is not familiar with it to appreciate all the beauties of English literature, or even to write the English tongue as a native. Most of our Catholic literature has, at least to one not brought up a Catholic, something of a foreign air, and lacks the peculiar graces of the English idiom, that home character which is one of its greatest charms."

23. *Early Life,* pp. 4, 8.

24. In concluding his treatise on Brownson (*Four Independents*, New York: Sheed and Ward, 1935) Daniel Sargent remarked: "On Easter Monday, 1876, the Herculean Brownson with his twelve tasks died . . ." (p. 243).

25. *BrQR* (April 1844), p. 278. His deep attachment to the state of Vermont is also indicated in many articles, such as "Beecher's Norwood," *The Catholic World*, X (December 1869), *Works*, XIX, pp. 533-544.

26. *The Convert*, p. 6.

27. Russell Blaine Nye, *The Cultural Life of the New Nation* (New York: Harper's, 1960), p. 219.

28. *The Convert*, p. 5.

29. *Ibid.*, p. 6.

30. John Henry Newman, *Apologia Pro Vita Sua* (London: Longmans, Green, and Co., 1890), p. 7.

31. *The Convert*, pp. 5-6.

32. *Ibid.*, pp. 7-8.

33. *Ibid.*, p. 8.

34. *Ibid.*, p. 9.

35. Workers of the Federal Writers Project of the State of Vermont, *Vermont, The American Guide Series* (Boston: Houghton Mifflin Co., 1937), p. 31.

36. *Early Life*, pp. 9-10.

37. *The Catholic Historical Review*, XLIX (January 1964), p. 529. This letter of Sir John Acton's to his tutor in Munich, Ignaz Döllinger, is perhaps the most interesting discovery of Brownson material for some decades. It is all about Brownson. In reporting his four-day interview — Acton also had had an extensive conversation with Brownson at his home in Boston two weeks previously — Acton was very free in giving his judgment on matters that might well have called for the competency of a more mature mind. Acton at the time was only twenty years of age. After meeting many of the very first men in church and state in the country, and so many of the literati, he said of Brownson: "No American I have seen comes near him intellectually" (p. 527).

38. *The Convert*, p. 10.

39. April 18, 1876, p. 7.

40. According to a letter from Rev. Reuben Smith, dated August 22, 1841, it is evident that young Orestes had had a "sleeping room" in the printshop. *Early Life*, p. 419. It is not improbable that the lodgings taken by his mother were not roomy enough to include a convenient place for the boy.

41. *The Convert*, p. 9.

42. Dr. Elhanan Winchester (1751-1797) had begun his career as a Calvinistic Baptist minister, and had gained a wide reputation as a zealous, fervent and eloquent preacher, almost such as to rival the famous George Whitefield, one of the original Oxford Methodists. But at the very height of his fame, he began to doubt the doctrine of endless punishment. His resulting belief in universal restoration caused him the loss of his pastorate. Thereafter he preached with success in England (1787-1794). Although it was "that eccentric Irishman, John Murray," who first avowedly preached universal salvation in the United States, Brownson asserts that Dr. Winchester must be regarded as "the founder of American Universalism." *The Convert*, pp. 20-21.

43. *The Convert*, pp. 20-27 and *passim*.

44. *Ibid.*, pp. 9-10.

45. "Dr. Brownson," *The Catholic World*, XXIII (June 1876), p. 370.

## CHAPTER 2

1. *The Convert*, p. 11.

2. *Orestes A. Brownson: A Pilgrim's Progress* (Boston: Little, Brown and Co., 1939), p. 10. Mr. Schlesinger reissued this biography of Brownson in paperback in 1966, reversing the title: *A Pilgrim's Progress: Orestes A. Brownson*. Nothing was changed in the text, but a new introduction was added.

3. *The Convert,* p. 12.

4. Microfilm of the *Brownson Papers,* roll 10. Notebook of Reflections. Brownson's papers in the archives of Notre Dame University were recently recalendared and microfilmed. The project was begun in 1965 and completed in 1967. There were originally nineteen rolls of microfilm in all. More recently, in 1970, supplementary roll 1 was added.

5. *Ibid.*

6. *Ibid.*

7. *Ibid.*

8. *The Convert,* p. 18.

9. *Ibid.,* pp. 11-12. Brownson's unhappy recollections of Calvinistic discipline were to abate little during his lifetime. In 1870 he wrote: "We shall never forget the odious tyranny to which Calvinism subjected our own boyhood. Life for us was stern, gloomy, hedged round with terror. We did not dare listen to the joyous song of a bird, nor to inhale the fragrance of an opening flower. Whatever gave pleasure was to be eschewed, and the most innocent pleasures were to be accounted deadly sins. We cannot even now, in our old age, think of our own Calvinistic childhood, which was by no means exceptional, without a shudder." "Civil and Political Liberty," *Works,* XIII, pp. 207-208. (Originally published in *The Catholic World,* X [March 1870], p. 725.)

10. *Ibid.,* pp. 13-19 and *passim.*

11. *Ibid.,* p. 16.

12. *Ibid.,* p. 19.

13. *Orestes Brownson, Yankee, Radical, Catholic* (New York: The Macmillan Co., 1943), p. 8. It is true that Reuben Smith (who had been pastor when Brownson was received as a Presbyterian at Ballston Spa) returned a flat denial in the *Princeton Review,* XXX (1858), pp. 390-392, to Brownson's statement in regard to the vote that had been taken — and repudiated also his description of the Ballston Spa Presbyterians. But Maynard himself throws suspicion on the objectivity of Reuben Smith when he states that Smith "could be tolerant toward Brownson when he was merely a Unitarian, but grew bitter towards him when he became a Catholic" (*ut supra,* p. 12, n. 18).

14. *BrQR* (April 1847), p. 208, n.

15. "Brownson's Exposition of Himself," *The Biblical Repertory and Princeton Review,* Philadelphia (January 1858), pp. 117-150.

16. "The Princeton Review and Ourselves," *BrQR* (April 1858), p. 253; *Works,* V, p. 213.

17. *Ibid.,* p. 287; *Works,* V, p. 246. It is not certain just who wrote the review of Brownson's autobiography in the *Princeton Review,* but it would not seem improbable that it was written by the editor at the time, Dr. Charles Hodge, D.D., professor of the Theological Seminary, Princeton. If so, he was to meet Brownson again as a very formidable adversary when Brownson reviewed his *Systematic Theology,* Vol. I, in *The Catholic World,* January 1872. Concerning the vigorous review Brownson wrote of Hodge's *Systematic Theology,* Father Augustine Hewit, C.S.P., remarked: "The review of Dr. Hodge is about as complete and masterly as I have ever seen, in fact the best in so small a compass. He will have but a very little circle to argue in after this, about as small as Napoleon III at Sedan." *Latter Life,* pp. 569-570. (See also "The Protestant Rule of Faith," *Works,* VIII, pp. 418-439.)

18. He referred to William Warren Sweet's *Religion in the Development of American Culture: 1765-1840* (New York: Charles Scribner's Sons, 1952), p. 207.

19. *Orestes A. Brownson's Road to Catholicism* (New York: The Humanities Press, 1970), p. 26. Much less surprising is the fact that Presbyterians have in our own times been doing what they can to water down the Calvinistic dogma of unconditional election and reprobation. The Southern Presbyterian Church, meeting in Dallas, Texas, on April 29, 1961, moved to soften its offensive features. *New York Times* (April 30, 1961), p. 41.

20. Microfilm of the *Brownson Papers,* supplementary roll 1.

21. *BrQR* (October 1875), pp. 564-565.

22. *Orestes A. Brownson's Road to Catholicism, ut supra,* p. 36.

23. *An Essay on the Development of Christian Doctrine* (London: James Toovery, Piccadilly, second ed., 1845). See Advertisement, pp. IV-X.

24. *BrQR* (April 1855), p. 245; *Works,* I, p. 322.

25. *The Convert,* p. 20.

26. *Early Life,* p. 10.

27. *Ibid.,* pp. 17-18.

28. *Ibid.,* p. 19.

29. *Apologia Pro Vita Sua* (New York: Longmans, Green, and Co., 1890), pp. 241-242.

30. *Ibid.,* p. 242.

31. Brownson's diary, or Notebook of Reflections.

## CHAPTER 3

1. He was not, however, without some previous acquaintances with Universalism. Per Sveino has unearthed from the *Gospel Advocate* that Brownson had attended a Universalist meeting while a Presbyterian, and that he "was admitted to the Lord's Supper in his own church only after due apologizing and without even having a chance of explaining and defending himself." *Orestes A. Brownson's Road to Catholicism* (New York: The Humanities Press, 1970), p. 42, n. 16.

2. *The Convert,* p. 20.

3. *Religion in the Development of American Culture: 1765-1840* (New York: Charles Scribner's Sons, 1952), p. 197.

4. *The Convert,* pp. 21-22.

5. *Ibid.,* pp. 22-25.

6. *Early Life,* p. 20.

7. *BrQR* (July 1875), p. 432.

8. *The Convert,* p. 30.

9. *Early Life,* p. 21; *The Convert,* p. 30.

10. *The Convert,* p. 32.

11. *Ibid.*

12. *Orestes A. Brownson and the American Republic* (Washington, D.C.; Catholic University of America Press, 1971), p. 5; *Early Life,* pp. 24-25.

13. *The Convert,* p. 33.

14. *Ibid.,* pp. 33, 35.

15. *Ibid.,* pp. 34-35.

16. *Ibid.,* p. 39.

17. *Ibid.,* p. 37.

18. *Ibid.,* pp. 36-37; *Early Life,* p. 58.

19. *Early Life,* p. 58.

20. Walter M. Abbott, S.J., *The Documents of Vatican II* (New York: America Press, 1965), p. 165.

21. *Works,* II, pp. 1-100.

22. Wilfrid Ward, *The Life of John Henry Cardinal Newman* (New York: Longmans, Green, and Co., 1912), II, p. 296. Concerning the knowledge of the existence of God, St. Thomas Aquinas wrote: "If the only way to us for the knowledge of God were solely that of reason, the human race would remain in the blackest shadows of ignorance. For then the knowledge of God, which especially renders men perfect and good, would come to be possessed by only a few, and these would require a great deal of time in order to reach it." *The Truth of the Catholic Faith, Summa Contra Gentiles* (Garden City, New York: Hanover House, 1955), Book I, chapter 4, n. 4.

23. *Early Life,* p. 59. Near the end of his life Brownson said: "We were personally led to deny the existence of God by the sensist philosophy as expounded by Locke and Hume, and by Dr. Thomas Brown." *Works,* XX, p. 429.

24. *Ibid.,* pp. 59-60.

25. *Ibid.,* p. 61.

26. *An Essay in Aid of a Grammar of Assent* (Garden City, New York: Doubleday, Image Books, 1955) chapter 5, pp. 100-101 in particular.

27. *Apologia Pro Vita Sua* (New York: Longmans, Green, and Co., 1890), pp. 198, 204.

28. *Charles Elwood; Or the Infidel Converted*, p. 196. This book has been incorporated into volume IV of his *Works*, pp. 173-313. In 1834 and 1835 Brownson wrote a series of reflections under the title: "Letters to an Unbeliever in Answer to some Objections to Religion." In 1840 he worked them over into a novel or work of fiction, and gave the result the title: *Charles Elwood; Or the Infidel Converted*. Its purpose was to describe under the name of another some of his own past experiences, particularly his period of unbelief and the means by which the recovery of his faith was effected. Speaking of the book, he said in the preface: "The characters introduced are of course fictitious, yet I may say that I have had an intellectual experience similar to that which Mr. Elwood records, and what he has said of himself would perhaps apply in some degree to me. I am willing that the public take the book as an account which I have thought proper to give of my own former unbelief and present belief. So far as it can be of any use, I am willing that what is here recorded should have the authority of my own experience."

Of this work E. A. Poe remarked: "In logical force, in comprehensiveness of thought, and in the evident frankness and desire for truth in which it is composed, we know of few theological treatises which can be compared to it." "A Chapter on Autography," *Graham's* Magazine, November-January, 1842; Poe, *Works*, IX, p. 201. Yet Brownson himself became quickly dissatisfied with it and would not allow a second edition. A London publisher, however, issued five editions of it. (See New York *Times*, obituary article on Brownson, April 18, 1876, p. 7, column 5.)

29. *Charles Elwood, Works*, IV, p. 176.

30. *Ibid.*, p. 314.

31. *Early Life*, pp. 423ff.

32. *The Nation*, "Orestes A. Brownson's Early Life," LXVII (September 1898), p. 205.

33. *Early Life*, pp. 424-425.

34. *Ibid.*, pp. 426-427. He based his argument on the nature of absolute ideas, drawn at the time from the philosophy of Victor Cousin. His son Henry called the argument "lame and unsatisfactory," but asserts that it still contains in germ his father's elaborate *Essay in Refutation of Atheism* published thirty years later.

35. *Ibid.*, p. 425.

36. *Ibid.*, pp. 480-481; *Middle Life*, p. 468. Brownson's *Middle Life* is the second volume of three in Henry's biography of his father.

37. *Ibid.*, p. 481.

38. *Ibid.*, p. 485.

39. *Works*, IV, p. 188. Elizabeth, however, was instructed by her pastor, Mr. Smith, never to give her heart to Charles unless he consented to be converted. On which point Brownson appended this footnote: "One of the most common methods resorted to by revivalists (when I was a young man) was to make the love which a young man had for a young woman, and the love he hoped for in turn, the means of his conversion to the church. My own case was not a singular one. The girl was instructed to throw her arms around her lover's neck, and entreat him, by all his affection for her, to join the church; but at the same time to assure him, that she could never consent to be his unless he gave evidence of his conversion. There was some knowledge of human nature in this, and these fair apostles were not unfrequently successful as well as eloquent pleaders for God, especially when seconded by the burning passions of their youthful admirers." *Ibid., Charles Elwood*, p. 209.

40. *Ibid*, p. 241. All of which reminds us of the famous saying of Blaise Pascal: "The heart has reasons of which reason itself knows nothing." H. F. Stewart, *Pascal's Pensées*, with an English translation (New York: Pantheon Books, 1950), pp. 342-343.

41. *Early Life*, p. 485.

42. *The Convert*, p. 40. After speaking at length on Julian the Apostate late in

life, Brownson remarked that "there is some temptation to one who stands outside the Church, whose heart has never been touched by the Christian spirit . . . to treat Christianity as low and unintellectual, as the work of fishermen. In my ante- and anti-Christian days I felt the temptation, and considered Christianity too weak and puerile, too low and vulgar for a man of ordinary intelligence and some self-respect to treat otherwise than with supreme disdain and contempt." "Early and Recent Apostates," *BrQR* (July 1874), pp. 397-398.

43. *Early Life,* pp. 56-61.

44. *The Convert,* p. 40.

45. *Early Life,* pp. 26-27, 29.

46. *The Convert,* p. 39. Perhaps it is more of verbal than written criticisms that Brownson was speaking.

47. Both Brownson and Newman had a strong belief in the sovereignty and power of truth. In his *The Present Position of Catholics in England* (London: Longmans, Green, and Co., 1889) Newman wrote: "I have an intense feeling in me as to the power and victoriousness of truth. It has a blessing on it from God. Satan himself can but retard its ascendancy, he cannot prevent it" (p. 386). Many other such passages could be quoted from both writers.

48. Yet a person may be a great and good man without having the perfection of a saint. Newman also said as a Catholic: "I have no tendency to be a saint — it is a sad thing to say." Cited in Meriol Trevor, *Newman, The Pillar and the Cloud.* (New York: Doubleday and Co., 1962), p. 509.

49. *The Convert,* p. 46.

50. *Ibid.,* p. 47.

51. *Ibid.,* p. 48.

52. Alexander Pope, *Complete Poetical Works,* (Boston and New York: Houghton Mifflin Co., 1903), Epistle IV, p. 225.

53. *Early Life,* pp. 30-34.

54. *Ibid.,* p. 30.

55. *Gospel Advocate,* VII (September 5, 1829), pp. 282-283.

56. Per Sveino brings out that Doubleday had sharply criticized Brownson for his "course" toward "atheism," and states that his successor, Mr. Dolphus Skinner was unwilling to engage Brownson as editor. Offense had been taken, too, by Doubleday inasmuch as Brownson had attended one of the meetings of Fanny Wright and had "held out to her the hand of fellowship and became attached to the *Free Enquirer.*" *Orestes A. Brownson's Road to Catholicism, ut supra,* p. 43, n. 66.

57. *Early Life,* p. 39.

58. *The Convert,* p. 40.

59. *Works,* VI, p. 528.

60. Notre Dame University has just acquired this letter, and it is still in the department of rare manuscripts. Perhaps it was lately discovered in some book the Rev. Whitman left behind.


## CHAPTER 4

1. *The Convert,* pp. 37, 41.

2. *Works,* IV, p. 383.

3. *Ibid.,* p. 226.

4. *The Convert,* p. 41.

5. Herbert Somerton Foxwell, Introduction to Anton Menger's *The Right to the whole Produce of Labor* (New York: August M. Kelley, Publishers, 1962), p. XC.

6. *The Convert,* pp. 41-42.

7. J.F.C. Harrison, *The Quest for the New Moral World* (New York: Charles Scribner's Sons, 1969), p. 164.

8. *Ibid.,* pp. 139-145.

9. *The Convert,* pp. 42-43.

10. *Ibid.,* p. 43.

11. *Transcendentalism in New England* (New York: G. P. Putnam's Sons, 1876), p. 129.

12. *The Convert*, p. 49.

13. *Ibid.*, pp. 50-51.

14. "Liberalism and Socialism," *BrQR* (April 1855), p. 191; *Works*, X, p. 534.

15. *The Great Encyclical Letters of Leo XIII* (New York: Benziger Brothers, 1903), p. 222.

16. *The Convert*, p. 49.

17. *Works*, IV, p. 241. Joseph Dorfman calls Brownson "a Christian Socialist" in his *The Economic Mind in American Civilization, 1806-1865* (New York: Viking Press, 1946), II, p. 661.

18. *The Convert*, pp. 51-57.

19. *Ibid.*, pp. 53, 56.

20. *Ibid.*, p. 64. In an undated letter, written apparently after he had become a Catholic, Brownson frankly acknowledged that his early radicalism had stemmed from Godwin: "A newspaper recently in a neighboring city," he wrote, "accuses me of borrowing some of my early radicalism from Godwin's *Inquiry concerning Political Justice* . . . the ablest work I have ever met with on that side of the question." Microfilm of the *Brownson Papers*, roll 8. Condercet also exerted a pronounced influence on him in his early years — a fact generally overlooked by biographers and commentators. *BQR* (July 1842), p. 281, n.

21. Paul R. Boher reedited it (Cambridge: Harvard University Press, 1963).

22. William Randall Waterman, *Frances Wright* (New York: Columbia Press, 1924), pp. 57, 68.

23. *Ibid.*, pp. 88, 90, 96. Her plans were also submitted to former President Monroe and Chief Justice Marshall for their consideration. She was also in correspondence with Benjamin Lundy, the great emancipationist of the day. *Ibid.*, p. 91.

24. J.F.C. Harrison, *Quest for the new Moral World, ut supra*, pp. 167-168.

25. Jean Pierre Boyer (1773-1850), a mulatto, became the first President of the Republic of Haiti (1822) after the protracted struggle for complete independence was won. He was responsible for much progressive legislation introduced into the government, including the basic law codes of the nation, but was ousted from office in 1843.

26. *The Convert*, pp. 57-58.

27. *Ibid.*, p. 58.

28. *Early Life*, p. 40.

29. *The Convert*, p. 59. Brownson did not exaggerate. Mrs. F. M. Trollope, mother of the novelist, who witnessed Miss Wright's appearance on the platform at Cincinnati, Ohio, wrote of her: "It is impossible to imagine anything more striking than her appearance. Her tall and majestic figure, the deep and almost solemn expression of her eyes, the simple contour of her finely formed head, unadorned, except by its own natural ringlets; her garment of plain white muslin, which hung about her in folds that recalled a Grecian statue, all contributed to produce an effect, unlike anything I have ever seen before, nor ever expect to see again." *Domestic Manners of the Americans* (London: Whittaker, Treacher and Co., 1832), I, p. 98.

30. *Early Life*, p. 41.

31. W. R. Waterman, *ut supra*, p. 187.

32. Issue of January 10, 1929.

33. Issue of January 17, 1929.

34. *Early Life*, p. 42.

35. *The Convert*, p. 29.

36. *Early Life*, p. 41.

37. *The Convert*, p. 59. *The Working Man's Advocate*, a weekly journal, was also published by the Free Enquirers to make a more direct appeal to the working class as the *New Enquirer* was tainted with infidelity and radicalism. W. R. Waterman, p. 201.

38. *Early Life*, pp. 41-42.

39. *The Convert*, p. 63; *Early Life*, p. 43. When marrying Mary Jane Robinson on April 12, 1832, Robert D. Owen observed nothing more than "a mutual agreement

in writing." In marrying William Phiquepal rather hurriedly Miss Wright was marrying the father of her expected child. Perkins, Alice J.G., and Wolfson, Theresa, *Frances Wright: Free Enquirer. The Study of a Temperament* (New York: Harper and Brothers, 1939), p. 318.

40. "An Earnest Sowing of Wild Oats," A Chapter of Autobiography (*Threading My Way*) *The Atlantic Monthly*, XXX (July 1874), p. 73.

41. W. R. Waterman, p. 63.

42. *The Convert*, p. 63.

43. *Ibid.*, pp. 60-62 and *passim.*

44. *Ibid.*, p. 63.

45. Matthew Carey (1760-1839), born in Ireland, fled to France as a political refugee when a young man where he made the acquaintance of Benjamin Franklin and the Marquis de Lafayette. Later he emigrated to America and settled in Philadelphia. With the aid of money given him by Lafayette he founded the *Pennsylvania Herald* (1785) and the *Columbia Magazine* in 1786. The money given him by Lafayette was repaid forty years later when the French aristocrat was in need. Carey became a noted American bookseller as well as publisher. His *Holy Bible* was the first American Douay edition. He was influential in both Philadelphia politics and banking. (See also *Early Life,* p. 45.)

46. *The Convert*, pp. 63-64.

47. *Ibid.*, p. 64.

48. *Early Life*, pp. 45-46.

49. Helen L. Sumner in J. R. Common's *History of Labor in the United States* (New York: The Macmillan Co., 1918-1935), I, pp. 234-237.

50. *Ibid.*, p. 257.

51. *Ibid.*, p. 267.

52. *Ibid.*, p. 274.

53. *The Convert*, p. 65.

54. *Ibid.*, p. 65.

55. The Great Encyclical Letters of Leo XIII, *ut supra*, p. 218.

56. *The Convert*, pp. 55-57.

57. The Great Encyclical Letters of Leo XIII, *ut supra*, pp. 218-219.

58. *Orestes A. Brownson's Road to Catholicism* (New York: The Humanities Press, 1970), p. 51.

59. *The Spirit-Rapper: An Autobiography* (Detroit: Thorndike Nourse, Publisher, 1884). Also in *Works,* IX, with identical pagination, pp. 1-234.

60. Arthur M. Schlesinger, Jr., *Orestes A. Brownson: A Pilgrim's Progress* (Boston: Little, Brown and Co., 1939), p. 51.

61. *The Spirit-Rapper, Works,* IX, p. 226. This became all the more credible in the light of what he said in a letter to Rev. Bernard Whitman already on June 13, 1831. After speaking of skeptics close to himself at the time, he added: "I fell in with some of their leaders. I heard Miss Wright lecture, finally became a corresponding editor of the Free Enquirer. I remained there but a short time. I now had a chance to look around on skepticism, and being among its friends, I saw its deficiency." Letter in the Archives of the University of Notre Dame (hereafter cited as *AUND*).

62. *Ibid.*, pp. 226-227. Explaining how it was that he was intellectually prepared to join Frances Wright and her followers when they appeared, Brownson said: "Like most English and Americans of my generation, I had been educated in the school of Locke. From Locke I passed into the Scottish school of Reid and Stewart, and adhered to it without well knowing what it was, until overthrown by Dr. Thomas Brownson, who, in the introductory lectures to his philosophy, revived the scepticism of Hume, and drove me into speculative atheism, by resolving cause and effect into invariable antecedence and consequence, thus excluding all idea of creative power or productive force. Still young, I rushed into pure sensism and materialism, and was prepared intellectually to join Frances Wright and her followers, when they appeared." *The Convert*, pp. 125-126.

63. *The Convert*, pp. 65-66.

64. *Ibid.*

65. W. R. Waterman, pp. 221, 231.

66. *Webster's Biographical Dictionary* (Springfield, Massachusetts: G & C Merriam Co., 1943), p. 1134.

67. *Works,* IV, p. 226.

68. *The Convert,* p. 66.

69. *Works,* IV, p. 214.


## CHAPTER 5

1. *Early Life,* p. 367.

2. "Dr. Brownson in Boston," *The Catholic World,* XLV (July 1887), p. 466.

3. *The Christian Register,* II (July 30, 1831), p. 121.

4. *The Convert,* pp. 68, 71.

5. Here it would appear that his excommunication was really retroactive, issued only after his departure.

6. *Early Life,* pp. 50-55.

7. *The Convert,* pp. 69-70.

8. *BrQR* (January 1857), p. 144.

9. "Lacordaire and Catholic Progress," *BrQR* (July 1862), pp. 312, 316; *Works,* XX, pp. 258, 262.

10. *Works,* IV, pp. 141-142.

11. *The Convert,* p. 66.

12. *Ibid.,* p. 78.

13. *Ibid.,* p. 71.

14. *Early Life,* pp. 57-58.

15. Doctoral dissertation by Charles Carroll Hollis (unpublished): *The Literary Criticism of Orestes Brownson* (Ann Arbor: University of Michigan, 1954), preface, p. vii. This excellent treatise will be referred to hereafter as Hollis's *Literary Criticism.*

16. *Early Life,* pp. 69-76 and *passim.*

17. *Four Independents* (New York: Sheed and Ward, 1935), p. 238.

18. Microfilm of the *Brownson Papers,* roll 8. Quote undated and unsigned.

19. Hollis's *Literary Criticism,* p. 8. Hollis gives no reference for his statement. Often did Brownson refer to this measure as being used against the independent preacher as though he was smarting from personal recollections. *BQR* (October 1840), pp. 456-457.

20. *BrQR* (October 1874), p. 548; *Works,* XX, p. 435.

21. Cited in Walter Elliot's *The Life of Father Hecker* (New York: Columbia Press, 1894), p. 182.

22. *Early Life,* p. 61. Brownson did not own *The Philanthropist;* its proprietor was H. J. Grew. (See letter of Brownson to Rev. B. Whitman, June 13, 1831. *AUND.*)

23. *Orestes A. Brownson's Road to Catholicism* (New York: The Humanities Press, 1970), p. 74.

24. *The Convert,* p. 71.

25. Microfilm of the *Brownson Papers,* roll 9.

26. *Early Life,* p. 85.

27. *Our Liberal Movement in Theology* (Boston: American Unitarian Association Press, 1882), p. 86.

28. Microfilm of the *Brownson Papers,* roll 9.


## CHAPTER 6

1. *The Convert,* p. 71.

2. "The Eclipse of Faith," *BrQR* (October 1853), p. 429; *Works,* VII, p. 289.

3. *Early Life,* p. 367.

4. *Ibid.*, p. 516.

5. *The National Catholic Register* (January 23, 1944).

6. "The French Republic," *BrQR* (July 1851), p. 382; *Works*, XVI, pp. 271-272.

7. *Early Life*, p. 86.

8. *Rhetoric in the Works of Orestes Brownson*, a valuable unpublished dissertation by Leonard James McCarthy, S.J. (New York: Fordham University Press, 1961), p. 93.

9. Charles Carroll Hollis, Introductory note, page 1. Hollis notes that there are of course some alterations in Brownson's standards of criticism as he passed from liberal to conservative. This explains some changing judgments, though not pronounced in most cases, on such authors as Emerson, Edward Lytton Bulwer, Edmund Burke, Wordsworth and others. In his opening chapter on Brownson's conservative period Hollis "discusses Brownson's formulation of a Thomistic aesthetics, a task in which he was definitely a pioneer in American thought." Introductory note, Part II, p. 1. *Literary Criticism of Orestes Brownson* (Ann Arbor: University of Michigan, 1954).

10. *BrQR* (October 1874), p. 571.

11. James Jeffrey Roche, *The Life of John Boyle O'Reilly* (New York: Cassell Publishing Co., 1891), p. 152.

12. *Early Life*, p. 89.

13. Cited in F. O. Matthiessen, *The American Renaissance* (New York: The Oxford University, 1941), p. 19, n. 6. When escorted around Harvard University on his visit to America in 1953, Sir John Acton found it disappointing by German standards. Referring apparently to the library, he remarked: "It is incomplete. History is ignored here. There seems to be no call for accurate learning here." *The Catholic Historical Review*, XLIX (January 1964), p. 525.

We get a fairly good idea of how slowly libraries grew in the country from the fact that, although the White House has today an excellent library, it had few books in 1850. When Millard Fillmore became President following the death of Zachary Taylor in 1850, he could not find even a Bible in the White House for the inaugural ceremony. His wife, Abigail Powers Fillmore, a former schoolteacher who loved books and reading, converted a large room on the second floor of the White House into a library. On March 3, 1851, Congress passed an appropriations act which "authorized for purchase of books at the Executive Mansion two hundred and fifty dollars to be expended under the direction of the President of the United States."

14. *Ibid.*, pp. 10, 18, 23.

15. *Early Life*, p. 71.

16. *Ibid.*, pp. 373, 381.

17. "Dr. Brownson and the Workingmen's Party Fifty Years Ago," *The Catholic World*, XLV (May 1887), p. 204.

18. "Dr. Brownson in Boston," *The Catholic World*, XLV (July 1887), p. 466.

19. "Brownson: A Man of Men," *The Catholic World*, CXXV (September 1927), p. 760.

20. *The Evening News* of St. Louis, January 9, 1854, p. 2.

21. *Early Life*, pp. 89, 374.

22. *The Unitarian* (March 1834).

23. *Early Life*, pp. 90-91.

24. *Ibid.*, p. 93.

25. "Dr. Brownson," *The Catholic World*, XXIII (June 1876), p. 370.

26. *Early Life*, p. 98.

27. Walter M. Abbott, S.J., ed., *The Documents of Vatican II* (New York: America Press, 1966), p. 241.

28. *Early Life*, pp. 99-100.

29. *Ibid.*, pp. 100-102.

30. "Memoir of Saint-Simon," *The Unitarian* (June 1834).

31. *Early Life*, pp. 106-108.

32. *Ibid.*, pp. 95-96.

33. *Ibid.*, p. 104.

34. H. Daniel Rops, *A Fight for God* (New York: E. P. Dutton and Co., 1966), p. 294.

35. *Early Life,* pp. 105-106.

36. Microfilm of the *Brownson Papers,* roll 9.

37. *Early Life,* pp. 109-110.


## CHAPTER 7

1. Adin Ballou, *Autobiography* (Lowell: Vox Populi Press, 1896), p. 254.

2. *Early Life,* p. 110.

3. C. C. Hollis, *Literary Criticism of Orestes Brownson* (Ann Arbor: University of Michigan, 1954), p. 204.

4. *Ibid.,* p. 16.

5. "Dr. Brownson and the Workingmen's Party Fifty Years Ago," *The Catholic World,* XLV (May 1887), p. 204.

6. *Early Life,* pp. 111-112.

7. *Ibid.,* p. 117.

8. *Ibid.,* pp. 114-115.

9. *Ibid.,* p. 118.

10. *Ibid.,* p. 110.

11. *Ibid.,* p. 121.

12. *The Dial,* I, p. 25.

13. *Early Life,* pp. 123-125; see also C. C. Hollis, *Literary Criticism,* p. 25.

14. *Early Life,* pp. 125-126. Brownson's letters to Everett have not been preserved. But Everett evidently took close notice of Brownson's English style. It seems that the first high encomium on Brownson's English style came from him. In an article on Brownson, Augustine Walsh remarked: "The celebrated American orator and master of polished diction, Edward Everett, once said: 'There is a young man in Boston who writes the best English in America.'" *The Placidian,* IV (January 1927), p. 37.

Of Brownson's literary style Walsh himself remarked: "One point is evident in all his writings: he tries to present his thought in such a manner that no one may mistake his meaning. . . . Brownson is the greatest exponent of plain English in American literature; he is not an Emerson, to give confused ideas yet more confusing expression. He is not remarkable for the music of his phrases; he is a writer, not a singer; a philosopher, not a poet. His words are strongly set, more like crystal rocks than liquid stream." *Ibid.,* pp. 42-43.

15. *Early Life,* p. 111.

16. C. C. Hollis, *Literary Criticism,* p. 25.

17. *Thoreau, The Poet and Naturalist* (Boston: C. E. Goodspeed Press, 1902), p. 32. Brownson at the time was not a member of the School Committee. He had been the year before. Kenneth W. Cameron is of the opinion that Thomas French, leader of the School Committeemen that year, "probably" asked Brownson to examine Thoreau. "Thoreau and Orestes Brownson," *Emerson Society Quarterly, A Journal of the American Renaissance* (1968), p. 54.

18. "Thoreau and Orestes Brownson," *Emerson Society Quarterly, ut supra,* p. 60.

19. *Early Life,* p. 204.

20. *Thoreau* (Boston: Houghton Mifflin Co., 1939), p. 58.

21. *Early Life,* p. 204.

22. *Orestes Brownson, Yankee, Radical, Catholic* (New York: The Macmillan Co., 1943), p. 60, n. 35.

23. "Thoreau and Orestes Brownson," *Emerson Society Quarterly, ut supra,* pp. 60-61.

24. "Orestes A. Brownson, LL.D.: A Man of Courage and a Great American," *The Catholic World,* LXXIX (April 1904), p. 23.

25. C. C. Hollis, *Literary Criticism,* p. 23.

26. Henry F. Brownson, *Orestes A. Brownson's Latter Life* (hereafter cited as *Latter Life*) (Detroit: H. F. Brownson, Publisher, 1900), p. 1.

27. *Orestes A. Brownson's Road to Catholicism* (New York: The Humanities Press, 1970), pp. 114-115. Per Sveino says: "Brownson's own [asserted] attitude toward external nature is difficult to account for, since his writings do not contain any descriptions of scenery. But indirectly the reader gets the impression that Brownson was no great lover of nature" (p. 114). Brownson was a magazine writer, almost exclusively concerned with logical thought, not a poet or novelist. His writings simply did not call for descriptions of scenery.

It was on that score, too, that Brownson complained of the "wearisome descriptions of natural scenery" in authors where the description simply did not fit. Yet Sveino sees this as another argument against Brownson's asserted love of external nature. Brownson never complained of descriptions of natural scenery in such authors as Lord Byron or in anyone else where they fit.

28. *BQR* (January 1841), p. 132.

29. Copies of it are still extant in the Houghton Library of Harvard, the Yale Library, and the Library of Congress, though the first mentioned is incomplete. "Thoreau and Orestes Brownson," *Emerson Society Quarterly*, p. 72.

30. "Thoreau and Orestes Brownson," *Emerson Society Quarterly*, pp. 59, 72. Kenneth Cameron demurs to Henry Brownson's statement that Thoreau spent "one summer vacation" with his father (*Early Life*, p. 204), and seemingly on good grounds. Thoreau's letter to Brownson speaks of only "six weeks" spent in the Brownson *household*. Cameron acknowledges, however, that Thoreau may have taught school and boarded elsewhere in town for a longer period. During that time Thoreau and Brownson could have kept up their communings. *Ibid.*, p. 72.

31. *Ibid.*, pp. 67-71.

32. *A Thoreau Handbook* (New York: New York University Press, 1959), pp. 119-120.

33. *The Convert*, p. 74. As Brownson observed: "Truth is older than error, and monotheism — the belief and worship of one only God — is older than polytheism, older than fetichism, and is, in fact, the earliest form of religion recorded in history." *Ibid.*, p. 74.

34. *Ibid.*, pp. 74-76 and *passim*.

35. *The Transcendentalists, An Anthology* (Cambridge: Harvard University Press, 1950), pp. 85-86.

36. *Early Life*, pp. 126-134.

37. *AUND*.

38. "Thoreau and Orestes Brownson," *Emerson Society Quarterly, ut supra*, p. 66.

39. Cited by Daniel J. V. Huntoon in his *History of the Town of Canton, Massachusetts* (Cambridge: John Wilson and Son, University Press, 1893), p. 564.

40. C. C. Hollis, *Literary Criticism*, p. 26.

41. Microfilm of the *Brownson Papers*, supplementary roll 1.

## CHAPTER 8

1. *Early Life*, pp. 137-138. He abandoned the enterprise after three years, but resumed it in 1842. *BQR* (July 1842), p. 367.

2. The report appeared in the *Boston Daily Advertiser*, and was reprinted in the *Christian Register* (March 25, 1836). See Per Sveino's *Orestes A. Brownson's Road to Catholicism* (New York: The Humanities Press, 1970), p. 119, n. 45.

3. *The Convert*, pp. 76-77.

4. *The Transcendentalists* (Cambridge: Harvard University Press, 1950), p. 45.

5. *The Convert*, p. 77.

6. *Literary Criticism of Orestes Brownson*, doctoral dissertation (Ann Arbor: University of Michigan, 1954), p. 32.

7. *The Convert*, pp. 82-83.

8. *Early Life*, p. 313.

9. *The Convert*, p. 78.

10. *Ibid.*, pp. 78-79.

11. *Ibid.*, pp. 80-82.

12. *Ibid.*, pp. 86-87.

13. Microfilm of the *Brownson Papers*, roll 10.

14. *BrQR* (April 1845), p. 259.

15. *The Convert*, pp. 92-100.

16. *Early Life*, pp. 138-139.

17. *Ibid.*, p. 142ff.

18. *Ibid.*, pp. 139, 145.

19. *The Prose Writers of America* (Philadelphia: A. Hart, late Casey and Hart, fourth ed., 1853), p. 422.

20. Microfilm of the *Brownson Papers,* roll 10.

21. *Ibid.*

22. *Ibid.*

23. *BQR* (July 1842), p. 258.

24. Harriet Martineau, *Society in America* (London: Saunders and Otley, 1837), II, p. 412.

25. *Ibid.*, p. 358. But Brownson did not reciprocate her admiration. He spoke of her as "that queen of gossips," and remarked that "Harriet is a bundle of contradictions" (*BQR*, 1839, pp. 259, 392). But he had measured praise for her *The Hour and the Man,* 2 vols. *Ibid.*, 1841. p. 260.

26. *Early Life*, p. 140.

27. Fr. Isaac Hecker, "Dr. Brownson in Boston," *The Catholic World,* XLV (July 1887), p. 471.

28. *The Convert*, p. 83.

29. *Early Life*, p. 146.

30. *Ibid.*, p. 146ff.

31. *BQR* (July 1842), p. 367.

32. *Early Life,* pp. 152-153.

33. *Ibid.*, p. 157. Miss Elizabeth Palmer Peabody was a sort of bluestocking of the "Hub," though not on the same level as Margaret Fuller. Her bookshop on West Street was a center at which many of the literati met to converse. "Dr. Channing . . . came every morning to the shop to read the papers. He stayed for the sake of the people he would meet, Orestes Brownson, George Ripley, and above all Theodore Parker." (See Louise Tharp, *The Peabody Sisters of Salem* [Boston: Little, Brown and Co., 1950], p. 208.) Elizabeth P. Peabody was also very active in the educational field, being mistress of private schools over a number of years. In 1860 she opened the first kindergarten in America. She also lectured at Amos B. Alcott's Concord School of Philosophy, and, besides other literary works, wrote her *Reminiscences of Rev. Wm. Ellery Channing* (Boston: Roberts Brothers, 1880) (Webster's Biographical Dictionary). She was also a great admirer of Brownson; her letters to him stretch over a long span of years. She was likewise sister-in-law to Nathaniel Hawthorne.

34. *The Convert*, p. 43.

35. *Ibid.*, pp. 83-84.

36. *Works,* IV, pp. 2, 59.

37. *Ibid.*, "The Church of the Future," p. 59.

38. "Brownson's Works," *The Dial* (1840), p. 25.

39. "The Church of the Future," *BQR* (January 1842), p. 2.

40. *The Convert*, pp. 87, 89.

41. *Works,* IV, pp. 23-24.

42. *The Convert*, p. 88.

43. *Works,* IV, pp. 28, 31-32.

44. *Ibid.*, pp. 9-11.

45. Genesis, I, p. 31.

46. *Romans*, VII, p. 23.

47. *Orestes A. Brownson's Road to Catholicism, ut supra*, pp. 126-127.

48. *The Convert*, pp. 84-85.

49. *Works*, IV, p. 25.

50. *The Transcendentalists*, pp. 114-115.

51. *Literary Criticism*, pp. 31-32.

52. *The Convert*, pp. 80-82.

53. Here and there an echo was heard of this longing for Christian unity. As Per Sveino records, the *Cumberland Presbyterian* journal gave expression to this longing when it said: "We believe that all true Christians will yet be united. The present generation may not witness a consummation so glorious; but so true as the Bible is the word of God, so surely will all who are in Christ Jesus be encircled in the embraces of brotherly love. Sectarianism and separatism and every other ism is destined to an early grave, whilst the whole Church of Christ shall yet constitute a harmonious brotherhood." *The Christian Register*, XV (February 27, 1836). (See Sveino's *Orestes A. Brownson's Road to Catholicism*, pp. 115-116).

54. *Works*, IV, pp. 55-56.

55. *The Convert*, p. 122.

## CHAPTER 9

1. *Early Life*, p. 161.

2. Microfilm of the *Brownson Papers*, roll 10.

3. Leonard Gilhooley, *Orestes Brownson and the American Idea, 1838-1860*, an excellent doctoral dissertation (New York: Fordham University Press, 1961), p. 66.

4. *Early Life*, p. 250, n.

5. *Ibid.*, p. 160.

6. Microfilm of the *Brownson Papers*, roll 10.

7. *Eary Life*, p. 192.

8. *Oration before the Democracy of Worcester* (Boston, 1840), p. 17.

9. *Babylon is Falling, A Discourse Preached in the Masonic Temple on Sunday, May 28, 1837* (Boston, 1837), p. 7.

10. *Early Life*, p. 171.

11. *Ibid.*, pp. 172-173.

12. Vatican Council II in its document on *The Church Today* proposes an examination of conscience in this matter for Christians. After mentioning various factors which may have contributed to the genesis of a widespread atheism in our modern world, the document remarks: "Yet believers themselves frequently bear some responsibility for this situation. For, taken as a whole, atheism is not a spontaneous development but stems from a variety of causes, including a critical reaction against the Christian religious beliefs, and in some places against the Christian religion itself. Hence believers can have more than a little to do with the birth of atheism. To the extent that they neglect their own training in the faith, or teach erroneous doctrine, or are deficient in their religious, moral, or social life, they must be said to conceal rather than reveal the authentic face of God and religion." (See Walter Abbot, *The Documents of Vatican II* [New York: America Press, 1966], p. 217.)

It is also to be noted that the text of the document refers specifically to the defects of a social conscience among Christians. Pope John XXIII evidently had cogent reasons in mind for the strong emphasis he laid on the social obligations of Christians when he declared forthrightly in *Mater et Magistra:* "We affirm strongly that Christian social doctrine is an integral part of the Christian conception of life." *Ibid.* p. 217, n.

13. "An English View of Brownson's Conversion," *The Catholic World*, LXIX (April 1899), p. 28.

14. *Early Life*, p. 173.

15. *Ibid.*, pp. 173-174.

16. *Ibid.*, pp. 174-178.

17. *Ibid.*, pp. 179, 190.

18. *Ibid.*, p. 182. Per Sveino believes that this line of thought is consonant with Edmund Burke's distinction between a representative's duty to his constituents and his responsibility to higher authority. Speaking in the House of Commons to his compeers, Burke said: "It is his duty to sacrifice his repose, his pleasures, his satisfactions, to theirs [his constituents']; and above all, ever, and in all cases, to prefer their interests to his own. But, his unbiased opinion, his mature judgment, his enlightened conscience, he ought not to sacrifice to you, to any man, or to any set of men living. These he does not derive from your pleasure; no, nor from the law and the constitution. They are a trust from Providence, for the abuse of which he will be deeply answerable." *Orestes A. Brownson's Road to Catholicism* (New York: The Humanities Press, 1970), p. 140.

19. Microfilm of the *Brownson Papers*, roll 9. A xerox copy of this letter was found more recently among the *Bancroft Papers* in the University of Cornell.

20. *The Age of Jackson* (Boston: Little, Brown and Co., 1946), p. 256.

21. *Society in America* (London: Saunders and Otley, 1837), I, p. 150.

22. Schlesinger, *The Age of Jackson*, p. 170.

23. *Early Life*, pp. 184-188.

24. *BrQR* (July 1853), p. 397. This matter is discussed by Lee H. Weaver in "Nathaniel Hawthorne and the Making of the President," *Historical New Hampshire,* XXVIII, Spring issue, 1973, pp. 21-34. Hawthorne freely volunteered to write the favorable biography for his friend Pierce. There was no offer of a *quid pro quo*, but when Pierce was elected, Hawthorne was appointed U.S. consul to Liverpool, England.

25. *Early Life*, p. 212.

26. "An American Marxist before Marx," *Sewanee Review,* XLVIII (July-September 1939), p. 14.

27. *Babylon is Falling* (Boston, 1837), p. 14.

28. *Orestes A. Brownson: A Pilgrim's Progress* (Boston: Little, Brown and Co., 1939), pp. 167-168.

29. *Ibid.*, p. 287. Schlesinger also said in his article, "An American Marxist before Marx," *Sewanee Review* (July-September 1939): "Brownson was compelled by his inexorable logic to become a Catholic, and his name quickly dropped out of American history. But before he went over to Rome he anticipated virtually all the slogans and shibboleths that every depression has since resuscitated, and he applied the tool of economic analysis to the scene before him with a skill that few later commentators have attained . . ." (p. 322).

30. "Popular Government," *Works,* XV (May 1843 in the *Democratic Review*), pp. 284-285. It is to be noted that Brownson vigorously denounced at once the dishonesty of the banks in the same terms in a "Discourse on Lying" in the Masonic Temple in the winter of 1837-1838. (See *BQR* [October 1840], p. 413. The sermon was republished in 1940 as a filler.)

31. *Ibid.*, p. 285.

32. *Early Life*, pp. 190-196.

33. "Education of the People," *The Christian Examiner,* XX (The Third Series), II, pp. 153-169.

34. *The Convert*, p. 90.

35. *Literary Criticism*, p. 33.

36. *BQR* (October 1839), p. 518.

37. "Brownson's Writings," *The Dial*, I, pp. 30-31.

38. Microcilm of the *Brownson Papers*, roll 9.

## CHAPTER 10

1. "Introductory Remarks," *BQR* (January 1838), pp. 3, 5-6.

2. *Ibid.*, p. 6. At the end of the second volume of the *BQR*, Brownson again

remarked: "I must say that one great end I have had in view in this work has been, to suggest trains of thought, which should lead even the skeptical to a firm belief and living faith in God, Christ, and immortality." *BQR* (October 1839), p. 518.

3. *Early Life*, p. 206.

4. *BQR* (January 1838), p. 8.

5. O. B. Frothingham, *Transcendentalism in New England* (New York: G. P. Putnam's Sons, Frothingham said more fully: "Mr. Brownson was a remarkable man, remarkable for intellectual force, and equally intellectual wilfulness. His mind was restless, audacious, swift; his thoughts came in floods; his literary style was remarkable for freshness, terseness and vigor" (p. 128).

6. *Early Life*, p. 114.

7. *The Literary Criticism of Orestes Brownson*, doctoral dissertation (Ann Arbor: University of Michigan, 1954), p. 35.

8. *Early Life*, p. 218. Edgar Allen Poe addressed the second of his poems "To Helen" (Sarah Whitman, *née* Power). Besides her own poems, she published as his defender *Edgar Poe and his Critics* (1860).

9. Microfilm of the *Brownson Papers*, roll 8. Roll 8 contains many newspaper clippings. In most cases there is no indication of who the author of the clipping was, or from what newspaper it was taken. Each clipping must stand on its own for what it is worth.

10. *Literary Criticism*, p. 36.

11. *The American Democracy* (New York: Viking Press, 1948), p. 664.

12. *Orestes Brownson and the American Idea* (New York: Fordham University Press, 1961), p. 74, n. 106.

13. Microfilm of the *Brownson Papers*, roll 1.

14. Pope John XXIII in his *Pacem in Terris* and Vatican Council II, particularly in the document on *Religious Freedom*, had much to say on the growing consciousness in the modern world of the dignity of the human person and the inalienable rights that inhere in every human being.

15. "The American Democrat," *BQR* (July 1838), p. 372.

16. *Democracy in America* (New York: New American Library Mentor Books, 1955), p. 114.

17. "Democracy," *BQR* (January 1838), p. 43; *Works*, XV, p. 9.

18. *Ibid.*, p. 65; *Works*, XV, p. 27.

19. *Ibid.*, p. 72; *Works*, XV, p. 32.

20. *The Convert*, p. 123. Brownson at this time seems to have still had a belief in the power of ideas to actualize themselves by their own intrinsic power, but he had long since abandoned the belief by the time he wrote *The Convert*.

21. "Democracy," *BQR* (January 1838), pp. 72-73; *Works*, XV, p. 33.

22. *Orestes Brownson and The American Idea*, pp. 48-49. In this paragraph Leonard Gilhooley refers to the title of Arthur M. Schlesinger, Jr.'s article in the *Sewanee Review*, XLVI (July-September 1839), "Orestes Brownson, An American Marxist before Marx." In a letter to me, dated September 11, 1969, Mr. Schlesinger remarked: "You are right that 'A Marxist before Marx' was a catch phrase for the article." Leonard Gilhooley also refers to C. C. Hollis's *The Literary Criticism of Orestes Brownson*, p. 98. Reference is also made to R. W. B. Lewis's *The American Adam* (Chicago: University of Chicago Press, 1955), pp. 178-187.

23. "Religion and Politics," *BQR* (July 1838), pp. 329-330.

24. *Literary Criticism*, p. 85.

25. *Ibid.*, p. 97.

26. "The American Democrat," *BQR* (July 1838), pp. 361-363.

27. *Ibid.*, p. 362.

28. *Ibid.*, p. 365. Brownson was here developing his doctrine on the inalienable rights of the human person. In this he was pioneering in the work Vatican Council II proposed to itself when it said: "Over and above all this, the council intends to develop the doctrine of recent popes on the inalienable rights of the human person and the constitutional order of society." Walter Abbott, *The Documents of Vatican II* (New York: America Press, 1966), p. 677.

29. "The American Democrat," *BQR* (January 1838), pp. 363, 365.

30. *Ibid.*, p. 366. Commenting on Brownson's review of Cooper's *The American Democrat*, C. C. Hollis also observes: "There are lengthy quotations or excerpts [from Cooper], the first one is the famous passage 'Aristocrat and Democrats,' which has been reprinted in almost every American literature anthology of this century. Apparently Brownson was the first to isolate this passage for separate consideration, although the quite limited circulation of the *Review*, both at the time and later, hardly warrants any accolades to him as a King-maker." Hollis says quite the same of another passage quoted from Cooper on "On the Manners of a Gentleman" which Brownson also isolated in his review of the book. *Literary Criticism*, p. 92.

31. This statement that "power has a perpetual tendency to extend itself," reminds one of Lord Acton's later famous dictum: "Power tends to corrupt and absolute power corrupts absolutely." When reviewing "Chevalier's Letters," *BQR* (April 1838), Brownson again remarked: "The possession of power almost always corrupts" (p. 222).

Is there a connection here between Brownson and Acton in this matter? It is by no means unlikely. In a remarkable letter Sir John Acton (later Lord Acton) wrote Brownson on May 13, 1854, after his visit with him in America the previous year, Acton reminded Brownson at the end of his letter: "I hope you have not forgotten your promise of collecting for me a complete set of your *Review* . . . (*Middle Life*, p. 477)." It can scarcely be doubted that Brownson redeemed his promise; and if so, there was that sentence in Brownson's *Review*: "The possession of power almost always corrupts." A little twist would give the world Acton's famous dictum. Acton at the time of his visit to the U.S. and subsequent letter to Brownson was in his early twenties. He was an ardent admirer of Brownson as his letter shows.

32. Cooper had expressed some regret over the growing neglect of the social distinction between cooks and ladies and footmen and gentlemen, and Brownson is here a bit impatient with Cooper for being less concerned about something so much more important, namely, safeguarding the basic rights of every individual.

33. "The American Democrat," *BQR* (July 1838), pp. 375-376. Brownson would have applauded to the echo former President Nixon's proposal to start a flow of power back to the states.

34. *Ibid.*, p. 377.

35. "Religion and Politics," *BQR* (July 1838), p. 326. Brownson's line of thought here anticipated the document of Vatican Council II on *Religious Freedom*.

36. "Slavery-Abolitionism," *BQR* (April 1838), p. 239; *Works*, XV, p. 45.

37. Microfilm of the *Brownson Papers*, roll 10.

38. "Abolition Proceedings," BQR (October 1838), pp. 496-497; *Works*, XV, p. 82.

39. *Ibid.*, p. 497; *Works*, XV, p. 82.

40. "Slavery-Abolitionism," *BQR* (April 1838), p. 256; *Works*, XV, p. 59.

41. "Abolition Proceedings," *BQR* (October 1838), pp. 494-495; Works, XV, pp. 80-81.

42. Microfilm of the *Brownson Papers*, roll 8. The letter was published in the *Catholic Historical Review* for April 1894. Whether or not it has been more recently acquired by *AUND*, it does not seem to have been drawn on by any previous biographer or commentator.

43. *BQR* (January 1838), pp. 35-36; *Works*, XV, p. 3.

44. "The Tendency of Modern Civilization," *BQR* (April 1838), p. 221.

45. *Ibid.*, p. 237.

46. "The Sub-Treasury Bill," *BQR* (July 1838), p. 360; *Works*, XV, p. 107.

47. "Democracy and Christianity," *BQR* (October 1838), pp. 444-473. Per Sveino tells us that Dr. Joseph Tuckerman, whose book Brownson mentioned, "dedicated much of his life to working in the slums of Boston." *Orestes A. Brownson's Road to Catholicism* (New York: The Humanities Press, 1970), p. 151.

Brownson greatly admired Lamennais's fight against tyranny and oppression, and in a letter to Victor Cousin in December 1838, asked if he could procure for him Lamennais's address. (Microfilm of the *Brownson Papers*, roll 9.) It was never sent. Perhaps it was difficult to obtain.

48. Brownson was by no means singular in holding at this time the coincidence of Christianity and democracy. As he remarked in *The Convert*: "It was substantially the doctrine of Dr. Channing, and that section of the Unitarians that took him for their leader; and it was held more or less distinctly by the whole movement party of the time, both in Europe and America. . . . It had penetrated very widely into the Catholic camp," and in the year 1848 there were priests in France and Italy who were ready to assert the identity of Christianity and democracy. "Even the pious and philosophical Rosmini seemed in the *Five Wounds of the Church* to look toward it. . . . It is as the Cardinal Archbishop of Rheims has well remarked, 'the great heresy of the nineteenth century' " (p. 102).

49. *Ibid.*, p. 465. Brownson quoted this same passage as a Catholic to reinforce his thought in the article "Lacordaire and Catholic Progress," *BrQR* (July 1862), pp. 309-310; *Works*, XX, p. 255. That is, "with slight modifications," as he said.

We find an echo in our day of the passage just quoted from Brownson, among others, in the thought of Archbishop Helder Camara: "For three centuries, Dom Helder points out, the church has 'accepted the ethic of slavery' and 'acquiesced in the social order — really social disorder — that keeps millions of human creatures in subhuman conditions.' If the church does not now 'join the battle for the development of social justice,' people will later say that it 'deserted them in their hour of need' and, if that happens, the church will suffer the consequence." *Current Biography Yearbook*, 1971, p. 79.

50. *BQR* (January 1838), p. 125.

51. "Specimens of Foreign Literature," *BQR* (October 1838), p. 439.

52. "Grund's Americans," *BQR* (April 1838), pp. 161-192.

53. *Literary Criticism*, p. 75.

54. *The American Adam* (Chicago: University of Chicago Press, 1955), p. 185.

55. "Grund's Americans," *BQR* (April 1838), pp. 162ff.

56. *Ibid.*, p. 163.

57. *Ibid.*, p. 163. In referring to "Old Harvard" in the quoted passage, it was no policy of Brownson to be baiting that venerable seat of learning. When reviewing H. W. Longfellow's *Hyperion, A Romance* (October 1841), p. 519, he also said: "By the by, we are inclined to think opposition to Cambridge may be carried a little too far. It is hardly just for men, who claim to be men of free thought, to condemn the only respectable Institution of this country, free from sectarian rule. True, we wish old Harvard would throw aside a few of her aristocratic airs, and conform to the liberal spirit — we were about to say of the age, but we check ourselves and add — of the *Boston Quarterly Review*. But with all her aristocracy, we should like to know: What institution in our country sends out freer, bolder, or more liberal scholars? After all, Old Harvard! we fancy that we reformers owe thee more than we care to tell, and we will say, God's blessing on thee."

58. *Ibid.*, pp. 165-166.

59. Harriet Martineau, *Society in America* (London: Saunders and Otley, 1837), I, pp. 13-14.

60. "Grund's Americans," *BQR* (April 1838), p. 167.

61. "Emerson's *Essays*," *BQR* (July 1841), p. 300.

62. Perry Miller, *The Transcendentalists* (Cambridge: Harvard University Press, 1950), pp. 86-88.

63. "Transcendentalism — Concluded," *BrQR* (October 1846), p. 438; *Works*, IV, p. 112.

64. "Transcendentalism, or the latest Form of Infidelity," *BrQR* (July 1845), p. 298; *Works*, VI, p. 25.

## CHAPTER 11

1. *The Periodicals of American Transcendentalism* (Durham, North Carolina: Duke University Press, 1931), p. 11.

2. Perry Miller, *The Transcendentalists* (Cambridge: Harvard University Press, 1950), p. 8.

3. Perry Miller tells us that "the Transcendental movement is most accurately to be described as a religious demonstration," that it was an "effort to create a living religion without recourse to what it supposed the obsolete jargon of theology." *Ibid.*, pp. 8, 11. Brownson himself said: "The real aim of the Transcendentalist is to ascertain a solid ground for faith in the reality of the spiritual world." *BQR* (July 1840), p. 272.

4. Thomas Wentworth Higginson, *Margaret Fuller Ossoli* (New York: Houghton Mifflin Co., 1884), pp. 141, 143. Higginson says that Brownson was known in the Club for his "gladiatorial vigor," this being perhaps the reason why he was not liked by Frederic Hedge. Hedge later remarked: "Brownson met with us once or twice, but became unbearable, and was not afterward invited." Lindsay Swift, *Brook Farm* (New York: The Macmillan Co., 1900), p. 7. Upon which Arthur M. Schlesinger has remarked: "Brownson no doubt proved unbearable to some; for the lesser Transcendentalists luxuriated in a windy and diffuse thought of a kind calculated to drive the logical Brownson to fury." *Orestes A. Brownson: A Pilgrim's Progress* (Boston: Little, Brown and Co., 1939), p. 46.

5. Joel Myerson, "A Calendar of the Transcendental Club Meetings," *American Literature*, Vol. 44, no. 2 (May 1972), pp. 197-207. Mr. Myerson lists each meeting of the Club and gives generally the theme chosen for discussion. Frederic H. Hedge may have felt a sort of quasi authority over the Transcendental Club since he was the one who first moved for its formation in a letter to Emerson already in June 1836, and who also called the first meeting in Willard's Hotel on September 8, 1836. *Ibid.*, pp. 197-198.

6. This sentence apparently explains why Brownson never took altogether to Transcendentalism. It was, among other things, a new version of Pelagianism with no explanation of the problem of evil. Moreover, speaking on the occasion of the establishment of *The Dial* in 1840, Henry Brownson remarked: "Brownson did not at that time quarrel with the transcendentalists, but he saw that their philosophy was pantheistic, and would lead to infidelity. The result was that Brownson's intercourse with them became less frequent than before, though there was no change in the warmth of his and Ripley's mutual friendship." *Early Life*, p. 308.

7. O. B. Frothingham, *George Ripley* (New York: Houghton Mifflin Co., 1882), p. 55.

8. Brownson said of Emerson's *Nature*: "We prophesy it is the forerunner of a new class of books, the harbinger of a new literature as much superior to whatever has been, as our political institutions are superior to those of the Old World." *Boston Reformer* cited in the microfilm of the *Brownson Papers*, roll 10.

9. *The Transcendentalists*, p. 107.

10. *The Dial*, I, p. 30.

11. Clarence L. Gohdes, *The Periodicals of American Transcendentalism*, p. 40.

12. *The New England Quarterly*, XV (December 1942), pp. 652-680.

13. *The Literary Criticism of Orestes Brownson*, dissertation (Ann Arbor: University of Michigan, 1954), pp. 21-22.

14. *BrQR* (January 1844), p. 8.

15. Microfilm of the *Brownson Papers*, roll 9.

16. *Early Life*, pp. 121-122.

17. *Periodicals of American Transcendentalism*, p. 41.

18. *Ibid.*, pp. 33-34.

19. *Ibid.*, p. 42.

20. *Literary Criticism*, pp. 26-28.

21. *The Convert*, pp. 91-92.

22. Although O. B. Frothingham in *Transcendentalism in New England* named Amos Bronson Alcott the leader of the American Transcendentalists, not Emerson (pp. 257-258), Brownson dubbed Emerson the high priest and Margaret Fuller the high priestess of the movement. *BrQR* (October 1857), p. 468. Perry Mill-

er seems to agree with Brownson that Emerson was the leader of the movement. *The Transcendentalists,* p. 107.

23. O. B. Frothingham, *Theodore Parker* (Boston: J. R. Osgood and Co., 1874), p. 106.

24. "Mr. Emerson's Address," *BQR* (October 1838), p. 501.

25. *Ibid.,* pp. 504-510.

26. *Ibid.,* p. 512.

27. *Ibid.,* pp. 511-513.

28. *American Literature and Christian Doctrine* (Baton Rouge, Louisiana: State University Press, 1958), p. 55. Sidney E. Ahlstrom remarked that "with the Divinity School address Emerson became America's first 'death of God' theologian. . . ." *A Religious History of the American People* (New Haven: Yale University Press, 1972), p. 603.

29. *BrQR* (January 1848), p. 69; *Works,* XIX, p. 242.

30. "Mr. Emerson's Address," *BQR* (October 1838), pp. 513-514.

31. *Literary Criticism,* pp. 109-110.

32. "Bulwer's Novels," *BQR* (July 1839), p. 272.

33. F. O. Matthiessen, *The Transcendental Renaissance* (New York: The Oxford University Press, 1958), p. 61, n.

34. *The Transcendentalists,* p. 84.

35. "Norton on the Evidence of Christianity," *BQR* (January 1839), p. 87.

36. *Ibid.,* pp. 99-100.

37. *Ibid.,* p. 103.

38. *Ibid.,* p. 105.

39. *Ibid.,* p. 110.

40. *Ibid.,* pp. 110-111.

41. *The Transcendentalists,* II.

42. *Ibid.,* p. 240.

43. "Two Articles from the Princeton Review," *BQR* (July 1840), p. 269.

44. *Ibid.,* pp. 270, 272.

45. *The Transcendentalists,* p. 241.

46. "Two Articles from the Princeton Review," *BQR* (July 1840), pp. 322-323.

47. *BQR* (January 1840), p. 11.

48. Microfilm of the *Brownson Papers,* roll 9.

49. Thomas Wentworth Higginson, *Margaret Fuller Ossoli, ut supra,* pp. 143, 148.

50. "The Political Ideas of Orestes A. Brownson," *Philological Quarterly,* XII (July 1933), p. 289. Ladu mistakenly, but significantly, refers to Brownson's "Democratic Review."

51. *Literary Criticism,* p. 36.

52. *BQR* (October 1839), pp. 517-518.

53. Microfilm of the *Brownson Papers,* roll 8.

54. *New Views, Works,* IV, pp. 28-29.

55. *Ibid.,* p. 27. See *Orestes A. Brownson's Road to Catholicism* (New York: The Humanities Press, 1970), p. 131.

56. "Unitarianism and Trinitarianism," *BQR* (July 1839), p. 381.

57. *Orestes Brownson and the American Idea,* doctoral dissertation (New York: Fordham University, 1961), p. 137.

58. Ralph Waldo Emerson, *Complete Works* (Cambridge, Massachusetts, Riverside Edition, 12 vols., 1883), III, p. 206.

59. "Romanticism in America: The Transcendentalists," *The Review of Politics,* XXXV (July 1973), p. 318.

## CHAPTER 12

1. *The Convert,* p. 40.

2. *The Literary Criticism of Orestes Brownson,* dissertation (Ann Arbor: University of Michigan, 1954), p. 135.

3. "Emerson's Phi Beta Kappa Oration," *BQR* (January 1838), p. 107.

4. *Ibid.*, p. 115.

5. "American Literature," *BQR* (January 1839), p. 19.

6. *Ibid.*, pp. 25-26.

7. "Bulwer's Novels," *BQR* (July 1839), p. 291.

8. "Wordsworth's Poems," *BQR* (April 1839), p. 165.

9. "Prospects of Democracy," *BQR* (January 1839), p. 134.

10. "Bulwer's Novels," *BQR* (July 1839), p. 297.

11. *Ibid.*, p. 275.

12. *Ibid.*, p. 270.

13. *Ibid.*, p. 269.

14. *The Periodicals of American Transcendentalism,* dissertation (Durham, North Carolina: Duke University Press, 1931), p. 49.

15. "The Kingdom of God," *BQR* (July 1839), p. 344. The first time Brownson made his distinction between the Christianity of Christ and the Christianity of the Church was in his *New Views of Christianity, Society, and the Church, Works,* IV, p. 1. What he evidently meant was that he was entirely satisfied with the Christianity of Christ but did not find it implemented in institutional Christianity.

16. *Ibid.*, pp. 348-349.

17. *BQR* (January 1838), p. 73.

18. "Pretensions of Phrenology," *BQR* (April 1839), p. 228; *Works*, IX, p. 253. This is a powerful statement of the case for tradition. Leonard Gilhooley remarks on this passage: "Burke never put the case more cogently, perhaps, than this 'pre-Marxian Marx.'" *The American Idea and Orestes Brownson,* dissertation, (New York: Fordham University Press, 1961), p. 69.

19. *Literary Criticism*, p. 148. As M. A. Fitzsimons has observed: "Few of the Transcendentalists had Brownson's knowledge and respect for the real world, including the social world." "Brownson's Search for the Kingdom," *The Review of Politics,* 16 (January 1954), p. 31.

20. "Subtreasury Bill," *BQR* (July 1838), pp. 345-346; *Works*, XV, p. 95.

21. *Early Life,* p. 320.

22. "Distribution and the Public Lands," *BQR* (April 1841), pp. 220-256; *Works,* XV, pp. 149-170.

23. "The Distribution Bill," *BQR* (January 1842), pp. 84-119); *Works,* XV, pp. 202-231. See also *Early Life,* p. 325.

24. *Early Life,* pp. 325-326. Reference in the quote is made to Lord Brougham in England. His statement also appears in newspaper clippings in the microfilm of the *Brownson Papers,* roll 8. These clippings are mostly undated.

25. *Early Life,* pp. 321-322.

26. "Acton and Brownson: A Letter from America," *The Catholic Historical Review,* XLI (January 1964), p. 530.

27. Richard Hofstadter, *The American Political Tradition* (New York: Vintage Books, a division of Random House, 1948), p. 74.

28. "The Democratic Princple," *BrQR* (April 1873), p. 241; *Works*, XVIII, p. 228.

29. "Philosophy and Common Sense," *BQR* (January 1838), p. 103; *Works*, I, p. 17.

30. "The Democratic Princple," *BrQR* (April 1873), p. 236; *Works*, XVIII, p. 223.

31. "Democracy and Reform," *BQR* (October 1839), p. 510.

32. "The Democratic Principle," *BrQR* (April 1873), p. 236; *Works*, XVIII, p. 223.

33. "Democracy and Reform," *BQR* (October 1839), p. 506.

34. *Ibid.*, pp. 509-510.

35. *Ibid.*, pp. 516-517. During this brief alignment with the Democratic party Brownson saw the advantages of working with a political party. His refusal to do so generally may possibly explain why he did not have a greater visible influence on politics and government in his day.

36. "Education and the People," *BQR* (October 1839), pp. 408ff. Brownson was here speaking strongly in favor of localism and educational voluntarism. He argued

that Horace Mann was ignoring the unique variety of American cultural life, and wished to destroy that variety by imposing a uniform culture on a diverse clientele. Two recent books have noted Brownson's stance in this matter: Michael B. Katz, *Class, Bureaucracy, and School: The Illusion of Educational Change in America* (New York: Frederick A. Praeger, 1971), pp. 3-56; and Peter Witonski, *What Went Wrong with American Education and How to Make It Right* (New Rochelle, New York: Arlington House, 1973), pp. 175-176.

37. *Ibid.*, p. 430.

38. *Ibid.*, p. 432.

39. "American Literature," *BQR* (January 1840), p. 64; *Works*, XIX, pp. 57-79.

40. Microfilm of the *Brownson Papers*, roll 8.

41. "American Literature," *BQR* (January 1840), p. 64; *Works*, XIX, p. 27.

42. *Ibid.*, pp. 74-75; *Works*, XIX, pp. 35-36.

43. *Ibid.*, p. 76; *Works*, XIX, p. 37.

44. *The American Democracy* (New York: Viking Press, 1948), p. 744.

45. "Chevalier's Letters," *BQR* (April 1840), p. 214.

## CHAPTER 13

1. Samuel Rezneck, "The Social History of an American Depression, 1837-1843," *The American Historical Review*, XL (July 1935), p. 662.

2. "The Laboring Classes," *BQR* (July 1840), p. 365.

3. *Ibid.*, pp. 362, 365.

4. *Ibid.*, pp. 366-368.

5. *Ibid.*, p. 368. But the day would come when Brownson would eat his own words in saying that slave labor was preferable to the system of wages. He castigated Henry Reed in 1862 for a similar sentiment, and added: "We ourselves once gave utterance to a similar sentiment; but we beg pardon of God and man for our folly. . . . We were moved more by our sympathy with the working men of the North, and our hostility to the great mercantile and industrial system of the modern world than we were by any wish to defend or palliate negro-slavery." *BQR* (April 1862), p. 267.

6. *Ibid.*, p. 270. In speaking of industrial "nabobs," Brownson must have had in mind the Appletons, the Lawrences and the Lowells, and the textile mills of Lowell. Those Boston associates had already established a "most complicated series of interlocking directories" that constituted a huge monopoly in various parts of Massachusetts, if not of New England. Hannah Josephson, *The Golden Threads* (New York: Duel, Sloan and Pearce, 1947), p. 101.

7. *Ibid.*, p. 370. Eric Gill's indictment of the factory system is no less fierce than Brownson's. Much in his *Autobiography* reads like transcripts from Brownson's essay on "The Laboring Classes." In short, he said: "The factory system itself is in itself so inhuman, subhuman and anti-human an institution . . . that, were we not so used to it, had we not been born in it, did not so many of us derive profits or wages from it, we should, as we some day shall, find it impossible to understand the frame of mind of the nations that endure it or the writers and policians who applaud it, and of the Christian clergy who seek every excuse to avoid condemning it." *Autobiography* (New York: The Devin-Adair Co., 1941), pp. 145-146, 152-153, 202-203, 171-173, 296-298.

8. *Ibid.*, p. 372.

9. Alexis de Tocqueville, *Democracy in America* (New York: New American Library Mentor Books, 1956), p. 220.

10. "The Laboring Classes," *BQR* (July 1840), p. 373.

11. Here we note a resemblance between Brownson and William Cobbett (1763-1835) who, decidedly hostile to the factory system, devoted his energies to restoring his ideal of a rural England which was being transformed by the industrial Revolution into the world's foremost manufacturing country. He wanted an England in which the factory system did not exist, and labored long and hard to bring about changes in the political and economic system looking in that direction. *The Encyclopedia Britannica* (1968), Vol. 4, pp. 409-410. Brownson's views in this matter were

also in line with the Jeffersonian tradition which had opted for a rural or agricultural America.

12. "The Laboring Classes," *BQR* (July 1840), pp. 373-374.

13. *Ibid.*, pp. 374-375. Was Brownson here drawing partly on the indictment of the clergy Rev. Samuel C. Allen had made in his letter to him on August 18, 1834? The thought is very similar. (See Chapter 7 of this book.)

14. *Ibid.*, p. 376.

15. *The National Catholic Register* (June 9, 1968), p. 1.

16. *The Church and Colonialism: The Betrayal of the Third World* (Danville, New Jersey: Dimension Books, 1969), pp. 102, 107.

17. "The Laboring Classes," *BQR* (July 1840), p. 376.

18. *Ibid* pp. 378-381. But he had good words for priests, too, when he said: "Mankind came out of the savage state by means of the priests. Priests are the first civilizers of the race." But "for the wild freedom of the savage, they substituted the iron despotism of the theocrat." Yet he was not without hope: "Though man's first step in civilization is slavery, his last step shall be freedom." *Ibid.*, p. 383.

On the same page Brownson seems to betray the influence of Rousseau when he writes: "In what a world does man even now find himself, when he first wakes and feels the workings of his manly nature . . . loaded all over with chains. . . ." Rousseau's opening sentence in his *Social Contract* is: "Man was born free, but is everywhere in bondage."

19. *Ibid.*, pp. 384-385. It seems quite strange that a man who knew the Sacred Scriptures so intimately as did Brownson should have attempted to deny that Christ ever instituted a priesthood. A critic in the *Methodist Quarterly Review* in the article, "The Rich against the Poor," XXXIII (January 1841), argued the case with him, pp. 110-112. In a letter to Dr. Channing two years later, Brownson claimed that he was here inveighing against "man-made priests, priests after the order of Aaron, not those after the order of Melchisedec." *Works*, IV, p. 171. Arthur M. Schlesinger, Jr., remarks that "Brownson's disgust with the conservatism of the church led him to exaggerate the villainy of the priesthood, just as a century later radicals were moved by their hatred of reactionary newspaper-owners to overrate the influence of the press." *Orestes A. Brownson: A Pilgrim's Progress* (Boston: Little, Brown and Co., 1939), p. 96.

20. *Ibid.*, p. 387.

21. *Ibid.*, pp. 388-391.

22. Helen S. Mims remarked: "The trenchancy of Brownson's style and his freedom from fears that paralyzed the elder Channing helped him in introducing the vocabulary of 'social Christianity' in America." "Democratic Theory and Orestes Brownson," *Science and Society, A Marxian Quarterly*, III, no. 2, Spring, 1939, p. 182.

23. "The Laboring Classes," *BQR* (July 1840), pp. 391-392. Hugh Marshall has given us some enlightening thoughts on this matter, and assures us that Brownson was in good company in holding these views. He asserts that "old John Adams had long ago held these judgments of the banking system. There were no national banks until the Civil War years, and the Second Bank of the United States had been destroyed by President Jackson. No restraints on the state banks now existed to force them to serve the public as solid financial institutions. Regulated only by state legislatures which were eager to get extensive credit for canal building, and by state legislators who were unwilling to thwart their constituents' desire for easy credit and increasing inflation, solid financial growth was impossible. Paper money was printed into the millions of dollars by recently chartered state banks which might have no gold or silver backing at all. Politicians were embarrassingly involved in scandalous bankruptcies that enriched themselves and the bankers at the expense of honest depositors. It was this unstable state of finances that brought on the Panic of 1837 in which thousands of state banks failed when they could not supply the increasing demand for gold dollars in exchange for their printing press dollars. This is the banking system Brownson condemns." *Orestes Brownson and the American Republic* (Washington, D.C.: Catholic University of America Press, 1971), p. 29, n. 77.

24. "The Laboring Classes," *BQR* (July 1840), pp. 394-395.

25. *Ibid.*, p. 395. Thomas T. McAvoy, C.S.C., has remarked that the thrust of Brownson's position in his "Laboring Classes" was "very Marxian" in its "proposals." Orestes Brownson and American History," *Catholic Historical Review,* XL (October 1954), p. 259. True, but we should keep well in mind that Brownson held to the right of private property.

26. *Ibid.*, pp. 393-394, n.

27. Elizabeth P. Peabody, *Reminiscences of Rev. Wm. Ellery Channing* (Boston: Roberts Brothers, 1880), pp. 415-416.

28. *Early Life,* p. 379. Miss Lynch, a person of some education, was one of Brownson's greatest admirers. In introducing herself to him in her first letter, dated December 28, 1839, she said: "I should apologize for introducing myself, but it appears to me that men like yourself belong to their country — their age, nay to *Humanity.* The discovery of truth is confined to such minds, and do I err in believing they are willing to dispense it? And more — we dare to approach the Deity and utter our praise and doubts and to ask for wisdom, and dare we not do the same to men?" Microfilm of the *Brownson Papers,* roll 1. She came in time to call him "my Rev. Confessor." However, as Brownson moved ever more to the right, she no longer found herself in full agreement with his thought, and wrote from Providence, Rhode Island (her home), on August 4, 1842: "To me you were really and in truth greater than Moses and the prophets . . . and I did not hesitate to tell you. . . . Of late your views have changed." *Early Life,* pp. 495, 497.

29. *Ibid.*, p. 216.

30. O. B. Frothingham, *Theodore Parker* (Boston: J. R. Osgood and Co., 1874), pp. 134-135.

31. Emerson's *Letters,* II, p. 373.

32. *The Transcendentalists* (Cambridge: Harvard University Press, 1950), pp. 447, 449.

33. *Middle Life,* p. 208.

34. "The Rich against the Poor," *Methodist Quarterly Review,* XXXIII (January 1841), pp. 92-122.

35. *Ibid.*, p. 98.

36. Hugh Marshall is not quite accurate when he says: "The workers could either quietly accept their deteriorating condition, or rebel and overthrow the whole structure. Brownson urged the latter course as did Marx a few years later." *Orestes Brownson and the American Republic* (Washington, D.C.: Catholic University of America Press, 1971), p. 29, n. 79. Per Sveino is more accurate when he says: "Even if the author of 'The Laboring Classes' felt sure of a coming class war, he tried to ward off the impending conflict by proposing the adoption of measures already mentioned." *Orestes A. Brownson's Road to Catholicism* (New York: The Humanities Press, 1970), p. 222.

37. "The Rich against the Poor," *Methodist Quarterly Review,* pp. 99, 101.

38. *The Convert,* pp. 118-119.

39. Bancroft to McAllister (August 5, 1840), *Bancroft Papers.*

40. *Memoir of Charles Sumner,* II, p. 168.

41. John Quincy Adams, "An Oration," *BQR* (April 1838), p. 152.

42. John Quincy Adams, *Memoir,* X, p. 345.

43. *The Convert,* p. 106. Brownson also remarked that his essay had been received with "one universal scream of horror." *Ibid.*

44. "Calhoun and the Baltimore Convention," *BQR* (April 1844), p. 262; *Works,* XV, p. 477.

45. *Early Life,* p. 249.

46. Arthur M. Schlesinger, Jr., *Orestes A. Brownson: A Pilgrim's Progress* (Boston: Little, Brown and Co., 1939), p. 106.

47. The sermons were: "Progress our Law: A Discourse," pp. 397-409, and "A Discourse on Lying," pp. 409-420. *BQR* (October 1840).

48. *The Convert,* pp. 120-121.

# CHAPTER 14

1. *The Convert*, p. 120.

2. *Rhetoric in the Works of Orestes Brownson* (New York: Fordham University Press, 1961), p. 141.

3. "The Laboring Classes," *BQR* (October 1840), p. 422.

4. *Ibid.*, pp. 422-425.

5. *Ibid.*, p. 427. The real mischief that resulted from his essay was not just what he had said. In a time of great political excitement what he said was sure to be twisted by unscrupulous politicians to serve their own nefarious purposes. So dastardly was its distortion that Brownson said: "What we complain of in our Whig friends, is their gross perversion of our views, and after having, by misrepresentation and misinterpretation concocted a set of doctrines, as abhorrent to us as to themselves, then charging those 'horrible doctrines' on the administration. The doctrines published in the newspapers and electioneering hand-bills, resemble ours about as much as night resembles day." *Ibid.*, p. 508.

6. *BQR* (October 1840), p. 519. That Brownson really had intended to discontinue his *Review* with the October edition of 1840 is supported by other evidence. In a letter to him, dated July 12, 1840, his friend Anne C. Lynch, remarked that she had previously heard that "the next number would close the *Boston Quarterly*" — which she was loathe to hear. She added a tidbit when she told him that a Mr. Peace had informed her that his *Quarterly* "is more read than any other periodical in the reading room of Philadelphia." Microfilm of the *Brownson Papers*, roll 1.

7. *The Convert*, p. 114.

8. "The Laboring Classes," *BQR* (October 1840), p. 428.

9. *Ibid.*, p. 429.

10. *Ibid.*

11. *Ibid.*, p. 430. Here we see again the prescient nature of Brownson's thought. More than a century after he was talking about *democratizing* the Church, a measured degree of a more democratic representation has come to the Church with the progressive movement of Vatican Council II.

12. *Ibid.*, pp. 430-432.

13. *Ibid.*, pp. 433-434.

14. *Works*, IV, p. 50. See also *BQR* (April 1838), pp. 216-217.

15. "The Laboring Classes," *BQR* (October 1840), p. 437. As Leonard J. McCarthy has observed, this is the only new matter Brownson brought into the second essay on the laboring classes. The rest was a rebuttal, point by point, of objections that his assailants had brought. *Rhetoric in the Works of Orestes Brownson*, p. 106.

But it is not certain that Brownson was consistent in giving his reasons for a single organization. In *The Convert* he stated: "I had not the least conception [he said, speaking of this very time] of a created order of supernatural existence, or of life above the natural; and with only a single organization of life, the double organization of mankind could not and cannot be defended. This is defensible only on the condition that there are two orders, the one natural and the other supernatural, and that man lives or may live in this world a natural and a supernatural life" (p. 112). Yet when he reviewed Theodore "Parker's Discourse" *BQR* (October 1842), he said: "We have always, ever since known to this community [he came to Boston in 1836], in the strictest, the most orthodox sense of the word, believed in supernaturalism" (p. 456). Perhaps he could reconcile the two statements. He also maintained that his doctrine of the single organization "had many friends among the profoundest thinkers and most approved writers of the country." *The Convert*, p. 112. Dr. Thomas Arnold, the famous headmaster of Rugby, strongly contended for the same. Lytton Strachey, *Eminent Victorians* (New York: Capricorn Books, 5th. ed., 1963), pp. 215, 217.

16. *Ibid.*, pp. 437-438.

17. *Ibid.*, pp. 438-439.

18. *Ibid.*, p. 441.

19. "Catholicity and Political Liberty," *BrQR* (April 1848), p. 175.

20. "The Laboring Classes," *BQR* (October 1840), p. 444.

21. *Ibid.*, pp. 455-457.

22. *Ibid.*, pp. 460-462. It may be that Brownson did overdraw in dark colors the conditions of the laboring classes, but he was to have his counterpart twenty years later in that great and good man of literary fame, John Ruskin, who stirred up a worse storm than did Brownson by his espousal of the cause of the laboring classes. Looking on their degradation and misery, Ruskin said: "I will endure it no longer quietly; but henceforward, with any few or many who will help, do my best to abate this misery." Leaving the field of art, he wrote four essays in which he pleaded for a more socialistic form of government in which reforms would be possible for the relief of the oppressed and downtrodden. The essays were published in the *Cornhill Magazine,* of which W. Makepeace Thackery was the editor. They aroused such a wild storm of protest that further publication had to be discontinued. Ruskin then had the essays published in book form, with the title *Unto the Last.* When he further discussed the principles of capital and labor and the evils of the competitive system in another book, *Munera Pulveris,* he was denounced as a visionary and madman. See William J. Long, *English Literature* (New York: Gin and Co., 1909), p. 537; also J. Ev., John Ruskin, *Encyclopedia Britannica,* Vol. 19, pp. 766-768.

23. *Ibid.*, pp. 464-466.

24. *Ibid.*, pp. 467-468.

25. *Ibid.*, pp. 468-469.

26. *Ibid.*, pp. 471-472. In other words, he saw industrialization harming all classes. He would no doubt have agreed with Matthew Arnold that industrialization has the effect of "materialising our upper class, vulgarising our middle class, and brutalising our lower class." *Mixed Essays* (New York: The Macmillan Co., 1903), p. 87.

27. *Turner's Address,* "The Significance of the Frontier in American History," (first delivered in 1893), ed. with introduction by Harold P. Simon (New York: Frederick Ungar Publishing Co., 1963), pp. 7, 12.

28. "The Laboring Classes," *BQR* (October 1840), pp. 473-474.

29. *Ibid.*, pp. 473, 475.

30. *Ibid.*, pp. 474, 476.

31. *Ibid.*, pp. 475-476. Later he again expressed his misgivings about the *laissez-faire* policy. He said: "The duty of government is not simply to let us alone, leave us to ourselves, and content itself with merely maintaining an open field for the full play of our natural selfishness. This would be for government to abdicate itself. We hold it to be the duty of government often to take the initiative, and by a wise and sound policy to foster and direct the industry of the country." *Works,* XV, p. 465, n.

32. *Ibid.*, p. 476.

32. *Ibid.*, pp. 477-480.

34. *Ibid.*, p. 481.

35. *The Convert,* p. 97.

36. "The Laboring Clases," *BQR* (October 1840), p. 488. We have no evidence that Brownson ever changed his notions about the hereditary descent of property. When he reviewed in a conciliatory spirit *Hereditary Property Justified, Reply to Brownson's Article on the Laboring Classes* (*BQR*, July 1841, pp. 390-391), he emphasized that he had only thrown out the proposal for *discussion,* but added with a touch of acerbity that he thought "possibly it might after a series of ages be adopted" (p. 391). In 1842 he was optimistic enough to say that the change would one day be effected "not by the direct action of civil government in assuming the initiative, but through moral and religious influences, creating a higher order of civilization, and involving a new and different organization of the race — an organization resting for its foundation, not on wealth, nor military force, nor accidents of birth, but on *capacity. BQR* (January 1842), p. 56.

37. *Ibid.*, pp. 496-497.

38. "The Laboring Classes," *BQR* (July 1840), pp. 369-370. The great sympathy of Brownson for the factory worker is somewhat paralleled in our times by that so graphically expressed by Pope John XXIII. His words of sympathy were reportedly addressed to some Sisterhoods that had gathered in Rome. To them he said:

"I have asked you to come down with me, with my priests and laity, from our

ivory towers. What do I mean? Sitting here at my desk, I look down on the broad ex-
panse of the Villa della Conciliatione. Simple workmen, dressed in worn shirts and
tattered pants, are crossing the avenue and disappearing into the early shadows of
the morning. These poor workmen have problems which you and I do not have. They
are slaves.

"They work each day and when they are old, they are discarded like used-up
machines or rejected tires. You and I have an obligation to that poor little factory
worker who just rode across the piazza on his bicycle. He is subhuman. He is under-
paid. He is frustrated by what he calls the rat-race. At this moment he is on his way
to be chained to a machine for 10 hours in a factory.

"Last night, look at the way he cycled. He was half drunk with cheap wine. He had to
to get drunk to blot out his monotony. His rags, his emaciated children with their
beautiful eyes, his human loneliness as he goes it alone, his lack of love.

"Yes, Christ loves him. Christ even weeps when his famished children sit down
to bread and water. Christ would willingly slit his cloak to put another blanket on
their shivering bed."

39. Hannah Josephson, *The Golden Threads* (New York: Duel, Sloan and
Pearce, 1949), p. 193. Apparently in gratitude for her defense of the Lowell mills,
Miss Farley within a year had become the object of benevolence of Amos Lawrence,
the "self-constituted Grand Almoner" of America, *Ibid.*, pp. 194-195.

40. *Ibid.*, pp. 223-224.

41. *Ibid.*, pp. 224-225.

42. "The Laboring Classes," *BQR* (July 1840), pp. 261, 264.

43. "The Laboring Classes, *BQR* (October 1840), pp. 507-508.

44. *Orestes A. Brownson* (Boston: Little, Brown and Co., 1939), p. 95.

45. "France, its King, Court and Government." By an American. *BQR* (October
1840), p. 519. This work was attributed to Governor Lewis Cass, then American
Minister at the Court of France. Brownson lashed him severely for his sycophantic
siding with French royalty against the cause of the people or popular rights — the
last thing of which a representative of democratic America should be found guilty at
a foreign court. *Ibid.*, pp. 515-518. Again in 1852 he excoriated Cass for his many political meanderings and tergiversations. He was glad to see him "laid on the shelf."
*BrQR* (October 1852), p. 555.

46. *Orestes Brownson and the American Idea* (New York: Fordham University Press, 1961), pp. 82-83.

47. *Orestes A. Brownson: A Pilgrim's Progress, ut supra,* p. 100.

48. Arthur M. Schlesinger, Jr., "An American Marxist before Marx," *Sewanee
Review,* XLVIII (July-September 1939), p. 319. An intriguing question here is,
whether Brownson may possibly have influenced the thought of Karl Marx. Is any
connection likely? Theodore Maynard, noting certain similarities between these two
world reformers, observed: "There is, however, no evidence that Marx ever read
Brownson, though as Dr. Menger remarks, Marx often went to some pains to conceal
his indebtedness to his predecessors, and yet studied everything that might contribute grist to his mills." *Orestes Brownson, Yankee, Radical* (New York: The
Macmillan Co., 1943), p. 92. Robert E. Moffit is not entirely satisfied with this statement. He admits that Maynard's "essential point is probably accurate, but that this
statement is *not* entirely true." To the contrary, he asserts, "there *is* evidence that
Brownson's work attracted Marx's attention. The evidence at hand, however, only
pertains to Brownson's position in the context of the American Civil War. Marx's
minor reference to Brownson appears in *Die Presse,* Vienna, November 7, 1861. The
citation can be found in Marx and Engel's *The Civil War in the United States*
[New York: International Publishers, 1969], pp. 82-83." Moffit continued: "It is not
unreasonable to suggest that Marx should have been more than casually familiar
with Brownson, a well known and outspoken social critic of the day, given that the
American was well known to other, more esteemed European thinkers, such as Victor Cousin, Pierre Leroux, John Cardinal Newman, and the great British historian,
Lord Acton." *Metaphysics and Constitutionalism: The Political Theory of
Orestes Brownson.* Chapter I: Brownson and His Age (Tucson: University of Ar-

izona Press, 1975), p. 53, n. 101. Count Montalembert might also be added to the list of names. But perhaps the most likely of all connections here is Lord Brougham, a most ardent admirer of Brownson already in the 1830s. It can scarcely be doubted that Marx knew definitely of Brougham, one of the great European reformers of the day, and through him may well have learned of Brownson's early socialistic writings.

49. Harold J. Laski, *The American Democracy* (New York: Viking Press, 1948), p. 405.

50. *Ibid.*, p. 310.

51. Anton Menger, *The Right to the Whole Produce of Labor.* Introduction by H. S. Foxwell (New York: The Macmillan Co., 1899), pp. ixxxix-xc.

52. As Vatican Council II observed: "Private ownership or some kind of dominion over material goods provides every one with a wholly necessary area of independence, and should be regarded as an extension of human freedom. Finally, since it adds incentive for carrying on one's function and duty, it constitutes a kind of prerequisite for civil liberties." Walter Abbott, *The Documents of Vatican II* (New York: America Press, 1966), p. 280.

53. *The Convert*, pp. 119-120.

54. *Ibid.*, p. 310.

55. Fr. Walter Elliott, *The Life of Father Hecker* (New York: Columbia Press, 1894), p. 179.

56. "Chevalier's Letters," *BQR* (April 1840), p. 221.

57. *BQR* (January 1841), p. 131.

58. *Literary Criticism*, p. 150.

59. "The Laboring Classes," *BQR* (July 1840), pp. 388-389.

60. Walter Abbott, *Documents of Vatican II, ut supra*, p. 243.

61. Leonard Gilhooley, *Orestes Brownson and the American Idea*, pp. 75, 85.

62. *The Convert*, p. 121.

## CHAPTER 15

1. *The Convert*, p. 120.

2. George Parsons Lathrop, "Orestes Brownson," *Atlantic Monthly*, LXXVII (June 1896), p. 774. It must have been of this period in Brownson's life that M. J. Harson spoke when he said: "The influence of Brownson on the thought of the country of the day — political, social, philosophical, and religious — was not exceeded by that of any other man in the country at the time, and his influence in individual cases was wide and far-reaching." *The Catholic World*, LXXIX (April 1904), p. 6.

3. "The Distribution Bill," *BQR* (January 1842), p. 108; *Works*, XV, p. 221.

4. Microfilm of the *Brownson Papers*, roll 8.

5. "Dr. Brownson and His Works," *Irish Ecclesiastical Record*, IX (September 1888), p. 806.

6. *The Convert*, p. 121.

7. *Ibid.*

8. "Popular Government," *Works*, XV, p. 286. (First published in the *Democratic Review*, May 1843.)

9. "Democracy and Liberty," *Works*, XV, p. 259. (First published in the *Democratic Review*, April 1843.)

10. "Liberalism and Progress," *BrQR* (October 1862), p. 464; *Works*, XX, p. 356.

11. "The Democratic Principle," *BrQR* (April 1873), p. 237; *Works*, XVIII, p. 224.

12. *The Convert*, p. 122.

13. *Ibid.*

14. John Henry Newman, *A Letter to His Grace, The Duke of Norfolk* (London: B. M. Pickering, 1875), p. 71. Even later in life (1885), he exclaimed in a letter to his friend, Dean Church: "What a dreadful thing this democracy is! How I wish Gladstone had retired into private life, as he seems to have contemplated some ten years ago." Wilfrid Ward, *The Life of John Henry Newman* (London: Longmans, Green, and Co., 1912), II, p. 513.

15. "Democracy and Liberty," *Works,* XV, p. 279.

16. "Social Evils, and their Remedy," *BQR* (July 1841), p. 289.

17. "Constitutional Government," *BQR* (January 1842), pp. 27-59; *Works,* XV, pp. 231-258.

18. "The Democratic Principle," *BQR* (April 1873), p. 237; *Works,* XVIII, pp. 224-225.

19. "Executive Patronage," *BQR* (July 1841), p. 354; *Works,* XV, p. 171.

20. "The President's Message," *BQR* (July 1841), p. 372; *Works,* XV, p. 187.

21. "Our Future Policy," *BQR* (January 1841), pp. 68-112; *Works,* XV, pp. 111-149.

22. Microfilm of the *Brownson Papers,* roll 8.

23. "Our Future Policy," *BQR* (January 1841), p. 170; *Works,* XV, p. 114.

24. *Ibid.,* pp. 81-82; *Works,* XV, p. 124.

25. *Ibid.,* pp. 82-83; *Works,* XV, p. 125.

26. *Ibid.,* pp. 82-85; *Works,* XV, pp. 124-127.

27. *Ibid.,* pp. 92, 112; *Works,* XV, p. 129.

28. *Ibid.,* pp. 86-90; *Works,* XV, pp. 128-131.

29. "Executive Patronage," *BQR* (July 1841), p. 369; *Works,* XV, p. 184.

30. "Our Future Policy," *BQR* (January 1841), pp. 89, 91-92; *Works,* XV, pp. 130, 132.

31. "The President's Message," *BQR* (July 1841), p. 386; *Works,* XV, pp. 198-199.

32. *The Ordeal of the Union* (New York: Charles Scribner's Sons, 1947), I, pp. 152-153.

33. "Social Evils, and their Remedy," *BQR* (July 1841), pp. 279-281.

34. "Bancroft's History," *BQR* (October 1841), p. 512.

35. *Ibid.,* p. 514.

36. *Ibid.,* p. 516.

37. *Ibid.,* p. 517.

38. "Constitutional Government," *BQR* (January 1842), p. 29; *Works,* XV, pp. 232-233.

39. "Executive Patronage," *BQR* (July 1841), p. 368; *Works,* XV, pp. 183-184.

40. "Constitutional Government," *BQR* (January 1842), p. 43; *Works,* XV, p. 244.

41. "The Distribution Bill," *BQR* (January 1842), pp. 84-118; *Works,* XV, pp. 202-231.

42. "Constitutional Government," *BQR* (January 1842), p. 43; *Works,* XV, p. 245.

43. *Ibid.,* pp. 44-46; *Works,* XV, pp. 245-247.

44. *Ibid.,* pp. 46-48; *Works,* XV, pp. 247, 249.

45. *Early Life,* p. 467.

46. It is perhaps putting the matter a little too strongly to say that Brownson gave Calhoun's nullification doctrine "full approval." See Hugh Marshall, S.T., *Orestes Brownson and the American Constitution* (Washington, D.C.: Catholic University of America Press, 1971), p. 59, n. 35. Brownson said distinctly in the article to which Marshall refers that he "merely" states Calhoun's doctrine, that he hoped in time to take it up at length, and determine, if possible, "its soundness or unsoundness." "The Life and Speeches of John C. Calhoun," *BQR* (January 1844), p. 124; *Works,* XV, p. 467. A more thorough investigation of the matter in 1847 led Brownson "to doubt both its theoretical soundness and its practical efficacy." "Slavery and the Mexican War," *BQR* (July 1847), p. 353, n.; *Works,* XVI, p. 45, n.

47. "The President's Message," *BQR* (July 1841), p. 386; *Works,* XV, p. 198.

48. "Popular Government," *Works,* XV, pp. 290, 293. (Published in the *Democratic Review,* May 1843). See also Margaret Coit, *John C. Calhoun* (Boston: Houghton Mifflin Co., 1950), p. 528ff.

49. "The Democratic Principle," *BrQR* (April 1873), pp. 241-242; *Works,* XVIII, p. 229.

50. "Social Evils, and their Remedy," *BQR* (July 1841), p. 282.

51. "The Distribution Bill," *BQR* (January 1842), p. 92; *Works,* XV, p. 208.

52. *Ibid.,* p. 103; *Works,* p. 217.

53. "Executive Patronage," *BQR* (July 1841), pp. 354-355; *Works,* XV, p. 172.

54. *Early Life,* pp. 281-287.

55. "An Address to Workingmen," *BQR* (January 1841), pp. 112-127. This address was written partly as an electioneering device in the national elections of 1840.

The term "Locofoco" had a bizarre origin. At a meeting in Tammany Hall, New York, on October 29, 1835, a battle ensued between the right-wing and the left-wing Democrats as to whose choice would be seated as chairman. When the left-wing Democrats, the workingmen's party, won out, the right-wing members left the hall, went downstairs and turned off the gas. This left the hall in total darkness. But the workingmen's party had come prepared. Taking out candles they lit them with loco-foco matches just then coming into use, and continued their meeting. Since these matches had come to the rescue of the workingmen, the next day the *Courier* and the *Enquirer* (Whig newspapers) labeled the workingmen the Locofocos.

56. "Conversations with a Radical," *BQR* (January 1841), p. 14.

57. "Early American Democratic Theory and Orestes Brownson," *Science and Society, a Marxian Quarterly,* III, no. 2, Spring (1939), p. 189. Bellamy's most noted work was of course *Looking Back.*

58. "Conversations with a Radical," *BQR* (January 1841), pp. 156-157.

59. "Social Evils, and their Remedy," *BQR* (July 1841), p. 289.

60. "The Distribution Bill," *BQR* (January 1842), p. 92; *Works,* XV, p. 208.

61. Charles C. Hollis, *The Literary Criticism of Orestes Brownson* (Ann Arbor: University of Michigan, 1954), p. 433, n. 57.

62. Microfilm of the *Brownson Papers,* roll 8.

63. "Social Evils, and their Remedy," *BQR* (April 1841), pp. 273, 276.

64. *Ibid.,* p. 276.

65. *Ibid.,* p. 291.

66. "Our Future Policy," *BQR* (January 1841), p. 78; *Works,* XV, p. 121.

67. *Early Life,* pp. 300-301.

68. *Ibid.,* p. 233.

69. *Ibid.,* pp. 302-303. It is an undoubtable fact that Calhoun wrote Brownson a number of letters, understandably so since he was so active later in the promotion of Calhoun's candidacy for the presidency. In his letters to Brownson, Calhoun refers to at least two letters he had received from Brownson (*Early Life,* pp. 302, 323). Yet no single letter of Brownson to Calhoun has shown up in recent biographies of Calhoun, neither in the three volumes of Charles M. Wiltse nor the one volume of Margaret C. Coit. There is a theory, not implausible, that Calhoun himself, or his literary executor, removed from Calhoun's literary remains all papers of a certain nature which bore on Calhoun's possible candidacy for the presidency. In speaking to Brownson of his possible candidacy in one of his letters, he reminded him that what he had written was to be held in "strict confidence, intended only for yourself." *Early Life,* p. 305. Calhoun might well have wished deleted any evidence of the unsuccessful attempt to make him President of the United States.

70. "Dr. Brownson and the Workingmen's Party of Fifty Years Ago," *The Catholic World,* XLV (September 1887), p. 207.

71. *Early Life,* p. 308.

## CHAPTER 16

1. "Brook Farm," *The Democratic Review,* IX (November 1842), p. 488.

2. Octavius Brooks Frothingham, *George Ripley* (New York: Houghton Mifflin Co., 1882), p. 74.

3. Lindsay Swift, *Brook Farm* (New York: The Macmillan Co., 1900), p. 9.

4. John T. Codman, *Brook Farm: Historic and Personal Memoir* (Boston: Arena Publishing Co., 1894), pp. 240-241.

5. Swift, p. 17.

6. *Ibid.,* p. 9.

7. *Ibid.,* p. 10. Emerson was a trifle flippant in speaking of the Brook Farmers. Codman castigated him for jokingly pretending that clothespins fell out of the pock-

ets of young men during their dances at Brook Farm. Codman, *Brook Farm*, p. 188.

8. *Ibid.*, pp. 16-17.

9. Codman, p. 49.

10. Frothingham, *George Ripley*, p. 128.

11. Swift, *Brook Farm*, p. 47.

12. Codman, *Brook Farm*, p. 91.

13. Swift, p. 59.

14. *Ibid.*, p. 257. In contrast to Cranch's popularity at the Farm, that of Margaret Fuller was less conspicuous. John Van der Zee Sears felt that her monologues and general experience at the Farm "were rather disappointing to her." Too many yawns from those present. *My Friends at Brook Farm* (New York: D. FitzGerald, Inc., 1912), p. 157.

15. Codman, p. 177.

16. John Van der Zee Sears in his *My Friends at Brook Farm* remarks that the soil of Brook Farm was "sandy where it was not rocky and rocky where it was not sandy" (p. 302).

17. Codman, p. 177.

18. "Brook Farm," *The Democratic Review,* IX (November 1842), p. 488.

19. *Early Life,* p. 500.

20. Microfilm of the *Brownson Papers,* roll 9.

21. *Early Life,* pp. 308-310. This letter is explanatory of their future relations. Brownson later met Mr. Garland, a Virginian, when he lectured in St. Louis in 1852. Brownson gave five lectures on "Catholicity and Civilization" which were unfavorable to Protestantism. Subsequently citizens of St. Louis asked Mr. Garland to give five lectures on "Protestantism and Government." Being still a great admirer of Brownson, he avoided any appearance of *replying* to Brownson. Brownson, however, reviewed his five lectures when they were sent to him. *BrQR* (April 1852), pp. 262-278; *Works,* X, pp. 411-426.

22. *Ibid.*, pp. 313-314.

23. *Letters from Brook Farm 1844-1847,* ed. by Amy L. Reed (Poughkeepsie, New York: Vassar College, 1928), p. 38.

24. "Dr. Brownson in Boston," *The Catholic World,* XLV (July 1887), p. 471.

25. "Parker's Discourse," *BQR* (October 1842), p. 488.

26. Swift, p. 116.

27. *Ibid.*, p. 117.

28. *Orestes A. Brownson: A Pilgrim's Progress* (Boston: Little, Brown and Co., 1939), p. 153.

29. *Years of Experience* (New York: G. P. Putnam's Sons, 1887), p. 147. Much that Mrs. Kirby relates concerning Brownson may be good comic relief, but Lindsay Swift, speaking of *Years of Experience* (relative to Brook Farm), remarks that "it has been intimated that her recollections betray signs of unfairness and an acid temper." He also spoke of her "palpable errors" and her "imperfect recollection of things." *Brook Farm*, p. 77. Evidently Mrs. Kirby is not the most reliable of historians. For reasons that seemed to her good or bad, she was hostile to Catholicity, and disliked Brownson's catholicizing tendencies.

30. *Middle Life,* p. 96.

31. Brownson's repeated efforts to convert Ripley reminds one of John H. Newman's persistent efforts to convert his dear friend, Edward B. Pusey, but with no better results. (See Paul M. Thureau-Dangin, *The English Catholic Revival in the Nineteenth Century* [New York: E. P. Dutton and Co., 1899], II, p. 352ff.)

32. Fr. Walter Elliott, *The Life of Father Hecker,* 2nd. ed. (New York: Columbia Press, 1894), p. 90.

33. *Early Life,* p. 337.

34. Swift, p. 221.

35. Marianne Dwight Orvis, *Letters from Brook Farm 1844-1847,* ed. by Amy Reed (Poughkeepsie, New York: Vassar College, 1928), pp. 122-123.

36. Codman, p. 177.

37. Elliott, *The Life of Father Hecker, ut supra,* p. 47.

38. Swift, p. 123.

39. *Early Life,* p. 314.

40. *Early Letters of George W. Curtis to John S. Dwight* (New York: Harper and Brothers, 1898), p. 9. There were two Curtis brothers at Brook Farm, George and Burrill. Ora Gannet Sedgwick tells us that they were so handsome that Ripley called them "two Greek gods." "A Girl of Sixteen at Brook Farm," *Atlantic Monthly,* LXXXV (March 1910), p. 402.

41. *Hawthorne's Notebooks* (New Haven: Yale University Press, 1932), p. 292.

42. In *Blithedale Romance,* chapter XXIV, cited by Ora G. Sedgwick in the article listed in n. 40, p. 339, in the Sedgwick article. Emerson referred to Hawthorne's *Blithedale Romance* (Hawthorne's story of Brook Farm) as "that disagreeable story," "which it truly is," added John Codman in his *Brook Farm,* p. 220. Brownson reviewed *Blithedale Romance* in the October 1852 issue of his *Quarterly,* pp. 561-564.

43. *Early Life,* pp. 316-317. William Sturgis who wrote to Brownson arranging these matters was one of the three "richest and best-known of the merchant princes of the East India and Northwest trade." Hannah Josephson, *Golden Threads* (New York: Duel, Sloan and Pearce, 1949), p. 128. This would indicate that at least a few of the wealthy attended Brownson's congregation.

44. *Ibid.,* p. 414.

45. Frothingham, *George Ripley,* p. 109.

46. Swift, p. 221.

47. An undated memorandum among the *Hecker Papers,* Paulist archives, New York City.

48. *The Life of Father Hecker,* p. 22. When Isaac wanted to go to Brook Farm, John Hecker, Isaac's eldest brother (with whom Isaac was staying at the time), wrote Brownson a letter on January 7, 1843, telling Brownson that he left it up to him to decide whether or not Isaac should go to Brook Farm. *Early Life,* pp. 501-503.

49. *Ibid.,* p. 55.

50. *Ibid.,* p. 31.

51. Vincent F. Holden, C.S.P., *The Yankee Paul, Isaac Thomas Hecker* (Milwaukee: Bruce Publishing Co., 1958), pp. 51, 58.

52. Elliott, *The Life of Father Hecker, ut supra,* p. 56.

53. Brownson did not favor Isaac's going to Fruitlands. On September 2, 1843, he wrote Isaac: "These communities after all are humbugs. We must rehabilitate the Church and work under its direction." Fr. Holden, *The Yankee Paul, Isaac Thomas Hecker, ut supra,* p. 69, n. 19.

Brownson was of course fairly acquainted with the three promoters of Fruitlands, especially with Alcott and Lane. In one of his conversations with Lane, taking pen and paper in hand, Lane tried to bring the discussion to a head by asking Brownson to name the three most profound men in America. When Brownson named himself in the third place, Lane gravely added his name to the other two. Upon Lane's report of the incident to Emerson, Emerson remarked: "Brownson never will stop and listen, neither in conversation, but what is more, not in solitude." R. W. Emerson, *Journals,* VI, p. 297.

When reviewing Arthur M. Schlesinger's biography of Brownson in the book review section of the New York *Times* (April 23, 1939), Henry Steele Commager remarked on the incident: "When he [Brownson] listed himself among the three most profound men in America there were those who took him seriously" (p. 3).

54. Clarence L. F. Gohdes, *Periodicals of American Transcendentalism* (Durham, North Carolina: Duke University Press, 1931), p. 270.

55. Swift, p. 270.

56. Amelia Russell spoke of the "absolute necessity" there was to try Fourierism or to resort to "some bold effort." "Home Life of the Brook Farm Association," *Atlantic Monthly,* XLII (1878), p. 461. Looking back, she admired Ripley in that his face had worn no evidence of the anxiety which almost crushed him." *Ibid,* p. 462.

57. "Brook Farm," *The Democratic Review,* IX (November 1842), p. 489.

58. Codman, p. 26.

59. *The Idyll of Brook Farm* (Boston: Trustees of the Public Library, 1937), pp. 27, 33.

60. *Ibid.*, p. 37.

61. John H. Noyes, *History of American Socialism* (Philadelphia: Lippincott, 1870), p. 37.

## CHAPTER 17

1. Fr. Vincent F. Holden, C.S.P., has done a fine piece of work in correcting some errors in the course of five articles Fr. Hecker wrote on Brownson in the *Catholic World,* 1887. Fr. Hecker asserted it was "somewhere about 1834" that Brownson had come to New York City to lecture, at which time he had apparently met him for the first time. But Fr. Holden has shown that it was not until 1841 that Brownson had come to New York to lecture, and that it was not until that year that young Hecker had apparently met him for the first time. In explanation of Fr. Hecker's inaccuracies as to time and place, Fr. Holden said: "These articles were written more than fifty years after the occurrences they chronicle, by a very sick man who died the following year." Rev. Vincent F. Holden, C.S.P., *The Early Years of Isaac Thomas Hecker (1819-1844),* (Washington, D.C.: Catholic University of America Press, 1939), p. 45ff.

2. *Early Life,* p. 510. Writing on September 6, 1843, Fr. Hecker acknowledged a deep sense of gratitude to Brownson when he said: "I feel too often that I am not within two hours' ride of your presence when heart and head are full to overflowing, but I feel inexpressible gratitude and unfathomable thankfulness for your kindness toward me and the great benefit of your influence — may my conduct be accordingly." *Early Life,* p. 337.

3. F. Byrdsall, *The History of the Loco-foco Party or Equal Rights Party* (New York: Clement and Pachard, 1842), p. 39.

4. Holden, *The Early Years of Isaac Thomas Hecker (1819-1844), ut supra,* pp. 37-38.

5. Fr. Isaac Hecker, "Dr. Brownson and the Workingmen's Party Fifty Years Ago," XLV, *The Catholic World* (May 1887), p. 203.

6. New York *Evening Post* (March 5, 1841). Brownson must have lectured in Philadelphia shortly before he had come to New York to lecture. The *Evening Post* carried a notice on February 27, 1841, which read: "Mr. Brownson's lectures have been listened to with general admiration at Philadelphia, judging from the accounts in the journals."

*Some* of the reports in the New York newspapers on Brownson's lectures here quoted are taken from Fr. Holden's *The Early Years of Isaac Thomas Hecker (1819-1844)* who pioneered in digging out the reports. *Some* of Brownson's letters to Isaac Hecker, now in the Paulist archives, quoted by Fr. Holden, are also used in this chapter. It is assumed that Fr. Holden did very careful and honest work in these fields.

7. Hecker, "Dr. Brownson in Boston," *Catholic World,* XLV (July 1887), p. 205.

8. "The Democracy of Christianity," *BQR* (October 1838), p. 468.

9. *The Convert,* p. 102.

10. *Ibid.,* p. 101.

11. The New York *Evening Post* (March 5, 1841).

12. Hecker, "Dr. Brownson in Boston," XLV (July 1887), p. 466.

13. Hecker, "Dr. Brownson and the Workingmen's Party Fifty Years ago," *The Catholic World* (May 1887), p. 206.

14. From a xerox copy of the oration in Harvard College Library, pp. 2-4.

15. Holden, *The Early Years of Isaac Thomas Hecker,* pp. 48-52.

16. *Ibid.,* p. 57, n. 47.

17. Holden, *The Yankee Paul, Isaac Thomas Hecker* (Milwaukee: Bruce Publishing Co., 1958), p. 49.

18. Hecker, "Dr. Brownson and the Workingmen's Party Fifty Years ago," *ut supra,* p. 206.

19. Hecker, "Dr. Brownson in Boston," *ut supra*, pp. 468-469.

20. *Early Life*, pp. 305, 326.

21. "The Distribution Bill," *BQR* (January 1842), pp. 93-94; see also "Mr. Calhoun and the Baltimore Convention," *BrQR* (April 1844), p. 257.

22. *Early Life*, pp. 327-329.

23. *Ibid.*, p. 334.

24. *Ibid.*, p. 335.

25. *Ibid.*

26. *Hecker Papers*, Letters to Father Hecker, XV, f.

27. *Early Life*, p. 336.

28. *Ibid.*, pp. 336-338.

29. *Ibid.*, pp. 338-339. Charles M. Wiltse also called the pamphlet Brownson had furnished for the occasion "excellent." (See *John C. Calhoun, Sectionalist* [Indianapolis: Bobbs-Merrill Co., Inc., 1951], III, p. 144.)

30. *Ibid.*, p. 339.

31. *Hecker Papers*, Orestes Brownson to Hecker (September 18, 1843), XLV, f.

32. *Hecker Papers*, Brownson to Hecker (September 2, 1843).

33. *Early Life*, pp. 340-341.

34. *Ibid.*, pp. 339-340.

35. *Hecker Papers*, Letters to Father Hecker, XLV, f. Brownson to Hecker (October 3, 1843).

36. C. C. Hollis, *The Literary Criticism of Orestes Brownson* (Ann Arbor: University of Michigan, 1954), p. 161.

37. "The Dial, A Magazine for Literature, Philosophy, and Religion," *BQR* (January 1841), pp. 131-132.

38. O. B. Frothingham, *Theodore Parker* (Boston: J. R. Osgood and Co., 1874), p. 139.

39. Clarence L. F. Gohdes, *Periodicals of American Transcendentalism*, (Durham, North Carolina: Duke University Press, 1931), p. 81.

40. *BQR* (October 1842), pp. 513-514.

41. *The American Democracy* (New York: Viking Press, 1948), p. 664.

42. *The Transcendentalists* (Cambridge: Harvard University Press, 1950), pp. 180-181.

43. *Early Life*, p. 344.

44. *Prose Writers of America* (Philadelphia: A. Hart, late Casey and Hart, 1853), p. 39.

45. *History of American Magazines* (Cambridge: Harvard University Press), I, 1741-1850 (1939), p. 684.

## CHAPTER 18

1. Microfilm of the *Brownson Papers*, roll 1.

2. *Ibid.* Letter dated July 5, 1842. He had said in a previous letter dated June 20: "I had no idea that on your publisher's part there would be any disposition to be unreasonable and unfair." Julian Hawthorne described O'Sullivan as "a cosmopolitan of Irish parentage on his father's side, and one of the most charming companions in the world." *Nathaniel Hawthorne and his Wife* (Cambridge: Harvard University Press, 1884), p. 160.

3. Microfilm of the *Brownson Papers*, roll 1. Letter dated August 5, 1842.

4. Arthur M. Schlesinger, Jr., *The Age of Jackson* (Boston: Little, Brown and Co., 1945), p. 372. It had as contributors such other celebrities as Bryant, Hawthorne, Thoreau, Whittier, Walt Whitman, Poe, Longfellow, Lowell, Bancroft and others. *Ibid.*, p. 372.

5. Microfilm of the *Brownson Papers*, roll 1.

6. Brownson received three dollars per page. He was to furnish an article of fifteen to twenty pages, more or less, for each month. A generous offer was also made for anything more that he might write.

7. Hugh Marshall is scarcely altogether accurate when he says: "If he [Brownson] had not been a legitimist who held firmly to the form of government legally existing in his country, he surely would have repudiated all popular institutions." *Orestes Brownson and the American Republic* (Washington, D.C.: Catholic University of America Press, 1971), p. 42. In April 1859, Brownson wrote: "We need not say that we are attached to our American institutions as they were left us by our fathers. What we oppose is the substitution of Jacobinical democracy for true American republicanism." "Politics at Home and Abroad," *BrQR* (April 1859), p. 225; *Works,* XVI, p. 580. In April 1862, he again affirmed: "We love our country with all her faults, for she is *our* country; but we love her institutions, because we have studied them, and believe them the wisest and the best the world has yet seen." "State Suicide, State Rebellion," *BrQR* (April 1862), p. 215; *Works,* XVIII, p. 248. In October 1873, he again wrote: "Corrupt as our politicians and no small part of the people certainly are, we know no actually existing government on earth for which we would exchange our own." "At Home and Abroad," *BrQR* (October 1873), p. 544; *Works,* XVIII, p. 544.

8. "Democracy and Liberty," first published in the *Democratic Review* (April 1843), Brownson's *Works,* XV, pp. 259-260.

9. *Ibid.,* p. 260.

10. *Ibid.,* p. 261.

11. *Ibid.,* pp. 261-263.

12. *The Democratic Review* (April 1843), p. 391.

13. Microfilm of the *Brownson Papers,* roll 2. Letter dated April 6, 1843. *The Democratic Review* had a subscription list of three thousand five hundred in 1843. See *The Age of Jackson, ut supra,* p. 373.

14. Brownson maintained that our form of government is not a democracy but a constitutional republic. A constitutional republic he defined to be "*a government in which power is held as a trust from the commonwealth, to be exercised for the public good, according to a prescribed law,* whether actually exercised by one man called king or emperor, or by the few called the nobility or aristrocracy, or by the many called the people. . . .*" "Origin and Ground of Government," *Works,* XV, pp. 375-376.

Democracy he defined: "A democracy, understanding the term strictly, is a government, not only administered by the people, but in which *the people,* or the major part, practically considered, *are sovereign, and their will, whenever, wherever, or however expressed, is THE SUPREME LAW." Ibid.,* p. 376.

He emphasized that our government was not called a democracy from the beginning. There was no party known as the Democratic party until the time of Jackson, Jefferson, Madison, Monroe and other fathers of the party, did not call themselves Democrats, but Republicans. Brownson added: "I myself remember well, when members of the party regarded it as a foul reproach to be called Democrats." *Ibid.,* pp. 375-378.

15. "Origin and Ground of Government," Brownson's *Works,* XV (September 1843), p. 332. Brownson's three articles in the *Democratic Review* on the "Origin and Ground of Government" were eventually incorporated into his *Works,* Vol. XV. Reference hereafter will be made to that volume.

According to Brownson's outright rejection of majoritarian democracy, he would scarcely have favored Frederick Grimke's theory of the power of the people operating "outside the doors of government." Frederick Grimke, *The Nature and Tendency of Free Institutions,* reedited by John William Ward (Cambridge: Harvard University Press, 1968), pp. 12-13. Grimke first published his work in 1848, then in 1856. A third edition was published after his death in 1871. Though of some pretension (it runs to seven hundred pages in this new edition), it seems to have received scant attention when appearing in the first three editions. Brownson himself never took any notice of it, although he did review Francis Lieber's *Manual of Political Ethics, designed chiefly for the Use of College and Students of Law,* 2 vols. He called it a "quack treatise on Political Ethics." *BQR* (January 1839), pp. 113-123; (April 1840), pp. 181-193.

16. *Ibid.*, p. 335.

17. *The American Adam* (Chicago: University of Chicago Press, 1955), p. 186.

18. "The Origin and Ground of Government," *Works*, XV (September 1843), p. 337.

19. *Ibid.*, p. 340.

20. *Ibid.*, p. 347.

21. *Ibid.*, p. 341.

22. *Ibid.*, p. 335.

23. *Ibid.*, p. 344.

24. *Ibid.*, p. 346. Like his friend Calhoun, Brownson was for getting as far as at all possible the will of the *whole people* represented in government, not just the majority: "Here is the great wisdom of our institutions, and, in this fact, that they are so contrived as to collect the sense of a larger proportion of those who are their subjects, than the institutions of any other country, do I find their glory. Thus far I go with my democratic friends, and find room for the freest and fullest action, of what the *Washington Globe* calls 'the Democracy of Numbers.' " "Origin and Ground of Government," *Works*, XV (October 1843), pp. 393-394.

25. Russell Kirk, *Randolph of Roanoke: A Study in Conservative Thought* (Chicago: University of Chicago Press, 1951), p. 41.

26. *Ibid.*, p. 4.

27. *Ibid.*, p. 22.

28. *Ibid.*, p. 55.

29. *Ibid.*, p. 60.

30. *Ibid.*, p. 80.

31. *Ibid.*, p. 33.

32. *Ibid.*, p. 38. There is also some similarity of thought in this matter between Brownson and Irving Babbit in his *Democracy and Leadership*, though there are dissimilarities, too. Babbit warned against arbitrary majority rule when he said: "The notion in particular that a substitute for leadership may be found in numerical majorities that are supposed to reflect the general will is only a pernicious conceit." *Democracy and Leadership* (Boston: Houghton Mifflin Co., 1924), p. 16.

33. "Origin and Ground of Government," *Works*, XV (September 1843), pp. 341-342.

34. *BrQR* (January 1844), p. 2.

35. "Popular Government," *Works*, XV, p. 283.

36. Microfilm of the *Brownson Papers,* roll 2. Letter dated April 7, 1843. A writer of the time gives us an interesting insight into the charge of frequent changes made against Brownson: "Indeed, if he [Brownson] had been less candid he might have preserved more apparent consistency. . . . Mr. Brownson has probably changed and modified his opinions no oftener than most intellectual men in the progress of his studies; but the greater part of mankind acquire the habit of concealing the different states of their progression, while Mr. B[rownson] has continually discovered to the world the successive struggles and achievements of his active mind. Perhaps he has not always been understood. It must be apparent, however, that there is a decided unity of results amidst the multiplicity of his enterprises." *Ibid.*, November 1842, signed simply "T."

37. *Early Life,* pp. 342-344; *Works,* XV, pp. 322, 508, 510; also "The Suffrage Party in Rhode Island," *BrQR* (October 1844), pp. 532-544.

38. "Popular Government," *Works*, XV (May 1843), p. 292.

39. "Democracy and Liberty," *Works*, XV (April 1843), p. 278.

40. *Ibid.*, pp. 280-281.

41. "Popular Government," *Works*, XV (May 1843), p. 282.

42. "Origin and Ground of Government," *Works*, XV (October 1843), p. 386.

43. "Popular Government," *Works*, XV (May 1843), p. 290.

44. *The Convert,* pp. 102-103. That Brownson was here dealing with a very abstruse and controversial question in his articles on the origin and ground of government should not be overlooked. As Russell Kirk has remarked: "Of all those vexed questions in what Coleridge called 'the holy jungle of metaphysics,' perhaps none has

been more hotly debated than that concerning the basis of authority in government." *Randolph of Roanoke: A Study in Conservative Thought, ut supra,* p. 17.

45. "Origin and Constitution of Government," *BrQR* (January 1844), p. 242; *Works,* XV, p. 433.

46. *Early Life,* p. 356.

47. Per Sveino has rightly observed: "While John Henry Newman in his pre-Catholic phase was particularly impressed by the church of the first centuries, Brownson in his pre-Catholic period was above all fascinated by medieval Catholicism. Already in his *New Views* [1836] he had contrasted the constructive work of Catholicism with the disintegrating character of Protestantism. Yet with his growing desire for a strong government, medieval Catholicism with its theocratic theories and practice appealed even more to him." *Orestes A. Brownson's Road to Catholicism* (New York: The Humanities Press, 1970), p. 304.

48. "The Origin and Ground of Government," *Works,* XV (October 1843), p. 348. Brownson was to do brave battle for this same church-state relationship in the years 1853 and 1854 in particular. (See *BrQR* for the years 1853 and 1854.)

49. *Ibid.,* p. 349.

50. "Brownson, the Philosophical Expounder of the Constitution," *Proceedings of the Meeting of the American Catholic Philosophical Association* (St. Louis University: Catholic University of America Press, 1931), p. 151.

51. "Origin and Ground of Government," *Works,* XV (October 1843), p. 353. This reminds one of Edmund Burke's statement: "We know, and, what is better, we feel inwardly, that religion is the basis of authority. . . . We know, and it is our pride to know, that man is by his constitution a religious animal." *Reflections on the Revolution in France, Works* (Boston: Little, Brown and Co., 1871), III, pp. 350-351.

(See Allen Guttman, *The Conservative Tradition in America* [New York: The Oxford University, 1967].) But Guttman does not present Brownson's doctrine on church and state in America entirely correctly (p. 85ff.); Brownson always most heartily approved as a Catholic of the church-state relationship that does exist in America. In February 1868, he said distinctly again: "In a word, we approve and urge the continuance of the relations between church and state which subsist in this country." "Separation of Church and State," *Works,* XII, pp. 437-438. Many other quotes from his writings might be made to the same effect. The American churchmen whom Guttman quotes (John Hughes, Gibbons, Ireland and John T. McNicholas), as having adopted the "liberal theory" of church and state in America only followed in the train of thought set by Brownson (who was himself in harmony with Archbishop John Carroll).

The ideal or Catholic doctrine on the matter (where the conditions are propitious) is the union of church and state, rightly understood, that is, their mutual cooperation for the common good or welfare, the church promoting directly the spiritual, and the state promoting directly the temporal welfare of the citizens. This doctrine was set forth by Pope Leo XIII in 1885 in his encyclical, *The Christian Constitution of States.* He compared the ideal union of the two to "the union of soul and body in man." *The Great Encyclical Letters of Pope Leo XIII* (New York: Benziger Brothers, 1903), pp. 107-134; p. 115 in particular.

Brownson saw a good approach to the ideal union of church and state as it exists in America: "For ourselves personally, we are partial to our American system, which, unless we are blinded by our national prejudices, comes nearer to the realization of the true union as well as distinction of church and state than has heretofore or elsewhere been effected; and we own we should like to see it, if practicable there, introduced — by lawful means only — into the nations of Europe." *Works,* XIII, May 1870), p. 272. (First published in the *Catholic World.*)

52. *Ibid.,* pp. 396-400.

53. *Ibid.,* pp. 400-403.

54. *Ibid.,* "Origin and Ground of Government," *Works,* XV (August 1843), pp. 296-297.

55. Thesis: *Orestes Augustus Brownson on the Nature and Scope of Political Authority* (Tucson: University of Arizona Press, 1971), p. 29. Charles Merriam,

*American Political Ideas: 1865-1917* (New York: The Macmillan Co., 1929), p. 373.

56. "Origin and Ground of Government," *Works,* XV (August 1843), pp. 298-299.

57. *Ibid.,* p. 300.

58. *Ibid.,* pp. 300-301.

59. *Ibid.,* (October 1843), pp. 401-402.

60. *Ibid.,* p. 404.

61. *Early Life,* p. 348.

62. "Origin and Ground of Government," *Works,* XV (October 1843), p. 374.

63. *Ibid.,* p. 375.

64. *Ibid.,* p. 385.

65. Fr. Isaac Hecker, "Dr. Brownson in Boston," *The Catholic World,* XLV (July 1887), p. 466.

66. Charles Merriam, *American Political Ideas: 1865-1917, ut supra,* p. 2.

67. "Origin and Ground of Government," *Works,* XV (October 1843), p. 404.

68. *Early Life,* pp. 505-506.

69. Microfilm of the *Brownson Papers,* roll 2. One of the happy results of Brownson's connection with the *Democratic Review* is the likeness of him that has come down to us from its pages, inserted with his first article. The philosophic cast of his features in this likeness distinguishes it from other images of him. That it is a true likeness of him at the time we have from one of his contemporaries (the name is not given). Speaking of Brownson and the *Democratic Review,* this contemporary remarked with an evident touch of humor at the end: "That journal [*The Democratic Review*] regaled his friends and readers with a beautifully engraved and faithful likeness of the great man, even to the arrangement of his flowing locks and the exact locality of his gold spectacles upon his well-formed democratic nose." Microfilm of the *Brownson Papers,* roll 8.

## CHAPTER 19

1. Fr. Isaac Hecker, "Dr. Brownson and Bishop Fitzpatrick," *The Catholic World,* XLV (April 1887), p. 202.

2. *Early Life,* p. 426.

3. Dogberty Runes, ed., *Dictionary of Philosophy* (Totowa, New Jersey: Littlefield, Adams and Co., 1962), p. 70. Henry Brownson tells us: "Before he [his father] became acquainted with Cousin's writings, like pretty much everybody in the United States, he accepted Locke's philosophy without much question. The study of Cousin led him into the direction which he afterwards followed in philosophy." *Early Life,* p. 403.

4. *Metaphysics and Constitutionalism: The Political Theory of Orestes Brownson* (Tucson: University of Arizona Press, 1975), p. 120.

5. Per Sveino, *Orestes A. Brownson's Road to Catholicism* (New York: The Humanities Press, 1970), p. 176.

6. *The Convert,* p. 126.

7. "Charles Elwood Reviewed," *BQR* (April 1842), p. 162; *Works,* IV, p. 344. Also *Early Life,* pp. 421, 427.

8. *Ibid.,* p. 163; *Works,* IV, p. 344.

9. Microfilm of the *Brownson Papers,* roll 1.

10. *BQR* (January 1840), Introduction, p. 19.

11. "Specimens of Foreign Literature," *BQR* (October 1838), p. 443.

12. Microfilm of the *Brownson Papers,* roll 9.

13. *Sumner's Journal* (March 9, 1838), Edward Pierce, *Memoir and Letters of Charles Sumner,* I, p. 265.

14. *Sumner to Story* (May 21, 1838), *ibid.,* p. 295.

15. Cousin's *Works,* Tom. I, p. vi (3rd ed.); *Early Life,* p. 393.

16. *Early Life,* p. 301.

17. *Ibid.,* pp. 235-236.

18. Microfilm of the *Brownson Papers,* roll 9.

19. "Charles Elwood Reviewed," *BQR* (April 1842), pp. 163-165; *Works,* IV, pp. 344-346; *The Convert,* pp. 128-129.

20. *Ibid.,* pp. 175-176; *Works,* IV, p. 355. To this Brownson added an interesting footnote when he said: "We know very well that this was not the real doctrine of Kant; that it was only demonstrated by him to be the result, to which all philosophy must come that is *based on pure reason.* He himself relied on practical reason, that is to say, on plain common sense; and his purpose in writing critiques of pure reason, was to demonstrate the unsatisfactory character of all purely metaphysical speculations. A wise man, after all, was that same Emmanuel Kant." *Ibid.*

21. "The Minor Transcendentalists and German Philosophy," *The New England Quarterly,* XV (December 1843), p. 671.

22. "Charles Elwood Reviewed," *BQR* (April 1842), pp. 180-181; *Works,* IV, p. 359.

23. *BQR* (January 1842), pp. 126-127. Brownson said further: "M. Leroux does not always do justice to M. Cousin, and differs in fact less from him than he fancies; but he is unquestionably the profoundest philosophical writer France can boast. . . . He is a profounder and more vigorous and inspiring writer than Cousin, though less chaste, elegant, and polished." *Ibid.*

24. *The Convert,* p. 127.

25. Microfilm of the *Brownson Papers,* roll 9.

26. *The Convert,* p. 127.

27. *Orestes A. Brownson's Road to Catholicism* (New York: The Humanities Press, 1970), p. 122.

28. *The Convert,* p. 126.

29. "Charles Elwood Reviewed," *BQR* (April 1842), p. 178; *Works,* IV, p. 357.

30. *Ibid.,* pp. 178-179; *Works,* IV, p. 357.

31. *Ibid.,* p. 182; *Works,* IV, pp. 360-361.

32. "Reform and Conservatism," *BQR* (January 1842), p. 61; *Works,* IV, p. 80.

33. "Leroux on Humanity," *BQR* (July 1842), pp. 260-261; *Works,* IV, p. 102.

34. "The Philosophy of History," *Works,* IV, p. 378. (Originally published in the *Democratic Review,* May and June 1843.)

35. *Metaphysics and Constitutionalism: The Political Theory of Orestes Brownson* (Tucson: University of Arizona Press, 1975), p. 139.

36. "The Philosophy of History," *Works,* IV, pp. 382-383.

37. "Reform and Conservatism," *BQR* (January 1842), p. 69; *Works,* IV, p. 86.

38. "The Mediatorial Life of Jesus," *Works,* IV, p. 172.

39. "Reform and Conservatism," *BQR* (January 1842), pp. 64, 68; *Works,* IV, pp. 82-83. Whatever Brownson's criticisms of Cousin's philosophy, he remained ever grateful to him for having taught him the distinction between the *le-moi* and the *le non-moi.* As Robert E. Moffit has emphasized: "Cousin's chief contribution to Brownson's thought, however, a contribution withered neither by time nor the criticisms of his numerous and vociferous critics, was the notion that there is a real distinction between the *le moi* and the *le non-moi* in consciousness. Thought, or consciousness, was nothing less than a 'synthesis of distinct subject and distinct object in relation,' as he was to recall in his 'Essay in Refutation of Atheism in 1873.' " *Metaphysics and Constitutionalism: The Political Theory of Orestes Brownson, ut supra,* p. 121.

Brownson stressed his original debt to Cousin all the more when he said: "Every philosopher does and must begin by the analysis of thought, that is, in the language of Cousin, the fact of consciousness, and there is no other way." "Victor Cousin and His Philosophy," *Works,* II, pp. 310-311.

40. J. B. Bury, *The Idea of Progress, An Inquiry into its Origin and Growth* (New York: Dover Publications, Inc., 1955), pp. 318-319.

41. "Leroux on Humanity," *BQR* (July 1842), p. 272. (Some parts of this article were not included as incorporated into vol. IV of the *Works.*)

42. *The Convert,* p. 129; *Works,* "Synthetic Philosophy," vol. I, p. 68. (The latter treatise was first published in the *Democratic Review,* December 1842, and January and March 1843.)

43. *Ibid.*, p. 129.

44. "Leroux on Humanity," *BQR* (July 1842), pp. 292-293. The mutual solidarity of all men, as advanced by Leroux, Brownson explained by asserting that in actual association the subject and the object are not only placed in juxtaposition, mutually acting and reacting upon each other, but become intimately united, *soldered together,* or amalgated as the acid and the alkali in the formation of a new salt, so that separation in time and space is impossible without destroying life itself. The *actual* object of each man is his family and his country, his *virtual* or possible object towards which he aspires, and should be free to aspire, is all men. "Each man is an undivided and indivisible part of the life of all men, and the life of all men and of each man is an undivided and indivisible part of the life of each man." *Ibid.* pp. 296-297.

45. *The Convert,* pp. 130-131.

46. *Ibid.*, p. 133.

47. *Ibid.*, p. 132.

48. "A Discourse on Matters pertaining to Religion," *BQR* (October 1842), p. 448. Professor A. Robert Caponigri has discussed lucidly Brownson's theory of the unique historical incursion of Christ the Mediator into human affairs in his article "Brownson and Emerson: Nature and History" in the *New England Quarterly,* XVIII (September 1945), p. 450 in particular.

49. *The Convert,* p. 132.

50. "Leroux on Humanity," *Works,* IV, p. 111.

51. *The Convert,* p. 145. Brownson varied in naming his providential men.

52. "A Discourse on Matters pertaining to Religion," *BQR* (October 1842), p. 450. George K. Malone has made a number of critical observations on Brownson's doctrine of *life and communion* in his dissertation on *The True Church: A Study in the Apologetics of Orestes Augustus Brownson* (Chicago: St. Mary of the Lake Seminary, Mundelein, 1957). While the dissertation as a whole has its merits, it seems a bit captious in parts. Malone makes a great deal of the point in particular that in the years 1842 and 1843 Brownson did not recognize Christ as the *sole* mediator between God and man (p. 73). If Brownson did not emphasize the divine mediatorship of Christ more clearly during those years, what is the explanation? We will probably find it in the fact that of all people whom he hoped to draw after him into the Catholic Church his own Unitarian fellow ministers stood no doubt first. His policy may well have been to lead them gradually to see the divine mediatorship of Christ. Moreover, there are passages in his writings during those years in which Brownson seems to assert the divine mediatorship of Christ quite clearly. Already in July 1841, he declared: "The conclusion to which our inquiries have led us is, that the Savior was very God and very man, and in him we see the union of perfect God and perfect man, Christ is one with God, was God, and the Christ, the true God, was incarnated in the man Jesus, true man, and type of the perfect man." Brownson was here reviewing a book, and added: "We do not find the Savior in it; the Son of God, one with the Father, through whom *alone* we can be cleansed from sin, and presented blameless at the last day." (Italics mine.) *BQR* (July 1841), p. 392. See also his letter to Dr. Channing, *Works* (1842), IV, pp. 143-144, 160. A number of Malone's references in dealing with this matter are faulty.

53. "The Mediatorial Life of Jesus," *Works,* IV, p. 157.

54. *Ibid.*, pp. 164-165.

55. *Ibid.*, p. 162.

56. *Early Life,* pp. 443-444.

57. *Our Liberal Movement in Theology* (Boston: Roberts Brothers, 1882), p. 86.

58. *The Convert,* pp. 151-152. Later Brownson remarked: "Protestanism, which has broken the life of humanity, and severed the present from the past, has deprived us alike of ancestors and of posterity, of the past and the future." *BQR* (July 1863), p. 382.

59. R.W.B. Lewis, *The American Adam* (Chicago: University of Chicago Press, 1955), p. 184.

60. *The Convert,* p. 143.

61. "Reform and Conservatism," *BQR* (January 1842), p. 78; *Works,* IV, p. 94.

62. *Ibid.,* p. 76; *Works,* IV, p. 92.

63. "The Mediatorial Life of Jesus," *Works,* IV, p. 149.

64. *The Convert,* p. 144.

65. *Ibid.*

66. "The Mediatorial Life of Jesus," *Works,* IV, p. 142.

67. *The Convert,* p. 19.

68. *Ibid.,* p. 135.

69. "Orthodoxy and Unitarianism," *BrQR* (July 1863), pp. 288-289.

70. *The Convert,* pp. 135, 139.

71. "Religious Orders," *Works,* VIII, p. 262. This article was originally published serially in the *Ave Maria* (1871).

72. "The Philosophy of History," *Works,* IV, p. 421. This treatise was first published in the *Democratic Review,* May and June 1843.

73. The present writer gave some notice of this treatise in two articles he contributed to the *Irish Ecclesiastical Record,* vol. LXXXV (January and February 1956) under the title, "Orestes A. Brownson and Historiography," pp. 10-17, 122-130.

74. *BrQR* (October 1852), pp. 421-459; *Works,* XIX, pp. 384-418.

75. "The Philosophy of History," *Works,* IV, p. 396.

76. *Ibid.,* p. 416.

77. *Ibid.,* pp. 403-404. Brownson spoke also of Sir Walter Raleigh's *History of the World* (incomplete) as "written with great vigor and majesty of thought, with a pathos, a richness and magnificence of style and language, hardly surpassed, if equalled, by any thing of the kind we are acquainted with." *Ibid.*

78. *Ibid.,* pp. 409-410. Referring to how God's revealed truth spread among the heathen nations, John Henry Newman spoke of that "vague and unconnected family of religious truths, originally from God, but sojourning, without sanction of miracle or a definite home, as pilgrims up and down the world, and discernible and separable from the corrupt legends with which they are mixed, by the spiritual mind alone." *An Essay on the Development of Christian Doctrine* (London: James Toovery, 1846), p. 118.

79. *Ibid.,* p. 410.

80. *Ibid.,* p. 418.

81. "Leroux on Humanity," *BQR* (July 1842), p. 293. (Paragraph not in vol. IV of *Works.*)

82. "Reform and Conservatism," *BQR* (January 1842), p. 77; *Works,* IV, pp. 93-94.

83. *Ibid.*

84. *Ibid.,* pp. 79-80; *Works,* IV, pp. 95-96.

85. "Emerson's Essays," *BQR* (July 1841), pp. 298-300.

86. *Ibid.,* pp. 301-302.

87. *Ibid.*

88. *Ibid.,* pp. 303-304.

89. *Ibid.,* pp. 307-308.

90. *The Literature of the American People, An Historical and Critical Survey* (New York: Appleton-Century-Crofts, Inc., 1951), pp. 266-267. Although Brownson treated Emerson with uniform tenderness, it is scarcely credible that Emerson found Brownson's criticisms very palatable. Leonard J. McCarthy, S.J., no doubt put the matter fairly correctly when he opined that while Emerson respected and admired Brownson, "he found him too argumentative and aggressive." *Rhetoric in the Works of Orestes Brownson* (New York: Fordham University Press, 1961), p. 81.

91. *Early Life,* p. 164.

92. *Literary Criticism of Orestes Brownson* (Ann Arbor: University of Michigan, 1954), p. 157.

93. *The American Adam, ut supra,* pp. 192-193. To C. C. Hollis Brownson seemed to belong to a "third movement" between the "rationalism that had become respectable (under Unitarian robes) in capitalistic Boston," and the thinking of

Emerson and others "who returned to the mystical tradition of the Puritans while rebuffing Puritanism itself." *Literary Criticism, ut supra,* p. 118.

94. The first article, "The Transient and the Permanent in Christianity," *BQR* (October 1841); the second, "A Discourse pertaining to Matters of Religion," *BQR* (October 1842). Alvin S. Ryan observes that the revolution in Brownson's thought between these two articles is "almost total." "The Critique of Transcendentalism," in *American Classics Reconsidered,* ed. by Harold J. Gardner (New York: Charles Scribner's Sons, 1958), p. 110.

95. "Zanoni," *BQR* (July 1842), p. 357. It is probably true to say that some of Brownson's thought was still quite ambivalent. While turning more to the right in most of his thought, he still also inclined to the left in some respects. In his article on "Modern French Literature" he declared, "All modern literature . . . is insurrectionary and rebellious. We, whose sympathies are always with the rebels, of course approve this literature." *BQR* (April 1842), p. 236; *Works,* XIX, p. 53. (By rebels in this case he probably meant nothing more than those who were striving to recover their lost rights.) He was also now reversing judgments he had formerly pronounced on various authors, particularly that on Walter Scott, whose writings now marked a "revolution in literature, and contain even a social revolution." *Ibid.,* p. 234; *Works,* XIX, p. 52. He had his qualified praise for the leading French writers of fiction of the day, such as Honoré de Balzac, Alexandre Dumas, but especially Victor Hugo and George Sand, alias Madame Dudevant. Arguing against Madame Dudevant and others, he declared that "marriage by its own nature is absolutely indissoluble." *Ibid.,* p. 245; *Works,* XIX, p. 61.

96. *Ibid.*

97. *Ibid.,* p. 360.

98. *Ibid.,* pp. 358-359.


## CHAPTER 20

1. "The Church of the Future," *BQR* (January 1842), pp. 1-27; *Works,* IV, pp. 57-78.

2. "Charles Elwood," *BQR* (April 1842), pp. 129-183; *Works,* IV, pp. 316-361.

3. *The Convert,* p. 138.

4. "The Mediatorial Life of Jesus," *BQR* (July 1842), p. 384.

5. "The Mediatorial Life of Jesus," *Works,* IV (June 1842), p. 384.

6. "An Introductory Address, or Remarks made by the Editor on resuming his Labors as a preacher of the Gospel," *BQR* (July 1842), pp. 366-368.

7. *Ibid.,* p. 370.

8. *Theodore Parker* (Boston: Beacon Press, 1947), p. 44. Arthur M. Schlesinger, Jr., has a whole page in his biography of Brownson detailing how Parker in these earlier years reproduced much of Brownson's thought in his own words on many of the social and religious questions of the day. *Orestes A. Brownson: A Pilgrim's Progress* (Boston: Little, Brown and Co., 1939), p. 104. But Parker was later to say many hard things about Brownson after he had become a Catholic.

9. *The Convert,* pp. 155-156.

10. *BQR* (October 1841), pp. 436-474.

11. *The American Adam* (Chicago: University of Chicago Press, 1955), pp. 182-183.

12. *The Convert,* pp. 182-183. In further comparison Brownson said: "He [Parker] was mad at religion, and, as *Sartor Resartus* would say, he wished to turn men in utter nakedness out into this bleak and wintry world, to rely upon themselves alone, and to support themselves as best they might from their own native resources. But I had long since got through that state of my disease, had long since subdued my wrath, and now longed to approach nearer and nearer to the Christian world, not to remove further and further from it. I had learned to loathe doubt, to have a horror of unbelief, and was now ready to be an orthodox believer the moment I

would see my way to believe without violence to my human nature or the abnegation of my reason." *Ibid.*, pp. 156-157. R.W.B. Lewis deals with the sharp divergence of the theological thought of Brownson and Parker at some length in *The American Adam, ut supra*, pp. 174-193.

13. "A Discourse on Matters pertaining to Religion," *BQR* (October 1842), p. 465.

14. "The Mediatorial Life of Jesus," *Works*, IV, p. 169.

15. Microfilm of the *Brownson Papers*, roll 1.

16. *Ibid.*, roll 1.

17. *The Convert*, p. 155.

18. "Liberalism and Socialism," *BrQR* (April 1855), p. 184; *Works*, X, p. 527.

19. *The Convert*, p. 159. Newman, too, in these times wanted a Catholicity without the pope. (See Meriol Trevor, *Newman, The Pillar of the Cloud* [New York: Doubleday and Co., 1962], I, p. 220.)

20. "A Discourse on Matters pertaining to Religion," *BQR* (October 1842), pp. 495-502. A very interesting comment on Brownson's review of "Parker's Discourse" is contained in a letter of Joseph Coolidge Shaw to St. Ives, minister of the Second Church in Roxbury, Massachusetts, dated April 30, 1844. The brief letter is on the title page of Brownson's *Boston Quarterly Review* for October 1842. It reads: "My dear St. Ives: With Mr. Parker's 'Discourse on Religion' I send you Brownson's review of it, which I think will interest you. It will show you how near he is to the Church. How certainly he would return to her bosom, did he but understand her. He is longing for what she is, not knowing that she is it." *Propaganda Fide: America Centrale*, vol. XIII, p. 572. (Microfilm copy in *AUND*.)

21. "Leroux on Humanity," *BQR* (July 1842), p. 318; *Works*, IV, p. 136.

22. "A Discourse on Matters pertaining to Religion," *BQR* (October 1842), p. 510.

23. *Latter Life* (this is the third volume of Henry Brownson's *Life* of his father), p. 555.

24. "Parker's Discourse," *BQR* (October 1842), pp. 510-511.

25. *Ibid.*, p. 508.

26. *The Convert*, p. 100.

27. "Introduction," *BrQR* (January 1844), pp. 5-6.

28. *Early Life*, p. 349.

29. *BrQR* (January 1844), pp. 4-5.

30. *An Essay on the Development of Christian Doctrine* (London: James Toovery, 1845), p. 39.

31. *BrQR* (January 1844), pp. 3-4.

32. "The Mediatorial Life of Jesus," *Works*, IV (June 1842), p. 140.

33. *BrQR* (January 1844), pp. 9-10.

34. *Ibid.*, p. 15.

35. *Ibid.*, p. 14.

36. *Ibid.*, p. 12.

37. *Ibid.*, p. 15.

38. *Ibid.*, pp. 16-17.

39. *Ibid.*, pp. 24-25. A variant on the old formula that *Man* against *Money* has no chance.

40. *Ibid.*, pp. 26-27.

41. *Ibid.*, pp. 27-28.

42. *Ibid.*, p. 19.

43. *Ibid.*, p. 18.

44. *BrQR* (January 1844), pp. 84-104.

45. *BrQR* (January 1844), pp. 21-22.

46. "Demagoguism," *BrQR* (January 1844), pp. 90-93; *Works*, IV, pp. 438-441.

47. "The Life and Speeches of John C. Calhoun," *BrQR* (January 1844), pp. 125-126; *Works*, XV, p. 468.

48. *Ibid.*, p. 128; *Works*, XV, p. 444.

49. *The Convert*, pp. 122-123.

50. *BrQR* (January 1844), p. 136.

51. "The Church Question," *BrQR* (January 1844), p. 64; *Works*, IV, p. 467.

52. *Ibid.*, pp. 59-82 and *passim*; *Works,* IV, pp. 463-482.

53. *Ibid.*, p. 82; *Works,* IV, p. 482.

54. "The Nature and Office of the Church," *BrQR* (April 1844), pp. 243-244; *Works,* IV, pp. 484-485.

55. *Ibid.*, p. 245; *Works,* IV, p. 486.

56. *Ibid.*, p. 246; *Works,* IV, p. 486.

57. *Ibid.*, p. 247; *Works,* IV, p. 487.

58. Walter M. Abbott, S.J., *The Documents of Vatican II* (New York: America Press, 1966), pp. 33-34.

59. "The Nature and Office of the Church," *BrQR* (April 1844), pp. 249-250; *Works,* IV, p. 490.

60. "Dr. Brownson in Boston," *The Catholic World,* LV (July 1887), p. 472.

61. "The Nature and Office of the Church," *BrQR* (April 1844), p. 252; *Works,* IV, p. 491.

62. *Ibid.*, p. 250; *Works,* IV, pp. 490, 495.

63. *BrQR* (January 1844), p. 16.

64. "No Church, No Reform," *BrQR* (April 1844), p. 175; *Works,* IV, p. 496.

65. *Ibid.* pp. 175-194; *Works,* IV, pp. 496-512.

66. *The Convert,* p. 124.

67. "No Church, No Reform," *BrQR* (April 1844), pp. 189-190; *Works,* IV, p. 508. Here a sentence descriptive of Gilbert Keith Chesterton could be applied to Brownson: "He [Chesterton] found sanity and creativity in a God-centered world; in an informed heart, not in rationalism or irrationalism." A. Herbold, "Chesterton, Gilbert Keith," *The New Catholic Encyclopedia,* III, p. 553.

68. *BrQR* (April 1844), pp. 278-280.

69. *Ibid.*, p. 279.

70. *Early Life,* pp. 382-385. It is interesting to note that substantially the same thought expressed in these lectures was (as related by Henry Brownson) first expressed by Brownson in his review of *The Life of Cardinal Cheverus, Archbishop of Bordeau. BQR* (July 1839), pp. 387-388. This goes to show Brownson's fairness to the Catholic Church already at that earlier date (1839). This review has been unfairly overlooked by biographers.

71. *Works,* IV, p. 67.

72. *Early Life,* p. 503.

73. *BrQR* (April 1844), pp. 278-279.

74. Max Weber, *The Protestant Ethic and the Spirit of Capitalism* (London: George Allen and Unwin, 1930).

75. *The New England Mind: The Seventeenth Century* (New York: The Macmillan Co., 1939), p. 43.

76. *BrQR* (April 1844), p. 280.

77. "Mr. Calhoun and the Baltimore Convention," *BrQR* (April 1844), p. 262; *Works,* LX, p. 477.

78. *Early Life,* p. 362.

79. *Ibid.*, p. 360.

80. "The Church Question," *BrQR* (January 1844), p. 64; *Works,* IV, p. 467.

81. *The Convert,* p. 160. According to Per Sveino, Brownson "dramatized matters a little" when speaking of his eighth essay. Per Sveino states that the editor of *The Christian World,* George G. Channing, had refused "to insert a reply from Brownson to James Freeman Clarke, finding the debate [between the two] 'subversive' of the original plan of the journal. This refusal made Brownson unwilling to write his last article of the series for *The Christian World.*" *Orestes A. Brownson's Road to Catholicism* (New York: The Humanities Press, 1970), p. 287.

82. *Ibid.*, p. 161.

83. *The Nation,* LXVII (September 1898), p. 206.

84. *Apologia Pro Vita Sua* (New York: Longmans, Green, and Co., 1890), pp. 231-232.

85. Wilfrid Ward, *The Life of John Henry Cardinal Newman* (New York: Longmans, Green, and Co., 1912), p. 76.

86. *The Convert*, p. 93.

87. *Ibid.*, pp. 162-163. This view of Brownson reminds one of Newman's remarks on the eve of his conversion: "No one can have a more unfavorable view than I have of the present position of Roman Catholics." Meriol Trevor, *Newman, The Pillar of the Cloud* (New York: Doubleday and Co., 1962), I, p. 341. Anglican Archdeacon Manning, later convert and cardinal, felt a decided repugnance at the thought of being ordained a Catholic priest, due to the low social and cultural status of Catholics at the time. Paul M. Thureau-Dangin, *The English Catholic Revival in the Nineteenth Century* (New York: E. P. Dutton and Co., 1899), II, pp. 46-47.

88. *BrQR* (April 1854), pp. 157-158; *Works*, XI, pp. 211-212.

89. *The Convert*, p. 163.

90. *Ibid.*, p. 166.

91. "Archbishop Hughes on the Catholic Press," *BrQR* (January 1857), p. 137; *Works*, XX, p. 68.

92. *The Convert*, p. 121.

93. After becoming a Catholic, as Perry Miller tells us, his former Transcendentalist associates, Emerson, Parker, Channing, etc., "virtually entered into a tacit conspiracy to expunge his name from the record." *The American Transcendentalists: Prose and Poetry* (New York: Doubleday and Co., 1957), p. 39.

94. *The Convert*, p. 121.

95. "Explanations to Catholics," *BrQR* (October 1864), p. 489; *Works*, XX, p. 380.

96. *The Convert*, pp. 166, 168.

97. *Our Liberal Movement in Theology* (Boston: Roberts Brothers, 1882), pp. 87-88.

98. *Apologia Pro Vita Sua, ut supra*, p. 231.

## CHAPTER 21

1. Rowland Edmund Prothero Ernle, *The Life and Correspondence of A. P. Stanley* (New York: Charles Scribner's Sons, 1894), II, p. 398.

2. "Catholic Magazine and Ourselves," *BrQR* (April 1845), p. 260.

3. Bishop Fenwick belonged to the Society of Jesus. After having held high positions in the dioceses of New York, Baltimore, and Charleston, South Carolina, and having been twice president of Georgetown College, Georgetown, as well as procurator general of the Society of Jesus in the United States, he was finally elected to the see of Boston on May 10, 1825.

4. "The late Bishop of Boston," *BrQR* (October 1846), pp. 520-523; *Works*, XIV, pp. 471-475. See also *The Convert*, p. 169. Brownson made no mention in *The Convert* of his visit with Bishop Fenwick in the spring of 1843. That he had two initial visits with Bishop Fenwick in the spring of 1844 before beginning preparations to be received into the Catholic Church is evident from his letter to Isaac Hecker, dated June 6, 1844.

5. Fr. Walter Elliott, *The Life of Father Hecker* (New York: Columbia Press, 1894), pp. 146-147. From this letter it is quite evident that Fr. Hecker was not accurate when he said: "I presented myself to him [Bishop Fitzpatrick] some months before Dr. Brownson did, for reception into the Church." "Dr. Brownson and Bishop Fitzpatrick," *The Catholic World*, XLV (April 1887), p. 2. As already noted, Fr. Hecker's memory was failing in his last two years.

6. "No Church, No Reform," *BrQR* (April 1844), p. 194; *Works*, IV, p. 512.

7. "Come-outerism; or the Radical Tendency of the Day," *BrQR* (July 1844), pp. 369-374; *Works*, IV, pp. 543-548.

8. *State of Mind, A Boston Reader*, Robert Carter, "The Newness" (New York: Farrar, Straus and Co., 1948), pp. 200-201.

9. *Ibid.*, p. 378; *Works*, IV, p. 551.

10. "Come-outerism," *BrQR* (July 1844), pp. 369, 371, 376; *Works*, IV, pp. 544-550.

11. *Ibid.*, p. 381. It is not improbable that he was here thinking of the reaction he had encountered to his "Laboring Classes" essay. It was after that essay that he had

reexamined his own principles and had adopted more conservative premises. He was wholly convinced at the time he wrote his famous — or notorious — essay that he was only following out principles widely held by his own countrymen. And behold the reaction! It had rankled in his bosom.

12. Microfilm of the *Brownson Papers*, roll 10.

13. "Church Unity and Social Amelioration," *BrQR* (July 1844), p. 320; *Works*, IV, p. 520.

14. *Ibid.*, p. 320; *Works*, IV, p. 520.

15. *Ibid.*, p. 319; *Works*, IV, pp. 519-520.

16. *Ibid.*, p. 326; *Works*, IV, p. 525.

17. *The Convert*, p. 49.

18. "Church Unity and Social Amelioration," *BrQR* (July 1844), p. 326; *Works*, IV, pp. 325-326.

19. "Hildreth's Theory of Morals," *BrQR* (July 1844), pp. 330-331; *Works*, XIV, pp. 237-239.

20. *Ibid.*, p. 333; *Works*, XIV, pp. 420-421. Besides the strafing Brownson here gave Benthem he again referred to him later as "that grave and elaborate humbug." "Liberalism and Progress," *BrQR* (October 1864), p. 463; *Works*, XX, p. 354.

21. *Ibid.*, p. 338; *Works*, XIV, p. 245.

22. Leonard Gilhooley, *Contradiction and Dilemma: Orestes Brownson and the American Idea* (New York: Fordham University Press, 1972), p. 102.

23. Microfilm of the *Brownson Papers*, roll 2.

24. *Ibid.*

25. *Early Life*, p. 413.

26. "The Minor Transcendentalist and German Philosophy," *The New England Quarterly*, XV (December 1942), p. 670.

27. Microfilm of the *Brownson Papers*, roll 9.

28. "Kant's Critic of Pure Reason," *BrQR* (July 1844), pp. 282-283; *Works*, I, pp. 162-163. In view of this close examination Brownson gave Kant's philosophy, Per Sveino is scarcely correct when he says: ". . . Brownson hardly ever undertook any serious study of German philosophy at first hand." *Orestes A. Brownson's Road to Catholicism* (New York: The Humanities Press, 1970), p. 300.

29. *Ibid.* (October 1844), p. 437; *Works*, I, p. 203. William J. Haggerty, Jr., worked out a doctoral dissertation on Brownson's philosophy entitled: *Realism in the Philosophy of Orestes A. Brownson* (Boston University, 1960), unpublished. Chapter III of the dissertation, "The Influence of Kantian Idealism on the Development of Brownson's Realism" was reproduced in substance in an article in the *Delta Epsilon Sigma* publication, IX (March 1964), under the heading: "Brownson and Kant: The Objectivity of the Pre-empirical Element in the Knowledge Situation."

30. *Ibid.* (July 1844), pp. 308-309; *Works*, I, pp. 184-185.

31. *Ibid.* (October 1844), p. 499; *Works*, I, p. 213.

32. *Middle Life*, pp. 64-65.

33. "Bishop Hopkins on Novelties," *BrQR* (July 1844), pp. 353-354; *Works*, IV, pp. 530-531.

34. *Ibid.*, p. 336; *Works*, IV, pp. 541-542.

35. Dr. Samuel Seabury was the grandson of Rev. Samuel Seabury (1729-1796) who was the first bishop of the Protestant Episcopal Church in the United States. He had been an active loyalist during the Revolutionary War and was arrested. When released, he became chaplain to the British forces in New York. The war over, he went to England to seek consecration as an Episcopal bishop, but encountered difficulties. He then went to Scotland where he received consecration from nonjuring Episcopal prelates on November 14, 1784. Seabury, Samuel (W.W.Ms), *Encyclopedia Britannica*, University of Chicago, 1968, vol. 20, pp. 120-121.

36. *The Convert*, p. 138.

37. "The Anglican Church Schismatic," *BrQR* (October 1844), pp. 512-513; *Works*, IV, pp. 587-588.

38. "Sparks on Episcopacy," *BrQR* (July 1844), pp. 386-387; *Works*, IV, pp. 558-559.

39. "The Right Reverend Benedict Joseph Fenwick, second Bishop of Boston," *BrQR* (October 1846), p. 522; *Works*, XIV, pp. 474-475.

40. *Ibid.*, p. 524; *Works*, XIV, p. 475.

41. *The Convert*, p. 170.

42. *Ibid.*, pp. 16, 18-19.

43. *Ibid.*, p. 171.

44. "The Catholic Magazine and Ourselves," *BrQR* (April 1845), p. 262.

45. Microfilm of the *Brownson Papers*, roll 5.

46. "Victor Cousin and His Philosophy," *Works,* II, pp. 327-328. (Originally published in the *Catholic World,* June 1867.) It is by no means certain, however, that Cousin refused to answer Brownson's further letters just because Brownson had become a Catholic. We should not forget that it was already in 1842 that Brownson had laid his grave strictures on Cousin's philosophy when reviewing *Charles Elwood; Or the Infidel Converted, BQR* (April 1842), pp. 129-183. That criticism, and subsequent criticisms, were without doubt very unpalatable to Cousin, especially after Brownson had praised him as a philosopher rather lavishly.

47. *The Convert*, pp. 171-172.

48. *Ibid.*, p. 170.

49. *Ibid.*, p. 169.

50. John Delaney and James Tobin, *The Dictionary of Catholic Biography* (New York: Doubleday and Co., 1961), p. 424.

51. Lord Acton, "Lord Acton's American Diaries," *Fortnightly Review,* CXI (1922), p. 68. With such an estimate of Bishop Fitzpatrick on the part of Brownson, it is not likely that Arthur M. Schlesinger, Jr., is entirely accurate when he remarks that Brownson went through his instructions under Bishop Fitzpatrick "smothering his instinctive dislike for his tutor." *Orestes A. Brownson: A Pilgrim's Progress* (Boston: Little, Brown and Co., 1939), p. 187. Bishop Fitzpatrick had been a brilliant student at the seminary in Montreal where he carried off many prizes, and was then sent to St. Sulpice, Paris, to continue his studies. (See Sister Loyola, S.H., S.N.D. "Bishop Fenwick and Anti-Catholicism," *Historical Records and Studies,* vol. 27, p. 190.) Bishop Fitzpatrick was likewise a great shepherd of his flock. They familiarly called him "Bishop John." When Lord Acton visited him on his tour of the United States in 1853, he related: "I spent an hour with him and he was called out at least twenty times by poor people who wished to see him. This goes on all day; he cannot close his door." "Lord Acton's American Diaries," *Fortnightly Review,* CXI (1922), p. 70.

52. Acton to Döllinger: "Acton and Brownson: A Letter from America" (Monday, July 21, 1953), *Catholic Historical Review,* XLIX (January 1964), p. 529.

53. "The Late Bishop of Boston," *BrQR* (October 1846), p. 523; *Works*, XIV, p. 475.

54. "Answers to Objections," *BrQR* (October 1874), p. 451; *Works*, XX, pp. 405-406.

55. *The Convert*, p. 172.

56. "Dr. Brownson and Catholicity," *The Catholic World,* XLVI (November 1887), p. 231.

57. Wilfrid Ward, *The Life of John Henry Cardinal Newman* (New York: Longmans, Green, and Co., 1912), II, p. 57.

58. John Henry Newman, *Apologia Pro Vita Sua* (New York: Longmans, Green, and Co., 1890), pp. 193-195.

59. *The Convert*, p. 177.

60. "Catholic Popular Literature," *BrQR* (April 1873), p. 196; *Works,* XIX, p. 586.

61. *Ibid.*, p. 193; *Works* XIX, p. 583.

62. "The Christian Register's Objections," *BrQR* (October 1852), p. 462; *Works,* VII, p. 232.

63. "Archbishop Hughes on the Catholic Press," *BrQR* (January 1857), p. 136; *Works*, XX, p. 232.

64. *The National Catholic Register,* September 3, 1967, p. 5.

65. "Mrs. Gerald's Niece," *Works,* XIX, pp. 556-557. (Originally published in *The Catholic World,* January 1871.) This does not mean, however, that he experienced no pangs as he saw a gulf opening between himself and his former associates on the occasion of his conversion. It is plain, says his son Henry, that "when he separated himself from the Unitarian ministry to seek a home with those who had been strangers, though he did not choose to expose to the world the sacrifice he made for the sake of truth, yet it was not without anguish of heart that he saw the ties severing which had united him so closely with the most intelligent men and women of New England." *Middle Life,* pp. 208-209.

66. *Orestes A. Brownson: A Pilgrim's Progress* (Boston: Little, Brown and Co., 1939), p. 185.

67. "Catholic Popular Literature," *BrQR* (April 1873), p. 192; *Works,* XIX, p. 582.

68. *Middle Life,* pp. 157-166.

69. George Parsons Lathrop, "Orestes Brownson," *The Atlantic Monthly,* LXXXVII (June 1896), p. 779. Oran had been a Mormon. Brownson told Lord Acton during their four-day conversation at Mt. St. Mary's College, Emittsburg, Maryland, right after Brownson had delivered his lecture there before the Philomathian Society, in June 1853, that "they [the Mormons] had once hoped to make a Mormon of us and let me know all the secrets and true story." Acton's letter to Döllinger, XLIX, *Catholic Historical Review* (January 1964), p. 529.

Brownson asserted the very same thing in *The Spirit-Rapper* (1854). After describing the mysterious origin of Mormonism, and his close association with the Mormon prophets and Elders, he added: "They hoped to make me a convert, and spoke to me with the utmost frankness and unreserve." *Works,* IX, pp. 88, 100.

This is all the more credible on the ground that both Joseph Smith, the founder of Mormonism, and himself, were natives of Vermont. Brownson wound up by saying that "Mormonism is literally the synagogue of Satan." *Ibid.,* p. 100.

70. Microfilm of the *Brownson Papers,* roll 2.

71. *Ibid.*

72. M. J. Harson, "Orestes A. Brownson, LL.D.," *The Catholic World,* LXXIX (April 1904), p. 2. With at least one other member of his family becoming a Catholic, Brownson fared much better than John Henry Newman. After Newman's conversion his two married sisters, Harriet and Jemima, grew cold to him, not to say bitter. Jemima and her husband did not even want him to have any contact with their children, and the husband "more or less showed him the door." Meriol Trevor, *Newman, The Pillar of the Cloud* (New York: Doubleday and Co., Inc., 1962), pp. 349, 351, 523. Concerning an absolutely frigid visit Jemima paid her brother John Henry when she happened to be passing through Birmingham, see Charles Stephen Dessain, *The Letters and Diaries of John Henry Newman* (London: Thomas Nelson and Sons, 1964), p. 504. After Newman's death his brother Frank published a "most horrible brochure" on him, entitled: *The Early Life of Cardinal Newman.* Meriol Trevor, *Newman, Light in Winter* (New York: Doubleday and Co., Inc., 1963), II, p. 598.

73. *Ibid.*

74. Microfilm of the *Brownson Papers,* roll 3.

75. Theodore Maynard, *Orestes Brownson: Yankee, Radical, Catholic* (New York: The Macmillan Co., 1943), p. 140.

76. *Early Life,* pp. 519-520. In mentioning to Brownson the advantages he would enjoy in choosing Bradford in Concord for his tutor, Isaac added: "And last but not least in my mind is that I shall not be *so* very *far* from the invaluable *influence of your mind*; this last will be to me a means of gaining more in one moment than in days of indefatigable toil."

77. Fr. Vincent Holden, *The Early Years of Isaac Thomas Hecker* (Washington, D.C.: Catholic University of America Press, 1939), p. 213.

78. *Early Life,* pp. 516, 519.

79. Fr. Walter Elliot, *The Life of Father Hecker* (New York: Columbia Press, 1894), p. 90.

80. *Ibid.*

81. *Early Life,* pp. 538, 547. Hence Per Sveino is not quite accurate when he says, "He [Fr. Hecker] and Thoreau had even made plans for a trip to Europe, but their youthful plans did not materialize." *Orestes A. Brownson's Road to Catholicism* (New York: The Humanities Press, 1970), p. 301.

82. "Catholic Popular Literature," *BrQR* (April 1873), p. 192; *Works,* XIX, p. 502.

83. M. J. Harson, "Orestes A. Brownson, LL.D.," *The Catholic World,* LXXIX (April 1904), p. 9.

84. *Early Life,* p. 226.

85. Microfilm of the *Brownson Papers,* roll 10. Yet it was not in Brownson's nature to cultivate friendships overly much. George Parsons Lathrop, who knew him personally, has given us an explanatory thought on the matter when he wrote: "One impression of Orestes Brownson is that he was self-absorbed — as a man who had so much to study, to think of, and to write about might well be — he had no bosom friends. If he had no such friends in the sense of permanent cronies, he made up for the lack by his devoted affection for his family and the overflowing abundance of his kindness to mere acquaintances or strangers who sought his advice." "Orestes Brownson," *Atlantic Monthly,* LXXVII (June 1896), p. 779.

86. "Questions of the Soul," *BrQR* (April 1855), pp. 209-210; *Works,* XIV, pp. 538-539.

87. "A few Words on Dr. Brownson's Philosophy," *Dublin Review,* LXXVII (January 1876), p. 55.

88. "Dr. Brownson and Catholicity," *The Catholic World,* XLVI (November 1887), p. 235.

89. Under the heading, "Brownson, Orestes A.," the *Dictionary of American Biography,* vol. III, pp. 178-179, remarks: "He [Brownson] was still so much identified, in men's minds, with liberalism that his conversion to Catholicism in October 1844 came with much of the same shock that the conversion of Newman was to bring just a year later."

90. *Early Life,* p. 528.

91. Parker to Miss C. W. Healey, April 1843, John Weis, *Life and Correspondence of Theodore Parker* (New York: D. Appleton and Co., 1864), I, p. 353.

92. Microfilm of the *Brownson Papers,* roll 2. He added in his letter of July 28, 1843: "I never maintain controversy with you — as well might Portugal declare war against England and hope success to her arms."

93. *Early Life,* pp. 325-326.

94. Microfilm of the *Brownson Papers,* roll 2. To R. W. B. Lewis, however, Brownson's conversion was by no means without rhyme or reason. Boiling matters down Mr. Lewis remarked: "Whether his [Brownson's] trust in logic hastened his decision about Rome, one cannot easily determine. His brand of logic was of a sort indulged in far more by Romanists than by romanticists. And yet logic may not, perhaps, be the quickest path to traditional theology for any one who begins quite outside theology. The fact anyhow is this: that Brownson came to his opinion about 'communion' — and hence to his opinion about the value of tradition, and hence, belatedly, to the Church of Rome, not out of emotional ecstasy, or because of sentimental attachment to the art and architecture, but because the traditional doctrines were the ones that made sense to him." *The American Adam* (Chicago: University of Chicago Press, 1955), p. 186.

95. Dr. James A. Corcoran, "In Memoriam: Orestes A. Brownson," *American Catholic Quarterly Review,* I (July 1876), p. 567.

96. *BrQR* (January 1847), p. 136. O. B. Frothingham relates that Brownson's former associates adopted the agreeable notion of ascribing his "steadfastness to Romanism to his fatigue of intellectual traveling." *Transcendentalism in New England* (New York: G. P. Putnam's Sons, 1876), p. 129.

97. *Early Life,* p. 467.

98. *Latter Life,* p. 218.

99. "Dr. Brownson and Catholicity," *The Catholic World,* LXV (November 1887), p. 234.

100. *Orestes A. Brownson: A Pilgrim's Progress* (Boston: Little, Brown and Co., 1939), p. 283.

101. *Early Life,* p. 546.

102. It was this independent fearlessness in proclaiming the truth that made him such a unique Catholic apologist. Speaking of Brownson's services to the Catholic Church, Virgil Michel, O.S.B., said: "He probably rendered his greatest service by the fearlessness of tone in which he defended the down-trodden religion he had adopted." "Brownson: A Man of Men," *The Catholic World,* CXXV (September 1927), p. 757.

103. Microfilm of the *Brownson Papers,* roll 2.

104. "A Study of Dr. Brownson," *The Catholic World,* LXXVI (June 1903), p. 312.

105. Paul M. Thureau-Dangin, *The English Catholic Revival in the Nineteenth Century* (New York: E. P. Dutton, 1899), I, p. 249.

106. Newman's *Apologia Pro Vita Sua, ut supra,* p. 34.

## CHAPTER 22

1. "The Catholic Magazine and Ourselves," *BrQR* (April 1845), p. 259.

2. *Middle Life,* p. 3.

3. *Early Life,* pp. 544, 546.

4. *Middle Life,* p. 4.

5. *Orestes A. Brownson: A Pilgrim's Progress* (Boston: Little, Brown and Co., 1939), p. 107.

6. *Four Independents* (New York: Sheed and Ward, 1935), p. 237.

7. "Orestes Brownson," *The Atlantic Monthly,* LXXVII (June 1896), p. 237. This article is probably the most comprehensive magazine essay on Brownson's life and thought ever written. Brownson's son Henry furnished some of the content of the article.
   Speaking of Brownson's logical powers, the distinguished Dr. James Andrew Corcoran, theologian and orientalist, also said: "His logical power is simply wonderful; no sophistry, no specious reasoning of error or unbelief can stand before it." "In Memoriam: Orestes A. Brownson," *The American Catholic Quarterly Review,* I (July 1876), p. 563.

8. *The New World* (Catholic Newspaper of Chicago), April 15, 1938, p. 14.

9. J. R. Lowell, "Fable for Critics," *Works,* IX, pp. 44-45.

10. *Works,* II, p. 361 (originally published in *The Catholic World,* November 1867).

11. *Four Independents,* p. 238.

12. Vol. XLIII (May 1876), p. 690.

13. *Middle Life,* p. 641. Horace Greeley, editor of the New York *Daily Tribune,* rated Brownson "the ablest of all writers who use the English language." *Latter Life,* p. 373, n.

14. *Latter Life,* pp. 554-555. In a footnote to these pages Henry Brownson quotes a letter he had received from his elder brother, Orestes, Jr., in which he had commented on his father's literary style. He said: "You know better than I do the wonderful scope and power of his mind. He told me once, 'if I am a success in life, I owe it to my knowledge and use of my mother tongue, of English, Anglo-Saxon English,' and I find it so. There is such a command of language, such a felicity of expression, always the best word in every case, and withal such enthusiasm that although I never could and cannot yet agree with all his conclusions, I am lost in admiration at his language and infallible logic. (His example does more to prove a divine essence in faith than all else I have witnessed)." *Ibid.*

15. *Rhetoric in the Works of Orestes Brownson,* dissertation (New York: Fordham University Press, 1961), pp. 7-8, 218, 254.

16. Ray Allen Billington, *The Protestant Crusade 1800-1860* (New York: The Macmillan Co., 1938).

17. *Ibid.*, p. 346.

18. John Henry Newman, *Lectures on the Present Position of Catholics in England,* 6th. ed. (New York, 1889), p. 82.

19. Billington, pp. 74-75.

20. *Ibid.*, pp. 223-230. During the three days of mob rule thirteen persons were killed and more than fifty were wounded.

21. *Ibid.*, p. 226.

22. *Ibid.*, p. 89.

23. Sargent, p. 216.

24. Billington, pp. 231-232.

25. *Ibid.*, p. 181.

26. *The Flowering of New England,* 1815-1865 (New York: E. P. Dutton and Co., 1936), p. 248.

27. Theodore Maynard, *Orestes Brownson: Yankee, Radical, Catholic* (New York: The Macmillan Co., 1943), p. 210, n. 2.

28. "Brownson's Review," *Mercersburg Quarterly Review,* II (January 1850), p. 37.

29. "The Catholic Magazine and Ourselves," *BrQR* (April 1845), p. 260.

30. "The Catholic Press," *BrQR* (January 1849), p. 24; *Works,* XIX, p. 292.

31. "The Great Question," *BrQR* (October 1847), p. 430; *Works,* V, p. 549.

32. *The Story of American Catholicism* (New York: The Macmillan Co., 1941), p. 580.

33. O. A. Brownson, *The Spirit-Rapper, an Autobiography* (Boston, 1854), p. 73.

34. *The New England Mind, The Seventeenth Century* (New York: The Macmillan Co., 1939), pp. 112, 439.

35. "Cardinal Wiseman's Essays," *BrQR* (October 1853), p. 532; *Works,* X, p. 453.

36. *Orestes Brownson; Yankee, Radical, Catholic,* p. 165.

37. "The Christian Examiner's Defense," *BrQR* (July 1850), pp. 310-311; *Works,* VII, p. 210.

38. "Reply to the Mercersburg Quarterly Review," *BrQR* (April 1850), p. 191; *Works,* III, p. 51. *The Mercersburg Quarterly Review* was the journal of Mercersburg Seminary, Mercersburg, Pennsylvania, which had combined with Marshall College. Here appeared, says Sidney E. Alhstrom, "one of the most brilliant constellations of religious thinkers in American history." He further asserts that the *Mercersburg Review,* "at least during the years of Nevin's editorship [1849-1853], [was] one of the great theological journals of pre-Civil War America." He speaks of the charge of "Romanizing tendencies" brought against the Mercersburg Movement, and states that Dr. Nevin himself "for a while teetered on the verge of Roman Catholicism." *A Religious History of the American People* (New Haven: Yale University Press, 1972), pp. 616, 618-619, 621.

39. "Brownson's Quarterly Review," *The Mercersburg Quarterly Review,* II (January 1850), p. 36.

40. John Murphy, "Dr. Brownson and His Works," *The Irish Ecclesiastical Record,* IX (September 1888), p. 809.

41. *Middle Life,* pp. 97, 639-641.

42. *Ibid.*, pp. 97-98. Theodore Maynard misrepresented this matter when he suggested that this was an outburst on Brownson's part because he found "the Friday penance was so great as to make him irritable," that he "ate vast quantities of meat," etc. *Orestes Brownson: Yankee, Radical, Catholic,* p. 186, n. 9. There is no evidence at all to support such statements, nor does Maynard give any. Henry Brownson reports this incident as a highly deliberate piece of strategy on the part of his father in an effort to raise the morale of Catholics, which he gradually dropped when he noticed Catholics were becoming less apologetic about their religion.

43. Robert Speaight, *The Life of Hilaire Belloc* (New York: Farrar, Straus and Co., 1957), p. 204.

44. *The Convert* (New York, 1857), pp. 173-174.

45. *The Prose Writers of America,* 4th ed. (Philadelphia, 1853), p. 423.

46. "Dr. Brownson and Bishop Fitzpatrick," *The Catholic World,* XLV (April 1887), pp. 5, 7.

47. *Ibid.,* p. 7.

48. *The Yankee Paul, Isaac Thomas Hecker* (Milwaukee: Bruce Publishing Co., 1958), p. 441, n. 31.

49. *Orestes Brownson: Yankee, Radical, Catholic,* pp. 145, 162. Per Sveino has likewise been misled in this particular matter, perhaps by incautiously following Theodore Maynard. See *Orestes A. Brownson's Road to Catholicism,* p. 306.

50. "Hildreth's Joint Letter," *BrQR* (July 1845), pp. 349-350; *Works,* XIV, p. 263.

51. Microfilm of the *Brownson Papers,* roll 9.

52. *Orestes Brownson and the American Republic* (Washington, D.C.: Catholic University of America Press, 1971), p. 81.

53. "Dr. Brownson and His Works," *The Irish Ecclesiastical Record,* IX (September 1888), pp. 797-798.

54. "The Catholic Magazine and Ourselves," *BrQR* (April 1845), pp. 259-260.

55. "Lacordaire and Catholic Progress," *BrQR* (July 1862), p. 306; *Works,* XX, p. 252.

56. *The Convert,* p. 173.

57. "Morris on the Incarnation," *BrQR* (July 1852), p. 286; *Works,* XIV, p. 142.

58. Fr. Hecker, "Dr. Brownson and Bishop Fitzpatrick," *The Catholic World,* XLV (April 1887), p. 4.

59. "Brownson's Quarterly Review," *Mercersburg Quarterly Review,* II (January 1850), p. 49.

60. "Orestes A. Brownson, LL.D., a Man of Courage and a Great American," *The Catholic World,* XXIV (April 1904), 10, p. 11.

61. "Popular Objections to Catholicity," *BrQR* (July 1857), pp. 324-325; *Works,* VIII, p. 455.

62. Guide to Thomas Aquinas (New York: Pantheon Books, 1962), p. 40.

63. "Protestantism ends in Transcendentalism," *BrQR* (July 1846), p. 386; *Works,* VI, p. 131.

64. "The Christian Examiner's Defense," *BrQR* (July 1850), p. 301; *Works,* VII, p. 200.

65. "The Conflict of Science and Religion," *BrQR* (April 1875), pp. 157-158; *Works,* IX, p. 551.

66. *Middle Life,* p. 635. This incident has been misrepresented by Brownson's last three biographers, by Mr. Maynard, *Orestes Brownson: Yankee, Radical, Catholic,* p. 155; by Per Sveino, *Orestes A. Brownson's Road to Catholicism,* p. 169; and by Hugh Marshall, *Orestes Brownson and the American Republic,* p. 80. It is not at all improbable that the latter two biographers simply took their data from Maynard's misrepresentation in the matter. All three assert that Hoover was attacking the *Catholic Church.* No such thing. He was "violently abusing" Brownson personally, calling him a traitor, another Benedict Arnold, for having become a Catholic. No one of the three mention that Brownson had first given the man a fair warning of what he would do if he did not stop his violent abuse. When Hoover defiantly continued his violent abuse, only then did he get his due come-uppance. To tell the incident as these three have done (perhaps the latter two innocently) is to make a great bully out of Brownson. It may make the story racy, but it is simply not history. Either give the incident with its antecedents, or not at all. See *Middle Life,* p. 534.

67. *Ibid.,* p. 634.

68. *Ibid.,* p. 638.

69. *Latter Life,* pp. 272, 274.

70. "Brownson: A Man of Men," *The Catholic World,* XXV (September 1927),. p. 757.

71. *Lord Acton's Diaries, Fortnightly Review,* CXI (1922), p. 68.

72. "Acton's Letter to Ignaz Döllinger," *The Catholic Historical Review,* XLIX (January 1964), p. 525.

73. *Ibid.,* pp. 527-528.

74. *Early Life,* p. 477.

75. "Steps of Belief," *Works,* VIII, p. 380 (originally published in *The Catholic World,* December 1870).

76. *BrQR* (January 1847), pp. 129-130.

77. *The United States Catholic Magazine and Monthly Review,* IV (March 1845), pp. 155-156.

# CHAPTER 23

1. Arthur M. Schlesinger, Jr., *Orestes A. Brownson: A Pilgrim's Progress* (Boston: Little, Brown and Co.), p. 293.

2. *Middle Life,* pp. 13-14.

3. "The Church against No-Church," *BrQR* (April 1845), p. 194; *Works,* V, p. 395. Both Dr. Wiseman (later cardinal) and Spencer Northcote urged Newman, too, to write out a "succinct account of his reasons" for becoming a Catholic, or to put it in a formula. But he was afraid his meaning would be twisted and misunderstood. To Northcote he replied: "If I said for instance, 'I have become a Catholic, because I must be either a Catholic or an infidel,' men would cry out, 'so he has flung himself into the arms of the Catholic Church to escape infidelity,' whereas I should only mean that Catholicism and Christianity had in my mind become identical, so that to give up the one was to give up the other." W. Ward's *Life* of Newman, I, p. 121. More than twenty years after his conversion, he said: "I was converted simply because the Church was to last to the end of time, and that no communion answered to the Church of the first ages but the Roman communion, both in substantial likeness and actual descent. And as to my faith, my great principle was: *Securus judicat orbis terrarum.*" *Ibid,* II, p. 234.

4. Letter dated January 15, 1849. Microfilm of the *Brownson Papers,* roll 2.

5. *Ibid.*

6. *Ibid.*

7. "Thornwell's Answer to Dr. Lynch," *BrQR* (April 1848), p. 198; *Works,* VI, p. 427; see also *Middle Life,* p. 15.

8. *Middle Life,* pp. 16-19.

9. "Thornwell on Inspiration and Infallibility," *BrQR* (July 1848), p. 294; *Works,* VI, p. 473.

10. *Middle Life,* p. 19. Dr. Lynch was himself an able controversialist who became bishop of Charleston in 1857.

11. "Thornwell against Infallibility," *BrQR* (October 1848), p. 452; *Works,* VI, p. 519.

12. Microfilm of the *Brownson Papers,* roll 2.

13. "The Church an Historical Fact," *BrQR* (April 1846), pp. 153-154; *Works,* V, p. 462.

14. *Ibid.,* pp. 159-171; *Works,* V, pp. 468-469.

15. "The two Brothers; or, Why are you a Protestant," *BrQR* (April 1847), pp. 146-159; *Works,* VI, pp. 292-304.

16. *Ibid.,* p. 160; *Works,* VI, p. 305.

17. "The Church an Historical Fact," *BrQR* (April 1846), pp. 164-165; *Works,* V, pp. 473-474.

18. St. John's Gospel, 2, v. 48.

19. "The Church and the Republic, or The Church necessary to the Republic, and the Republic Compatible with the Church," *BrQR* (July 1856), p. 274; *Works,* XII, p. 2.

20. *BrQR* (October 1845), pp. 514-530; *Works,* X, pp. 1-16.

21. *Ibid.* (January 1845), pp. 76-98; *Works,* X, pp. 17-37.

22. "Native Americanism," *BrQR* (January 1845), p. 91; *Works,* X, p. 31.

23. "Catholicity necessary to Democracy," *BrQR* (October 1845), p. 516; *Works,* X, pp. 2-3.

24. "Native Americanism," *BrQR* (January 1845), p. 94; *Works*, X, pp. 34-35.

25. Ray Billington, *The Protestant Crusade: 1800-1860* (New York: The Macmillan Co., 1938), pp. 70, 124-125. Brownson's two articles were really a reply to Dr. Lyman Beecher who already in 1830 began a series of fiery anti-Catholic lectures in his Park Street church in Boston (popularly called "Brimstone Corner") in which he attempted to show that "Catholicism and despotism were definitely allied and equally opposed to American principles of republicanism" (Billington, p. 70). Beecher was scarcely outdone by any man of his day, unless by Samuel F. B. Morse, in his virulent attacks on the Catholic Church. As Sister Loyola, S.N., has observed in her study entitled "Bishop Fenwick and anti-Catholicism," Beecher's lectures "on the wickedness of 'Popery,' his denunciation of 'Romanism,' his impassioned, conglomerate ideas on 'Papism,' in his *Plea for the West*, indicate the bias and prejudice of the Presbyterian divine." *Historical Records and Studies*, XXVII, pp. 194-195. His incendiary speeches and the writings of Samuel F. B. Morse were the main incitements to the wild mob violence that laid the Ursuline Convent, Mt. Benedict, Charlestown, Massachusetts, in ashes, in 1834.

26. *The Course of American Thought* (New York: The Ronald Press Co., 1943), p. 55. R. H. Gabriel mistakenly refers to *Brownson's Quarterly Review* as his *Democratic Review*. Others have significantly made the same mistake.

27. "The Dangers of Jesuit Instruction," *BrQR* (January 1846), p. 86.

28. *BrQR* (April 1845), p. 265.

29. *BrQR* (January 1846), p. 57, n.

30. Milwaukee: Bruce Publishing Co., 1950, p. 296.

31. Robert C. Cross, *The Emergence of Liberal Catholicism* (Cambridge: Harvard University Press, 1958), p. 37.

32. "Transcendentalism — Concluded," *BrQR* (October 1846), p. 409; *Works*, VI, p. 82.

33. "Protestantism ends in Transcendentalism," *BrQR* (July 1846), p. 370; *Works*, VI, p. 115.

34. "Transcendentalism — Concluded," *BrQR* (October 1846), p. 437; *Works*, VI, p. 111.

35. *BrQR* (October 1844), p. 546.

36. *State of Mind, A Boston Reader*, ed. by Robert N. Linscott (New York: Farrar, Straus and Co., 1948). (See "Portrait of a Blue Stocking," Ralph Waldo Emerson, p. 216, n.) As correspondent of the New York *Tribune*, Miss Fuller went abroad in 1846, and met and married the Marquis Angelo Ossoli. Both took part in the Roman revolution of 1848. Sidney E. Ahlstrom tells us that Margaret "was a warm admirer of Mazzini and while in Italy served as a nurse in the Roman Republic uprising." *A Religious History of the American People* (New Haven: Yale University Press, 1972), p. 607. On a return trip to America, Margaret with her husband and child were lost in a wreck off Fire Island, New York, on July 19, 1850.

37. *BrQR* (April 1845), p. 273; *Works*, VI, p. 220.

38. *BQR* (January 1841), p. 129.

39. *BrQR* (April 1845), p. 254; *Works*, VI, pp. 225-226. Apparently this eloquent tribute goes mainly to Sally Healy, his wife. If so, it is one of the grandest that could be paid her. Later he wrote: "Men are but half men, unless inspired and sustained in whatever is good and noble by woman's sympathy and cooperation." *BrQR* (April 1873), p. 258; *Works*, XVIII, pp. 244-245.

40. "Brownson and the Woman Question," *The American Benedictine Review*, XIX (June 1968), pp. 211-219.

41. *BQR* (January 1841), p. 129.

42. *The Convert*, p. 99.

43. *Fascinating Womanhood* (Santa Barbara, California: Pacific Press, 1970).

44. *Latter Life*, p. 592.

45. *Ibid.*, p. 521; *Works*, XVIII, pp. 481-497.

46. *BrQR* (October 1873), pp. 509-529; *Works*, XVIII, pp. 398-417.

47. "Miss Fuller and the Reformers," *BrQR* (April 1845), p. 257; *Works*, VI, p. 229.

48. *BrQR* (July 1845), p. 273; *Works,* VI, p. 1.

49. "Transcendentalism, or the latest Form of Infidelity," *BrQR* (July 1845), pp. 304-305; *Works,* VI, pp. 31-32.

50. *Ibid.,* p. 315; *Works,* VI, p. 42.

51. "Transcendentalism — Concluded," *BrQR* (July 1846), p. 428; *Works,* VI, p. 102.

52. *Literary Criticism of Orestes Brownson* (Ann Arbor: University of Michigan, 1954), p. 328.

53. *BrQR* (July 1846), p. 369; *Works,* VI, p. 113.

54. "Protestantism ends in Transcendentalism," *BrQR* (July 1846), pp. 383-389; *Works,* VI, pp. 127-128, 134.

55. "Transcendentalism, or the latest Form of Infidelity," *BrQR* (October 1845), p. 441; *Works,* VI, p. 82.

56. *The Transcendentalists* (Cambridge: Harvard University Press, 1950), p. 8.

57. "Protestantism ends in Transcendentalism," *BrQR* (July 1846), pp. 391-392. This paragraph would seem to indicate that Brownson was personally a little more sympathetic to former associates, the Transcendentalists, than Theodore Maynard would seem to suggest. (See Maynard's *Life* of Brownson, New York: The Macmillan Co., 1943, pp. 172-173.) "Error is never harmless, and in no instance to be countenanced," was ever Brownson's premise, and he proceeded accordingly to demolish it. Nor is Maynard correct when he remarks relative to Brownson's thoroughgoing refutation of Transcendentalism, "Reading this in his Redemptorist novitiate in Belgium, Isaac Hecker must have winced" (p. 173). Isaac Hecker never saw a single copy of Brownson's *Review* in his Belgium novitiate. See Vincent Holden, *The Yankee Paul* (Milwaukee: Bruce Publishing Co., 1958), n. 31, pp. 441-442.

58. "Questions of the Soul," *BrQR* (April 1855), p. 215; *Works,* XIV, p. 544. Per Sveino asserts that insofar as the Transcendentalists rejected "the sensist philosophy of Locke and believed in the capacity of the soul to perceive intuitively ideas transcending the world of the senses, Brownson throughout his life remained a 'Transcendentalist.' " *Orestes A. Brownson's Road to Catholicism,* p. 158. This is an interesting statement, but may possibly be open to question. Certainly Brownson rejected Abbé Gioberti's faculty of the superintelligible, calling it "inadmissible," and "indeed a contradiction in terms." See *Works,* II, p. 276; see also vol. I, p. 469. To support his view Per Sveino quotes O. B. Frothingham, who claimed that Brownson was "essentially a Transcendentalist" when he wrote *The Convert,* and quoted from p. 135.

59. "Protestantism ends in Transcendentalism," *BrQR* (July 1846), p. 339. The last ten pages of this article were excised when the article was transferred to the *Works.*

60. "Transcendentalism — Concluded," *BrQR* (October 1846), pp. 438-439; *Works,* VI, p. 112.

61. "A Joint Letter to O. A. Brownson, and the Editor of the North American Review," *BrQR* (July 1845), p. 341; *Works,* XIV, p. 225. C. C. Hollis interestingly remarks on Brownson's alertness for correcting grammatical errors: "At first glance it may seem somewhat odd that Brownson should consider himself something of an expert on grammar. Yet the early limitations of his formal training had certainly a great deal to do with the unique situation. There is no other critic of like position and stature who goes so consistently out of his way to review judicially books and even elementary school texts on grammar and who corrects at such length (both seriously and humorously) the grammar of translators and writers of the day. Without the confidence in handling language that formal education might have provided, he kept grammar-guides at his desk always throughout his career as editor. Well into adult life, when most writers would probably scorn the practice, he made constant references to such guides for his own writing, and it doubtless pleased him to catch others napping." *Literary Criticism of Orestes Brownson,* dissertation (Ann Arbor: University of Michigan, 1954), p. 273.

62. *Ibid.,* p. 343; *Works,* XIV, p. 257.

63. *Ibid.,* p. 344; *Works,* XIV, p. 257.

64. *Ibid.*, pp. 345-346; Works, XIV, p. 257.

65. "Jouffroy's Ethical System," *BrQR* (January 1845), p. 60; *Works, XIV,* p. 273.

66. "Hildreth's Joint Letter," *BrQR* (July 1845), pp. 350-351; *Works, XIV*, pp. 264-265.

67. Brownson has been criticized for the statement that "Faith is not possible without the Church." (Encyclical letter of Pope Pius IX, *Quanto conficiamur moerore,* dated August 10, 1863, has been cited.) Perhaps, however, it has not been cited correctly if the article is looked at closely. In this article he is elucidating the conditions requisite for eliciting an act of public and *Catholic* faith. He did not deny the possibility of eliciting an act of theological faith outside "the ordinary course of God's gracious providence," such as was "no doubt elicited by individuals under the old dispensation, and for aught we know, is so elicited by individuals under the new." *BrQR* (January 1846), p. 25; *Works, V,* p. 447.

68. *BrQR* (April 1846), pp. 272-327; *Works,* V, pp. 481-531.

69. "Acton and Brownson: A Letter from America," The Catholic Historical Review, XLIX (January 1964), p. 529.

70. Maynard's *Life* of Brownson, Introduction, p. XIV.

71. Sidney A. Raemers, M.S., Ph.D., *America's Foremost Philosopher* (Washington, D.C.: St. Anselm's Priory, 1931), p. 23.


## CHAPTER 24

1. *The Literary Criticism of Orestes Brownson,* a dissertation (Ann Arbor: University of Michigan, 1954), p. 233. Mr. Hollis does not set much store by Fr. Virgil Michel's *The Critical Principles of Orestes A. Brownson* (Catholic University, 1918). He points out that only the first third of the thesis really concerns Brownson, and was prepared merely as a springboard for the presentation of his "own notions of what a philosophy of art should be. What he does in the last two thirds of his paper is provocative and stimulating, but really has no connection with Brownson's literary criticism" (pp. VIII, IX).

2. "American Literature," *BrQR* (July 1847), p. 390; *Works,* XIX, p. 208.

3. Norman Wegand, ed., *Immortal Diamond* (New York: Sheed and Ward, 1949), p. 41.

4. *BrQR* (January 1849), pp. 129-130.

5. "Dana's Poems and Prose Writings," *BrQR* (October 1850), p. 477; *Works,* XIX, p. 329.

6. *BrQR* (April 1849), p. 275.

7. *BrQR* (January 1849), pp. 130-131.

8. "American Literature," *BrQR* (July 1847), p. 396; *Works,* XIX, p. 213.

9. "Dana's Poems and Prose Writings," *BrQR* (October 1850), p. 466: *Works,* XIX, p. 318.

10. "The Works of Daniel Webster," *BrQR* (July 1852), pp. 365-366; *Works,* XIX, p. 366.

11. *BrQR* (January 1847), p. 136.

12. *The Brownson Reader* (New York: J. P. Kenedy and Sons, 1955), p. 174.

13. "Literature, Love and Marriage," *BrQR* (July 1864), p. 318; *Works,* XIX, p. 496.

14. "R. W. Emerson's Poems," *BrQR* (April 1847), p. 264; *Works,* XIX, p. 191.

15. *Ibid.*, pp. 275-276; *Works,* XIX, pp. 201-202.

16. *Orestes Brownson: Yankee, Radical, Catholic* (New York: The Macmillan Co., 1943), p. 216.

17. G. P. Lathrop, "Orestes Brownson," *The Atlantic Monthly,* LXXVII (June 1896), p. 780.

18. "The Works of Daniel Webster," *BrQR* (July 1852), p. 345; *Works,* XIX, pp. 346-347. Brownson asserted that the common law was the basic Palladium of our American liberties rather than the American Constitution, and should be guarded as

such. Leonard Gilhooley expresses the opinion that in his lusty fulminations against "Jacobinism" in the 1840s and 1850s Brownson was not so fearful of overt violence here in America as a subtle undercutting of the principles of the common law. "Since the effect of either violence or slow subversion of the law might ultimately be the same, Brownson feared that Americans might ridicule the possibility of violent revolution here, and overlook the similarly effective but more hidden threat of the gradual erosion of personal liberties." *Orestes Brownson and the American Idea* (New York: Fordham University Press, 1961), p. 321.

19. *Ibid.*, pp. 366-377 and *passim*; *Works*, XIX, pp. 366-377 and *passim*.

20. "Dana's Poems and Prose Writings," *BrQR* (October 1850), pp. 483, 487; *Works*, XIX, pp. 335, 339.

21. *Ibid.*, pp. 484-485; *Works*, XIX, pp. 336-337.

22. *Ibid.*, pp. 485-486; *Works*, XIX, pp. 337-338; also "Wordsworth's Poetical Works," *BrQR* (October 1855), pp. 532-533; *Works*, XIX, p. 425.

23. "Wordsworth's Poetical Works," *BrQR* (October 1855), p. 536; *Works*, XIX, p. 429.

24. "Dana's Poems and Prose Writings," *BrQR* (October 1850), p. 486; *Works*, XIX, p. 338.

25. *BrQR* (July 1856), p. 398.

26. *BrQR* (April 1850), p. 269. Brownson acknowledged that God had given John G. Whittier "noble gifts," but that he used them mostly in the service of unworthy causes. *BrQR* (October 1850), p. 540.

27. "The Vision of Sir Launfal," *BrQR* (April 1849), p. 269; *Works*, XIX, p. 312.

28. *Ibid.*, p. 272; *Works*, XIX, p. 315.

29. *Works*, IV, p. 423.

30. "The Sea-Lions," *BrQR* (July 1847), p. 399.

31. *Literary Criticism of Orestes Brownson* (Ann Arbor: University of Michigan, 1954), pp. 300-301.

32. *Ibid.*, p. 455, n. 23.

33. *Ibid.*, p. 306.

34. *Ibid.*, p. 313.

35. "The Scarlet Letter," *BrQR* (October 1850), p. 529.

36. *Ibid.*, pp. 529-530.

37. *Ibid.*, p. 530.

38. *Ibid.*, p. 531.

39. Randall Stewart, *Nathaniel Hawthorne, a Biography* (New Haven, 1948), pp. 97-98.

40. "The Scarlet Letter," *BrQR* (October 1850), p. 530.

41. *BQR* (April 1842), p. 252.

42. *BrQR* (October 1852), p. 561.

43. *BrQR* (January 1853), pp. 135-136.

44. *Ibid.* (July 1853), p. 413.

45. "Catholicity and Literature," *BrQR* (January 1856), pp. 76-77; *Works*, XIX, p. 460.

46. "Religious Novels," *BrQR* (January 1873), p. 67; *Works*, XIX, p. 573.

47. *Ibid.*, p. 63; *Works*, XIX, p. 569; also *BrQR* (January 1875), p. 150.

48. *Select Discourses from Newman's Idea of a University*, ed. by May Yardley (Cambridge: Harvard University Press, 1931), Discourse IX, p. 126.

49. "Grantley Manor," *BrQR* (October 1848), p. 50; *Works*, XIX, p. 263.

50. *Works*, XIX, "Mrs. Gerald's Niece," pp. 546-547 (from *The Catholic World*, January 1871).

51. "Recent Publications," *BrQR* (April 1847), p. 218; *Works*, XIX, p. 157.

52. "Thornberry Abbey," *BrQR* (October 1846), p. 539; *Works*, XIX, p. 136.

53. "Grantley Manor," *BrQR* (October 1848), pp. 482-506; *Works*, XIX, pp. 244-268.

54. *BrQR* (October 1853), pp. 413-414.

55. "Mrs. Gerald's Niece," *Works*, XIX, pp. 544-559 (from *The Catholic World*, January 1871).

56. *BrQR* (October 1850), pp. 537-538.

57. "Bancroft's History of the United States," *BrQR* (October 1852), pp. 423-424; *Works,* XIX, pp. 383-384.

58. *BrQR* (April 1853), p. 280.

59. *BrQR* (January 1855), pp. 136-137.

60. *BrQR* (January 1852), p. 139.

61. *BrQR* (January 1855), p. 142.

62. *BrQR* (October 1856), pp. 514-524; *Works,* XX, pp. 40-50.

63. *BrQR* (January 1858), p. 133.

64. *BrQR* (January 1857), p. 143.

65. *Middle Life,* p. 604. It is a curious fact that Newman in all his writings seems never to have referred to his contemporary Catholic historian, John Lingard, author of the eight-volume *History of England.*

66. *Tristam Shandy* (New York: E. P. Dutton and Co., 1915), Book III, Chapter XII, p. 131.

67. *BrQR* (January 1858), p. 134.

68. George H. Miles, "Alladin's Palace" in the volume, *Said the Rose and other Lyrics* (New York: Longmans, Green, and Co., 1907), pp. 99-100. Brownson himself seems to have been able to take literary criticism in good spirit, even in good humor as is seen in his review of "The Yankee in Ireland," *BrQR* (January 1860), pp. 126-127; *Works,* XX, pp. 89-90. Brownson once wrote: "If I know myself, which is very doubtful, I am more pleased with 'admonition and rebuke' than praise, of which I have had more than I desire." *Middle Life,* p. 493. This was evidently said on the score that enlightened criticism afforded him further opportunity for self-improvement. It reminds one of another of his statements: "He who helps me to correct my error is my friend." *Works,* IV, p. 2.

Newman seems to have felt a little differently about this matter. Writing to a friend, he said: "I wish to thank you for your favorable critique. I have been so bullied all through life for what I have written that I never publish without forebodings of evil. . . . There must be always that in what I write which really deserves criticism, yet I am more pleased when people are kind to me than when they are just." Paul M. Thureau-Dangin, *The Catholic Revival in England in the Nineteenth Century* (New York: E. P. Dutton, 1899), II, p. 248.

69. Microfilm of the *Brownson Papers,* roll 3.

70. *The Spirit-Rapper* (Detroit: Thorndike Nourse, Publisher, 1884), preface, pp. 1-2.

71. *Ibid.,* p. 83.

72. *BrQR* (July 1856), p. 406.

73. *Works,* IX, pp. 352-365 (from *The Catholic World,* March 1872).

74. Milwaukee: Bruce Publishing Company, 1933, preface, pp. xiv-xv.

## CHAPTER 25

1. Ignaz Döllinger regarded Newman "as the greatest living authority on the history of the first three centuries of the Christian era." Wilfrid Ward, *The Life of John Henry Cardinal Newman* (New York: Longmans, Green, and Co., 1912), I, p. 444.

2. "Newman's Development of Christian Doctrine," *BrQR* (July 1846), p. 347; *Works,* XIV, p. 6. Brownson admitted development in Newman's sense in discipline and the science of theology.

3. Ward's *Life* of Newman, I, pp. 160-161.

4. *Middle Life,* p. 35. Purcell then worked on Bishop Fitzpatrick of Boston to get Brownson into action against Newman's book. *Ibid.,* p. 483.

5. Microfilm of the *Brownson Papers,* supplementary roll 1. The other letter referred to is in this same microfilm division.

6. *Middle Life,* pp. 53-59.

7. *Fortnightly Review,* CXI (1922), p. 70.

8. Microfilm of the *Brownson Papers,* supplementary roll 1.

9. Paul M. Thureau-Dangin, *The English Catholic Revival in the Nineteenth Century* (New York: E. P. Dutton, 1899), I, p. 389.

10. *Fortnightly Review,* CXI (1922), p. 67.

11. "The Church and the Civil Power," *BrQR* (July 1875), p. 335.

12. *An Essay on the Development of Christian Doctrine,* second edition (London: James Toovery, 1846), p. 167; see also "Newman's Theory of Christian Doctrine," *BrQR* (January 1847), p. 69; *Works,* XIV, p. 58.

13. *Ibid.,* p. 27; "The Development Theory," *BrQR* (July 1846), pp. 349-350; *Works,* XIV, pp. 8-9.

14. Ward's *Life* of Newman, I, p. 184.

15. Charles Stephen Dessain, *The Letters and Diaries of John Henry Newman* (London: Thomas Nelson and Sons, 1962), XII, p. 42.

16. *Middle Life,* pp. 561-562; see also "Döllinger and the Papacy," *BrQR* (January 1873), p. 35; *Works,* XIII, pp. 352-353. Dr. Jeremiah W. Cummings, however, really directed Brownson's attention to the Latin wording of the Catholic Church's solemn definition of the Immaculate Conception. On February 26, 1855, he wrote Brownson: "By the way, have you read the Encyclical letter on the Immaculate Conception? Have you paid attention to the statement that the Church received the deposit of faith full and entire, in a reference to which 'nihil addit, nihil demit, nihil minuit' — and the other, that however a dogma may be illustrated and explained according to the mind of the Fathers, 'numquam crescit nisi in genere suo'? In other words, no dogma grows or develops that did not exist before, and however much it may thus grow and develop, it never 'grows' another dogma? Where, pray, are our old friends the Developmentists now?" *Middle Life,* p. 613.

17. "The Development Theory," *BrQR* (July 1846), p. 366; *Works,* XIV, p. 25.

18. "Newman's Theory of Development," *BrQR* (January 1847), pp. 39-86; *Works,* XIV, pp. 28-74.

19. *Middle Life,* pp. 41-53.

20. Ward's *Life* of Newman, I, p. 60.

21. Wilfrid Ward, *William George Ward and the Oxford Movement* (New York: The Macmillan Co., 1889), pp. 293-312.

22. Wilfrid Ward, *William George Ward and the Catholic Revival* (London: Longmans, Green, and Co., 1912), p. 9.

23. *BrQR* (January 1847), p. 130.

24. *Middle Life,* p. 43.

25. *Ibid.,* pp. 46-47.

26. *Ibid.,* pp. 68-69.

27. *Ibid.,* pp. 56-57.

28. *Ibid.,* p. 48.

29. *Ibid.,* p. 58.

30. Ward's *Life* of Newman, I, p. 553. Newman felt himself exempt from entering the field of controversy over his writings on the score that Truth eventually defends itself, and falsehood eventually defeats itself. He quoted Crabbe's lines to sustain his sentiments:

> "Leaving the case to Time, who solves all doubt,
> by bringing Truth, her glorious daughter out."

31. Ward's *Life* of Newman, I, p. 174.

32. "The Dublin Review on Developments," *BrQR* (October 1847), pp. 485-486; *Works,* XIV, p. 75.

33. *Ibid.,* p. 267; *Works,* XIV, pp. 118-119.

34. "The Dublin Review and Ourselves," *BrQR* (April 1848), p. 269; *Works,* XIV, p. 122.

35. *Middle Life,* p. 53.

36. Charles Stephen Dessain, *The Letters and Diaries of John Henry Newman, ut supra,* XV (1964), p. 495.

37. "Newman's Theory of Christian Doctrine," *BrQR* (January 1847), pp. 85-86; *Works,* XIV, p. 74.

38. *Ibid.*, p. 85; *Works*, XIV, p. 73.

39. *A Preface to Newman's Theology* (St. Louis: B. Herder Co., 1945), pp. 113-156. This matter is more thoroughly discussed in detail by Edward E. Kelly in his scholarly article, "Newman, Wilfrid Ward, and the Modern Crisis," *Thought*, XLVIII (1973), pp. 508-519. It is a rather amazing article in its disclosures. When Pius X condemned Modernism in his encyclical *Pascendi Gregis*, in 1907, Wilfrid Ward, who spent twenty-two years "almost buried in Newman's life and thought" preparatory to writing his biography, positively thought that Newman's "most characteristic teachings" were included in the condemnation of Modernism (pp. 511, 515). When Ward again wished to publish a third volume of Newman's letters, Newman's literary executors refused permission on the score that he considered Newman's thought condemned by *Pascendi*. Alfred Loisy held that Newman was "the spiritual father of the Modernists, and the initiator of the movement" (p. 518). Both George Tyrrell and Paul Sabatier asserted that Newman was implicated in the condemnation of *Pascendi* (p. 515). Even Cardinal Mercier advised Ward, when he was writing his two-volume *Life* of Newman, not "to try to defend Newman's Modernist connections" (p. 518).

Edward E. Kelly ends his article by asserting that although Newman's theory of doctrinal development was invoked a number of times in Vatican Council II, yet "very little has been done to contrast or even to relate this theory or Newman's other theological views with those of the Modernists, especially as they are represented in *Pascendi*. The tendency is to forget or ignore these things, just as Ward did in his biography. A thorough theological study of these relationships still needs to be written."

Yet, whatever the claim of the Modernists that Newman belonged in their company, we have the assurance of Pius X that the Modernists could not justly in any sense claim him. (See letter of Pius X to Bishop O'Dwyer of Limerick, Ireland, in Christopher Hollis' *Newman and the Modern World* [New York: Doubleday and Co., 1968], p. 200.)

40. W. Ward's *Life* of Newman, I, p. 16. Newman's former Oxford friend, Whately, then Anglican archbishop of Dublin, Ireland, thought Newman's book "more likely to make skeptics than Romanists. . . . Nor do I think," he added, "the R[oman] Catholics will like it at all." Meriol Trevor, *Life* of Newman, I, p. 370.

41. Edmund D. Benard, *A Preface of Newman's Theology* (St. Louis: B. Herder Co., 1945), p. 99.

42. Meriol Trevor, *Newman, The Pillar of the Cloud* (New York: Doubleday and Co., 1961), I, p. 401. It seems it was Bishop Michael Power of Toronto, Canada, who, when he came to Rome, brought to Newman the first two articles Brownson had written against his theory. In a letter to T. R. Knox, dated May 10, 1847, Newman wrote: "The other day the Bishop of Toronto was here. . . . He asked me if I intended to do anything about Mr. Brownson. I said I would answer categorically any question from a *theologian* — but that Mr. Brownson was a layman, moreover a layman who had lately been converted — who made him judge of good and bad tendencies of latent errors, of dangerous schools, etc., etc.? . . . Indeed I think he ought to go through a course of divinity before he attempts to decide on difficult points in theology." Dessain, XII (1962), pp. 77-78, n. Newman of course did not know that Brownson had gone through a systematic course in theology under Bishop Fitzpatrick of Boston, and that the bishop was backing him (not openly) on the stand he had taken.

43. "The Dublin Review on Developments," *BrQR* (October 1847), pp. 522-523; *Works*, XIV, pp. 112-113.

44. "Morris on the Incarnation," *BrQR* (July 1852), pp. 318, 320-321; *Works*, XIV, pp. 173-174.

45. *Ibid.*, pp. 320-321; *Works*, XIV, p. 175.

46. In a letter to J. M. Capes, founder of the *Rambler*, Newman said: "I am opposed to laymen writing on theology, on the same principle I am against amateur doctors, and still more, lawyers — not because they are laymen, but because they are *aútodidaktoi*. For this reason I am disgusted with Brownson." *Lord Acton and His Circle*, ed. by Abbot Gasquet, O.S.B. (London: Burns and Oates, 1906), p. xxiv.

Later Newman wrote: "It requires an explanation when a layman writes on theology." M. Trevor, II, p. 194. Brownson expressed his sentiments on this subject quite differently when he said: "Even the theological opinion of a layman is entitled to more weight than that of a priest or a bishop, if he is more richly endowed by nature, and has superior theological learning and science. The grace of orders confers the power of performing sacerdotal functions, which the layman cannot perform, but it is no part of Catholic faith or doctrine that it increases the quantity or quality of a man's brain, or the sum of his science and learning. Some bishops are great theologians, some can hardly be called theologians at all. The same may be said of some priests." "The Church is not a Despotism," *BrQR* (April 1862), p. 148; *Works*, XX, p. 225.

47. *Middle Life*, pp. 386-390.

48. In this respect, the comment of the distinguished English convert, Richard Simpson, in a letter to Fr. Isaac Hecker, concerning the controversy over Newman's theory, is interesting. He wrote: I think posterity will judge of their quarrel as it has done of that between Plato and Aristotle; that the latter, though the most acute and most formally logical, has failed to see what the other intended, and had therefore misapprehended him." *Middle Life*, p. 396.

Though sincere efforts for a mutual understanding seem to have been made on both sides, Brownson and Newman never did come to understand each other. It was basically a difference of temperament. The one was an American of Americans, the other an Englishman of Englishmen. "I would rather be an Englishman (as in fact I am), than belong to any other race under heaven," said Newman (*Apologia*, p. xvi). And so the twain ne'er did meet — not really. Brownson disliked particularly — and cordially — the Oxfordian philosophy Newman had brought with him into the Catholic Church. To rest certitude on a series of probabilities was to him unsatisfactory. It seemed too much like substituting guesswork for certainty in matters of religion. He remarked: "Dr. Newman confesses that his philosophy can only prove the probable existence of God, though the Holy See decides that it can be proved *with certainty* by reason." *Latter Life*, p. 575. Brownson evidently referred here to Vatican Council I of 1870 which declared that "the one true God, the Creator, can be known certainly by the natural light of human reason," thus asserting the rights of the human intellect and the validity of its operations. See Cuthbert Butler, *The Vatican Council* (New York: Longmans, Green, and Co., 1930), I, p. 276. Of Newman's *Essay in Aid of a Grammar of Assent* Brownson remarked that he could "make neither head nor tail." "Catholic Popular Literature," *BrQR* (April 1873), p. 202; *Works*, XIX, p. 592.

49. "Saint-Bonnet and Social Restoration," *BrQR* (October 1851), pp. 462-463; *Works*, XIV, p. 207.

50. *BrQR* (October 1854), p. 525.

51. When writing in October 1864, what must have appeared to him at the time his farewell to his fellow Catholics as Editor of *Brownson's Quarterly Review* ("Explanations to Catholics") he was perhaps slightly disposed to proffer peace offerings here and there. Although in that article he asserted that he had long suspected that he had done Newman injustice in the interpretation he himself had given his theory (*BrQR*, October 1864, p. 480; *Works*, XX, pp. 371-372), he reverted outright in 1873 to his original stand on the theory. "Catholic Popular Literature," *BrQR* (April 1873), p. 202; *Works*, XX, p. 592.

52. W. Ward's *Life* of Newman, I, p. 292.

53. "Fathers of the Desert," *BrQR* (July 1853), pp. 381-382. About this time, November 1852, Cardinal Wiseman wrote Newman assurances that his theory of development was in keeping with the traditional Catholic theology. This could be regarded as a sop thrown to Cerberus. Wiseman certainly had a real bill to settle with Newman. The assurances could well have been given partly in reparation for the calamity he had allowed to come upon Newman insofar as he himself had failed to produce the documents of evidence he had vouched for to Newman, and which would have forestalled the terrible Achilli trial (terrible to Newman). Newman himself referred to

Wiseman as the *origo mali* in the case. Wilfrid Ward, *The Life and Times of Cardinal Wiseman* (London: Longmans, Green, and Co., 1912), II, pp. 39-43.

About this time Cardinal Wiseman also expressed his great admiration for Brownson. After a visit with Wiseman on his travels abroad in 1854, George H. Miles wrote his godfather, Dr. McCaffery of Mt. St. Mary's College, Emmitsburg, Maryland, on December 4, that the cardinal "is full of Brownson, and longs to see him." Mary Meline and E. F. X. McSweeney, *The Story of the Mountain* (Emmitsburg, Maryland, 1911), I, p. 490.

54. *BrQR* (July 1875), pp. 335-336.

55. *Ibid.*, p. 335.

56. "Saint- Bonnet and Social Restoration," BrQR (October 1861), p. 462; *Works,* XIV, p. 207.

## CHAPTER 26

1. "Recent Publications," *BrQR* (April 1847), pp. 216-249; *Works,* XIX, pp. 155-189.

2. "The Great Questions," *BrQR* (October 1847), pp. 413-458; *Works,* V. pp. 531-576.

3. *BrQR* (July 1849), pp. 277-407; *Works,* X, pp. 207-238.

4. *BrQR* (April 1874), pp. 220-245; *Works,* V, pp. 578-584.

5. "Answer to Objections," *BrQR* (July 1874), pp. 433-460; *Works,* XX, pp. 393-414.

6. *Ibid.*, p. 439; *Works,* XX, p. 394.

7. *Ibid.*, p. 451; *Works,* XX, p. 406.

8. *BrQR* (January 1846), p. 136.

9. Said Brownson: "It is seldom we meet a Catholic, man or woman, priest or layman, who will permit us to say 'out of the Church no one can be saved,' without requiring us to qualify the assertion, or so to explain it as to make it *meaningless* [italics mine] to plain people who are ignorant of the subtilties, the nice distinctions, and refinements of the theologians." *BrQR* (April 1874), p. 221; *Works,* V, p. 578.

10. "Archbishop Spalding," *BrQR* (January 1874), p. 110; *Works,* XIV, pp. 503-504.

11. "Recent Publications," *BrQR* (April 1847), p. 234; *Works,* XIX, p. 173.

12. "Native Americanism," *BrQR* (October 1845), p. 530. The Hoover dramatic incident has already been mentioned, chapter I, vol. II.

13. "Answer to Objections," *BrQR* (October 1874), pp. 458-459; *Works,* XX, p. 413.

14. *BrQR* (July 1849), pp. 288-289; *Works,* X, pp. 217-218.

15. "Membership in the Church," CXII (January 1944), pp. 278-305.

16. "The Great Question," *BrQR* (October 1847), pp. 451-452; *Works,* V. pp, 569-570.

17. "Answer to Objections," *BrQR* (October 1874), p. 438; *Works,* XX, p. 394.

18. "Recent Publications," *BrQR* (April 1847), p. 234; *Works,* XIX, p. 173.

19. "The Great Question," *BrQR* (October 1847), p. 445; *Works,* V, p. 563.

20. "Answer to Objections," *BrQR* (October 1874), p. 443; *Works,* XX, p. 398.

21. "The Great Question," *BrQR* (October 1847), p. 441; *Works,* V, p. 559.

22. "Protestantism anti-Christian," *BrQR* (October 1873), p. 470; *Works,* VIII, p. 470.

23. "Life of Eliza A. Seton," *BrQR* (April 1853), p. 181. That this article was written by Archbishop Patrick Kenrick we know from Brownson himself. (See *BrQR,* "Answer to Objections," [October 1874], p. 439; *Works,* XX, p. 394.) Brownson asserted in 1874 that Archbishop Kenrick had turned out to be more strict in that article in his interpretation of the Catholic Church's claim of exclusive salvation than he himself had ever been. "While seeming in the outset," said Brownson, "to make the most liberal concessions to the latitudinarian theologians who would seem to hold that no one but bad Catholics is in danger of being damned, he concluded by being more rigid and exclusive if possible, than the *Review* had ever been."

24. "Answer to Objections," *BrQR* (October 1874), pp. 446-447; *Works*, XX, pp. 401-402. When the Roman theologian, Fr. Perrone, S.J., sent him his *Il protestantisemo e la regula de fede* for review, Brownson, while praising it highly, could not agree with the author in supposing so generally the good faith of Protestants. "He has never been a Protestant," he remarked, "and lends to them more of the qualities of his own Catholic heart than we believe them entitled to. . . . Their ignorance is crass and supine rather than invincible." *BrQR* (January 1854), p. 129.

A theologian who reviewed Fr. Gury's *Moral Theology (BrQR* [January 1853]), after minimizing the validity of what some regard as invincible ignorance, added: "It is worthy of remark, that Protestants never plead invincible ignorance as an excuse for refusing to believe" (p. 70).

25. "Extra Ecclesiam nulla Salus," *BrQR* (April 1874), p. 227; *Works*, V, p. 583.

26. "The Great Question," *BrQR* (October 1847), pp. 442-443, n.; *Works*, V, p. 562, n.

27. "The Great Question," *BrQR* (October 1847), pp. 444-445, n.; *Works*, V, pp. 562-563, n.

28. *BrQR* (January 1851), p. 130.

29. *Ibid.* (April 1861), p. 268. Pertinent to this Brownson said: "He who sacrifices the truth sacrifices charity, and he who sacrifices the truth needed — the precise truth needed — by his age or country, does sacrifice it. If the truth be offensive, and he tells it, it will offend, whatever the soft phraseology in which he tells it." *BrQR* (October 1847), p. 423; *Works*, V, p. 542.

30. "Answer to Objections," *BrQR* (October 1874), p. 459; *Works*, XX, p. 414.

31. "Civil and Religious Toleration," *BrQR* (July 1849), p. 283; *Works*, X, p. 212. Referring to the fact that Rousseau had asserted that this dogma is antisocial, Brownson set about explaining why it should not be so regarded: "Even though the dogma be asserted, our religion forbids us to judge any one. And no one knows how many now visibly outside the Church, may yet be joined to the Church at least invisibly, and so depart this life, while an undetermined number of those who live visibly in the Church may be eventually cast into exterior darkness." *Ibid.*, pp. 302-303; *Works*, X, pp. 231-232. The difficulty seems to be that at least to some the dogma appears to be asserted in a partisan spirit. Not so at all. All that is asserted is that no one can be saved except through Christ, and simply that the Catholic Church is Christ in society. The American bishops put the matter succinctly in their *Collective Pastoral Letter* (January 11, 1968, p. 33): "Outside of Christ, there is no salvation. . . . Outside the Church, no salvation."

The Catholic Church itself has never expressed any opinion on the number of those who, though living outside the Church, may be saved by being invisibly joined to the Church. It is interesting to note that the great Newman wrote a Dominican Mother Prioress in 1871 that he was disposed to believe that no more than seven thousand souls would be saved in each generation. Ward's *Life* of Newman, II, p. 344. This of course is vestigial evidence of his Calvinistic upbringing which will scarcely find any acceptance in modern thinking.

32. "The Great Question," *BrQR* (October 1847), p. 433; *Works*, V, pp. 551-552.

33. "Let us," he said, "love our countrymen too much to be ingenious in inventing excuses for them. . . . Let us from a deep and tender charity, which when need is, has the nerve to be terribly severe, or, if we are not Boanerges, breathe in soft but thrilling accents, in their ears, in their souls, in their consciences, those awful truths which they will know too late at the day of judgment. . . . Tell the truth in your own way, and by all means in a manner as little offensive as possible; but *tell it.*" "The Great Question," *BrQR* (October 1847), pp. 456-457; *Works*, V. pp, 574-575.

34. *BrQR* (January 1851), p. 130.

35. *BrQR* (January 1873), Introduction, p. 3; *Works*, XX, p. 383.

36. "Answer to Objections," *BrQR* (October 1874), pp. 437-451; *Works*, XX, pp. 392-406. When he reviewed Dr. Hawarden's *Charity and Truth*, who seemed to allow for exceptions, he observed: "To say then there are exceptions and some can be saved outside the Church, would be to say no less than that there are exceptions to salvation by Christ Our Lord, and give the lie to the Apostle when he says there is

none other name under heaven among men whereby we can be saved. If a single soul can get to heaven without the Catholic Church, it can get there without Christ, and the Incarnation is not necessary in the economy of salvation." *BrQR* (April 1861), pp. 267-268.

37. *Ibid.*, pp. 435-437; *Works*, XX, p. 392.

38. "Brownson, Hecker, and Hewit," *The Catholic World*, CLIII (July 1941), p. 402.

39. *Historical Records and Studies*, XLII (1954), p. 48.

40. *Latter Life*, p. 144.

41. Theodore Maynard, *Orestes Brownson: Yankee, Radical, Catholic* (New York: The Macmillan Co., 1943), p. 168.

42. "Civil and Religious Freedom," *BrQR* (July 1864), p. 283; *Works*, XX, pp. 217-218.

43. Maynard, p. 390.

44. "Civil and Religious Toleration," *BrQR* (July 1849), pp. 288-289; *Works*, XX, pp. 217-218.

45. "Recent Publications," *BrQR* (April 1847), pp. 216-249; *Works*, XIX, pp. 155-189.

46. "The Great Question," *BrQR* (October 1847), pp. 413-458; *Works*, V, pp. 531-576.

47. Maynard, p. 390.

48. "Answer to Objections," *BrQR* (April 1874), p. 448; *Works*, V, p. 403.

49. "Extra Ecclesiam nulla Salus," *BrQR* (April 1874), p. 226; *Works*, V, p. 577.

50. *Orestes Brownson and the American Republic* (Washington, D.C.: Catholic University of America Press, 1971), pp. 79-80.

## CHAPTER 27

1. *BrQR* (January 1849), p. 136.

2. "De Maistre on Political Constitutions," *BrQR* (October 1847), p. 468; *Works*, "Political Constitutions," XV, p. 566.

3. *Ibid.*, p. 473; *Works*, XV, p. 561.

4. *Ibid.*, p. 472; *Works*, XV, pp. 559-560.

5. *Ibid.*, p. 469; *Works*, XV, pp. 556-557.

6. *Ibid.*, p. 474; *Works*, XV, p. 562.

7. *The American Republic* (Detroit: H. F. Brownson, Publisher, 1895), p. 3.

8. "De Maistre on Political Constitutions," *BrQR* (October 1847), p. 478; *Works*, XV, p. 566.

9. *Ibid.*, pp. 468, 485; *Works*, XV, pp. 556, 573.

10. *BQR* (October 1842), p. 357.

11. "Works of Daniel Webster," *BrQR* (July 1852), p. 377; *Works*, XIX, pp. 376-377.

12. "Acton and Brownson: A Letter from America," *Catholic Historical Review* (January 1964), p. 530.

13. *Ibid.* (January 1838), pp. 33-74.

14. "Conservatism and Radicalism," *BrQR* (October 1847), p. 476; *Works*, "Legitimacy and Revolutionism," XV, p. 561.

15. *Ibid.*, pp. 454-467; *Works*, XVI, pp. 61-79. Brownson took the term *rebellion* in its strict sense. Replying to a contemporary writer who had used the word loosely, he said: "Justifiable resistance to tyranny there undoubtedly may be; but such resistance is not properly rebellion, for the tyrant is necessarily a usurper, and therefore without legal authority. To resist him is not to resist legitimate government, or government in the legitimate exercise of its power. But a *legitimate rebellion* is a contradiction in terms, and is as much as to say that law may be *legally* violated." *BrQR* (July 1848), p. 413.

Nor did Brownson fail to acknowledge that the current European revolutions had been provoked, and that tyrannical sovereigns had only themselves to blame. He remarked: "Our constant readers know perfectly well that we have no sympathy, republican as we are, with the European revolutions of the last century and the present; but they may not have observed that we have always maintained that those revolutions were, though not justified, provoked by the despotism and corruption of morals and manners which preceded them. Their causes, aside from the inborn corruption of human nature, are to be sought in the tyranny and licentiousness of the royal and imperial courts of Europe." "The Spiritual not for the Temporal," *BrQR* (April 1853), pp. 155-156; *Works,* XI, p. 54.

16. *Ibid.,* p. 477; *Works,* XV, p. 76.

17. Perhaps it was his disgust (momentary or otherwise) with the everlasting revolutions of the day that made him write to his friend Montalembert, on June 30, 1851: "Whether the American revolt from the British Crown in 1776 was justified or not, I am not in my own country called upon to discuss. In my own personal judgment, it was not; and I date the legality of our proceedings from the acknowledgment of our independence by Great Britain in 1783. . . ." *Middle Life,* pp. 327-328.

18. "Conservatism and Radicalism," *BrQR* (October 1848), pp. 478-479; *Works,* XVI, p. 78.

19. *Ibid.*

20. In his article "The French Republic," Brownson asserted that the old order in France had been broken up, and that therefore the French people were entirely free to reconstruct government in a form they judged best adapted to serve the nation. *BrQR* (July 1851), p. 365; *Works,* XVI, p. 225.

21. "Conservatism and Radicalism," *BrQR* (October 1848), p. 455; *Works,* XVI, p. 62.

22. "Democracy," *The Boston Quarterly Review* (January 1838), p. 36.

23. *Middle Life,* p. 176. John Henry McCaffrey was one of the more distinguished priests of the United States at the time. He was president of Mt. St. Mary's College and Seminary, Emmitsburg, Maryland, 1837-1872. In the meantime he was offered successively three bishoprics, that of Natchez, Savannah and Charleston. That his correspondence with Brownson lapsed with the approach of the Civil War may be at least partly explained by the fact that his views were quite pro-Southern and Brownson was an adamantine Unionist. "McCaffrey, John Henry," G. D. Mulcahy, *The New Catholic Encyclopedia,* Vol. 9, pp. 5-6.

24. "The Republic of the United States," *BrQR* (April 1849), p. 182; *Works,* XVI, p. 88.

25. *BrQR* (January 1847), p. 135.

26. Allen Nevins, *Ordeal of the Nations* (New York: Charles Scribner's Sons, 1947), p. 217.

27. "The Republic of the United States," *BrQR* (April 1849), pp. 182, 184; *Works,* XVI, pp. 88-89.

28. *Ibid.,* pp. 183-184; *Works,* XVI, pp. 88-89.

29. *Ibid.,* pp. 182-183; *Works,* XVI, p. 89.

30. "The Works of Fisher Ames," *BrQR* (October 1854), p. 512; *Works,* XVI, p. 389.

31. *Madison Papers,* p. 753; "The Republic of the United States," *BrQR* (April 1849), p. 193; *Works,* XVI, pp. 99-100.

32. *Ibid.*

33. "The Republic of the United States," *BrQR* (April 1849), p. 193; *Works,* XVI, pp. 99-100.

34. "Cooper's Ways of the Hour," *BrQR* (July 1851), p. 276; *Works,* XVI, pp. 329-330.

35. "Works of Fisher Ames," *BrQR* (October 1854), p. 512; *Works,* XVI, p. 388.

36. "The Republic of the United States," *BrQR* (April 1849), pp. 193-194; *Works,* XVI, pp. 100-101. Lawrence Roemer in his *Brownson on Democracy and the Trend toward Socialism* (New York: Philosophical Library, 1953) demonstrates how intelligently and courageously Brownson sought to interpose a demurrer in his day between our distinctive American type of democracy and the strong trend toward irresponsible democracy or socialism. Mr. Roemer has less admiration for

Brownson's *The American Republic* than for his other political writings. He feels that more of Brownson's vitality and personality went into his political articles written under the stimulus of the occasion, whereas *The American Republic* was written in a sort of a philosophical vacuum. Yet such a dispassionate disquisition should have favored a clearer and more systematic exposition of the whole body of his political principles. Every disadvantage has its advantage. But it is true that much of Brownson's best writing was done under the stimulus of the occasion. John H. Newman remarked that his *Essay in Aid of a Grammar of Assent* was the only work he himself had ever produced that had not been called forth by a challenge of one kind or another. Henry Tristam, *Newman's Autobiographical Writings* (New York: Sheed and Ward, 1957), p. 272.

37. "Slavery and the Mexican War," *BrQR* (July 1847), p. 363; *Works*, XVI, pp. 54-55.

38. *BrQR* (January 1846), pp. 62-89.

39. *BrQR* (July 1848), pp. 305-334.

40. *BrQR* (July 1848), pp. 415-416.

41. *Middle Life*, p. 125.

42. *BrQR* (January 1851), p. 135.

43. *BrQR* (January 1849), p. 136.

44. "The Licentiousness of the Press," *BrQR* (October 1849), pp. 536, 538; *Works*, XVI, pp. 139-140.

45. *Middle Life*, p. 226.

46. *Ibid.*, p. 143.

47. "The Licentiousness of the Press," *BrQR* (October 1849), pp. 539-540; *Works*, XVI, pp. 140-141.

48. *Ibid.*, pp. 536-537; *Works*, XVI, p. 138.

49. "Ventura's Funeral Oration," *BrQR* (April 1848), pp. 256-257; *Works*, X, pp. 70-71.

50. "The Licentiousness of the Press," *BrQR* (October 1849), pp. 541-542; *Works*, XVI, pp. 142-143.

51. *Middle Life*, pp. 227-228.

52. *BrQR* (January 1849), pp. 81-127; *Works*, X, pp. 79-110.

53. *BrQR* (April 1849), pp. 209-239; *Works*, X, pp. 136-168.

54. *BrQR* (October 1849), pp. 438-475; *Works*, X, pp. 169-206.

55. "Socialism and the Church," *BrQR* (January 1849), p. 93; *Works*, X, p. 81.

56. *Ibid.*, pp. 99-103; *Works*, X, pp. 88-91.

57. *The Roots of American Order* (Open Court, La Salle, Illinois, 1974), p. 458.

58. "Socialism and the Church," *BrQR* (January 1849), p. 108; *Works*, X, p. 92. This was probably more true of socialism in its rise and initial progress. It seems to have sloughed off somewhat its Christian habiliments or pretensions.

59. *Ibid.*, p. 108; *Works*, X, pp. 93-94.

60. *Middle Life*, p. 175.

61. "Catholic Yankee: Resuscitating Orestes Brownson," *Triumph*, IV (April 1869), p. 26.

62. *BrQR* (July 1850), p. 395. Speaking of his former days of "wildest radicalism," he said: "Our doctrine was even then, as it is now, that evils existing under a social or political order are to be removed by and in consonance with that order, never by its destruction, and, when not so removable, are to be patiently submitted to as the less evil of the two. . . . We were never of the no-government sect; we were never, strictly speaking, a revolutionist. . . . We never suffered ourselves to maintain that it is lawful to do evil that good may come. . . ." *Ibid.*

63. *Ibid.*, pp. 396-397.

64. "The Higher Law," *BrQR* (January 1851), pp. 85-87; *Works*, XVII, pp. 6-7.

65. *Ibid.*, p. 87; *Works*, XVII, p. 7.

66. *Ibid.*, pp. 87-88; *Works*, XVII, p. 8.

67. St. Paul to the Romans (chapter 13, verses 1 and 2).

68. "The Higher Law," *BrQR* (January 1851), p. 89; *Works*, XVII, p. 9.

69. *Ibid.*, p. 90; *Works*, XVII, p. 10.

70. "The Fugitive Slave Law," *BrQR* (July 1850), pp. 385, 393; *Works,* XVII, pp. 21-22.

71. *Ibid.*, p. 401; *Works,* XVII, p. 29.

72. "Sumner on Fugitive Slaves," *BrQR* (October 1854), p. 489; *Works,* XVII, p. 39.

73. "The Higher Law," *BrQR* (October 1851), p. 94; *Works,* XVII, p. 14.

74. *Ordeal of the Nation* (New York: Charles Scribner's Sons, 1947), II, pp. 61-62. Arthur M. Schlesinger, Jr., gives us the following interesting fact: "In 1854 the House demanded a copy of the Ostend Manifesto and related expansionist documents from President Pierce. The State Department, before sending over the papers, thoughtfully deleted an inflammatory page in which the Secretary of State instructed the American minister in Madrid to detach Cuba from Spain. Many years later an historian came upon the missing page in the files." *The Imperial Presidency* (Boston: Houghton Mifflin Co., 1973), p. 50.

75. "The Cuban Expedition," *BrQR* (October 1850), pp. 493, 496; *Works,* XVI, pp. 275, 277.

76. *Ibid.*, p. 496; *Works,* XVI, p. 278.

77. *Middle Life,* pp. 315-316.

78. *Ibid.*, pp. 301-302. His son George had also passed from this life on March 26, 1849. In a letter to her sister Betsy, dated March 26, 1850, the mother Sally wrote: "I often think, Betsy, of Rachel and those women that mourned for their children [two years old or younger] whom Herod slaughtered. . . . They refused to be comforted because their children were not." Microfilm of the *Brownson Papers,* roll 3.

79. "Austria and Hungary," *BrQR* (April 1852), pp. 195-226; *Works,* XVI, pp. 209-226.

80. "Webster's Answer to Hülsemann," *BrQR* (April 1851), p. 201; *Works,* XVI, p. 181.

81. *Ibid.*, pp. 199-200; *Works,* XVI, p. 180.

82. *Ibid.*, pp. 215-216; *Works,* XVI, p. 195.

83. "The Cuban Expedition," *BrQR* (October 1850), p. 497; *Works,* XVI, pp. 278-279.

84. "Austria and Hungary," *BrQR* (April 1852), pp. 226-227; *Works,* XVI, p. 225.

85. "The Message of the President of the United States to both Houses of Congress, December 2, 1851," *BrQR* (January 1852), pp. 132-139.

86. "Kossuth in New England: A full Account of the Hungarian Governor's Visit to Massachusetts," *BrQR* (October 1852), p. 551. Brownson claimed that Webster wrecked his chances for the presidential nomination at the time by his official support of Kossuth, that his letter to Hülsemann and his after-dinner speech and toast at the Kossuth banquet turned against him the whole influence of Henry Clay and his friends.

87. *Middle Life,* pp. 338-339.

88. "Webster's Answer to Hülsemann," *BrQR* (April 1851), pp. 229-230, *Works,* XVI, pp. 208-209.

89. Sidney A. Raemers, *America's Foremost Philosopher* (Washington, D.C.: St. Anselm's Priory, 1931), p. 22.

## CHAPTER 28

1. *BrQR* (October 1854), p. 537.

2. *Ibid.*

3. *Middle Life,* pp. 231-232.

4. *Ibid.* Mrs. James Sadlier, *née* Anne Madden, migrated from Ireland to Canada in 1844, and there married the publisher, James Sadlier. She wrote some sixty popular novels, most with Irish backgrounds, prominent among which are *The Red Hand of Ulster, The Confederate Chieftains, Willy Burke, Eleanor Preston, The Old House by the Boyne,* and *The Blakes and the Flanagans.* The last mentioned Brownson gave a full-length review. *BrQR* (April 1856), pp. 195-212; *Works,* XXIX, pp. 23-29.

5. *Ibid.*, pp. 233-234.

6. *Ibid.*, pp. 235-237.

7. *Ibid.*, pp. 137, 198.

8. *Ibid.*, pp. 192-198.

9. *Ibid.*, p. 237.

10. *Ibid.*, pp. 126-127. Dr. Cummings also wrote Brownson on January 28, 1849, to say: "I consider that I have a right to dislike here and there some of the little accompaniments of the principles you enunciate, but I take this occasion to say that as a *Roman* Catholic, I defy any theologian in the United States or any other states, to lay his finger on any statement (in the numbers of the *Review* I have seen) written by your pen since you mended it with the Catholic pen-knife, which can prove to be *unsound* in doctrine, or *unedifying* in tendency." *Ibid.*, p. 188.

11. *Ibid.*, p. 195.

12. *Ibid.*, p. 190.

13. *Ibid.*, p. 238.

14. "Brownson, Orestes, Augustus," *Appleton's Cyclopedia of American Biography* (New York, 1887).

15. *History of American Magazines*, vol. I, 1741-1850 (Cambridge: Harvard University Press, 1939), p. 688, n. 17.

16. *BrQR* (January 1853), p. 136. His friend Fr. McCaffrey wrote him: "I have noticed that even those, who always find you ultra, grow less cautious and timid in upholding the truth by reading your *Review*." *Middle Life*, p. 145.

17. *Ibid.* (July 1849), p. 412.

18. *Ibid.*, pp. 411-412.

19. Microfilm of the *Brownson Papers*, roll 3.

20. Albert S. Foley, S.J., *Bishop Healy, Beloved Outcast* (New York: Farrar, Straus and Co., 1954), p. 37.

21. *Ibid.*, pp. 20-21, 47.

22. *Ibid.*, pp. 29-30.

23. Microfilm of the *Brownson Papers*, roll 2. Regarding Brownson's sons who had entered the seminary, his close friend, George Allen, wrote him on August 22, 1852: "I well understand what a disappointment it must have been to you to find that your sons had not the vocation with which you hoped they had been honored." *Ibid.*

George Allen, a former Episcopalian minister in Vermont, became a Catholic in 1847. He was widely known for his classical, scientific and artistic attainments. He was made professor of Greek in the University of Pennsylvania. *Middle Life*, p. 166, n.

24. *Ibid.*

25. Microfilm of the *Brownson Papers*, supplementary roll 1.

26. Microfilm of the *Brownson Papers*, roll 3.

27. *Ibid.*

28. "Protestantism and Government," *BrQR* (April 1852), p. 264; *Works*, X, pp. 411-412. After Hugh A. Garland had completed his course of lectures in St. Louis, he sent a copy of them to Brownson, and he reviewed them in the article here referred to, in which, after giving the author credit for wide reading, and some reflection, he found his thought to be undigested and chaotic in nature, and the principles he unconsciously asserted to be such as would overthrow his proposed thesis.

29. *Middle Life*, pp. 340-344.

30. "Protestantism and Government," *BrQR* (April 1852), p. 264; *Works*, X, p. 412.

31. Katherine Burton, *Three Generations* (New York: Longmans, Green, and Co., 1947), pp. 84, 174.

32. *Early Life*, pp. 308, 311.

33. *Middle Life*, pp. 354-355.

34. Microfilm of the *Brownson Papers*, roll 3.

35. *Middle Life*, p. 360.

36. *Ibid.*, pp. 137-138, 351.

37. Microfilm of the *Brownson Papers*, roll 3.

38. *Ibid.*

39. Microfilm of the *Brownson Papers,* roll 9.

40. We have another thumbnail sketch of Brownson as he appeared on the lecture platform by an anonymous writer in the *Evening News* of St. Louis, January 9, 1854 edition. Said the writer: "We have listened, with much interest, to the lectures delivered by Dr. Brownson, on different subjects, before the Catholic Institute, and though we differ widely from him, we do him the credit to say, that we know few men who could discuss, with more ability, any subject presented to their mind. His intellect is of the highest order, and his attainments of a varied character. His appearance can hardly be improved upon, and his delivery fills exactly our idea of what it should be in a popular orator."

41. *The Republican,* of January 8, 1854, said: "In commenting on Dr. Dewey, Dr. Rice, and Dr. Brownson, we have to object to them, that they devote their time, their talent and their learning to the discussion of what may be justly termed mere sectarian divisions upon religious creeds and tenets." The writer thought them "productive of injurious results to society." The aim of Brownson was to eliminate "sectarian divisions" by working for religious unity, whatever the aim of the other two.

42. *The Shepherd of the Valley* (January 14, 1954), p. 4.

43. *Middle Life,* p. 443.

44. *Ibid.,* pp. 525-526.

45. *Ibid.,* pp. 608-609.

46. *Ibid.,* p. 612. Much of the data in the following paragraphs is taken from Dagmar LeBreton's article on "Orestes Brownson's Visit to New Orleans in 1855," *American Literature,* XVI (May 1944), pp. 110-114. To him goes the credit of having dug out the newspaper reports at the time on Brownson's lectures there.

47. *BrQR* (July 1858), pp. 413-424. Of Dr. Clapp Brownson said: "He is a man of large native powers, kindly and agreeable manners, a pleasing address, a cultivated mind, and much natural benevolence of heart." *Ibid.,* p. 414.

It is a matter of some surprise that there seems to be no evidence that the well-known Louisianan, Adren Rouquette, visited Brownson while he was in New Orleans. He was a great admirer of Brownson and his writings, and frequently quoted from his *Review* when he wrote *La Thébaide en Amérique,* a copy of which he sent to Brownson. Rouquette's religious epic of America, *L'Antoniade,* which he wrote in 1855, contains many references and tributes to the genius and courage of Brownson. Perhaps Rouquette was absent from the city on the occasion of Brownson's visit. *Middle Life,* pp. 565-566.

48. *Middle Life,* p. 525.

## CHAPTER 29

1. "You go too far," *BrQR* (January 1854), p. 102; *Works,* XI, p. 109.

2. "The Temporal Power of the Pope," *BrQR* (October 1855), p. 435; *Works,* XI, p. 154.

3. "Papal Infallibility," *BrQR* (July 1873), p. 326; *Works,* XIII, p. 416.

4. "The Edinburgh Review on Ultramontane Doubts," *BrQR* (October 1851), pp. 526-556; *Works,* X, pp. 328-356.

5. "The two Orders, Spiritual and Temporal," *BrQR* (January 1853), pp. 26-62; *Works,* XI, pp. 1-36.

6. *Ibid.,* p. 53; *Works,* XI, p. 27.

7. *Ibid.,* pp. 28-32; *Works,* XI, pp. 3-6. See also "The Papal Power," *BrQR* (July 1860), p. 275; *Works,* XII, p. 352.

8. "Temporal Power of the Popes," *BrQR* (April 1854), p. 202; *Works,* XI, p. 122.

9. "Newman's Reply to Gladstone," *BrQR* (April 1875), p. 238; *Works,* XIII, p. 506. In 1875 in his *Letter to the Duke of Norfolk* Newman, too, as Brownson noted, had accepted "as of divine right the pope's deposing power." *Ibid.,* p. 235; *Works,* XIII, p. 503. This was after the solemn definitions of Vatican Council I on the papal prerogatives of supremacy and infallibility.

Although Brownson freely owned that the deposing power was of "impracticable" application to the modern state of Christendom, he still felt that its use would be far preferable to the anarchical proceedings of "a Parisian or Berlin mob." "Gallicanism and Ultramontanism," *BrQR* (July 1874), pp. 323-324; *Works*, XIII, p. 471.

10. As Douglass Woodruff remarked when discussing *Church and State*: "The picture remains as it always has been, that the Church is exceedingly slow and reluctant to say anything that could trouble the minds of the faithful about their duty as citizens, or about indicating to individuals that they should refuse to obey a command of their sovereign." *Church and State* (New York: Hawthorn Books, 1961), p. 81.

11. "Uncle Jack and his Nephew," *BrQR* (October 1854), p. 416; *Works*, XI, p. 258.

12. "Temporal Power of the Popes," *BrQR* (April 1854), p. 194; *Works*, XI, p. 121.

13. *Ibid.*, p. 211; *Works*, XI, p. 129.

14. "The Spiritual not for the Temporal," *BrQR* (April 1853), pp. 151-152; *Works*, XI, p. 50.

15. "Temporal Power of the Popes," *BrQR* (April 1854), p. 211; *Works*, XI, p. 129.

16. "You go too far," *BrQR* (January 1854), p. 103; *Works*, XI, p. 110.

17. "Temporal Power of the Popes," *BrQR* (April 1854), p. 190; *Works*, XI, p. 117.

18. James Broderick, S.J., *Robert Bellarmine* (New York: Longmans, Green, and Co., 1950), I, pp. 258-276.

19. *Middle Life*, p. 516. Bakewell may have overstated the case a bit.

20. Bishop Michael O'Connor was reputed to be one of the ablest theologians in the country — "One of the glories of the American Church." See John G. Shea, *History of the Catholic Church in the United States* (New York, 1892), IV, pp. 68, 364, 419.

21. *Middle Life*, pp. 434, 487.

22. "Temporal Power of the Popes," *BrQR* (April 1854), p. 202; *Works*, XI, p. 123. Brownson remarked that he would not, though he still could do so consistently with the doctrine he was maintaining in his *Review*, take the oath of allegiance to the British Crown required of Irish and English bishops.

23. *Middle Life*, p. 488.

24. "Brownson's Review for January, Art. IV. 'You go to far,' " *Metropolitan Magazine* (March 1854), p. 110. Bishop O'Connor's first article against Brownson appeared in the February issue of the *Metropolitan Magazine*, 1854, pp. 53-54. In it he confined himself to a flat denial of the indirect power of the pope in the temporal order as inherent in his office.

25. *Ibid.*, p. 115.

26. *Ibid.*, p. 115.

27. *Ibid.*, p. 117.

28. *Ibid.*, p. 111.

29. *Ibid.*, p. 113.

30. *Ibid.*, p. 113.

31. "Temporal Power of the Popes," *BrQR* (April 1854), pp. 188, 191; *Works*, XI, pp. 115, 118.

32. *Ibid.*, pp. 188-189, 215-216; *Works*, XI, pp. 115-116, 119, 133-134.

33. *Ibid.*, p. 194; *Works*, XI, p. 121.

34. "Brownson's Review for April, Art. III. 'The Temporal Power of the Popes,' " *Metropolitan Magazine* (July 1854), p. 355. In rejecting the doctrine that the popes in the Middle Ages deposed tyrannical rulers by divine right, Bishop O'Connor may possibly have been somewhat influenced by the great John England, Bishop of Charleston, South Carolina (1820-1842), who held that it was only by a concession of secular princes that they exercised that right. Peter Guilday, *The Life and Times of John England* (New York: America Press, 1927), I, p. 368.

35. *Ibid.*, p. 359.

36. *Ibid.*, p. 362.

37. *Middle Life,* pp. 489-493.

38. *Ibid.,* pp. 492-498 and *passim.*

39. *Pittsburgh Catholic* (August 12, 1854), p. 182.

40. "You go too far," *BrQR* (January 1854), pp. 93-94; *Works,* XI, pp. 101-102.

41. "Gallicanism and Ultramontanism," *BrQR* (April 1874), p. 320; *Works,* XIII, p. 468.

42. Letter to the present writer dated March 7, 1936.

43. *Middle Life,* p. 502.

44. *Ibid.,* pp. 503-509.

45. Microfilm of the *Brownson Papers,* supplementary roll 1.

46. *Ibid.*

47. *Dublin Review,* 1900, p. 191.

48. *Middle Life,* pp. 500-501.

49. *Ibid.,* pp. 610-611.

50. Microfilm of the *Brownson Papers,* roll 3.

51. "Uncle Jack and his Nephew," *BrQR* (October 1854), pp. 429-430, n.; *Works,* XI, p. 136.

52. *Latter Life,* p. 147.

53. "Temporal Power of the Popes," *BrQR* (April 1854), p. 218; *Works,* XI, p. 136.

54. *Latter Life,* p. 92.

55. *BrQR* (July 1853), p. 410.

56. *Middle Life,* p. 508.

57. "The Church and the State," *BrQR* (July 1873), p. 367; *Works,* XIII, p. 440. Robert Bellarmine, too, had had a hard fight in his own day in defense of the deposing power of the Sovereign Pontiffs. After stating Bellarmine's doctrine, his biographer says: "The greater part of his life was spent in justifying it, and so far was he from being frightened by the clamor it raised that he wrote the following strong words in his unpublished book against Roger Widdrigton:

" 'Quamvis enim fortasse quaeri possit utrum sententia negans (Papae potestatem deponendi reges) sit proprie dicenda haeresis directe et principaliter, tamen dubitari non potest quin sit temeraria, erronea et heretica saltem reductive et secondario, ita ut sine pericula fidei catholicae defendi nequeat.' " James Broderick, *Robert Bellarmine* (New York: Longmans, Green, and Co., 1950), I, p. 267.

Brownson's statement parallel to this was: "We have said that we believe Catholic dogma requires us to maintain at least the *indirect* temporal authority of the popes, or to forswear our logic: by which we evidently mean, not that it is a Catholic dogma, but a strict logical deduction from it. This may be the case, and yet one who denies it not be a heretic; for the Church does not hold a man to be a heretic because he happens to be a poor logician." *BrQR* (April 1854), p. 191; *Works,* XI, p. 118.

58. "Gallicanism and Ultramontanism," *BrQR* (July 1874), p. 329; *Works,* XIII, p. 476.

59. "The Constitution of the Church," *BrQR* (July 1875), pp. 297-298; *Works,* XIII, p. 527.

60. "The Temporal Power of the Pope," *BrQR* (October 1855), p. 442; *Works,* XI, p. 161.

61. "Gallicanism and Ultramontanism," *BrQR* (July 1874), p. 323; *Works,* XIII, p. 470.

62. "Brownson's Works," *The Irish Ecclesiastical Record,* V (1884), pp. 13-21.

63. "Acton and Brownson: A Letter from America," *Catholic Historical Review,* XLIX (January 1964), p. 527.

64. *Latter Life,* p. 274.

## CHAPTER 30

1. *BrQR* (October 1875), p. 579; *Works,* XX, p. 437.

2. *Middle Life,* Detroit, Michigan, 1899.

3. *Orestes A. Brownson: A Pilgrim's Progress* (Boston: Little, Brown and Co., 1939).

4. *Orestes Brownson: Yankee, Radical, Catholic* (New York: The Macmillan Co., 1943).

5. *Granite for God's House, The Life of Orestes Augustus Brownson* (New York: Sheed and Ward, 1941).

6. "Native Americanism," *BrQR* (January 1845), p. 84; *Works*, X, pp. 23-24.

7. Coleman J. Barry, O.S.B., who made a close study of the immigrant Catholic racial groups of the last century, says: "Between 1830-1870 the Irish immigrants had come in the largest numbers, up to 50 percent above the German totals. But by 1865 the German had equalled the Irish influx and, from 1870-1890, the Germans led the field until the Italian immigrant movement began in earnest in the last decades of the century and thence continued as the dominant immigrant movement in the Church of the United States for many years." *The Catholic Church and the German Americans* (Milwaukee: Bruce Publishing Co., 1952), p. 7.

8. "Native Americanism," *BrQR* (July 1854), p. 339; *Works*, XVIII, pp. 385-386.

9. *Ibid.*, p. 337; *Works*, XVIII, p. 284. George Potter's book, *To the Golden Door, The Story of the Irish in Ireland and America* (Boston: Little, Brown and Co., 1960) describes in chapter 13, "The Icicles of Yankee Land," how the Irish were received in New England, particularly in Boston. Regarding the Yankee objections to Irish clannishness, Potter quoted the Boston *Pilot*, 1839, as saying: "We hear a great complaint against the Irish 'because they do not mingle with the people among whom their lot is cast, because they adhere to favorite customs, and enjoy their national likings and antipathies without the consent of the majority. But what does this amount to, but that they set the Yankees an example they would do well to follow, *minding their own business*'" (p. 277).

10. *Ibid.*, pp. 352-353; *Works*, XVIII, pp. 298-299.

11. *Ibid.*, pp. 346-347; *Works*, XVIII, p. 293.

12. *Ibid.*, p. 346; *Works*, XVIII, p. 293.

13. *Ibid.*, p. 345; *Works*, XVIII, p. 291.

14. *Ibid.*, p. 342; *Works*, XVIII, p. 289.

15. *Ibid.*, p. 347; *Works*, XVIII, pp. 292-293.

16. *Ibid.*, p. 351; *Works*, XVIII, p. 298. He had changed somewhat in this matter from his first article on Native Americanism in which he had said: "But what is the effort to confine political functions incident to citizenship to native-born Americans, but the attempt to found an aristocracy of birth, even a political aristocracy, making the accident of birth the condition of political rights? Is this Americanism? Shame on the degenerate American who pretends it." *BrQR* (January 1845), p. 80; *Works*, X, p. 20. But Brownson would claim that times had changed. And they had.

17. *Ibid.*, pp. 340-341; *Works*, XVIII, p. 287.

18. Arthur M. Schlesinger, Jr., *Orestes A. Brownson: A Pilgrim's Progress* (Boston: Little, Brown and Co., 1939), p. 215.

19. *Middle Life*, pp. 534-539.

20. "Aspirations of Nature," *BrQR* (October 1857), p. 500; *Works*, XIV, p. 574. It may be of interest to recall here that Brownson's wife, Sally Healy, was of Irish descent, at least partly. She was a cousin of the well-known John Healy, law partner of Daniel Webster, and one of the very best lawyers in Boston. Brownson himself often consulted him on legal matters. *Middle Life*, p. 468.

21. *Middle Life*, pp. 569-570.

22. Microfilm of the *Brownson Papers*, roll 4.

23. *Middle Life*, pp. 582-585.

24. "The Know-Nothings," *BrQR* (October 1854), p. 469; *Works*, XVIII, p. 321.

25. "Introduction to the last Series," *BrQR* (January 1873), pp. 3, 5; *Works*, XX, p. 321. Yet there is no question he remained American to the core to the very end. Writing on Brownson in the June edition of *The Atlantic Monthly*, 1896, George Parsons Lathrop, a former editor of that journal, quoted an old acquaintance of Brownson's as saying that he was "as intense an American as Washington, Jackson, or Lincoln," an assertion that will strike anyone as banal who has read his writings or

studied his character. If he was one of the acutest critics ever of things American, it was his deep patriotism that goaded him on to labor for improvement. "His observations on society," remarked Arthur M. Schlesinger, Jr., "has a profundity no other American of the time approached." *Orestes A. Brownson, ut supra*, p. 294.

26. "The Know-Nothings," *BrQR* (October 1854), p. 464; *Works*, XVIII, p. 316. As Robert E. Moffit has remarked: "He [Brownson] was unable to fathom the depth and bitterness of the Celtic rejection of the Anglo-Saxon 'way of life.' " *Metaphysics and Constitutionalism: The Political Theory of Orestes Brownson*, chapter I, p. 94.

27. "Native Americanism," *BrQR* (July 1854), pp. 353-354; *Works*, XVIII, pp. 298-299. The Irish came back at Brownson with an anonymous pamphlet titled *Brownson's Review Reviewed: Being a Mild and Vigorous Vindication of the Rights and Privileges of Adopted Citizens against the Assaults and Aspersions of Dr. O. A. Brownson by the Catholic Press of the United States* (Boston, 1854).

28. "Thébaud's Irish Race" *BrQR* (October 1873), p. 504; *Works*, XIII, p. 563. Not a single biographer of Brownson has even as much as referred to this article of Brownson on the Irish race, not even his son Henry in his three-volume *Life*. Yet it is of no small importance in the way of rounding out the thought of Brownson's July 1854 article on Native Americanism. In the October 1854 issue of his *Review*, p. 569, Brownson said point-blank: "Our Irish brethren were right in holding that to Americanize is to protestantize, and we were wrong in holding the contrary, at least at present."

29. *Ibid.*, pp. 492-493; *Works*, XIII, pp. 551-552. Yet some Irish journalists were not satisfied with Brownson's encomiums. In reply Brownson said: "No man has more ably defended the Irish than we did in our review of Father Thébaud's *Irish Race in the Past and Present*, for which more than one Irish journalist roundly abused us. Our warmest and most intimate friends are, and always have been with the Irish, but we sometimes feel it necessary to rebuke some Irish journalists who are perpetually obtruding their nationality upon us, and, in doing so, we do but remind them that it is they, not we, who are making national distinctions." "Protestant Journalism," *BrQR* (October 1875), p. 459; *Works*, XIII, p. 584.

30. Paulist Archives. Paulist Generale, Scarsdale, New York.

31. "Native Americanism," *BrQR* (July 1854), p. 351; *Works*, XVIII, p. 299.

32. The author of the article, "Theological Errors of the Day," *Dublin Review* (January 1864), after remarking that Brownson's "antipathy to the Irish race is well known, and breaks out here and there," added a footnote: "Dr. Brownson on more than one occasion charges the Irish (especially Edmund Burke) with having corrupted the English language. We believe that he could name no eminent Irish writer whose style has less of the Saxon or Anglo-Saxon in it than that of Milton, and the contemporary of Burke, Dr. Johnson; and that he could name no English writer in whom it is more conspicuous than Swift and Goldsmith. Among the writers who have taken their places as classics in our literature, decidedly the most un-English are the Scotch — Hume, Robertson, Sir James Macintosh, etc. — the latter especially in his history of England." pp. 92-93., n.

When he lectured in New Orleans in 1865 the *Daily Orleanian* resented his attitude toward the Irish and declared itself as "dissenting widely from Doctor Brownson in national views and opinions." Dagmar Renshaw LeBreton, *American Literature*, XVI, p. 212, 410-414.

33. *The Irish Ecclesiastical Record*, VII (1900), p. 476. Brownson was certainly not anti-Irish; if anything, he was slightly pro-Irish. Yet statements he made at times lent themselves to misunderstanding. How does one otherwise explain the charges which were to recur intermittently to the end of his life?

In a fragment of an undated letter, with no indication to whom it was addressed, Brownson wrote: "You dislike the Anglo-Saxon race. I do not. I dislike the English government in its practice since it became Protestant, but the Anglo-Saxon race I do not dislike, for I dislike no race. I believe that God made of one blood all the nations of men." Microfilm of the *Brownson Papers*, roll 3.

(Cf. the present writer's article, "Orestes A. Brownson and the Irish," *Mid-America,* July 1956, pp. 156-172.)

## CHAPTER 31

1. "The Know-Nothings," *BrQR* (October 1854), pp. 448-449, 466, 486; *Works,* XVIII, pp. 301, 318-319, 337.

2. *Ibid.,* pp. 450, 485; *Works,* XVIII, pp. 303, 336. But in dealing with national susceptibilities, was Brownson right when he said: "Questions which touch national feelings and habits, are, no doubt, delicate things to deal with, but we believe it the wisest way, when they must be dealt with, to approach them in a bold, straightforward, and manly manner, and deal them such a blow that no second blow need be struck"? *Ibid.,* p. 452; *Works,* XVIII, p. 304. This may well have been one of his serious errors of judgment.

3. *Ibid.,* pp. 450-451; *Works,* XVIII, pp. 303-304.

4. *Ibid.,* pp. 457-458; *Works,* XVIII, pp. 309-311.

5. John G. Shea, *A History of the Catholic Church within the Limits of the United States* (New York: John G. Shea, 1892), IV, pp. 360-362.

6. "The Know-Nothings," *BrQR* (October 1854), pp. 455-457; *Works,* XVIII, pp. 308-310.

7. *Ibid.,* p. 460; *Works,* XVIII, p. 312.

8. *Ibid.,* pp. 468-469; *Works,* XVIII, pp. 320-321. It was of Americanism in its political connotation that Brownson was speaking. It was a false tendency in Christian doctrine and spirit that Pope Leo XIII condemned under the term "Americanism" in his encyclical *Testem Benevolentiae.* It was so called only because the false tendency and spirit arose among some Catholics in America.

9. *Ibid.,* pp. 478-483; *Works,* XVIII, pp. 329-334.

10. Microfilm of the *Brownson Papers,* roll 3.

11. "The Know-Nothings," *BrQR* (October 1854), p. 483; *Works,* XVIII, p. 334. Of those trying to undercut and destroy his influence he certainly considered James Alphonse McMaster, editor of *The Freeman's Journal,* one of the most active and persistent offenders. In two letters Brownson wrote him, in July 1853, he complained to him bitterly of the knavish treatment he was receiving at his hands: "I complain," he said, "with justice of your rash assertions, your misrepresentations, and your statements and insinuations derogatory to my character as a man and my loyalty as a Catholic reviewer." After his narrative of complaints, he asked: "What is it, Mr. McMaster, that you wish? Do you wish to put down my *Review* and elevate yourself on its ruins? . . . I am at a loss to explain the motives of your attacks on me begun without any provocation on my part, when I was suffering no little reproach for calling myself your friend, and continued after your most solemn promises to discontinue." Microfilm of the *Brownson Papers,* roll 3.

12. "Native Americanism," *BrQR* (July 1854), pp. 338-352; *Works,* XVIII, pp. 285-289. Speaking of the Know-Nothings' anti-foreign accomplishments, Oscar Hanlin remarks: "The most prominent achievement was the disbanding of the Irish military companies which annoyed natives particularly because they carried off prizes at drills." *Boston's Immigrants* (New York: Atheneum Publishers, 1972), pp. 202-203.

13. *Middle Life,* pp. 528-529.

14. Ray Billington, *The Protestant Crusade, 1800-1860* (New York: The Macmillan Co., 1938), pp. 326-327.

15. "The Know-Nothings," *BrQR* (January 1855), pp. 127-134; *Works,* XVIII, pp. 350-356.

16. *Ibid.,* pp. 130-131; *Works,* XVIII, pp. 352-353.

17. *Ibid.,* pp. 120-121; *Works,* XVIII, pp. 343-344.

18. *Ibid.,* pp. 133-134; *Works,* XVIII, pp. 348-349.

19. *Ibid.,* pp. 133-134; *Works,* XVIII, pp. 355-356.

20. "A Know-Nothing Legislature," *BrQR* (July 1855), pp. 394-395. This article was not incorporated into Brownson's *Works.*

21. *The Protestant Crusade, ut supra,* p. 388.

22. *Ibid.,* p. 413.

23. *Ibid.,* pp. 414-415.

24. "A Know-Nothing Legislature," *BrQR* (July 1855), pp. 396-405.

25. *The Flowering of New England, 1815-1865* (New York: E. P. Dutton and Co., 1937), p. 248.

26. "The Know-Nothings," *BrQR* (October 1854), pp. 472-473; *Works,* XVIII, p. 324.

27. *Middle Life,* pp. 548-550.

28. Billington, p. 408.

29. *Ibid.*

30. "The Temporal Power of the Pope," *BrQR* (October 1855), p. 417; *Works,* XI, p. 137.

31. John M'Clintock, D.D., *The Temporal Power of the Pope* (New York, 1855), p. 120.

32. *Middle Life,* pp. 518-520.

33. *Ibid.,* p. 563.

34. Dom Edward Cuthbert Butler, *Vatican Council I* (New York: Longmans, Green, and Co., 1930), II, p. 6.

35. "The Power of the Pope," *BrQR* (October 1855), pp. 421-423; *Works,* XVIII, pp. 141-142.

36. *Ibid.,* pp. 423-424; *Works,* XI, pp. 142-143.

37. *Ibid.,* pp. 426-432; *Works,* XI, pp. 145-146. In his April edition of this year, 1855, Brownson also refuted with his accustomed power and logic two books, *Romanism in America,* and *The Papal Conspiracy Exposed,* respectively pp. 145-182 and pp. 246-270, which fostered the idea there was some recondite conspiracy on the part of Rome or Catholics "to take over" America.

38. "The Know-Nothing Platform," *BrQR* (October 1855), pp. 482-483; *Works,* XVIII, pp. 365-366. This is the precise distinction to which Cardinal Capalti, one of the presidents of Vatican Council I, endeavored to hold the fiery bishop of Bosnia, Joseph G. Strossmayer, in one of the most dramatic scenes that ever occurred in a General Council of the Church. Edward Cuthbert Butler, *ut supra,* II, pp. 270-272.

39. *Ibid.,* pp. 479, 486; *Works,* XVIII, p. 369.

40. *Middle Life,* pp. 553-559. Maurice John Farge did a thesis on Brownson relative to this whole matter under the title: *Orestes A Brownson as a Catholic Nativist,* 1962. Page one reads: "A thesis submitted in conformity with the requirements for the degree of Master of Arts in the University of Toronto, Spring, 1962." Joseph R. Frese, S.J., published a study of Brownson's articles on Know-Nothingism in *Historical Records and Studies,* 1939, XXVII, pp. 52-74.

## CHAPTER 32

1. Ray Billington, *The Protestant Crusade: 1800-1860* (New York: The Macmillan Co., 1938), p. 388.

2. Microfilm of the *Brownson Papers,* supplementary roll 1.

3. *Ibid.*

4. *Ibid.*

5. *Ibid.*

6. *Ibid.*

7. *Middle Life,* p. 589.

8. *Ibid.,* p. 590

9. *BrQR* (April 1845), pp. 263-266; *BrQR* (October 1859), pp. 540-544.

10. Microfilm of the *Brownson Papers,* supplementary roll 1.

11. *BrQR* (April 1855), p. 580.

12. *Middle Life,* p. 592.

13. *Ibid.,* pp. 592-593.

14. *Ibid.,* pp. 593-596.

15. *Ibid.*, pp. 521-522.

16. *Ibid.*, pp. 522-523.

17. Microfilm of the *Brownson Papers,* supplementary roll 1.

18. *Ibid.*

19. The novels of Huntington that Brownson had criticized were *Alban, or the History of a young Puritan,* and a sequel to *Alban,* entitled *Forest.* Though Brownson praised them in some respects, he did not agree with the author's theory of art. *Middle Life,* pp. 402-404.

20. *Middle Life,* pp. 601-606.

21. *Ibid.*, pp. 587-588.

22. *The Protestant Crusade, ut supra,* p. 407.

23. Microfilm of the *Brownson Papers,* supplementary roll 1. Henry tells us also in this same letter that his father had decided to move out of the state of Massachusetts if Catholics were disfranchised. One anti-Catholic plank in the Know-Nothing platform in 1855 called for the disfranchisement of Catholics. "The Know-Nothing Legislature," *BrQR* (July 1855), p. 396. This affair, therefore, could have had a little something to do with his removal to New York in this same year. Yet Brownson tried to dissuade Catholics from leaving the country for Canada because of the ugly doings and threats of the Know-Nothings.

24. Microfilm of the *Brownson Papers,* roll 4. Archbishop Francis Patrick Kenrick of Baltimore no doubt stated fairly correctly the reasons why the more eminent prelates in the country had feared or hesitated to go along with the high-toned papal doctrine Brownson had been proclaiming when he said in a letter to his brother, Peter Richard Kenrick, archbishop of St. Louis, on March 14, 1854:

"The Bishop of Pittsburgh has written [a paper] on the power of the Pope to repudiate the opinion of Brownson. He [Brownson] is piling up trouble for us, defending that temporal power for the Pope, which is generally not accepted [as essential to the Pope's office]. He does this in a style that is not temperate; and insinuates that it is the one genuinely Catholic teaching which we fear to handle. Later on non-Catholics will make [just] such charges against us." F.E.T., *The Kenrick-Frenaye Correspondence* (letters chiefly of Francis Patrick Kenrick and Marc Antony Frenaye, 1830-1862, Philadelphia, 1920, pp. 365-366).

## CHAPTER 33

1. *Middle Life,* pp. 579-580.

2. *Ibid.*, pp. 469-470. Referring for his evidence to a letter Newman had written Cardinal Wiseman on February 1, 1854, Fergal McGrath, S.J., concludes that the first invitation to become lecturer extraordinary at the university was extended by Newman to Ignaz Döllinger, then at the height of his fame as professor of canon law and church history at the University of Munich, and a member of the Frankfort Parliament. *Newman's University, Idea and Reality* (New York: Longmans, Green, and Co., 1951), pp. 215-216. But this is incorrect. Newman said distinctly in his letter to Brownson: "You are the first person to whom I have applied." *Middle Life,* p. 471. But it is true that Newman's letters to Brownson and Döllinger were written on the same day, December 15, 1853. (See Charles Stephen Dessain, *The Letters and Diaries of John Henry Newman* [London: Thomas Nelson and Sons, 1964], XV, pp. 504-506.) McGrath could find no evidence that Döllinger ever replied to Newman. He did reply on July 15, 1854, exactly seven months later, a much longer delay than Brownson's. *Ibid.*, XVI, pp. 225-226, n.

3. *Ibid.*, p. 471.

4. "Rights and Duties," *BrQR* (October 1852), pp. 523-550; *Works,* XIV, pp. 290-316. "Uncle Jack and his Nephew, Or Conversations of an Old Fogie with a Young American," *BrQR* (January, April 1854), pp. 1-30, 137-166; *Works,* XI, pp. 165-221.

5. *Middle Life,* pp. 471-478.

6. *Ibid.*, p. 479.

7. This letter has just recently been obtained by the present writer from the

archives of Newman's Birmingham Oratory, England, through the courtesy of Fr. Charles Stephen Dessain. It was not among the *Brownson Papers.*

8. *Middle Life,* pp. 479-480.

9. "Protestant Journalism," *BrQR* (October 1875), p. 448; *Works,* XIII, p. 574.

10. This letter has also been just recently obtained by the present writer from the archives of Newman's Birmingham Oratory, England. It was not among the *Brownson Papers.*

11. Newman, *My Campaign in Ireland,* p. xxxiv.

12. *Middle Life,* pp. 481-482. Newman says here that he "received letters from different places which have perplexed me very much." I applied to the Birmingham Oratory in quest of any letters Newman may have received protesting Brownson's appointment to the university staff. Little has been found. Only a note which Archbishop Cullen (of Dublin) added when he returned Brownson's letter to Newman which Newman had sent him (for inspection). Cullen's note, written on August 21, 1854, reads: "I inclose a letter from Dr. Donnelly now collecting in America [for the University]. He is of the opinion that Dr. Brownson should not be appointed professor. I believe Dr. Kenrick and Dr. O'Connor are of the same opinion. It would be well to weigh the matter well before you make any appointment." Dessain, XVI, p. 234, n. 3. Cullen said: "I believe Dr. Kenrick [Baltimore] and Dr. O'Connor [Pittsburgh] are of the same opinion." No doubt he was right about O'Connor, but it is much more likely that Archbishop Hughes (New York) and/or Archbishop Purcell (Cincinnati) were of that opinion rather than Archbishop Kenrick, Brownson's true and constant friend.

13. McGrath, pp. 216-217. There was a reason why Bishop Walsh had made his representations to Brownson "as delicately" as he could. Brownson had given Walsh's latest production, *The Catholic Offering: A Gift Book for all Seasons,* a favorable notice in the January 1852 issue of his *Review,* p. 140. He had also made use of the occasion to urge his readers to contribute to the university fund as collections had already begun in this country.

Fergal McGrath is unjust to Brownson when he says that "though an able and sincere man, he had picked quarrels with almost every one in America" (p. 216). Almost all of Brownson's battles were simply defenses against attacks made on doctrines he had advanced, such as those on the papal prerogatives, his interpretation of the dogma *Extra Ecclesiam nulla Salus,* the doctrines advanced against the false liberalism of the day, both religious and political. He did not go about picking quarrels with others as the sentence of McGrath would lead others to believe. If there is any exception to be made in the matter, it is his attack on Newman's theory of the development of Christian doctrine. Yet we must here remember that he was urged to the course he adopted by bishops. There is no question, however, that he was a dogged, dauntless battler for truth and justice as he saw it.

14. "Morris on the Incarnation," *BrQR* (July 1852), p. 293; *Works,* XIV, p. 148.

15. Rev. Walter Elliott, *The Life of Father Hecker* (New York: Columbia Press, 1894), p. 181.

16. "Morris on the Incarnation," *BrQR* (July 1852), p. 320; *Works,* XIV, p. 175. (This passage was also partly quoted in ch. 3, Vol. II, pp. 21-22, but as it is so meaningful in both contexts of the narrative its repetition seems called for.)

17. Cullen received this letter while he was rector of the Irish College in Rome, written on July 27, 1846. *Records of the American Catholic Historical Society of Philadelphia,* VII (1896), p. 456.

18. McGrath, p. 218, n. McGrath asserts that the signature of the author of the letter has become illegible, but that it came from a person evidently in authority. On page 188 (a note) he says the letter came from Rhode Island, but the note on page 218 seems to imply that it came from Baltimore. He quoted the correspondent as saying (p. 188, n.), "Dr. Newman has no greater admirer in America than Archbishop Hughes, and the Archbishop thinks somehow that he has had a great hand in Dr. N[ewman]'s appointment to the post of Rector."

19. "Native Americanism," *BrQR* (July 1854), pp. 329-354; *Works,* XVIII, pp. 281-300.

20. McGrath, p. 218. If he had been unjust to Newman in his description of his men-

tal powers, he now endeavored to make up for it generously when reviewing Newman's *Loss and Gain.* He said: "His [Newman's] powers are far more varied than we had supposed, and he is endowed with a genius of a far higher order than we had given him credit for. The book is a masterpiece of art. It is a genuine work, deep, earnest, free from all cant, from all sham, or artifice, and says just what should be said, and no more, and says it in the proper place and the most fitting words. . . . We are most happy that such a man as its author is the Rector of the new Irish University." *BrQR* (October 1854), p. 526.

21. Charles Stephen Dessain, *The Letters and Diaries of John Henry Newman,* XVI, p. 238. The postscript was marked "private."

22. McGrath relates that Arthur Griffith declared Dr. MacHale to be "the greatest of Irish archbishops of the nineteenth century." A man of great intellectual force, he was a good classical and Hebrew scholar, fluent in French, German and Italian, as well as his own native Gaelic, in which he had published his translations of the *Iliad,* parts of the Scriptures, and the *Melodies* of Thomas Moore. Having been professor at Maynooth, he had a wide knowledge of theology, history and literature, and was possessed of a "devastating dialectical power." He was foremost in organizing relief during the years of the tragic famine of 1846-1847. A Protestant nationalist, Mitchell Henry, spoke of him in the House of Commons as "that venerable man . . . whose name, for half a century, has been a household word wherever Irishmen are to be found." He was reputedly dubbed by Daniel O'Connell as "the Lion of the fold of Judah."

He appreciated what the illustrious name of Newman meant to the university, but he wanted its management left in the hands of the Irish bishops. Data taken from McGrath, pp. 91-93, 124, n., 199, n., 200.

23. McGrath, pp. 187-188.

24. *Ibid.,* p. 188.

25. *Middle Life,* p. 484.

26. Doran Whalen, *Granite for God's House* (New York: Sheed and Ward, 1941), p. 321.

27. Charles Carroll Hollis, *The Literary Criticism of Orestes Brownson,* dissertation (Ann Arbor: University of Michigan, 1954), p. 438, n. 89.

28. McGrath, p. 217. Newman also sent a letter of inquiry concerning Brownson's appointment to Robert Ornsby very similar to the one sent to Henry Wilberforce, on November 23, 1853. Dessain, XV, pp. 482-483. Ornsby in turn asked Frederick Lucas what he thought of the matter. Lucas, making certain observations, replied that he thought it "a good plan to invite him."

Robert Ornsby was assistant editor of the *Tablet,* and one of the three counselors Newman came to relay upon in organizing the university, the other two being Henry Wilberforce and Frederick Lucas, founder and editor of the *Tablet.* Newman appointed Ornsby professor of classical literature in the new university. McGrath, pp. 126, 322.

29. McGrath, p. 507.

30. *Ibid.,* p. 331.

31. *The Imperial Intellect, A Study of Newman's Educational Ideal* (New Haven: Yale University Press, 1958), p. 162.

32. McGrath, pp. 251-252.

33. *Ibid.,* pp. 188, n. 253.

34. *BrQR* (October 1859), p. 555. McGrath relates that in a letter of August 18, 1854, Newman remarked: "We shall have, I suppose, 'the nations' in distinct houses. We expect soon, not at once, from 60 to 100 Yankees" (p. 343). In a letter of February 1, 1857, he gave as random figures that England had contributed to the university fund altogether three thousand pounds while America's figure was sixteen thousand pounds. He added: "Ireland, however, has contributed the bulk, and contributes yearly" (p. 435).

35. Microfilm of the *Brownson Papers,* roll 4. Regarding the author of this letter, Meriol Trevor tells us: "Tom Arnold's mother and wife Julia were almost more horrified at his going to *Newman's* University than at his conversion, even though

they regarded Newman as responsible for that terrible event too." Julia continued to write Newman abusive letters "in spite of the fact that all he did was to find jobs for her husband." On one occasion Newman referred to her as "Xanthippe." The Catholic faith of her husband grew wobbly and tumbled on the occasion of the publication of the *Syllabus of Errors* (1864), "but he came back and died in the Church." Meriol Trevor, *Newman, Light in Winter* (New York: Doubleday and Co., 1963), II, pp. 151, 262, 369.

36. In a letter given in *Middle Life* which Brownson wrote on September 12, 1854, in response to Newman's request that he postpone his visit to Dublin, but which letter was never sent, he said: "The postponement you request would not put me to the least inconvenience, and is in fact what I desired and should myself have requested. I could not possibly have made arrangements to visit Europe during the next year, and I want at least a year to prepare my son to take care of my *Review* during my absence" (p. 482).

37. Sir John Acton, "Letter to Ignaz Döllinger," *The Catholic Historical Review* (January 1864), pp. 524-531.

38. *Middle Life,* pp. 471-478.

39. Dešsain, XVI, n. 2.

40. Hugh A. MacDoughall, O.M.I., *The Acton-Newman Relations: The Dilemma of Christian Liberalism* (New York: Fordham University Press, 1962), p. 12.


## CHAPTER 34

1. *Middle Life,* p. 478.

2. *Latter Life,* p. 1.

3. *Middle Life,* pp. 635-636. Fr. John Roddan, "an extremely capable and versatile priest," was the first Boston priest to be educated in Rome at the College of the Propaganda. Having lived in Rome during the days of the revolutionary movements there, he had come back to Boston with leanings toward radical theories. Through his great friendship with Brownson, however, he gradually came to a belief in more conservative ideas. After a fine record as pastor in Quincy, Massachusetts, he became the helmsman of the Boston *Pilot.* As the *Pilot* was not an official organ of the diocese, he enjoyed all the more fredom. When he died in 1858, his post was taken over by Fr. Joseph M. Finotti. Both priests did much for the *Pilot* in making it a scholarly publication. Roddan was deep and clear in his thought, while Fr. Finotti, with his great love for literature, brought to its pages many of the best Catholic writers of the times. Robert H. Lord, John E. Sexton, and Edward T. Harrington, *The History of the Archdiocese of Boston,* three volumes (New York: Sheed and Ward, 1944), III, pp. 744-745.

4. *Ibid.,* pp. 356-357. Although Fr. O'Callaghan was regarded as somewhat "eccentric," he was a "man of unusual talents," and was promoted to the office of procurator in the first synod of the diocese, held in August 1842. Michael J. Scanlan, *A Brief History of the Archdiocese of Boston,* p. 25. Fr. O'Callaghan was called "the Apostle of Vermont," the territory of his labors.

5. *Ibid.,* p. 637.

6. Microfilm of *Brownson's Papers,* roll 9.

7. *Orestes A. Brownson: A Pilgrim's Progress* (Boston: Little, Brown and Co., 1939), pp. 209-210.

8. *Orestes Brownson: Yankee, Radical, Catholic* (New York: The Macmillan Co., 1943), p. 151, n. 85, 193, 274.

9. Microfilm of the *Brownson Papers,* roll 9.

10. *BrQR* (April 1862), p. 140; *Works,* XX, p. 217.

11. *A History of the Catholic Church in the United States* (Notre Dame, Indiana: University of Notre Dame Press, 1969), p. 180.

12. "Liberalism and Socialism," *BrQR* (April 1855), p. 193; *Works,* X, pp. 535-536. This article of Brownson was on the Essay of Donoso Cortes, Marquis of Val-

degamas on *Catholicity, Liberalism* and *Socialism* (Madrid, 1851), and also on Pierre Leroux's *De L'Humanitie.* The Marquis of Valdegamas had been brought to Brownson's attention in a letter Montalembert wrote him on Easter Sunday, 1851. The Marquis was at the time Spanish ambassador to Paris, and was conspicuous among European intellectuals of the day. He belonged to a group that was planning a European quarterly review. Others of the group were Montalembert himself, Louis Veuillot, and De la Tour. Montalembert invited Brownson to become a contributor, urging that he would thus become more widely known in European circles. *Middle Life,* pp. 326, 405.

13. *Middle Life,* p. 31.

14. *Ibid.,* p. 29.

15. "Liberalism and Socialism," *BrQR* (April 1855), p. 185; *Works,* X, p. 528.

16. *Ibid.,* pp. 183, 206-211; *Works,* X, pp. 526, 538-543.

17. Microfilm of the *Brownson Papers,* roll 4.

18. *BrQR* (July 1855), pp. 316-322 (not included in the *Works*).

19. "Lacordaire and Catholic Progress," *BrQR* (July 1862), p. 323; *Works,* XX, p. 268.

20. "Le Correspondant," *BrQR* (January 1856), pp. 121-124.

21. "Le Correspondant," *BrQR* (July 1856), pp. 399-400.

22. *BrQR* (October 1856), p. 540. Neither did Newman have much liking for the ways of Veuillot. See Meriol Trevor, *Newman, Light in Winter* (New York: Doubleday and Co., 1963), II, pp. 198, 476.

23. "Religious Liberty in France," *BrQR* (July 1857), p. 398; *Works,* XVI, pp. 522-523. When Brownson criticized the *Univers* and its adherents in his article on "The Outlook at Home and Abroad," *BrQR* (October 1874), pp. 551-552, William Seton wrote him from Bozen, Tyrol, Austria, on October 31, 1874: "You are not a bit too severe on Louis Veuillot. He is the religious bully of European Catholics. He whips them into any shape he pleases." Microfilm of the *Brownson Papers,* roll 7.

24. *Latter Life,* pp. 54-56.

25. *Ibid.,* p. 57.

26. *BrQR* (July 1856), pp. 273-307; *Works,* XII, pp. 1-32.

27. *Latter Life,* pp. 57-58.

28. "The Church and the Republic," *BrQR* (July 1856), pp. 273-274, n.; *Works,* XII, pp. 1-2, n.

29. *BrQR* (January 1857), pp. 1-29; *Works,* XII, pp. 33-58.

30. *BrQR* (January 1858), pp. 102-127; *Works,* XII, pp. 79-102.

31. "Brownson on the Church and the Republic," *BrQR* (January 1857), pp. 1-2; *Works,* XII, pp. 33-34.

32. Wilfrid Ward, *The Life of John Henry Cardinal Newman* (New York: Longmans, Green, and Co., 1912), I, p. 584.

33. "Recent Publications," *BrQR* (April 1847), pp. 240, 247; *Works,* XIX, pp. 180, 187-188.

34. *Latter Life,* pp. 59-60.

35. Microfilm of the *Brownson Papers,* roll 4.

36. "The Rambler," *BrQR* (July 1856), pp. 400-402. *The Rambler,* first a weekly and then a monthly periodical, was founded by John Moore Capes, assisted by friends in 1848, and was mainly the organ of lay converts, mostly former Oxford men of a liberal cast of mind. Sir John Acton was the chief non-convert connected with it. Richard Simpson was one of the main contributors, and became its editor. Newman got himself into a peck of trouble when in a moment of crisis in the history of the magazine he briefly assumed the editorship. When it collided with ecclesiastical authority, its directors transformed it in 1862 into *The Home and Foreign Review* without any alteration in its animus. The *Munich Brief* and the *Syllabus of Errors* brought it to an end in 1864. (See Josef Altholz, *The Liberal Catholic Movement in England, The Rambler and its Contributors, 1848-1864* [London: Burns and Oates, 1962].)

How far Brownson was influenced by this liberal Catholic group, or influenced them, may not be easily determined. In 1856 he called *The Rambler* "by far the best

Catholic monthly in our language," so far superior to "your quiet, safe, humdrum periodicals." *BrQR* (July 1856), pp. 400-401. It is safe to say that Brownson was in sympathy with the general views and aims of the conductors of *The Rambler*. He wrote: "We may not accept their theology or their philosophy. We believe they mistake, in some measure, the means to the end they seek; but as to the end itself, the recognition of the science and literature of the age, and the enlistment of both in the service of the faith, we are with them, heart and soul." *BrQR* (April 1863), p. 159; *Works,* III, p. 595.

37. *Middle Life,* p. 15. Brownson's refutation is contained in five articles under the heading, "Derby's Letters to his Son," *Works,* VII, pp. 335-457.

38. Microfilm of the *Brownson Papers,* roll 3. This letter has been misplaced in the microfilms. It is with the letters of 1851, roll 3, but it should be with the letters of 1857, roll 4. The preparator of the Brownson papers evidently misread 1857 for 1851, the number seven being somewhat indistinct. The letter must necessarily belong to 1857 since Brownson did not complete his review of Derby's book until that time.

39. Paul M. Thureau-Dangin, *The English Catholic Revival in the Nineteenth Century* (New York: E. P. Dutton and Co., 1899), pp. 62-63, 70, 81.

40. *Ibid.,* p. 233.

41. "The Church and Modern Civilization," *BrQR* (October 1856), pp. 462-486; *Works,* XII, pp. 117-136.

42. "The Church in the Dark Ages," *BrQR* (July 1849), pp. 330-357; *Works,* X, pp. 239-266.

43. *Ibid.,* p. 339; *Works,* X, p. 248.

44. *Ibid.,* p. 338; *Works,* X, p. 247.

45. *Ibid.,* p. 340; *Works,* X, p. 249.

46. "Romantic and Germanic Orders," *BrQR* (October 1859), pp. 493-526; *Works,* XII, pp. 258-269.

47. *Ibid.,* pp. 495-496; *Works,* XII, pp. 240-241.

48. *Ibid.,* pp. 502-526; *Works,* XII, pp. 247-269.

49. *BrQR* (January 1853), p. 132.

50. "Romantic and Germanic Orders," *BrQR* (October 1859), p. 507; *Works,* XII, p. 251.

51. "Religious Liberty in France," *BrQR* (July 1857), p. 403; *Works,* XVI, p. 526.

52. "Conversations of Our Club," *BrQR* (July 1859), pp. 314-324; *Works,* XI, pp. 542-551.

53. *The Convert* (September 1857), p. 2.

54. "Dr. Brownson's Road to the Church," *The Catholic World,* XVI (October 1887), pp. 3-4. The chasm between the natural and the supernatural cannot, humanly speaking, be bridged, i.e., by reason, but no doubt what Fr. Hecker meant is that Brownson showed the harmony between the two by removing philosophically any seeming antagonism.

55. *Orestes A. Brownson's Road to Catholicism* (New York: The Humanities Press, 1970), p. 304.

56. *The Convert,* p. 171.

57. "Answers to Objections," *BrQR* (October 1874), p. 459; *Works,* XX, p. 413.

58. *The Convert,* p. 181.

59. *Ibid.,* pp. 189-190.

60. Microfilm of the *Brownson Papers,* roll 4.

61. *Ibid.*

## CHAPTER 35

1. "The Most Rev. John Hughes, D.D.," *BrQR* (January 1874), p. 78; *Works,* XIV, pp. 485-486.

2. F. D. Cohalan, "Hughes, John Joseph," the *New Catholic Encyclopedia,* VII, pp. 196-198.

3. *Orestes Brownson: Yankee, Radical, Catholic* (New York: The Macmillan Co., 1943), p. 248.

4. *BrQR* (April 1862), p. 78; *Works*, XX, p. 217.

5. *Latter Life*, p. 67. In his *Life of the Most Reverend John Hughes*, D.D., first archbishop of New York (New York: D. Appleton and Co., 1866) John R. G. Hassard says that Hughes made a number of "hostile and ironical remarks" to the speaker "vastly to the entertainment of the audience" (p. 383).

6. *Latter Life*, pp. 67-72.

7. *Ibid.*, p. 73.

8. *Ibid.*, pp. 73-74.

9. *United States Documents in the Propaganda Fide Archives* (Rome), first series, vol. II, ed. by Finbar Kenneally, O.F.M., Academy of American Franciscan History, Washington, D.C., 1966. Folio (letter) no. 1034. (Microfilm copy in the University of Notre Dame archives. The letter was originally in French.)

10. "The Most Rev. John Hughes," *BrQR* (January 1874), pp. 81-82; *Works*, XIV, p. 489. However, in speaking so often against foreignism in the Catholic Church, he may well at times have appeared to favor a native clergy.

11. *Latter Life*, pp. 80-82.

12. "The Most Rev. John Hughes," *BrQR* (January 1874), pp. 85-86; *Works*, XIV, p. 493.

13. "Archbishop Hughes and the Catholic Press," *BrQR* (January 1857), p. 121; *Works*, p. 56.

14. Wilfrid Ward, *The Life of John Henry Cardinal Newman* (New York: Longmans, Green, and Co., 1912), I, p. 14.

15. "Mission of America," *BrQR* (October 1856), pp. 409-412; *Works*, XI, pp. 551-554.

16. *Ibid.*, p. 414; *Works*, XI, p. 556.

17. *Ibid.*, p. 483; *Works*, XI, p. 579.

18. *Latter Life*, pp. 82-83.

19. *Ibid.*, p. 77.

20. "Archbishop Hughes and the Catholic Press," *BrQR* (January 1857), p. 134; *Works*, XX, p. 66.

21. *Ibid.*, pp. 129-132; *Works*, XX, pp. 60-65.

22. Letter to Ambrose St. John, dated October 30, 1856. F. McGrath, *Newman's University, Idea and Reality* (New York: Longmans, Green, and Co., 1951), p. 424.

23. *Latter Life*, p. 67.

24. *Ibid.*, pp. 71-72.

25. *BrQR* (April 1855), p. 211; *Works*, XIV, p. 540.

26. "Archbishop Hughes and the Catholic Press," *BrQR* (January 1857), pp. 131-132; *Works*, XX, pp. 60-64.

27. *Latter Life*, pp. 171-172.

28. *Ibid.*, p. 77.

29. Microfilm of the *Brownson Papers*, roll 4.

30. In regard to this matter, Leonard Gilhooley knowingly remarked: "It should also be noted here that Brownson calls Isaac Hecker the 'godfather' of this article, and says that the latter 'inspired' it. . . . Nevertheless, a reader must note, *mutatis mutandis*, the closeness of its argument [in 'Mission of America'] to the American Idea of Brownson's youth." Dissertation, *Orestes Brownson and the American Idea* (New York: Fordham University Press, 1961), p. 276, n. 69.

31. Microfilm of the *Brownson Papers*, roll 7.

32. "Most Reverend John Hughes," *BrQR* (January 1874), p. 81; *Works*, XIV, p. 489.

33. Quoted in "Archbishop Hughes on the Catholic Press," *BrQR* (January 1857), p. 118; *Works*, XX, p. 54.

34. *BrQR* (October 1857), pp. 492, 494-495; *Works*, XIV, pp. 566-567, 569.

35. "Archbishop Hughes on the Catholic Press," *BrQR* (January 1857), p. 139; *Works*, XX, pp. 70-71.

36. *Latter Life*, pp. 70-71.

37. *BrQR* (July 1857), pp. 349-374; *Works*, XII, pp. 136-160. See also Josef Al-

tholz's *The Liberal Catholic Movement in England,* The Rambler and its Contributors, 1848-1864 (London: Burns and Oates, 1962).

38. *Latter Life,* p. 119.

39. *The Yankee Paul, Isaac Thomas Hecker* (Milwaukee: Bruce Publishing Co., 1958), pp. 321-322.

40. *Latter Life,* p. 119.

41. *Ibid.,* p. 214.

42. Microfilm of the *Brownson Papers,* roll 4.

43. *Ibid.*

44. *The Yankee Paul,* p. 324.

45. *BrQR* (October 1857), p. 496; *Works,* XIV, p. 570.

46. Paul M. Thureau-Dangin, *The English Catholic Revival in the Nineteenth Century* (New York: E. P. Dutton and Co., 1899), II, pp. 196-197.

47. Microfilm of the *Brownson Papers,* roll 4, letter dated September 29, 1857.

48. *Ibid.*

49. Archives of the Paulist Fathers, New York (hereafter cited as *APF), Hecker Papers,* an audience with the Holy Father on December 18, 1857.

50. "Aspirations of Nature," *BrQR* (October 1857), p. 502; *Works,* XIV, p. 576.

51. Microfilm of the *Brownson Papers,* roll 4.

52. *Latter Life,* pp. 128-129. His lecture in the Academy of Music, New York, netted him, all expenses paid, $1,018.65. The testimonial letter accompanying the check read: "Your audience on the occasion numbered, as near as can be ascertained, five thousand three hundred and sixty six persons; and in respectability and intelligence not inferior to any that assembled within the noble edifice in which it [the lecture] was delivered."

He also received at this time a generous sum from a company of twenty-four priests who signed their names to this testimonial of esteem:

"Dear Mr. Brownson: Please accept the enclosed small present which a few of your friends have given me to present to you. They wish you to regard it as a mark of esteem and of their appreciation of your labors of love for the Church of God. They hope also that this expression of their esteem and appreciation may cheer you up in the hour of literary toil and in the hour of chivalrous fight for the cause of truth. Please accept it, seeing the spirit in which they offer it, and enroll them among the number of your friends and well-wishers. Allow me also to express to you my own sincere regard and to subscribe myself yours, Thomas Farrell." *Ibid.*

Brownson also received now and then scattered individual gifts. Archbishop F. P. Kenrick sent after him $50 when he left Baltimore hurriedly after lecturing there in May 1857. When Fr. Hecker was on a mission in Savannah, Georgia, in January 1857, some anonymous donor handed him $50 to be given to Brownson. Microfilm of the *Brownson Papers,* roll 4.

53. *Latter Life,* pp. 127-128.

54. *Ibid.,* pp. 126-127.

55. *Ibid.,* pp. 92-93.

56. Microfilm of the *Brownson Papers,* roll 4.

57. Arline Boucher and John Tehan, *Prince of Democracy: James Cardinal Gibbons* (Garden City, New York: Hanover House, 1962), p. 36.

58. "Most Rev. John Hughes," *BrQR* (January 1874), p. 84; *Works,* XIV, p. 492.

59. *Latter Life,* p. 197.

60. "Brownson: A Man of Men," *The Catholic World,* CXXV (September 1927), p. 503.

61. Microfilm of the *Brownson Papers,* roll 9.

## CHAPTER 36

1. Wilfrid Ward, *The Life of John Henry Cardinal Newman* (New York: Longmans, Green, and Co., 1912), I, p. 585. Newman found that his efforts at improvement were taken as "an insult."

2. *BrQR* (January 1858), pp. 91-102.

3. "Rights of the Temporal," *BrQR* (October 1860), p. 494; *Works,* XII, p. 403.

4. "Conversations of Our Club," *BrQR* (October 1858, Chapter IX), pp. 443-444; *Works,* XI, p. 410. This judgment of Brownson was quoted approvingly in an article in *The Rambler,* February 1859. (See John Coulson's introduction to the book, "On Consulting the Faithful in Matters of Doctrine" [New York: Sheed and Ward, 1961], p. 12.)

The first Catholic schools were evidently much inferior to the fine system of parochial schools that was developed as rapidly as could be expected.

5. "Public and Parochial Schools," *BrQR* (July 1859), pp. 325-330; *Works,* XII, pp. 200-204.

6. *Ibid.,* pp. 330-331; *Works,* XII, p. 204.

7. *Ibid.,* p. 332; *Works,* XII, p. 205. In a letter to Count Montalembert, dated December 27, 1858, Brownson had unconsciously revealed that foreignism in the Catholic Church was for the moment becoming something of a phobia with him when he wrote: "The design of the movement here in behalf of Catholic schools is a movement to train up our children in anti-American sentiments, to perpetuate the low and servile sentiments generated by despotism and to keep the population simply a foreign colony in the country." No such thing. Microfilm of the *Brownson Papers,* roll 9.

8. *Ibid.,* p. 334; *Works,* XII, p. 207.

9. *Middle Life,* p. 497.

10. "Public and Parochial Schools," *BrQR* (July 1859), p. 337; *Works,* XII, p. 210. He gave another reason for not being unfriendly to the public school system. This country, he said, is one day to be Catholic, and then Catholics will have a fine system of schools ready-made to their purpose. "Wait a little, and the educational and all other institutions of this noble country, will peaceably pass into the hands of an enlightened and virtuous Catholic population." "Conversations of Our Club," *BrQR* (April 1859, Chapter XIV), p. 152; *Works,* XI, p. 214.

11. *Ibid.,* p. 341; *Works,* XII, p. 214. Brownson's criticisms of Catholic education (always meant constructively) were dealt with by Edward J. Power, Ph.D., in three articles: "Orestes A. Brownson," *Records of the American Catholic Historical Society of Philadelphia,* LXII (June 1951), pp. 47-94; "Brownson's Attitudes Toward Catholic Education," *ibid.,* LXII (June 1952), pp. 110-128; and "Orestes A. Brownson on Catholic Schools," *The Homiletic and Pastoral Review,* LV (April 1955), pp. 563-570.

The late Fr. Thomas T. McAvoy, C.S.C., had an article in *The Review of Politics,* XXVIII (January 1966), pp. 19-26, on "Public Schools vs. Catholic Schools and James McMaster [Editor of the *Freeman's Journal*]." McMaster's stance was extremely condemnatory of the public schools, but he was instrumental in obtaining from the Holy See the *Instruction of 1875* directing that Catholic schools must be established where possible in parishes. The decision on when the children of Catholic parents would be excused from attending was left to the judgment of the respective bishop.

12. *BrQR* (January 1959), pp. 141-142.

13. *Latter Life,* pp. 171-172.

14. Microfilm of the *Brownson Papers,* roll 4.

15. Harold Gardiner, S.J., ed., *American Classics Reconsidered,* "Orestes Brownson," "The Critique of Transcendentalism" (New York: Charles Scribner's Sons, 1958), p. 99.

16. "Present Catholic Dangers," *BrQR* (July 1857), pp. 363-364; *Works,* XII, p. 150.

17. *BrQR* (October 1858), pp. 455-466; *Works,* XI, pp. 421-426.

18. *Ibid.*

19. *BrQR* (April 1860), pp. 254-255.

20. *Ibid.,* pp. 259, 270.

21. "Mary Lee, or the Yankee in Ireland," *BrQR* (January 1860), pp. 118-130; *Works,* XX, pp. 83-93.

22. "Greek Meets Greek," *Commonweal*, XX (1934), pp. 40-42.

23. "Mary Lee, or the Yankee in Ireland," *BrQR* (January 1860), p. 127; *Works*, XX, p. 90.

24. *BrQR* (April 1860), p. 272.

25. *BrQR* (July 1860), pp. 308-310.

26. *Ibid.*, p. 319.

27. *BrQR* (July 1859), p. 415.

28. *New York Tablet* (July 21, 1860), p. 12; also *Metropolitan Record* (July 21, 1860), p. 5.

29. Microfilm of the *Brownson Papers,* roll 9.

30. "Rights of the Temporal," *BrQR* (October 1860), pp. 463, 491; *Works*, XII, pp. 376, 400.

31. "Catholic Education in the United States," *BrQR* (October 1860), p. 41.

32. "Vocations to the Priesthood," *BrQR* (October 1860), pp. 503-504. Fr. Jeremiah Cummings (b. in Washington, D.C., April 15, 1814, d. January 4, 1866) had his roots deep in American soil. His ancestors, Northern Protestant Irish, had emigrated to the U.S. and settled (c. 1782) in Washington, D.C. His maternal granduncle, Capt. Worthy Stephenson, was one of the founders of Washington, and was grand marshal when General Washington laid the cornerstone of the Capitol. As already noted, Fr. Cummings himself became the first pastor of St. Stephen's parish in New York City, and made it one of the most prominent in the city. Florence D. Cohalan, "Cummings, Jeremiah W." *The New Catholic Encyclopedia*, IV, p. 533.

33. *Ibid.*, p. 505.

34. *Ibid.*, p. 507.

35. "Seminaries and Seminarians," *BrQR* (January 1861), pp. 113-115.

36. *Ibid.*, pp. 115-117.

37. "Vocations to the Priesthood," *BrQR* (October 1860), p. 506.

38. Henry Walshe, *Hallowed were the Gold Dust Trails* (Santa Clara, California: University of Santa Clara Press, 1946), p. 39. Bartholomew Woodlock succeeded Newman in the rectorship of the Catholic University of Ireland in April of 1861. Fergal McGrath, S.J., *Newman's University: Idea and Reality* (New York: Longmans, Green, and Co., 1951), p. 468.

39. Microfilm of the *Brownson Papers,* roll 5.

40. W. Ward's *Life* of Newman, I, pp. 512-518.

41. "Vocations to the Priesthood," *BrQR* (October 1860), pp. 507-512.

42. *Latter Life,* p. 198.

## CHAPTER 37

1. W. Ward, *The Life of John Henry Cardinal Newman* (New York: Longmans, Green, and Co.), I, p. 581.

2. *Ibid.*, p. 526.

3. "The Roman Question," *BrQR* (October 1859), p. 527; *Works*, XVIII, p. 418.

4. *Ibid.*, p. 538; *Works*, XVIII, p. 428.

5. *Ibid.*, p. 529; *Works*, XVIII, p. 420.

6. "Ventura on Christian Politics," *BrQR* (April 1860), pp. 222-227; *Works*, XII, pp. 338-340.

7. "The Papal Power," *BrQR* (July 1860), pp. 292-293; *Works*, XII, pp. 366-368.

8. *Ibid.*, pp. 298-299; *Works*, XII, pp. 372-373.

9. *Latter Life,* pp. 198-199.

10. "Rights of the Temporal," *BrQR* (October 1860), p. 463; *Works*, XII, pp. 376-377.

11. *Ibid.*, pp. 377-378; *Works*, XII, pp. 378-379.

12. *Difficulties of Anglicans,* II, p. 81. Some of the Roman officials took offense at this statement also.

13. *Latter Life,* p. 273.

14. "Faith and Theology," *BrQR* (January 1863), p. 21; *Works*, VIII, p. 20.

15. "Rights of the Temporal," *BrQR* (October 1860), p. 467; *Works,* XII, p. 379.

16. W. Ward's *Life* of Newman, II, p. 127.

17. "Rights of the Temporal," *BrQR* (October 1860), pp. 470-472; *Works,* XII, pp. 383-384.

18. *Ibid.,* p. 478; *Works,* XII, p. 389.

19. *Ibid.,* p. 486; *Works,* XII, p. 396.

20. *Ibid.,* p. 480; *Works,* XII, p. 391.

21. *Ibid.,* p. 483; *Works,* XII, p. 394.

22. *Ibid.,* p. 490; *Works,* XII, p. 399.

23. Newman, too, considered it unfair "that laymen should be allowed no voice in deciding about the education of their sons." Meriol Trevor, *Newman, Light in Winter* (New York: Doubleday and Co., 1963), II, p. 356.

24. "Rights of the Temporal," *BrQR* (October 1860), p. 491; *Works,* XII, p. 400.

25. "Conversations of Our Club," *BrQR* (October 1858), pp. 446-447; *Works,* XII, p. 413.

26. "Rights of the Temporal," *BrQR* (October 1860), p. 473; *Works,* XII, p. 385.

27. F. McGrath, *Newman's University, Idea and Reality* (New York: Longmans, Green, and Co., 1951), pp. 444, 447.

28. Josef Altholz, *The Liberal Catholic Movement in England, The Rambler and its Contributors, 1848-1864* (London: Burns and Oates, 1962), p. 101.

29. "Rights of the Temporal," *BrQR* (October 1860), pp. 492-493; *Works,* XII, pp. 401-402.

30. "Editor's Comments," *BrQR* (October 1874), p. 539; *Works,* XX, p. 426.

31. "Rights of the Temporal," *BrQR* (October 1860), p. 495; *Works,* XII, pp. 503-504.

32. *BrQR* (October 1860), pp. 516-522. Brownson would no doubt have been well pleased with Hilaire Belloc's *How the Reformation Happened.*

33. *Ibid.,* pp. 521-522.

34. *BrQR* (January 1861), p. 135.

35. *Ibid.,* p. 136.

36. *BrQR* (October 1860), pp. 538-540.

## CHAPTER 38

1. *Latter Life,* pp. 206-207.

2. *Ibid.,* pp. 208-218.

3. *Ibid.,* pp. 219-220.

4. *Ibid.,* p. 298.

5. *Ibid.,* pp. 221-225.

6. *BrQR* (January 1861), pp. 134-135.

7. *Latter Life,* pp. 225-231.

8. Microfilm of the *Brownson Papers,* roll 5.

9. *Latter Life,* pp. 250-251.

10. William H. Elder (1819-1904), born in Baltimore, had studied at the Urban College in Rome, Italy. After ordination to the priesthood he became professor of dogmatic theology and rector of St. Mary's College and Seminary at Emmitsburg, Maryland. In 1857 he became bishop of Natchez, Mississippi. He was the only native clergyman in his diocese. During the Civil War, in 1863, when ordered by the commander of the union forces occupying Natchez, Brig. Gen. Y. M. Tuttle, to insert a special prayer in the Mass for the President of the United States and for the success of the North, he refused, and on April 7, 1864, wrote "a masterful statement of his position to President Lincoln." When Tuttle was replaced by Brig. Gen. M. Brayman, the new general ordered Elder to Vidalia where he was confined for seventeen days, and where he wrote a second statement to Secretary of War Edward M. Stanton, which again elicited no official action. Elder became archbishop of Cincinnati, Ohio, on July 4, 1883, succeeding Archbishop John B. Purcell. C. R. Steinbicker, the *New Catholic Encyclopedia,* vol. V, pp. 238-239.

11. "Catholic Polemics," *BrQR* (July 1861), pp. 358-360; *Works*, XX, pp. 110-112.

12. *Latter Life*, p. 239.

13. "Catholic Polemics," *BrQR* (April 1861), pp. 371-372; *Works*, XX, pp. 123-124.

14. *Latter Life*, p. 227.

15. *Ibid.*, p. 237.

16. *Ibid.*, p. 197.

17. Microfilm of the *Brownson Papers*, roll 5.

18. *Ibid.* Sorrow had also come to the family when Brownson's twenty-nine-year-old son John Healy Brownson walked out of a window apparently in his sleep and fell to his death in St. Paul, Minnesota, on December 4, 1858.

19. Microfilm of the *Brownson Papers* roll 9.

20. *Ibid.*, roll 5.

21. *Latter Life*, p. 205.

22. "Ward's Philosophical Introduction," *BrQR* (January 1861), p. 11; *Works*, XIV, p. 358. Although this article was not published until January 1861, it was written in October 1860. (See *Latter Life*, pp. 320-321.)

23. Microfilm of the *Brownson Papers*, roll 5.


## CHAPTER 39

1. *BrQR* (July 1861), pp. 371-372; *Works*, XX, pp. 123-124.

2. W. Ward, *The Life of John Henry Newman* (New York: Longmans, Green, and Co., 1912), I, p. 503, and II, pp. 128, 168-169.

3. "Separation of Church and State," *BrQR* (January 1861), pp. 75-76; *Works*, XII, pp. 416-417.

4. *Ibid.*, pp. 90, 95; *Works*, XII, pp. 431-436.

5. Microfilm of the *Brownson Papers*, roll 5.

6. *Ibid.*

7. *BrQR* (January 1861), p. 136.

8. "Pope and Emperor," *BrQR* (April 1861), pp. 181-182; *Works*, XII, pp. 456-457.

9. "Sardinia and Rome," *BrQR* (July 1861), p. 404; *Works*, XVIII, p. 432.

10. *Ibid.*, p. 406; *Works*, XVIII, p. 434.

11. *Ibid.*, 415; *Works*, XVIII, p. 443.

12. *Latter Life*, p. 250.

13. *Ibid.*, p. 250.

14. *Ibid.*, pp. 253-254.

15. This letter was included with a covering letter of Fr. George M. McCloskey to Brownson, on July 19, 1861. *AUND.* Given in *Latter Life*, pp. 258-259.

16. *Latter Life*, pp. 259-260. It is an interesting sidelight that while Cardinal Barnabò admired Brownson greatly, he did not take to Newman. He even mimicked him. (See Meriol Trevor, *Newman, Light in Winter* [New York: Doubleday and Co., 1963], II, p. 105.)

17. Microfilm of the *Brownson Papers*, roll 5. Apropos of the service Fr. Cummings was here rendering Brownson., Fr. John Talbot Smith, LL.D., remarks in his *History of the Catholic Church in New York* (New York and Boston: Hall and Locke Co., 1905) II, p. 393: "Dr. Cummings was a man of independent and imperious temper, and had held his own against the great Dr. Hughes; he had also championed the cause of Brownson at Rome, with Cardinal Barnabò and Cardinal Franzelin, and had won for his client the favor of these two great men."

18. Microfilm of the *Brownson Papers*, roll 9. This letter was not available to previous biographers of Brownson. It was recently unearthed in the Archives of the Sacred Congregation Propaganda Fide, by the late Fr. Thomas McAvoy, C.S.C., and was used in his article "Orestes A. Brownson and Archbishop Hughes," in the *Review of Politics*, XXIV (January 1962), pp. 19-47.

19. Microfilm of the *Brownson Papers*, roll 5.

20. *Latter Life*, pp. 257-258.

21. Microfilm of the *Brownson Papers*, roll 9. Neither has this letter been available to previous biographers. It was likewise recently obtained by Fr. Thomas T. McAvoy, archivist of the University of Notre Dame, from the archives of the Propaganda Fide, Rome.

22. "Brownson: A Man of Men," *The Catholic World*, CXXV (September 1927), p. 756.

23. *Latter Life*, pp. 284-287.

## CHAPTER 40

1. Microfilm of the *Brownson Papers*, roll 5. Brownson reprinted Gresselin's entire letter in the October 1861 issue of his *Review*, pp. 417-420; *Works*, XX, pp. 130-132.

2. "At Home and Abroad," *BrQR* (October 1873), p. 538; *Works*, XVIII, pp. 538-539.

3. Chapter 13, verses 1, 2.

4. "The Church not a Despotism," *BrQR* (April 1862), p. 141; *Works*, XX, p. 219.

5. W. Ward, *The Life of John Henry Cardinal Newman* (New York: Longmans, Green, and Co., 1912), I, p. 498.

6. "Introduction to the Last Series," *BrQR* (January 1873), p. 2; *Works*, XX, p. 381.

7. *The American Quarterly Review*, VI (Spring, 1954), p. 20.

8. *Ibid.*, p. 31.

9. Microfilm of the *Brownson Papers*, roll 5.

10. *Latter Life*, p. 262.

11. "Present Catholic Dangers," *BrQR* (July 1857), pp. 352-353; *Works*, XII, p. 140.

12. *Ibid.*, p. 355; *Works*, XII, p. 142.

13. "Catholic Polemics," *BrQR* (July 1861), p. 355; *Works*, XX, p. 108.

14. W. Ward's *Life* of Newman, II, p. 49. Newman's supreme effort to meet the non-Catholic mind was made of course in his *Essay in Aid of a Grammar of Assent*. It was attacked along scholastic lines by the Jesuit, Fr. Harper, in successive articles in *The Month. Ibid*, p. 269.

15. "Catholic Polemics," *BrQR* (July 1861), p. 360; *Works*, XX, pp. 112-113.

16. *Ibid.*, pp. 364, 368; *Works*, XII, pp. 116, 120. Brownson developed this distinction at length in his article on "Faith and Theology," *BrQR* (January 1863); *Works*, VIII, pp. 1-28.

17. *Ibid.*, p. 367; *Works*, VIII, p. 119.

18. W. Ward's *Life* of Newman, II, p. 254.

19. *Ibid.*, II, p. 436.

20. "Catholic Polemics," *BrQR* (July 1861), pp. 371-372; *Works*, XX, pp. 123-124.

21. "The Church and the Republic," *BrQR* (July 1856), p. 300; *Works*, XII, p. 27.

22. *The Dublin Review* coined the word "minimizers" as designating those who tended to minimize the content of divine faith. W. Ward's *Life* of Newman, II, p. 83.

23. *BrQR* (October 1862), p. 545.

24. W. Ward's *Life* of Newman, II, p. 167.

25. Microfilm of the *Brownson Papers*, roll 5.

26. October 1856 issue, p. 315.

27. *BrQR* (July 1856), p. 400. Both Brownson and Newman had a high opinion of the *Home and Foreign Review* on the score of literary merit. Newman called it "the ablest publication we have, though I don't quite trust its conductors." W. Ward's *Life* of Newman, I, p. 539.

28. Microfilm of the *Brownson Papers*, roll 9. This letter was recently unearthed in the archives of Downside Abbey, near Bath, England.

29. In a letter to Richard Simpson, dated June 31, 1862, Sir John Acton remarked in reference to Brownson: "I wish you joy of the perversion of Brownson. Certainly,

when I knew him in his prime, nine years ago, the light was not kindled in him, and I thought it never would come, because of his imperfect education and his unhistorical mind. He is not yet sixty, and his decay is pitiful and premature; his letter to one who knew him, very melancholy." *Lord Acton and His Circle* (London: Burns and Oates [no date given]), letter CXXXIII, p. 289.

This writer had wondered in the past over just what could have been the occasion of Acton writing the above remarks to Richard Simpson. They are in strange contrast, if not contradictory, to the exceedingly laudatory letter Acton had written Brownson on May 13, 1854, after his extended conversations with him on his visit to the United States. *Middle Life*, pp. 471-478. It now appears that in speaking of Brownson's "very melancholy" letter, Acton had reference to the above letter that Brownson had written Simpson on May 21, 1862. Simpson must have sent the letter or showed it to Acton, and Acton replied with the above letter of the next month (June 31, 1862). Any way the matter is viewed, Acton's comments are a bit puzzling since he himself was a simon-pure liberal, at least ecclesiastically speaking. It could be that Acton was irked a trifle at this particular time by Brownson because of his adamantine fight for the Union cause during the Civil War. Acton himself had opted for the Southern Confederacy.

30. Gasquet, *Lord Acton and His Circle*, p. lxv.

31. *Latter Life*, p. 200.

32. *BrQR* (July 1861), p. 408; *Works*, XVIII, p. 436.

33. *BrQR* (April 1856), pp. 225-252; *Works*, XVI, pp. 489-513.

34. *Latter Life*, pp. 35-46. The Count's letters to Brownson were generally written in a very good English style. His mother's name was Forbes, perhaps more Scotch than English, and the Count himself had lived in England till he was twenty years old. He claimed that through his mother he was of Irish extraction. "Count Montalembert," *BrQR* (July 1874), p. 291; *Works*, XIV, pp. 516-517.

35. Letter dated May 24, 1857. This letter was recently found in the Château de la Roche-en-Brenil, France. Transcripts were graciously furnished the AUND by Viscomte de Meaux. Brownson had begun a reply to the Count's letter of July 8, 1856, in August of 1856, but apparently the letter was never finished or sent. Microfilm of the *Brownson Papers*, roll 9. (See also *Latter Life*, pp. 46-48.)

36. "Reform and Reformers," *BrQR* (April 1863), p. 234; *Works*, XX, p. 299.

37. *Latter Life*, p. 304.

38. *Ibid.*, p. 278.

39. "The Church not a Despotism," *BrQR* (April 1862), p. 144; *Works*, XX, pp. 221-222.

40. *Ibid.*, p. 147; *Works*, XX, p. 224.

41. *Ibid.*, p. 163; *Works*, XX, p. 240. Newman was saying the same thing in 1864: "Why was it that the Medieval Schools were so vigorous? Because they were allowed free play. . . . As far as I can make out this has ever been the rule of the Church till now, when the French Revolution having destroyed the Schools of Europe, a sort of centralization has been established at headquarters." W. Ward's *Life* of Newman, II, pp. 49-50.

42. "Lacordaire and Catholic Progress," *BrQR* (July 1862), pp. 325-326; *Works*, XX, pp. 270-271. Again Newman wrote: "Nothing great or living can be done except when men are self-governed and independent; this is quite consistent with full maintenance of ecclesiastical supremacy." W. Ward's *Life* of Newman, I, p. 367.

43. Microfilm of the *Brownson Papers*, roll 5, letter dated February 10, 1862.

44. *Ibid.*, letter dated September 4, 1861.

45. *BrQR* (January 1862), p. 133.

46. *Latter Life*, pp. 287-291.

47. *Ibid.*, p. 291.

48. "Catholicity, Liberalism and Socialism," *BrQR* (October 1862), p. 534; *Works*, XX, p. 280.

49. "The Church not a Despotism," *BrQR* (April 1862), p. 143; *Works*, XX, p. 221.

50. "Reading and Study of the Scriptures," *BrQR* (October 1861), p. 502; *Works*, XX, p. 181.

51. W. Ward's *Life* of Newman, I, p. 409.

52. "Various Objections Answered," *BrQR* (October 1861), pp. 430-432; *Works*, XX, pp. 140-143.

53. "The Church not a Despotism," *BrQR* (April 1862), p. 141; *Works*, XX, p. 219.

54. Microfilm of the *Brownson Papers,* supplementary roll 1. A. Hechinger to H. F. Brownson, December 1890.

55. *BrQR* (October 1861), pp. 547-548.

56. W. Ward's *Life* of Newman, I, pp. 579-581.

57. Meriol Trevor, *Newman, Light in Winter* (New York: Doubleday and Co., 1963), II, p. 331.

58. "Faith and Theology," *BrQR* (January 1863), p. 27; *Works*, VIII, p. 26.

59. "Various Objections Answered," *BrQR* (October 1861), p. 436; *Works*, XX, p. 147.

60. He asserted that such questions concerning eternal punishment were still unanswered by the Catholic Church — which leaves opinion free.

61. *Latter Life*, p. 258.

62. *Ibid.,* p. 377.

63. W. Ward's *Life* of Newman, II, pp. 125-126.

64. "Papal Infallibility," *BrQR* (July 1873), p. 332; *Works*, XIII, p. 442.

65. "Lacordaire and Catholic Progress," *BrQR* (July 1862), p. 311; *Works*, XX, p. 257.

66. *Ibid.,* p. 333; *Works*, XX, p. 278.

67. "Religious Orders," *Works*, VIII, p. 221.

68. "Saint-Worship," *Works*, VIII, p. 146.

69. In 1871 Brownson wrote: "I must myself confess, to my shame and deep sorrow, that for four or five years, ending in 1864, I listened with too much respect to these liberal or liberalizing Catholics, whether at home or abroad, though I had previously written against them, and sought to encourage their tendency as far as I could without absolutely departing from Catholic faith and morals. I had been taught better, and my better judgment and my Catholic instincts never went with them; but I was induced to think that I might find in the more fondly cherished tendencies of my non-Catholic countrymen a *point d' appui* for my arguments in favor of the teaching of the church, and by making the distance between them and us as short as possible greatly facilitate their conversion. . . . All I gained was a distrust of a large portion of the Catholic public. . . ." "Religious Orders," *Works*, VIII, pp. 220-221, n.

70. J. W. Smith and A. L. Jamison, eds., "Catholicism in the United States," *Religion in American Life: The Shaping of American Religion,* I (Princeton, New Jersey, 1961), p. 79.

71. *Ibid.*, p. 115; *American Christianity,* ed. by H. S. Smith et al (New York, 1963), II, pp. 514, 536-542.

72. Charles A. and Mary R. Beard, *The Rise of American Civilization,* IV (New York, 1948), pp. 232-233, 256-263.

73. A review of the *Brownson Reader,* ed. by Alvan Ryan, in *The Catholic Worker* (October 1955), reproduced in the *Emerson Society Quarterly* (1963), no. 32, part 3, p. 37.

74. *Latter Life,* p. 3.

75. *Works,* XI, p. VII.

## CHAPTER 41

1. Arnold Whitridge has written: "No historian has yet accounted for the failure of this great weight of public opinion [against the outbreak of the Civil War] to make itself felt during the critical period between Lincoln's election and the firing on Sumter. At no time in their history have the American people seemed so incapable of controlling their destiny." *No Compromise: The Story of the Fanatics Who Paved the Way to the Civil War* (New York: Farrar, Straus and Co., 1960), introduction, p. 10.

2. "Slavery and the Mexican War," *BrQR* (July 1847), p. 334; *Works*, XVI, p. 25.

3. "Slavery and the Incoming Administration," *BrQR* (January 1857), pp. 89-93; *Works*, XVII, pp. 54-57.

4. "Politics at Home and Abroad," *BrQR* (April 1859), pp. 215-216; *Works*, XVI, pp. 570-572.

5. "The Slavery Question once more," *BrQR* (April 1857), p. 248; *Works*, p. 77.

6. *Ibid.*, p. 249; *Works*, XVII, pp. 77-78.

7. *Ibid.*, pp. 257-258; *Works*, XVII, pp. 84-85.

8. *Ibid.*, p. 275; *Works*, XVII, p. 92.

9. *Ibid.*, pp. 272-277; *Works*, XVII, pp. 92-94. An anonymous writer in *The Metropolitan Magazine* of Baltimore, writing under the heading, "Dr. Brownson and the Supreme Court of the United States," launched a tirade on Brownson's observations on the majority opinion Judge Taney had handed down on the Dred Scott case, accusing him of setting himself up "as a sort of a super-Supreme Court of Appeals." He bitterly assailed Brownson as tending to destroy the authority of the Supreme Court by controverting its reasoning and denying its conclusions. Of the questions involved, said the writer: "No questions have ever excited so much irreconcilable antagonism of opinion in the country, or involved so much bitter sectional hostility, as those considered by the Court in the Dred Scott case." Vol. V (April 1857), pp. 208-215. Brownson made answer to this onslaught in "Conversations of Our Club," *Works*, XI, pp. 378-381.

10. *Latter Life*, pp. 413-414.

11. "Explanations to Catholics," *BrQR* (October 1864), pp. 471-472; *Works* XX, pp. 363-364. Fr. Charles Gresselin, S.J., gave the other side of this case in a letter he wrote Brownson on February 19, 1862. *Latter Life*, pp. 417-418. His letter was in answer to a letter Brownson had written him about the whole affair. Brownson's letter to Fr. Gresselin has unfortunately been lost. In the latter 1860s Fr. Gresselin moved to Canada and died there shortly thereafter, and all his papers were lost. In his letter to Brownson, dated February 19, 1862, he said: "I pass now to the concluding paragraph of your letter. It is truly affecting, full of manliness and simplicity." Microfilm of the *Brownson Papers*, roll 5.

12. *Latter Life*, p. 413.

13. This statement came originally from the late Fr. Joseph P. Donovan, C.M., erstwhile rector of Kenrick Seminary, St. Louis, Missouri, who had a wide knowledge of all that concerned Brownson.

14. "Slavery and the War," *BrQR* (October 1861), p. 525; *Works*, XVII, p. 159.

15. *Latter Life*, p. 411.

16. Carl Sandburg, *Abraham Lincoln, The War Years* (Vol. II) (New York: Charles Scribner's Sons, 1939), pp. 4, 171.

17. *Ibid.*, p. 124.

18. *Latter Life*, pp. 411-412. Congressman Kelley was a genuine patriot. *The Dictionary of American Biography* tells us that "although exempt from military service, he answered the emergency call of September, 1862, and joined an artillery company just before the battle of Antietam, but never took part in the engagement. He favored a vigorous prosecution of the war and boldly criticized the dilatory practices of General McClellan."

19. "Slavery and the War," *BrQR* (October 1861), p. 520; *Works*, XVII, p. 154.

20. "The Great Rebellion," *BrQR* (July 1861), pp. 378-379; *Works*, XVII, pp. 121, 135.

21. "Essays on the Reformation," *BrQR* (October 1862), p. 420; *Works*, XII, p. 577.

22. Allan Nevins, *The Emergence of Lincoln, The War Years* (New York: Charles Scribner's Sons, 1950), pp. 1, 21-27.

23. "Slavery and the War," *BrQR* (October 1861), pp. 518, 521; *Works*, XVII, pp. 152, 155.

24. Carl Sandburg, *Abraham Lincoln, The War Years* (Vol. III) (New York: Charles Scribner's Sons, 1939), pp. 5, 178.

25. "Slavery and the War," *BrQR* (October 1861), p. 520; *Works*, XVII, pp. 153-154.

26. "The Great Rebellion," *BrQR* (July 1861), p. 401; *Works*, XVII, p. 142.

27. "Slavery and the War," *BrQR* (October 1861), pp. 539-540; *Works*, XVII, pp. 145, 173. Brownson had begun his powerful article on "Slavery and the War" with a notice of Augustin Cochin's work on *The Abolition of Slavery* (two volumes). A reviewer of the first volume of Cochin's work for the *Atlantic Monthly*, March 1863, remarked: "It is worth while to note that the most logical and effective assailants of slavery that these years have produced have been devout Catholics — Augustin Cochin in France, and Orestes A. Brownson in America" (p. 397).

28. "The President's Message and Proclamation," *BrQR* (January 1864), p. 106; *Works*, XVII, p. 531.

29. "Slavery and the War," *BrQR* (October 1861), p. 540; *Works*, XVII, p. 174.

30. Microfilm of the *Brownson Papers*, roll 5.

31. Brownson's friend, Dr. Henry Hewit, wrote him from New York on October 16, 1861: "The Archbishop is *wroth* — in fact savage; and if times had not changed, you and your *Review* would have the pleasure of contributing to the brilliancy of a wood-pile in full blaze." Microfilm of the *Brownson Papers*, roll 5.

32. "Archbishop Hughes on Slavery," *BrQR* (January 1862), pp. 38-39; *Works*, XVII, pp. 183-184. (See also "Slavery and the War," *BrQR* [October 1861], p. 512; *Works*, XVII, p. 146.)

33. John R. G. Hassard, *The Life of the Most Reverend John Hughes, D.D.*, first archbishop of New York (New York: D. Appleton and Co., 1866), pp. 436-437.

34. "Archbishop Hughes on Slavery," *BrQR* (January 1862), p. 59; *Works*, XVII, pp. 203-204.

35. *Latter Life*, p. 363.

36. Hassard, p. 437.

37. *Latter Life*, p. 363.

38. Hassard, pp. 436-437, n.

39. Microfilm of the *Brownson Papers*, roll 5.

40. *Ibid.*

41. *Latter Life*, p. 373, n. The New York *Tribune* also said of the communication in the *Herald* on Brownson's same article: "It is an attempt to parry the blows which Dr. Brownson powerfully deals at Slavery and Rebellion by scurrilous attacks on him personally. Such a mode of treating this grave question is, in itself a confession, on the part of the friends of secession, of their incapacity to meet Dr. Brownson in fair debate." *Ibid.*, p. 367.

42. "Archbishop Hughes on Slavery," *BrQR* (January 1862), p. 66; *Works*, XVII, p. 210.

43. *Latter Life*, pp. 372-374.

44. Microfilm of the *Brownson Papers*, roll 5.

45. *Latter Life*, pp. 425-426.

46. *Ibid.*, p. 381.

47. *Ibid.*, p. 424.

## CHAPTER 42

1. "Slavery and the War," *BrQR* (October 1861), p. 544; *Works*, XVII, pp. 177-178.

2. "Archbishop Hughes on Slavery," *BrQR* (January 1862), pp. 63-64; *Works*, XVII, p. 207.

3. "The President's Message," *BrQR* (January 1863), p. 91; *Works*, XVII (title changed to "The President's Policy"), p. 388.

4. Lincoln had probably been considerably influenced by the report of Cassius Clay, just back from the Russian Legation, who told him that "over Europe he found the governments ready to recognize the Confederacy, anxious to intervene, that an emancipation proclamation now would block these European autocracies." Carl Sandburg, *Abraham Lincoln, The War Years* (Vol. I) (New York: Charles Scribner's Sons, 1939), pp. 3, 573. This visit of Clay to Lincoln was made apparently in

the forepart of the summer of 1862. No precise date is given by Sandburg. Clay's report was confirmed at the time by J. L. Motley, Minister to Vienna, and Carl Schurz, Minister to Madrid. *Ibid.*

5. *Latter Life,* p. 395. Fr. Charles Raymond McCarthy, C.S.P., in his dissertation on *The Political Philosophy of Orestes A. Brownson* (University of Toronto, 1962) asserts that Brownson made two trips to the White House to urge on Lincoln his views on the matter (p. 75).

6. *Abraham Lincoln, The War Years* (Vol. I), *ut supra,* pp. 3, 555-577.

7. *BrQR* (October 1861), pp. 511-512; *Works,* XVII, p. 147. (See also *Abraham Lincoln, The War Years* [Vol. I], pp. 3, 580-582.)

8. J. G. Randall, *Lincoln the President* (New York: Dodd, Mead and Co., 1945), II, p. 154 (Welles, Diary I, pp. 70-71).

9. *Latter Life,* p. 396.

10. Carl Sandburg, *Abraham Lincoln, The War Years* (Vol. II) (New York: Charles Scribner's Sons, 1939), pp. 4, 15-16.

11. "The President's Message and Proclamation," *BrQR* (January 1864), p. 97; *Works,* XVII, p. 522.

12. *Ibid.,* p. 95; *Works,* XVII, p. 520.

13. "Confiscation and Emancipation," *BrQR* (July 1862), p. 393; *Works,* XVII, p. 313. In 1875 Brownson asserted that it was Lincoln's eventual adoption and proclamation of emancipation as a war measure that "was the decisive measure that caused the final collapse of the Confederacy" by working a gradual disorganization of the South's labor system. *BrQR* (October 1875), p. 543; *Works,* XVII, p. 578.

14. "The President's Message," *BrQR* (January 1863), p. 91; *Works,* XVII (title changed to "The President's Policy"), p. 388.

15. *Abraham Lincoln, The War Years* (Vol. I), *ut supra,* pp. 3, 566-567.

16. *Latter Life,* p. 421.

17. Marie De Mare, *G.P.A. Healy, American Artist* (New York: David McKay Co., Inc., 1954), introduction by Eleanor Roosevelt, p. 209.

18. *Latter Life,* p. 421.

19. Marie De Mare, pp. 209-210.

20. Microfilm of the *Brownson Papers,* roll 6. Cochin sent his congratulations to Brownson through a letter to Mary L. Booth, dated April 2, 1864. *Ibid.*

21. "Are Catholics Pro-Slavery and Disloyal?" *BrQR* (July 1863), p. 373.

22. "What the Rebellion Teaches," *BrQR* (July 1862), p. 340; *Works,* XVII, pp. 279-280.

23. "Catholics and the Anti-Draft Riots," *BrQR* (October 1863), p. 387; *Works,* XVII, p. 414.

24. *Ibid.,* pp. 388, 401; *Works,* XVII, pp. 415, 428. In this same article of October 1863, Brownson also gave considerable attention to a letter Pope Pius IX had sent to Archbishop Hughes of New York (a similar one was sent likewise to Archbishop J. M. Odin of New Orleans) calling upon him and the American bishops to do all in their power to dispose the American government and its people to peace, and to put an end to the further effusion of blood. The letter had just been published (though dated October 1862). Brownson took the view that the letter had either been forged in the name of the Supreme Pontiff or had been solicited and obtained under false representations. The lawful government of the country and its people were simply resisting an attack on the life of the nation; they had never wanted war in the first place. Hence there was no call to try to dispose them to peace. Peace could be had the moment the real culprits in the case, the rebel states, laid down their arms and ceased their attack. Expressing the greatest respect and reverence for the noble intentions of the pope in the matter, as the common spiritual father of all, Brownson feared that those who had obtained the letter would use it to no good against the Union cause. The great body of Catholics were in the North, and to preach peace to them might only cool their attachment to the government in its desperate effort to put down the rebellion. *Ibid.,* pp. 436-441.

25. "Conscription and Volunteers," *BrQR* (January 1863), p. 64.

26. "Are Catholics Pro-Slavery and Disloyal?" *BrQR* (July 1863), p. 370.

27. *Ibid.*, pp. 376-377. Although the number of Brownson's *Review* is not identified, it is evident enough that it was this edition of July 1863 with the article "Are Catholics Pro-Slavery and Disloyal?" that L. B. Binsse, Consul of the Propaganda Fide to the United States (a layman) sent to Cardinal Barnabò, Prefect of the Propaganda Fide, Rome, with an accompanying letter dated September 18, 1863. He remarked that he had "marked specially" the article. Finbar Kenneally, O.F.M., ed., *Documents in the Propaganda Fide* (Washington, D.C.: Academy of American Franciscan History, 1966).

28. "Faith and Reason — Revelation and Science," *BrQR* (April 1863), pp. 159-160; *Works*, III, p. 595.

29. *Works*, II, pp. 101-182.

30. "Faith and Theology," *BrQR* (January 1863), p. 26; *Works*, VIII, p. 25.

31. He had made all that very clear in a sizable footnote to his article, "An A Priori Autobiography," in the January 1850 issue of his *Quarterly*, pp. 28-29; *Works*, I, pp. 241-242. His criticism of Gioberti was even more severe in his *Spirit-Rapper*, 1854, *Works*, IX, pp. 112-117. He in no sense endorsed the man or his writings without grave reservations, though he admired his genius — and that was enough to get him into a peck of trouble.

32. *BrQR* (January 1863), p. 128.

33. Microfilm of the *Brownson Papers*, roll 6.

34. *Ibid.*, roll 5.

35. "Essays on the Reformation," *BrQR* (July 1862), p. 302; *Works*, XII, p. 565.

36. *BrQR* (July 1875), p. 422.

37. *Ibid.* (July 1863), p. 127.

38. *Latter Life*, pp. 366-367. He stressed this same interpretation of the war in his essay, "The Struggle of the Nation for Life," *BrQR* (January 1862), pp. 114-115; *Works*, XVII, pp. 213-214.

39. "The Return of the Rebellious States," *BrQR* (October 1863), p. 481; *Works*, XVII, p. 448.

40. "State Rebellion, State Suicide," *BrQR* (April 1862), p. 200; *Works*, XVII, p. 233. Brownson held to the end that "state rebellion is state suicide," but when he wrote *The American Republic* he modified the opinion that he had "too hastily expressed, that the political death of a state dissolves civil society within its territory and abrogates all rights held under it, and accept[ed] the doctrine that the laws in force at the time of secession remain in force till superseded or abrogated by competent authority. . . ." *Works*, XVIII, p. 4.

41. Microfilm of the *Brownson Papers*, roll 5. Brownson and Senator Charles Sumner had by this time become political bedfellows. This Sumner is the same who as a young man had brought back from Paris the intelligence that Victor Cousin was anxious to see Brownson appointed to the chair of philosophy at Harvard University. Sumner had with the passing of the years become a rather rabid Free-Soil and abolitionist agitator, and had on that score drawn some critical fire from Brownson. *BrQR* (October 1854), pp. 487-514; *Works*, XVII, pp. 39-53. He was perhaps the foremost leader in Congress among the opponents of slavery. His vitriolic attacks upon slavery and its defenders brought upon him a physical assault by Representative Preston S. Brooks of South Carolina in retaliation for a verbal attack upon his uncle, Senator Andrew Butler. Sumner never did fully recover from the wounds inflicted on the occasion. Brownson's views on slavery, in contrast to Sumner's were always fairly balanced and moderate. Sumner, too, like Brownson, made visits to the White House to urge on the President an emancipation proclamation. Sumner was so dignified in appearance and manner that Lincoln remarked that, of all persons, Sumner reminded him most of a bishop. The Civil War over, Brownson and Sumner drifted apart. In 1866 Brownson wrote his son: "I have lost all sympathy with Sumner, he has nigger on the brain worse than ever." *Latter Life*, p. 481.

42. "State Rebellion, State Suicide," *BrQR* (April 1862), p. 211; *Works*, XVII, pp. 244-245.

43. *Ibid.*, p. 217; *Works*, XVII, p. 251.

44. "The Return of the Rebellious States," *BrQR* (April 1863), pp. 490-491;

Works, XVII, pp. 456-457. (See also "The Federal Constitution," BrQR [January 1864], pp. 19-22; Works, XVII, pp. 484-490.)

45. "Are the United States a Nation?" BrQR (October 1864), pp. 391-393; Works, XVII, pp. 566-567.

46. "The President's Message," BrQR (January 1863), p. 99; Works, XVII (title changed to "The President's Policy")), p. 396.

47. Carl Sandburg, Abraham Lincoln, The War Years (Vol. III) (New York: Charles Scribner's Sons, 1939), pp. 5, 81.

48. "The President's Message and Proclamation," BrQR (January 1864), p. 86; Works, XVII, p. 511.

49. Ibid., p. 91; Works, XVII, p. 516. Brownson considered it a mistake for the administration to have anticipated the problem of reconstruction. "Reconstruction," he said, "while the rebellion is in full force, and as a means of putting it down, is absurd, and therefore it is absurd to suppose it can be done under the war power. Reconstruction of the state governments, as well as the Union itself, is the work not of war but of peace, and is practicable only after the rebellion has been suppressed, and hostilities have ceased." "Mr. Lincoln and Congress," BrQR (October 1864), p. 443.

50. "The President's Message," BrQR (January 1863), pp. 97-98; Works, XVII, p. 395.

51. Ibid., pp. 103-104; Works, XVII, pp. 400-402.

52. "The President's Message and Proclamation," BrQR (January 1864), pp. 90, 97-98; Works, XVII, p. 522.

53. Ibid., p. 92; Works, XVII, p. 517.

54. "The Seward Policy," BrQR (October 1862), p. 512; Works, XVII, p. 377.

55. "The President's Message and Proclamation," BrQR (January 1864), p. 103; Works, XVII, p. 527.

56. Ibid., pp. 100-101; Works, XVII, p. 525.

57. The Catholicism of Orestes Brownson (Albuquerque, New Mexico: University of New Mexico Library, 1955), p. 254.

58. Abraham Lincoln, The War Years (Vol. III), ut supra, pp. 5, 125-138. (See also "Mr. Lincoln and Congress," BrQR [October 1864], p. 434.)

59. Microfilm of the Brownson Papers, roll 5. Later decisions of the Supreme Court upheld the views of Brownson and Sumner on this matter. (See J. G. Randall, Constitutional Problems under Lincoln [Urbana: University of Illinois Press, 1951], pp. 41-44.)

60. "The President's Message and Proclamation," BrQR (January 1864), p. 106; Works, XVII, pp. 529-530.

61. Latter Life, p. 397, n.

62. "What the Rebellion Teaches," BrQR (July 1862), p. 339; Works, XVII, pp. 278-279.

63. "State Rebellion, State Suicide," BrQR (April 1862), p. 215; Works, XVII, p. 248.

64. "Our Programme," BrQR (January 1864), pp. 1-12.

65. Microfilm of the Brownson Papers, roll 6.

66. "Civil and Religious Freedom," BrQR (July 1864), p. 262; Works, XX, p. 313. Brownson had enunciated this same sound doctrine, perfectly in harmony with the doctrine of Vatican Council II on religious freedom, already in 1838 in his article on "Religion and Politics" in his Boston Quarterly Review in the July issue, pp. 310-333.

67. Mr. McMahon had a more extended letter on this matter also in The Commonweal, the issue of December 3, 1964, Correspondence, p. 260.

68. Abraham Lincoln, The War Years (Vol. II), ut supra, pp. 4, 569.

69. BrQR (January 1864), pp. 112-121.

70. Microfilm of the Brownson Papers, roll 6.

71. "Military Matters and Men," BrQR (July 1864), pp. 243-244.

72. "Lincoln or Fremont," BrQR (July 1864), pp. 339-370.

73. Microfilm of the Brownson Papers, roll 9.

74. Abraham Lincoln, The War Years (Vol. I), ut supra, pp. 3, 344.

75. *Latter Life,* p. 450.

76. *Latter Life,* p. 452, n. He also counseled the general public to vote for Lincoln. (See *Works,* XVII, p. 536.)

77. Microfilm of the *Brownson Papers,* roll 6.

78. *Latter Life,* pp. 434-436.

79. Microfilm of the *Brownson Papers,* roll 8.

80. *Latter Life,* p. 438.

81. BrQR (October 1861), p. 547.

82. On November 5, 1862, Brownson actually wrote his friend Fr. Sorin of Notre Dame to ascertain what terms could be granted him should he decide to accept a professorship there, saying that in such an event he would discontinue his *Review.* This was only a few months after Richard Simpson, founder with Sir John Acton of the *Home and Foreign Review* (July 1862) had asked him to become a contributor.

83. "Explanations to Catholics," *BrQR* (October 1864), p. 489; *Works,* XX, pp. 380-381.

84. Microfilm of the *Brownson Papers,* roll 6. In a letter to Count Montalembert (June 1865), Brownson expressed his regrets for his pages critical of the Jesuits "because they can do no good, and have been and will be misunderstood." Microfilm of the *Brownson Papers,* roll 6. Brownson differed from the Jesuits in theology and philosophy and in these matters, as in others, he claimed the fullest measure of freedom in expressing his honest convictions. He had the highest veneration for the Jesuits individually, and counted many of them among his truest and warmest friends. And few have been the persons who have said things more laudatory of the Society. But he did not think the Society was free from all corporate imperfections any more than any other society.

85. Microfilm of the *Brownson Papers,* roll 6. Archbishop Francis Patrick Kenrick, archbishop of Baltimore, however, felt that Brownson's *Review* was "lacking in variety" by "presenting the face of one writer only to its readers." But the difficulty in the matter for Brownson was to find contributors who would make offerings that comported with the high standard of his sedate *Quarterly.* A solicitous friend wrote him on July 7, 1857, remonstrating with him against the introduction into his *Review* in the past of articles "fit only to injure the *Review.* . . . We would rather pay the double of our subscription and have essays always from your pen or worthy of it." *Latter Life,* pp. 90-91. It is not surprising, then, that Brownson "insisted perseveringly" with such a scholar as Archbishop F. Patrick Kenrick himself that he write for the *Review.* And the archbishop in turn kept urging his brother, Peter Richard Kenrick, archbishop of St. Louis, that he do the same. But it does not appear that he ever did. (See F.E.T. *The Kenrick-Frenaye Correspondence, Letters Chiefly of Francis Patrick Kenrick and Marc Antony Frenaye* [selected from the Cathedral Archives of Philadelphia], 1830-1862, pp. 221, 292, 318.)

Archbishop F. Patrick Kenrick, however, did try to add variety to Brownson's *Review* by such articles as: "Christian Ethics" (April 1846), pp. 137-153; "Gerard College" (April 1849), pp. 162-175; "Guevara on the Veneration of Images" (January 1850), pp. 39-56; "Bishop England's Works" (April 1850), pp. 137-159; "Life of Mrs. Eliza A. Seton" (April 1853), pp. 165-184; "Prayer Books" (April 1857), pp. 184-190; and "The Mortara Case" (April 1859), pp. 226-246.

After Bishop John Bernard Fitzpatrick of Boston, Archbishop F. Patrick Kenrick was Brownson's best friend in the American hierarchy. When he had understood that Brownson was to discontinue his *Review* at the end of 1861, he was solicitous to provide a pension for him, and wrote his brother on August 23, 1861: "Brownson, tired out with contradictions, and suffering from his eyes, will give up his work [the *Review*] in the month of October. He will be in need of the means to sustain life. It would be an excellent thing to fix a pension for him of at least six hundred dollars a year. If the bishops favor this, it can be done easily." *Kenrick-Frenaye Correspondence, ut supra,* p. 462.

## CHAPTER 43

1. Microfilm of the *Brownson Papers,* supplementary roll 1. This is the same Louis B. Binsse who had been consul of the Propaganda Fide, Rome, to the United States.

2. *Latter Life,* pp. 443-444.

3. *Ibid.,* pp. 444-446.

4. Microfilm of the *Brownson Papers,* roll 9. A copy of this letter was recently obtained from the archives of the Château de la Roche-en-Breny, France, by the late archivist of Notre Dame University, Thomas T. McAvoy, C.S.C.

5. Microfilm of the *Brownson Papers,* roll 6.

6. *Ibid.*

7. Unpublished dissertation of Leonard James McCarthy, S.J., *Rhetoric in the Works of Orestes Brownson* (New York: Fordham University Press, 1961), pp. 160-161. This dissertation contains an excellent commentary on Brownson's literary style in his book, *The American Republic.* He sees the philosophical style as the perfect style to match the genre of the book. Lawrence Roemer, on the other hand, seems to think that the style, among other facts he also mentions, lessens the merits of the book, making it neither "his last nor his best book." He asserts: "*The American Republic* cannot possibly be the best Brownson wrote." *Brownson on Democracy and the Trend toward Socialism* (New York: Philosophical Library, 1953), pp. xiv-xv. Charles Raymond McCarthy, C.S.P., has given Roemer's half-page estimate of Brownson's *The American Republic* a valid four-point rebuttal in his dissertation on *The Political Philosophy of Orestes A. Brownson* (University of Toronto, 1962), pp. 11-14. This, however, is not to say that the rest of Roemer's book does not have its distinctive merits.

Fr. McCarthy wrote his dissertation to inquire "to what extent there are two political philosophies in Brownson" (p. 14). That is, the one of his Transcendental period, and a different one later. He thinks that the failure to note the difference between the earlier and the later political philosophy may well be the reason why "Brownson's political philosophy has been treated too much as if it were one piece, to the detriment of both his philosophies" (p. 233).

Although Fr. McCarthy's dissertation contains many good insights, he is not accurate when he says that "after 1842 Brownson rejected Transcendentalism and, for a time, ceased to write dealing with political theory. When he began to write once again on political thought, a period of seven years had elapsed" (p. 14). Brownson wrote five political articles in 1843, including the three articles on the "Origin and Ground of Government," which were later to form the basis of *The American Republic.* (See *Early Life,* p. 348.) He wrote another on the "Origin and Constitution of Government" in 1844. To mention no others, Brownson's very important article on "Political Constitutions" was written and published in 1847. Whether or not Fr. McCarthy establishes his thesis that there are two political philosophies in Brownson's writings, both Lawrence Roemer and Robert Emmet Moffit see no "radical break" in Brownson's political thoughts subsequent to his conversion to the Catholic Church in 1844. (See Moffit's *Orestes Augustus Brownson on the Nature and Scope of Political Authority* [Tucson University of Arizona Press, 1971], p. 170. All the articles of Brownson here referred to are contained in Vol. XV of his *Works.*)

8. *The University Bookman* (Spring, 1973), p. 52.

9. *BrQR* (July 1873), pp. 419-420.

10. "Home Politics," *BrQR* (October 1875), p. 544; *Works,* XVIII, p. 579. Speaking of the confusion regarding where sovereignty resides in the American political system that prevailed during the Civil War, he further said that only "some three or four members of congress understood the question, but they were lost in the dense fog that enveloped the rest, the administration, and the people." "Constitutional Law — the Executive Power," *BrQR* (July 1874), p. 383; *Works,* XVIII, p. 276.

11. *The American Republic, Works,* XVIII, p. 7. There are various editions of *The American Republic* with varying pagination. References hereafter will be made to the book as incorporated in volume XVIII of the *Works.*

12. *Ibid.*, p. 2.

13. *Latter Life*, p. 451.

14. *The American Republic*, p. 2. Although Lawrence Roemer does not agree, as we have noted, Aaron I. Abell says of this statement of Brownson: "It proved in fact to be his last word in the sense that thereafter he added nothing constructive to the body of political theory." This seems correct except possibly in regard to some of Brownson's thought on amendments to the Constitution which he did not treat in *The American Republic*. (See "Brownson's 'The American Republic': The Political Testament of a Reluctant Democrat," *Records of the American Catholic Historical Society of Philadelphia*, LXV [June 1955], p. 127.)

15. *Ibid.*, p. 3.

16. *Ibid.*, pp. 7-8.

17. *Rhetoric in the Works of Orestes Brownson*, p. 253.

18. *The American Republic*, p. 12.

19. *Ibid.*, p. 11.

20. *BrQR* (April 1863), p. 245.

21. *The American Republic*, pp. 3, 9, 11. This alteration in Brownson's thought has been noted neither by Aaron I. Abell in his article listed in footnote 14, nor by Hugh Marshall in his book, *Orestes Brownson and the American Republic* (Washington, D.C.: Catholic University of America Press, 1971), p. 52. Abell says simply: "In Brownson's view America's providential constitution — the constitution of the state and civil society — was fundamentally the British Constitution minus the hereditary House of Lords and the hereditary monarchy" (p. 121).

22. *Ibid.*, p. 130.

23. *Ibid.*, p. 131.

24. *Ibid.*, p. 3. The eminent constitutional historian, Charles Howard McIlwain, has noted: "There is no medieval doctrine of the separation of powers. . . . It is a figment of the imagination of eighteenth-century doctrinaires who found it in our earlier history only because they were ignorant of the true nature of that history. These political balances were unknown before the eighteenth century, were almost untried before the nineteenth." *Constitutionalism, Ancient and Modern* (Ithaca, New York: 1947), pp. 142-143. Cited by Arthur M. Schlesinger, Jr., in *The Imperial Presidency* (Boston: Houghton Mifflin Co., 1973), p. 423, n. 1.

25. *Ibid.*, p. 132. The division of power, he insisted, is not between a *national* government and state governments, but between a *general* government and particular governments. "The general government, inasmuch as it extends to matters common to all the states, is generally called the government of the United States, and sometimes the federal government, to distinguish it from the particular or state governments, but without strict propriety; for the government of the United States, or the federal government, means, in strictness, both the general and the particular goverments, since neither is in itself the complete government of the country." *Ibid.*, p. 131.

26. *Ibid.*, p. 9.

27. *Ibid.*, pp. 9-10.

28. Sister M. Felicia Corrigan, S.L., is the first one who reported this in her dissertation on *Some Social Principles of Orestes A. Brownson* (Catholic University of America Press, 1939), p. 15. She wrote: "Woodrow Wilson is also said to have stated in a summer course at John Hopkins University, that any one who knows anything about works on the Constitution, knows that *The American Republic* is the greatest treatment ever written thereon; but he added that Brownson was a Catholic. This information was brought out during discussions at the seventh annual meeting of the A.C.P.A. in 1931. As far as the present writer is aware, there is no printed evidence of the fact" (p. 15, n.). She most probably obtained this information from Fr. Joseph P. Donovan, C.M., J.C.D., who read a paper on Brownson's political thought at that meeting.

29. *The American Republic*, p. 5.

30. *Ibid.*, p. 15.

31. *Ibid.*, pp. 28-29.

32. *Ibid.*, p. 29.

33. "The American Republic and Western Christendom," *Historical Records and Studies*, XXXV, 1945, p. 10.

34. *The American Republic*, pp. 29-30.

35. *Ibid.*, pp. 30-33. Brownson really examined closely eight theories which purport to explain the origin of government, namely: (1) Government originates in the right of the father to govern his child. (2) It originates in convention, and is a social compact. (3) It originates in the people, who, collectively taken, are sovereign. (4) Goverment springs from the spontaneous development of nature. (5) It derives its rights from the immediate and direct appointment of God. (6) It derives its rights from God through the pope, or visible head of the spiritual society. (7) It derives its rights from God through the people. (8) It derives its rights through the natural law.

The last two of these theories Brownson found acceptable. The first of the two, the Thomistic-Suárez theory, derives government from God through the people; the second, the one Brownson seemed to prefer, develops government from God to the people through the natural law.

Robert Emmet Moffit has made a close examination of Brownson's analysis of these eight theories in his thesis *Orestes Augustus Brownson on the Nature and Scope of Political Authority* (Tucson: University of Arizona, 1971). His thesis is an excellent contribution to a growing literature on Brownson's political philosophy.

There is also an excellent treatise on the origin of government in *Robert Bellarmine*, by James Broderick, S.J. (New York: Longmans, Green, and Co., 1950), in Volume I, Chapter XI, "Princes and People," presenting in particular the Bellarmine-Suárez doctrine versus Rousseau's "social contract."

36. *Ibid.*, pp. 74-75. Brownson, however, rebuked De Maistre for his exclusive monarchical views, and for excluding human agency from the formation of the civil polity. *Ibid.* He accordingly rejected also De Maistre's doctrine that constitutions are "fixed and unalterable."

37. Stanley Parry, C.S.C., "The Premises of Brownson's Political Theory," *Review of Politics*, XVI (April 1954), p. 197.

38. Ross J. S. Hoffman, "The American Republic and Western Christendom," *Historical Records and Studies*, XXXV (1946), pp. 10-11.

39. *Ibid.*

40. *The American Republic*, p. 126.

41. *Ibid.*, p. 113. Brownson remarked: "State sovereignty broke the nation into pieces, and destroyed not only the life of the whole, but the life of each of the parts." "The Federal Constitution," *BrQR* (January 1864), p. 22; *Works*, XVII, p. 487.

Stanley Parry gives here the difference between Brownson's thought and that of Aristotle on what is required if a written political constitution is to work well: "The good political constitution is that which Aristotle says 'is the best in relation to actual conditions.' (Politics, Bk. IV, ch. I, 1288b) In reasoning to this conclusion, however, Brownson's minor premise is quite different from Aristotle's. He uses the political argument of Aristotle: that a constitution out of joint with its society will not work and therefore is not good for the society. But this is not ultimate in his thinking. The real reason why such a constitution is bad is that it is the product of secondary causality operating out of harmony with the primary effects of Providence. Thus it violates the basic law that human action must conform to the patterns created and developed by Divine Action." "The Premises of Brownson's Political Theory," *The Review of Politics* (April 1954), p. 200.

42. *Ibid.*, pp. 139-140.

43. St. Paul's Letter to the Romans, Chapter 13, v. 2; also *The American Republic*, pp. 61-62.

44. *The American Republic*, p. 66.

45. *Ibid.*, p. 25.

46. *Ibid.*, p. 45.

47. This is taken from a newspaper clipping made when Dr. Toynbee lectured in this country in 1955. The name of the paper is not indicated. The heading of the article

reads: "Historian says life based on technology does not jibe with religious foundation."

48. *The American Republic*, p. 153.

49. *Ibid.*, p. 38ff. Brownson spoke of the state as "a mysterious existence." (See "The Federal Constitution," *BrQR* [January 1964], p. 36; *Works*, XVII, p. 501.)

50. *The American Political Mind: A Textbook in Political Theory* (New York: McGraw-Hill, 1949), p. 279.

51. *The American Republic*, p. 178.

52. *Ibid.*, pp. 182-184.

53. "The American Republic and Western Christendom," *Historical Records and Studies*, XXXV, 1845, p. 9. Their counterpart today would be such types as the Berrigan brothers, their sympathizers, *et id omne genus*.

54. *The American Republic*, p. 185.

55. *Ibid.*, p. 186.

56. *Ibid.*, p. 187.

57. "Orestes A. Brownson," *The American Republic, The Review of Politics*, IV (April 1942), p. 182.

58. *The American Republic*, pp. 109-113. "The key to the mystery [the political nature of the states]," he said, "is precisely in this appellation *United States*, which is not the name of the country, for its distinctive name is America, but a name expressive of its political organization." *Ibid.*, p. 115.

According to Hugh Marshall, John Hurd's best service to Brownson in his book, *The Law of Freedom and Bondage in the United States*, was in directing Brownson's mind to "historical fact" in the case, as opposed to the legal and political theories current about where sovereignty lay in the American system. *Orestes Brownson and The American Republic* (Washington: Catholic University of America Press, 1971), p. 202.

Paul R. Conroy does not accept Brownson's tenet that the American states (previously the colonies) were never sovereign severally. He says: "A glance at any standard history of the United States shows that the colonies certainly thought they were sovereign after they secured their independence from Great Britain, and proceeded to act as such." Conroy seems to think it was only the Civil War that made us one nation. (See "The Role of the American Constitution in the Political Philosophy of Orestes A. Brownson," *The Catholic Historical Review*, XXV [October 1939], p. 248.)

But Conroy paid a great tribute to the perennial value of Brownson's political writings when he said: "If dates were deleted from his articles, one might easily suppose they had been written in our own times for our own generation. They have a peculiarly modern ring, for Brownson was a disillusioned man who lived and wrote a half century before our age of disillusionment." *Ibid.*, p. 286.

59. "Brownson, the Philosophical Expounder of the Constitution," *Proceedings of the Seventh Annual Meeting of the Catholic American Philosophical Association* (St. Louis: St. Louis University, December 29, 1931), p. 162.

60. *The American Republic*, pp. 24, 152-153. When Brownson wrote his review of *Fr. Thébaud's Irish Race* (1873), he said: "Were we writing our 'American Republic' now, after having read Father Thébaud . . . we would . . . correct, in some respects, our definition of Barbarism." *BrQR* (October 1873), p. 497; *Works*, XIII, p. 556.

Brownson also stated that to claim the elective franchise as a natural right of man is only to assert the fundamental principle of barbarism. It is a political trust, not a natural right, which the state may extend to whom it will. But he made clear that he was not for a restrictive suffrage: "To restrict suffrage to property holders helps nothing, theoretically or practically. Property has of itself advantages enough, without clothing its holders with exclusive political rights and privileges, and the laboring classes any day are as trustworthy as the business classes. The wise statesman will never restrict suffrage, or exclude the poorer and more numerous classes from all voice in the government of their country. General suffrage is wise. . . .

*Ibid.*, p. 24. He included in this the Southern blacks also. (See Brownson's letter dated December 24, 1865, *Latter Life*, p. 468.)

61. Microfilm of the *Brownson Papers*, roll 6.

62. *The Growth of American Thought* (New York: Harper and Brothers, 1951), p. 474.

63. *The American Republic*, pp. 190-191.

64. "Catholic Yankee; Resuscitating Orestes Brownson," *Triumph*, IV (April 1969), p. 26.

65. *The American Republic*, p. 198. Professors Cook and Leavelle cite the Roosevelt-Churchill eight-point "Atlantic Charter" as exemplifying Brownson's political realism in foreseeing the role the United States was destined to play in European affairs. "The American Republic," *The Review of Politics*, IV (April 1942), p. 89, n.

66. *Ibid.*, p. 221.

67. *Ibid.*, p. 199.

68. *Ibid.*, p. 221.

69. "The American Republic and Western Christendom," *Historical Records and Studies* (1946), p. 8.

70. *The American Republic*, p. 221.

71. "The American Republic," *Review of Politics*, IV (1942), p. 191.

72. *The American Republic*, p. 211.

73. *Ibid.*, p. 217.

74. "The American Republic," *Review of Politics*, IV (April 1942), p. 191.

75. *BrQR* (July 1873), p. 420.

76. "The American Republic and Western Christendom," *ut supra*, p. 7.

77. Cf. n. 28 above.

78. *The American Republic*, p. 4.

79. Microfilm of the *Brownson Papers*, roll 4.

80. But he did this also forthrightly as a Protestant. (See his forthright statement on Christianity as the basis of politics and government in his article on the "Origin and Ground of Government," *Works*, XV, p. 353.)

81. A Thesis, *Orestes Augustus Brownson on the Nature and Scope of Political Authority* (Tucson: University of Arizona, 1971), pp. 164-165.

82. *The American Republic*, p. 192. Brownson always maintained that the American state is founded on old Catholic principles. The Founding Fathers, he said, "were so directed and overruled by Providence that they retained from the old civilization of Europe only those principles which harmonized with Catholicity, and added to them only those principles which the Popes for ages had been urging in vain on European statesmen." "The Constitution of the Church," *BrQR* (January 1856), p. 17; *Works*, VIII, p. 543. He referred particularly of course to the principle of the incompetence of the state in spiritual matters and a recognition of the inalienable rights of man. Two articles have been written by distinguished scholars which point to evidence that the Catholic democratic doctrine of medieval divines, particularly that of Robert Bellarmine, may well have influenced the thought of the Founding Fathers. The one entitled "The Virginia Declaration of Rights and Cardinal Bellarmine," which appeared in the *Catholic Historical Review* (October 1917), pp. 276-289, is by Gaillard Hunt, then head of the Department of Manuscripts in the Library of Congress. The other is by Professor Alfred A. Rahilly, and is entitled "Sources of English and American Democracy," *Studies, An Irish Quarterly Review* (June 1919), pp. 189-207. Among other evidence in the case, both authors bring out the fact that Jefferson's copy of Sir Robert Filmer's *Patriarcha* is still in the Library of Congress. Filmer was an inveterate royalist, and on the opening page of his treatise he epitomized the democratic doctrine of Bellarmine only for the purpose of refuting it. There it was on the first page when Jefferson opened his volume.

Thomas R. Ryan, C.PP.S., *The Sailor's Snug Harbor; Studies in Brownson's Thought* (Westminster, Maryland: The Newman Book Shop, 1952), has an article on "The Church and the American Constitution" pp. 98-106.

83. *Ibid.*, p. 140.

84. "The Democratic Principle," *BrQR* (April 1873), p. 243; *Works*, XVIII, p. 230.

85. *The American Republic*, p. 142.

86. *Ibid.*, p. 96.

87. *Ibid.*, p. 81.

88. "Home Politics," *BrQR* (October 1875), p. 548; *Works*, XVIII, p. 583. Commented on in *The American Republic*, p. 171.

89. *The American Republic*, pp. 170-173.

90. *Ibid.*, p. 164.

91. "Constitutional Guarantees," *BrQR* (April 1874), p. 208; *Works*, XVIII, p. 256.

92. *Ibid.*, pp. 205-206; *Works*, XVIII, p. 254.

93. "Home Politics," *BrQR* (October 1875), p. 547; *Works*, XVIII, p. 582.

94. *Ibid.*, p. 546; *Works*, XVIII, p. 581. He was growing a trifle pessimistic about the way the Constitution was being managed, or rather mismanaged: "Our own experience proves that the people are not safe guardians of the Constitution, for they have in numerous instances sanctioned its violation, and in several [cases] violated it themselves. It was violated by Congress in the case of the creation of the state of West Virginia out of the state of Virginia; for the pretense that the Pierrepont government was competent to give the consent of Virginia was too ridiculous to be seriously considered. Not one of the states that seceded from the Union has been reconstructed on constitutional principles, yet the ruling people approved the unconstitutional laws." *BrQR* (April 1874), p. 204; *Works*, XVIII, p. 253.

95. "Brownson, the Philosophical Expounder of the Constitution," *The Proceedings of the Seventh Annual Meeting of the American Catholic Philosophical Association, ut supra*, p. 162.

96. "The Role of the American Constitution in the Political Philosophy of Orestes A. Brownson," *Catholic Historical Review*, XXV (October 1939), p. 275.

97. (Judge) Peter H. Burnett, "The American Theory of Government," *BrQR* (July 1873), p. 430.

98. *Ibid.*

99. A doctoral dissertation, *Metaphysics and Constitutionalism*, Chapter VII, *Brownson and the Democratic Theory* (Tucson: University of Arizona Press, 1975), p. 625.

100. "The American Republic," *The Review of Politics*, IV (January 1942), p. 77.

101. Augustus M. Kelley, ed., *The American Republic* (Clifton, New Jersey: Augustus M. Kelley, Publishers, 1972).

102. Americo D. Lapati, ed., *The American Republic* (New Haven, Connecticut: College and University Press, Publishers, 1972), p. 19. Joseph P. Donovan, in an article in *Columbia* (April 1927), "Giant among Giants," called Brownson's *The American Republic* "the greatest book on general politics that has ever come from the American press" (p. 36).

103. "Orestes Brownson," *The Atlantic Monthly*, LXXVII (June 1896), p. 777.

## CHAPTER 44

1. *Latter Life*, p. 451.

2. *Ibid.*, p. 576.

3. Sidney A. Raemers, M.A., Ph.D., *America's Foremost Philosopher* (Washington, D.C.: St. Anselm's Priory, 1931), foreword, pp. xv-xvi.

4. Microfilm of the *Brownson Papers*, roll 9.

5. *Ibid.*, roll 5.

6. *BrQR* (July 1873), p. 416.

7. *Ibid.* (July 1852), p. 420.

8. "The Christian Register's Defense," *BrQR* (October 1852), p. 460; *Works*, VI, p. 230. Fr. Francis P. Siegfried, professor of philosophy at Charles's Seminary, Overbrook, Pennsylvania, though not accepting what he called Brownson's "basal principle" in philosophy, remarked: "Now, no one acquainted with Dr. Brownson's

works and the English literature of philosophy will deny that he has few peers, if he has one, among philosophers who have used our mother tongue as the vehicle of their thought." "A Recent Work on Faith and Science," *The American Ecclesiastical Review*, XIV (January 1896), pp. 66, 72.

9. *Middle Life*, pp. 214-218; *Works*, I, pp. 215, 240-241.

10. Microfilm of the *Brownson Papers*, roll 9.

11. *Latter Life*, p. 556.

12. *BrQR* (January 1854), pp. 56-57; *Works*, I, pp. 301-302.

13. "Primitive Elements of Thought," *BrQR* (January 1859), p. 68; *Works*, I, p. 418.

14. "The Giobertian Philosophy," *BrQR* (April 1864), pp. 135-136; *Works*, II, pp. 217-218.

15. "Primitive Elements of Thought," *BrQR* (January 1859), p. 72; *Works*, II, p. 421.

16. He was still standing by the Giobertian formula in the last year of his *Review* (1875). Among the solutions to the epistemological problem offered by philosophers, whether ancient or modern, Christian or heathen, he preferred that of Gioberti as the key to the epistemological mystery. He added: "We do not cite Gioberti as authority for holding the doctrine, but as the author who first formally stated it and defined it. We hold the doctrine for reasons independent of Gioberti, and of every other philosopher, ancient or modern; for reasons which we have heretofore given and regard as conclusive." *BrQR* (April 1875), pp. 274-275; *Works*, II, pp. 500-501.

17. *Orestes A. Brownson: A Pilgrim's Progress* (Boston: Little, Brown and Co., 1939), p. 231.

18. "An A Priori Autobiography," *BrQR* (January 1850), pp. 21, 23; *Works*, I, p. 236.

19. "The Existence of God," *BrQR* (April 1852), p. 163; *Works*, I, p. 274.

20. *Middle Life*, p. 215.

21. "An A Priori Autobiography," *BrQR* (January 1850), pp. 28-29; *Works*, I, pp. 241-242, n.

22. Letter to this writer, dated September 12, 1947.

23. "Ward's Philosophical Introduction," *BrQR* (January 1861), pp. 1-32; *Works*, XIV, pp. 348-379.

24. *Latter Life*, p. 326.

25. *Ibid.*, pp. 323-324.

26. *Ibid.*, p. 327.

27. "A Few Words on Dr. Brownson's Philosophy," *Dublin Review*, XXVI (January 1876), pp. 36-55. It was not very logical on Ward's part to call for a clearance of Brownson's philosophy after confessing he could not get at an understanding of it. If he failed to understand it, how could he know it was unsound?

28. "Catholic Popular Literature," *BrQR* (April 1873), pp. 201-202; *Works*, XIX, pp. 591-592.

29. "Brownson's Works," *The Irish Ecclesiastical Record*, I (January 1884), pp. 14-15.

30. *Ibid.*, pp. 14-15.

31. "The Existence of God," *BrQR* (April 1852), p. 163; *Works*, I, p. 274.

32. *Middle Life*, p. 213.

33. *Ibid.*, p. 633.

34. *Ibid.*, pp. 212-213.

35. Fr. Joseph Herman Koop, C.M., was professor of philosophy at the Seminary of Our Lady of Angels, Niagara County, New York. In a letter to Brownson, dated January 17, 1872, he said: "I must sincerely acknowledge, and always have and always will acknowledge my great indebtedness to you for any knowledge of philosophy I have." Microfilm of the *Brownson Papers*, roll 7.

36. Letter to this writer, dated August 7, 1941.

37. Raemers, p. 109.

38. *Orestes Brownson's Approach to the Problem of God* (Washington, D.C.: Catholic University of America Press, 1950), p. 130.

39. Microfilm of the *Brownson Papers,* roll 9.

40. *Latter Life,* p. 330.

41. *Ibid.,* p. 555. In his article "Rationalism and Traditionalism," *BrQR* (October 1860), p. 429, *Works,* I, pp. 505-506, Brownson rejected in particular the tenet of the Louvain professors, as represented by Abbé Lefebvre, that we have an innate *idea* of God.

42. "Primitive Elements of Thought," *BrQR* (January 1859), pp. 60, 74; *Works,* I, pp. 409, 422.

43. "Schools of Philosophy," *BrQR* (January 1854), pp. 31-32; *Works,* I, pp. 277-278.

44. *Recent Philosophy: Hegel to the Present* (New York: Random House, 1966).

45. In another letter, dated August 23, 1970, Fr. Maurer referred to the high estimate the late noted philosopher, Gerald B. Phelan (1895-1965), set upon Brownson as a philosopher. He wrote: "I knew Fr. Phelan well and am aware that he had a great admiration for Brownson. I once heard him say that he thought Brownson was the best philosopher produced by the United States."

46. Fr. Maurer added here the footnote: "Brownson ascribes the condemned propositions to unnamed 'Louvain professors' and denies that he himself teaches it in the sense in which it is condemned." "Refutation of Atheism," I, pp. 11, 52. (See "The Giobertian Philosophy," II, pp. 260-261. *Recent Philosophy, ut supra,* p. 489, n. 48.)

47. *Recent Philosophy,* p. 583. Fr. Maurer adds here another footnote: "An Old Quarrel," II, p. 304. In reply to a letter by H. S. McMurdie, Brownson comments on each of the seven propositions concerning ontologism and pantheism condemned by Pius IX in 1861, and he denies that he teaches them. (See T. T. McAvoy, "Brownson and Ontologism," *The Catholic Historical Review,* XXVIII [1943], pp. 376-481. On the same page as above, p. 489.)

Robert Emmet Moffit, who has been doing work on Brownson's thought for the past several years at the University of Arizona, remarked on Brownson's philosophy in a letter dated May 22, 1974: "Those who have read ontologism into his [Brownson's] writings have failed to consider his psycho-epistemological problem: if we fail to intuitively discern *necessity* in the act of thought, as an element of thought, then there is absolutely no way for the mind to account for the laws of logic, the necessity which underlies mathematical and physical principles, geometry, and the simple principle of non-contradiction which hovers about us every day. Certainly our knowledge of these things is not empirical. He only claimed to have an intuitive knowledge of real and necessary being, not God. This alone releases him from the ontological charge. The necessity of things in the world is a *participated* necessity, which exists by virtue of the *creative* act, which Brownson holds is essentially mysterious."

Daniel R. Barnes, professor of English at Ohio State University, also stated the case clearly for Brownson when he said in a remarkable article: "In so denying that we can know the existence of God by intuitive means alone, and in affirming that such knowledge comes only after reflecting upon the data intuitively furnished, Brownson at one and the same time establishes clearly his own view of the relation of the roles of reason and intuition in the cognitive process and exonerates himself of the charge of ontologism." "Brownson and Newman, The Controversy Re-examined," *Emerson Society Quarterly,* no. 50 (First Quarter, 1968), p. 14.

48. "Faith and Theology," *BrQR* (January 1863), pp. 24-26; *Works,* VIII, pp. 23-24. (See also "Hill's Elements of Philosophy," *BrQR* [October 1875], p. 491; *Works,* II, p. 507.)

49. "A Study of Dr. Brownson," *The Catholic World,* LXXVII (June 1903), p. 316.

50. "What Reason Can Do," *BrQR* (April 1855), p. 243; *Works,* I, p. 320.

51. "Primitive Elements of Thought," *BrQR* (January 1859), p. 71; *Works,* I, p. 420.

52. "Rationalism and Traditionalism," *BrQR* (October 1860), p. 414; *Works,* I, p. 494.

53. "Conversations of an Old Man with Young Friends," *BrQR* (October 1850), p. 520; *Works,* X, p. 320.

54. "Various Objections Answered," *BrQR* (October 1861), p. 424; *Works,* XX, p. 137.

55. *Ibid.*

56. "Hill's Elements of Philosophy," *BrQR* (October 1875), p. 502; *Works,* II, p. 518.

57. In the quote above, n. 45; p. 583 in *Recent Philosophy.*

58. "Vincenzo Gioberti's Philosophy of Revelation," *BrQR* (July 1861), p. 281; *Works,* II, p. 140.

59. *Latter Life,* p. 525. This is another instance of the oscillatory tendency of Brownson's mind. His great enthusiasm sometimes carried him too far, and he would then retreat. If enthusiasm has its advantages, it also has its disadvantages.

60. *The Convert,* vol. V, p. 126.

61. "The Giobertian Philosophy," *BrQR* (April 1864), pp. 137-138; *Works,* II, p. 219.

62. "The Philosophy of Religion," *BrQR* (October 1861), p. 486; *Works,* II, p. 20. In a letter dated April 23, 1974, George N. Shuster remarked: "The German Catholic encyclopedias I have [researched] state pointblank that he [Gioberti] taught Ontologism and that his last idea was to make a synthesis of Plato and Hegel."

63. "Rationalism and Traditionalism," *BrQR* (October 1860), p. 419; *Works,* I, p. 498.

64. "Schmucker's Psychology," *Works,* I, p. 42. (This article was first published in the *Democratic Review,* October 1842.)

65. "Hill's Elements of Philosophy," *BrQR* (October 1875), p. 502; *Works,* II, p. 518.


## CHAPTER 45

1. *Latter Life,* p. 498.

2. "Saint-Worship," *Works,* VIII, p. 174.

3. *Ibid.*, p. 120. Brownson had also dealt with this same charge of Mariolatry in a previous article in 1853 on "The Worship of Mary," *BrQR* (January 1853), pp. 22-23. It was at a time when, as Fr. Edward Day, C.SS.R., has observed, spiritualism had become a common cult in Boston that Dr. Brownson chose to set down the teaching of the Catholic Church on the Mother of God. He did so to brace and confirm the faith of Catholics. "While sneering at the Mariolatry of their chambermaids, Boston's best families saw nothing incongruous in straining the silence of a séance for tappings of spirits from the great beyond." Fr. Edward Day, "Orestes Brownson and the Motherhood of Mary," *The American Ecclesiastical Review,* XXXIX (July 1953), pp. 20-27. Rappomania (a coined word meaning "spirit rapping") was sweeping New England and, as an editorial in the Boston *Pilot* stated: "Scarcely a village can be found which is not infected with it." Herbert Thurston, S.J., *The Church and Spiritualism* (Milwaukee: Bruce Publishing Co., 1933), p. 49.

4. *Ibid.*, p. 185; *Latter Life,* pp. 497-501.

5. Microfilm of the *Brownson Papers,* roll 6.

6. *Ibid.*

7. *Latter Life,* p. 506.

8. Microfilm of the *Brownson Papers,* roll 6.

9. M. R. Daily, "Gillespie, Angela, Mother," the *New Catholic Encyclopedia,* VI, pp. 489-490.

10. "Catholic Schools and Education," *BrQR* (January 1862), pp. 66-85; *Works,* XII, pp. 496-514.

11. In childhood Mother Angela had been Eliza Maria Gillespie, and was cousin to James Gillespie Blaine, later the famed "Plumed Knight." They grew up together as next-door neighbors and playmates. She was also niece to Senator Thomas Ewing, and was related to the Shermans of Ohio and other prominent families of the Middle

West. After having distinguished herself in the academic world, she was one of the first to answer the call that burst forth during the Civil War for volunteer nurses on the battlefield. Fr. Sorin accompanied her to Washington, D.C., and introduced her to President Lincoln. The extensive work she did in caring for the sick and wounded won her a high place among the "Angels of the Battlefield." When she died on March 4, 1887, her funeral was a real event. Messages of condolence poured in from many parts of the country. One addressed to the Hon. H. Ewing read: "Your message is a sad one to me. Communicate my deepest sympathy to Aunt Mary and your mother." It was signed "James G. Blaine." "James G. Blaine's Religion," *Historical Records and Studies* (1938), XXIX, pp. 75, 78.

12. *Latter Life,* pp. 499-500. Fr. Bonaventure Stefun, O.F.M., published two articles on the Mariological thought of Brownson in the *American Ecclesiastical Review* under the heading, "The Mother of God in Brownson's writings." The one in the May 1956 issue and the other in the July 1956 edition. They are worthy of the subject.

13. *Latter Life,* pp. 507-508.

14. *The History of American Magazines,* 1865-1885 (Cambridge: Harvard University Press, 1938), III, p. 329.

15. *Latter Life,* p. 514.

16. *Ibid.,* pp. 512-513.

17. Microfilm of the *Brownson Papers,* roll 9 (September 26, 1871).

18. *Ibid.*

19. *Ibid.*

20. *Ibid.*

21. *Ibid.*

22. *Ibid.*

23. Microfilm of the *Brownson Papers,* roll 6.

24. *Ibid.*

25. *Ibid.*

26. Microfilm of the *Brownson Papers,* roll 9. Brownson wrote his son Henry on February 1, 1869: "Fr. Hecker wants me to write according to his mind not only [in] the *Catholic World,* but also in the *Tablet.* The excellent man is utterly unconscious of the despotism he would exercise. . . . But I shall write as I please or not at all." Microfilm of the *Brownson Papers,* roll 6.

27. Microfilm of the *Brownson Papers,* roll 6.

28. *Ibid.* This is the same Cantu who had pronounced Brownson "North America's best prosewriter." (See *BrQR* [July 1856], p. 398.)

29. Microfilm of the *Brownson Papers,* roll 9.

30. *Ibid.*

31. Microfilm of the *Brownson Papers,* roll 6.

32. Microfilm of the *Brownson Papers,* roll 9.

33. "Why a Brownson Revival?" *Acolyte,* III (March 1827), p. 7. We have already noted that the most extensive study ever made of Brownson's doctrine on church and state is that made by Professor Francis E. McMahon, which appeared in the June 1954 issue of *Theological Studies* (Woodstock, Maryland), XV, no. 2, under the heading, "Orestes Brownson on Church and State."

34. Microfilm of the *Brownson Papers,* roll 9.

35. *Ibid.* We can understand better his lament over having fulfilled none of his "mighty plans" when we recall what he wrote his son Henry on March 2, 1866: "I am about to commence another work, *The Problem of the Age,* designed to show the principle in which [the following] meet and are reconciled: Faith & Reason, Revelation & Science, Theology & Philosophy. I wish to do some thing for my age similar to what St. Augustine did in his *de Civitate Dei* for his age, & St. Thomas in his *Contra Gentiles* did for his age. You see my ambition is great, greater than my ability, but I will do the best I can." Microfilm of the *Brownson Papers,* roll 9.

36. *BQR* (January 1838), p. 3.

37. *Latter Life,* pp. 539-540.

38. Microfilm of the *Brownson Papers,* roll 9.

39. *Ibid.*

40. *Latter Life,* p. 564.

41. Microfilm of the *Brownson Papers,* roll 7.

42. Microfilm of the *Brownson Papers,* roll 9.

43. *Ibid.*

44. *Latter Life,* p. 566.

45. Microfilm of the *Brownson Papers,* roll 7.

46. Fr. Hewit in turn accused Brownson later in the *Catholic World* of ontologism. Brownson's forceful rebuttal is given in his *Review,* "Ontologism and Psychologism" (July 1874), pp. 360-363; *Works,* II, pp. 471-473.

47. Microfilm of the *Brownson Papers,* roll 9.

48. *Ibid.*

49. *Ibid.*

50. Microfilm of the *Brownson Papers,* roll 7.

51. Microfilm of the *Brownson Papers,* roll 9.

52. *Ibid.*

53. Microfilm of the *Brownson Papers,* supplementary roll 1. Strange as it may seem, I have been unable to find any report of this event either in the religious or secular press of the city.

54. *Latter Life,* p. 545.

55. Microfilm of the *Brownson Papers,* roll 9. The late Fr. Vincent Holden, C.S.P., Fr. Hecker's biographer, was no doubt correct when he remarked in a letter to the present writer, dated October 21, 1958: "At this juncture it seems quite clear to me that the real quarrel was between Hewit and Brownson and not Hecker."

56. "Personal Reminiscences," *The Catholic World,* I (April 1915), pp. 50-55.

57. Microfilm of the *Brownson Papers,* roll 7. William Seton was a grandson of Mother Seton. He studied at St. John's College (now Fordham University), at St. Mary's College, Emmitsburg, Maryland, and abroad. He was admitted to the bar in New York City. During the Civil War he fought with the Union forces, and was twice wounded at the battle of Antietam. After the war he devoted himself to writing. Among his novels are *The Romance of the Charter Oak,* and *The Pride of Lexington.* Brownson reviewed the latter in his *Quarterly* (April 1874), pp. 273-274.

58. *Ibid.*

59. Microfilm of the *Brownson Papers,* roll 6. (See also *Latter Life,* p. 549.) She translated from the Spanish the *Essay on Catholicism, Liberalism, and Socialism* of Don Juan Donoso Cortes, Marquis of Valdegamas. She was then Madeleine Goddard. Brownson praised her translation highly. *Works,* XVIII, p. 281. She also translated from the French *The Executive Power of the United States,* by the Marquis of Chambrun, highly praised again by Brownson. *Works,* XVIII, p. 269. She was also the author of "numerous novels and books of travel," such as *South Sea Sketches* and *Lights and Shadows.*

Brownson also carried on a correspondence to a lesser degree with Mrs. William Tecumseh Sherman. He was present in the fall of 1874 at the wedding in Washington, D.C., of General Sherman's daughter, Minnie. Joseph T. Durkin, S.J., *General Sherman's Son* (New York: Farrar, Straus and Co., 1959), p. 32.

60. *Latter Life,* pp. 549-554.

61. Nelson J. Callahan, *A Case for Due Process in the Church, Father Eugene O'Callaghan, American Priest of Dissent* (Staten Island, New York: Alba House, 1971), pp. 30-31.

62. *Latter Life,* pp. 368, 559-560.

63. Microfilm of the *Brownson Papers,* roll 9.

64. *Latter Life,* pp. 548-549.

65. *The National Catholic Register* (September 3, 1967).

66. *Latter Life,* pp. 561-562.

67. *Ibid.,* p. 523.

68. Microfilm of the *Brownson Papers,* roll 6. Fr. Luke Wimmer, O.S.B., was the nephew of Fr. Boniface Wimmer who founded the St. Vincent archabbey, college and seminary in Beatty, Pennsylvania.

69. *Ibid.*

70. Vol. XV (1870), pp. 244-246. In extending this praise, the author of the notice referred to the article on "Theological Errors of the Day — Brownson's Review," in the *Dublin Review,* XIV (January 1864), pp. 58-95, and endeavored to soften a bit the asperities of the article which was calculated to be quite damaging to Brownson's reputation with anyone who knew little about the man and his writings. Theodore Maynard in his *Life* of Brownson (pp. 268, 314, n. 29) ascribes the article, "Theological Errors of the Day," to William G. Ward. But this appears to be mere guesswork on the score that Ward was at the time editor of the *Dublin Review.* John Murphy in an article on "Dr. Brownson and His Works," in the *Irish Ecclesiastical Record* (September 1888, pp. 797-813), says categorically that the article was written by Dr. Patrick Murray, distinguished professor of Maynooth Seminary, Ireland, author of *De Ecclesia* and other works. Murphy remarked that Dr. Murray's attack on Brownson is a good example of what happens when Greek meets Greek. Murray attacked Brownson in particular for some of his remarks on Froschammer and Gioberti — with great vigor and effect, said Murphy. But according to Murphy:

". . . A close perusal of both Reviews would lead one to think that Dr. Murray did not do full justice to his opponent. He makes no mention of Brownson's explicit and repeated condemnation of Gioberti's leading doctrines. Then the work of Gioberti which Brownson most admired was one that was not published for some years after the condemnation of his other works. Of this work Brownson argued that, though it was rendered 'suspected' by the previous condemnation of the author's works, yet it might be considered on its own merits inasmuch as it was not involved directly in the condemnation" (p. 812).

It is in no sense surprising that Dr. Murray missed some things in Brownson's writings. He acknowledged at the outset that he had read only certain issues of Brownson's *Review,* a perilous starting point when one attempts to write an elaborate review. It seems quite probable that Dr. Murray was the same who took notice of Brownson's *Liberalism and the Church* in the *Dublin Review,* judging from the manner in which reference is made to the article, "Theological Errors of the Day."

71. Microfilm of the *Brownson Papers,* roll 6.

72. *The Daily Journal* of Elizabeth, New Jersey, issue of April 11, 1872, carried the following notice: "The wife of Dr. O. A. Brownson, who died Tuesday last in the 69th year of her age was buried this morning from St. Mary's (R.C.) [Roman Catholic] Church. Several distinguished clergymen from New York were present at the funeral ceremonies. Monsignore [sic] Seaton [sic] as celebrant, Rev. Father [Augustine J.] Thébaud [S.J.] as deacon, Rev. Father Vonsilger as sub-deacon and Rev. Father Cody as master of ceremonies. Rev. Father Hewit [C.S.P.] preached the funeral sermon; in the sanctuary were Rev. Fathers Hecker and Timot of New York, Salome of Red Bank and Lyon of St. Patrick's in this city.

"The choir consisted of a quartette from St. Patrick's Cathedral in Newark."

The name of the monsignor is misspelled. Monsignor Robert Seton, celebrant of the Mass, was a grandson of Mother Seton, and had been made a prothonotary apostolic in 1867, the first priest in the United States to receive that honor. He was later to become titular archbishop of Heliopolis. (See C. D. Hinrichsin, "Seton, Robert, Archbishop, Author," the *New Catholic Encyclopedia,* XIII, pp. 136-137.)

Although the Brownsons attended different churches during the years in Elizabeth, they seemed to have been mainly associated with St. Mary's parish. In the history of the parish occurs the following notation: "One of St. Mary's parishioners was Dr. Orestes A. Brownson, LL.D., who lived on Pearl street below Bridge street with his wife [Sally] and daughter, Miss Sarah Brownson, who married Judge Tenney, father of the late Police Chief, George C. Tenney. Dr. Brownson had a pew rather far up on the right hand of the middle aisle. He was a most distinguished convert to the church and a man of towering intellectual genius. To quote Lord Brougham, 'He was one of the first thinkers and writers not merely of America but of that age.' " Miss Emma I. Shea (daughter of John Gilmary Shea, the noted Catholic historian), "Historical Review of St. Mary's Parish," no name of publisher, 1915, pp. 13-14. This review is included in a "Golden Jubilee" booklet of the parish, 1865-1915.

73. *BrQR* (January 1873), p. 2; *Latter Life,* p. 580.

74. Both Brownson and Newman were "under a cloud" particularly in the early 1860s and in a large measure for much the same reasons. But as the late Fr. Joseph P. Donovan, C.M., remarked in an article in *Columbia* (April 1927), "Giant Among Giants," in Newman's case "the *Apologia* and the cardinalate brought him back into popularity" (p. 36). Brownson never had any such adventitious aids to restore him to the fullest confidence of his fellow Catholics. Brownson's autobiography, *The Convert,* was not written in 1857 under the dramatic circumstances under which Newman's *Apologia* was written in 1864.

75. Microfilm of the *Brownson Papers,* roll 9.

76. *Ibid.*

## CHAPTER 46

1. *Latter Life,* pp. 584-585.

2. Microfilm of the *Brownson Papers,* roll 7.

3. *Ibid.* Another great admirer of Brownson, Michael R. Keegan, wrote him to say that he now sees him "as once more putting on the armor of St. Michael to fight nobly with the leader of the heavenly hosts against all the enemies of God and his Christ." *Ibid.*

4. Microfilm of the *Brownson Papers,* supplementary roll 1.

5. *BrQR* (January 1873), p. 8. The *Review* had seventeen hundred subscribers in the first year, but then fell back to twelve hundred in the second year.

6. "Walworth's Gentle Skeptic," *BrQR* (July 1863), pp. 312-341; *Works,* IX, pp. 254-268. In the *Works* the title is changed to "Science of Sciences."

7. Articles in the *Works,* Vol. IX, between pp. 268-456.

8. "Walworth's Gentle Skeptic," *BrQR* (July 1863), p. 313; *Works,* IX, "Science of Sciences," pp. 255-256.

9. *Orestes A. Brownson: A Pilgrim's Progress* (Boston: Little, Brown and Co., 1939), p. 263.

10. "Religion and the Sciences," *BrQR* (April 1874), pp. 192-193; *Works,* III, pp. 531-532.

11. *Ibid.,* p. 195; *Works,* III, p. 534.

12. "Professor Tyndall's Address," *BrQR* (January 1875), p. 19; *Works,* IX, p. 546.

13. "Positivism and Christianity," *The Catholic World* (October 1871), *Works,* II, pp. 429-430.

14. "Primeval Man not a Savage," *BrQR* (April 1873), pp. 206-207; *Works,* IX, p. 458.

15. "True and False Science," *BrQR* (July 1873), p. 398; *Works,* IX, p. 528.

16. "Faith and Science," *The Catholic World* (September 1867), *Works,* IX, p. 274.

17. "Darwin's Descent of Man," *BrQR* (July 1873), pp. 349-351; *Works,* IX, pp. 494-496.

18. "Education and the People," *BQR* (September 1839), p. 402.

19. The articles are all in volume XIII of the *Works.* "Church and the Civil Power," *BrQR* (July 1875), pp. 344-370, is a reprint from the *Review* (January 1853), the article, "Temporal and Spiritual," *Works,* XI, pp. 1-36.

20. *BrQR* (April 1873), p. 288.

21. *BrQR* (October 1873), p. 436; *Works,* II, p. 4. Newman wrote in his last years: "I have all that time [the last fifty years] thought that a time of widespread infidelity was coming, and through all those years the waters have in fact been rising as a deluge. I look for the time, after my life, when only the tops of the mountains will be seen like islands in the waste of waters." W. Ward's *Life* of Newman, Vol. II, p. 416.

22. Microfilm of the *Brownson Papers,* roll 7.

23. "Count de Montalembert," *BrQR* (July 1874), pp. 292-293; *Works*, XIV, p. 519. The fact that the Count never answered his last letter of June 25, 1865, may have made Brownson feel a bit more free to criticize what he considered to be the Count's shortcomings. Could it be that the Count became a trifle indifferent to his friend since Brownson could no longer throw his influence on the Count's side through his *Review* (now defunct)? Brownson wrote of him: "In a word, Count Charles de Montalembert, a noble-minded man, of chivalric disposition, pure and disinterested, pious and devout even, was an orator, historian, scholar, publicist, statesman, rather than a philosopher or theologian, and viewed the Church rather in her political and social relations, than in her relation as the body of Christ, the visible representation of the Incarnation, to the salvation of the soul, or the beatitude of heaven." *Ibid*, pp. 308-309; *Works*, XIV, p. 534. The letter the Count wrote shortly before his death against papal infallibility (see E. E. Y. Hales, *Pio Nono*, New York: P. J. Kenedy and Sons, 1954, pp. 289-290), Brownson could not but regard as his fall, though he extolled in the highest terms his eminent abilities and the splendid services he had rendered the Catholic Church and the true interests of his fellowmen in the past.

24. Microfilm of the *Brownson Papers*, roll 9.

25. *BrQR* (October 1873), pp. 496-498; *Works*, XIII, p. 556.

26. *BrQR* (July 1873), pp. 416-418.

27. "Father Hill's Philosophy," *BrQR* (April 1875), pp. 270, 271; *Works*, II, pp. 497-498.

28. "Hill's Elements of Philosophy," *BrQR* (October 1875), pp. 495, 503; *Works*, II, pp. 512, 519.

29. *Latter Life*, pp. 607-608.

30. "Hill's Elements of Philosophy," *BrQR* (October 1875), p. 490; *Works*, II, p. 506.

31. *Ibid.*, pp. 490-491; *Works*, II, p. 507.

32. *Ibid.*, p. 499; *Works*, II, p. 515.

33. *Ibid.*, p. 501; *Works*, II, p. 517.

34. *Ibid.*, p. 503; *Works*, II, p. 519.

35. Microfilm of the *Brownson Papers*, supplementary roll 1.

36. Microfilm of the *Brownson Papers*, roll 7.

37. Wilfrid Ward, *The Life of John Henry Cardinal Newman* (New York: Longmans, Green, and Co., 1912), I, pp. 166-167.

38. "Count de Montalembert," *BrQR* (July 1874), pp. 305-306; *Works*, XIV, pp. 530-531.

39. "Letter to the Editor," *BrQR* (October 1874), p. 543; *Works*, XX, p. 430.

40. "The Use and Abuse of Reading," *The Catholic World* (January 1866), *Works*, XIX, p. 517.

41. *BrQR* (October 1875), p. 571.

42. *BrQR* (October 1875), p. 135.

43. "Religious Novels," *BrQR* (January 1873), pp. 53-54; *Works*, XIX, p. 560.

44. *BrQR* (January 1873), p. 130.

45. *Latter Life*, pp. 605-606.

46. *Early Life*, p. 496.

47. *Latter Life*, pp. 606-607. Yet Brownson defended in the next issue of his *Review* what he had said, remarking that when "a woman, nun or not, enters the field of literature, we recognize the author only. If she expects nothing, we deny her nothing on the score of sex, or her religious profession. . . . Our dear Sister M. Frances Clare, whose books sell by the hundreds and thousands, should not feel it any thing more than a useful mortification, if there happens to be one old man who stands aloof from the crowd of her flatterers, and refuses to puff what he regards as her light-weighted wares." Quite true, but there was still no call to reflect directly on Sister M. Frances Clare's lack of the virtues of a true religious. (See *BrQR* [April 1873], pp. 286ff.)

48. She published her autobiography under the title, *The Nun of Kenmare* (Boston: Tricknor and Co., 1889). With permission of the Holy Father she founded a Sisterhood known as the Sisters of Peace. They located in Jersey City, New Jersey. But

nothing prospered. Her family name was Margaret Cusick, and she herself was a convert. Upon inquiry the following information about her was obtained from Sister M. Philomena of the Kenmare Sisterhood, Ireland, on May 14, 1973:

"Her story is a tragic one and much research has been done into her life in recent years. On leaving her mission in America she reverted to the Baptist religion and lectured against the Pope and the Blessed Virgin Mary although while a member of the Kenmare Community she had written and published two comprehensive and orthodox volumes defending the Catholic teaching regarding them both. She returned to her Protestant relatives in England and died in Leamington Spa, Warwickshire, in June 1899. We have letters written by Mercy Sisters who visited her there. She gave them Mass offerings and expressed a wish to see them privately, but her relatives would not allow it.

"The order she founded exists still — well known as 'St. Joseph's of Newark.' It was nurtured and inspired by a Sister M. Evangelist, an Irish Sister who was received by the Nun of Kenmare. . . . They have again assumed the title, 'Sisters of Peace.'

One researcher has also remarked: 'There is reason to hope from letters preserved in the archives of the Kenmare Convent, and from a statement made by a dying priest, that she died reconciled to the Church.' "

49. "Women's Novels," *BrQR* (July 1875), p. 370; *Works,* XIX, p. 595.

50. "Religious Novels," *BrQR* (January 1873), pp. 61, 63; *Works,* XIX, pp. 567, 569.

51. *Ibid.*, p. 68; *Works,* XIX, p. 574.

52. "Mrs. Gerald's Niece," *The Catholic World* (January 1871), *Works,* XIX, p. 548.

53. "Religious Novels," *BrQR* (January 1873), pp. 61, 63; *Works,* XIX, pp. 567, 569.

54. Microfilm of the *Brownson Papers,* roll 7.

55. *Latter Life,* p. 607.

56. "Mrs. Gerald's Niece," *Works,* XIX, pp. 544, 559. (Article originally published in *The Catholic World,* January 1871.)

57. "Dr. Brownson," *The Catholic World,* XXIII (June 1876), p. 371.

58. Sister M. Felicia Corrigan, S.L., M.A., *Some Social Principles of Orestes A. Brownson* (Washington, D.C.: Catholic University of America Press, 1939), p. 16.

## CHAPTER 47

1. Augustine F. Hewit, "Dr. Brownson," *The Catholic World* (June 1876).

2. A Xerox copy of this letter is in my possession. Mrs. Lawrence Peiffer of Dubuque, Iowa, a granddaughter of Orestes, Jr., is the possessor of the original. (Letter to this writer, dated April 20, 1972.)

3. Microfilm of the *Brownson Papers,* roll 7.

4. All these letters are in the microfilm of the *Brownson Papers,* roll 7.

5. This information has been obtained from Sister M. Arsenia, O.S.F., Dubuque, Iowa, a granddaughter of Orestes, Jr.; Sister Margaret Brownson, S.S.N.D., Mequon, Wisconsin, another granddaughter; and Mrs. Lawrence Peiffer of Dubuque, another granddaughter.

6. The leaflet listing the particulars of this program was obtained from Loras College, Dubuque. The J. J. (John Joseph) Brownson, M.D., just mentioned, was the son of Professor Orestes, Jr., and eventually became quite distinguished in the medical profession. As a young man he had been principal of the Old Dodge Street School, later known as the Bryant School, but afterwards took up the study of medicine in Iowa City and then practiced medicine in Dubuque for more than half a century. He was the first to adopt new methods, new ideas, new practices in medicine and surgery. He was the first physician in Dubuque to perform an appendectomy. He became dean of the Dubuque medical fraternity and was known as the pioneer user of antiseptic surgery west of the Mississippi River. On the completion of his fiftieth

year of medical practice the University of Iowa erected a golden plaque in his honor. He was a devout Catholic, highly civic minded, and also became president of the Midwest Antiquarian Association, national sponsors of the Columbia Museum. (See the obituary notice of him in the *Daily Catholic Tribune,* issue of June 29, 1938.)

The same J. J. Brownson, M.D., named one of his sons after his grandfather, the original Orestes A. Brownson. This son also became well known in the medical profession. After studying at St. Raphael's Academy in Dubuque and the Jesuit College in Prairie du Chien, Wisconsin, he entered the College of Physicians and Surgeons of St. Louis, Missouri, and was duly graduated in 1906 with the degree of Doctor of Medicine. He made surgery his specialty, and took a postgraduate course at the College of Physicians and Surgeons in Chicago. After practicing medicine for some years in Dubuque he finally established headquarters in Los Angeles where he died of a heart attack. He was an eye, ear and nose specialist. (Letter of Mrs. Agnes Peiffer, dated March 26, 1973.)

7. Microfilm of the *Brownson Papers,* roll 9.

8. He died on April 29, 1892, and was buried from St. Joseph's Church, Key West, Iowa. Key West is four miles from Dubuque, in Dubuque County. Orestes and family, however, lived one mile from Rockdale which is three miles from Dubuque.

9. This is stated in a letter of his mother to her sister Betsy, dated March 13, 1853. Microfilm of the *Brownson Papers,* roll 3.

10. Microfilm of the *Brownson Papers,* roll 9. Henry carried out with true filial affection the charge his father had given him. In a letter Josephine Brownson, Henry's daughter, wrote Fr. S. A. Raemers, on October 14, 1930, she stated that her father had put all the money of the family into the publication of his father's writings. Microfilm of the *Brownson Papers,* supplementary roll 1.

11. *Ibid.*

12. *Faith and Science* (Detroit: H. F. Brownson, Publisher, 1895).

13. Microfilm of the *Brownson Papers,* supplementary roll 1. After stating that Henry F. Brownson (b. Canton, Massachusetts, August 8, 1835, d. Detroit, December 19, 1913) graduated from Georgetown College at the age of sixteen, and mentioning many other very interesting facts in his career, the *National Cyclopedia of American Biography* adds: "Major Brownson was among the foremost scholars of the United States. His literary taste was unfailing and his reading extensive. As a linguist he was familiar with Hebrew, Greek, Spanish, Italian, Dutch, French and German. . . . The thoroughness and variety of his knowledge were amazing. . . . He was not less remarkable for his modesty, however, than his learning, and no less conspicuous for his piety in private life than for bravery on the field of battle." Vol. XVI, p. 436.

14. *BrQR* (January 1859), pp. 140-141.

15. Doran Whalen, *Granite for God's House: The Life of Orestes Augustus Brownson* (New York: Sheed and Ward), p. 141.

16. Microfilm of the *Brownson Papers,* roll 9.

17. Microfilm of the *Brownson Papers,* roll 6. It has been argued whether or not this letter was really sent. Whatever the case, it contains the father's sentiments on the matter. It may be that Sarah wore out her welcome a bit in her long visit with brother Orestes and family. Later when it came to dividing up what money and property the father had left (he made no will), Sarah's letters to Henry show clearly enough that she had no great love for her brother Orestes. She said in a letter, dated April 27, 1876, that Orestes "always considered that he should have the lion's share." Microfilm of the *Brownson Papers,* supplementary roll 1.

18. Microfilm of the *Brownson Papers,* roll 9.

19. *Ibid.*

20. *Ibid.*

21. Microfilm of the *Brownson Papers,* roll 7.

22. Microfilm of the *Brownson Papers,* roll 1.

23. As has been observed, Brownson was by this time a giant in decay, ailing badly now for a whole decade; and Sarah had been of infirm health for some time. In a letter to Henry, dated April 24, 1867, the father had spoken of her ill health (microfilm, roll 9). Again in a letter to Henry, dated August 15, 1869, the mother had spoken of her

poor health (microfilm, supplementary roll 1). Her early death, therefore, could not have been wholly unexpected.

24. Microfilm of the *Brownson Papers,* supplementary roll 1.

25. *Ibid.*

26. *Ibid.*

27. *Ibid.*

28. *Ibid.*

29. *Ibid.*

30. *Ibid.*

31. *Ibid.*

32. *Ibid.* Judge William J. Hewett Tenney, born in Newport, Rhode Island, in 1811, son of Caleb Jewett Tenney and Ruth Channing, had a fairly good cultural background. He had graduated from Yale College in 1830, and in 1842 studied medicine in Boston, but abandoned it for the law, which he studied in New Haven, Connecticut, and opened an office in New York City. He was connected with the *Journal of Commerce* in 1841, and the *Evening Post,* 1842-1843 and 1847-1848. In 1843 he edited the *Mining Magazine;* the same year he entered the employment of D. Appleton and Company, and there edited the *Annual Cyclopedia* from its incorporation, 1861, until his death. He was author of the *Military and Naval History of the Rebellion of the United States,* and also author of *Grammatical Analysis,* 1866. He was for fourteen years a member of the city council of Elizabeth, New Jersey, and two years presiding judge of the criminal court of Brooklyn, New York. He died in Newark, New Jersey, on September 20, 1883. He was a convert to the Catholic faith. (See *Appleton's Cyclopedia,* 1883; also the *Adjutant-General* of New Hampshire.)

33. Microfilm of the *Brownson Papers,* supplementary roll 1.

34. *Ibid.* Donald Capps has remarked of Brownson: "Following her death [Mrs. Brownson's], he engaged in frequent drinking bouts and boasted of his forthcoming marriage to his Chambermaid." "Orestes Brownson: The Psychology of Religious Affiliation," *Journal for the Scientific Study of Religion* (Fall, 1968), Vol. VII, p. 206.

Capps' remark about Brownson's "drinking bouts" is absolutely gratuitous. Capps neither could nor did he attempt to offer an evidence for his statement. *No one* at the time ever accused Brownson of any excess in drinking. Although he did say something to his daughter, Sarah, about marrying again [apparently at least partly in teasing], he never once named his "chambermaid," Agnes, nor did he ever marry again.

35. *Orestes Brownson: Yankee, Radical, Catholic* (New York: The Macmillan Co., 1943), p. 419.

36. *Early Life,* p. 91.

37. *The Catholic Historical Review,* XLIX (January 1964), p. 529.

38. "Review of Maynard's Life of Brownson," *Books on Trial* (December-January issue, 1943-1944), p. 406.

39. Microfilm of the *Brownson Papers,* supplementary roll 1.

40. *Ibid.*

41. Microfilm of the *Brownson Papers,* roll 9.

42. Microfilm of the *Brownson Papers,* supplementary roll 1.

43. Microfilm of the *Brownson Papers,* roll 9.

44. Microfilm of the *Brownson Papers,* supplementary roll 1 (letter dated July 9, 1874).

45. Microfilm of the *Brownson Papers,* roll 9.

46. *Ibid.*

47. Microfilm of the *Brownson Papers,* roll 9.

48. "Valedictory," *BrQR* (October 1875), pp. 578-580; *Works,* XX, pp. 436-438.

49. Microfilm of the *Brownson Papers,* roll 7.

50. "Valedictory," *BrQR* (October 1875), p. 579; *Works,* XX, p. 437.

51. "A Few Words on Dr. Brownson's Philosophy," *Dublin Review,* LXXVIII (January 1876), p. 37.

52. "Valedictory," *BrQR* (October 1875), pp. 579-580; *Works,* XX, pp. 437-438.

53. Letters in roll 9 of the microfilmed *Brownson Papers.*

54. Microfilm of the *Brownson Papers,* roll 9.

55. *Latter Life,* pp. 613-614.

56. Microfilm of the *Brownson Papers,* supplementary roll 1 (letter dated March 12, 1876).

57. *The Convert (Works,* V), p. 5.

58. A number of these facts were gathered in conversation from Elizabeth Brownson, daughter of Henry, or from correspondence with her. She lived in Detroit and passed away there in August 1969, the last surviving member of the family.

Her sister, Josephine (b. Detroit, Michigan, 1880; d. 1942, Grosse Pointe, Michigan), was a distinguished catechist. After a notable academic career, she founded the Catholic Instruction League in Detroit in 1916 for the benefit of children attending public schools. This organization was finally incorporated into the Detroit Archdiocesan Confraternity of Christian Doctrine in 1939. In that same year she was awarded the Laetare Medal by the University of Notre Dame, Indiana, and was named a member of the American Social Service Mission to Venezuela. She had been honored in 1933 by the papal decoration *Pro Ecclesia et Pontifice* and the LL.D. degree from the University of Detroit. (See M. A. Frawley, "Brownson, Josephine Van Dyke, teacher, author," the *New Catholic Encyclopedia,* Vol. II, p. 827.)

Another sister of Elizabeth and Josephine Brownson, Sarah, daughter of Henry, entered the Sisterhood of the Sacred Heart, and became dean of Manhattanville College, New York City, and was known as Mother Sarah Brownson.

The second child of Sarah Brownson, wife of Judge Tenney, born shortly before Mrs. Tenney died in 1876, and christened Mary, also entered the Sisterhood of the Sacred Heart. She, too, became dean of Manhattanville College, and had a notable career in the history of the college.

59. *Latter Life,* p. 615.

60. Taken from George N. Shuster's review of Theodore Maynard's *Life* of Brownson, "A Yankee Philosopher and His Era," New York *Times* (issue of February 20, 1944), book review section, p. 3.

## CHAPTER 48

1. *Orestes A. Brownson: A Pilgrim's Progress* (Boston: Little, Brown and Co., 1939), p. 297.

2. "Reade's Very Hard Cash," *BrQR* (April 1864), p. 227.

3. "Archbishop Spalding," *BrQR* (January 1874), pp. 113-114; *Works,* XIV, p. 507.

4. *Latter Life,* pp. 587-589.

5. "Orestes A. Brownson," the *Encyclopedia Britannica* (11th. ed.), Vol. IV, pp. 674-675. The celebrated Jesuit theologian, Cardinal Franzelin, was deputed to conduct the examination into Brownson's writings and to pass judgment. They were found to be above censure.

6. Microfilm of the *Brownson Papers,* roll 6.

7. "Dr. Brownson," *The Catholic World,* XXIII (June 1876), p. 371.

8. *Ibid.,* pp. 374-375.

9. *Transcendentalism in New England* (New York, 1876), p. 129.

10. "A Few Words on Dr. Brownson's Philosophy," *Dublin Review,* LXXVIII (January 1876), pp. 54-55.

11. *Princeton Review,* XXX (April 1858), p. 392.

12. "A Study of Dr. Brownson," *The Catholic World* (June 1903), p. 318.

13. "Dr. Brownson's Valediction" (November 1875).

14. "Dr. Brownson and His Works," *The Irish Ecclesiastical Record* (September 1888), p. 810.

15. *The Catholic World,* XXIII (June 1876), p. 375.

16. Frank Luther Mott, *The History of American Magazines,* Vol. I: 1741-1850 (Cambridge: Harvard University Press, 1939).

17. *Ibid.,* p. 691.

18. D. J. Scannell O'Neil, *Watchwords from Dr. Brownson* (Techny, Illinois: Society of the Divine Word, 1910), p. 8.

19. "Archbishop Hughes on the Catholic Press," *BrQR* (January 1857), p. 136; *Works,* XX, p. 68.

20. "Dr. Brownson," *The Catholic World,* XXIII (June 1876), pp. 366-377.

21. "In Memoriam: Orestes A. Brownson," *The American Catholic Quarterly Review,* I (July 1876), pp. 560-566.

22. *Our Liberal Movement in Theology* (Boston: American Unitarian Association, 1882), pp. 87-88.

23. This newspaper clipping was given to me in 1968 by Helena W. Odiorne, the great-granddaughter of Brownson, granddaughter of Mrs. Tenney.

24. *Latter Life,* p. 615.

25. "A National Brownson Memorial," *Historical Records and Studies,* XXXII (1941), p. 111. However, Harson may well have drawn considerable inspiration in the matter from Henry F. Brownson whom he met at the first National Catholic Lay Congress, held at Baltimore, Maryland, on November 11 and 12, 1889, with whom he served together with Peter L. Foy on the Committee on Papers. *Ibid.*

26. *BrQR* (July 1873), pp. 352-354.

27. M. J. Harson, "Orestes A. Brownson, LL.D.," *The Catholic World,* LXXIX (April 1904), p. 19.

28. *Ibid.,* pp. 20-21.

29. "A National Brownson Memorial," *ut supra,* pp. 111-114.

30. James McGurrin, Bourke Cockran (New York: Charles Scribner's Sons, 1948), pp. 307-308.

31. New York *Times* (issues of July 1 and 5, 1937).

32. "A National Brownson Memorial," *ut supra,* pp. 111-114.

33. Microfilm of the *Brownson Papers,* supplementary roll 1. Mrs. Brownson said of the Healy portrait: "Healy's portrait is a very exact likeness, but it is not his [Brownson's] best expression. A hundred years hence, if no other likeness was taken, it would not do him justice." Letter to son Henry, dated September 26, 1869. *Ibid.*

Bishop John Moore of St. Augustine, Florida, reported that "the strong features of Dr. Brownson struck him [Pope Leo XIII]," when looking at a picture of him in the *Church History* of the United States by Fr. Benedict Joseph Spalding. This information is contained in a letter of Bishop Moore to Lawrence Kehoe, publisher of the *Catholic World,* dated April 13, 1885, telling of his presentation of the volume of *Church History* to the Holy Father. The letter was printed on the back cover of the *Catholic World* (October 1885). This matter has come to light through the courtesy of Kenneth W. Cameron, editor of the *Emerson Society Quarterly.*

34. Americo D. Lapati, *Orestes A. Brownson* (New York: Twayne Publishers, Inc., 1965).

35. New York: The Humanities Press, 1970.

36. Washington, D.C.: Catholic University Press of America, 1971.

37. New York: Fordham University Press, 1972.

38. *The Conservative Mind* (Chicago: Henry Regnery, 1953), p. 213.

39. *Orestes A. Brownson: A Pilgrim's Progress, ut supra,* p. 297.

# BIBLIOGRAPHY

## PRIMARY SOURCES

### 1. Manuscript Material

Microfilm of the Brownson Papers. In 1965 and 1966 the Brownson Papers in the archives of the Notre Dame University Library were re-calendared and microfilmed under the sponsorship of the National Historical Publications Commission. The project was directed by Thomas T. McAvoy, C.S.C., Ph.D., late archivist, and was carried through by Lawrence J. Bradley, LL.B., M.A., as the manuscript preparator. The work consisted originally of nineteen rolls of microfilm. Subsequently another roll was added entitled *Supplementary Roll One*. In 1966 a pamphlet was published by the archives as *A Guide to the Microfilm Edition of the Orestes Augustus Brownson Papers*.

### 2. Works Published by Brownson

*An Address on the Fifty-Fifth Anniversary of American Independence Delivered at Ovid, Ithaca Co., New York, July 4, 1831.* Ithaca, 1831.

*An Address on Intemperance.* Keene, New Hampshire, 1833.

*An Address Delivered at Dedham on the Fifty-Eighth Independence.* Dedham, 1834.

*Babylon is Falling.* Boston, 1837.

*Oration before the Democracy of Worcester and Vicinity, Delivered at Worcester, Mass., July 4, 1840.* Boston: E. Littlefield. Worcester: M. D. Phillips, 1840.

*An Address on the Fourth of July,* Washington Hall, New York City, July 5, 1841. A Xerox copy was graciously furnished by the Harvard College Library.

*An Address on Social Reform.* Boston, 1844.

*The American Republic: Its Constitution, Tendencies, and Destiny.* New York: P. O'Shea, 1866.

*Boston Quarterly Review.* Vols. 1-5, 1838-1842.

*Brownson's Quarterly Review.* 1844-1864, 1873-1875.

*Charles Elwood; Or the Infidel Converted.* Boston: C. C. Little and J. Brown, 1840.

*Conversations on Liberalism and the Church.* New York: D. & J. Sadlier, 1870.

*The Convert; Or Leaves from My Experience.* New York: D. & J. Sadlier, 1857.

*Essays and Reviews, Chiefly on Theology, Politics, and Socialism.* New York: D. & J. Sadlier, 1852.

*The Mediatorial Life of Jesus.* Boston: C. C. Little and J. Brownson, 1842.

*New Views of Christianity, Society, and the Church.* Boston: C. C. Little and J. Brown, 1836. This is the first book Brownson ever wrote.

### 3. Compilations of Brownson's Works

*The Brownson Reader.* Edited by Alvin S. Ryan. New York: P. J. Kenedy and Sons, 1955. *Brownson's Works.* Edited by Henry F. Brownson, Detroit: Thorndike Nourse, 1882-1887, twenty volumes. These volumes are a collection of Brownson's main writings as a Catholic with the exception of volume 4. Volume 4 contains what Henry Brownson considered his father's more important writings before his conversion, especially those leading in the direction of the Catholic Church. The twenty volumes, however, according to Charles Carroll Hollis, represent only "about one third of his total output." *The Literary Criticism of Orestes Brownson*, unpublished doctoral dissertation, University of Michigan, 1954, p. vi.

*Literary, Scientific, and Political Views of Orestes A. Brownson.* Edited by Henry F. Brownson, New York: Benziger, 1893.

*Orestes A. Brownson's Early Life* (1803-1844). Edited by Henry F. Brownson. Detroit: H. F. Brownson, 1898.

*Orestes A. Brownson's Middle Life* (1845-1855). Edited by Henry F. Brownson. Detroit: H. F. Brownson, 1899.

*Orestes A. Brownson's Latter Life* (1855-1876). Edited by Henry F. Brownson. Detroit: H. F. Brownson, 1900. C. C. Hollis asserts that this three-volume *Life* of Brownson by his son Henry is "still the most essential for all subsequent studies," and remarks that the work is "more scholarly and objective than family relationship might indicate." *Literary Criticism of Orestes Brownson,* p. vii. (I have often referred to letters contained in the three volumes rather than to the microfilms on the score that the reader will find the three volumes more accessible than the microfilms.)

*Orestes Brownson: Selected Essays.* Edited by Russell Kirk. Chicago: Henry Regnery Co., 1955.

*Watchwords from Dr. Brownson.* Edited by D. J. Scannell O'Neill. Techny, Illinois: The Society of the Divine Word, 1910.

## SECONDARY SOURCES

Abell, Aaron I. "Brownson's 'The American Republic'; The Political Testament of a Reluctant Democrat." Records of the American Catholic Historical Society of Philadelphia, LXVI (1955), pp. 118-127.

Abbott, Walter M. *The Documents of Vatican II.* New York, 1966.

Acton, Lord. "Lord Acton's American Diaries." *Fortnightly Review,* CX (1921), pp. 727-742, and CXI (1922), pp. 63-83.

Adams, John Quincy. *Memoirs* (ed. by Charles Francis Adams), 12 vols. Philadelphia, 1874-1877.

Ahlstrom, Sidney E. *A Religious History of the American People.* New Haven, Connecticut, 1972.

Allen, Joseph. *Our Liberal Movement in Theology.* Boston, 1882.

Altholz, Josef L. and Victor Conzemius. "Acton and Brownson: A Letter from America." *Catholic Historical Review,* XLIX (1964), pp. 524-531.

──────── . *The Liberal Catholic Movement in England.* London, 1962.

Altholz, Josef L., Damian McElrath and James Holland. *The Correspondence of Lord Acton and Richard Simpson.* Cambridge, England, 1973.

*American Catholic Quarterly Review.* "In Memoriam: Orestes A. Brownson," I (1876), pp. 560-566.

*American Quarterly Church Review.* "Orestes A. Brownson as a Philosopher," XIX (1868), pp. 532-547.

Andelin, Mrs. Helen B. *Fascinating Womanhood.* Santa Barbara, California, 1970.

Babbit, Irving. *Democracy and Leadership.* Boston, 1924.

Ballou, Adin. *Autobiography.* Lowell, Massachusetts, 1896.

Bancroft, Frederic. *The Life of William Seward,* 2 vols. New York and London, 1900.

Barcus, James E. "Structuring the Rage within: the Spiritual Autobiographies of Newman and Orestes Brownson." St. Bonaventure University, New York; *Cithara,* XV (November 1975), pp. 45-57.

Barnes, Daniel R. "Brownson and Newman: The Controversy Re-examined," *Emerson Society Quarterly,* L (1968), pp. 9-20.

Baumgartner, A. W. *Catholic Journalism: A Study of its Development in the United States (1789-1930).* New York, 1931.

Beard, Charles and Mary. *The Rise of American Civilization.* New York, 1948.

Beitzinger, Alphonse J. *A History of American Political Thought.* New York, 1975.

Benard, Edmond D. *A Preface to Newman's Theology.* St. Louis, Missouri, 1945.

Bernard, Leon. "Orestes Brownson, Montalembert, and Modern Civilization," *Historical Records and Studies,* XIII (1954), pp. 23-48.

Bertin, Farrel, C.P. *Orestes A. Brownson's Approach to the Problem of God.* Dissertation. Catholic University of America, 1950.

Billington, Ray Allen. *The Protestant Crusade, 1800-1860: A Study of the Origins of American Nativism.* New York, 1938.

Birdsall, F. *The History of the Loco-foco Party or the Equal Rights Party.* New York, 1842.

Boucher, Arline and John Tehan. *Prince of Democracy* (James Cardinal Gibbons). New York, 1962.

Broderick, James, S.J. *Robert Bellarmine.* London and New York, 1950.

Browne, Edythe H. "Brownson, A Militant Philosopher," *Commonweal,* III (1926), pp. 627-628.

*Brownson's Review Reviewed. Being a Mild and Vigorous Vindication of the Rights and Privileges of Adopted Citizens against the Assaults and Aspersions of Dr. O. A. Brownson by the Catholic Press of the United States.* Pamphlet. Boston, 1854.

Brownson, Henry F. *Faith and Science.* Detroit, 1895. This book is mainly a reproduction of his father's thought on the relation of faith to science.

Burton, Katherine. "A man of Our Day," *Commonweal,* XXVII (1948), p. 719.

_____. *Paradise Planters: The Story of Brook Farm.* New York, 1939.

_____. *Three Generations.* New York, 1947.

Butler, Dom Edward Cuthbert, *Vatican Council I.* 2 vols. London and New York, 1930.

Callan, Nelson U. *A Case for Due Process in the Church: Father Eugene O'Callaghan, American Pioneer of Dissent.* New York, 1971.

Camara, Helder. *The Church and Colonialism: The Betrayal of the Third World.* New Jersey, 1969.

Canby, Seidel. *Thoreau.* Boston, 1939.

Capognigri, A. Robert. "Brownson and Emerson: Nature and History," *New England Quarterly,* XVIII (1945), pp. 368-390.

Capps, Donald. "Orestes Brownson: The Psychology of Religious Affiliation," *Journal for the Scientific Study of Religion,* VII (1968), pp. 197-209.

Carleton, T. F. "The Workingmen's Party of New York City," *The Political Quarterly,* XXII (1907), pp. 401-415.

Channing, William Ellery (ed.). *Thoreau, the Poet Naturalist.* Boston, 1902.

Channing, William Henry. *Memoir of William Ellery Channing,* 8th ed. 3 vols. Boston, 1860.

*Central-Blatt.* "Brownson, An Early Social Thinker," XXXII (1937), p. 119.

Clarke, James Freeman. "Orestes A. Brownson's Argument for the Catholic Church," *Christian Examiner,* XLVIII (1850), pp. 227-240.

Coakley, Thomas F. "Orestes A. Brownson." *America,* XV (1916), pp. 549-550.

Codman, John. *Brook Farm: Historical and Personal Memoir.* Boston, 1894.

Coit, Margaret. *John C. Calhoun.* Boston, 1950.

Commager, Henry S. *Theodore Parker.* Boston, 1947.

Commons, John R., and Associates. *History of Labor in the United States,* I. New York, 1940.

Conroy, Paul. "The Role of the American Constitution in the Political Philosophy of Orestes A. Brownson," *Catholic Historical Review,* XXV (1939), pp. 271-281.

_____. *Orestes A. Brownson: American Political Philosopher.* Unpublished Ph.D. dissertation. St. Louis University, 1937.

Cook, Thomas I, and Arnaud B. Leavelle. "Orestes Brownson's *The American Republic,"* *Review of Politics,* IV (1942), pp. 77-90, 173-193.

Corrigan, Sister M. Felicia, S.L. *Some Social Principles of Orestes A. Brownson.* Dissertation. Catholic University of America, 1939.

Cox, Harvey. *The Secular City.* New York, 1966.

Cross, Robert C. *The Emergence of Liberal Catholicism.* Cambridge, Massachusetts, 1958.

Culler, Dwight. *The Imperial Intellect: A Study of Newman's Educational Ideal.* Yale University, 1958.

Daley, Sister Benita, C.S.J. "The Marian Message of Orestes A. Brownson," *Magnificat,* LXXXI (1948), p. 191.

Day, Edward, C.SS.R. "Orestes Brownson and the Motherhood of God." *American Ecclesiastical Review,* CXXIX (1953), pp. 20-27.

De Mare, Marie. *G.P.A. Healy, An American Artist.* New York, 1954.

Dessain, Charles Stephen. *The Letters and Diaries of John Henry Newman.* Vols. XI, (1961), XII (1962), XIII (1963), XIV (1964), XV (1965), XVI (1966), XVII (1967), XVIII (1968). London.

Donovan, Joseph P., C.M. "Why a Brownson Revival," *Acolyte,* VI (1927), pp. 6-7.

——————. "Brownson: Giant Among Giants," *Columbia,* VI (1927), p. 36.

——————. "Matchless Interpreter of Peerless Constitution," *Homiletic and Pastoral Review,* XLVIII (1948), pp. 494-502.

——————. "Brownson, the Philosophical Expounder of the Constitution," *American Catholic Philosophical Association: Proceedings of the Seventh Annual Meeting* (1931), pp. 148-165. St. Louis, Missouri.

*Dublin Review.* "Orestes A. Brownson's Early Life," CXXIII (1898), pp. 560-562.

——————. "Orestes A. Brownson's Middle Life," CXXVII (1900), pp. 196-198.

——————. "Orestes A. Brownson's Latter Life," CXXIX (1901), pp. 189-190.

Dwyer, Archbishop Robert, J. "Just a Little Timid of the Ghost of Big Bear," *National Catholic Register* (September 1967), p. 3.

Earls, Michael. "Greek meets Greek," *Commonweal,* III (1934), pp. 40-42.

Elliott, Walter. *The Life of Father Hecker.* New York, 1894.

——————. "Personal Reminiscences," *Catholic World.* CI (1951), pp. 190-198.

Ellis, John Tracy. *American Catholicism.* New York, 1955.

Emerson, Ralph Waldo. *Journals.* Boston and New York, 1911.

——————. "The Portrait of a Bluestocking" in *State of Mind: A Boston Reader,* pp. 216-224. New York, 1948.

Enderton, Colonel Herbert Bronson. *The Bronson, Brownson, and Brunsun Families. Some Descendants of John, Richard, and Mary Bronson of Hartford.* Place of publication not given, 1969.

Farge, Maurice J. *Orestes A. Brownson as a Catholic Nativist.* M.A. dissertation, University of Toronto, 1962.

——————. "Brownson and the Common Schools: Nativism in an American Catholic," *Canadian Catholic Historical Association Report,* XXIX (1962), pp. 25-40.

Fenton, Joseph C. "Use of the Terms Body and Soul with Reference to the Catholic Church," *American Ecclesiastical Review,* CLX (1944), pp. 48-57.

——————. "Extra Ecclesiam Nulla Salus," *American Ecclesiastical Review,* CX (1944), pp. 300-306.

——————. "Membership in the Church," *American Ecclesiastical Review,* CXX (1945), pp. 278-305.

F.E.T. *The Kenrick-Frenaye Correspondence, 1830-1862.* Philadelphia, 1920.

Fitzsimmons, M. A. "Brownson's Search for the Kingdom of God: The Social Thought of an American Radical," *Review of Politics,* XVI (1954), pp. 22-36.

Foley, Albert B., S.J. *Bishop Healy, Beloved Outcast.* New York, 1954.

Foxwell, H. H. Introduction of Anton Menger's *The Right to the Whole Produce of Labor.* New York, 1962.

Fredrickson, George M. *The Inner Civil War: Northern Intellectuals and the Crisis of the Union.* New York, 1965.

Frese, Joseph R., S.J. "Brownson and Know-Nothingism," *Historical Records and Studies*, XXVII (1937), pp. 52-74.

————. "The Hierarchy and Peace in the War of Secession," *Thought*, XVIII (1943), pp. 293-305.

Frothingham, Octavius B. *Transcendentalism in New England*. New York, 1876.

————. *Theodore Parker*. Boston, 1874.

Gasquet, Abbot, O.S.B. (ed.). *Lord Acton and His Circle*. London, 1906. This is a volume of Lord Acton's letters addressed to a wide variety of persons. In 1904 Herbert Paul had edited a collection of some of Acton's letters which exhibited him in an attitude somewhat critical of the Catholic Church, under the title: *Letters of Lord Acton to Mary Gladstone, Daughter of Right Hon. W. E. Gladstone*. In an effort to redress the balance in the case, Gasquet edited this other volume of letters.

Gabriel, Ralph H. *The Course of American Democratic Thought*. New York, 1943.

Gildea, William L. "An English View of Brownson's Conversion," *Catholic World*, LXIX (1899), pp. 24-31.

Gilhooley, Leonard, C.F.X. *Brownson and the American Idea, 1838-1860*. PH.D. dissertation. Fordham University, 1961.

————. *Contradiction and Dilemma: Orestes Brownson and the American Idea*. New York, 1972.

Gill, Eric. *Autobiography*. New York, 1941.

Gohdes, Clarence L.F. *The Periodicals of American Transcendentalism*. Durham, North Carolina, 1931.

Gorman, Robert. *Catholic Apologetic Literature in the United States, 1784-1858*. Catholic University of America, 1939.

Griffin, John J. "Brownson's Philosophy of Family Life," *Ave Maria*, LXVII (1948), pp. 551-557.

Griswold, Rufus. *Prose Writers of America*, 5th ed. Philadelphia, 1853.

Guilday, Peter. "Gaetano Bedini," *Historical Records and Studies*, XXIV (1933), pp. 87-137.

————. *The Life and Times of John England*. New York, 1927.

Guttman, Allen. "From Brownson to Elliot: The Conservative Theory of Church and State," *The American Quarterly Review*, XVII (1965), pp. 483-500.

————. *The Conservative Tradition in America*. New York, 1967.


Haggerty, William J., Jr. "Brownson and Kant," *Delta Epsilon Sigma Bulletin*, IX (1964), pp. 7-15.

————. "Orestes A. Brownson: Faith and Reason," *Delta Epsilon Sigma Bulletin*, XI (1966), pp. 79-91.

Hanlin Oscar. *Boston's Immigrants*. New York, 1938.

Harastzi, Zoltan. *The Idyll of Brook Farm*. Boston, 1937.

Harson, M. J. "Orestes Brownson, LL.D., 'A Man of Courage and a Great American,' " *Catholic World*, LXXIX (1904), pp. 1-21.

Harrison, J. F. C. *Quest for the New Moral Order*. New York, 1969.

Hassard, John R. G. *The Life of the Most Reverend John Hughes, D.D.* New York, 1866.

Hawthorne, Julian. *Hawthorne and His Wife*. Cambridge, Massachusetts, 1884.

Healy, John. "Brownson's Works," *Irish Ecclesiastical Record*, V (1884), pp. 13-22.

Hecker, Isaac, T. "The Transcendental Movement in New England," *Catholic World*, XXIII (1876), pp. 528-537.

————. "Dr. Brownson and Bishop Fitzpatrick," *Catholic World*, XLV (1887), pp. 1-7.

————. "Dr. Brownson and the Workingmen's Party Fifty Years Ago," *Catholic World*, XLV (1887), pp. 200-208.

————— . "Dr. Brownson in Boston," *Catholic World,* XLVI (1887), pp. 466-472.

————— . "Dr. Brownson's Road to the Church," *Catholic World,* XLVI (1887), pp. 1-11.

————— . "Dr. Brownson and Catholicity," *Catholic World,* XLVI (1887), pp. 222-235.

Hewit, Augustine F. "Dr. Brownson," *Catholic World,* XXIII (1876), pp. 366-377.

Higginson, Thomas Wentworth. *Margaret Fuller Ossoli.* Boston, 1892.

Hildreth, Richard. *A Joint Letter to Orestes A. Brownson and the Editor of the North American Review in which the Editor of the North American Review is proved to be no Christian and little Better than an Atheist.* Pamphlet. Boston, 1844.

Hoffman, Ross. "The American Republic and Western Christendom," *Historical Records and Studies,* XXXV (1945), pp. 3-17.

Hofstadter, Richard. *The American Political Tradition.* New York, 1948.

Holden, Vincent F., C.S.P. *The Early Years of Isaac Thomas Hecker (1819-1844).* Washington, D.C., 1939.

————— . *The Yankee Paul, Isaac Thomas Hecker.* Milwaukee, 1958.

Hollis, Charles Carroll. *The Literary Criticism of Orestes Brownson.* Ph.D. dissertation. University of Michigan, 1954.

Hunt, Gaillard. "The Virginia Declaration of Rights and Cardinal Bellarmine," *Catholic Historical Review,* III (1917), pp. 276-289.

Huntoon, Daniel, J.V. *History of the Town of Canton.* Cambridge, Massachusetts, 1893.

Hurd, John C. *The Law of Freedom and Bondage in the United States,* 2 vols. New York, 1858-1862.

Hurley, Daniel A. *Orestes Augustus Brownson's Way to the Catholic Church.* Unpublished M.A. dissertation. St. Bonaventure College, 1946.

*Irish Ecclesiastical Record,* VII (1900), a review of *Middle Life,* p. 476.

Josephson, Hannah. *The Golden Threads.* New York, 1949.

Kelly, Edward E. "Newman, Wilfrid Ward, and the Modernist Crisis," *Thought,* XLVIII (1973), pp. 508-519.

Keneally, Finbar, O.F.M. *Documents in the Propaganda Fide; Academy of Franciscan History.* Washington, D.C., 1966. Archives of Notre Dame University.

Kirby, Georgiana Bruce. *Years of Experience.* New York, 1887.

Kirk, Russell. *Randolph of Roanoke: A Study in Conservative Thought.* Chicago, 1951.

————— . "Two Facets of the New England Mind: Emerson and Brownson," *The Month,* IV (1952), pp. 208-217.

————— . *The Conservative Mind: From Burke to Santayana.* Chicago, 1953.

————— . *Orestes Brownson: Selected Essays.* Chicago, 1955.

————— . "Catholic Yankee: Resuscitating Orestes Brownson," *Triumph,* IV (1969), pp. 24-26.

————— . *Roots of American Order.* La Salle, Illinois, 1974.

Ladu, Arthur I. "Political Ideas of Orestes A. Brownson, Transcendentalist," *Philological Quarterly,* XII (1933), pp. 280-289.

Lapati, Americo D. *Orestes A. Brownson,* New York, 1965.

————— . *The American Republic.* (A reissue in paperback of Brownson's *The American Republic* with a knowledgeable introduction.) New Haven, Connecticut, 1972.

Lapomarda, Vincent A. "Orestes Augustus Brownson: A 19th. Century View of Blacks in American Society," *Mid-America,* LIII (1971), pp. 160-169.

Laski, Harold. *The American Democracy: A Commentary and An Interpretation.* New York, 1948.

Lathrop, George Parsons. "Orestes Brownson," *Atlantic Monthly,* LXXVII (1896), pp. 770-780. This article, as a single article, furnishes probably the most comprehensive data on Brownson and his writings that has ever been written. It was written in collaboration with Brownson's son Henry.

LeBreton, Dagmar Renshaw. "Orestes Brownson's Visit to New Orleans in 1855," *American Literature,* XVI (1944), pp. 110-114.

Lewis, R. W. B. *The American Adam: Innocence, Tragedy, and Tradition in the Nineteenth Century.* Chicago, 1955.

*Lincoln Day by Day: A Chronicle, 1800-1865.* The Washington Congressional Library.

Linscott, Robert (ed.). *State of Mind: A Boston Reader.* New York, 1948.

Long, William. *English Literature.* New York, 1907.

Lord, Robert H., John E. Sexton, and Edward T. Harrington. *History of the Archdiocese of Boston.* New York, 1944.


MacDoughal, Hugh A., O.M.I. *The Acton-Newman Relationship, The Dilemma of Catholic Liberalism.* New York, 1962.

Malone, George K. *The True Church: A Study in the Apologetics of Orestes Augustus Brownson.* Dissertation. St. Mary of the Lake Seminary, Mundelein, Illinois, 1957.

Marshall, Hugh. *Orestes Brownson and the American Republic.* Washington, D.C., 1971.

_____ . "Brownson and the Church," *University Bookman,* XII (1973), pp. 67-69.

Martineau, Harriet. *Society in America,* 2 vols. London, 1837.

Matthiessen, Otto F. *The American Renaissance.* London and New York, 1841.

Maurer, Armand A. "Orestes A. Brownson: Philosopher of Freedom." Delivered at the 50th Anniversary Meeting of American Philosophical Association in New York City, April 2-25, 1976.

Maurer, Armand A., Etienne Gilson and Thomas Langan. *Recent Philosophy: Hegel to the Present.* New York, 1966.

Maynard, Theodore. *Orestes Brownson: Yankee, Radical, Catholic.* New York, 1943.

_____ . "Orestes Brownson, Journalist," *Commonweal.* XXXVII (1943), pp. 390-393.

_____ . *The Story of American Catholicism.* New York, 1941.

McAvoy, Thomas, C.S.C. "Brownson's Ontologism," *Catholic Historical Review,* XL (1942), pp. 376-381.

_____ . "Brownson and American History." *Catholic Historical Review,* XL (1954), pp. 257-268.

_____ . "Orestes A. Brownson and Archbishop Hughes," *Review of Politics,* XXIV (1962), pp. 19-47.

McCarthy, Charles Raymond, C.S.P. *The Political Philosophy of Orestes Brownson.* Unpublished Ph.D. dissertation. University of Toronto, 1962. The author attempts to demonstrate that there are two different philosophies in Brownson's political thought, one proper to his transcendental years, and another adopted later as a Catholic. In his attempt to establish this thesis he is not exact in some of his statements.

McCarthy, James Leonard, S.J. *Rhetoric in the works of Orestes Brownson.* Unpublished Ph.D. dissertation. Fordham University, 1961. This dissertation contains an excellent discussion of the various literary styles Brownson adopted in his writings.

McCarthy, Jay David. *A Catholic Voice on the Civil War, 1861-1864.* An unpublished M.A. dissertation. University of Notre Dame, 1956.

McDonnell, James M. *Orestes A. Brownson and Nineteenth Century Catholic Education.* Unpublished Ph.D. dissertation. University of Notre Dame, 1975.

McGrath, Fergal, S.J. *Newman's University: Idea and Reality.* London and New York, 1951.

McGrath, James W. *The Catholicism of Orestes Brownson.* Unpublished Ph.D. dissertation. University of New Mexico, 1955.

McLaughlin, J. Fairfax. "A Study of Dr. Brownson," *Catholic World,* LXXVII (1903), pp. 310-319.

McMahon, Francis E. "Brownson and Newman," *America,* LXXXIX (1953), pp. 45-47, 79-80.

————— . "Orestes Brownson on Church and State," *Theological Studies,* XV (1954), pp. 175-228. This article is by far the most elaborate treatise ever written on Brownson's doctrine on church and state.

————— . "Orestes Brownson: Always in Pursuit of the Right Answers," *Books on Trial,* XIII (1955), pp. 277, 322-324.

Meline, Mary, and D. F. X. McSweeney. *The Story of the Mountain.* 2 vols. Emmitsburg, Maryland, 1911.

*Mercersburg Review.* "Brownson's Quarterly Review." II (1950), pp. 33-80.

————— . "Brownson's Quarterly Review Again." II (1950), pp. 307-324.

Merriman, Charles. *American Political Ideas, 1865-1917.* New York, 1929.

McMaster, James A. "Brownson's Review," *Freeman's Journal,* July 1853, p. 40.

————— . "Brownson's Review — Its Value and Appreciation," *Freeman's Journal,* November 15, 1856, p. 4.

————— . "The Rambler on Brownson," *Freeman's Journal,* November 15, 1856, p. 4.

*Methodist Quarterly.* "The Rich Against the Poor: The Laboring Classes by O. A. Brownson," XXIII (1941), pp. 92-122.

————— . "Brownson's Quarterly Review," XXVII (1845), pp. 454-478.

*Metropolitan Magazine.* "Dr. Brownson and the Supreme Court of the United States," V (1857), pp. 209-215.

Michel, Virgil G., O.S.B. *The Critical Principles of Orestes Brownson.* Dissertation, Catholic University of America, Washington, D.C., 1918. Charles C. Hollis attaches little value to this treatise.

————— . "Brownson's Political Philosophy and Today," *American Catholic Quarterly Review,* XLIV (1919), pp. 193-202.

————— . "Orestes A. Brownson," *Catholic World,* CXXV (1927), pp. 499-505.

————— . "Brownson: A Man of Men," *Catholic World,* CXXV (1927), pp. 754-762.

Miles, George. *Said the Rose and Other Lyrics.* New York, 1907.

Miller, Perry. *The Transcendentalists, An Anthology.* Cambridge, Massachusetts, 1950.

————— . *The American Transcendentalists, Their Prose and Poetry.* New York, 1957.

Mims, Helen Sullivan. "Early American Democratic Theory and Orestes Brownson," *Science and Society, A Marxian Quarterly,* XXX (1939), pp. 166-198.

Moffit, Robert E. *Orestes Augustus Brownson on the Nature and Scope of Political Authority.* Unpublished M.A. dissertation. University of Arizona, 1971.

————— . *Metaphysics and Constitutionalism: The Political Theory of Orestes Brownson.* Unpublished Ph.D. dissertation. University of Arizona.

*Month.* "Brownson's Works," XLVII (1883), pp. 429-431.

————— . "The Works of Orestes Brownson," XLVIII (1883), pp. 439-442.

————— . "Brownson's Works," LIII (1885), pp. 444-448.

————— . "Brownson's Political and Literary Articles," LV (1885), pp. 439-443.

————— . "Dr. Brownson's Valediction," XXIII (CXXXVIII) (1875), pp. 366-369.

858

Moran, Vincent J. *The Relation of Brownson to the Philosophy of Kant.* Unpublished doctoral thesis. University of Toronto, 1954.

Mott, Frank Luther. *History of American Magazines.* 3 vols. New York, 1938.

Murphy, John. "Dr. Brownson and His Works," *Irish Ecclesiastical Record,* IX (1888), pp. 797-813. This article has been generally overlooked. I have not come across anyone who has ever referred to it. Yet it is a very important article. It gives an eminently fair and objective estimate of the man and his works.

Murray, Patrick. "Theological Errors of the Day — Brownson's Review," *Dublin Review,* LIV (1864), pp. 58-95. This unsigned critical article has invariably been attributed to William George Ward. The attribution has apparently been made on the score that Ward was at the time editor of the *Dublin,* and was Bronson's old adversary of former days. But John Murphy in his article, "Dr. Brownson and His Works," asserts categorically that the article was written by Patrick Murray, distinguished professor of Maynooth Seminary, Ireland, and author of *De Ecclesia Christi* (three volumes), and a number of other works.

Myerson, Joel. "A Calendar of the Transcendental Meetings," *American Literature,* XLIV (1972), pp. 197-207.

*Nation.* "Orestes A. Brownson's early Life," LXVII (1898), pp. 205-206.

_____. "Orestes A. Brownson's Middle Life," LXXI (1899), p. 77.

_____. "Orestes A. Brownson's Latter Life," LXXIII (1900), pp. 16-17.

Neil, Thomas P. *They lived the Faith.* Milwaukee, 1950.

Nevin, J.W. (See *Mercersburg Review,* above.)

Nevins, Allen. *The Ordeal of the Union.* New York, 1947.

_____. *The Emergence of Lincoln.* New York, 1950.

Newman, John Henry. *An Essay on the Development of Christian Doctrine.* London, 1846.

_____. *Apologia Pro Vita Sua.* New York, 1890.

_____. *The Present Position of Catholics in England.* New York, 1889.

_____. *An Essay in Aid of a Grammar of Assent.*

_____. *My Campaign in Ireland.* (Privately printed.)

_____. *A Letter to His Grace, The Duke of Norfolk.* London, 1875.

Newman, Josephine K. *Changing Perspectives in Brownson's Philosophical Thought.* Unpublished doctoral thesis. University of Toronto, 1971.

Nye, Russell Blaine. *The Cultural Life of the Nation.* New York, 1960.

O'Brien, John A. *Giants of the Faith.* New York, 1957.

Orvis, Marianne Dwight. *Letters from Brook Farm, 1844-1847* (ed. by Amy L. Reed). Poughkeepsie, New York, 1928.

Owen, Robert Dale. *Twenty Seven Years of Biography: Threading My Way.* New York, 1874.

Parsons, Wilfrid, S.J. "Brownson, Hecker, and Hewit." *Catholic World,* CLIII (1941), pp. 396-400.

Peabody, Elizabeth P. *Reminiscences of Rev. Wm. Ellery Channing, D.D.,* Boston, 1880.

Perkins, Alice, J.G., and Theresa Wolfson. *Franics Wright: Free Enquirer: The Study of a Temperament.* New York and London, 1939.

Pfulf, Otto, S.J. "Orestes Brownson: Ein grosser Gedächtnistag für die Kirche der Vereinigten Staaten," *Stimmen aus Maria-Laach,* LXV (1903)," 145-165. The author rates Brownson the greatest son the United States has given to the Catholic Church.

Pieper, Joseph. *A Guide to Thomas Aquinas.* New York, 1962.

Pierce, Edward L. *Memoir and Letters of Charles Sumner.* 4 vols. Boston, 1877-1893.

Pius XII, Pope. *Mystici Corporis.* Rome, 1943.

Potter, George. *To the Golden Door: The Story of the Irish in Ireland and America.* Boston, 1960.

Power, Edward J. *The Educational Views and Attitudes of Orestes A. Brownson.* Unpublished Ph.D. dissertation. University of Notre Dame, 1949.

Quinn, Arthur Hobson (ed.). *The Literature of the American People.* New York, 1951.

Raemers, Sidney A. *America's Foremost Philosopher,* Ph.D. dissertation, St. Anselm's Priory, Washington, D.Č.

Rahilly, Alfred H. "Sources of English and American Democracy." *Irish Quarterly Reivew,* VIII (1919), pp. 189-209.

*Rambler.* "Brownson's Quarterly Review," XVIII (1865), pp. 315-317.

Randall, James Garfield. *Constitutional Problems under Lincoln.* Urbana, Illinois, 1951.

—————. *Linoln the President.* New York, 1946.

Reidy, John P. "Orestes A. Brownson: 'Conservative Mentor of Dissent,' " *The American Benedictine Review,* XXI (1970), pp. 224-239.

Rezneck, Samuel. "The Social History of an American Depression, 1837-1843," *American Historical Review,* XL (1935), pp. 662-687.

Ripley, George. "Brownson's Writings," *Dial,* I (1840), pp. 22-46.

Roemer, Lawrence. *Brownson and Democracy and the Trend Toward Socialism.* New York, 1953.

Rowland, James P. "Brownson and the American Republic." New York, 1953.

Runes, Dogbert (ed.). *Dictionary of Philosophy.* New Jersey, 1962.

Russell, Amelia A. *Home Life of the Brook Farm Association.* Boston, 1900.

Ryan, Alvin S. *The Brownson Reader.* New York, 1955.

—————. "Orestes Brownson: The Critique of Transcendentalism," in Harold C. Gardner, *American Classics Reconsidered: A Christian Appraisal.* New York, 1958.

Ryan, Edwin. "Brownson and Newman," *American Ecclesiastical Review,* LII (1915), pp. 406-413.

—————. "Orestes Augustine [*sic*] Brownson," *Downside Review,* XLIV (1926), pp. 115-124.

Ryan, Thomas R., C.PP.S. "Brownson, The Catholic," *Acolyte,* X (1934), pp. 7-8.

—————. "The Constitution and the Church," *Catholic World,* CXLVIII (1938), pp. 75-80.

—————. "Why Continue to Smear Brownson?" *Acolyte,* XVII (1941), pp. 11-14.

—————. "Brownson Speaks of England," *Catholic World,* CLIV (1942), pp. 426-429.

—————. "Brownson on the Papacy," *American Ecclesiastical Review,* CXII (1946), pp. 114-122.

—————. "Brownson on Salvation and the Church," *American Ecclesiastical Review,* CXVII (1947), pp. 117-124.

—————. "Brownson's Technique in Apologetics," *American Ecclesiastical Review,* CXVIII (1948), pp. 12-22.

—————. "Brownson's Love of Truth," *Catholic World,* CLXII (1948), pp. 534-544.

—————. "Whence Comes Freedom?" *Catholic World,* CLXVII (1948), pp. 491-497.

—————. "Brownson on Salvation and the Church," *American Ecclesiastical Review,* CXXIX (1953), pp. 155-169.

—————. "Orestes A. Brownson and Historiography," *Irish Ecclesiastical Record,* LXXXI (1956), pp. 10-17, 122-130.

—————. "Orestes A. Brownson and the Irish," *Mid-America,* XXXVIII (1956), pp. 156-172.

_____ . *The Brownson Reader.* Edited by Alvin S. Ryan. *New England Quarterly,* XXIX (1956), pp. 114-116 (a book review).

_____ . "Brownson and the 'Higher Law,' " *Homiletic and Pastoral Review,* LXI (1961), pp. 1054-1059.

_____ . "Brownson in the Theological Field," *A Catholic Dictionary of Theology,* I (1961); pp. 302-304. London. This series of volumes is a work that was "projected with the approval of the Catholic hierarchy of England and Wales." The subject matter of volume 1 runs from A to C.

_____ . *Orestes Brownson on Saint Worship, the Worship of Mary* (ed.). Paterson, New Jersey, 1963.

_____ . "Some Critical Principles of Orestes A. Brownson," *Irish Ecclesiastical Record,* XCVII (1962), pp. 233-240.

_____ . "Brownson and the Modern Novel," *Irish Ecclesiastical Record,* XCVIII (1962), pp. 232-240.

_____ . "Brownson and Poetry," *Irish Ecclesiastical Record,* XCVIX (1963), pp. 248-255.

_____ . *Orestes A. Brownson's Road to Catholicism.* By Per Sveino. *Theological Studies,* XXXIII (1972), pp. 70-72 (a book review).

_____ . *Contradiction and Dilemma: Orestes Brownson and the American Idea.* By Leonard Gilhooley. *Thought,* CXC (1973), pp. 418-419 (a book review).

_____ . "Brownson and the American Polity," *University Bookman,* XIII (1973), pp. 61-66.

_____ . "Newman's Invitation to Orestes A. Brownson to be Lecturer Extraordinary at the Catholic University of Ireland," *Records of the American Catholic Historical Society of Philadelphia,* LXXXV (1974), pp. 29-47.

Sandburg, Carl. *Lincoln, The War Years,* Vols. I, II, III, IV. New York, 1941.

Sargent, Daniel. *Four Independents.* New York, 1935.

Schlesinger, Arthur, M., Jr. *Orestes A. Brownson: A Pilgrim's Progress.* Boston, 1939. (Reissued in paperback in 1966.)

_____ . *The Age of Jackson.* Boston, 1945.

_____ . "Orestes Brownson, An American Marxist before Marx," *Sewanee Review,* XLVII (1939), pp. 317-323.

_____ . *The Imperial Presidency.* Boston, 1973.

Schwartz, Michael. "Democracy: For Catholics Only," *Triumph,* VIII (1973), pp. 24-25. This article is largely an exposition of Brownson's thought in his treatise: "Catholicity necessary to sustain Popular Liberty," *BrQR* (1845), pp. 515-530.

Sedgwick, Ora Gannet. "A Girl of Sixteen at Brook Farm," *Atlantic Monthly,* LXXXV (1900), pp. 394-404.

Shaughnessy, Sister Jerome. *Dr. Brownson and the Philosophy of Nationalism.* Unpublished M.A. dissertation. University of Notre Dame, 1926.

Shea, John Gilmary. *History of the Catholic Church in the United States.* Vols. III (1890), and IV (1892), New York.

Shuster, George N. "A Yankee Philosopher and His Era," *New York Times,* February 20, 1944, p. 3. This is a review of Theodore Maynard's biography of Brownson.

Sibley, Mrs. Harriet Bronson. *The Bronson Lineage, 1636-1917.* Oregon, 1929.

Siegfried, Joseph P. "A Recent Work on Faith and Science," *American Ecclesiastical Review,* XIX (1896), pp. 61-73.

Simon, Harold. "Frederick Jackson Turner: The Significance of the Frontier in American History." (Address delivered in 1893.) Introduction by Harold Simon, New York, 1963.

Smith, Duane. "Romanticism in America: The Transcendentalists," *Review of Politics,* XXXV (1973), pp. 302-325.

Smith, John Talbot. *History of the Catholic Church in New York.* New York and Boston, 1905.

Soleta, Chester A. "The Literary Criticism of O.A. Brownson," *Review of Politics,* XVI (1954), pp. 334-351.

Speaight, Robert. *The Life of Hilaire Belloc.* New York, 1957.

Stanlis, Peter J. "Orestes A. Brownson, The American Republic," *University Bookman,* XIII (1973), pp. 52-60.

Stefun, Bonaventure, O.F.M. "The Mother of God in Brownson's Writings," *American Ecclesiastical Review,* CXXXIV (1956), pp. 316-323, 395-403.

————— . "Orestes Brownson: Apologist," *Homiletic and Pastoral Review,* LXIII (1962), pp. 40-47. In this article Stefun presents Brownson as "a dissenter who furthered unity."

Stewart, Randall. *Nathaniel Hawthorne, A Biography.* New Haven, 1948.

————— . *American Literature and Christian Doctrine.* Baton Rouge, Louisiana, 1958.

Styles, Daniel. *The Town of Waterbury.* Concord, New Hampshire, 1959.

Sveino, Per. *Orestes A. Brownson's Road to Catholicism.* New York, 1970.

Sweet, William Warren. *Religion in the Development of American Culture: 1765-1840.* New York, 1952.

Swift, Lindsay. *Brook Farm.* New York, 1900.

Swidler, Arlene, "Brownson and the 'Woman Question,' " *American Benedictine Review,* XIX (1968), pp. 211-219.

Thomas, Abell C. *Civilization and Roman Catholicism. A Review of O.A. Brownson's Four Lectures.* Pamphlet. Philadelphia. 1851.

Thomas, Charles Grandison. *Hereditary Property Justified. Reply to Brownson's Article on the Laboring Classes. By One Whose Personal Experience Should Enable Him to Feel the Wants and Sympathize with the Condition of the Laborer.* Pamphlet. Cambridge, 184I.

Thomas, M.F. "A Brownson National Memorial," *Historical Records and Studies,* XXXII (1941), pp. 111-114.

Thureau-Dangin, Paul M. *The English Catholic Revival in the Nineteenth Century.* 2 vols. London and New York, 1899.

Thurston, Herbert, S.J. *The Church and Spiritualism.* Milwaukee, 1933.

Trevor, Meriol. *Newman.* 2 vols. *The Pillar of the Cloud,* 1961; *Light in Winter,* 1963. Garden City, New York.

Tristram, Henry (ed.). *John Henry Newman, Autobiographical Writings.* New York, 1956.

Trollope, Frances, *Domestic Manners in America.* 2 vols. London, 1832.

*United States Catholic Magazine and Monthly Review.* "Brownson's Quarterly Review," IV (1845), pp. 152-164.

*United States Magazine and Democractic Review.* "Mr. Brownson's Recent Articles in the Democratic Review," XIII (1843), pp. 653-660.

Van der Zee Sears, John. *My Friends at Brook Farm.* New York, 1912.

Walsh, Augustine, O.S.B. "Orestes Augustus Brownson," *Placidian,* IV (1927), pp. 37-43.

————— . "Brownson on War," *Placidian,* IV (1927), pp. 240-246.

————— . "Glossary of Brownson on War," *Placidian,* IV (1927), pp. 377-381.

Walshe, Henry. *Hallowed were the Gold Dust Trails.* Santa Clara, California, 1946.

Ward, Wilfrid. *The Life and Times of Cardinal Wiseman.* London, 1887.

————— . *William George Ward and the Oxford Movement.* London, 1890.

————— . *William George Ward and the Catholic Revival.* London, 1893.

————— . *The Life of John Henry Cardinal Newman.* 2 vols. London, 1912.

Ward, William George. "Brownson's Quarterly Review," *Dublin Review,* XIX (1845), pp. 390-400.

_____. "Mr. Brownson on Developments," *Dublin Review*, XXIII (1847), pp. 373-405.

_____. "A Few Words on Dr. Brownson's Philosophy," *Dublin Review*, LXXVII (1876), pp. 36-55.

Waterman, William Randall. *Frances Wright*. New York, 1924.

Weaver, Lee H. "Nathaniel Hawthorne and the Making of the President," *Historical New Hampshire*, XXVIII (1973), pp. 21-34.

Wegand, Norman (ed.). *Immortal Diamond* (Gerard Manley Hopkins). New York, 1949.

Weis, John. *Life and Correspondence of Theodore Parker*. 2 vols. New York, 1864.

Wellek, René. "The Minor Transcendentalists and German Philosophy," *New England Quarterly*, XV (1942), pp. 652-680.

Whalen, Doran. (Pen name used by Sister Rose Gertrude Whalen, C.S.C., in memory of her father.) *Some Aspects of the Influence of Orestes A. Brownson on His Contemporaries*. Ph.D. dissertation. University of Notre Dame, 1933.

_____. *Granite for God's House, The Life of Orestes Augustus Brownson*. New York, 1941. Joseph P. Donovan, a learned Brownsonian, remarked that the author of this *Life* of Brownson wrote well of him "on his human side." But she did not document her narrative, nor succeed in avoiding all inaccuracies.

_____. "Review of Maynard's Life of Brownson," *Book on Trial*, I (December-January 1943-1944), pp. 406-407.

Yardley, May. *Selected Discourses from Newman's Idea of a University*. Cambridge, England, 1931.

# INDEX

## • A •

## • B •

Brownson, Relief Metcalf, Orestes's mother — 17-18, 302.
Brownson, Sally — 68, 81-82, 301, 420, 430, 557, 582, 693, 708, 713, 732, 843 (n. 72).
Brownson, Sarah Nicolena — 301, 420, 582, 703-704, 708, 712-718, 720-721.
Brownson, Sylvester Augustus, Orestes's father — 16-17.
Brownson, Thorina — 17, 303, 736 (n. 13).
Brownson, William Ignatius — 96, 301, 420, 422, 642.
Buchanan, James — 307, 618-619.
Bulwer-Lytton, Sir Edward — 148, 155, 261, 358-360, 705.
Burke, Edmund — 234, 261, 352, 393-394, 502, 651.
Byron, George Gordon — 155, 359, 363.

## • C •

Caesarism — 517-518, 526-527, 552, 604, 655.
Carey, Matthew — 56, 743 (n. 45).
Calhoun, John Caldwell — 131, 157-158, 173, 197, 200, 205, 223-225, 273, 282-283, 307, 520, 614, 634, 651, 654-655.
Calvin, John — 27, 276, 384.
Calvinism — 30-31, 97, 150-152, 256, 543, 690, 738 (n. 9).
Cameron, Kenneth Walter — 88-89, 94.
Canton (Massachusetts) — 81-82, 94-95.
Cantu, César — 353, 682-683.
Carbonari of Italy — 56, 476.
Carlyle, Thomas — 146, 150, 155, 164, 189, 340, 355, 361, 501.
**Catechism of the Council of Trent** — 100.
Catholic Church — 49-50, 92, 107-108, 152, 213, 215, 239, 251, 257, 262-263, 270, 272, 281, 283-284, 286, 288, 291, 298-299, 303, 309, 333, 369, 438, 444, 469, 471, 521, 527-528, 535, 646, 662.
**Catholic Polemics** — 580, 592, 601.
Catholic University of Ireland — 508, 513.
Catholicism — 31, 106, 212, 281, 298, 318, 339, 598-599, 629.
Catholicity — 17, 79, 100, 267, 285-286, 288, 321, 339, 343, 401, 419, 424, 441, 463, 466, 468, 471, 482-483, 499, 517-518, 523, 527, 544.
Cavour, Count — 560, 562, 587.
Channing, William Ellery — 9, 17, 64-65, 68, 77, 79-82, 94-95, 99, 103, 112, 116, 120, 157, 207, 253-256, 263-264, 266-267, 269, 278-279, 404.
Channing, W. H., nephew to William Ellery — 125, 138, 172, 207, 213-216, 228, 244.
**Charles Elwood** — 39-40, 47-50, 61, 68, 87, 740 (n. 28), 743 (n. 39 and n. 61).
Chateaubriand — 64, 505.
Chelsea (suburb of Boston) — 96, 142, 192, 223, 264, 321, 422, 514.
Chesterton, Gilbert K. — 322.
**Christian Examiner** — 73, 87, 120, 124, 126.
Christianity — 64, 78, 85, 92, 96, 100, 102, 114, 120, 135, 156, 168-169, 177, 209, 279, 402, 405, 424, 535, 615.
Christians — 22, 79, 132, 169, 177.
**Church and the Republic** — 520-521, 538.
**Church Not a Despotism** — 515, 532, 604.
Church of the Future — 92, 97-99, 121, 273, 276.
**Church Question** — 274-277.
Civil War — 435, 613, 617-618, 647.
**Civiltà Cattolica** — 384, 503, 544, 553, 638.
Clarke, James Freeman — 80, 141-142, 320, 327.
Clay, Henry — 157, 233, 243, 406.
Clerk, George Edward — 417-418, 428, 462-463, 473.
Cochin, Augustin — 603, 622-623, 630.
Codman, John T. — 208, 296.
"Come-Outerism" — 289, 296.

Fenwick, Benedict Joseph, Bishop of Boston — 287-288, 296-298, 300, 780 (n. 3).

Fitzpatrick, Bp. John Bernard — 74, 288, 297-300, 305, 314-318, 321-323, 325, 367-368, 372, 382-383, 416, 442, 446, 453, 488, 513-514, 516, 523, 527, 530, 532, 547, 555, 604.

Forbes, Dr. John M. — 503, 535, 604-605.

Fordham University — *See* St. John's College.

"Fourierism" — 215-216, 278.

"Fourierists" — 216, 291.

France — 73, 97, 108, 137, 242, 401, 403-404, 423, 517-519, 526, 539, 542, 551, 587, 611, 620, 631, 712, 725.

Free-Soilers — 406, 408-410.

French Revolution (1789) — 51, 106, 261, 399, 558.

Frothingham, Octavius Brooks — 9, 49, 76, 125, 142, 208, 726.

Fruitlands — 210, 215, 303, 767 (n. 53).

Fugitive Slave Law (1850) — 405-411.

Fuller, Margaret — 125, 141, 145, 151, 172, 209, 215, 340-342.

Fullerton, Lady Georgiana — 361, 366, 706.

## • G •

Gallicanism — 402, 423, 438-441, 444, 450, 479, 498, 518, 592.

Garesche, Alex J. — 424, 430, 434-435.

Garland, Hon. Hugh A. — 210-211, 213, 427, 434.

Garrison, W. Lloyd — 134, 289, 654.

Gavazzi, Padre Alessandro — 285, 459, 470, 477.

George III, King — 395, 414, 481.

Germany — 97, 108, 120, 137, 242, 510, 725.

Gibbons, Card. James — 340, 547.

Gilhooley, Leonard T. — 111, 126, 128, 153, 187, 190, 292, 733.

Gioberti, Abbé Vincenzo — 248, 502, 604, 631, 648, 665, 674, 687-688, 699.

Glover, Fr. Thomas, S.J. — 294-295, 373.

Gosselin, Jean-Edmé-Auguste — 439, 442, 451.

Gratry, Père — 503, 603, 699, 728,

Greeley, Horace — 215, 623, 629.

Gresselin, Fr. Charles, S.J. — 552-553, 559, 583, 586, 597, 606, 674.

Griswold, Rufus W. — 101, 228.

Guizot, Francois M. — 117, 179, 361.

Guy, Fr. Robert, O.S.B. — 584, 667.

## • H •

Haggerty, William J., Jr. — 508, 672.

Harrison, William Henry — 173, 192, 194, 233.

Harson, M. J. — 88, 304, 326, 729.

Harvard — 89, 115, 137, 141, 145, 154, 247.

Hawthorne, Nathaniel — 118, 208-209, 214, 268, 350-351, 356-357.

Healy, Bp. James Augustine — 422.

Healy, John — 41, 422, 453, 523, 668-669, 822 (n. 18 of Ch. 38).

Healy, Sally — 40-41.

Hecker, Isaac T. — 62, 68, 75-76, 103, 189, 205, 422, 467, 480, 507, 513, 517, 522, 528, 539, 543-545, 599, 644-645, 665, 676, 679-683, 685-686, 688-689, 712, 727 and *passim.*

Hewit, Augustine F., C.S.P. — 25, 77, 522, 539, 632, 678-679, 681-685, 687-689, 693, 707-708, 725, 727 and *passim.*

Hildreth, Richard — 292-293, 343-345.

Hill, Fr. Walter, S.J. — 701-703.

Hilton, Judge G. H. — 462, 498, 520.

Hobbes, Thomas — 130, 241, 392, 650-653.

Holden, Fr. Vincent, C.S.P. — 221, 323, 563, 768 (n. 1).

Hollis, Charles Carroll — 10-11, 65, 76, 84, 87, 94, 98, 108, 121, 125-126, 137, 154, 157, 189, 226, 260, 343, 348, 355, 357, 509 and *passim*.

Hughes, Bp. John — 280-282, 301, 303, 308, 314, 317, 323, 428, 493, 515, 517, 530-532, 534-535, 537, 541-545, 547-548, 553, 556-559, 562, 565, 568, 577-578, 580, 593, 597, 608, 610, 615, 620, 623, 630, 727-728, 732.

Huntington, Jedediah Vincent — 357-358, 363, 494-495.

Hyacinthe, Père — 673, 699.

McCloskey, Archbp. John — 304, 308, 314, 342, 373, 416, 645, 695, 699.

Marx, Karl — 49, 128, 172, 187-188, 404, 762 (n. 48).

Maynard, Theodore — 30, 88, 319, 323, 346, 389-390, 456, 514-515, 532, 716, 733.

Michel, Virgil — 76, 329, 547.

Middle Ages — 31, 108, 152, 239, 281-282, 439, 443, 452, 498, 523, 588, 603, 605.

Miller, Perry — 9, 92, 97, 108, 142, 150-151, 192, 228, 282, 319, 343.

Mission of America — 534-535, 540, 544.

Moffit, Robert Emmet — 241, 245, 250, 658, 661, 733.

Montalembert, Count de — 389, 401-404, 415, 423, 502, 505, 516-519, 542, 551-552, 587-588, 599, 603, 611, 623, 631, 638, 643, 646, 699.

Montesquieu, Baron de — 241, 271.

Mott, Frank Luther — 229, 419, 678.

Munich (Germany) — 23, 158, 450, 500-501, 505-506, 512, 598, 689, 712.

• **N** •

Napoleon III, Emperor — 429, 458, 517, 526-527, 551, 560, 605, 622, 630.

Native American party — 456, 459, 461, 465, 468, 477.

Native Americanism — 334, 455-457, 460-462, 464, 469, 472-473, 507, 509.

Native Americanism — 334, 338, 456.

Nevin, Dr. John W. — 318, 320, 326.

Nevins, Allen — 197, 397, 619.

New Views of Christianity, Society and the Church — 87, 105-107, 109, 263.

New York City — 217, 513, 515-516, 519, 531-532, 547, 602, 630.

Newman, Card. John Henry — 10, 21, 31-32, 38-39, 47, 193, 269, 284, 286, 299-300, 309, 316, 359, 367-380, 428, 447, 500-512, 522, 528, 535, 538, 544, 548, 559-560, 563, 566, 585, 591, 598, 601-602, 606, 609, 611, 667, 699, 703, 727.

No Church, No Reform — 277, 289-290.

Norton, Andrews — 148-150, 342.

Notebook of Reflections — 26, 738 (n. 4).

• **O** •

Obituary notice (1876), Brownson's — 23-24.

O'Callaghan, Fr. Eugene — 690-692.

O'Connell, Daniel — 402-403, 458.

O'Connor, Bp. Michael — 370-371, 373, 442, 447, 451, 488, 491-492, 494-496, 530.

Odiorne, Mrs. Thomas (Helena H.) — 714-715, 730.

Origin and Ground of Government — 232-233, 238, 241-242, 772 (n. 51).

Ossoli, Margaret Fuller — See Fuller, Margaret.

O'Sullivan, John L. — 228, 230-237.

Owen, Robert Dale — 48, 52, 209, 269, 365, 397.

• **P** •

Paine, Thomas — 57, 234, 392.

Paris (France) — 246-247, 404, 423, 439, 503, 594, 728.

Parker, Theodore — 9, 125, 141-142, 144-145, 172, 227, 261, 265, 267, 306, 409-410.

Paul, St. — 93, 107, 238, 253, 307, 410, 598, 701.

Peabody, Miss Elizabeth Palmer — 104-105, 176, 293, 748 (n. 33).

Perrone, Giovanni, S.J. — 369-371, 377.

Peter, St. — 37, 267, 276, 402, 452-453.

Philosophy of Brownson — 75, 839 (n. 47).

Pierce, Franklin — 118, 411-412, 473, 497.

Pierce, Isaac B. — 306, 423.